1809.

HISTORY

OF

ASHLAND COUNTY,

OHIO,

WITH

ILLUSTRATIONS AND BIOGRAPHICAL SKETCHES,

BY

GEORGE WILLIAM HILL, M. D.

PUBLISHED BY

WILLIAMS BROS.

1880.

This volume was reproduced
from a personal copy located in
the Publishers private library

All rights reserved. No part of this publication may be reproduced,
stored in a retrieval system, transmitted in any form, posted
on the web in any form or by any means without the
prior written permission of the publisher.

Please direct all correspondence and book orders to:
SOUTHERN HISTORICAL PRESS, Inc.
1071 Park West Blvd.
Greenville, SC 29611

Originally Printed 1880
New Material Copyright 2025 by:
 Southern Historical Press, Inc.
ISBN #978-1-63914-645-1
Printed in the United States of America

TO THE PEOPLE
OF
ASHLAND COUNTY, OHIO,

WHOSE DEEDS ILLUSTRATE DEVOTION

TO

INDUSTRY, LITERATURE AND RELIGION,

THE PERPETUATION

OF

AMERICAN FREEDOM, PURE GOVERNMENT,

EQUALITY OF TAXATION,
FREEDOM OF OPINION AND AN
ENLIGHTENED PRESS,

THIS VOLUME

IS RESPECTFULLY DEDICATED

BY

THEIR FELLOW CITIZEN,

GEO. W. HILL.

ASHLAND, O., April 10, 1876.

CONTENTS.

HISTORICAL.

GENERAL HISTORY.

CHAPTER.	PAGE.
I.—Pre-historic History	9
II.—The Stone Era	10
III.—Ashland City—Earthworks, the extent and probable origin	12
IV.—The Eries, or the Cat Nation	17
V.—The Wyandots	19
VI.—The Ottawas	20
VII.—The Mohegans	22
VIII.—The Mingo villages of the Mohican	24
IX.—Major Rogers on the soil of Ashland County	27
X.—The Moravians	28
XI.—Crawford's Expedition	31
XII.—The legend of Helltown	34
XIII.—Indian Trails	35
XIV.—Indian Customs	36
XV.—Indian Characteristics	38
XVI.—Indian Navigation and Theology	41
XVII.—Treaties and Surveys	43
XVIII.—The Survey—An adventure	45
XIX.—The erection of Fairfield County	49
XX.—Pioneer History	50
XXI.—The War of 1812	53
XXII.—Occurrences during the War	55
XXIII.—The Settlers take Refuge in Block-houses	58
XXIV.—Military Expeditions	61
XXV.—Victory brings joy	63
XXVI.—Organization of Wayne and Richland Counties	65
XXVII.—After the War of 1812	68
XXVIII—Township Organization	71
XXIX.—Early Grist-mills	73
XXX.—The Villages and Towns of Ashland County	76
XXXI.—Education and Institutions of Learning	79
XXXII.—Religious Societies and Churches	83
XXXIII.—The Pioneers of the year 1825	94
XXXIV.—The erection of Ashland County	98
XXXV.—The Militia and Soldiers of 1812	100
XXXVI.—Ashland County in the War of 1861-5	102
XXXVII.—Newspapers, Benevolent Societies and Banks	114
XXXVIII.—Statistics	116
XXXIX.—Medicine and Law	118
XL.—The County Officers from 1846 to 1880	122
XLI.—A list of the Justices of the Peace	124

BIOGRAPHICAL.

	PAGE.
Armstrong, Captain	130
Armstrong, Dr. Harrison	170
Armstrong, Dr. David	171
Andrews, James	203
Andrews, Alanson	205
Andrews, Lorin, LL. D.	208
Armentrout, Abraham	237
Alberson, James	254
Andrews, Mrs. Sarah H.	263
Alberson, W. T.	265
Beall, General Reason	142
Bird, Sparks	152
Bailey, Abel	154
Bryte, David	154
Bryte, John	155
Burns, Hugh	156
Beach, Daniel	178
Bowerice, George W.	180
Bushnell, Sterling G., sr.	191
Bull, Hon. George W.	207
Beer, Rev. Thomas	221
Brothers, Henry	224
Bishop, John	229
Berry, Col. John	249
Berry, Jacob	249
Burgan, Laban	251
Beer, William	254
Beer, Richard	254
Beer, Captain Robert	255
Brubaker, Peter	258
Burns, Peter	260
Bechtel, Joseph	262
Beer, Hon. Thomas	380
Bull Family	383
Coulters, The	146
Chandler, Joseph	148
Carter, Daniel, sr.	149
Chandler, Robert F.	151
Carter, Daniel, jr.	159
Cliff, Dr. Joseph	167
Clark, Dr. P. H.	170
Clark, Dr. Bela B.	170
Clark, Dr. W. R. S.	170
Crane, Dr. Isaac L.	171
Chase, Hon. James E.	173
Charles, John	175
Copus, Wesley	177
Coffin, Frederick W.	177
Carver, Aldrich	179
Carter, Norman	180
Clark, Nathaniel	181
Curry, George W.	183
Chapman, John	183
Culler, Michael	203
Chamberlain, Jesse	214
Cole, Thomas, sr.	223
Cory, John	230
Carr, John, sr.	231
Clark, James	231
Crouse, Jacob	234
Church, Henry	237
Crall, Jacob	238
Campbell, Arthur, jr.	239
Cordell, Samuel	257
Culberson, Robert	259
Campbell, James	380
Dowdee, Billy	153
Deming, Dr. William N.	169

CONTENTS.

Name	Page
Davidson, Dr.	169
Doty, James	174
Dougherty, Hon. John	176
Dunlap, Thomas	181
Doty, Abraham	219
Davis, Hugh	222
Donley, John	255
Donley, Thomas	255
Davis, Isaac	257
Eagle, William and Thomas	145
Elliott, Patrick	182
Emerson, Rev. R. D.	215
Emerson, William A. G.	217
Fast, Christian, sr.	133
Foulks, George and Elizabeth	138
Finley, Alexander	143
Ford, Elias	164
Fuller, Dr. Ephraim B.	167
Fulkerson, Major R. P.	172
Ferris, Abraham	180
Frees, Jacob	213
Frazee, William C.	227
Fast, William	251
Fluke, Henry	261
Fast, Jacob	383
Greenlee, John	150
Gates, Isaac	159
Greenlee, William	162
Glass, Dr. Samuel	171
Grubb, Jacob H.	173
Grinold, James	180
Gallup, Josiah	197
Graham, Francis	206
Gibson, Jacob	243
Graham Francis	250
Harvuot, Joseph	160
Hiffner, Jacob, sr.	164
Hildreth, Dr. Joseph	168
Huff, Peter	177
Haskell, Nathaniel	178
Huffman, Abraham	197
Hamilton, William	206
Helbert, Jacob	219
Hughes, Rev. William	220
Heltman, William G.	380
Hill, Dr. George W.	between 126 and 127
Ilgor, William W.	245
Ingmand, Luke	252
Ingmand, Judge Edmund	252
Jerome, Baptiste	127
Jonacake, Solomon	129
Jennings, Jacob O.	238
Jones, Judge John D.	380
Kinnaman, Dr. Jacob B.	171
Kilgore, James	232
Lyons, Thomas	130
Lucas, Jacob	164
Luther, Dr. Joel	167
Lambright, John	176
Latta, William	212
Latta, Moses	213
Luther, Hulbert	222
Link, Adam	228
Leidigh, Samuel	381
Mason, Andrew	157
Mason, Mrs. Elizabeth	157
McCarty, Dr. Oliver	172
McCutchin, Joseph	181
Murray, Patrick	198
Markley, Joseph	199
Metcalf, Vachel	199
McConnell, John	204
McGuires, The	211
Metcalf, Edward	212
Metcalf, Thomas	212
Mason, Martin, sr.	214
Moody, Rev. Samuel	216
Mercers, The	226
Markel, Solomon	226
McCombs, John H.	240
Mansfield, Martin Henry	244
Myers, Michael	246
Morr, Michael	261
McClain, John	261
McConnell, John	382
Newman, Andrew	166
Newell, Robert	173
Nelson, Robert	202
Nelson, John S.	213
Oliver, Lewis	160
Oesterlen, Dr. Gustavus	169
Oliver, Allen	183
Osborn, Judge William	203
Offineer, James A.	383
Priest, James Loudon	161
Paullin, Z. T.	176
Poag, James	180
Pipe, Captain	193
Porter, John	212
Parker, Rev. Joseph Seeley	215
Parmely, Sylvanus	233
Peck, Homer	236
Rice, Ebenezer	162
Roorback, Jacob	180
Richards, Samuel	181
Robertson, Samuel	182
Reed, Asa S.	214
Robinson, Rev. John, D. D.	217
Robison, John	221
Ramsey, William	224
Riddle, Michael, sr.	224
Ralstons, The	227
Ramsey, John	246
Scott, John	155
Shopbill, Jacob	166
Scott, Dr. Andrew J.	167
Slocum, Dr. Willard	169
Sutherland, Thomas Smith	178
Sturtevant, Bradford	179
Sacket, Harvey	179
Smith, Henry	181
Sprott, Thomas	187
Slocum, Elias	192
Smith, Thomas	201
Sheets, Joseph	204
Sultzer, Frederick	204
Springer, John	210
Strickland, Joseph	211
Sheets, Joseph	220
Swineford, John	222
Swineford, George	245
Smith, James W.	247
Summers, Daniel	247
Stull, Isaac	249
Sprengle, Louis Jefferson	253
Smith, John	256
Smith, Mr. Samuel	256
Stentz, Peter	260
Sheller, Henry	262
Sprott, Thomas, jr.	381
Stubbs, Joseph D.	381
Slocum, General Willard	384
Thomas, Peter	158
Tannehills, The	163
Tilton, John	165
Taylor, William	165
Thomas, Josiah	176
Taylor, Mr. Enoch	219
Taylor, William, and Sons	241
Thomas, Michael	258
Urie, Colonel George W.	183
Urie, Solomon	189

	PAGE.		PAGE.
Van Arnan, Charles S.	181	Winbigler, Richard	207
Van Nest, John	214	Wallack, Eli W.	227
Van Nordstrand, Peter, sr.	225	Whitmore, Judge Daniel W.	241
Vantilburg, Daniel, sr.	246	Welch, Ephraim	246
Vance, Solomon	248	Willson, Charles	254
Williams, Abram	128	Westheffer, William	258
Walker, Captain Alanson	174	Young, Jacob	235
Weston, Roswell	180		

TOWNSHIP SKETCHES.

	PAGE.		PAGE.
Green	273	Jackson	338
Lake	284	Orange	341
Hanover	291	Milton	348
Vermillion	299	Sullivan	353
Clearcreek	310	Mohican	356
Mifflin	315	Montgomery	364
Perry	323	Ruggles	379
Troy	336		

ILLUSTRATIONS.

	PAGE.		PAGE.
"Appleseed Johnny," portrait	facing 184	Smith, J. W., portrait	facing 247
Brubaker, J., portrait	facing 364	Sprott, Thomas, portrait	facing 381
Culler Michael, portrait	between 202, 203	Thomas, Josiah and wife, portraits, with biography	facing 176
Culler, Barbara, portrait	between 202, 203	Urie, G. W., portrait, with biography	facing 189
Culler, John P., portrait	between 206, 207	Welch, Jane, residence and portraits	facing 273
Culler, Samuel, portrait	between 206, 207	Priest stockade, 1812	facing 55
Carter, David, portrait, with biography	facing 149	The attack on the Copus cabin by Indians, morning of September 15, 1812	facing 56
Donley, John and wife, portrait	facing 254		
Fluke Family, portraits	between 260, 261	Blockhouse at Jeromeville, 1812	facing 60
Hill, Dr. George W., portrait (steel), with biography	between 126, 127	The Zimmer cabin, 1812	facing 55
McCombs, J. H., portrait, with biography	facing 230	Indian village of Greentown, 1812	facing 34
Markel, I. F., portrait, with biography	facing 326		

PREFACE.

There seems to be a general desire among the people of this county to investigate and become conversant with its local history. To this end I have attempted to rescue from oblivion memorials of unpublished facts, reminiscences, personal adventures and traditions, and particularly the memory of the primitive days of our fathers, their frontier life, privations and struggles in the forests of the valleys of Mohican.

In the preparation of this volume I have encountered many embarrassments. The thoughtless destruction of township pioneer records, the conflicting statements of the living, and the tendency to embellish, on the part of many, made it exceedingly difficult to reconcile dates and narrations. Determined to arrive at the truth, and at the same time let the follies of the dead sleep, I have discarded, as far as possible, all doubtful statements.

The temptation to exaggerate, round up and adorn personal adventure and family history, is such that the larger part of the world, if we are to judge from an heroic standpoint, descended directly from the gods. The love of parents and ancestry is a laudable trait; and if all the children of the pioneers demonstrate their veneration for the past by transmitting unstained histories to their descendants, a great and noble work will have been achieved—worthy of all admiration and imitation.

The major part of this volume is derived from pioneer and border history, public documents, private records and living witnesses, who still linger among us. The task of compiling their narrations has been difficult and protracted. I have aimed to obtain the truth in all things, without prevarication or bias; and am happy to have met and interviewed so many aged gentlemen and their wives, before they have taken their final departure, to dwell no more amongst us.

In the biographical department I have been assisted by the friends of the parties—by family records, and the traditions of their associates. This department is rich in personal adventure, border experiences and captivities. Many thrilling incidents are preserved, that in a few years "would have slept the sleep that knows no waking." These adventures have never been published, and I believe it a work of merit to present them to the public that they may be treasured in our libraries.

As most of the streams of this county have derived their names from the tribes once dwelling upon their banks, I take especial pride in giving very full sketches of the leading chiefs and hunters of the *Mohegans*, *Delawares* and *Mingoes*, as well as some account of the *Eries*, *Wyandots* and *Ottawas*, who preceded them in the occupancy of these beautiful valleys from one to two hundred years. Their names will be familiar to the early settlers.

Let us preserve these memories while we may. Ere long the last of the pioneers will be garnered by the relentless reaper. Even now they are departing almost weekly, and soon the village bell will have tolled the knell of the last tottering frontiersman. The red man that met and welcomed him to these fertile valleys, has long since gone to the great hunting-ground, or now roams, old and feeble, towards the setting sun. While meditating upon these changes, I sometimes feel like exclaiming with Omar, the Tent Maker:

> The worldly hope men set their hearts upon
> Turns ashes—or it prospers; and anon
>   Like snow upon the desert's dusty face
> Lighting a little hour or two, was gone.
>
> Think, in this batter'd caravansera
> Whose portals are alternate night and day,
>   How sultan after sultan with his pomp
> Abode his destined hour, and went his way.
>
> They say the Lion and the Lizard keep
> The courts where Jamshid gloried and drank deep;
>   And Bahram, that great hunter—the Wild Ass
> Stamps o'er his head, but cannot break his sleep!
>
> I sometimes think that never blows so red
> The Rose, as where some buried Cæsar bled;
>   That every Hyacinth the Garden wears
> Dropt in its lap from some once lovely head!
>
> And this reviving herb, whose tender green
> Hedges the river-lip on which we lean:
>   Ah! lean upon it lightly, for who knows
> From what once lovely lip it springs unseen!
>
> Ah! my beloved! fill the cup that clears
> To-day of past regret and future fears!
>   *To-morrow?* Why, to-morrow I may be
> Myself with yesterday's seven thousand years!

Grateful acknowledgments are due to the many friends who have furnished information concerning the early settlement of this county. Of these are Alexander and Miss Rosella Rice, of Green; John Greenlee, of Lake; Major Ben. Tyler, of Mohican; Joseph Chandler, of Perry; Jacob Fast, of Jackson; William Fast, of Orange; Colonel George W. Urie, Daniel Carter, jr., Andrew Mason, Isaac Stull, and Rev. John Robinson, D. D., of Montgomery; Thomas Bushnell, W. W. Scott and W. O. Porter, of Vermillion; Lewis Oliver and Rev. William Hughes, of Green; Colonel John W. Bull and Dr. A. J. Scott, of Loudonville; Daniel Hoover, Wesley Copus, and Mrs. Sarah Vail, of Mifflin; John Nelson, Hugh Burns, and Mrs. Thomas Smith, of Milton; John Bryte, Hugh Elliott, and Miss Huffman, of Clearcreek; Daniel Beach and James Grinald, of Ruggles; Charles Vanoonam and Henry Summers, of Troy; James Dunlap, Hamilton Porter, and Mrs. Parmely Mann, of Sullivan.

I am also indebted to General L. V. Bierce, of Akron; Colonel Charles Whittlesey, of Cleveland; Hon. Andrew H. Byers, of Wooster; Isaac Smucker, of Newark; Colonel George C. Johnson, of Piqua; General R. Brinkerhoff and Dr. William Bushnell, of Mansfield; Dr. James P. Henderson, of Newville; General Leslie Combs, of Kentucky; Hon. William Walker, of Kansas; Mr. Harbaugh, former, and H. H. Robinson, present, State librarian, for valuable aid and encouragement.

In preparing the historical narration, I consulted Bancroft's History of the United States; Western Annals, by James H. Perkins; Henry Howe's Virginia; Sherman Day's Pennsylvania; Schoolcraft's Indian Tribes; Conspiracy of Pontiac; Stone's Life of Brandt; Heckewelder's Indian Missions; Colden's Five Nations; Loshiel's Missions; Finley's Missions; Taylor's History of Ohio; Brown's History of the War of 1812; McAfee's History of the War of 1812; Bosman's Maryland; Price's Fort Wayne, and numerous other volumes, deemed authentic.

With these statements and acknowledgments, this volume is respectfully submitted to the public.

May, 1876. G. W. H.

Publishers' Notice.

We are enabled to place this volume in the hands of its readers much sooner than was anticipated at the time when we concluded to undertake its publication. The people of Ashland county have seemed averse to pictorial representations of themselves or their homes in this history of their county, and as we have consequently had very little engraving to do for the book, we have been able to do it quickly.

Although we have published, we think, every line of manuscript which the author has furnished us, the volume does not embrace as many printed pages as the author and publisher at the outset estimated the narrative would make. However, the history as given, is complete, and embraces a detailed and thorough record of the events comprising the history of Ashland county. The publishers have never issued a volume so rich in biographical history. The author has seemingly omitted no citizen or pioneer settler of the county in his treatment of this department of the work.

We believe a book so valuable, so replete with historic lore, prepared with so much skill, labor and painstaking, and withal so complete and authentic a record, will be most acceptable to the people of Ashland county. The author has executed his task faithfully and well, and if his important work be not fully appreciated now by his fellow-citizens of Ashland county, he can rest assured that the memory thereof will be gratefully treasured in the hearts of a generation yet unborn.

As publishers, we have endeavored to consummate our part of the undertaking conscientiously, and trust this verdict will be accorded us by those who are to be our judges.

WILLIAMS BROTHERS,
Publishers.

Cleveland, Ohio, September 21, 1880.

HISTORY OF ASHLAND COUNTY, OHIO.

CHAPTER I.

PRE-HISTORIC HISTORY.

A Definition of History.—Speculative and Proper.—Some Conjectures Upon the Pre-Historic Races of Northern Ohio.—Their Strongholds. —Their Numbers.—Their Contact with other Warlike People.

HISTORY is defined to be a narration of past and present events in relation to peoples, nations and empires. It is of two classes—speculative and proper. By speculative history is meant such theories as are derived from deduction or inference. For instance, there was what is denominated the "Stone age or period," in the history of the human race. We infer this from the fragments of their rude arts found in almost every country on the globe. We have no means of learning from whence that people came, how long they existed, and under what circumstances they disappeared, and by whom they were succeeded.

Again, by deduction, we may trace the occupation and temper of extinct races by their monuments, their military defences, and their systems of internal improvements.

The historian is largely dependent upon this species of conjecture for an outline of the pre-historic periods of this country. The monuments found in South America, in Mexico, and along the valleys of the Mississippi, the Ohio, and other rivers of the United States, throw much light upon the character and occupations of the early races that inhabited those regions.

In North America, the Mound Builders, so called, seem to have had possession of a number of very strong positions, from which their settlements radiated in all directions. The most prominent establishment of that race was undoubtedly in the valleys of Mexico, from which they gradually diffused themselves over Texas, New Mexico, and the valleys of the Mississippi, the Missouri, the Red river, the Ohio, the Muskingum, and their tributaries, as well as the Susquehanna, the Potomac, the Chesapeake bay and the Hudson, forming, at all strong points, vast settlements and cities defended by earthworks.

In Mexico, Central and South America, the Mound Builders must have shown a wonderful degree of proficiency in the arts of civilization. Great cities, containing, perhaps, hundreds of thousands of people, existed; and when the Spanish conquered that region over three hundred years ago, the population of those countries was quite dense; and the ancient sites of their cities are still to be seen. Their monuments, military defences, and temples erected to the "Sun;" and their culture of the soil, and researches in the finer metals, evince the fact, that they were as a people, immense in numbers, as well far advanced in the arts of civilized life.

A distinguished and reliable Spanish historian, who accompanied the expedition of Cortez, named Bernard de Sahagua, says at that time a tradition existed among the natives of Florida, that a foreign colony had arrived on their shores more than two thousand years before, and proceeded across the Gulf of Mexico and landed in Yucatan, where they founded cities, now in ruins, the greatest of which had been destroyed over a thousand years before the arrival of the Spanish expedition. When the Spanish subdued Mexico, Montezuma re-asserted that tradition by assuring Cortez, the Spanish general, that the ancestors of the Mexican race came from the rising sun.

That the ancestors of the Mound Builders were of Asiatic origin, scarcely admits of a doubt. In Yucatan, the remains of civilization are Egyptian and Assyrian in character, and seem to have been erected prior to the arrival of the Incas and the Aztecs of the line of the Montezumas. The principal deity of Peru was said to have been called Chon, the same in name as the deity of the ancient Phœnicians, who was called Baal-Chon, or Saturn. Query: Were the Mound Builders the actual descendants of the ancient Phœnicians, or was the similarity in the names of their deities accidental?

Traveling further north into the Valley of Mexico, the temples and pyramids are more strikingly Egyptian and Assyrian. The great pyramid at Cholula was evidently a copy of those along the Nile, and dedicated to the same deity worshipped in the East. Can it be said, also, that the pyramidal system of both hemispheres is accidental, like the name of the deities worshipped in both? Or, have we here evidence that at some period in the history of the world, intercourse between the eastern and western continents must have been frequent?

The next stronghold of the Mound Builders in their march northward, was opposite St. Louis, Missouri, where a group of pyramids was erected and which seems to have been the capital of a great empire, like the city of Mexico. From this point they slowly advanced up the Mississippi, the Ohio, the Muskingum, the Scioto and the Wabash, continuing their settlements and constructing mounds and immense earthworks for defence. In the valleys of the Scioto, the Muskingum and the Licking the most of these ancient intrenchments are found, within the limits of Ohio. West of Newark, in Licking county, are found two circular entrenchments of considerable extent. Half a mile west of that city is found the most curious, enclosing thirty acres of ground, and surrounded by another entrenchment, which has been almost obliterated by plowing. Some three miles west of that point is another system of earthworks enclosing three times as much ground, in circular form, and having a number of gateways. These works must have been the seat of a large population; for their construction would require the united efforts of a great number of people for many years.

From that point their settlements seem to have radiated northward through Knox, into the river portions of Holmes, to Richland, up the Black fork to the south parts of Wayne and Ashland counties, and thence to the lake shore.

The migration of that strange people was undoubtedly resisted by another powerful race, composed of nomadic tribes having some sort of government; for the erection of the earthwork defences, found all along their course from Mexico northward, conclusively show that they were met at every point by a warlike people, who had prior claims to the soil. This would furnish occasion for the erection of the earthworks as a place of retreat and safety from the incursions of an enemy, as well as a place to pay their devotions to their deities. The small mounds found in the neighborhood of these extended entrenchments may have been used as so many signal sites to announce the approach of an enemy.

These grand central points must have held for a long series of years, and been cultivated by the inhabitants with great success; for the lands are composed of the richest soils, and by culture, yield large crops.

Many of the rude implements of warfare used by that people have been found scattered all over northern Ohio; and are exhibited in the cabinets of the antiquarians and are really curious and ingenious in workmanship. Evidence of the existence of a race somewhat advanced in the arts of military defence, anterior to the appearance of the Caucasian, is found in almost every part of this county. Mounds and intrenchments at all the great valleys and commanding points are very numerous. The principal streams along which the earthworks are found are the Muddy, the Jerome, the Black and Clear forks of the Mohican.

CHAPTER II.

THE STONE ERA.

The Period of Stone Axes, Fleshers and Arrow Points, Etc.—By whom made.—Skill and Patience shown in their Manufacture.—Their use for Domestic as well as for Warlike Purposes.—Others for Ornament only.—Implements Found in Ashland County.—By whom Constructed and for what Purposes Used.

THE archæologist is furnished a wide field in Ohio. Almost every county in the State abounds in evidence of the former presence of an extinct race. The question as to when the Mound Builders took possession of North America, how long they flourished, and under what circumstances they disappeared, is unsettled. It is equally uncertain whether the presence of that race constituted the "Stone Era," or, whether the race by whom the battle-axes, spear heads and flint darts were manufactured, preceded or succeeded the Mound Builders. The presumption, however, is, that the rude implements of warfare, such as battle-axes and flint arrow-heads, were made by the Mound Builders, or a race that was cotemporary with them. This inference gains strength from the fact that the aforesaid implements are found in and about the mounds and earthworks throughout Ohio, and other States, and must have been abundant during that period. So numerous were these implements, that in almost every section of the State they continue to be plowed up by the farmers while preparing for their crops.

The writer of this article has many rare and curious specimens of the war-like implements of the Stone age, which evince high architectural skill in their preparation. We know not, at this time, how such weapons were manufactured. The extreme hardness of the flint and granite out of which they are made, and the evident absence of all knowledge of iron and steel, will suggest to the archæologist the amount of skill and patience exercised by the race by whom they were prepared. It seems to be generally conceded that large numbers of arrow-heads, spear-heads, stone axes, and the like, were manufactured in the vicinity of the flint ridge, in Licking county, Ohio, and from thence scattered all over the State in the chase and in warlike incursions. This inference gains strength from the quantity of spalls and broken arrow-heads found in that region, as well as from the admitted identity of the material. We have certain proofs that the Indian tribes found on this continent by the early settlers and missionaries, had a knowledge of the manufacture of such implements, and may have prepared them for the chase and for war. They seem to have readily adopted them for hunting purposes, using them as arrows, with elastic bows and raw-hide thongs, in their incursions against each other.

The Ohio Indians undoubtedly manufactured stone axes, stone knives and arrow-heads of flint, before the French and English introduced fire-arms, and perhaps long since.

The remarkable resemblance between the stone axes, spear heads, arrow points, stone wedges, stone images and the like, found on this continent, and those found in Europe and Asia, would suggest a like origin and age. Mr. Evans, an able English archæologist, enters into a full discussion of the implement manufactured during the Stone age in England, Ireland, and Scotland, from the hard and unmanageable rock known as flint. In his work the important suggestion is thrown out that they were not used for the purposes of warfare alone, but for purposes of husbandry, the chase, domestic use, and personal ornament; and that they worked up the materials found in these plains and valleys, consisting of flint and granite. He cites the fact that the Celts manufactured, from flint, implements for felling trees, hewing canoes, hoes, harrows, scrapers for preparing skins, arrow points for shooting birds and other small game, knives, gouges, saws, pounding-stones, chisels, hammer-axes, picks, and instruments for grinding stones and dressing their flint arrows. He also says that rings, amulets, spindle-whorls, pestles, needles of bone, drilled by flint, were found in caves.

A large number of the implements mentioned seem to be of little use further than ornament, because of their fragile structure. They are, he says, exquisitely polished and ground, and evince a wonderful degree of useless toil, if they were designed for warfare. Neither could they have been available for hard work, such as cutting down trees or working timber, for they do not exhibit any sign of fracture or even of scratching, which would not be the case if they had been used for cutting, as tools or weapons. He further declares that many of these implements are made of Asiatic stones of beautiful colors and capable of taking high polish. To students in archæology, this suggestion will furnish a strong argument in favor of the eastern origin of the Stone age, for it is improbable that the human race appeared simultaneously on the eastern and western continents. That the course of the nations of that era was from India into Asia, Europe and North and South America, is as well settled as any hypothetical problem can be. This is again suggestive of the origin of the primitive races of this continent. That there must have been some connection between Asia and North America admits of scarcely a doubt.

STONE IMPLEMENTS.

Several classes of implements are found, in great numbers, within this county. They seem to have been scattered broadcast over the hills and valleys. One class consists of highly polished stone pestles, stone axes, weighing from six or eight ounces to five or six pounds—stone fleshers, stone implements pick-shaped, with a neatly drilled hole in the middle, stone beads, and flat, variagated stones, from one to two inches wide, six or seven long, and half an inch thick, with rounded ends, highly polished, and generally with a neatly drilled hole in the center, have been found in and about these ancient works.

Another class of more recent date, consists of thousands of flint arrow-heads from a half to seven inches in length. These were unquestionably made by the modern tribes that overspread northern Ohio, and most of the material was procured from the ridges in Licking county. One such nest was plowed up in Sullivan township, three years since, by Mr. S. W. Riggs, containing two hundred and one pear-shaped arrow-heads, neatly finished and of an unsual style, having no notch for fastening them to the shaft, and had the appearance of being intended for cutting.

It is claimed that the polished stone implements were used by an earlier race than the *Eries*. It will be difficult to substantiate that assertion. It is not certain that the *Eries* ever saw European arms, and they undoubtedly never used them. It is equally certain they occupied an advanced position in the art of self defence, and like the civilized races, began to gather into fortified towns. It is reasonable, then, to suppose they were equally skilled in preparing arms for the defence of their country. The stone axe would be easy of construction. The flesher would follow in the preparation of their clothing, which consisted of dressed skins. The polished stones were doubtless used for ornamental purposes, as were the beads and other stone badges.

In a treaty at Lancaster, Pennsylvania, held June 26, 1644, Canassatego, a distinguished Iroquois chief, said;

"Indeed, we have some small differences with the English, and during these, some of their young men would, by way of reproach, be telling us, that we should have perished, if they had not come into the country, and furnished us with strowds (shawls) and hatchets and guns, and other things necessary for the support of life ; but we always gave them to understand, that they were mistaken, that we lived before they came amongst us, and as well, or better, if we may believe what our forefathers have told us. We then had room enough, and plenty of deer, which were easily caught; and though we had not knives, hatchets, or guns, such as we have now, yet we had knives of stone, and hatchets of stone, and bows and arrows. and these served our uses as well then, as the English ones do now." *

There can be no doubt as to the fact that the *Iroquois, Eries, Delawares*, and other tribes, continued to manufacture stone axes, fleshers, hammers, war-clubs, headed with stone, and arrow-heads, until, and even after, English arms were introduced. The *Creeks* and *Blackfeet*, of Red river, Canada, still continue to manufacture very beautiful stone axes and fleshers.

If these works were constructed by a more ancient race, the growth of forests proves nothing, unless it may be, that all the timber of these valleys was destroyed by the Mound Builders; for the trees found in and upon these fortifications, were of the same size and character as those of the surrounding forest. Two hundred and seventy-five or three hundred years would be a sufficient length of time for the growth of the trees found in and upon these works. These fortified places, and polished implements, may have been constructed by the *Eries*, then, to protect their people from sudden invasion by the *Iroquois*, while cultivating the soil; for that nation must have been too numerous to depend alone upon the chase.

If done by an earlier race, the swarms of red men, of Tartar descent, who passed Behring's Straits, and poured down the shores of our northern chain of lakes, may have compelled their erection, as a means of defence, until their occupants were driven south, or exterminated, by the wild, nomadic tribes, who overran and, subsequently, occupied, all northern Ohio.

It has been urged that the red races did not possess

* See Colden's "Five Nations," second part, page 105.

tools or implements to erect such stockades. It is true we are unable to designate the manner of their construction. That proves nothing. An examination of the most extended railroad track and embankment in Ohio, might not lead to the discovery of a single plow, shovel, mattock, cart, horse, or wheelbarrow. Still the fact would exist, that all these were employed in the construction of our railways. If the aborigines used wooden, flint, or stone shovels, bark buckets, or copper tools, in erecting their stockade, they probably carried them away. The races that lived and flourished, and contended for their soil and homes, had passed away years before the Caucasian discovered the western world. Their deeds of heroism disappeared with them, and no Homer, Virgil, or native bard, sung or related their achievments.

They were followed by the fierce and untamed red men, who still linger in the far west. They, too, are passing away. The light canoe of the *Wyandot*, the *Mohegan*, and the *Delaware*, are no more seen upon our waters. They are remembered only by the most aged of the white race. Armstrong, and Pipe, Lyons, and Johnnycake, have long since gone to the great hunting-ground, and their descendants have found homes on the headwaters of the distant Missouri.

As we have seen in the history of the Mound Builders strong indications of Asiatic civilization, so in the striking resemblance of the stone implements found in the East and West, we discover other links of the great chain that connected the races of America, Europe and Asia, as well as another evidence that man progressed westward as the populations of the earth pushed him forward in pursuit of a new home and enterprises. How long the people of the "Stone age," may have inhabited this continent, will doubtless ever remain an unsolved problem. To continue such an inquiry would be like the toil of dropping buckets in empty wells, and growing old in drawing nothing up; for the aboriginal races, found here by our fathers knew nothing of their ancestors worth preservation. We know that such a people existed along the streams, and upon the uplands of this county, because stone images, implements of warfare, battle-axes, arrow-heads, and the like, are yet found in our fields and in the forests. The presence of these rude images is conclusive that the primitive races inhabiting this region venerated objects of idolatry. A year or two since, an image, cut from granite, representing a sort of ape, was plowed up on Honey creek in this county, by a farmer! Query:—Did the people of the "Stone age," venerate the ape like those surrounding the sacred groves of Benares? Did they pay devotions to idols, or is this simply a rude representation of a household pet? We have no evidence that the Indian tribes of Ohio were ever idolaters. Their history shows that they had very correct conceptions of a Supreme Being, or Great Spirit, from whom they derived life, happiness and prosperity. Idolatry came from the east. In the early ages, in the East, almost every object in nature was invested with divine power, and was inovked by the ignorant devotee. Were these images brought to this continent as household gods by the Mound Builders or their successors? It seems useless to speculate upon the subject. No ray of history has, as yet, penetrated the gloom of that era, and we will have to content ourselves with believing that such a people once roamed over the hills and through the valleys and along the streams of this county.

CHAPTER III.

ASHLAND COUNTY EARTHWORKS.

A Description of the Forts.—Tyler's Fort.—Ramsey's Fort.—Metcalf's Fort.—Winbigler's Fort.—The Glenn Fort.—Gamble's Fort.—Sprott's Hill.—Bryte's Fort.—Stoner's Fort.—Shambaugh's Fort.—The Parr Fort.—Darling's Fort.—The Origin of the Works.

TYLER'S FORT.

On section twenty-four, now in Wayne county, a short distance below the junction, upon the heights northeast of Tylertown, and east of the stream, is an ancient intrenchment. It overlooks the valley, which here is about one and a half miles wide, and gives an extended view, up and down the Mohican. The work is situated on an elevated spur of the ridge, on the lands of Benjamin Tyler; is circular in form, and contains about three acres. When Mr. Tyler located in 1814, he found the work destitute of grown timber. The ridge, in and about the intrenchment, had the appearance of having been often burned over. He found the embankment about four feet high, and about ten feet in diameter, at the base, and completely covered with hazel-brush, about as high as his head. He states, that he stood in the center of the work, and could overlook the Mohican valley for many miles. The work is now covered by a growt' thrifty young white oak, ranging from fifty to seventy feet in height, and ten to fifteen inches in diameter. Unlike most of the earthworks of this county, there was no spring in its immediate vicinity. From the center of the work, a grand view of the Mohican valley, for many miles dotted with fertile farms, may be had. The work was evidently one of defence, and was calculated to repel a large force, as access to it, from every side, was up a declivity.

RAMSEY'S FORT.

Ascending the Muddy fork, about fifteen miles, we find another intrenchment upon the lands of John Ramsey, on the southwest quarter of section twenty-eight, in Jackson township. The valley of the stream, the entire distance, is very fertile and was once a favorite resort of the *Delawares*. This work is situated on the western side of an elevated ridge, overlooking the valley. The eastern line of the entrenchment reaches the summit facing the valley. The work is quadrangular, and estimated to contain a fraction over two acres. When first discovered, the embankment was about three feet in height, and from eight to ten in diameter at the base. The timber within the fort was equal in size to that of the forest around it, and was of the same character. The area of the fort has been cultivated about twenty-five years, and the embankment is nearly obliterated by the plow. While plowing within the fort, a highly polished stone, five inches long, two inches at the base, and one and one-half inches at the point, encircled in the middle by a groove, was found. The implement is known as the stone hammer. The ravines in the vicinity contained water sufficient to supply the wants of the fort if beleagured by an enemy.

Two mounds were found in the north part of Perry township, about one mile from the fort. They were about thirty feet apart, and occupied level ground near a brook. The larger one was about five feet high, and twenty-five feet in diameter, at the base. The smaller one was probably twelve feet in diameter, at the base, and three and a half feet high. William Hamilton extirpated the larger one in digging a cellar; and about four feet below the natural surface found a triangular wooden post, and three human skeletons, one of unusual size, embedded in sand. On exposure the smaller ones dissolved. He also found a highly polished stone, six inches long, one and a half inches wide, and half an inch in thickness, rounded at the ends. It was converted into a whetstone by a German of the vicinity.

METCALF'S FORT.

By returning to the Jerome fork, and ascending that stream about one and a half miles, we approach a fort on the lands of the late William Metcalf, south of the stream, on an elevated plateau, facing the valley on section twenty-one. It was circular in form and contained about three acres. It was near a spring. When first discovered in the forest, in 1812, the embankments were about four feet in height, and the base about ten feet in diameter. Large trees grew in and upon the work. It commanded an extensive view. The fort at Tyler's, some four miles down the stream, could be easily seen by the naked eye. By the means of assault probably used by the race that then inhabited these valleys, it would have been difficult to capture it.

WINBIGLER'S FORT.

On an elevated point, two and a half miles north, and across the Jerome fork, was another fort on the lands of Henry Winbigler, on the northeast quarter of section nine. It contained about four acres of land, was circular in form, and was much more defensive than Metcalf's, because the ground around it was steep and more difficult of ascent. The embankments were also somewhat higher than the former work, and ten feet thick at the base. When first discovered it was covered with large timber—a sort of ridge oak, of slow growth, and must have been abandoned for a long series of years. It had a gate-way looking to the north and one to the south, and was near an excellent spring. From this fort a good view of Metcalf's was had. By the use of torches or other signals, the Tyler fort could have been alarmed at the same time. Nearly due west of this fort, on section thirteen, in Vermillion township, is a large mound which was used as a burial site by the *Mohegans* and *Delawares;* but was, doubtless, erected as a signal point by the same race that constructed the forts. West of it, about four miles, on section fourteen, and near the town of Hayesville, is another large mound, at the head of the valley reaching the Mohican. It was also most likely used as a signal point.

THE GLENN FORT.

About one and a half miles nearly east of the Winbigler fort, on an elevated plateau, is found, near the center of section eleven, a square fort, the north side being two hundred and thirty-six feet long, the east side one hundred and ninety-five, the south two hundred and six, and the west one hundred and thirty-nine feet. The north side is thirty-six feet greater than the south, and the east fifty-six feet greater than the west side, so that the square is rather oblong. There is a gate-way at the northwest corner, fifteen feet wide, with a guard or embankment extending out about thirty-five feet, which terminates in a small mound, probably the post of a sentinel. A wing about ninety feet long extends from the northeast corner, and one one hundred and fifty feet long, from the southeast corner. There is a mound a few rods southwest of the center of the work, thirty-one feet in diameter and about three and a half feet in height. This work overlooks the Tyler, Metcalf, and Winbigler forts, and gives a good view of the valley for many miles. A number of stone and flint instruments have been found in the vicinity of this work. Mr. J. N. Glenn, jr., has made, also, a curious collection of fragments of ancient pottery found in the vicinity of the fort, resembling those relics excavated from the mounds of central Ohio. In plowing he has also found many ingeniously constructed pot-holes, sufficiently large to contain eight or ten gallons of water, neatly paved with small bowlders, much burned and roasted. This may have been the work of modern tribes, but the earthworks evidently belonged to another race.

GAMBLE'S FORT.

Continuing up the Jerome fork, which rises in the summit, in the north center of the county, is found a beautiful valley, from three to six miles wide, through which that stream meanders, fed by numerous smaller ones, on either side. As we approach Ashland, an elevated point of land, on the north of the town, on section eight, southwest quarter, is seen overlooking the whole surrounding country, for a distance of from four to seven miles. This work is above the town, and there is a gradual descent from it in all directions. It is a strong military position. The practical eye of the engineers of the ancient race that once swarmed in these valleys, selected it as a defensible position of value. A circular embankment, two thousand one hundred and forty-five feet in length, containing an area of eight and one-fourth acres, surrounded the brow of the hill. When the late Henry Gamble entered upon this land, in 1815, the fort was covered by large trees, such as were found in the forests of the neighborhood. The embankments were very nearly four feet high, in the center, and ten or eleven feet wide at the base. The work must have required a considerable body of men a long time to construct it. It had a gate-way at the southwest side, facing a deep ravine; and near the gate, a very excellent spring. In taking the dimensions of the fort, I was assisted by Colonel George W. Urie, and Major Richard P. Fulkerson, who examined the work nearly fifty years ago, when much of the large timber was standing. The New York, Pennsylvania & Ohio railway passes down the ravine just south of the fort, and the spring now supplies the water-tank. The embankments have been plowed over for nearly fifty years, and exhibit but slight traces of their outlines.

In looking down the valley some two miles, a large mound can be seen, which has recently been opened and found to contain human bones, charcoal and woody fibre, clearly evincing the presence of fire. The mound is situated on the northeast part of section nine, and is composed of sand and drift. The excavation from which it was taken, about one hundred yards away, can be plainly seen. On section three, in a northeast direction from the above mound, about a quarter of a mile distant, near a fine spring, stood another small mound, which contained human bones, a few arrow heads and one or two stone axes and fleshers. These were turned up by the plow. The site of the mound is now obliterated. Other small mounds have been found in Montgomery township, the contents being similar to the ones described. Four miles northeast of the Gamble fort, on section twenty-eight, in Orange township, is found the Norris mound, near the village of Orange. It has been examined and found to contain human bones, large quantities of red and yellow ochre, charcoal, a few shells and a pure copper needle seven inches long, with a well-tempered point. If the forest were removed this mound could be plainly seen from the fort. It was evidently a burial site. The presence of charcoal, and the oily condition of the hard-pan, ochre and sand, would suggest that vast quantities of animal oil had been used in its sacrificial ceremonies. It may have been a signal point also. Large trees grew around and upon this mound, its height being about five feet and diameter thirty. It was evidently the work of a race that preceded the red man. This locality must have been the home of a people in advance of the Indian. Many curious relics have been found within a short distance of the mound.

About thirty-five years since, while engaged in cutting a bluff, on the bank of the creek, east of the residence of the late Patrick Murray, for the purpose of improving the trail-road alluded to, a number of human skeletons were unearthed, among which was one supposed to have been over seven (?) feet high, when erect. The bones were in a good state of preservation. This giant must have loomed up among his aboriginal kinsmen like a Colossus, as he headed their war-files along the forest paths, on the margin of the streams of this county. If he wielded authority in proportion to his immense physical dimensions, he must have more than rivalled Pipe, Logan or Tecumseh. Colonel Oldshue, who discovered the remains, found no difficulty in passing the under-jaw over his face! The cranium and other bones showed, that this relic of another age must have been a man of unusual size and power.

In the year 1850, George Barrick, in digging a well for Isaac Stull, near his residence, half a mile south of the village of Orange, after having dug down about five feet below the surface, came upon an earthen vessel that would hold, perhaps, about two gallons. Before discovering this singular relic, he unfortunately stepped upon, and broke it. It was found mouth up, and resembled, in many respects, a two-gallon crock. The rim around the top was artistic, and intended to aid in lifting the vessel. It was formed of a bluish earth, and seemed to have been subjected to the influence of heat. It was ornamented, all over the exterior surface, by finely pulverized white flint, somewhat resembling rice grains, which adhered firmly to it. A short time afterwards, in plowing in a field, northwest of his house, Mr. Stull turned up a fragment of the same kind of vessel, as large as his hand.

In the fall of 1872, Harvey Roberts, residing a short distance west of the Stull farm, on an elevation, just north of the creek, while engaged in excavating for the foundation of a small building, came upon two human skeletons, some three feet beneath the surface, in a sitting posture, in a good state of preservation. These remains were undoubtedly those of *Wyandots*, who had died during their annual residence and hunting excursions along the Mohican, over sixty years ago. Another old Indian cemetery was found, on the premises of Jacob Young, about half a mile southeast of Mr. Roberts, and many of the graves, being very shallow, were exposed, in his garden, and on the bank of the creek. The most of those on the lands of Mr. Young, we believe, were buried in a horizontal position. We do not, as yet, find the precise reason for this difference. It may be, that the parties found by Mr. Roberts may have been chiefs, or members of another tribe.

SPROTT'S HILL.

On the northeast quarter of section thirty-five, in Clear Creek township, and about two and a half miles northwest of Gamble's fort, is Sprott's hill. This hill is about ninety feet high, and contains, at its base, an area of about five acres. It is composed of alluvium, mixed with gravel and rounded boulders. The top is about sixty by ninety feet, and is nearly flat. Upon this two mounds were erected, each about twenty-five feet in diameter, and four or five feet high. When Thomas Sprott settled there, some fifty years since, large trees grew upon and about these mounds, which were about thirty feet apart. From these mounds a good view of the Gamble fort and the mound at Orange can be had.

In examining the south mound some thirty years ago, Thomas Sprott and a brother came upon a sort of stone coffin, constructed of flat stones set on the edges, which contained the skeletons of some six or eight Indians, neatly cleaned and packed, in a good state of preservation. On the flat stones constituting the lid of the coffin, over a peck of red vermillion was found. These relics were replaced by Mr. Sprott.

BRYTE'S FORT

is situated about one and a half miles northwest of the Sprott mound, on section twenty-six. This work is quadrangular in shape. Its longest sides face the east and west, and are very nearly five hundred feet each in length, while the north and south ends are each about two hundred and fifty feet long, making the whole length of the embankment about fifteen hundred feet. Near the southwest corner was a gate-way leading to a very fine spring, some four or five rods distant. A deep ravine encircles the west side and the south end of the work, while there is a gradual descent from the north end and eastern side, showing that it was erected for defensive purposes. The view from the fort in all directions, is very fine, and takes in an area of four or five miles. The Orange mound and those of Sprott's hill, were plainly discernible. When Mr. John Bryte commenced to clear his farm some fifty-four years ago, he found large oak trees and other timber growing on the embankment, and often walked upon it in hunting squirrels. When he first saw it the walls were between three and four feet high, and perhaps ten or eleven wide at the base. He has been cultivating the fort for nearly fifty years, and the embankment is nearly obliterated. For defensive purposes the site was a good one. The water of the adjoining spring would supply a large army. It is situated on the summit, where the brooks divide to flow north to Lake Erie, and south to the White-woman, the Muskingum and the Ohio.

Many stone axes, fleshers, arrow-heads, polished and perforated stones, and pipes, have been found in the vicinity of the foregoing work.

STONER'S FORT.

Ashland county must have been, in pre-historic times, the home of a numerous people. From evidences to be found in many parts of the county, its people lived in large fortified villages, and from the nature of the places chosen for settlement, capable of making a vigorous defence against the attacks of a beleaguering enemy. High and commanding points were prepared. The localities are generally found at the head of valleys, at a prominent point; many of the ancient earthworks overlook a wide valley, and give a commanding view of the surrounding country. In this manner, no doubt, the inhabitants were enabled to detect the approach of an enemy and guard against sudden attacks and surprise. It is a curious question to determine by what means, or in what manner these villages were protected from attack and dispersion by the enemy. How were they fortified? The early French explorers say the ancient *Eries*, a remnant of the Mound Builders, no doubt, resided in castles or towns fortified by picket or palisade; the intrenchments were thrown up in circular or square form. This county possesses, perhaps, twelve or fifteen such works, ranging in area from two to eight acres in quantity. The remnants of these fortified places found in the forests when the first pioneers commenced to clear up the country, some seventy years since, were generally about three to five feet high in the center, and about ten feet across the base, having in many places large oak and other timber, ranging in a growth from three hundred to six hundred years. It will be easily observed that intrenchments of this kind, without pickets, would furnish no possible defence against the attacking forces of an enemy; for the red warrior could easily leap over such an earthen wall and assault the village. It is equally difficult to fix, with precision, the date of these works, and the kind of people who built them; judging from the timber and its slow growth, they may have ranged these valleys fifteen hundred years ago. It is equally difficult to determine the cause of their disappearance; they may have been succeeded by the fierce red man, or driven by force to a less rigorous climate for protection. The traditions of the Aztec race fixes their former residence in the far north, possibly in Ohio, Indiana and in Missouri, from whence they were expelled by a fiercer and more warlike race, finally finding a home in Mexico. The habits of the red man are different; they are opposed to physical exertion, and never could have been the means of fortifying great military works. They are very warlike, full of strategy, and very destructive to their enemies. The race they expelled must have been organized into a sort of government, and either by coercion or arrest employed large numbers in the erection of their stupendous earthworks in different parts of Ohio. Many of their works seem to have been erected in the absence of timber; in fact, the whole country seems to have been almost destitute of timber, from what cause we are unable to determine. The growth of our timber has largely occurred within six hundred years. Acorns planted by design or accident, on the very intrenchments of the forts, have grown into lofty oaks, three to four feet in diameter, and perhaps six hundred years old.

With these prefatory remarks, we desire to call the attention of the pioneers to an ancient earthwork or intrenchment on lands of John and David Stoner, in southeast quarter of section twenty-eight, in Milton township. Sixty-seven years ago the pioneers of Milton had their attention drawn to this work then in the forest, and nearly as when left by those who erected and occupied it. It is a few hundred yards west of Mr. Stoner's house, and is partly within a plowed field. It forms nearly a complete circle. The length of the circle is about one thousand nine hundred feet; it contains nearly eight acres of land. The east half of the circle has been plowed over for, perhaps, forty years, and is nearly obliterated. The west half of the circle can be distinctly traced, and has many trees upon it. Among these were noticed some three or four white oaks, very tall, that are over three feet in diameter, that have grown upon the embankment, that are at least six hundred years old. In the location of the work it is surrounded by ravines east, west, and northwest, possessing sufficient water for all practical uses. Early settlers state that before the removal of the forest the work was about three feet high, and nine or ten feet at the base, and may have been originally a strong stockade, and been the residence of hundreds of people. The view from the fort is very fine; it overlooks the valley of the Black fork to the west and northwest for a long distance. The locality in Richland county known as High Hill, comes clearly into view from the fort, and constitutes a striking feature of the landscape. This seems to be a continuation of the same class of works found on the farm of the late John Bryte, in Clear Creek township, and doubtless erected by the same race, for defensive purposes. Mr. John W. Fry of Ashland, accompanied me in viewing and taking the dimensions of the work, and is of the opinion that it was much more distinct when he first saw it, many years ago. From the fort we passed to land of Mr. Henry Pifer, about half a mile northwest, where we viewed the remains of an ancient mound, probably connected as a burial site, with the fort, in the valley, near the Black fork. While no bones have been reached in plowing, different strata of earth have been turned up, such as tough yellow clay, black, tough hard-pan and sand, and gravel in great abundance. By excavating eight or ten feet deep, it was discovered that large numbers of human bones may be found encased in muck, like those recently found in the John Green mound. In plowing farther south, along the Black fork, Mr. Pifer is of opinion that other burial places and excavations will came to light. It will then appear that to erect and complete such a village, with the mound to be used for burial purposes, it must have taken the joint labor of a vast number of men. To accomplish so much with the feeble means employed, it will appear that this county must have teemed with human beings long before the white man arrived.

SHAMBAUGH'S FORT.

Returning to the south end of the county we ascend the Black fork of Mohican. At the farm of Lewis Oliver, and one or two points below, were found mounds of five or six feet in height, and about thirty feet in diameter, at the base. A little southwest of Perrysville, on the road leading to Newville, on the summit, above the village, was a mound overlooking the valley, the size of the ones described.

Passing up the stream to near the old Indian village of Greentown, to the lands of Mr. John Shambaugh, on the north side of the stream, on section eighteen, we find another circular fort, containing very nearly two acres, with a gate-way looking to the west. In the center was a mound, about four feet high, which had probably been an altar or lookout. When first discovered, the embankment was about three and a half feet high, and ten wide at the base. It is difficult to conjecture for what purpose the work was constructed, as it was situated on the bottom, fully a quarter of a mile from the elevated lands on either side of the stream. A small brook flowed by it, from which, no doubt, water was obtained. Timber—such as oak, hickory and elm, grew upon and within the work, the larger trees being over three feet in diameter. The lands along the streams are very fertile; and the site of the fortification having been plowed over for half a century, the embankments are merely traceable.

THE PARR FORT.

About one mile distant from the work alluded to, on section nineteen, is found what is known as the Parr fort. It is also a circular work, the embankment, when first discovered by the pioneers, being about seven feet high, and twelve or fourteen in diameter, at the base. It enclosed an area of about three acres, and had a gateway at the west. Very near it, on the east side, stood a large mound from which copper beads and stone implements have been taken.

I am informed by Dr. J. P. Henderson, of Newville, that this mound was opened some fifty years ago. In it were found human bones, charcoal, decayed wood, a stone pipe, the stem of which was wrapped with copper wire and a copper wedge. This last produced quite a sensation at the time, as it was supposed to be gold; but on being taken to Wooster, and examined by a silversmith, it depreciated in value, and was disposed of for a mere trifle. The mound was of peculiar structure. It was built of large flat stones in a circular form, like a shot-tower, and filled up and around with earth; and was a cone in appearance. The fort was well situated, and should have made a good defence. Many stone axes, stone fleshers, and polished stone plates have been found in the vicinity of these works.

DARLING'S FORT.

About two and a half miles south of Parr's fort, near St. John's church, on the north bank of the Clear fork of the Mohican, is found another very strongly situated work. It is circular, and contains an area of nearly three acres. It had embankments from the gate on the south side (as I am informed), leading down to the bank of the stream. When first discovered, by Judge Peter Kinney and others, it was covered with large timber, and the embankment was over three feet high. It comma. a full view of the valley for many miles, and was doubtless used as a defensive work. Many very choice stone relics have been plowed up along the valley by farmers, and are now in the cabinet of Dr. James P. Henderson, of Newville. It will be seen then, that, Green township contained three defensive works, and is rich in archæological remains.

We find no other remains until we reach the village of Mifflin. On the level land, a little northwest of the village, is a large mound. The top is slightly flattened, and was, no doubt, used as a burial spot by the *Delawares*. It has not been excavated, and its contents are only a matter of conjecture. Many stone axes, stone heads, flint arrow-heads, and pick-shaped implements of stone highly finished, have been plowed up by the farmers all along the valley of the Black fork.

There are, perhaps, twenty or thirty smaller mounds scattered over the county to which my attention has not been called. The mounds of this county are invariably truncated and none exceed ten feet in height. I am inclined to the opinion that many of the smaller ones were the center of an encampment, and were erected for sacrificial purposes. Such a mound existed in the center of the council house at Greentown. The venison and bear meat, for their great feasts, was boiled in large copper kettles upon the mound. This may account for the charcoal, ashes, and charred bones so frequently found in small flat mounds. I have reason to believe, also, the tent or wigwam of the ruling chief was sometimes placed on a central mound of similar structure.

THE ORIGIN OF THE WORKS.

Two hundred and thirty years ago, when the French Jesuit missionaries, La Moyne, Father Joseph De la Roche, D'Allyon, Brebœuf, Chamount, and Sayard, were endeavoring to establish missionary stations among the *Hurons, Ottawas*, and the *Five Nations* known as the *Iroquois*, the *Eries*, a powerful nation, owned all the territory south and adjoining Lake Erie, and gave name to the lake. This nation was able, single-handed, to repel the assaults of the *Five Nations*. Its borders extended along the lake shore, from the *Senecas*, near Buffalo, to the *Miamis*, southwest of the lake, one of their fortified positions, according to Schoolcraft, being on what is now known as Kelley's Island. Like the *Hurons*, they are supposed to have occupied densely populated villages, well fortified by ditch and palisade. They owned the territory out of which the Western Reserve was erected, and many suppose the earthworks of this region were constructed by that people. When the missionaries were first permitted to enter the eastern part of their territory, they had twenty-eight villages, and twelve large towns or forts, which contained twelve thousand people and four thousand warriors. From 1634 to about 1660, a fierce and relentless war raged between the *Eries* and the *Iroquois* or *Five Nations*, in which the *Iroquois* finally triumphed and expelled the *Eries* from the country.

If it be true, as conjectured, that the *Eries* erected the earthworks of northern Ohio, it must have taken place about that period. If we take the growth of forest trees as evidence of so recent an occupation of these fortified places, it will make it tolerably certain that they were constructed by that nation. The peculiar structure of the embankments strengthens the supposition that they once contained a stockade. They are too low to have afforded protection in case of assault, and only upon the theory of having been palisades can we imagine they were used for military defence. If it be true, that two hundred and fifty years ago, as suggested by Mr. Shea, the *Hurons, Eries*, and other nations occupied fortified places, it may be reasonably inferred that the *Eries*, about the beginning of the year 1600, occupied and fortified this region.

It may be said they were destitute of implements to construct such fortifications. We know not what implements were used, or how long it took to throw up such embankments, nor the number of men employed in their construction. The earth was found *in situ*, and only had to be heaped against each side of a palisade. How the stakes were obtained for such a purpose is a matter of conjecture. The trees may have been felled, and the stakes separated in suitable lengths by fire.

CHAPTER IV.

THE ERIES OR THE CAT NATION.

The Aborigines of Northern Ohio.—Their Antiquity.—They Yield to the Encroachments of the Whites.—The Eastern and Western Tribes arrayed against each other.—The Eries.—They give their Name to the Lake North of Ohio.—Their Works and their Character as a Nation.—Vanquished by the Iroquois.—Does a Remnant of the Tribe still exist?

Two hundred years ago the territory composing the State of Ohio was unexplored by the white man. The Indian tribes were the undisputed lords of the soil, and dwelt along its rivers and streams and fertile valleys. Although the children of the forest possessed no written records, tradition assures us that their history teemed with tragic events. We have no means of determining when the red man took possession of the lake shore, and the valleys of the Miami, the Muskingum and the Ohio. That they roamed over the hills, amid the valleys, and rowed their birch canoes upon the beautiful rivers of this State, ages before the arrival of the white man in this region, is undisputed.

Upon the appearance of the European upon the eastern shores of New England, Virginia, Maryland, Delaware, New York, and New Jersey, and his attempt to take possession of the territories inhabited by the Indian tribes, jealousies and collisions soon sprang up and culminated in a fierce and bloody border war, in which many of the most powerful Indian tribes were severely chastised, and broken in strength and numbers, and finally compelled to seek new hunting-grounds in the west.

The rivalry between Great Britain and France in establishing colonies in North America, resulted in arraying the Indian tribes of the west against those of the east, and contributed to their dispersion and final extinction in many of the older States. The tribes recognized as the original proprietors of the soil on the south shores of Lake Erie, enter chiefly into a history of the territory composing Ashland county. It is generally conceded that the *Cat Nation*, or *Eries*, sometimes called in the early annals of the country, the *Kahkwahs*, were once the lords of the soil of all Northern Ohio, and inhabited this region. It is the opinion of the early Jesuit missionaries, as well as of Mr. Bancroft, that the *Cat*, or *Erie* nation suggested the name of Erie, to the beautiful lake that fringes the northern border of the State. The chief seat of their power seems to have been located near the southeastern shore of Lake Erie; while the tribe had a wide range extending from the Miami of the lake to the Allegheny in western Pennsylvania, and south to central Ohio. They do not seem to have been a war-like race, but from the strength of the tribe, constituted a sort of human wall to break the incursions of the *Sioux* and *Illinois* from the west, as well as the expeditions of the *Five Nations*, occupying northern New York and a part of northern Pennsylvania. Occupying a sort of middle ground, and being one of the most powerful tribes in the confederacy, known as the neutral nation, they excited the jealousy and revenge of the *Five Nations*, and finally fell before the victorious *Mohawks*. The details of the struggle that led to their conquest are very obscure.* The names of the leading men, and the exact strength of the nation on the battle-field, are all buried in uncertainty. We are indebted to the early Jesuit missionaries for all the information we possess concerning the *Eries*.

The Canadian shores of the lake were first visited by those self-sacrificing christian messengers, with a view of propagating the tenets of the Catholic church, and the spread of French authority among the red men of the Canadian forests. They penetrated almost every portion of that region, pushing their enterprise west to Wisconsin, over the wild prairies of Illinois, to the Mississippi, to central Ohio, along the Muskingum, the Scioto, the Miami, into the wilds of Indiana to Vincennes, as well as northern New York.

The first mention of the *Eries* is by Father Le Moyne and Claude Dablon, in 1657, who were then missionaries among the *Mohawks* and *Senecas* of northern New York, by whom it is stated that the savage tribes composing the *Five Nations* were carrying on a war of extermination against the *Eries*, bringing back great numbers of prisoners to the villages to be delivered to the flames, or adopted into the *Five Nations*. This war of extermination was continued by the savage *Mohawks*, and their confederates, until the broken and vanquished *Eries* were driven back to Kelley's Island and subjugated and their way opened to the *Miamis*, the *Illinois*, and the *Sioux*. These authorities inform us that the *Mohawks* were furnished arms and ammunition to accomplish the ruin of the *Eries* by the British colonists, in the hope of breaking French influence among the tribes of the West. The *Five Nations*, according to Schoolcraft, made war upon the neutral nation, west of them, composed probably of the *Hurons*, the *Ottawas*, a remnant of the *Alleghans*, the *Andastes* or *Kahwahs*, and the *Eries*; and, after the conquest of the *Hurons*, or *Wyandots*, then established on the borders of Lake Huron, the *Five Nations* invaded the *Andastes* and the *Eries* in 1655, and, after they had been forced westward to their stronghold on Kelley's Island, the relentless *Iroquois*, known as the *Five Nations*, followed them thence and laid siege, using their canoes as scaling ladders, and, leaping down like tigers among the defenders, butchered them without mercy.†

The greater part of the nation was involved in the massacre, and a remnant carried back with the victors and incorporated with the conquerers or consigned to the flames, a few escaping to other tribes. This misfortune befell the poor *Eries*, doubtless because they were at the head of the confederation called the neutral nation. The *Eries*, being at the head of the neutral nation were seldom engaged in war with their neighbors of the East or West; and with the *Miamis* on the west, and the *Andastes*, their kinsmen, on the east, they held sway over the larger portion of Ohio, and pursued the buffalo, the elk, the deer, and other game through our forests and over the plains undisturbed by foreign foes, until the rage of the bloody *Mohawk* marked the nation for destruction. Schoolcraft is of the opinion the *Eries* had developed the laws of civilization so far as to desire peace with the surrounding tribes, and seemed intent on making progress in the arts of civilized life. After their destruction by the *Iroquois*, it was found that their intrenchments on Kelley's Island were very strong, and of a character unlike anything found among other tribes. The intrenchments were on the southern shore of the island and were composed of two crescent shaped embankments, and seemed to be intended to inclose and defend their villages. One of them had a front of four hundred feet, and the other six hundred and fourteen feet on the rocky margin of the lake. Adjacent is a rock thirty-two by twenty-two feet on the surface, on which a great variety of figures are deeply cut. It presents the most extensive and well sculptured inscriptions of the antiquarian period found in America. The characters are pictographic and easily interpreted. If his conjectures be correct, the ancient *Eries* had made greater progress in recording their history than any of the Indian tribes found in the valleys of the Ohio and Mississippi; and their conquest by the relentless and untamed *Mohawks* is to be greatly regretted because they came nearer connecting the Indian tribes with the ancient Mound Builders than any of the tribes found within the limits of the State, by the first settlers and missionaries. In visiting the waters emptying into the Muskingum and the Ohio, we have no doubt the ancient *Eries* made Ashland county a part of the great highway leading to central Ohio. We are led to this conclusion because it was a part of their territory, and because the sides of the stream along which they must have journeyed are dotted with the relics and ruins of ancient stockades and earthworks.

In his history of the condition of the Indian tribes, part second, 86-7—he expresses the opinion that the inscriptions found on Kelley's Island allude to the occupation of that basin of the lake by the *Eries*, the coming of the *Wyandots*, of the fatal triumph of the *Iroquois*, and the flight of the people who have left their name to the lake. If such is a correct interpretation of the inscriptions, the *Eries* were not exterminated, as some suppose, by the *Iroquois;* for this record must have been placed there after the conquest. General Lewis Cass, of Michigan, concurs in this opinion, and says the Canadians term the *Shawanese* the "Cat Nation." He also expresses the opinion that the *Kickapoos* and *Catawbas* are remnants of the vanquished *Eries*. Mr. Taylor, in his history of Ohio, first part, page 520, says a people who were called *Erierions* by the *Wyandots*, and *Kahkwahs* by the *Iroquois*, may have had many other names from other tribes; and that a remnant of the nation called the "Cat" or "Eries," may still be in existence somewhere among the Indian tribes of the West.

---

*Colonel Charles Whittlesey, in a letter addressed to the author, concerning the ancient *Eries*, and their final overthrow and dispersion says:

"I have made another effort to learn more of the *Eries*, whom the *Iroquois* exterminated between 1650 and 1655. The town which was the scene of the final battle, was somewhere in the interior of Ohio, called Kointown—probably near a river—but cannot be identified."

†Mr. Schoolcraft's conjectures concerning the residence of the *Eries* on Kelley's Island are not regarded as authentic.

CHAPTER V.

THE WYANDOTS.

The Wyandots as Successors of the Eries.—Some Account of their Conquest and Expulsion from the Shores of Lake Huron by the Iroquois. Their occupancy of Michigan and Northern Ohio.

ABOUT the year 1615, while engaged in establishing missions among the Indian tribes of northern New York, Father Sigard visited the *Quatoghee* or *Wyandot* nation, then occupying the southern shores of Lake Huron. At that time they called themselves *Yendots*, but were called *Hurons* by the French, because of their location on the shores of that lake. The nation at that time consisted of five confederated tribes or clans, as follows: *Ataronch-ronons,* four villages; the *Attiquenongnahai,* three villages; the *Attignaouentan,* twelve villages; the *Ahrendah-ronons,* three villages; and the *Tionontate,* nine villages. According to Father Gabriel Lallemand, these thirty-one villages occupied a territory of about sixty miles in extent, adjoining the *Five Nations,* and lying about one hundred miles south of the mouth of the Ottawa, or French river. About that time, Champlain, an eminent Frenchman who afterward became governor of Canada, spent some time with the *Ahrendah-ronons,* the most northeastern tribe. The Jesuit, Father Sigard, resided with the nation some years, and succeeded in making a favorable impression upon the tribes.

In 1639, the whole nation was scourged by small-pox, and about twelve hundred fell victims to that abhorrent disease. The Jesuit missionaries took advantage of the scourge, to visit every village, to administer to the wants of the afflicted, and baptize their dying children. In their labor of charity and love, they went to almost every cabin, and succeeded in influencing great numbers of *Wyandots* to unite with the Catholic church. They estimated the number of cabins, at that time, at seven hundred, and the number of families at two thousand, and the whole population at about twelve thousand. The year before the appearance of the small-pox, the Jesuit, Jean de Brebœuf, while a missionary among the *Wyandots,* near Lake Huron, became acquainted with a remarkable warrior, named Ahasistari, who related to the missionary a singular dream, concerning the white man's deity, and afterwards became a zealous member of the church. Many other *Wyandots* followed the example of Ahasistari, and joined the missionaries in the erection of chapels, and in the ceremonies of the church. The *Wyandots* willingly embraced the doctrines of the Jesuits, and made rapid advancement in civilization; particularly in agriculture, to which they paid a good deal of attention. They were more amiable than the tribes of the *Five Nations,* and were more readily induced to embrace the tenets of the Catholic church, as expounded by Father Brebœuf and his successors. By the advice and instruction of the missionaries, a **number of churches and schools were established, in their most populous villages, and stockades erected to protect them from surprise by the *Five Nations.* The villages of St. Louis and St. Ignatius were esteemed the most important.**

It was the custom of the *Wyandots* to make annual visits to Quebec, then a small French village, to consult the Jesuit teachers, exchange furs for goods, and renew their devotion to the king of France. They returned by the way of the Ottawa and the rivers that interlock with it.* Their journey was more than sixteen hundred miles, through dense forests, and along shoaly rivers; and all day long the missionaries and the *Wyandots* were compelled to wade or handle the oar. At night they had no food but a scanty measure of Indian corn mixed with water, and their couch was upon the earth or the rocks! In this long journey they passed thirty-five water-falls, and carried their canoes upon their shoulders many leagues through the forests, and dragged them by hand through shallows and rapids over sharp stones; and while thus proceeding on their journey homeward, accompanied by Father Isaac Joques, in August, 1649, a band of *Mohawks,* whose war parties, fearlessly strolling through the forest, were ever ready to fall suddenly upon their foes, lay in wait for the pilgrims as they ascended the St. Lawrence.† Ahasistari, the pilot of the pilgrims, landed, and upon examination, declared there were only three canoes, and added there was nothing to fear. The party proceeded, and the *Mohawks* from their ambush attacked the canoes as they neared the land. *Wyandots* and Frenchmen alike hastened to the shore to seek security in the forest. The pious Joques might have easily escaped, but among the wounded were converts who had not yet been baptized, and caring not for his own safety, he proceeded to discharge his duty to the dying *Wyandots*. Ahasistari succeeded in gaining a hiding place, but observing Joques to be a captive he hastened to him, saying: "My brother, I made oath to thee that I would share thy fortune, whether death or life; here am I to keep my vow." Joques, Rene Goupil, Ahasistari and other captives were carried through the *Mohawk* villages, where Goupil was tomahawked and Ahasistari suffered the most horrible tortures, and finally, death by being burned at the stake, while Joques was unexpectedly spared.

Thus a new war sprang up between the *Wyandots* and the *Five Nations,* who had long been jealous of the influence of the *Wyandots* with the neutral nation, and who had stood in their path to the Illinois and the Mississippi. By frequent surprises by the *Mohawks,* communication by the Ottawa river with Quebec was cut off, and after repeated repulses elsewhere, the *Wyandots* became dispirited in consequence of the loss of so many of their warriors, and abandoned the small villages and concentrated in the large ones. This seemed to exasperate the *Five Nations,* and the *Wyandots* were a doomed race. In 1654 the combined forces of the *Five Nations* resolved on the destruction of the *Wyandots,* invaded their country and attacked and took the most of their stockaded villages, and massacred large numbers of the inhabitants. The attack was renewed the next year, and the *Wyandot* nation was completely scattered, some seeking a refuge by the Ottawa, under the walls of Quebec, whither they were pursued

---
*Bancroft.
†Father Joques, in "French Relations."

by the relentless *Mohawks*. Several bands were captured and incorporated in the *Five Nations*; a remnant of the nation fled to the country of the *Chippewas* of Lake Superior. Other bands fled to the upper part of Michigan and other remote quarters. As we have already seen, the *Five Nations* then opened a war of extermination against the *Andastes* and the *Eries*. About the year 1671, that part of the *Wyandot* nation which had taken refuge among the *Chippewas*, was induced by Father Marquette to return to the Peninsula of Michigan, where they united their fortunes with a dispersed remnant of their brethren near Detroit, with perhaps a remnant of the *Andastes*, and the *Eries*, who had sought refuge in that quarter.

About the close of the thirty years' war between the French and the *Five Nations*, when the strength of the latter had been broken, and their incursions into Ohio successfully checked, the *Wyandots* took quiet possession of the ancient territory of the ill-fated *Eries*, claiming sovereignty over all the country between Lake Erie and the Ohio river. We find the *Wyandots*, in 1740, sufficiently strong to offer an asylum on the Muskingum to a part of the *Delaware* nation which had fled from the intrusions of the white man in Pennsylvania.* The *Wyandots* probably obtained the territory of the *Eries* through French influence. The *Wyandots* occupied a commanding influence over the western tribes as late as the treaty of Greenville. Mr. Taylor says the *Wyandots* dwelt upon the waters of Sandusky and Maumee in 1750. The principal seat of the nation was opposite Detroit, Michigan, and the Ohio settlements were in the nature of colonies from the peninsulas bordering on Lake Huron. The *Wyandots* unquestionably stood at the head of the Ohio Indians for bravery, intelligence and capability of adopting the laws of civilized life. President Harrison, who was a military officer in the northwest, became well acquainted with the *Wyandots*, declared that neither surprise nor sudden disaster in battle cowed their courage. At the battle of the rapids of the Miami, where he won a noted battle over the confederated tribes, he says the *Wyandots* lost thirteen chiefs, notwithstanding which, they fought with the most constant and unflinching courage. It was one of the characteristics of the *Wyandots* that they would never be taken in battle. In the appropriate place, it will be seen that they took a leading part, under British influence, in the warlike incursions in the eastern and western parts of this county, and aided in the destruction of the property of the early settlers, as well as in menacing their safety.

---

* Heckewelder.

NOTE.—The reader will remember that after the war of 1812-14 the *Wyandots* resided on their reservation at Upper Sandusky, occupied in the pursuit of agriculture, and making considerable advancement in education and the arts of civilized life, until 1842-43, when they were assigned a new reservation by the general government, in the territory of Kansas, to which they removed, and where they now reside.

CHAPTER VI.

THE OTTAWAS.

The Ottawas and their Expulsion by the Iroquois.—Their Flight to the Upper Lakes.—Their Return to Michigan and Ohio.—As Confederates of the Hurons or Wyandots.

WHEN the *Five Nations* had conquered and dispersed the *Wyandots* in 1655, they immediately assailed the *Ottawas*, another branch of the neutral nation occupying the shores and islands on the Ottawa river, in Canada. The invasion was conducted by the relentless *Mohawks*, with their usual vigor and cruelty, until the unfortunate *Ottawas*, unaccustomed to war, were compelled to abandon their homes and seek refuge on the Bay of Saginaw, opposite the territory of Michigan.* Here they found the scattered *Wyandots*, for whom they had borne the strongest attachments; and, uniting with them, removed to the deserts north of Lake Superior in 1665, near the *Chippewas*, where they were visited by the Jesuit missionary, Allouez.

When first visited by the missionaries, about the year 1615, they occupied an island on the Ottawa river, as well as the territory adjacent to the river, and although disposed to be on peaceful terms with their neighbors, they exacted a sort of tribute or toll from all the Indians navigating that river, which seems to have been willingly assented to by the *Wyandots* and other fur-trading tribes. We may infer, therefore, that they were the original proprietors of the islands and the shores of that river. At that time their chief occupation was fishing, hunting, raising corn, and trading with the nations, using the river as a sort of commercial highway. In fact, the early missionaries supposed the term "Ottawa" originally meant in their language, a trader.

About the year 1680, La Salle a distinguished French explorer, visited the *Ottawas* at the Bay of Saginaw and found them and the *Huron*s or *Wyandots*, confederated against the *Five Nations*, and engaged in cultivating corn, which was their ordinary food, and fishing upon the borders of the lake. He purchased an abundance of "whitings" and some "trouts" of extraordinary size of them. Father Hennepin, a Franciscan, also visited them at their new home about the same time, and joined them in fishing in the bay, by breaking holes in the ice, and by means of several large stones, sunk nets to catch fish, which he did in great abundance, and adds, "these made our Indian wheat go down the better, which was our ordinary diet." He also relates that at that time the *Ottawas* were greatly in dread of the *Iroquois* or *Five Nations*, who had a short time before taken an entire family of twelve souls into slavery, and otherwise greatly distressed their people, while others had fled to the French at Quebec for protection and food. It seemed difficult for the *Ottawas* to escape the raids and malice of the *Five Nations* who sought the fugitives wherever they attempted to conceal themselves. In the year 1701, after the peace between the French and the *Five Nations*, a settlement by the French was commenced at Detroit by De la Matte Cadillar, with a Jesuit missionary

---

* Bancroft.

and one hundred Frenchmen. A fort was erected for the protection of the new settlers, and Detroit soon became the center of trade with the Indians. The *Ottawas* and *Wyandots*, after a residence of over fifty years in Upper Canada, joined the new settlement by returning to its vicinity. The French were ambitious to hold the ascendency over the British in the territories of Illinois, Michigan, Indiana and Ohio, and to do so, encouraged the *Wyandots* and *Ottawas* to pass down the western shores of Lake Erie.

In the year 1750, nearly one hundred and fifty years after the expulsion of the *Ottawas* from the home of their fathers on the Ottawa river, we find the French engaged in constructing a fort at Sandusky. It is not known with certainty how many French occupied the new fort, but their influence was speedily seen on the Indians of Ohio, who were encouraged by presents and jealousy to make savage raids on the border settlements of Pennsylvania and Virginia. The principal settlements of the *Ottawas* were on the Maumee, along the lake shore, at Plymouth, Huron county, the mouth of Huron river, on the Black river, and a large village at or near Cuyahoga Falls. After the decay of French influence in Canada, when the *Ottawas* and all the other northwestern tribes in Ohio gave in their adhesion to the British, and during the Revolution and the war of 1812–15, the *Ottawas* were known by the first settlers of this and the surrounding counties, as "Canada Indians," and were generally adherents of the British cause; and encouraged in their predatory incursions on the border settlements, by presents in compensation for the scalps they were able to exhibit on their return from their expeditions.

While the *Ottawa* nation seems to have been almost entirely destitute of great war chiefs and leaders, it must be admitted that in what may properly be termed "Indian diplomacy," it ranked as a nation or tribe with most of the Ohio Indians. In the history of Ohio, it is noticeable that the British and French often employed *Ottawa* emissaries to influence the other tribes to join their cause, and frequently with considerable success. As a people, the *Ottawas* were without true courage, and relied upon their cunning and dissemblance for success. The *Wyandots* were a frank, brave and fearless people, while the *Ottawas* were timid, treacherous and uncertain, as enemies or friends.

The only really great man ever produced among the *Ottawas* was the gallant war-chief, Pontiac, who was supposed to be the son of an *Ojibwa* woman, while his father was an *Ottawa*.* It is not known with certainty, whether Pontiac was born during the residence of his tribe near the upper lakes, or after his people had settled on the Maumee, in Ohio. Pontiac was a strong friend of the French; and when their colonists were contending for the occupation of Michigan, the valleys of Ohio, the Wabash, and the Miami, he rallied the red men of the forest against the British, and fought with distinguished courage, side by side with the French. Watchful, fearless, indomitable, he was ever on the alert to foil the advance of the "Long-knives," the Pennsylvanians and the "Red coats" aiding their advance into these territories.

When, in 1760, Canada surrendered to the English, by the French governor, Vaudrueil, Major Robert Rogers, a native of New Hampshire, and an associate of Putnam and Stark, was ordered to take possession of the western forts. * He left Montreal with two hundred rangers, well trained as hunters and woodsmen, armed like Indians, with hatchet, gun, and knife. He embarked at Presque Isle, up Lake Erie, in fifteen whale boats; and when, from bad weather, he was compelled to put into the mouth of the Geauga, or Grand, river, Ohio, he met an embassy of *Ottawas*, who told him the chief or king was a short distance away, coming, and desired him to halt for a talk. The request was complied with, and Pontiac met him; and, after the first salutation, demanded to know his business in his country, and wished to know how it happened that he dared to enter it without his leave? When Major Rogers told him he had no desire to injure the Indians, but came to remove the French out of the country, Pontiac told him he stood in his path, and would give him a final answer the next day. The next day, Pontiac agreed that Rogers might proceed, accompanied by himself and the *Ottawas*, as a guard, on his journey to remove the French. To carry out this agreement, he sent one hundred warriors, with bags of parched corn and other necessaries, to protect, and assist in driving, one hundred cattle, which Rogers had brought for the use of the detachment from Fort DuQuesne; at the same time, dispatching messages to the several Indian towns on the south side of Lake Erie, to inform them that Rogers had his consent to come into the country. Pontiac constantly accompanied the Major, until the expedition arrived at Detroit, and was the means of preserving the detachment from the fury of the Indians, who had assembled at the north of the strait, to cut the expedition off. Rogers regarded Pontiac as an extraordinary man, possessing great strength of judgment and a wonderful thirst for knowledge. He was desirous of learning how the English manafactured cloth, iron, guns, and other things peculiar to civilized life; and even expressed a strong desire to visit England.

The Indians in northwestern Ohio, Indiana and Michigan submitted sullenly to British dominion. The French were unable to cope with the English, and the Indians were forced to submit to their new masters, although strongly attached to and sympathizing with their fallen friends, the French. The fierce hatred of Pontiac had not been subdued, and regarding the British as intruders into his country, he silently awaited a suitable opportunity to strike a fatal blow at the new invaders. He nursed his aversions towards the British, and cited his Indian allies in the west to the encroachments of the English emigrants from Pennsylvania and Virginia, and the pretended grants of his territory to the newcomers.

---

*Perkins ii, 223.

*Roger's Journal.

The English failed to keep their engagements with the Indians, and this aided in fanning the flames of disaffection until it reached the height of an insurrection. Pontiac was at the head of the great conspiracy. He was a chief of great genius, possessing qualities only equaled by the most distinguished of his race, such as Tecumseh, King Philip, Powhatan, Cornstalk and Logan. He proceeded from tribe to tribe, organizing his grand conspiracy, and seemed to wield the power of an emperor among his people. He had fought in behalf of the French in the Acadian war of 1747, at Braddock's defeat 1755, and at the surrender of Fort DuQuesne, and he claimed to speak by the inspiration of the Great Spirit, who he declared had "told him not to suffer those dogs in red clothing to enter his country and take the land given him." "Drive them from it! Drive them! When you are in distress, I will help you, said the Great Spirit."

According to the papers of J. H. Perkins, in May, 1763, the great drama commenced. By a simultaneous movement the Indians precipitated themselves upon and captured nearly every settlement from Michilimackinack to Fort Pitt, while the border streams of Virginia and Pennsylvania again ran red with human gore. The fort at Detroit held out, but was closely beleaguered by six hundred Indians led by the indomitable Pontiac. He continued the siege of Detroit until June, when the fort was reinforced, and Pontiac retired to the Maumee in Ohio.

In October a royal proclamation was issued which eventually pacified the Indian tribes of the leagues. This proclamation prohibited further settlements in the territory until the pleasure of the crown. Pontiac yielded a sullen submission on the Maumee in August, 1765, to General Croghan, and agreed no longer to stand in the path of the English; but denied that by taking possession of the French forts they gained any right to the country. He said the French occupied and lived upon their land by sufferance only. Croghan declared that Pontiac was a "shrewd, sensible Indian, of few words, and commanded more respect among his own nation than any Indian he ever saw." About the year 1769 the great Pontiac disappeared from the Maumee, proceeding to the country of the *Illinois*, and thence to the French garrison at St. Louis. He was warmly received by St. Ange, then commander of the fort, where he remained for two or three days. He appeared in the full uniform of a French officer. Hearing that a number of Indians were assembled on the opposite side of the Mississippi, and drinking and engaged in other amusements, he said he would cross over and see what was going on. St. Ange endeavored to convince him that those Indians were the friends of the British, and might injure him. Pontiac proudly replied, "Captain, I am a man! I know how to fight. I always fought openly. They will not murder me. If any one attacks me as a brave man, I am his match." He crossed the river, found the Indians in a carousal, drank deeply, strode down the village to the adjacent woods, was followed by a *Kaskaskia* Indian (who had been bribed by an English trader named Williamson with a barrel of rum), who stole near him in the forest and buried his tomahawk in his brain.

According to the compilation of Mr. Taylor, Pontiac was buried by his friends, the French officers, with warlike honors, near the fort at St. Louis; and about his grave a great city has risen, and the race whom he hated now tramples over his forgotten grave. After the close of the war of 1812-15 the major part of the *Ottawas* sought and obtained permission of the British to return to their ancient homes on the Ottawa river, where many of them are yet to be seen. In the proper place it will be shown that the *Ottawas* were familiar with the territory of this county, and that their great chief, Pontiac, may have traversed it frequently to rouse the *Delawares*, the *Mohegans* and the *Mingoes*, against the encroachments of the white man.

CHAPTER VII.

THE MOHEGANS.

A Remnant of the Connecticut Mohegans Locate on a Branch of White Woman's River and give Names to all the Streams Emptying into it from the Northwest.—They Erect a Village Under the Chiefship of Mohegan John, on the Jerome Fork of Mohican.

WHEN the English landed in New England they were heartily welcomed and treated with much consideration and kindness by the native Indians inhabiting her coasts. The English colonists made a show of purchasing the lands of the Indians, closing their purchases and treaties in writing, which the natives neither understood nor could read. By these repeated contracts and sales, they narrowed the domains of the children of the forest, and thus artfully crowded them into narrow and sterile tongues of land until they feared starvation and extermination. Thus, the English villages and settlements drew nearer and nearer their hunting grounds, and the natives were constantly pressed upon and forced back from the homes and graves of their fathers. They resisted, but in vain! Their tribes were broken and scattered by the "psalm-singing Puritans," and compelled to seek refuge up the St. Lawrence and among the *Five Nations* in northern New York.

The *Mohegans* of Connecticut, once owning the eastern part of that State, the most of Rhode Island, and the country between the banks of the Connecticut and the Hudson, fell victims to the avarice of the white settlers by being stripped of their lands and driven from their homes. The most of them fled up the St. Lawrence under French protection, where they probably incorporated themselves with the *Iroquois* and became a mixed race. From Canada they found an asylum in the wild territories of Ohio by passing the domains of the *Five Nations* or through Michigan down the western coast of Lake Erie. The precise period of their arrival in Ohio is not known with certainty; but by reference to Pownall's map, we find that the *Mohegans*, remnants of the old Connecticut tribe, occupied the west branch of the Muskingum as early as 1755.

These, last of a race made famous in the early annals of New England, seemed to have been fused with *Canadians* and *Iroquois*, and had emigrated a short time before, from near Montreal. One of their villages was Tullihas, and was situated about twenty miles above the principal forks of the Muskingum, near the junction of the Vernon and Mohican rivers, on the borders of Knox and Coshocton counties. As nearly all the rivers and streams in Ohio received a name from the Indian tribe or nation located on their margin, may not the name of the "Mohican" and its branches, have been derived from the tribe long resident at Tullihas and afterwards at Jeromeville? This meagre account of their early settlement in Ohio, is mostly derived from Heckewelder and Drake's "Life in a Wigwam."*

That the customs and manners of the *Mohegans* and other tribes inhabiting the territories of Ohio at an early period, may be properly understood by the reader, we deem it proper to introduce the narrative of James Smith, who was captured when about eighteen years of age, by three Indians, near Bedford, in western Pennsylvania, in the spring of 1755, a short time before the crushing defeat of General Braddock. He was compelled to run the gauntlet on the banks of the Allegheny, opposite Fort Du Quesne, now Pittsburgh, where he nearly lost his life by being felled by a blow from a stick or tomahawk handle, and on attempting to rise was almost blinded by having sand thrown into his eyes. He was then taken in an unconscious condition into the fort, and tenderly cared for by a French physician, until he had recovered from his wounds.

After remaining in the fort nearly a month, where he heard of the defeat of Braddock and Washington, and witnessed the exultation of the French, and the savage brutalities of the Indians towards their captives, and expecting the same fate himself, he was taken by his captors on a long journey through the forests to the village of Tullihas, on the west branch of the Muskingum, about twenty miles above the forks. The village was occupied by *Mohegans, Caughnewagos* and *Delawares.*† Here he was adopted by the Indians. In his journal he says:

"The day after my arrival at the aforesaid town, a number of Indians collected about me, and one of them began to pull the hair out of my head. He had some ashes on a piece of bark, in which he frequently dipped his fingers in order to take the firmer hold, and so he went on, as if he had been plucking a turkey, until he had all the hair clean out of my head, except a small spot about three or four inches square on my crown. This they cut off with a pair of scissors, excepting three locks, which they dressed up in their own mode. Two of these they wrapped around with a narrow beaded garter, made by

---

*As early as the year 1762, a number of them (*Mohegans*) had emigrated to the Ohio, where I became acquainted with their chief, who was called by the whites "Mohican John."—*Heckewelder's Indian Nations*, page 77. He probably visited Mohican John at his village, three-fourths of a mile southwest of Jeromeville, in Mohican township, as a missionary.

† It has been supposed that the village alluded to was on the present site of Roscoe, Coshocton county; but if, as Smith states, it was twenty miles from the junction of the Tuscarawas, up the Whitewoman, or west branch of the Muskingum, it was somewhere near the junction of the Lake fork of the Mohican with Vernon rivers, or Owl creek.

themselves for that purpose, and these they plaited at full length, and then stuck it full of silver brooches. After this they bored my nose and ears, and fixed me off with ear-rings and nose-jewels. Then they ordered me to strip off my clothes and put on a breech-clout, which I did. They then painted my head, face and body, in various colors. They put a large belt of wampum on my neck, and silver bands on my hands and right arm; and so an old chief led me out on the street, and gave the alarm, "Hallo!" Coo-wigh—several times, repeated quick; and on this, all that were in the town came running and stood around the old chief, who held me by the hand in their midst. As I at that time knew nothing of their mode of adoption, and had seen them put to death all they had taken, and as I never could find that they saved a man alive at Braddock's defeat, I made no doubt but they were about putting me to death in some cruel manner. The old chief, holding me by the hand, made a long speech, very loud, and, when he had done, he handed me to three young squaws, who led me by the hand down the bank, into the river, until the water was up to our middle. The squaws then made signs to me to plunge myself into the water, but I did not understand them. I thought the result of the council was that I should be drowned, and these young ladies were to be the executioners. They all three laid violent hold of me, and I for the time opposed them with all my might, which occasioned loud laughter by the multitude that were on the bank of the river. At length one of the squaws made out to speak a little English (for I believe they began to be afraid of me), and said, 'No hurt you.' On this, I gave myself up to their ladyships, who were as good as their word; for though they plunged me under water, and washed and rubbed me severely, yet I could not say they hurt me much. These young women then led me to the council house, where some of the tribe were ready with clothes for me. They gave me a new ruffled shirt, which I put on, also a pair of leggins done off with ribbons and beads, likewise a pair of moccasins, and gaiters dressed with beads, porcupine quills, and red hair—also a tinsel-laced cappo. They again painted my head and face with various colors, and tied a bunch of feathers to one of those locks they left on the crown of my head, which stood up five or six inches. They seated me on a bear-skin and gave me a pipe, tomahawk, and polecat-skin pouch, which had been skinned pocket-fashion, and contained tobacco, killigenico, or dry sumach leaves, which they mix with their tobacco; also spunk, flint, and steel. When I was thus seated, the Indians came in, dressed and painted in their grandest manner. As they came in, they took their seats, and for a considerable time there was a profound silence—every one was smoking; but not a word was spoken among them. At length one of the chiefs made a speech, which was delivered to me by an interpreter, and was as follows: 'My son, you are now flesh of our flesh and bone of our bone. By the ceremony which was performed this day, every drop of white blood was washed out of your veins; you are taken into the *Caughnewago* nation, and initiated into a warlike tribe; you are adopted into a great family, and now received with great seriousness and solemnity in the room and place of a great man. After what has passed this day, you are now one of us by an old strong law and custom. My son, you have now nothing to fear—we are now under the same obligations to love, support, and defend you, that we are to love and defend one another; therefore, you are to consider yourself as one of our people. At this time I did not believe this fine speech, especially that of the white blood being washed out of me; but since that time I have found that there was much sincerity in said speech; for, from that day, I never knew them to make any distinction between me and themselves, in any respect whatever, until I left them. If they had plenty of clothing, I had plenty; if we were scarce, we all shared one fate. After this ceremony was over I was introduced to my new kin, and told that I was to attend a feast that evening, which I did. And as the custom was, they gave me also a bowl and wooden spoon, which I carried with me to the place, where there was a number of large brass kettles full of boiled venison and green corn; every one advanced with his bowl and spoon, and had his share given him. After this, one of the chiefs made a speech, and then we began to eat."

The names of the chiefs of *Tullihas*, were Tecanyaterighto and Asallecoa. The next evening Smith was invited to a sort of Indian dance which he describes thus:

"The young men stood in one rank, and the young women in another, about one rod apart, facing each other. The one that raised the tune, or started the song, held a small gourd or dry shell of a squash in his hand, which contained beads or small stones, which rattled. When he began to sing, he timed the tune with his rattle; both men and women danced and sung together, advancing towards each other, stooping until their heads would be touching together, and then ceased from dancing, with loud shouts, and retreated and formed again, and so repeated the same thing over and over, for three or four hours, without intermission. This exercise appeared to me at first irrational and insipid; but I found that in singing their tunes ya-ne-no-hoo-wa-ne, like our fa-sa-la, and though they have no such thing as jingling verse, yet they can intermix sentences with their notes, and say what they please to each other, and carry on their tune in concert. I found that this was a kind of wooing or courting dance, and as they advanced stooping with their heads together, they could say what they pleased to each other's ear, without disconcerting their rough music, and the others, or those near, not hear what they said."

Smith remained at Tullihas until the following October, when he accompanied his adopted brother, whose name was Tontileaugo, and who had a *Wyandot* wife, on the shores of Lake Erie. Their route was along an old trail up the lake fork, to near the present village of Tylertown, thence up the Jerome fork through the townships of Mohican, Montgomery and Orange, to the south borders of Sullivan, and across the same, to the head branches of the Black river, called by the Indians Canesadooharie, traveling Medina and Lorain counties, to where it falls into the lake, some distance north of Elyria, where they found a large camp of *Wyandots*, and the wife of Tontileaugo. Smith remained with the *Wyandots*, *Ottawas* and *Mohegans*, traveling over various parts of northern and western Ohio, to Detroit, Montreal and Presque Isle, for about four years, and then escaped, and returned to his home in Pennsylvania. It will be seen, then, that Smith was probably the first white man that ever penetrated the forests of Ashland county. At any rate, we have no authentic account of such an adventure by a white man, prior to his forced visit along the fertile valleys of the goodly Mohican.

About the year 1762, two years after the escape of James Smith from the *Wyandots*, "Mohican John," a noted chief, with a band of Connecticut *Mohegans*, emigrated to Ohio and established a village on the west side of the Jerome fork, upon a site subsequently covered by the farms of Rev. Elijah Yocum and Judge Edmund Ingmand. These Indians were evidently under the influence of the French, at, or soon after they located on the Jerome fork; for, upon the arrival of the earliest settlers in Mohican township, John Baptiste Jerome, a Frenchman had married an Indian woman and was residing in the vicinity of the village, and subsequently within the present limits of Jeromeville. The number of Indians accompanying Mohican John to their new hunting grounds is not clearly set forth, but from the frequent mention of the village in after times, may have been from one hundred and fifty to two hundred.

CHAPTER VIII.

THE MINGO VILLAGES OF THE MOHICAN.

The Name Mingo.—How Applied.—The Mingoes visited by General Gage and George Croghan.—William Johnson Negotiates a Treaty.—George Washington Visits the Tribe.—The Location of some of their Villages.—They are Friendly with other Tribes.—Logan, the great Mingo Chief.—His Career.—His Immortal Speech.

ACCORDING to Heckewelder, and other Indian authorities, the name, "*Mingo*," does not apply to any distinct nation or tribe of Indians, but is applicable, principally, to the *Cayugas*, a colony springing from the *Five Nations*, intermixed with *Delawares*, *Mohegans*, *Cachuewagas*, and *Iroquois*.

It is not certain whether the *Mingoes*, or *Cayugas*, separated from the parent nation during the attempt of the *Five Nations* to exterminate the *Alleghans*, the *Andastes*, the *Eries*, the *Wyandots* and the *Ottawas*, or during the period when the *Delawares* along the Susquehanna were "made women" by the great New York confederacy, or whether, at a subsequent period, they selected the teeming forests of Ohio for their new hunting-grounds.

As early as 1750, straggling parties of the New York Indians were often met along the shores of Lake Erie, and a *Mingo* village was found at the mouth of Beaver, and one near the present site of Steubenville, Ohio.

In consequence of the Indian raids on the border settlements, General Thomas Gage, in 1764, ordered Colonel John Bradstreet to chastise the Ohio Indians. In obedience to orders, he advanced toward Presque Isle, and was met by ten *Mingoes*, representatives of the New York tribes settled in Ohio, near that place. Pownall's map places a *Mingo* village at Cuyahoga Falls, after which, doubtless, Cuyahoga county was named, they being of the New York tribe of *Cayugas*.

In 1765, George Croghan, a sub-commissioner of Sir William Johnson, who had just held a council with the Indians on German flats, in New York, was empowered to visit the Ohio Indians, for the purpose of fixing a boundary for the white settlements. He embarked at Pittsburgh, in May, intending to visit the Wabash, the Miami, and other regions in Ohio. On the north side of the Ohio, near where Steubenville now stands, at the mouth of Cross Creeks, he passed a Mingo village.

In 1768, Sir William Johnson negotiated a treaty at Fort Stanwix, in central New York, with the deputies of the *Five Nations*, the *Delawares*, *Shawnees*, and *Mingoes*, of Ohio.

In 1770, George Washington, then a young man, with a surveying party, made a trip down the Ohio to the mouth of the Great Kanahwa for the purpose of fixing certain boundaries and locating military lands. He also passed the Mingo village at Indian Cross Creeks and interviewed its settlers. During his stay he observed they viewed the settlements on the Ohio with a jealous eye, and claimed that they should be compensated for their right to the soil, if the settlers persisted in locating thereon.

As early as 1774 the migration of the white settlers on the west side of the Ohio had been so great that the *Delawares*, *Mingoes* and other tribes were compelled to retire further into the wilderness to obtain more extended hunting grounds. This was the occasion of much jealousy, ill-temper and resentment on the part of the Indians. As a general thing, the conduct of the white people only tended to arouse the hostility of the Indian tribes until they were compelled, in self-defence, to league themselves against the encroachments of the "Long Knives;" and then their pent up rage burst forth with savage fury at the inexcusable and unaccountable assassination of the family of Logan by Greathouse and his party. This act of cruelty and murder was the cause of Dunmore's sanguinary war.

Sometime between the years 1755 and 1761 a small village of *Mingoes* was located on the east bank of the Jerome fork, nearly north of where Mohican John afterwards placed his village and council house on the west side of said stream.

From the few scraps of history that relate to the *Mohegans, Delawares* and *Mingoes*, we are inclined to think they intermarried and were on the most intimate terms. They hunted together, went to war together, raised cattle, and hogs, and corn, and adopted many of the customs of the whites. From this circumstance we are of opinion that the *Mingoes* of the Jerome fork, and of Greentown, were really a branch, if not a part of the tribe formerly resident on the Susquehanna, at Presque Isle and Beaver, Pennsylvania, at Cuyahoga Falls and Indian Cross Creeks, Ohio, some of whom fled hither after the assassination of the wife and children of poor Logan and the dispersion of his village in 1774. Their inclination to raise cattle, hogs and corn, seems conclusive that they had previously learned their value from the pioneers on the Ohio and in western Virginia and Pennsylvania.*

As the history of the great *Mingo* chief, John Logan, may be somewhat connected with this county, it will, doubtless, be interesting to the reader to peruse a concise sketch of his wonderful career, which, with that of Pontiac, Powhatan, Cornstalk, King Philip, and Shikillimus, has attracted the admiration of statesmen and scholars in Europe and America.

From Heckewelder the Indian historian and Moravian missionary who spent the major part of his life among the *Delawares* and *Mingoes*, and who was well acquainted with the father of Logan, we learn that the ancestors of the great *Mingo* chief resided nearly a century before on the banks of the Susquehanna, and had suffered many wrongs through the treachery and duplicity of the whites; so much so, that his tribe was broken of its strength, and a portion only remained by sufferance. Their chief, when the Moravian missionaries visited them in 1742 at Shomokin, a populous Indian town on the Susquehanna, was Shikillimus, a *Cayuga* or *Mingo*, who afterwards became a convert to the Moravian faith, and was attended in his last moments by David Zeisberger in 1749. Logan is declared to have been the second son of this chief, and was called after John Logan, secretary of the province, for whom Shikillimus entertained a very high regard. Logan left Shomokin, with others of his tribe, when a young man, and spent a number of years within the present limits of Mifflin, Pennsylvania. It is probable that Logan married while he resided in Mifflin, near what is known as the "Logan Spring." Many anecdotes are related by the pioneers of that section concerning the great *Mingo* chief prior to his departure to the territories west of the Ohio. Judge Brown, long a resident of Mifflin and well acquainted with Logan, declared he was "the best specimen of humanity he ever met with, white or red."—Heckewelder describes him as tall and imposing in appearance, and as possessing "superior talents and correct sentiments" He was first met, after leaving Mifflin, by Heckewelder in 1772, encamped with a number of *Mingoes* at the mouth of Beaver. Heckewelder again visited him the next spring, and was treated "with every civility from such of the family as were at home."

A short time prior to the opening of Dunmore's war, Logan seems to have joined his Mingo friends at Cross Creeks. About this time, one Dr. John Connelly asserted the claims of Virginia to Fort Pitt and its vicinity. He was arrested by Arthur St. Clair, who represented the proprietors of Pittsburgh, but was afterwards discharged and again re-asserted the claims of Virginia, and took possession of the fort, which he repaired and called Fort Dunmore. He immediately commenced a series of annoyances and aggressions upon the Ohio Indians, which were resented. Under his influence, May 4, 1774, Greathouse and Michael Cresap, officers in command, assembled at the house of one Baker (who had settled on the Virginia side), with thirty-two persons who had gathered from the neighborhood, just opposite the Indian encampment on the Ohio side. By invitation, five Indian men, one woman and a little child, crossed over in a canoe to Baker's. Greathouse gave them whiskey, and three of the men became drunk. The woman and the other two Indians refused to drink. These the inhuman followers of Greathouse instantly shot and killed, and afterwards tomahawked those they had caused to become intoxicated—saving none but the infant. It is due to the volunteers to state that this barbarous act was perpetrated by but five or six of the party of Greathouse, while the others protested against it as an atrocious murder.

The Indians at Yellow creek hearing the firing, sent two Indians in a canoe to see what had happened. These were shot down as soon as they landed. Others attempted to pass over and were likewise shot and wounded. Among the first party were probably the wife and other relatives of Logan. They were cruelly assassinated by the Baker party. Up to that time Logan had been the friend of the whites, and but a few days before had advised the Indians to be on terms of peace with the "Long Knives" and the Pennsylvanians. This act of wanton cruelty changed his whole nature; and from a warm friend he became the deadly enemy of the white settlers. His relations were now all dead! No one cared for poor Logan! He resolved to avenge the death

---

*The *Mohegans* and *Delawares* dwelt together in what is now Carbon county, Pennsylvania, in 1746, from whence they may have accompanied the *Delawares* to the branches of the Muskingum.—Egle's History of Pennsylvania, page 491.

of his relations by killing an equal number of the settlers. He selected eight warriors, and penetrated to the settlements on the waters of the Monongahela, where he took many scalps and several prisoners, and eluded pursuit. These he carried to an Indian town near Dresden, on the Muskingum, where William Robinson, one of the prisoners, was condemned to be tortured to death. Logan made an eloquent speech in his behalf, but in vain, for the Indians were determined to burn him. While tied to the stake Logan rushed forward, cut his thongs, and threw a belt of wampum around him, and then led him in safety to his own wigwam, where he was adopted in place of a brother whom the Baker party had killed at Yellow creek.

Logan then visited nearly all the Indian tribes in Ohio, and endeavored to induce them to join a great defensive league to prevent the encroachments and settlements of the whites. In making this effort it is not unlikely that he visited the *Delawares*, *Mingoes* and *Mohegans* of this county; and in his final retreat to Detroit may have resided some time at Mohican Johnstown. He succeded in inducing some of the *Wyandots*, *Delawares*, *Mohegans*, *Mingoes*, and a large number of the *Shawnees* to join his league.

In August of the same year, Lord Dunmore, then governor of Virginia, resolved on punishing the Indian tribes west of the Ohio, and compelling a peace with the leagued tribes. On the seventeenth of October, 1774, the memorable battle of Point Pleasant, at the junction of the Kanawha with the Ohio, was fought. The Indians occupied a strong position in the midst of dense underbrush, behind fallen trees and logs, where they fought with desperate courage from early in the morning until nearly night, when they withdrew across the Ohio. The numbers on each side were nearly equal, being about twelve hundred. The Virginians lost half their officers, while the killed and wounded were fully one-fourth the army engaged. The Indian loss is reported at two hundred and thirty-three. Indian authorities assert that Logan, Cornstalk, Ellenipsco, Red Hawk, and many other celebrated chiefs participated in that great battle.

After crossing the river the allied Indians retreated in the direction of Pickaway plains. Dunmore with his army descended the Ohio to the mouth of Hockhocking, and having erected Fort Gower, and leaving a garrison, ascended Hocking to Logan, the present county seat, and then marched westward to within seven miles of the present site of Circleville. Here he halted for a council, and built a fort called camp Charlotte. The Indians were encamped at a point called Old Chillicothe. Cornstalk, who had been at the battle of Point Pleasant, was now anxious for a permanent peace. He met Dunmore in council and, undaunted by past reverses, spoke with peculiar emphasis concerning a cessation of hostilities. While this was going on, Logan approached John Gibson, an interpreter of Dunmore, and asked him to walk out with him. He did so, and while sitting down, Logan talked over the murder of his relations at Yellow Creek, at the same time shedding many tears, declaring that up to that time he had always been the friend of the white man, and opposed the war. It was at this interview that he delivered to Gibson the speech that has made his fame world-wide. It was as follows:

"I appeal to any white man to say, if ever he entered Logan's cabin hungry, and he gave him not meat; if ever he came cold and naked, and he clothed him not? During the course of the last long and bloody war, Logan remained idle in his cabin, an advocate for peace. Such was my love for the whites, that my countrymen pointed as they passed, and said, "Logan is the friend of the white man." I had even thought to have lived with you, but for the injustice of one man, Colonel Cresap, the last spring, in cold blood and unprovoked, murdered all the relations of Logan, not even sparing my women and children. There runs not a drop of my blood in the veins of any living creature. This called on me for revenge. I have killed many. I have fully glutted my vengeance. For my country, I rejoice at the beams of peace. But do not harbor a thought that mine is the joy of fear. Logan never felt fear. He will not turn on his heel to save his life. Who is there to mourn for Logan? Not one."

The treaty was concluded, but Logan did not attend; and the *Mingoes*, though assenting to its terms, were not parties to it. After the peace, Logan, heart-broken, melancholy—at times laboring under a mania, wandered from tribe to tribe, mourning over his misfortune in the loss of his wife, children and relations, and finally, in an Indian camp near Detroit, Michigan, while sitting with a blanket over his head, before a camp-fire, his elbows resting on his knees, and his head upon his hands, buried in profound reflection, an Indian who had taken some offence, stole behind him, and buried his tomahawk in his brains! Thus fell Logan, greatest of Indian orators, and bravest of their heroic chiefs, the last of his race, with no one to shed a tear over his grave.

NOTE.—The reader will perceive by reference to histories of the war of 1812, that there are two Logans of note. The first being John Logan, the *Mingo* or *Cayuga*, and Logan, the *Shawnee*. Upon the services of the *Shawnee* Logan, Mr. Flint observes:

"In 1812 the Indian tribes that remained faithful to the United States, and whose wish to join our standard had been hitherto refused, by an arrangement with the executive, were permitted to take a par the war. Logan, a warrior of distinguished reputation, joined General Harrison, with seven hundred warriors. There was some severe skirmishing of the enemy with the advance of General Winchester's force, in which Logan, the friendly chief, after conducting with great personal bravery, was mortally wounded."

In a letter addressed to the author of these notes, General Leslie Combs, of Kentucky, who was present when Logan No. 2 was brought into camp, wounded, says: A *Shawnee* chief being at Wappakenetta, now a railroad station in Ohio, not far from Piqua, who joined General Harrison, with a few followers, at St. Marys, early in September, 1812, where I first saw him. A very fine-looking man, about forty years of age, and full six feet high, weighing about one hundred and eighty pounds. I next saw him the night he was mortally wounded, on the twenty-second of November, 1812, when I was a cadet in the army of the Northwest, at camp No. 3, six miles below old Fort Defiance, on the Maumee. He died in a few days at that place, and was sent home to his family, by a special delegation. General Combs yet survives (1879), and resides at Lexington, Kentucky. He is now eighty-five years old.

CHAPTER IX.

MAJOR ROGERS ON THE SOIL OF ASHLAND COUNTY.

The Return of a Part of the Expedition of Major Robert Rogers from Detroit, through the Forests of Ohio, in 1761.—A Correct Outline of his Route along the Old Huron Trail to Pittsburgh, or Fort Pitt.—A Hunting Scene on the Mohican.

AFTER coasting up the south shores of Lake Erie, under the lead of the brave and sagacious Pontiac, in 1760, we find Major Robert Rogers and his two hundred rangers in possession of the fort at Detroit, the French commandant, Monsieur Beleter, having yielded that post without resistance, on the twenty-ninth of November. While his rangers were resting, and recruiting from their toilsome expedition up the lake, against wind and current, the Major visited Lakes Huron and St. Clair, making observations upon their location, the condition of the Indian tribes upon their shores, and the influence of the French in that quarter.

After providing for the garrison, which took possession of the fort at Detroit, on the twenty-third of December he commenced his return by land for Pittsburgh, marching along the west coast of the lake, until January 2, 1761, when he arrived safely at "Lake Sandusky," or Sandusky bay.

It is not known how many rangers accompanied Rogers on his return; but, being well convinced that the apparent welcome of Pontiac was a carefully-conceived piece of dissemblance to throw him off his guard, many *Ottawas* and *Wyandots* having yielded a reluctant consent to British authority in that quarter, he did not, probably, leave Detroit with less than one hundred and twenty or twenty-five men, to encounter the new dangers that might beset him on his way, in case of the treachery of Pontiac and his friends, who still remembered the French as their friends and protectors.

That the reader may have an opportunity of verifying the route by the map of Ohio, and, at the same time, learn the condition of the northern part of the State, one hundred and fifteen years ago, we will quote from the journal of the Major a full description of the trip from Castalia, in Erie county, to the "Long Meadow, or Prairie," in Wayne county.

The narrative begins:

"On January 3d, southeast by east three miles, east by south one mile and a half, southeast a mile through a meadow, crossed a small creek about six yards wide, running east, traveled southeast by east one mile, passed through Indian houses southeast three quarters of a mile, and came to a small Indian town of about ten houses. There is a remarkably fine spring at this place, rising out of the side of a small hill with such force that it boils above the ground in a column three feet high. I imagine it discharges ten hogsheads of water in a minute.* From this town our course was south southeast three miles, south two miles, crossed a brook about five yards wide, running east southeast, traveled south southeast two miles, crossed a brook about eight yards wide. This day we killed plenty of deer and turkeys on our march, and encamped.

"On the fourth, we traveled south southeast one mile, and came to a river about twenty-five yards wide, crossed the river, where are two Indian houses, from thence south by east one mile, south southeast one mile, southeast one mile, south southeast one mile and a half, southeast two miles, south southeast one mile, and came to an Indian house, where there was a family of *Wyndots* hunting, from thence south by east a quarter of a mile, south five miles, came to the river we crossed this morning;* the course of the river here is west northwest. This day killed several deer and other game, and encamped.

"On the fifth, traveled south southeast half a mile, south one mile, south southeast three quarters of a mile, south half a mile, crossed two small brooks running east, went a south southeast course half a mile, south half a mile, southeast half a mile, south two miles, southeast one mile, crossed a brook running east by north, traveled south by east half a mile, south southeast two miles, southeast three quarters of a mile, south southeast one mile, and came to Maskongam creek,† about eight yards wide, crossed the creek and encamped thirty yards from it. This day killed deer and turkeys in our march.

"On the sixth, we traveled about fourteen or fifteen miles, our general course being about east southeast, killed plenty of game, and encamped by a very fine spring.‡

"The seventh, our general course about southeast, traveled about six miles, and crossed Maskongam creek, running south, about twenty yards wide.§ There is an Indian town about twenty yards from the creek, on the east side, which is called the Mingo cabins. There were but two or three Indians in this place, the rest were hunting. These Indians have plenty of cows, horses, hogs, etc.‖

"The eighth, halted at this town to mend our moccasins and kill deer, the provisions I brought from Detroit being entirely expended. I went a hunting with ten of the rangers, and by ten o'clock got more venison than we had occasion for.

"On the ninth, traveled about twelve miles, our general course being about southeast and encamped by the side of a long meadow, where there were a number of Indians hunting."*

From this point he continued to travel in a southeasterly direction until the thirteenth, when he arrived at a Delaware town called Beaver town, afterwards Tuscarora, on the west side of the "Maskongam river," where he found the residences of many leading chiefs and one hundred and eighty warriors. He found about three thousand acres of cleared ground around this town.

Perkins, in his Western annals, page 3, speaks of the route of Major Rogers as being the common one from Sandusky to the fork of the Ohio. He says: "It went from Fort Sandusky, where Sandusky city now is, crossed the Huron river, then called Bald Eagle Creek, to "Mohickan Johnstown," upon what we know as Mohican creek, the northern branch of Whitewoman's river, and thence crossed to Beaverstown, a Delaware town on the west side of the "Maskongam creek," opposite "a fine river," which we presume was Sandy creek."

Mr. Knapp, in his history of Ashland county, page 14, says: "The "Mingo Cabbins" were probably upon the Indian village of Green Town;" and also suggests, from information derived from "Dr. Bushnell, of Mansfield, who has been familiar with the country for a period of upwards of forty years, that the "fine spring" mentioned does not probably lie somewhere between Vermillion and Montgomery townships," as Mr. Taylor supposes, but was probably one of the "Quaker springs," two or three miles southeast of Hayesville.

The theory of Mr. Knapp is involved in many difficulties. By a careful examination of the route of Major Rogers, we are of opinion he crossed the Black fork in the southwest part of Weller township, in Richland

---
* Castalia or Cold Spring, Erie county.

* The Huron river.
† The Black fork.
‡ Probably McCammon's spring, in Montgomery township.
§ The Jerome fork, near Jeromeville.
‖ This village must have been located near the west end of Main street, in the village of Jeromeville, perhaps near the site of Winbigler's grist-mill. It is uncertain when the *Mingoes* settled there.

* In Plain townshtp, Wayne county.

county, and, that after continuing his course a few hours, he struck what has since been denominated "Bealls' trail," following the same to the farm lately owned by Mr. John McCammon, where he found the "very fine spring," and halted for the night. From this spring he continued in a southeast direction about seven miles and crossed the Jerome fork of the Mohican.

If the reader will carefully examine the general course of the trail of Major Rogers, it will be seen that it was nearly southwest from Castalia, in Erie county, where he found the remarkable spring, alluded to by him, in the beginning of his journey. To suppose the latter spring to be one of the "Quaker springs," would take him too far south for the "Mingo cabbins," on the Jerome fork, opposite where Mohican Johnstown was afterwards located, about which there is no dispute. To suppose the "Mingo cabbins" alluded to, were those of "Greentown," increases the difficulty, for Major Rogers would have been compelled to face about, and travel directly southwest nine or ten miles, to reach that locality, where he would have found the "Mingo cabbins" on the north, instead of the east, side of the Black fork.

Again, if he had kept directly down the Black fork, as some suppose, it would have carried him away from the route noted in his journal, and placed him on the north side of that stream, and prevented his passage of the north branch of "Maskongam creek," otherwise, the Jerome fork of the Mohican.

The course of Rogers was east southeast from the Jerome fork, or north branch of "Maskongam creek," to the "Long meadow," in Plain township, Wayne county, about which there is no difficulty. If he had crossed the Black fork at "Greentown," his route would not have been continuously southeast, but directly northeast for at least twenty miles, to reach the "Long meadow"; so that, upon any rational theory, the route of Major Rogers cannot be placed at "Greentown," nor his "fine spring" in the southeast part of Vermillion township.

Upon a full investigation of the whole subject, we are inclined to the opinion that the theory of Mr. Perkins, that Major Rogers followed the well-known Indian trail, afterwards Bealls' trail, from Sandusky to the forks of the Muskingum, by way of the Jerome fork, and crossed the same at the point where Mohican John subsequently established his village and council house, is correct. Presuming upon the accuracy of the foregoing deductions, we have to award to Milton, Montgomery, Vermillion, and Mohican townships, the honor of being traversed by the first "armed troops" that ever penetrated the wilds of northern Ohio; and the east part of Vermillion, and the township of Mohican, as furnishing the first "deer hunt" for the "red coats" to replenish their exhausted stores.

The change in this region since 1761—one hundred and nineteen years—has been wonderful. The red men of the forest have disappeared, and the "Mingo cabbins" and "Mohican Johnstown" are only remembered as relics of the past. Where Pipe, Killbuck, Lyons, Logan, Johnnycake, and other leading spirits of the Indian tribes, roamed in pursuit of the wild game of the forest, are now found fertile farms and the happy homes of the descendants of the pioneers.

CHAPTER X.

THE MORAVIANS.

The Removal of the Moravians by Captain Pipe of the Delawares, and Half-King of the Wyandots.—Affecting Scenes at the Moravian Towns, and Hardships on their Route.—Their probable Route to Sandusky.—The Return of a part of the Converts, and their Inhuman Slaughter by Williamson and his Men.

THE Moravian missionaries commenced their labors among the *Mohegans* on the Connecticut, as early as 1740. A devout member of the denomination named Rauch, was the first to introduce the Moravian faith to the *Mohegans*, who at that time were hopelessly sunk in misery, drunkenness, and every vice and crime that could defile and degrade human nature. The *Mohegans* at first rejected his teachings; but finally, a leading chief embraced the new faith, and then he assisted in opposing the traders who had demoralized the poor savages by their traffic in intoxicating liquors. Thus a good work was accomplished. From this, a new mission was formed at Bethlehem, in Pennsylvania, among the *Delawares* along the Susquehanna. In 1742 Count Zinzindorf, chief bishop of the Moravians in Europe, visited the missions of America; and with some of the leading teachers went through the Indian territories in Pennsylvania and northern New York, and preached to a great number of tribes. He made a good impression upon the *Iroquois* and *Delawares*, and returned to Europe in 1743. The missionaries ordained by him continued their work with varied success, making it a rule to earn their livelihood by bodily toil, to promote the object of their mission—at the same time practicing moderation in all things—and when they failed they received help from Bethlehem. They lived and dressed in Indian style, and Frederick Post, one of their most influential teachers, married a baptized Indian woman.

At Bethlehem, as in Connecticut, the missionaries had to contend against the white traders, who insisted on selling intoxicating liquors to the savages. The visit of Count Zinzindorf to the *Six Nations*, resulted in the conversion of *Cayugas* or *Mingoes*, who finally settled with their Delaware brethren on the Susquehanna, and were the ancestors and kinsmen of the great Indian orator, John Logan. The Moravian teachers translated the Bible into the various dialects of the Indian tongue, and taught their converts and children to read the scriptures. The teachers mingled freely among the Indians, and participated in all their rural labors, and thus a strong affection grew up between teachers and savage. Opposed to war, the Moravians sought to tame and subdue the wild fury and resentments of the savage, and turn his thoughts to the nobler pursuits of civilized life.

About the year 1755 a sect of fanatics sprang up in

Pennsylvania who conceived it to be their duty to exterminate the Indian tribes, and contended that the vengeance of Heaven would rest upon them if they failed to extirpate the Indians, as the Jews had the native races of Palestine. Their fury was also directed towards the Moravian teachers who were declared enemies of the British government. Attacks were soon made upon the Moravians at Bethlehem, and many of the non-resisting brethren were slain. In 1755 a clan of white savages denominating themselves the "Paxton rangers," in revenge for injuries inflicted on the western border, fell upon the *Conestoga* Indians who had long been the faithful friends of the whites, and were rapidly becoming Moravians, and a general massacre followed, the victims being mostly women and children! These drunken rangers made it a rule to shoot down the Moravian Indians wherever they met them. Soon after, one hundred and forty christian Indians were removed to Philadelphia to secure their protection. The rioters then hastened to Lancaster jail, and murdered a number of Indian converts who had been placed there for protection. The principal Moravian settlements were Gnadenhutten, Shomokin, Bethlehem, and Friedenshutton. The entire community in 1772 removed to Beaver river and then to Shoenbrun on the Muskingum, known now as the Tuscarawas. They were accompanied by John Heckewelder, David Zeisberger and other teachers. The *Delawares* were informed of the arrival of their kinsmen from the Susquehanna and gave them a hearty welcome. In 1768 Zeisberger had visited the site of Shoenbrum and was the means of converting a noted chief called Isaac Glikhikan, a *Delaware*, who afterwards became a warm friend of the Moravians, and in 1770 had invited them to settle at the mouth of Big Beaver, which many did, calling the new station Friedenstadt. Shoenbrum was about two miles below the present site of New Philadelphia, and was inhabited principally by *Delawares*. Under the lead of the veteran Zeisberger, Gnadenhutten was established about seven miles south of Shoenbrun on the Tuscarawas, and was inhabited mostly by *Mohegans*. The total number of emigrants in the two villages was estimated at about one-hundred and sixty-nine. These villages were regularly laid out, and each had a log chapel and a school-house where the Indians and Moravians were taught by their preachers and teachers. They cleared fields for the cultivation of corn and vegetables, raised cattle and hogs, and thus soon had enough to live comfortably.

When the *Wyandots* and other warlike tribes of northwestern Ohio made incursions against the border settlements of western Virginia and Pennsylvania, on their return they stopped at these villages, often bringing clothing and other stolen articles which they exchanged for corn and provisions. This exasperated the border settlers and led them to believe that the Moravians secretly aided the *Wyandots* who were the friends of the British in their raids on the border settlers. On the other hand, the quiet demeanor of the Moravian Indians excited the suspicions of the *Wyandots* and their allies among the *Six Nations* who demanded their removal. In 1775 Heckewelder estimated the number of the Christian Indians in Ohio at four hundred and fourteen; and there can be but little doubt that these converted Indians were the means of saving the colonies from subjugation by the British, for the *Wyandots, Shawanese* and warlike *Delawares* were constantly neutralized by the pacific principles of the Christian *Delawares* and *Mohegans*, who always stood in their path. Heckewelder and Zeisberger were unceasing in their efforts to indoctrinate the tribes along the Tuscarawas and at the forks of the Muskingum; but almost from their first settlement their location made them a sort of half-way point between the borders of the States and the *Wyandots*, and hence, the poor Moravians were constantly under the ban of suspicion from both sides; and while Heckewelder was establishing schools and churches the Moravian Indians were quietly cultivating their fields and abstaining from war or hostility towards either party.

In 1777 the *Wyandots* had expressed a determination to sustain Governor Hamilton, of Detroit, against the cause of the rebellious colonies. He endeavored to form an alliance with all the Ohio tribes, but was foiled in his efforts by Colonel George Morgan (whose Indian name was Tamenend), who succeeded in neutralizing many of the tribes. Captain Pipe and White Eyes, famous Delaware chiefs, separated on the question of aiding the British, and Pipe removed with his supporters to the Tymochtee, near Upper Sandusky, and joined the fortunes of Half King and the *Wyandots*. Just before this Heckewelder founded a new village near the forks of the Muskingum, which he called Lichtenau. The chiefs of the *Delawares* in the vicinity of the village desired that their children might be taught the gospel of peace. While laboring here Half King and his warriors came to destroy the settlement; but the calm manner of Heckewelder and the Christian Indians excited the compassion of Half King, and the little settlement rested four years from further disturbance.

In 1781 Shingess, a famous Delaware chief, sometimes called Bockingehelas, demanded the surrender of all the Christian chiefs, that they might be removed until after the war which seemed about to break out, to a place of safety, declaring that the border settlements intended to exterminate the Moravian Indians on the Muskingum. His demand was rejected, because Heckewelder and his converts thought his opinions erroneous. The *Wyandots* became clamorous for their removal to Sandusky. The *Six Nations* held a great council at Niagara, and handed over to the *Ottawas* and *Chippewas* the Christian Indians on the Muskingum to make broth of. These tribes being relations of the *Delawares*, refused to make war on the *Moravians*. Captain Pipe and Half King, with three hundred warriors, led by a noted chief called Wingenund, soon appeared (with a British flag carried by the notorious Captain Elliot) at Salem, a settlement of the *Moravians*, and proposed a council to be held at Gnadenhutten. At first the *Moravians* declined; but Elliot pressed the matter, and Half King was ready to use force if they did not consent to be removed. After suffering some violence from the *Wyandots*, the *Moravians* consented to abandon their settlement and return with Half King and Pipe.

On the tenth of September, 1781, they were ordered to get ready. The command was obeyed. By this removal they lost, says Loskiel, "three beautiful settlements—Gnadenhutten, Salem and Schoenbrun, and the greatest part of their possessions in them. They had about two hundred head of cattle, four hundred hogs, and three hundred acres of corn, besides potatoes, cabbages and garden fruits, worth about twelve thousand dollars. They were most pained at the loss of their books and writings, which were all burned by the Indians." On the thirteenth they arrived at Goshocking and tarried a few hours. Here Elliott left them. They then commenced the ascent of the Walholding, partly by water and partly by land along its banks. On the nineteenth, six days after they left Goshocking (Coshocton) two of their best canoes, heavily laden with provisions, sank in a violent storm of wind and rain, and the women and children suffered severely. Half King halted to dry their clothes, after which they again proceeded on their way and at Gook-ho-sing, a branch rising in Knox county and emptying into the Walholding, called the habitation of owls, from the rugged nature of the uplands on its margin, they left the river, traveling by land, and on the eleventh of October they arrived at the Sandusky river, three miles southeast of the present Upper Sandusky, where they "pitched upon the best spot they could find in the dreary waste, and built small huts of logs and bark, to screen themselves from the cold, having neither beds nor blankets, and being reduced to the greatest poverty and want, the savages having by degrees stolen everything, both from missionaries and the Indians, on their journey."

As it has long been a mooted question whether the Moravians passed up "Owl creek," in Knox county, or ascended the Walhonding and the Black fork of Mohican, we deem it appropriate to quote Heckewelder. In his narration, page 277, he says: "Our course was now up the Walhonding river, otherwise called the Whitewoman's creek; but the river being at this season low, and in some narrow places obstructed by driftwood, the workmen had to cut a passage before they could pass on, which caused us to move slowly. Those who traveled by land, having their provisions in the canoes, were frequently obliged to wait an hour, or longer, until the canoes came up, which obliged us to make but short journeys each day. Continuing our journey for a number of days after the manner we had done, we arrived at Gook-ho-sing (habitation of owls), where we left the river, traveling by land across the country, for Upper Sandusky; and suffered much on our way, through the ill will of the *Wyandots*, who, by this time, had become impatient to get home." Page 283, it will be observed that neither Loskiel nor Heckewelder states that the route was up the Owl creek or Kokosing, in Knox county. On the contrary, on reaching the mouth of that stream, they left it, and traveled across the country. When Heckewelder wrote his narrative in 1820, Knox county had been organized over twelve years. If the Moravians had passed up the Owl creek, it is not unlikely he would have so stated. On the contrary, we find, so late as 1808, that Heckewelder preferred to travel the old Huron trail, on the Black fork.

The Black fork has always been regarded as the main branch or head of the Walhonding, and has been so called by many early writers; and after a careful analysis of the route, it seems probable that they passed up that stream to near the modern site of Greentown. This opinion seems to be confirmed by Mary Heckewelder, daughter of the missionary, John Heckewelder, who was living at Bethlehem, Pennsylvania, as late as 1843, and who, according to Perkins, page 253, says: "Our journey was exceedingly tedious and dangerous; some of the canoes sunk, and those that were in them lost all their provisions, and everything they had saved. Those that went by land drove the cattle, a pretty large herd. The savages now drove us along, the missionaries with their families usually in their midst, surrounded by their Indian converts. The roads were exceedingly bad, leading through a continuation of swamps. We went by land through Goseuchguenk (Coshocton), to the Walhonding, and then, partly by water and partly along the banks of the river, to Sandusky creek." The nature of the ground from the Black fork, by the route described, conforms to the idea of Mary Heckewelder.

The company were seven days in traveling the first twenty-five or thirty miles. They reached the branches of the Sandusky on the eleventh of October, twenty days after the storm. A fair estimate of the distance traveled the first seven days, would bring them to the old *Huron* or *Wyandot* trail at the mouth of Clear fork, in Hanover township, and the eighth day would place them near the modern site of Greentown, on Armstrong's creek, or the Black fork of the Mohican. The route from thence would conform to the recollection of Mary Heckewelder, being full of ponds, marshes and bogs, and difficult of passage. This was the common route of the *Wyandots*, and was the favorite route of the *Delawares* as late as the appearance of the white settlers.

Now, if as supposed, the Moravians turned up the Lake fork, when they left the Walhonding, they probably followed the Black fork until they reached the mouth of the Rocky fork, where they struck an ancient trail that followed that stream by the present site of Mansfield, to the site selected for their village, on the branch of the Sandusky. Regarding both routes as not freed of difficulty, and, therefore, unsettled, we resume the thread of our discourse.

A party was sent back to gather the corn yet standing in the fields, and returned with about four hundred bushels. About one hundred and fifty Moravians returned in February, 1782, and divided so as to work at the three deserted towns in the cornfields. Elliott, Girty, and McKee accused the missionaries of a want of fidelity to the British, and had them removed to Detroit, where they were tried, and acquitted by the testimony of Captain Pipe, who declared that he believed that they had acted faithfully as neutrals.

Soon after the removal of the Moravians, a number

of depredations were committed along the borders of Pennsylvania, by small bands of *Wyandots*, which exasperated the people to madness and revenge. Colonel David Williamson organized a volunteer expedition to go to the Muskingum, with a view of punishing the Moravians, who were charged with harboring and encouraging the *Wyandots*. In a brief time, his irregular forces were ready to march to the villages. In March, 1782, about ninety volunteers, under command of Williamson, assembled in the Mingo bottom, just below the site of Steubenville. They proceeded rapidly to Gnadenhutten, and entered the town, where they found a large body of Indians in a field, getting corn. They told the Indians they had come to take them to Fort Pitt for protection. The Indians were pleased at the prospect of removal, and delivered their arms, which they used in hunting, and commenced to prepare breakfast for the soldiers. An Indian messenger proceeded to Salem, to inform the brethren there, and returned with them. The treacherous soldiers then proceeded to secure the Indians, by binding and confining them in two houses, well guarded. The Salem Indians were also fettered, and divided between the two prison houses, the males in one, and the females in the other. The number thus confined was about ninety-six, including old men, women, and children. The infuriated soldiers of Williamson then held a council, to determine how the Moravian Indians should be disposed of. After some discussion, Colonel Williamson put the question, whether the Moravian Indians should be taken prisoners to Fort Pitt, or put to death, requesting those who were in favor of saving their lives to step out, and form a second rank. Only eighteen voted for mercy! The balance resolved to murder the Christian Indians in their custody! The soldiers were deaf to all pleas of mercy and protection! The poor Moravians were ordered to prepare for death. The sound of the Christian's hymn and the Christian's prayer, soon found an echo in the surrounding forest, but no response from the unfeeling bosoms of their determined executioners. With gun, and spear, and tomahawk, and scalping knife, the work of death progressed, in these slaughter-houses, until not a sign or moan was heard, to proclaim the existence of human life within. All were murdered, save two boys, who escaped, as if by miracle, to be witnesses, in after times, of the savage cruelty of the soldiers of Williamson. Of the number killed, between fifty and sixty were women and children, some innocent babes. No resistance was made. The whites finished the tragedy, by setting fire to the town, including the slaughter-houses with the bodies in them, and all were consumed. The people of Schoenbrun, hearing the news of the dreadful tragedy, fled, and saved their lives. This act of inexcusable cruelty and cowardice, shocked the border settlers, and called down upon Williamson and his men the execrations of every humane person in the country. The only excuse offered, in palliation of these wanton murders, was the fact that a few garments, formerly belonging to the settlers, some of them stained with blood, were found in the houses of the Moravians.

These articles, doubtless, had been purchased of the hostile Indians, in exchange for provisions, while on their return through the villages. This act of barbarity cannot be justified. It leaves an ineffaceable stain upon the character of the border volunteers of Pennsylvania; and the judgment of the Almighty soon overtook many of the actors in that sanguinary tragedy, on the plains of Sandusky, in the subsequent disaster that overtook Crawford and his army.

CHAPTER XI.

CRAWFORD'S EXPEDITION.

Expedition of Colonel William Crawford to Upper Sandusky in 1782.—His Disastrous Repulse and Flight.—His Capture, Torture, and Death at the Stake, by Captain Pike.—The Object of the Expedition.—The Route of the Expedition Through the Forests of Ohio.

The massacre of the Moravian Indians on the Tuscarawas intensified the hate of Captain Pipe towards the border settlers, because they were mostly *Delawares* and his kinsmen. Although he had opposed the pacific principles and faith of the Moravian Indians, and had, to some extent, assisted in persecuting and annoying them in consequence of their refusal to go upon the war-path, yet, when they were attacked by the Pennsylvania volunteers and barbarously slaughtered, his sympathies were aroused in their behalf, and he resolved to avenge the death of the inoffensive brethren who had been wantonly murdered by the blood-thirsty rangers of Williamson at Gnadenhutten. The *Wyandots*, the *Shawnees*, the *Ottawas*, the *Miamis*, the *Mingoes*, and the *Mohegans* rallied to his support, and the borders of Virginia and Pennsylvania were threatened with invasion by the savages of the northwest. Pipe and Half King went from tribe to tribe calling for assistance, and several thousand warriors were collected in the vicinity of Sandusky plains ready to measure arms with the "Long Knives," and go upon the war path to visit summary vengeance upon the whites for the inhuman treatment of the Christian *Delawares*.

In the meantime, the border counties of Pennyslvania and Virginia became greatly excited over the impending danger of an Indian invasion. Volunteers were invited to join a new expedition then organizing to march into territories of Ohio to attack the new settlement of the Christian Indians on the Sandusky, as well as the *Wyandot* and *Delaware* towns located thereon. The enterprise was conducted with as much secresy and rapidity as possible, the volunteers furnishing their own outfits, and mostly mounted on horses, were supplied with arms and ammunition by the authorities of Washington county, Pennsylvania.

About the twentieth of May, 1782, the volunteers crossed the Ohio river and rendezvoused at the deserted *Mingo* village below what is now Steubenville. An election for a commanding officer took place. The candidates were Colonel David Williamson and Colonel

William Crawford, the confidential friend of General Washington. Colonel William Crawford received a majority of the votes, and was declared the commander, although he is said to have accepted the command with much reluctance. Colonel Williamson accompanied the expedition in command of a company of volunteers.

On the twenty-fifth of May the army, numbering about four hundred and eighty men, departed for the Sandusky, following the Williamson trail, and on the fourth day reached Shoenbrun, on the Tuscarawas, then the Muskingum, and found sufficient corn in the field for their horses. They continued down the Tuscarawas, and, on the thirtieth, discovered, a few hundred yards in advance, two Indians skulking through the forest, apparently watching the movements of the troops. They were fired at but escaped. The soldiers were thrown into a fever of excitement and confusion over the circumstance, and expected an ambush and attack; and Colonel Crawford is said to have expressed apprehensions of the worst consequences, from the evident want of discipline and subordination on the part of the rangers, and afterwards lost all confidence in their courage and capacity to cope with any considerable force of Indians. He, as an experienced soldier, was impressed with the fact that the two Indians were acting as spies, and had stealthily followed him from the Ohio river, and were fully aware of his destination and the number of troops composing the expedition, all of which had doubtless been communicated to the villages in their advance, and to Pipe and Half King. Colonel Crawford found all the Indian villages on his route deserted, and the impression prevalent that no quarter was to be given to an Indian, whether man, woman, or child.

On his route from the Tuscarawas, he passed through White Eyes plains, across the north part of Holmes and the south part of Wayne counties, and over the townships of Lake and Green, in Ashland county, near the present residences of Warring Wolf, David Hunter, Thomas and Benjamin McGuire, north of Alexander Rice, George Guthrie and old Greentown, to the Rocky fork, and up it to where Mansfield now is; thence to Spring mills, and thence to near Pipestown, where they found the Moravian huts or cabins on the sixth of June, deserted, and nothing but desolation to mark the spot. The site was surrounded by tall grass, and the remains of a few huts were seen. It was well—for the human tigers that had feasted on Christian blood at Gnadenhutten, intended to make a dash at the towns of the Moravian *Delawares* and *Wyandots* upon the Sandusky, where no Indian was to be spared—friend or foe—every red man was to die! This, then, might be considered a second Moravian campaign, as its object was to finish the sanguinary work of murder and plunder commenced on the Tuscarawas. Having had a taste of blood and plunder, there, without risk and loss, they had entered upon the new campaign with high hopes of easily extirpating the *Delawares* and *Wyandots*.

Finding the Moravian village deserted, the officers called a halt, and held a council, in which the propriety of advancing was fully discussed. Some desired to turn back, as their horses were much wearied by the long and toilsome journey, and needed rest and proper forage. It was finally decided that the army should advance one day further, and, if an enemy could not be discovered, to retreat. The army was again put in motion, and, having crossed the Sandusky, advanced about one mile west to a point about three miles north of Upper Sandusky, where the guard, about two o'clock, was attacked and driven in by the Indians, who were discovered in large numbers in the high grass with which the plain was covered. The Indians attempted to take a piece of woods to conceal themselves behind the trees, but were prevented by the rapid movements of Colonel Crawford's forces, and the battle commenced by heavy firing from both sides. The Indians were driven from the timber, and the battle continued with incessant and heavy firing until dark, when both armies kindled large fires along the line of battle to prevent surprise, and rested on their arms during the night. In the morning the battle was not renewed, but the Indians were seen during the day in large numbers traversing the plains in various directions. A council of officers was held, and a speedy retreat resolved on as the only means of saving the army. Captain Williamson proposed to take one hundred and fifty men and march directly to Upper Sandusky. The proposition was rejected, under the belief that it would weaken the forces so as to allow them to be cut off in detail, and result in the capture of an empty town. During the day, the dead (three in number) were buried, and arrangements for carrying the wounded were made. At a given signal the retreat was to commence in the evening, after dark. The route is not clearly pointed out, but seems to have been in the direction of Upper Sandusky, the only open point in the Indian lines. The forces moved forward, but were soon thrown into great confusion by an attack by the Indians. While some three hundred men moved forward as directed, Capt. Williamson, with about forty men, seems to have separated from the main body and broken through the Indian lines under a severe fire, with some loss, and, on the second day, overtook the army on its retreat. The main army probably passed through Upper Sandusky without pursuit, and then, wheeling to the left, kept up the stream a short distance, crossed over, and continued to retreat in an easterly direction until it again struck the trail by which it had advanced, and followed the same with as much rapidity as possible to the Tuscarawas, and thence to the Ohio river, pursued by the Indians, who cut off all the stragglers found on the route. When the retreat commenced, a large number of soldiers believing it to be safer to separate from the main army, scattered over the plains, and were all captured or killed by the Indians. Colonel Crawford having delayed while the troops were passing, in search of his son and other relatives, was joined by Dr. Knight, the surgeon, and failing to meet or hear of the young men, and, having no confidence in the courage of the army, he, Dr. Knight, and two others, changed their course northward, guided by the north star, and continued to travel in that direction for nearly an hour, and then, turning east, soon crossed the Sandusky, and pressed forward until daybreak, when their horses failed and were abandoned. Continuing their journey on foot they soon fell in with Captain Biggs, who had generously surrendered his horse to a wounded officer, Lieutenant Ashley, and was walking by his side with a rifle in his hand and a knapsack on his shoulders. At three o'clock in the afternoon a heavy rain fell, which compelled them to encamp. They constructed a temporary shelter by barking several trees, after the manner of the Indians, and spread the bark over poles. Here they passed the night. In the morning they resumed their route and were so fortunate as to find the carcass of a deer neatly sliced and bundled in the skin, and a mile further on fell in with a white man, who had kindled a fire. They breakfasted heartily after the fatigues and abstinence of thirty-six hours, and continued their march. By noon they had reached the path by which the army had marched a few days before, in their advance upon the Indian towns, and some discussion took place as to the propriety of taking that route homeward.* Biggs and Knight strenuously insisted upon continuing their course through the woods, and avoiding all paths, but Crawford overruled them, representing that the Indians would not continue the pursuit beyond the plains, which were already far behind. Before they had advanced a mile, a party of *Delaware* Indians sprang up near Colonel Crawford and Dr. Knight, who were some distance ahead of their comrades, and ordered them, in good English, to stop. They surrendered —the rest fled; but Biggs and Ashley were overtaken and killed the next day.† Crawford and Knight were taken to an Indian encampment near by, where they found nine other prisoners.

On the next morning, all were conducted toward the Tymochtee, by Pipe and Wingenund, *Delaware* chiefs, except four of them, who were killed and scalped on the way, they being about thirty-three miles from Sandusky, on the trail by which the army had advanced. When they arrived at a *Delaware* town on the Tymochtee, a few miles northwesterly from the site of Upper Sandusky, preparations were made for the burning of Colonel Crawford. In the vicinity the remaining five of the prisoners were tomahawked and scalped by squaws and boys. The relations of Crawford were executed by the *Shawnees* on the Scioto. Upon the arrival of Colonel Crawford on the Tymochtee, he endeavored to enlist the sympathies of the notorious Simon Girty, who was then living with the Indians, but Girty would not or could not exert any influence in his behalf. Indeed, it is said that Captain Pipe rebuked him for his interference, with a threat of burning him also if he again mentioned the matter. A post about fifteen feet high was set in the ground, where the prisoner was to be burned; and a large pile of hickory poles, about six yards from it, had been burned in the middle, so as to make a bed of coals and fagots to torture him. When the colonel approached the spot, he was surprised at these preparations, and, Heckewelder says, when Wingenund came up, Crawford addressed him in regard to their intentions, and desired his influence on the ground of a long acquaintance, and warm friendships. Wingenund said he sympathized with him, and admitted the force of his arguments for mercy; but that Captain Pipe could not be appeased for the cruel death of his Moravian kinsmen on the Muskingum, and was determined to make a victim of the colonel. When reminded that Colonel Crawford had no part in that dreadful tragedy, he said if they could have captured Williamson he thought the life of Crawford would have been spared. But, as the matter then stood, he could do nothing, and would retire from the spot.

Dr. Knight says, when we "went to the fire, the colonel was stripped naked, ordered to sit down by the fire, and then beat him with sticks and their fists. Presently after, I was treated in the same manner. They then tied a rope to the foot of the post, bound the colonel's hands behind his back, and fastened the rope to the ligature between his wrists. The rope was long enough for him to sit down or walk round the post once or twice, and return the same way. The colonel then called to Girty, and asked if they intended to burn him? Girty answered yes. The colonel said he would take it patiently." Upon this, Captain Pike made a speech to the Indians, about thirty or forty men, and sixty or seventy squaws and boys. At its conclusion, the Indians gave a hideous yell of assent; and the Indian men then took up their guns and fired sixty or seventy loads of powder into the colonel's body, from his feet as far up as his neck. They then crowded about him and mutilated him; and then, three or four Indians by turns, took up the burning pieces of the poles and applied them to his naked body, already blacked with the powder. Some of the squaws took boards and poured burning coals and hot embers on him, so that in a short time he had nothing but coals to walk upon. In the midst of these extreme tortures, he begged Girty to shoot him—but the hardened wretch derisively replied he had no gun, at the same time turning about to an Indian, laughed heartily, and seemed delighted at the horrid scene. "Colonel Crawford, at this period of his sufferings, besought the Almighty to have mercy on his soul, spoke very low, and bore his torments with the most manly fortitude." He continued to survive under these extreme tortures for over two hours, when an Indian removed the doctor to Captain Pipe's house, about three quarters of a mile from the place of the colonel's execution. The next morning the doctor was untied and painted black, to be taken to a *Shawnee* town, some forty miles distant, to be burned. He was taken, bound to an Indian post, the spot where the colonel had been burned, and says: "I saw his bones lying among the remains of the fire, almost burned to ashes. I suppose, after he was dead, they laid his body on the fire. The Indians told me that was my big captain, and gave the scalp halloo." On the way to

---

* After a careful analysis of the course of Colonel Crawford and his comrades, we are inclined to believe that this parley took place nearly on the line of the Pittsburgh & Fort Wayne railroad, some two or three miles northwest of Mansfield, a distance of about thirty-three or thirty-four miles east of the Sandusky river.

† It is probable that Captain Biggs and Lieutenant Ashley were killed somewhere in the east part of Milton or the west part of Montgomery township, in this county.

the Shawnee town, through the forest, the doctor made his escape, and finally got safely to Pittsburgh. Thus ended the disastrous campaign of Colonel Crawford. His death was the penalty demanded for the slaughter of the Moravians. He is described as an amiable, intelligent, and chivalrous officer; and the intelligence of his death sent a shudder of horror over the border counties of Pennsylvania and Virginia.*

* In a letter addressed to the author, Hon. A. H. Byers, of Wooster, who had a relative in the command of Colonel Crawford, says:

"Crawford's route from Shoenbrun, two miles south of New Philadelphia, to Odell's, or Mohican John's lake, was nearly west. My opinion is that the expedition continued nine or ten mile west, up Sugar creek, the mouth of which must be very near where Shoenbrun stood, the valley being for that distance nearly east and west, broad and level, and beautiful. The south branch falls in there, having run some distance from the west, not far from the line between Wayne and Holmes counties; thence the army may have passed down the Salt creek to Killbuck, near Holmeville, from thence to Mohican John's lake; and thence continued more westerly not far from Loudonville, thence up that branch of Mohican, past Greentown. Since writing the foregoing, I have looked at a map, and find my route between Shoenbrun and Odell's lake would be rather more north than west, but still it seems to me a very probable one."

The actual route was about one and a half miles north of Loudonville, and about one mile north of the Indian village of Greentown, which was not established until 1783. In other words, Colonel Crawford simply followed the old Huron trail leading from Sandusky to the forks of the Muskingum and Fort Du Quesne.

CHAPTER XII.

THE LEGEND OF "HELLTOWN."

A Legend concerning the Abandonment of "Helltown" in 1782, on the Approach of Crawford's Army, and the Founding of "Greentown" in 1783, by the Lenni-Lenapes or Delawares, by the Aid of a White Tory.

THE precise period of the location of the *Delaware* and *Mingo* village of Greentown, on the Black fork, some three miles west of the present village of Perrysville, in Green township, cannot be fixed with entire certainty. The location of that village was on the north side of the Black fork or Armstrong's creek, and on the present site of the farm of John Shambaugh. The weight of authority would seem to fix the date of location of the Greentown Indians as early as 1783, one year after Crawford's expedition, and some thirty-five years before the appearance of the white settlers in that region.

The legend connected with the settlement of the village is very interesting, and is based upon the recollections of an old pioneer of Mohican township, Mr. Benjamin Tyler, of Tylerstown, Ohio.* In the spring of 1782, when Colonel William Crawford invaded the Indian settlements of Upper Sandusky, he passed up the old Indian trail through White Eyes plains, in Tuscarawas county, and across the counties of Wayne, Holmes, Ashland, Richland and Crawford. As he approached the banks of the Mohican, he was closely watched by the Indians who beleaguered his path. At that time, an Indian village by the name of "Helltown," existed near the south line of what is now Green township, on the

*Died in 1876.

banks of the Clear fork of the Mohican. Its inhabitants having learned the fate of the poor Moravians, their relatives, on the banks of the Tuscarawas, some months prior to the new invasion, fled to Upper Sandusky for safety. This village was the home of Thomas Lyon, Billy Montour, Thomas Jelloway, Billy Dowdy, Thomas Armstrong—chief—and other leading *Delawares;* and the occasional residence of the noted Captain Pipe, who aided in the execution of the unfortunate Colonel William Crawford.

The village probably derived its name from a Pennsylvania captive, who spoke the German language, "Hell," in that vernacular, signifying clear, light or transparent. It was, therefore, the village of the clear stream.

Tradition, as derived from the noted Thomas Lyon, in a conversation with Judge Peter Kinney, fixes the location of Greentown the year following Colonel Crawford's expedition, "Helltown" being abandoned as a village site. Thomas Armstrong, the ruling chief, with the original inhabitants of the village on the Clear fork, constituted, with a few *Mingoes* and *Mohawks*, the proprietors of the new village. It was situated on a bluff or tongue of land extending to the north banks of the Black fork or "Armstrong's creek," and pretty nearly surrounded by alder marshes east, south, north and west, and was a strong position. The village site covered from three to four acres. The huts numbered perhaps from one hundred and fifty to two hundred, and were constructed of poles, and covered with bark, and were irregularly placed on the knoll, and surrounded a very handsome play-ground, at the west side of which was a council house and a cemetery in a grove.

From 1783 to 1795 this village was a point on the route from Upper Sandusky to Fort Pitt, and many trembling captives passed through it on their way to Detroit or other points in the Indian country. Many captives on their return east mention "Greentown" and "Mohican Johnstown," places to which they were conducted during their captivity.

Having, for a long time, been curious to learn why the village should have been named "Greentown," the author accidentally ascertained that Mr. Benjamin Tyler and his ancestors had information concerning the fall of Wyoming that was, as yet, unwritten. We called upon him for the information desired. He stated that his parents had resided at an early day in the Mohawk valley, where he was born. Mr. Tyler came into Mohican township in 1814, and is now eighty-four years of age. In 1804 his father, Benjamin Tyler, sr., resided in Cayuga county, New York, and was visited by one Thomas Green, whom he had formerly known in New England, in company with two Delaware Indians from Ohio, who asked and obtained leave to stay all night. Mr. Tyler, having been acquainted in his boyhood in Connecticut with Mr. Green, desired to learn, during the conversations of the evening, where he had been for the twenty-five years prior to that time. Mr. Tyler had known that Green was regarded as a tory, and had sympathized with the British and Indians in the destruction of the beautiful valley of Wyoming, and had fled to the

INDIAN ✦ VILLAGE ✦ OF ✦ GREENTOWN, ✦ 1812

territory west of the Ohio river and made his home among the *Delawares*. In response to the inquiry, Green gave Mr. Tyler, in the presence of his sons, the late Major Tyler and Benjamin, a full recital of his adventures, among other things stating that he had founded a village on the waters of Mohican, which the Indians in honor of himself called "Greentown;" and that he possessed a great deal of influence over his Indian brethren. In a few days Green and his companions returned to the wilds of the Black fork, and were never again seen by Mr. Tyler.

Mr. Benjamin Tyler thinks Green subsequently died among the Greentown Indians, and now rests in the old Indian cemetery.

Mr. Tyler is regarded as a truthful man, and the fact that Billy Montour, Thomas Jelloway, and Thomas Lyons were at the destruction of Wyoming, gives weight to the legend as detailed by him. We are of opinion his statement is reliable. We may conclude then that the founding of Greentown took place in the year 1783, and that it was so named in honor of Thomas Green, a Connecticut tory who joined the Indians.

CHAPTER XIII.
INDIAN TRAILS.

Ancient Indian Trails in Ashland County, from the period of the expeditions of Major Rogers and Colonel Crawford.

AN examination of the maps and trails of the territory of Ohio throws much light on the expeditions of the Indians against the border settlements in Pennsylvania and Virginia. A knowledge of those trails enabled the early settlers to trace the flight of the Indians to their villages on the Muskingum, and at Sandusky, after committing depredations upon the persons and property of the pioneers. It was along these trails or paths that in subsequent years many of the first settlers in Ohio traveled to locate lands, and finally reached their new homes, in the absence of roads through the forests.

It is a subject of remark that the Indian trails, as well as those of the buffalo, have furnished the best location for canals and railroads, not only in Ohio, but west of the Mississippi, where those trails have been followed through the mountain gorges, and along the streams and rivers until the Pacific has been reached. Fremont and Carson, and in fact all the earlier emigrants to the Pacific slope, were well aware of the superior engineering qualities of the Indian and the buffalo, and did not hesitate to follow the paths marked out by them.

In former numbers we have alluded to certain expeditions, and paths of adventure through and across this county. It will, therefore, be interesting to notice the early Indian trails amid the forests and along the streams flowing through this county, and this, because along these trails many of the pioneers reached their future homes.

The first great trail was from fort DuQuesne to Sandusky. It commenced opposite the present site of Pittsburgh and ran a little north of west to the mouth of Big Beaver, twenty-five miles; from thence to the junction of Sandy and Tuscarawas creeks at the south line of Stark county, ninety-one miles; from thence to the east line of Paint township in Wayne county, thence a little northwest through east Union township, along the south side of where Wooster now is, and crossed Killbuck three or four rods north of the bridge on the Ashland road, and continued along south of Little Killbuck, crossing the Muddy fork of Mohican near the present site of Reedsburgh thence to Mohican Johnstown, where it crossed the Jerome fork of Mohican, fifty miles; * thence probably by the route of Rogers to Junandot or Wyandot Town, (Castalia) in the county, forty-six miles; thence to Fort Sandusky, on Sandusky bay, four miles; thence to Fremont on Sandusky river, twenty-four miles;—the entire distance from Fort DuQuesne being two hundred and forty miles by said trail. † We are inclined to the opinion that this was a much traveled trail for perhaps a century before the forests of Ohio had been penetrated and taken possession of by the European.

It is also quite certain that from Mohican Johnstown this trail branched off a little south of east passing through Plain township by the "Long Meadow," or perhaps a little south, by Mohican John's Lake in Clinton township, in Wayne county, thence across Killbuck some twelve miles south of Wooster, where Rogers crossed that stream, and where we feel quite certain that Colonel Crawford also crossed, and encamped a short distance north of what is now known as Odel's lake, then known as Mohican John's Lake, on his expedition to the Moravian settlement on Sandusky creek, in Crawford county.

From Mohican Johnstown there was also a trail, running southwest, to the Delaware village of Greentown, by or near the former site of Goudy's old mill, to the Quaker springs, in Vermillion township; thence, continuing southwest, over Honey creek, to the west part of Green township, to a point about three miles west of Perrysville. This trail was, subsequently, known as the old Portage road,‡ and was traveled by many of the pioneers to their new homes in Green township. The trail continued thence, in the direction of the present site of Lucas, to near Mansfield.

From Mohican Johnstown there was also another trail, running up the east side of the Jerome fork, much traveled by the *Mohegans*, in their hunting excursions on the Black river; and, in the north part of this county, to the junction of the Catotaway, in the eastern part

---

* We are indebted to Hon. H. Byers, of Wooster, for the course of the trail through Wayne county. Having access to the papers of Joseph H. Larwill, now deceased, he finds a map, which was made at the land office at Cincinnati at a very early day for Mr. Larwill's own use, and is no doubt positively accurate, as it was made from the field notes of the surveyors of whom he was one.

† See Taylor's History of Ohio, page 163.

‡ The late Judge Peter Kinney helped survey and open this path from New Lisbon, Wooster, Jerome's place, Greentown, Fredericktown, and Clinton, Knox county, Ohio, as early as 1810. They followed the trail.

of Montgomery township, where it crossed, and passed near the residence of Moses Latta and Burkholder's mill, and thence up the creek, past the old Gierhart farm. Here resided a proud old Indian hunter, named Catotawa, after whom the stream was undoubtedly named. Some of the pioneers of Montgomery remember him well.

At, or near, the former residence of the late Mr. Samuel Burns there was another path, or trail, which ran past the residence of Mr. Newell, continuing up the creek, to the former residence of Daniel Carter, sr., a few hundred yards north of the bridge on the Harrisburgh road; thence, up the stream, to the present residence of Mr. David Sloan; thence to Mr. Leo Wertman's; thence to near the old Cunningham residence; and from thence to the Vermillion lake, and down the Vermillion river, in the direction of the Huron, into Richland county. This trail does not seem to have been traveled as much as that of the Catotaway.

There was also a trail passing down the east side of the Black fork from some point above Mifflin, to Greentown, where it met the trail from the direction of Lucas. From Greentown, as we are informed by colonel John Coulter, Mr. Alexander Rice and Mrs. Otho Simmons, who were among the earliest settlers in Green township, a trail passed down by the north side of the present site of Loudonville, nearly on the line of the Pittsburgh railroad, continuing down the valley through the lands of the Priests, in Holmes county, towards the Lake fork of the Mohican.*

Another trail kept down the south side of the Black fork from Greentown to the Walhonding proper, and then to the forks of the Muskingum; and probably was the path of the Moravians when they were *enroute* to their new home on Sandusky creek. These trails at the arrival of the early settlers were well marked, and were traveled by hunting parties from Upper Sandusky; and were evidently their great highways to the Muskingum, as well as Tullihas, Gnadenhutten, Shoenbrun, and Fort DuQuesne, and the Indian village on Killbuck, called Beaver.

Like the buffalo, the Indians always march single file; and their regular trails soon became so worn and distinct that they could easily be followed from point to point. When Rodgers passed over this country in 1761, he found the Indians in possession of horses, cows and hogs and it is tolerably certain that the *Wyandots* and *Mohegans* sometimes traveled with horses, and this circumstance also added to the distinctness of their trails. We are inclined to think that the elk and the buffalo had nearly disappeared from this region when Rodgers passed through to Pittsburgh, as they are rarely mentioned at that period.

---

* Another trail passed by the north shore of Odell's lake, thence a little northwest till it reached Priest's prairie, thence in a northwest direction north of the gap, passing near the residence of Warring Wolf, thence across the north part of the lands of Hunter, Thomas McGuire, and near Carey's corners, thence north of George Guthrie's, thence to Mr. Boughman's old farm, thence to and up the Rocky fork. It was by this trail that Colonel Crawford marched to Sandusky in 1782.

CHAPTER XIV.

INDIAN CUSTOMS.

Manners, Customs, and Religion of Northern Ohio Indians. Their Wigwams and Tents. Making Sugar.—Planting Corn.

BEFORE entering upon the pioneer history of the county, we deem it appropriate to discuss, at some length, the customs, habits, social relations and religion of the Indians of northern Ohio. The red men of this part of the State displayed many traits worthy of admiration by the civilized races. When we consider that for ages the Indian tribes in this region had lived in ignorance of the laws and customs of the enlightened races of mankind, we are amazed at the purity of their morals, their comparative freedom from the vices of the white race, and their lofty conceptions of a Supreme Being, and of an existence after their departure, by death, from the hunting-grounds and forests of earth. The Indian of Ohio was proud, high-toned and chivalrous in a remarkable degree. The territories he inhabited, the streams along which he roamed, and the shores of the great lakes, were regarded as his property, given him by the Great Spirit as an inheritance for himself and his children forever. When he beheld the white race seizing and occupying his lands without adequate compensation, it is not a matter of surprise that he promptly resented such encroachments with all the means within his possession. Our fathers, for like reasons, repelled British authority in 1776, and demanded self-government and independence. We offered no terms to the Indian, but submission or death.

WIGWAMS AND TENTS.

For a description of the wigwams and tents of the northern Ohio Indians, we return to the narrative of James Smith.* The winter cabin was generally about fifteen or twenty feet long, and constructed of small logs laid upon each other, posts being driven into the ground at each end to keep them together, the posts being tied at the top with bark, and by this means the wall was raised about four feet high; and in the same manner, another wall was raised opposite, about twelve feet distant; they then drove forks into the ground in the middle of each end, and laid a strong pole from end to end on them, and from the walls to the pole they set up small poles for rafters, and on these tied small poles for laths, and covered them with lynn bark, which was peeled in wide strips, and carried off the rain, and kept the hut quite dry. The bark was raised by the tomahawk near the top of the tree in strips five or six inches broad, and sometimes a piece would be thirty or forty feet in length. This was cut in suitable lengths to cover a cabin. At the ends of the walls split timber was set, so that the sides and ends were enclosed by timber, excepting a door at each end, over which a bear skin was suspended. At the top an open place was left for the escape of smoke. Bark was laid down as a floor, and bear skins spread for beds. From one end of the hut to the other, in the winter season, in the center, the squaws made fires of

---

* Frost and Drake's History of Indian Wars and Captivities in the United States.

dry, split wood. The holes between the logs were carefully closed with moss, gathered from old logs. This species of cabin was mostly used by the *Wyandots, Delawares, Mingoes,* and *Mohegans,* and is described by Smith and other captives, as being very comfortable during the severest winters. The *Ottawas* had a very useful and artistically constructed tent, which was made of flags plaited and stitched together in such manner as to turn rain or wind. Each mat was fifteen feet long, and about four feet wide. In order to erect this kind of tent, a number of long straight poles were driven into the ground so as to form a circle, the upper ends approaching together, so as to be tied. The mats were then spread on these poles, beginning at the bottom and extending up, leaving a small hole at the top to answer the place of a chimney. A fire of dry, split wood was made in the center, and bark and skins spread for beds, on which the Indians slept in a crooked posture, around the fire. For a door they lifted one end of the mat, and crept in, letting it fall down behind them. These tents were warm and dry, and generally quite free from smoke. Their fuel was generally split and prepared in the fall by the squaws, and kept under inverted birch canoes, where it was dry and free from rain. When the *Ottawas* traveled from one part of the forest to another, they took down their tents, and put them in large rolls, being very light; and they were removed by the squaws. This tent resembled those now in use in our armies on the plains, in many respects; and was superior to the far-famed Sibley tent. In the construction of tents, therefore, the children of the forest have evinced wonderful skill, taking into account the materials out of which they were made.

MAKING SUGAR.

About the first of March the Indians commenced to tap sugar trees and make sugar. The sap was generally boiled in large brass or copper kettles which they purchased from the French or English in exchange for valuable furs. The manner of securing the water was very ingenious and successful. As elm bark will strip or run in the winter season, squaws cut down elm trees, and with a crooked stick, broad and sharp at the end, peeled the bark in wide strips, and made vessels in a curious manner that held two or three gallons each. Of these they made one or two hundred; and then cut a sloping notch in the sugar tree and stuck a tomahawk at the end of the notch and drove in a long chip or spile to carry the water to the bark vessel. They generally selected the larger trees for tapping, as the water was deemed stronger and produced the most sugar. They also made bark vessels for carrying water, which held about four gallons each. Having generally two or three, and sometimes six or seven, large kettles, they boiled the water very rapidly. When sap was produced faster than they could boil it away, they prepared vessels of bark that held about one hundred gallons each for the remaining water. Thus, they made sugar rapidly, and were always busy during the season. This sugar was generally mixed with bears' oil or fat until the fat was nearly as sweet as the sugar; and into this the Indians dipped their roasted venison. Sugar was sometimes kept in skins, but more frequently in bark vessels prepared for that purpose by the squaws. Bears' fat, when mixed with sugar, was put in vessels made of deer skins, which were pulled over the neck without ripping. The hair was then removed, and the skin gathered into small plaits round the neck and drawn together like a purse; and in the center a pin was put, below which a string was tied; and when the skin was wet it was blown up like a bladder, and let remain so until it was dry, when it appeared nearly in the form of a sugar loaf. One of these vessels would hold four or five gallons. In such vessels they carried bears' oil also.

PLANTING CORN.

When the season for planting corn arrived, the Indian women busied themselves in clearing a spot of rich soil for that purpose. Having prepared the ground with their rude hoes, they planted and cultivated it, and kept down the weeds with wonderful industry, until it had matured sufficiently for use. Their cornfields were mostly in the vicinity of the villages, and in favorable seasons yielded plentifully. The squaws took charge of the culture of corn exclusively. When Smith was among the *Wyandots*, the squaws requested him one day to take a hoe and help them. He did so, and says:

The squaws applauded me as a good hand at the business, but when I returned to the town, the old men, hearing of what I had done, chided me, and said I was adopted in the place of a great man, and must not hoe corn like a squaw. They never had occasion to reprove me again, as I never was extremely fond of work.

It was the task of the Indian women to cultivate corn, pound and prepare the hominy, cut and carry wood, and, in fact, do all the drudgery, while the men pursued and captured the game, defended the wigwams and went to war. After the corn had ripened, it was parched, put in a rude wooden mortar, or on a flat stone, and pounded into a sort of meal, which was mixed with sugar, and sometimes a little bears' fat, and put in skin and bark vessels for future use; and is said to have been a palatable and nourishing food.

As corn (zea) was indigenous to this continent, and never seen in Europe until about the year 1495, it may be interesting to recite the Indian legend concerning its origin and use.* The legend runs thus:

In times past, a poor Indian was living, with his wife and children, in a beautiful part of the country. He was not only poor, but inexpert in procuring food for his family, and his children were all too young to give him assistance. Although poor, he was a man of kind and contented disposition. He was always thankful to the Great Spirit for everything he received. The same disposition was inherited by his eldest son, who had now arrived at the proper age to undertake the ceremony of the Ke-ig-nish im-o-win, or fast, to see what kind of a spirit would be his guide and guardian through life. Wunzh, for this was his name, had been an obedient boy from his infancy, and was of a pensive, thoughtful, and mild disposition, so that he was beloved by the whole family. As soon as the first indications of spring appeared, they built him the customary little lodge, at a retired spot, some dis-

---

*Indian Tales and Legends, by Henry R. Schoolcraft, volume 1, page 122. Of course, this is a myth, but is nevertheless exceedingly interesting, and evinces some of the mental characteristics of the Indian. The boundaries between truth and fiction are but feebly defined among the aborigines of this continent. All their knowledge is made up of the misty recollections of tradition, and reads more like a fairy tale than reality.

tance from their own, where he would not be disturbed during this solemn rite. In the meantime he prepared himself, and immediately went into it and commenced his fast. The first few days he amused himself in the mornings, by walking in the woods, and over the mountains, examining the early plants and flowers, and, in this way, prepared himself to enjoy his sleep; and, at the same time, stored his mind wtih pleasant ideas for his dreams. While he rambled through the woods, he felt a strong desire to know how the plants, herbs, and berries grew without aid from any man; and why it was, that some species were good to eat, and others possessed medicinal or poisonous juices. He recalled these thoughts to mind, after he became too languid to walk about, and had confined himself strictly to the lodge; he wished he could dream of something that would prove a benefit to his father and family, and to all others. "True!" he thought, "the Great Spirit made all things, and it is to him that we owe our lives. But could he not make it easier for us to get our food, than by hunting animals and taking fish? I must try to find out this in my visions."

On the third day he became weak and faint, and kept his bed. He fancied, while thus lying, that he saw a handsome young man coming down from the sky, and advancing toward him. He was richly and gaily dressed, having on a great many garments, of green and yellow colors, but differing in their deeper or lighter shades. He had a plume of waving feathers on his head, and all his motions were graceful.

"I am sent to you, my friend," said the celestial visitor, "by that Great Spirit who made all things in the sky and on the earth. He has seen and knows your motives in fasting. He sees that it is from a kind and benevolent wish to do good to your people and to procure a benefit for them, and that you do not seek for strength in war or the praise of warriors. I am sent to instruct you and show you how you can do your kindred good." He then told the young man to arise and prepare to wrestle with him, and it was only by this means that he could hope to succeed in his wishes. Wunzh knew he was weak from fasting, but he felt his courage rising in his heart, and immediately got up, determined to die rather than fail. He commenced the trial, and, after a protracted effort, was almost exhausted, when the beautiful stranger said: "My friend, it is enough for once; I will come again to try you;" and, smiling on him, he ascended in the air in the same direction from which he came. The next day the celestial visitor re-appeared at the same hour and renewed the trial. Wunzh felt that his strength was even less than the day before, but the courage of his mind seemed to increase in proportion as his body became weaker. Seeing this, the stranger again spoke to him in the same words he used before, adding, "To-morrow will be your last trial. Be strong, my friend, for this is the only way you can overcome me and obtain the boon you seek. On the third day he again appeared at the same time and renewed the struggle. The poor youth was very faint in body, but grew stronger in mind at every contest, and was determined to prevail or perish in the attempt. He exerted his utmost powers, and after the contest had been continued the usual time, the stranger ceased his efforts and declared himself conquered. For the first time he entered the lodge, and sitting down beside the youth, he began to deliver his instructions to him, telling him in what manner he should proceed to take advantage of his victory.

"You have won your desires of the Great Spirit," said the stranger. "You have wrestled manfully. To-morrow will be the seventh day of your fasting. Your father will give you food to strengthen you, and it is the last day of trial, you will prevail. I know this, and now tell you what you must do to benefit your family and your tribe. "To-morrow," he repeated, "I shall meet you and wrestle with you for the last time; and, as soon as you have prevailed against me, you will strip off my garments and throw me down, clean the earth of roots and weeds, make it soft, and bury me in the spot. When you have done this, leave my body in the earth and do not disturb it, but come occasionally to visit the place to see whether I have come to life, and be careful never to let the grass or weeds grow on my grave. Once a month cover me with fresh earth. If you follow my instructions you will accomplish your object of doing good to your fellow creatures by teaching them the knowledge I now teach you." He then shook him by the hand and disappeared.

In the morning the youth's father came with some refreshments, saying, "My son, you have fasted long enough. If the Great Spirit will favor you, he will do it now. It is seven days since you have tasted food, and you must not sacrifice your life. The Master of life does not require that." "My father," replied the youth, "wait till the sun goes down. I have a particular reason for extending my fast to that hour." "Very well," said the old man, "I shall wait till the hour arrives, and you feel inclined to eat."

At the usual hour of the day the sky visitor returned, and the trial of strength was renewed. Although the youth had not availed himself of his father's offer of food, he felt that new strength had been given to him, and that exertion had renewed his strength and fortified his courage. He grasped his angelic antagonist with supernatural strength, threw him down, took from him his beautiful garments and plume, and finding him dead, immediately buried him on the spot, taking all the precautions he had been told of, and being very confident at the same time, that his friend would come to life. He then returned to his father's lodge and partook sparingly of the meal that had been prepared for him. But he never for a moment forgot the grave of his friend. He carefully visited it throughout the spring, and weeded out the grass, and kept the ground in a soft and pliant state. Very soon he saw the tops of the green plumes coming through the ground; and the more careful he was to obey his instructions in keeping the ground in order, the faster they grew. He was, however, careful to conceal the exploit from his father. Days and weeks had passed in this way. The summer was now drawing towards a close, when one day, after a long absence in hunting, Wunzh invited his father to follow him to the quiet and lonesome spot of his former fast. The lodge had been removed, and the weeds kept from growing on the circle where it stood, but in its place stood a tall and graceful plant, with bright-colored silken hair, surmounted with nodding plumes and stately leaves, and golden clusters on each side. "It is my friend," shouted the lad; "it is the friend of all mankind. It is Mondawmin. We need no longer rely on hunting alone; for, as long as this gift is cherished and taken care of, the ground itself will give us a living." He then pulled an ear. "See, my father, said he, "this is what I fasted for. The Great Spirit has listened to my voice and sent us something new; and henceforth our people will not alone depend upon the chase or upon the waters."

He then communicated to his father the instructions given him by the stranger. He told him that the broad husks must be torn away as he had pulled off the garments in his wrestling; and having done this, directed him how the ear must be held before the fire till the outer skin became brown, while all the milk was retained in the grain. The whole family united in a feast on the newly-grown ears, expressing gratitude to the Merciful Spirit who gave it. So corn came into the world, and has ever since been preserved.

CHAPTER XV.

INDIAN CHARACTERISTICS

Indian Endurance.—Bear Hunting.—Indian Courtship and Marriage.—Matrimonial Fideliy.—Wampum.—Indian Doctors.

NOTHING is more astonishing in the Indian character than their powers of endurance. They have been known to travel one thousand miles through the trackless forests, over mountains, wide spreading prairies and across numberless streams and rivers, on the most meagre supply of food, sleeping upon the ground at night, with nothing to protect them but a blanket wrapped around their bodies, and a small fire at their feet. With a belt or girdle drawn around their bodies, a little sack or pouch of parched corn swung by their side, with rifle and ammunition, they pushed boldly along, and thus accomplished the most surprising journeys in an incredibly short period. That the reader may be able to judge the accuracy of this statement, and fully comprehend Indian endurance as compared with a most striking example of fleetness among the white race, we will allow James Smith to relate an adventure with his Indian brother Tontileaugo, while a captive in 1756 among the *Mohegan*s, *Ottawas* and *Wyandots* of northern Ohio. At that time the part of the tribe to which he was attached, was encamped on the Canesadooharie or Black river, not a great ways from the present site of Elyria, in Lorain county. Food was excessively scarce in that region, and Tontileaugo proposed to Smith to take a hunt on the head branches of that stream where they interlock with the Mohican and other branches of the Muskingum. Smith expressed a willingness to accompany him, knowing that he was an expert hunter. Having put up some sugar and bears' oil, and a little dried venison, they ascended the east branch of the Canesadooharie or Black river, about thirty-five miles and encamped. This was about the close of the winter months. They succeeded remarkably well in procuring game. While engaged in hunting, they discovered a stray horse, mare and colt that had been running in the woods all winter, and were in very good order. There was plenty of grass in that region all winter under the snow, and horses accustomed to feeding in the woods could work it out. These animals had become very timid and wild in consequence of not meeting with Indians or white people. Tontileaugo poposed to run them down. We will now permit Smith to relate, in his peculiar style, the balance of the enterprise. He says:

"Tontileaugo one night concluded that we must run them down. I told him I thought we could not accomplish it. He said he had run down bears, buffaloes and elks; and in the great plains, with only a small snow on the ground, he had run down a deer; and he thought that in one whole day he could tire or run down any four-footed animal except a wolf. I told him that though a deer was the swiftest animal to run a short distance, yet it would tire sooner than a horse. He said he would at all events try the experiment. He had heard the *Wyandots* say that I could run well, and now he would see whether I could or not. I told him I never had run all day, and, of course, was not accustomed to that way of running. I never had run with the *Wyandots* more than seven or eight miles at a time. He said that was nothing, we must either catch these horses or run all day. In the morning early we left camp, and about sunrise we started after them, stripped naked excepting breech-clouts and moccasins. About ten o'clock I lost sight of both Tontileaugo and the horses, and did not see them again until about three o'clock in the afternoon. As the horses run all day in about three or four miles square, at length they passed where I was, and I fell in close after them. As I then had a long rest, I endeavored to keep ahead of Tontileaugo, and after some time I could hear him after me calling chako, chako-anaugh, which signifies, pull away, or do your best. We pursued on, and, about an hour before sundown, we despaired of catching the horses, and returned to camp, where we had left our clothes. I reminded Tontileaugo of what I had told him; he replied he did not know what horses could do. They are wonderful strong to run; but withal we have made them very tired. Tontileaugo then concluded he would do as the Indians did with wild horses when out at war; which is, to shoot them through the neck under the mane, and above the bone, which will cause them to fall and lie until they can halter them, and then they recover again. This he attempted to do; but, as the mare was very wild, he could not get sufficiently near to shoot her in the proper place; however, he shot, the ball passed too low, and killed her. As the horse and colt stayed at this place, we caught the horse, and took him and the colt with us to camp."

We incline to the opinion that this remarkable race took place within the present limits of Sullivan township, in this county, and the west part of Homer township, in Medina county, on the east branch of Black river. If the reader will take a rule, and measure by townships, from a point a mile or two above Elyria, on Black river, thirty-four or thirty-five miles, in a southwesterly direction, he will strike that branch in Sullivan and Homer townships. Concluding that the locality is accurately ascertained, we will have to yield to Sullivan township the honor of the first horse-race within the limits of Ashland county.

BEAR HUNTING.

The Canesadooharie or Black river had been famous among the aborigines of northern Ohio, for the number and largeness of its bears, for more than half a century prior to the arrival of the pioneers. Some of the pioneers, yet surviving, of this county, visited the sources of Black river in search of bruin nearly fifty years ago, and relate many stirring adventures in search of him. It may not be known to the reader, that it was the habit of those animals, in the early part of winter, to select holes in large trees, or make a lair or nest in the alder-bush jungles, where they remained three or four months without eating or drinking! This may appear incredible, but it is declared to be a well-known fact among experienced pioneer hunters. In ascending large trees to reach the holes, the bark was scratched or torn by these animals in climbing, and the hunter had but little difficulty in ascertaining where they had lodged for the winter. The Indian hunters had observed all these signs, and rarely failed to rouse the bear from his comfortable home. Tontileaugo and Smith resorted to the following piece of strategy, which was the common mode of half a century after he left the Black river region. They felled a sapling or small tree against or near the hole; and it was the business of Smith to climb up and drive out the bear, while Tontileaugo stood ready with his gun and bow. They once found a bear about forty feet up in an elm. Tontileaugo got a long pole and some dry decayed wood, which he tied in bunches with bark, and climbed the tree, carrying with him the decayed wood, pole and fire. He then placed his rotton wood on the end of the pole, and setting it on fire, thrust it into the hole. He soon heard the bear snuff, and then descended rapidly to the ground, seized his gun, and waited until it came out; but it was then too late to see the sights of his gun, and setting it down by a tree, he instantly bent his bow, took an arrow, and shot the bear behind the shoulder, and it soon fell to the ground. Occasionally they resorted to the expedient of cutting down large trees with their tomahawks, to secure their game.

The attack of those animals within the jungles was more dangerous, but it was rare that they escaped the unerring aim of the Indian hunter. At the season of the year when those animals ascended large trees to their holes, the bark was scratched or torn by the bear in climbing, and the hunter had but little difficulty in ascertaining where his game had lodged for the winter. Those animals were generally very fat, and were prized very highly by the Indians for their oil and flesh, the mode of preparing which has heretofore been described. The skin was carefully stretched, cleansed and dried, and was used as a bed, and frequently as clothing in the winter by the Indians. Having secured a quantity of flesh and a number of skins, Tontileaugo constructed a canoe of elm bark, and having placed his meat and skins therein, embarked for the falls near the present site of Elyria, where he arrived in safety in one day, being thirty-four or thirty-five miles; while Smith, mounted on his captured horse, with a bear-skin saddle and bark stirrups, proceeded by land to the falls, where his Wyandot and Ottawa friends were encamped. The *Wyandots, Ottawas* and *Mingoes* were generally quite successful in hunting bruin, and were well versed in his mode of seeking and securing winter quarters. They relished his flesh, and feasted upon his oil or fat; and a morsel of venison dipped in sweetened oil was regarded as a dainty dish by friend or stranger.

INDIAN MARRIAGES.

The Indian mode of courtship differed considerably from that of the European or white race. The chief or head of the family generally regulated the marriage relation, presenting the daughter to his choice of the young braves or hunters. When the daughter was allowed to select her own husband, it was not uncommon for her to press her suit with a young man, though the first address may have been by another young man. This was somewhat akin to the leap-year liberty of the white race, in which it is allowable for the young ladies to invite young gentlemen to call upon them, go pleasure trips or accompany them to suppers and refreshments, the young ladies footing the bills. Among the *Wyandots* and *Delawares* advances of that sort were not deemed immodest or improper; in fact, the young braves rather regarded such calls as a delicate piece of flattery, and encouraged their lady loves to continue their suit. The marriage relation seems to have been an agreement or contract between the parties to live with, and adhere to each other as long as domestic unity and fidelity prevailed between man and wife. As a general thing the *Wyondots* and *Delawares* kept their marriage vows with much faithfulness. The *Ottawas* were not regarded as being entirely free from immodesty; and very often, by their words and actions, put young men to the blush. The Ottawa men seem to have possessed more modesty than the women; yet many of the young squaws appeared really modest; genuine it must have been—for they had but little restraint by the laws of education and example. The *Wyandots* and *Delawares* prided themselves upon their virtue, hospitality and bravery; and we know of no well authenticated case where their female captives were insulted or misused. They always evinced the utmost modesty toward their unfortunate female captives. Among these tribes domestic infidelity was severely reprimanded and punished. Respect for parents and for age, fraternal affection, self-denial, and endurance under fatigue or suffering, were uniformly inculcated. These qualities have been applauded and acknowledged in their wigwams, in the mazes of the wilderness, and around the council fire.

WAMPUM.

Wampum is an Iroquois word, meaning a muscle; and a number of these muscles, strung together, is called a string of wampum; which, when a fathom long, was a belt of wampum; but the word string is commonly used, whether it be long or short. These belts were esteemed very valuable by the Ohio Indians, and were very difficult to make; for, not having the proper tools, or instruments, the Indians spent much time in finishing them. When the Europeans commenced trading with the Indians, and ascertained the value attached to wampum, they soon contrived to cut the shells, and perforate the pieces, and then make strings of wampum, both neat and elegant. These they bartered with the Indians for their furs, peltry, and venison, and found the traffic quite profitable. The muscles were mostly found on the coast of Virginia and Maryland, and were valued according to their colors, which were brown, violet, and white. They were first sawed into square pieces, about a quarter of an inch in length, and an eighth in thickness, then ground round, or oval, upon a common grindstone. The hole was bored lengthwise, through each, large enough to admit a wire, or whip-cord, or any cord, to string them like beads; when they were ready for traffic. Four such strings, joined in breadth, fastened together with fine thread, made a belt of wampum; being about three or four inches wide, and three feet long, containing, perhaps, four, eight, or twelve, fathoms. This was determined, by the importance of the subject which the belts were intended to explain, or confirm, or by the dignity of the person to whom they were delivered. Everything of moment transacted at solemn councils, either between the Indians themselves, or with Europeans, was ratified, and made valid, by strings and belts of wampum. Black or brown wampum meant war or warning; red, with a hatchet in the middle, meant, also, to undertake war; and white meant peace. None but the war-belt showed any red color. By these belts, they also remembered the exact words of their treaties. This was a sort of Indian pnemonics; and, forty years afterward, the very words of a treaty could be repeated by the chiefs making it. *

INDIAN PHYSICIANS.

No part of Indian history is more interesting than their mode of treating diseases. In fact, they evinced a wonderful degree of skill in combating the distempers that assailed their race. In this respect they were, generally, quite as successful as the majority of the physicians of the white race. The favorite remedy for nearly all disorders, among the *Delawares, Wyandots, Ottawas, Mohegans,* and *Mingoes,* was the sweat-house. For this purpose, in every town, or near it, they built, of stakes or boards, covered with sods, a sweat-house; or dug a hole in the side of a hill; or drove down four stakes, and covered them with blankets or skins. Large flat, or round stones were heated red-hot, and placed in the center of the sweat-house; when the patient crept, naked, into the structure. Water was poured upon the hot stone, and, the sweat-house being closed, the patient was soon thrown into a profuse sweat; and, as soon as he found himself too hot, he crept out, and plunged into cold water, where he remained one or two minutes, and again returned to the oven, or sweat-house. This process was repeated about three times, when the patient smoked his pipe with composure, and, in most cases, the cure was complete.

---

* George Henry Loskiel, in his "American Missions," p. 26.

They used herbs extensively in their rude practice. Old men, too feeble to hunt, became medicine men, and healed diseases to procure a comfortable living. One made the study of herbs a specialty, another examined and tested the virtues of every species of bark. They generally made a profound secret of their knowledge. The administration of their remedies was always accompanied by mysterious ceremonies, to operate upon the superstitious mind of the patient, and to make the effect appear supernatural.

They had remarkable success in healing wounds, old sores and ulcers. In fractures and dislocations of bones their surgery was as ingenious as original. If an Indian dislocated his foot or knee when hunting alone, he crept to a small tree, and tying one end of a strap to it, he fastened the other to the dislocated limb, and lying on his back, continued to pull until it was reduced.

In burns and chilblains, they used a decoction of beech bark and leaves, as a speedy and successful cure. In bleeding, a small, sharp pointed flint was fastened to a wooden handle, and placed upon the vein, and struck until the blood gushed out. Their medicine men extracted teeth very much as white surgeons do, with a sort of pincers. Rheumatism was treated by sweating and scarification. The bark of the white walnut, pulverized when green, was often applied to the painful part until an eruption was produced. This remedy was extremely acrid, and produced a most pungent pain on the skin where it was applied. For a headache or a toothache, this bark was applied to the temples or the cheek. A strong decoction was also used in fresh wounds, as a styptic, and prevented swelling.

The bite of poisonous serpents was treated by the Indian doctors with wonderful success. They used the leaf of the rattlesnake root—*polygala senega*—as a most efficacious remedy. Indeed, they were so well convinced of the certainty of that antidote, that many Indians would suffer themselves to be bitten for a glass of whisky or brandy. A quantity of the leaves were chewed and immediately applied to the wound, and a small portion swallowed, producing intense thirst, which would relieve the effects of the bite. They also used the Virginia snake root—*serpentinea virginiaenses*—as a poultice for wounds of that description. A decoction of the buds of the white-ash—*fraxemus carolina*—taken inwardly, was believed to be a certain remedy for such wounds.

As tonics and stomachics, they used a decoction of the bark and root of the thorny ash—*aralia spinosa*—the dogwood—*cornus florida*—the wintergreen—*pyola umbellaa*; while the native jalap—*convolvular jalappa*—which grew in abundance, was used as a purgative. They had a knowledge of ginseng—*panox quinque folium*—and it was regarded as a good tonic.

It is a subject of remark, that more than one hundred years before the whites discovered spring or fossil oil, now carbon oil, the Indians used it extensively as an ointment.

CHAPTER XVI.

INDIAN NAVIGATION AND THEOLOGY.

Indian Navigation.—Indian Theology and the Great Spirit.—Tecaughretanego, the Indian Philosopher.—His Remarkable Utterances Concerning the Great Spirit.

IN continuing a discussion of the customs, manners and religion of the Indians of northern Ohio, it will be interesting to notice their modes of navigation. The precise period of the invention of canoes is a matter of conjecture. Canoes seem to have been abundant as a means of transportation and travel on the shores of the northern lakes on the appearance of the earliest Jesuit missionaries, and other adventurers in search of new discoveries. These vessels, wherever seen, bore a striking resemblance as to form, material and use. It is probable they were invented at a very remote period in Indian history, as a means of navigating the rivers and lakes of the north. The birch-bark canoe was a model of beauty and symmetry; and so constructed, that it glided over the waves like a thing of life; and journeys of sixty or seventy miles a day were often made down Lake Erie by a fleet of such vessels, with light sails made of flags, stitched after the manner of their tents. Their largest canoes were about four feet wide, three feet deep, and thirty-five feet long; and could carry heavy loads. They were ingeniously constructed over a wooden frame, by stitching the bark so as to prevent leak and danger of sinking. They were often ornamented with rude paintings and colors, and a fleet of such vessels presented a strange spectacle. They were so light, that after a trip down the lake shore, they could be carried by four men many miles over the summit ridges, and again launched on the head-waters of the Ohio and Muskingum. When the Indians encamped any length of time they carried their canoes up the banks of the streams along which they hunted, and inverting them, converted them into dwelling houses, and making fires before them cooked their provisions, while they stored their baggage and meat and slept beneath these little houses which turned the rain and kept them dry. On the smaller streams and rivers these vessels were paddled by two or four men, and moved along with surprising speed. In the fall of the year the Indians buried their canoes, bottom up, on the banks of a stream, and uncovered them in the spring, when they were apparently uninjured by the frosts of winter, and ready for use again.

HOSPITALITY AND FIDELITY.

Smith relates that when encamped on the Conesadooharie or Black river, and Tontileaugo, his Indian brother, was out hunting, he was visited by a Wyandot, to whom he gave a shoulder of roasted venison that he had prepared for himself, which the Wyandot received gladly, telling him he was very hungry, and thanked him for his kindness. When Tontileaugo returned he related what he had done; he said it was very well, and added he supposed Smith had given him sugar and bears' oil to eat with it. Smith said he had not, as those articles were down in his canoe. Tontileaugo reprimanded him severely, by saying "he had just behaved like a Dutchman," and told him when strangers came to their camp he ought to give them the best they had. Smith admitting he had done wrong, Tontileaugo said "he must learn to behave like a warrior, and do great things, and never be found in such little actions." Indian hospitality was proverbial among the Ohio tribes; and while Williamson and his men were preparing to murder the poor Moravians at Gnadenhutten, they were engaged in cooking and getting breakfast for his volunteers. Could the contrast be greater? When white men or Indians were invited to their feasts, or to accept shelter or nourishment within their cabins, they were sure of protection, and a fair division of food. In fact, when the members of one tribe visited another, it was regarded as a suitable occasion for feasting and good cheer, until all their supplies of provisions had been consumed. In this respect they surpassed most of our own race. If a white man or an Indian refused to eat with them when invited, it was interpreted as a symptom of displeasure, or, that those refusing were angry and disliked those who had invited them to eat. No Indian was allowed to pass the camp of a hunter without being invited to eat and refresh himself, and to do otherwise was regarded a shame, and an evidence of excessive meanness. If all the food had been consumed prior to a request for it, the statement of that fact was always deemed an honorable apology. While it was deemed excusable among Indians to carry off the property of the "Long Knives," in war, no Indian was allowed to steal from another. This rule was adhered to with much severity until they learned to cheat, swear and steal, from their white neighbors.

An Indian never forgot an injury nor a benefit. When Simon Kenton had been captured, and thrice condemned by the *Shawnees* to be burned, Logan, whose kindred had been cruelly murdered by the Baker party on the Ohio river, approached him while the Indians were evincing their anger and menacing his life, and told him to fear not, for he would arrange the matter and save his life. He was always as humane as he was brave. The next morning he told Kenton he would send two young men to Upper Sandusky to speak a good word for him. When the young men returned Kenton was taken by them a prisoner to Upper Sandusky. Logan was then on the Scioto. Before leaving, Logan shook hands with Kenton, but gave no intimation of his fate. When he and his guards arrived at Upper Sandusky, the Indians, young and old, came out to welcome the warriors, and view the prisoner. He was again compelled to run the gauntlet. A grand council was immediately held. This was the fourth time his life was suspended in the balance. When it was organized, Peter Druyer, a Frenchman, then a captain in the British service, made his appearance in the council. He was British agent and interpreter in Indian affairs. It was to him Logan had sent Kenton for protection. He addressed the council in behalf of Kenton. He urged that Kenton be sent to Detroit, where he would be useful to the British in giving information of the movements of the whites in Ohio and Kentucky. He then offered them one hundred dollars in rum and tobacco. The Indians agreed, and Kenton was sent to Detroit, where he was detained and exchanged as a prisoner of war.* The character of Logan only serves to illustrate the acts of hundreds of others who interfered to save white men from impending death by torture at the stake. These instances of Indian fidelity are rarely excelled by the white race. When we consider how often the untutored children of the forest were deceived and wronged by bad white men, we do not marvel that their resentments were carried to the utmost severity. We would not apologize for, nor attempt to extenuate, any of their extreme cruelties, but must admit that, while their mode of torturing prisoners seemed unnecessarily cruel, it was their law of retaliation against implacable enemies. While we condemn the practice of burning helpless captives, what must we say concerning those Christian denominations that have felt it to be their duty to roast each other at the stake because of a difference of opinion on creeds, or assumed powers of enchantment, denominated witchcraft?

INDIAN THEOLOGY.

Had the aborigines of Ohio a theology? We believe they had. James Smith relates a conversation he had with his elder Indian brother, Tecaughretanego, concerning the Great Spirit, and his dealings with the red men of the forest. After hunting two days without eating, Smith returned late in the evening, faint and weary. Tecaughretanego asked him what success. Smith told him not any. This Indian brother had prepared him a kind of soup from some fox and wildcat bones which lay about the camp, and which the ravens and buzzards had picked. He told him he was much refreshed. His Indian brother then handed him his pipe and pouch, and told him to take a smoke. After doing so, he informed Smith that he had something of importance to tell him, if he was now composed and ready to hear it. Being willing to hear him, Tecaughretanego proceeded thus:

He said the reason he deferred his speech, was because few men are in a right humor to hear good talk when they are extremely hungry, as they are generally fretful and discomposed, but as I appeared now to enjoy calmness and serenity of mind, he would now communicate the thoughts of his heart, and those things I knew to be true.

"Brother—as you have lived with the white people, you have not had the same advantage of knowing that the Great Being above feeds his people, and gives them their meat in due season, as we Indians have, who are frequently out of provisions, and yet are wonderfully supplied, and that so frequently that it is evidently the hand of the great Owaneeyo (God) that doeth this. Whereas, the white people have commonly large stocks of tame cattle, that they can kill when they please, and also their barns and cribs filled with grain, and therefore have not the same opportunity of seeing and knowing that they are supported by the ruler of heaven and earth.

"Brother—I know that you are now afraid that we will all perish with hunger, but you have no just reason to fear this.

"Brother—I have been young, but am now old; I have been frequently under the like circumstances that we now are, and that some time or other in almost every year of my life, yet I have hitherto been supported, and my wants supplied in time of need.

"Brother—Owaneeyo (God) sometimes suffers us to be in want, in order to teach us our dependence upon Him, and to let us know that we are to love and serve him; and likewise to know the worth of the favors we receive, and to make us more thankful.

"Brother—be assured that you will be supplied with food, and that just in the right time; but you must continue diligent in the use of

---

* Howe's History of Ohio, page 311.

means. Go to sleep, and rise early in the morning and go a hunting; be strong, and exert yourself like a man, and the Great Spirit will direct your way."*

These are sentiments worthy a philosopher; and Tecaughretanego but uttered the prevailing idea of the *Wyandots* and *Delawares* concerning the existence of God and his overruling providence. At this time this great Indian was over sixty years of age, very much crippled, and unable to hunt; and depended upon the goodness of the Great Spirit to feed him and his little son. Smith arose early the next morning and proceeded slowly about five miles and saw deer, but the crust of the snow made a great noise and they fled before he came in reach of them. Keeping up his courage he soon discovered buffalo tracks, and hastening into a small glade he killed a very large cow; kindled a fire; roasted some of the meat; abated his hunger; made haste and packed up all the meat he could carry and returned to the cabin of his Indian brother. When they were all refreshed, Tecaughretanego delivered a speech upon the necessity and pleasure of receiving the necessary supports of life with thankfulness, knowing that Owaneeyo (God) is the great giver. Such a speech from an Indian may be thought by those who are unacquainted with them altogether incredible. But when we reflect that the person who thus discoursed was no ordinary Indian, but in his sphere as great as Socrates among the educated Greeks, we are not surprised that he should deliver such a discourse upon patience, fortitude and faith.

---

*Frost and Drakes' Indian Captivities.

CHAPTER XVII.

TREATIES AND SURVEYS.

A Brief Discussion of the Indian Policy of William Penn, and the United States.—Perfidy upon all Sides.

In the year 1758, the French surrendered to the British authorities Fort DuQuesne, and, with it, fell French dominion in Ohio, Indiana, Illinois, and Michigan. In September, 1760, the French governor, Vaudrueil, surrendered the fort at Detroit to Major Robert Rogers, who left an English garrison to hold and defend it. The French never regained their possessions in Ohio, although they intrigued, through Pontiac and his savage allies, for their recovery.

In 1768, a treaty was held by Sir William Johnson, at Fort Stanwix, in central New York, in which the Indian title to the lands between the Alleghanies and the eastern boundaries of Ohio, was extinguished, and came under the jurisdiction of Pennsylvania. By this treaty, the colonists of Virginia were greatly gratified, by having their territory extended beyond the Ohio; although the *Shawnees, Miamis,* and many of the *Wyandots,* resisted the extension of the territorial dominion of Virginia, and it required many sanguinary campaigns to subdue their opposition. The Indians of Ohio continued to make incursions upon the frontiers of Pennsylvania and Virginia, often capturing many prisoners, and killing the helpless pioneer settlers. To soften their hostility, and obtain their good will, it was thought best to send agents among them, to hold talks and make presents.

In 1775, congress organized an administration of Indian affairs, and Captain James Wood proceeded to the territory of Ohio, by authority of the general assembly of Virginia, to invite a council at Fort Pitt, formerly Fort DuQuesne. In the meantime, Governor Hamilton, of Canada, used all his arts, through secret agents, to enlist the Indian tribes in the cause of Great Britain. Captain Wood found much difficulty in inducing the Ohio savages to meet him in council at Fort Pitt, but finally succeeded. Congress appointed Franklin, Henry, and Wilson, commissioners, to meet the Indians at Fort Pitt. The conference, in effect, accomplished nothing.

About that time Colonel George Morgan, a gentleman of undoubted courage, discretion and experience, was appointed Indian agent, and by his influence the hostility of the Ohio tribes was neutralized, and the horrors of impending invasion averted during the dreary years of the revolution. Morgan personally visited nearly all the hostile tribes, and finally brought about a conference at Fort Pitt, in October, in which nearly all the tribes were divided in their support of the British, and agreed to abstain from hostility against the border settlements. By presents, false representations, and intrigue in 1779, British influence had so far triumphed with all the western tribes except the *Delawares* and a few *Wyandots,* that it held the ascendency until 1783, when the tribes were humbled by the colonial forces, being abandoned by the British, who were compelled to retire before the victorious legions of the colonists. In 1784, a new treaty with the *Six Nations* took place at Fort Stanwix, at which those tribes were informed that Great Britain had yielded by treaty, to the United States, all claims to the country south and west of the great northern rivers and lakes, as far as the Mississippi, making no reservation in favor of any Indian nation, but leaving their tribes to seek for peace with the United States upon such terms as might be deemed reasonable and just. The chiefs of those powerful tribes expressed much surprise at the conduct of the British authorities, claiming that they had risked all for their great father, the British king. There were many chiefs from the *Wyandots, Delawares, Ottawas, Shawnees* and other western tribes present at the conference. That treaty extinguished the claims of the *Six Nations* to all the lands west of the Ohio, and defined their future possessions in northern New York and Pennsylvania. In 1775, the treaty of Fort McIntosh was held, and the *Wyandots, Delawares, Chippewas* and *Ottawas* were represented. By that treaty those tribes acknowledged themselves and all their tribes, to be under the protection of the United States. The boundary between those tribes was fixed by the commission. Citizens of the United States were prohibited from settling on their lands; many persons having crossed from Pennsylvania into Ohio, were ordered to return and vacate their improvements.

While upon this topic, the reader will pardon a short digression upon the Indian policy of our fathers. The character of William Penn has been panegyrized alike by orator, poet, and painter. The picture has been sadly overdrawn, and William Penn placed in a false light. Let us examine his policy. It is asserted that he made a treaty with the Indians under a great elm at Shackamaxon, in which he made an ostentatious purchase of the lands of the aborigines. West, the painter, has drawn an imaginary picture of the scene, and the features of Penn, and the red men of the forest surrounding him. He is represented as purchasing their lands for a few yards of British broadcloth, a few beads and other tinsels. * Thus millions of acres of land were purchased for a few hundred dollars, and a homiletic snivel upon war and conquest delivered. History presents no authentic evidence of such a treaty! It is simply a myth drawn from Quaker tradition, and never had any real existence. † That Penn had a talk with the Indians of Shackamaxon, now Philadelphia, and that he distributed a few presents in cloth, and discoursed on the wickedness of war, is doubtless true. All such sales to Penn, or any other party were void. But admitting they could enter into a contract. The consideration offered them for their lands was a fraud upon its face.

These criticisms may be regarded as too severe, by the friends of the old Quaker, but to show the superficial charity of the Penns in their Indian policy, we will add a few more facts of history. A son of William Penn, John, governor of Pennsylvania, in 1764, by proclamation, offered a premium for Indian captives and scalps. "For the capture of any male above ten years, one hundred and fifty dollars, or for his scalp, being killed, one hundred and thirty-four dollars; and for every female captured, one hundred and thirty dollars, or for the scalp of such female killed, fifty dollars."‡ Thus the fine theories of the good William were disregarded in the first generation of Penns. And because the Indians resented the loss of their lands, the venality and cruelty of the whites, Governor Penn proposed to hunt them, like wolves, by offering a price for their scalps! This was the occasion of the relentless Indian incursions, that desolated western Pennsylvania in later years.

When Lord Calvert purchased the right of occupation of the aborigines of St. Mary's, in Maryland, for a consideration which seems to have given general satisfaction, he carefully cultivated their friendship, and perfect amity prevailed. He gave the Indians in exchange for the liberty of occupying their land, axes, hoes and clothing, thereby endeavoring to introduce among them the first rudiments of civilization—the implements of agriculture.§ Yet, we have no Wests painting fine pictures of him, and his new-made aboriginal friends.

* Chalmer's Annals, page 207.
† Clarkson's Biography of Pennsylvania.
‡ See Craig's History of Pittsburgh, page 97.
§ Bozman's "History of Maryland," volume II., page 569.

So, when Great Britain deserted her Indian allies in Ohio, Michigan, and the northwest, she did a cowardly thing. Her pretended ownership of their soil fell to the ground, and the United States were finally compelled to admit that the Indians were the owners of the soil, and obtained the same by conquest, treaty, and purchase, although the remuneration fell far below the just value of their lands. In 1786 the treaty at Fort Finney, at the junction of the Miami river with the Ohio, was held, and resulted in placing the *Shawnees* and other tribes under the protection of the United States, and admitting their sovereignty over all the land over which the Indians roamed.

Under her colonial charter, Virginia had claimed all the lands between the thirty-fourth and forty-fifth degrees of north latitude, which included all the territories of Ohio, Indiana, Illinois, Wisconsin, and Michigan. A counter-claim to a part of the territory northwest of the Ohio was set up by Connecticut. Other colonies complained that Virginia was about to take possession of nearly all the western territory, while the twelve remaining colonies had assisted in wresting it from the common enemy; and urged that those territories should be considered as common property, and sold as prescribed by Congress, for the common benefit, to be erected into free States for admission into the Union. In 1784, in order to settle all disputes concerning the territory west of Ohio, Virginia authorized her delegates in Congress to make a deed of cession to the United States of the territory in dispute, asking indemnity for her expenses of subduing the British posts in said territory. On the twenty-ninth of April, 1784, Congress accepted the cession, and the States subsequently endorsed the same, with a stipulation prohibiting slavery. In 1786 Connecticut also ceded to the United States her claims on the lands lying in northern Ohio, for the common benefit.

On the thirteenth of July, 1787, Congress passed the celebrated ordinance organizing the territory of the Ohio, now constituting five of the most prosperous States west of the Ohio river. The territory was organized under the ordinance; and General Arthur St. Clair was appointed governor of the Northwestern territory, on the fifth of October, 1787.* The intrusion of settlers had forced a public system of survey and sale of land upon the attention of Congress as early as May, 1785. An ordinance prescribing the mode of survey and sale of western lands was passed. It provided that a corps of surveyors—one from each State, and appointed by Congress—should be placed under the direction of Thomas Hutchins, geographer of the United States, and instructed to divide the territory into townships of six miles square, by lines running due north and south, and others crossing these at right angles, as far as practicable. The first line running north and south was to begin at the Ohio river, at a point due north from the western termination of the southern boundary of Pennsylvania; the first line running east and west was to begin at the same point and extend through the territory. The townships, whole or

* Taylor's history of Ohio.

fractional, were to be numbered from south to north—the ranges of townships progressively westward. The townships were to be subsequently divided into thirty-six sections, each containing a mile square, or six hundred and forty acres. The survey has since been carried to half sections, quarter sections, and eighths, and in some cases to sixteenths. Jackson, Perry, Mohican and Lake townships are in the fifteenth range from the western boundary from Pennsylvania; and Hanover, Green, Vermillion, Montgomery and Orange in the sixteenth range, while Mifflin, Milton and Clearcreek are in the seventeenth range of townships. Ruggles, Troy and Sullivan were surveyed out of the Connecticut Western Reserve, and do not range with the sectional survey of this county. It was provided that where the survey of seven ranges of townships had been completed, plots should be returned to the board of the treasury, and the Secretary of War was to reserve, by lot, one-seventh part for the use of the late continental army, and so of every subsequent seven ranges, when surveyed and returned. Lots eight, eleven, twenty-six and twenty-nine, in each township, were reserved to the United States for future sale; lot sixteen, for the maintenance of public schools within the townships.

The Connecticut Western Reserve is situated in the northeast quarter of the State, between Lake Erie on the north, Pennsylvania east, the parallel of the forty-first degree of north latitude south, and Sandusky and Seneca counties on the west. It extends one hundred and twenty miles from east to west, and is about fifty miles wide. It contains about three million eight hundred thousand acres. It is surveyed into townships of five miles square each. About five hundred thousand acres of the west end was set apart by the State of Connecticut to sufferers by fire during the revolution. These lands were donated in 1792. The townships being five miles square were subdivided into four quarters, and these into lots of from fifty to five hundred acres each to suit the purchaser. Hanover, Green, Mifflin and Milton townships were surveyed by James Hedges, deputy United States surveyor, and a citizen of Virginia, in 1807. Vermillion, Montgomery, Lake, Mohican and Perry were surveyed by Jonathan Cox, deputy surveyor, under Mansfield Ludlow in 1807. Clearcreek, Orange and Jackson townships were surveyed by Mansfield Ludlow in 1807. The three northern townships, Ruggles, Troy and Sullivan, being part of the Western Reserve and "gore," were surveyed about the time that territory was divided into townships. At the period when these surveys took place, the territory now constituting the limits of Ashland county had not a single pioneer within it; but was used as a free hunting ground by the *Wyandots, Ottawas, Delawares, Mohegans* and *Mingoes*. The first land office for the entry and purchase of lands was established at Canton, Ohio, soon after the survey was completed; and a majority of the lands of this county were entered at that office. Subsequently an office was established at Wooster, Ohio, where the pioneers purchased the remaining lands of the county, subject to entry.

CHAPTER XVIII.
THE SURVEY.—AN ADVENTURE.

Notes of the Surveyors.—A Description of the Timber, the Quality of the Lands, the Size and Direction of Streams —The Indian Villages. —An Adventure with Two old Chiefs, Pipe and Armstrong.

HAVING access to the field-notes and observations of the surveyors, by whom the sectional subdivisions of this county were made (now in possession of the county surveyor), we find many topics noted, worthy of preservation, and of deep interest to the people who now occupy the lands alluded to by the surveyors. The names of the parties accompanying these surveys, are not mentioned in the field-notes. The surveyors seem to have carried tents, and encamped during the nights and rainy days, doing their own cooking, after the manner of hunters and soldiers. Their provisions were purchased, generally, at the village of Clinton, Knox county, and carried through the forests on pack-horses, requiring two or three days to perform the journey.

The distance traveled, in making the surveys, varied from six to eighteen miles, depending much on the nature of the forests and the marshes, per day. In passing, the sectional lines were blazed, and the corners marked by trees or posts; and the character of the soil, and the kind of timber, carefully noted, as well as the number, size, and direction, of the brooks, creeks, and other streams, to enable the purchaser of the lands to ascertain the value of the soil, of which he was to become possessed.

Range fifteen, composed of Lake, Mohican, Perry, and Jackson townships, was first run. The lands along the east range line, in Lake, Mohican, and the south part of Perry, are described as generally level, and the timber much burnt by fire, with barrens, and a few scattering trees. This was the work of the Indians, in pursuit of game. In Lake township, the range line, or eastern boundary, was surveyed by William Ludlow, in 1806; and the sectional subdivisions were made in March and April, 1807, by Jonathan Cox, deputy United States surveyors. In the sectional survey, we find that Lake township had been pretty much all burned over, and that the principal timber was small white oak, burr oak, hickory, dogwood, and hazel. The surveyors continued their work on Sundays, the same as other days.

The major part of Mohican township was burnt over, and the timber much destroyed. In the swampy marshes, alder-bushes and willows were the principal timber. The timber on the uplands was generally white oak, hickory, dogwood and ash, much injured by fire. Indian trails leading down the Mohican, and out of the northwest, northeast, and southwest parts of the township, are often mentioned by the surveyors. The Indian village of "Mohican Johnstown," on section eighteen, containing "about fifteen" persons, is noted. This was probably about one-fourth of the actual population, the balance being engaged in hunting. The Indian reservation in Mohican township consisted of four sections (seven, eight, seventeen and eighteen), of which they retained the title until about the year 1818, when the general government purchased their lands, and subdivided them into quarter sections, and they were sold at the Wooster land office to purchasers. The sectional subdivision of this township was surveyed by Jonathan Cox, and completed on the tenth of December, 1806, shortly after the range line had been run.

The survey of Perry township was commenced on the second of October, and completed on Sunday, November 15, 1806, by Jonathan Cox. In running the south boundary, going west, at the southwest corner of the thirty-sixth section, they crossed a well worn and much used Indian trail, known as the *Wyandot* trail, extending from Sandusky to Fort Pitt or DuQuesne. It passed through section thirty-six in a northeasterly direction, over the Muddy fork of Mohican John's creek, which was fifty-eight links wide, and ran southeast. The land here is described as level, and grown up with brush eight feet high, with but few trees of common size, having been often burned over by the Indians. The whole south line was pretty much burned over, leaving much brush and undergrowth, and but few large trees. On the sixth mile they came upon an Indian trail or path, much used, bearing northwest; and then to a creek (Jerome fork of Mohican John's creek), seventy-five links wide, running southeast. In running the east boundary, the land is described as being mostly level; the timber, white oak, hickory, sugar, maple, and some ash. The land in this township varies from rich to second and third rate, and is gently rolling, with oak, hickory, sugar, walnut and cherry timber.*

Jackson township was surveyed by Maxfield Ludlow, who commenced on the south boundary line on Saturday, October 4, 1806. In running the south line, going west, he came to the Muddy fork of Mohican John's creek, sixty links wide, and running southeast and heads north west. The land, second rate; from the creek, gentle ascents and descents; timber, beech, oak, sugar, hickory, and undergrowth throughout the whole line. In subdividing into sections, he commenced on the first mile north of the southeast corner of the township, on the east boundary. On the second tier of sections, south side of the township, Mr. Ludlow struck a blazed road † which starts from the center of the fourth township and range in the United States military lands, and leads to the mouth of the Kayahoga (Cuyahoga). The fifty-seventh mile-tree bears northeast and southwest. This road subsequently became the Cleveland road, and passing through the north corner of Perry township, enters Montgomery at the late residence of James Boots, passing by the farm of Aaron Markley, through Ashland, and southwest to Mansfield. It passed between sections nineteen and twenty and eight and nine in Jackson township, where it intersected the Connecticut Western Reserve line. The land of this township is described as good, and the timber is especially praised by Mr. Ludlow.

RANGE SIXTEEN

is composed of Hanover, Green, Vermillion, Montgomery and Orange townships. Hanover was surveyed by James Hedges, who commenced March 15th, and ended March 25, 1807. The east boundary had much burnt woods. On the fifth mile going south, came to an old Indian boundary line, being perhaps the north line of the Jelloway reservation, in Knox county. The line runs southwest across the township, and passes out nearly in the middle of section thirty-one. In subdividing the township, between sections one and two, he touches Armstrong's creek, one hundred and fifty links wide, running southwest. This creek is so named from Captain Armstrong, an Indian chief who resided at the village of Greentown, some eight miles higher up on the stream. It is also described by other surveyors as the Muddy or Black fork of Mohican John's creek, but more properly known as the Black fork or principal head of the Walhonding or White-woman's river. The junction of the Clear fork with the Black fork is mentioned, the width being one hundred and forty links. In running the south boundary, going west, came to an old Indian path or trail leading north and south—perhaps to the Jelloway settlement on the Walhonding. The land of Hanover is described as being rugged and poor, with stunted timber, much burnt on the northeast part of the township.

Green township was also surveyed by James Hedges in April, 1807. In running the south and east boundary of this township Mr. Hedges seems to have been much embarrassed over the variations in his compass. In order to test the accuracy of the survey the lines were re-surveyed. He could not determine the cause of the variation. Along the south line, land rolling and timber much burnt, underbrush plenty. On the west boundary, going north, came to Mohican John's creek (Clear fork) one hundred and fifty links wide—runs east from northwest. On the fourth mile to Muddy fork of Mohican John's creek one hundred and fifty links wide, runs southeast. Crossed over and came to an Indian village in the line. This was the village of Greentown or Armstrong's village, located on section eighteen. Here a section post was stuck in a cornfield. The number of Indian families residing at this village is not given, but must have been fifty or sixty. The village was situated on a rolling slope of land extending down to a bend in the Black fork; and the spot upon which the graveyard and village were placed must have contained from four to five acres. These Indians offered no resistance to the surveyors. Indian trails, much used, were found leading northwest and down the stream. The land of Green township, down the valley, is regarded as prime, though wet and marshy. The timber in the valley and on the hills adjacent was much burnt, and the undergrowth thick and difficult to pass. Tim-

---

*About the year 1808, Joseph Larwill, of what is now Wooster, surveyed the sectional subdivisions of Perry township. While thus engaged, "Captain Pipe" and several of his warriors came upon the surveying party and ordered them to desist, saying: "You go tick-tuck, tick-tuck, all day. Me cut your legs off, then how you go tick-tuck, tick-tuck?" In the meantime, his warriors seized and ran away with the chain, and thus put a stop, for a while, to the work.—*Letter to the author by Hon. A. H. Byers, of Wooster, Ohio.*

† This was the line of the old Cuyahoga road, which had been surveyed and blazed from Franklinton, in Franklin county, Ohio, to the mouth of the Cuyahoga river, some time previous to the range and section surveys.

ber—white oak, burr oak, dogwood and ash. Balance of the township rolling land, second rate.

Vermillion township was surveyed by Jonathan Cox, in April, 1807. In running the south boundary, which was done in October, 1806, James Hedges, by whom it was done, became greatly confused over the variations of the length of the line. He re-surveyed it three times and observes: "I am at a loss to know what cause to attribute the increased length of the south boundary line of said township twenty-one, range sixteen. The chaining on said boundary must be imperfect, or the variation must operate very partial in running south on west line of said town." On the third survey he says: "I find the chaining correct. I am now much perplexed to know the cause of my westing or inclining south. The variation must operate very partial, or my compass must have been unluckily altered." He then re-surveyed the west boundary, and coming to the southwest corner of said town observes: "Here I experience troubles of a new kind, having already spent two days and a half waiting on an Indian chief* who appeared hostile to our business; also laboring under the difficulty of a hand being absent thirteen days on a tour for provisions, in the meantime having lived eight days upon boiled and parched corn, I now find my camp robbed of some necessary articles, and two hands that I left to keep the same revolted and run away; these difficulties increased my range and town lines not being finished, expecting shortly other surveyors after me to subdivide; all conspire to make me unhappy. No alternative remains but to proceed to Owl creek and get hands and provisions. This being the twentieth day of October, 1806." This suspended operations until April, 1807, when Jonathan Cox proceeded to subdivide the township into sections. In running along the east boundary Mr. Cox came upon Indian trails much traveled, running northeast and opposite. These trails doubtless passed over to Greentown, along what is now known as the old Portage road, and led from Mohican Johnstown. About one mile south of the northeast corner he found a path much traveled leading northwest and opposite.† Along the west boundary in the southwest corner of the township were also much traveled Indian paths. The land of the township is described as mostly of gentle ascents and descents; timber—oak, hickory, sugar, maple, ash, some walnut, chestnut and dogwood.

The range boundaries of Montgomery township were surveyed by Maxfield Ludlow, in October, 1806. In running the south boundary, going west, seventeen chains and twenty links from the third mile stake, he came to an Indian path or trail running southeast and northwest. This path is described as a well worn road or trail. This is the well known path of the *Wyandots*, which was followed by Major Robert Rogers, in 1761, in his route to the forks of the Muskingum, on his return to Pittsburgh, or Fort DuQuesne; as well as by General R. Beall in his expedition to Sandusky. This trail passed over the farm known as the late residence of John McCammon, thence across the Ryal farm, in Milton township, into Richland county, in a northwesterly direction, through Bloominggrove township. The east boundary of the township is noted as "flat, and marshy, with bottoms subject to overflow;" the timber, elm, maple, sugar, swamp-oak and alder-bush. On the third mile going north, a plain, much traveled Indian path or trail, leading northwest, was seen. This path passed by the old Newell farm, thence to near the covered bridge on the Wooster road, where it divided, one branch leading up the Catotaway, and the other near the bridge on the Harrisburgh road, by the old residence of Daniel Carter, subsequently known as the John Mason farm. The lands of Montgomery township on the east are described as level and rich; in the middle and west part of the township, as rolling and of good quality. The timber—ash, walnut, oak, hickory, cherry, sugar and maple, with considerable undergrowth, and a number of glades. The subdivision into sections was surveyed by Jonathan Cox, in November, 1806.

ANTIQUITIES.

On surveying the fifth tier of sections, Mr. Cox passed an ancient intrenchment or earthwork, containing about eight acres, on what is now known as the Gamble farm, on the north side of Ashland. This earthwork was circular in form, and had a gate-way looking to the southwest. The embankment walls were between three and four feet high, and perhaps eight feet wide at the base. A forest of timber—oak, hickory, sugar, maple and ash grew in and about this old fort, showing that it had not been used for centuries. By whom, and when, this work was thrown up, and for what purpose, will, perhaps, never be clearly ascertained. This curious old fort is yet remembered by the old settlers, though it is scarcely traceable, from the fact that it has been plowed over for more than fifty years. It was located on the plateau, just north of the residence of the late Henry Gamble. The Orange township boundary and sectional subdivisions were surveyed by Maxfield Ludlow in October 1806. In tracing the south boundary, going west, on the third mile, crossed an Indian trail bearing northwest and southeast; and about half a mile west came to a creek sixty links in width, and running south. This was where James Wright formerly lived. The trail crossed the stream at the bridge near Jacob Young's house, and passed up the west side of the stream east of the residence of the late Patrick Murray, thence northwest near the shore of Vermillion lake. From the point where it struck the south line of Orange township, the trail passed by the Crouse school-house and cemetery over the old farm of Peter Thomas, to near the residence of Stephen Wolf, thence in a southeasterly direction across the Catotoway to Rowsburgh, and from thence to a point where it intersected the old trail leading from Mohican Johnstown to near the present site of Wooster; and was much traveled by the *Wyandots* and *Ottawas* in their excursions to the east part of the State. About the year 1816, that path was surveyed by Rev.

---

*Probably Captain Thomas Armstrong of the Greentown village on the Black fork.

†This was the old Huron or Wyandot trail leading across Vermillion, Montgomery and Milton townships.

James Haney, of Savannah, who was a practical surveyor, to Rowsburgh, and from thence to Wooster, the late Samuel Urie, sr., being one of the viewers, and was opened as a road, and was the common highway of the early pioneers of Orange and Clearcreek townships.

The evidences of Indian occupation in many parts of Orange township, at that period, were numerous. The aborigines, it seems, were accustomed to assemble annually in the spring, in large numbers, upon the lands subsequently owned by Isaac Mason, Jacob Young, Jacob Heifner and Peter Biddinger, to make sugar and hunt, which custom they kept up until as late as 1815 or 1816. Mr. Biddinger, being a gun-smith, was often visited by them for repairs to injured or broken flint-locks.

The soil and timber of Orange township do not differ materially from Montgomery. The land is described as level, and of gentle ascents and descents.

RANGE SEVENTEEN.

After an absence of six days, Mr. Hedges returned from Owl creek, having secured hands and provisions to continue the range and subdivision lines. He commenced operations about the twenty-eighth of October, 1806, and concluded the sectional surveys about the second day of December. In running the south boundary of township twenty-two (Milton), he says the line passes over steep hills, amid "timber much burnt, with much underbrush, vines and briers;" timber, oak, chestnut, hickory and dogwood. On the second mile going west, "passed over a small wet prairie, and then crossed Black or Muddy fork of Mohican Johnscreek," afterwards called by him, Armstrong's creek. He says: "This stream promises fair for navigation, being a dead, still current, one hundred and forty links wide, runs southeast." The Black fork is now the boundary between Richland and Ashland counties in Mifflin township. Small flat boats, we believe, have been propelled as high as Perrysville in early times. Mr. Hedges then proceeded to verify the east boundary line of the township, running north. This line was mostly over hilly land, the timber being oak, elm, beech and hickory, with much brush and grape-vines. He experienced some of the difficulties occurring on the south line of Vermillion in the third and fourth miles of this line. He says the "needle appeared not to work well, but the converging of the line to the one formerly run appeared to be nearly uniform throughout the six miles. The cause of my falling so far to the west when running south is to me not known." It may be that his compass had received some injury, but it seems to have been all right in the sectional subdivisions. Query: Was there some metallic influence arising from iron ore in the southwest corner of Vermillion township? Mr. Hedges failed to comprehend the phenomena. Who will find valuable ores in that neighborhood? The supposed rich ores are found in the lakes of Mifflin, and are bog ores. In running the sectional subdivisions the land in the east part of the township is described as hilly, and the soil generally good. The western part was composed of level land, part bottoms and wet prairies. In section twenty-six he reaches Armstrong's creek, one hundred and eighty links wide. From this point, he calls the Black fork, Armstrong's creek." In section twenty-three he finds a small lake, and a stream ten links wide flowing into the north and out of the south side of it. An old Indian path or trail enters the south part of the township, a few rods east of the Black fork, and continues northwest near the little lake, thence across the old Ruffner farm to the lands of Joseph Charles, continuing up the Black fork into the southwest part of Milton township, where it passed over into Butler township in Richland county, and probably united with the old Wyandot trail.

Milton is a fractional township, two miles of which, on the western side, were not annexed to this county when it was created. The sectional subdivisions were surveyed by James Hedges, who commenced the work November 4th, and ended November 20, 1806. Mr. Hedges failed to note many things of interest in his surveys, and, in this respect, fell far behind Mr. Ludlow and Mr. Cox. These surveyors not only noted carefully the kind and quality of timber, but also the direction and size of the streams, the Indian trails, villages, and other objects of curiosity. The south boundary of Milton is noted as uneven and hilly, land second rate, and timber composed of oak, beech, and hickory. The east boundary is noted as generally level, soil good; timber the same as on the south line, with sugar maple, dogwood, and an occasional wild cherry. The land of the township is described as of gentle ascents and descents, some places level; soil good for farming, and, generally, more or less clayey. It has an abundance of water, flowing from clear, pure, and never-ceasing springs. In the neighborhood of the Short farm is to be found one of the strongest springs in the county.

Clearcreek township was surveyed, and subdivided into sections, by Maxfield Ludlow, in the fall of 1807. It is, also, a fractional township, being only four miles wide, from east to west. In running the south boundary, the land is described as level, and second rate; timber, white oak, hickory, sugar, beech, and the usual undergrowth. In the subdivisions, the lands are regarded as generally level and rich, and the timber of good quality. In some sections, he passes over beautiful farming land. In sections thirteen and twenty-four, he came to the bank of a lake, which bears northwest and southeast; turned, and made an offset south; found the lake to be twenty-three chains south of the line, and twenty chains wide, from east to west; found an old Indian path, bearing northwest and southeast, on south side of said lake. This trail kept down the Vermillion river, which heads at the northwest corner of the lake, and runs northwest. In sections thirteen and fourteen, he again strikes the lake, which bears northwest three-quarters of a mile; crossed the head branch of Vermillion, twenty links wide; again crosses the Indian path, bearing northwest and southeast; again, between sections one and twelve, came upon another Indian path, leading northwest and southeast. This path must have branched at the lower end of the lake.

In April, 1808, after completing the subdivisions, Mr. Ludlow proceeded to re-survey the Connecticut line, being the south boundary of the Western Reserve. He commenced at the east line of range fifteen, and ran to the west line of range seventeen. He commenced at the eighty-third mile west, from the east range, or range one. This line had been surveyed prior to that time, by a Mr. Pease. On the eighty-fourth mile west, he reached the present boundary between Ashland and Wayne counties. About one-sixth of the ninety-first mile, going west, he struck an old Indian path or trail, north and south. This was in section two, on the north boundary line of Orange township. On the ninety-seventh mile, he came to a plain Indian path, bearing northwest and southeast. This was in section two, on the north boundary of Clearcreek, according to Ludlow; but Mr. Pease makes it in section four, in Orange township. On the ninety-eighth mile, he crossed Vermillion river, forty links wide, and came to west boundary of Ashland county on the ninety-ninth mile, going west.

CHAPTER XIX.

THE ERECTION OF FAIRFIELD COUNTY.

The County Created.—Its Great Extent.—Andrew Craig and Wife.—He is the First Settler in Ashland County.—Alexander Finley and Wife.—Thomas Eagle and Family.—The Primitive Forests.

AFTER the territory of this county had been surveyed into ranges, townships, and sections, in 1806-7, the territory now composing the counties of Fairfield, Licking, Knox, Richland, parts of Morrow and Ashland, was erected into one county, with the seat of justice at Lancaster. The inhabitants of Licking, Knox, and Richland counties, were then very few, and the settlements far apart. The region about Newark, Granville, Utica, Clinton, Bellville, and Mansfield, had but few residents, and the latter, perhaps, none. The whole of Knox, the greater part of Licking, and the whole of Richland, was thickly covered with the original forest, and was the favorite hunting-ground of the Indian tribes of the Northwest. No white man had settled within the limits of this county at that period.

The great extent of Fairfield county rendered it very inconvenient for the pioneer settlers in the most remote portions of the county to visit the seat of justice, located at Lancaster. As early as 1806 the question of a division of the territory into smaller counties was agitated, and many petitions were sent the legislature, then in session at Chillicothe. The senator and representatives of Fairfield county favored the proposed division, and, in 1808, a bill passed both branches of the legislature, creating and fixing the boundaries of Licking, Knox, and Richland counties. The county of Richland, including most of the present limits of Ashland county, was left under the jurisdiction of Knox until the legislature should deem it proper to organize it into a separate county. In February, 1808, a commission, under a joint resolution of the legislature, fixed the seat of justice for Knox county at Mount Vernon, where the people of Richland county would have to attend court until that county should have a sufficient number of inhabitants to locate a seat of justice, and establish a court in her midst. Under this arrangement, in April, 1808, the entire population of Knox and Richland counties was requested to assemble at Mount Vernon and vote for a county commissioner, a sheriff, a coroner, township trustees, and other officers. We find that the greatest number of votes cast at that election was thirty-six; so that the aborigines of the forest were ten times more numerous than their white neighbors.

It is a mooted question as to who was the first white settler in Ashland county. Mr. Knapp is disposed to award the honor to Alexander Finley, who came from the present site of Mt. Vernon, and located at the present site of Tylertown, in Mohican township, April 17, 1809. He says: "At the time Mr. Finley settled in Mohican township, himself and family were the only white inhabitants within the limits of the territory that now constitutes the territory of Ashland." Mr. Norton, in his history of Knox county, awards the honor to one Andrew Craig. He gives the following description of Craig and wife, with the reasons for his location at Greentown in 1809:

"From our research into early statements, we are led to believe that Andrew Craig was the first white man who located within the present county limits. He was, at a very early day, a sort of frontier character, fond of rough-and-tumble life, a stout and rugged man—bold and dare-devil in disposition—who took delight in hunting, wrestling and athletic sports, and "hail fellow well met" with the Indians then inhabiting the country. He was from the bleak, broken, mountainous region of Virginia, and as hardy a pine knot as ever that country produced. He was in this country when Ohio was in its territorial condition, and when this wilderness region was declared to be in the county of Fairfield,* the sole denizen in this entire district, whose history is now written, tabernacled with a woman in a rough log hut, close by the little Indian field, about half a mile east of where Mt. Vernon now stands, and at the point where Center run empties into the Ko-ko-sing. There Andrew Craig lived when Mt. Vernon was laid out, in 1805—there he was upon the organization of Knox county, its oldest inhabitant—and there he continued until 1809. Such a harum-scarum fellow could not rest easy when white men got thick around him, so he left and went to the Indian village—Greentown—and from thence migrated farther out upon the frontier, preferring red men for neighbors."

While we are willing to award Mr. Finley all the honor to which he is entitled as a pioneer, we incline to the opinion that Mr. Craig was the first white man that settled within the present limits of Ashland county (excepting Baptiste Jerome and Thomas Green); and that Greentown, instead of Tylertown, furnished a home for the new adventurer. Greentown, at that period, contained from eighty to one hundred Indian families, many of whom resided in comfortable cabins. Mr. Heckewelder, in his account of the Indian nations,† says:

---

* Fairfield county was created by a proclamation of Governor Arthur St. Clair, December 9, 1800; and originally contained nearly all the territory of Licking, Knox, Morrow, Richland and Ashland counties.

† See transactions of the historical and literary committee of the American Philosophical Society, volume one,—printed in Philadelphia, 1818, pages 132-3.

In the year 1808, while I was riding with a number of gentlemen through Greentown (an Indian town in the State of Ohio), I heard an Indian in his house, who through a crevice saw us passing, say in his language to his family: See! what a number of people are coming along! What, and among all these not one "Long Knife" (Virginian). "All Yengees!"—then probably observing me, he said to himself, "No! one Qua-kel (Quaker)!"

How often the good Moravian missionary, Rev. John Heckewelder, passed through Greentown in his missionary tours among the *Delawares*, we are not informed; but the trip made in 1808 throws much light upon the condition of the inhabitants of Greentown, and goes far to show that when James Copus acted as occasional preacher among the people of that village in 1809-10-11-12, they were not unaccustomed to the presence of the white missionary; and that the Armstrongs, the Jelloways, Thomas Lyon and other leading Indians were prepared to listen attentively to the heralds of the truths of the Christian religion.

When Alexander Finley and family arrived at their new home on the Mohican, their nearest neighbor, as he supposed, was Benjamin Miller, who resided on the present site of Wooster. William and Joseph Larwill, now deceased, were then boarding in the family of Mr. Miller, and were young men. Thus, then, the valleys of the Black fork and Mohican were first selected for settlement, Messrs. Craig, Eagle and Finley arriving about the same period, in 1809. These valleys at that period were nearly destitute of underbrush and small timber. It had been the custom of the Indians for a long time to burn the undergrowth in Mohican, Lake and Green townships, to facilitate the pursuit of game. Some portions of the hills below Greentown were entirely bare of timber, while in Lake and Mohican timber was scarce and much injured by fire. In the early part of the summer the soil in these townships was covered with sedge-grass and peavines, which afforded an abundance of provender for cattle and horses, and when cut and properly cured, a very nourishing food for winter.

In May, 1809, Thomas Eagle and family arrived and located on a farm subsequently owned by Henry Treace, near the present site of Mohicanville. There were many Indians in the neighborhood at the time of his arrival. The Indian village of Mohican Johnstown had, perhaps, about one hundred families, composed of *Mohicans, Delawares, Mingoes*, and a few *Shawnees*. Mr. Eagle described them as being generally harmless, and friendly to himself and family.

Mr. Eagle, and Finley, were under the necessity, for some years, of obtaining their supplies of food from Shrimplin's mill, near Mount Vernon. To do so, they descended the Lake fork and passed up Owl creek in canoes, with small quantities of corn or wheat, which, having been ground, was re-conveyed to their homes after an absence of several days.

The forest abounded in an abundance of game, and these early pioneers could easily supply their families with a sufficient quantity of flesh, though salt to cure and preserve it was a rare article. While Messrs. Finley and Eagle were engaged in erecting their cabins, and clearing a small piece of ground around them for cultivation, Captain Pipe, Crane, Jelloway, Killbuck, the Armstrongs, Jonacake,* Buckwheat, Catotaway, and Thomas Lyon were roaming up and down the Jerome fork, the Lake fork, the Black fork, the Walhonding, and the shores of the Ko-ko-sing on hunting excursions. For three years the neighborhood of Messrs. Finley and Eagle remained undisturbed by the children of the forest.

---

* This name was originally spelled "Johnny cake," but, we think, incorrectly. The "cake" from which he was doubtless named was known by Virginians as "journey-cake," from which "Jonacake" is derived, and is the correct way of spelling it. See Zell's Encyclopedia.

CHAPTER XX.

PIONEER HISTORY.

The Pioneers from 1809 to 1812.—Two Indian Feasts at Greentown.—Curious Indian Ceremonies.—The White Persons Present.—Old Captain Pipe, Armstrong and Lyon.

A FEW weeks after the arrival of Andrew Craig and wife, he erected a camp cabin about one and a half miles southeast of the Indian village of Greentown, where he resided when James Copus and family landed, some weeks afterward, on his way to his forest home in the south part of Mifflin township. Mr. Copus was born in Greene county, Pennsylvania, about the year 1775. He married in his native county in 1796. In March, 1809, he removed to the Black fork in Richland county. His family consisted of himself, wife and seven children. His route of travel was through Wheeling, Cambridge, Zanesville, Coshocton, and up the banks of the Walhonding through the Indian village of Greentown. He located at first about three-quarters of a mile northeast of the present site of Charles' mill, on what was afterwards known as Zimmer's run, and erected a small camp cabin of poles. The cabin was constructed by planting two forks in the ground about twenty feet apart, and placing a ridge pole on them, and then leaning split timber against the pole, making a sort of shed roof, the base being about twelve feet wide, leaving a small opening at the top for the escape of smoke. The ends were closed by setting poles in the ground, leaving a door at one end. The cracks were carefully closed with moss gathered from old logs. The floor consisted of the smooth, well packed earth. In this rude structure James Copus and family resided for a period of about eighteen months. Though often visited, in the meantime, by the Greentown Indians, he felt entirely safe, and remained on the most friendly terms with Captain Armstrong and his people. Being a stout, fearless and industrious man, he set to work at once to clear and prepare a few acres for corn, and soon had a small field fenced with brush, and otherwise prepared to plant. Having brought a "yoke of oxen" and a cow or two along with him, he felt certain that his family could survive the hardships of pioneer life, aided by his industry. At that time the forests abounded in the most luxuriant growth of sedge-grass, pea-vines and other growths upon which horses and cattle could feed and grow fat. In July he had the misfortune to see his field of corn bitten by the frost and greatly injured. However, though soft, it turned out better than he anticipated. In the meantime he visited Andrew Craig, and purchased a hog or two from him, and by their increase and the use of his trusty rifle he procured meat enough to pass the first winter in safety. In the spring of 1810 he erected a cabin in the vicinity of an excellent spring, about three-quarters of a mile south of the camp cabin, on the Indian trail leading to Greentown. Here he cleared about twenty acres and enclosed the same with a good rail fence. Here he resided when the war of 1812 commenced between the United States and Great Britain. In the meantime, being an exhorter and local preacher in the Methodist Episcopal church, he was often invited to address the Indians at Greentown, by whom he was listened to with great attention. He soon became intimate with Captain Armstrong, the chief, and the leading men of the village, among whom were Montour and Jelloway.

INDIAN FEAST.

In the fall of 1809 he attended an Indian feast at Greentown, where he met James Cunningham and other new settlers. Cunningham was a native of Maryland, and had emigrated to Licking county, Ohio, in 1804, and from thence to the vicinity of Greentown in May, 1809. His neighbors were Samuel Lewis, Henry McCart and Andrew Craig. The refreshments (?) consisted of boiled venison and bear meat, somewhat tainted, and not very palatable to the white guests. The ceremonies took place in the council house, a building composed of clap-boards and poles, some thirty feet wide, and perhaps fifty feet long. When the Indians entered the council house, the squaws seated themselves on one side and the men on the other. There was a small elevation of earth in the center, eight or ten feet in diameter, which seemed to be a sort of sacrificial mound. The ceremonies were opened by a rude sort of music, made by beating upon a small copper kettle, and pots, over the mouths of which dried skins had been stretched. This was accompanied by a sort of song, which, as near as could be understood, ran; "Tinny, tinny, tinny, ho, ha, ho, ha, ho"—accenting the last syllables. Then a tall chief arose and addressed them. During the delivery of his speech, a profound silence prevailed. The whole audience observed the speaker, and seemed to be deeply moved by the oration. The speaker seemed to be about seventy years of age. He was tall and graceful. His eyes had the fire of youth, and blazed with emotion while he was speaking. The audience frequently sobbed, and seemed deeply affected. Mr. Copus could not understand the language of the address, but presumed the speaker was giving a summary history of the *Delawares*, two tribes of which, the "Wolf" and the "Turtle," were represented at the feast. Mr. Copus learned that the distinguished chief who had addressed the meeting, was "Old Captain Pipe," of Mohican Johnstown, the executioner of the lamented Colonel Crawford. At the close of the address dancing commenced. The Indians were neatly clothed in deer skin and English blankets. Deer hoofs and bear claws were strung along the seams of their leggins, and when the dance commenced, the jingling of the hoofs and claws gave a rude sort of harmony to the wild music made upon the pots and kettles. The men danced in files or lines, by themselves around the central mound, and the squaws followed in a company by themselves. In the dance there seemed to be a proper sense of modesty between the sexes. In fact, the Greentown Indians were always noted for being extremely scrupulous and modest in the presence of each other. After the dance, the refreshments were handed around. Not relishing the appearance of the food, Mr. Copus and the other whites present, carefully concealed the portions handed them until they left the wigwam, and then threw them away. No greater insult could be offered an Indian, than to refuse to accept the food proffered by him. So those present had to use a little deception to evade the censure of the Indians.

In the spring and summer of 1810, the population of Green township was increased by the arrival of George Crawford, David Davis, Frederick Zimmer, sr., Frederick Zimmer, jr., Philip Zimmer, John Lambright, Peter Kinney, Edward Haley, John Davis (a widower), Charles Tannahill, Bazel Tannahill, John Coulter, Melzer Coulter, Archibald Gardner, and their families. These settlers commenced improvements along the Black fork, the Clear fork, and the Rocky fork of the Mohican, each erecting a small cabin, and clearing a few acres of ground for corn. The majority of these settlers were of German descent, and had come directly from the western counties of Pennsylvania, Virginia, Maryland, and the eastern part of Ohio; and had found the way to their new homes up the branches of the Mohican, and by Indian trails. Many of them had entered their lands at Canton, Ohio, without seeing them, and had followed their neighbors into these wilds.

While these settlers were erecting new homes along the Black fork, Alexander Finley and Thomas Eagle were being joined, in 1810, by James Loudon Priest, Nathan Odell, Joshua Oram, Benjamin Emmons, John Baptiste Jerome, Ezra Warner, Elisha Chilcoat, Benjamin Bunn, James Conley, Amos Norris, William Metcalf, John Newell, Westel Ridgely, Vatchell Metcalf, Josiah Crawford, and John Shinnabarger. The Odells, Orams, Priests, and Metcalfs, settled in the present limits of Lake township. Mr. Emmons settled in Perry, and Mr. Warner in the lower part of Vermillion. These settlers were mostly from the border States, and from Jefferson county, Ohio. They had found their way to their new homes like the settlers on the Black fork, and commenced the erection of cabins, and clearings, in the same way. Corn was generally purchased and ground, the first year, in Knox county; and the new settlers either packed it on horses, or descended the Mohican in canoes, and transported it in that way. The hominy block was in universal requisition among the early settlers; and jonacake, or journey-cake, pork, and wild game, furnished the principal solid food, while spicewood and sassafras tea, and milk, furnished the balance of nourishment.

In 1811, Calvin and Joseph Hill, Allen Oliver, Ebenezer Rice, Joseph Jones, Melzer Tannahill, sr., Lewis Hill, Solomon Hill, Moses Adzit, Jeremiah Conine, Sylvester Fisher, Thomas Coulter, Otho Simmons, and their families, came into the Greentown settlement, along the Black fork. These families were from Pennsylvania, Virginia, New York, Vermont, Maryland, and eastern Ohio. Soon the woodman's ax was heard in every direction, and cabins commenced to spring up, and fields were cleared and fenced, and crops planted. The most friendly relations existed between the new pioneers and the Indians.

ANOTHER INDIAN FEAST.

In 1811, about two years after the first feast attended by Mr. Copus and Cunningham, another one took place at Greentown. It was conducted very much like the one in 1809. John Coulter,* who was present, and who is now (1873) in his eighty-third year, gives me the following description of the feast, which Alexander Rice and others confirm:

The feast was prepared and held in the large council house. In the center of the building was a mound of earth, perhaps eight or ten feet across and two feet in height. The kettles for cooking the supper were placed around the edge of the mound, over small fires, and bear's flesh and venison put in them. In the center of the mound a large fire was kindled, which blazed with great brilliancy. While the supper was being cooked an occasional choice morsel was thrown into the large fire as a sacrifice to the Great Spirit. A great number of distinguished chiefs and warriors from Upper Sandusky, Jerometown and other parts, were present and participated in the ceremonies. While the supper was being cooked the leading chiefs and warriors commenced to move in a solemn procession around the altar, sometimes singing, sometimes delivering short speeches in their native tongue. While this was going on the balance of the audience were arranged in lines two or three deep around the inside of the council house, which, according to Mr. Howe, was about sixty feet long and twenty-five feet wide, one story high, and enclosed by clapboards. The singing was a sort of low, melancholy wail accompanied by a sort of grunt, contortions of the face, and singular gesticulations of the arms. The exact meaning of the speeches and other performances was not understood by Mr. Coulter and the other guests. The chiefs and other distinguished warriors present made a fine display as they marched around the altar, arrayed, as they were, in costume which exhibited many gay colors, arranged so as to produce a fine effect. As on the former occasion, their leggins were ornamented with dry deers hoofs, which produced a rattling noise as they marched around the central mound. These ceremonies produced a profound impression on all present. Whether it was a recital of the history and achievements of the *Delawares*, or whether it portended future trouble, and was an offering to avert the calamities of war, could not be divined by those of the white race present. The ceremonies lasted two or three hours, and then the cooked venison and bear's meat were distributed among the audience and the ceremonies closed with a general hand-shaking, congratulations and other friendly tokens. Mr. Coulter, Wesley Copus and other invited guests, feel confident that they met "old Captain Pipe" of Jerometown, there. There were from three to four hundred Indians present, and Wesley Copus says that Thomas Lyon, who was a warm friend of his father (James Copus), prepared a choice bit of venison for him. We are compelled to believe that "old Captain Pipe" was present. This was the last we hear of him at any public gathering in this region; and we are inclined to think this feast foreshadowed the calamitous war of 1812, which commenced a few months after that feast.

Along the Jerome fork and the brooks that flowed into it, in the same year (1811) we find John Carr, James Collyer, James Slater, James Bryan, Joseph Chandler, sr., Robert Newell, Robert Finley, George Eckley, Jonathan Palmer, James Wallace, Thomas Newman, and perhaps a few others and their families.

At this time there was not a white man in Montgomery, Milton, Clearcreek, Orange, Jackson, and the three northern townships. The number of the cabins in the lower part of Vermillion, in Lake and Perry, as well as all over Mohican, was rapidly on the increase; and the prospect for a large influx of settlers in 1812 was fair. The pioneers were keenly alive to their interests, and traveled far and near to aid each other in raising cabins, felling the forest, rolling logs and fencing new fields. Many hardships were encountered the first year or two, by reason of unripe grain, and the great distance to be traveled in reaching mills. Still, those difficulties were met with fortitude and soon overcome.

The spring of 1812 saw the tide of emigration on the increase. At that period a war was impending between Great Britain and the United States. This checked the influx of the pioneers, for it was evident the Indians of the northwest would be invited to assist the enemy. In fact, it had been observed for nearly two years, that the Greentown and Jerometown or Mohican Johnstown Indians had been in the habit of making frequent visits to Upper Sandusky, and always returned with new blankets, tomahawks and ammunition in abundance. Indeed, it was suspected that British agents were busily at work sowing the seeds of disaffection among the northern Ohio Indians.

A few families settled on the Black fork in 1812, among whom were Samuel Hill, Simon Rowland, (single) Martin Ruffner, Richard Hughes, Henry Smith, (single) Archibald Gardner, and Michael Ruffner, (single).

On the Jerome fork and vicinity, we find the population increased by the addition of the families of Thomas Carr, William Bryan, and perhaps one or two others.

In January, 1812, Daniel Carter, sr., located about one mile northeast of the present site of Ashland; Christopher Crickle at the east end of Ashland, where Markley's brick house formerly stood; Benjamin Cuppy near the Orange road, on the farm owned by the late David Sloan, and Jacob Fry near the present residence of Leo Wertman, on the Troy road, while Robert Newell located on the old McGuire farm, near where the brick house now stands. All north of this region was a dense forest, and had not been disturbed by the presence of the white hunter or settler. Messrs. Carter, Cuppy, Fry, Newell and Trickle put up small cabins, soon to abandon them for a home in the Jeromeville block-house.

---

* Since deceased.

CHAPTER XXI.

THE WAR OF 1812.

War Declared against Great Britain.—The Concentration of Troops in Northwestern Ohio.—The Disgraceful Surrender of General Hull.—Threatening Aspect of the Border.—Removal of the Jerome and Greentown Indians.

On the eighteenth of June, 1812, the United States declared war against Great Britain and her dependencies. The national pride of England had been deeply wounded by the treaty of 1783, that gave independence to the colonies. The events of the Revolutionary war forcibly constrained Great Britain, reluctant as she was, to surrender all control over the thirteen colonies; yet, she refused to execute the treaty in good faith, and availed herself of every equivocation to justify her perfidy. She agreed to vacate all the western ports from Oswego to Michilimacinac; but, contrary to the express terms of the treaty, retained forcible possession of them. This breach of faith subjected the United States to the expense of a long and bloody Indian war. In that war, the Indians were supplied with the means of death from those very ports. The governor-general of Canada, Lord Dorchester, was industrious in instigating Indian hostilities all along our frontiers. His agents were distributing arms, ammunition, food and blankets among the Indians during the campaigns of Harmer, St. Clair and Wayne. McKee, Girty and Henry, were busy in their efforts to excite the whole Indian race against the pioneers, and offered liberal rewards for every scalp brought by the Indians to Malden. To aggravate the matter, a systematic rule of impressment was adopted in the British navy during the French war, and large numbers of our sailors and seamen were torn from American vessels on the high seas, and forced into the British service. The administration of Jefferson and Madison had protested in vain against these outrages, and war became inevitable. The British agent, Mr. Henry, was dispatched through the New England States with power to corrupt and detach them from the Union, and re-annex them to the British empire.

While these things were transpiring, war was declared. Mr. Madison made haste to meet the storm. The waters of lakes Erie, Huron and Michigan, as well as the territory of Michigan, northwestern Ohio and northern Indiana, were in a defenceless condition. The Executive of the United States determined to display a respectable military force on the borders of the straits separating the lakes. In April, 1812, a requisition was made by the President for one thousand two hundred of the militia of the State of Ohio, who were to be found by the Fourth regiment of United States regular troops, then on their way from Vincennes, Indiana. In obedience to the call, Governor Meigs, with his usual promptitude, issued orders to the major-generals of the western and middle divisions, to furnish their respective quotas of men, who were to rendezvous at Dayton on the twenty-ninth of the same month. In a few days the requisition was more than complied with. Citizens of the first distinction were among the foremost to enroll their names. With a celerity never equaled in a new country, volunteers collected from every part of the State. They rendezvoused at Dayton, as required. An election for officers took place, and Duncan McArthur was elected colonel of the First regiment; James Finley, of the Second, and Lewis Cass, of the Third. By the middle of May the troops were provided with blankets, tents, and other necessary camp equipage, and had become expert in military evolutions and the manual of arms. Brigadier General William Hull, of the United States army, was appointed by the government to conduct the expedition. Governor Meigs having assembled the troops in obedience to the orders of the Secretary of War, now surrendered their command to General Hull.

Everything being in readiness for the departure of the troops, they took their line of march on the first of June. On the nineteenth the army passed through the Auglaize region. On the fourth of July the army reached the Huron river, twenty miles from Detroit. The British and Indians gave no trouble up to this period. On the fifth of July the army encamped at Spring wells, three miles below Detroit. Detroit contained about two hundred houses and twelve hundred inhabitants at that period. General Hull and his army took possession of the fort, which stood upon a handsome eminence of moderate height, about two hundred yards in the rear of the town. The fort had well constructed ramparts of earth, surrounded by a ditch, defended by a double line of pickets; between this and the town was a stockade enclosing about two acres of ground. The area of the fort was about one and a half acres. There were also extensive commons in the rear of the fort, skirted by boundless and almost impenetrable forests, which offered an easy and safe retreat for the Indians. General Hull remained in the fort at Detroit, making an occasional feint as if he intended to invade Canada, at one time sending forward a few soldiers, and in a few days recalling them, until the sixteenth of August, 1812, when he surrendered his army to the British commander, Major General Isaac Brock! The circumstances attending the surrender were of the most suspicious character. It was alleged that Hull was under the influence of liquor, that his conduct was cowardly in the extreme, and that he had been acting under a bribe from the British! * The number of the troops surrendered amounted to about two thousand and five hundred men. The same number of arms was stacked on the esplanade and in the arsenal. There was also an abundance of fixed ammunition. In the magazine was sixty barrels of powder and one hundred and fifty tons of lead. There were twenty-five pieces of iron ordnance, and eight brass field pieces. Hull had also an abundance of flour, and

---

* The day before the surrender, the fifteenth of August, General Hull pitched a markee in the centre of the encampment, of a most singular appearance, with red and blue stripes painted on the top and sides, which gave it a strong resemblance to the British flag! As the general had not erected a tent in camp since the fourth of July, this became an object of surprise, and was evidently portentous of the issue. See Brown's History of the second war for Independence, page—76.

A court matrial convened at Albany, New York, in the winter of 1814, sentenced General Hull to be shot; but appealing to his revolationary record and services, against the charge of treason, Mr. Madison remitted the sentence of the military court.

three hundred head of cattle. The army was composed of brave and patriotic men, officered by such men as McArthur, Cass, Finley and Miller; yet the fort was surrendered without resistance! The news of the surrender of Detroit was so unexpected, that it came like a clap of thunder to the ears of the American people. The disastrous event blasted the prospects of the campaign, and opened the northern and western frontiers of Ohio to savage incursions. The news of the disaster soon reached the pioneers of Richland and Ashland counties, and they were deeply alarmed at the appalling prospect of soon hearing the yells of the Indians of the northwest in their midst. Governor Meigs and the authorities of Washington, made haste to furnish protection for the border states, and to renew the struggle with the now triumphant British and Indians.

At the time of the surrender, two thousand militia under Major General Payne, a battalion of mounted riflemen under Colonel R. M. Johnson, from Kentucky, a brigade of militia under the orders of Brigadier General Tupper, and nearly one thousand regulars under the command of General Winchester, were advancing to support General Hull, and had reached the St. Mary's, when the news of the capture was received. But for the timely arrival of the above force, a wide scene of flight, misery, bloodshed and desolation must have ensued in the border settlements. Nearly half the territory in Ohio must have been depopulated, or its inhabitants fallen victims to the tomahawk and scalping knife. This force was sufficient to arrest the tide of savage invasion; but it became necessary not only to repel invasion, but to subdue the foe. The governor of Kentucky brevetted William H. Harrison a major general and he took command of the army of the northwest and marched to the relief of Fort Wayne, which was invested by Indians and British from Malden, on their way to the frontiers of Ohio. The Indians and British fled at his approach. This was early in September, 1812. Soon after the surrender of Hull, two block-houses were built on what is now the public square of Mansfield. The first was built by the company of Captain Shaeffer, from Fairfield county, and the other by the company of Captain Williams of Coshocton. About three and a half miles below Mansfield, on the Rocky fork, another block-house was built, and the company of Captain Martin, of Tuscarawas county, was stationed there. The block-house was named after Mr. Jacob Beam, who had located on the Rocky fork in the spring of 1811, and put up a log cabin and cleared a small piece of ground. In the fall of 1811 he put up a small log mill which had one run of stones. It was probably the first mill in Richland county. Mr. Beam was born in the State of Pennsylvania.

During the summer of 1812 Andrew Newman put up a small saw-mill on the same stream two and one-half miles below Mr. Beam, and was engaged on the race when the Zimmer-Ruffner tragedy occurred, and sought protection at the Mansfield block-house.

In the meantime John Baptiste Jerome was arrested, by order of General Beall, and confined some weeks in the block-house at Wooster, to prevent him from communicating with the Indians, as was alleged.

About this time, Captain Douglas was dispatched with his company, by Colonel Samuel Kratzer, who had arrived in Mansfield with his command, from Knox county, to remove the Indians from Jerometown and Greentown, as a measure of safety to the settlers, to some other part of the State. Captain Douglas proceeded quietly to their villages, but when he arrived at Greentown, Captain Thomas Armstrong, the chief, hesitated about obeying the order of removal. He had about eighty warriors under his command, and could have made a vigorous resistance. Fearing trouble, Captain Douglas, before attempting to use force, proceeded to the residence of James Copus, some two and a half miles further up the Black fork, and requested him to accompany him and his guard to Greentown, to use his influence to induce the Indians to depart without further trouble. Mr. Copus had the confidence of Armstrong, and felt that he would be doing injustice to his Indian neighbors to interpose in the matter, without the most positive assurance from Douglas that their property would remain safe until peace, and that no violence would be offered his Indians on their way to Urbana, the point to which they were to be removed. On receiving these assurances, he and his three sons (Henry, James, and Wesley) accompanied Douglas to Greentown. When they arrived, Armstrong and his people were greatly excited, and fears of a fight were entertained. Armstrong was an old man, and much esteemed by his people. He trembled with excitement when the consultation took place. On appealing to Mr. Copus, as to whether their property would be safe, he responded that Douglas had pledged him that it would be, and, though he was sorry they had to leave, he thought all would be safe. Prior to this, the Indians had assured Peter Kinney, a neighbor, that, if permitted to remain, they would surrender all their guns and war-like weapons, and answer to a roll call every day; but Douglas insisted that his orders were to remove them, and he intended to obey them. Accordingly, after the assurances of Mr. Copus, Captain Armstrong held a consultation with his leading advisers, and consented to go. A schedule of their property was taken by James Cunningham and Peter Kinney, and they took up their line of march across the Black fork, to the new State road, and proceeded thence to Lucas, and from there to Mansfield, and encamped in the ravine southwest of the public square. A few of Douglas' soldiers, perhaps eight or ten, remained in the village until Armstrong and his people had disappeared in the forest, and then, to the surprise and horror of Mr. Copus and his three sons, deliberately set fire to the village, and nearly everything in it was consumed in their presence.* This is the statement of Wesley Copus (died in 1876, at the age of

---

*Mrs. James Irwin, daughter of Judge Peter Kinney, who was near the village and conversant with the history of the removal, states that only part of the huts were burned by the soldiers of Douglas, and that the remaining huts were burned by the army of General Crook, who encamped some days on the site of the village. The army devoured the balance of the Indian corn, hogs, and cattle.

PRIEST·STOCKADE·1812.

THE·ZIMMER·CABIN.
1812.

seventy-four years), who was present and saw it. He attributes the untimely death of his father to this piece of perfidy on the part of Douglas and his men. After being joined by a few Indians from Jerometown, including the wife and daughter of Baptiste Jerome, a Frenchman, Colonel Kratzer and his command conducted the Indians through Berkshire, and across Elm creek, in Delaware county, to Urbana, where the settlers were more numerous, and where many peaceable Indians resided; and left Captain Armstrong and his people, as well as the Jerometown Indians—and the wife and daughter of Baptiste Jerome, who soon died from exposure, and were never again permitted to see husband and father! Jerome lamented the fate of his wife and daughter for many years, and often shed tears over their sad separation.

CHAPTER XXII.

OCCURRENCES DURING THE WAR.

A Part of the Greentown Indians, and a Number of Wyandots, Return.—The Murder of Martin Ruffner, Frederick Zimmer and Family, on the Black Fork.—The Tragedy at the Cabin of James Copus, and His Death.—The Rescue of His Family.

ABOUT two weeks after the removal of the Green and Jerometown Indians, the murder of Martin Ruffner and the family of Frederick Zimmer, sr.,* took place. Mr. Ruffner and a brother-in law, named Richard Hughes, erected cabins not a great ways apart, in the spring of 1812, about half a mile north of west of the present village of Mifflin, into which they moved. The mother of Mr. Ruffner, and a brother, aged about nineteen years, named Michael, accompanied and boarded with Richard Hughes. The wife and child of Martin Ruffner came on late in the summer. They had all resided in Fairfield county, Ohio, for several years, from whence they had gone to Canton, Ohio, and entered their lands. Mr. Zimmer located his tract about two and a half miles southeast of Mr. Ruffner, and, having put up a cabin, moved into it with his wife, daughter Catharine, and son Philip, aged about nineteen years. Being an old man, he was unable to do much work. Desiring to rapidly prepare some fifteen or twenty acres for corn, he hired Michael Ruffner, brother of Martin, to assist him. In the meantime, Martin Ruffner and a bound boy named Levi Berkinhizer, kept bachelor's hall in his cabin, working and doing their own cooking.

Early in September, one afternoon, while Michael Ruffner was on his way, on the old Indian trail leading from the cabin of Frederick Zimmer to the cabin of his brother, through the forest, he met two Indians who were well armed with guns, knives, and tomahawks, and seemed very friendly to him. Stopping him, they asked if the Zimmers were at home. He replied, they were. They then passed into the forest; and he hastened on and stated to his brother the occurrences on the way. Martin Ruffner suspected mischief—took down his gun—mounted a very fleet mare,* and rode rapidly down the trail to put Zimmer on his guard, and notify the other settlers in the vicinity. He arrived before the Indians, and Philip Zimmer was dispatched to inform James Copus, who lived about two miles further south, on the trail. Having notified Mr. Copus, he hastened from thence to inform John Lambright, who resided about two miles further south. Lambright returned with him, and, joined by Mr. Copus, they all proceeded to the cabin of Mr. Zimmer, where they arrived in the early part of the evening.† Finding no light in the cabin, and all being silent, fears were entertained that the Indians had killed the inmates. Mr. Copus moved cautiously around to a back window and listened a moment, but hearing no movements he crept slyly around to the door, which, on examination, he found partially ajar, and, pressing upon it, found some obstruction behind it. He at once suspected the family had been murdered, and, on placing his hand upon the floor, found it wet with blood! Hastening back to Philip and Lambright, who were concealed a short distance from the cabin, he stated his convictions, when Philip became frantic with grief and excitement, and desired to rush into the cabin to learn the whole truth concerning the fate of his venerable parents and sister. Suspecting Indians were concealed in the cabin, awaiting his return, Messrs. Lambright and Copus induced him to accompany them. On arriving at his cabin, Mr. Copus hastily took his wife and children and poceeded with Mr. Lambright to his residence. There they were joined by his wife and children. From thence they pressed on to the cabin of Frederick Zimmer, jr., brother of Philip, and he and his brother joined the fugitives, and they hastened along an Indian path near where the village of Lucas now stands, and stopped at the cabin of David Hill, where they remained until the next morning. Hill and family then accompanied them to the block-house

---

* Mr. Zimmer purchased his land at Canton, in the spring of 1812, for which he obtained a deed, or patent, signed by President Madison, October 2, 1812. It was recorded in the land office, in the name of Philip Zimmer—by modern settlers pronounced Semour or Seymour.

*Statement of Daniel Hoover, a neighbor of Martin Ruffner in Fairfield county, Ohio, who now resides in Richland county, about three miles northwest of Mifflin, on the west side of the Black fork. He is now (1873) seventy-nine years of age. He came from Rockingham county, Virginia, and settled on the waters of Rush creek, in Fairfield county, about the year 1803, with the family of his father. He had known Martin Ruffner in Shenandoah county, Virginia. Ruffner moved to Pleasant township, Fairfield county, Ohio, in 1807, accompanied by his mother, brother Michael, and a sister, who married one Richard Hughes. Martin Ruffner returned to Virginia a year or two before he moved to Richland county, and married. He and his relatives located on what is now Staman's run, half a mile below Mifflin, in the spring of 1812. Mr. Hoover was in Mansfield, on his way to Ruffner's, when Hull surrendered; and, taking into view the excitement produced by that disaster, thought it prudent to return home, where he remained until 1814, and then removed to and commenced improvements on the farm upon which he now resides. He says: "Michael Ruffner, on his return to Fairfield, in 1812, gave him a full statement of the Ruffner-Zimmer affair, which is substantially the same as given in the foregoing sketch."

† Statement of Wesley Copus, who remembered the occurrence very distinctly. He died in 1876, aged seventy-four years.

at Jacob Beam's, where they arrived safely and gave the alarm. Mr. Copus, Philip and Frederick Zimmer, Hill, Lambright and a number of soldiers, well armed, proceeded by the most direct route, through the forest, to the cabins of Martin Ruffner and Richard Hughes.* They found that the cabin of Ruffner had not been disturbed, and that Levi Berkinhizer, the boy, had slept there, alone, the night before, and that the cabin of Hughes had also been undisturbed. Ruffner had, a short time prior to this, on learning of the surrender of Hull, sent his wife and child to Licking county in company with young Berkinhizer, to reside with Mr. Laird, an uncle, who lived about one and a half miles from Utica. After the return of the boy, they did their own cooking. Ruffner was a large, fearless man--had been on good terms with his Indian neighbors—in fact, when he came on to locate his land, in passing through Greentown an Indian volunteered to show him the piece he entered, telling him "it was good land—had Indian huts on it; had apple trees, good water, and other advantages." He had cleared, and planted four or five acres of corn, which was attended by himself and Berkinhizer.

After the murder of the old people, Philip Zimmer, May 1, 1815, and wife Elizabeth, before Thomas Mace, justice of the peace of Pickaway county, deeded the old farm to Michael Culler, who took possession of it, and resided upon the land until his death, in 1876. This deed was plainly signed by Philip and Elizabeth Zimmer, his wife.

But to return. When they arrived at Ruffner's cabin, young Berkinhizer, Michael Ruffner and Hughes joined the company, and hastened down the trail to the cabin of Mr. Zimmer. On entering it, they found the old gentleman, the old lady and Catharine all dead and dreadfully mangled by the savages. Ruffner was found in the yard dead. He had, apparently, made a desperate effort to save the family, during which he had succeeded in reaching the front yard. His gun was bent nearly double, from clubbing it in the cabin. Several of his fingers had been cut off by blows from a tomahawk; and the struggle had finally ended by his being shot twice through the body. Ruffner and the Zimmers had been scalped by the Indians. It seemed from appearances, that the table had been set with refreshments for the savages, as the most of the food remained.† The attack must have been very sudden and unexpected; for Ruffner, with his trusty rifle, was more than a match for two Indians. Indeed, there can be scarcely a doubt that eight or ten Indians were engaged in the tragedy. It is also probable that the Indians that committed those murders had resided at Greentown, and had a personal spite to avenge on Mr. Zimmer and family. The older pioneers say the Indians often complained that the Zimmers had maltreated their ponies by tying clapboards to their tails, when they were feeding around their fields, to frighten them away; and they had possibly taken this way to complete their retaliation. Their fences were mostly made of brush, and the corn was very tempting to the Indian horses. Any injury to their dogs and ponies was always remembered and resented.

Martin Ruffner and the Zimmers were buried on a little knoll, a few rods from the scene of the tragedy, in one grave, where they now rest quietly in the dream of death. The farm is now owned by Michael Culler (since deceased), and the site of the grave is pointed out by him. After performing the last sad ceremonies over the remains of the murdered pioneers, they returned to the block-house at Beams, and Michael Ruffner, his mother, and Hughes and family, removed to Fairfield county, Ohio, from whence, we are informed, they never returned.*

About five days after the return of Mr. Copus to the blockhouse, becoming weary of staying there, and believing the Indians entertained no ill will towards him, he insisted on returning with his family to the Black fork. Captain Martin protested that he was incurring much danger in doing so; but Mr. Copus insisting on going back, nine soldiers were detailed to conduct him and his family home. They all arrived safely in the afternoon, and found the cabin and stock secure. In the evening Mr. Copus invited the soldiers to sleep in the cabin; but the weather being yet quite warm, they preferred to take quarters in the barn, which stood four or five rods north of the cabin, on the trail, that they might have a better opportunity to indulge in frolic and fun, and be less crowded and under less restraint. Before retiring, Mr. Copus cautioned them against surprise by Indians who might be lurking about. During the afternoon, Sarah, a little daughter of Mr. Copus, aged about twelve years, went into the cornfield, a few rods south of the cabin, and while there saw an Indian, in the edge of the forest, skulk behind a brush heap, but neglected to relate the circumstance to her father † That night the dogs kept up a constant barking, and Mr. Copus had many unpleasant dreams. Before daylight he invited the soldiers into the cabin, telling them he feared some great disaster was about to overtake himself and family. He again lay down to rest; and when daylight began to appear, the soldiers insisted on going to the spring, about three rods away, to wash. The spring is one of finest in the country, and gushes from the base of the hill in a large current. He again cautioned them of impending danger, telling them that Indians were certainly in the

---

* Statement of Daniel Hoover.

† There is a tradition among the early settlers, that about the year 1815-16, two Indians were arrested in the east part of the State for some crime, and imprisoned at New Philadelphia; and that while there, one of them—Philip Konotchy—a Greentown Indian, stated that he had killed Kate Zimmer after she had prepared supper for the Indians. That after Ruffner and the old people had been killed, the balance of the Indians desired to save Kate, but he returned and finished the work by sinking his tomahawk into her brains. While many of the pioneers relate this story, we are not able to verify it by anything on record. For a further description of this Indian, see also, personal sketch of Robert F. Chandler.

*Statement of Daniel Hoover.

† Mrs. Sarah Vail, now a widow seventy-eight years of age, relates this occurrence, and says the reason she did not inform her father of it is, that he was a very strict man in regard to the truth, and fearing she might have been deceived, did not wish to incur his displeasure by creating a false alarm, and therefore did not relate the circumstance.

neighborhood, or his dogs would not have made so much noise; and said "if they went to the spring, they should take their guns along," which they promised to do; but on passing out leaned them against the cabin, and started for the spring. They had scarcely reached it, when the Indians rushed from their concealment in the cornfield with a terrific yell, and cutting off all retreat, began to shoot and tomahawk the soldiers. Mr. Copus, upon hearing the uproar, sprang from his bed, seized his gun and rushed for the door. Just as he opened it, he met a ferocious looking savage, and both fired at the same instant, and both were mortally wounded. The ball passed through the leather strap that supported the powder-horn † of Mr. Copus, and penetrating his breast, caused him to fall, when he was supported to his bed, where he expired in about an hour, while begging the soldiers to bravely defend and save his poor family from the cruel fate that seemed to await them. Two of the soldiers fled to the forest, pursued by the Indians, and were soon overtaken, killed and scalped; the third had nearly escaped his pursuers, when they fired after him, and shot him through the bowels and foot. He ran about six hundred yards, and becoming weak through loss of blood, sat down, and leaning against a tree, stuffed his handkerchief into the wound and expired. Mr. Geo. Dye, another soldier, (from Morgan county), made a desperate effort and regained the cabin, but was shot through the thigh just as he entered. The killed were Geo. Shipley, John Tedrick, and Mr. Warnock, who fled into the forest. The ground on the east of the cabin was quite precipitous and rose about seventy-five or eighty feet high. It had a small growth of dwarfed timber, and furnished a good lodgment for the Indians. A few stunted oaks stood along the brow of the hill, behind which the Indians partially concealed themselves as they loaded their guns. The door of the cabin was soon riddled with balls; and the soldiers tore up the puncheons and placed them against it, to prevent the balls from entering the room and killing or wounding the family. Volley after volley was fired into the building, until the logs were honey-combed with leaden balls. From the elevation obove the cabin, the Indians fired through the roof, in the hope of hitting the inmates. Nancy Copus, a little girl, was shot through the door, above the knee, producing a painful wound. George Launtz, a soldier, had his arm broken by a ball, up stairs, as he was removing the clay and chinking, to enable him to get a "crack" at an Indian! Very soon he saw the "head of the red fiend protruding from behind a small scrub oak, that stands yet on the brow of the hill, above the cabin, and "let drive at it," and the "Indian bounded into the air and rolled down the hill into the trail."

The battle continued about five hours, when the savages, despairing of success, withdrew and carried off their wounded and buried their dead. The exact number could not be ascertained; neither could the point where they buried their dead be pointed out. As a sort of farewell salute they emptied their guns into a flock of sheep belonging to Mr. Copus that had, from fright, huddled together on the brow of the hill above the cabin, and killed most of them.* As soon as the Indians disappeared, one of the soldiers up stairs cautiously separated the clapboards of the roof, and passing out, made the utmost speed to inform the soldiers at the block-house at Beam's of the disasters of the morning, and crave immediate assistance. Before leaving the block-house, the day before, Captain Martin agreed to call at the Copus cabin the same evening, with a number of soldiers, and stay all night. But he and his soldiers having been out on a scout all day, and failing to find Indian signs concluded that all apprehensions of danger were frivolous; therefore neglected to appear as agreed. He encamped above the Black fork, and on the morning of the disaster, moving leisurely down the trail from the region of Ruffner's, reached the scene of the fight too late to render aid in the fearful struggle. On approaching the cabin, he and his soldiers were awe-struck on beholding the work of death around them. The captain and his men attended at once to the wounded, and the grief-stricken family of Mr. Copus, who was then lying cold in death, surrounded by his terrified wife and children. Search was then made for the Indians; but from the trail in the rich weeds that grew luxuriantly about the hill, it was found they had retreated around the southern brow of the bluff, and gone up a ravine about a quarter of a mile away, and fled in the direction of Quaker Springs in Vermillion township; and hence, pursuit was abandoned. Mr. Copus and the murdered soldiers were buried by the command, in a large grave at the foot of an apple tree, a rod or two from his cabin, where their bones yet repose.

Captain Martin and his soldiers then took the family, and the wounded, and, proceeding up the valley about half a mile, stopped for the night, and placed pickets around the camp to prevent surprise. In all, there were about one hundred persons in the camp that night. The wounded were carried on poles, over which linen sheets had been sewed, making a sort of stretcher. The next morning, the little army passed up the trail near the deserted cabin of Martin Ruffner, and crossed the Black fork, about where the State road is now located; that being the route by which Martin and his men had advanced. The whole party reached the block-house that evening, and were again safe. About six weeks after this, Henry Copus, and five or six soldiers, returned to the cabin, and found Mr. Warnock leaning against a tree (as before stated), dead; and buried him near the spot where he was found. The two Indians, the one in the

---

† This powder-horn, a very large on, is yet in the possession of the family of Mr. Wesley Copus, and is a rare relic of the days of the pioneers

* These transactions were narrated by Wesley Copus and Mrs. Sarah Vail, his sister, who were old enough at the time to observe and retain a most vivid recollection of them. It was found on examination that forty-five fires had been kindled in the edge of the forest, just south of the cornfield, from which Sarah had seen the Indians. These fires had been kindled in a small hole scooped out of the ground, to prevent their being seen. She thinks the Indians had probably dined the evening before the murders, on roasted corn. The number of fires would indicate that forty-five Indians were engaged in the assault.

front yard, and the one at the foot of the hill, were still in the position they had been left; and were, doubtless, afterwards devoured by the wolves that existed in great numbers in the forests at that time.

Mrs. Copus and her children, after remaining in the block-house some two months, were removed to Guernsey county, Ohio, by Joseph Archer and George Correll, who resided near Claysville, in that county, where they remained until the spring of 1815, and then returned through the old village of Greentown, where, to their alarm, they found many of the Indians had re-erected their cabins, and had again settled.

This tragedy is believed to have occurred on Tuesday morning, September 15, 1812. Mr. Lewis Oliver is very certain it so occurred, and cites facts to prove it.

CHAPTER XXIII.

THE SETTLERS TAKE REFUGE IN BLOCK-HOUSES.

The Flight of the Pioneers.—The Erection of Block-houses.—Preparations to Meet and Repel the Savages.—The Depot at Clinton, Knox County.—Beam's Block-house on the Black Fork.

In a few hours the painful intelligence of the assassination of Martin Ruffner and the Zimmer family reached the settlers along the branches of Mohican creek. A panic ensued; and the yells of the furious Indian hordes of the northwest, led on by the relentless Tecumseh, were momentarily expected. The situation was comprehended at a glance, and a general flight of the pioneers to the block-houses and other safe retreats, took place. Pack-horses, wagons and carts were in demand—in fact, every means of conveyance was put into speedy requisition; and such articles of bedding and wearing apparel as could not be dispensed with, were put in packs and conveyed along with the fugitives. As near as can be remembered, the following families fled to Clinton: Ebenezer Rice and family, Joseph Jones and family, Calvin Hill and family, Moses Adzit and family, Abraham Baughman and family, Allen Oliver and family, and J. L. Hill and family. There were in all about thirty persons, and they made their way, as rapidly as possible, along the paths leading through the forests to the village of Clinton, near the present site of Mt. Vernon, then a sort of depot for supplies for the army. A difference of opinion existed among pioneers as to the propriety of the flight, and the necessity of seeking protection among the Clintonites, some asserting that it seemed cowardly, while others contended that the Greentown Indians entertained none but the kindest feelings for their pioneer neighbors, and that if they should return would do them no harm*

The upper settlement on the Black fork hastened to the block-house on the Clear fork, owned by Samuel Lewis. At that time, some twenty or thirty soldiers, under Lieutenant Barkdall, were there as a guard. Those seeking refuge there were Peter Kinney and family, James Cunningham and family, Andrew Craig and family, David Davis and family, John Davis, William Slater and family, John Wilson and family, Peter Zimmerman and family, Harvey Hill and family, Henry McCart and family, and Henry Nail and family. Most of these families made a temporary stay at the block-house, returning to their cabins frequently, during the fall months, to keep watch over such household goods as were left in them, and to take care of their abandoned stock.

The next day after the flight to the Lewis block-house, Harvey Hill and John Coulter, who aided the fugitives in driving along most of their cattle, returned; and by the aid of the Tannahills and others, whose names are not now remembered, the roof of the cabin of Thomas Coulter was thrown off, and a second story put on, and the cabin thereby became "Coulter's block-house." We learn from Mr. Alex. Rice, who was then a boy, that the Coulter cabin was perhaps sixteen by eighteen feet, built for their first dwelling in the fall of 1810, the overjutting part being put on as referred to above. It stood at the base of a bold bluff, on the bank of the Black fork, near where the mill-dam now is, about half a mile southeast of the village of Perrysville, and furnished a safe retreat for the neighbors of Mr. Coulter, when endangered by the savages. As soon as this block-house was completed, the following persons occupied it: Thomas Coulter and family, Allen Oliver and family, Melzer Tannahill and family, Jeremiah Conine and family, and George Crawford and family. When the foregoing families had gathered in, Thomas Coulter and Harvey Hill volunteerd to go to Wooster, through the forest, to secure soldiers to defend the settlement against Indian incursions. They succeeded in obtaining a guard of eleven soldiers, under the command of Lieutenant Winterringer, of the Tuscarawas militia, of the army of General Beall, then collecting at Wooster, for an expedition to Upper Sandusky. The guard accompanied them home, and in the day-time skirmished about the hills, and up and down the valleys for Indian signs, and then stood guard at night to prevent an attack by the Indians.

While a resident of the block-house, the wife of Jeremiah Conine died and was buried in the cemetery at Perrysville. She was the second person interred in that ground, the first being Mr. Samuel Hill who died the preceding June.

The settlers along the Jeromefork and its branches were also greatly excited and alarmed over the murder of Ruffner and the Zimmers. Thomas Eagle hastened to Wooster for assistance. The block-house at Wooster, then a mere village, was under the command of Captain Stidger, whose company constituted a part of the army of General Beall. The company of Captain Nicholas Murray, composed of about sixty soldiers, immediately hastened to the relief of the Jerome settlement.

---

*Early in November, 1812, the families that fled to Clinton, returned to Green township, and made Coulter's block-house their place of retreat when threatened by Indian invasion. The cabin of Allen Oliver being quite safe, he and his family spent but a night or two at Coulter's.

A block-house was erected by his men, a short distance northeast of the present site of the mill, on a gentle rise of ground, where the settlers commenced at once to concentrate. Mr. Eagle also conducted a guard of eight or ten men to protect a small block-house or cabin at the Finley and Collyer settlement, about five miles down the Jerome fork, near where Tylertown now stands.

In the meantime, Robert Newell and family, George Eckley and family, Jonathan Palmer and family, James Wallace and family, Christopher Trickle and family, James Bryan and family, Ezra Warner and family, and David Noggle and others, not now remembered, gathered at the new block-house. The families of Benjamin Cuppy and Jacob Fry did not remain at the fort, but passed on east. It was noticed, when all had gathered in, that Daniel Carter and family were missing. Much uneasiness was evinced concerning the safety of Mr. Carter and family. He resided up the stream, about nine miles from the block-house, and one mile northeast of the present site of Ashland. Absolom Newell, the eldest son of Robert Newell, volunteered to go and inform Mr. Carter and family of the danger that threatened them. Being an active young man, he soon reached the cabin of his father, some five miles up the Jerome fork, which he found almost consumed by fire. Supposing Indians had set it on fire, and were concealed in the vicinity, he hastened back and related the circumstance to the company at the block-house. David Noggle, a warm friend of Mr. Carter, at once offered to undertake the hazardous task of reaching him on horseback. Thirty soldiers were detailed for the expedition. Mr. Noggle and the soldiers followed a trail cut through the forest by Mr. Carter when he removed his family to his new cabin, which passed south of Newell's, thence over lands more recently owned by Mr. Smucker, Samuel Swinford, and the late farm of Daniel Carter, jr., and so on to his cabin. Mr. Noggle reached the cabin some time before the soldiers, and found Mr. Carter at work with his team, all safe. From circumstances afterwards developed, it appears that a body of Indians had that very morning* passed through the cornfield near the cabin, but had offered no harm to Mr. Carter and his family. He had always made it a rule to treat the Indians kindly and offered them food when they visited his cabin; and it was doubtless owing to this circumstance that their lives were spared that morning. Mr. Carter hastily placed such clothing and bedding on his wagon as he could conveniently remove, and taking his family, accompanied Mr. Noggle. They had gone but a short distance when they met the guard. The soldiers continued in the direction of the deserted cabins of Cuppy and Fry, and on approaching the former, found it yet burning, and some of the soldiers discovered the rear guard of the Indians skulking in a cornfield. On looking towards the cabin of Mr. Fry, a half-mile west, they could see the smoke ascending from it. They then turned about, and retraced their steps to the block-house at Jerome's place, where Mr. Carter and family had arrived a short time before. Mr. Carter and family did not remain at the block-house; but passed on through Wooster to New Philadelphia, Tuscarawas county, where he and his family remained until February, 1813.

The band of Indians that burned the cabins of Newell, Cuppy and Fry was undoubtedly the same that the day before made the assault on the Copus cabin. They had passed through the forest in the hope of wreaking vengeance upon these families; and if they had been found at home the tomahawk of the savages would have done its work. Fortunately they had all fled on gaining intelligence of the Ruffner-Zimmer tragedy, which took place some five days prior to the Copus murders. It is somewhat remarkable that Mr. Carter and his family should have remained in his cabin after the departure of Cuppy, Fry and Trickle.* No satisfactory explanation has ever appeared concerning the course of Mr. Carter, unless it be that he felt confident the Indians would do him no harm. A very strong friendship existed between Mr. Carter and Thomas Lyon, a famous old Delaware warrior, who accompanied the expedition, but who always denied that he had aided in killing Ruffner, the Zimmers and Copus. Mr. Carter never failed to invite hungry Indians into his cabin and offer them food when they called on him. These acts of hospitality made him feel confident and secure, although at that time he resided nine miles farther in the Indian country than his Jerome neighbors. Acts of hospitality have always been remembered by the red man of the forest, and many instances are recorded, where years after, the Indian warrior interposed to save the white prisoner from the fagot. Assuming such to be the true explanation of the motives of Mr. Carter in remaining in his cabin, all incoherence is removed, as well as the apparent indifference of his fugitive neighbors.

At this time there were six or eight families in the Vachel-Metcalf settlement, some two and a half miles southeast of the fort on Jerome's place, among whom were those of William Bryan, James Conley, Elisha

---

* Mr. Daniel Carter, jr., now a resident of Ashland, states that some time after the flight, Thomas Lyon, a well-known Delaware warrior, in conversation with himself and father, inquired whether they had seen Indian tracks in the cornfield that morning. On assuring him that they had, he said he was with the *Wyandots* that passed up the creek, and could see Carter's family from the corn. Carter asked him why he did not stop? Lyon replied, "Some strange Injin with me. Me 'fraid scare you. Me pass on." It is probable the presence of Lyon saved the family of Carter from the deadly tomahawk of the strange *Wyandots*.

*Andrew Mason, now well advanced in years, states, that in a conversation with his father, Martin Mason, now deceased, at his mill where the mill of Mr. Lidigh now stands on the Troy road, some four miles north of Ashland, about the year 1816. Thomas Lyon told his father "that being present at the Copus affair, but taking no part in the murder, and learning that it was the intention of some Greentown and Wyandot Indians to pass up the Jerome fork and kill all the settlers, he had gone through the forest and notified Mr. Cuppy of his danger." If this statement be not erroneous, Thomas Lyon, as is believed by the Copus family, was present at both those tragedies. In a conversation with Mrs. Copus after the return of herself and children in 1816, Lyon admitted that he knew all about the affair, but asserted that he was innocent of taking a part in the horrors of that morning.

If it be true as asserted by Lyon, that he was not disposed to alarm Mr. Carter and family, it is conclusive that he was restrained by gratitude for past hospitality, as well as by friendship and fidelity.

Chilcote, Benjamin Bunn, James Slater, and James Bryan. These met and constructed a fort two stories high, the walls of the second story projecting beyond the first on all sides. The floor and sides of the second story were pierced with port-holes. The pioneers, with ox teams, axes and strong arms soon erected the fort. The lower story had strong doors securely fastened, and was to be occupied by women and children, while the men, with trusty rifles, were to occupy the second story in hours of danger and alarm. About one-fourth of an acre of ground was cleared around the fort and enclosed by a palisade twelve feet high, with a strong gate; and all the families of the settlement gathered into the fort, while their horses and cattle were placed within the palisade. Mr. Metcalf and his neighbors remained in the fort during the winter of 1812-'13 and part of the summer of 1813, while cultivating, by occasional visits, small patches of corn and vegetables, with pickets, to prevent surprise.

In Lake township, Messrs. James Loudon Priest and William Greenlee had located very near the old Indian highway known as the Wyandot or Crawford's trial leading to Upper Sandusky from the Tuscarawas. When they first landed, the Jerome and Greentown Indians were peaceable and inclined to be quite friendly, and passed up and down the trail in large numbers on hunting excursions. Early in the spring of 1812, it was noticed that the Indians were quite uneasy, and that large numbers passed up the trail painted and armed for war. * Mr. John Greenlee, son of William, now aged seventy-two years from whom we obtain these particulars, says at the time of the murders on the Black fork, he and the son of a neighbor were at Shrimplin's mill in Knox county to obtain a small grist of corn meal, and upon their return were greatly surprised at finding all the settlers gathered at the cabin of Mr. Priest, busily engaged with ox-teams hauling logs and split timber to build a fort. The fort was erected near the banks of the Mohican, not a great way from the point where the Pittsburgh, Fort Wayne and Chicago railroad crosses that stream. A new extension was added to the strong cabin of Mr. Priest making it a double log house with an entry passage between the wings. The wings were about forty feet long and twenty feet wide. The fort was surrounded by a picket of heavy split timber about twelve feet high and enclosed about one fourth of an acre of ground. It had a strong gate suspended on wooden hinges. In case of necessity, the horses and cattle of the settlers could be brought within the enclosure. The families of James L. Priest, William Greenlee, William Hendrickson, Nathan Odell, John Oram, Thompson Oram, Joshua Oram and Mordecai Chilcote forted here some three months during the fall of 1812; but were not visited by any of the hostile red men of the northwest. In a few days after the construction of the fort, Samuel Marvin and John Hendrickson and their families departed for Wheeling, Virginia, leaving but seven families in the little colony. During the continuance of the war in 1813-14 the little settlement remained stationary as to numbers and undisturbed.

THE BLOCK-HOUSE.

It may be interesting to the reader to learn something of the construction of the early block-houses, or wooden forts. They were generally constructed of hewn logs, closely jointed or fitted together, two stories high; the length and width of the building being about twenty by thirty feet. The logs resting on each other, prevented the balls from entering the cracks or crevices. The corners were carefully notched and fitted, so that the building was really quite strong. There was but one door, or entrance, made of thick planks or puncheons, hung on strong wooden or iron hinges, and bolted or fastened on the inside, so as to prevent ingress unless much force should be used,—the door being thick enough to prevent ordinary musket or rifle balls from passing through it. The first story was generally about eight or nine feet high. Sometimes the floor consisted of well packed earth. The second story generally projected over the lower one, about three feet, on the sides and ends. This over-jut rested upon logs or joists, which were allowed to project over the first story. The second story was about seven or eight feet high, and was perforated with numerous port-holes, pointing in every direction, so as to guard against the approach of an enemy. The floor of this story was thick and strong, and had port-holes pointing downward, so that if an enemy came under the projection, to set fire to the building, he could be shot from above. There were also port-holes in the lower story, from which the savages could be seen and cut off before they reached the building. The roof was of clapboards, supported by logs. These little forts, or block-houses, were generally placed in an open space, upon some slight elevation of ground, so as to prevent the approach of a hostile force without being seen by the inmates. The next point in the location of a block-house was to secure good water; and hence, they were always placed near a pure, sparkling spring.* In such a fort, or block-house, twenty-five or thirty families could be accommodated with tolerable quarters, by spreading their beds upon the floors, and sleeping thereon. During the day, the inmates could pass in and out; and, most of the time, attend to business without being molested by the Indians,—their raids being only semi-occasional, and very sudden and unexpected. We do not learn that more than two block-houses of this county, were surrounded by stockades.

Life in the block-houses was exceedingly irksome and monotonous; and the inmates were always pleased when assured they could safely return to their deserted cabins and stock. Of course, hours and weeks were spent in reciting and reiterating stories of revolutionary adventure, and pioneer hardships, until all could repeat them. Thus, the tedium of the fort was wiled away for two or three months. The scarcity of flour, meal, salt, and other provisions, sometimes rendered the situation exceedingly unpleasant; nevertheless, all was borne with

---

* Mr. Greenlee died since this sketch was written.

* The one at Jeromeville had a well within it.

BLOCKHOUSE AT JEROMEVILLE 1812

patience until November, when most of the pioneers again returned to their cabins. A few soldiers continued to patrol the neighborhood, sleeping at the block-houses at night.

CHAPTER XXIV.

MILITARY EXPEDITIONS.

The Expeditions of Generals Beall and Crooks.—Their Trails Across Ashland County.—The Artillery Train of Colonel Anderson.—The Aid Extended to the Inhabitants of the Block-houses on the Branches of the Mohican.

THE battle at the cabin of James Copus having taken place Tuesday morning, September 15, 1812, after which the pioneers fled to the block-houses, the military expeditions forming in the eastern part of the State hastened the time of their departure to aid General Harrison, who was then at Upper Sandusky awaiting the arrival of reinforcements and army stores. About the twenty-fifth of September, General Rezin Beall commenced to raise a brigade of soldiers in the vicinity of New Lisbon, Canton and the village of Wooster, with a view of furnishing protection to the border settlers of Wayne and Richland counties, as well as to aid General Harrison in repelling British invasion. The entire brigade was composed of about two thousand men. A portion of the brigade, in detached companies, and parts of companies, preceded, by some weeks, the advance of the main army, to guard the block-houses of the border settlers. Early in October, General Beall, with two regiments, commenced to advance. The brigade had been a short time at Canton in organizing. The route from Canton to the village of Wooster, led through the forest, and was very rough. When the army reached Wooster, where the advance had put up a block-house, it was joined by two or three new companies. From that point the army proceeded to the west bank of the Killbuck and encamped over night, cutting a path wide enough to permit the baggage-wagons to pass. From thence, by the most direct route, a trail was cut to Jerome's place, and the army passed over it. After remaining in the vicinity of the block-house one or two days, General Beall crossed the Jerome fork, and his pioneers opened a path along the old Wyandot trail, in a northwesterly direction, to the banks of a small stream, where they formed a camp. This location was subsequently known as the Griffin farm. The camp received the name of "Mercer," in honor of Major Musser, who commanded one of the regiments. The distance of this camp from the present site of Jeromeville, was about three miles. Here the army remained about two weeks.

While encamped at Mercer, a ludicrous scene occurred one night, from a false alarm. One of the guards, Jacob Ostler, saw some object cautiously approaching in the darkness, and immediately suspecting "injuns," cried "halt." The invader ceased not to advance slowly upon the guard. Suspecting the insidious enemy, Mr. Ostler leveled his musket and blazed away, and down tumbled the enemy! The whole camp was aroused at the report, and the cry "to arms, to arms!" rang through the darkness. Agitated and frightened soldiers expected momentarily to hear the hideous yells of the red fiends of the forest, and to feel their scalps disappearing in the hands of the savages. While the soldiers were uttering brief reflections of—"Now I lay me down to sleep"—the sentinels rushed in and reported the enemy upon them! The drums beat to arms, horses neighed, bugles sounded. The ground trembled with the dull tread of squadrons. The order was given to "fire," and never before or since was such a noise and din heard in Vermillion, as there was that eventful night. The cavalry (old wagon horses) charged in the direction of the supposed enemy, but finding no person or thing, returned from the charge, and reported that the foe had retreated; but when the first gray of morning appeared, the outposts discovered that they had been firing upon a herd of cattle belonging to the settlers, which had been roaming through the woods, and had slaughtered seventeen. This was afterward known among the settlers as "The battle of the Cowpens."* It was while General Beall tarried at this camp, that he ordered the removal of the wife and daughter of Baptiste Jerome to Urbana, where they soon died from exposure.† This act was deemed, at the time, extremely cruel, and not demanded by the exigencies of the occasion. The wife of Jerome was a full Indian; but had learned the customs of the whites. The daughter was an interesting girl of fourteen or fifteen.

From Camp Mercer, General Beall sent forward twenty pioneers, well guarded, to cut a road along the old Huron or Wyandot trail, through the north part of Vermillion, the south part of Montgomery, and across Milton, in a northwesterly direction, into Richland county, which, afterwards, was known as "Beall's trail," and was used for many years as a common highway by the settlers. In about one month, the road was completed through the present site of Olivesburgh to Shenandoah, in Richland county.

In the meantime, General Beall moved forward, and erected a camp on a small stream, a short distance from the present site of Olivesburgh, which he called Camp Whetstone, owing to the quality of the stone found there, which made excellent whetstones. There he remained about one week, and then moved forward to the present site of Shenandoah. From thence, he turned southwest about one and a half miles, and erected a camp on a small stream. This he called Camp Council. Here he awaited further orders from General Wadsworth, who had rendezvoused at Cleveland. The army had remained at Camp Council about six weeks, when one evening a strange officer and his guard rode into the camp. One of the guard, a Mr. Hackathorn, at first refused to let him pass; but, on further examination, the

---

* Knapp's History, page 256.

† The weight of pioneer tradition says Captain Douglas removed Jerome's wife and daughter with the Greentown Indians, some weeks prior to the arrival of General Beall.

stranger turning out to be General Harrison, let him and his guard pass in. His arrival was timely, for the soldiers of General Beall were in open revolt. Their rations were about exhausted, and the means of obtaining more, precarious; besides, the time of heir enlistment was about to expire. Many of them were making arrangements to return home. Some of them had already packed their knapsacks with clothing and a few rations, and were ready to march away! General Harrison, the next morning, ordered a parade of the army. A hollow square was formed, around a huge stump, upon which the general mounted, and addressed the disaffected troops. He told them the dangers that environed the border settlers and their helpless families, painted in vivid colors the horrors of invasion by the savages, and deprecated the conduct of the soldiers who would abandon the settlements to the tomahawks of the ruthless foe. One by one, the knapsacks disappeared from the backs of the discontented soldiers; and, by the time he had concluded his address, the army of General Beall was ready to move forward, and endure all manner of hardships, to shield the border settlements from impending ruin.

From Camp Council General Beall proceeded with his army to Camp Avery, which was located about six miles above the mouth of the Huron river. Here he was tried by court-martial for disobeying the orders of General Wadsworth. This was about the first of January, 1813. It seems that General Wadsworth outranked General Beall, and had ordered him to rendezvous at Cleveland instead of going the route he did. General Beall believed he could render the settlements on the branches of the Mohican more secure by cutting his trail. Hence he refused to obey the order of General Wadsworth, and for this he was court-martialed. Upon a full hearing of the charges, General Beall was acquitted. He was then ordered to reinforce General Winchester who was then in the neighborhood of the river Raisin, but only succeeded in reaching Lower Sandusky, where he was ordered to return to Camp Avery and disband his army. The soldiers made their way along the route of his advance to their homes about Wooster, Canton, New Lisbon, and along the Sandy and Tuscarawas rivers.*

EXPEDITION OF GENERAL ROBERT CROOKS.

While Governor Meigs was exerting himself to obtain troops to reinforce General Harrison in the northwest, the war department at Washington city ordered the governors of Pennsylvania and Virginia, each to dispatch two thousand men to aid General Harrison. The order was promptly obeyed, and the Pennsylvanians were placed under the command of Brigadier General Robert Crooks, and ordered to rendezvous at Pittsburgh, and, as soon as equipped, to hasten to the relief of General Harrison. The artillery and army stores not being ready, General Crooks was ordered to move as rapidly as possible by way of New Lisbon, Canton, and Wooster, to Mansfield, and there remain until the artillery and army stores should arrive, under the direction of the quartermaster. The brigade under the command of General Crooks numbered about two thousand men—western Pennsylvanians. The brigade moved slowly down the west bank of the Ohio, from Allegheny City, some forty miles, thence, turning westward, moved on through New Lisbon, Canton, and Wooster. In the meantime its movements were much impeded by the rough roads, then mere paths cut through the forest. The army was put in motion about the middle of October, 1812, and arrived in Wooster about three weeks after the departure of General Beall to Jerome's place. The train of wagons connected with General Crooks' brigade numbered, as near as can be remembered, some twenty-five or thirty six-horse teams, the wagons being covered by canvas, and filled with army stores of all kinds.

After halting a day or two at Wooster to repair broken wagons and allow the jaded teams to rest, the brigade was again put in motion. It reached the block-house and log cabin, afterwards known as Jerometown, in one day. Here the army of General Crooks passed the Jerome fork and turned to the southwest. The brigade passed up a small stream, by what was afterwards known as the site of Goudy's mill, and commenced to cut a path, now known as the "old Portage road." The pioneers cut the road along an old Indian trail, as far as the Quaker springs, the first day, where General Crooks and his brigade encamped for the night. The next day the pioneers continued along the old trail, in a southwest direction, cutting a path large enough for the teams to pass, reaching the deserted village of Greentown in the evening, and the brigade coming up, encamped there for the night. Nearly all the Indian huts had been burned prior to this time, by order of another command. At Greentown the brigade crossed the Black fork, and proceeding southwest a short distance, struck a new blazed road leading to the west. The pioneers again kept in advance of the brigade, cutting the road, filling up gulches, and preparing the crossings over small streams until they reached the cabin of David Hill, on the present site of Lucas, where the brigade again encamped for the night. The next morning the pioneers continued to penetrate the forest, and in the afternoon reached the present site of Mansfield, where they found two block-houses, and a few cabins and dwelling houses. In the evening General Crooks and his men encamped on what is now the public square of Mansfield, where he remained some weeks awaiting the arrival of the quartermaster's train. About the fifteenth of December General Crooks was ordered to proceed to Upper Sandusky to assist in fortifying that point. The quartermaster had as yet failed to reach Mansfield. General Crooks moved forward under the guidance of Jacob Newman, an old hunter and a citizen of the village, to Upper Sandusky.

About three weeks after the departure of General Crooks and his brigade from Allegheny City, Colonel James Anderson, acting quartermaster, was ready to

---

*We are indebted for these details to Patrick Murray, John Clay, Henry Gamble, Thomas Hewey and Samuel White, (all deceased), who were soldiers under General Beall; and an interesting history of Richland county now being published by General R. Brinkerhoff.

march *en route* to Mansfield and Upper Sandusky. His command was composed of the following officers: Captain Gratiot, engineer of equipments; Captain Paul Anderson, forage-master; Captain Wheaton, pay-master; Captain Johnston and ninety men, and Lieutenant Walker,* with forty men, as a guard.

Colonel Anderson had, for conveyance to Upper Sandusky, twenty-five iron cannon, mostly four and six pounders. They, and the balls fitting them, were placed in covered road wagons, and drawn by six horses to each. The cannon carriages, twenty-five in number, empty, were each drawn by four horses. The cartridges, canister, and other necessary ammunition, were put in large covered wagons. There were fifty covered road wagons, drawn by six horses each. They were loaded with such army stores as would be serviceable in the expedition.

Equipped in this manner, Colonel Anderson left Allegheny City about the first day of November, 1812, and camped nine miles down the west side of the Ohio, the first night. The second night, he reached General Wayne's Legionville. The third night, encamped thirty miles down the river from Allegheny. The fourth night at Greersburgh, forty-two miles from Pittsburgh. The fifth night, fifteen miles further on their journey. The sixth night, at New Lisbon, seventy-five miles from Pittsburgh, where he stayed three days to repair broken wheels and wagons. The tenth night, the command had advanced fifteen miles further. The eleventh night, Colonel Anderson reached the village of Canton. Here he tarried ten days, repairing wagons, shoeing horses, and obtaining provisions. On the twenty-first night he reached Hahn's swamps, and was three or four days in passing over the same, to Wooster, owing to the fact that Beall and Crooks' road was badly cut up with their wagons. Part of the route from the swamps to Wooster, Colonel Anderson had a new road cut. At Wooster, Colonel Anderson's men beheld an object of curiosity in the new block-house, the first they had seen. About the tenth of December, Colonel Anderson left the village of Wooster, pursuing the route of Beall and Crooks, and the first evening reached a block-house and cabin on the east side of the Jerome fork of the Mohican, where he encamped for the night. On the eleventh he crossed the Jerome fork, taking the trail of General Crooks, which he followed through the forest, crossed the Black fork, and encamped for the night on the present site of Lucas. On the twelfth he reached the village of Mansfield, where they found two block-houses, a tavern, and one store.

General Crooks and his brigade had left before the arrival of Colonel Anderson. The teamsters being volunteers, at twenty dollars per month, and their time having expired, desired to return home. Colonel Anderson being ordered to follow General Crooks to Upper Sandusky, offered to pay the teamsters one dollar per day, if they would continue in the expedition until he arrived at Upper Sandusky. These terms were accepted, and each teamster was furnished a gun to be kept in the feed

---

* Lieutenant Walker was unfortunately killed, when out hunting, by an Indian, while General Crooks was quartered at Upper Sandusky.

trough, to defend himself against an apprehended attack of the Indians. The command had scarcely got out of sight of the village of Mansfield when it commenced to snow, and continued to do so until it was two feet deep. The ground being unfrozen, the situation became very embarrassing. The heavy wagons cut into the soft earth, and the horses were unable to draw them. A council was held, and fifteen gun carriages were sent ahead to break the path, and let it freeze, so that the heavy teams could pass without crushing through. By this means they made a few miles a day; and when one team gave out, it turned aside and another took its place. At night the soldiers were compelled to work two or three hours shoveling off a suitable place to pitch their tents, build fires to cook their food and keep them from freezing. The soldiers cut brush and threw their blankets over it, and by that means, while sleeping, were raised above the mud, water and snow. After some two weeks of such travel and hardships, the command reached Upper Sandusky (New Year's Day), January 1, 1813. After a brief rest the teamsters, under a guard, took the horses of the expedition to Franklinton, one mile west of the present city of Columbus, to be fed and kept until spring.*

---

* We are indebted for the items of this sketch to the excellent memory of Captain Robert Beer, now eighty-three years of age (1876), a resident of Pittsburgh, Pennsylvania, who accompanied Colonel James Anderson as teamster, and took charge of one of the cannon carriages. This sketch never having appeared before in print, is very valuable as a personal and historic reminiscence, and we know the reader will thank Captain Beer for it, although it is somewhat foreign to an exact home history of Ashland county. Mr. Beer died in Alleghany City, Pennsylvania, May 4, 1880, aged about eighty-seven years.

CHAPTER XXV.

VICTORY BRINGS JOY.

Adventures of the Pioneers, and Life in the Block-houses.—The Collyer Affair.—Cultivating the soil under a Guard.—The Heroic Defence of Fort Meigs.—The Gallantry of Major Croghan at Fort Stevenson.—The Naval Victory of Perry.

THE commands of Generals Crooks and Beall, that passed through this region in the fall of 1812, as related in a former chapter, were left in the vicinity of Upper Sandusky about the first of January, 1813. The time of service of General Beall's troops having expired, most of them returned and dispersed. General Winchester having advanced with his forces to the river Raisin, and the position at Upper Sandusky being regarded as critical, the brigade of General Crooks was induced to volunteer one more month to defend the borders of the northwest. His brigade, after finishing the intrenchments at Upper Sandusky, was ordered to Fort Meigs, with an artillery train and stores, which were dragged through the mud and snow by the soldiers. In doing so, they had to endure the most incredible hardships—part of the time wading through mud and water two or three feet deep, and being compelled to cut brush and logs to lift them above the water when they encamped at night. General Winchester had advanced with his army, about one thousand strong, to within eighteen miles of Malden, where he was surprised by General Proctor, with his British and Indians, and a battle ensuing on the twenty-second of January, 1813, Winchester was defeated with great slaughter. The loss of the Americans was about four hundred in wounded, killed and missing, being fully one-third of all the force engaged in the battle! General Winchester was taken prisoner in the commencement of the engagement; and many of his soldiers, after having surrendered, were butchered by the savages in the most wanton manner, without the interference of the British commander to prevent it! This misfortune disconcerted all the plans of General Harrison for the spring campaign; and compelled him to fall back to Fort Meigs, until the troops ordered into the field by Governor Meigs, should arrive. While these bloody scenes were transpiring, the people of Richland, Wayne and Knox counties were again compelled to seek safety in the block-houses, not knowing what moment the infuriated savages, led on by Tecumseh, might appear in their midst. Along the Black fork and Clear fork the fugitives that found safety at Clinton, the fall before, had returned to their homes in the vicinity of Coulter's block-house, and that of Samuel Lewis, on the Clear fork; though they had spent most of the winter at their own cabins. Their corn crops, though small, had been secured and safely stored; their cattle and swine were under their control. The mills in Knox county, and below Wooster, had been visited and a stock of corn meal laid in for the winter. So that they had an abundance of corn-bread and meat; and by the aid of hominy-blocks, there was no imminent danger of starvation, though the situation was rather exciting.

Along the Jerome fork, the majority of the fugitives remained in the block-house during the winter. In the fall of 1812, when Captain Nicholas Murray, with a company of sixty men, was ordered by General Beall to advance to Jerome's place, to build a block-house, just after he had crossed the Killbuck, he met the fugitive families of John Carr, Christopher Trickle, Matthew Williams, Robert Newell, Ezra Warner, Daniel Carter, Jacob Fry, and Benjamin Cuppy. Captain Murray offered all these families protection, and they all returned with him to Jerome's place, except Mr. Carter and family, who continued their flight to New Philadelphia, Tuscarawas county. These families remained in and around the block-house during the winter. About the middle of February, 1813, Daniel Carter and family returned from New Philadelphia, and again occupied his old cabin, one mile northeast of the present site of Ashland, where he found everything as he had left it the fall before. His corn was yet standing in the field undisturbed, except what had been devoured by deer, wild turkeys, and small animals.

A pioneer gives the following version of the Collyer affair:

"About the first of March, 1813, in the morning, four strange Indians appeared at the cabin of James Collyer, then residing about two miles above the junction of the Jerome and Muddy forks of Mohican, a short distance from Finley's bridge, and asked for something to eat. They appeared to be well armed, and his suspicions were excited. There had not been an Indian seen in that neighborhood for several months, the last of the *Mohican John* Indians having been sent away by order of General Beall, when he cut his trail the fall before. Putting on an air of confidence and calmness, he invited them into his cabin, entering which, they leaned their guns against the wall near the door, and were seated. Mr. Collyer told his wife, who was much alarmed, to set some cold victuals on the table for them to eat. She did so, putting on a lot of meat, corn-bread and such other articles as she had at hand. Mr. Collyer motioned for them to sit down and eat. They went to the table and were seated, and began to eat heartily of the food. While they were eating Collyer moved cautiously to the point where he kept his gun, which was always loaded, and securing it, placed himself, unobserved, between the Indians and the door, and carefully raising his gun so as to get a range on two of them, prepared to fire, seeing which, Mrs. Collyer shrieked out, and fainting, fell to the floor. This alarmed the Indians, and they sprang to their feet, but seeing the threatening attitude of Collyer, raised their hands and begged him to spare their lives, saying, "me Goshen Injin, me no harm you." Thereupon Collyer withheld his fire, still keeping his gun pointed at them—his intention having been after killing or wounding two of them at the table, to club it over the other two, and thus secure them all—he being a powerful man and having had a good deal of experience as a hunter, and in Indian warfare. They continued to protest their innocence of any intended harm to him and his family, when he told them he would spare them on condition of retiring from the cabin and leaving their guns within, when he would remove the flints and priming, and hand them the balance of the food on the table, out at the window, when they should immediately leave the neighborhood and not return again. They accepted these conditions, and retired at once from the cabin. After securing the door, Mr. Collyer placed his wife on a bed, and proceeded to remove the priming and flints from the guns of the Indians, and having done which, he passed them out at a small window; after doing so, he handed them the balance of the food, and they disappeared in the forest. After waiting until he was satisfied they had gone, and were not intending to attack him, he took his wife and such valuables as he possessed, and hastened to the "Eagle" block-house, a strong cabin prepared by Thomas Eagle for himself and neighbors.

The news of this exploit soon reached the block-house at Jerome's place, and word of it being sent to Daniel Carter, he again took leave of his cabin, never to return to it, for he was compelled to remain at the block-house until the spring of 1814. A few days after this, a number of Indians appeared in view of Eagle fort, and made some hostile demonstrations, but owing to the strength of Eagle's force, they retired in the direction of Jerome's place, killing a number of hogs on their way, and finally disappeared from the neighborhood without doing further mischief. This added to the excitement produced by Winchester's defeat, the particulars of which were now understood at the block-house.

On the approach of the season for planting corn, a few fields were put out by the pioneers of the block-house. John Carr had about twenty acres cleared; Ezra Warner had about the same number of acres ready; and Jerome had some thirty acres, on the bottom beyond the block-house. Mr. Carter had four or five acres near the old Indian village, across the Jerome fork. These fields were plowed, and the planting was done, by the residents of the block-house, as a community. While part of them planted and cultivated the corn, during the summer, the others patrolled the forests in the vicinity of the fort, to prevent surprise and capture by the Indians. When the corn had become sufficiently matured for use, the same vigilance prevailed in and about the neighborhood, to prevent surprise. When the crop was gathered, it proved to be quite large.

The summer months, in this way, seemed to pass slowly. The inmates could rarely get news from the frontiers. The defence of Fort Meigs by General Harrison, and his victory of the fifth of May, 1813, sent joy to the block-houses along both forks of Mohican. Harrison and his army had endured, in the most heroic manner, the fierce assaults and cannonading of the British army, and finally compelled them to march down the Maumee river. In August, the monotony of the block-house was again removed by the reception of the intelligence of the splendid defence of Fort Stevenson (Lower Sandusky) by the heroic Major Croghan and his men. The signal repulse of the British, under Proctor, and their hasty retreat from that locality, gave renewed hope and confidence. On the tenth of September, Commodore Perry captured the whole British fleet on Lake Erie, and by that great achievement the territory of Michigan passed into the possession of the American forces. So great was the joy of the people of this region over the victory on Lake Erie, that a pioneer (Mr. John Greenlee) now seventy-five years of age, who was then a boy, assures us he thinks he could hear the echo of Perry's guns during the conflict, amid the forests of what is now Lake township, in this county!

In the month of June, Mrs. Anna Carter, wife of Daniel Carter, and his son James, a lad of six years of age, died in the block-house at Jerome place, and were buried in the Carr cemetery near the fort. In September, Christopher Trickle also died in the block-house, and was buried in the same cemetery. These deaths were occasioned from malaria and want of proper medical attendance, there being no physicians within the present limits of the county, at that time.

Upon the recurrence of autumn, the pioneers along the Black fork, the Clear fork, the Lake fork and the Jerome fork, busied themselves in storing their meagre crops for winter. Stibbs' mill, and one or two other mills on the Vernon river, each running one set of buhrs, some of which were "nigger-head," were visited by pioneers with pack-horses and small canoes, loaded with shelled corn, to be converted into meal. Their food consisted of corn-bread, journey-cake, mush and milk, potatoes, vegetables, and principally wild meat, cattle and swine being very scarce. "Store tea" and coffee, were exceedingly rare and very costly. "Store goods" were a thing of note; and the calicoes of that day were a luxury few could afford. Home-spun and woven linsey-woolsey, and flax or linen garments were the best to be seen; and many a daring, whole-souled pioneer felt proud, clothed in such garments. Salt and flour were luxuries that few could use profusely. Salt was purchased at Zanesville and Pittsburgh, and from its price had to be used sparingly. Ammunition, such as lead and powder, was obtained from the supplies furnished the soldiers left to guard the block-houses. So far, then, as food was concerned, the inmates of the block-houses "fared sumptuously"—to use an expression of an old gentleman who was quartered in one about two years. Nothing happened in the fall of 1813 to materially disturb the quiet of the pioneers of this region.

CHAPTER XXVI.

ORGANIZATION OF WAYNE AND RICHLAND COUNTIES.

The Pioneers from 1813 to 1815.—The Situation.—Roads.—Currency.—A Trip for Salt.

WAYNE was the third county established in the territory ceded by the Indian tribes to the United States at the treaty of Greenville in 1795, and was the largest county in the United States. Its original limits embraced nearly all of Ohio, Indiana, Illinois, Wisconsin, and Michigan. Governor Arthur St. Clair erected Wayne county by proclamation, about ten years before the township and sectional surveys were made by the United States. As early as 1808 the site of Wooster was purchased at the land office at Canton, and was laid out by the proprietors—John Beaver, William Henry, and Joseph H. Larwill. Shortly after, a few cabins were erected, and among the first settlers were William Larwill, Joseph H. Larwill, John Larwill, and Abraham Miller. In 1809-10, James Morgan, John Beaver, Joseph Stibbs, William Smith, Hugh Moore, Jesse Richards, Michael Switzer, and a few others, located within the county. In 1811-12, a few scattering settlements were formed, among which was the Odell colony in Lake, and the original families in Mohican, the Finleys, the Metcalfs, the Eagles, the Carters, the Carrs, the Bryans, and others. Range fifteen was included within the jurisdiction of Wayne county. When Wooster became the seat of justice, the whole of Wayne county was comprised in one township, which was called Killbuck, after a noted Delaware chief, whose village was on a stream of that name, ten miles south of the present site of Wooster. In 1810 the census gave the whole number of heads of families in this township at forty-six.

In discussing the erection of Fairfield county, it was stated that the inhabitants of Licking, Knox, and Richland counties were much scattered. The great extent of Fairfield rendered it inconvenient for the settlers of most remote parts to attend the seat of justice at Lancaster. In 1808 the counties of Licking and Knox were erected by the legislature, and their boundaries defined. Their seats of justice were located at Newark and Mount Vernon. The boundaries of Richland were also defined, and the citizens, for civil purposes, left under the jurisdiction of Knox county, until her population had become sufficiently large to resume the home government.

In 1813, the population having reached about five hundred, it was deemed proper to take the incipient steps for county organization. The people met and consulted, and concurred in the necessity of a home government. The commissioners established the seat of justice at Mansfield, and converted one of the block-houses, that had been erected in the public square, into a hall of justice, and, in August, Thomas Coulter and Peter Kinney, of what is now Green township, Ashland county, and William Gass, of Mansfield, being associate judges, held the first session of the court of common pleas, for the administration of estates, and other purposes. The jurisdiction of this court extended over ranges sixteen and seventeen, in what is now Ashland county.

We again return to the condition of the pioneers in the years 1813 and 1814.

After the splendid naval achievement of Commodore Perry on Lake Erie, on the tenth of September, 1813, General Harrison prepared for the immediate invasion of Upper Canada. The army under Generals Cass, McArthur, Ball, Shelby, Johnson and Hill, embarked on board Perry's vessels for Malden, which they entered without opposition, on the twenty-eighth of September, and found the British and Indians under Proctor and Tecumseh had just evacuated the town and fort, setting fire to the latter to destroy the work and stores. General McArthur with his forces was dispatched to take possession of Detroit, which was also abandoned by the British. General Harrison pursued General Proctor's retreating army up the river Thames, on the second of October. On the fifth the great battle, two miles below the Moravian town, known as the battle of the Thames, was fought, in which General Harrison's forces gained a signal victory over Proctor, in which the noted Indian warrior, Tecumseh, fell under the sure aim of Colonel Richard M. Johnson. The death of that daring and wily chief was a great disaster to his Indian allies, for they immediately lost all courage, and all hope of ever regaining their old hunting-grounds in northwestern Ohio. This blow completely humbled nearly all the Indian tribes that had aided the British in their invasion, and assisted in perpetrating revolting cruelties upon our soldiers at Detroit and the river Raisin; and Walk-in-the-water, Between-the-legs, and other chiefs of the *Ottawas, Chippewas, Miamis, Kickapoos* and *Pottawatomies* gladly accepted peace at the hands of General Cass. This success of the army of General Harrison put an end to all active hostility in Michigan territory, Indiana and Ohio; and on the twenty-third of October, 1813, General Harrison, with all his disposable force, embarked on board Perry's fleet and sailed for Buffalo, in obedience to orders from the Secretary of War. Previous to his departure, he appointed Lewis Cass provisional governor of Michigan territory. General Cass was left with about one thousand men, who were employed at once in preparing winter quarters at Detroit. From this period the war was transferred to northern New York, and the borders of Lower Canada.

At the close of the year 1813, we left the pioneers of the Upper Black fork, at Beam's block-house—those of the Greentown neighborhood, at Lewis' block-house—those in the region of the Rices', at Coulter's, with the exception of a few families who had strong cabins for self-defense—a few families in the vicinity of Odell's, Oram's and Priests, who collected in a strong cabin in that neighborhood—a few families, among whom were those of Alexander Finley and James Collyer, at Thomas Eagle's or John Shinnabarger's, and all the pioneers up the Jerome fork, at the Jerome block-house. The inmates of these retreats remained there until the spring of 1814.

After the death of Ruffner, Zimmer's and Copus, that settlement was abandoned for nearly two years, and the small fields cleared by them were overrun with tall weeds and underbrush; and wild game had an undisturbed range along the valley. The Carter, Cuppy, Fry, Newell and Trickle clearings in Montgomery had again become a wild waste, where deer, turkey and bear roamed at will. The Trickle cabin, where Markley's brick house was subsequently erected, was the pioneer mansion of Uniontown. There was not a cabin north of it containing a white family. Neither was there a house in any of the now villages of this county, except the cabin of Jerome, near the block-house. The *Wyandots* and *Delawares* had a free hunt during the fall of 1813 and the winter of 1814; for the inmates of the block-house did not venture many miles into the forest, unless compelled to do so to visit the mills. The danger of returning to their cabins, however, was more imaginary than real; for, after the battle of the Thames, the Indians of the northwest were shorn of their power to inflict serious mischief upon the settlements, many of the *Delawares, Wyandots* and *Shawnees* voluntarily having joined the army of General Harrison.

Early in the spring, the inmates of the block-houses prepared to return to their cabins and put out crops. The woodman's axe was again heard in the forest, and new cabins began to appear in every direction. The tide of emigration, though not rapid in the spring, during the summer and autumn increased considerably, and the settlers were greatly encouraged.

In the spring of 1814 all the territory in ranges sixteen and seventeen, within the present limits of Ashland county, for civil purposes, comprised one township—Green; and all the territory in range fifteen, within the present limits of the county, was under the jurisdiction of Mohican, for civil purposes, no other township having been, as yet, organized.

We learn, from pioneer tradition, that in 1813, 1814, 1815, the following new settlers arrived on the Black fork: Trew Pettee, William Brown, John Shehan, Ahira Hill, Asa Brown, Lewis Crossen, Stephen Vanscoye, Noah Custard, David Hill, John Crossen, H. W. Cotton, Lewis Pierce, Adam Crossen, William Slater, Jeremiah Conine, Moses Jones, Sylvester Fisher, John Totton, William Irvin, John Murphy, Henry Naugh, John Pool.

William and Asa Brown started the first dry-goods store on the present site of Perrysville.

In what is now Hanover, we find Stephen Butler and Caleb Chapel, with their families.

In Mohican, William Metcalf, William Ewing, Major Tyler, John Bryan, John Naylor, Christian Deardorf, William Vaughn, Adam Teener and John Lake, with their families.

In Lake, John Newkirk and family.

In Perry, Hugh Carr, Cornelius Dorland, Thomas Johnson, Joseph Chandler, Arthur Campbell, John Raver, Richard Smalley, Henry Worst and John Pittinger, with their families.

In Jackson, Joseph A. Dinsmore, John Chilcote, Isaac Lyons and Noah Long, and their families.

In Vermillion, Lemuel Boulter, Samuel Hutchins, William Black, George McClure, Daniel Harlan, William Reed, Robert Jackman, John Vangilder, William Harper, William Karnahan, William Ryland, Joseph Workman, George, William and Thomas Hughes, John McCrory and Joseph Strickland, with their families.

In Montgomery, Jacob Crouse, Daniel Mickey, Samuel Burns, Henry Baughman, Joseph Markley, Widow Trickle, John Carr, Benjamin Cuppy, Robert Newell, Daniel Carter, William McNaull, Henry Gamble, James Kuykendall, David Markley, John McNaull, Michael Springer, William Montgomery, John Heller, Conrad Kline, Robert Ralston, and John Smith, and their families.

In Orange, John Bishop, Jacob Young, Amos Norris, Vachel Metcalf, Jacob Mason, Joseph Bishop, Martin Hester, Lot Todd, Solomon Urie, John McConnell, Martin Mason, Jacob Mason, Patrick Murray, Christian, William, David, and Nicholas Fast, Henry Hampson, Mordecai Chilcote, and William Patterson, and their families.

In Milton, Alexander Reed, John Clay, Robert Nelson, Andrew Stevenson, Henry Keever, Michael Smeltzer, John Hazlet, William Dickey, S. King, F. Sultzer, J. Hoover, Peter and Benjamin Brubaker, John Hewey, A. Doty, A. A. Webster, J. Church, and J. Crawford, and their families.

In Mifflin, George Thomas, James Ford, Jacob Snyder, Jacob Keifer, Leonard Croninger, Daniel Harlan, Michael Culler, and David Braden, and their families.

In Clearcreek, David Burns, John Richard, and W. Freeborn, James Haney, William Shaw, Abraham Huffman, Peter Vanostrand, and Isaac Vanmeter. The records of the settlers are very imperfect, and our record of early settlers is mostly a matter of tradition, and, hence, it may be quite imperfect.

The year before Mr. Thomas and his family arrived at their new home, Peter Thomas, now a resident of Montgomery township, made a trip from near Cadiz, Ohio, through the forest, unarmed, accompanied only by a faithful watch dog, to the cabin of his uncle, Jacob Beam, on the Rocky fork, where the block-house had been built in 1812, and where his uncle had subsequently built a mill with one run of buhrs. He stayed all night at Stibbs' mill, below Wooster, and the next night at what was afterwards known as John Raver's cabin, southeast of the present site of Rowsburgh, the only house he found between Wooster and Beam's block-house. From the cabin on the Muddy fork, he followed horse trails, by the way of Jerome's place, until he reached the cabin of his uncle, which took one day. He is unable to point out the precise route, but remembers that he traveled hard all day, with his faithful dog at his side, and neither feared Indians nor wild animals. His brother, George, was at Beams' when the Ruffner-Zimmer-Copus murders took place, and helped bury the dead. In 1814 he was returning from Cadiz with his family, by the way of Odell's lake, when he took sick and died, and was buried there—his wife and children subsequently reaching the residence of Mr. Beam with their goods.

In the fall of 1814, John Coulter and Ebenezer Rice contracted with the State commissioners to cut a road on the old survey, from Trickle's cabin, at the east end of the present site of Ashland, to what is now Windsor, in Richland county—ten miles—for ninety dollars. The Trickle cabin was then deserted; Mrs. Trickle having sold it to Mr. Markley, who had not yet taken possession. When the road was cut, it became the duty of Melzer Coulter and Alexander Rice, then boys, to supply the laborers with food. On pack-horses, they passed down the old Portage road to near the Jerome block-house, and then took the Beall trail to near the present residence of James Newman, and then followed a path through the forest to the present site of Ashland. On one of those trips, while passing down the old Portage road, Alexander Rice found an axe setting beside a log, with the letters "U. S." stamped upon it, which had probably been left there by the pioneers of General Crooks. He took the axe home, and used it for a number of years; finally having it made into a wedge, which he yet has in his possession, as a memento of the days sixty years agone.

The territory along the branches of Mohican remained undisturbed during the fall of 1814, and emigrants in large numbers visited the country, to select sites for their new homes. A glance at the financial condition of this region, therefore, may be interesting.

The only currency in circulation among the pioneers of this region in 1814 was gold and silver, and that in very limited quantities. The supplies furnished the army of the northwest, kept a small amount of specie in circulation. But when the sums paid the soldiers for their services had been invested in small tracts of land, money became very scarce. "Necessity" is said to be the "mother of invention," and Pennsylvanians, Virginians, and Yankees, alike, were driven to "invention." Falling back to the common remedy for all evils—the constitution of the State—the pioneers held, that in consequence of the scarcity of money, they had the right to have charters granted for the establishment of a bank or banks by the legislature. Insisting upon such right, articles of association were drawn for the establishment of a bank at Mt. Vernon, with a capital of two hundred and fifty thousand dollars, in shares of fifty dollars each. In December, 1814, articles of association were submitted to a meeting held in Mt. Vernon, and it was resolved that an institution, to be called the "Owl Creek Bank of Mt. Vernon," be established; and certain commissioners were appointed, to open stock books. Petitions for a charter were presented to the legislature, which was refused; and then the stockholders "went it alone," and planting themselves upon their assumed constitutional rights, they formed themselves into a company and established the "Owl Creek Bank of Mt. Vernon." This institution issued shinplasters, from the denomination of six and one-fourth cents, up to ten dollars, and the country was soon flooded with them. In fact, the settlers of Richland county, and the people of what is now Ashland county, were compelled to take it or nothing for their surplus produce. In a few years, the Owl Creek currency became worthless, and much distress, with unlimited recrimination, followed. Samuel Williams, a merchant of Mansfield, got up a sort of rival currency, upon which he had printed a coiled rattlesnake. A good many of such shinplasters were thrown into circulation. Finally, Jacob Beam, who had purchased about a section of land in the vicinity of his mill, and was the owner of a fine six-horse team, which was used to haul produce to Pittsburgh, and bring back salt, nails, iron, dry-goods and the like, for the use of the settlers, became involved in the meshes of Williams, and was subsequently stripped, by litigation, of his wealth. Such was the beginning and effect of the wild currency of 1814.

Many anecdotes are related concerning the "Owl Creek Bank," and its worthless notes. The Indians visiting Mt. Vernon and Mansfield, were frequently offered the "Owl Creek" shinplasters, on which was the figure of an owl, in exchange for venison and furs, but they invariably refused to take them, saying: "Too much hoo, hoo, hoo, hoo." On one occasion, an enemy of the bank killed a large owl, which he deposited on the counter of the bank, saying "he had killed its president."

Salt was extremely scarce among the pioneers, so much so, that neighbors often borrowed pints. Corn-bread, hominy and mush were exceedingly unpalatable without salt. This article was generally brought from Zanesville on pack-horses, or in small boats up the Muskingum and its branches. Late in the fall of 1814, William Ewing,* then a young man, living two miles below the present site of Jeromeville, fitted out a four-horse team, taking a small load of shelled corn, and money enough to purchase a load of salt and plow-castings, and started for Zanesville. He passed up the old Portage road to Greentown, thence to near Lewis' block-house, on the wagon trail leading to the village of Clinton, one mile north of Mt. Vernon. The day he started it was clear and cold, and he made good progress until he reached the Clear fork. That stream was unusually full and rapid. In crossing it, he struck the opposite bank obliquely, and in attempting to ascend it the hind part of his wagon was overturned, emptying the greater part of the corn, which was in sacks, into the stream. For a time he thought his wagon would be drawn into the current, and his horses entangled and drowned. Fortunately, he had a fifth-chain along, which he fastened to the coupling poll, and, hitching two horses to it, and at the same time encouraging his wheel horses, he succeeded in righting the hind wheels and dragging the wagon up the bank to dry land. The next effort was to fish out his sacks of corn and food, which had become completely saturated with

* Mr. Ewing died in Montgomery township, in 1874, aged about eighty years.

water. After considerable exertion, he finally replaced his corn in the wagon, when, to use his own language "the only dry spot on him was the collar on the back of his neck." Being much chilled and benumbed, it was with difficulty he could hitch his horses in their proper places in the team. This he finally succeeded in doing; and again started on the path through the forest. He continued along it until after dark, expecting to lay out during the night, and probably freeze before morning; but, as he was about to lose all hope, the light of a cabin window was seen in the distance. Pressing on, he soon reached it, wet, cold and hungry. He was welcomed to its shelter. His horses being arranged about the feed-trough, and fed, he found his new landlady had prepared him a bowl of warm mush and milk, for which he was exceedingly thankful. The fire kept up a cheerful blaze until he had dried his clothing and recovered from his numbness. He slept soundly, rose bright and early, and started on his way whistling. In about ten days he returned safely to his cabin, with a load of salt and castings. We give this incident to illustrate the hardships endured by the pioneers.

CHAPTER XXVII.

AFTER THE WAR OF 1812.

The Close of the Tour.—Peace Declared.—A Rush of Pioneers to the Branches of the Mohican.—Cabin Raising.—The Woodman's Axe.—Log Rolling.—Planting.—Social Bearing of the Pioneers.—Sugar Making in 1815.

AFTER the departure of General Harrison for Buffalo, New York, the humbled Indian tribes of the northwest were earnest in their desire for an early peace. The government of the United States appointed General Harrison and General Cass commissioners to negotiate a treaty with the Indian tribes. The commission met at Greenville, July 2, 1714; and the tribes were represented at that place by their head men, chiefs, and warriors, and a treaty was agreed upon, which was ratified by the Senate of the United States, and signed by President Madison, December 1, 1814. In the treaty, the *Wyandots, Delawares, Shawnees, Senecas* and *Cayugas*, being friends of the United States, granted peace to the *Miamis, Pottawatomies, Ottawas, Kickapoos, Chippewas* and other tribes aiding the British. The treaty was signed by Killbuck, White Eyes and Captain Pipe of the *Delawares*, and one hundred and ten other chiefs and heads of Indian tribes. The various bands or tribes mentioned in the treaty, agreed to place themselves under the protection of the United States, and aid in all wars against Great Britain. This brought a speedy reconciliation among the Indians of Ohio, and averted all danger of subsequent difficulties, by fixing boundaries to the tribes and regulating their intercourse with the whites who had settled in their midst. In the meantime, commissioners on the part of the United States and Great Britain met at Ghent, in Belgium, and on the twenty-fourth of December, 1814, agreed to articles of a treaty of peace and unity between the two countries; but before it had been received and ratified by the two governments, the brilliant victory over the British forces under Packingham, at New Orleans, had been won by General Andrew Jackson and his gallant army, on the eighth of January, 1815, the treaty being ratified and signed February 18, 1815. Thus ended the second war for independence, after the United States had shown ability, for nearly three years, to cope successfully with the mother country by land, lake and sea. The war having closed, pioneers from all the States east, with their families, goods and valuables hastened to occupy a portion of the paradise west of the Ohio river; and in 1815 the forests of this region echoed with the sturdy blows of the new settlers.

A pioneer, Michael Culler, who was among the first settlers within this region, assures us that in the months of April, May, and June, the forests along the various streams of this county presented a scene of unrivaled beauty. The banks of the streams resembled a vast greenhouse, where choice flowers, flowering shrubs, and plants of every variety peculiar to this climate, might be seen growing in wild luxuriance, diffusing their fragrance on the passing gale. The trees being in full leaf, with an undergrowth of shrubbery, pea-vines, and sedge grass, intertwined by wild grape-vines; and, in the glades, black haw, red haw, and plum trees, in abundance; and all echoing with the merry songs of birds, and the chatter of squirrels, leaping from branch to branch, saluting the pioneer or hunter, rendered the scene a veritable paradise. He says: "Nothing could be more lovely and inviting; though to the town and city people of the present day, a scene of this description would possess but few charms." After a trip to the Black fork to select his future home, he returned to Maryland to report what he had seen in the far west, and to invite a fair young lady, of that State, to accompany him to his cabin, to share his joys and sorrows, in his newly discovered paradise of flowers, beautiful streams, blooming forests, and rich land, in which dwelt Indians, wild animals, and serpents of all kinds! "Telling the whole truth, the old people thought it extremely hazardous to make choice of such a home;" but the little lady he had left behind him had a strong will and a brave heart, and said "she would freely go to the wilds of Ohio, and share his joys and griefs, amid the serenades of wolves, and the terific screams of the wild cat." She did come; and, for over half a century, dwelt upon the banks of the Black fork, sharing the prosperity and happiness of a faithful husband, surrounded by her family, until the benevolent Father of all, in 1873, called her hence. The old man still lingers, with gray locks and trembling gait, and is now waiting to join her in that better land.* Since they came to the Black fork, what a change! The unbroken forests have been leveled by the woodman's axe, and the village and farm are now seen, where then all was wild luxuriance. This is the story of hundreds of pioneers, now old and feeble, residing in this county; and, though romantic, is, nevertheless, real life.

The first task of the pioneer was the erection of a comfortable cabin for the reception of his family. The first cabins were generally made of round logs, which were cut in suitable lengths, and dragged by oxen to the spot selected for the erection of a house. Those who had ox-teams hauled the logs, while the axe-men cut them in suitable lengths. While this was being done, others were riveing clap-boards of oak for the roof. They were made six or eight inches wide, and about four feet long, and a half to three-quarters of an inch thick. Though mechanics were very scarce, almost any pioneer could use a frow, an adz, a broad-axe and a drawing knife. When the logs were collected, the task of raising commenced. A good axe-man was placed at each corner to notch the logs, while other hands shoved or lifted them into position. When the first story was completed, straight saplings were placed across for joists, and upon which rested a clap-board loft. From the second story the logs were gradually cut shorter, and the ends tapered so as to form the roof, by placing straight logs three or four feet apart, upon which the clap-boards rested, the last log of the main round jutting over about fifteen inches for the eaves, upon which a log was placed for the first course of clap-boards. As each course of boards was placed in position, it was secured by a roof-pole, supported by blocks of the proper length, extending from pole to pole. The chimneys were very ample, and built on the outside, of split timber, and lined with stone and clay. A section of the logs was cut out for a door, chimney, and a small window or two. The floor was made of split timber, hewed into what were known as puncheons. Many of the cabins had only earth floors for the first year or two. In this manner the first cabins were erected near a good spring. Having thus completed a cabin for the new settler, and congratulated him on his new home, all hands dispersed. In such rude cabins, the pioneers of Ashland county lived many happy years. The occupants of those humble homes were always distinguished for their hospitality and manhood.

The dense forests seemed to defy the efforts of man to remove them. The aggregated strength of a community always triumphed. It was the custom, for miles, to assemble in aid of each other, to cut and heap the logs. The hands were divided into squads, so that they could work to advantage, and by the use of strong ox-teams, the logs were easily heaped into piles, where they could be consumed by fire. These gatherings furnished excellent opportunities for the display of strength, and the herculean woodsmen of that day were not backward in seeking the championship. The rugged men of those times overflowed with fun and frolic. After a hard day at a cabin raising or a log rolling, it was not uncommon to wind up with a foot-race, a wrestle, or even a trial of skill in boxing. If blows followed, the parties were compelled to shake hands, take a drink, and agree to be

---

*Deceased in 1875.

good friends. These little frolics were esteemed trivial, and only meant a sort of friendly how do you do. To hold resentment after such an adjustment, was regarded as cowardly, and hence, discountenanced. These exhibitions of fun and merriment were thought to be but the outcroppings of a whole-souled, courageous and spirited nature. Very few new communities possessed a more rugged, go-ahead class of backwoodsmen than the branches of Mohican, and nowhere in Ohio could be found a more generous and hospitable people.

The rarest sport was found at the corn huskings, flax scutchings, and quiltings. The corn was plucked from the stalks, hauled and piled in a long row, near where it was to be cribbed. An invitation was then extended to the hardy settlers and their sons to assemble in the evening and husk corn. At these gatherings captains were chosen, and the hands divided as nearly equal as possible, and the long pile of corn measured, and the center marked by a rail. The captains were placed next the rail to maintain fair play, and keep it in position until the pile had been husked. At a given signal all hands entered briskly upon the contest. The rivalry was generally very exciting, and the golden maize was unshucked with astonishing rapidity. Interest was increased by an occasional song and a little whiskey. It was thought that a little music and whiskey added freshness and vigor. Shouting and hurrahing were in order. Thus hours passed, until the pile had disappeared. In the meantime, it was not unusual for some sly contestant, if the night were dark, to conceal many bushels of unhusked corn, that his side might excel. Such performances, if not discovered at the time, were esteemed allowable, and evidence of shrewdness. When the task was completed, supper was announced, and the huskers assembled in the cabin of the pioneer, where a plain meal had been prepared. To the surprise (?) of all, a large company of married and unmarried ladies confronted the huskers. They had assembled in the afternoon to aid a neighbor friend in preparing a quilt. While the huskers had been enjoying themselves over their contest, the quilting ladies had been arranging and bringing upon a table a steaming supper. After the huskers had satisfied their hunger, the tables were removed, and some native violinist appeared. "French fours," and "Old Virginia reels" were then in order. The puncheon floors received additional polish by the brogans of the rustics.

The cottons, calicoes and other goods used at that time were scarce and costly. This deficiency was supplied by home manufacture. Flax was extensively cultivated by the early settlers, and when manufactured into linen, largely used for shirting, pantaloons, and other wearing apparel. When combined with wool, the article was called "linsey-woolsey," and was very generally worn by both sexes. What were known as "hunting-shirts" with a cape, a belt, and fringed around the edges, were worn by the men. They were large and flowing, and were much esteemed in their day. Almost any housewife at that era could spin and preside at the loom, and much of the family wearing apparel was spun and woven by them.

The flax scutchings, therefore, were of prime necessity, and the young men and women regarded such gatherings as highly useful and honorable. It was on such occasions that the flax was broken, the shives separated therefrom and made fit for spinning and weaving. These frolics, so called, furnished much amusement for the young people, and generally wound up with a merry cabin dance. Everything tended to practical utility. The hardy mothers, fathers, sons and daughters of that period entered heartily into the pursuits of active life.

For several years, Beall's trail, and the Portage, cut by General Crooks, were the principal roads in the county, along which many emigrants reached their new homes in the wilderness. The roads diverging from these trails were mere paths, being only ten or twelve feet wide. The undergrowth had been cut, and removed to the sides of the road. Owing to the sparseness of the settlers, the roads were, for several years, very rough and poorly kept. To keep them, even in a passable condition, required a good deal of labor. The supervisor of highways was a man of considerable importance. If he properly filled his office, he was regarded as a public benefactor. From the importance of the position, it was customary to select the most energetic man as supervisor. For a long time, the only bridge fund was the strong muscle of the pioneer. By him, the ruts were filled, and the marshes spanned by corduroy bridges.

On the arrival of the early settlers, in 1810-11-12, there were a good many black bear, deer and wolves in the forests. In a few years the bear and wolves disappeared. The deer and turkey remained until within the last thirty-five years. When the dense forests began to be cut away, gray foxes appeared. Hunting deer and other game was regarded as rare sport. A majority of the hunters kept hounds for deer and fox hunting. Foxes were esteemed for their fur. In pursuit of this game the baying of the hounds, as they wound up and down the valleys and over the uplands, was deemed charming music by the hunters. The head branches of Black river were the usual resorts for game. Deer, bear and wolves were found there in abundance. Solomon Urie, John McConnell, Christopher Mykrantz, and Jacob Young were among the most noted hunters. Many anecdotes are related concerning their exploits with the rifle.

Sugar was one of the luxuries of the early settlers. The forests of this county abounded in maple and sugar trees. Along the Black fork and Jerome fork and their branches, there was one continuous camp of sugar trees. For a long time prior to the appearance of white settlers, these regions were the favorite resort of the *Delawares*, *Wyandots* and *Mingoes*, in the season for making sugar; and numerous huts and small camps of Indians were seen along the banks of the various streams of this county. The Indian mode of tapping sugar trees, securing the sap, and boiling it down, and granulating sugar, has been fully described in a former article. After the treaty of 1814, the *Wyandots*, *Delawares*, *Ottawas*, and *Mingoes* or *Senecas*, returned to this region in the spring of 1815 to make sugar and hunt. The white settlers and the Indians were frequently neighbors during the season for making sugar, and exchanged visits, and generally got along on friendly terms. This custom, in some parts of the county, continued for twelve or fourteen years, when the Indians finally disappeared, never to return. Some of the pioneers who had lost relatives during the war, did not entertain the most cordial affection for their red-skinned brethren, and occasionally one of the Indians known to have been very active in killing and scalping white people during and prior to the war of 1812, ceased to visit the settlements, and it was whispered about that they had probably fallen into Black river, or mired in some of the swamps about the Mifflin or Clearcreek lakes.

Making sugar was rare sport for the young people. Small camp-houses of poles were erected and covered with clapboards or bark, and a furnace of stones, cemented with yellow clay, and sufficiently long to receive eight or ten large iron kettles, in which the sugar water was speedily evaporated, and prepared for granulation. When large iron kettles could not be obtained, iron pots, brass kettles and other cooking utensils were brought into requisition. The large iron kettles were generally purchased at Zanesville, Pittsburgh, and Portland. Large troughs, dug-outs of white ash, holding two or three hogsheads, were made for the surplus water in a good run. The usual mode of tapping, sugar trees being abundant, was to notch, and bore a hole so as to intersect the inner part of the notch, which sloped down and back, so as to fit in a spile of elder or alder to convey the water into a trough or other vessel. The troughs were generally made of black and white ash, dug out, and would hold two or three gallons each. It was not uncommon for a pioneer to tap from three hundred to six hundred trees, and make from one thousand to one thousand five hundred pounds per season. Sugar, in those days, ranged in price from eight to eighteen cents per pound, and hundreds of pioneers paid for their farms by making sugar. The utmost hilarity and good cheer prevailed in the camps, and it was not uncommon for parties of young, and even middle-aged people, to travel four or five miles about the neighboring camps to serenade, sing, tell anecdotes, romp and frolic. Thus, the friendly Indian and the white settlers gathered a harvest of sweets for many recurring springs, as neighbors.

CHAPTER XXVIII.
TOWNSHIP ORGANIZATION.

Organization an Anglo-Saxon Characteristic.—Mohican Township.—The First Justice of the Peace.—Green Township.—Lake.—Perry.—Jackson.—Hanover.—Vermillion.—Montgomery.—Orange.—Mifflin—Milton.—Clearcreek.—Ruggles.—Troy.—Sullivan.

ORGANIZATION seems to be the highest characteristic of the Anglo-Saxon. Wherever enough adventurers or pioneers are found to locate, the first prominent idea is, to call a meeting and organize for self government. In the midst of the warlike excitement of 1812-15, the pioneers of the branches of Mohican failed not to remember that self government was the boon for which their revolutionary fathers contended. As rapidly as the population would permit, they proceeded to organize townships, and elect magistrates to enforce the laws and preserve order. Wayne county was comprised in one township, which was called Killbuck.

MOHICAN TOWNSHIP.

On the twelfth of April, 1812, the commissioners of Wayne county, one of whom was John Carr, then a resident of what is now Mohican township, divided Wayne into four townships, the western part including what are now Jackson, Perry, Mohican and Lake, and part of Washington in Holmes, and the west half of Clinton, Plain, Chester and Congress townships in Wayne; and organized this territory into one township under the name of Mohican. This was a large township. John Carr was one of its principal citizens, and one of the first commissioners of the county.

The first justices of the peace are believed to have been Nathan Odell and James Loudon Priest, who were succeeded by John Weatherbee and John Newkirk in 1815. A new justice was added in 1815, and William Metcalf was elected.

GREEN TOWNSHIP

was erected in 1812; prior to that time, Richland county constituted but a single township, which was named Madison. That township was authorized to elect several justices of the peace. As early as 1810, Archibald Gardner was elected a justice in what became Mifflin; and Henry McCart in 1811, and Peter Kinney in 1812, in what subsequently became Green; and James McClure and Andrew Coffinberry in 1814, in the balance of Madison township. In 1812 this arrangement was deemed inconvenient, and the township was divided on the seventeenth range, giving the territory in ranges sixteen and seventeen to the jurisdiction of the new township, which was called Green. It is asserted by some, that it was named after General Nathaniel Greene, of revolutionary fame; but probably received the name of the Indian village in the west part of the township. Peter Kinney was acting as a justice when the township was organized.

LAKE TOWNSHIP

was organized by the commissioners of Wayne county, in September, 1814; and in 1824, upon the organization of Holmes county, a strip from the south side of the township was ceded to that county. In 1814 the population of Lake was very sparse. The settlements were east of the Lake fork, in the region of Odell's lakes, and were composed, principally, of those who forted at Priest's in 1812. Nathan Odell and James Loudon Priest are believed to have been acting as justices of the peace at the organization of Lake.*

PERRY TOWNSHIP

was organized at the same session of the commissioners with Lake, in September, 1814, and had jurisdiction over the territory of Jackson until 1819. The pioneers of Perry at that time (1814), are believed to have been John Carr, John Ewing, Joseph Chandler, Aaron Cory, John Cory, John Raver, Benjamin Emmons, James Scott, Richard Smalley, Henry Worst, Arthur Campbell, Cornelius Dorland, and John Jackson, who was the first justice of the peace.

JACKSON TOWNSHIP

was organized by the commissioners of Wayne county in February, 1819. The township, at that period, was thinly settled. The pioneers of that date are believed to have been Noah Long, Isaac Lyons, John Chilcote, John Jackson, John Davault, Charles Hey, Jacob Berry, Thomas Cole, James A. Dinsmore, Jonas H. Gierhart, Josiah Lee, Jesse Mathews, Michael Richel and Mathias Richel. The pioneers concur in the statement that John Jackson was the first justice of the peace for Jackson township.

HANOVER TOWNSHIP

was organized by the commissioners of Richland county in 1818. The major part of the township being exceedingly rugged and difficult of cultivation, retarded settlement. At the period of its organization it is believed the following heads of families constituted the majority of the settlers: William Burwell, Thomas Taylor, Robert Dawson, George Davidson, George Snider, Amos Harbaugh, William Webb, Abner Winters, Stephen Butler, Abel Strong, John Hilderbrand, John Burwell, and —— Chapel. Stephen Butler was the first justice of the peace.

VERMILLION TOWNSHIP

was organized in December, 1816, by the commissioners of Richland county. It is difficult to ascertain the precise number of the heads of families at that time, the township records not being in existence. It is believed the following families resided in the township as early as 1818: Ezra Warner, George Eckley, James Wallace, Robert Finley, Samuel Bolter, Jonathan Palmer, George McClure, William Harper, William Karnahan, William Reed, William Ryland, Joseph Workman, Peter and John Vangilder, Joseph Strickland and sons, Mr. Harlan, Mr. Lattimer, Mr. Crabb, Mr. Beabout, Mr. Beck, and the late John Scott, sr. James Wallace was the first justice of the peace.

MONTGOMERY TOWNSHIP

was organized by the commissioners of Richland county in 1816. Prior to that time Vermillion and Montgomery each elected one justice of the peace and acted as one township. The pioneers of Montgomery, at the period of its organization, are believed to have been Robert Newell, Daniel Carter, Jacob Fry, Benjamin Cuppy, Henry Baughman, Samuel Burns, Daniel Mickey, Solomon Urie, Samuel Urie, Jacob Figley, William Montgomery, Jacob Crouse, James Kuykendall, Joseph Markley, John McNaull, Michael Springer, John Springer, Henry Springer, Daniel and Henry Vautilburg, and probably a few others not now remembered. The first justice of the peace was Robert Newell, who was succeeded by Daniel Carter, sr.

ORANGE TOWNSHIP

was organized by the commissioners of Richland county in 1818. The pioneers of that date are believed to have been Christian Fast and sons, Martin Mason and sons, Jacob Young, Vachel Metcalf, Amos Norris, John McConnell, Patrick Murray and sons, Jacob Mason, Joseph Bishop, John Bishop, Frederick Heiffner and sons, Thomas Green, Mordecai Chilcote, Philip Fluke and sons, James Clark, William Patterson, and probably others not now remembered by the present generation. The first justice of the peace was Vachel Metcalf.

MIFFLIN TOWNSHIP

was organized by the commissioners of Richland county in 1815. The pioneers at that date, as near as can be ascertained, were John Lambright, Leonard Croninger, David Braden, Michael Culler, Daniel Harlan, George Thomas and sons, Jacob Keiffer and sons, James and Wesley Copus, sons of Rev. James Copus, Daniel Hoover, Elijah Hart, sr., William B. James, Peter Deardorf, Samuel Lewis, and many others not now remembered. The first justice of the peace in Mifflin, was Archibald Gardner, who served one term, and was succeeded by William Gardner.

MILTON TOWNSHIP

was organized in 1816, by the commissioners of Richland county. The pioneers of that date are believed to have been Jacob Foulks, Alexander Reed, Robert Nelson, Benjamin Montgomery, James Andrews, Peter Brubaker, John Clay, Henry Keever, Frederick Sultzer, John Hazlett, Joseph Charles, Andrew Stevenson, David Markley, James Crawford, David Crabbs, Elijah Charles, David McKinney, John Ferrell, Abel Montgomery, William Houston, George Burget, and possibly a few others. Prior to 1816, Milton had been under the jurisdiction of Mifflin. The first justice of the peace was Robert McBeth, from what is now Clearcreek, then under the jurisdiction of Milton.

CLEARCREEK TOWNSHIP

was organized by the commissioners of Richland county in 1820.* The pioneers at that period are believed to have been David Burns, John Richards, John Freeborn, James Haney, William Shaw, Abraham Huffman, Peter Vanostrand, Isaac VanMeter, Elias Ford, Thomas Ford, John Bryte, Nathaniel Bailey, Daniel Huffman, James Burns, Abraham Clayberg, Jacob Foulks, Richard Freeborn, Thomas Haney, John Haney, Abel Bailey, John

---

* John Greenlee so states.

*This is the recollection of Mr. John Bryte. See "Biographical Sketches."

Bailey, Thomas Wright, John McMurray, John Cuppy, Patrick Elliott, Isaac Harvuot, John McWilliams, John Aten, Robert McBeth, and perhaps others, not now remembered. Robert McBeth, who had been justice during the jurisdiction of Milton over Clearcreek, was also the first justice of the peace for Clearcreek.

RUGGLES TOWNSHIP

was organized in 1826, by the commissioners of Huron county. It was called after Judge Almon Ruggles, who surveyed the Fire Lands. It was erected from the Fire Lands, and was five miles square, and subdivided into four quarters, each being again subdivided into lots containing from fifty to five hundred acres. The jurisdiction of Bethel township was extended over Ruggles until her population was sufficient for home rule. At the time of the organization, in 1826, the following heads of families are believed to have resided in the township: Bradford Sturtevant, Daniel Beach, James Poag, Harvey Sacket, Aldrich Carver, Norman Carter, Enoch Taylor, Reuben Fox, Jacob Roorback, Perry Durfee, A. Bates, C. Sanders, Abraham Ferris, Ezra Smith, T. Hendrix, D. J. Parker, Justus Barnes, and, perhaps, a few others, not now remembered. Harvey Sacket is believed to have been the first justice of the peace after Ruggles assumed self-government.

TROY TOWNSHIP

was organized by the commissioners of Huron county, in 1835. It was erected out of territory known as the "Gore," and was four miles wide and five miles long. At the time of its organization it abounded in forests, and was the resort of wild game. It had been attached, for purposes of civil rule, to the township north of it, in Huron county. The pioneers, at the date of its organization, are believed to have been: Joseph Parker, Nathaniel Clark, Benjamin Moore, Christian Bush, David Mason, Ralph Phelps, Nicholas Fast, Christian Fast, and Sanford Peck. Benjamin Moore was the first justice of the peace after the township assumed its organized condition.

SULLIVAN TOWNSHIP

was organized in 1819 by the commissioners of Lorain county. It is divided into lots in the same manner as Ruggles, being five miles square. This township was originally heavily timbered and abounded in wild game. The Canesadooharie, or Black river, famed as the region of deer and bear in Indian times, rises in Sullivan township. The pioneers at the date of its organization were,—Sylvanus Parmely, John Parmely, Asahel Parmely, Jesse Chamberlain, Abijah Chamberlain, Thomas Rice, James Palmer, Aretas Marsh, George Mann, J. M. Close, Henry Close and Rhesa Close. These were followed in 1818, by Whitney Chamberlain and Mr. Durfee. John Gould is believed to have been the first justice of the peace in Sullivan.

This concludes the organization of the various townships, and shows their original position in the counties, from which they were, at a later day, detached.

CHAPTER XXIX.

EARLY GRIST MILLS.

Hominy Blocks.—The Coffee Mill.—The Horse Mills.—Water Mills.—Chop Mills.—Mill-wrights.

"Oh, who has not seen Kitty Clyde,
She lives at the foot of the hill,
In a sly little nook by the babbling brook,
That carries her father's old mill."

When the pioneers entered the forests of what is now Ashland county, and commenced to erect cabins and remove the sturdy oak and the tangled undergrowth, they experienced many privations and inconveniences. A majority of the first settlers were in moderate circumstances, and had to depend upon their own strong arms and the smiles of Providence for subsistence. Their food was exceedingly plain, and their habits industrious and economical. Their clothing was generally of the most primitive character, and spun and woven by the faithful pioneer mothers.

From 1809 to 1813 there were but two grist-mills within a radius of some thirty-five miles. These mills were owned by Messrs. Shrimplin and Stibbs, and were of hewed logs and quite primitive in appearance. The former was located on Owl creek, some distance below Mt. Vernon. This mill could be reached by descending the branches of Mohican to the Walhonding, and ascending Owl creek, or by Indian paths through the forest. By either route it took several days. Stibbs' mill, near Wooster, was less distant, and could be reached by wagon or bridle paths. Pack-horses, ridden by small boys, generally made the trip to Stibbs' in from two to three days, depending upon the throng for their grist. These settlements being somewhat earlier in their improvements, generally had surplus corn crops, and were able to supply the new settlers on the branches of Mohican.

HOMINY-BLOCKS.

In consequence of the difficulties attending pioneer life, the great distance of grist-mills, the failure of the corn crops to mature, and the economic habits of the people, the pioneers were compelled to resort to the use of hominy-blocks. This method of preparing meal was, perhaps, the oldest in the world. The red races that preceded the pioneers have left many relics of the mortar and pestle. The hominy-block was very simple in its construction. It was generally made of a section of a beech tree, fifteen or eighteen inches in diameter, and three or four feet long, in one end of which holes were bored, forming a sort of hopper, the inside being removed by burning or a chisel, and the surface polished or made smooth. This rude receptacle was placed upright, and the corn, in the mortar, was pulverized by hand or the spring-pole. An iron wedge inserted in the end of an upright shaft and secured by a ring, formed the pestle. By the use of such an instrument, corn was rapidly crushed. In a few hours an active hand could prepare from one to three pecks of hominy meal. Many of the pioneers brought from the settlements wire sieves for the separation of meal from the coarse portions of the cracked corn, while others occasionally used home-made sieves, of perforated deer skins, drawn over a hoop. The finer meal was made into mush or journey-cake, and the coarse made excellent hominy.

THE COFFEE-MILL.

The labor of preparing meal in the foregoing manner, was so great that a more expeditious method had to be adopted. Ingenious native mechanics soon began the construction of what were known as "hand-mills." Two or three neighbors joined in the purchase of such a mill. They were made from a large bowlder, much after the fashion of the coffee-mills now in use. A hopper was drilled in a "nigger-head," and made in the shape of an inverted cone; a cylinder of the same material, exactly fitting the hopper, perforated through the center by a shaft, and also regularly grooved, was placed therein, on a pivot, and propelled by the aid of a lever, by one or two hands, as necessity required. The meal was received in a box below, and sifted by hand. It operated much like the modern coffee-mill. The hopper was stationary and generally artistically finished. About the same time an improved hand-mill made its appearance. Small "nigger-head" buhrs were used. They were placed within a hoop, very much as in the larger mills of the present day. The buhrs were grooved in the same manner, and the meal, being somewhat finer than that produced by the coffee-mill, was secured and sifted in the same manner. They were adjusted for fine or coarse work, and required from two to four men to turn them so as to greatly increase the quality of meal produced. They were not in extensive use, and were soon superseded by

THE HORSE-MILL.

A number of these were erected in many parts of the county. They were rude affairs, requiring great numbers of cogs, wheels and other curious machinery. They were propelled by horse-power much as the modern threshing machine or cider-mill. Many produced very good meal and flour, and generally had hand-bolts. A description of their machinery would occupy more space than can be allotted in these notes. They were in very general use for a period of about fifteen years. The buhrs of the horse-mills were made, mostly of bowlders or "nigger-heads," and fitted and secured much like the buhrs now in use in the water and steam grist-mills. The horse-mills were succeeded by improved

WATER-MILLS.

The numerous small streams throughout the county, during the earlier settlement, furnished valuable mill sites; and a great number of enterprising pioneers erected small grist- and saw-mills upon them. Before the removal of the heavy forests that covered most of the county, sufficient water was obtained to propel one or two set of buhrs, in the smaller mills, the major part of the year; but since the forests have been cut away, the water produced by heavy showers is rapidly conveyed by brooks and small streams to the larger ones, while the moisture left on the surface soon evaporates; the result being, that nearly all the smaller mills were compelled to suspend work three-fourths of the year. The consequence is, that while, in our earlier history, every little stream had a grist- or saw-mill, the number has gradually diminished, until there are not over a dozen good mills left, and these are chiefly propelled by steam.

It will be interesting to note the history of our mills, from the earlier settlements to the present time.

It is generally conceded that the first grist-mill within the present limits of Ashland county, was erected by Benjamin Cuppy, on a small stream one and a half miles northeast of Ashland, on what is now the Orange road, in March, 1816. It had one run of stones, and ground very slowly, not exceeding four bushels of corn per day.* It long since disappeared, and was replaced by the present mill, which has for many years been a great convenience to the farmers. It is now run by steam.†

About four weeks after the completion of the Cuppy mill, Martin Mason finished a small water-mill upon the present site of Samuel Leidigh's mill, on the Troy road, four miles north of Ashland. It had one run of hard-head stones. It was of hewn logs. It was a convenient neighborhood mill for many years, and did fair work. It passed through many hands, and the site is now owned by Mr. Leidigh. About the year 1870 he constructed a new and elegant frame mill, which is partly propelled by water, and partly by steam. It is doing a fine business.

About the year 1817, John Raver put up a small grist- and saw-mill on a run about one-fourth of a mile northeast of the present site of Rowsburgh, in Perry township. It run about one-third of the time, had an under-shot wheel and one set of stones and a hand-bolt. It stood several years, and was replaced by a mill built some years later by John Pittinger, east of Rowsburgh, on the Muddy fork of Mohican, since owned by the late Dr. A. Ecker, and is yet doing a prosperous business.

During the fall of 1817, it is believed that Constance Lake, of Jeromeville, erected a small log grist-mill, where what is now known as Goudy's mill, was subsequently built. The Goudy mill was accidentally burned about 1850. It had sustained a good reputation, and was a great loss to the community. It was not rebuilt, and the site is abandoned.

Conrad Kline, about the year 1819, built a small horse-mill one and a half miles northeast of Ashland, near the late residence of John Mason. It was constructed in the usual form of such mills, had one run of stones and a hand bolt. It made good meal and flour. It long since tumbled into ruins.

Jabez Smith, in 1820, erected a saw- and grist-mill half a mile south of the present site of Mohicanville, in Lake township. He sold it to R. F. Chandler, who kept the mill moving until the spring of 1875, when it accidentally burned. It was long a convenience to the farming community, and its destruction was much regretted.

Robert Crawford, a rugged, enterprising pioneer, put

---

*The Cuppy mill had "nigger-head" stones and was a poor affair. It was soon succeeded by a larger and better mill, erected near the same site by Thomas Oram, the millwright being John Brown, of Clearcreek township.

†The steam-mill was accidentally burned in the fall of 1875, since which time the site has remained unimproved.

up a large and expensive horse-mill on the present land of Albert Tilton, in the southeast part of Orange township, in 1820-21. It had one run of stones, a fine bolt, and did a large business for those times. It was finally abandoned about the year 1837.

About the year 1823 Thomas Ford put up a small horse-mill near what is now known as Ford's meeting-house, in Clearcreek township. It was a neighborhood mill, and did some business for a number of years. It has long since given way to the march of improvement.

It is believed that Oliver Sloan put up a saw- and grist-mill two miles southeast of Hayesville, about the year 1830. It had one run of stones and a bolt, and did a good deal of neighborhood work. It was conducted, for some years, by a Mr. Vangilder. It is now in ruins.

John Hendricks built a water-mill on Vermillion creek, about one mile west of Savannah, in 1823. It had one run of stones, and a bolt, and did some business. He subsequently sold to the late Joseph Roop, who caused a deep ditch, at heavy expense, to be dug from the lower lake, in the hope of increasing the flow of water; but only succeeded in draining the lower lake. The enterprise was a financial failure, and the mill went down.

Conrad Kline erected a small grist-mill, about two miles east of Ashland, at the foot of Roseberry hill, in Montgomery township, in 1825. It did some business, and was carried on some eight or ten years, when it was abandoned.

John Haney built a small horse-mill, on a run east of the village of Savannah, in Clearcreek township, in 1825. It was chiefly used for chopping, in connection with a distillery. It stood but a few years, and went to ruin.

David Weitzel erected a small saw- and grist-mill on the present site of the Ashland woollen-mills, about the year 1825. It had a pair of coffee-mill stones and was used chiefly for chop-work. It had also a hand-bolt. It subsequently became the property of the late John Jacobs, and was by him considerably improved. It was superseded by the large brick flouring-mill now owned by John Damp & Company. This mill is propelled exclusively by steam, and its work has long been classed among the finest in the county. It has a fine run of stones and can produce seventy-five barrels of flour per day.

Andrew Newman built what is now known as the Hershey mill, on the Black fork, two and one-half miles northwest of the village of Mifflin, in the year 1820. It is regarded as one of the best of its kind. It is chiefly a neighborhood mill, does fine work, and is run by water. It is now owned by Stamen Brothers.

Silas Longworthy built a small water-mill three miles southwest of the village of Mifflin, on the Black fork, in 1825, and sold to John Hewhey, he to Charles Lewis, and he to Daniel Kauffman. It was carried on until 1845, when Daniel Kauffman, a skilful millwright, tore it down and erected a valuable mill which he sold to John Charles. It is propelled exclusively by water, and is regarded as one of the best in the county. It has a saw mill attached.

It is believed that James Neely erected a grist-mill, on Zimmer's run, two and one-half miles southeast of Mifflin, as early as 1825. The mill is still in operation, and is doing a fair neighborhood business, when it has water. It is now owned by W. W. Matthews.

Jonathan Harvuot built a small horse-mill, about one mile northwest of Ashland, on lands recently owned by James Wells, about the year 1830. It had a brief career, and was used mostly as a chop-mill by the farmers.

Joseph Sellers put up a small water-mill, on Clearcreek, two miles west of Savannah, in 1830. It struggled along a few years and went down.

Colonel John Murray erected, for himself, a grist- and saw-mill, on Mohican creek, one and a half miles north of Orange, in 1831. It did considerable business in wet seasons, but finally became of little value, because of a want of water.

George McCartney constructed a small water-mill in connection with a carding machine—on lands since owned by the late Samuel Urie, in Milton township, in 1830. It had insufficient power, and the enterprise failed and brought disaster upon its owner.

William Goudy and sons put up the present large grist-mill at Jeromeville, about the year 1836. It has passed through many hands,—Eli Zimmerman, N. G. Glenn, R. McMahan, G. W. Basford, 1851, John Webster, 1856, R. M. Winbigler & Co., 1871, and in 1873, R. M. B.,— and is yet regarded as a valuable property. It has fine water power, and does a fair business. It has a good saw-mill connected with it.

Armstrong Meanor erected a small grist-mill three miles north of Loudonville, on the Hayesville road, near a small stream, about the year 1831. It was subsequently rebuilt, and is yet doing a fair business.

About the same time (1831), Mr. Newman built a grist-mill three miles northeast of Hayesville, on a small stream in the Finley settlement. It was carried on for many years, and did a prosperous business. A new mill, now known as Smith's mill, was erected in the neighborhood some twenty years since, and the old mill is going to decay.

Jacob Mason built a small undershot mill about four miles north of Ashland, on Leidigh's run, in 1831. It was used principally as a chop-mill for a distillery. It has long since disappeared.

Daniel Beach built a saw-mill in 1824, and a grist-mill on Vermillion river one mile north of Ruggles corners, in 1832. It run to about 1858, and is now in ruins. It passed through four or five hands.

Daniel Carter, jr., put up a water-mill two miles east of Ashland, near the Wooster road, in 1832. It did a fair business eighteen or twenty years. It is now in ruins.

The Loudonville mill—a frame—two run of stones, was built by Alexander Skinner in 1818; Caleb Chapel was carpenter and first miller. He died in 1821, and T. J. Bull became the owner of the mill; he sold to Thomas Carlisle; and in 1835 the mill became the property of Gray & Freeman, of Cleveland. They run it until 1845; then it passed into the hands of James Christmas and John C. Larwill, and in 1861, A. A. Taylor, who erected a new mill. It is run, principally, by steam, and has nine run of stones, and manufactures seventy-five thousand barrels of flour annually.

Hanvey and Smith, from Rochester, New York, put up a large flouring mill on the Lake fork, three miles southeast of Mohicanville, in 1836. It is now known as the "Rochester mill." It has fine water power, and does an excellent business.

Michael Diblebess erected, in 1840, a small water-mill where the Berkholder mill now stands, on the Catotaway, in Montgomery township. It made some flour, and had a hand-bolt.

Thomas Stringer erected a large grist-mill, on the Black fork, about one mile below Perrysville, in 1839. He owned it but a short time. It has had a stirring career, and has passed through many hands. It is a valuable property, and capable of doing a large business.

John Scott, sr., put up a valuable grist-mill one mile north of Hayesville, on the Ashland road, in 1846. It has a good location, and when the seasons are favorable, does a fair business. The stream is gradually failing, and the mill will eventually have to be run by steam.

In 1874 Messrs. Roop, Coble and Myers erected a large brick mill in Ashland. It is driven by steam, and is complete in all its machinery. It is capable of producing one hundred barrels of flour per day. It was put in motion early in 1875, and has already become noted for its excellent work. It is one of the most valuable mills in northern Ohio.

CHOP-MILLS AND WHISKEY.

As reference has frequently been made to chop-mills, in connection with distilleries, it is proper to state that our pioneers were not particularly noted for intemperance. Distilleries, like mills, were a necessity. There was a surplus of corn and rye, while there were neither purchasers nor a market. Transportation by wagons to Portland, Cleveland, and Pittsburgh, was attended with much expense. The only way the surplus corn and rye could be made available was to convert them into whiskey, which could be exchanged for groceries, salt and goods. The whiskey thus manufactured was put into barrels and hauled to market. The result was that many distilleries sprang up in every part of the country, and chop-mills came into use. It will be seen, therefore, that good rye whiskey soon became a "legal tender" in the market. Improved modes of conveyance have long since disposed of the chop-mills and the numerous distilleries. Whiskey is an institution, nevertheless. It pays an enormous revenue, and is feared alike by the politician and the moralist.

It was said in classic times, that "the mills of the Gods ground slow, but exceedingly fine." It will be observed that the earlier mills of the pioneers not only ground exceedingly slow, but also exceedingly coarse.

I have adverted to the earlier mills, because many of the mill-boys of sixty years agone are yet with us. Many pleasant memories cluster about those days. Trips of thirty miles, on pack-saddles, through the forests, along the winding paths, were not without interest. Sleeping on the mill floors upon an empty sack—the delay to obtain a grist, and the lively jokes and songs of those days, must often come to recollection. As the aged mill-boys now meander through the country, by the old mill seats, I have no doubt they are often led to exclaim—

"Here's the path by the long deserted mill,
And the stream by the old bridge, broken still,
And the golden willow boughs bending low,
To the green sunny banks where the violets blow;
The wild birds are singing the same sweet lays,
That charmed me in dreams of the dear old days."

MILLWRIGHTS.

John Horrick made most of the nigger-head hominy mortars, and coffee mill-stones.

Colonel John Murray was the most noted millwright in this part of the county. When a young man, he learned his trade in Louisville, Kentucky. He is said to have been a very ingenious workman. Colonel George W. Urie and Isaac Stull, both citizens of Ashland, learned of Colonel Murray.

Abraham Holmes, who resided near Windsor, in Richland county, constructed a good many mills along the Black fork and in other localities.

Daniel Kauffman, who built the Charles mill, was regarded as a good mechanic. He resides in Richland county.

John Brown, of Millbrook Wayne county, built the Carter Mill, and some others, in the county. He is said to have beeen a good mechanic.

NOTE.—In writing the foregoing sketch it was impossible to obtain the exact date of the erection of all the mills, many of the parties having long since removed or deceased.

CHAPTER XXX.

THE VILLAGES AND TOWNS OF ASHLAND COUNTY.

Loudonville.—Perrysville.—Jeromeville.—Ashland.—Mifflin.—Savannah.—Orange.—Hayesville.—Perrysburgh.—Mohicanville—Sullivan—Lafayette.—Polk.—Ruggles Center.

IN the long future, it may be interesting to recur to the appearance, growth, and decay of villages and towns within the limits of this county. We will, therefore, proceed to notice the location and survey of each.

LOUDONVILLE,

in Hanover township, was laid out August 6, 1814, by James Loudon Priest and Stephen Butler, and contained at the census of 1870, a population of eight hundred and eleven. It is located in the northeast corner of the township, on the banks of the Black fork of the Mohican, which was navigable, for many years, for small craft. The Pittsburgh and Fort Wayne railroad passes through it, and adds thrift and enterprise to the place. The road was constructed in the years 1852 and 1853, and, since its completion, the town has grown quite rapidly. Recently, many fine brick buildings have been constructed along its principal business streets, and a number of handsome and valuable brick residences put up, in different parts of the original town, and several very showy ones in a new addition above the depot. During the construction of the Walhonding canal, some thirty-five years ago, it was proposed to continue it up the lake and Black fork; and Loudonville was made a point. After that enterprise was abandoned, the village failed to improve, until the completion of the railroad. A good deal of business is now transacted in the town. It furnishes a good market for all the surplus grain and stock of the southeast part of the county. It has a spirited population, and contains two good hotels, a bank, several dry goods establishments, a drug store, a tin and hardware store, a foundry, a carriage manufactory, a large tannery, an excellent steam grist-mill, clothing stores, blacksmith shops, lumber yards, cabinet shops, shoe stores, a gunsmith, five or six fine churches, a newspaper, several physicians, and a lawyer. The country around the town is healthy, and the hills and valleys are quite romantic; and many legends are related, concerning the red men that roamed up and down the streams of Hanover, three-quarters of a century agone.

PERRYSVILLE,

in Green township, from the victory of Commodore Perry, September 10, 1813, was the second village in the present limits of Ashland county. It was laid out June 10, 1815, by Thomas Coulter. Its growth for many years was moderate. In the days of the construction of the Ohio canals, this village had large expectations concerning the route of the extension of the Walhonding canal. It is located on the Black fork, which was navigable to within a little distance of the village. As early as 1822 a number of flat-boats were built in its vicinity, loaded with the surplus products of Green township, and sent south. Since the completion of the Pittsburgh, Fort Wayne & Chicago railroad, which passes through the town, its growth has been quite rapid. It has a station and warehouse, and large quantities of grain, and the surplus stock of the southeast part of the county are here purchased and shipped west. This adds greatly to the thrift and enterprise of the town. Its population is estimated at about five hundred. The village contains three stores, a foundry, a fine grist-mill, a tavern, a post-office, one Presbyterian, one Baptist, and one Methodist church, two blacksmith shops, a carriage and wagon manufactory, four physicians, and an excellent institution of learning. The town is surrounded by a rich valley of land, which is cultivated by hundreds of thrifty and prosperous farmers. The outlook for the future is very flattering. Her academy, under the management of Professor J. C. Sample, is an ornament to the town, and cannot fail to contribute to the intelligence and prosperity of her people.

JEROMEVILLE,

in Mohican township, named after John Baptiste Jerome, the original proprietor of the land upon which it was surveyed, was the third town within the present limits of Ashland county, having been laid out February 14, 1815, by Christian Deardorff and William Vaughn; and is now estimated to contain a population of about four hundred. It is eligibly located in the northwest part of the township, on the old and much traveled road from Wooster to Mansfield, and prior to the construction of railroads, had a large patronage from the traveling public, and was a good business town. The interests of the town would be greatly enhanced by the construction of a railroad up the valley to Ashland, which project is now being considered by her most enterprising citizens. It contains two or three small stores, two hotels, a carriage manufactory, two cabinet shops, a harness shop, three blacksmith shops, several shoe shops, one wagon shop, a tailor, several groceries, two physicians, a fine mill, and an excellent school. It also has one Presbyterian, one Methodist and one Disciple church. It is surrounded by fine farming land and industrious farmers, whose patronage adds to the prosperity of the town. No better agricultural lands can be found in the State than those along the branches of Mohican; and all the farmers need is access to a ready market for all their surplus products, to make them wealthy and independent.

ASHLAND,

formerly Uniontown, in Montgomery township, was laid out by William Montgomery, July 28, 1815, and was the fourth town within the present limits of Ashland county. It retained the name of Uniontown, until the establishment of a post-office, in 1822, which was called Ashland, because there was another Uniontown in the State. The village thereupon received the name of Ashland. Mr. Frank Graham, now (1876) eighty-five years old, was the first postmaster.

Ashland is situated on sections seven, eight, seventeen and eighteen, and is estimated to contain a population of three thousand. In 1822, the village contained about twenty log cabins, one small dry goods store, a blacksmith, two distilleries, a tannery, a shoemaker, a tailor, a hatter, a cooper, a wheelwright, a small tavern, and one physician. The inhabitants of the village were William Montgomery, farmer; Philip Shaffer, shoemaker; Elias Slocum, tavern keeper; Alanson Andrews, farmer; George W. Palmer, distiller; Samuel Urie, blacksmith; Joseph Sheets, tailor; Joseph Markley, distiller; David Markley; Amos Antibus, hatter; Ebenezer D. Nightingill, hatter; Mr. Barr, cooper; Francis Graham, storekeeper; John Croft, tanner; Alexander Miller, cabinet-maker; Joel Luther, physician. This was really the beginning of the village. The principal street was very crooked, and the cabins were ranged along either side of it. A grist- and saw-mill or two, all propelled by water, soon appeared. Jacob Grubb, an excellent cabinet-maker, and other mechanics, soon erected dwellings. A demand for more goods introduced other business men, and more stores were opened. The original plat filled rapidly, and more room was required. Markley's addition was laid out, and, in a few years, Alanson Andrews, Francis Graham, Joseph Sheets and Christopher Mykrantz added their additions. Then, in 1846, Ashland became the seat of justice, and South Ashland was laid out. More recently, the additions of Rocky, Cowan & Myers, and Willis, have been added. Some of the original streets have been straightened and considerably extended, while Main and Orange streets have been paved and guttered with bowlders. The original cabins and frame structures have gradually disappeared, and been replaced by fine brick buildings along Main and other streets. For many years Ashland was noted for its excellent academy. This was suffered to be merged into the union school system in 1850. At present, her schools are in a prosperous condition. The town contains ten churches, nine Protestant and one Catholic. It has three banks, an Odd Fellows' hall, and a masonic lodge, two manufactories of agricultural implements, four blacksmith shops, two large steam grist-mills, three carriage and wagon manufactories, two steam saw-mills, two lumber yards, two large tanneries, four harness and saddle shops, four shoe stores, three hardware stores, three clothing stores, two hotels, five dry goods stores, four provision stores, three stove and tin stores; two silverware and jewelry stores, two bakery establishments, two printing offices, one gun store, three butcher shops, two furniture stores, one furniture manufactory, sixteen physicians, two dentists, thirteen lawyers, three livery establishments and two book stores.

The county buildings add to the business of the place during the sessions of the court, and the payment of taxes. The New York, Pennsylvania & Ohio railroad, with its warehouses and depot, is within the northern limits of the town, and adds to its property wealth. All in all, we conclude that in the future, as in the past, Ashland will go steadily forward in the increase of her population, in wealth, and number of valuable improvements. It is surrounded by a fine, productive country, and can sustain a much greater population.

MIFFLIN,

formerly called Petersburgh, in Mifflin township, was laid out by William B. James, Peter Deardorff, and Samuel Lewis, June 16, 1816. It was located on the old State road leading from Wooster to Mansfield. For many years it was very thrifty, and, under the old stage era, and during the early settlement of Richland county, was well patronized by the traveling public. George Thomas erected the first tavern, which he conducted until about 1820. The removal of the old stage lines, and the construction of railroads, diverted travel to other lines, and for many years the village has been sustained almost exclusively by the patronage of the farmers of Mifflin. It has one tavern, one store, one cabinet shop, one blacksmith shop, one grocery, a post-office, an excellent district school, one church, one physician, and one shoe shop. It contains a population of about one hundred and fifty.

SAVANNAH,

formerly Vermillion, in Clearcreek township, was laid out December 25, 1818, by John Haney. It is situated on a beautiful plateau, on the old Vermillion road, and contains a population of about four hundred. It has five churches, two dry goods stores, one tavern, two grocery stores, a wagon and carriage shop, a tannery, two blacksmith shops, a saddle and harness shop, a tailor shop, a cabinet shop, a tin shop, and a number of mechanics. It has, also, a fine academy, which is well patronized, and adds thrift and spirit to the town. Its inhabitants are, largely, the descendants of Scotch-Irish, intermixed with people of New England birth. The town is noted for its adhesion to total abstinence from every form of intoxicating drinks, and, in this respect, is a safe resort for young men seeking an education, and preparing for future usefulness.

ORANGE,

in Orange township, was laid out by Amos Norris and John Chilcote, April 22, 1828. It is located on section twenty-eight, on a branch of Mohican creek, in the midst of splendid farming lands. It was for many years a flourishing village; but its nearness to the county-seat has somewhat checked its growth. It contains one hotel, one dry goods store, one or two groceries, a blacksmith shop, two tanneries, a shoe shop, a harness manufactory, a tailor shop, a post-office called Nankin, a physician, a Presbyterian and a Methodist church, and a good school. The New York, Pennsylvania & Ohio railway passes near the village and has a small station and telegraph office. The village is estimated to contain two hundred and fifty inhabitants.

HAYESVILLE,

situated near the center of Vermillion township, was laid out October 26, 1830, by John Cox and Linus Hayes. The State roads running from Wooster to Mansfield and from Ashland to Loudonville, intersect each other in the center of the town, and constitute its principal streets. It contains two dry goods stores, a wagon and carriage manufactory, two or three blacksmith shops, a cabinet shop, a shoe shop and store, two or three groceries, two hotels, one or two boarding houses, a good district school, one Presbyterian, one United Presbyterian, and one Methodist church, post-office, two physicians, and many pleasant residences. The population and business are on the increase. In 1875, a newspaper was started, in connection with Vermillion institute, which has for many years been the ornament of the town. The population of Hayesville is estimated at about six hundred. It is surrounded by a good farming community, and must continue to increase in wealth and population.

PERRYSBURGH,

in Jackson township, was laid out October 13, 1830, by Josiah Lee and David Buchanan. It has a population of about one hundred and fifty. It has one tavern, two small stores, a shoe shop, a blacksmith shop, a wagon manufactory, a cabinet shop, a tailor, and one church. The post-office is named Albion. The village has had a gradual growth, and is supported by a good farming community.

MOHICANVILLE,

in the southwest part of Mohican township, was laid out July 2, 1833, by Simeon Beall and Henry Sherradden.

It contains a population of near two hundred, and has three churches, a hotel, one store, a grist-mill propelled by steam and water, a woollen manufactory a wagon shop, a shoe shop, a harness manufactory. a carriage shop, a paint shop, a cabinet shop, a good school, a post-office, and two physicians. The people of the village are wide-awake and prosperous. The village has very fine water-power, and is healthfully located in the midst of excellent farming lands. It has a fair trade, and is mostly supported by the farmers.

SULLIVAN,

situated in the center of Sullivan township, was laid out in 1836 by Sylvanus Parmely, Ira Palmer, Joseph Palmer and Joseph Carlton, whose lands formed the corners of the center. It contains one tavern, one dry goods store, one shoe shop, one grocery, one carriage shop, one blacksmith shop, one cabinet shop, one harness shop, one steam saw-mill, four good churches, a good school, and is eligibly situated. Its population is about two hundred, and mostly from New England. The post-office bears the name of the village. Its principal support is derived from the neighborhood trade. The population of the township is largely engaged in the dairy business and grazing.

ROWSBURGH,

in the center of Perry township, was laid out by Michael D. Row, April 15, 1835. It is situated on the main road from Ashland to Wooster, and has a population of about two hundred and fifty. It has two stores, one tavern, one wagon and blacksmith shop, a large tannery, a cabinet shop, two harness manufactories, three churches, a fine school and a post-office. It also has one physician. The country about the village contains many valuable farms, and the patronage of the farmers contributes largely to the growth and prosperity of the town. There is also considerable travel.

LAFAYETTE,

in the north part of the township of Perry, was laid out in the spring of 1835, just prior to the platting of Rowsburgh. The original proprietors were William Hamilton and John Zimmerman. The location of the village at that time, gave promise of a fair business and considerable growth, being situated on a much traveled road. The country around the village is very productive, and is filled by industrious, frugal, and prosperous farmers. It has one store, a blacksmith, a cabinet-maker, a shoemaker and other mechanics, a good school and one or two churches. The population has not increased of late years.

POLK,

in Jackson township, was laid out May 4, 1849, by John Kuhn. It is located near the New York, Pennsylvania and Ohio railway, and contains about one hundred and fifty inhabitants. It has a good store, a tavern, a steam saw-mill, a harness manufactory, a blacksmith shop, a post-office, a railroad station, two churches, a good school and two physicians. Its growth for the last few years has been quite rapid.

TROY CENTER,

in the center of Troy township, became a village in 1851, upon the addition of Norris division. The corners were re-surveyed and consolidated in 1868, and platted. Its post-office is called "Nova." It has one tavern, one store, a blacksmith shop, a steam saw-mill, a shoemaker, a cabinet-maker, a tailor, a tin shop, a harness maker, and about forty dwelling houses, one church and school-house. It also has one lawyer and a physician. The roads from Sullivan and from Ashland cross at right angles, and form the principal streets. It has a fair neighborhood trade.

RUGGLES CENTER

is located on the intersection of the Ashland, New London and Sullivan roads, and contains a post-office, a grocery store, a blacksmith shop, two shoe shops, one Methodist and one Congregational church, a school, and twelve residences. The old point of trade in the township was the corner west of the center; but since the old trade route to Mohican has been abandoned, in consequence of the completion of the Atlantic & Great Western railway (now the New York, Pennsyluania & Ohio), through Ashland, it has gone down.

CHAPTER XXXI.
EDUCATION AND INSTITUTIONS OF LEARNING.

A Description of the First School-Houses.—Early Teachers.—What Branches Taught.—School Amusements.—Improved Methods and Progress.—School Statistics for 1875.—Ashland Academy.—Ashland Union Schools.—Vermillion Institute.—Loudonville Academy.—Savannah Academy.—Perrysville Academy.—Ashland College.—Ashland City Church.

IN the early settlement of the territory now constituting Ashland county, the system of education adopted by the pioneers was very ineffective. The schools of that period were supported almost exclusively by individual subscriptions, the only aid being a nominal sum received in each township, from leases on section sixteen. Teachers were employed for low wages, or it would have been impossible for the sparse settlers to have maintained or supported any schools. At first, a few pupils were collected in a cabin of one of the pioneers, for instruction, by a volunteer teacher, deemed capable of imparting a knowledge of the elementary branches. In examining the pioneer records, it is found that, in many localities, the first teachers were single or married ladies, and that the amount received for tuition, from the parents of the pupils, was used to defray the expense of clearing and preparing a homestead. They were noble sisters and exemplary wives.

The first school-houses were of round logs, and were erected by the joint voluntary efforts of the citizens residing within the district, which was generally large. These "backwoods colleges," as they were sometimes denominated in jest, had puncheon floors, benches of split timber, writing desks of planed boards, placed in front of a long window, formed by cutting out a log, while the light was reflected through oiled paper; and benches, the legs of which, for some unexplained reason, were generally quite lengthy. The fire-place was very broad, and the chimney generally erected against the end of the school-house, and formed of split timber, lined with stone and clay. The fuel was of large, round logs for "back sticks," and smaller ones for "fore-sticks," which rested upon a stone or andirons. The school-house, by such a fire, could be made quite comfortable, in all the stages of winter. The fuel was delivered in a sort of voluntary frolic, with teams of oxen and horses, while the axe-men cut and prepared it. In this way, for many years, the earlier schools were supplied with fuel.

The earlier teachers were from Pennsylvania, New York, Maryland, and the New England States. Sometimes an educated Irishman sought and obtained employment as a teacher. In a general way, good order, in school hours, was rigidly enforced; and if a ready compliance, on the part of the pupil, was not yielded, an application of birch readily induced the recreant scholar to comply. The theory of moral suasion was not so popular then as now. The commands of the teacher were obeyed, much as those of the military officer, where no argument, as to the right or wrong of a command, is permitted. The modern theory is: More argument, and less birch. Both systems have their advocates.

The course of instruction in those days was generally limited to the elementary branches, such as spelling, reading, writing, arithmetic, geography, and English grammar. These branches were carefully and thoroughly taught. In penmanship, the old fashioned round hand prevailed. The Spencerian was unknown. In spelling, the scholar champion often spelled every word in the book. In arithmetic, every problem was solved. In fact, the scholars of those days illustrated the adage—"beware of the man of one book," because they knew all that their school books contained. The brains of the student were not addled, like the over-tasked scholar of the present, with six or eight half-mastered, and ill-digested branches. The speculation in new text books had not been introduced.

The amusements of those days consisted in a game of "town ball," somewhat like the modern "base ball," "corner ball," "chase the fox," leaping, running, and wrestling. These athletic sports were harmless, and entered into at recess and noon, with much spirit and good humor, and were supposed to add vigor to both body and mind. Spelling schools were conducted with a good deal of enthusiasm, and rival schools, from adjoining neighborhoods, often competed for the championship.

At the approach of the holidays, it was the custom of the larger boys and girls to insist upon the enforcement of the immemorial usage of exacting a "treat" from the teacher. This generally consisted in the donation of a bushel of apples, a gallon or two of cider, and a lot of pies or cakes. As a general rule, the teacher yielded to the custom, but sometimes refused. Upon refusal, the sport of "barring" the door and windows, to exclude the teacher, was the next resort. The issue being thus joined, either the teacher or scholars had to surrender. A good deal of strategy followed on both sides. If the teacher—an Irishman—gained admission, a beech or hickory rod soon enforced obedience. Sometimes the boys, being large and rugged, seized the teacher and expelled him by force. In that case the obstinate "master" compromised by agreeing to donate a bushel of apples, while the courageous scholars would remit the cider and pies. The apples were distributed, and after a good deal of merriment and many practical jokes, steady habits and hard study were resumed.

But a change was rapidly approaching. Farmers were becoming wealthy. The school lands were sold, and the deficiency of funds was supplied by direct taxation. The next grand improvement was the erection of neat, commodious, well painted and furnished school-houses in every district in the county. Township school boards enforced this system by local taxation, and the standard of qualification for teachers was raised, until our common schools now rival, in number of branches, the academies of forty years ago.

The names of a few of the early teachers are well remembered. Miss Elizabeth Rice, afterwards Mrs. John Coulter, taught a little subscription school in a cabin near the present site of Perrysville, in the summer of 1814. She yet survives, and lives in the village of Congress, in Wayne county, Ohio. In the winter of 1816 Asa Brown had a school about one mile north of Perrysville. In the summer of 1817 Mrs. Patrick Elliott taught a small school in her cabin home in Clearcreek. In the winter of 1817 Robert Nelson taught in a cabin on the premises of the late Abraham Huffman, in Clearcreek. In 1818 Rev. John Hazard taught a small school in what is now known as the "Crouse" district, in Montgomery. He was followed by the late Sage Kellogg, in 1819-20. In 1818 John G. Mosier is believed to have taught the first school in Perry. About the same time L. Parker taught a small school in the Priest neighborhood, in Lake. At a later period John Bryte, of Clearcreek, Hugh Burns, of Milton, Therygood Smith, of Montgomery, the daughters of Sterling G. Bushnell, of Vermillion, Chandler Foot and Lorin Andrews, of Montgomery, were among the noted teachers. The thoughtless destruction of township records makes it impossible to extend, accurately, a list of the early teachers. It is proper to state, in this connection, that many of the better educated pioneers instructed their own families in the elementary branches.

The common schools of this county are now in a flourishing condition. The amount annually appropriated for the employment of competent teachers, insures a continuous school, in each district, of from four to six months each year.

The total number of scholars enrolled in common schools for 1875 was.. 5,041
The total number enrolled in the high schools for 1875, was.. 1,306
The total number of teachers in the common and high schools in 1875, was.. 231

The total value of school-houses in 1875, was.................$89,800
The total value of high school property, in 1875 was.......... 71,500
The total amount paid teachers of common schools, in 1875, was 42,258
The total amount paid teachers in high schools, in 1875, was.. 36,357
The total number of school-houses, in 1875, was.............. 118
The total amount for defraying expenses in the erection of high
    school buildings in 1875, ... $2,905
The amount received from section 16, Fund in 1875.......... 1,686
The amount of Western Reserve fund received in 1875......... 65

From the foregoing statistics, it will be seen, that the neglect to give each member of a family, at least a good common school education, is growing unpopular; and to be illiterate, amid so many school advantages, is regarded as inexcusable. Mental culture and intellectual development bring out the latest sparks of genius, and enable civilized communities to advance in all that conduces to the peace, prosperity and happiness of man.

We will now direct attention to the higher institutions of learning, and see that the people of Ashland county have placed a proper estimate upon the importance and value of a finished education.

ASHLAND ACADEMY.

In the year 1838, Professor Samuel McClure, of Cuyahoga Falls, taught a select school in Ashland, which attracted a good deal of interest. Public attention was directed by Professor McClure and others, to the project of erecting and organizing, under trustees, an Academy at Ashland, with a view of attracting a large number of foreign students. In the years 1838–9, through the efforts of the principal citizens of Ashland, and other villages in what is now Ashland county, a handsome brick structure, two stories high, was erected, and dedicated as Ashland academy.

The board of trustees was as follows: Rev. Robert Fulton, president; John P. Rizner, John Jacobs, William S. Granger, Joseph Wasson, Francis Graham, James Stewart, Abraham Huffman, Joseph McComb, Daniel W. Brown, Willliam McComb; Jones Stout and Silas Robbins, secretaries; and John L. Lang, treasurer.

The board elected Rev. Robert Fulton, A. M., principal; Rev. R. R. Sloan, assistant; and Miss Jane E. Coulter, preceptress of the ladies department. They entered on the discharge of their duties in May, 1839. Professor R. Fulton died in 1841, and was succeeded by Rev. Samuel Fulton, of Pittsburgh. Professor Sloan and Miss Coulter continued as assistants about two years, under the new principal. Professor Samuel Johnston succeeded Rev. S. Fulton, and a sister, Cecilia, became preceptress in lieu of Miss Coulter, who became Mrs. Sloan; and Lorin Andrews succeeded Professor Sloan. In 1844 Professor Johnston resigned, and Professor Lorin Andrews became principal, Professor A. M. Fulton, assistant, and Miss Lisle, preceptress. She remained about one year, and Miss Jane M. Becket became preceptress of the ladies' department. Professor A. M. Fulton resigned about 1846, and was succeeded by Professor John M. Rankin, who continued about eighteen months. In 1847 Professor Andrews resigned to engage in the union school enterprise. He was succeeded by Rev. John M. Rowe in 1848, who was aided by Professor T. V. Milligan. After a struggle of about one year the labors of Professor Rowe terminated, and the academy was discontinued; and the buildings finally merged into the union school.

Ashland academy had a very successful career of over ten years, during which it sustained a high reputation at home and abroad. Very few academic institutions of Ohio can furnish a roll of scholars containing more influential and leading men, as teachers, attorneys, physicians, men of science, and politicians.

ASHLAND UNION SCHOOL.

Under the act authorizing the erection of union schools, the electors of the Ashland school district, in 1850, adopted that system and proceeded to erect buildings. A large central building was constructed, adjoining the old academy, for the high school, while the latter was occupied for the primary branches. Professor John Lynch was elected by the board the first superintendent. He resigned in 1852, and was succeeded by Professor Seth M. Barber. Professor Barber continued until 1861, when he resigned to take a captain's position in the army. He was temporarily succeeded by Professor C. W. Mykrants. Professor George L. Mills succeeded Mr. Mykrants in September, 1862. Professor Mills was succeeded by Professor Foose, and he by Professor S. E. Pearree, and he, in 1867, by Professor Barber, who continued as superintendent until 1872, when he resigned, and Professor T. J. Bartin was elected. In 1875 Professor J. A. Beattie was elected. In 1874-'5 a large central building was erected at an expense of thirty-two thousand dollars. It maks a fine appearance.

VERMILLION INSTITUTE.

Those in Vermillion township who desired advanced educational training beyond the facilities furnished in the common schools, were compelled to send their children to the academy at Ashland or to more distant institutions. The enterprising people of Hayesville and Vermillion township, upon a full discussion of the subject, concluded that the establishment of a high school or academy at Hayesville would reduce the expense of sending their youth to distant schools, and at the same time contribute to the growth and interest of the village. By the joint efforts of her citizens, a sufficient amount of stock was subscribed to warrant the erection of an academic building. In 1842 a high school was opened by Rev. Lewis Granger, of Granville, who was elected principal. The school was non-sectarian. Rev. J. L. McLean took a deep interest in the school, and it prospered beyond expectation. In 1845 a charter was granted by the legislature erecting the school with Vermillion institute, and authorizing it to confer degrees. The erection of a suitable building for the institute was commenced, and on the fourth of July, 1845, the corner stone was laid. Upon the completion of the building, Rev. J. L. McLean was elected president, with assistants W. J. Booth and others. The institute course of studies was the same as a collegiate routine. The machinery was too intricate for the patronage, and the institution resumed the academic course. Under this arrangement the institution had a prosperous career for about five years.

In 1850, the presbytery of Richland, and, in 1854, Wayne and Coshocton, joined in the purchase of the institute, and elected trustees, who employed the professors. At first there were ten trustees, but when Wayne and Coshocton joined Richland, in 1854, in its management, the number was extended to fifteen. By this arrangement the institution came under the management of the Presbyterians. Professor S. Diefendorf, a learned and accomplished scholar, was selected as principal, and W. W. Colmary and W. T. Adams assistants. Professor W. J. Booth took charge of the mathematical branches, under President McLean, and resigned in 1850 and removed to Athens. Professor Diefendorf, after being absent about one year, resumed his place as principal in 1851, and continued until 1866, when he resigned and moved west. In 1867 Professor J. Simpson took charge of the school, but remained only a short time. Professor A. F. Ross became principal in the fall of 1868, but remained only a few months, and resigned. In 1869 Professor Diefendorf again resumed his old position, but soon withdrew. In 1870-71 Professor W. J. Brugh became principal. In 1872 Professor John Martin succeeded Professor Brugh; he remained but a short time. In 1873 Professor J. A. Bower was elected principal. Owing to disputes arising in the board of trustees, the institution was transferred, in 1874, to its original owners, and passed from the management of the presbytery.

In 1875 the institution again became non-sectarian, and is now managed by new trustees. Under this management Professors W. J. Ward and J. B. Paine became teachers, and continued until the close of the session of 1876, when they retired. The institution, after a checkered and restless career, is again under the management of the accomplished and learned Professor Diefendorf. The institute property is estimated to be worth about six thousand dollars. May it again flourish.

LOUDONVILLE ACADEMY.

This institution originated from a high school taught by the late Professor John McCormick, about the year 1848. It was erected by the joint efforts of the citizens of Loudonville. The location of the academy was very pleasant. The school was well patronized for the first four or five years. Professor McCormick remained about two years, and was succeeded by Professor Andrew J. Scott, who continued until 1852, and was succeeded by the author of these notes, who continued one session, and resigned in consequence of ill health. From 1853, the school languished under a number of changes, and was finally consolidated with the high schools.

SAVANNAH ACADEMY.

This institution was the result of a voluntary subscription on the part of the citizens of Clearcreek township. Those favoring the enterprise formed a joint stock company, agreeing to name the institution, "The Savannah Male and Female Academy." The required stock was secured and the necessary buildings erected. A board of trustees was elected, consisting of Dr. John Ingram, Dr. Thomas Hayes, Rev. Alex. Scott, A. F. Shaw, Daniel G. Templeton, Rev. R. Newton, Rev. A. Rumfield, John R. Bailey, Rev. John Bryte, Samuel Gault, James Heant, Jared N. Slonaker, Joseph McCutchin, Dr. W. S. Shaw, S. Shaw, and Mead Fancher. One-third of the board served three years, one-third two, and one-third one year. Daniel G. Templeton was elected president, Rev. A. Riverfield vice-president, Dr. J. Ingram secretary, and Mead Fancher treasurer. The school was to be non-sectarian. The board elected Professor E. J. Rice, of Sullivan, principal; Miss — Foster and Miss — Rice, graduates, took charge of the female department. Rev. A. Scott was elected professor of moral science, Rev. R. Newton of history, and Dr. John Ingram of natural science. The course of study in the male department was quite thorough, and that of the female department was preparatory for graduation. Professor Rice served about two years, and was succeeded by Rev. A. Scott as principal, and Dr. J. Ingram as assistant. Miss — Stafford and Miss — Rutan had charge of the female department. In 1862, Professor C. K. Geddes was elected principal, while Miss M. Boynton took charge of the female department. Upon the resignation of Professor Geddes, Rev. Samuel F. Boyd became principal and Professor Elias Fraemfelter associate. Miss Mattie Franks took charge of the female department. Upon the resignation of Professor Boyd, Professor J. Peoples became principal, and, upon his retirement, Professor J. A. Brown took charge of the institution. The academy came under the control of the presbytery of Wooster in 1875. A committee of five was appointed to co-operate with the original trustees, who continue to be elected as in the organization of the institution. The property is valued at about four thousand dollars.

PERRYSVILLE ACADEMY.

This institution was erected in 1871. It is thirty-two by forty-five feet, two stories high, and cost about three thousand five hundred dollars. It is eligibly situated, and deserves a liberal patronage. Professor J. C. Sample has been the principal since the erection of the academy. It originated from a select school, in 1869, under Professor Sample. He opened the school and met with flattering success. The project of erecting an academy was put on foot, and resulted in that institution. The average number of students is about seventy-five. The advanced branches are taught, and many teachers are departing from the school annually. Their influence is felt in many parts of the county.

ASHLAND COLLEGE.

For many years the Church of the Brethren (Tunkers) had under consideration the propriety of establishing an institution for the higher education of the sons and daughters in that denomination, and had made a number of attempts in this direction at Berlin, and at Plum Creek, Pennsylvania, and at Bourbon, Indiana, all of which efforts had failed; but the friends of the movement in northeastern Ohio, undaunted by previous reverses, determined to make their enterprise a success, and solicited S. Z. Sharp, their professor in Marysville college, Tennessee, to sever his connection with that institution and throw his entire energy into this new enterprise. After several refusals, he at last consented, and in June, 1877, made a tour through a part of this State in search of a suitable location. The choice of himself and friends was nearly unanimous in favor of Ashland, and when this was well discussed by the friends of the movement, the matter was laid before some of the most influential citizens of Ashland, who at once caught the spirit, called a meeting in the city hall, where an unusually large and enthusiastic audience was addressed by the present president of the college, S. Z. Sharp, who set forth the object of the founders to be to establish a college equal to any in the State; that it would be under the care of the Church of the Brethren to the same extent that other colleges were under the care of their religious bodies; that among the prominent features of the institution would be thorough scholarship, and the cultivation of a sentiment among the students to appreciate solid worth rather than vain show; and that plain, neat attire, and a richly stored mind, were better than a gaudy dress and an empty mind. After hearing the plan and aims of the proposed institution, the citizens of Ashland unanimously endorsed the project, and at once raised ten thousand dollars towards the erection of the college building. The most beautiful site in this part of the State was selected. A campus of twenty-seven acres of land was bought for six thousand three hundred and thirty-three dollars, and a building erected which is at this writing nearly completed, and will cost, including material, work, supervision, furniture, apparatus and cabinet, sixty thousand dollars. The college building is one hundred feet front, one hundred deep, four stories high, built of brick, roofed with slate, and, for substantial construction and convenience, has few equals. There is also a boarding hall one hundred and ten feet long, forty feet wide and four stories high, which, when completed, will cost between ten and eleven thousand dollars.

A charter was obtained February 22, 1878, by which the institution is placed under the care of members of the church of the Brethren, and put upon an equal footing with any other college in the State. The charter provides for the following courses of instruction: classical, philosophical, normal and commercial.

The college was formally opened September 17, 1879, with a full corps of instructors, as follows: Elder S. Z. Sharp, A. M., president, professor of mental and moral philosophy; L. Huber, A. M., professor of Latin and modern languages; J. E. Stubbs, A. M., professor of Greek language and literature; David Bailey, A. M., professor of mathematics; Jacob Keim, Ph. D., professor of natural science; J. C. Ewing, professor of music; Mrs. C. P. Chapman, teacher of painting and drawing.

The first term closed December 24, 1879, with one hundred and twelve pupils enrolled, and was regarded as a decided success in every respect.

ASHLAND CITY CHURCH.

The Ashland City Church of the Brethren (Dunkard) was organized May 22, 1879, with S. Z. Sharp as elder in charge, and S. H. Basher, assistant in the ministry. J. H. Worst was also called to the ministry, on the day of organization; and J. N. Roop and E. J. Worst, deacons. The membership enrolled at that time was forty-three, which has increased since to sixty-five. The congregation worships every Sabbath in the chapel of Ashland college, and has a Sunday school of over one hundred members. The *Gospel Preacher*, having a circulation of about five thousand, and *Our Sunday School*, a juvenile weekly, having nearly six thousand subscribers, are published in Ashland, under the auspices of the Brethren church.

CHAPTER XXXII.
RELIGIOUS SOCIETIES AND CHURCHES.

The Eckley Church.—The Presbyterians.—Methodist Episcopal Churches.—The Evangelical Lutheran.—Baptists and Disciples.—German Baptists, or Tunkers.—The Evangelical Association.—German Reformed.—Catholics.

IN the early settlements of the territory now composing Ashland county, there were but few organized churches. An occasional minister, of the Presbyterian or Methodist persuasions, traversed this region. The pioneers, for a number of years, assembled in a log cabin to hear preaching. If the weather permitted, people often gathered in the forest, and sometimes in a log barn to hear a new minister. As the country improved, and the settlements became more densely populated, religious societies of kindred faith, by voluntary contributions of labor, prepared timber, and other necessary materials, began the erection of small hewed log churches, and employed a preacher to deliver an occasional discourse. In this way, all the early organizations struggled along from year to year, until Providence enabled them to build more elegant structures for public worship.

The name of the first organized religious association, within the present limits of the county, remains in some uncertainty. The Eckley church, a log building, in the northeast part of Vermillion township, was undoubtedly the first church edifice erected within the county. We understand, however, that it was a union building, and free to all Protestant ministers, and was long so used by all denominations. The Methodists being much more numerous, occupied the building the major part of the time for many years.

THE PRESBYTERIANS.

Upon carefully comparing traditions, we are inclined to the opinion that the first organized congregation was within the present limits of Montgomery township. The membership was largely composed of the residents of Milton township. It was organized by the settlers of 1815-16, who were the descendants of the Scotch-Irish. In 1816 these people, mostly from western Pennsylvania, were visited by Rev. Joshua Beer, who preached a few sermons in the cabins of the pioneers, and became a candidate for settlement among the congregation then organizing. About the same time Rev. William Mathews also became a candidate for employment. Upon consultation, the members gave Mr. Mathews the preference, and employed him one-third of the time. The balance of the time was divided between Mt. Hope, in Perry, and Jeromeville, in Mohican township, where a few Presbyterians were beginning to organize, with a view of erecting churches. In 1817 the Hopewell congregation was organized, and twenty-two persons received on certificates and twelve on examination. In 1818 Robert Nelson and Abraham Doty were elected elders, ordained and installed. The members, so far as we can learn, were Robert Nelson, Abraham Doty, David McKinney, William Huston, David Pollock, Abel Montgomery, William Andrews, George Ryall, Samuel Burns, David Burns, Jasper Snook, James Clingin, James Ferguson, Hance Hamilton, Thomas Cook, Robert Culbertson, Isaac Mathews, Jesse Mathews, William Lions, John Hall, George Hall, Samuel Urie, James Black, William Shilling, and their wives, and Mrs. Jane Burgett, Mrs. Mary Stevenson, Mary Vanoshand, Susan Vanmeter, Nancy Owens, Margaret and Mary Owens, Mary Callen, Nancy Starret, Obediah Ferrell, John Crabs, John Prosser, Joseph Scott, Elisha Kelley, and Cornelius Eaton.

In 1819 a hewed log church, thirty by thirty-five feet, was erected one and a half miles west of Uniontown, now Ashland, on what is now the Olivesburgh road. According to the recollection of Mr. John Nelson, son of Robert, "the building had a cabin roof, plank floors and door, plank benches without backs or cushions, the windows very high from the ground, the pulpit elevated after the old style, four or five steps, and boarded as high as a man's shoulders. The church was heated, in winter, by a large box-stove, capable of receiving four-foot wood. The building was erected by the voluntary efforts of the pioneers and members, some furnishing a quota of hewn timber, others, plank and boards, and others, clapboards, sash, glass and nails, while others, with teams, hauled the materials to the ground where the church was to be erected. William Andrews and George Ryall, excellent singers, were chosen to conduct the music. They were stationed near the pulpit, on a platform, where they read two lines of a psalm or hymn—

> "And are we wretches yet alive,
> And do we yet rebel?"

and sang, the congregation joining as the leaders proceeded to read and sing."

These services—reading, singing, and preaching—began about ten o'clock in the forenoon, and continued until about twelve o'clock, when there was a recess, after which the services were renewed for one or two hours. In the absence of the pastor, a reader was selected from among the church officers, who read a printed or written discourse for the edification of the members. This task frequently fell upon Elder Robert Nelson, who is said to have been a fluent reader. It was not uncommon, at that period, for members and others to ride or walk three or four miles, along the forest paths, to attend day and evening meetings.

We have been thus careful in the description of the early practices of the pioneers, for the reason that all other denominations passed through a similar routine until their organization and membership were sufficient to warrant the erection of denominational church buildings.

The Rev. William Mathews continued, a portion of his time at Hopewell, until 1821, and was succeeded by Rev. Robert Lee, who remained until 1826, when he was succeeded by Rev. William Mathews, who devoted one-third of his time, until 1833, when he was succeeded by Rev. James Robinson, who gave half his time, until 1837, the congregation, in the meantime, increasing to about one hundred and fifty members. In 1837–38 a lot was purchased in Ashland, and a large frame church erected thereon, and the old church was abandoned.

The minister officiating at that time was Rev. Samuel Hare. In 1839 Rev. S. N. Barnes supplied the pulpit. He was succeeded by Rev. Robert Fulton, then principal of Ashland academy. He remained until 1841, and was succeeded by Rev. James Robinson, who remained until 1843, when he was succeeded by Rev. Samuel Moody, who was pastor until his demise, in 1856.

The church building, soon after, became the property of the Catholics, the congregation having dissolved and connected with other churches.

The Jeromeville Presbyterian church, in point of time, succeeds Hopewell. The congregation was organized as early as 1817, and Rev. William Mathews divided his time with Rehoboth, as it was called in 1820, and Hopewell. The first church edifice was erected in 1820. Mr. Mathews was succeeded, in 1820, by Rev. Robert Lee, and he, in 1829, by Rev. R. Brown, who remained until 1832. He was succeeded by the following, in the order named: Revs. Robert Fulton, Samuel Fulton, William Colmary, S. Diefendorf, and Thomas Beer. The last named remained until 1857, and was succeeded by Rev. James Bower. In the meantime, after 1830, Revs. Samuel Baldridge, Joseph Wylie, Benjamin Lowe, and J. W. Knott are believed to have acted as supplies. The membership is thirty-five.

The Mt. Hope Presbyterian church, in the northeast part of Perry township, was organized in 1820, and a small log building erected. At that period, it was known as the "Muddy Fork church," being situated near that stream. In 1831, the name was changed. Its first pastor was Rev. William Mathews, who, at that time, had charge of Hopewell, near Ashland. He was succeeded by Rev. Robert Lee. In 1829, Rev. R. Brown became pastor. He preached also at Congress and Jeromeville. In 1834, Rev. Thomas Beer took charge of the church. In 1836, the building was accidentally burned. In 1841, a new church was built. Mr. Beer remained until 1857, when he was succeeded by Rev. T. B. VanEmmons. The church ceased to exist in 1861–2, having lost its membership by emigration.

The Perrysville Presbyterian church was organized as early as 1818, by Rev. S. Baldridge. He remained some time, and was succeeded by Rev. William Hughes, in 1829. The present church building was erected in 1865, and is thirty-four by fifty-five feet, and has a bell. The building is neat, and cost three thousand dollars. The church also possesses an organ. The original elders were Thomas Coulter, John VanHorn, and George Crawford. The Rev. William Hughes, who filled its pulpit for thirty-seven years, retired in 1866, in consequence of age and feeble health. He states that, when he came, there were no church buildings in either Hanover or Lake, and but one in Green township. The membership is one hundred and twenty-five.

The Lake Fork Presbyterian church was organized in 1826, through the efforts of Rev. Samuel Baldridge. The congregation met in the cabins of the pioneers, until 1831, and in 1832 erected a church. The congregation, always small, ceased to exist in 1858, since which time there has been no regular service.

The Savannah Presbyterian congregation was organized by Rev. Robert Lee, in 1833. He and Rev. William Mathews are believed to have supplied the church, occasionally, as ministers, until 1840, when Rev. F. A. Shearer succeeded to the pastorship of the church, and continued two years. In 1845, Rev. W. C. Kniffin became pastor, remaining three years; and in 1848, Rev. W. T. Adams became the pastor, and remained two years. In 1856, Rev. A. Scott became its pastor, and remained until 1872. In the interval between 1850 and 1856, Rev. William Bonar, Rev. James Anderson, and Rev. Jacob Coon, labored as supplies. The membership, at present, is one hundred and seventy-eight; and Rev. John Kelley is pastor. In 1861, the church building was considerably enlarged and improved.

The Orange Presbyterian church was organized in 1834, principally through the efforts of Rev. William Mathews. In 1835, Rev. Nathaniel Cobb was pastor; and in 1841, Rev. F. A. Shearer became pastor, devoting one-third of his time. In 1843, Rev. Samuel Moody became its pastor, dividing his time equally between Hopewell and Orange. He continued until his decease, in 1856; when Rev. A. Scott become its pastor, and continued until 1872. Rev. S. T. Boyd, the present pastor, was his successor. The number of members is about eighty.

The United Presbyterian church of Hayesville was organized in 1838, by Rev. Samuel Hindman. He had preached in Hayesville occasionally, one or two years prior to that time. He devoted one-fourth of his time to Hayesville, and the balance to Mansfield, Iberia, and Savannah. He retired in 1842. In 1844 Rev. J. L. McLain took charge of the congregation, dividing his time equally between Mansfield and Hayesville. He retired in 1855. From that period until 1856, the church had occasional supplies. In 1856, Rev. J. Y. Ashenhust became the pastor, dividing his time equally between Savannah and Hayesville. In 1859, after the union of the associate reformed churches, Mr. Ashenhust confined his services to Hayesville. The present membership is about eighty.

The First Presbyterian church of Ashland, in consequence of a division in Hopewell, on the subject of music and modes of worship, was organized in 1841. The congregation of Hopewell opposed choir music. Those concurring in the propriety of a choir, after a number of conferences and consultations, withdrew from the mother church, and established a new one, which received the name of the First Presbyterian church of Ashland.

The new congregation erected a fine free-stone building, forty-three by sixty-five feet, and fifteen years afterward increased its length to eighty-four feet, and otherwise greatly improved it. It has a large bell and a good organ. It was served by Rev. Robert and Samuel Fulton, as supplies, until 1843, when Rev. John Robinson became the pastor, and has continued ever since, a period of over thirty-one years. It has prospered greatly under his ministry, and now contains a membership of about three hundred and twenty.

The Second Presbyterian church of Ashland was removed in 1879, and a new and handsome brick church built by the congregation, at an expense of about twenty-five thousand dollars, on the old location. The present structure presents an imposing appearance, and retains the old bell.

The Presbyterian church of Hayesville was organized in 1846, through the efforts of Rev. Benjamin T. Lowe, who divided his time between the churches of Jeromeville and Hayesville. Rev. William W. Calmary succeeded the former, and remained until 1850, when he was succeeded by Rev. S. Diefendorf. In 1852, he was succeeded by Rev. Jacob Coon. In 1853 he resigned, and the church remained without a stated minister until 1854, when Rev. Diefendorf again supplied the pulpit. In 1859, a new frame building was erected by the congregation, and Mr. Diefendorf continued, as supply. The church, at present, has no minister. The membership is about one hundred.

The Mifflin Presbyterian congregation was organized in 1851, through the efforts of Rev. W. T. Adams. The membership being too feeble to erect a church building, worshipped in the union church, which was erected in 1851, and occupied by the Baptists, Albrights, Methodists, and Presbyterians, jointly. The congregation ceased to exist, through inability to sustain the preaching of the gospel, in 1854.

The Free Presbyterian church of Savannah was organized in 1851, by Rev. F. M. Finney. It had but fourteen members at its organization. The congregation still occupies the Associate Reform church. It has not increased largely in members, and at present has no minister.

The United Presbyterian church of Savannah was organized in 1858. Its membership was derived from the union of the Associate and Reformed Presbyterian churches. The membership is now believed to be about one hundred. The first pastor was Rev. J. Y. Ashenhust. In 1861 Rev. William Bruce became the stated supply. The congregation occupies the Free Presbyterian church, and the present pastor is Rev. Mr. Miller.

The Associate Reformed Presbyterians of Savannah organized as early as 1831, the Rev. James Johnson being the first minister. He was succeeded by Rev. James Arbuthnot. The congregation erected a house of worship in 1834, and a new and more commodious one in 1845. Originally the church was the strongest in Clearcreek township, having among its members some of the most influential of the pioneers, among whom were the McMeekins, the Welshes, the Hearsts, the Paxtons, the Dunlaps, the Marshalls, Longbridges and Craytons, of Scotch-Irish descent. We are unable to give the exact number of members.

The Presbyterian church of Savannah, presided over by Rev. Kelley, removed their old church in 1879, and built a new one at an expense of about five thousand dollars. It is a frame, has a bell, and presents a fine appearance. It is located a little east of the old church on another lot.

The Presbyterians of the village of Polk, in Jackson township, formerly connected with the Orange church, erected a handsome frame edifice in 1875. The exact number of members we are unable to give. The minister is Rev. Samuel T. Boyd.

The Loudonville Presbyterian church was organized in 1873. The pastor was Rev. Homer Sheely. In 1874 he resigned, in consequence of ill health. In 1875 a neat church edifice was erected. The membership is about fifty. The present pastor is the Rev. F. R. Davis.

METHODIST EPISCOPAL CHURCHES.

The first Methodist preachers held their meetings in the cabins of the pioneers until a sufficient number of members were obtained to form a class, with leaders. When the membership became sufficiently numerous, small log or frame churches were erected, and their congregations speedily enlarged. As communities improved in wealth and means, a new era dawned, log churches disappeared, and neat frame or brick structures took their place. The circuits were large, and traveled on horseback. The early preachers were proverbial for their good horses. Strong, active animals were chosen. In making the round of their circuits through the forests, across the valleys and amid the hills of Ohio, in the inclement seasons of the year, these animals often carried their faithful riders across swollen streams and through bogs and swampy paths to their appointments. The characteristic hat, white cravat, and Quaker coat, of the Methodist preacher, enabled the pioneer to recognize his mission. The zeal and energy manifested by the early Methodist preachers captivated the plain settlers; and small classes were formed in almost every section of the country.

The first church building occupied by the Methodist people of this county, is believed to have been erected by George Eckley and his neighbors, in the northeast part of Vermillion township, in 1816 or 1818, and was free to all Protestant denominations. Mr. Eckley was a member of the Methodist Episcopal church, and that people being the most numerous in the settlement, occupied the church—a plain log building,—the major part of the time. At an early day, a number of quarterly conferences were held at this church. The members from a distance prepared and brought food from home, upon which to subsist during the progress of the meetings. In fact, Methodism radiated from "Eckley's" to every part of the county, and that church must be credited with being the originator of Methodism in this region. The old church has long since tumbled into ruins; and a more showy frame structure, known as "Newman's church," occupies its place. The membership is small.

The Methodist Episcopal church of Ashland, was organized in 1823. The first class was composed of the following members: Jacob Grubb and wife, James Hull and wife, Elijah Oram and wife, James Kent and wife, Therygood Smith and wife, James Swaney and wife, John Smith and wife, Mrs. Henry Gamble, Belinda and Mary Smith. James Swaney was the first class leader. The class was organized by Revs. James Hazard and James Haney. It met at the house of John Smith, (which stood near the site of the brick residence of the late Christopher Mykrantz,) for a number of years. In the meantime, Father Goff McIntire, and Rev. H. O. Sheldon, are remembered as having traveled this circuit. In 1835—6, the congregation erected a large freestone church in which they worshipped until 1847, when it was disposed of to the county commissioners for a temporary court house. In 1848, a new brick church was commenced. It was about ten years before it was completed throughout. It is fifty by eighty-five feet, and has a basement for class rooms and official meetings—a choir and melodeon and a good bell. The church is frescoed and the seats are neatly arranged and finished. The membership is about three hundred.

In this, as in all the other Methodist churches of this county, it is impracticable to give a full list of ministers, owing to the fact that they have been changed every one or two years.

The Methodist Episcopal church of Orange was organized in 1830, and a small church erected. In 1853 the present edifice, forty by sixty feet, was built. Vachel Metcalf and John Sloan were very active in organizing the first class. The Reverends Elmer Yocum and John Jaynes were the first circuit preachers. The early members were John Sloan, Vachel Metcalf, Jacob Fluke, John, Isaac and Andrew Mason, Wesley Richards, Isaac Gordon, Thomas Richards, Henry Gill, George Koontz, John Fluke and their wives. The present membership is about one hundred and fifty.

The Jeromeville Methodist Episcopal church was organized in 1820, and a log church built. The first class was composed of the following members: Luke Ingmand, Edmund Ingmand, Robert Copels, Samuel Warner, John Naylor and their wives, Mrs. Ezra Warner and daughters. Preaching was at first held in cabins, and sometimes in the forest, until the first church was built. The congregation, in 1858, erected a new frame church. The membership is now about one hundred.

The Hayesville Methodist Episcopal church was organized about the year 1830. A class had been formed prior to that time, and preaching held in the cabins of the pioneers. The first church was of logs, twenty-eight by thirty-five feet. In 1855 the congregation erected a new frame church thirty-eight by fifty feet. The present number of members is one hundred and fifty.

The Ford Methodist Episcopal church, of Clearcreek township, was erected in 1830, by the voluntary contributions of the pioneers of Clearcreek. From about the year 1821 the cabin of Thomas Ford was the prominent place for public worship. A large class was formed, principally through the exertions of Father Goff and Rev. James Haney. Thomas Ford was a zealous and influential member. When the new church was completed the quarterly conferences were held in it for several years. We are unable to give the present number of members, probably about fifty.

The McKay Methodist Episcopal church was organized by the formation of a class in 1834, and in 1837, after having had preaching in cabins for some time, a neat church was erected at the corners. The church subsequently became a union church, owing to its feeble membership, and is now free to all Protestant denominations.

The Loudonville Methodist Episcopal church was organized in 1834, by the formation of a class, by Rev. Elijah Yocum. The class and congregation met in the warehouse of Thomas McMahon. A church twenty-four by thirty-six feet was erected in 1836. In 1856 a new church, forty by fifty feet, was built. The membership is about one hundred.

The Mohicanville Methodist Episcopal church was organized by Rev. Elijah Yocum, as a class, in 1828. The congregation, for some years, met in cabins and a log school-house, near the village. In 1844 the congregation built the present church. Its members number about seventy.

The Rowsburgh Methodist Episcopal church was originally organized, as a class, in 1822, at the house of the late John Helman, north of the village, and continued to meet, for preaching, at his house, for about thirty years. In 1854 a church, thirty-eight by fifty feet, was built in the village. The present number of members is about seventy.

The Perrysville Methodist Episcopal church was built in 1871, and cost one thousand five hundred dollars. It has a good bell, and is neat in all its arrangements. It is thirty-two by fifty feet, and heated by a furnace. Its membership is about seventy-five.

The Polk Methodist Episcopal church was organized some time prior to 1839, as a class. In that year a church was built. The congregation, at that time, belonged to the Ashland circuit. Its leading members were the Bryans, Chilcotes, Richards, Proudfits, Ruffcorns, Gordons and Barracks. It has now about sixty-five members.

The Perrysburgh Methodist Episcopal church was organized in 1839 by Rev. John Mitchell. Its members were the Coles, Buchanans, Bryans, Berrys, Withouts, Reeds, Smiths, and others. The church was built in the year 1839. Its membership numbers about seventy-five.

The Lake Fork Methodist Episcopal church was erected in 1838. It is twenty-eight by thirty-four feet. A class had been formed some time prior to that time. Elijah Yocum was quite active as a local preacher in that part of the county, and was influential in the promotion of many classes, which subsequently increased in numbers until a small church was built. The present membership is small. In 1876 a new church was built, which cost two thousand five hundred dollars. It is finely finished and frescoed.

The North Orange Methodist Episcopal church was erected in 1848, and had but eleven members. It is twenty-five by thirty feet. The members now number about sixty.

The Hammond Methodist Episcopal church, in the northwest part of Vermillion township, was erected in 1852. It is a neat frame building. The membership numbers about sixty.

The Sherradden Methodist Episcopal church, in the east part of Montgomery township, was erected sometime between 1830 and 1835. It was torn down about 1870, and a neat frame, twenty-five by thirty-five feet, erected. The membership is not large.

The Methodist Episcopal church of Savannah was erected in 1838. It was deeded to John Freeborn, Adam Smith, Thomas Ford, Anthony McLaughlin, and A. G. Richardson, as trustees, from James Burgan, being lot ninety-nine. It has been repaired at different times, and is now known as in Savannah circuit. Its present membership is about fifty. Mr. Joseph McCutchin, our informant, has been a member and leader for twenty-five years. The congregation have also a parsonage, which was erected in 1868.

The Ruggles Methodist Episcopal church, thirty-six by fifty-two feet, was built in 1873, and has a good bell. The building is a neat frame. The membership is sixty.

The Troy Center Methodist Episcopal church, a neat frame, forty by sixty feet, with a good bell, was erected in 1870. The membership is about one hundred and sixty.

The Troy Center United Brethren church, thirty by forty-five feet, with a bell, was erected in 1874. The members number sixty.

The South Troy Union church, thirty by forty-five feet, mostly occupied by the United Brethren, was erected in 1870. Membership small.

In addition to the ministers already mentioned, we are informed that the following have traveled curcuits and been located within this county: Russell Bigelow, William B. Christie, Henry O. Sheldon, Elmer Yocum, Edward Thompson, H. L. Harris, Thomas Barkdull, John H. Power, Adam Poe, J. McMahon, David Gray, Peter Sharp, John Wheeler, John Mitchell, James McNabb, Jesse Warner, Joseph Kennedy, Philip R. Roseberry, James Sutherland, John Sloan, Joshua Carr, James Fast, James A. Kellam, H. L. Parish, H. G. Duboise, L. Parker, E. Bush, T. Hildreth, E. C. Gault, Hiram M. Shaffer, Rolla H. Chubb, P. B. Stroup, and A. L. Yourtee. The majority of the foregoing ministers were noted for their talents and efficiency in the pulpit. Of course, there were many others, but want of space prevents the appearance of their names.

THE EVANGELICAL LUTHERANS.

The membership of the Lutheran church is largely composed of Pennsylvanians, and the descendants of Germans. It is a strong denomination, and its ministers are now generally educated in colleges founded by the Lutherans.

The Ashland Lutheran church is believed to have been organized in 1839. It originated from the efforts of Rev. W. J. Sloan, who became its first minister. The late Christian Miller, sr., and Jacob Young, were among its leading members. The first church was located one mile north of Ashland, on the Troy road. In 1842 the congregation purchased a small church from the Universalists on the corner of Orange and Third streets, which was occupied until 1852, when the present brick church, forty by sixty feet, was erected on Third, between Orange and Church streets. It is a good building, neatly seated, and has a bell. The ministers have been: W. J. Sloan, E. Eastman, J. J. Hoffman, William A. G. Emerson, S. Ritz, Isaac Culler, Samuel McReynolds, V. A. G. Emerson, A. H. Myers, J. W. Swick, and M. L. Wilhelm. The church is in a prosperous condition. The membership is about two hundred and eighty:

The following is an extract from the sermon of Rev. O. Wilhelm, on the history of the Lutheran church in Ashland:

About 1820 Father Stough preached to the scattered Lutherans of this county. The Masons, Crouses, Youngs, and Branderberrys were among the membership. He introduced revivals, and the doctrine that "for every drop of intoxicants distilled the distillers would have to sweat drops in hell." He is now dead.

About 1830 F. J. Ruth came and preached in school-houses, dwellings, and in the open air to the Lutherans and citizens, catechised, and held revival meetings with great success. He still lives in Galion, Ohio, and preaches regularly. Rev. Shew organized a congregation of Germans about the same time, and built the Neff church, one mile north of Ashland, on the present site of Peter Dessenberg's residence. All that remains of that congregation has been absorbed in this congregation.

Rev. W. J. Sloan came about 1838, and organized this congregation in 1839, preaching in the Neff church a short time, then in a school-house in Ashland, then the brewery which stood on the southwest corner of Orange and Third streets was purchased and converted into a church. W. Imhoff and —— Weber were deacons, Alexander McClelland and Father Young, elders, in this organization. Father Sloan still lives in Wooster, Ohio.

Rev. E. Eastman succeeded in 1844, and continued two years. He is now dead.

Rev. Hoffman came in 1846, and continued one year. He is also dead, and his memory sacred.

Rev. W. A. G. Emerson took charge in 1847. During his ministry great meetings were held, and many converted. The present building was erected at a cost of three thousand dollars. Alexander McClelland, Henry Woods, and S. Bauchman, were the building committee; Henry Woods, carpenter; S. Bauchman, brick-mason. Rev. Richard Emerson preached the dedication sermon. A. McClelland, B. Grosscup, D. Grosscup, W. Imhoff, Jacob Stoner, and S. Bauchman, were among the contributors. The Sabbath school was organized at this time; W. A. G. Emerson was the first superintendent, and Abraham Hoffman the first lay superintendent.

Rev. S. Ritz followed, and continued two and one-half years, with great success, directing his efforts against formalism and drunkenness. He left in 1853, and has since gone over the river.

Rev. Isaac Culler came in 1855, and continued two years. He is now living in Richland county, Ohio.

Rev. S. W. McReynolds took charge in 1858; continued two and one-half years, leaving January 1, 1861. To him is due the honor of instituting the church records. He found eighty-four members, and added forty-three.

Rev. W. A. G. Emerson was recalled April 1, 1861, and continued to labor to October 1, 1862, when he entered the army as chaplain. He added sixty-four to the church.

Rev. A. H. Myers took charge October 1, 1862, and continued four and one-half years. During this time, the civil war raged. Seventy-six were added to the church. He is now dead, having died most gloriously in our common faith.

Rev. J. W. Swick took charge May 1, 1866, continuing to December 1, 1874, making a term of eight years and seven months. During his ministry the church was extensively repaired, the present parsonage built, and two hundred and seventy-three added to the church. He still lives, and preaches in Leetonia, Ohio.

Rev. M. L. Wilhelm, your present pastor, took charge June 20, 1875, having been here one year. Fifty-four have been added, and concord prevails. This makes thirteen pastors who have served this charge, six of whom are dead, seven still living. During this time, fifty-four members have died.

There have been not less than eight hundred connected with the church; two hundred and eighty-nine answer to their names now, five hundred have died, or been dismissed by letter to unite elsewhere, and wandered we know not where. Where, O! where are the five hundred? There has been not less than an average of one thousand dollars contributed each year to the necessities of the church, making in all thirty-seven thousand dollars. Let the congregation but maintain the principles of its origin and history, and its future will be alike glorious for, first, piety; second, temperance; third, benevolence. Its means of success, first, prayer; second, labor; third, sacrifice. Do but this and the future will surpass the past.

Prior to 1839, say from 1825, the German Reformed and Lutherans, new school, had formed an organization in Ashland, to which the German Reformed ministers preached. About 1832, Rev. Francis Ruth, new school, preached alternately with a German Reformed minister, to a small number of members, who assembled in a brick school-house in Ashland. Mr. Ruth preached until Rev. Mr. Coon, German Reformed, took charge of the organization. Under Mr. Sloan, the Evangelicals and German Reformed separated, and formed the new church.

The Hanover Evangelical Lutheran and German Reformed church, in the southeast part of Hanover township, was built in 1846. The Evangelical Lutherans subsequently occupied the church. The Rev. M. Hartsbarger has been the regular minister. The membership is small.

The Loudonville Lutheran church was built in 1861, on the site of the German Reformed church, which had been accidentally burned in 1860. The minister was Rev. M. Hartsbarger. The membership is small.

The new German Reformed church, of Loudonville, was built in 1861, and Rev. Mr. Greenline became its minister. It is feeble in point of membership.

The German Evangelical, or Mennonite, church, of the northwest part of Vermillion township, was erected in 1847. The late Rev. John Risser was the first pastor. The church subsequently became the property of the Germans and Lutherans. The building is twenty-eight by thirty-six feet.

The German Reformed and Lutheran church in the Finger settlement, in Orange township, twenty-eight by fifty feet, was built in 1859. The original German Reformed church was built in 1832. Rev. D. R. Moore was the stated minister for several years. The membership is about seventy-five.

The Canaan German Reformed and Lutheran church, on lands of Samuel Maxhammer, in Orange township, was built in 1850. It is thirty by forty-five feet. The membership is small, and they have no stated minister.

The St. Jacob's German Reformed, in the east part of Orange township, was built in 1853. It is twenty-four by thirty-six feet. It has about fifty members. It has, at present, only occasional preaching.

The Evangelical Lutherans, of Jeromeville, built a church in 1850, thirty-six by forty-six feet. It has been very prosperous. The present number of members is one hundred.

The German Reformed church, of Mohicanville, was organized in 1859. It has seventy members. The minister is Rev. H. H. Sandoe.

The Evangelical Lutherans organized under Rev. W. J. Sloan, in Rowsburgh, in 1842, and erected a church thirty by forty-five feet. Mr. Sloan continued to preach for some time. Rev. Richard D. Emerson subsequently took charge of the congregation. The membership is now about one hundred and twenty-five.

The German Reformed and Lutherans built a church on the present site of the village of Polk, in Jackson township, in 1830. A small congregation organized in 1827. In 1840-41, the members of Orange township withdrew, and those remaining in Jackson town erected a new church, thirty-five by forty feet, half a mile west of Perrysburgh. It has about seventy-five members.

The Evangelical Lutherans, of Mifflin, organized soon after the separation of the German Reformed, and erected a church, which was accidentally burned in 1860. A new church has since been built. The late Michael Culler, a wealthy and zealous member, contributed largely to the support of the church. Its early ministers were Revs. F. Ruth and W. A. G. Emerson.

The German Lutherans, about 1840, built a good frame church four miles southwest of Ashland, on the Mansfield road. Its membership is small, and there is no regular minister.

The Lutherans of Ruggles township built a church in 1852, twenty-six by thirty feet, in which irregular services are held. The congregation is small.

THE BAPTISTS AND DISCIPLES.

The Baptists, in the early history of the county, were quite numerous, and had a number of small churches in which their people assembled for preaching. Sometime prior to 1824, the Baptists organized a small congregation in Ashland. Rev. John Rigdon became the stated minister. His labors were successful, and the church was prosperous. Sometime after the organization in Ashland, Alexander Campbell, of Bethany, Virginia, became the leader and exponent of certain reforms in the doctrines and modes of church government in the Baptist organization. Those adopting his views were admitted into what is now known as the Disciple or Christian church, having withdrawn from the Baptist organization. Mr. Rigdon passed under censure for accepting and teaching the ideas advocated by Mr. Campbell, withdrew and joined in organizing the present Disciple church of Ashland.

Those adhering to the Baptist organization, met at the Neoff church, on the Troy road, one mile north of Ashland, until about 1849, when the congregation ceased to exist, because of the migration of its members to the west. Rev. Solomon Neoff was the last pastor. In 1860 a few Baptists, who had in the meantime located in and about Ashland, through the efforts of Rev. I. N. Carman, erected a neat frame church in South Ashland. He was its pastor for some years. It is feeble in membership, and has no stated minister at present.

The Baptist church of Taylor's corners, in Green township, was erected in 1837. It was of brick, thirty-five by forty-four feet. The organization prospered, and some thirty-two years afterward—1869, the old church was torn down, and a neat frame, thirty-two by forty-six feet, built. The McGuires, Gladdens, Rices, and other leading families, are active members. Rev. Mr. Tulloss, of Knox county, was recently the minister. It has about sixty members.

The Perrysville Baptist church was erected in 1865, and is thirty-four by fifty feet. It is a neat structure, and cost two thousand five hundred dollars. It has about sixty members. The present minister is Rev. Mr. Wiley.

The Loudonville Baptist church was formed as early as 1839. It was organized by Rev. Mr. Willson. The building is a frame, forty by forty-five feet, and was erected in 1843. The ministers have been Revs. Willson, Stearns, Thomas, Lecte, Eddy, and Seigfried.

The Hayesville Baptist church was erected in 1842. Rev. John Cox, late of Mansfield, was perhaps the earliest minister at Hayesville. Rev. Granger, of Granville, preached occasionally at this church. The church some years since, owing to a feeble membership, ceased to exist.

The Baptist church at Weddel's corners, in Vermillion township, was organized in 1869, and a neat frame building, thirty by forty feet, erected. It has about one hundred members. Rev. S. Stanley is the minister.

The Sullivan Baptists organized about 1830, and held their meetings in the town hall, until 1837, when, under the exertions of Elder Freeman, a frame church was erected, in which the congregation still worships. The membership is small.

The Baptists organized and erected a small church in Savannah about 1830, which continued to exist until about 1850. It finally yielded to the zeal of the Disciples. Elder Andrew Barnes was among its latest preachers.

The Disciple church was organized in Ashland in the fall of 1836, by James Porter, and erected a building in 1842 on Orange street. Prior to the erection of said church, the congregation met in the Universalist church at the corner of Third and Orange streets (subsequently the property of the Lutherans), and at the residence of John Mykrants, west of Ashland, and that of Michael Riddle, four miles east of Ashland. The original members were Frederick Sulcer and wife, John Anderson and wife, Mother Matthews and two daughters, Barbara Sigler, Mary Hazlet, Mr. Justus and wife, John Gilkerson and wife, Jonas Stough and wife, Mary Redburn, John Horick and wife, Michael Riddle and wife, John Mykrants and wife, Elizabeth Luther, Michael Shoup and wife, Isaac Van Nood Straud. Elders, Michael Riddle and John Gilkerson. Deacons, John Horick and Mr. Justus.

The Disciple or Christian church, of Ashland, was erected in 1842. We are unable to give room for a disquisition on the tenets of the church. It is sufficient to state that the modes of worship and baptism are nearly identical with the Baptists. The Disciples, however, appear to have no printed creed, each member reading and interpreting the Scriptures for himself. The ministers or elders of the church in Ashland have been John Rigdon, James Porter, John Reed, Abner Woods, Judson Benedict, Andrew Barnes, I. N. Carman, Isaiah Jones, Leroy Norton, James L. Parsons, John F. Rowe, S. E. Pearree, John Lowe, Arius Rumfield, N. P. Lawrence, M. Riddle, and others occasionally.

The Jeromeville Disciple church was organized in 1854. The church building is thirty-five by fifty feet. The Hootmans, Winbiglers and Wilsons were among the organizing members. Elder Arius Rumfield was, until recently, the minister. The church is strong in its membership.

The Clearcreek Disciple church was organized as early as 1830. It is on the southwest line of the township, and known as Bryte's church. The present church building, a neat frame, thirty by forty feet, was erected in 1853. The late David Bryte, Joseph Harvuot, Abner Mercer, Peter Vanostrand, and Philip Shriver, were among its early members and officers. Elder John Bryte has been the principal speaker for many years. The membership is about sixty.

The Sullivan Disciple church was organized about 1835. Its first members were Sylvanus Parmely, Milo Carlton, Parmely Mann, and their wives and daughters. These members seceded from the Baptist organization, and the new church was organized by Elders Almond Green and Sutton Hayden. These members were soon followed by others. In 1850 the present church was erected. The present number of members is about ninety.

THE GERMAN BAPTISTS OR TUNKERS.

As this organization has recently appeared in this region, it may be interesting to give some explanation of its faith and mode of worship, for which I am indebted to the courtesy of Professor S. Z. Sharp and David Westman, speakers in the church, who are regarded as authority in that denomination. Professor Sharp states that the following synopsis, published in the Ashland *Times*, contains a fair statement of the history and religious teachings of that people:

At the present time there are in the United States about one hundred thousand people whose religious faith and practice are very imperfectly understood by the generality of American readers, and in Europe, very little is known of them. Many papers have gone forth purporting to give a correct account of their religious tenets, and some of their peculiar principles, but, so far, have been vague and often very incorrect. This article can be strictly relied upon as being correct, and is likely the most complete account of that people that has yet been published, and is intended to set forth some of their arguments by which they defend their faith and practice, along with many of their peculiarities, for which they are noted.

In history they are generally known by the name of German Baptists, but, more commonly, among outsiders, Dunkers, or, as it is more generally spoken, Dunkards. The latter, however, are nick-names, derived from a German word, meaning *to dip*, and is somewhat expressive of their manner of baptizing. Among themselves they are known as Brethren, taken from the declaration of Christ on a certain occasion when he said: "All ye are brethren." (Matt. 23: 8).

The origin and history of this reformatory movement dates from the year 1708; having taken its rise in Germany about that time, in a portion of country where Baptists are said to have been unknown. Some eight persons in number, who had been bred Presbyterians, excepting one who was a Lutheran, became much dissatisfied with the then prevailing religious principles of the day, consorted together, in order to prayerfully read the Bible and comfort one another, and, if possible, find the old path, and walk therein, for as yet they knew not that there were any Baptist churches in existence.

After a careful study of the sacred word, they were fully convinced that faith and strict obedience in all things laid down in the perfect law of liberty, were essential to salvation, and agreed to "obey from the heart that form of doctrine once delivered unto the saints." Consequently, in the year 1708, they all repaired to the river Eder, by Schwarzenau, and were buried with Christ in baptism. They all were baptized by trine immersion, organized themselves into a church, and chose Alexander Mack for their minister. Though Alexander Mack was chosen as their first minister, yet the church has never recognized him as the originator of either their faith or practice.

They increased rapidly; their doctrine spread far and wide, and soon excited the hatred of persecution, by which they were driven from place to place, until the year 1719, when they commenced emigrating to America, and settled in the vicinity of Philadelphia and Germantown. In 1829 nearly the whole church found herself quietly settled down in the western world. Among these was their first preacher, Alexander Mack, who, though formerly a man of considerable property, was now poor in this world's goods, yet rich in grace and knowledge. He quietly settled himself on a small lot near Germantown, in the vicinity of Philadelphia. He did not live long to enjoy the quietude of a home in the new world, for only six years after his arrival in America closed his labors on earth. And now in the Brethren's public burying-ground in Germantown, the stranger is shown the spot where rests the remains of this humble and venerable reformer. He is said to have been a man of great influence in his own family. All his sons united with the church in their seventeenth year, and some of them lived to be useful men in their Master's cause.

It may be proper to observe that all the Dunkards in America have sprung from the little band of eight souls, who started up in Germany in the year 1708, and that, too, in a portion of the country where no Baptist had lived in the memory of man, and even now, none e. there. Most all reformatory movements have usually been introduced and kept up by some one of great influence and talent, but not so in this. This movement was put on foot by men and women who occupied humble positions in life, and, consequently, at the head of the organization is no man to whom the body can appeal for human authority or precedent, and, hence, in all their faith and practice they are under the necessity of appealing directly to the Scriptures, the only infallible source of correct information, for all their authority in religious practices.

This little leaven has spread itself far and wide till now nearly every State and territory has its members. They are, however, most numerous in Pennsylvania, Maryland, Virginia, Ohio, Indiana, Illinois, Kansas, Iowa and Missouri.

But while the present organization dates its history from the movement in Germany, the careful reader will observe that the rise of their faith and practice generally is hid in the remote depths of Christian antiquity.

Owing to the fact that they have never published any denominational statistics, it is somewhat difficult to determine their exact number. Those, however, who are acquainted with the entire body, state that their number is not far from one hundred thousand. As this estimate was made several years ago, it is likely short of their number, for in various localities they have increased in numbers very fast, and it is perhaps safe to place their number considerably above one hundred thousand.

The larger majority of them are farmers, and where they settle to any great extent, they are sure to make a well improved country. Many of them are mechanics, while a small number are professional men. Such a thing as a Dunkard lawyer is wholly unknown. They are usually in good circumstances, and many of them are men of considerable wealth. As it is a part of their religion to inculcate industry and frugality, abstaining from all extravagance and worldly display, they are likely to become in possession of property. By abstaining from superfluities of all kinds, they not only improve their health, and increase their wealth, but set before the world a good example of plainness and frugality.

They have no written creed, save the New Testament, which they regard as an only rule of their religious faith and practice. They consider this to be all that was used by the primitive Christians in the first century, and by virtue of the same is sufficient now. The minutes of their annual councils are published, from year to year; this is by not a few innocently regarded as their discipline, but they do not regard it as such, but recieve it as advice from those who are assembled on that occasion. Lately they have collected and published all the minutes of their annual councils and bound them in book form.

They believe in the Trinity—that there are three divine persons or powers in the Godhead. They accept the entire Old and New Testaments as being of divine inspiration, and strongly contend for a literal interpretation of the same, as we would interpret the language of other books, so far as it may appear in harmony with the general tenor of the Bible. They believe in future rewards and punishments—that the wicked, those who wilfully disobey the gospel, "shall go away into everlasting punishment, but the righteous into life eternal."—Matt. 26: 26.

They believe that all idiots, all infants, and persons who die before they arrive at the years of knowledge—to know good from evil—will be saved without obedience, being sufficiently atoned for by the death of Christ. They are, however, strong opposers of infant baptism, believing like the Baptists in general, that baptism is intended for believers only, and as infants cannot believe, and are not required to do so, they are perfectly safe without it. It is further believed by them that baptism in connection with faith and repentance is for the "remission of sins" (Acts 2 : 38), that is, actual sins committed—and as the children have committed no actual sin against a law of which they know nothing, they are fit subjects for heaven without being baptized. It being further maintained that baptism is "the answer of a good conscience towards God" (1st Peter 3 : 21), cannot apply to children as they know nothing of baptism and cannot, therefore, have any conscience in the matter.

Faith, repentance and baptism are considered essential to salvation and for the remission of sins. "Without faith it is impossible to please God." He that believeth not shall be damned." "Except ye repent ye shall all likewise perish." "Repent and be baptized every one of you, in the name of Jesus Christ for the remission of sins." "Except a man be born of water and of the Spirit, he cannot enter into the kingdom of God." None are recognized as members until after baptism.

First in order of the ordinances is baptism, which is to be observed immediately after the exercise of true repentance, according to the command, "Repent and be baptized." The mode of baptism is peculiar, is called trine immersion, and their general service attending it is as follows: At the water-side they kneel down, especially the applicant and the administrator, and the administrator then offers up a short prayer to God. This being over, they both go down into the water to a proper depth, and the applicant kneels down. The administrator then asks the following questions, all of which the applicant answers in the affirmative : Dost thou believe that Jesus Christ is the Son of God, and that He has brought from Heaven a saving gospel? Dost thou willingly renounce Satan, with all his pernicious ways, and all the sinful pleasures of this world? Dost thou covenant with God, in Christ Jesus, to be faithful unto death? Then he proceeds: "Upon this, thy confession of faith, which thou hast made before God and these witnesses, thou shalt, for the remission of sin, be baptized in the name of the Father" (then bends the applicant forward until he is wholly immersed), "and of the Son" (dipping him the second time), "and of the Holy Ghost" (dipping him the third time). After this, and while the applicant is yet kneeling, the administrator lays his hands upon the applicant's head, and offers up a short prayer to God, in his behalf. Baptism makes the recipient a member of the church, and is never repeated for the same individual. Excommunication does not impair the validity of the baptism, so that they can be received again, on proper repentance and reformation, without the re-administration of the ordinance.

In defence of their practice it is maintained by them that the commission—"Baptizing them into the name of the Father, of the Son, and of the Holy Ghost," is very elliptical, and when filled up agreeable with the rules of the English as well as the Greek language, will read as follows: "Baptizing them into the name of the Father, and baptizing them into the name of the Son, and baptizing them into the name of the Holy Ghost." This is claimed to be the grammatical import of the language —amply sustained by all the ancient Greeks of Christian antiquity who have written on the subject. It may be in place to remark that Chrysostom, the most renowned Greek scholar of antiquity, and who lived and wrote in the fourth century, says: "Christ delivered to his disciples one baptism in three immersions of the body, when he said unto them, 'Go teach all nations, baptizing them in the name of the Father, and of the Son, and of the Holy Ghost.'" The Greek portion of Christendom, who received the gospel directly from the apostles themselves, to this day, amid all their speculations and ceremonies, still retain the use of the three-fold immersion, which is an unanswerable argument in defence of the antiquity of the trine immersion as now practiced by the German Baptists. As they believe in the Trinity—that there are three persons in one Godhead, they maintain that there should also be three actions in the one baptism. Their method is invariably performed by the forward motion of the body in the water, believing that backward immersion is a human invention, and cannot be traced beyond its origin among the English Baptists in the sixteenth century (Judson on Baptism, page 112). They hold that as baptism is an act of obedience, like all other obedience, must be forward and not backward, and being in the likeness of Christ's death, which took place on the cross where He bowed His head (forward), they in like manner must bow forward in the water.

Next in order is the ordinance of feet-washing. The authority is from the incident of Christ washing His disciple's feet, narrated in John 13. They believe the command in the fourteenth and fifteenth verses of this chapter to be as literally binding as the commands elsewhere for the observance of the communion. It is observed as a preparation for the love-feast and communion, according to the statement of Christ to Peter in the tenth verse. In the observance of the ordinance the brethren wash the feet of the brethren only, and the sisters of the sisters. The sexes never, under any circumstances, wash the feet of each other, as has sometimes been charged. Everything connected with the ordinance is done decently and in order. It is observed at every love-feast and communion. It is proper to observe, however, that those who perform the service of feet-washing are not "chosen" from the members, but any member may perform this service, which is always a purely voluntary one.

Next is the love-feast. The authority for this is predicated upon the fact that before Christ instituted the communion, on the night of His betrayal, He first partook of a supper with His disciples. They make this a real meal. There is no limit as to kind or quality of food. The only requirement is, that it be a real supper. After this, and immediately preceding the communion, is the salutation of the kiss, which they claim was observed by the apostles and Christian churches following them. In this ordinance the brethren salute each other, and the sisters the same. The sexes do not interchange salutations.

In the observance of the communion, which is the ordinance next in order, the sisters all have their heads covered with plain caps, and the brethren with heads uncovered. Thanks are given both for the bread and wine. The minister breaks the bread to the brethren, and they to each other. The minister breaks to the sisters also, but they do not break to each other; and the same is the case in passing the wine. The communion and its attendant ordinances are always observed at night, as this was the hour of their institution by Christ. It is observed usually once or twice a year in every church.

In addition to these ordinances, is that of the laying on of hands, and anointing the sick with oil; founded on James, 5: 14, 15. It is done only at the request of the sick person, and always by an elder, if one is within reach; but if it is not convenient to secure the presence of an elder, the ordinance is then administered by a minister. To perform this ceremony, two are always required,

The church government is republican in form. Each church has its council, to which all matters of difference, and questions of difficulty, must first be submitted. If not settled here, they are carried to the council of the district. These districts generally include about twenty churches, sometimes less; and the council is composed of delegates from each church. If not settled here, and is a matter of general interest, it is taken to the national council, or conference; but no local matter is allowed to come up before that body. In some cases, the national council appoints persons to confer with the local councils, and, in this way, assists in the settlement of difficult cases.

The national conference is composed of two delegates from each district. One of the two serves on the standing committee, which has important offices to perform; and the other attends more particularly to the matters before the conference. But, while these delegates constitute the official conference, opportunity is given to all members present to speak, and participate in the proceedings. In the lower councils, all matters are decided by vote, and the sisters are allowed the same privileges as the brethren, in this respect; but in the national conference, the decisions are by common consent, and the sisters do not participate in the official deliberations.

The special object of this national conference is to decide matters for which no "Thus saith the Lord" can be found. Questions naturally arise which cannot be decided by reference to the Bible teachings, and the object of this annual conference is to take all such questions into consideration and decide upon them. A clerk keeps a careful record of all the proceedings, and at the close the record is printed and sent to each church, and becomes the final authority, so far as advice is concerned, on all the subjects considered.

Their mode of worship does not differ materially from that of other people, save in the use of the Lord's prayer, which they repeat at the end of each prayer. In case two ministers are together, one offers up a prayer and the other repeats the Lord's prayer. Meeting generally opens with singing and prayer, after which a chapter is read. Then follows preaching by one or more of the ministers present. If no minister is present, the meeting is generally conducted by one of the deacons. The services are closed in the same way they are opened, by singing and prayer. They do not use the benediction. The minister usually says: "We are dismissed in the name of the Lord," or some similar phrase.

During services the sisters are required to have their heads covered with a plain covering, in compliance with Paul, who says: "It is a shame for a woman to pray or prophesy with her head uncovered." The men keep their heads uncovered at all times during services.

The Dickey church may be regarded as the pioneer denomination of Dunkers, in what is now Ashland county, and the late Joseph Roop, as the pioneer who was instrumental in introducing the first "Dunkard" speakers to Montgomery township. As early as 1839-'40 he invited Mr. Tracy, one of their speakers, to address a few hearers at his (Mr. Roop's) residence, in the east part of the township. These meetings were frequently addressed by Mr. Tracy and other speakers, and finally resulted in the organization of a small society, which continued to meet frequently at the residence of Mr. Roop, and being joined by others, finally became sufficiently numerous to erect what is now known as the "Dickey church," one of the leading speakers being the late Elias Dickey. The church was a neat frame, in the east part of Montgomery township, and was erected about 1860; but a new and larger one was erected by the same congregation in 1877, forty by eighty feet.

The Ashland City church assembles at the chapel in the new college of the Dunkards. The congregation was organized during the summer of 1879, and mostly addressed by Professor S. Z. Sharp, David Wertman and Bashor. The members number about fifty, and are increasing.

The Lafayette church, in the north part of Perry township, was organized in 1856. The congregation is mostly made up of Pennsylvanians, who speak the German language and conform to the faith of the Dunkards. Mr. Snowlarger, a member of that denomination and a man of wealth, donated the church building.

The Maple Grove or Beighley church was organized in 1850. The church was erected four or five years earlier than the Dickey church, say about 1855. The Beighleys, Roops and Myers were among the first and leading members. The members number about one hundred and fifty.

The Hershey or Oak Grove church, in the northwest part of Vermillion township, was purchased from the German Reformed Lutherans about 1870, and has about twenty members. It is a branch of the Dickey congregation, and increasing in members, and evinces prosperity.

The Burns organization, in Milton township, is a branch of the Maple Grove or Beighley church, and meets at the Burns school-house. It has about twenty members.

The speakers at the Beighley church and its branches are: William Sadler, George Worst, Isaac Rudy and Alphus Dickey.

The speakers for the Dickey church and its branches are: David Whitmer, Henry Kilheffner, David Workman, Dillon Parker and Isaac Kilheffner.

The Loudonville, or Workman church, in Green township, was built about 1863. It is thirty by forty feet, and has about one hundred members. The speakers are Morton Workman, William Workman and J. Workman.

It is proper to state that the speakers for the Dunkards receive no salary; but if the speaker be a poor man, and devote his time and talents to the spread of their faith, the Dunkards regard it as incumbent to reward their speaker by gifts.

THE UNITED BRETHREN.

The United Brethren church of Ashland was erected in 1867. It is a neat frame. The members number about two hundred. The present minister is Rev. David Sprinkle.

The United Brethren church, of Mohican, near the Lake fork, was built in 1847. It is thirty by thirty-eight feet, and known as Fairview chapel. The membership is about sixty.

The Oak Grove United Brethren church is some three miles north of Fairview. The building is twenty-six by thirty feet. The membership is about seventy-five.

The United Brethren, of Lafayette, have a small frame church. There is also a small church near the south line of Perry township. The number of members in each is believed to be about forty.

The United Brethren church, of Jackson township, known as Otterheim chapel, thirty by thirty-six feet, was built in 1861. It has about thirty members, and has occasional preaching.

THE EVANGELICAL ASSOCIATION.

This church has been represented in Ashland by a few members for upward of forty years. Occasional preaching has been held in private dwellings. The Heltmans and Michael Thomas were early members. When Michael Thomas moved to Ashland a class was formed, consisting of himself, C. Kreisher, H. Campbell, Joseph Heltman, Mr. Rebman, Mr. Wenrick, William, Daniel and Philip Morr, Mr. Shaffer, and M. Proudfit. In 1875, the society built a very fine brick church, thirty-eight by sixty-six feet, in modern gothic style, with a tower and fine bell. It is beautifully frescoed, and cost over six thousand dollars. Rev. Dr. D. H. Resenburg is the pastor, and the new church is the result of his zeal. The membership is now about sixty in town; and five miles east he has another class called Trinity society, consisting of one hundred and ninety-six members. This class was formed in 1832 by Andrew Morr, Daniel Morr, Mr. Shreffler, Benjamin Myers, Jacob Myers, Michael Morr, Jacob Morr, John Myers, Adam Echelbarger and others. The first ministers were Revs. C. Hammer and J. J. Kopp. In 1850, a neat frame church was erected. In 1870 a new frame superseded the old one. It is thirty-six by fifty feet, and has a good bell. This church is under the care of the Ashland station. Its members are wealthy farmers, and possess a good deal of enterprise and Christian zeal.

At Lafayette a class was formed in 1830, by Henry Zimmerman, John Betts, Henry Kiplinger, Henry Shaffer, Nicholas Shaffer, Mr. Swaisgood and George Walkey. Preaching was held in cabins till 1846. At that time a log church, thirty by thirty-five feet, was built. In 1858, this was vacated, and a new frame church built, and again remodeled and enlarged, in 1865, to a fine church, thirty-six by fifty feet, with a steeple and bell. The membership is now about one hundred and fifty. The people are very harmonious and prosperous.

In Jackson township, in section twenty-two, a fine frame church, thirty by forty feet, with a tower and bell, was erected in 1873. The leading members are John Swaisgood, Mr. Landis, Mr. Stelzer, Mr. Nickle, Jones, and Isaac Eshelman. The entire membership is about fifty-six.

Near Lakeville, in Lake township, is another church, which was organized in 1840. It has now about one hundred and fifty members. The building is a neat frame.

In the southwest corner of Green township is another church of the same denomination. It was organized about 1846. The church is a neat frame. The members number about seventy.

It is proper to observe that the Evangelical Association, in its doctrines, modes of church organization, and appointment of classes and ministers, resembles the Methodist Episcopal church. The ministers are appointed by the annual conference of the Association.

The Evangelical Association was originally formed by Rev. Jacob Albright, of Pennsylvania, and the members of the church are known in some localities as "Albrights." Jacob Albright was born May 1, 1759. He joined the Lutheran church in 1791; and subsequently joined the Methodist Episcopal church and was licensed to preach. He lost his place by absence from class. He began to preach as an independent, in 1796, and in 1800 the formation of the Evangelical Association took place. He was then thirty-seven years old. He died May 18, 1808, aged nearly fifty years. The present membership of the Association is one hundred thousand.

THE CONGREGATIONAL CHURCH.

In 1827 a small Congregational society formed in Ruggles Center. The minister was Rev. E. T. Woodruff; the members Harvey Sackett, E. D. Smith, Reuben Fox, Tholia Sackett, Norman Carter, Rachel Curtiss, Sarah Sturtevant, Lorinda Beach, Jerusha Peck, Mina Fox and Cynthia Smith. The ministers have been Revs. Joseph Treat, E. T. Woodruff, S. Robinson, Benjamin Judson, E. P. Salmon, S. Dunton, W. L. Buffett, O. W. Mather, E. P. Sperry, W. T. Milikan, G. C. Judson, James Wilson, John McCutchin, H. L. Howard, and G. V. Fry. The services were held in the cabin of Mr. Sackett, and in a school-house for several years. In 1838 a church was erected by the congregation and township. In 1854 a new church was erected. The members number about ninety-five.

THE CATHOLICS.

St. Peter's Catholic church, of Loudonville, was built in 1871. It is of brick, seventy by forty feet, and thirty-five feet high in the clear. The corner-stone was laid by Rev. Father Verlet, of Massillon, June 25, 1871, assisted by Father Ankly, of Wooster. Father Magenhann sang high mass in Loudonville on the occasion. The building was completed in 1872, and Rev. Father Schmitz took charge. It has a membership of thirty-five families, and is a neat, comfortable church. It cost about twelve thousand dollars. It has no school as yet.

The Catholic church, of Ashland, St. Edward's, was organized in 1863. Mass had been said as early as 1853, by Father Brennan, who came from Wooster, Ohio, saying mass in private houses. He was followed by Fathers O'Neill and Molony, and Rev. J. F. Gallagher, of Wooster, in 1863, in which year the Presbyterian church was purchased, for six hundred dollars; and from that time the organization of the congregation may be dated. Rev. J. Kuhn took charge in 1865, attending every four weeks, from Mansfield, Ohio. About this time, the church, a wooden structure, quite old, was repaired, at an expense of about five hundred dollars. The congregation consisted, at that time, of about thirty members. By the time of the completion of the Atlantic and Great Western railway, it had a less membership. Father Kuhn continued in charge until 1867, when Rev. A. Magenhann, of Mansfield, took charge. At this time, the old church burned down. A new church (brick) was built in 1870, thirty-six by fifty feet, at a cost of three thousand five hundred dollars; and in 1872, Rev. M. Schmidt, of Loudonville, took charge, and has continued ever since. Mass is said every five weeks. St. Edward's has no school, and has never had a resident pastor.

GERMAN REFORMED.

About the year 1838, a small congregation of Evangelical Lutherans and German Reformed Lutherans organized in the Gierhart settlement, on the east line of Montgomery township, and erected a brick church. Rev. Mr. Wolf was the first preacher. The Rev. Adam Staump preached at the same time, the congregation being partly Lutheran and partly German Reformed. The Rev. William Gilbraith subsequently took charge of the congregation.

The German Lutherans of Ashland, having organized some time prior, erected a neat brick church in 1868. The first minister was Rev. Mr. Schmidt. The present minister is C. R. O. Muehler. The members number about thirty.

The German Reformed Lutherans of Ashland, having organized some time prior, erected a new frame church in 1867. The membership is about fifty. The present minister is Rev. Mr. Mutsinger.

The Winebrenarians erected a church, near the east line of Vermillion township, in 1835. It has now about seventy-five members. The early ministers were Rev. Thomas Hickerall and Jacob Keller.

CHAPTER XXXIII.

THE PIONEERS OF THE YEAR 1825.

The Settlements in the Various Townships.—Lake.—Mohican.—Perry. —Jackson.—Green.—Vermillion.—Montgomery.—Orange.—Mifflin. —Milton.—Clearcreek.—Ruggles.—Troy.—Sullivan.

In the settlement of the various townships prior to 1825, the arrival of pioneers has been fully detailed; and, since we will not have space for a personal notice of each pioneer, at a later period, we have concluded to give the name of each voter and male citizen, so far as possible, at that date.

That the list may be properly arranged, we will first give the townships in the fifteenth range—Lake, Mohican, Perry and Jackson.

Lake.—Nathan Odell, L. D. Odell, William Greenlee, William Hendrickson, Elijah Balling, John Greenlee, John Emrick, Jacob Emrick, John Emrick, jr., Andrew Emrick, George Emrick, John Ewalt, William Ewalt, George Marks, Ephraim Marks, William Marks, George Marks, jr., William Green, Asahel Webster, Joshua Oram, Elijah Oram, Thomas Oram, Henry Oram, John Wetherbee, Justus Wetherbee, Jabez Smith, Peter Wycoff, William Wycoff, John Riddle, J. C. Young, James Green, Jesse Green, William Green, John Green, William Green, jr., John Newkirk, Henry Newkirk, Reuben Newkirk, James Gray, Thomas Baker, John Smith, and Robert Chandler.

Mohican.—The property holders were: Austin Ambrose, Robert Andress, James Arnold, Silas Allen, Kendal Beard, Calvin Beard, Calvin Beard, jr., Charles Beard, Asa Beard, John Bivins, Henry Bivins, Frederick Blew, John Blew, Simon Bell, William Bryan, Joseph Botterfield, Mary Brown, John Black, James Bryan, Benjamin Bunn, Thomas Brown, Aaron Beard, William Boils, James Cameron, Edward Church, Charles Cliff, Jacob Cook, Matthew D. Cully, Charles Collins, Francis Carothers, Robert Caples, Thomas Carnes, George Clark, George Conkel, Lewis Crum, James Collier, John Cully, Isaac Cangman, Carpenter David, James David, Nathan Daily, Thomas Dallas, Henry Dubbs, John Ewing, Thomas Eagle, Jacob Ewing, James Ewing, William Ewing, Michael Ensminger, George Ensminger, David Ensminger, John B. Eagle, William Eagle, Samuel Freeman, Luther Freeman, Alexander Finley, Hannah Finley, John Glenn, sr., Joshua Glenn, George Gear, John Gorsuch, Isaac Gill, Frederick Gill, James Greer, Alexander Greer, John Gilbreath, Daniel Heller, John Harpster, sr., George Harpster, Henry Hopkins, Jacob Houser, John Harpster, George Hart, Samuel Heller, Cyrus Harry, John Hiser, William Helper, Richard Hargrave, Isaac Hallinger, William Hayne, John Heaney, Luke Ingmand, Isaac Ingland, Edmond Ingmond, sr., Edmond Ingmand, Heman Isable, Charles Isable, Henry Jackson, James Kelley, Archibald Kennedy, Frederick Kiser, Jacob Lybarger, John Laix, George Laix, Jacob Leathers, Alexander Mitchell, David Murdock, George Martin, Josiah Metcalf, John Mitchell, Edward Metcalf, John Musgrove, Benjamin Martin, John McMurray, Joseph McCombs, John Mickmacken, John H. Metcalf, Allen Mackenon, Melinda Metcalf, John Metcalf, Thomas Metcalf, Thomas McClure, Equiler Nailer, Thomas Newel, Charles Newel, William Norris, William Newbrough, Joseph Norris, Joseph Noggle, John Nailor, David Noggle, Thomas Newman, John Otto, Matthias Otto, Jonathan Potts, Richard Owens, Robert Richey, Absalom Rice, James Reed, Jacob Raub, Richard Ridgeley, Henry Riley, Thomas Smurr, John Smith, John Shinabarger, Thomas Selby, Hugh Skilling, James Slater, Jacob Steel, Adam Steel, David Strouse, Nathaniel Sheldon, Frederick Strouse, Jacob Stoler, Jacob Trease, Benjamin Tyler, Major Tyler, Sarah Tyler, Francis Winbigler, Richard Winbigler, John Woods, John Wonder, George Winbigler, Samuel Warner, John Winbigler, Daniel Wissamore, Thomas Wissamore, William Wible, and Thomas Wissinger.

Perry.—John Allison, sr., John Allison, jr., James Allison, William Akrite, Robert Ason, John Adams, William Adams, Alexander Allison, James Anderson, Henry Buffenmyer, David Buffenmyer, William Buffenmyer, Mathias Buffenmyer, George Buffenmyer, Joseph Clark, Thomas Cunningham, David Cunningham, David Cunningham, jr., George Carey, David Clark, David Cline, John Carr, Nicholas Carr, Hugh Carr, Aaron Cory, John Cory, Mathias Campf, Arthur Campbell, Joseph Chandler, Jacob Countryman, Philip Clodfelter, Charles Cliff, James Dorland, Garrett Dorland, James Dickason, Samuel Deardorf, Abraham Echer, James Ewing, John Ellison, Adam Eichelburger, John Ewing, Jacob Ecker, Conrad Friedline, John Fry, Henry Gierhart, Henry Grindle, Henry Grindle, jr., William Hamilton, John Hern, Samuel Y. Hayes, John Hillis, William Hillis, Robert Hillis, Conrad Hare, John Helman, Christopher Heffler, John Hileman, John Hamilton, John Ihrig, David Johnson, Thomas Johnson, Isaac Jackson, William Kelley, Jacob Klingman, John Klinger, John Kelley, William Kiplinger, Robert Laughlin, John Long, Lazarus Lowry, Francis Lowry, Zacheus Lash, Jacob Lash, Peter Lash, Henry Lash, John Lattimore, John McLain, Hugh Meloy, Edward McFadden, John Maurer, Philip Mang, Samuel Mang, Peter Mang, Solomon McMiller, William Morgan, Benjamin Moyer, Valentine Mogle, David McConahey, Samuel Neal, James Nelson, William Nelson, jr., Jacob Onstott, John Pittinger, Thomas Pittinger, Nathaniel Paxton, Peter Pittinger, Daniel Pittinger, Jonn Pittinger, John Raver, Jacob Rauch, Robert Robinson, Christian Rice, Michael Row, Michael Row, jr., John Smith, David Smith, Henry Sapp, Phineas Summerton, Frederick Shawn, Remember Stockwell, John Shissler, Richard Smalley, John Smalley, James Scott, William Spencer, George Strouse, James Shinnebarger, Henry Smalley, Thomas Selby, John Shisler, William Shisler, John Scott, David Swash, Isaac Smalley, Henry Smalley, John Thomas, John Tarryer, Samuel White, David Williams, Jacob White, Jacob White, jr., William Williams, James White, Henry Worst, John White, Daniel Williams, Frederick Wise, Jacob Weggardt, Charles Wilson, George Worley, Henry Zimmerman.

Jackson.—William Anderson, John Bryan, Shadrach Bryan, Daniel Bryan, William Prosser, Jacob Berry, Tate Brooks, Philip Brown, Adam Bruge, Peter Berk, Peter Bowman, John Berry, Joseph Chilcote, Samuel Chacey, Thomas Cole, Thomas Cole, jr., Stephen Cole, Henry Culler, Thomas Copley, Benjamin Drodge, James Durfee, James A. Dinsmore, Samuel Dyarman, John Davoult, Robert Dyarman, John Duncan, Henry Eldridge, Martin Fast, James Fulton, Francis Fast, Michael Foreman, Daniel Goodwin, Jonas H. Gierhart, James George, John George, Thomas Green, William Harris, Jacob Hellman, Hanson Hamilton, Peter Henry, John Harbaugh, Chas. Hoy, Adam Henry, John Johnsonbaugh, Jacob Kiplinger, John Kiplinger, Adam Keny, Michael Kiplinger, Peter Kiplinger, Moses Kitchin, Peter Kane, John Kelley, Henry Kiplinger, Henry Kiplinger, jr., John Kuhn, Jacob Kramer, Job King, John Keen, George Long, Isaac Lyons, Noah Long, Nathaniel Lyons, Josiah Lee, John Lafler, John M. Livingston, Peter Loucks, Samuel Landis, John Langherry, Michael Markle, Thomas McBride, Jesse Mathews, John Meason, Amos McBride, Solomon Mokle, Samuel McConahey, Isaac Mickey, James F. McMeekin, Alexander McConnell, Frederick Miller, Henry Moyer, James McCoy, John Nelson, Jacob Oxenrider, Hankey Priest, David Proudfit, William Prosser, John Priest, Mathias Rickle, John Rickle, Michael Rickle, Peter Rickle, John Ramsey, John Raker, William Ramsey, William Ruffcorn, Solomon Raser, Martin Shaffer, Lawrence Swape, John A. Smiley, Robert Smiley, Nicholas Shaffer, Thomas Smith, William Smith, Henry Shisler, David Sprinkle, David Tucker, John Tarryer, John Vavolman, Thomas Urie, Conrad Weaver, Peter Yearick, John Young.

We will return to range sixteen, and give a list of property holders and voters in Hanover, Green, Vermillion, Montgomery and Orange townships, in 1825.

Hanover—Isaac Y. Askew, William Burwell, Stephen Butler, John Burwell, George W. Bull, Thomas J. Bull, Ransom Clark, William Cunningham, Robert Dawson, George Davidson, George Davidson, jr., Samuel Garrett, Amos Harbaugh, John Hildebrand, Samuel Hendricks, Calvin Hibbard, Edward S. Hibbard, Nathaniel Haskell, John Lisar, William Kay, Mark Mapes, John McCoy, Gilbert Pell, William Robinson, John Reno, George Snyder, Thomas Shearer, Andrew Smith, Abel Strong, Chester Spafford, Thomas Taylor, William Webb, Abner Winters, Anthony Zeers.

Green.—The following list is as nearly accurate as tradition can make it: Moses Adsit, James Ady, Isaac N. Ayres, William Brown, Joseph Byers, James Byers, John Bailey, Thomas Coulter, sr., Jonathan Coulter, John Coulter, David Coulter, Caleb Chapel, Noah Castor, Conrad Castor, Pelham Cook, John Chambers, George Crawford, James Cunningham, Adam Crosser, Michael Crosser, Aaron Crosby, Jeremiah Conine, Richard Conine, Robert Davidson, George Davidson, Isaac Doney, William Darling, Nathan Dehaven, Robert Irwin, James Irwin, William Irwin, Sylvester Fisher, Joseph Gwin, Azariah Gwin, James Gwin, Uriah Gee, John Glass, William Guthrie, Richard Guthrie, John Guthrie, George Guthrie, C. Guthrie, Samuel Guthrie, Samuel Graham, James Gladden, Calvin Hill, Harvey Hill, Josiah L. Hill, Andrew Humphrey, William Hunter, James Hunter, Joseph Hill, Joseph Jones, Moses Jones, William Johnson, Aaron Kinney, John Kinney, William McNaull, Benjamin Murphy, Isaac Martin, Almarine Marshall, James McFall, James McNaull, Isaac Menor, John Neptune, John Oliver, Daniel Oliver, Lewis Oliver, Moses Odle, Trew Pallee, Joseph Parish, Lewis Pearce, Andrew Pearce, William Pearce, John Palmer, Alexander Rice, James Rowland, Simon Rowland, John M. Rowland, Jedediah Smith, Chandler Smith, Otho Simmons, Alexander Skinner, Joel Stroud, John Shambarger, Jacob Shambarger, David Snyder, Philip Shambaugh, William Simmons, Joseph Studley, Melzer Tannehill, Charles Tannehill, Basil Tannehill, William Taylor, Stephen Vanscoyce, Jonathan Vanscoyce, John Vaughn, John Van Hoon, Jesse Van Zile, Peter Van Hoon, Samuel White, Joshua White, A. Winter, William Wallace, John White, Isaac Wolf, Warring Wolf.

Vermillion.—Andrew Byerly, Nathaniel Baker, Aquilla Bennett, John Bennett, Peter Bennett, Abraham Bennett, Michael Bennett, John Brown, Daniel Block and sons, John G. Blurt, William Bell, Sterling G. Bushnell, William, Collins, Jotham, Homer and Thomas Bushnell, John Cox, sr., John, James E. and Thomas Cox, William and Samuel Craig, John Clapper, James Campbell, Joseph Dawson, Robert Dawson, Joseph Duncan, John Duncan, Ephraim Davis, Edward Dalton, Peter Dragon and sons, George Ewing, William, John and Walter Emery, Philip, Frederick, Christian, Samuel, George and Andrew Eihinger, George Eckley, Ephraim, Jeremiah, and David Eckley, James, Lewis, William, jr., Henry, George, Titus, Stephen, David and John Ewing, William Ewing, sr., Philip, Michael, Jacob and George Friend, John Farver, Robert, Hugh, Isaac and Daniel Finley, William, Thomas, George and James Goudey, William, John, William, jr., and Thomas Galloway, Michael, Joseph, David, John and Thomas Grubaugh, Jacob Huff, Daniel, Samuel, John, Samuel, jr., and Peter Harman, Daniel Harlan, John, Thomas and William Harper, Thomas Hewey, Nathaniel Hammond, John Hall, Linus, George and Titus Hayes, John Howard, George Hersh, William Hervey, Andrew and William Humphrey, Aaron, Enoch and Isaac Hoagland, Samuel Harlan,

Reuben Hill, David Hazlett, Joel Hughes; Linus, Walter, Lucius and Edwin Insign; Richard, Henry, Robert and Samuel Jackman, John Johnson and sons, Abraham Johnson, Uriah Johnson, John King, Isaac Kilmer, John Kirk, Patrick Kelley, William, Robert and John Lemon, William McCrary, George Marshall, William McLaughlin, John McNabb, Thomas McGuire, Mashem Metcalf, John McCrory, James McCrory, David and John Matthews, John Mowdy, George Marshall, jr., Andrew, William and James Newman, James Nealy, William and George North, Aquilla Naylor, John and Daniel Porter, Peter M. Purdy, Jonathan Palmer, James Palmer and sons, William Reed, Jacob Reed, William Ryland and sons, Abraham Roarick, George Shriver, Stephen and James B. Smith, William Scott, William Spirter and sons, Henry Sigler and sons, John Steel, John Stover, Joseph Strickland and sons, Mahlon, Joseph and William S., David Sherrick, Nathan, John and Thomas Stafford, Andrew, William and John Scott, John Scott, sr., Weekly W. and John Scott, jr., Azariah Vanzile, John, Peter, Jeremiah and George Vangilder, Thomas Vanzile, Alfred Vanzile, Robert Williams, Joseph, Thomas and Stewart Workman, John Wilson, J. H. Williams, Robert Williams, jr., James Whittington and sons Samuel and John, Solomon Updegraff.

The foregoing list, although very full, may not contain all the settlers of 1825. In obtaining the list, we had to rely mostly upon tradition.

Montgomery.—John Aten, Richard Aten, Amos Antebus, Alanson Andrews, Richard Beer, David Barr, Thos. H. Brown, James Boots, Samuel Burns, John Brubaker, Seth Benton, Henry Baughman, Samuel Baughman, Abraham Baughman, George Butler, Elias Bailey, John Baughman, Joshua Brooks, John Carr, Jacob Crouse, Ludwig Cline, Jonas Cline, Daniel Carter, Daniel Carter, jr., Jesse Callehan, James Cole, Conrad Cline, Jacob Cline, Seth B. Cook, Richard Clark, Philip Cline, Benjamin Cuppy, James Cuppy, Joseph Conley, William Drumb, Uriah Drumb, Andrew Drumb, Levi Dunaway, Aaron Dolby, Benjamin Emmons, Jacob Figley, Henry Gierhart, Martin Griner, Francis Graham, Henry Gamble, Josiah Gallup, Jacob Grubb, Michael and Jonathan Grubaugh, John Hough, John Herriman, David Herriman, Daniel Herriman, John Heller, Jacob Heller, John Hull, Abraham Holmes, Jonathan Harvuot, Asa Ingland, John Jacobs, Isaac Jones, Wells Kellogg, Sage Kellogg, Burr Kellogg, James Kindall, Moses King, John Keller, James Kuykendall, John Kuykendall, Ezekiel Knight, David Lockhart, Adam Link, William McCune, Abraham Myers, Daniel Mickey, John McNaull, Joseph Markley, David Markley, Aaron Markley, Jonathan Markley, William Mathews, Jacob McClusky, John Mullen, Hugh Moore, Christopher Mykrants, John Mykrants, Jacob Mykrants, John Mason, John McCommon, Andrew Mason, Michael Myers, Alexander Miller, William Montgomery, Elijah and Elisha McKeral, Thomas Maize, Robert Newell, Joseph Newell, Samuel Newell, E. D. Nightingill, Daniel Oldshue, Thomas Oram, James Proudfit, John Proudfit, Andrew Proudfit, George W. Palmer, Joseph Palmer, Robert Ralston, Robert Ralston, jr., James Ralston, John Rowland, Michael Riddle, Samuel Rowland, Andrew Rutter, David Robinson, sr. David Robinson, jr., Benjamin Sirkel, John Smith, Therygood Smith, Nicholas, Jacob, Peter, and John Shaffer, Elias Slocum, Benjamin Shearer, Peter Swineford, John Swineford, George Swineford, Samuel Swineford, Henry Springer, John Springer, Thomas Smith, William Skilling, Solomon Shearer, Samuel Sheets, Joseph Sheets, Willard Slocum, Paul Sherradden, John Sutherland, James Swaney, Wesley Swaney, David Swaney, Jacob Stair, William Sheets, Abraham Sherradden, Solomon Sherradden, Michael Thomas, Peter Thomas, Leonard Thomas, George Thomas, Solomon Urie, Samuel Urie, David Urie, Solomon Urie, jr., James Urie, George W. Urie, Henry Vantilburg, Daniel Vantilburg, Franklin White, Samuel White, John Wolf, Samuel B. Whiting, Jacob Wolf, William Wallace, Simon Wertman, Alanson Walker, Henry, George, and Jacob Wachtell, Peter Zimmerman.

Orange.—Adam Artman, Solomon Artman, John P. Anderson, John D. Baker, Peter Biddinger, Thomas Brown, Isaac Biddinger, Philip Biddinger, John Y. Burge, Samuel C. Bowlsby, Henry Baughman, John Bishop, John N. Bowman, Nathaniel Bryte, Martin Boyer, Christian Bush, Henry Bishop, Joseph Bishop, Masham Bowman, Silas A. Bryan, William Bryan, Joshua Carr, Robert Culbertson, Aaron Cunningham, Robert Campbell, Daniel Campbell, Elijah Chilcote, James Campbell, John Cassel, George Campbell, James Clark, Mordecai Chilcote, John Chilcote, Humphrey Chilcote, Thomas Donley, Abraham Erb, Christian Fast, sr., Jacob Fast, William Fast, David Fast, George Fast, Nicholas Fast, Abraham Fast, Philip Fluke, Henry Fluke, Samuel Fluke, William Fitzgerald, John Fluke, Philip Fluke, jr., Jacob Fulmer, John Fulmer, Valentine Hiffner, Henry Hiffner, Frederick Hiffner, Jacob Hiffner, David Hiffner, Jacob Hiffner, jr., George Hall, John Hartman, David Hartman, John Heister, Nicholas Jones, John Krebs, Mathias Krebs, Christian Krebs, James Kilgore, Jacob Krebs, Jacob Kendig, Henry Krepps, John Linard, Joel Mackerill, George McConnell, Patrick Murray, Edward Murray, Thomas McConnell, John McConnell, Vachel Metcalf, Samuel Metcalf, Jacob Mason, William Murray, John Murray, James Murray, George Murray, James McLaughlin, Robert McLaughlin, Hugh Murray, William McDowell, John McDowell, Hance McMeekin, Martin Mason, sr., James McDowell, Amos Norris, William Patterson, Samuel Richards, Daniel Reaser, Jacob Ridenour, John Richards, Michael Ridenour, James Richards, Christopher Ricket, Daniel Summers, Michael Sheets, Joseph Snyder, John Sibert, Jacob Switzer, John Stull, Isaac Stull, John Singer, Jacob Shroder, John Tilton, Aaron Tilton, Samuel Tilton, James A. Tilton, Josiah Thomas, Jonathan Tucker, Josiah Tucker, Henry Tucker, David Tucker, Thomas Urie, sr., Thomas Urie, jr., Valentine Vance, Ephraim Welch, Jacob Young.

We will now enumerate the pioneers of range seventeen, which includes the greater part of the townships of Mifflin, Milton and Clearcreek.

Mifflin.—Francis Andrews, John Andrews, John and Michael Autsbarger, Isaac Abey, David Bolles, Henry Brubaker, Joseph Bolles, Peter Baum, John Brubaker, Jonas Bolyeat, Samuel Braden, Robert Bentley, David Brubaker, Jacob Baum, John Beninghoff, Benjamin Bare, Aquilla Bennett, Jacob, Henry and Stephen Bolyeat, Benjamin and Leonard Croninger, Fred Cotner, Joseph Charles, John Charles, Michael Culler, James Copus, jr., Wesley Copus, James Chew, Phillip Culler, Frederick Deal, Joseph Doty, Philip Deter, Isaac Davis, James Doty, Peter Egner, Francis Enos, C. Edwards, William Gardner, John Gongwer, John Gates, Christian Hahn, Joseph Hughes, Benjamin Hershey, Joseph Hoover, Daniel Hoover, Hugh Hazles, Martin Kagy, Samuel Kagy, Isaac Kagy, Daniel and John Kauffman, Jacob Keever, Jacob Koogle, John Landis, John Lemon, William Lattimore, Samuel Lewis, John Lambright, Lewis Lambright, Charles and Nathan Lewis, Robert Lemon, Jacob Markley, Calvin Morehead, John McCrony, Daniel and Martin Matthews, William Newman, Jonathan Pettet, Andrew and John Richey, Charles M. Reed, Henry Sunday, Samuel Scott, Jacob Stehman, Jacob Sheller, John Stofford, Samuel and Joseph Simpson, Henry Smith, John Sunday, Christian Vesper, James, Solomon and John Vail, John Vautilburg, Joseph and Jacob Will, Solomon Walters, John Woodhouse, David Young, Michael Young, Joshua and John Yehman, Henry and David Young, Isaac Zehner, Samuel Zehner, Mathias Zehner.

Milton.—John Anderson, James Anderson, Hugh Anderson, Lemon Armstrong, James Andrews, George Albert, Obed Andrews, Elijah Andrews, Daniel Arnold, Joseph M. Anderson, Thomas Braden, Benjamin Brubaker, Jacob Blughlauger, Adam Baum, Peter Brubaker, Andrew Burns, sr., Samuel Baum, Jacob Baum, Robert Barr, Stephen Barr, Peter Bechtel, Joseph Bechtel, David Barr, Peter Brubaker, Andrew Barnes, jr., Hugh Burns, Jacob Baum, Benjamin Brubaker, John Clay, David Crawford, Joseph Charles, Lewis Corts, John Chambers, John Campbell, David Clay, William Callin, Hugh Callin, Henry Campbell, Jacob Cotner, Jacob Culler, James Crawford, Abraham Doty, John Doty, Samuel Doty, James Ferrell, Obediah Ferrell, George Garber, Jacob Gebhart, Peter Greenawalt, John Holderman, James Hall, Samuel Hilburn, Jacob Hiller, John Hall, Amos Hilburn, John Hazlett, Nottingham Houston, George Hall, James Hilburn, Joseph Heltman, John Hilton, John Imhoff, Peter Imhoff, William Imhoff, Theodore Imhoff, John Kauffman, Henry Keever, James Kelley, John Klingan, William Kelley, Adam Link, William Lockhart, Jacob Lora, Allen Lockhart, Alexander Lockhart Franklin Mercer, A. E. Mercer, Jackson Mercer, John Myers, Levi Mercer, Abraham Myers, Benjamin Miskin, John Myers, James McConoughey, Joseph Mellinger, Jacob Myers, Samuel Motter, Robert McCrory, George McCartney, Robert McCartney, John McCrory, John Nusbaum, Henry Neal, John Neal, Peter Neese, Peter Nusbaum, Robert Nelson, John Nelson, Scott Nelson, John Neal, Archibald Owens, David Pollock, John Pollock, Joseph Pollock, James Pollock, Nicholas Perrine, George Ryall, Alexander Reed, John Ryall, Nicholas Rutan, Frederick Rienhart, Abraham Rutan, John Souser, John Stout, David Stout, Thomas Smith, Michael Smeltzer, John Smeltzer, Frederick Sulcer, David Stoner, John Starrett, James Short, Samuel Thomas, David Teel, James Wharton, John Wharton, Isaac Williams, Ebenezer Williams, Abel A. Webster, Benjamin Whitmarsh, Joseph Williams, Robert Williams, John Woodburn, Henry Zehner, Peter Zehner, Samuel Zehner, David Zehner.

Clearcreek.—John Aten, James Anderson, William Andrews, Jacob Akright, Jeremiah Abbott, John Bryte, David Burns, John Brown, Nathaniel Bailey, David Blann, John Bennett, Thomas Brink, John Bailey, Abel Bailey, George Beymer, Thomas C. Cook, John Coonelson, Lewis Crow, John Cuppy, Abraham Clayburg, John Cooper, Job Casey, John Cook, Joel Crampton, George Downer, John Downer, Moses Dayhuff, Joseph Davis, Patrick Elliott, Joseph Fast, John Freeborn, Richard Freeborn, William Freeman, Samuel Freeman, Jacob Foulks, Henry Fisher, Thomas Fisher, Thomas Ford, Elias Ford, Elijah Ford, William Gilchrist, James Gribben, Nicholas Goldsmith, Vincent Goldsmith, Matthew Harper, James Haney, John Haney, Thomas Haney, John Hendricks, Robert Houston, Abraham Huffman, Samuel Huffman, Isaac Harvuot, Joseph Harvuot, Joseph Harvuot, jr., John Jackson, Joseph Jackson, James Jackson, Sylvanus Kellogg, James Laughton, Matthew Laughton, Thomas Munhollen, Hance McMeekin, Joseph Marshall, Robert Merfert, Jacob McClain, Robert McBeth, William McMeekin, William McMeekin, jr., Joseph McKibben, Alexander McCready, John McWilliams, John Owens, James Poag, Alexander Porter, Ephraim Palmer, Robert Patterson, Elijah Potter, William Price, John Prosser, Nicholas Peterson, John Rigdon, Thomas Ross, William Shaw, John Smith, Adam Smith, David Stratten, Joseph Scott, Casper Snook, John Scott, Alfred Skinner, Thomas Sprott, Thomas Sprott, jr., Jared N. Slonaker, Isaac Vanmeter, Peter Vanostrand, Joseph Wright, Casper Wagner, Thomas G. Whitlock, Thomas Wright, Mr. Youngblood.

Ruggles.—The voters and property holders of this township, in 1825, were as follows: Truman Bates, Justus Barnes, Daniel Beach, Norman Carter, Aldrich Carver, Perry Durfee, Reuben Fox, Abraham Ferris, Jacob Roorback, Harvy Sacket, Bradford Sturtevant, Ezra D. Smith, and shortly after, Solomon Weston, Enoch Taylor, Samuel Monroe, Samuel Camp, John Hall, and J. Gates.

Troy.—It is believed there was not a single white inhabitant within the township in 1825. At that period it was a common hunting-ground for Indians, and the pioneer hunters, of what now constitutes the county of Ashland.

Sullivan.—Henry Close, Benjamin Close, R. M. Close, Jesse Chamberlain, Abijah Chamberlain, Whitney Chamberlain, Richard Chamberlain, John Hooker, Daniel Tillotson, John Munson, ——Durfee, A. Mann, Sylvanus Parmely, John Hendryx, William Woods, John Parmely, Asahel Parmely, Ashley Parmely, John Parmely, jr., James Palmer, Thomas Rice, Joseph Carlton, Isaac

Diamond, George Mann, Uriah Chapman, Abijah Marsh, John Gould, Aretas Marsh, and Harris Hooker.

It will be seen by consulting the foregoing lists, that the population of the territory now constituting Ashland county, in 1825 was much larger than is supposed by many. If we estimate six members to each family, the aggregate number of people in this region must have reached nearly eight thousand. When we reflect that in 1812 the entire population did not exceed one hundred and fifty souls, the settlement of the wilds of Richland county, for the next thirteen years, must have been exceedingly rapid; while the erection of cabins and improvements dotted almost every part of the forest.

CHAPTER XXXIV.
THE ERECTION OF ASHLAND COUNTY—PHYSICAL FEATURES.

Formation of County.—Location of County-Seat.—Erection of Jail.—Geological Formation.—Area.—Streams.—Soil.—Lakes.—Minerals.

THE legislative act creating Ashland county was enacted February 24, 1846. It was formed of the territory of Richland, Huron, Lorain, and Wayne counties. The fractional townships of Mifflin, Milton and Clearcreek, and the full townships of Hanover, Green, Vermillion, Montgomery and Orange, were from Richland county, while Ruggles was from Huron, and Troy and Sullivan from Lorain, and the fractional townships of Jackson, Perry, Mohican, and Lake from Wayne county.

On the first Monday of April, 1846, the county-seat was located at Ashland, by a vote of the electors, the citizens of Ashland agreeing to donate suitable grounds, and five thousand dollars to erect county buildings thereon.

In 1847-48, the present jail was erected, by Ozias S. Kinney, architect, and cost the county about fourteen thousand dollars. An old stone church, purchased on the site of the grounds selected for the erection of county buildings, was occupied some seven years as a court house. It stood about midway between the present court house and jail, and had been erected by the Methodist denomination. The new court house was commenced by Ozias S. Kinney, architect, in 1851, and completed in 1853; and cost the county about twenty thousand dollars. The infirmary was erected by Sylvester Alger and George W. Urie, architects and builders, in 1849, and cost about four thousand dollars.

Geologically considered, Ashland county presents evidence of having shown dry land at a very remote period in the history of the globe. Her soils and hills are older than the carboniferous, or coal and limestone periods; and if ever either existed within the limits of this county, they were worn away by the glacial flow from the north; or, during the emptying of the great northern seas through the valleys of the Ohio, Mississippi and the Hudson, after the elevation of the Appalachian chain of mountains, by the cooling and shrinking of the crust of the earth.

How long this region may have been covered by the northern seas, will doubtless never be known by man, but that such seas enveloped this part of the globe for an extended period of time, must be apparent to all careful observers. It is very probable that the great chain of lakes extending from northern New York to the Lake of the Woods, is but a remnant of the mighty sea that covered a large portion of the States of New York, Pennsylvania, Ohio, Michigan, Indiana, Illinois, Wisconsin, and Minnesota. The hypothesis, that during the "glacial period" huge mountains of ice were forced southward from high, northern regions, and in their advance, plowing deep valleys, and wrenching granite rocks from their position, and crushing, and rolling, and rounding them into boulders by erosion, receives much strength, on careful examination. It is possible that during the "drift period" great quantities of what are called "nigger-heads,"—boulders, were carried by ice, thousands of miles, thawed out, and dropped in the position they are now found. These granite boulders are found scattered all over northern Ohio, in sizes ranging from three or four pounds, to tons in weight, gradually diminishing in size as they recede from the lake shore.

Further evidence of the existence of a great sea is found in the deposit of immense quantities of petrified shells, among the surface rubbish of the freestone formation. It is quite certain that these shells were deposited slowly, and that an immense period of time was exhausted in their petrifaction. The freestone rocks are in strata; and their beds range in thickness from three to twenty feet. The sandstone formation crops out at a later period. Petrified shells are not so frequently found above or beneath the sandstone. The sandstone is found on the highest land east of Ashland, commencing at Roseberry's hill, and extending nearly south to Lake township. It is also found on the elevated tract of land running from Milton, through Mifflin and Green townships, to Hanover. These stones are found in abundance, and form a useful and durable material for walls, bridges and buildings.

Ashland county contains an area of about four hundred square miles. It is divided into two principal slopes, or water-sheds, by a range of upland, extending in a northeast direction, across the south part of Clearcreek and the north part of Orange and Jackson townships; thus forming a dividing ridge, that separates the heads of the streams flowing south to the Muskingum, and north to Lake Erie.

The streams on the south side of the dividing ridge, rising mostly from strong springs, flow in a southern direction, until they form a junction with larger ones, out of the county. The streams south of the dividing ridge are: the Black fork, fringing the western border of Milton and Mifflin townships, and passing across Green and Hanover; the Jerome fork, rising in the northwest and northeast parts of Orange township, passes over Montgomery, the western part of Mohican and the eastern part of Lake, and joins the Black fork in Holmes county; the Muddy fork rises in the northeastern part of Jackson township, and flows in a southwesterly direction across Perry, into Mohican, and thence into the Lake fork. These streams are fed by a number of smaller ones—the Catotaway, Honey creek, and a branch or two in Vermillion and Lake townships, and assume a considerable size before they form a junction with the Lake fork; and in early days were navigable for small flat-boats as high as Perrysville, Findlay's bridge, and Rochester mills. The uplands, south of the dividing ridge, slope gently to the south, presenting fine views for residences, and most desirable lands for agricultural purposes. At many points on the uplands, a landscape of eight to ten miles in circuit sweeps before the vision, giving as lovely a view as can be found elsewhere on the globe.

The range of lands on the western slope is composed of clay soil, second bottom loam, and rich alluvium along the streams, giving every variety of soil; the same is the character of the soils in the middle and eastern ranges throughout the county, except in Hanover, where the upland is more rugged, the soil more sandy and less productive. The direction of the streams in that township is from the west, and though her hills antedate the carboniferous periods, they must have been elevated, like small islands, above the surface of the great sea, centuries before the region in and about Hayesville, Ashland, Savannah and Orange.

The Vermillion river rises in the small lakes near Savannah, and is fed by numerous small rivulets and brooks on its winding way to Lake Erie. The Black river rises in the northern part of Sullivan township, and also empties into Lake Erie.

The townships north of the dividing ridge dip slightly towards the north, and possess a stiff clay soil, better adapted to grazing than agricultural purposes, and many fine cattle are produced for the market by the farmers.

The lakes in Ashland county are five in number. Two of these are found a short distance southeast of Savannah, in a basin formed by the dividing ridge, and are fed by springs. The upper, and larger lake, contains about one hundred and sixty acres, and the lower one, which has been partially drained, about eighty acres. They contain many of the varieties of fishes usually found in the streams of this State, and are of great depth, and evidently the remains of a much larger body of water. They are often resorted to for the sport of fishing in canoes, and as a pastime for picnic parties.

There are also three small lakes about two miles southwest of Mifflin. The larger one contains about fifty acres, the middle one about thirty, and the smaller one about ten. They constitute a sort of basin, and are fed by numerous springs. They abound in the same varieties of fishes found in the Vermillion lakes. These lakes were once the favorite resort of the Indians for fishing purposes, and their bark canoes were often floated over the glassy surface of these hill-hedged basins of water, known as the "mimic lakes of Mifflin."

There are a number of noted springs in the western part of the county. In Milton and Mifflin, the largest are found. In the neighborhood of the Nelsons, in Milton, is found one of extraordinary power, pouring forth a volume of water sufficiently large to turn a mill, if properly directed. Near the residence of Mr. Copus, in Mifflin township, are also found several springs, throwing out copious quantities of pure, cool water. Many sections of Green, Lake, and Mohican townships possess springs of great strength; and few counties in the State have a better supply of pure, sparkling, healthful water, than this.

The timber of this county consists of oak, walnut, black and white ash, cherry, beech, sugar, maple, hickory, chestnut, elm, and the usual undergrowth found in other parts of the State. In Troy, Ruggles and Sullivan, on the northern slope, a few scattered poplars were found in early days, but have been long since converted into lumber.

Ashland county is exceedingly limited in its mineral productions. A few pieces of coal, and a little slate, found on the dividing ridge north of Ashland are all the evidences of coal that are seen within its limits.* It is believed that the county is totally deficient in limestone and iron ore. Attempts have been made, in the deep valleys of Hanover, to discover coal oil by boring; but such attempts have been unsuccessful, so far.

If it be true, that the nature of the soil nearly always determines the occupation of a people, the inhabitants of this county, with but few exceptions, must pursue the delightful and manly avocation of tilling the soil, raising fine horses and cattle, and flocks of sheep, surrounded by abundance, with homes blessed of God, and made comfortable by industry, and the fruits of toil.

Evidence exists on all sides that when the red man of the forest roamed unchecked over plain, and hill, and along our lakes and streams the dappled deer in numerous groves, with the elk, the wild turkey and other game, marched up and down these wilds in native freedom, disturbed only by the savage with his bow and arrow; and long since with him, have traveled toward the setting sun, and ere long will be swept before the remorseless march of the white man, into oblivion.

---

*A small vein of coal was found on the farm of Cyrus Miller in the lower part of Hanover township in 1875.

CHAPTER XXXV.

THE MILITIA AND SOLDIERS OF THE WAR OF 1812.

The First Regiment of the First Brigade.—First Officers.—Reorganization.—Regimental Musters.—Free Fights.—The Rifle Regiment.—Roster of Ashland Soldiers in the War of 1812.

THE military history of Ashland county is quite meagre. Prior to its separation from Richland county, in 1846, it had a regiment of militia and a regiment of rifles. The militia regiment was formed about the year 1824, and consisted of ten full companies. The rolls of the companies have been destroyed, and we are compelled to accept a traditionary history. The organization was known as the "First regiment, of the First brigade, of the Eleventh division, of the Ohio militia." The regimental officers were:

FIELD AND STAFF.

Colonel John Oldshue.
Lieutenant Colonel William Scott.
Major William Roller.
Adjutant Sage Kellogg.
Surgeon Joel Luther.

COMMISSIONED OFFICERS.

Captain Burr Kellogg, Montgomery.
Captain Absalom Newell, Montgomery.
Captain James Doty, Mifflin.
Captain Hugh Burns, Milton.
Captain John Woodburn, Milton.
Captain Thomas Ford, Clearcreek.
Captain John McWilliams, Clearcreek.
Captain Joseph Bishop, Orange.
Captain William Patterson, Orange.
Captain Joseph Strickland, Vermillion.

During the existence of the first organization, many changes took place in the regimental and company officers. John Latta, Zachariah Newell, Christian Bush, Burr Kellogg, and Jacob Heckard acted part of the time as captains.

REORGANIZATION.

In 1834 the regiment was reorganized, but retained its original place in the Ohio militia. Colonel John Oldshue resigned, and was succeeded by Alexander Miller; Major William Roller resigned, and was succeeded by Richard P. Fulkerson. The regimental officers then were:

FIELD AND STAFF.

Colonel Alexander Miller.
Lieutenant Colonel William Scott.
Major Richard P. Fulkerson.
Adjutant Ephraim R. Eckley.
Surgeon Joel Luther.

COMMISSIONED OFFICERS.

Captain Richard P. Fulkerson, Montgomery.
Captain Alanson Walker, Montgomery.
Captain Zachariah Newell, Montgomery.
Captain James Doty, Mifflin.
Captain John Woodburn, Milton.
Captain Hugh Burns, Milton.
Captain Christian Bush, Orange.
Captain Joseph Bishop, Orange.
Captain Thomas Ford, Clearcreek.
Captain Joseph Strickland, Vermillion.

In a short time, Samuel W. Russell succeeded William Scott as Lieutenant Colonel; and Colonel Alexander Miller having resigned, Lieutenant Colonel Russel became Colonel, and John Madden Lieutenant Colonel. In the meantime, Adjutant Ephraim R. Eckley resigned, and Paschel Whiting was appointed to fill the vacancy. When Captain Richard P. Fulkerson became major, William Sheets was elected to fill the vacancy. There were other changes not now remembered.

This regiment maintained its organization until about the year 1844, when the militia system of Ohio practically expired.

Colonels Oldshue and Russell, and Major Madden removed west. Colonel Alexander Miller died in 1860. Adjutants Kellogg and Whiting, Dr. Luther and Colonel Scott, and a majority of the captains, have responded to the last roll-call, and gone to a grand encampment across the great river. Captain Alanson Walker served honorably in the war of 1861-5; and Major Richard P. Fulkerson accompanied the "Squirrel Hunters" to Cincinnati, during the apprehended invasion of General Kirby Smith, of Kentucky.

The regimental musters, for many years, took place on a small prairie below the village of Mifflin, on the banks of the Black fork. This field gave ample room for maneuvering and regimental display. The privates were destitute of fire-arms on train day, and the performance was a mere pastime, and regarded as a dry affair. For many years the companies were conditionally kept in existence. The privates, under the law, could either train or work two days on the public highway. Many preferred to repair the roads, and this sapped the vitality of the organization.

Train days, however, were not wholly destitute of excitement. Such assemblages gave an opportunity for the "roughs" to concentrate their forces to settle old griefs and grudges. In the earlier years of the militia system, there seems to have been a bitter feud between the pugilistic chiefs of the Clear fork and the Whetstone. The Clearcreek chiefs consisted of the Slaters and Brawdys, and their backers, while those of the Whetstone were led by the Montgomerys, Burgetts, Bradens and others. There were also many game men on the military quarters in Montgomery and Orange townships, known as members of the "sixteen nations," who were ready, on all occasions, to see a fight well regulated, and generally took a hand in such contests. When the great chiefs of the Whetstone and the Clear fork met, their friends accompanied them. They were, generally, men of large size and famous for their muscle and courage.

At the dismissal of the companies in the evening, the respective chiefs, fired by bad whiskey, and eager for the fray, assembled their hosts. In a few moments the champions opened the contest, when large numbers of sympathizers would be drawn into the struggle to see fair play. A hand to hand contest followed. Parties were knocked right and left, and the victims of the "manly art of self-defence" were found in every quarter, with bruised faces, and gouged eyes and bitten fingers, stained with blood. It was no child's play. The heavy blows made fearful havoc. The war ended. The braves and their friends marched to a brook, washed their faces, and then proceeding to a neighboring still-house, drank friends and buried the hatchet. These sturdy warriors are all gone. Their places are now filled by men of peace. Reason, instead of blows, sways public gatherings, and intelligence, instead of brute force, rules along those beautiful streams.

About the year 1852 an effort was made to revive the militia organization of the county, and create a brigade. To this end Captain John S. Fulton and Colonel George W. Urie visited the officers of the old regiment, who voted for Captain Fulton as their choice for brigadier general. He was accordingly commissioned by the governor as brigadier general, and appointed his staff officers. The brigade officers were:

Brigadier General John S. Fulton,
Brigade Inspector George W. Urie,
Quartermaster Jacob Crall.

The other members of the staff were from Huron county. The attempt thereafter to revive the militia system was abandoned.

THE RIFLE REGIMENT.

About the year 1826, a rifle regiment was formed within the territory now composing Ashland, Morrow, and Richland counties. It was known as the First regiment, of the First brigade, of the Eleventh division of Ohio militia. The regimental and company officers were:

FIELD AND STAFF.

Colonel Samuel G. Wolf.
Lieutenant Colonel John Murray.
Major George W. Urie.
Adjutant William Stevens.
Surgeon William Bushnell.

COMMISSIONED OFFICERS.

Captain George Murray, Orange.
Captain Joseph Gladden, Green.
Captain Hugh Martin, Springfield.
Captain Jacob Lynn, Franklin.
Captain Ezekiel Chew, Blooming-grove.
Captain N. S. Henry, Lucas.
Captain Robert W. Mitchell, Bloomfield.
Captain John Baughman, Bellville.

It will be seen that the regiment was composed of eight companies, which were elegantly uniformed and armed, and the glitter of their burnished rifles, and their gay dresses, made a fine display in the field. The regimental and company officers attracted much attention in consequence of their size and soldier-like bearing. The regimental officers were superbly mounted, and their regalia was quite expensive.

The first company was composed of volunteers from Clearcreek, Orange and Montgomery. The first captain was John Murray. He was succeeded by John Sprott, and he by George W. Urie. The company then disbanded, Captain Urie having been promoted to major. A new company was then formed. Jacob Oldshue was elected captain, and sometime afterward resigned. George McConnell succeeded him, and upon his resignation George Murray was elected captain, and remained in command until the regiment disbanded.

Upon the resignation of Colonel Samuel G. Wolf, Lieutenant Colonel John Murray became colonel, and upon the resignation of Colonel Murray in 1840, Major Urie was elected colonel of the regiment. Colonel Urie appointed John Sherman, now Secretary of the Treasury of the United States, adjutant. He is said to have possessed a good deal of military spirit. He rode a spirited horse, and, being elegantly uniformed, excited a good deal of admiration by his promptness, neatness, and officer-like bearing.

Colonel Samuel G. Wolf, at a recent period, was a citizen of Richland county, and, if alive, is well advanced in years. He is said to have been a very fine officer. His personal appearance and excellent voice enabled him to acquit himself with marked efficiency.

Colonel John Murray possessed a good deal of military spirit, and made an industrious and influential officer. He served as county treasurer for Richland from 1837 to 1841. He removed to Missouri and died about 1858. He is well remembered by all the old citizens, for his fine personal appearance, genial manners and industrious habits.

Colonel George W. Urie resides in Ashland, and although well advanced in years, the shrill tones of a fife, the sound of a drum or a military parade excites the martial fires that once blazed in his organization. During the war of 1861–65, it was difficult for him to refrain from taking a hand in the "scrimmage." Advancing years and failing health alone kept him from the fray.

Very few company officers survive. Captain Gladden, Captain Lynn, Captain George McConnell and Captain John Sprott are believed to be all of the old organization that remain.

Many pleasant memories cluster about the old train days. To keep those reminiscences ever green is the principal object of this sketch. Of course, it is not pretended that this history is complete. The unfortunate destruction of the old company rolls and other records, make it impossible to travel out of tradition.

About the year 1841 a company of lancers was formed in Ashland, composed of boys from fifteen to eighteen years of age, of which the late Bolivar W. Kellogg was captain. The members of the company possessed all the enthusiasm of regular soldiers, were handsomely uniformed and made a fine display. It survived some three or four years.

About the same time a light infantry company was formed, and the late William Johnston, of Mansfield, was elected captain. This company survived until about 1846, when it was merged into a new organization, sometimes called the Ashland guards. Captain Scott, Richard Emerson, John S. Fulton and Anthony Jacobs successively became its captains. It expired in 1852.

SOLDIERS OF THE WAR OF 1812.

During the pioneer period of Ashland county many soldiers of the war of 1812 located amid the forests of this region. Very few of these brave old men survive. At this time (1880) the only ones able to answer roll-call are: Abraham Armentrout, of Hayesville, James Kilgore, of Orange, E. Halstead of Indiana, Nathaniel Clark and J. S. Parker, of Troy, Jacob Helbert, of Mohicanville, R. D. Emerson, Missouri, and Jacob Shopbell, of Orange. The rest have passed over the great river to a grand encampment in a better land. The following is believed to be a complete roll of the worthy braves who settled within the present limits of Ashland county:

Solomon Urie, Samuel Burns, David Burns, John Clay, Samuel White, Joshua Glenn, Henry Gamble, William Reed, Patrick Murray, James Murray, John Tilton, Jacob Hiffner, jr., George Hilkey, James Pollock, Abraham Doty, Andrew Stevison, Thomas Donley, John Proudfit, Francis Graham, Peter Whitright, Jacob Zigler, James Dickason, George Remley, Allen Lockhart, Thomas Miller, James Short, James A. Dinsmore, William Hunter, Abraham Armentrout, John Galloway, Enoch Taylor, John Taylor, Michael Riddle, Robert Nelson, Richard Winbigler, George Martin, Thomas Henry, Thomas Urie, Samuel Urie, Andrew Byerly, Isaac Smalley, James Andrews, Adam Link, Thomas McConnell, Samuel Fulton, R. Richey, W. Richey, Calvin Hibbard, Sage Kellogg, John McConnell, Jacob Jackson, James Kilgore, Thomas Willey, James Campbell, Jacob Mykrantz, Charles Hoy, George McFadden, Daniel Porter, William Craig, George Cornell, E. Halstead, Nathaniel Clark, J. S. Parker, John Hazlett, Thomas Smith, John Woodburn, Joseph Workman, John Smith, Hugh Adams, Case Macumber, Charles Tannehill, Elijah Hart, Sterling G. Bushnell, Abraham Johnson, David Stephens, Joseph Strickland, Samuel Taylor, William Burwell, John Burwell, Matthew Palmer, Mordecai Lincoln, Nicholas Shaffer, George Winbigler, James Cameron, George Richart, Jacob Shopbell, John Chambers, Abraham Huffman, Jacob Ridenour, Jacob Crouse, Rudolph Brandeberry, Philip Brandeberry, William Shaw, John Weltman, John Davoult, John Lambright, Henry Neal, Harvey Sackett, Salmon Weston, Brahmon Johnson, Samuel Monroe, Daniel Beach, Samuel Camp, Jacob Roorback, Abraham Ferris, John Hall, Joseph Gates, Elias Slocum, Rev. Richard D. Emerson, Philip Markley, Jacob Switzer, Robert Ralston, sr., Jacob Helbert, Levi Mercer, sr., Wesley Richard, Thomas Pittinger, James Allison, Charles Hoy, Christopher Rice, John Smith, James Dickson, Samuel Cordell, Peter Burns.

REVOLUTIONARY SOLDIERS.

There were two in Perry: John Shriner, from Maryland, who died in 1855, and John Scott, from Pennsylvania, who died about 1853 or 1854.

CHAPTER XXXVI.

ASHLAND COUNTY IN THE WAR OF 1861-5.

A Complete Roll of all the Commissioned and Non-commissioned Officers and Privates, with a History of the Company and Regiment in Which they Served, and the Casualties Attending the Service.

WHATEVER may be the judgment of future historians as to the avoidance or necessity of the great civil war of 1861-65, it must be conceded that the soldiers and officers who served in the campaigns of that struggle, acquitted themselves promptly, efficiently and bravely, and are entitled to a just meed of praise.

Ashland county furnished a just proportion of volunteers and officers, and the number of deaths, the scars and missing limbs of the surviving, show that her sons did not cower in the presence of the enemy.

It is therefore deemed appropriate, in sketching the history of this county, to record the soldierly bearing of the sons of the pioneers, in the late war. The want of space alone, prevents a full narration of the achievements of our volunteers on the ensanguined fields of the far south.

During the late war, the State of Ohio furnished three hundred and ten thousand six hundred and fifty-four soldiers, who were enlisted in the various counties in proportion to the draftable population. This enormous force was embodied into one hundred and ninety-eight regiments of volunteer infantry, thirteen regiments of volunteer cavalry, twenty-six independent batteries, one regiment light artillery, two regiments of heavy artillery, one regiment of colored volunteer infantry, and a number of independent companies of sharpshooters, light guards, squadrons of cavalry, etc., etc.

These combined regiments make an army equal to some of the larger empires of Europe, and came from a State that three quarters of a century ago, contained a population of less than fifty thousand. How amazing has been the growth of Ohio in population and wealth within the last fifty years! Her sons won imperishable laurels on every battlefield of the war, and commanded most of the armies of the Republic. McDowell, Sherman, McClellan, Grant, Sheridan, McPherson, Morgan, Rosecranz, Buell, and hundreds of other prominent officers, were the sons, or the adopted sons, of the Buckeye State.

THE SIXTEENTH REGIMENT, OHIO VOLUNTEER INFANTRY.

Of the seventy-five thousand enlisted soldiers of April 15, 1861, Ohio furnished twelve thousand three hundred and fifty-seven. Ashland county had one company of volunteers for the three months' service. The officers were:

Captain John S. Fulton; First Lieutenant Thomas J. Kenny; Second Lieutenant William B. McCarty.

The company rendezvoused at Camp Jackson, near the city of Columbus, Ohio, April 23, 1861, where it was enrolled to the eighteenth day of August 1861. On the third day of May, 1861, Captain John S. Fulton was promoted to lieutenant colonel, and Thomas J. Kenny to be captain of company B. On the seventh of May William B. McCarty was commissioned first lieutenant, Samuel L. Wilson, second lieutenant; William P. Wright, ensign.

NON-COMMISSIONED OFFICERS.

First Sergeant Warren H. Wasson.
Second Sergeant William W. Brown.
Third Sergeant Buel Walcott.
Fourth Sergeant Silas Gould.
First Corporal James Lafferty.
Second Corporal John Sloan.
Third Corporal Nelson Smith.
Fourth Corporal Henry Dudley.

PRIVATES.

Albert Briggs, John Brothers, Nathan Blue, John Bird, Elzie Bean, Nelson Blue, Alonzo Brown, John F. Cordell, Gates F. Carnes, Stephen Carney, George V. Coner, David R. Crance, Robert N. Cross, Harrison Campbell, Josiah Closson, James Campbell, Robert M. Campbell, Le Grand G. Drown, William Daniels, John B. Darrow, James W. Delano, Ambrose S. Eldred, Samuel N. Ecker, Nathaniel L. Eddie, Porter M. Ford, Luther M. Fast, John Grissinger, Windom Garst, John Hickle, Oscar Harrington, Christian N. Hershey, John Hyman, David Hunt, William C. Hodge, Andrew Hornstine, Frederick Heitz, Celestus Jenkins, Cyrus W. Johnston, Samuel Kidwell, Theodore W. Krisher, Joshua B. Krebs, James H. Landis, Joseph Lockhart, Arteus Marsh, George McConnell, Lucius Mead, Albert McCurdy, Samuel Miller, George McNabb, William Mater, George Miller, George Mitchelton, Thomas McMurray, Lot McSweeney, Allen McCall, Lewis Markley, William Noggle, John S. Nickson, Hamilton Oldroyd, Thomas B. Onstall, Franklin Otts, Hezekiah Potter, William A. Power, James F. Potter, Jerome Potter, James Peacock, Ransom Pearson, William H. Porter, John S. Plunk, John Richards, John W. Rathbun, Daniel Ranhouser, Lincoln S. Rice, Milton Randall, Wilber F. Robinson, Geo. Riggs, William H. Rowe, Joseph Spencer, John M. Scott, William G. Scott, Gates Scoby, George W. Slover, Joseph Steinbruser, Charles Smith, Michael Sprinkle, Daniel W. Sue, Andrew Shoemaker, John D

Scatchell, Harman Thomas, George Tuttle, William Tuttle, Benjamin F. Upton, Christopher C. Warner, and William Zimmerman—ninety-four men.

The company became a part of the Sixteenth regiment, at Camp Jackson, Columbus, in May, 1861, under the command of Colonel James Irvine; John S. Fulton, of Ashland, being lieutenant colonel by promotion. The regiment was immediately ordered to Bellaire, and thence to Grafton, West Virginia, where it met the Fourteenth, under Colonel James B. Steedman, and the Fifteenth, under Colonel Lorin Andrews, and a regiment of West Virginians under Colonel Kelley. The Confederate forces, on the approach of these regiments, retired from Grafton in the direction of Philippi, and were pursued to that point, where a sharp skirmish ensued with Colonel Porterfield, who again retreated, and West Virginia was practically liberated. From Bellaire to Grafton the railroad track had been greatly damaged by the Southern forces, and the Ohio regiments immediately commenced repairs, and put the road in proper condition, placing guards to prevent further injury. To accomplish the task of restoring the road, the Sixteenth Ohio performed arduous duty. A short time after the affair at Philippi, General McClellan made a demonstration in the direction of Laurel Hill, but, from delays, and want of concert in movement, nothing was accomplished beyond marches and counter-marches. The Fourteenth regiment, under Colonel Steedman, was the first to cross at Parkersburgh, and the Sixteenth, under Colonel Irvine, at Bellaire.

The company was mustered out August 18, 1861, at Columbus, Ohio.

THE TWENTY-THIRD REGIMENT, OHIO VOLUNTEER INFANTRY.

The Twenty-third was commanded by Colonel E. P. Scammon. Under the call of July 22, 1861, for five hundred thousand men, Ohio furnished eighty-four thousand one hundred and sixteen men. These volunteers were divided among the various counties in the ratio of draftable men. Ashland county raised two full companies, which were incorporated in the Twenty-third regiment. The roster shows the following officers, promotions and men:

COMPANY G—THREE YEARS SERVICE.
COMMISSIONED OFFICERS.

Captain Willard Slocum, resigned July 17, 1861.
Captain James B. Drake, resigned September 24, 1862.
Captain Henry G. Hood, mustered out.
First Lieutenant Henry G. Hood, promoted captain.
First Lieutenant C. E. Reichenbach, promoted captain.
First Lieutenant B. F. Cooper, mustered out.
First Lieutenant George W. Stevens, promoted captain.
First Lieutenant D. K. Smith, promoted captain.
First Lieutenant M. B. Deshong, promoted captain.
Second Lieutenant Addison Snively, mustered out.
Second Lieutenant George W. Stevens, promoted first lieutenant.
Second Lieutenant D. K. Smith, promoted first lieutenant.
Second Lieutenant B. F. Cooper, promoted first lieutenant.
Second Lieutenant W. A. Stoner, mustered out.
Second Lieutenant C. A. Towslee, mustered out.
Second Lieutenant M. B. Deshong, promoted first lieutenant.
Second Lieutenant L. R. Gray, killed at Winchester.
Second Lieutenant Henry M. Beer, mustered out.
Second Lieutenant James M. Craig, mustered out.

NON-COMMISSIONED OFFICERS.

First Sergeant John McNaull.
Second Sergeant Charles A. Towslee.
Third Sergeant Milton B. Deshong.
Fourth Sergeant Frederick F. Koonse.
Fifth Sergeant John M. Simonton.
First Corporal James S. Brown.
Second Corporal Alfred O. Long.
Third Corporal Edward P. Carr.
Fourth Corporal Mark Slonaker.
Fifth Corporal Andrew B. Jackson.
Sixth Corporal Abram Gipe.
Seventh Corporal Willard E. Slocum.
Eighth Corporal George A. Kellogg.
Fifer Patrick Fleaharty.
Drummer James A. Huffman.
Bugler John Zimmerman.
Wagoner Philip Martin.

PRIVATES.

William Arthur, Alfred Arthur, Edwin Arthur, Edward Albright, William Brown, Joseph A. Brown, Andrew M. Burton, Abner G. Byron, Theodore Belding, John M. Benton, John Buchan, Daniel Chapman, Rodney H. Carr, Theodore Coffin, Eugene Coffin, Oscar F. Crall, John M. Clugston, Joseph J. Cratty, Milton N. Campbell, W. A. Critchfield, William S. Crepps, Josiah M. Closson, Lawrence Donivan, Charles Dean, William H. Eichner, John B. Fulkerson, James Finley, Bartholomew Fitzgerald, John Foll, John Gault, John N. Galleher, Lewis R. Grey, John Goss, Christian Gillgen, Francis M. Grimes, Charles Goodfellow, Jacob Hisey, Henry Hildebrand, David Hart, Samuel Harman, Jacob B. Hoke, Silas Hall, Alfred Hall, Thomas J. Hargrave, Charles W. Hoffman, Oliver P. Jackson, Amos Kirkwood, Herbert Kilburn, John W. Kiser, Jeremiah Linard, Solomon Linard, Cyrus McConnell, Hugh Moore, Philip Michael, Samuel W. McClain, David Mercer, Thomas Micks, John McKinley, Francis R. McClintock, Earhart V. Miller, George W. Mock, George W. Mercer, John Melheim, Christian Miller, John Neff, William Neff, Levi Owen, John W. Oswald, Michael O'Brien, William O'Brien, John S. Pinney, Solomon Richwine, Joseph J. Roop, Perry Romine, William A. Stoner, James Strong, William Strick, John Sughrue, William A. Snively, Frederick Stewart, George W. Smith, George K. Smith, Andrew F. Saner, Henry P. Shutt, William E. Sefton, William Stover, John Spitler, Milton Simonton, Christian Stoner, Charles Sanders, Michael S. Treace, Wesley J. Taylor, George M. Towslee, John Vangilder, Newton VanNimman, David V. Wherry, Daniel Whisler, Henry O. West, William H. Whitcomb, and Alexander Wright.

The company was organized in Ashland, by Captain Willard Slocum, and went to Camp Chase, Columbus, Ohio, June 7, 1861; and on the 11th, was mustered into service. July 25th, it was ordered to West Virginia. It participated in nearly all the engagements against Generals Lee, Jackson and Floyd. In 1862, it was at the engagement at Jumping Branch. In May, it was at the battle of Pearisburg. It was next in Pope's campaign. In September, it helped expel the enemy from Frederick City, and participated in the great battles at South Mountain and Antietam. In October, it returned to the Kanawha valley, and aided in expelling the Confederate forces. In February, 1863, it was engaged in watching the approach of the noted Confederate raider, General John Morgan.

In the long and arduous service of this company, the wounded and mortality list is quite heavy. The following members of the company died in hospital or were killed during engagements: Mark Slonaker, killed at South Mountain; William S. Crepps, killed at South Mountain; David Hart, died in hospital; John W. Kiser, John S. Penney, and Daniel Whisler, killed at South Mountain; W. H. Whitcomb, died in hospital; William H. Eichner, killed at Cloyd Mountain; Lewis R. Gray, killed at Winchester; Charles Goodfellow, wounded at Winchester, taken prisoner, and died while in captivity; George W. Mercer and Charles Sanders, killed at Cloyd Mountain; George M. Towslee, killed at Cabletown, Virginia.

COMPANY H—THREE YEARS' SERVICE.

This company was organized by Captain James L. Drake, and recruited in Hanover, Lake and Green townships, and was mustered in at Camp Chase, Columbus, Ohio, June 12, 1861. The officers and privates were:

COMMISSIONED OFFICERS.

Captain James L. Drake.
First Lieutenant John P. Cunningham.
Second Lieutenant DeHaven K. Smith.

NON-COMMISSIONED OFFICERS.

First Sergeant Charles E. Reichenbach.
Second Sergeant Bently Leggitt.
Third Sergeant George W. Ramage.
Fourth Sergeant James M. Craig.
Fifth Sergeant George W. Smith.
First Corporal William F. Leopold.
Second Corporal Benjamin S. Brown.
Third Corporal Lewis D. Hughes.
Fourth Corporal Elisha Harris.
Fifth Corporal George W. Shaffer.
Sixth Corporal Emanuel Stoffer.
Seventh Corporal William Brown.
Eighth Corporal John Elder.
Musician Elias Robinson.
Musician Richard Lightner.
Wagoner Aaron Sigafoos.

PRIVATES.

John Atherton, William C. Barnes, Benjamin F. Bell, Lorenzo D. Bell, Samuel Bell, David Briggs, John Campbell, Samuel G. Clark, Henry H. Cramer, Benjamin F. Cooper, Albert Carmichael, Joseph Cramer, Isaac R. Crawford, Christian Cremmel, Conrad Doup, Lewis Doup, Francis M. Drake, John B. Fisher, Frank I. Gardner, Barnard Gillespie, David Grenbaugh, James W. Green, George W. Harper, Henry Henderson, Florian F. Howriens, Christian Kelser, Jacob J. Kelser, Airne Lechot, Harrison Leggett, Harrison H. Leggett, Henry Lichtner, Daniel Long, Joshua W. Mattocks, James McClain, James L. McClaren, Samuel E. McGinley, Thomas McIntire, Immer A. McMillen, William H. Northway, Charles Oats, Daniel I. Onstoll, James W. Poulson, Henry W. Parsons, Wilson B. Patterson, Elijah Pealer, Francis V. Pecant, James Pinkerton, Joseph Pinkerton, William W. Peck, David J. Richardson, Jacob E. Rife, Joseph Rawlinson, Henry Saner, Walter B. Selby, Christian Shank, David Shanklin, William H. Snyder, Samuel B. Spencer, Stephen Spurgeon, John W. Turner, John C. Wareham, Isaac N. Whitney, Robinson Wiggins, Thomas H. Williams, John Dunn, Charles Jones, John Moore, Jacob Moore, Stephen Mullony, John Seven, John Smith, Jeremiah Sutton and William Truax.

George W. Shaffer was killed at South Mountain; Richard Lichtner died in hospital; Joseph Cramer was drowned in the Kanawha river; Henry W. Parsons died of wounds received at South Mountain; Joseph Pinkerton died in hospital; David J. Richardson died from wounds received in battle; Isaac N. Whitney was killed in action September 14, 1862; and Robinson Wiggins fell in the same battle.

Company H appears to have been mustered out at Cumberland, Maryland, July 26, 1865.

THE TWENTY-THIRD REGIMENT.

The Twenty-third was organized at Camp Chase, Ohio. Colonel William S. Rosecranz commanded. During the campaign in West Virginia he was promoted to the position of brigadier general, and Lieutenant Colonel Scammon promoted to the vacancy.

On the twenty-fifth of July, 1861, the regiment was ordered to Clarksburgh, West Virginia. On the twenty-seventh of July, it was ordered to Weston. Here it performed arduous duty in fighting guerillas. The regiment next marched to Carnifax Ferry, where General Rosecranz found the Confederates under General Floyd, who retreated to Gauley river. Long marches and counter-marches ensued, in which the Twenty-third suffered severely. The regiment returned to Camp Ewing, on New river, and the winter of 1861-2 was devoted to drill and discipline. In the spring of 1862, Rosecranz advanced to Princeton. On the eighth of May, General Heth attacked and defeated the Northern forces. The Twenty-third fell back to Flat-top mountain, suffering severely from exposure, sickness, and want of healthy food. It subsequently returned to Parkersburgh and took the cars for Washington city. It marched under General McClellan toward Frederick city, from which the Confederates were driven. General McClellan then marched to Middletown, where the battle of South Mountain began, and was succeeded by the great battle of Antietam, which took place September 17, 1862. The Twenty-third participated in both battles. It lost, in wounded and killed, nearly two hundred men, and its colors were riddled with bullets. In October, the Twenty-third returned to West Virginia. During the campaign of 1862 it marched about six hundred miles. It wintered at the falls of the Great Kanawha, in West Virginia. In 1863 the Twenty-third was quartered, for some time, at Charleston, to watch the operations of General Morgan and the Confederate cavalry. In the spring of 1864, the Twenty-third entered upon an expedition that terminated in a battle at Cloyd Mountain on the ninth of May. The regiment then returned to Staunton, enduring many hardships; thence to Brownsburgh, and thence to Lexington, where another engagement took place. Here the military academy and residence of Governor Letcher were burned against the protests of the officers of the Twenty-third. The affair at Lynchburgh soon followed, and the Twenty-third retreated to Liberty; thence to Salem; thence to Big Sewell mountain, and thence to Charleston, enduring many hardships the entire route. On the tenth of July, 1864, the Twenty-third accompanied the division of General Crooks to Martinsburgh, to aid in repelling the invasion of General Early. The battle of Snicker's Ferry ensued, and the Twenty-third being surrounded, cut its way out. The battle of Winchester took place July 24th, and the Twenty-third lost one hundred and fifty men and ten officers, and retreated to Martinsburgh. It next participated in the battles of Berryville, Opequan, North Mountain and Cedar Creek, in September and October, 1864. It then returned to Cumberland, and to Grafton, where it remained on duty until March, 1865. July 26, 1865, it returned to Camp Taylor, near Cleveland, Ohio, where the men were paid and mustered out.

FORTY-SECOND REGIMENT OHIO VOLUNTEER INFANTRY.

The Forty-second was organized at Camp Chase, near Columbus, Ohio, in September, October and November, 1861. Colonel James A. Garfield commanded. Ashland county furnished two full companies for the three years' service. The company officers were:

COMPANY C.

COMMISSIONED OFFICERS.

Captain Tully C. Bushnell, resigned October 22, 1862.
First Lieutenant J. D. Stubbs, promoted assistant quartermaster and mustered out November 13, 1862.
First Lieutenant William N. Starr, promoted captain October 22, 1862.
Second Lieutenant John R. Helman, promoted first lieutenant June 11, 1862.
James S. Bowlby promoted second lieutenant October 22, 1862, and resigned January 9, 1864.

NON-COMMISSIONED OFFICERS.

First Sergeant James S. Bowlby.
Second Sergeant Reuben D. Kiplinger.
Third Sergeant George McCrea.
Fourth Sergeant William H. Marteen.
Fifth Sergeant Daniel Grosscup.
At the promotion of James S. Bowlby to second lieutenant all the sergeants were promoted—Frank Otto to fifth sergeant.
First Corporal Benjamin F. Beer.
Second Corporal Jacob D. Hilman.
Third Corporal John R. Shriver.
Fourth Corporal George Lee.
Fifth Corporal Andrew J. Snowbarger.
Sixth Corporal Albert H. Chambers.
Seventh Corporal William B. McBride.
Eighth Corporal William S. Brown.

PRIVATES.

John Ankeny, William L. Aten, James Anderson, John Albright, Earnest Aller, Samuel G. Brown, David W. Brandt, George Burd, Chas Bundy, Israel Border, James A. Beer, George Cassel, W. S. Chamberlain, Royce S. Crial, Edward Clarke, John E. Campbell, Chester Drake, John B. Darrow, James H. Doll, James R. Dinsmore, Horace Dibler, Marcus Deinoss, Daniel Draek, Abraham C. Echer, Zachariah Emery, John P. Ely, Adam Emmons, David Eicker, David B. Elson, Josiah Fike, Daniel Fike, Henry J. Fooney, John Fisher, Lewis Fullington, Jacob Freidline, George Foll, Alpheus A. Hamilton, Henry F. Hettinger, Edmund I. Heiser, Oren I. Howard, Jesse Hines, Jacob Helman, James Hull, Jeremiah Johnson, Samuel Kopp, Jacob Kait, John P. R. Kramer, Levi Kiplinger, William J. Lowerie, Charles G. Martin, John C. Musser, William Mish, James C. McConnell, Adam Maurer, William Maxhammer, Benjamin F. Martin, David Munsdorf, Benjamin F. Nelson, Jacob W. Over, Eli L. Over, Robert Patterson, Joseph Palmer, George Pomroy, Thomas H. B. Patterson, Tyler D. Park, Robert Pollock, John Pollock, Herbert Parsons, Aaron Plank, Milton Randall, Peter Rote, William B. Rudd, John Rote, Lewis Rote, Harry Simmons, Robert Smilie, Joseph Swartz, John Shafer, John Sadler, John Sowers, John M. Smalley, John B. Switzer, Samuel Switzer, Isaac Shockey, Rudolph Sutor, Abel D. Smalley, Russel Smith, Edmund P. Smith, Milton Shriver, Jacob Snowbarger, Robert Thompson, Paul Trauger, Andrew Utz, Dennis Vanderhoof, John B. Wiles, Abel D. White, John Wise, Jeremiah Mish.

The mortality list is as follows:

Died in hospital, John B. Darrow, James Doll, Abraham C. Ecker, Daniel Fike, John M. Smalley, James A. Beer, Lewis Fullington, Israel Border, Milton Shriver, Aaron Plank, Russel Smith, in Sullivan, John Albright; Abel D. Smalley, killed May 1, 1863; Earnest Aller, killed May 16, 1864; David Munsdorf, killed December 29, 1862; Jacob Friedline, Adam Emmons, Rudolph Suter, Isaac Shockey, Samuel Switzer, David Eicker, William J. Lowerie, Peter Rote, George Foll, died in hospital.

The company was mustered into the service at Camp Chase, Columbus, Ohio, September 25, 1861, and discharged at the same camp, September 30, 1864.

COMPANY H, FORTY-SECOND REGIMENT.

This company rendezvoused at Camp Chase, Columbus, Ohio, November 27, 1861, and was mustered into the United States service for three years. The following are the commissioned and non-commissioned officers and privates of said company, as enrolled:

COMMISSIONED OFFICERS.

Captain Seth M. Barber, resigned June 11, 1862, and transferred to Veteran Reserve corps, March 6, 1864.
Captain John R. Helman, transferred from company C, and promoted captain, June 3, 1864.
First Lieutenant William S. Spencer, resigned June 5, 1862.
First Lieutenant Peter Miller, transferred to company H, and promoted first lieutenant, January 22, 1864.
First Lieutenant Charles B. Howk, promoted first lieutenant, November 26, 1862; resigned October 23, 1863.
Second Lieutenant Edwin C. Leach, resigned June 5, 1862.
Second Lieutenant John F. Robinson, assigned to company H November 25, 1862, and transferred and promoted major Third infantry, June 6, 1863.
Second Lieutenant Charles B. Howk, promoted first lieutenant.

NON-COMMISSIONED OFFICERS.

First Sergeant John F. Robinson.
Second Sergeant Charles B. Howk.
Third Sergeant George B. Masters.
Fourth Sergeant LeGrand Brown.
Fifth Sergeant Joseph D. Moody.
First Corporal George Mitchelson.
Second Corporal William H. Mason.
Third Corporal Thomas B. White.
Fourth Corporal John Griffith.
Fifth Corporal H. J. Bowman.
Sixth Corporal Henry O. Biggs.
Seventh Corporal Charles Wickham.
Eighth Corporal Alvin I. Stanley.
Drummer A. G. Case.
Fifer W. A. Smith.
Wagoner Arthur Leach.

PRIVATES.

David Buffrime, John Buckley, Elisha Beggs, Andrew J. Burns, Wm. J. Buchan, Jacob Buzzard, Henry Burton, Henry Burge, Solomon Barrick, Jacob Barrick, Frederick Byers, William Chambers, Byron D. Clugston, James F. Crawford, Charles Crozier, James L. Chapman, Robert M. Cellers, Christian Dell, John Davidson, William Davidson, James A. Darrow, Elmore Evans, Luther M. Fast, William B. Fasig, Franklin A. Ford, George Full, Jacob Griffith, David Garver, Jacob Hines, James O. Humphrey, Nelson S. Hendryx, Austin Hayes, Adam Innis, David Kiplinger, D. E. Long, Frederick Long, Andrew McComb, William Maxhammer, Jacob Newcomer, David Onstott, William Robinson, George Peters, George W. Ryall, Hiram Raker, George M. Reed, George Riggs, Peter Royer, Tobias Spiker, David Schroll, Joseph B. F. Sampsell, jr., William Sloan, James B. Smith, John D. Schumaker, Joseph Spencer, William Swineford, Elisha Starkweather, George Taylor, Lewis Taylor, George Vanostrand, John Wells, John Warren, Richard P. Wooehouse, Eli Westenbarger, Reuben Wall, Philip Youngblood.

The following is the mortality list as derived from the company rolls: James Crawford, died in hospital; Christian Dell, in hospital; Jacob Hines, in hospital; Adam Innis, in hospital; David E. Long, at home; Andrew McComb, at home; George N. Ryall, of wounds received in battle; Elisha Starkweather, in hospital; Tobias Spiker, at home; Charles D. Towslee, in hospital; George Vanostrand, at home; Jacob Griffith, in hospital.

This company was mustered out at Camp Chase, Columbus, Ohio, December 2, 1864.

In an engagement near Memphis, Tennessee, Captain Seth M. Barber had the misfortune to be wounded in the foot, which subsequently required amputation, and was the occasion of his resignation, and subsequent assignment to the Veteran Reserve corps.

THE FORTY-SECOND REGIMENT.

General Garfield appointed Peter B. Johnson, of Ashland, then over sixty years of age, train master. He served three years in Virginia, Kentucky, and Tennessee, and was honorably discharged.

In December, 1861, the Forty-second was ordered to Kentucky. In January, 1862, it arrived near Paintville, and on the eighth marched under Lieutenant Colonel Sheldon to the fortified position of General Humphrey Marshall, and found the works evacuated and provisions carried away or destroyed. Colonel Garfield followed Marshall, and on the ninth the battle of Middle Creek took place, and Marshall again retreated and burned his stores. The Forty-second returned and passed up the Big Sandy and took possession of Pound Gap. The campaign was disastrous to the volunteers of the Forty-second, eighty-five of whom died through exposure and disease. In March the Forty-second was ordered to Louisville, where it was attached to the brigade of General George W. Morgan, and moved by rail to Lexington, and from thence marched to Cumberland Ford, with only three hundred and fourteen men fit for duty. In June it marched to the rear of Cumberland Gap, amid continued skirmishing. On the fifth of August, the Forty-second engaged and held back the advance of General Kirby Smith. General Morgan, after consultation, finally evacuated the Gap and fell back to, and crossed, the Ohio river at Greensburgh. The retreat was very rapid, and the men suffered severely for the want of clothing, proper food and rest. In the month of November, Morgan's brigade passed down to Memphis, Tennessee.

In December, the Forty-second was ordered to the Yazoo, and led the advance against Vicksburgh. For three days the regiment held its position in line, when the army was compelled to retire. In January, 1863, the forces proceeded to White River, and thence to Arkansas Post, and captured Fort Hindman with seven thousand prisoners, all the guns, small arms and stores. The Forty-second then returned to the rear of Vicksburgh. In the engagements which followed, the regiment sustained heavy loss. After the surrender of Vicksburgh the Forty-second marched to Jackson, and participated in its capture, and then entered the Department of the Gulf. It remained at Thebodeaux during the winter of 1864, and in the spring went on an expedition to Clinton, Louisiana, where it participated in a severe engagement. It was also in several other small expeditions, and returned to Camp Chase where it was mustered out September 30, 1864. The Forty-second was engaged in eleven battles, in which it lost one officer and twenty men killed, and eighteen officers and three hundred and twenty-five men wounded. Its tattered banners show hard service.

SIXTY-FIFTH REGIMENT, OHIO VOLUNTEER INFANTRY.

The Sixty-fifth was a part of the brigade raised at Mansfield by Hon. John Sherman, and organized at Camp Buckingham, and mustered into service December 1, 1861. Its term of service was three years. The regiment was commanded by Colonel Charles G. Harker. Part of a company from Ashland county entered the Sixty-fifth under the following officers:

COMMISSIONED OFFICERS.

Captain Orlow Smith.
First Lieutenant Charles Gregg.
Second Lieutenant Charles O. Tannehill.

NON-COMMISSIONED OFFICERS.

First Sergeant Dolson Vankirk.
Second Sergeant Nelson Smith.
Third Sergeant Hamilton C. Oldroyd.
Fourth Sergeant John C. Zollinger.
Fifth Sergeant W. H. H. J. Gorham.
First Corporal R. A. Chapel.
Second Corporal Brewer Smith.
Third Corporal George W. Gordon.
Fourth Corporal Augustus Reimlin.
Fifth Corporal Joseph Crow.
Sixth Corporal H. C. Jennings.
Seventh Corporal Ezekial Moore.
Eighth Corporal John Mellony.

PRIVATES.

Samuel Alderge, James Anderson, James Atlerholt, Adam Apple, John Boyd, Daniel Black, Jacob Biehamme, John Brown, C. F. E. Blaich, John Cobon, Peter Clemmens, Robert Cross, Daniel Carmack, William Clark, Charles Carpenter, Martin Casey, George W. Curtis, C. W. Curtis, E. Drumheller, William Donelson, David Drumheller, James Delano, A. Eminger, Oliver Evans, John E. Earnest, Lewis Eckhart, Isaac Fisher, Jacob Tiks, Joseph Fellman, J. G. Gorham, Daniel Gregory, Jacob Garsht, David Grubaugh, John Guidman, Theodore Geisey, Harrison Hazen, C. C. Hess, David Hoff, Samuel Huber, Horace Heliker, Robert Heliker, Calvin Jordan, S. Johnson, Clark Jordan, Harrison Johnson, William Kolhorst, Jasper Karns, Frederick Koegele, Henry Lyon, Lewis Laubaugh, Henry Leidkie, George McClellan, James Mitchell, John McGuire, Andrew Mumper, George McKinley, James Murtz, John Murphy, John Murts, A Markham, Michael Nash, John V. Nicholai, James Nolan, Jesse Potter, George W. Philo, John S. Pennill, E. S. Russell, James Swassick, Peter Sharp, William B. Sturdevant, Reuben Sigler, Clinton Strine, Lewis K. Sheehand, John Sullivan, Peter Selner, J. C. Weedemier, William Walsh.

Company G was mustered into the United States service at Camp Buckingham, Mansfield, Ohio, November 25, 1865, and discharged at Victoria, Texas, November 30, 1865.

The mortality list was not included in the roll, and, hence, cannot appear here. It is certain, however, that the company performed arduous duty in the far South, and was considerably diminished by disease and death before its discharge.

THE SIXTY-FIFTH REGIMENT.

Captain Orlow Smith was promoted to lieutenant colonel, October 10, 1865, and to colonel, November 24, 1865.

The Sixty-fifth was employed some months, in 1862, in Kentucky, repairing and guarding roads, and then marched into Tennessee to Columbia, and thence to Savannah, Georgia, and from thence to Pittsburgh Landing, and participated in that battle. It next moved to Corinth, and was at the siege, and returned to Louisville, Kentucky. It was ordered to march toward Stone River, and was in the battle of December 29, 1862. In June, 1863, it was ordered to Chattanooga, and participated in that battle. The Sixty-fifth passed on to Mission Ridge, and took part in that engagement. Then came the Atlanta campaign—the affair at Lookout Mountain, Resaca, Dallas, Marietta, Kenesaw, Peachtree Creek, and Jonesborough, in which the Sixty-fifth took a part. On the twenty-ninth of November, it was in the battle of Springfield; on the thirtieth, in the battle of Franklin, and afterwards, in the battle of Nashville. In June, 1865, the regiment was ordered to Texas, and remained at San Antonio until December, and was ordered to

Camp Chase, Ohio, where it was mustered out January 2, 1866. The Sixty-fifth came out of the service scarred veterans.

THE EIGHTY-SECOND REGIMENT, OHIO VOLUNTEER INFANTRY.

The Eighty-Second was recruited in Ashland, Logan, Marion, Union and Richland counties, for three years. It was commanded by Colonel James Cantwell, who was killed in the second battle of Manassas. The regiment was mustered into service December 31, 1861, and contained nine hundred and sixty-eight men. Ashland county had one company, K. Its officers were:

COMMISSIONED OFFICERS.

Captain David S. Sampsell, resigned July 30, 1862.
Captain Francis S. Jacobs, resigned.
First Lieutenant John S. Fulton, died April 30, 1862.
First Lieutenant Francis S. Jacobs, promoted to captain.
First Lieutenant John A. McClusky, resigned.
First Lieutenant James J. Beer, killed May 3, 1863.
First Lieutenant Warren Wasson, resigned.
First Lieutenant George W. Youngblood, mustered out.
Second Lieutenant Francis S. Jacobs, promoted first lieutenant.
Second Lieutenant James J. Beer, promoted first lieutenant.
Second Lieutenant Warren Wasson, promoted first lieutenant.
Second Lieutenant George W. Youngblood, promoted first lieutenant.

NON-COMMISSIONED OFFICERS.

First Sergeant James J. Beer.
Second Sergeant William W. Brown.
Third Sergeant John A. McClusky.
Fourth Sergeant Alonzo Mingus.
Fifth Sergeant James I. Nelson.
First Corporal James Campbell.
Second Corporal James N. Chandler.
Third Corporal Albert Hines.
Fourth Corporal George H. McNabb.
Fifth Corporal William Moore.
Sixth Corporal Thomas Hallam.
Seventh Corporal John A. Arnold.
Eighth Corporal Thomas K. Jacobs.

PRIVATES.

John Aten, Henry M. Brown, William H. Bush, Edward Butcher, Henry Bushaw, John Bonebright, Reuben Blue, George Buchanan, David Colerman, Sigman Crabell, Dennis Dove, Charles Deatrick, Abner Ewing, W. A. G. Emerson, Charles F. Engle, John F. Fennell, Richard Frankhauser, Samuel Framer, Harmon Fulton, Franklin Fisk, Otis Friend, John Y. Greenlee, Philip Helwigg, John Houston, George Hibberts, Adolphus Huickle, A. Johnson, Edward Justice, William Knight, John C. Koutzman, Hiram Lockhart, James Lafferty, Daniel Lile, Joseph Low, William C. Layton, Charles Merling, Philip Martin, Joseph Maize, Elias Marshall, Wilson Motter, Cyrus Markley, James Mushland, Franklin Myers, Hankey Priest, Leroy Park, James C. Pittinger, John W. Powers, William H. Russell, Samuel Reuben, Albert Rose, Daniel Sental, George Shultz, Lorin S. Saner, Warren J. Sales, Isaiah Spitler, F. J. Studebaker, Peter Topper, Isaac Thralekill, Charles Tucker, D. H. Toff, Warren H. Wasson, Grafton White, Alanson Walker, John Williams, John Walters, William Weygandt, Washington Weygandt, Washington Wineland, William Woods, Jesse Vanosdall, Gutelius I. Yearick, Jacob Zapp.

Company K was mustered out at Louisville, Kentucky, July 24, 1865. We are unable to make out the mortality list from the roll; but by reference to the regimental service, which follows, it will be seen that company K performed arduous duty, and that its ranks were greatly thinned by disease and the casualties of war.

THE EIGHTY-SECOND REGIMENT.

In January, 1862, the Eighty-second was ordered from Kenton, Ohio, its place of rendezvous, to West Virginia, and went into camp near the village of Fetterman, for instruction and drill. In the spring the regiment, in the brigade of General Robert Schenck, was sent to various points in pursuit of guerillas, after which it was ordered to go to the aid of General Milroy, near McDowell. The Confederate forces were attacked by Generals Schenck and Milroy near Bull Pasture mountain, and compelled them to retreat. The Eighty-second then joined General John C. Fremont, and passed by rapid marches through Petersburgh, when the battle of Strasburgh occurred, and the enemy again retreated under Stonewall Jackson. The column passed on to Cross Keys, where a running fight ensued, and Jackson crossed the Shenandoah, destroying the bridge and marched leisurely away, having scattered the forces of General Shields. The tardiness of Fremont in the pursuit of Jackson, practically ended his military career. Severe campaigning followed. The troops returned to Middletown, and General Siegel took command of the division. The Eighty-second was transferred to an independent brigade, commanded by General Milroy. On the seventh of August Siegel's corps moved to Culpeper; and on the ninth toward Cedar Mountain, where a battle was going on. Milroy moved to the front to relieve exhausted troops; and on the night of the tenth, the enemy retreated. The Eighty-second destroyed Waterloo Bridge, and skirmished continually for ten days. The second battle of Manassas took place, and Colonel Cantwell, in leading a charge, was killed. The Eighty-second was much exposed and suffered severely in the battle. The National forces were finally compelled to withdraw to Centerville. In September the Eighty-second moved to Fort de Kalb, Siegel's headquarters. On the twenty-fifth it advanced to Fairfax Court House, and the campaign closed with the attempt to capture the heights of Fredericksburgh. The Eighty-second was transported to the division of General Schurz, and by him designated as a battalion of sharpshooters. In April, 1863, the Eleventh corps moved on the Chancellorsville campaign, crossing the Rappahannock, at Kelley's Ford, and the Rapidan, at Ely's Mills; and on the thirtieth arrived within three miles of the battle ground. The battle opened May 2nd, and the Eighty-second and others deployed with fixed bayonets, and fell back to the rifle-pits. The Eighty-second held its position; but regiment after regiment was pressed back under the terrible charge of the forces of Stonewall Jackson, and it finally fell back. It took a new position, having but one hundred and thirty-four men with the colors. Here Captain James J. Beer, a gallant young officer from Ashland county, fell. After the battle, the remaining members of the Eighty-second returned to its old camp near Stafford. In June, the Gettysburgh campaign commenced. The Eighty-second participated in that arduous campaign. It was ordered to move over the plain to assail, with its brigade, the Confederate works. In the attempt it lost twenty of its remaining men. The gaps were promptly filled, and the Eighty-second advanced within seventy-five yards of the Confederate lines. It went into the battle with twenty-two commissioned officers, and two hundred and thirty-six privates, and of these, nineteen officers and one hundred and forty-seven men were killed, wounded, or captured.

The balance of the regiment brought the colors, tattered and torn by shot and shell, safely from the field. After the retreat of the Confederate forces, the Eighty-second performed patrol duty at Catlet's station. It was then attached to the army of the Cumberland, and was in the battle of Mission Ridge. Then came a defeat and a retrograde movement to Knoxville. General Longstreet, of the Confederate army, retreated on the approach of the Northern forces. The ranks of the Eighty-second were so thinned by disease and battle that when General Sherman reached Goldsborough it was consolidated with the Sixty-first Ohio. These regiments continued with Sherman until his army reached Washington city, by way of Richmond and Alexandria, on the nineteenth of May, 1865; and then proceeded by rail to Louisville, Kentucky, and on the twenty-fifth of July returned to Camp Chase, Ohio, where it was paid and discharged on the twenty-ninth. No regiment in modern times performed more arduous duty than the Eighty-second. Very few of its young heroes survived the horrors of the battle field and returned to the family circle.

EIGHTY-SEVENTH REGIMENT, OHIO VOLUNTEER INFANTRY.

This regiment rendezvoused at Camp Chase, Columbus, Ohio, in June, 1862, and was a three months' organization. It was under the command of Colonel Henry B. Banning, of Mount Vernon. The organization of the regiment was completed by the twelfth of June, 1862, at which time it was ordered to repair to Baltimore, Maryland, and report to Major General Wool, commander of that post. It arrived in Baltimore on the fifteenth of June, and was assigned to a camp north of the city, where it was drilled some weeks by Colonel Banning.

COMPANY B.

COMMISSIONED OFFICERS.

Captain Henry H. Otis.
First Lieutenant William H. Johnston.
Second Lieutenant James A. Landis.

NON-COMMISSIONED OFFICERS.

First Sergeant W. J. Terrell.
Second Sergeant Dwight L. Wilber.
Third Sergeant John B. Smith.
Fourth Sergeant David Barnhisel.
Fifth Sergeant William W. Gibson.
First Corporal Adam J. Snook.
Second Corporal Charles D. Graham.
Third Corporal Anson H. Fast.
Fourth Corporal Oscar Crall.
Fifth Corporal Porter Stevens.
Sixth Corporal Crustus E. Fast.
Seventh Corporal George A. Bemis.
Eighth Corporal John Sleigh.
Musician Charles M. Steer.
Musician Fernando S. Pond.

PRIVATES.

Charles Archibald, Edward H. Alder, Harrison W. Atwood, James Blair, Ralph K. Beebe, Richard H. Bear, Abel Bailey, Michael C. Bronsch, James Buell, Herbert T. Bushnell, Edwin Bryant, Edward Bensinger, James M. Baughman, Ira R. Baldwin, Irwin W. Carpenter, William W. Calhoun, Isaac W. Cressinger, Newton Chalker, William H. Chalker, Orville Campbell, Perry D. Coner, William N. Callahan, William Decker, George H. Dulin, Bela D. Dudley, Jasper Dalton, James K. Elder, Henry M. Eells, James Elliott, Henry A. Frarey, Richard Gailey, Elbert Gillett, Hezekiah S. Griffiths, Norman Gilbert, John W. Grant, Ezra Greiselman, William H. Herrick, Albert Hamilton, Henry Hallbock, Elisha Halsted, James T. Hazard, James T. Hervey, William A. Holmes, Henry S. Humphrey, Henry S. Hiskey, Henry L. King, Manuel G. Kanauss, Morgan Langley, Joseph Lockhart, James Mathews, William D. Mathews, Charles McCluskey, Smith A. Marvin, James S. McClain, James P. Moore, Robert K. Moore, Burwell Neff, Henry Nemming, Upton Newman, Thomas B. Onstott, Oscar Patch, Alexander Pruden, David Pyle, Thomas L. Phillips, Luther S. Pilgrim, Henry A. Pilgrim, Henry Roberts, Harrison Robison, Everel S. Smith, William T. Sweet, John Saddler, Levi Shultz, Augustus W. Springer, Edward Sither, Scarett J. Terrell, Samuel Utz, Samuel A. Wierman, Robert L. Wilson, Samuel White, Henry C. Webster, Aaron Walters, Addison Walcott, Henry B. Wier, Willis W. Woodruff.

In the latter part of July, 1862, the Eighty-seventh received orders to report to Colonel Miles at Harper's Ferry. It was stationed on Boliver Heights, and subjected to rigid drill. It remained there until the siege of the Ferry by "Stonewall" Jackson, and at the surrender was included with the National forces. The various companies were subsequently released from their paroles, and were mustered out at Delaware, Ohio, on the twentieth of September, 1862.

*The muster out roll fails to detail the casualties of company B.

THE ONE HUNDRED AND SECOND REGIMENT, OHIO VOLUNTEER INFANTRY.

The One Hundred and Second enlisted under the call of July 1, 1862, for three hundred thousand men. It was recruited from Ashland, Holmes, Richland and Wayne counties, and was commanded by Colonel William Given. It was organized at Camp Mansfield, on the eighteenth of August, 1862. Ashland county furnished two full companies. The officers were:

COMPANY B.

COMMISSIONED OFFICERS.

Captain John McNaull, resigned December 20, 1862.
First Lieutenant Joseph R. Folwell, promoted captain December 20, 1862, and discharged.
First Lieutenant William A. Beer, of Company K, promoted captain in 1864.
Second Lieutenant Holiday Ames, promoted first lieutenant December 20, 1862.
Second Lieutenant John T. Robert, promoted second lieutenant December 20, 1862.

NON-COMMISSIONED OFFICERS.

First Sergeant William H. White.
Second Sergeant Oscar Swineford.
Third Sergeant Samuel R. Smith.
Fourth Sergeant William Green.
Fifth Sergeant David Carr.
First Corporal Reuben Richards.
Second Corporal R. H. Ridgely.
Third Corporal William Langden.
Fourth Corporal Hiram A. Kellogg.
Fifth Corporal Henry Krebbs.
Sixth Corporal John McCun.
Seventh Corporal Dilman Newman.
Eighth Corporal H. C. Buffenyer.
Drummer B. F. Ridgely.
Wagoner George Lundy.

PRIVATES.

Henry Albright, Livingston Anderson, John Brown, John H. Bender, Joseph Biggs, Stephen Boyd, Adam Bahn, Franklin Bailey, Henry A. Bailey, John W. Brubaker, Porter Craig, James W. Crone, David M. Ecker, Nathaniel Eddy, William Fasig, Daniel Fisher, Daniel Fisher, jr., William H. Fisher, Henry France, Michael Fleaharty, John Grosh, George Goudy, Gancin Hall, Jacob Hilderbrand, jr., John W. House, Samuel Hamer, Edmund Hough, Isaac Hough, Lewis Hough, James

B. Hull, George Hull, David Hamilton, John Hartsell, John F. Kailaver, Theodore Kiser, Samuel Kyle, Christian Keener, Pollis D. Lacey, Joseph Lucas, Alexander McKinney, Jacob McCauley, James McCready, Andrew J. Michle, Franklin Mish, James M. Mercer, Madison Mercer, Levi M. Mercer, William Martin, William Maxwell, Albert Pittinger, William Pittinger, Silas Potter, David Pryor, Alexander Ritchy, Jeremiah Smith, Peter Smith, Henry Saner, John Smith, Samuel Staker, John M. Scott, Harrison Spafford, Henry Swaisgood, William Swaisgood, John Sulcer, Joseph Smutz, Samuel Scruly, Alfred M. Sheets, Solomon Sheets, Daniel Smalley, Paul Sherradden, Benjamin F. Shrock, James W. Wells, Johnston Winters, Matthew Woods, John Wycoff, Asa Webster, Ephraim Whissamore, Abraham Whissamore, Charles Whingate John Wagoner, and Joseph Wells.

Company B was enlisted in Ashland county for three years, by Captain John McNaull.* It went into Camp Mansfield August 20, 1862, and was armed with Austrian rifles on the third of September, and, on the fourth, left camp by rail for Cincinnati, and crossed the Ohio river and arrived at Covington, Kentucky, and on the sixth was mustered into the United States service by Captain P. H. Bresslin. It served three years, and was discharged at Columbus, Ohio, July 8, 1865.

The mortality list, so far as we are able to gather from the rolls, is as follows: Stephen Boyd, David M. Ecker, William Faher, Edmund Hough, Lewis Hough, William Maxwell, Jeremiah Smith.

COMPANY K.

COMMISSIONED OFFICERS.

Captain John M. Sloan.
First Lieutenant William A. Beer.
Second Lieutenant Jerome Potter.

NON-COMMISSIONED OFFICERS.

First Sergeant Daniel W. Kagey.
Second Sergeant George McConnell.
Third Sergeant Andrew Proudfit.
Fourth Sergeant Joel Berry.
Fifth Sergeant William A. Fast.
First Corporal Robert W. Alberson.
Second Corporal Michael H. Sprinkle.
Third Corporal David R. Crantz.
Fourth Corporal Edmund D. Stentz.
Fifth Corporal Wilson A. Fast.
Sixth Corporal Watson W. Anderson.
Seventh Corporal James M. Campbell.
Eighth Corporal William Molter.
Musicians Chandler Powers and C. A. Wilcox.
Wagoner Jacob Stoner.

PRIVATES.

William A. Barker, John Barker, Joseph B. Bechtell, William Beck, Isaac Boyer, George M. Bowlby, Daniel Braden, Henry Bradley, John F. Bryan, Elijah Bullard, Caleb Budd, Henry Bunt, George B. Carney, John Cassel, Anderson N. Cook, Elias Cyle, John Dall, Thomas Donley, Alexander Dunlap, Jacob Ely, Isaac Fast, James B. Gibson, Andrew Gorden, Isaac Grubaugh, John F. Hartman, Jacob Holtzman, Josiah Hoover, John F. Imhoff, Charles Kanauss, John F. Kauffman, Samuel Kerstetter, David Kiplinger, Lorenzo Keller, Jacob Kissel, Luther N. Lane, Oliver Lee, James Lee, Reuben Leidigh, Abraham Lutz, Aretus Marsh, James H. McKee, Aaron Mitchell, John Molter, Charles Molter, Jacob Moore, Hugh Murray, Peter S. Myers, John D. Myers, Henry Myers, Elmore Y. Norris, Charles E. Ogden, Solomon Philips, Calvin C. Rice, Wesley Reddick, Henry Robinson, John Romine, Benjamin F. Ross, Frederick Rockenfelder, Peter Rutan, John Sattler, George Sattler, Samuel Signs, William Silance, Jeremiah Singer, Josiah A. Shultz, Annias Shultz, Josiah Shultz, Joseph N. Shaver, Amos Sprinkle, Henry Starrett, Abraham Stayman, George Steinmetz, Joseph Stofer, John Tracey, George G. Topping, John Vanosdall, Simon B. Vanosdall, James Walker, John Walker, John Wolf, Joseph Wolf, Benjamin F. Yonk, Samuel Youngblood.

Company K was mustered out at Nashville, Tennessee, June 30, 1865.

The mortality list as gathered from the rolls is as follows:

Daniel W. Kagey, died of small pox; Andrew Proudfit, died a Bowling Green; David R. Crantz, died at Nashville; Anderson Watson, died at Jefferson barracks; Joseph B. Bechtell, died at Vicksburgh; William Beck, died at Tullahoma; George W. Bowlby, died at Bowling Green; Caleb Budd, died at Nashville; John Cassel, lost on Sultana; Jacob Ely, died at Huntsville; James B. Gibson, died at Huntsville; Andrew Gordon, died at Nashville; Isaac Grubaugh, died at Clarksville; John F. Hartman, lost on Sultana; Jacob Holtzman, died at Russelville; John F. Imhoff, died at Bowling Green; Reuben Leidigh, lost on Sultana; Aretus Marsh, died at Clarksville; Elmore Y. Norris, died at Andersonville; Charles E. Ogden, lost on Sultana; John Romine, died at Andersonville; Frederick Rockenfelder, died at Nashville; John Sattler, died at Clarksville; Jeremiah Singer, lost on Sultana; Annias Shultz, died at Bowling Green; George Steinetz, lost on Sultana; Simon Vanosdall, died at Andersonville; Samuel Youngblood, died at Clarksville; Henry W. Bunt, died at Bowling Green.

THE ONE HUNDRED AND SECOND REGIMENT.

The One Hundred and Second was ordered to Kentucky, and mustered into service at Covington, September 6, 1862. It was ordered to Louisville, and went into the trenches to defend that city. In October, it marched to Shelbyville, Franklin, and Perryville, and thence to Crab Orchard; thence to Bowling Green. From thence it was ordered to Clarksville, Tennessee, for drill and camp duty. In September, 1863, it returned to Shelbyville, to aid in repelling the invasion of General Wheeler, of the Confederate army. It returned to Nashville, and went into winter quarters. In April, 1864, the One Hundred and Second marched to Tullahoma, and thence to Bellefonte, Alabama. Here it was ordered to patrol the Tennessee river, from Stevenson to Seven Mile island, a distance of fifty miles. On this line it erected twelve block-houses and one fort. The regiment was frequently assailed by guerillas, and suffered considerably from exposure and sickness. Shortly after the completion of its fort and other works, General Forrest, of the Confederate army, made a dash upon the One Hundred and Second with his cavalry, and captured a portion of its men under Colonel Elliott, near Athens, after a severe fight. Six months afterward the prisoners were paroled, and placed on board the ill-fated Sultana, at Vicksburgh, and eighty-one men of the One Hundred and Second were lost. On the twenty-fourth of October, General Hood, of the Confederate forces, attacked the garrison at Decatur, Alabama, in which the remaining companies of the One Hundred and Second were on duty, and were conspicuous in the fight. After the evacuation of Decatur, the One Hundred and Second continued in active duty in Tennessee until June 30, 1865, when it was mustered out at Nashville; returned to Camp Chase, Ohio, and was paid and discharged July 8, 1865. The regiment was noted for its prompt obedience of orders, and gallantry in the face of the enemy.

---

*NOTE.—When Captain John McNaull resigned, First Lieutenant John R. Falwell was promoted to be captain. Upon his resignation, some four months prior to the close of the enlistment, in 1865, Captain Anderson Beer, of company K, was transferred, and took command of company B. Davilla Bender, second sergeant of company B, was discharged for disability December 10, 1862.

THE ONE HUNDRED AND TWENTIETH REGIMENT, OHIO VOLUNTEER INFANTRY.

This regiment was organized at Camp Mansfield, under the call for three hundred thousand men, in August, 1862. The regiment was recruited from Ashland, Holmes, Richland, and Wayne counties, and contained nine hundred and forty-nine men. It was commanded by Colonel Daniel French. Ashland county furnished two full companies.

COMPANY C.
COMMISSIONED OFFICERS.

Captain John F. McKinley.
First Lieutenant Thomas Armstrong.
Second Lieutenant William Harvey.

NON-COMMISSIONED OFFICERS.

First Sergeant William Hughes.
Second Sergeant Robert F. Wallace.
Third Sergeant Samuel Harlan.
Fourth Sergeant James Gillis.
Fifth Sergeant David Hunt.
First Corporal William J. Hunter.
Second Corporal George Guinther.
Third Corporal Samuel Budd.
Fourth Corporal Henry Sweringen.
Fifth Corporal Joseph Seibert.
Sixth Corporal Henry B. Davis.
Seventh Corporal William J. McCreary.
Musicians John Reading and William Robinson.
Wagoner John P. Woodhull.

PRIVATES.

William S. Anderson, William Buzzard, Joseph Byerly, Eli Bell, William Budd, John E. Buckley, Aaron Buckley, Jonathan Black, Riley Black, Michael Bitner, Crawford Byers, John L. Beard, Gibson Craig, John M. Crabb, John W. Cole, George B. Cole, John Cole, John Casey, William Cipher, Thomas C. Coke, Silas Cotter, Samuel Christine, Stephen Davis, Marion Dalton, Amos M. Ely, John Eberhart, John France, Harrison Fisher, John Gray, William L. Gray, Henry B. Grindle, Anthony L. Gettle, Daniel Henney, John A. Henney, Lester L. Haxen, John S. Hankins, Christopher C. Huber, Henry Harpster, Franklin Hayes, William Harman, Jacob Houker, James Jarvis, Amasa Jones, James Latimer, Abner Marshall, Archibald Marshall, Lewis W. Miller, Wilton McCreary, Franklin McMaster, Henry McClay, James F. McClure, John S. Petty, Joseph Risser, John J. Rodenheber, David Rhodes, Henry Rhodes, Thomas C. Stevens, John C. Scott, William S. Shambaugh, Alonzo Shambaugh, Henry Shambaugh, Daniel Stauffer, Alonzo M. Stearnes, Marion Sigler, Jared Sigler, Thomas J. Spade, Jonathan C. Terrence, John Tanney, Thomas C. Tanney, William Vangilder, Semin Whitamore, William Wilson, James Wilson, Samuel Weerick, Elliott Winters, Lucius Weatherbee, Jackson Weatherbee.

Company C rendezvoused at Camp Mansfield, and was mustered into the United States service on the seventeenth of October, 1862, for three years.

It is impossible to gather from the original rolls of the organization, the mortality that attended company C, which was undoubtedly very large.

COMPANY F.
COMMISSIONED OFFICERS.

Captain Henry Buck, resigned February 15, 1863.
First Lieutenant Robert M. Zuver, resigned June 14, 1863.
Second Lieutenant John Sloan, promoted captain February 20, 1863.

NON-COMMISSIONED OFFICERS.

First Sergeant Elias Framfelter, promoted First Lieutenant March 15, 1863.
Second Sergeant Henry Berry.
Third Sergeant John Ambrose.
Fourth Sergeant Peter Heckert.
Fifth Sergeant Charles H. Dorland.
First Corporal David George.
Second Corporal David Crumrine.
Third Corporal Franklin Emery.
Fourth Corporal Daniel Lair.
Fifth Corporal David Pollock.
Sixth Corporal John Switzer.
Seventh Corporal Samuel Sloan.
Eighth Corporal Andrew Nunemaker.
Musician John Herbrand.
Musician Arthur Coffin.
Wagoner Franklin Welch.

PRIVATES.

Emanuel Albright, Leonard Burkholder, Richard Biggs, William Brown, John Brindle, Jacob Black, Richard Barr, Andrew Clinger, Israel Crull, Henry Delancy, William Dow, Frederick Elsor, Samuel Freeman, Michael France, Thomas Gribben, Martin Gardner, John Gable, George Gast, Solomon Houser, Aaron Hilyard, Jonathan Holmes, William Hettinger, Robert J. Harris, William Hildebrand, Isaac Judd, John Heiffner, Emanuel Lutz, Jacob W. Myers, William Myers, Benjamin Myers, George H. Mentor, Adam Mish, Daniel Mohler, John W. Millington, James McCaleb, Samuel McCullough, James McClain, William P. Martin, John Maxwell, Charles Nixon, Henry Over, John Palmer, Cyrus Plank, Morgan Rhees, James Richard, Francis Reckard, George Reckard, William Rickel, Peter P. Rickel, George W. Saltzman, William Stametz, John W. Smalley, Thomas H. Sloan, Henry Stauffer, Alfred Sturges, George Shriner, Thomas H. Smith, Richard Smilie, John Spigle, Albert Thompson, Joseph P. VanNest, Marion Vanoonam, Frederick Wagoner, Hugh Weaver, George W. Weitman, Abraham Yearick, Isaac Yearick, Edward Zartman.

The mortality list for company F is as follows: Charles H. Dorland, died at St. Louis; David Crumrine, died in hospital; Daniel Lair, at Keokuk, William Brown, killed in Arkansas; John Brindle, killed in Mississippi; Israel Crull, died at Nashville; William Dow, died in Louisiana; Samuel Freeman, died in Arkansas; Martin Gardner, died at St. Louis; John Gable, died in Louisiana; William Hettinger, died in Louisiana; Emanuel Lutz, died in Louisiana; William P. Martin, died at St. Louis; Morgan Rheese, died in hospital; William Stametz, died in Louisiana; John W. Smalley, died at St. Louis; Thomas H. Sloan, died in Louisiana; Marion Vanoonam, died in Louisiana; George W. Weitman, died in Louisiana.

Company F was mustered into the United States service at Camp Mansfield, October 14, 1862, and on the twenty-fifth departed by rail for Covington, Kentucky, where it arrived on the twenty-sixth. The meanderings of the Twelfth will exhibit the history of its compa:

THE ONE HUNDRED AND TWENTIETH REGIMENT.

At the organization of the One Hundred and Twentieth, Lieutenant Willard Slocum acted as adjutant, and was promoted to major February 18, 1863, and lieutenant colonel September 8, 1863, and brevetted after the close of the war. Captain John McKinley was promoted to major September 8, 1863, and transferred to the One Hundred and Fourteenth Ohio volunteer infantry, when he was promoted to lieutenant colonel and mustered out.

The One Hundred and Twentieth reported to General Wright at Cincinnati, on the twenty-fifth of October, 1862, for duty, and crossed to Covington, Kentucky. In November it was ordered to Memphis, Tennessee, where it entered the brigade of General George W. Morgan, and moved to the mouth of the Yazoo river, and thence to Johnson's landing to attack the fortifications defending Vicksburgh. The attack commenced on the twenty-sixth, the One Hundred and Twentieth participating. It was actively engaged during the siege, and suffered severely in consequence of malaria and exposure. The regiment was ordered to Arkansas Post in January, 1863. When Fort Hindman had been surrounded, the One Hundred and Twentieth made a direct charge upon the works—the enemy displayed a white flag and surrendered—the One Hundred and Twentieth having the honor of first entering the fort, as Sergeant Robert Wallace scaled the parapet and planted the colors, for which he was promoted to first lieutenant. The regiment returned to Young's Point, where it suffered severely from malarious fever for nearly two months, more than half the privates being on the sick list. In consequence of delays, several of the officers resigned. Early in the spring of 1863 the regiment was ordered to different points along the Mississippi, and finally to Fort Gibson, which was captured, the One Hundred and Twentieth losing one-eighth of its men in the battle. Jackson and Raymond were next captured, and the regiment remained at the latter place until May, 1863. The One Hundred and Twentieth returned to the rear of Vicksburgh and participated in the siege. In July it was ordered on another expedition to Jackson, and, during its investment, Colonel Spigel was severely wounded, and the regiment considerably cut up by the artillery of the enemy. It returned to the Black River bridge in July, and went into camp at Vicksburgh. In September the regiment passed down the Mississippi and returned to Plaquemine, one hundred and ten miles above New Orleans, where it remained until March, 1864, when in joined the expedition under General N. P. Banks to invade Arkansas. At Red River Bend, near Snaggy Point, the "City Belle," on which the regiment was crossing the river, was suddenly attacked by about five thousand Confederates concealed behind the levee, who poured a murderous fire into the boat. It was soon disabled by the artillery of the enemy and floated to the opposite side of the river, where it displayed a white flag and surrendered. Colonel Spigel fell, and Captains Elias Fraunfelter, Rummel, and Miller, and two hundred privates fell into the hands of the Confederates, and were marched off to Camp Ford, near Tyler, Texas, where they remained in a miserable prison about one year. Those who escaped formed a battalion of three companies under Lieutenant Colonel Slocum, and, after a march of twenty-three hours, arrived safely at Alexandria and joined the forces of General Banks. In May General Banks began his retreat. The regiment returned to Morganza, Louisiana, and remained until September, and moved up White river to St. Charles, Arkansas, and thence to Duvall's bluff. In November the One Hundred and Twentieth and One Hundred and Fourteenth Ohio were consolidated, Lieutenant Colonel Kelley, of the One Hundred and Fourteenth, becoming colonel, and Major McKinley, of the One Hundred and Twentieth, lieutenant colonel of the new regiment. Lieutenant Colonel Slocum was honorably discharged, his position being rendered supernumerary by the consolidation of the regiments. This ended the career of the One Hundred and Twentieth regiment. It was organized in 1862 with nine hundred and forty-nine men, and, in 1864, received one hundred and fifty recruits, making ten hundred and ninety-nine men. At its discharge it contained only four hundred and forty men, showing a loss of six hundred and fifty-nine men during the service. The toil and suffering of this regiment were borne throughout with unshrinking fortitude. Like the Eighty-second, the One Hundred and Twentieth returned scarred and worn veterans, to the firesides of their friends.

THE ONE HUNDRED AND SIXTY-THIRD REGIMENT OHIO VOLUNTEER INFANTRY.

This regiment was mustered into the United States service at Camp Chase, Ohio, May 12, 1864, under Colonel Hiram Miller, and on the thirteenth proceeded to Washington city, D. C., under orders from General Heintzelman, commanding the department of the Ohio. The regiment remained at Fort Reno, when it was ordered to the front, and proceeded on transports to White House, Virginia, and thence to Bermuda Hundred. It then reported to General Butler at Point of Rocks, and on the twelfth and fourteenth of June was in the reconnoissance of the Petersburgh & Richmond railroad. On the fifteenth two hundred and fifty men were engaged in a heavy skirmish. On the sixteenth the regiment proceeded to Wilson's Landing. It assisted in building Fort Pocahontas. On the twenty-ninth the regiment was relieved from further duty and returned to Columbus, Ohio, and was mustered out September 10, 1864. Company I was from Ashland county.

COMPANY I.
COMMISSIONED OFFICERS.

Captain Joseph R. Remley.
First Lieutenant Corpus C. Funk.
Second Lieutenant Isaiah Mowry.

NON-COMMISSIONED OFFICERS.

First Sergeant Emanuel Kauffman.
Second Sergeant James R. Glenn.
Third Sergeant William P. Williams.
Fourth Sergeant Thomas Glenn.
Fifth Sergeant F. Wilson.
First Corporal Nicholas Glenn.
Second Corporal Alva Ingmand.
Third Corporal Henry F. Grindle.
Fourth Corporal John B. Remley.
Fifth Corporal John Gardner.
Sixth Corporal James H. Allison.
Seventh Corporal Jacob Fasig.
Eighth Corporal Hugh Hamilton.
Drummer Harrison McHose.
Fifer Charles T. Allaman.

PRIVATES.

Caleb S. Anderson, William Ambrose, John H. Blew, Henry M. Buffenmire, Peter Barkley, Henry Barkley, Arthur Campbell, John Campbell, George W. Culbertson, Robert M. Cross, William Dieffenderfer, John Dalton, George B. Eagle, Harrison Friedline, Samuel Friedline, Benjamin Funk, Plummer Fetterman, Franklin Gardner, Levi Gardner, William R. Garst, William Gill, William M. Gill, John Goudy, David Goodman, Alexander Gault, Michael Harpster, W. H. Huff, Bradford D. Harris, Abram Householder, David Hackett, Isaiah Hartman, James Henry, Jeremiah Johnson, Haynes Jones, Samuel Kahl, Jonas Kiplinger, Samuel Lash, John D. Maurer, Benton McCrary, James W. McCarthy, Charles C. McBride, James A. McGuire, George W. Palmer, Finley Pocock, James Patterson, William Ryland, Valentine Robb, William Royer, James Rennie, Samuel W. Ray, John Springer, James Springer, Michael Seibert, John W. Snyder, Enoch G. Selby, Henry C. Smalley, John W. Smalley, Milton H. Selby, Michael W. Stauffer, William Stauffer, John Troxell, David Wiler.

The company was mustered into the one hundred days' service, but served a few days over time. Samuel Friedline was transferred. George B. Eagle died at Wilson's Wharf, Virginia, June 8, 1864. Nicholas G. Glenn died in hospital at Fortress Monroe, Virginia.

THE ONE HUNDRED AND NINETY-SIXTH REGIMENT, OHIO VOLUNTEER INFANTRY.

This regiment was organized at Camp Chase, Ohio, for one year, and mustered into service March 25, 1865. Colonel R. P. Kennedy commanded. It contained part of a company, thirty men, from Ashland county. The officers were:

COMMISSIONED OFFICERS.

Captain Warren H. Wasson.
First Lieutenant P. M. Cowles.
Second Lieutenant James Campbell, promoted first lieutenant.

NON-COMMISSIONED OFFICERS.

First Sergeant Thomas Bisby.
Second Sergeant P. T. Kissane.
Third Sergeant Christian Clark.
Fourth Sergeant William W. Gibson.
Fifth Sergeant Samuel S. Hare.
Sixth Sergeant John Furnish.
Seventh Sergeant Oscar Hayes.
First Corporal David S. Sampsel.
Second Corporal Valentine Greenewald.
Third Corporal Andrew Greenewald.
Fourth Corporal James J. Pike.
Fifth Corporal Frank Campbell.
Sixth Corporal Charles Bemenderfer.
Seventh Corporal Thomas Dupler.
Eighth Corporal George W. Hamilton.

Not being personally acquainted with the men composing that part of company A enlisted in Ashland county, we copy the entire roll, as recorded by the adjutant general.

PRIVATES.

Daniel Arnold, James M. Andrews, Franklin P. Alderman, Elias Arnold, Adnund M. Barnes, Henry Bennett, John Bowman, William Biddison, Thomas R. Bisby, Isaac Betts, jr., Edward Baker, John M. Bost, Aaron Buffenmyre, Charles H. Bemenderfer, John Corliss, David E. Chandler, James Campbell, Christian H. Clark, Jay Chatfield, Thurston P. Cowell, David Campbell, Orison Chatfield, James Cook, Frank Campbell, Peter S. Clark, James A. Crandall, John S. Cramer, Daniel H. Crowell, Elijah Diale, Alexander Darler, Maxwell Drunan, Thomas Duplex, Lafayette Dains, Samuel A. Davis, Marion Dargetz, Owen Evans, Elmore Ewing, David F. Ford, John L. Furnish, James W. Finley, George Finney, James W. Falls, Andrew Greenwald, Valentine Greenwald, William W. Gibson, Jacob Gross, George W. Hamilton, Austin Hayes, David Holmes, Samuel S. Hare, Lorin Hildebrand, John B. Hoat, James F. Henry, Alanson W. Hamilton, Otis Hodge, Isaac Johns, William H. Johns, John Kauffman, William H. Kosht, Persifer F. Kissam, Wallace King, N. W. Lattimore, Charles H. Metcalf, Charles W. Moody, John D. Moore, William McCarter, Hugh J. McGuire, Charles S. McGown, Jeremiah H. Neff, Ezram Ohl, Eli Ohl, James J. Pike, A. E. Peck, E. M. Pease, A. G. Reamish, Charles Radcliff, George W. Rowland, Martin S. Ruther, M. H. Snyder, David S. Sampsel, jr., F. W. Stibbins, Solomon Sheets, David Smalley, John Springer, Minor W. Swineford, H. T. Scoby, Jacob Soudler, Orin G. Thayer, John J. Wirt, John Wilson, Norman Wertman, Norrel Whitney, William W. Walker, Silas E. Wright, James Winkler, Orin A. Wirt, Albert White, and Charles G. Young.

This company was mustered into the United States service at Camp Chase March 25, 1865, for one year, and was mustered out at Baltimore, Maryland, September 11, 1865. The roll does not give the mortality list. It was probably small, as the service was not active.

THE ONE HUNDRED AND NINETY-SIXTH REGIMENT.

The regiment was immediately ordered to West Virginia, where it was attached to the Ohio brigade at Winchester. It was subsequently called to Baltimore, and assigned to duty in the fortifications around the city. It was mustered out September 11, 1865. The regiment performed but little field duty; but had the reputation of being a well drilled organization.

The officers and men of the One Hundred and Ninety-sixth were all veterans, having served in the other organizations over two years. More than two-thirds of the men had belonged to other regiments, and had been honorably discharged for wounds or expiration of term of service.

FIRST REGIMENT OHIO LIGHT ARTILLERY.

This regiment was composed of twelve batteries, and mustered into service for three years, September 3, 1861. It was commanded by Colonel James Barnett. The command was organized and equipped at Camp Dennison and sent to the field. Battery D was principally raised in Ashland county. Its officers were:

BATTERY D.

COMMISSIONED OFFICERS.

Captain Andrew Conkle.
Senior First Lieutenant Paul H. Rohrbocher, resigned January 1, 1862.
Junior First Lieutenant Lemuel P. Porter, promoted First Senior Lieutenant January 1, 1862.
Senior Second Lieutenant William H. Pease, promoted junior first lieutenant January 1, 1862.
Junior Second Lieutenant Henry C. L. Lloyd, promoted senior second lieutenant January, 1862.

NON-COMMISSIONED OFFICERS.

First Sergeant Nathaniel N. Newell, promoted second junior lieutenant January 1, 1862.
Second Sergeant William O. Beebe, quartermaster sergeant.
Third Sergeant Edward T. Pritchard, secretary.
Fourth Sergeant Joseph B. Charles, promoted captain in 1864 and resigned.
Fifth Sergeant Henry C. Grant.
Sixth Sergeant William J. Patterson.
Seventh Sergeant Josiah Brown.
Eighth Sergeant Moses Y. Ransom, promoted first sergeant January 1, 1862.
Ninth Sergeant William Zimmerman.
First Corporal George B. Newberry.
Second Corporal Joseph L. McLeaf.
Third Corporal John Patterson.
Fourth Corporal Cornelius Linehan, promoted sergeant November, 1862.
Fifth Corporal Henry Farnsworth, promoted sergeant January 1, 1862.
Sixth Corporal Martin J. Bender.
Seventh Corporal Samuel C. Fry.
Eighth Corporal Gates P. Carny.
Ninth Corporal Frederick Heitz.
Tenth Corporal John Starrett.
Eleventh Corporal Edgar M. Baird.
Twelfth Corporal John B. Deshong.
Musicians Addison D. White and Frederick Neff.
Bugler John Brestel.
Wagon Artificers Charles Houp, John B. Lyons, and Adam Taggart.

PRIVATES.

Daniel Ackerman, Thomas C. Atwater, Justus Angel, John F. Adams, George H. Brown, Frederick W. Boon, Thomas B. Blackburn, Hezekiah Brown, James Budd, John Budd, John R. Bennighoff, David R. Buck, Jacob Beule, Cyrus Benjamin, Alexander H. Baldwin, James L. Baker, Henry A. Baker, Orrin C. Baker, Russell J. Butler, George Blakeslee, William Boyd, jr., James H. Bateman, Henry E. Butler, Edward Crane, James E. Chapman, Perez G. Clark, John Condon, John L. Campbell, Jacob A. Campbell, John F. Cordell, William Cosgrove, Chauncey Crow, William E. Chamberlain, George Chart, Dennis Condon, Albert Clark, George W. Curtiss, Charles E. Curtiss, George W. Cover, Adam Coyer, Joseph Color, Anthony Color, Frederick T. Coffin, Jerome Coon, Charles C. Carson, Lawrence O. Craig, Charles Costello, Peter Caviner, William D. Cumberworth, Jacob Dunterman, William Daniels, Asa Daniels, Franklin A. Daniels, Thomas Dixon, John Davis, William Delong, John H. Eldridge, Joseph Elmrick, William Everett, Thomas Fisher, Jacob Fulker, William Fink, Edwin Fuller, jr., Samuel Gaylord, Edward Gevehard, Christian Groff, Joseph H. Gould, William N. Gaylord, Amos E. Griffith, Warren H. Goss, Martin Gale, jr., Hiram T. Gilbert, Aaron J. Hart, William Hails, George Huber, Ambrose Hind, Asa D. Hatch, Edward G. Hinman, Thomas Hadfield, Andrew W. Hall, Jacob L. Hagenbuch, John Hyman, Charles Herberth, Franklin H. Hitchcock, Wayland S. Hough, Michael Honodale, Harvey Hull, Rufus M. Hinman, Thomas Holness, Burton J. Hoadley, Joshua Haldeman, Delos Hartson, George A. James, Hermann Koch, Samuel Kelso, Josiah A. Kellogg, William Killop, Michael Kenny, John G. King, Chester King, Jared V. Kidney, Charles E. Lewis, William B. Lowery, Lucius Lyons, George Lovell, Horace Loomis, James Mackin, Michael Merkle, William Murphy, William R. Mooney, Zebulon McAlpine, Lewis Mack, William Matthews, Daniel Mooney, John McNarney, Frederick Moe, James R. Neeley, Zetus L. Numbers, Christian Owen, Christopher Post, Henry Patterson, Edward T. Pritchard, Levi D. Post, Jesse A. Post, Andrew Poe, Gustavus Russert, Wilber F. Robinson, John B. Rinear, John F. Remmy, Ashbel Root, Addison H. Richardson, Martin Sefling, Timothy R. Sanford, Jacob Senn, Alfred Sperry, Henry Stackhorn, Leonard F. Sisenger, John Scutchell, St. Clair Steel, George Smith, Charles Stair, Martin Schrady, Daniel Stair, Henry J. Slitt, James Sangster, James Southwood, Albert Smith, Charles H. Stearns, Henry F. Steward, James R. St. Clair, Sylvester Silsby, Henry A. Thompson, Harrison Thomson, Martin A. Terrell, Wentzel Threedollar, Luke Usher, Chauncey C. Vermilya, Henry Victor, Henry Vanheising, Wesley A. Wells, Willibald Wagner, William P. Wright, David R. Watson, James W. Whiting, John H. Webster, Fulton Wait, Philip Young, George Yanders, George W. Yanders, Eli Yarrian, and Benjamin Yarrian.

The mortality list is as follows: John Condon died October 28, 1861; Chauncey Crow, June 12, 1862; Frederick T. Coffin was killed in battle at Stone River, Tennessee; William Delong died January 17, 1863; William Frink died December 10, 1861; Samuel Gaylord died February 5, 1862; Jacob L. Hagenbuch died in hospital; William R. Mooney died January 14, 1862; James R. Neely died at Nashville, Tennessee; Chauncey C. Vermilya died June 18, 1862; John Patterson died March 11, 1862; Gates P. Carney was discharged and has since died.

About one-half of the men in battery D were enlisted in Ashland county; hence the whole roll has been copied that the strength of the battery may be exhibited. Corporal John B. Deshong was promoted to second lieutenant of battery D, and was transferred and promoted to first lieutenant in battery H; and Sergeant William Zimmerman was promoted to first lieutenant and transferred to battery G, of colored troops. Sergeant Joseph B. Charles was promoted to captain, and took command of battery H, colored troops.

Battery D left Camp Dennison in November, and reported to Brigadier General William Nelson, in Kentucky, and marched with his command up the Big Sandy to Piketon. It returned to Louisville, and thence to Mumfordsville. In February, 1862, the battery reported at Nashville and moved to Pittsburgh Landing, thence to Corinth, Mississippi, and to Athens, Alabama. In September it returned to Mumfordsville, where it was captured by the Confederate forces, paroled and sent to Camp Chase, and exchanged in January, 1863. The battery was reorganized at Columbus, Ohio, and joined the Third brigade at Lexington, Kentucky, in March. In June, 1863, it went on a raid to East Tennessee, under Colonel Saunders, and burned many bridges, a large amount of ordnance and commissary stores. In July it marched with General Burnside to Cumberland Gap, which was captured. In August and September the battery went on a raid into Kentucky and Tennessee, with Colonel Woolford's cavalry. It next marched to Knoxville and participated in the siege. The battery re-enlisted and was sent on a thirty days' veteran furlough to Ohio. The ranks being recruited in January, 1864, it marched to Atlanta, Georgia, and joined the forces of General Sherman, and was in all the engagements of that campaign. It was also in the battles of Franklin and Nashville, and went to Wilmington, North Carolina, and was finally mustered out at Cleveland, Ohio, July 15, 1865.

FIRST REGIMENT HEAVY ARTILLERY (COLORED).

This regiment was organized at Knoxville, Tennessee, in January, February, and March, 1864. It contained two companies commanded by officers from the veterans of 1861–64, who had been promoted in other batteries for meritorious services. They were:

COMPANY G.
COMMISSIONED OFFICERS.

Captain John T. Collins.
Senior First Lieutenant W. Zimmerman.
Junior First Lieutenant C. H. W. Beecher.

COMPANY H.
COMMISSIONED OFFICERS.

Captain Joseph B. Charles.
Senior First Lieutenant John B. Deshong.
Junior First Lieutenant L. G. Bigelow.

The foregoing companies were employed for a long time constructing and extending the fortifications about Knoxville, besides being detailed on guard duty. In January and February, 1865, these companies went on an extensive forage expedition to East Tennessee. Guerillas were often met on the route, but fell back. In March, 1865, companies G and H were ordered to the department of the Cumberland, and served as infantry under General Stoneman. After the surrender of General Lee, the regiment was ordered to Chattanooga upon garrison duty, where it was mustered out in March, 1866.

THE "SQUIRREL HUNTERS."

In July and September, 1862, during the apprehended siege of the city of Cincinnati by John Morgan, the noted Confederate raider, an appeal was made to the farmers and laboring men within a proper distance of the city to aid in its defence. A large number of men from the rural districts hastened to the rescue. On the second of September Governor Tod issued a proclamation authorizing General Lew Wallace to complete the organization, and stating that none but armed men would be received, and also providing for their transportation by rail at the expense of the state. The Queen City was speedily put in a position of defence by General Wallace. General Morgan failed to commence the siege, and the "Squirrel Hunters" were dismissed. Ashland county sent one hundred and four men. By a resolution of the legislature, in the winter of 1863, discharges, in due form, were furnished the "Squirrel Hunters" of 1862.

SURGICAL DEPARTMENT.

The following physicians from Ashland county served in the army:

Isaac L. Crane, M. D., as surgeon in the Twenty-second regiment, three months in 1861, and in the Sixty-third regiment from October, 1861, to January 28, 1863, when he resigned. He also acted as brigade surgeon.

John Ingram, M. D., as surgeon in the Seventy-fifth from the first of November, 1863, until he resigned.

P. H. Clark, M. D., as assistant surgeon in field hospitals from June, 1862, at Farmington and Iuka, Mississippi, and temporarily in the Forty-third regiment. In 1863 he was transferred to Cumberland and to Camp Parol prison in Annapolis, Maryland, and remained until fall. In December, 1862, he was appointed pension surgeon, which position he now fills.

Oliver C. McCarty, M. D., acted as assistant surgeon in the One Hundred and Sixty-ninth during the one hundred days' service in 1864, and was transferred to the One Hundred and Eighty-first, where his time expired November 2, 1864.

Dr. John D. Skilling acted as assistant surgeon in the hospitals at Cumberland and Clarysville, Maryland, from 1862 to 1865, the close of the war.

NOTE.—In preparing the foregoing sketch of Ashland county in the war, a special effort has been made to secure accuracy and impartiality.

CHAPTER XXXVII.

NEWSPAPERS, BENEVOLENT SOCIETIES, AND BANKS.

The Mohican Advocate.—The Ashland Herald.—The Ohio Globe.—The Western Phœnix.—The Ashland Standard.—The Ashland Democrat.—The Ohio Union.—The Ashland Times.—The Independent.—The Loudonville Advocate.—Masonic Lodges.—Odd Fellows.—The First National Bank.—The Farmers' Bank.—The Loudonville Bank.

THE *Mohican Advocate and Hanover Journal* is believed to have been the first newspaper published within the present limits of Ashland county. The office was established in Loudonville, in October, 1834. The editor and proprietor was a Mr. Rogers. The paper failed after the issue of the sixth number, and further operations were suspended. The sparseness of the settlement and the limited number of subscribers no doubt contributed to the failure.

The *Ashland Herald* appeared December 30, 1834, some three months after the Loudonville *Advocate*, and was published by J. C. Gilkison. It was neutral in politics. The *Herald* continued some eight or nine months, and suspended. It seems to have had a fair share of advertising. We find in its list the names of L. M. Pratt, P. M., Granger & Campbell, merchants, S. Moulton, merchant, John P. Rejnor, insurance agent, Rejnor, Luther & Deming, merchants, A. W. Melsheimer, Golden Eagle hotel, etc.

The *Ohio Globe* was established by Joshua H. Ruth, in Ashland, a few weeks after the suspension of the *Herald*. It was the advocate of Democratic principles.

In 1836 it sustained the nomination of Martin VanBuren for the presidency. The advertisers in the *Globe* were William Wasson, tanner; Ruth & Jacobs, merchants; Rejnor & Luther, merchants; Hugh Davis, tanner; Samuel B. Whiting, carpenter; Granger & Lang, merchants; R. P. Fulkerson, blacksmith. The *Globe* lived about one year.

The *Western Phœnix* was established by Thomas White and Samuel McClure, now judge of common pleas, of Akron, Ohio, a short time prior to the close of the presidential campaign of 1836. It was the advocate of the principles of the National Whigs, and sustained the nomination of General W. H. Harrison. It survived until sometime in 1837, and suspended because of financial embarrassments.

The *Ashland Standard* was established by R. V. Kennedy, in the spring of 1846, after the organization of Ashland county. It was intended to be the exponent of the bank wing of the Democratic party, as opposed to a hard currency, and was conducted with spirit and ability until the spring of 1849, when it suspended, and Mr. Kennedy removed west.

The Ashland *Democrat* was established by William A. Hunter and Jonathan Moffett, in the spring of 1846. The *Democrat* was the advocate of the most ultra, or hard currency, wing of the Democratic party. A bitter and protracted personal warfare was at once initiated, between the editors of the *Democrat* and *Standard*. Mr. Kennedy was a racy and accomplished writer, and a practical printer; while Messrs. Hunter & Moffett were attorneys, and had no knowledge of the printing business. They were unaccustomed to the duties of editorial life. The editorial department of the *Democrat*, therefore, failed in ability and polish. Mr. Hunter, in his best moods, resented, with a good deal of strength, the ironical assaults of his neighbor. In February, 1848, Mr. Hunter sold his interest in the *Democrat* to Mr. Moffett, and removed to Williams county, Ohio.

In April, 1848, Mr. H. S. Knapp, of the *Kalida Venture*, purchased from Mr. Moffett the *Democrat*, and from William T. Jackson, the *Standard*; and, having blended the material, changed the names of the papers to the *Ohio Union*. He continued to edit and publish the *Union* until the fall of 1853, when the paper was purchased by Dr. John Sheridan, and Mr. Knapp took charge of the *Ohio State Democrat*, at Columbus, Ohio.

In November, 1855, Collins W. Bushnell purchased the *Ohio Union*, and changed the name to the Ashland *Union*, and continued to edit and publish it until his decease, in 1856.

In January, 1857, Mr. H. S. Knapp, having returned from Columbus, re-purchased the establishment, and continued its publication until May 30, 1860, when it was purchased by John J. Jacobs. Mr. Knapp declined to support the nomination of Stephen A. Douglass, preferring the platform and principles upon which John C. Breckenridge was nominated. Not desiring to enter the campaign, and having many fears as to the future peace of the country, Mr. Knapp preferred to enter, for the time being, the ranks of private life.

The *Union* was edited and published by J. J. and F. S. Jacobs for about two years, and John W. McCord became part proprietor. In the fall of 1864, John W. McCord, Benjamin F. Nelson, and John M. Landis, became the proprietors, J. J. and F. S. Jacobs retiring. McCord and Nelson soon after retiring, the paper became the property of John M. and James H. Landis, brothers, who continued to edit and publish the same until April 1, 1868, when the concern was purchased by Dr. George W. Hill.

Dr. Hill continued to edit and publish the paper, under the name of the *States and Union*, until August 1, 1872. During the stormy political contests of 1868 to 1872, the question was, "Shall we have such a Union as was intended by the instrumentality of the constitution bequeathed us by our fathers, or shall the old Union be ignored and exchanged for a military government, subject to the whims of future military despots?" Pending reconstruction, after the conquests of the war of 1861–'5, the *States and Union* was the advocate of the equality of the States, the liberty of speech, the freedom of the press and the maintenance of the Union.

August 1, 1872, the *States and Union* was purchased by Messrs. Benjamin F. Nilson and William H. Gates, of Ashland. These gentlemen again changed the name of the paper to the *Press*. Alberson & Heltman are the present proprietors. The paper has a large list of subscribers, and is well supported. It is Democratic.

The *Ashlander* was established by William B. McCarty, in the summer of 1850, and continued two years under his management. The press and material, after the suspension of the *Ashlander*, at the close of the presidential campaign of 1852, passed into the possession of L. J. Sprengle. The *Ashlander* was a Whig journal.

The Ashland *Times* succeeded the *Ashlander* as a Whig organ in July, 1853, L. J. Sprengle being the proprietor, and William Osborn, editor. In 1855 Mr. Osborn retired, and was succeeded by Josiah Locke, as editor. He continued to edit the *Times* until 1857, when Mr. Sprengle became the editor and proprietor, Mr. Locke having removed to another part of the State. Mr. Sprengle, November 15, 1875, sold the *Times* to J. C. Stubbs & Co. J. C. Stubbs & Brother are the present editors and proprietors.

The *Independent*, neutral, of Loudonville, was established in 1867 by Rev. Robert Lockhart, and continued until the fall of 1874, when the paper was transferred to Mansfield, where, in a few months, it suspended publication. The *Independent* was the organ of temperance reform and prohibition, and was very extreme in its ideas.

The Loudonville *Advocate*, neutral, was established by Joshua H. Ruth in the fall of 1872, and is still published by him as editor and proprietor. It is a neat and handsomely printed journal, and contains a fine selection of reading matter each week. Mr. Ruth is one of the oldest practical printers in this part of the State, having edited the *Ohio Globe* at Ashland in 1835–6.

In the summer of 1875 the Hayesville *Journal*, neutral, was established, Mr. J. B. Paine, editor, and E. T. Fairchilds, local editor. The paper is owned by a joint stock company. It has a patent outside, is neat in appearance, and contains eight pages. The *Journal* is intended to forward the interests of the Vermillion Institute, and is mainly devoted to literature and news.

BENEVOLENT INSTITUTIONS.

MASONIC LODGES.

Hanover Lodge, No. 115, at Loudonville, was established by a dispensation from the Grand lodge in 1843, George H. Stewart, Adolph Klemm, Nathaniel Haskell, John Ewalt, W. J. Cullen, P. B. Griffith, E. B. Fuller, and Jacob Booth, being petitioners. On the evening of October 28, 1844, the first regular officers were installed. They were, George H. Stewart, W. M.; N. Haskell, S. W.; P. B. Griffith, J. W.; W. J. Cullen, S. W.; E. B, Fuller, S. D.; A. Klemm, J. D.; Jacob Booth, Treas.; ———, Sec.; L. E. Huston, T. At that time there were fifteen members. The lodge now contains about seventy-five members.

Ashland Lodge, No. 151, was established by a dispensation of the Grand lodge, which met at Zanesville October 19, 1846, Charles R. Deming, Lorin Andrews, Benjamin F. Whitney, William A. Hunter, Luther M. Pratt, James McNulty, Bela B. Clark, George W. Urie, Sage Kellogg, and Wells Kellogg being petitioners. Charles R. Deming was appointed first M., Lorin Andrews, first S. W., and B. F. Whitney, first J. W. At a meeting held May 7, 1847, a constitution and by-laws were adopted. The first lodge met in the third story of the county jail until 1859, when the lodge was transferred to the Miller building, on Main street, where it remained until 1875, when a new room was completed and occupied in the Cowan block, on the corner of Main and Orange streets. Ashland lodge now contains about one hundred members.

Ashland Chapter, No. 67, was formed by a warrant of dispensation granted by the M. E. G. H. Priest, to companions C. R. Deming, G. W. Urie, R. H. Chubb, H. Humphrey, Wells Kellogg, Henry Spafford, Andrew Miller, H. D. Ruth, and Daniel Campbell, June 13, 1855. Rev. Rolla H. Chubb was appointed first H. P.; Charles R. Deming, the first K.; and George W. Urie, the first S. The chapter occupied the lodge room in the jail, until it was transferred to the John Miller hall, on Main street. The first meeting was held June 19, 1855. The chapter adopted a constitution and by-laws, which were approved by the Grand Chapter October 2, 1872. The stated meetings are held on the first Tuesday evening of every month.

Sullivan Lodge, F. and A. M., No. 313, was chartered October 20, 1859. The charter members were: Harlow P. Sage, George W. Kilburn, DeWitt Prince, Alexander Masters, Henry Summers, James Beever, John Campbell, A. H. Palmer, Thomas Parker, Shadrach Bryan, Calvin Bryan, Leonard Brown, C. B. Houck, Daniel Campbell, jr., and Hiram Thurston. The present number of members is about fifty.

ODD FELLOWS.

The dispensation for Mohican Lodge, No. 85, of the Independent Order of Odd Fellows, at Ashland, was granted by the Grand lodge of the State of Ohio, to Matthew Clugston, James Sloan, Jackson Wolverton, John Clark, S. and J. Hayes, and John Musser, petitioners, December 26, 1846. The lodge was organized May 10, 1847, by Thomas C. McEwen, D. D. G. M.; but five members were present. The first officers were: John Clark, N. G.; Jackson Wolverton, V. G.; John Musser, R. S.; H. J. Hayes, P. S.; James Sloan, Treas. The lodge room was in the third story of the Boffenmyre, or Freer, block, on the north side of Main street, below the Miller house, until 1875, when it was transferred to a new and elegant room over the First National bank, on the corner of Orange and Main streets. The present number of members is ninety.

Concord Lodge, No. 325, at Hayesville, was established by a dispensation from the Grand lodge of Ohio, May 14, 1857, J. Kinninger, William L. Smith, William G. Galloway, Nicholas McCool, and M. McLaughlin petitioners. The lodge was instituted July 27, 1857, by R. W. G. Alexander E. Glenn. The first officers were: Joseph Kinninger, N. G.; W. L. Smith, V. G.; M. McLaughlin, recording secretary; W. G. Galloway, treasurer. The present membership is about sixty.

Sylvan Lodge, No. 240, was established at Loudonville, by charter from the Grand lodge of the State of Ohio, April 20, 1854, John Taylor, David E. Stockman, A. P. Mather, C. Hilderbrand, and Aaron Yarnell petitioners. The lodge is in a flourishing condition. The members are mostly of German descent, and number about sixty.

BANKS.

The First National bank of Ashland originated in the "Ashland Bank," an institution of discount and deposit, established in 1851, under the name and style of Luther, Crall & Co.—the partners then being Hulbert Luther, Jacob Crall, James Purdy, William S. Granger, George H. Topping, and Jacob O. Jennings. The institution was ably managed until 1863, when, under a law of Congress, it was merged into the First National bank of Ashland, with a capital of fifty thousand dollars, secured in United States bonds deposited in the treasury at Washington. It was authorized, under the law, to issue bank notes to the amount of forty-five thousand dollars, for circulation. The First National bank has been wisely managed, and sustains a high reputation as a business institution. Its quarterly statements show that its resources are ample to meet promptly all its liabilities. For the quarter ending December 31, 1875, the total amount of its resources was four hundred and fifty-three thousand five hundred and ninety-two dollars and ninety cents. This sum includes loans and discounts, two hundred and sixty-nine thousand nine hundred and forty dollars and fifty-eight cents; United States bonds, sixty thousand and fifty dollars; due from other banks, thirty-two thousand five hundred and thirteen dollars and forty-six cents; due from United States treasury, two thousand two hundred and fifty dollars; banking house, safe, and fixtures, forty thousand dollars; other real estate, three thousand four hundred and fifty-seven dollars and fifty cents: expenses, and cash on hand, forty-five thousand three hundred and eighty-one dollars and thirty-six cents. The present stockholders are: Ashland—Jacob Crall, J. H. McCombs, Jonas Freer, J. O. Jennings, Sherman W. Beer, L. J. Sprengle, R. D. Freer, Jacob Cohn, William Osborn; Mansfield—William Bird and Nancy Mitchell; Loudonville—J. H. Sanborn. Jacob O. Jennings, president; Joseph Patterson, cashier.

The Farmer's bank was established in Ashland in the summer of 1875, and is owned by Jonas and Randolph Freer, brothers, the former being president and the latter vice-president. The liability of the stockholders is unlimited. It is a bank of discount and deposit. It is located on the south side of Main street, three doors west of the town hall building. N. B. Dressler is cashier.

The Loudonville bank was organized about the year 1867, by a joint stock company as a bank of discount and deposit, Nathaniel Haskell being the principal stockholder and president. At his decease, a nephew, Mr. George C. Haskell, by will of Nathaniel Haskell, became the principal stockholder and manager of the bank. At his decease, in January, 1875, the institution was reorganized under the name and style of the Loudonville Banking company, with a capital and assets of three hundred thousand dollars. G. Schauweker, president; William Garrett, vice-president, and J. L. Quick, cashier.

CHAPTER XXXVIII.
STATISTICS.

The Population of Ashland County.—The Value of Real and Personal Property.—The Industries of the County.—The Amount of Taxation.—The Future of the County.

THE population of the county has fluctuated considerably in the last twenty years. This is attributable to many causes, among which is the late war. Prior to 1860, the size of farms averaged from forty to one hundred and sixty acres. There were also many families occupying small farms. At the opening of the war, and during its progress, the major part of the able bodied young and middle aged men entered the service. For the first eight years after the opening of the contest, all the surplus products of the farmers commanded unusually high prices, and the agriculturalist was enabled to purchase the smaller farms adjoining the homestead. The inferior buildings, previously erected thereon, were removed or destroyed. The result was, that at the close of the war hundreds of returning soldiers were compelled to quarter in the villages and towns, or remove from the county. This and the mortality attending the war, reduced the population about two thousand in the decennial period between 1860 and 1870. The voluntary migration of a portion of our people westward is another cause. The actual population of the county by townships, in 1880, is as follows:

Montgomery, including towns			4,628
Orange,	"	"	1,451
Vermillion,	"	"	2,209
Green,	"	"	2,289
Hanover,	"	"	2,317
Jackson,	"	"	1,488
Perry,	"	"	1,493
Mohican,	"	"	1,695
Lake,	"	"	886
Mifflin,	"	"	849
Milton,	"	"	1,194
Clearcreek,	"	"	1,154
Ruggles,	"	"	726
Troy,	"	"	715
Sullivan,	"	"	817
Total			23,811

The population of Ashland city, Montgomery township...... 3,004

From the first settlement of the territory now constituting Ashland county, the people have progressed quite rapidly in all that contributes to their intelligence, prosperity and contentment. The agriculturalist occupies fertile lands that yield abundantly; and few counties, of the same area, can exhibit more culture and wealth. The county is estimated to contain two hundred and sixty-seven thousand four hundred and forty-three acres of land, which is divided as follows:

	ACRES.
Lands subject to annual cultivation, including villages and towns	160,359
Meadows and pasture lands	31,894
Wood and uncultivated lands	75,190
The value of these lands in 1874	$ 8,045,010
Value of estate in towns	1,067,034
Value of chattel property	4,247,987
Total	$13,360,031

The actual cash value of the real and personal property will exceed twenty million dollars. The best farm lands sell readily from sixty dollars to one hundred dollars per acre, depending somewhat upon their location.

The question of taxation is one of much importance to a free people. Taxes, economically expended, in the enforcement of just and equitable laws, cannot be the subject of criticism and complaint on the part of the tax payer. The grand duplicate of Ohio shows that in 1874 Ashland county was required to pay the following taxes:

For State sinking fund	$ 10,688 02
For general revenue	6,680 02
For asylum fund	12,024 02
For common school fund	13,360 03
For county purposes	16,032 04
For poor purposes	8,016 02
For bridge purposes	9,352 02
For road purposes	12,287 27
For township purposes	8,453 38
For township and sub-district school-house and for school purposes	51,669 17
For other special taxes	3,602 15
For city, town, and village	10,710 41
Total	$162,874 55

It will be seen that much the greater proportion of this amount arises in local taxation. It will, therefore, be, in the future, a question for the economist to investigate and settle so as to prevent abuses in that direction.

Very few men fully appreciate the effect of adding five or ten mills to the aggregate of taxation, but when the subject is fairly presented, and the effect of such increase shown, it will be less difficult to enforce lessons of economy.

No subject can be more interesting than that of the industries of the county. The prosperity and happiness of the people depend largely upon the industry, frugality and intelligence of the farmer and mechanic. Let us look at some of the results of each of these branches of industry:

	VALUE.
Horses, 8,507	$ 544,743
Cattle, 21,200	293,245
Mules, 89	6,850
Sheep, 56,154	140,810
Hogs, 20,131	48,881
Carriages, 4,178	168,170
Watches, 955	13,853
Pianos	24,225
Merchants' stock	201,923
Manufacturers' stock	74,540
Non-taxable bonds	16,805
Moneys	416,384
Book's credits	1,151,162
Stocks not taxable	4,000
Dogs taxed, 825	4,130
Banks and other corporations	2,399,154
Other taxable personal property	276,565
Total	$4,164,048

This is a stupendous sum, but falls short of the actual value of the property enumerated perhaps a half million of dollars. This discrepancy arises from the fact that no property is valued at its actual cash value for taxation. There are other branches of industry equally interesting to all classes; and we will now give further details.

The following are the products for 1874:

Wheat,	acres,	24,727	bushels, 386,444	$386,444
Corn,	"	21,512	" 725,830	435,498
Oats,	"	15,583	" 464,988	232,494
Barley,	"	229	" 4,231	4,231
Rye,	"	350	" 3,711	3,711
Irish potatoes,	"	915	" 63,718	50,974
Sweet	"	21	" 1,096	1,096
Hay	"	16,148	tons 16,091	112,637
Clover	"	14,287	bush. seed 4,456	17,824
Flax	"	1,666	" " 9,873	19,746
Tobacco,	pounds,		30	2
Butter,	"		644,897	128,979
Cheese,	"		1,033,668	103,366
Sorghum,	gallons,		532	532
Maple sugar,	pounds,		51,577	3,610
Maple molasses,	gallons,		10,823	10,823
Wool,	pounds,		251,821	100,728
Apples,	bushels,		184,274	46,468
Peaches,	"		130	320
Pears,	"		1,356	1,356
Grapes,	pounds,		156,720	94,032
Wine,	gallons,		172	250
Total				$1,767,709

The greater proportion of the foregoing products is sold and consumed within the limits of the county. From these exhibits it will be seen that the occupation of our people is largely agricultural. It is true, that the manufacture of wool, leather, and machinery, forms a part of the industries of our people; and it would be interesting to give those items, if it were possible to obtain the figures. In gathering statistics, these items have been overlooked by statisticians, and we deprived the pleasure of their publication.

In conclusion, it will be seen that while our people possess fertile lands, pure water, and a healthful climate, they are rapidly advancing in all the arts of civilization, and can look with pride to the future.

CHAPTER XXXIX.
MEDICINE AND LAW.

The Early Physicians.—A List of Those who have Practiced in the County.—Medical Societies.—Ashland County Lawyers.

THE history of Ashland county would be incomplete without a notice of the learned professions. The healing art is the custodian of the highest interests of the people, and the educated physician, properly devoted to his profession, has it within his power to contribute largely to the elevation of society. It has been truly observed, that every scholar realizes, in whatever direction his energies may be employed, there is still much beyond his reach, and, that in advancing, he discerns ever more clearly his own mental deficiencies. This is especially true of the learned and accomplished physician. None but the charlatan or mountebank rushes in where the accomplished physician would hesitate to advance. So long, therefore, as the people place more value upon a horse or a cow than upon the life of a human being, professional accomplishments will be antagonized by the sounding clatter and impositions of the pretender. If a farmer have a house, a barn or a mill to construct, he seeks to employ a skilful and trustworthy mechanic. If a member of his family becomes ill, why not act upon the same principle, and employ the educated physician? The charlatan always finds friends, and those who practice delusions and impositions in medicine, are ingenious in the adoption of means to entrap the credulous. Their nostrums, like the frogs of Egypt, are emptied into the very bread-trays of almost every family. It is in vain that true men warn the public against the flattering deceptions practiced by patent nostrum venders.

For the first six or eight years after the pioneers began to locate along the rich valleys of this county, they were compelled, in critical cases, to go to Wooster, Mt. Vernon, or Mansfield, for a physician.

The prevailing diseases of that period were agues and bilious fevers. These were caused from the exhalations of decaying vegetable matter, in ponds and marshes, during the summer and autumnal months. They rarely proved fatal. Home cures were the remedy. Butternut bark pills—a decoction of wild cherry bark, dogwood bark, boneset, and black alder were used freely.

Some surgically inclined pioneer was armed with an old-fashioned pair of forceps, commonly called "pullicans" or "turnkeys," to extract the aching fangs of the people, with a peculiar nervous twist, almost painful to call to recollection.

Some settler in almost every neighborhood acted as professional phlebotomist; and blood-letting was regarded as a sovereign remedy for many ills. It is remarkable that the process that destroys the life of an ox, should ever have been adopted as a means of prolonging human life.

About the year 1818 one or two educated physicians located within the present limits of this county. In a few years these were followed by others, and ere long, every village and township contained from one to a half dozen doctors. Among the number were to be found many who had true professional pride and high attainments.

Of late years the medical profession of this county has advanced rapidly in scientific attainment; and public sentiment is being educated to a better appreciation of the responsibilities of the true physician. This may result in elevating the educated physician to his appropriate sphere among the people.

The earlier physicians frequently changed location, and it is now quite impossible to follow the meanderings of each. Their number has been "legion;" and the schools from which they emanated are equally varied in practice. Indeed, this county has been an open field for every species of medical theory. The public have tried all.

ASHLAND.

Drs. Joel Luther, 1816*; Joseph Hildreth, 1824*; William N. Deming, 1825*; A. L. Davidson, removed; George W. Cochrane, died; Gustavus Oesterlin, 1834; Peoples, 1836, killed; Burr Kellogg, 1842, died 1863; Willard Slocum, 1834, removed; John Hanna; Marshall, 1839, removed; N. S. Sampsell, 1844, removed; J. F. Sampsell, 1845; Bela B. Clark,* 1846, died 1858; W. R. S. Clark, 1846, removed; Jacob W. Kinnaman, 1847, died 1874; Benjamin F. Whitney, 1849, removed; P. H. Clark, 1850*; David S. Sampsel, 1851; I. L. Crane, 1856, died 1867*; J. P. Cowan, 1859; Jeremiah Hahn, 1846, removed; Jacob Myers, 1849, removed; J. M. Diller, 1853; Samuel Riddle, 1853; Paul W. Sampsell, 1851, removed; P. M. Miller, 1849, died 1852; George W. Hill, 1861; Thomas S. Hunter, 1867; Samuel Glass, 1867, died 1873*; William S. Allen, 1869, removed; Benjamin Myers, 1870; Robert Kinnaman, 1872; David S. Sampsell, jr., 1873; G. B. Cole, 1874; J. C. Campbell, 1874; Lamartine Greenwald, 1872; Frank Cowan, 1874; Joseph Sheets, 1862, died 1866; John P. Cowan, 1874; W. K. Foltz, 1868; Dr. Gascia, 1872, died 1873; J. E. Roop, 1875; J. H. Stoll, E. N. Dunham, H. P. Nelson, E. V. Cobb, A. L. Sherrick.

A majority of the foregoing were graduates.

HAYESVILLE.

Drs. Cliff 1822, H. Armstrong 1832, J. L. McCully, J. Vautilburg, Constance Lake, Samuel Miller, Austin Rogers, Gilbert Rogers, David Armstrong, Samuel Glass,

---

*See Biography.

James E. Yocum, E. V. Kendig, O. C. McCarty, N. Waddle, Joseph Sheets, Thomas S. Harter, Lewis Armstrong. Drs. Yocum and Kendig are the only physicians at the present time.

SAVANNAH.

Drs. Cliff 1821, Thomas Hayes, James E. Hayes, William Langhendge, Charles Johnston, John Ingram, John Sheridan, W. C. Cook, James W. McKee, William S. Shaw, D. R. Francis, H. H. Ford, David Crowell.

ORANGE.

Drs. John Hanna 1834, William Deming 1835, A. J. Pyle, A. Alden, Richard Powers, I. P. Hall, John Lambert, W. C. Leach, A. J. Norris, A. G. McClelland, Josiah Deal, Jeremiah Hahn, and T. P. Crowell. Dr. T. P. Crowell is at present the only physician in the village.

JEROMEVILLE.

Drs. Cliff, Moses Owens, Vailes, Church, O. H. Edwards, A. E. Page, David Young, J. P. Cowan, J. Sheridan, John Cowan, E. J. Roberts, John M. Waddle, Frank Wilson, L. Greenewald, and S. Z. Davis. Drs. Wilson and Davis are at present engaged in practice.

MOHICANVILLE.

Drs. Thomas A. Eagle, Thomas Moore, Samuel Riddle, A. J. Scott, — McKonkey, Ivery Cole, George W. Parr, Samuel Eberhard, A. Glasscol, Harvey Smith, Russel Thayer, S. Z. Davis, Samuel McClain, French Armentrout, John A. Wolf, — Beggs, — Kimball, A. Ransom, and A. Emerick. Dr. A. Emerick is the principal physician near the village.

LOUDONVILLE.

Drs. J. S. Irvin 1821, — Cliff 1823, — Clendenin 1825, E. B. Fuller 1831, — Harrison, — Cass, J. H. Smith, Samuel Smith, Charles Kesselmeyer, E. W. Lake, M. E. Barnitz, A. N. Barnes, B. F. Whitney, — Vanderberg, C. Sapp, O. H. Edwards, J. C. McBeth, — Kalar, S. P. Fouts, A. R. Anderson, W. H. Myers, Jesse L. Fouts, Augustus Case, H. C. Newkirk, William Fox, C. Hubert, Augustus E. Gasche, Andrew J. Scott, Amos B. Fuller, W. H. Wertz, S. S. Mills, J. W. Riggs, and J. M. Wertz. A large proportion of these remained but a short time.

PERRYSVILLE.

Drs. Robert Irvin, T. G. V. Simmons, B. F. Whitney, W. C. Harrison, T. C. Turner, John Lambert, — Wineman, Alfred Lee, H. Croninger, — Johnson, J. Palmer, J. W. Griffith, James Miller, W. Downing, John Vantilburg, Tyler, Ransom, Riggs, Christie, G. W. Parr, J. F. Johnston, S. F. Griffith, and M. Pocock.

MIFFLIN.

Drs. John Hanna, J. Chandler, John Lambert, James Miller, Samuel Miller, Samuel Glass, J. W. Griffith, James E. Yocum, John Houke, H. Buchanan, Jeremiah Hahn, and John McCray. Dr. H. Buchanan, a fine physician, has the entire practice.

RUGGLES CENTER.

Drs. George W. Paddock, A. J. Rutan, Cyrus Paine, W. W. Parker, J. Deal, and O. L. Andrews. Dr. Andrews is, at present, the only physician in the township.

ROWSBURGH.

Drs. Abraham Ecker, John Ecker, W. C. More, P. M. Miller, A. S. Long, James Knox, Harvey Tidd, Henry Buck, George Greener, Peter Shearer, Andrew Connell, J. S. Cole, Frank Cowan, and George Gregg. Dr. Gregg is the only physician in practice, the rest having removed or deceased.

POLK.

Drs. Oliver C. McCarthy, David Young, Andrew Pyle, Richard Powers, Levi Ballard, John Campbell, J. E. McDonald, D. W. Rumbaugh. Drs. McCarty and Rumbaugh are the only practitioners in the township at present.

SULLIVAN.

Drs. William Mead, Fowler, A. E. Wigton, A. B. Sampson, McCook, Jacob Gillett, William Bunce, John Campbell, William S. Shaw, J. E. McDonald, H. E. Black, and D. G. Hart. Drs. Hart and Black are the only practitioners.

TROY CENTER.

Drs. William B. Young, Andrew J. Norris, George Weedman, and John D. Skilling. Dr. George Weedman, a very successful physician, had, for a long time, no opposition. He has now a competitor in the person of Dr. Richards.

MEDICAL SOCIETIES.

About the year 1850, a county medical society was organized, with the expectation of elevating the standard of medical practice and education. The society met considerable opposition, and, after one or two years, disbanded. Its organization was beneficial.

In April, 1864, the physicians of Ashland and other towns within the county, organized a new medical society, in order to advance the interests and usefulness of the medical profession, and the social relations and courtesies that belong to professional gentlemen. A constitution and by-laws, setting forth the object and government of the society, were adopted. The members of the society as organized were: Doctors Gustavus Oesterlin, Jacob P. Cowan, P. H. Clark, George W. Hill, Joseph Sheets, Jacob W. Kinnaman, David S. Sampsel, Isaac L. Crane, Samuel Glass, Oliver C. McCarty, William S. Shaw, Thomas S. Hunter, David R. Francis, S. J. Davis, Benjamin Myers, Robert C. Kinnaman, Jeremiah Hahn, Andrew J. Scott, A. B. Fuller, John Campbell, W. S. Allen, I. S. Cole, T. P. Crowell, E. V. Kendig, George W. Parr, William H. Wirt, John Cowan, Jacob Crabbs, Alexander Emerick.

The society has existed about twelve years, and has, to a considerable degree, softened the old rivalries in the profession.

Drs. Joseph Sheets, J. W. Kinnaman, Isaac L. Crane, and Samuel Glass have deceased.

At the last regular election, Dr. J. P. Cowan was elected president; William S. Allen, vice-president; R. C. Kinnaman, secretary; Gustavus Oesterlin, treasurer; Drs. Cole, Hill, and Cowan, censors.

THE LEGAL PROFESSION.

Prior to the erection of Ashland county, regularly admitted attorneys were few. Elias Slocum,* Sterling G. Bushnell,* Silas Robbins, jr., Erastus N. Gates, and J. W. Smith, of Ashland, and Nicholas M. Donaldson, of Loudonville, were pretty extensively employed in justices' courts, and occasionally in the court of common pleas at Mansfield.

Since Ashland became the seat of justice for this county, the resident attorneys have been: Erastus N. Gates, James W. Smith, John S. Fulton, Bolivar W. Kellogg, John H. McComes, William A. Hunter, Jonathan Moffitt, James Sloan, John W. Rankin, John Clark, Harvey H. Johnson, Ohio F. Jones, Willard Slocum, S. W. Shaw, J. Vincent, A. M. Fulton, Albert L. Curtis, Alexander Porter, Thomas J. Kenney, William Osborn, John W. Fry, Almer R. Campbell, A. V. Watts, S. D. Gault, J. S. Wertman, F. C. Semple, T. J. Smilie; Geo. W. Geddes, of Hayesville; Nicholas M. Donaldson, of Loudonville; Wm. Henry, of Savannah; and, subsequently, Thomas J. Bull, of Loudonville; Amos Norris, of Orange; George W. Carey, of Rowsburgh; John J. Gurley, of Hayesville; William Cowan, of Green; Francis Kenyon, of Savannah, and John Scott, jr., of Hayesville, became practicing attorneys.

About the year 1849, William B. Allison, T. J. Kenny, George W. Hill, George H. Parker, William B. McCart, and Robert Beer were admitted, and, shortly after, the list was enlarged by the names of John J. Jacobs, Robert M. Campbell, C. S. Van Arnam, J. D. Stubbs, and William T. Johnston; and has since been increased by the addition of the names of George B. Smith, H. S. Knapp, H. S. Lee, J. P. Devor, John D. Jones, D. S. Sampsell, J. Hahn, John McCray, Henry McCray, Byron Stilwell, William O. Porter, Peter S. Grosscup, and Charles Dorland.

In point of ability and learning the bar of Ashland will compare favorably with those of the surrounding counties.

The bane of the lawyer is politics. Whenever an attorney devotes more attention to party discussions, and efforts to obtain political promotion, than to the study of the principles and practice of law, the result will soon be apparent. The politician becomes rusty and demoralized, while the industrious practitioner and legal student always advances in knowledge and efficiency.

No signal achievement has ever followed a professional man who neglects to be a laborious and continued student. Many brilliant men have destroyed their usefulness by want of application, and by attempting too many things at the same time.

The man of many books, ill digested, will prove to be a smatterer in all. One thing well done is worth more than many ill undertakings.

Erastus M. Gates was a native of Massachusetts. He practiced several years in Ashland, accumulated a handsome property, sold, and removed to Newton, Iowa.

John S. Fulton, a native of Pennsylvania, was prosecuting attorney one term, served as captain and colonel in the late war, and deceased in 1862. He was a good lawyer, and had strong military tastes.

John H. McComes is a native of Washington county, Pennsylvania, and is a graduate; was admitted about 1839. He has settled more estates than any attorney in the county. He has withdrawn from practice.

Bolivar W. Kellogg was a native of Ashland. He was a gentleman of good literary and legal attainments, and was the third prosecuting attorney of the county. He deceased in 1856, of pulmonary consumption.

James Sloan, a native of Pennsylvania, located in Ashland in 1846. He was a gentleman of excellent habits. His literary attainments were fair. He was rapidly advancing in his profession. He died of pulmonary consumption in the spring of 1855.

John W. Rankin, a graduate of Jefferson college, Pennsylvania, came to Ashland in 1846, and removed to Iowa in 1850, where he subsequently became a common pleas judge. He was a gentleman of fine attainments.

James W. Smith located in Ashland in 1842. He attended school at the Ohio university of Athens. He is a native of Wayne county. He is engaged in practice.

John Clark located in Ashland in 1847. He removed to Iowa in 1850, where he is still engaged in practice. He was register of one of the land districts of that State during the administrations of Pierce and Buchanan.

Harvey H. Johnson, a native of New England, located in Ashland about 1848. He was a fair lawyer. He was elected to Congress in 1852, and defeated for re-election in 1854. He removed to Minnesota in 1855.

William A. Hunter, a native of Pennsylvania, located in Ashland in 1846, as one of the editors and proprietors of the Ashland *Democrat*. He continued in the *Democrat* until 1848, and also in the practice of law. In 1849 he removed to Williams county, Ohio, and became treasurer. He served in the late war. He has since gone west.

Jonathan Moffett, a native of Ohio, was one of the editors and proprietors of the Ashland *Democrat*, in 1846-8, and the legal partner of William A. Hunter. He removed to Wyandot county in 1849, and subsequently was elected auditor two terms.

Willard Slocum, a native of Ashland, has been engaged in law for many years. He was among the earliest attorneys after the erection of Ashland county. He served in the late war and was promoted through all the grades from captain to brigadier general.

William Osborn, a native of Columbus, Ohio, located in Ashland about 1847. He edited the Ashland *Times*, and has a good reputation in the legal profession. He has served one term as common pleas judge in this district.

George W. Geddes is a native of Knox county, studied with Columbus Delano, and practiced law in Hayesville one or two years. He removed to Mansfield about 1849, where he became a successful attorney. He was subsequently elected judge of the court of common pleas, and served about fifteen years on the bench. He is in practice.

* See biographical sketch.

Albert L. Curtis, a native of the State of New York, located in Ashland about the year 1849. He acted as deputy clerk in the court of common pleas, under Jacob O. Jennings, three years; and after the adoption of the new constitution, was elected probate judge six years. He has also been mayor of Ashland and prosecuting attorney of the county.

Alexander Porter, a native of Lorain county, Ohio, located in Ashland in 1852. He served as prosecuting attorney one term. In 1853 he was appointed postmaster at Ashland. He removed to New London, and deceased. He was a man of unusual fluency as a speaker.

Thomas J. Kenny, a native of Buffalo, New York, was admitted in 1850. He has served as prosecuting attorney one term, and one term in the State senate. He is now serving as common pleas judge for this district, having been elected in 1874. He was captain of a company in the Sixteenth regiment of Ohio volunteer infantry, in 1861.

George W. Carey remained at Rowsburgh as an attorney for several years. Visited California and made a handsome property, after which he located in Green township, and served one term in the Ohio legislature and died of pulmonary consumption in 1865.

John J. Gurley, a native of Pennsylvania, had an office two or three years in Hayesville about 1852, and was justice of the peace. He removed to Morrow county. He was there elected probate judge and served as a member of the constitutional convention of 1873-4. He is a gentleman of fair attainments.

William B. Allison, a native of Perry township, in this county, was admitted in 1850, formed a partnership with J. W. Smith, and afterward with B. W. Kellogg, and again with William Osborn, and practiced at the Ashland bar about eight years, and removed to Iowa, where he was elected three terms to Congress, and is now serving in the Senate of the United States.

Nicholas M. Donaldson, of Loudonville, was elected the first prosecuting attorney after the erection of Ashland county. He served one term and removed to Wisconsin. He was a fair lawyer.

George W. Hill, a native of Marshall county, Virginia, came to Ashland, as a student, under Lorin Andrews, of the academy, in 1845; was admitted to practice in 1849; was in Columbus and Washington city, District of Columbia, in the department nine years; returned, and was elected prosecuting attorney two terms, 1862 to 1866; from 1868 to 1872, was editor and proprietor of the *States and Union*. In 1873-4, served in the Ohio constitutional convention.

William B. McCarty, a native of Pennsylvania, located in Ashland about 1851, as editor of the Whig journal, the *Ashlander*. He subsequently read law, and practiced some fifteen years at the Ashland bar. He served, in the meantime, two or three terms as justice of the peace. He served as lieutenant in the late war. He resides, now, in Michigan. He was a fine writer, and a polished speaker.

Robert Beer, a native of Ashland county, was admitted about 1853. He was a good scholar, but lacked legal tastes. He subsequently studied for the ministry, in the Presbyterian church, and located in Indiana. He has become a very eloquent and effective minister.

John J. Jacobs, a native of Ashland, was admitted about 1857. He was, when a student at the academy, regarded as an eloquent speaker. He was twice elected prosecuting attorney. He also edited the Ashland *Union* about four years. He died at about the age of thirty-seven years.

Robert M. Campbell, born in Orange township, attended school at Hayesville, Vermillion institute; studed law with Judge F. J. Kenny; admitted in 1863; was elected county auditor in 1866, re-elected in 1868, and is now in practice.

William T. Johnston, a native of the Western Reserve, was admitted about 1856. He served one term as prosecuting attorney, and commanded a company in the late war. He removed, about 1870, to the State of Nebraska, where he is rising in his profession.

J. S. Wertman was born March 13, 1845, on a farm three and one-half miles north of Ashland; attended school at Savannah academy, and graduated at Wittenberg college, Springfield, Ohio, class of 1869. He taught school until 1871. Practiced surveying and engineering for two years. Studied law with B. F. Davis, of Indianapolis, Indiana, and began the practice in that city. Came back to Ashland in August, 1877, and has been practicing here ever since.

Peter S. Grosscup, a native of Milton township, Ashland county, attended school at Wittenberg college and graduated in 1872. He then entered the law department of the Boston university and graduated in 1873, and was admitted to the Boston bar. Returned to Ashland and was appointed city solicitor. He is now the partner of Judge William Osborn.

John McCray, a native of Washington county, Pennsylvania, was admitted about 1869. He was elected prosecuting attorney in 1871, and served two terms. In 1875 he was elected clerk of the court of common pleas of Ashland county.

Henry McCray, a native of Washington county, Pennsylvania, studied with Thomas T. McCray, a brother, at Wooster, Ohio, and was admitted about 1866; came to Ashland in 1872, and removed to Loudonville in the spring of 1874. He is now in practice.

John D. Jones, a native of Pennsylvania, was elected sheriff in 1852, and served four years. He subsequently served as probate judge six years; has been, also, elected justice of the peace three times. He was admitted to the bar some time after the expiration of his term as probate judge.

Jacob P. Devor, a native of Pennsylvania, was admitted to the bar about 1861. He has served nine years as justice of the peace. He is engaged, generally, in the settlement of estates in the court of probate.

Byron Stilwell, a native of Holmes county, Ohio, came to Ashland about 1871. He is a young man of fair attainments. He was elected prosecuting attorney in 1874.

George B. Smith, a native of Ashland, attended school at Kenyon college, Knox county, two years; studied law with his father, James W. Smith, and was admitted in 1869. He is at present a partner with J. W. Smith. He is a young gentleman of fine literary tastes.

H. S. Lee, born in the city of New York, August 13, 1821; attended school in the city; came to Ohio in 1842; engaged in mercantile business in Savannah; was elected clerk of the court of common pleas in 1857, and served two terms; was admitted to the bar in 1864.

Charles Dorland, a native of Perry township, Ashland county, was admitted in 1875. He is a young gentleman of industrious habits, and will succeed in his profession.

William O. Porter, a native of Vermillion township, Ashland county, was educated at Vermillion institute, was sheriff of the county four years, and was admitted to the bar in 1873. He is now farming, and occasionally acting as attorney.

Silas Robbins, jr., the first educated attorney who settled in Ashland, about the year 1828 or 1829, was a native of the New England States, and a gentleman who sustained the reputation of being "an honest lawyer." He served about six years as justice of the peace for Montgomery township. He had a fair practice at the Mansfield bar, and accumulated considerable property. He died in 1842.

CHAPTER XL.
THE COUNTY OFFICERS FROM 1846 TO 1880.

Commissioners.—Auditors.—Treasurers.—Recorders.—Infirmary Directors.—Legislative.—Organization of the Courts.—Associate Judges.—Probate Judges.—Clerks of Common Pleas.—Prosecuting Attorneys.—Sheriffs.—Constitutional Convention of 1873-4.

COUNTY COMMISSIONERS.

After the erection of the county in 1846, three commissioners were elected, one for one year, one for two years, and one for three years. Since that period the same order has been observed in electing their successors. The following is a complete list to 1880:

Abner Crist, of Ruggles, 1846 to 1847; Edward S. Hibbard, of Hanover, 1846 to 1848; Josiah Thomas, of Orange, 1846 to 1849; Aldrich Carver, of Ruggles, 1847 to 1850; James M. Hammett, of Mohican, 1848 to 1851; Christian Newcomer, of Mifflin, 1849 to 1852; Luke Selby, of Mifflin, 1850 to 1853; George McConnell, of Orange, 1851 to 1854; Amos Hilburn, of Milton, 1852 to 1855; Luke Selby, of Mifflin, 1853 to 1856; George McConnell, of Orange, 1854 to 1857; Hervey Fenn, of Ruggles, 1855 to 1858; William S. Strickland, of Vermillion, 1856 to 1859; Jacob Emerick, of Lake, 1857 to 1860; John Berry, of Jackson, 1858 to 1861; Daniel Pocock, of Mohican, 1859 to 1862; Jacob Emerick, of Lake, 1860 to 1863; John Berry, of Jackson, 1861 to 1864; Robert Cowan, of Vermillion, 1862 to 1865; John VanNest, of Perry, 1863 to 1866; Henry Wicks, of Jackson, 1864 to 1867; William Cowan, of Green, 1865 to 1868; John VanNest, of Perry, 1866 to 1869; Henry Wicks, of Jackson, 1867 to 1870; William Cowan, of Green, 1868 to 1871; James Dunlap, of Sullivan, 1869 to 1872; John P. Smalley, of Perry, 1870 to 1873; William M. Crowner, of Hanover, 1871 to 1874; James Dunlap, of Sullivan, 1872 to 1875; John P. Smalley, of Perry, 1873 to 1876; William M. Crowner, of Hanover, 1874 to 1877; Stephen Barrack, of Orange, 1875 to 1878; J. J. Wolf, 1877 to 1880.

COUNTY AUDITORS, 1846 TO 1880.

Hugh Burns, of Milton, 1846 to 1850; Aldrich Carver, of Ruggles, 1850 to 1852; Isaac Gates, of Mifflin, 1852 to 1856; James Swineford, of Montgomery, 1856 to 1860; Johnson Oldroyd, of Mohican, 1860 to 1862; Isaac Gates, of Mifflin, 1862 to 1866; Robert M. Campbell, of Orange, 1866 to 1870;* Emanuel Finger, of Orange, 1870 to 1874; William T. Alberson, of Orange, 1874 to 1876; E. Grosscup, 1876 to 1880.

COUNTY TREASURERS, 1846 TO 1880.

George W. Urie, of Montgomery, 1846 to 1850; James W. Boyd, of Mohican, 1850 to 1854; Jacob Crall, of Montgomery, 1854 to 1856; John Jacobs, of Montgomery, 1856 to 1860;† Reuben N. Hershy, of Mifflin, 1860 to 1864; Henry Hershy, of Mifflin, 1864 to 1866; William G. Heltman, of Milton, 1866 to 1870; Gutelius I. Yearick, of Jackson, 1870 to 1874; Michael Miller, of Montgomery, 1874 to 1876; G. Ullman, elected in 1877.

COUNTY RECORDERS, 1846 TO 1880.

Asa S. Reed, of Mohican, 1846 to 1855; Robert Scott, of Montgomery, 1855 to 1859; George Johnston, of Montgomery, 1859 to 1865; George W. Urie, of Montgomery, 1865 to 1874; John P. M. Goodman, of Mohican, 1874 to 1883.

COUNTY SURVEYORS, 1846 TO 1880.

John Keene, jr., of Jackson, 1846 to 1858; Orlow Smith, of Milton, 1858 to 1861; George W. Ryall, of Milton, 1861 to 1864; John Keene, jr., of Jackson, 1864 to 1867; George W. Ryall, of Milton, 1867 to 1867;‡ Henry Pifer, of Milton, 1868 to 1871; George W. Ryall, of Milton, 1871 to 1874; John B. Weddell, of Milton, 1874 to 1877; John Weddell, 1877 to 1880.

INFIRMARY DIRECTORS.

After the completion of the infirmary, in 1850, it was organized by the appointment of Joseph McCornes, of Mohican, John Scott, of Vermillion, and Elias Ford, of Clearcreek, as directors. Their successors, under the constitution of 1851, were:

1852, David Bryte, of Montgomery, one year, Joseph H. Miller, two years, George Boldorf, of Mohican, three years; 1853, David Bryte, three years; 1854, Patrick Kelley, of Vermillion, three years; 1855, Hugh McGuire, of Montgomery, three years; 1856, George Boldorf, three years; 1857, Henry Hough, of Montgomery, three years; 1858, Joseph Strickland, of Vermillion, three years; 1859, D. K. Hull, of Vermillion, three years; 1860, Holiday Ames, of Montgomery, three years; 1861, Johnston Martin, of Montgomery, three years; 1862, Joseph Strickland, of Vermillion, three years; 1863, D. K. Hull, of Vermillion, part of a term; 1864, William Craig, of Vermillion, part of a term; 1865, James McNaull, of Montgomery, three years; 1866, William Craig, of Vermillion, three years; 1867, Moses Latta, of Montgomery, three years; 1868, William Galloway, of Vermillion, three years; 1869, William Craig, of Vermillion, three years; 1870, Moses Latta, of Vermillion, three years; 1871, William Galloway, three years; 1872, George Myers, of Perry, three years; 1873, Joseph Strickland, of Vermillion, part of a term; 1874, Clark A. Barton, of Vermillion, two years; 1874, Andrew Jackson, of Perry, three years; 1875, C. A. Barton, three years; 1876, Andrew Jackson, three years; 1877, George Smith; 1878, T. Miller; 1879, Benjamin McGuire.

The superintendents of the infirmary since 1852, have been:

Edward Moore, 1852 to 1863; W. S. Strickland, 1863 to 1864; William Crowner, 1864 to 1865; Samuel Rowland, 1865 to 1865; William Miller, 1865 to 1872; T. J. Mopes, 1872 to 1876.

---

* In the fall of 1870 Robert M. Campbell resigned, and Emanuel Finger was appointed to fill the unexpired term.

† John Jacobs, having deceased before the expiration of his first term, F. S. Jacobs was appointed to fill the vacancy; and was elected in 1858, one term.

‡ John Keene, jr., having deceased in August, 1867, George W. Ryall was appointed to fill the unexpired term of deceased. Messrs. Smith and Ryall had acted as deputies under Mr. Keene for a number of years.

REPRESENTATIVES, 1846 TO 1880.

George W. Bull, of Hanover, session of 1846-7-8; Charles R. Deming, of Montgomery, session of 1848-9-50; Jacob Miller, of Perry, session of 1850-1-2; Richard D. Emerson, of Montgomery, session of 1852-3-4; Jacob P. Cowan, of Mohican, session of 1855-1856; Jacob P. Cowan, of Mohican, session of 1857-1858; George McConnel, of Orange, session of 1859-1860; * John Taylor, of Green, session of 1859-1860; John Taylor, of Green, session of 1861-1862; George W. Carey, of Green, session of 1862-1864; William Larwill, of Hanover, session of 1865-1867; William Larwill, of Hanover, session of 1868-1869; James E. Chase, of Jackson, session of 1869-1870; James E. Chase, of Jackson, session of 1871-1872; Benjamin Myers, of Perry, session of 1873-1875; Benjamin Myers, of Perry, session of 1876-1877; John M. Bull, session of 1878-1880.

SENATORS, 1846 TO 1878.

George W. Bull, of Hanover, session of 1849-1850; Joseph Musgrave, of Montgomery, session of 1855-1857; Thomas J. Kenney, of Montgomery, session of 1859-1861; Samuel Glass, of Vermillion, session of 1862-1864; John Cowan, of Mohican, session of 1869-1870; T. M. Beer, session of 1876-1878.

During this period Ashland and Wayne—Ashland and Richland, and Ashland, Richland, Lorain, and Medina counties constituted the senatorial district.

THE COURTS.

At the organization of the county, in 1846, Judge Parker, of Mansfield, was president judge of the district.

The governor appointed and commissioned Edmund Ingmand, of Mohican, George H. Stewart, of Hanover, and John P. Reznor, of Montgomery, associate judges.

The court, thus constituted, appointed Daniel W. Brown, of Ruggles, clerk *pro tem.*

James Hunter, of Montgomery, was appointed deputy clerk, under Mr. Brown.

At the expiration of the time for which Daniel W. Brown was appointed clerk, in 1847, the question of appoining a successor arose. The applicants were Jacob O. Jennings, of Mohican, and Daniel W. Brown, of Ruggles. In the contest, it appears that Judge Parker agreed to cast his vote for the candidate for whom a majority of the associate judges should vote. Judges Ingmand and Stewart voted for Jacob O. Jennings, and Reznor for Daniel W. Brown. Judge Parker, therefore, gave his vote for Mr. Jennings, who qualified and entered upon the duties of his office, and continued in the same until the adoption of the constitution, in 1851, when a successor was elected and qualified.

Albert L. Curtis, of Millersburgh, Holmes county, an experienced clerk, was chosen, by Mr. Jennings, as deputy, and he continued in that capacity until 1852.

Soon after this contest Judge John P. Reznor resigned, and Daniel W. Brown was appointed his successor, and, at the expiration of his time, in 1849, John C. Myers, of Clearcreek, was appointed and commissioned associate judge, and successor to Daniel W. Brown. Ingmand, Stewart, and Myers continued in office until the adoption of the constitution of 1851.

PROBATE JUDGES.

The constitution of 1851 abolished the office of associate judge and substituted therefor the office of probate judge. Prior to that period, the associate judges met at fixed periods for the appointment of administrators, executors and guardians, and the settlement of estates.

* Decennial increase under constitution of 1851.

The clerk of the court of common pleas kept a record of their proceedings. The new constitution, in creating a probate court, transferred all administration questions to that court, making the probate judge his own clerk.

The following list exhibits all the probate judges who have served in that court, from its commencement to the date of this volume:

Albert L. Curtis, of Montgomery, 1852 to 1858; John D. Jones, of Mohican, 1858 to 1864; William A. G. Emerson, of Montgomery, 1864 to 1864; Edmund Ingmand, of Mohican, 1864 to 1867; Tully C. Bushnell, of Montgomery, 1867 to 1870; Daniel W. Whitmore, of Milton, 1870 to 1876; John Taylor, of Green, 1876 to 1882.

The election of William A. G. Emerson was contested by Edmund Ingmand, and resulted in favor of the contestant. Judge Ingmand deceased in 1867, and Tully C. Bushnell was elected to fill the vacancy. Collins W. Bushnell, of Montgomery, was elected probate judge at the fall election of 1857, but deceased a short time after he had taken his office, and John W. Jones, of Mohican, was appointed to fill the vacancy.

COUNTY CLERKS, 1846 TO 1880.

Daniel W. Brown, of Ruggles, 1846 to 1847; Jacob O. Jennings, of Mohican, 1847 to 1852; John Sheridan, of Clearcreek, 1852 to 1855; Jacob O. Jennings, of Mohican, 1855 to 1859; Henry S. See, of Clearcreek, 1859 to 1865; William G. Heltman, of Milton, 1865 to 1865;* Seth M. Barber, of Montgomery, 1865 to 1867; Edwin T. Drayton, of Montgomery, 1867 to 1870; William C. Frazee, of Montgomery, 1870 to 1876; John T. McCray, of Ruggles, 1876 to 1882.

PROSECUTING ATTORNEYS, 1846 TO 1880.

Nicholas M. Donaldson, of Hanover, 1846 to 1847; John S. Fulton, of Montgomery, 1847 to 1849; Boliver W. Kellogg, of Montgomery, 1849 to 1853; Alexander Porter, of Sullivan, 1853 to 1855; Thomas J. Kenny, of Montgomery, 1855 to 1857; John J. Jacobs, of Montgomery, 1857 to 1859; William T. Johnston, of Montgomery, 1859 to 1861; George W. Hill, of Montgomery, 1861 to 1867; Albert L. Curtis, of Montgomery, 1867 to 1869; John J. Jacobs, of Montgomery, 1869 to 1871; John T. McCray, of Mifflin, 1871 to 1875; Byron Stilwell, of Montgomery, 1875 to 1877; George B. Smith, present incumbent.

SHERIFFS, 1846 TO 1880.

James Doty, of Mifflin, 1846 to 1848; Isaac Gates, of Mifflin, 1848 to 1852; John D. Jones, of Mohican, 1852 to 1856; John J. Hootman, of Mohican, 1856 to 1860; James McCool, of Montgomery, 1860 to 1864; John G. Brown, of Montgomery, 1864 to 1866; Levi H. Kiplinger, of Jackson, 1866 to 1868; William O. Porter, of Vermillion, 1868 to 1872; John J. Winbigler, of Mohican, 1872 to 1876; Joseph Moore, 1876 to 1880.

When James Doty was sheriff, Isaac Gates acted as deputy. When Isaac Gates was elected, John D. Jones was his deputy. When James McCool became sheriff, John G. Brown was his deputy. It will be seen that the deputies were generally in the line of promotion.

CORONERS, 1846 TO 1880.

Michael Riddle, 1846 to 1848, Montgomery; Justus Weatherbee, 1848 to 1852, Mohican; John G. Brown, 1852 to 1854, Montgomery; John Woodburn, 1854 to 1858, Milton; George W. Crozier, 1858 to 1860, Sullivan; S. P. Crozier, 1860 to 1862, Sullivan; John Woodburn, 1862 to 1864, Milton; William J. Vermilya, 1864 to 1866, Ruggles; Israel Markel, 1866 to 1868, Orange; Dr. A. Emerick, 1868 to 1872, Lake; Daniel Ambrose, 1872 to 1876, Montgomery; Dr. F. H. Wilson, 1876 to 1878, Mohican; Daniel Ambrose, present incumbent.

CONSTITUTIONAL CONVENTIONS.

In electing delegates to the constitutional convention of 1851, Ashland and Wayne counties constituted a

* The election of William G. Heltman was contested by Seth M. Barber, and decided in favor of the latter gentleman by the court of common pleas. Mr. Barber entered upon the duties of his office in June, 1865.

district. Ashland county elected John J. Hootman; while Wayne county elected Elza Wilson and Dr. Leander Firestone, and upon his resignation, John Larwill.

In the convention of 1873, for remodeling the constitution of 1851, each county elected the same number of delegates to which it was entitled for representatives in the house. Ashland county was represented by Dr. George W. Hill.

CHAPTER XLI.
A LIST OF THE JUSTICES OF THE PEACE.
Vermillion.—Green.—Hanover.—Orange.—Mifflin.—Milton.—Clearcreek.—Lake.—Mohican.—Perry.—Jackson.—Sullivan.—Troy.—Ruggles.

THE following is a list of the justices of the peace who have served in the different townships from the early settlement to the present time:

MONTGOMERY TOWNSHIP.

Robert Newell, 1814; Robert Ralston, 1816; Daniel Carter, 1817; Jonas Kline, Solomon Sherradden, Josiah Gallup, Jonas H. Gierhart, David Robison, Silas Robins, jr., William Dwyre, Wells Kellogg, Erastus N. Gates; Charles R. Deming, 1840; Joseph Madden, 1845*; Charles R. Deming, 1847; Stephen Wolf, Daniel W. Brown, 1848; Charles R. Deming, 1850; John A. McClusky, 1850; David Bryte, 1851; William Millington, 1852; John A. McClusky, 1853; William B. McCarty, 1854; Francis Graham, 1856; Jacob P. Devor, 1856; William Willson, 1857; John A. McClusky, 1859; Francis Graham, Jacob P. Devor, 1860; Robert McMurray, 1862; Henry Burns, Jacob P. Devor, 1863; Robert McMurray, 1864; James W. Smith, Andrew Mason, 1866; Robert McMurray, 1868; John D. Jones, John A. McClusky, 1869; Robert McMurray, 1870; Sterling G. Bushnell, H. B. Pancoast, 1872; John D. Jones, 1874; Sterling G. Bushnell, H. B. Pancoast, 1875; John D. Jones, Cyrus Plank and M. H. Marietta, 1880.

VERMILLION TOWNSHIP.

James Wallace, 1814; James Walters, 1815; Joseph Workman, 1817; James Walters, 1818; Ephriam Eckley, Stephen Smith, 1821; Ephriam Eckley, 1824; Stephen Smith, 1825; William McCrary, 1828; William W. Irwin, Jared Irwin, 1831; Robert Cowan, 1834; John Harmon, Robert Cowan, 1837; Peter Eckley, 1838; John Harmon, Robert Cowan, 1840; Joseph Strickland, jr., Archibald Gillis, 1841; Andrew Scott, David Ciphers, 1842; John Harmon, 1843; Oliver Sloan, 1844; David Ciphers, 1845; John Harmon, George Buchanan, 1846; David Ciphers, 1848; John J. Gurley, George Buchanan, 1849; John M. Rowland, 1851; David Ciphers, 1851; George Buchanan, 1852; William S. Strickland, N. G. Swaringen, 1854; James B. Smith, 1855; Joseph Kinninger, 1857; William S. Strickland, James B. Smith, 1858; McClure Davis, William S. Strickland, 1861; McClure Davis, D. K. Hull, 1864; William S. Strickland, 1866; William G. Galloway, 1867; David Fox, 1868; William G. Galloway, 1870; H. C. Johnson, 1871; William G. Galloway, 1873; Henry Butcher, 1874; W. W. Armstrong, David Fox, and Joseph Heichel, 1880.

GREEN TOWNSHIP.

Henry McCart, 1810; Peter Kinney, 1812; Thomas Coulter, 1812; Peter Kinney, 1815; James Rowland, 1818; Jonathan Coulter, 1819; Trew Pattee, 1821; Jonathan Coulter, 1822; Ahira Hill, 1822; Simon Rowland, 1824; Jonathan Coulter, 1825; William Taylor, 1827; Jonathan Coulter, 1828; William Taylor, 1830; John Coulter, 1831; Thomas Andrews, Simon Rowland, 1833; John Coulter, 1834; Thomas Anderson, Simon Rowland, 1836; Thomas W. Coulter, 1837; John M. Rowland, Isaac Martin, jr., 1838; Thomas W. Coulter, 1840; John M. Rowland, Isaac Martin, jr., 1841; Thomas W. Coulter, 1843; Hugh Martin, William Reed, 1844; Philip H. Plummer, 1846; Hugh Martin, William Reed, 1847; Philip H. Plummer, 1849; Hugh Martin, William Reed, 1850; Phillip H. Plummer, 1852; Elias Groff, Abraham Dehaven, William Reed, 1853; Thomas Calhoun, George W. Carey, 1856; John Taylor, Paul Oliver, 1859; William Cowan, Paul Oliver, 1862; William Cowan, Paul Oliver, 1865; John Taylor, William Cowan, 1868; John Taylor, Warring Wolf, 1871; John Taylor, Warring Wolf, 1874. Mr. Taylor resigned in February, 1876, to fill the position of probate judge, to which he was elected at the October election of 1875. Silas C. Parker was his successor. Joseph Mumper was elected in 1880.

HANOVER TOWNSHIP.

Stephen Butler, 1818; Stephen Butler, 1821; Abel Strong, John McCoy, 1824; Abel Strong, Gilbert Pell, 1827; Abel Strong, Thomas Shearer, 1830; Edward S. Hibbard, William McMillan, 1833; John Kennedy, 1834; Edward S. Hibbard, James Willson, 1836; John Kennedy, John A. McFall, 1837; George W. Bull, Edward S. Hibbard, 1839; John A. McFall, 1840; George W. Bull, Edward S. Hibbard, 1842; Peter Yost, 1843; George W. Bull, 1845; James M. Ayers, Peter Yost, 1846; George W. Bull, 1848; James M. Ayers, Peter Yost, 1849; Thomas J. Bull, 1850; Solomon Givler, James L. Drake, William Garrett, 1851; George W. Bull, 1852; Jacob Hublitz, John Taylor, 1853; William Garrett, A. U. Bishop, 1854; Isaac S. Bishop, John Strong, 1855; Joseph B. Sanborn, 1856; J. B. Cummings, 1857; A. C. Kile, Morrell Rust, 1859; William Garrett, Morrell Rust, 1862; Stephen Mapes, Morrell Rust, 1865; Stephen Mapes, Morrell Rust, 1868; Stephen Mapes, Morrell Rust, 1871; George Wolf, John C. Gaines, 1874, and 1877; W. M. Crowner, 1877.

ORANGE TOWNSHIP.

James Murray, 1816; Vachel Metcalf, Jacob Mason, 1818; Vachel Metcalf, Jacob Mason, 1821; Vachel Metcalf, Jacob Mason, 1824; William Patterson, 1827; John Murray, 1828; Daniel Campbell; John Murray, 1831; John Smurr, Daniel Campbell, 1834; John Smurr, Daniel Campbell, 1837; John Smurr, Daniel Campbell, 1840; John Smurr, 1843; John Smurr, 1846; Robert Culbertson, 1843; Robert Culbertson, 1846; Daniel Campbell, 1849; John Smurr, 1850; William Rigby, A. C. Fast, 1852; James Alberson, 1854; Daniel Campbell, jr., John Warren, 1855; Daniel Campbell, jr., John Warren, 1858; Israel Markel, 1860; Robert Culbertson, James Alberson, 1861; James D. Hamilton, James Alberson, 1864; David Biddinger, 1866; James Alberson, 1867; George Miller, 1869; James Alberson, 1870; George Miller, 1872; James Alberson, 1873; David Biddinger, 1878; and James Alberson, 1879.

MIFFLIN TOWNSHIP.

Archibald Gardner, 1814; William Gardner, 1817, and continuously until 1841; John Fleming, 1836; James Doty, 1838; John Fleming, 1839; James Doty, 1841; Isaac Gates, 1842; James Doty, 1844; Isaac Gates, 1845; George Roberts, Charles Boals, 1846; Samuel Culler, 1847; Isaac Gates, Elijah Hart, 1848; Samuel Culler, 1850; Elijah Hart, 1851; Samuel Culler, 1853; John Charles, Samuel Culler, 1856, John Charles, Samuel Culler 1859; Henry Blust, Joseph Doty, 1862; Joseph Doty, Henry D. Ruth, 1865; Dilman Switzer, John F. Beninghoff, 1868; Harrison Funk, John F. Beninghoff, 1871; Solomon Doty, 1872; George W. Rebman, 1874; Solomon Doty, 1875; Samuel Culler, and Paul Keightley, 1878.

MILTON TOWNSHIP.

Robert McBeth, Benjamin Montgomery, 1816; Robert Nelson, Benjamin Montgomery, 1819; Robert Nelson, Samuel King, 1822; Joseph Arnold, Robert Nelson, 1825; Joseph Arnold, Isaac Charles, 1828; Thomas Smith, Isaac Charles, 1831; William Taggart, Thomas Smith, 1834; James Andrews, Thomas Smith, 1837; James Andrews, Thomas Smith, 1840; James Andrews, Thomas Smith, 1843; Amos Hilborn, Thomas Smith, 1846; Thomas Smith, Benjamin Grosscup, 1849; Samuel Smith, Andrew Barnes, jr., 1852; James Andrews, 1853; Samuel Smith, 1855; James Andrews, 1856; Samuel Smith, 1858; Daniel Grosscup, 1859; Samuel Smith, 1861; Daniel W. Whitmore, 1862; Obed Andrews, 1863; James McCrea, 1865; Daniel W. Whitmore, 1866; Benjamin Wenrick, 1868; Daniel Whitmore, 1869; Elisha Barton, 1870; Benjamin Wenrick, 1871; James McCrea, Benjamin Wenrick, 1874; Enoch Wertman, George Hartman, 1880.

CLEARCREEK TOWNSHIP.

Robert McBeth, 1816; Robert McBeth, 1819; Elias Ford, 1822; Elias Ford, 1825; James Haney, 1825; Dr. Porter, 1828; Dr. Porter, 1831;

---

*The records having been lost, we are unable to give the year of the election of the foregoing justices, and the number of terms which they served respectively.

John Musser, 1834; John Musser, 1837; John C. Myers, 1840; John C. Myers, John Musser, 1843; John Musser, 1846; John C. Myers, 1847; A. F. Shaw, John Musser, 1849; Thomas Hayes, John Aten, 1850; Thomas Hayes, John Aten, 1853; A. F. Shaw, 1855; John Aten, Thomas Hayes, 1856; A. F. Shaw, 1858; Thomas Hayes, George S. Shriver, Daniel G. Templeton, 1859; Thomas Hayes, George Shriver, D. G. Templeton, 1862; George S. Shriver, H. M. Dodd, 1865; R. J. Simonton, George S. Shriver, John M. Sloan, 1868; W. J. Vermilya, George S. Shriver, R. J. Simonton, 1871; Arius Rumfield, George S. Shriver, Benjamin Crabbs, 1874; David Greagor, 1875; J. B. Vermilya, George B. Masters, 1879.

LAKE TOWNSHIP.

James Loudon Priest, 1815; James Loudon Priest, John Newkirk, 1818; John Weatherbee, John Newkirk, 1821; John Weatherbee, 1824; William Wicoff, 1835; Martin Wolf, William Wicoff, 1838; Robert Naylor, William Wicoff, 1841; Henry Maurer, William Wicoff, 1844; Martin Wolf, William Wicoff, 1847; Henry Maurer, Elijah Oram, 1850; Henry Maurer, Elijah Oram, 1853; Henry Maurer, Elijah Oram, 1856; Henry Maurer, Elijah Oram, 1859; George W. Brubaker, Allen Metcalf, 1862; Allen Metcalf, George W. Brubaker, 1865; Robert Marks, 1867; George W. Brubaker, 1868; Robert Marks, 1870; Adam Long, 1871; Robert Marks, 1873; Adam Long, 1874; Sparks Burd, 1877; John Kantzer, 1879.

MOHICAN TOWNSHIP.

Nathan Odell, 1812; John Newkirk, 1815; William Metcalf, 1814; Aaron Beard, 1816; Aaron Beard, Edmund Ingmand, 1819; Alexander Finley, 1820; Aaron Beard, 1821; Aaron Beard, 1824; Francis Corrothers, 1825; Jacob Lybarger, 1827; Francis Corrothers, 1828; Jacob Lybarger, 1830; Francis Corrothers, 1831; Elza Wilson, 1833; Edmund Ingmand, 1834; David Hazlett, 1836; Edmund Ingmand, 1837; David Kauffman, 1840; David Kauffman, Henry Winbigler, 1843; Henry Winbigler, Johnson Oldroyd, 1846; James W. Boyd, Johnson Oldroyd, 1849; Henry Winbigler, 1851; William Campbell, 1852; Henry Winbigler, 1854; William Campbell, 1855; Christopher Hootman, J. T. Smith, 1857; Heman Alleman, 1859; William H. Hill, 1860; John J. Winbigler, 1862; William F. Hill, 1863; John J. Winbigler, 1865; J. D. Mumper, 1866; J. N. Slater, 1868; J. D. Mumper, 1869; J. W. Slater, 1871; A. J. Lybarger, 1872; Joseph Heickel, 1874; A. J. Lybarger, 1875; Joseph Heickel, 1877, and A. Ingmand, 1879.

PERRY TOWNSHIP.

John Jackson, 1816; Thomas Johnston, 1818; John Ihrig, 1819; Thomas Johnston, 1820; John Smith, 1822; John A. Kelley, 1824; John Smith, 1825; John Herr, 1827; John Ihrig, 1828; John Allison, 1830; John Ihrig, 1831; John Allison, 1833; John Ihrig, 1834; John Allison, 1836; John Ihrig, Jacob Miller, 1837; John Allison, 1839; John Smith, 1840; Isaac Cahill, 1842; John Smith, 1843; John Ecker, 1845; Jacob Miller, 1846; John Ecker, 1848; John Van Nest, 1849; John Cory, 1851; John Van Nest, 1852; Columbus C. Coulter, 1854; John Van Nest, 1855; Alexander Hamilton, 1856; Hugh Hamilton, 1857; John Van Nest, 1858; Hugh Hamilton, 1860; Henry Buck, 1861; John A. Shidler, 1863; John Van Nest, 1864; John A. Shidler, 1866; Solomon Hohenshill, 1867; J. G. Bringolf, 1869; Solomon Hohenshill, 1870; Andrew Jackson, John Van Nest, 1873; P. R. Greenlun and Thomas Sefton, 1879.

JACKSON TOWNSHIP.

Charles Hoy, Jonas H. Gierhart, 1819; John Keene, Michael Debolt, 1831; Michael Debolt, Thomas Smith, 1834; Philip Shutt, Robert Buchanan, 1835; John Keene, 1837; Robert Buchanan, 1838; James Culbertson, David Young, 1840; James McCoy, 1841; James McCoy, 1844; David Young, 1845; Christian Fast, John Keene, jr., 1846; James Stephenson, 1848; Philip Shutt, 1849; Joseph C. Bolles, Charles Hoy,* 1851; Jacob Fast, 1852; Joseph C. Bolles, 1854; Jacob Fast, 1855; Joseph C. Bolles, Jacob Fast, 1857; Edward McFadden, Jacob Fast, 1860; William Berry, David Biddinger, Jacob Fast, 1863; William Berry, Jacob Fast, 1866; William Berry, Thos. M. Dearman, 1869; John Berry, Jacob Fast, 1872; John Berry, Jacob Fast, 1875; John Berry, Jacob Fast, 1878.

SULLIVAN TOWNSHIP.

John Gould, Henry M. Close,† J. W. Spencer, 1846; Francis Frink, 1847; Hamilton Porter, 1850; John J. Wright, 1851; Joseph J. Wright, 1849; Joseph J. Wright, 1852; Hamilton Porter, 1853; A. H. Palmer, 1855; Hamilton Porter, 1856; A. H. Palmer, 1858; Hamilton Porter, 1859; Rhesa Close, 1861; Hamilton Porter, George Philpot, 1862; Hamilton Porter, George Philpot, 1865; Hamilton Porter, George Philpot, 1868; Marcus De Moss, Hamilton Porter, 1871; Marcus De Moss, Hamilton Porter, 1874; Marcus De Moss, Hamilton Porter, 1877.

TROY TOWNSHIP.

Benjamin Moore, 1835; Benjamin Moore, 1838; Benjamin Moore, 1841; Christian Bush, 1844; Christian Bush, 1847; David F. Young, 1848; J. M. Bruce, 1850; D. F. Young, 1851; B. F. Fulton, 1852; Henry Summers, 1854; Francis Frink, 1855; John W. Carn, 1858; F. Frink, 1858; Henry Summers, 1860; E. P. Philips, 1861; Henry Summers, 1863; E. P. Philips, 1864; Henry Summers, 1866; Cornelius Bishop, 1867; Charles S. Vanoonam, 1868; Henry Summers, 1869; R. D. Kiplinger, 1871; Henry Summers, 1872; R. D. Kiplinger, 1874; D. V. Bailey, Henry Summers, 1875—failed to qualify, and John Smith was elected in 1876; John Taylor, 1878; and John D. Phelps, 1879.

RUGGLES TOWNSHIP.

The justices of this township, prior to 1846, were Harvey Sacket, Daniel Beach, Salmon Weston, Stanley Weston, Albert G. Buell, Daniel W. Brown, Thomas Grinald, Jacob Roorback, Aldrich Carver,‡ Erastus Rathbun, George W. Paddock. After that date the following:

Edward Lee, J. W. Spencer, Norman Carter, 1846; W. J. Vermilya, 1847; Erastus Rathbun, 1848; Edward Lee, 1849; W. W. Parker, W. J. Vermilya, 1850; Edward Lee, Homer Peck, 1853; D. J. Allen, 1854; Edward Lee, W. J. Vermilya, Alexander Bowman, 1856; Homer Peck 1858; Edward Lee, Alexander Bowman, 1859; Homer Peck, O. L. Andrews, 1861; Edward Lee, 1862; Laban Ford, 1863; Homer Peck, 1864; R. W. McCready, 1866; Homer Peck 1867; R. W. McCready, 1869; U. W. Barker, John Thorn, 1870; Charles Crittenden, 1872; John Thorn, 1873; Homer Peck, 1875, and 1878; William W. Beach, 1880.

---

* Declined to serve.

† We are unable to give the time of service of the foregoing justices, as Sullivan was attached to Lorain county for several years, and the records are lost.

‡ It is now impossible to give the dates of their election and the time of service, as the records are not to be had.

BIOGRAPHICAL HISTORY
OF
ASHLAND COUNTY.

THE PIONEERS,

"Who, departing, left behind them
Footprints on the sand of time."

AND

SKETCHES OF SOME OF THE MOST NOTED INDIANS RESIDING ON THE BRANCHES OF MOHICAN, FROM 1808 TO 1824.

AUTOBIOGRAPHY OF DR. GEORGE W. HILL.

George William Hill, of Ashland, was born in Marshall county, Virginia, April 22, 1823. His ancestors were Scotch-Irish. His great-grandfather settled in the Shenandoah valley, Virginia, in about the year 1750. His grandfather, Edward Hill, settled about four miles west of Mt. Pleasant, in Westmoreland county, Pennsylvania, in the year 1794, a region prior to that time claimed as a part of the territory of Virginia, where John Hill, father of George W. Hill, was born in 1801. In the fall of 1822 John Hill located in Marshall county, Virginia, where he married Catharine Grandstaff, of German descent, and where George William Hill, their first child, was born. In 1824 John Hill removed to Richhill township, Muskingum county, Ohio, on the head waters of Wills creek, then a wild and sparsely settled region. In 1830, he removed to near Brownsville, in Licking county, where he remained until 1834, and then located near Hartford, in the same county, in the midst of the forest of that region, where deer and other game could be seen almost daily ranging through the deep woods, and commenced to prepare a new home. After making some improvements upon his farm, he sold it and again located near Newark in 1836, and in September of the same year his wife deceased and was buried in the old cemetery of Newark. John Hill then returned with his children, seven in number, to Richhill, in Muskingum county. In March, 1840, while engaged in business, John Hill died at Providence City, in the Maumee region. In 1842 the administrator of his estate became a bankrupt, and took the benefit of that law, and the children of John Hill were left penniless, owing to the defects of the administration laws of the State at that time. Without money and in the possession of a few books, having a limited common school education, the subject of this sketch apprenticed himself to learn the trade of a tanner, and served about three years, on the principle that every young man should have a trade or occupation to warrant success in life.

In 1845 he entered Ashland academy, then under the superintendence of the lamented Lorin Andrews, one of the most successful instructors in Ohio, and who afterwards became president of Kenyon college, in Knox county, Ohio. Mr. Hill remained at that school three years, paying his way by working nights, mornings, and during vacations. In 1848 he became deputy for the auditor and treasurer, and remained in the county offices until 1851. In 1850, having read law at nights after office hours, he was admitted to the bar as a practicing attorney. In 1852 he was principal of Loudonville academy, which position he held until failing health compelled him to resign. In 1853-4 he was official reporter for the Ohio senate. In August, 1854, he was appointed a deputy in the office of the State auditor, that office being presided over by Hon. William D. Morgan, now of Newark, Ohio. In November, 1855, he was appointed to a first-class clerkship in the treasury of the United States. In 1859, he graduated in medicine in the medical department of Georgetown college, District of Columbia, lecture hours occurring after office hours in the treasury, thus enabling him to attend lectures without losing time. In July, 1861, he was at the first battle of Bull Run, as a volunteer surgeon. In January, 1862, he returned to Ashland, Ohio, and entered upon the practice of medicine, and continued in that profession until the fall of 1867. In 1862 he was elected prosecuting attorney of Ashland county, and was re-elected in 1864. In the winter of 1868-9, he was official reporter of the house of representatives of Ohio. In April, 1868, he purchased the Ashland *Union*, the Democratic organ of the county, and changed its name to *The States and Union*. He continued to edit said paper until August, 1872, when, differing with his party on the policy of nominating Horace Greeley for President, he sold said paper.

In 1872 he was a delegate from the fourteenth district to the Baltimore convention, but refused to act with his delegation as to the time-serving policy of selecting a candidate from the ranks of the Republican party to head the National Democratic ticket for President. In disgust he retired, selling to men who thought they sacrificed no principle in advocating the claims of Greeley for President, although he had often stated in the *Tribune*, that he "would not say that every Democrat was a horse thief, but would say that every horse thief turned out to be a Democrat." The people of the United States refused to sustain his nomination, and defeat and disaster overtook the old man, and from disappointment, he soon became a hopeless wreck, and died. Such is the end of ambitious and ill-balanced men! In the spring of 1873, Mr. Hill was elected a member of the Ohio Constitutional convention held at the cities of Columbus and Cincinnati in the summer of 1873 and winter of 1874, and served upon several committees in the convention, and was chairman of the committee of accounts and expenses. He made a number of speeches, all of which are printed in the volumes of the debates. He was active in opposing all schemes to deplete the treasury, and increase the burthens of the people, and finally voted against the constitution, feeling convinced that it was not what the people wished. On the fourth of July, 1876, at a town meeting, the people selected him to deliver the Centennial address for Ashland county. A large assemblage of people was present to hear the address, which was published in both the county papers. In 1875-6-7-8 he wrote the sketches of Marion, Wyandot and Allen counties, with a full history of the ancient *Wyandotts, Delawares* and *Shawnees*, including their final removal west. In 1880 he finished, for publication, the history of Ashland county.

Mr. Hill married Miss Rebecca Draper, daughter of John Draper, formerly from near Boston, Massachusetts, May 17, 1850. His family consists of three children: Margaret Amanda, Ida Rena and William Duane Hill, all of age.

George W. Hill, M. D.

BAPTISTE JEROME.

John Baptiste Jerome was born near Montreal, Canada, of French parents, in the year 1776 or 1777. When seventeen or eighteen years of age he crossed the lake with some French emigrants, and settled among the Indians at the mouth of Huron river. He married an Indian girl, supposed to have been the sister of a noted Indian known as George Hamilton. After remaining on the Huron a few years, he moved to Upper Sandusky, and resided among the Indians until the campaign of General Anthony Wayne. In company with Captain Pipe, of the *Delawares*, he was engaged in a number of battles against the American forces, and was at the famous battle of "Fallen Timbers." At the time of his residence in this county, he often related anecdotes concerning that battle, describing the amazement of the Indians at the rapidity and violence of the movements of Wayne's army—the Indians comparing him to a huge "black snake," and ascribing almost supernatural powers to him. He asserted, that for a long time, the very name of "Mad Anthony" sent a chill of horror through the body of an Indian. They had, prior to the appearance of General Wayne, baffled the armies of the American generals, and committed many barbarities upon the wounded and dead soldiers left upon the battle field; but, when he came, like a huge anaconda, he enclosed and crushed the warriors in such a frightful manner that they abandoned all hope of resisting his victorious march, and were glad to stop his ravages by making peace.

After the treaty at Greenville in 1795, Jerome, Captain Pipe, and a number of the *Delawares* left the northwest and settled at what was formerly Mohican Johnstown, on the south side of the stream, about three quarters of a mile from the present site of Jeromeville. The stream was thenceforth known as the Jerome fork, which name it doubtless received from Jerome. The precise period of this migration can not be accurately fixed, but was doubtless as early as 1796 or 1797. Jerome crossed the stream and built a cabin a little southeast of the present site of the mill, where Joseph H. Larwill found him, his wife and daughter, while surveying, in 1806-7. Captain Pipe built a wigwam and located south of the stream, and about one mile from Jerome, near what is now the Hayesville road. When the first settlers came into Killbuck, now Mohican township, Jerome resided in the aforesaid cabin, and had some thirty-five or forty acres of land cleared along on the bottom, on the banks of the stream, which he cultivated in corn.* He resided in his cabin with his wife Mary or Munjela, who was about fifteen years old when the war of 1812 was declared. A short time prior to the declaration of war, Captain Pipe and all his *Delawares*, except three or four friendly and harmless families, quietly slipped away and joined their friends in the northwest. When Captain Murray came to Jerome's place to build the block-house, it is asserted by some of the pioneers, that by order of General Beall, Jerome was arrested and sent to the block-house at Wooster, where he was confined for a short time as a precaution against furnishing aid and comfort to the Indians who might be found prowling about the forest; and that while he was at Wooster, Captain Murray sent his (Jerome's), wife and daughter to Urbana, where they subsequently died from exposure. Another statement is, that when Captain Douglas removed the Greentown Indians the wife and daughter of Jerome, with others, accompanied them, Jerome voluntarily remaining to take care of his stock, of which he was well supplied, and his cabin and household goods; and that he was not confined at Wooster. We accept the latter statement as being the most probable; for there were no Indians at the arrival of General Beall to be sent away, and we have no account of a separate expedition from that of Douglas to convey the Indians to Urbana.

Jerome is said to have been warmly attached to his wife and daughter, and deeply mourned his separation from them; and often reproached the military for enforcing so cruel an edict. He never looked upon their faces again; for, long before the close of the war, they were both in the grave. Prior to his being separated from his wife, Jerome was noted for his hospitality—his wife being an excellent cook and housekeeper, considering her opportunities, Jerome being her only instructor as to domestic duties. During the prevalence of the war, Jerome remained at the block-house among the pioneers who sought protection there in 1812-'13-'14. The loyalty of Jerome was beyond question. On several occasions he evinced as much zeal in protecting the neighboring cabins as his pioneer companions of the block-house. He was a small man—vivacious and positive. Though impulsive, and at times irritable and bitter in his resentments, he was generous and brave, and firmly attached to his friends. He was endowed with a good understanding, and could converse in French and Indian, and sufficiently well to be understood in English. Before his separation from his wife and daughter his circumstances were prosperous, being in possession of a lot of cattle, hogs and horses—a few fields of cleared land, with a comfortable cabin. At the close of the war, everything went wrong with him—his property was dispersed and his affairs began to go to ruin. He married a German woman on the Clear fork, with whom he lived until he sold his farm. He sold the farm, occupying the present site of Jeromeville, in the winter of 1815, to Christian Deardorf and William Vaughn, and purchased the farm upon which Goudy's mill was subsequently erected, about two miles southwest of his old farm. He remained here some time, and sold the land to Joseph Workman, who sold it to Constance Lake for a mill site. Jonathan Palmer was his neighbor for three years, and always spoke kindly of Jerome. About the year 1817 Jerome and his German wife removed to his old residence at the mouth of Huron river, where he died a few years afterwards, in indigent circumstances, leaving his wife and one child, who returned to Rich-

---

*When the old Portage road was surveyed in 1810, Peter Kinney, afterward Judge Kinney, was one of the party, and found Jerome's cabin as above stated, near the foot of Main street, in Jeromeville, on the south side. See also, biography of Alexander Finley and letter of James Finley.

land where they remained. Jerome is believed to have been the first white settler within the present limits of Ashland county, his arrival antedating that of Alexander Finley and Andrew Craig some eight or nine years.

ABRAM WILLIAMS.

Among the wigwams of Greentown when the pioneers of 1809-10 entered the township, was that of Abram Williams, an irritable, morose old Indian, who had formerly married a white captive on the Sandusky river, from whom he separated in consequence of the violence of his temper and long continued jealousy and cruelty. The story of this unhappy marriage, as near as I can learn, is as follows:

About the year 1785 a family by the name of Martin and a Mr. Castleman were neighbors in Beaver county, Pennsylvania, and resided near the east bank of the Ohio river. It had been the custom of these families, for several years, to cross the river in the spring to make sugar on the bottoms. They had been engaged several days during the spring alluded to; when Castleman's horses strayed from their enclosure. He went in search of them on the river bottoms. During his absence, Martin returned from the camp and requested Mary Castleman, aged about thirteen, and Margaret, about nine, to accompany him to assist in boiling and gathering sugar water.

Mrs. Castleman hesitated for some time to let them go; but Martin being quite positive there were no Indians in the vicinity, she finally consented to let them return with him. A short time after they crossed the river Mrs. Castleman heard the explosion of guns in the vicinity of the camp, and being alarmed for the safety of her daughters, hastened to the river side and called aloud, but received no reply. Returning to her cabin she alarmed the neighbors, and a number of men assembled on the east bank of the river, but dared not pass over, for fear of an ambush. On the succeeding morning, a number of volunteers crossed in a canoe, and found Martin and his wife dead and scalped.

The Castleman girls, and a little daughter of Martin, were nowhere to be found. The volunteers concluded they had been captured and carried away by the Indians. Pursuit was now useless, as the savages were doubtless many miles away. Years after, it was learned that there were but three Indians at the capture. In skulking along the banks of the Ohio, they happened on Martin's camp, and finding it defenceless, concluded to kill him and his wife, and take the girls to Sandusky.

After they had killed Martin and his wife they secured the girls. While they were engaged in the fiendish murder of the two old people, Margaret attempted to conceal herself in a hollow sycamore log, while Mary fled to the river and got into a canoe and began to push it from the shore, but one of the Indians instantly pursued her into the water and dragged the canoe back again, and secured her. He asked her how many men were at the house, and knowing that the safety of her mother and family depended upon her strategy, she answered nine.

The Indians then took up their line of march for Greentown, on the Black fork. After several days they arrived at the Indian village, where they met some traders from Detroit. They passed up the ancient trail from Fort Pitt, by way of Jerometown, now known as the Portage trail. A trader at Greentown, by the name of McIntosh, was much pleased with the appearance of Margaret, and purchasing her for twenty-five dollars, took her home with him to Detroit, where she remained a number of years as a member of his family, and attended school. Her father, through the traders, finally learned of her whereabouts, and went to Detroit and took her home.

The Indians took Mary and the Martin girl to Sandusky, where they remained. The history of the Martin girl, during her residence among the *Delawares*, is a blank. Mary Castleman grew up to womanhood among the Indians, learning all their customs and language. During her residence among the Indians at Sandusky, she became acquainted with Abram Williams, a half-blood, to whom she was married. She had by him two children, George and Sally. Williams was a jealous, tyrannical and cruel husband, and he and his white squaw lived very unhappily.

Williams, in his paroxysms of rage and jealousy, often maltreated his wife, and threatened to kill her. Fearing he would put his threat into execution, she resolved, if possible, to make her escape and seek refuge among her friends in Beaver county. By the traders, who often visited Fort Pitt, she conveyed intelligence of her situation to her father, and her desire to be relieved. The attempt to rescue her would be attended with much danger. If not successful, it would result in bringing upon her the vengeance of her exasperated husband, and might terminate in great suffering and death.

Mr. Castleman made arrangements with a man by the name of George Foulks, a neighbor, to go to Sandusky to obtain the release of Mary. In his youth, Mr. Foulks had been captured by the Indians, taken to Sandusky and adopted, where he resided for many years, and became versed in their language and customs. He was well acquainted with all the Indian trails, and it was presumed by Mr. Castleman, that Foulks was just the man to secure the liberation of his long missing daughter.

Mr. Foulks, after some preparation, set out for Sandusky, passing up the old trail to Jerometown; thence near where Olivesburgh now stands, through Bloominggrove, in Richland county, to the place of his destination. He soon found Williams and his wife. After spending a few days with them he proposed to Williams to let Mary accompany him on a visit to her friends in Beaver county. The jealousy of Williams was at once aroused. He refused to permit his wife to leave, and menaced the life of Foulks if he persisted in making such a request.

Mr. Foulks determined to carry out his intentions to bring Mary home. The rage of Williams was to be baffled by strategy. Affecting to acquiesce in the unwillingness of the dusky husband, he alleviated his fears. Mr.

Foulks then went to an old Indian acquaintance and friend, and proposed to give him a barrel of whiskey and other presents if he would aid him in getting Mary away from Williams. The Indian feared the resentment of his Indian neighbor, and at first refused; but the "fire water" was a tempting prize.

At the next interview he entered heartily into the project, and agreed to go with Mary. The plan was, for Foulks to keep away from Williams, and remain about the Indian camp. The confederate then took Mary and started down the old Jerometown trail, while Foulks remained a day in the camp, and then started by another trail to meet his Indian friend and Mary at Jerometown. When he arrived near the Indian village he gave the signal, and Mary and his friend soon appeared in the forest, and she was then taken home by Mr. Foulks and restored to her friends and civilized society.

Some time after this desertion Williams came to Greentown, built a wigwam, and was residing there with his children, George and Sally, when the first pioneers came into the neighborhood. Sally was then a young woman, and had many admirers among the dusky warriors. Mrs. James Cunningham, Mrs. James Irwin, Mrs. Sarah Vale, and others, called at the wigwam of Williams to see what kind of a housekeeper Sally appeared to be. These ladies were all young then. They found the wigwam of Williams neat and clean, and Sally a pleasant young lady.

SOLOMON JONACAKE.

A short time before the removal of the Greentown Indians, a good-natured, fine-looking Delaware warrior, by the name of Solomon Jonacake, located among the tribe, and soon became fascinated with the charming Sally Williams. He proffered her his hand in marriage, saying: "Me want squaw velly bad. Me like squaw. Me want Sally for squaw." The proffer was accepted on condition that the marriage ceremony should be after the manner of the whites, and by a white man. Sally exacted these conditions on the ground that she had already been twice married to recreant young warriors, and the Indian ceremony had failed to "stick."

Jonacake was but too happy to comply, for he "wanted Sally velly bad." There being no minister in that region authorized to perform the ceremony, they went to the cabin of Peter Kinney, who was justice of the peace, and he married them. It was a good job, for Jonacake proved a kind and faithful husband. Abram Williams was very proud of the choice of Sally, and stated to Mr. Elijah Harter, of Mifflin, that "Jonacake was a good Indian. He no heathen Indian. He Moravian Indian. He be kind to Sally. He velly good Christian Indian."

When the Greentown Indians were removed, in 1812, to Urbana, Williams, Jonacake and wife accompanied their friends. After the war, they and many other Greentown Indians returned annually to hunt, for ten or twelve years. Jonacake hunted a good deal in what is now Lake township, placing his wigwam near a good spring, where Sally presided like an Indian queen. Many of the brooks in Lake yet bear his name.

In 1819, he encamped in the spring and fall, on a bottom west of the Black fork, in the vicinity of the present residence of Daniel Hoover, some three miles northwest of the village of Mifflin. While there, Mrs. Hoover visited the bark wigwam of Jonacake, and spent some hours with Sally, who could converse very well in German. At that time Jonacake had two interesting little boys, aged respectively about five and seven years. Mrs. Hoover says Sally was an interesting woman, and her children were very neatly kept. Her little boys were handsomely clothed in dressed deer-skin, after the Indian style. Everything exhibited an air of comfort and contentment.

During the interview, Sally complained of being surfeited on venison, and expressed a wish for salt pork. Mrs. Hoover agreed to exchange pound for pound. Sally was delighted. A few mornings after the visit, Jonacake appeared very early at the door of Mr. Hoover's cabin with a load of fresh venison. Hoover went to his smoke-house and selected the pork which he proposed to exchange, and having weighed it, handed it to Jonacake. The good-natured hunter appeared much pleased with the trade. Breakfast being then ready, Mr. Hoover politely invited Jonacake to eat. He readily consented, and took a seat at the table. He behaved with becoming modesty, and handled his knife, fork and cup with as much skill as a white man.

Mr. Hoover says Jonacake was a tall, fine looking Indian, and would weigh, perhaps, one hundred and sixty or one hundred and seventy pounds. He seemed to be imbued with the doctrines of the Moravians. Sally was a firm believer in that faith; and Jonacake and his family observed the Sabbath much more faithfully than the semi-christianized borderers who surrounded them. Mr. Hoover regarded his Indian neighbor as harmless, and as possessing integrity to a remarkable degree. He often met him in the forest hunting, and says he was always courteous and good-humored. Sally was, in his opinion, a remarkable woman, considering the fact that she never had any of the advantages of civilized life.

Mr. Knapp refers to the residence of Jonacake in Clearcreek township at a late date. In 1824, in the spring, Jonacake had a wigwam in the vicinity of the present site of Savannah. While there, one Sabbath, Hance McMeekin and Andrew Clark visited his wigwam, and entered into conversation with Sally. McMeekin was a merry, fun-making sort of a pioneer, and relished a good joke. After saluting Sally and her little boys, he inquired as to the success of Jonacake in hunting.

Sally—"Not very good. Last Sunday, Jonacake saw a number of deer, while hunting his horses that had strayed away; but being without a gun, they escaped."

McMeekin—"Without his gun! Why did he go without it?"

Sally—"He never carries his gun on Sunday."

McMeekin—"What do you know about Sunday? Do you know when that day comes?"

Sally—"Do you suppose I am an animal? I am a human being, and know when Sunday comes as well as the white people."

McMeekin—"Do all the Indians know when Sunday comes?"

Sally—"They very generally do; but, like most of the white people, fail to keep it."

This retort satisfied McMeekin, and he ceased to poke his fun at Sally.

McMeekin often related this adventure with great glee, and conceded that Sally was rather spicy in her dialogue with him.

Jonacake and other Indians, at that period, often visited the mill of Martin Mason, where Leidigh's now stands, to purchase corn-meal in exchange for pelts and venison. Andrew Mason remembers him distinctly.

In the treaty of 1817, at the Maumee rapids, a reservation, three miles square, south of the *Wyandots*, was allowed the remnant of *Delawares* from Jerometown and Greentown. Jonacake is named as one of the joint proprietors.

In 1829, when the *Delawares* were removed to their new home, west of the Mississippi, Jonacake and his family went along.

Jonacake died on the Delaware reservation, in Kansas, leaving two or three sons. In the war of the Rebellion of 1861–5, three grandsons of Jonacake served in company M, Sixth regiment of Kansas volunteer infantry, under Captain John W. Duff. Their names were: John, Benjamin, and Philip Jonacake. Captain Duff says they were excellent soldiers.

CAPTAIN ARMSTRONG,

of Greentown, whose Indian name was Pamoxet, is first mentioned in the treaty of Fort Industry, on the Maumee river, July 4, 1805. The object of the treaty was the final relinquishment of all Indian title to the lands of the Western Reserve. We are inclined to the opinion that he was a chief of the Turtle tribe, and that he located at Greentown fifteen or sixteen years before Pipe made his residence near the village of Mohican Johnstown. He was there when the first settlers of Green township commenced the erection of their cabins, in 1808–9; and seemed to exercise a very controlling influence over the Indians of that village, among whom were *Delawares, Mingoes, Mohawks*, and a few *Shawnees*.

From the year 1800, up to 1812, Knox county furnished a favorite resort for Armstrong and his tribe, in the fall of the year, as a site for hunting. Mr. Banning, in his history of Knox county, says the Indians congregated at Greentown, at the periods mentioned above, numbering from three to five hundred. During the summer seasons, various acts of hostility were attributed to Armstrong's band, of which they were doubtless innocent. Collisions, therefore, between the white settlers of Knox county and the Greentown Indians, became frequent. The major part of the tribe, on the rumor of the approaching war, voluntarily left Greentown; but Armstrong and many others were loth to leave the hunting grounds of their youth—the graves of their fathers—the homes of their race. So Major Kratzer determined that Armstrong and his people should be removed to Urbana, as before described.

At the time James Copus, John Coulter, and Ebenezer Rice, first met Armstrong, he appeared to be about sixty-five years of age; was a small man, slightly stooped, rather dignified and reticent; dressed in full Indian costume, and appeared to advantage. He had two wives; one an old squaw, by whom he had James and Silas, and probably other children. He married a young squaw about 1808, by whom he had children. He frequently visited the first cabin of James Copus, where he made sugar the first spring after his arrival.

James and Silas often shot at a mark, with bows and arrows, with James and Wesley Copus, in the sugar camp. They also amused themselves by hopping, wrestling, and other boyish sports. Armstrong had two Indian servants or slaves, both deaf. They were of some other tribe. Armstrong appeared to be a harmless old chief, and treated his pioneer neighbors very kindly. At his request, James Copus preached a number of times to the Greentown Indians. After Douglas removed the Indians, Captain Armstrong settled with the *Delawares* in the Upper Sandusky region, and never returned to Greentown. The boys, James and Silas, frequently came back. The old chief was a good Indian doctor, and could talk very good English.

His descendants—the Armstrongs—intermarried with the *Delawares* and *Wyandots*, and finally removed, in 1828–29, west of the Mississippi.

It is believed that Captain Armstrong was born in Pennsylvania, of white parents, and was captured, when quite young, and adopted by the *Delawares*, and, becoming a leading warrior, was promoted to the office of chief.

There is a current legend among the pioneers of Green township, that Armstrong received his name, when a young man, from a successful contest with a black bear, just prior to his promotion to the chiefship. It runs thus: "Pamoxet was in the forest, hunting. He met and wounded a large black bear. The ferocity of the animal was aroused. It rushed upon him, and, in an erect posture, seized his left arm and commenced to lacerate it. His gun being emptied, he seized a bowlder, and when the bear began to gnaw his arm, he used the bowlder upon its head. He soon compelled it to desist, and it fell dead at his feet. The Indians immediately recognized his heroic conduct, and called him Captain Strong Arm, or Armstrong."

He died about the close of the war of 1812–15, on the Delaware reserve.

THOMAS LYONS.

When the pioneers of 1808–9 began to settle in what are now known as Green and Mifflin townships, in this county, they found a tall, lean, aged Delaware, by the name of Thomas Lyons. From conversations held with James Cunningham, Peter Kinney, James Copus, Lewis Oliver, and John Coulter, it was learned that Lyons was born in New Jersey, near the Delaware line. It was impossible to gather from him any definite idea of the date of his birth. When interrogated on that subject, his response generally was: "One hundred fifty years." In conversation with others concerning the length of a year, "Tom" considered the winter and the summer each a year. That would make him about seventy-five years of age, in 1810. Most of the settlers, however, concur in the opinion that he was the oldest Indian they had ever met. He was probably near one hundred years old when he left the country.

Lyons informed Judge Peter Kinney that he was at the massacre of Wyoming, in 1778. Colonel John Butler, at the head of eleven hundred *Mohawks*, and a few white tories who had joined the British, entered the lovely valley of Wyoming, in northern Pennsylvania, July 2, 1778. Most of the strong men were then away on distant duty, and families and homes found defenders only in aged men, tender youths, resolute women, and a few trained soldiers and friendly *Delawares*. These were marched up the valley to drive back the invaders, but the savage *Mohawks* soon put them to flight, a large portion being slain or made prisoners. A few escaped to a fort near Wilkesbarre, where families for long distances around had fled for safety. The invaders soon appeared before the fort. They were sweeping onward towards the Susquehanna with resistless fury, carrying carnage and death in their train. The night after the battle, the yells of the infuriated savages echoed through the forests, and death seemed impending over the beleagured refugees within the little fort. An agony of suspense rested upon all during the slowly passing hours of that dark and dreary night. Morning came, but contrary to expectations, the leader of the savages (John Butler) appeared near the fort and offered terms of safety to the inmates if they would surrender. The gates were thrown open, and most of the families were permitted to return to their homes. During the day the *Mohawks* scattered up and down the valley. Before sunset, all the inhabitants were doomed. Scarcely had the shades of night appeared, before their burning dwellings threw a lurid glare over forest and field, and the work of death began. The terrified people fled to the mountains and the forests to escape the hatchet and the scalping knife; but, alas! the red fiends, led by the inhuman Butler, left that fair valley blackened with the ruins and cinders of the homes of the pioneers, while their bodies, scalped and mutilated, were scattered through the forest, to become food for wild beasts.

After this dreadful disaster, Tom Lyons and several other friendly Indians fled to their Delaware friends, on the Tuscarawas and the branches of the Mohican. Tom Lyons dwelt among the Moravians some time at Gnaddenhutten, and continued to revisit that favorite spot of the Christian *Delawares* to the close of his life. When Colonel Crawford invaded the Sandusky country in 1782, Thomas Lyons, Thomas Armstrong, Billy Montour, Thomas Jelloway and a number of the *Delawares* are believed to have had a village on the Clear fork, about one mile west of the old Lewis block-house, in Richland county. The name of this town was German, and signified clear, light or transparent. It was Helltown. In German the word "hell" signified light or clear. The name probably originated from some Pennsylvania captive, as the village on the Clear fork or Clear water. Upon the approach of Colonel Crawford, the inhabitants of the village fled, and when his army returned from its disastrous defeat, Armstrong and his associates located a new village called Greentown, on the banks of the Black fork, and the stream was known to the surveyors and early settlers as Armstrong's creek. This village was the home of Lyons, when Andrew Craig, James Copus, the Coulters and Olivers came into the township in 1808-'9-'10.

It has been asserted that Thomas Lyons was a chief. He was only a warrior. On a few occasions he related his military achievements. He had been in many battles on the border, and taken many scalps. When under the influence of "fire water" he related many acts of extreme cruelty, and a few of his barbarities, inflicted upon the wives and children of the border settlers. Like most of his race, he delighted in the excitements of war, and was easily induced to join his red brethren in their attempt to expel the pale faces from the beautiful hunting grounds of Ohio. When Harmar, St. Clair and Wayne invaded the Indian country of the northwest in 1791-'2-'3-'4, Tom Lyons joined Captain Pipe, Armstrong and other Delaware chiefs in an effort to expel the invaders. On one occasion, while stopping a night with Allen Oliver, father of Lewis and Daniel, in Green township, he gave a very graphic description of the battle of "Fallen Timbers." Lyons, Pipe, Armstrong, Montour, Baptiste Jerome, and other Greentown and Jerometown Indians were in the fight. Lewis Oliver, now eighty-one years of age, relates the conversation thus:

Allen Oliver.—"You say you were at the battle with Wayne. What do you think of Wayne as a white chief?"

Tom Lyons. "Him be great chief. He be one devil to fight. Me hear his dinner horn—way over there go toot, toot; then way over here it go toot, toot—then way over other side, go toot toot. Then his soldiers run forward—shoot, shoot; then run among logs and brush. Indians have got to get out and run. Then come Long Knives with pistols and shoot, shoot. Indians run, no stop. Old Tom see too much fight to be trap—he run into woods—he run like devil—he keep run till he clear out of danger. Wayne great fight—brave white chief. He be one devil."

Mr. Lewis Oliver states that while "Old Tom" was going through this description of the fight, he gesticulated, grimaced and expressed as much emotion as if he had been in the midst of the battle. In fact, terror was evinced in the whole of the mimic battle he was then fighting over. Add to this the fact that he was perhaps the ugliest Indian ever seen by the border settlers, and some idea of his emotions may be gleaned. Mr. Oliver thinks he was "about six feet high, quite lean—very like a mummy in the consistence and color of his skin, with a long protruding chin, some missing teeth, short upper lip, a low forehead, a protruding crown, jet eyes, very fierce and piercing, and wore a dress, never very tidy nor clean." This was old "Tom Lyons." The war-like fire of his youth had ceased to blaze. He was now an old man. He had long since given up the idea of driving back the pale faces. At this period, 1811-12, he was quite friendly to the new settlers. He had no wife. His two sons, George and James, occasionally visited the pioneers. George had the reputation of being a cruel and ill-tempered Indian; though he never molested the pioneers. Before the war of 1812, Tom Lyons, as I am informed by Mrs. James Irwin, daughter of Judge Peter Kinney, often came to her father's house in great haste, requesting him to hurry to Greentown and enforce quiet among the Indians, who were quarreling, and evinced an inclination to scalp each other. Mr. Kinney was then a justice of the peace, and was quite an influential man among his red-skinned neighbors.

When Captain Douglas and Cunningham removed the Greentown Indians, in the fall of 1812, Tom Lyons accompanied his people to Urbana*. A short time after the removal of the Indians, the Ruffner-Zimmer-Copus murders took place. The Greentown Indians were blamed for that invasion and those wanton assassinations.

After the war, a number of Greentown Indians returned and erected cabins on the site of their old village, and continued to hunt for six or eight years. Among these were Tom Lyons, Billy Dowdee, Jonacake, Buckwheat, and others not now recollected. Thomas Lyons visited his old friends in the neighborhood of Greentown, among others, Mrs. James Copus and her children, at the cabin where Mr. Copus had been killed. Mrs. Copus (as I am informed by Mrs. Sarah Vail, now seventy-six years of age, and daughter of Mrs. Copus,) inquired of Tom Lyons whether he was present and helped the Indians kill her husband on that frightful morning. Tom Lyons said he was not; but he knew who did it, but could not help it, as many strange Indians were along. He manifested many regrets over the tragedy; said, he and Mr. Copus were good friends. On that fatal day, the same band passed by Newell's, in Montgomery township, burned his cabin, and early next morning, through Carter's cornfield, to Cuppy's cabin, burned it; then to Fry's, and burned it; and continued on towards Sandusky. Several years after, Tom Lyons explained this adventure to Daniel Carter, sr., who was undisturbed. He stated also, to Martin Mason, who originally had a mill where Leidigh's now stands, that he notified Fry and Cuppy several days before, to leave, which was speedily done, and their families were saved from torture and death.

This singular old Indian continued to hunt in different parts of the county up to about the year 1823. He often visited the pioneers on his way to and from Goshen, in Tuscarawas county. He, on several occasions, brought cranberries and a wild turkey which he had shot, to be dressed, stuffed and roasted by Mrs. Copus, after the manner of the whites. She always complied; and when it was done, with many words of gratitude, "old Tom" would bundle it in his deer-skin pouch and proceed on his way to Goshen or to Sandusky, as the case might be.

He, on several occasions, accompanied by other Indians, stopped at the shop of Solomon Urie, father of Colonel George W. Urie, in Orange township, to have their guns and tomahawks repaired. From there they proceeded to Mason's mill, to obtain meal and other provisions, in exchange for venison. Thence they would proceed to John Bryte's distillery, in Clearcreek, and then strike out through the forest.

About the fall of 1822, Lyons visited Mrs. Irwin, in Green township, for the last time. He had a strong attachment for his old friend, Peter Kinney. Almost as soon as he entered the house, he inquired if Mrs. Irwin had recently heard from Judge Kinney, who had removed to Illinois some years before. Mrs. Irwin says the poor old fellow put down his head, and muttered to himself: "My poor friend Kinney, I never see him any more. Peter Kinney was a good friend. Poor Peter Kinney, I never see him any more." After remaining a few hours, the old man departed. That was fifty-eight years ago. She says she never saw the old man again. He always behaved well at their house, and seemed to possess many good traits, although he had been reared amid the wilds of the forest, and among untamed savages. He never fully explained the reason that he received the name of Thomas Lyons. She thinks he had very little, if any, white blood in his veins. He at one time requested Judge Kinney to go with him to the Wyoming valley, in Pennsylvania, to act as his agent, where he said he owned a large tract of land, for which the Government had never compensated him. But, for some reason, Judge Kinney could not accompany him.

At a treaty, in 1814-17, territory six miles south of Upper Sandusky was set apart, as a reservation for the Jerometown and Greentown Indians. A village was built there, called Pipetown, in honor of Captain Pipe, jr., who, in conjunction with Silas Armstrong, son of Captain Thomas Armstrong, was made a half-chief over the remnant of *Delawares* there located.

Thomas Lyons resided at Pipestown, in Marion county, in 1821-22-23, and in company with his son Tom, Billy Dowdee, and other Delawares, often hunted along the Whetstone or Olentangy. The old settlers along those streams, the Sharracks, Beckleys, and others, were often visited by him in their cabin homes. Old Tom was very fond of repeating his war exploits along the Delaware, the Schuylkill, the Wyoming valley and other localities in Pennsylvania, before the removal of the *Delawares* to the branches of the Mohican, in Ohio.

Old Thomas Lyons is believed to have died on this reservation, some time in the winter or spring of 1824.

---

*Some authorities say Piqua. The latter place was the headquarters of the friendly *Shawnees*, and possibly of the Jerome and Greentown *Delawares*.

It is now believed that the stories of his assassination by white hunters, are destitute of foundation, and that the old warrior died a natural death.

CHRISTIAN FAST, SR.

As the full particulars of the capture of Christian Fast, by the *Delawares* of Sandusky, have never appeared in print, it may be interesting to the pioneers of west Pennsylvania and Ohio to peruse a brief sketch of his life among the red men of the Tymochtee.

In the month of June, 1781, an expedition, composed of Indians and Canadians, destined to invade Kentucky, moved from their places of rendezvous at Detroit, the Sandusky, the Miami and the Wabash. The salient point of the campaign was the falls of the Ohio, or Louisville, then containing only a few cabins, and a station for soldiers to protect the scattered settlements of Kentucky against Indian invasion.

Colonel George Rogers Clark, the hero of Kaskaskia and St. Vincent, learning that an expedition, composed of British and Indians, was about to invade that region, stationed a small body of troops at the village of Louisville, to intercept the passage of war parties on their way to the interior of Kentucky. His command was soon increased by the arrival of one hundred and fifty Pennsylvanians and Virginians, under the command of Colonel Slaughter.

Colonel Archibald Loughery, of Westmoreland county, Pennsylvania, raised a corps of about one hundred men, who volunteered to accompany General Clark on the expedition. These volunteers embarked in boats at Wheeling, and moved down the river, in order to join the troops of General Clark at the falls of the Ohio. On the twenty-fourth of August, Colonel Loughery and his party passed the mouth of the Great Miami river, and soon afterward one of the boats was taken to the Kentucky side of the river, and a number of men, under the command of Captain William Campbell, went ashore for the purpose of cooking and eating some buffalo meat. The river was low, and the boat was fastened near a sand-bar. While on shore, Colonel Loughery's forces were attacked by a large body of Indians, and after a brief resistance the small expedition was forced to surrender. Forty men were killed. Colonel Loughery was made prisoner, tomahawked and scalped. Sixty of his men were captured and taken to Detroit. See Dillon's history of Indiana, pages 173-4.

For reasons never fully explained, the British expedition, commanded by Colonel Byrd, on reaching the mouth of the Great Miami, changed its destination; and when the boats conveying his troops, cannon and military stores, arrived on the Ohio river, instead of descending its rapid current, turned up the stream, and ascended the Licking to its forks, where he landed his men and munitions of war. It is probable the destination of Colonel Byrd was changed in consequence of his advanced Indian spies and scouts coming in contact with the forces of Colonel Slaughter in their descent of the Ohio.

Some thirty-five or forty miles above the falls, the boats of Colonel Slaughter, which were conveying horses and a few soldiers, became separated from the main body of the expedition in the night. At daylight the advanced boats drove an occasional stake near the shore, and attached written directions thereto, to guide the boats in the rear.

The boats thus abandoned being deprived of proper rations for the soldiers, had no alternative but to supply themselves with such game as could be obtained from the forest. Perceiving a buffalo heifer leisurely feeding a short distance from shore, the larger boat was shoved to a shoal and the heifer shot. It was hastily skinned, a fire was built, and the soldiers proceeded to prepare breakfast.

While in the act of cooking the flesh of the heifer, the party was attacked by Indians, who were probably drawn to the spot by the sound of the guns. The frightened soldiers, who had neglected to station pickets, fled to the boat which had been stranded on the shoal, just as the smaller boats were making toward the shore for breakfast. They were unable to shove the boat to the current, and the Indians rushed down the shore firing into the boat, wounding and killing several of the men and horses.

All was consternation. Many of the soldiers endeavored to save themselves by leaping overboard and attempting to swim to the opposite side of the river, but, on reaching it, were again fired upon. Among those who fled to the opposite shore was Christian Fast, a youth of about seventeen years of age, who had volunteered as a cavalry-man, from what is now Fayette county, Pennsylvania, then a part of Westmoreland county.

Young Fast was an expert swimmer. As the Indians rushed upon the men, he leaped over the opposite side of the horse boat, and struck out boldly for the Kentucky shore, which he reached in safety. Just as he was about to arise from the water and ascend the bank, two or three Indians approached him, saying:

"Come on, brother, we will use you well," at the same time reaching out their hands in token of friendship.

Knowing the savage character of the red man, he doubted their pacific intentions, and speedily turning about, started for the middle of the river. He had scarcely got in motion, when they commenced to fire after him, a ball passing so near his head that it stunned him for a moment, by its concussion in the water, while another ball passed through the fleshy part of his thigh, making a painful wound, notwithstanding which, he succeeded in reaching the center of the river.

On reaching the main current, he found the boats had floated some distance from the stranded one from which he had fled, and he resolved to swim after and overtake a small horse boat which was a few rods in the rear of the rest. After a vigorous exertion, aided by the current and a shower of bullets from shore, he reached the boat just as she surrendered. The Indians boarded it at once, and the prisoners were taken on shore, and the plunder secured.

After the prisoners had been deprived of all means of defence, the savages proceeded to strip them of such wearing apparel as they desired. In fact, the majority of the captives were left almost nude. The military suits with which the soldiers were clothed were deemed a God-send to these children of the forest. The appearance of the captives was most distressing; nevertheless resistance would have been rewarded with a cruel, lingering death by torture.

When the exulting savages had secured such plunder as they could carry away, it was put up in bundles and their new prisoners were compelled to pack it. The whole party proceeded through the forest in the direction of Upper Sandusky. The level lands along the Ohio and the Miami, at that season, abounded in rank, almost impenetrable, weeds, briars and nettles. The journey was a severe ordeal.

Young Fast was small, had hair as black as a raven, dark eyes, and a swarthy skin; was exceedingly agile, and very slim and straight. His appearance pleased the Indians, and an old Delaware claimed him as his prisoner. The leader of the band was old Thomas Lyons. On the route to Upper Sandusky, which was principally up the Great Miami until they reached the portage, the poor prisoners endured many hardships and cruelties.

Having been deprived of their clothing, the nettles, briars, weeds and undergrowth made fearful havoc with their uncovered bodies, so much so, that on one occasion, after they had been some hours in the forest, young Fast put down his head and refused to proceed, telling his Indian master to tomahawk him. The old warrior took pity on him, and returned most of his clothing. His wound was becoming quite painful. The old warrior assisted in dressing it until it healed.

After the war party had been two or three days in the forest, the Indians built a camp-fire and cleared a spot for a dance. The prisoners were all tied so as to prevent their escape. The savages engaged in the dance with much spirit, singing, hopping, leaping, brandishing their tomahawks and scalping knives, and grimacing in a most frightful manner. Their music was a sort of wail, between a shout and a moan, while a kind of time was beaten on a brass kettle by a warrior.

When the Indian dance had ended, the prisoners, one by one, were untied and requested to give an exhibition of their agility. With bodies torn and bruised, half famished for want of food, wearied with the journey, and almost nude, they endeavored to comply, knowing that a refusal would incur the hate and severity of their savage masters. When the time came for young Fast to dance, he felt it impossible to do so, in consequence of his painful wound, but fearing to incur the censure and vengeance of the warriors, he said to his comrades: "Boys, I can't dance and run on my feet, but I can run on my hands." So, limping into the ring, when the Indian music began, he proceeded a few steps, and then springing upon his hands, he elevated his feet, and commenced a sort of bear dance, accompanied by sundry singular manœuvres on his hands, turning an occasional somersault, and yelling like an Indian!

At first the savages seemed amazed at his performances, but soon began to applaud by the most uproarious laughter and shouts, some of them actually rolling on the ground in their merriment. After he had passed around the ring in this gymnastic manner, several of the warriors who had been most delighted with his antics, put their hands on the ground and desired him to "do so more." He pointed to his wound and refused, saying, he was "too lame." His singular vivacity and good nature captivated the Indians, and from that time on, he was the hero of the party, and was no longer tied at night.

On reaching the Shawnee towns on the Great Miami, the prisoners were compelled to run the gauntlet for the amusement of the old *Shawnees*, the squaws and youth. Several of the prisoners were severely beaten. A man by the name of Baker, a silversmith by trade, from Westmoreland county, Pennsylvania, was beaten almost to death. In his desperation, he ran past the council-house two or three times, being blinded by the blows and fright, and was about to sink, when a friendly voice directed him to enter the door. He did so and was spared. When this performance was going on, the old warrior who had young Fast in charge, shoved him back among the Indians, and he did not have to undergo the punishment of the gauntlet.

When the party arrived at Upper Sandusky, the prisoners were again compelled to undergo the ordeal of running the gauntlet. They were all handled very severely, but none of them were killed. Young Fast was again excused from the gauntlet by his Indian master. His wound, by this time, had nearly healed. The surviving prisoners soon recruited from their fatigue, and were exchanged at Pittsburgh, and on the Muskingum.

Young Fast was retained, and adopted into an old Delaware family, in lieu of a son who had lost his life in a border skirmish. His hair was plucked out in the usual manner, leaving a small scalp-lock about the crown; his white blood was all washed away; his ears and the cartilage of his nose were perforated, and brooches placed therein. After this, he was dressed in Indian costume, his hair roached up, and filled with gaudy feathers. Being taken to the council-house, he was regularly indoctrinated as the son of the tribe. He received the name of Mo-lun-the, and was taken to the cabin, or wigwam, of his new parents.

Young Fast resided on the banks of the Tymochtee about two years. He was treated very kindly by his Indian mother. He had an Indian brother, by the name of Ke-was-sa, to whom he became much attached. They often hunted coon and other game. On one occasion, Ke-was-sa invited young Fast to accompany him to hunt bear. After traveling some distance in the forest, they discovered evidences of the ascent of a bear up a large elm, which was hollow near the top. After trying some time, in vain, to rouse the bear from its retreat, it was proposed that a tree, which stood at a proper distance from the elm, should be felled, in such a manner as to lean against the elm, to enable young Fast to climb to the hole, and smoke bruin out with punk and rotten wood. The tree was cut, and fell against the elm. Young Fast, being expert in climbing, ascended it to the proposed point, and commenced operations with a view of smoking bruin into a surrender. Kewassa placed himself in a position, gun in hand, where he could welcome the bear, on its appearance, to a smell of powder. Young Fast lighted the dry tinder and threw it into the hole, but bruin failed to make his appearance. While engaged in this fruitless enterprise, a strong breeze struck the leaning tree, and it fell to the ground. Here was a dilemma. Young Fast was some forty feet from the ground, on a large elm. He could not grasp his arms around it, so as to safely descend. Kewassa was alarmed for his safety. There could be no help, for the only tree in the vicinity had been cut. After gazing at young Fast some time, without being able to offer assistance, he hastened to the camp, several miles away, expecting that his new brother would be dashed to pieces.

Taking in the situation at a glance, young Fast concluded that he only hazarded his life by remaining where he was; and the attempt to descend could result in nothing more than death, but might terminate in safety. Summoning all his strength, he grasped the rough bark with his hands, at the same time making good use of his feet and legs, and commenced the descent, moving cautiously, until he came within fifteen or eighteen feet of the ground, when his strength so far failed him, that he was compelled to relax his grip and slid down, mangling his hands, and the inside of his arms and legs badly. On reaching the ground he was considerably stunned, but soon revived and started for the camp, where he arrived amidst the grief of his Indian mother and brother, who had given him up as lost.

On one occasion, after he had been a captive over a year, when all the warriors were absent from the village, his Indian mother having also left the camp for a short time, he became very melancholy. Thoughts of home stole upon him. He left the wigwam and proceeded a short distance into the forest, and seating himself upon a log, soon became absorbed in meditation. While thus musing, he was interrupted by a stranger, who suddenly appeared and confronted him. Discovering his embarrassment and dejection, the stranger said in the Delaware language :

"Ah, young man, what are you thinking about?"

Fast.—"I am alone, and have no company, and feel very lonesome."

Stranger.—"That is not it, you are thinking of home. Be a good boy and you shall see your home again."

After some further conversation, he learned that the stranger was none other than that terror of the pioneers, the renegade, Simon Girty. Young Fast afterward became well acquainted with Girty, and was the recipient of many favors at his hands. In fact, Girty's assurance that he would again see his home in Pennsylvania, greatly revived his drooping spirits and led him to believe that Girty, though often denounced by the pioneers as a villain, a demon in human shape, was not destitute of sympathy and kindness, though associating with the fierce red men of the northwest.

During the campaign of Colonel William Crawford, which ended so disastrously, Mr. Fast was with the *Delawares* on the Tymochtee. Captain Pipe and Wingenund, leading Delaware chiefs, resided, when in their villages, in that region of Ohio. After the rout of Crawford's army, when the Colonel was brought back a prisoner, Mr. Fast was present and saw him. He was in hearing distance when the *Delawares* tortured the Colonel, and could hear his groans. He was so much affected that he left the spot in company with his Indian brother and mother. Mr. Fast, in his lifetime, often related incidents connected with the unfortunate expedition of poor Crawford. As they have been repeated by Dr. Knight, Slover, and Heckewelder, it is unnecessary to narrate them here.

Shortly after the execution of Crawford, Mr. Fast was urged to marry a young squaw, a daughter of an Indian family of some distinction. He was then about nineteen years of age. It was a question of much delicacy, and required a good deal of tact to repel the proposal in such manner as to avoid offence. When the subject was again seriously pressed upon his attention, he intimated he was only a boy, and was too young to marry. The *Delawares* were greatly amused at his modesty, and his reason for refusing. He added as a further objection, that no man should marry until he had become a good hunter, and could provide meat. Not being the owner of a gun, it would be impossible for him to supply the quantity of game required for food. Moreover, he thought he could not get along without a cow, an essential to every person designing to marry. As soon as these could be procured he would gladly consent. He professed much admiration for the young squaws, and intimated he could easily select a wife from among them, if his terms could be met. It was agreed his ideas were correct, and that he should accompany the first expedition to the settlements along the Ohio, and the first gun captured should be his, and on returning he should be permitted to bring back a cow.

In August, 1782, there was a grand council at Chillicothe, on or near the Great Miami, in which the *Wyandots, Delawares, Ottawas, Mingoes, Shawnees, Miamis* and *Pottawatomies* participated. Simon Girty, Elliott and McKee were present, and addressed the assembled warriors. The council resolved to raise two armies, one of six hundred men, and the other of three hundred and fifty, the larger to march into Kentucky, and the smaller into western Virginia and Pennsylvania. By the last of August, the greater army appeared under the lead of Simon Girty, at Bryant's station, in the territory of Kentucky. The story is narrated in all the histories of Kentucky.

The Indian forces destined to operate against the border settlements of Virginia and Pennsylvania, delayed their march until a runner brought tidings of success from Kentucky. Some four hundred fierce warriors assembled on the Sandusky, and were armed and equipped by the agents of the British. The warriors were dressed and painted in the most fantastic manner, their hair, being gathered in a sort of cue and drawn through a tin tube, was ornamented by colored hawk or eagle quills. With scalping knives, tomahawks and guns, they presented a formidable appearance. For many days and nights before the expedition started, their wild orgies echoed through the forests. Speeches, dances, and the like, accompanied by threats of extermination against the white race, were common.

Young Fast was painted in true warrior style, his hair being put up in a cue and drawn through a tin tube, and ornamented with feathers. He was furnished a tomahawk, scalping-knife, and bow, and told he might accompany the expedition. Before departing, he buried, in a secure place, his fancy brooches and other ornaments of silver, so that if he ever returned he could reclaim them. The expedition passed down the old Wyandot trail through what are now Crawford, Richland and Ashland counties, by Mohican Johnstown; thence near the ruins of the Moravain towns on the Tuscarawas. Arriving at that point, a difference of opinion arose as to the exact destination of the expedition.

After some consultation in council, as the expedition to Kentucky was proving successful, it was decided that the Indian army should proceed to and attack the small fort or block-house at what is now the city of Wheeling, West Virginia. On the approach of the Indian army, the expedition was discovered by John Lynn, a noted spy and frontier hunter, who was scouting through the forests and watching the Indian paths west of the Ohio. He hastened to the stockade and gave the alarm. The stockade had no regular garrison, and had to be defended exclusively by the settlers who sought security within its walls. On the arrival of Lynn, all retired within the stockade, except a family of Zanes; and when the attack began, there were but about twenty efficient men to oppose nearly four hundred savages, led on by Simon Girty.

The Indian army soon crossed the Ohio river, and approached the stockade waving British colors. An immediate surrender was demanded. Colonel Silas Zane responded by firing at the flag borne by the savages. The assault was commenced by the Indians, and kept up briskly for three days and nights, but each attack was successfully repelled by the little garrison. While the men within were constantly engaged in firing at the enemy, the women moulded bullets, loaded and handed guns to the men, and by this means every assault was repulsed. The galling fire poured upon the savages exasperated them to madness. In the night they attempted to burn Zane's house, from which they had suffered most, but through the vigilance of Sam, a colored man, their intentions were thwarted.

On the return of light, on the second day, the savages, after some delay, renewed the siege. A wooden cannon, loaded with balls captured from a small boat on its way to the falls of the Ohio, was pointed towards the stockade, and, amid the yells of the infuriated Indians, discharged. They expected to see a section of the stockade blown to splinters, and an opening for the warriors created. The cannon exploded, and the fragments flew in every direction. Several of the warriors were wounded and a number killed, and all were appalled at the result. Recovering from their dismay, and being furious from disappointment, they again pressed to the assault with renewed energy. They were as often repelled by the deadly aim of the little garrison, and forced to retire.

The achievements of Elizabeth Zane, on this occasion, are matters of history, and too well known to require repetition in this article.

The third day the siege was renewed with terrible ferocity; but every attempt to storm the fort was successfully resisted. In the afternoon, despairing of success, the Indians resolved to change their programme. About one hundred warriors remained to annoy the stockade, lay waste the country, and scour the neighboring settlements. The balance of the army crossed the Ohio, and made a feint of returning to Sandusky, but the next morning re-crossed the river above the stockade, and divided into two parties, and hastened towards the settlements about Fort Rice, some forty miles away, in what is now Washington county, Pennsylvania.

On the third night of the siege, learning of the departure of a part of the Indian army, and presuming the savages were about to invade his old home, young Fast resolved, if possible, to effect his escape. Late in the night, while reposing beside his Indian brother on his blanket, on the ground, the memory of his home and dear friends came fresh to his recollection, and knowing the whole settlement was imperiled by the approach of his savage companions, intent on revenge and blood, he could not sleep. Ka-wa-sa, his Indian brother, wearied with the exertions of a three days' siege, slept soundly. Knowing the nature of an Indian, when profoundly slumbering, young Fast attempted to awaken his Indian brother, stating that he was very thirsty and desired him to go with him to the river for water. He refused to rise, telling Molunthe to wait until morning.

Permitting his brother to return to his state of stupor for some time, he again made an effort to arouse him, insisting that he could not wait, but must have water. The Indian, having full confidence in young Fast, as a brother, told him to go himself, as no one would harm him. He was but too happy to comply. Taking a small copper kettle, he hastened to the river bank and placed the kettle in a position that might imply that he had fallen into the stream, been drowned and floated down the current. Then carefully wending his way through the Indian lines, he proceeded across the hills and valleys in the direction of Fort Rice, on Buffalo creek, some fifteen or twenty miles from his old home. He groped his way among rocks, down declivities and across small streams, sometimes falling headlong down the embankments, and about daylight became exhausted from fatigue and want of food, and was compelled to seek repose at the base of a steep bluff, in a thicket of undergrowth; and while resting there, could distinctly hear the passing warriors conversing. A short distance hence the trail divided.

Carefully concealing himself until all the warriors passed, he again proceeded in the direction of the fort, taking a ridge midway between the trails. By a vigorous exertion he got in advance of the savages, and when within about two miles of the fort, he discovered a white man approaching with a bridle and halter in his hand. Springing behind a large tree, he waited until the settler arrived within a few feet of his concealment, when he stepped into the path and confronted him. The white man was taken by surprise and trembled with fear, and was about to flee for life, when the supposed warrior addressed him in English, briefly informing him who he was, where he was going, the approach of the warriors and the danger that environed the settlement. Calmed by the assurances of present safety, the white man caught his horses, which were near, and he and young Fast mounted and hastened to the fort and spread the alarm, and succeeded in gathering the settlers in the vicinity into it before the savages appeared. The fort consisted of a strong block-house, surrounded by several cabins of the settlers. When all the men were gathered in, there were only six.

The savages approached with much assurance, and offering to spare all the prisoners, if the little band would surrender. Young Fast assured the inmates that the cold steel of the tomahawk would be the price of such an indiscretion. Their proffers of safety were not accepted. A fierce assault at once commenced. The siege was kept up all day and night; but the little fort held out. Several of the savages were wounded, and the warriors finally despairing of success, suddenly withdrew and spread among the scattered settlements in detached parties, burning houses, and shooting cattle and hogs. They had probably learned the approach of Colonel Swearinger with relief for Wheeling, that was yet beleaguered by the red fiends.

After the retirement of the savages, young Fast hastened to his old home, painted and dressed as an Indian warrior. On arriving at the cabin of his parents in what is now Fayette county, he so nearly resembled a wild Indian warrior of the wilderness that his parents were unable to distinguish him. Indeed, they were much alarmed at his presence, fearing he was a genuine savage acting as a decoy. He attempted to calm their fears by assuring them, in their own tongue, that his name was Fast, and that he was really their own son! At length his mother, recalling some peculiarity about the pupils of his eyes, and some spots on his breast, recognized him, and rushing forward to embrace him in her arms, was told not to do so, as he was covered with vermin from the Indian camps. The tube in which his scalp-lock was enclosed was removed, and he repaired to an out-building where his infected garments were taken off and burned. Soap and water soon removed the encrusted paint and soil from his person, when he was presented with a clean suit of clothes, which restored him to his status as a white man. The joy of his parents on his safe return home, scarcely knew bounds. A full detail of his adventures was given, and often repeated to inquiring friends.

On arriving at manhood, Mr. Fast located in Dunker township, Greene county, Pennsylvania, where he married, and remained until the spring of 1815, when he removed with his family to what is now Orange township, Ashland county, Ohio, and settled about half a mile southeast of the Vermillion lakes. When Mr. Fast and family arrived at the lakes, he found a number of Indians encamped near where he subsequently erected a cabin. He built a fire and his wife proceeded to prepare supper, surrounded by a dense forest. While in the act of cooking, their little company was alarmed by the appearance of eight or ten Indians, headed by an old warrior who was extremely ugly, shriveled in flesh, and ferocious in appearance. They had just discovered their new neighbors, and came to see who they were. On approaching within a few feet of Mr. Fast and his children, who were seated on a log near where Mrs. Fast was preparing supper, the old Indian looked steadfastly at Mr. Fast for a moment, and then rushing forward exclaimed, Molunthe! at the same time offering his hand in token of friendship.

The old warrior was Thomas Lyons, who was present at the capture of Mr. Fast, on the Ohio, some thirty-five years prior to that time, and was along with the expedition to Wheeling when his favorite young warrior, Molunthe, made his escape. The Indians had never suspected him of desertion, but had always believed he had, in the darkness, fallen into the river and drowned. On finding him here alive, "old Tom," manifested much gratification, and gave many tokens of a friendship that remained very cordial up to 1822, the last appearance of the *Delawares* in this region. During the ensuing seven years, the *Delawares* often encamped in the vicinity, regarding Mr. Fast and family as of their tribe. They frequently went into his cabin in the evening and danced after the *Delaware* manner, making rude music by pounding on a stool and singing, while the dancers hopped about the room, flourishing their scalping-knives, shouting and keeping time to the music.

In the fall of 1819, old Thomas Lyons and a party of *Delawares* had a feast, on what is now known as the John Freeborn farm, southwest of Savannah, to which Mr. Fast and his sons were invited. Being unable to be present, his sons Nicholas and Francis, aged respectively twenty-five and fifteen, attended. The feast was in their camp. There were present some fifty or sixty Indians, and no whites, except the Fasts. A large black bear had been roasted and boiled. The body being roasted, was cut into small slices, and handed around on new bark plates. The head and feet, unskinned, were boiled in a copper kettle, and a sort of soup made therefrom, which was handed around in wooden ladles. Nicholas and Francis partook, courteously, with the Indians. The roast was elegant, but the soup was not relished. At the conclusion of the feast, Lyons insisted on painting Francis, Indian fashion. The boy readily submitted, for the fun of the thing. "Old Tom" laid on a good coat of vermillion, which gave him the appearance of a young Indian. The paint was so adhesive that, when he returned home, he was unable to remove it for a long time; and was afterwards known as "Indian Frank." Billy Montour, Jim Jirk, Monos, Jonacake, George and Jim Lyons, Buckwheat, Billy Dowdee, Captain George, and other well-known Delawares, were at the feast.

Christian Fast had nine sons, Jacob, Martin, William, Nicholas, David, Francis, George, Christian, and John; and four daughters, Margaret, Barbara, Isabel, and Christena. Jacob, aged 84, William 78, and George 65, remain in Orange township.

Christian Fast, sr., died, at his farm in Orange township, in 1849.

GEORGE AND ELIZABETH FOULKS.

About the year 1774, the parents of George Foulks located in the midst of the dense forest in the northwest corner of what is now Washington county, Pennsylvania, near the Ohio river. The family of Mr. Foulks consisted of three boys and two or three girls. He was quite poor, and had ventured to improve his fortunes amid the dangers surrounding the border settlers. He had lived some years in the city of Philadelphia, where most of his children were born. When he moved to his new home, the *Delaware* and *Wyandot* Indians visited that region in great numbers in search of game. The colonies had been greatly oppressed by Great Britain, and were just on the verge of a revolt. Her agents and traders were busy in alienating and exciting the savages against the rebel inhabitants of the colonies, as they were then denominated.

It was the custom of many of the settlers of that region, in the spring of the year, to cross the Ohio—which there runs nearly west for many miles—in canoes, to make sugar on the fine bottoms. John, George and Elizabeth Foulks, aged respectively nineteen, six and seventeen years, crossed the river in company with their father and erected a neat camp house of small poles, and a furnace, in which they placed kettles to boil sap.* After tapping a large number of sugar trees, Mr. Foulks re-crossed the river to his cabin, leaving John, Elizabeth, and George to gather and boil the sugar water. This was early in March, 1777. After they had been thus engaged several days, one evening about nine o'clock, while the moon was shining brightly, the camp-house was approached by five or six *Wyandot* Indians, well armed. They had been attracted by the camp-fire. When they arrived within a short distance of the camp John Foulks discovered their approach, and judging the visit to be hostile, fled in the direction of the Ohio river, where he hoped to cross in a canoe left near the north bank of that stream, leaving his little sister and brother to the mercy of the savages. The Indians followed him with a dog, and he had fled but a short distance, when they overtook him, and insisted on his surrender and return; but continuing to retreat, several of the warriors discharged their guns after him, and he was mortally wounded, fell, and soon expired. His scalp was taken, and they hastily returned to the camp, where George and Elizabeth had been taken without resistance.

The Indians hastily entered the forest in a westerly direction, ordering Elizabeth and George, in broken English, to follow. They were much terrified, but complied promptly. They traveled some miles, when their prisoners were secured, and all slept on the leaves. Early the next morning, the Indians arose, and broiled slices of venison, on which all breakfasted, and continued their flight nearly west all day, and again slept as they had done before. During their progress through the forest, they crossed a number of small streams on logs or poles. While crossing one, some three feet deep, an Indian who walked behind George, in sport, pushed him off the log, and he was thoroughly saturated. At this, the Indians all laughed heartily. George refrained from showing temper, but resolved to retaliate the first opportunity. The next day they came to another stream somewhat more swollen, and had to cross it on a log. The Indian who had pushed him in the day before, pointed to the log, desiring him to lead again. George refused the honor of leading, and fell in behind the Indian. They had gone about half over, when George caught the belt of the Indian, and giving him a sudden twitch, the savage fell into the stream nearly neck deep. He waded out, venting all sorts of threats and imprecations on George for his temerity. The Indian was thoroughly soaked, and his comrades gave vent to the most uproarious merriment over the incident. This calmed the fury of the enraged Indian, and changed his revenge to admiration. The little captive was regarded from that time with favor, and as much tenderness as if he were a real Indian. They traveled a little southwest until they reached the old trail which passed near the present site of Wooster, to a village then known as Mohican Johnstown, near the present site of Jeromeville, in Ashland county. They were several days in reaching this point, and being unaccustomed to the Indian mode of preparing food, which consisted almost wholly of venison, without salt, bread, or even parched corn, the prisoners were very hungry. They remained at Mohican Johnstown several days, and then continued along the trail in a northwest direction across what is now Ashland and Richland counties to Snipestown, an Indian village near the present site of Rome. Here they found a large number of *Wyandots* who rejoiced at the success of the captors, who proved to be of that nation or tribe. Here the scalp halloo was given, as at Mohican Johnstown, but at neither place were they required to run the gauntlet.*

They remained at Snipestown some days. This village was named after a leading warrior and chief who resided there, and was much esteemed by his people. From this village they continued along the old trail to

---

* George Foulks never became a citizen of this county. Two or three of his brothers settled in Richland county, one Jacob Foulks in Clearcreek, now Ashland county. We insert this sketch that the reader may learn the trials and actual condition of this territory from 1781 to 1795. This Castleman family located in the north part of Richland county, and the last of the girls (Mrs. Stoner) died in Clearcreek township, in this county, in 1874. George Foulks was born in Philadelphia, December 4, 1769.

* The chief, Captain Snipe, was very active in the removal of the Moravians in 1781 from the Tuscarawas. See Heckewelder's narrative of Indian missions.

Upper Sandusky, the principal town and headquarters of the *Wyandot* warriors. When they came in sight of the village, the scalp halloo was again given, and large numbers sallied out to meet the warriors. George was again spared the pain of running the gauntlet.

He was given to an old squaw who had some time before lost a son on an excursion to the Pennsylvania border. She was the reputed mother of seven sons, all brave warriors and noted among the *Wyandots*. His sister was claimed by another warrior, and was given to an Indian family in Lower Sandusky to be taught the manners and duties of a squaw. George remained at Upper Sandusky with his new mother, who treated him with much tenderness. He attracted a good deal of attention, and soon formed an acquaintance with the Indian youths of his village. He was clothed and habited in all respects as an Indian, and soon learned to talk their language, and became accustomed to their mode of preparing food, and their bark wigwams or huts. He was taught the use of the bow—their gymnastic exercises—wrestling—foot-racing—playing ball and other sports, and soon became contented with his new mode of life. He occasionally met his sister, who was equally fortunate in securing a good Indian mother, who did not require her to perform all the drudgery of a common squaw.

It was the custom of the *Wyandots*, in the spring of the year, to scatter to various points in the forest, in small bands, to make sugar. The first year or two after George had been captured, he was required to assist in gathering the sap in small bark buckets to be evaporated in brass and copper kettles by the squaws. Never relishing hard work, he disliked his new vocation. The water was caught in bark vessels prepared for the purpose, and when it flowed freely, the task of gathering it was quite laborious. After worrying several days in a vain effort to keep pace with the flow of sap, George conceived a plan of relieving a portion of his toil. When he emptied the vessels, he slightly perforated the bottom and a large share of the sap escaped. In this way his toil was reduced, to the confusion of the squaws, who were unable to penetrate the mystery. A discovery of his trick would have resulted in many stripes; but fortunately, the difficulty was not solved.

The following autumn the Indian mother and father of George, and a number of *Wyandots* were encamped near Snipestown. An incident occurred that made a very strong impression upon George. It was this: The Indians brought in a white boy who had been captured on the borders of Pennsylvania. The poor little captive was offered to an Indian woman whose son had been killed by the "Long Knives," in lieu of her child. She scornfully rejected the proposition, declaring "Me no take white rebel for my son." Upon consultation, the little boy was ordered to be executed, and the time and place fixed. Sometime in the afternoon, on the day prior to the time appointed, George and a number of Indian boys were playing a little distance from his mother's hut. She called him to her and told him the white boy was to be killed the next morning, and he should not be so merry. This reproof arrested his sport. His sympathies were deeply moved. The next morning the captive was bound to a log to be slain. At this time, a number of *Delawares* were encamped not a great distance from Snipestown. They somehow learned the *Wyandots* had determined to execute the rejected prisoner, and a warrior conceived the idea of rescuing him. He hurrried into the Wyandot camp, and coming to the place where the prisoner was bound, struck the cords by which he was fettered, with his tomahawk, and severing them, carried off the boy, to the astonishment of the *Wyandots*. The boy afterwards escaped and returned to his friends.

When George reached the proper age, he was adopted after the manner of the *Wyandots*, passing through all their ceremonies, and was given an Indian name, Ha-en-ye-ha, or my brother, which he retained. During the period of his indoctrination into Indian customs, modes of hunting and fishing, he often accompanied his Indian parents and other members of the tribe through the north part of what are now Richland, Ashland and Wayne counties; and sometimes nearly to Beaver county, Pennsylvania, during which excursions he learned the names of the streams, all the good camping points, the best springs and the principal resorts of game. In fact, he became a thorough woodsman, an accomplished hunter, and an Indian in taste, dress and habits. Snipestown was a favorite Indian village, and he spent a large share of his captivity there, occasionally visiting Upper and Lower Sandusky and Cranestown with the warriors and hunters.

Many times during his captivity the Indians suffered for food. After the hunting seasons, when they had plenty of venison and hominy, bear's oil and sugar, they lived extravagantly. For many weeks their chief occupation was visiting, dancing and feasting, which continued until their stores of provisions were consumed. At this point, the hunters and warriors were compelled to sally forth to renew their stores of venison and bear's meat. On many occasions George and his Indian mother were so nearly starved that they were compelled to gather the old bones about their wigwam, crack and reboil them for soup, after they had been bleaching in the sun and air for many months. These messes were, to him, very savory, and quite a luxury, at such periods.

The Indian women were very industrious, and hoed the corn, chopped the wood, did all the cooking, built the camp fires, and, in fact, were literally slaves for their red-skinned lords. They made sugar in the spring, fried out the bear's oil, jerked the venison and buffalo meat, pounded and prepared the hominy and parched corn for the haughty warriors.

Towards the close of the Revolutionary war George often accompanied the warriors to the borders, but was always very reticent about the mischief done during those excursions. In fact, he had been so thoroughly indoctrinated in Indian secresy, that very little, if anything, could be learned of him concerning the warlike expeditions of the *Wyandots*. He was at several Indian consultations at Cranestown, some four miles north of the present site of Upper Sandusky. He there met the noted Simon Girty and several British agents. Their council-house was of bark, and was seventy-five or one hundred feet long and perhaps twenty feet wide. Tarhe, or as he was sometimes called, King Crane, was rising into influence and power as a chief among the *Wyandots*. He there met many other chiefs and warriors, and learned the particulars of the capture and execution of Colonel William Crawford by the *Delawares*, being, himself, too young to witness that battle.

When he was about twenty years of age, he obtained a sort of furlough to hunt in the east, near the Ohio river, and stealthily visited his old home. He was then a complete Indian, in dress, language and manners; and loved the nomadic life of his people. His parents offered every motive for his return to civilized life, but in vain. He determined to return to the home of the red man. This was in the fall of 1786. He had then been with the Indians about twelve years.

In 1789–90 active hostilities were carried on between the Indians and the settlers in West Pennsylvania, Virginia, and Kentucky. It is believed that George Foulks accompanied the *Wyandots* and *Delawares* against Harmar and St. Clair, though he was always silent on the subject. In 1790 the *Wyandots* were very anxious on the subject of war then approaching. They feared the "Long Knives"—*Sarayumigh*, would prevail. One of their prophets or medicine men, took a lot of charcoal, and pounding it into a sort of powder, placed it upon a piece of bark, and then drew a rude map of the country, its rivers, lakes, Indian trails, and the probable route of the invaders. They then took a flint and steel and fired a piece of punk and applied it to the points where Harmar and his army would be most apt to attack the Indian territory. The fire gradually spread from the points ignited. The Indians watched it attentively. When the charcoal ceased to burn, the Indians formed into a double file and simultaneously fired their guns. After which they stood quietly watching a dark cloud that was floating over. In a few seconds, the sound of their guns was distinctly heard in the clouds. The Indians regarded this as a good omen and shouted over the result, stating that the white warriors would not succeed that year. They at once began to prepare for war. The result is too well known for repetition. Disaster met the frontier soldiers at every point.

About the year 1788, George Foulks was persuaded to marry a Wyandot woman, and fully identify himself with the fortunes of his people. He had two children by his Wyandot wife; but, like Jonathan Alder, finally tired of the Indian mode of living. His people were so frequently involved in war with the whites that there was great danger of final extermination. Looking the whole field over, he concluded to abandon the *Wyandots* and return to civilized life. The Wyandot warriors discovered by his manner that something was wrong, and watched his motions closely. The real difficulty was, the Indians insisted that he should become a real warrior, and accompany them against St. Clair and Wayne. He declined to do so, and slyly departing from his wigwam, took the most direct route for his old home in Washington county, Pennsylvania. The warriors soon discovered his desertion, and several of them took the trail and gave chase. Suspecting this, he traveled with the utmost speed, and when about exhausted, and likely to be overtaken in crossing a principal stream on the route, he concealed himself beneath driftwood, thrusting all but his head under the water. While in this retreat, several of the warriors walked on the drift, and gave utterance to their indignation, saying they would punish him severely if they caught him, for the perfidy of deserting his tribe. The sound of their voices gradually died away and all became quiet. He cautiously emerged, and finding the warriors had disappeared, proceeded on his way, and finally reached his old home in safety. He was soon noticed by Brady, Sprott, McConnell and other scouts in the government employ, and had some adventures. He did not enter very zealously, however, the field against the *Wyandots*. He had always been treated by them as if he had been born amongst them, and was a real Indian. After the battle of Fallen Timbers, and peace had been declared, the *Wyandots* frequently returned to hunt, fish, and sell their peltry in the city of Pittsburgh. After his return home he married a daughter of Henry Ullery, and located near the present site of the village of Darlington, in Beaver county, Pennsylvania.

Shortly after he located, he was requested by a Mr. Castleman to go to Upper Sandusky and rescue his daughters from captivity. Two daughters of Mr. Castleman, Mary, aged thirteen, and Margaret, aged nine, had been captured in a sugar camp near the banks of the Ohio river some years prior to the proposed rescue. The Indians had taken the captive girls to Greentown, on the Black fork, and sold the youngest to an English trader by the name of McIntosh, while Mary was taken to Upper Sandusky and adopted. Margaret was taken to Detroit, sent to school, and finally, through the traders, returned to her parents. Mary married a half-breed named Abram Williams, by whom she had two children, George and Sally. Williams loved fire-water, and, when under its influence, was jealous and very cruel to his wife. He often threatened to tomahawk her. Regarding her life as being in peril, she managed to convey word of her whereabouts to her parents, through the traders, who often visited Pittsburgh. George Foulks consented to attempt to rescue her from her perilous situation. He passed, alone, through the dense forests, up the well-worn Indian trails to Upper Sandusky, where he met Williams, and proposed to take his wife home on a visit. Williams became angry and threatened to scalp Foulks if he attempted such an enterprise. Foulks desisted from further interviews with Williams. From his long residence with the *Wyandots*, he had many confidential friends among the warriors. He, therefore, resorted to stratagem. He proposed to an old Indian if he would secretly take Mary away, he would give him a barrel of whiskey and a lot of trinkets. After some parleying, the Indian consented—the "fire-water" was so tempting he could not resist. The warrior, in company with Mrs. Williams, left the village without exciting suspicion, and passed down the old Wyandot trail which ran very near the present site of Olivesburgh to Jerometown, while Foulks remained one day and then proceeded by a circuitous route to reach the same place. On arriving near Jerometown he gave a signal, and the Indian and Mrs. Williams joined him in the forest. He had arranged with a trader for the whiskey and trinkets for the Indian upon his return. Foulks and Mrs. Williams continued along the trail near the present site of Wooster, and safely reached the residence of Castleman, in Washington county, Pennsylvania. Mrs. Williams regretted very much to leave her children, but an attempt to take them along would have proved fatal. She never met them again. Sally grew up and married a famous hunter by the name of Solomon Jonacake, who was well known to the pioneers of Ashland and Richland counties. This was the last Indian exploit of George Foulks.

Some time after this, his Indian wife and two children are reported to have visited him in Beaver county, to induce him to return to the *Wyandots*. He declined to do so; but visited Pittsburgh and purchased a number of blankets and such other articles as would be useful in their wigwam, and presented them to the squaw with a horse to bear them to their home on the Sandusky, which she accepted and never returned.

Mr. Foulks had a fine mill near Darlington, and afterwards became quite wealthy. He was a man of fine native abilities, and was often spoken of as a suitable person to be elected to the legislature or to fill any of the county offices. He, however, refused to accept any office, and steadily continued in business. During his captivity, he passed over the most valuable parts of what is now Richland county, and became acquainted with all the good agricultural locations. After the war of 1812, when the lands, in what is now Blooming-grove township, came into market, he entered eight or ten quarter sections, and induced his father-in-law, Mr. Ullery, to invest largely in lands. About the year 1830, Henry and George, sons of George Foulks, located near Rome, in Richland county. He had several daughters, some of whom yet survive. Jacob and William, brothers of George Foulks, also located in Blooming-grove. Jacob resided two or three miles northwest of Olivesburgh. George Foulks died in Beaver county, Pennsylvania, July 10, 1840, aged seventy-one years, and sleeps quietly in the cemetery near Darlington, where he lived many years, an influential and reputable citizen. Mrs. Foulks died at the residence of one of her sons in Richland county some years after his decease.

It may be interesting to the reader to learn the history of Elizabeth Foulks, who was captured with George, on the banks of the Ohio river. As before stated, she was taken to Lower Sandusky, where she was adopted by a kind squaw. As she grew to womanhood she became acquainted with a young man by the name of James Whittaker, who had been captured by the *Wyandots* when a child, in Virginia, and adopted by them. All his friends were killed. He had lost nearly all recollection of his parentage, and had become thoroughly initiated among the Indians, and had no desire to leave them. Whittaker became much attached to Elizabeth, and she to him. They were finally married after the Wyandot custom. Whittaker became an influential trader and interpreter among the Indians. On one occasion a number of Cherokee, Shawnee, and Wyandot warriors captured an emigrant boat on the Ohio river with a number of pioneers, among whom were a Mr. Skyles and Johnston, with one or two others who were brought to Upper Sandusky. A French trader, M. Duchonquet, purchased Johnson of the Indians, and Skyles finally escaped.

A few days afterwards, the *Cherokees* appeared with a Miss Flemming, who had been captured at the same time, and made preparations for her execution. The French trader took an interest in the fate of Miss Flemming, and invited Whittaker to accompany him to the Cherokee camp. He did so, and Miss Flemming recognized him as an old acquaintance. Whittaker had often visited, with the Indian hunters, her father's tavern near Pittsburgh. He was, therefore, very desirous of aiding her. Miss Flemming implored him to save her from death by torture, which was then impending. Whittaker tried to induce the *Cherokees* to release her for a consideration. They sternly refused. Whittaker determined to have Tarhe or King Crane, who was then the great Wyandot chief, intervene. Tarhe was at Detroit, and Whittaker took a small boat and hastened to see him. When he landed, Tarhe, with deep interest, heard his story. Whittaker said Miss Flemming was his sister, and was about to be killed by torture. He asked Tarhe to interfere for her rescue. The chief admitted that the enterprise was humane, and at once started for Sandusky and hastened to the Cherokee camp. The *Cherokees* were inflexible, and would not consent to release the prisoner, and heaped upon Tarhe charges of cowardice for interfering. The chief retaliated on the *Cherokees* for the inhuman attempt to torture a woman, and withdrew. The *Cherokees* were alarmed, and determined to kill their prisoner without delay. She was striped of her clothing, tied to a stake, and faggots placed around her, and left to suffer the horrors of impending death. She was to be burned early the next morning. Tarhe expected this, and to avert the tragedy took a number of young warriors, and at midnight entered the Cherokee camp. He found Miss Flemming tied to a stake, painted black and in a state of insensibility, moaning over her condition. Tarhe at once released her from her painful situation, re-clothed her and set her at liberty. An Indian whoop was then given, when the *Cherokees* were awakened and hurried to the spot. Tarhe told them he had rescued the prisoner, and that by the laws of conquest she was his property. Tarhe's warriors were the most numerous, and the *Cherokees* quietly admitted that he had the advantage. They then expressed a willingness to accept the offer of the day before—six hundred silver brooches. Tarhe consented and by the aid of the traders, furnished the brooches, and Miss Flemming, clothed as a squaw, was returned to her parents at Pittsburgh by two faithful *Wyandot* warriors.

Mr. and Mrs. Whittaker were employed as interpreters at the treaties of 1814–17 and at several other interviews between the whites and Indians. They are often mentioned for their humane acts by the *Wyandots* and *Delawares*. They remained in the Indian country about Malden, Detroit and Upper Sandusky long after the war of 1812. They had several children, sons and daughters. Some thirty years since a Miss Whittaker, daughter of Elizabeth, visited an uncle (Jacob Foulks) near Olivesburgh, and is said to have been a young lady of good education and fine address. The relatives treated her kindly and her visit was a pleasant one. Whittaker and his wife died many years since at Lower Sandusky, and their descendants are presumed to have gone west with the civilized *Wyandots* in 1842–3.

Such is the story of George and Elizabeth Foulks, as we have been able to glean from his acquaintances in Beaver county, Pennsylvania, and elsewhere. The larger part of the narrative was obtained from Mrs. Robert Starr, formerly of Washington county, Pennsylvania, now a resident of Blooming-grove township, Richland county, Ohio, two miles west of the village of Lafayette, and aged about eighty-seven years. Her mind is quite clear. She was intimately acquainted with Mr. Foulks in his lifetime, and has heard him repeat the story of his adventures a great many times. Mr. Foulks also related many hunting exploits, the outlines of which have escaped recollection. All in all, he was an extraordinary character—a bold woodsman—a thrifty business man and a noted pioneer.

GENERAL REASIN BEALL.

A sketch of his life was originally published in the Wooster *Democrat*, March 9, 1843, and which gives a good many interesting items of history. We republish it entire.

"To render the tribute of approbation to the merit and worth of departed friends, and indulge in expressions of regret at the bereavement we experience in their death, has, in some form or other, been a custom from the earliest ages. Independent of the incentive to noble actions which such a practice holds forth to the minds of youth, there is, on the part of those who may be called to the performance of the service, a kind of pleasing melancholy, which almost seems for the time to bring them again into the society of the friend whose final exit it is their misfortune to deplore.

"General Reasin Beall, who died at Wooster, Ohio, on the twentieth day of February, 1843, was born in Montgomery county, in the State of Maryland, on the third of December, 1769, and a few years thereafter accompanied his parents to Washington county, in the State of Pennsylvania, where they made a permanent settlement. The exact time of this settlement is not known, but it must have been some years before 1782, for in that year the father, Major Zephaniah Beall, was an officer in the unfortunate campaign made by a body of volunteer militia from western Pennsylvania, under the command of Colonel Crawford, against the Indians of Upper Sandusky.

"At the age of fourteen years, Mr. Beall entered the office of the Hon. Thomas Scott, at one time a member of Congress, a gentleman of considerable note in the public affairs of Pennsylvania, and then prothonotary of Washington county. With that gentleman he remained until he was twenty-one years of age, and on quitting his employ, received the most flattering testimonials of good conduct.

"The privations and sufferings which were experienced by the hardy and intrepid pioneers who first undertook to tame the forests west of the Alleghany mountains, has no parallel in anything of the kind that has ever existed. Favored with no government aid or protection, and without roads, other than such as they opened by their individual efforts, they had to scale a rugged mountain wilderness, of more than a hundred miles in extent; and when arrived on the western waters they, for a long time, had to subsist mainly by the chase. But this was not all; the treaty of peace, which acknowledged American independence, brought no peace to them. The Indian nations, who espoused the cause of the British during the war, were not content to desist from their depredations upon the western settlements, and such was the inefficiency of the government under the confederation, that it was not until the new organization under the present constitution, that measures were taken to repel their incursions. In 1790 an expedition was fitted out, and marched against the Indians on the heads of the two Miamis. The command of this corps was given to General Harmar. Mr. Beall served in the expedition as an officer in the quartermaster's department, and was with the army when a severe action was fought between a detachment under Colonel Harden and the Indians near Fort Wayne, in 1791. That expedition having failed of its object, the troops returned to the Ohio river, near to where the city of Cincinnati now stands, and Mr. Beall returned to his friends in Pennsylvania.

"Subsequently to this, General St. Clair marched a second force on the same route, and unfortunately met with an entire defeat. These repeated disasters determined the government to put forth all its energies in order to secure peace by the chastisement of the savages. On General Wayne's being appointed to the command of the northwestern army, Mr. Beall received a commission as ensign; and after some time spent in the recruiting service, repaired to headquarters, then at Legionville, on the north bank of the Ohio, near the site of the present town of Economy, in Beaver county, Pennsylvania. It was in the campaign which succeeded that Mr. Beall became acquainted with General, then Captain, Harrison, the late lamented President of the United States; an acquaintance in which the mutual friendship of the parties seemed to be increased rather than diminished by separation and time.

"Mr. Beall remained with the army until some time in the year 1793, when he resigned and returned to his friends in Pennsylvania to consummate a matrimonial engagement of long standing. Soon after his return, he married his late wife, then Miss Rebecca Johnston, and with whom he continued to live in the enjoyment of the greatest connubial happiness, until her death, which happened in the latter part of 1840. To the many excellent qualities and Christian virtues of that estimable lady he was, no doubt, much indebted for those Christian impressions which softened the death-bed pillow, and served as an effectual solace to his mind when looking to an eternal separation from all things here below.

"Like many enterprising men of his age, Mr. Beall fell in with the current of emigration which has constantly set to the west, and, consequently, several times changed his place of residence. In 1801 he removed with his family from Pennsylvania and settled for a short time in Steubenville, from which place he removed, in the fall of 1803, to New Lisbon, where he remained until 1815, in which year he removed to his late residence near Wooster.

"On his settlement at New Lisbon he received the appointment of clerk of the supreme and common pleas courts, which offices he held nearly the whole time he remained in the county. Although Mr. Beall had served but a few years in the regular army, it was sufficient to give his mind a military bias, and, previous to the late war, he took much pains to infuse into the militia of his county a military spirit, confidently anticipating that the difficulties then existing between this country and England would ultimately end in war. Soon after his settlement at New Lisbon he was chosen colonel of a regiment (being at that time the entire militia of the county), and, in a few years thereafter, a brigadier general. The war of 1812 found him in that capacity. On the surrender of General Hull at Detroit, a general panic seized upon the people of the sparsely settled counties to the west of Columbiana, and many were inclined to abandon their homes and seek places of greater safety. In this state of things all eyes were turned to General Beall for relief, and, to his great honor be it said, they were not in the least disappointed. Immediately on the receipt of the unwelcome news, which was communicated to him by express from Canton, he set about the organization of a detachment, and, in a very few days put himself at the head of several hundred men, and marched to the support of the frontier inhabitants of Wayne and Richland counties, and, ultimately, continued his route to Camp Huron, where he joined the troops from the Western Reserve, under General Wadsworth and General Perkins. At that place they were visited by General Harrison, the commander-in-chief, who attended in person to the reorganization of the corps, and, as the whole was not more than sufficient for a brigade, the command devolved on General Perkins as the senior officer. After this General Beall returned home, with the consolation of having done a good service by the promptitude of his march, which was a means of inspiring confidence among the people almost ready to surrender all hope of protection. Those who have never witnessed scenes like these can form a very imperfect idea of the difficulties which surround those who undertake to ward off such evils as were then impending. A frontier of more than a hundred miles was perfectly defenceless, abounding with all the facilities for an attack by a savage foe. Not a single company of government troops in the State; and no means either in money, provisions, or munitions of war within the reach or control of any officer who was called to the field.

In the spring of 1813, President Madison issued his proclamation for a special session of Congress, and the seat for the northern district being vacant by the death of Mr. Edwards, the member elect, General Beall was, at a special election, chosen to fill the vacancy. He served in Congress during that and the succeeding session, assisting to the full extent of his abilities, in providing ways and means for a vigorous prosecution of the war, then rendered extremely difficult by the prevalence of a reckless party spirit in various portions of the country.

But a congressional life did not suit his taste. He was naturally of a domestic turn of mind, and he longed to rid himself of a trust which compelled him to a separation, for so large a portion of his time, from his family.

The office of register of land office for the Wooster land district becoming vacant in 1814, General Beall was appointed, and resigned his seat in Congress, and in the following year removed to his late residence in the vicinity of Wooster. The office of register he resigned in 1824, when he retired from all public employment. But he was not permitted so to remain. At the great Whig mass convention at Columbus on the twenty-second of February, 1840, he was chosen to preside over its deliberations, and was afterwards chosen one of the electors of President and Vice-President, and had the honor as well as the pleasure of casting his vote in that capacity, for his old friend and military associate, General Harrison. No incident of his life seemed to give him so much pleasure as this; and with an ardent hope that in the performance of this last trust, confided to him by his fellow citizens, a foundation was laid for the lasting prosperity of his country, he considered his account closed with the public forever. How illusory are all earthly prospects and how vain are all human hopes."

ALEXANDER FINLEY.

Alexander Finley was born in Hartford county, Maryland, in the year 1770, of Scotch-Irish parents. His father was descended from one of seven brothers who emigrated to the north of Ireland during "King William's war." They subsequently emigrated to the State of New Jersey, from whence one of the brothers migrated to Hartford county, in the State of Maryland, about a century and a half ago. Here Alexander Finley was born. He attended the schools of his native county, and obtained a knowledge of the English branches. Upon reaching manhood, he located in Green county, Pennsylvania, where he married Miss Mary Smith, a relative of the Hon. Resolve Smith, president of the first bank organized in Philadelphia. In the fall of 1803, he emigrated, with his little family, to Fairfield county, Ohio, then including the counties of what are now Licking,

Knox, Richland and Ashland, and stopped the winter of 1803-4 in the cabin of Thomas Bell Patterson, on the present site of Mount Vernon. In the spring of 1804, he erected a cabin, about half a mile northwest of Mr. Patterson, on what is now the Fredericktown road, and resided there until April, 1809. On the fifteenth of April, 1809, he landed on the west bank of the Lake fork of Mohican, on the present site of Tylertown, where he quartered a few months in a camp cabin.

In May, Benjamin Bunn and family, William and Thomas Eagle and family arrived. These were the settlers in what is now Mohican township, in 1809. When Mr. Finley arrived, he was soon visited by the Indians of what was then known as Jerometown, a village on the Jerome fork of the Mohican, some five miles northwest of his cabin. The inhabitants of the Indian village were generally friendly. Mr. James Finley, of Marquand, Madison county, Missouri, from whom was obtained these particulars, says:

"As near as I can recollect, the Indian village contained perhaps about thirty bark and pole huts or wigwams. The names of the heads of families were, Aweepsah, Oppetete, Catotawa, Neshohawa, Buckanddohee, Shias, Ground-squirrel, Buckwheat, Philip Canonicut, and sometimes Thomas Lyons, Billy Montour, and Thomas Jelloway." The chief, Captain Pipe (Hobacon), resided some distance from the village. "He was a tall, dark, scowling old Indian, and seemed hostile to the whites. I seldom saw him. He did not associate with the whites of the neighborhood, but did his trading abroad. I learned that he and Armstrong, of Greentown, often made expeditions to attack emigrants on the Ohio river, on their way to Kentucky." "John Jerry Bettis Jerome had a cabin on the present site of Jeromeville, near the stream, when we moved to the country. He had been a trader among the Indians seventeen years in the northwest, and was a Frenchman; and, like most of the traders of that nation, married a squaw. He had a daughter ten years old, named Aweepsah. He had cleared some twenty-five or thirty acres—had horses, cattle and hogs, and often entertained the pioneers. After the declaration of war, his wife and daughter accompanied the Jerometown Indians to Piqua, where they died. Jerome sold his land and married a German woman, and removed to the mouth of Huron, on the lake, where he died some years afterward."

In 1809 the region along the Lake and Jerome forks of Mohican, was an unbroken forest. Jerome, and Benjamin Mills, who resided on the present site of Wooster, as Mr. Finley supposes, were the only white people in that part of Wayne county. He became quite intimate with Jerome, and exchanged many articles of food with him, and was indebted to him for many acts of friendship. The Indian village was about one mile southwest of Jerome's cabin, and surrounded on three sides by almost impenetrable marshes, filled with alder and other swamp growths. The emigrants of 1810-11, state, "that the wigwams or huts were scattered over a space of eight or ten acres, with the undergrowth cut away, and a smooth play-ground in the center, which was much used as a bowling ground. Here the hunters and warriors amused themselves. The council house was located northwest of the village, and was some twenty-five feet wide and fifty feet long, covered with clapboards and bark. It was of poles and split timber." Years before the arrival of Mr. Finley, this village was conspicuous in the annals of the border wars. It was located near the ancient trail leading from Pittsburgh to Upper Sandusky, and many trembling captives ran the gauntlet in passing through it, on their way to the Indian towns in the northwest. This was the headquarters of those warriors of the Wolf tribe that still followed the fortunes of Captain Pipe. At that period, the Greentown Indians seemed quite intimate with the Jerometown branch of the *Delawares*, and often associated with them in celebrating their feasts.

In 1810, Mr. Finley was joined by Vachel and William Metcalf, Thomas and Joshua Oram, Benjamin and John Mackerel, James and Joseph Conelly, Elisha Chilcote, John Shinnabarger, and their families.

When the war of 1812 came, and the Indians commenced hostile demonstrations, Mr. Finley, and some of his neighbors, forted in Wooster. In 1813, he joined families and forted with his neighbor, John Shinnabarger, who had a strong cabin with port holes, one mile northwest of the present site of Tylertown. Save the affair at Colyer's, elsewhere alluded to, the settlement remained undisturbed. James Finley relates a number of amusing incidents connected with the flight of the pioneers to Wooster, and other places of safety. After proceeding some distance along a circuitous path, with his family, his father remembered that he had left some young calves in pens, and, fearing they would starve, returned to let them to the cows, and then attempted to pass straight through the forest to Wooster, eleven miles away, but soon became confused, and was out three days before he got to the fort, his family, in the meantime, arriving safely. At the same time, a neighbor, Mr. Jacob Lybarger, rolled his infant daughter in a small bed and took it on his back, proceeding rapidly on his way, followed by his wife, through the forests by narrow Indian trails. From the speed made by her husband, Mrs. Lybarger supposed the danger very imminent. Calling to her husband, who was some distance in advance, she said: "Jake—Jake, are you afraid?" He promptly responded, "No," and they hurried forward in the narrow path. In his flight, he dropped the infant, and his wife, coming up in haste, stumbled over it, exclaiming: "Jake, Jake, you need not tell me you are not afraid, for you have lost Maria out of the bed, and you didn't know it." The little daughter was speedily replaced, survived the war, and, upon arriving at womanhood, became the wife of the late Justus S. Weatherbee.

After the close of the war, Mr. Finley continued to reside on his farm until December, 1825, when he deceased, aged about fifty-nine years. During the early part of his residence on the Lake fork, it was navigable for small craft to the present site of Tylertown, known as Finley's bridge, where a structure of that sort spans the stream. Here the pioneers landed, making their way by forest paths to Orange, Montgomery, Perry, Vermillion and Mohican townships.

His family consisted of James, Benjamin, John, Hannah, Sarah, Abner, Rachel, Elizabeth, and Mary. James resides in Madison county, Missouri; Benjamin and John are deceased; Hannah (widow Glenn,) resides in Urbana, Illinois; Sarah, wife of Daniel Pocock, resides near Hayesville; Abner lives near Plympton, Holmes county, Ohio; Rachel, wife of Sparks Bird, near Mohicanville, Ashland county, Ohio; Elizabeth, wife of James Pocock, in Hayesville, Ohio; Mary, wife of Elijah Pocock, died near Hayesville.

Mrs. Mary Finley, wife of Alexander Finley, deceased March 23, 1856, aged about seventy-nine years.

MINE LA-MOTTE, April 10, 1876.

George W. Hill, Esq.:

I was absent when your letter arrived, which accounts for not being answered sooner. Jerome settled on Mohican. When we came to the country, he was living at Jerometown, in a small cabin, a short distance from the Indian houses. He cultivated some six or eight acres of land, kept a few horses, cattle, and swine. He and the Indians did not get along well. They wished him to divide the products of his farm with them. This he refused to do, and the consequence was, when they got bad whiskey they whipped him. He built a cabin near the trail, on the east side of the stream, at the foot of Main street, in the present village of Jeromeville, having bought the land where Jeromeville now stands, where he kept a house of entertainment. In 1812, when the Indians were removed, he said he gave his squaw the privilege of going or staying with him. She chose to go with the Indians. He afterwards married a white woman. He sold his farm to Mr. Deardorff, and settled at Huron, in Huron county, and shortly after died. He commenced trading with the Indians when seventeen years old; but how long he continued a trader, I do not know. He was with the Indians in Wayne's campaign, but whether he was with them in Harmar's and St. Clair's, I do not know. The Indians did not have much cleared land. I never saw their field, but it was situated out of sight of the village. I think they had only a few small patches. The cleared land around the village was a lawn, well set with blue grass, and contained an occasional tree and a few shrubs—perhaps amounting to eight or ten acres. I was in the village during the residence of the Indians, some three or four times. It consisted of some fine cabins, about sixteen by eighteen feet, one story high, and a number of smaller huts or wigwams. The council house, I think, was a temporary building, built lodge fashion. I do not recollect of having seen it. I saw the wigwam of Captain Pipe. It was within the cleared space of the village. I have no recollection of wife or children. He appeared to be upwards of fifty years old. Was a tall, dark, and straight Indian. I never talked with him, perhaps father did, but I think not much, as Pipe was a surly, unrelenting enemy of the whites, and had little intercourse with them. I think he left early in the summer of 1812. I have no knowledge of Captain Pipe, jr. The Captain Pipe, jr., of Greentown, of whom you speak, must have been some other Pipe—perhaps a son. I know that the Captain Pipe I describe resided in Jerometown in the years 1809-10-11. I believe there were more Captain Pipes than one. I think Jerome said the Indians had been on Mohican about ten or twelve years previous to the white settlement; but of this I am not positive.

Very respectfully, yours,
JAMES FINLEY.

---

*The above is a letter from James Finley, in answer to one addressed him by the author, on the subject of the Indian settlement at Jerometown, asking him to be more definite concerning Jerome and Captain Pipe. It seems that Jerome had at first a cabin in or near the Indian village, but in consequence of bad whiskey, failed to agree with his red brethren. Mr. Finley remembers the wigwam of old Captain Pipe, but fails to recollect his wife or children. It is probable that Pipe lived alone. Captain Pipe, jr., of Greentown, was undoubtedly his son.

WILLIAM AND THOMAS EAGLE.

The following sketch was written by Dr. Thomas A. Eagle, jr., of Macon City, Missouri, in reply to a letter making certain inquiries concerning the first settlers of Mohican. It differs, in some degree, from the recollection of others, but, from his standpoint is, no doubt, reliable. He places the location of the Eagles in 1810. They were, undoubtedly, in Mohican in May, 1809. The forts alluded to were, probably, the Buren or Metcalf, and Shinabarger block-houses, and stockade.

"The whites commenced their first settlement in Mohican township in the spring of 1810. In that spring four families emigrated and settled in the rich and fertile valley of the Mohican. The first settlement was made on the west side of the stream, generally from one-half to one mile from it. Alexander Finley and family were the first emigrants. They arrived about two weeks before the families of Thomas Eagle and my father, William Eagle, who were met and cordially welcomed by Mr. Finley. Mr. Finley and family brought with them, for the use of father and family, a bucket of butter-milk and a fine corn-pone, which was quite a treat, and thankfully received. This was their first meeting and acquaintance. It was very pleasant and cordial, and ripened into an attachment that grew stronger from day to day, and was never chilled by jealousies or broils. Their limited means, dangers, and dependence upon each other, had the effect to cement the friendship. Their families imbibed the same feeling, and, to-day, the descendants of these pioneers look back to their childhood days, on the banks of the Mohican, with feelings of delight. Surrounded by dangers and enured to hardships, they learned to think for themselves, and acquired courage to accomplish the task they had undertaken. It was no place for faint hearts or irresolution. They were forty miles from the settlements and in the midst of red men, who generally treated them kindly until the war of 1812. The first settlers were, religiously, of the Methodists and Presbyterians. The Finleys and Eagles were exemplary members, and their children became members of one or the other of these churches. My father, William Eagle, remained in Mohican township, on the farm on which he settled, until the spring of 1855, when he removed to Iowa, and from thence to Missouri, and died in Kirksville, aged seventy-six years.

"In the winter of 1862 my mother died in her ninety-second year. They were natives of Virginia. They had seven children—four are dead, and three living: one, Elizabeth Culbertson, resides in Iowa—She was the first white child born in Mohican, February 20, 1811—Mary Montgomery, wife of Jonathan Montgomery, of Macon, Missouri, and myself.

"The *Delaware* Indians inhabited Mohican at the time of the opening of the war of 1812, and were regarded as hostile and treacherous. At that time the white settlers had become pretty numerous, and were much annoyed at the presence of the Indians. The alarms were frequent, sometimes well founded, and at others false. When the murders on the Black fork took place, by the Indians, the inhabitants of the Jerome fork erected two block-houses, one a few hundred yards north of my father's house (William Eagle), and one two miles north. The one north was known as the Hellar block-house. When it looked threatening, the settlers sought safety in the block-houses and stockades. The Indians were tampered by a Frenchman by the name of Jerome, who was married to a squaw. He had been trading with them several years, and had a post at what is now Jeromeville. The place was named after him. During the Indian troubles it was agreed that there should be no shooting at the block-houses unless in case of alarm, for the benefit of those at work on their improvements. Late one afternoon the citzens heard shooting at Hellar's block-house. They hastened to depart to General Beall's army at Wooster, as it was thought impracticable to reach the fort. Father, with his family, started. Mother Eagle was sick in bed, unable to travel on foot. Sometimes she was held on a horse, and at others carried on the route. My oldest sister (Mary) was then a small child, and also had to be carried. When they arrived at the Mohican, the canoe was on the opposite side. Mr. Finley had arrived and crossed, and concealed his family on the opposite side of the stream, supposing that the fleeing families were Indians in pursuit of him. Finding it impossible to cross, father went down the stream and the family secreted south of what is now Finley's bridge, for the night. I have often heard father relate this adventure while my childish fears were aroused. The family were not molested, and reached their destination in safety.

"After the close of the war, the settlers of Mohican were compelled to undergo many privations. For several years they had to go thirty or forty miles to mill, on pack-horses, following the Indian trails as best they could, or in canoes, down the Lake fork of Mohican and up Owl creek to Shrimplin's mill, and by-paths to Apple creek, in Wayne county. Some may conclude that the first settlers would be gloomy and despondent. Such was not the fact. Amidst toil and dangers they would have their sport. On one occasion, when there was an alarm, it was thought the Indians were approaching. The citizens convened at James Colyer's, about one mile east of the Mohican. In the night they heard a noise which they imagined to be the Indians. In great haste, each seized his gun and took position to be ready for the bloody contest; but one of their number, on attempting to place the guards, was found to be missing. The missing youth had professed great anxiety to meet the savage foe. Search was made, and the brave (?) boy was found secreted beneath a bed, half frightened out of his wits; when asked what he was doing, he said he was in search of the short gun. The gun was noted for its extreme shortness, and the brave young man was afterwards known as the "short gun hero."

As for myself, I was born April 5, 1819, in Mohican township. Read medicine in Ashland, under George W. How, M. D. I practiced several years in Mohican, Iowa, one year in California, two years in Fairfield, and in 1857 moved to Macon county, Missouri. I made, that year, the first "free soil" speech ever made in the county, for which my life was threatened. In 1864 I was elected to the legislature for two years, and re-elected in 1866, and served four years. In 1868 I was elected sheriff and county collector for two years. Since that time I have been engaged in the practice of medicine. I was the youngest of the family of William Eagle."

THE COULTERS.

Thomas Coulter was born August 9, 1766, in the State of New York. His father, John Coulter, was a native of Ireland, and came to America when a youth and married Abigail Parshall, a native of the State of New York. His paternal ancestors, therefore, were Scotch-Irish, and those on his mother's side were Hollanders, and were among the early settlers of New Amsterdam. The home of John Coulter and his wife, after leaving New York, was near Sunbury, Northumberland county, Pennsylvania, but in a short time they were driven thence by the Indians, at the time of the Wyoming massacre (1779), their house and grain being consumed by fire and their cattle driven away by the Indians and tories. The father of Tom Jelloway, since a Greentown Indian, was then living in the Wyoming valley, and, being friendly to the whites, warned them of their danger; and among the number saved was the Coulter family. As soon as the perils of the times were over they turned their faces toward the West, and made a home near Ginger Hill, in Washington county, Pennsylvania. In 1788, Thomas Coulter, and his father, John Coulter, took a cargo of flour, fruit, etc., down the Ohio river to Maysville, then Limestone, Kentucky, where they disposed of their load. While there, they were both attacked with small-pox, which proved fatal to the father. After Thomas was sufficiently recovered, he started for home, on foot, having previously sold the boat. One day, as he was pursuing "his solitary way," he was overtaken by the notorious renegade, Simon Girty, armed with all the weapons peculiar to the savage *Senecas*, with whom he then lived as an adopted member of the tribe. Mr. Coulter knew him, and not relishing or desiring his company, resolved to get rid of him by stratagem. Under some slight pretext he stepped behind Girty, cocked his rifle, and told him if he moved either to the right or left, or offered any resistance whatever, he would be a dead man. Girty was taken by surprise, and obeyed orders; and they marched all that day along the paths through an unbroken wilderness, until they reached a settlement, when Mr. Coulter gladly gave up his prisoner. Some time after his return he joined a volunteer company under Colonel Morgan, and went to White River, Indiana, to aid in subduing the Indians who were committing depredations upon the white inhabitants of the frontier settlements in Kentucky. After an absence of a few months he again returned home, and in a short time married Miss Nancy Tannahill, the marriage occurring August, 1789. In 1797 he moved to Butler county, Pennsylvania, where he remained until about the year 1806, when he settled in Jefferson county, Ohio. After remaining there a few years he finally emigrated to Richland county, then a part of Knox county, and settled near the present site of Perrysville, in Ashland county. The town of Perrysville was laid out by Thomas Coulter, June 10, 1813, with the intention of naming it Coulterville; but after Perry's victory on Lake Erie, he changed his intention, and called the village Perrysville, in honor of the naval achievement of Commodore Perry. When Richland county was organized, he was appointed one of the associate judges by the general assembly of Ohio. Mr. Coulter was a member of the Presbyterian church of Perrysville, and one of the first elders. He died as he lived—a consistent Christian, and zealous for the growth and prosperity of the church of his choice. He died October 24, 1844, and was buried in Perrysville cemetery, aged nearly seventy-nine years. He was the father of seven children, viz.: John, Rachel, Abigail, David, Melzer, Nancy, and Thomas.

John Coulter was born September 13, 1790, in Washington county, Pennsylvania, and was the oldest son of Judge Thomas Coulter. His education was obtained principally in the common schools of the time. He frequently spoke in the highest terms of one of his teachers, the Rev. Mr. McMillen, one of the pioneers of Presbyterianism in western Pennsylvania, and particularly in Washington county. Among the pupils of this good man was Rev. John Coulter, brother of Judge Coulter, who was pastor of the church of Concord, in the presbytery of Butler, more than forty years. Also, of Walter Lowrie, of blessed memory. John Coulter came to Richland, then a part of Knox county, in the fall of 1810, in company with Edward Haley, a young man employed by Judge Coulter to accompany him. They began their labors upon a farm a little southeast of the present site of Perrysville, in October, and continued their work until they had made several thousand rails, built a cabin, cleared out ten acres of ground, set out fruit trees, etc., after which they returned to their homes in Jefferson county, Ohio. In the following spring, 1811, John Coulter, and the rest of his father's family, removed to the cabin in the wilderness which had been erected the fall before. This cabin afterwards became the Coulter block-house, and, while used as such, John Coulter acted as one of the scouts to watch the proceedings of the Indians. Early in the fall of 1812 he went with a surveying party to open a road from Cleveland to Mansfield. This road is now known as the Harrisville and Cleveland road, and passes through the town of Ashland. On Saturday evening, after having commenced the survey, they had reached Chippewa lake, in Medina county, and were encamped for the night. Mr. McArthur, one of the commissioners to locate the road, was also captain of an independent company, and while there a messenger rode into camp with orders for Captain McArthur's company to return immediately to Cleveland, at the same time bringing the news of the surrender of General Hull at Detroit, this being the first intimation they had of the event, although it occurred on the sixteenth of August, 1812, some weeks prior to the survey. The surveying party was, therefore, disbanded, a part of which returned to Cleveland, and a part to the Black fork of the Mohican. Every one of the few settlements they passed on their way home was deserted, the cabins standing silent and tenantless. How their hearts must have sunk within them when they thought of the possible fate of their loved ones. But when they reached the block-house they found the several families of the settlers gathered there for safety, and learned that the Zimmer family had been murdered by the Greentown, or other Indians, the night before. While they were encamped at Chippewa lake, they heard the noise of chopping on the other side, and, as they afterward found the Harris settlement deserted, from which they supposed the noise to proceed, Mr. Coulter was strongly of the opinion that the Indians who killed the Zimmers were encamped there. The details concerning the great flight to the block-houses at Clinton's, Lewis', Beam's, Oliver's, Coulter's, Jerome's, Priest's, Eagle's, and Metcalf's, are given in the sketch of the war of 1812, where Mr. Coulter's experiences are referred to.

In the fall of 1813 Mr. Coulter and Captain Ebenezer Rice took the job of continuing the survey and opening of the same road, from Trickle's cabin, the late location of the Markley brick residence, just east of Ashland, to the Black fork. While thus employed, Mr. Coulter killed a large black wolf. After the completion of the contract, early in the year 1814, Captain Rice walked to Chillicothe to receive the money, ninety dollars, which was due them, also, four dollars which the law of Ohio allowed for each wolf scalp.

On the seventh of April, 1814, John Coulter was married by Rev. James Scott, a Presbyterian minister of Mount Vernon, to Betsey Rice, eldest daughter of Captain Ebenezer Rice. In September, 1814, the young couple moved to their own home, a cabin on a quarter of land which joined Captain Rice's. In the summer of 1815, Mrs. Coulter taught the first school in Green township, and, we believe, in what is now Ashland county, and took spinning and weaving as her pay for tuition. She said it was a great accommodation to her, as she did not understand spinning and weaving as well as teaching. Mrs. Coulter (Betsey Rice) was born January 27, 1797, in New Salem, Worcester township, Hampshire county, Massachusetts. She came with her father's family, Captain Ebenezer Rice, to Newark, Licking county, Ohio, in 1810, and, in February, 1811, he settled near the present site of Perrysville, in Ashland county, then part of Knox county. Mrs. Coulter is now (1878) a resident of Congress, Wayne county, and although far advanced in years, possesses perfectly all her mental faculties and a fair degree of physical force.

In June, 1814, John Coulter and his brother-in-law, James Moore, descended the Black fork, Walhonding, and Muskingum, in a canoe, to Zanesville, on a shopping expedition; and from the bill of goods we learn that six small dinner plates cost one dollar and fifty cents; six cups and saucers, one dollar and seventy-five cents; an earthen teapot, one dollar and twenty-five cents; a little blue creamer (still in existence), sixty-two and one-half cents, etc., etc. In the spring of 1815 he and David Hill went in a canoe to the mouth of Owl creek, to one of Johnny Appleseed's nurseries, and brought up five hundred apple trees, which produced excellent fruit.

Mr. Coulter was a man of sterling intergity, sound judgment, warm and true in his friendships; and in consequence of these qualities the people often honored him with office. When the project of erecting the new county of Vermillion was agitated, Mr. Coulter was sent to Columbus some two or three sessions of the legislature, to work up the claims of the new county. He afterwards served on the State board of equalization for real estate, and was the first assessor of personal property of the eastern half of Richland county, and was the first coroner. He was twice elected justice of the peace in Green township, Ashland county, and twice in Washington township, Richland county, besides to many minor offices, all the duties of which he discharged with fidelity and honor.

In November, 1817, he and his wife united with the Methodist Episcopal church, under the ministry of Rev. John Sommerville, and Mrs. Coulter and their eldest child, Rumina, were baptized the same day. A few years afterward they united with the Presbyterian church, in communion and fellowship of which they walked together until the death of Mr. Coulter, which occurred in Perrysville, October 2, 1873. He had reached the ripe old age of eighty-two years and seventeen days, and had lived with the wife of his youth nearly sixty years. The purity of his acts certified to the sincerity of his professions, and his long and busy life closed calmly and peacefully. His grave is made in Perrysville, where he spent the strength of his early manhood.

Mr. Coulter was the father of ten children, only four of whom survive, viz.: C. C. Coulter, of Perrysville, Captain J. N. Coulter, of Glidden, Carroll county, Iowa, Elizabeth R., wife of A. D. Zimmerman, of Shreve, Wayne county, Ohio, and Nancy L., wife of Rev. Franklin Eddy, of Congress, Wayne county, Ohio. The names of the deceased are: Cyrenius M., Rumina, wife of Dr. J. H. Register, Sebastian C., and Martha R., all buried at Perrysville, and Lucina, wife of David Ewing, of Hayesville, Martin Van Buren, who died at Miliken's Bend, Louisiana, in the One Hundred and Twentieth Ohio volunteer infantry, in 1863.*

JOSEPH CHANDLER

was born near Black Rock, Baltimore county, Maryland, May 20, 1798, and came with his parents to Jefferson county, Ohio, in 1809, where he resided a short time, and removed to Tuscarawas county, and settled near the village of New Philadelphia, and having purchased a piece of wild land at the office in Canton, he came to Perry township, then in Wayne, but now in Ashland county. He came with his father, Joseph Chandler, sr., and his brothers, Thomas and Robert F., to improve it, in the spring of 1812. The farm was situated about two miles north of the Indian village, then known as Mohican Johnstown. The village contained a council house and about sixty or eighty pole lodges or wigwams, and was located near the old Wyandot trail, and about one mile southwest of the present site of Jeromeville, and on the west side of the stream. At the same time he found a Frenchman named John Baptiste Jerome living with a squaw, a sister of the chief, George Hamilton, in a neat log cabin near the site of the present gristmill, at the west end of Main street. Mr. Chandler, in the summer of 1812, worked occasionally for Jerome, and considered him an impulsive, clever Frenchman. He had taught his wife to cook and keep house like the white women, and Mr. Chandler regarded her as a good housekeeper, considering her opportunities. Jerome seemed much attached to his Indian wife. He formerly lived as a trader in the village, but stated that the warriors got fire-water, and frequently abused him, hence, he cleared a small farm and raised horses and other stock, and cultivated a cornfield on the bottom. He entered one hundred and sixty acres of land, where Jeromeville now stands. He had great numbers of swine, horses and cows running in the forests. In fact, his stock ranged in the woods in great numbers. Jerome had a daughter, aged about fifteen years, named Mary or Mollie, who had received her name from a Catholic priest at her baptism, near Detroit, Michigan. Jerome repeatedly rehearsed his military exploits in the campaigns against Harmar, St. Clair and Wayne, in the presence of the whites, and stated that Captain Pipe and his *Delawares* had been in all those battles and glutted their vengeance against the white invaders.

Mr. Chandler thinks there is no doubt of the return of Captain Pipe to Jerome's village, one mile west of the stream, and of his having a wigwam at that point, where it was pointed out in 1812. Pipe, he thinks, went to the British in the spring of 1812, as he was not seen after the war began. His son resided at Greentown, until removed by Captain Douglass. After the assassination of the Zimmer, Ruffner, and Copus families on the Black fork, Jerome's wife and daughter were sent with the Greentown Indians to Urbana, where, during the winter of 1812-13, she and her daughter died from exposure, and Jerome was imprisoned for a short time in the block-house at Wooster. Jerome sold the village site, and married another wife, and removed to the mouth of the Huron river, where he died shortly afterwards.

In the fall of the year 1812, Joseph Chandler, sr., and sons returned to Tuscarawas county, where they remained until the close of the war, and then re-occupied their cabin in Perry, where his father deceased, May, 1815, aged sixty years, leaving a widow and six sons: Thomas, Robert F., Joseph, Shadrac, Jacob, and John; and four daughters: Rebecca, Eleanor, Henrietta, and Alice. Joseph Chandler resided, at the time of his

---

* NOTE.—We are indebted to Mrs. Rev. Eddy, of Congress, Wayne county, for most of the items of this personal sketch. It is quite valuable as a family reminiscence, and for the light it sheds upon the pioneer transactions of 1812.

DAVID CARTER,

son of Daniel Carter, sr., was born in Montgomery township, on the old homestead in section twenty-eight, March 18, 1815. He was the first white child born in the township. It has been heretofore stated, on what should have been good authority, that the first white child born in Montgomery township was Lorin Andrews, but this is a mistake, as he was not born until 1819, four years later than David Carter. Sarah Carter was born in 1816, and William Sheets in the early part of 1819, so that Lorin Andrews was the fourth instead of the first child born in the township.

Daniel Carter, sr., was born in Baltimore county, Maryland, December 25, 1776, and was married in Bedford county, Pennsylvania, to Ann Snyder. They came to Ohio in 1806, and she died in the block-house at Jeromeville in 1813, leaving eight children: John, William, Daniel, Rachel, Elizabeth, James, George, and Anna. Mr. Carter subsequently married Ruth Warner, March 9, 1814. She came with her parents to Mohican township in 1810 or 1811. Seven more children were the result of this marriage—David, Sarah, Mary, Samuel, Miranda, Milton, and Charles.

David Carter attended the subscription schools of the time, a few terms at the district schools, and one term at the Norwalk seminary, after which he became a teacher for one term. On December 26, 1837, he was married to Miss Elizabeth Griffith, of Fayette county, Pennsylvania, by whom he has had three children, all of whom died in infancy.

Mr. Carter was first lieutenant in a volunteer infantry company in 1841, and held that office some seven years. He was afterwards sergeant-major of the regiment, and finally became quartermaster. He was for some three years aide-de-camp to General Meredith, who commanded the First brigade of the Eleventh division of Ohio militia, of Richland county, in which capacity he served until the brigade was divided. In 1861 he volunteered as a private soldier in company I, of the Sixty-fourth Ohio volunteer infantry, in which he served until March, 1862, when he was ordered home on a discharge furlough, and was never ordered back to his regiment, nor was he discharged.

Mr. Carter and his wife are members of the Methodist Episcopal church. In politics he abides by the doctrines of Andrew Jackson. He now lives on the old homestead, within a few rods of the place where stood the old log cabin in which he was born. He has never known any home other than this.

death, on the old homestead. He often alluded to the wonderful change that had occurred in Perry township since his arrival in 1812, now sixty-eight years ago. First, he states that the first grist-mill was erected by John Raver, in Rowsburgh; second, the first school-house of round logs was in the west part of Perry; third, the first teacher was John G. Mosier, who died near Ashland in 1856; fourth, the first dry goods store, Michael Row, in Rowsburgh; fifth, the first blacksmith, Adam Tener; sixth, the first carpenters, Isaac Smalley and James Scott; seventh, the first carding machine, at Rowsburgh, by Mr. McConayha; eighth, the first tanner, George McFadden; ninth, the first wagon-maker, Andrew Casebeer, at Buchanan's corners; Tenth, the first church at Mt. Hope on Muddy fork; eleventh, the first Presbyterian preacher, Rev. Mr. Brown.

Mr. Chandler has always been a practical farmer, and resided on his father's old homestead. He was an exemplary member of the Methodist church for a period of over forty years, was a good citizen, and noted for his frugality and integrity. His family have all grown, and are much scattered. He saw the country when a wilderness, and has noted its wonderful changes, its wealth and prosperity, and trusted that the descendants of the pioneers would remember the hardships of their parents, and live frugal, moral and useful lives, and preserve the institutions of their fathers, untarnished by corruption and tyranny.

He was three times married. In 1825 to Amelia Jones, of Jefferson county, Ohio; she died in 1825. In 1827 he married Elizabeth Farnham, of Knox county. She died in 1850, and was the mother of Lafayette, John, Marion, Joseph, Farnham and Elizabeth. In 1852 he married Margaret Beattie, of Vermillion township. The children were Orin, Mitchell, and Franklin. His last wife still survives to mourn his loss.

Mr. Chandler suffered but a short time. He had grown greatly in flesh, and would weigh nearly three hundred pounds. He had been afflicted for several years with a chronic trouble, that finally cut short his days. He became a member of the Ashland County Historical Society in 1875, and took especial interest in rehearsing the early times and occurrences in the county. It will be difficult to fill his place in the society, as well as in the community, where he resided. He was a good man, and will be much lamented. Peace to his ashes and rest to his soul.

DANIEL CARTER, SR.,

was born in Baltimore county, Maryland, and moved, when young, with his mother to Huntingdon county, Pennsylvania, in the year 1774. He emigrated to near Canton, Stark county, Ohio, in 1806, and then to what is now Montgomery township, Ashland county, in January, 1812, stopping a few days with John Carr, who had a cabin adjoining the farm of Baptiste Jerome, until the erection of his cabin, and entered it with his family in February, 1812. The circumstances attending the erection of his cabin, and its first and second abandonment; his flight to New Philadelphia; his return, and his seeking safety, for several months, for himself and family, at the block-house at Jerome's place, now Jeromeville, have been described in former chapters. The death of his wife and son James, has also been spoken of in connection with his residence at the block-house. About the time he left the block-house he sold the tract of land northeast of the present site of Ashland, to Conrad Kline and John Heller, and purchased four quarters, some two miles south of his original purchase, upon one of which he located, having, in the meantime, married Miss Ruth Warner. Mr. Carter continued to reside on the new purchase until February 7, 1854, when, after a brief illness, he died at the advanced age of eighty years. Mrs. Carter, his second wife, survived him eight or nine years. Mr. Carter was an industrious, frugal and upright man. He had been a very faithful member of the Methodist church for over sixty years. His children, by his first wife, were—John, William, Daniel, Rachel, Elizabeth, James, George, and Anna; by his second—David, Sarah, Mary, Samuel, Miranda, Milton, and Charles. Daniel, David, and Samuel, are residents of Montgomery township, and three daughters reside within the county. All the rest have moved elsewhere.

Daniel Carter, jr., is a citizen of Ashland. His pioneer experiences are as exciting and interesting as those of any settler of that period. When about eleven years of age, he states his father dispatched him with a sack of shelled corn, on horseback, through the forest, to Odell's mill, in the south part of what is now Lake township, to have it ground into meal. This was early in the spring of 1812. Pipe and his *Delawares* had not yet left Mohican Johnstown. On his return in the evening, being belated by the difficulty of winding his way along the Indian paths, he reached the Indian village a little after dark, and seeing a number of Indians collected for a sort of council at the council house, he stopped to witness the performances. It was at this "pow-wow" that the "red-stick," of Tecumseh was rejected by "Old Captain Pipe." He returned to his father's cabin, however, without molestation by the Indians, who, at that time, were on friendly terms with their white neighbors. Mr. Carter relates many adventures, amid the forest, in his youthful days, of a thilling character. He married Miss Eliza Slocum, daughter of another leading pioneer of a later period.

David Carter was born March 18, 1815, on the homestead in section twenty-eight, Montgomery township. He is believed to be the first male child born in Montgomery township. He married Miss Elizabeth Griffith, of Fayette county, Pennsylvania, December 26, 1837. He resides on the old Carter homestead, and is a farmer by occupation. His children—three—deceased in infancy. He is a man of good natural attainments, and possesses a fund of pioneer experiences.

JOHN GREENLEE.*

John Greenlee was born in Crawford county, Pennsylvania, near French creek, in 1804. William Greenlee, his father, visited Ohio in the spring of 1811, and located a farm near James L. Priest, in that part of Lake township subsequently annexed to Washington township, Holmes county. In making that trip on horseback, he passed down the banks of the Ohio river to Wellsburgh, Virginia, crossed at the ferry, and traveled west to Cadiz, thence to Cambridge, thence to Zanesville, thence up the banks of the Muskingum river to the village of Coshocton, thence up the bank of the White-woman to the Lake fork, and thence through an unbroken forest, by Indian paths, to the cabin of James L. Priest. Mr. Priest had been a neighbor in Crawford county, Pennsylvania, and had located near what is now "Priest's Prairie," in the summer of 1809. After a stay of ten or fifteen days, Mr. Greenlee became so pleased with the country that he resolved to select and locate upon a tract of land near Mr. Priest. He returned to Pennsylvania, and arranged for removing his family to Ohio. By the first of October, 1811, he had completed his arrangements, and commenced his journey through the forests with one two-horse and one four-horse covered wagon, loaded with household goods, provisions, grain, and his family, consisting of his wife and seven children—six girls and one boy, John. He also brought a few head of cows. He crossed the Ohio river, and came by the trail through Canton, Massillon, and Wooster, all mere villages, the trail being narrow and but little traveled. There were but few cabins along the route, and he was compelled to camp by the way-side, pretty nearly the entire distance. When he arrived at the village of Wooster, he found no opened path to the Priest cabin, and hence preceded his teams with an ax, cutting the undergrowth and prepared a wagon road. In this way his progress was slow, and it took the major part of one month to perform the entire journey. He finally arrived safely, and was assisted by his old friend, and eight or ten friendly Indians, among whom were Thomas Jelloway, Tom Lyon, Billy Dowdee, Thick-necked John, Monos, and Billy Montour, and a few white men, in putting up a cabin.

The pioneer families within a circuit of six miles are believed to have been, at that time, Mr. Finley, Mr. Eagle, Samuel Marvin, William and John Hendrickson, Elijah Bolling, William Greenlee, and James L. Priest. The cabins of Messrs. Priest and Greenlee were near the old Huron trail, and great numbers of *Delawares*, from Sandusky, Green and Jerometown, passed on their way to and from the old Indian settlement on the Tuscarawas during the fall of 1811 and the spring of 1812, but all remained quiet and friendly until after Hull's surrender at Detroit, in August, 1812. This was followed by the removal of the Green and Jerometown *Delawares*, and the assassination of Ruffner, the Zimmers, and James Copus, by the hostile Indians from Sandusky. The pioneers, in the Priest neighborhood, converted Mr. Priest's double cabin into a block-house, and enclosed by pickets about one-fourth of an acre of ground around it. The fort was a few hundred yards west of the Lake fork, and near where the railroad crosses that stream. The settlers near Odell's lake joined those of the Priest settlement, in the erection of the stockade, and came there for safety. The families who entered the fort were those of James L. Priest, William Greenlee, William and John Hendrickson, Elijah Bolling, Samuel Marvin, Nathan Odell, Joshua and Thomas Oram, and Elijah Chilcoat. The settlers remained in the fort but a short time, and returned to their cabins. The fort, however, remained a sort of headquarters for the little colony during the continuance of the war, although the red men of the northwest failed to put in an appearance. While the war progressed, in 1813, Mr. John Greenlee relates that on the tenth of September he distinctly heard the roar of artillery in the naval engagement between Perry and the British commodore on Lake Erie; but, although the day was clear, supposed at first it was a heavy storm or hurricane in the northwest. In a few days the news of Perry's triumph was heralded over the country.

In a short time, the settlement was increased by the arrival of John, Henry, and Reuben Newkirk, James Gray, Thomas Baker, Mr. Ellsworth, John, Jacob, Alexander, and George Emrich, Peter Wycoff, John Smith, George Marks, Jabez Smith, and Robert Chandler. In 1824 William Greenlee sold his farm to Calvin Hibbard, and purchased the homestead on section fourteen, southwest quarter. Here William Greenlee died in 1854, aged eighty two years and three and a half months, and at his decease John Greenlee came into possession of the homestead. John Greenlee married Miss Susannah Warner, of Lake township, August 10, 1836, and resided on the homestead about sixty-three years. He was a successful and thrifty farmer, a good citizen, an upright and honest man. He did his full share in improving highways, building school-houses, erecting churches, and in supporting public charities. His family was numerous, consisting of thirteen children, a part of whom, with his beloved wife, survive him. Mr. Greenlee, after a brief illness, deceased on the eighteenth of June, 1877, and was followed to the grave, his final resting place, by a large number of his old neighbors and friends.

When he entered Lake township, that part of the county was covered with its native forest, and abounded in wolves, bear, deer, and in other wild animals. The shrill yells of the red man often echoed amid the wilds, as he passed up and down the ancient trails. These have long since disappeared, for new men and new ideas. Civilization, with school-houses, villages, churches, railroads, and other improvements, has taken possession of the land. How great the change, even in a life-time of sixty-four years! The Indian has gone toward the setting sun to find his last retreat; the forest and the hunter's sport have gone, in exchange for the delightful pursuits of agriculture, and the independence of a farmer's home.

---

* This sketch was prepared by a committee appointed by the Historical Society of Ashland county, consisting of Andrew Moss, George W. Urie, and George W. Hill.

ROBERT F. CHANDLER

was born in Baltimore county, Maryland, September 4, 1795, and removed with his father's family to Jefferson county, Ohio, in 1810, and shortly after, to Tuscarawas county, where he remained until the spring of 1812. At this time the father, Joseph Chandler, sr., and his sons Thomas, Joseph, jr., and Robert F., went to Perry township, then in Wayne county, to improve lands previously entered at Canton land office. The location is now where Joseph Chandler, jr., resides, about two miles north of Jeromeville, on the east side of Mohican. When the Chandlers landed, the *Delawares* were quite numerous, but harmless. They had a village about one mile southwest of the present site of Jeromeville, on the west side of the stream, known as Mohican Johnstown. The village contained a council house and about sixty or eighty pole lodges or wigwams, and was located near the old Wyandot trail. The village was a common resort of hostile *Wyandots* on their warlike excursions to western Pennsylvania and Virginia, in the days of the border wars. Many white captives had been led up the old trail, by the village, from 1780 to 1795. The Indians had cleared some fifteen or twenty acres of bottom land, which the squaws cultivated in corn, after the Indian manner. The village was west of the stream, on lands now owned by Dr. Yocum. About one mile northeast of the village, a Frenchman by the name of John Baptiste Jerome, resided in a comfortable cabin, having an Indian wife and a daughter aged about fifteen years. He also had horses, cattle and swine, and had cleared about thirty or forty acres of bottom land along the stream at the west side of what is now Jeromeville, on which he raised corn, and supplied many of the early pioneers with seed corn. When Mr. Chandler landed, the Indians, mostly *Delawares*, were quite friendly, and often came to see him in his cabin and clearing. He was a Quaker in dress and faith, and the Indians manifested a good deal of interest in his safety and success. The Chandlers immediately set about clearing a piece of land on the bottom, (near where they erected a cabin,) which he planted in corn.

About the time of Hull's surrender at Detroit, August 16, 1812, the friendly Indians notified Chandler of approaching danger, and he and his sons deemed it prudent to leave. They returned to Tuscarawas county, to near where New Philadelphia now stands, where they remained with the family until the close of the war. In the meantime, Robert F. returned to Jefferson county, where he remained until about 1815, when he again rejoined his father's family and returned to the Mohican, and continued improvements on their old homestead. In May, 1815, the Chandler family, father, mother and sons, removed to their wilderness home. Two years afterwards his father, Joseph Chandler, sr., sickened and died. His mother survived until 1852, and died at an advanced age. Robert F. continued to reside near Jeromeville until 1834, when he purchased and carried on what was then known as Smith's mill, near Mohicanville. This mill he continued, with certain improvements, to carry on about thirty years, and finally disposed of it and purchased the farm where he deceased, and turned farmer. Mr. Chandler was a friendly, genial pioneer, and in his primal days delighted to dwell upon the incidents of pioneer life sixty-eight or seventy years ago. Being a miller for many years, and possessing good conversational powers, he became acquainted with nearly all the early settlers of the south part of the county, and, when in the humor, a very interesting talker. He was never a member of any church, regarding it his duty to treat all men justly, and believing that when his career should end on earth, that the Supreme Ruler of the universe would reward such a life. He looked kindly upon all men, and desired to so live that he might have a conscience free of offence when called home.

He married young, when about twenty years of age, Miss Charlotte Jones, April 25, 1816. This lady deceased September 19, 1819; and in January, 1825, he married Miss Hannah Winbigler, who died February 25, 1875. His family consisted of Charles and Eleanor, of his first wife, and Robert, William, Joshua, Shadrac, Hannah, Joseph, Charlotte, Sarah, Rebecca, John, and Jasper, by his second wife. All these were living when this sketch was written, in 1876, except John and Jasper. His family are much scattered, and many reside in the far west.

Among the incidents of his life, Mr. Chandler took much pleasure in relating the following: When a young man, during his residence in Tuscarawas county, he became acquainted with a number of *Delaware* Indians, formerly from Greentown, upon the Black fork. At a hilarious gathering, near Goshen, in Tuscarawas county, a number of *Delawares* joined in the sport of wrestling, running and hopping. A tall, powerful Indian, formerly from Greentown, by the name of Philip Kennotchy, challenged Mr. Chandler to wrestle at arms-length—Indians never taking back-hold. Mr. Chandler being always full of conceit, and very ambitious and atheletic, and weighing at the time about two hundred pounds, accepted the banter. The parties selected the ground, and took hold as agreed, Mr. Chandler supposing himself superior to all rivals at arms-length; but the giant grasp of the big *Delaware* soon convinced him that he had a full match. They twisted, tripped and struggled for thirty or forty minutes, until nearly exhausted, without apparent advantage to either. Mr. Chandler became very much enraged and quite desperate, while Kennotchy remained calm and resolute, and finally compelled him to ask a cessation of the struggle, which Kennotchy was willing to do. Mr. Chandler said that at one time, that he was so much enraged that he felt like striking the Indian; but, in his calmer moments, he is now satisfied that he refrained from all violence, because the Indian would have undoubtedly overpowered and severely punished him. In connection with this Indian, he gave a very interesting detail of the Ruffner-Zimmer assassinations, on the Black fork, in the fall of 1812. Kennotchy was very fond of fire-water, and while under its influence, gave full particulars of the Black fork murders. He stated that he was one of the number that killed Martin Ruffner, Frederick Zimmer, the old lady, and Kate. After leaving the cabin and passing up the ravine, the Indians held a council, when Kennotchy returned and dispatched the white squaw, meaning "Kate," with his tomahawk, the other Indians protesting, when he claimed to have "brave heart." This is the most valuable information ever obtained concerning the particulars of that fearful tragedy.

SPARKS BIRD.

Sparks Bird, son of John and Cassandra Bird, was born at Redstone, Westmoreland county, Pennsylvania, February 9, 1797. His parents removed to Jefferson county, Ohio, about the year 1803, which, at that time, was very sparsely settled. The *Delawares* yet remained along the Tuscarawas river, in large numbers, and ranged the forests in quest of wild game. They often visited the cabin of the parents of Mr. Bird, but offered no threats or intimidations. In the spring of 1814, at the age of eighteen, young Bird left the parental roof in search of employment and fortune, and stopped a short time near the present city of Massillon. In the spring of 1815, he visited his uncle, General Beall, at Wooster, and obtained employment of him; and in 1816, in company with the general and the late Hon. Levi Cox, passed up the trail and visited the village of Loudonville, which at that time, contained but few cabins. They traveled over a good deal of the townships of Hanover, Green, and Lake, and he made choice of the southeast quarter of section seven, in Lake township, when he returned to Wooster and entered. He then entered the employ of General Beall, and worked at clearing and farming for some time. The farm of the general occupied most of the present site of Wooster, and Mr. Bird says he has plowed over the ground upon which some of the best residences of Wooster now stand. The old Wyandot trail, just at the south margin of the present city of Wooster, was then quite plainly marked by Indian travel. The trail was at that time much used by the *Delawares* and *Wyandots*, on their trading excursions to "Old Pitt," as the city was then called. It was not uncommon to see hundreds of red men, from the northwest, pass and re-pass the settlement about the block-house, every week, for four or five years after the war of 1812; but the spirit of the red man had been completely broken, and the hostiles had generally removed to Canadian soil, while the Montours, the Armstrongs, the Jonacakes, the Dowdees, and the Lyons still continued to range the forests of what is now Ashland county, in search of game.

During the period of his employment by General Beall, he became acquainted with the notorious John Driskel, who afterwards became the leader of a gang of desperadoes in Green township, of what is now Ashland county, that were the terror of law-abiding people. When Driskel first came to the settlement at Wooster, he was not considered a bad man, otherwise than somewhat quarrelsome when under the influence of corn whiskey. Associations and sprees with his gang of outlaws soon made him a dangerous man; and so rapid was his progress in crime that law-abiding citizens were compelled to defend themselves against the incursions of the villainous thieves and land pirates headed by him. The leading crimes of this bandit consisted in horse-stealing, incendiarism, and house-breaking. Driskel and his gang originated in Columbiana county, whence they gradually collected in Wayne county, and spread to Green township, in what was then Richland county. The boldness of their crimes created terror wherever they appeared. Driskel, the head of the banditti, is said to have been maimed by an encounter with Andrew Poe—having had the end of his nose bitten or cut off, which, added to his crimes, rendered him exceedingly repulsive in appearance. While residing in Wayne county, several of the gang were detected, convicted and sent to the penitentiary. Driskel was finally captured and sent to State prison; but, by some means, escaped, and, by the aid of his son John, and the two Brawdys, relations, and professional highwaymen and thieves, for a long time escaped recapture. Repeated acts of incendiarism in Green township, in which many barns, other buildings, hay and stock were consumed, and horses and cattle stolen, the indignant pioneers speedily organized a band of regulators, or a black cane company, to compel the Driskel gang to leave the country or suffer retaliation from an indignant and outraged community. The Driskel banditti, learning the state of public feeling, prepared to rejoin John Driskel, the head of the gang, who had been, in the meantime, captured, and on his way to Columbus had escaped and fled to Illinois, where his desperadoes hastened to rejoin him and renew their desperate vocations as a banditti, and where the Driskels finally expiated their crimes by being shot or hung by the regulators.

In September, 1820, Sparks Bird accompanied a surveying party to Michigan, as a chain carrier, and was employed in surveying several counties around Saginaw bay. On the return of the company, they were driven ashore in a violent snow storm; but all escaped from the wreck, suffering dreadfully from cold and wet. They finally reached Cleveland, almost exhausted, where they were kindly cared for. From thence he returned to Steubenville, and, in 1823, returned to Lake township, and commenced clearing and improving his farm, and put up a cabin. In 1824 he was joined by his brother William and family. He then commenced pioneer life in earnest—clearing, making rails, fencing, log-rolling, and raising cabins among the new settlers, being the chief employment. At this time wild game was quite abundant on Little Lake, and it was not uncommon for the pioneers to be serenaded by wolves. On one occasion, the Bird brothers had purchased a lot of chickens from a neighbor about one and a half miles distant, and, for convenience, had gone for them in the evening. After capturing them upon the roost, they had gone but a short distance along the winding paths in the directon of their own premises, when they were saluted by the unpleasant howl of wolves rapidly advancing upon their trail. The Bird brothers quickened their gait from a rapid walk to a run, as the wolves neared them in their flight. William Bird, being quite large and fleshy, kept up with Sparks, who was much lighter and more active, with difficulty. They hastened along the path, making all the speed of which they were capable, until Sparks caught his foot, tripped, and fell in some brush, but held his fowls, and finally escaped the wolves. He is of opinion that he must have made excellent time, for the voracious howlers remained about his cabin all night, in the hope of dining on his favorite poultry.

Mr. Bird was a good shot, and a successful hunter, and kept his table well supplied with both venison, turkeys, bear, and wild honey. His experiences as a hunter are much like other rangers of the forest in Ashland county. He often met Jonacake, Billy Dowdee, and other Indian inhabitants of Greentown, as they ranged over the hills of Lake.

He has lived continuously on his pioneer farm since he began to improve it in 1823-4. He has frequently been honored, by his fellow citizens, with township offices, having been elected trustee in 1838-9 and again from 1849 to 1855.

He married Eliza, daughter of the late Jacob Long, in 1832. She deceased in 1835. He married Charlotte Austin, of Jeromeville, in 1840. She died in 1860. In 1864 he married Rachel, youngest daughter of the late Alexander Finley, the first pioneer of Mohican.

In 1832 the parents of Mr. Bird located in Clearcreek township, and his mother, Mrs. Cassandra Bird, was one of the first organizing members of the Presbyterian church of Clearcreek, then a branch of "Old Hopewell," in Montgomery. John Bird, father of Sparks, resided near Savannah, from 1832 to 1839, and was a soldier under General St. Clair, in his disastrous expedition against the *Shawnees* and their confederates, on the Miami, November 4, 1791, but was so fortunate as to escape that massacre.

Sparks Bird, although far advanced in years, possesses a good deal of mental and physical vigor, and may survive to relate his pioneer experiences for many years.

BILLY DOWDEE.

The old Delaware hunter, Billy Dowdee, visited the cabin of Allen Oliver, father of Lewis, in the spring of 1812, a few months before the removal of the Greentown Indians. Dowdee, with his squaw and six or seven children, encamped at the mouth of a rivulet, half a mile above Mr. Oliver, where it empties into the Black fork. The old warrior had hunted for some time, over the hills and along the valleys of Green township, but with ill success. His squaw and children lived meagerly on hominy and venison. Dowdee was a humane Indian, and was much attached to his squaw and children. In his distress, he concluded that Mr. Oliver would be likely to sympathize with the "red hunter." He had met his new neighbor several times, and rightly conceived the true elements of his character. He hastened to the cabin of Mr. Oliver, when the following dialogue took place:

Dowdee—"How much you charge for big pot full mush and milk? My squaw and pappoose velly hungry."

Oliver—"How much will you give?"

Dowdee—"Me give one large buck-skin."

Oliver—"All right, bring them along."

Dowdee hastened to his wigwam to inform his squaw and children of the good news, and bring them to the cabin of Mr. Oliver.

In the meantime, Mrs. Oliver prepared a two-gallon pot of mush, and it was steaming hot when Dowdee and his family appeared at the cabin. On entering, "Billy" desired the pot to be placed in the middle of the floor, which was done; and the Indian family surrounded it, seating themselves on the floor. Tins, spoons and milk were provided, and Dowdee and his dusky family commenced their meal. The little Indians were remarkably voracious. The mush gradually disappeared. Finally the glossy skinned little fellows, with distended stomachs, began to hesitate. "Billy," talking to them in the Delaware tongue, urged them to "eat more." It was in vain, for their appetites had been fully glutted.

There they sat, nearly nude, with their yellow skins expanded almost to the point of explosion. One by one, they began to become drowsy, and nodded. The scene was exceedingly ludicrous. It was well worthy some native artist, and excited a smile from those who beheld it. The mush was at last consumed, and "Billy" produced the buckskin, and handed it to Mr. Oliver. He then roused his pappooses from their torpor, bade adieu to Mr. Oliver, and returned to his wigwam. The rivulet upon which he encamped, has since been known as "Dowdee's run."

A year or two after the war Dowdee returned to the Greentown settlement to hunt, and re-visited that region, annually, for several years, for the same purpose. The characteristic love of the Caucasian for mental culture existed among the early settlers of Green township. The children of the pioneers were gathered into a rude log school-house, and the services of a young lady secured as teacher. This was probably the first school ever taught in the township. The young lady who taught the young idea how to shoot still survives, and has nearly reached four score of well spent years. She informs me that, one drowsy, summer afternoon, when the little urchins under her charge were sleepily perusing their A B C's, and feeling perfectly secure, a large, copper-colored warrior stepped into the school-room and looked gravely at the children. Profound silence prevailed. The little fellows could almost feel their scalps disapapearing. The teacher looked enquiringly at the Indian. The little ones trembled in expectation of capture or the tomahawk. It was Billy Dowdee. He took in the whole scene at a glance Looking gravely at the teacher, he said: "Much pappoose—velly much pappoose." The young teacher blushed, visibly, at the insinuation, and felt greatly embarrassed. The point was, "Billy" intended to compliment her on possessing so large a family of pale-faced pappooses.

At the treaty at the Maumee rapids, in 1817, William Dondee, or Dowdee, is named as one of the proprietors in a reservation three miles square, south of Upper Sandusky, which was assigned to the Greentown and Jerometown Indians, formerly of Ashland county.

Billy Dowdee was a harmless old Indian, and is well remembered by the pioneers of Green township. He and his family accompanied the *Delawares* to their new reservation, west of the Mississippi, in 1829.

ABEL BAILEY

was born in Westmoreland county, Pennsylvania, July 24, 1799. In 1806, his father, in company with other emigrants, came down the Youghiogheny on a small flatboat to Pittsburgh. The family of Mrs. Bryte, mother of John and the late David Bryte, were also in the company. On departing from Pittsburgh, they attached the flat-boat to one of the river boats, and descended the Ohio to Steubenville, and located about eight miles northwest of the village, where they remained until 1809, when John Bailey and family located near New Lisbon and remained until 1816, and removed to Green township, Richland county, and settled near Honey creek. Here the family remained until 1818, when John Bailey, father of Abel, purchased the southeast quarter of section fourteen, in Clearcreek township, and located upon it. John Bailey and his son, Abel, visited and selected the quarter in 1817, one year prior to the removal. John Bailey, sr., father of John Bailey, jr., who was the father of Abel Bailey, was of English descent, and served during the Revolutionary war, from Rhode Island, and located with his family in Westmoreland county, Pennsylvania, where he deceased. John Bailey, father of Abel, died in Richland county, whither he had removed, about 1850. Mrs. Bailey died in Clearcreek at an advanced age. Abel married Miss Acsah, daughter of John Murphy, of Green township, in 1821, and in 1830 purchased the homestead in Clearcreek township of his father, and still resides thereon. When the Baileys removed to Clearcreek in 1818, they found the following pioneers in the township: Nathaniel Bailey, a brother of John, who located in 1817, Abraham Huffman, John McWilliams, David Barnes, Isaac Vanmeter, Peter Vanostrand, Robert McBeth, James Haney and his sons, Richard, John and Thomas, Richard and John Freeborn, Thomas Munholland, Patrick Elliott, Jacob Foulk, Thomas Ford and his sons, Elijah, Elias, Thomas and John, and John Bryte. These settlers were much scattered. The roads were mere paths, ill-worked, and, in wet seasons, difficult to travel. There were no churches or school-houses. There were a few Baptists and Methodists. Their meetings were held in the cabins of the pioneers for several years. The forests of Clearcreek were very dense, and the timber very tall and of unusual size. The first settlers performed a prodigy of labor in its removal. Mr. Bailey says, "The task was absolutely disheartening." By perseverance, however, fine farms were prepared, and many of the pioneers, now well advanced in age, are living in comfort and plenty. He remembers vividly the scenes, ludicrous and otherwise, that occurred at the early cabin raisings, log rollings, and making roads. Fired by corn whiskey, and an exuberance of animal spirits, the rugged pioneers were ambitious to excel in all that tested physical endurance and courage. Very few of the first settlers remain. Many of them have long since been gathered and garnered by the remorseless reaper. Mr. Bailey has long been a member of the Baptist denomination, and assisted in the erection of the first church in Savannah, in 1840. It is a neat frame, and in a good state of preservation. Upon the introduction of the reform of Alexander Campbell, the church was greatly weakened, many of the members having connected with the new church. The Baptists have no regular minister at present. The members number about thirty. The family of Mr. Bailey consists of Eli, of Van Wert, Ohio, and John, of Savannah. The daughters are Jane, wife of David Andrews, Ellen, wife of John Smith, and Aletha, wife of Simon Stentz. Mrs. Bailey died in 1873. Mr. Bailey resides on the homestead. He is in good health, and his memory unimpaired.

Mr. Bailey relates that when he came to the township in 1818, deer were very plenty, and the hunters could easily procure an abundance of wild meat. The most noted hunters of what is now Ashland county were Edward Wheeler, Elias Ford, James Kuykendall, Christopher Mykrants, Solomon Urie, John McConnell, and Jacob Young, most of whom are now deceased. They hunted along the Vermillion river, the Black river, and on the Fire Lands of the Reserve. At that time, large encampments of *Wyandots* and *Delawares* hunted annually along those streams, and frequently met and conversed with the white hunters. The last deer was killed as late as 1845, within the present limits of Troy township.

DAVID BRYTE.

Mr. Bryte was born in Fayette county, Pennsylvania, in December, 1806, and in 1807 his parents removed to Jefferson county, Ohio. In 1821, when sixteen years of age, he and a younger brother walked to Clearcreek township, in Richland county, and passed through the then village of Uniontown, now Ashland. At that time, fifty years ago, it contained but a few log cabins and one or two small stores. For a number of years he followed the occupation of teaching school. At that period he taught several terms in Milton and Montgomery townships. He then located in Mansfield, where he continued to teach until about the year 1840. About this time he became deputy under Sheriff McCullough, and served two terms, and was elected sheriff one term. Upon the erection of Ashland county in 1845-6, he removed to his farm three miles south of Ashland, and in 1850 was elected a justice of the peace. In 1853 he was elected infirmary director, and resigned to remove to Allen county, where he remained a few years.

Mr. Bryte had been twice married, and his second wife and five children, all grown, survive him. He was an acceptable and zealous member of the Christian church. He was a man of nervous temperament, and during his prime, a very ardent Democrat. His long residence in this vicinity enabled him to become acquainted with most of the pioneers of the county. He took great pleasure in recounting the exploits and adventures of the early settlers and their families. He lived to see great changes in men, and the general appearance of the country. He was buried in the cemetery in Ashland on Thursday, March 28, 1872.

JOHN SCOTT

was born in Washington county, Pennsylvania, in the year 1793. He continued to reside in that county until he was about twenty-six years of age. He attended the neighborhood schools until he had obtained a fair knowledge of the English branches. His father was a farmer, and had located in the wilds of Washington county after the close of the Revolution, and was of Scotch-Irish extraction. Mr. Scott grew up an active, robust, and intelligent young man, and evinced an inclination to locate amid the forests of the Ohio country, as this State was then called.

In October, 1818, he married Miss Matilda Weakley, of Cumberland county, Pennsylvania, and in the spring of 1819 removed to the west part of Vermillion township, Richland (now Ashland,) county, to the land now known as the Joshua Campbell farm, where he purchased some two hundred and twenty acres, erected a cabin, and commenced the arduous task of cutting away the forest to prepare fields for cultivation, and his future home. When he arrived the settlements in Vermillion were very sparse. When a cabin was to be erected, it required a circuit of many miles to procure hands sufficient to accomplish the task. When he commenced his pioneer home, it is believed that Peter and John Vangilder, Joseph Strickland and his sons, William S. and Joseph, William Reed, Mr. Harlan, Mr. Lattimer, George Eckley, Ezra Warner, Ephraim Eckley, Mr. Crabb, Mr. Beabout, Mr. Beck, Mr. Wallace, and a few others, were the only residents of the township. These families were very much scattered, and the only intercourse was in assisting each other in preparing cabins, rolling logs and the like. Mr. Scott continued active operations as a pioneer farmer about twelve years, and then located at Hayes' Cross Roads, where the town of Hayesville now stands, in the winter of 1831, and opened a small store. The store-room was in a log cabin on what is known as Armstrong's corner. He subsequently erected a more substantial building, and entered into partnership with Mr. Daniel Porter, in the dry goods business. The new firm was remarkably prosperous, and did an active trade for that day.

Mr. Scott was a quiet, clear-headed, far-seeing man, and gave his energies full scope. A want of suitable markets for the surplus products of the pioneer farmers greatly embarrassed them. Mr. Scott became convinced that he could greatly relieve these embarrassments by purchasing the surplus cattle and horses, and driving them to a suitable market. He entered largely into that enterprise, and by his promptness, fidelity and shrewd management, not only relieved the farmers—to their profit—of such stock, but greatly benefitted the firm. At a subsequent date, when Pittsburgh, Portland (now Sandusky City), Cleveland and Milan were the only markets for the surplus wheat of the township, which had to be hauled over rough roads at great expense, Mr. Scott came to the rescue of the farmers by erecting a mill in 1847, and converting a large quantity of wheat annually into first-class flour. In this, as in all other enterprises, fortune favored the brave. He continued in trade and the mercantile business about thirty years. In the meantime he sold his Armstrong corner to Jacob Kinnaman and purchased, in 1840, what is known as the Francis Graham brick building on the opposite corner south, and continued in business until 1846, when he sold to Messrs. Cox & Higbee, and practically retired from active mercantile business. In 1857 his son Weakley W. entered into business at the old stand and continued several years. Mr. Scott died in 1864, aged seventy-two years, and was buried on a beautiful Indian mound within the corporation of Hayesville, where Mrs. Scott and other members of the family were subsequently interred. Mr. Scott was a large man, full six feet high and of fine appearance. He was calm and dignified in his deportment. He was noted for his business integrity, good judgment, prudence and shrewdness. Very few men have accomplished as much, and none have distributed more benefits in this county. While he regarded business as a business man, and insisted upon promptness and integrity at all times, he was sympathetic and charitable to a remarkable degree; and while in business never distressed the poor. This excellent trait was rewarded by great fidelity on the part of those whom he befriended, so much so that he was accustomed to state "he rarely lost a cent by trusting a poor man."

Mr. Scott left three sons and one daughter at his decease—Mr. W. W. Scott, who resides near Hayesville, John Scott, a lawyer, who resides and practices his profession in Cleveland, Dr. David Scott, who married the only daughter of Governor Allen, and who resides at Fruit Hill, near the city of Chillicothe, and Miss Sidney Scott, of Hayesville.

William Scott, a brother of John, sr., emigrated to Vermillion township in 1822, and resided on what is known as the Michael Helbert farm. He married Miss Edwards, of Mifflin, and died in 1854, aged sixty years. He was distinguished among the pioneers as a fine marksman and a very successful hunter. Many anecdotes are related concerning his adventures.

JOHN BRYTE

was born in Westmoreland county, Pennsylvania, July 20, 1800. Michael Bryte, his father, removed to Jefferson county, Ohio, in 1807. The family consisted of three boys, John, Nathaniel and David, and three girls. In 1815, Michael Bryte died. John, after the decease of his father, returned to the Forks of the Youghiogheny, where he remained nearly four years, attending a district school in the winter, and laboring in the summer season. In 1819 he accompanied Mr. Nathaniel Bailey, a relative, to Clearcreek township, walking all the way from the "Yoh." On the route he passed through New Lisbon, Canton and Wooster, then new villages. Mr. Bailey had located in 1817, and Mr. Bryte, for a time, made the house of Mr. Bailey his home. When he entered the township the names of those who preceded him were: Nathaniel Bailey, Abraham Huffman, Daniel Huffman, David and James Burns, Abraham Clayburg, Jacob Foulks, Richard Freeborn, John and Thomas Henney, Abel Bailey, John Bailey, Thomas Ford, Elias Ford, John McWilliams, John Aten, Robert McBeth, and possibly a few others. At that period a great many *Delaware* Indians made annual visits in the spring and fall of the year to make sugar and hunt deer, which were quite numerous along the Black and Vermillion rivers and the branches of Mohican. They often encamped in different parts of the township, but were harmless and never interfered with their white neighbors. In these excursions the hunters were often accompanied by Thomas Lyons and Isaac George, two rather noted old Indians. Mr. Bryte frequently met the eccentric, but inoffensive, Johnny Appleseed, *alias* John Chapman, as he meandered over the country planting appleseeds and cultivating nurseries. Mr. Bryte was the second clerk of Clearcreek township, and held the office eleven years, the township having been organized in 1820. He was also trustee a number of times, and was a warm friend of the common school system at all times, being one of the earliest teachers in the township. He was a man of benevolent feelings, and in 1856 was appointed trustee of the Central Ohio lunatic asylum at Columbus, by Governor S. P. Chase, and continued in that position until 1862. In 1820 he became an active member of the Baptist church, near Ashland, and in 1835, united with the Christian church, and has been one of its speakers nearly forty years, and has adorned his profession by an upright life.

In 1824 he married Miss Elizabeth Ford, daughter of Thomas Ford, and in 1826 purchased a part of the farm —section twenty-six, on which he deceased. On this land he found an ancient earthwork containing over three acres. It is now nearly obliterated from long cultivation with the plow.

In 1874, Mr. and Mrs. Bryte celebrated the fiftieth anniversary of their wedded life, having all their children and friends present. In August, 1874, he went to California with his son Michael, who for many years had been a resident of that State. He returned in the fall, and until his decease loved to dwell upon what he saw and learned during his visit to the Pacific. He related the scenes and incidents of his journey in a manner so entertaining and earnest, that he never failed to deeply interest all who heard him. At the organization of the pioneer and historical society of Ashland county, on the tenth of September, 1875, Mr. Bryte presided as the first temporary president, and became an active member of the association. During the summer his general health began to fail, and he was confined to his room for some time. He again rallied, and hopes were expressed that he might be spared many more years; but he was again seized by sickness. He died of pneumonia, on Saturday evening, February 17, and was buried at Bryte's church, in Clearcreek township, on Monday, February 19, 1877. In his death Clearcreek lost a valuable citizen, and society an influential and exemplary member. Mr. Bryte was noted for his strong common sense, his integrity and love of truth and fairness between man and man. The pioneer society misses him very much, because he possessed an extraordinary memory, and remembered the history of his township very clearly. The obituary committee of the society adopted the usual resolutions concerning his decease.

HUGH BURNS

was born in Philadelphia, Pennsylvania, January 20, 1810, and emigrated with his parents to Milton township, Richland (now Ashland) county, Ohio, in 1820, and settled on what is now known as the Kelley farm. In the fall of the same year Andrew Burns, sr., father of Hugh, built a cabin on what is now known as the John Huzlet farm, then owned by his brother, Barnabas Burns, and resided in it until 1821, when he moved to a cabin near the present site of Yeaman's mill, in Mifflin township, where the family remained until 1823, and then located on the Richard Woodhouse farm in Milton. In 1829 Mr. Burns, father of Hugh, purchased what is now known as the Burns' farm, near the schoolhouse of that name in the west part of Milton township, where he resided until his death in 1857, at the age of seventy-seven years. He was born in Donegal, Ireland, and was a devout Catholic. He came to Philadelphia in 1801, and about 1812 located in Lancaster county, Pennsylvania. In 1820 he removed to Ohio. He had three sons, Hugh, Andrew, and Barnabas, and two daughters, Margaret and Sarah. Mrs. Burns died in 1851, aged seventy-five years.

Hugh attended the schools of the neighborhood, and obtained a fair knowledge of the English branches, and at an early day commenced his career as a teacher. While a young man he was elected township clerk, and the records show a very neat journal was made by him. At the organization of Ashland county in 1846, he was selected as county auditor, a position he held until 1851. He made an efficient, industrious and conscientious officer, and was much respected for his integrity and personal worth. At the expiration of his term of office he opened a dry goods store in Ashland; but the enterprise proved unfortunate, and he failed in business, losing pretty much all the capital he had invested. He then recommenced the life of a farmer, which seems most congenial to his nature. He purchased the west half of what is known as the Nicholas Rutan farm, near his old home in Milton, to which he removed in 1867. During his residence in Ashland he took an active interest in the public schools, and was repeatedly a member of the board of education.

When a young man he became a member of the Baptist church of Windsor, and in 1846 joined the Disciple church of Ashland, of which he remained a member until 1867, when he was transferred to the Clearcreek Disciple church, of which he is now an active member. Mr. Burns is regarded as an exemplary, high-toned and conscientious Christian.

When he arrived in Milton, in 1820, he recollects the following pioneers had preceded his father: Frederick Sulcer, James Kelley, James Andrews, Amos and Samuel Hilburn, Peter Lance, William Dickey, James Crawford, John Kent, Robert Andrews, Robert Nelson, and a few others. The first mill he attended was Reynold's near Windsor. In 1821 he attended Newman's mill to obtain grists. The first preachers, Presbyterian, were Robert Lee and Mr. Matthews; and of the Methodists, Mr. Haney and Mr. Hazard; and of the Baptists, Mr. Jones—say from 1820 to 1825.

ANDREW MASON

was born in Fayette county, Pennsylvania, February 4, 1801. His father, Martin Mason, emigrated with his family to Columbiana county in 1804. In August, 1814, in company with his brother Jacob, Jacob Crouse, Jacob Young, Martin Hester, Lot Tod, and Peter Biddinger, Martin Mason visited Orange township, then in Richland county, and put up six cabins. Jacob Mason was accompanied by his family, and boarded the above mentioned pioneers while engaged in erecting the cabins. In addition to his household goods, Jacob Mason brought a team and three cows. Upon the completion of their cabins, they returned to Columbiana county, and, in October, Martin Mason, Jacob Young, Jacob Crouse, Joseph Bishop, and Peter Biddinger, in wagons, suitably covered, removed with their families, household goods and their cattle, to their cabin homes in the forests of Orange and Montgomery townships. The little colony was composed of thirty-one persons, including women and children. The heads of families were all originally from western Pennsylvania. They followed Beall's trail, from four miles west of New Lisbon, through the village of Wooster, to the present site of Jeromeville, where they encamped on what is now the Samuel Naylor farm. From thence they cut a path on the east side of the stream to the residence of John Carr, in Montgomery township; and thence in a northwest direction across the present farm of Andrew Mason, to Young's bridge, on the Orange road, where they struck the old Indian trail, which they followed to the present site of Leidigh's mill. For a short time Mr. Mason located on what is now known as the Shopbell farm, and, in 1815, at the site of Leidigh's. The residences of Messrs. Crouse, Bishop, Young, and Biddinger, are well known.

At that period the new settlers were compelled to traverse the forest paths to Stibbs' mill, one mile east of Wooster, to obtain a supply of flour and meal, or use hominy blocks or hand-mills. During the winter of 1814-15, which was remarkably severe, the new settlers were nearly destitute of meat, and had to depend on the unerring rifle or friendly Indians for a supply of wild meat. Their cabins were imperfect, having puncheon floors, open chimney places and clapboard doors. Their bedsteads were made of poles fastened in the walls, and covered with clapboards, upon which their straw beds rested. The wheat and corn used was purchased mostly at New Lisbon and carried on pack-horses to Stibbs', to be converted into flour and meal, and again packed to the settlement in Orange.

In the fall of 1815 Martin Mason commenced the erection of a small grist-mill, which was completed in March, 1816. It had niggerhead or bowlder stones, and was quite an accommodation to the settlers. It was the second mill erected in this part of the county, Mr. Oram having completed a small mill one and one-half miles northeast of the present site of Ashland, a short time before, on the modern site of Ritter's mill.

Martin Mason died August 14, 1860, aged eighty-two years. He then resided in Richland county. His family consisted of John, Andrew, Margaret, Mary, Martin, and Anna. Andrew and Martin reside in Montgomery township, and are farmers. Andrew is a gentleman of good memory, and possesses a fair English education, having attended school in the log cabins of Orange township nearly sixty years ago. He retains a vivid recollection of pioneer life and its hardships, and we have drawn liberally from his stores of experience in other chapters of these sketches. As a farmer he has been successful, and possesses a fine homestead some two and one-half miles northeast of Ashland. He has served efficiently as a justice of the peace for Montgomery, and became a member of the Ashland county pioneer society organized on the tenth of September, 1875. He has been an active member of the Methodist Episcopal church for many years, and adorned his profession by an upright walk. The members of his family mostly reside within Ashland county. At this time (1879), Mr. Mason and his wife are in excellent health, and may survive to an advanced age.* They entered the forests of this region and have seen them leveled and the country dotted with thousands of happy homes.

MRS. ELIZABETH MASON.

Mrs. Mason, who was a daughter of Valentine Heiffner was born in Huntingdon county, Pennsylvania, March 19, 1807. Having relatives in Orange township, then Richland, but now of Ashland county, she came, when a young lady, on a visit to that region with Mr. Snider and wife, formerly of Pennsylvania. Her sister, Mrs. Barbara Rowland, had come to Orange some years prior to her trip, and not having good health, became very lonesome in that region, then comparatively an unsettled forest. The object was to aid her sister in recovering her health and contentment. The new settlers of

---

* His wife died in the spring of 1880. See biography.

that day were compelled to endure many hardships and privations in order to prepare homes. Christian Rowland and lady finally became residents of Uniontown, now Ashland, where they died about 1832, and are well remembered by old citizens of Ashland. During her residence with Mrs. Rowland, Elizabeth became acquainted with Andrew Mason, and in 1824 they were married, and she never returned to her native country to live. It is proper to note, as a pioneer reminiscence, that Mr. and Mrs. Mason were married by Rev. James Haney, who was the first Methodist preacher in this county, whose son, John Haney, was the proprietor of Haneytown, but now the village of Savannah, in Clearcreek township, in this county. Mr. and Mrs. Mason lived together as man and wife fifty-five years, three months and twenty-five days. She went through many hardships, having gone over the period since 1824 in which great changes have occurred in the wild regions of Richland, but now Ashland county. Cabins and forests were then found in all parts of the county. After a long struggle and enduring many hardships the first settlers succeeded in taming the wilds of the native woods, and now reside in comfortable homes, surrounded by desirable improvements, and the abundance furnished by rich lands, industry and genial climate to reward the industry, economy and frugal habits, for which the pioneers of this county are noted. Mrs. Mason passed through all these scenes a cheerful, industrious Christian lady, and like her husband, long an exemplary member of the church of her choice. At a pioneer meeting on their premises, in 1879, in which many of their neighbors joined, Mrs. Mason prepared, in the ancient way, a lot of corn bread, which was regarded quite a treat. She seemed much interested in the exercises of the pioneers, and became a member of the county society at that time. The pioneers are passing rapidly to that bourne from whence no traveler returns. As the gray-haired patriarchs are called to bid adieu to earth, we trust they may be found fully prepared for that great change, and welcomed to that rest prepared in that better country for all the good. Mrs. Mason was buried on Sunday, March 21st, in the Orange cemetery. Her remains were conducted to their last resting place by about seventy carriages which formed the procession, followed by relatives, neighbors and friends, making eight or nine hundred people present. The funeral discourse was preached by Rev. P. Roseberry from II. Corinthians v, 1, assisted by Rev. A. Lyon, presiding elder of the Methodist church.

Mrs. Mason was the mother of thirteen children, six of whom preceded her to the better land. She had twenty-eight grandchildren, one of whom had passed over the river of death before her departure. She had four great-grandchildren. She had been a Christian and a motherly pioneer, and an affectionate wife for over half a century, and we trust has found the reward of every Christian and faithful wife.

One evening she asked the friends to sing "Home of the Soul," and "I am so glad that Jesus loves me." She then broke out in joyous strains: "I am so glad that Jesus loves me." In a vision or dream she said she saw her little grandchild in the spirit land; she was very happy, and sent word to her parents to not mourn for her.

MEMORIAL.

Two more hands are gently folded
  On a faithful, silent breast;
Two more feet have ceased to journey
  Through life's howling wilderness;
One more head is freed from aching,
  One more heart has ceased to beat,
One more soul has left its casket—
  Gone to Heaven's safe retreat.

One dear face no more appearing
  When the breakfast table's spread;
One less kneeling at the altar
  When the evening prayers are said;
One more husband sad and lonely,
  One more family motherless,
One more singing hallelujah,
  In the regions of the blest.

Six dear, sainted little spirits
  Opened wide the golden gate,
When they saw their mother coming
  To enjoy their happy state.
Still the blissful chorus singing,
  Angels shout it loud and long,
"Welcome, welcome sainted mother,
  Welcome to this happy throng."

O, cheer up, dear father Mason,
  Soon *your* journey will be o'er,
Then you'll meet your dear companion
  Where sad partings are no more.
Children, serve your mother's Saviour;
  Heed your mother's dying prayer—
May the family reunited,
  Dwell forever with her there.
    —MRS. S. Z. KAUFFMAN.

Nova, Ashland county, March 22, 1880.

PETER THOMAS

was born in Somerset county, Pennsylvania, July 9, 1798. His father, George Thomas, emigrated with his family, to Harrison county, in the spring of 1807. In 1815 Peter Thomas, then sixteen years of age, traveled on foot, accompanied by the family watch-dog, a large and faithful mastiff, along a new path leading from Cadiz to the village of Wooster, and rested one night at Stibbs' mill. The next night he reached the cabin of John Raver, near the present site of Rowsburgh. The following morning he pursued his journey by paths until he struck Beall's trail, at Jerome's place, and thence along a blazed path partly opened, to Beam's mill, three miles below Mansfield, on the Rocky fork of Mohican. Jacob Beam, the owner of the mill, was an uncle. He remained a few weeks, and returned. In 1817, his father's family came on and erected a cabin on the present site of Mifflin, believed to have been the first shingled house in the township of Mifflin. When the tide of emigration commenced, after the close of the war, the road from Mansfield to Wooster, passed through Petersburgh, as the village was then called, and it became the principal route to Richland and other western counties for emigration. Mr. George Thomas, father of Peter, kept the first house of entertainment, which was well patronized for six or eight years. In 1823, George Thomas and family located on a farm now owned by Josiah Thomas, in Orange township. Peter Thomas purchased two hundred acres adjoining the homestead, in Montgomery township, and resided upon it until about 1860, when he removed to a new residence, one and a half miles northeast of Ashland, where he deceased, February 26, 1876. He was conscious of the approaching termination of his life, and was in the act of dictating a codicil to a will, when he became faint, and expired in a few moments, from paralysis of the heart. He had been three times married, and left a large and reputable family to mourn his loss. He had been a member to the Disciple church for a number of years, and adorned his profession by an upright and exemplary life. As a citizen, he was highly respected. He was a man of uncommon resolution and firmness when he had deliberately formed an opinion. He was high-toned and exact in all his transactions with men, and inflexibly opposed to every species of prevarication in morals, business and politics. He was never an office-seeker, but was always the advocate of a pure, economical and patriotic administration of the government.* He was a careful, frugal, and shrewd business man, and had acquired a handsome property. Few men have taken a deeper interest in the prosperity of the county, and none will be more lamented.

DANIEL CARTER, JR.,

was born in Butler county, Pennsylvania, May 23, 1802. He emigrated, with his father's family, in March, 1806, to Stark county, Ohio, where he resided until February 12, 1812, and then removed, by way of Jerome's Place, now Jeromeville, where they remained a few days at the cabin of the late John Carr until Daniel Carter, sr., erected a cabin in Montgomery township, half a mile northeast of the present site of Ashland.

Daniel Carter, sr., had entered at the land office in Canton three hundred and twenty acres of land in Montgomery, constituting the present lands of Peter Thomas, and what was recently known as the John Mason farm. The cabin was a frail affair. It resembled a camp house—was open at one end and made of poles and covered with clapboards. He moved into it in February, 1812. The family began active work on a clearing for corn, and got along quietly, being occasionally visited by Indians, until after Hull's surrender at Detroit, on the sixteenth of August. About this time several families quartered for a short time at the cabin of Robert Newell, in the lower part of Montgomery, recently known as the Hugh McGuire place. When General Harrison moved his army to the northwest, these families, Frys, Tridrels, Cuppys and Carters, returned to their cabins. In September, after the murders on the Black fork, most of these families fled to the block-house at Jerome's place.

Mr. Daniel Carter, sr., as has been elsewhere stated, took his family to Harrison county, and remained for some time at the cabin of a friend, Mr. William Rhodes, about four miles from New Philadelphia. In February, 1813, he returned to his cabin and remained until the fifth of March, when he received news of the Colyer excitement near Tylertown, a son of John Carr bringing him news of the appearance of Indians, when he fled with his family to the block-house at Jerome's Place, and remained there until the spring of 1814.

Daniel Carter, jr., retains a vivid recollection of the incidents of block-house life. His father, in the spring of 1814, purchased at Canton the farm upon which David Carter now resides, and removed to it.

The settlers, for several years in Montgomery, were very much scattered. The schools were indifferent, and the youth of that era were deprived of educational opportunities, except in the primary branches. Mr. Carter says he never attended school over three months. He grew up among the pioneers, attending cabin raisings, log rollings and other pioneer gatherings. He purchased one hundred and sixty acres of land on section sixteen, built a cabin and improved his farm. The farm had been entered by William Drumm. In 1829 he married Miss Elizabeth, daughter of Elias Slocum. His family consisted of two daughters—Amanda, wife of William M. Patterson, of Cleveland, Ohio, and Anna A., wife of Hon. William B. Allison, now a senator of the United States, from Iowa. Mr. Carter sold his farm in 1864, and now resides in Ashland. In 1850 he made a trip to California via. Panama, and remained about three and a half years. He never sought political promotion, but in sentiment was a Whig until that party disbanded, when he became a Republican, and still adheres to the principles of that party.

ISAAC GATES

Peter Gates was born in New Jersey, in 1778, of German descent, and emigrated to Washington county, Pennsylvania, in 1801, and married Sarah Spech in 1803. He removed to Mifflin township, Richland county, in 1830, and deceased in 1861, aged eighty-three years. His family consisted of Martin, Jacob, John, Isaac, Elizabeth, Eunice, Margaret, and Sarah. He was twice married, his second wife being Elizabeth, sister of Samuel Lewis, of Mifflin.

Isaac Gates, fourth son of Peter, was born near Hillsborough, Washington county, Pennsylvania, September 15, 1815. In 1830 he accompanied his father's family to Richland county, Ohio. Here he grew to manhood, attending the common schools of the neighborhood in the winter season, and labored on a farm in the summer. His father's family being in moderate circumstances, he was compelled to labor at wages to procure clothing and education, the schools at that period being sustained by individual subscriptions. In 1839 he was elected con-

---
*He was often elected school director, and was township trustee sixteen or eighteen times, but was always nominated and pressed into the service, against his own wishes.

stable of Mifflin township, and was re-elected five times successively. In November, 1834, he married Susan Newcomer, daughter of Christian Newcomer, who was subsequently commissioner of Ashland county. Mr. Gates moved to the village of Mifflin, where, in 1842, he was elected justice of the peace, and twice re-elected. In 1848 he was elected sheriff, and re-elected in 1850. In 1852 he was elected auditor, and re-elected in 1854. In 1862 he was again elected auditor, and re-elected in 1864. He now resides in Ashland. Since the expiration of his second term, as auditor he has followed the business of a public salesman or auctioneer. He has been an active member of the Lutheran church since 1847, and, much of the time, a deacon or elder. His family consists of Sarah J., Halstead, Margaret, deceased, Fannie E., Nelson, William H., Christian N., Reuben H., Arminda, Elizabeth, Frank and Martin L.

JOSEPH HARVUOT

was born in Chester county, Pennsylvania, in 1792. In 1818 he married Lydia Bruce, and removed to Clearcreek, Richland county, Ohio, in the spring of 1820, and located on section twenty-five, where he resided until his decease in 1843. He was a member of the Disciple church, and an elder. His family, at his decease, consisted of Isaac, Anne, Richard, Elizabeth, Lewis, Sarah, Joseph, and Mary, by his first wife, and William, by his second wife, having been twice married. The only member of the family left in Clearcreek is Isaac. Isaac is a dealer in money, and is accumulating a fortune. He is married, and resides in Savannah.

LEWIS OLIVER.

In the early settlement of the south part of this county, the pioneers were considerably embarrassed for a market for their surplus grain and other farm products. The ports on Lake Erie, Pittsburgh, and New Orleans were the principal markets. To reach the lake by teams, over the rough, new-cut roads, was toilsome and difficult, as well as quite expensive; while wheat, flour, and corn commanded a low price. In consequence of the inferior markets on the lake, at Zanesville and Pittsburgh several enterprising pioneers had boats constructed, which were loaded and conveyed to New Orleans.

In the spring of 1823, Lewis Oliver and John Davis, of Green township, purchased of Nathan Dehaven, a flat-bottomed boat, which had been built at the mouth of Honey creek on the Black fork, by Mr. Dehaven, near the modern site of his saw-mill. The boat was fifty-five feet long and fifteen feet wide, with rounded bows and a steering apparatus, and cabin. It was so covered as to protect its lading. This boat was conveyed up the Black fork to near the residence of Mr. Oliver, where it was partly loaded with wheat, flour, pork, whiskey, and chickens.

About the sixteenth of March, the new vessel passed slowly down the Black fork to Dehaven's, and the Loudonville mills, where a large amount of sawed cherry lumber and other articles were placed on board, to be conveyed to a southern market. The Black fork was a slow, tortuous stream, though the water was quite deep. Navigation was considerably impeded in consequence of the lodgment of driftwood in its winding course to the Walhonding. These difficulties were overcome by moving slowly and guarding the boat against accident.

The crew of the boat consisted of Lewis Oliver and John Davis, proprietors, and Amos Harbaugh and Timothy Wilson, as hands. On the seventeenth, "all hands aboard," the boat was floated leisurely down the Black fork to its junction with the Lake fork; then down the Walhonding to its junction with the Tuscarawas at the town of Coshocton; thence down the Muskingum to the city of Zanesville. There were on board, two skiffs, so that if the boat should be snagged, or otherwise injured by driftwood, the proprietors and hands could have means of escape. When the stream was sluggish and current slow, the boat was urged forward by setting-poles.

Upon their arrival at Zanesville, a formidable obstacle to their further advance was presented. The dam across the Muskingum at that place, was difficult to pass. It was seen at a glance, that it would require an experienced pilot to conduct the boat over it in safety. Mr. Oliver went ashore to procure the services of a suitable guide. An individual representing the craft, presented himself and offered to conduct the boat safely over the dam. On being asked his price for the job, he blandly informed Mr. Oliver it would be cheap at ten dollars. Mr. Oliver thought the charge rather extravagant. The valorous pilot feeling certain that he would ultimately get the job, declined to take a cent less.

Here was a quandary. Mr. Oliver returned to the boat and reported the result of his mission. After some consultation, Mr. Davis concluded they could conduct the craft over the dam without the aid of a professional pilot. By this time a large crowd of spectators had assembled on the river bank to see the fun. The fall over the dam was about ten feet, and the current was very rapid. Some fifteen or twenty rods below the dam, the Buckingham bridge, since the bridge of the national turnpike, supported by large stone piers, spanned the Muskingum river. If the boat moved straight forward, it would pitch upon its prow and be crushed or capsized; and if it escaped such a disaster, might strike a pier.

In this crisis Jersey wit and ingenuity triumphed. Mr. Oliver placed himself as steersman, at the stern, while Mr. Davis and the hands, by united efforts, swung the boat around so that it would pass obliquely over the dam, and strike and rise on the rolling current below, without stoving or capsizing. They held its course steadily, until it reached the dam, when it shot over like an arrow, rose and floated on the current, and narrowly escaped the pier. At this achievement, the large assemblage on shore, gave a tremendous shout, and declared a "Jersey Yankee," was equal to any emergency, and capable of any daring.

The boat floated slowly down to Duncan's falls, nine miles below Zanesville, where it was again compelled to encounter new dangers. They were less formidable, however, than the dam over which the boat had just passed. A point where the channel was deepest, was selected, and the little vessel cleared the falls in safety, and moved onward to Marietta, and entered the Ohio river. The hills and bluffs along its banks, covered with pine and other timber, rendered the voyage novel and interesting. The buds of the trees were just opening into leaf, and the banks of the river were lined with spring vegetation and flowers. Thus they glided toward the far south, where they were to find new and strange scenery.

They passed Cincinnati, now the queen city of the west. How great has been the growth of that beautiful city since 1823! Its markets were then easily glutted. Messrs. Oliver and Davis were compelled to go further south to dispose of their produce. Their little boat was shoved from the wharf into the main current of the Ohio, where it moved rapidly toward the falls at Louisville. On their way they overtook a stranded emigrant boat which was unable to move, in consequence of the drift-wood. There were several families, with their goods on it, *en route* to southern Illinois and Iowa. Seeing the situation, the owners of the boat from the Black fork volunteed their aid to relieve the emigrants.

On arriving at the falls, the boat passed through without accident, and the light-hearted owners pushed onward to the Mississippi, and down its dark-rolling current to New Orleans, the great southern market of that period. Here they found a ready market for their cherry lumber, at two dollars and twenty-five cents per hundred feet, and thirty-seven and one-half cents per gallon for their whiskey—a better article than now sells for five dollars per gallon in the same city. Times change, men change, and prices necessarily fluctuate. Our country and its wealth are much more potent now than they were fifty-two years ago, and hence a greater value is attached to "fire-water." The pioneers are pretty generally of the opinion that the article manufactured fifty years ago was much purer and less harmful in its effects than modern "fire-water."

Finding no demand for their wheat, flour, and pork, they concluded to transfer those articles to a schooner and proceed to Richmond, Virginia, for a market. This transfer was made, and, as soon as completed, the "wharf rats" of New Orleans captured and concealed the boat. It was never seen again by its owners. About the first of April they sailed for Richmond. Their voyage was a pleasant one. They coasted around to the Chesapeake bay, and passed up the James river to Richmond. They arrived there about the seventeeth of April. The grand outline of the southern coast, with its attractive scenery, was constantly under their gaze, and was the subject of many remarks and much admiration. As they passed up the James river, the ancient homes of the colonists frequently hove in view and excited comment. Along the banks of that now classic stream, nearly three hundred years before, the colonists contended with the "fierce red man," for a home.

On reaching the market, they obtained one dollar and thirty cents per bushel for their wheat, and eight dollars per barrel for salt pork. These prices were such as would reward them fairly for their toil and perseverance. They felt amply compensated.

After spending a few days in Richmond, they prepared for returning to the wilds of the Black fork. They had separated from their hands at New Orleans. Their route, from Richmond, was through Goochland, Louisa, and Albemarle counties, and over the Blue Ridge mountains to Harrisonburgh, in Rockingham county; thence across the Great North mountain, to Moorefield, in Hardy county; thence to the Old Fort Redstone, in Pennsylvania; thence to Wheeling, West Virginia; thence by Zanesville, Newark, and Mount Vernon, to the Black fork, making a journey of about nine hundred miles on foot. They met with no accident or incivility on their way, and arrived at home about the first of July.

Mr. Oliver is now about eighty-seven years of age, is quite active, and in the possession of all his faculties. He looks younger than many men of sixty-five. He informs me, that during the haying season of 1874 he drove a team and rode on the mowing-machine several days, and felt none the worse for it. Very few men, at his age, would think of performing any labor. He has always been noted for his integrity, industry, and uprightness, and says "he feels better to keep moving." He owns and resides upon the old homestead of his father, Allen Oliver, and has resided in the same locality sixty-four years.

JAMES LOUDON PRIEST,

from Crawford county, Pennsylvania, settled on the banks of the Lake fork, in what was then Wayne county, as early as 1810. At that period the Coshocton county line joined Wayne on the south and included the county of Holmes. At the erection of Holmes county, in 1824, the part of Lake township where Mr. Priest located became a part of Washington township, in Holmes county; and at the erection of Ashland county, in 1846, another slice, on the east side of the township, was annexed to Clinton township, Wayne county, leaving Lake one of the smallest townships in Ashland county. Mr. Priest, with his family, located in the spring of the year, and by the aid of Thomas Jelloway, and several other friendly Delaware Indians, put up a plain log cabin and moved into it. His nearest neighbor was Alexander Finley, who had located six miles further up the Lake fork, at a point now known as Tylertown, in 1809. Mr. Priest was indebted to Mr. Finley for his seed corn for his first crop, and many other favors. His next neighbor was Nathan Odell, who arrived in the spring of 1811, and located in that part of Lake township which is now known as Clinton township, Wayne county.

James Loudon Priest died about 1822, at an advanced age.

WILLIAM GREENLEE.

In the spring of 1811 Mr. Greenlee visited James L. Priest, a former neighbor, from Crawford county, Pennsylvania. Mr. Greenlee came by the way of Harrison county to Zanesville, then a new village, and up the banks of the Muskingum, the White-woman and the Lake fork on horseback. He found but few settlers between Mr. Priest and Zanesville. He selected and located a farm adjoining Mr. Priest, and returned for his family by the route he came. In October, 1811, he and his family, consisting of his wife, six daughters, and one son, started for the forests of Ohio. He had two teams, one with two and the other with four horses. The wagons were covered with linen canvas, and contained such household goods and provisions as were deemed essential to the comfort of a new settler. The route was through the village of Canton to what is now Wooster, and thence to the Lake fork. The trail was so narrow that Mr. Greenlee was compelled to widen it at many points before his teams could pass. His family slept in the wagons most of the way, doing their cooking by the side of the trail, nights and mornings. The route was wild and romantic, and it required some eight or ten days to complete the journey. He erected a plain log cabin, by the aid of Mr. Priest and a few friendly Indians, and moved into it. He resided on this farm until 1814, and sold it to Calvin Hibbard, father of Edward Hibbard, one of the first commissioners of Ashland county. He then purchased where John Greenlee, his only son, now resides. When he landed in Lake, there were but the families of J. L. Priest, Samuel Marvin, William Hendrickson, Elijah Bolling and John Hendrickson, in what is now Washington township, Holmes county. The next settlement was that of the Odells, which contained the families of Joshua Oram, Thomas Oram, John Oram, and Mordecai Chilcote, near Odell's lake.

On the morning of the tenth of September, 1813, John Greenlee went in search of his father's horses, which had strayed in the direction of Odell's lake. About the middle of the day, a heavy, roaring sound was heard in the northwest, amid the forest. It resembled distant thunder, and he feared a tremendous tornado was approaching. What excited his surprise was, the sky was clear and cloudless, and the roaring seemed a phenomenon. In the afternoon he abandoned the search and returned home, convinced that a great storm was approaching. His parents and others had heard the same rumbling sound, and were unable to account for it. In a few days the little colony learned the particulars of the victory achieved by Commodore Perry over Commodore Barclay and the British fleet; and this accounted for the mysterious rumbling of the 10th. The sound of Perry's guns had been conveyed down the valleys, a distance of over seventy miles. It is related that the heavy cannonading was heard at Cleveland, about the same distance. Mr. Greenlee is a man of intelligence and unquestioned veracity, and relates the incident with minuteness and patriotic pride.

William Greenlee died in 1854, aged about eighty-two years.

EBENEZER RICE

was born in Marlborough, Massachusetts, April 8, 1773. He was the eldest son of Samuel and Abigail Underwood Rice. Samuel was born in Sudbury, in November, 1752, and was the son of Gersham and Elizabeth Rice. Gersham was born in Sudbury, in June, 1703, and was the son of Ephraim and Hannah Livermore Rice. Ephraim was born in Sudbury, in April, 1665, and was the son of Thomas and Mary Rice. Thomas was born in 1611, and was the son of Edmund and Tamazine Rice, who came from Barkhamstead, England, in 1638-9, and settled in Sudbury, and lived and died there, on the beautiful old farm on the east side of Sudbury river, near the border of the extensive meadows through which that river flows in its course to the Merrimac. The old farm is now in the possession of the Hon. John Whitmore Rice.

Ebenezer Rice married Martha, daughter of Barnabas and Mary Clark Hammond, of New Salem, Massachusetts. She was born in September, 1776, and they were married May 5, 1796, and emigrated to Licking county, Ohio, from Essex county, New York, in the year 1810. The following February they came to Richland county, and entered the farm upon which Alexander Rice now resides, in Green township. Mr. Rice and his family experienced all the privations and anxieties of pioneer life in their forest home. He cheerfully aided the new settlers in the erection of cabins, at log-rollings and other gatherings. For several years the pioneers were mutually dependent upon each other, and the social relations were largely cultivated. The forests were to be cut away, farms to be opened, school-houses to be erected, and public highways to be constructed. Mr. Rice took an active and leading part in all these enterprises. He was particularly interested in the education of his children. He survived until 1821. His family, at his decease, consisted of eleven children—four girls: Elizabeth, Martha, Harriet, and Abigail; and seven boys: Ebenezer, Alexander, Clark, Orson, Reuben, Levi, and Samuel. Only four survive: Elizabeth, wife of the late John Coulter; Martha, of Wisconsin; Alexander, of Green township, and Samuel, of Iowa. The widow of Ebenezer Rice subsequently married Judge Thomas Coulter, and died in September, 1835.

Alexander Rice was born in Massachusetts, in August, 1801, and emigrated with his parents to Green township, in 1810. He grew up amid the wild and beautiful scenery of the hills and valleys fringing the Black fork of the Mohican, and a neighbor to the red men of the village of Greentown. His educational advantages at that early day, were extremely limited. Being a young man of excellent sense, he acquired much information after reaching manhood. He is noted for his practical ideas, and plainness of speech. He has resided about sixty-six years on the homestead, and been continuously engaged in cultivating the soil.

In 1826 he married Miss Sarah Johnson, of Vermillion township. Their children were—Rosella, Rosina, Orson, Reuben H., Isaac J., and Rosaline. Mrs. Rice died in 1844. Miss Rosella is a lady of talent and fine literary attainments, and has written a great deal for the eastern magazines.

Mr. Rice subsequently married Mary Vanscoyoc, by whom he had Russell B., Ida, Josephine, and Ada Lenore.

Mr. Rice is yet in the full possession of all his faculties, and is quite vigorous for a man of his age. He remembers very distinctly the early scenes in Green township—the excitement of cabin-raisings, log-rollings, cutting roads and constructing corduroy bridges over marshes and sloughs. He relates, with historic precision, the opening scenes of the war of 1812, the Indian tragedies on the Black fork, the erecting of block-houses, and modes of life from 1812 to 1815.

When about nine years of age, his father, mother and a number of neighbors, were invited by the Indians to attend a feast at their village. He accompanied the invited guests to witness the performance. "There were between three and four hundred Indians present. The invited guests were permitted to enter the council house, a building, perhaps thirty feet wide, and nearly sixty feet long. In the center of the building was a mound of earth about three feet high and eight or ten feet in diameter. Forks were driven into it and poles placed upon them. Upon these a number of copper kettles were suspended. They contained bear's meat, venison and the like, which was being boiled for distribution among the Indians and invited guests. The white and Indian boys remained outside the building." While gazing at the performance within, a young Indian came up behind young Rice, seized him around the arms and body and held him firmly. The alarm and amazement of young Rice were very great. He states that his first sensation on being unable to extricate himself, was that of despair. He thought he could almost feel his scalp disappearing. By the intervention of a squaw he escaped the grasp of the young savage, to the relief of his fears. Although this scene occurred sixty-four years ago he says he retains a most vivid recollection of his sensations on that occasion. Subsequently he became well acquainted with the Armstrong boys, young Pipe, a son of old Captain Pipe, Jonacake, Lyons, Dowdee and other Greentown Indians.

Mr. Rice possesses a most extraordinary memory for dates, and the author of these pages is indebted to him for many valuable reminiscences of the early settlements of Green township. Mr. Rice is yet (1880) residing on his homestead near Perrysville, aged nearly eighty years, and retains all his mental faculties and much physical vigor.

THE TANNEHILLS.

Melzer Tannehill, sr., was born in Frederick county, Maryland, July 12, 1716. He emigrated to what is now Allegheny county, Pennsylvania, and located near Pittsburgh in the year 1777, during the Revolutionary war. He married Miss Eleanor Lile, March 23, 1790. He emigrated to Jefferson county, Ohio, in 1805, and in September, 1811, removed to Green township, in what is now Ashland county, and located on section twenty-three, where he resided over fifty years. He was one of the first commissioners of Richland county in 1813. In 1812 he was assessor of Knox county. He was subsequently a justice of the peace for Green township. During the exciting scenes of 1812, after the assassinations on the Black fork, he took a vigilant part in preparing to repel any future assaults by the savages. He deceased April 24, 1851. He was an exemplary and upright man, and had been a regular attendant upon the services of the Presbyterian church for many years. His family consisted of five sons and five daughters. Two sons and three daughters yet survive.

Charles Tannehill was born in Allegheny county, Pennsylvania, January 30, 1792. He emigrated with his father's family in 1811, and assisted in improving the homestead in Green township. During the border troubles of 1812, he served as a soldier in a company recruited in Knox county, Ohio, by Captain Greer, and participated in all the dangers incident to border life. In June, 1814, he married Miss Mary, daughter of Allen Oliver, and located on section twenty-seven, where he resided over fifty years. He died at the residence of his son-in-law, Mr. Joseph Cathcart, in Portage county, Indiana, November 26, 1875, at the advanced age of eighty-four years. His remains were brought to Perrysville for interment, and now rest beside those of the wife of his youth, who had preceded him to the grave. He was a member of the Disciple church. His family consisted of twelve children, nine sons and three daughters. Four sons and two daughters survived him. Mr. Adamson Tannehill, the oldest son, resides in Hicksville, Defiance county, Ohio. He was born July 1, 1815, and is the oldest living native of Green township.

Melzer Tannehill, jr., second son of Melzer, sr., was born in Butler county, Pennsylvania, June 18, 1801, and removed with his father's family to Jefferson county, Ohio, and thence to Green township in 1811, and assisted in improving the old homestead. He is now seventy-five years old, and quite rugged. He writes a fair hand, and may survive many years. He is an influential farmer, and takes a lively interest in the improvement of the county. His recollections of the days of the pioneers are quite vivid. At the organization of the pioneer and historical society of Ashland county in 1875, he communicated many interesting incidents, and became a member. He says the following pioneers were citizens of Green township at the arrival of his father's family in 1811: "George Pierce, John Davis, George and Abram Baughman, John Murphy, Joseph Jones, Sylvester Fisher, Ebenezer Rice, Solomon Hill, Josiah L. Hill, Moses Adsit, Thomas Coulter, Allen Oliver and Jeremiah Conine, and their families. In the fall of 1812, when the Indians became hostile, the settlers erected strong cabins and block-houses for their protection. Some three or four families having friends at Clinton, Knox county, removed there for greater safety. There was no stampede, as some state. All the settlers, except the ones named, remained and occupied their own places of defence."

ELIAS FORD

was born in Washington county, Pennsylvania, in 1799. He came with his father, Thomas Ford, from Jefferson county, Ohio, to Clearcreek township, in 1819. His father had entered a quarter section of land in section twenty-two. They journeyed in a small, one-horse wagon, in which they brought the necessary provisions for their absence, and a few tools to erect a cabin. From Wooster they passed along the path to the present site of Rowsburgh, thence along the old trail to the house of Jacob Young, on the Mohican, northeast of Uniontown; thence, to near Mason's mill, and then, along a new cut road to section twenty-two, where they erected a temporary shelter, somewhat in the form of a camp house, with open front, and covered with bark. Their bunk upon which they slept was suspended by bark ropes from the roof and was about three feet from the ground. The fire place was immediately in front of this open cabin and fire was kept burning during the night to frighten away the wolves, and keep off the musquitoes. The wolves were uncommonly numerous and mischievous. Rattlesnakes, and other varieties of reptiles, were quite numerous. The bed being thus elevated secured the occupants from the reptiles. Mr. Ford was accompanied by a large watch-dog, who slept at the open doorway in front of the cabin, to alarm the occupants in case of intrusion or danger. Thomas and Elias Ford were well armed. Elias slept in the cabin while his father made his home at Thomas McConnell's, a son-in-law, in Orange township. At the time of the arrival of Mr. Ford and son, a large number of Delaware Indians were encamped in the neighborhood, engaged in making sugar and hunting. They were well armed but quite friendly. A strong attachment soon sprang up and continued until the close of the hunting season. At this date many *Wyandots* and *Delawares* hunted annually along the Vermillion river and in the vicinity of the Savannah lakes, and looked with suspicion upon the intrusion of the white settlers. After a few weeks, Thomas Ford returned to Jefferson county and removed with the balance of his family to Clearcreek. Elias had been engaged in clearing and fencing a field for corn, and in the absence of a team, carried rails on his shoulders to place them in a fence.

The family of Thomas Ford, at their arrival in 1819, consisted of four sons, Elias, Elijah, Thomas H., and John; and four daughters, Elizabeth, Rebecca, Susannah, and Belinda. In the meantime a larger and more commodious cabin had been erected by the aid of the scattered settlers. Elias, subsequently, September 9, 1821, married Miss Elizabeth Parks, of Jefferson county, and located on the late Daniel Huffneer farm. At this time there was neither a church nor school-house in the township. The people assembled at the cabin of Thomas Ford, for public worship, for many years. In 1830, Ford's meeting house was erected; it was a fine structure for that period, and was occupied by the Methodists as a place of worship. Thomas Ford died October 10, 1830; his funeral was preached by Rev. Elmer Yocum.

Elias Ford performed arduous labor in clearing and preparing his farm. For many years he experienced all the privations of pioneer life, but by industry and frugality accumulated a handsome property. Having disposed of his old homestead, he purchased a new home in 1845, and subsequently, about 1865, sold it, and removed to Troy township, where he deceased in the fall of 1874, aged about seventy-five years. Mr. Ford was a large man; would weigh about two hundred pounds. He had a fine head, and bore a striking resemblance to Daniel Webster. If he had possessed the advantage of a thorough collegiate course of training, he would have left a proud record. As it was, he was a leading man in his township, as a farmer and a citizen. He was a man of high moral attainments, and took a leading part in favor of the public schools. Thomas H. Ford, a younger brother, served in the Mexican war as a captain, and subsequently became lieutenant governor of Ohio. He was also a colonel in the war of 1861–5. He is dead. The balance of the family are somewhat scattered.

JACOB LUCAS,

was born in Fayette county, Pennsylvania, June 27, 1805. He is of German descent. His father was from Hessia, and came over in the British army during the American Revolution. He served about three years, and upon learning that the colonists were not really cannibals, as asserted by the British officers, deserted to the colonial side. At the close of the war he settled in Fayette county, Pennsylvania, where he died in 1833, aged seventy-three years.

Jacob Lucas, his son, emigrated to Perry township, Wayne county, in 1832, with his family. He served a time at the trade of a tanner, in Mt. Pleasant, Westmoreland county, Pennsylvania, in 1821–3, and was among the first of his craft in Perry township. He carried on business over forty years, and retired in 1872. He is a leading member of the German Baptists or Dunkards. His family consists of four sons, John, Albert, Joseph, and Hiram, and four daughters, Rebecca, Elizabeth, Mary, and Lydia—all married.

JACOB HIFFNER, SR.,

was born in Hessia, Germany, in 1752, and when about sixteen years of age emigrated with his father's family to the State of Maryland, and settled near the Pennsylvania line. In the fall of 1776 he volunteered to serve three years in the line of Maryland infantry in the American Revolution. He marched with the Maryland troops to Trenton and Princeton, and participated in the battles of December 27, 1776, and January 3, 1777. In the following August he was in the battle of Bennington, and in September, the battle of Brandywine. He was at the surrender of Burgoyne, in October 1777. He fought in the battle of Monmouth, in June, 1778. From that period to the close of his enlistment, he marched and countermarched with the army from point to point, participating in many skirmishes and hard fought battles. At the expiration of his enlistment he returned to the residence of his father, where he remained nearly two years. The long continuance of the contest was rapidly decimating the colonies of their able-bodied men. It became necessary to force recruiting. A new draft was ordered and Mr. Hiffner's name was drawn. Having seen hard service in the army, he was not inclined to renew his old toils, dangers and sufferings. His father aided him in procuring a substitute, by the payment of such sum as was demanded. At the close of the Revolution Mr. Hiffner removed to Huntingdon county, Pennsylvania, where he remained until the fall of 1817, when he removed to Orange township, Richland county, Ohio. At the time of his removal his family consisted of six sons, Jacob, Frederick, Henry, John, David and Valentine, and four daughters, Elizabeth, Mary, Martha and Catharine. Mr. Hiffner and his sons, several of whom were married and had families, were accompanied by Jacob Ridenour, a son-in-law, and his family. The little colony was transported through the wilderness, along trails and recently opened paths, by four four-horse teams, in covered wagons, in which the families slept at night, during their long trip, cooking by the side of the paths at the regular hours. They crossed the Ohio river at Steubenville, and passed, thence, by narrow, muddy paths to New Philadelphia, to Wooster, and the present site of Rowsburgh, thence along the old Indian trail and emigrant path, to Jacob Young's, in Orange, and thence through the forest by new cut paths to section fourteen, where they erected small cabins within a short distance of their present homes, and commenced to cut away the forests and prepare fields for culture. When Mr. Hiffner and his sons and son-in-law landed, they found the following settlers, who had preceded them one or two years: Rudy Brouderberry, Robert Wasson, Martin Hester, Jacob Fast, Solomon Urie, Vachel Metcalf, Amos Norris, Jacob Young, Mordecai Chilcote, Philip Fluke, and John Bishop, who subsequently married Elizabeth Hiffner*. Mr. Hiffner lived to see his children all possess comfortable homes. He deceased November 23, 1848, aged ninety-six years and two months. He was buried on a bluff of Mohican creek, in the family cemetery, where many of his kindred sleep. May his rest never be disturbed by American recreancy or a want of patriotic devotion to the institutions he helped inaugurate. The only survivors of the large family are Catharine, wife of Joseph, Bishop and David, aged (1876) seventy-three years. Jacob Hiffner, the oldest of the family, served three months in the war of 1812 at Black Rock. He died, aged about eighty years. Henry died, aged seventy-two years. Valentine died, aged sixty-six years.

---

*A short time after the arrival of Mr. Hiffner, in the fall of 1817, Thomas Lyons, and sixteen or seventeen Delaware Indians, visited his cabin and had a long talk on the history of the *Delawares* in Pennsylvania, and the noted land-marks in that state, as well as the beautiful valleys of the Wyoming. Old Tom was very civil and slept on a blanket in the cabin of Mr. Hiffner. It was the custom of the *Delawares* for the following six or seven years to hunt and make sugar along the streams in Orange and Jackson township.

JOHN TILTON

was born in Princeton, New Jersey, in 1760. He entered the army of the American Revolution when he was sixteen years old, in 1776. He served in a regiment commanded by Colonel Klon. He was in the battles of Princeton, January 3, 1777; Germantown, October 4, 1777; Monmouth, June 28, 1778; Sander's Creek, August 16, 1780; Jamestown, July 9, 1781; at the surrender of Lord Cornwallis, October 19, 1781, and in a number of heavy skirmishes and retreats. He was in the service nearly five years, during which he experienced all the privations and hardships incident to the Revolutionary war. At the expiration of his service he returned to New Jersey, and married.

In 1787 he removed to Washington county, Pennsylvania. His family, at that time, consisted of himself, his wife, and two children—Elizabeth and Ira.

In August, 1812, he removed to Stark county, Ohio. In 1814 he removed to Wayne county, where he remained until May, 1831, when he located on section thirty-five, in Orange township, Ashland county. He purchased the farm of Robert Crawford, upon which had been erected, by its owner, a noted horse-mill of the pioneer period.

Mr. Tilton enlisted, for a tour of three months, in the brigade of Colonel Robert Crooks, in the war of 1812, in the northwest, while residing in Stark county, and accompanied the Pennsylvania troops, under General Robert Crooks, from Pittsburgh to Jerome's place and Mansfield, late in the fall of 1812.

He possessed great bodily vigor, which he retained to an advanced age. He was inflexible in his purposes, and retained a clear intellect until the time of his death. He expired, after a brief illness, at his farm in Orange township, August 12, 1849, aged nearly ninety years. He was accompanied to his final rest, in the cemetery at Orange, by volunteer military companies under the command of the late Colonel Alexander Miller, Major R. B. Fulkerson, and Captain John S. Fulton, and hundreds of his old neighbors.

Mr. Tilton was regarded as an upright and valuable citizen. His services in the war of Independence, and of 1812, with Great Britain, won for him the esteem of all his patriotic neighbors.

Mrs. Tilton preceded him to the grave about four months, at the age of eighty-four years. The family consisted of Elizabeth, Ira, Sarah, Amy, Phebe, Deborah, Aaron, and James A. Of these, only two survive—Mrs. Phebe Camybell, aged eighty-five, and James Albert, aged sixty-five. The latter resides on the old homestead, and is remarkable for his extraordinary physical force and mental determination. He is a successful farmer and business man.

WILLIAM TAYLOR

was born in Bucks county, Pennsylvania, January 14, 1774. His father had emigrated from Ireland two or three years before the commencement of the American

Revolution. He removed, after the close of the war, into Huntingdon county, and subsequently into Bedford county near the iron works. Here William remained until manhood, and married. In August, 1821, he emigrated, with his family, to Richland county, Ohio, landing at Mansfield. He brought with him one five-horse, one four-horse, and one two-horse team. The large team was loaded principally with axes, grubbing hoes, wedges, corn hoes and other necessary tools, and one set of blacksmith tools, which were disposed of to the pioneers at a fair profit. His route was by Pittsburgh, then along Cook's and Beall's trails to Wooster, and thence through Jeromeville, Hayes' cross roads, Petersburgh, and to Mansfield along the old State road. In the fall of 1821, he purchased four quarter sections of land adjoining what is now the Carey farm in Green township. He improved this property, passing through all the struggles of pioneer life, and resided on it until March 7, 1851, when he deceased. This homestead, in point of soil and location, was one of the finest in the county. Mr. Taylor was twice married. His family consisted of eight sons—William, Thomas, Levi, James, Alexander, David, John and Andrew, and one daughter, Sarah, wife of Thomas McGuire, of Green. John has been repeatedly elected justice of the peace, has served two terms in the Ohio legislature, and was elected probate judge in 1875.

The family are all deceased but Levi, James, David, John, Andrew and Mrs. McGuire.

ANDREW NEWMAN

was born in Rockingham county, Virginia, in 1778. He was of German descent, the original name being Neumann. He emigrated to Richland, then Fairfield county, in 1806, and settled on the Rocky fork of Mohican, in Mifflin township, about three and a half miles below the present site of Mansfield. Here he was joined by Jacob Beam and other pioneers. When the war of 1812 was declared, and the border settlers menaced by the Indians on the Black fork and Jerome fork, Mr. Newman assisted in the erection of a block-house, known as "Beam's," to which the settlers fled for safety. At the time of the removal of the Green and Jerometown Indians, Mr. Newman was engaged in building a saw-mill on the Rocky fork. In this work he was aided by William and Richard Roberts, of Knox county. The night the Zimmers and Ruffner were slain by the Indians, Mr. Newman fancied that the savages were in the vicinity of his cabin, for the reason that his big dog kept up such a disturbance. The hands got their guns in readiness, expecting to be attacked momentarily. Newman labored under unusual excitement, and in attempting to load his gun spilled the powder. Mr. Newman called to his aid Mr. Shearer; exclaiming, "py sure I vill spill all my powter. Shearer, you loads mine gun." The guns were loaded, and the score-axes placed in reach, to repel the savages if they attempted to enter the cabin. There was no more sleep that night. The next morning James Copus, John Lambright, Frederick Zimmer, and Isaac Hill and families, arrived at Beam's block-house, and reported that Ruffner and the Zimmer family had been killed. Upon examination about the forebay of the mill-race, which had just been raised, several moccasin tracks were discovered, and the evidence was clear that the Indians had meditated an attack there, but feared the Newman party were too strong. There were but four men at Newman's—himself, Mr. Shearer, and the two Roberts brothers. Within an hour after hearing of the massacre, Newman got up his team and fled to the block-house at Mansfield. The Roberts brothers, with a few soldiers from Captain Martin's company, which was stationed at Beam's block-house, rode over and examined the scene at Zimmers, and helped bury the victims of Indian vengeance. Mr. Newman remained in Mifflin township until the fall of 1825, when he purchased of Samuel McBride the farm upon which he afterwards erected a grist-mill, being the property more recently known as the Joseph Boyd mill, in the northeast part of Vermillion township. After disposing of the mill property he purchased a farm near the south line of the township, where he deceased January 20, 1861, aged eighty-three years. The surviving members of his family were William and James H. Newman, neither of whom reside in this county. James removed in the spring of 1876 to the vicinity of Hillsboro, Ohio.

JACOB SHOPBELL

was born in Berks county, Pennsylvania, September 29, 1788. His father, Daniel Shopbell, was a Revolutionary soldier and served in the army about seven years. He was in the battles of White Plains, Brandywine, Bunker Hill, and other struggles. He died in 1806 in Northampton county, Pennsylvania. His grandfather, Eberhard Shopbell, was a soldier in the war between France and Germany, in which the French acquired the territory of Alsace and Loraine. He lost a brother by the guillotine, and many relatives in the war, and came to America and settled in Berks county, Pennsylvania, where he died at the age of one hundred and four years. The people of that county were largely German, and the schools were entirely in that language. Jacob Shopbell was educated in the German dialect, and although he speaks the English tongue, reads only the German language. He emigrated from Northampton county, Pennsylvania, to Orange township, Richland, now Ashland county, Ohio, in 1832. He located near what is now Leidigh's mill. He served three months in the war of 1812, at Black Rock, near the lake shore, under Colonel Irwin and Captain Joseph Dean. He was in no regular battle of small arms. He is now the oldest soldier of this region. He has always been a farmer, temperate, industrious and economical, and is yet remarkably vigorous for a man of his age. He has been twice married, and is the father of seventeen children, eleven girls and five boys. There were six children by his first wife, and eleven by the second. His sons are Andrew, of Michigan, Daniel, John, Samuel, and David, of Ashland county. He resides with a son-in-law, George Shidler.

DR. ANDREW J. SCOTT

was born in Richland county, Ohio, November 12, 1827. He obtained a liberal education, and upon reaching manhood became a successful teacher. He was principal of the Loudonville academy for some years. He read medicine in the office of Dr. E. B. Fuller, attended lectures at Starling medical college, Columbus, Ohio, at Buffalo university, at the medical department of Havard college, and college of physicians and surgeons. He opened an office in Loudonville, in 1853, and has been in successful practice to the present, 1876. Since his graduation he has become a member of the Ashland county medical society, and also of the Ohio State medical society. He is also corresponding member of the gynæcological society of Boston, and a member of the American medical association. He takes a deep interest in literary pursuits, and when a teacher, was regarded as one of the best mathematicians in the county. He has been three times married, twice to daughters of Dr. E. B. Fuller. He is of Scotch-Irish descent, and possesses all the enthusiasm of both races. Possessed of a strong will, he is resolute in the prosecution of whatever he deems right. If health permits, he has the attainments to achieve a fine reputation in the medical profession. He would acquit himself ably in any of the medical colleges of this State. He is a fluent conversationalist, a ready speaker, and a clear thinker.

DR. EPHRAIM B. FULLER

was born in Madison county, New York, July 8, 1799. He read medicine in the office of Dr. Parkis, of Tioga county, Pennsylvania, and commenced practice in 1823. He married Sarah Culver, of Elkland, Pennsylvania, in March, 1822. He practiced in Potter county, Pennsylvania until the spring of 1832, when he located in Loudonville, Richland (now Ashland,) county, Ohio.

Dr. Fuller was not a regularly educated physician, having read in a private office, and according to the statutes of New York, was examined and admitted to practice medicine and surgery under a certificate issued by the county censors. He was a man of marked industry, and possessed an iron will, which associated with a powerful physical organization, a love of his profession, and close attention to medical authorities enabled him to accomplish a great deal in the line of his calling. He had a most extensive practice, and was unusually successful in the treatment of the diseases of his locality. He practiced continuously over thirty-six years, sometimes under circumstances the most adverse, and in the face of a well arranged competition, always sustaining himself honorably in his profession. He should rank among the very best of the profession in the county. He died at Loudonville, December 23, 1867. He left a family.

Dr. Amos B. Fuller is a son, and Dr. A. J. Scott, a son-in-law. The son is said to possess many of the peculiarities of the father, and will probably succeed to a fair share of his practice.

DR. JOSEPH E. CLIFF,

a native of London, England, an energetic and spirited physician, well calculated to make himself known and felt in the community, settled in Loudonville in 1825. He studied medicine with Dr. Daniel McPhail, of Wooster, 1821-2 a Scotchman, and leading physician of Waynec ounty, for several years, in At that period Dr. McPhail frequently visited Clearcreek, Montgomery, Vermillion, and Mohican townships, accompanied by Dr. Cliff, who sometimes repeated the visits. He remained about two years at Loudonville, and returned to Wooster, and shortly afterwards departed for the gold mines in Brazil, South America. He landed in the midst of a revolution, and proceeding to the mines, remained several years, and became possessed of considerable wealth. In the meantime, his wife, a daughter of Dr. McPhail, supposing him dead, married Robert W. Smith, late of Mohican township. Dr. Cliff returned from South America and found his wife in the possession of another! Accepting the condition of things as philosophically as possible, he proceeded to provide liberally for his son, who afterwards read medicine, and now enjoys a wide reputation as Dr. D. B. Cliff, of Franklin, Tennessee. After this the old doctor returned to London, England, where he died some years since. This is highly romantic, but nevertheless true. It is obtained from the lips of his venerable wife, who still survives, and is now seventy-six years of age, and resides with her son, Edward P. Smith, near Ashland.

Money was very scarce, and the surplus products of the country, in 1825, had no market. High spirited and ambitious, the doctor hoped to better his fortunes in other countries. He was wholly deprived of the means of corresponding with his family, and the sequel shows that, while he accomplished the object of his adventure, he lost an amiable and accomplished wife.

DR. JOEL LUTHER.

On a pleasant evening in the fall of 1820, a young man of fair countenance, dark eyes, black hair, very erect and plainly habited, seated in a one-horse wagon, with a wooden box for a trunk, drove to the front of what was then known as the "Sheets' tavern," located on the lot now occupied by Jacob Weisenstine, in Uniontown, now Ashland, and asked permission to lodge for the night. It was granted, and the young man was soon seated for supper, while his jaded horse was carefully stabled and fed by the landlord, Mr. Joseph Sheets, who was also the principal tailor and merchant of the village. The new guest appeared to be a quiet, self-possessed, intelligent young gentleman, and Mrs. Sheets soon had him engaged in a lively conversation. Supper being over, the routine of finding out the birth-place, the financial resources, the destination, and the personal peculiarities of the stranger, was gone into in a systematic manner.

During this ordeal it was learned that the stranger was a native of Berkshire county, Massachusetts, was born about the year 1794, had attended a neighborhood school until he was of age, and then, like a true son of New England, had come west to seek his fortune, his parents being unable to extend further aid. It further transpired that he had gone to Troy, New York, about the year 1816, where he earnestly engaged in the vocation of teaching school, in the meantime studying medicine under a leading practitioner of that place, where, at the conclusion of his studies, he had been licensed to practice, and located, for a short time, at a place called Red Post, in the vicinity of Troy, but, finally, preferred to go further west, and that, with one hundred dollars in money, and his horse and wagon, he had reached Uniontown in the hopes of finding a new home.

Mr. and Mrs. Sheets gave it as their opinion that a physician might soon obtain a lively practice in this region, as there was no doctor nearer than Mansfield (Dr. Miller), which was about sixteen miles away. The young gentleman whom they addressed was Dr. Joel Luther, Berkshire, of Massachusetts.

The new doctor retired to bed feeling much encouraged over the idea of having found a good location and a pleasant home. About daylight the next morning the occupants of the Sheets house were aroused by loud knocking at the front door. Mr. Sheets hastily opened it and asked what was wanting. The man, who resided some three miles in the country, inquired if there was not a doctor in town, stating that a member of his family was very sick. Mr. Sheets replied that a young doctor had arrived the night before, was in the house, and had about concluded to locate in the village. Dr. Luther was urged to accompany the pioneer to his cabin. He was but too happy to do so. He was soon ready, mounted his horse and threaded his way along paths through the forest to the presence of his new patient. This was the first case of the first doctor; and having been successfully treated, the new physician soon obtained an extensive practice. The prevailing diseases of those days were autumnal fevers, bilious, bilious remittent, and the process of treatment was generally such as kills the modern bullock—copious blood-letting. Strong men required vigorous treatment, and they got it without stint. The lancet was an indispensable instrument; and when a physician could not be had, many private persons proffered their services as plebotomists, and human blood was abstracted freely. Times change, and men change. The sanguinary theory is now almost a dream.

The doctor erected an office a short distance above the present location of the McNulty house, where he continued to do business until about the year 1831, when he retired from the practice, owing to failing health, and soon after opened a dry goods establishment in which he was engaged until his decease in 1834. As a physician he had an extended and successful practice, and drew around him a large circle of friends. As a business man he was shrewd and exact and careful in all his dealings, and accumulated a fine property. He was genial and pleasant among his patients and friends, and not averse to a good practical joke.

In 1824 he was married to Miss Elizabeth, daughter of Christopher Mykrantz, who died April 19, 1880, aged seventy-two years, two months and twelve days, born in Westmoreland county, Pennsylvania. At his death he left one daughter who married Dr. J. F. Sampsell, and is now deceased.

DIPLOMA OF DR. JOEL LUTHER.

Be it known, that on the twenty-fifth day of September, A. D., 1817, Joel Luther was examined by the censors of Rensselaer medical society in the various branches of medical science, and received their approbation. Now, know ye, therefore, that by virtue of the powers in me vested, I do hereby authorize and license the said Joel Luther to practice physics and surgery, in the State of New York. In testimony whereof, I have set my hand to these presents, and caused the seal of the society to be hereunto affixed.

Done at Troy this twenty-fifth day of September, A. D., 1817.

HEZEKIAH E. DRAY, President.

J. M. HALL, Secretary.

STEUBEN COUNTY, CLERK'S OFFICE, } ss.
October 15, 1818.

A copy of the within diploma has been duly filed in the office of the clerk of the aforesaid county.

C. HOWELL, Clerk.

DR. JOSEPH HILDRETH.

About the year 1821, a young man from "York State" arrived in Ashland, and obtained employment at the distillery of Slocum and Palmer. He was dreadfully afflicted with obliquity of vision, a disease known as *strabismus*. One eye seemed to be so much affected as to be useless for all purposes, and the other, so distorted as to make it very difficult for him to read. His singular appearance attracted a good deal of attention, and many unfeeling witticisms were perpetrated at his expense. The young man attended promptly to the interests of his employers; and in deportment was habitually reserved. It was noticed, however, that he possessed quite a store of information, and could converse fluently when so disposed. He very soon engaged the attention and sympathy of Dr. Joel Luther, whose esteem he finally won. The doctor discovered, on further acquaintance, that the young man possessed a most retentive memory, and had talents of an unusual order. Thus he had been richly endowed with intellect to atone for all his physical infirmities, as in the case of Æsop and thousands of others. At the request of Dr. Luther, Mr. Hildreth commenced a course of medical studies, and made rapid progress. He continued in the office, as a student, some three years. At that period the laws of Ohio required all students, at the completion of their studies, before entering upon practice, to procure a license to do so. There being no medical school, the young doctor had to thread his way along rough roads and paths to the legislature, with a view of submitting to an examination by a special committee to be appointed by that body. On his arrival, he attracted a good deal of attention. The committee was appointed, and the time and place for examination designated. From the singular appearance of the applicant, it was believed that the committee would make a sort of frolic of the affair—have a good deal of fun and let the young man depart in disgust. The chairman of the committee, being a sort of doctor, turned out to be not so learned on anatomy as Horner, Wistor or Wilson. He had proceeded but a brief time in the examination, when the young doctor picked him up on the origin, insertion, and location of the sartorius. The next blunder was, in assigning the position of the liver and stomach in relation to the diaphragm. The young doctor triumphed. The principles of the theory and practice of medicine were hastily disposed of, and compatibles and incompatibles entered upon. By way of crowding the young doctor into a tight place, the chairman wished to know the result of a mixture of alkaline salts, water, and animal oil, in given proportions. After revolving the matter a moment, the young doctor said: "Gentlemen, I have studied with a view of practicing medicine, and not to follow the occupation of making soap." The laugh was on the wrong side again. The committee had caught a "Tartar," and was bound to bring in a favorable report, which was done; and the doctor returned fully authorized to practice his profession. He continued in practice, in Ashland, with fair success, some five or six years, and removed to Bellville, Richland county, where he resided many years. He subsequently studied law and located in Mansfield, where he deceased about two years since.

The doctor achieved a fine reputation as a leading member of the Masonic fraternity. He was, perhaps, one of the brightest Masons in the State, and many years ago was appointed by the Grand lodge a member of a committee to revise the work, a duty which he discharged with fidelity and rare ability.

As a physician, he understood clearly the principles of his profession, and, as a lawyer, he is said to have been well versed, but, owing to his infirmities of vision, he was unable to make such a display of his talents as would win public patronage.

He was the second physician in Ashland, and a man of note. He is an illustration of what can be accomplished by industry and untiring perseverance, notwithstanding the embarrassments of physical infirmities.

DR. WILLIAM N. DEMING,

from Medina county, Ohio, is believed to have been the third physician of Ashland. He arrived about the winter of 1826. He continued in an active practice until 1837, when he located in the village of Orange, where his brother, Charles, was engaged in the mercantile business. He resided in Orange about two years, when he became a member of the Methodist Episcopal church, during a revival, and prepared to enter the ministry. He attended conference, and was assigned to a circuit. Upon returning home he was taken suddenly very sick, and died, after a brief illness. The doctor is represented as having been an excellent physician, and a man of many accomplishments. His untimely demise was much lamented.

DR. DAVIDSON

arrived about the year 1829, and continued in practice until 1833, when he removed to Canton, Illinois. He is represented as a gentleman of good social bearing and fair medical attainments. His Christian name is not remembered.

DR. WILLARD SLOCUM.

Dr. Slocum arrived in 1833 from the State of New York, and succeeded to the practice of Dr. Davidson. He was a man of strong points, and soon made an impression, financially and professionally. He had considerable reputation, and is said to have been a bold operator. He closed his practice, and emigrated to Michigan, in the spring of 1846, where he deceased, after a residence of some two or three years. He was a relative of the late Elias Slocum.

DR. GUSTAVUS OESTERLEN.

Dr. Oesterlen was born in the kingdom of Wurtemberg, Germany, November 20, 1804. He attended a Latin and German school until he was sixteen years of age, and then entered a gymnasium at Stuttgardt, the capital of the state, where he remained four years, and was examined in the languages and admitted into the university of Tubingen, to study the different branches of medicine, and remained there five years. In 1829 he attended the Queen Catharine hospital, at Stuttgardt; was examined in the spring of 1830, and received his diploma. In the spring of 1830 he was appointed assistant surgeon in the army of Wurtemberg, and remained in said position until the fall of 1833. In the spring of 1834 he took passage for America, and in July arrived at Mansfield, Richland county, where he remained until about the first of October, and then located in Ashland, where he has been in practice nearly forty-one years. In size, the doctor is below the medium, his height being about five feet seven inches, and his weight about one hundred and twenty pounds. He is quite active, and in the full possession of all his faculties. He is very courteous and kind in his bearing towards the members of his profession. In the languages he is, perhaps, the best scholar of the medical profession of this region. He has had a good German practice for many years, and has met with excellent success. As a surgeon, he has had a good reputation, and in his prime was the best operator in the country. Of late years, from failing vision and nervousness, he has performed fewer operations. The doctor is a fine specimen of the old school German gentleman; and still adheres to many of the customs of the fatherland. As a citizen, he is law-abiding, quiet, and exemplary. As a business man, his integrity has never been disputed. Among the members of his profession he is much respected. He was among the first to aid in the formation of a medical society in this county, that courtesy, fraternity and professional zeal might be disseminated among his brethren.

For a period of nearly thirty years the doctor has been an active member of the Masonic order, and has been almost continuously the treasurer of the lodge. This speaks well for his fidelity and masonic bearing among his associates. Among the members of the lodge, as among the medical fraternity, he has been noted for his genial and unselfish disposition. He has always a kind word for the encouragement of the younger members of his profession. He is now the Nestor of his profession in this county. Learned, courteous, and proud of his profession, he hails every advancement in medical science as the harbinger of good to the race.

DR. BELA B. CLARK

was born in New Milford, Connecticut, October 1, 1796. He studied medicine in the same place, and attended lectures under Drs. Hosac, Francis and Mott, in New York city in 1817. He came to Medina, Ohio, in 1818, and was married to Sophia P. Searls, October 28, 1820. He practiced medicine in Medina county twenty-four years, and removed to the city of Columbus in 1842, where he practiced three years. During his residence in that city he became acquainted with several gentlemen from Ashland, who were laboring for the passage of an act for the erection of the new county of Ashland, and became identified with the measure. Upon the passage of that act, he removed to Ashland and entered upon his profession. He continued to practice medicine about fourteen years. When the enterprise of constructing the Atlantic & Great Western railway originated, Dr. Clark entered heartily into the project, and aided until it was nearly graded. He was among the first directors. Soon after his arrival in Ashland he was appointed one of the associate judges of the court of common pleas, and served until the adoption of the constitution of 1851. During his medical practice he received a diploma from the fellows of the Connecticut medical society in 1817; also one from the nineteenth medical district of Ohio, at Cleveland, May 25, 1824; and a license from the court of the third judicial circuit of Ohio, November 30, 1818, and another from the medical society of the eighth medical district of Ohio, November 5, 1818; and in 1841, Willoughby Medical college conferred an honorary degree of medicine, with diploma, upon him.

The doctor died from apoplexy, August 20, 1859, aged about sixty-three years. He had been an active member and ruling elder in the Presbyterian church for a number of years. He was an accomplished physician, a zealous advocate of education, and always active for the public weal. His family consists of his wife, who still survives; Dr. W. R. Clark, of Des Moines, Iowa, a successful physician; Elizabeth, wife of Dr. P. H. Clark, of Ashland, and Charles F. M., of Iowa.

DR. P. H. CLARK,

born in Wakeman, Huron county, Ohio, August 3, 1819; studied medicine and attended one course of lectures at Willoughby in 1839–40, and practiced in Allen county, Indiana, and in Wisconsin, for some time; removed to Ashland in 1850; was assistant surgeon in the late war in 1862–3 in the field hospitals. He attended a second course of lectures at the university of Buffalo, New York, in 1861–2, and graduated. He is a member of the Ohio State Medical society, and has been pension surgeon since December, 1862. He is now in practice.

DR. W. R. S. CLARK,

born November 26, 1821, in Medina, Ohio; attended school at Kenyon college; studied medicine with his father; attended lectures at Willoughby and Cleveland, where he graduated. He practiced in Lorain county and Ashland; removed to Bucyrus and practiced until the war, and was appointed surgeon, and subsequently removed to Des Moines, Iowa.

DR. HARRISON ARMSTRONG

was born near Wellsville, Columbiana county, Ohio, November 25, 1809. He was of Scotch-Irish descent, his grandfather having emigrated from the north of Ireland, and served as a soldier in the American Revolution. He removed with his father's family to Canaan township, Wayne county, in the year 1815. Here he attended the common schools of the neighborhood, and grew to manhood. He studied medicine under the instruction of the late Dr. L. F. Day, of Wooster, in 1828, and attended lectures in Cincinnati, at the Ohio Medical college, in the years 1830–1, and graduated. He practiced medicine in 1831 in company with Dr. Irvine, of Millersburgh, Holmes county, and in the spring of 1832 located in the village of Hayesville, in Ashland county, being the first regular physician who resided in that place. He soon won public confidence, and for a period of twenty years had a large and lucrative practice in Vermillion, Mohican, Green, and Mifflin townships. In 1853 he retired from practice, and devoted his time partly to the mercantile business, but chiefly to agriculture.

He owned a valuable farm in the vicinity of Hayesville, to which he removed, and brought to a high state of culture. He took great pride in the pursuits of agriculture, and was surrounded by all the comforts of a scientific farmer. He married in Hayesville, in 1837, Miss Margaret Cox, daughter of the late Rev. John Cox, of Mansfield, one of the pioneers of Vermillion township. His family consisted of nine children—six sons and three daughters. Two of his sons are dead.

DR. DAVID ARMSTRONG

graduated in Jefferson Medical college, Philadelphia, in 1850, and was a physician of much promise. He deceased in 1852, much lamented by his friends and the profession. The late Doctor Armstrong was a large, finely developed gentleman, ruddy, and of imposing appearance. He possessed many of the characteristics of his ancestry, both in sense, wit and humor, and enjoyed a little fun and a hearty laugh. As a physician and business man he stood deservedly high among his fellows, and was noted for frankness and directness in all his dealings with men. In politics, he was an old line Whig, and more recently a member of the Republican party.

For one or two years prior to his last illness he had been in feeble health. His last sickness was the result of heart disease. For three or four months prior to his decease, he was constantly distressed by the growing malady, all of which he bore with exemplary fortitude and patience. His sufferings were brought to a close on the morning of December 14, 1876, and his remains were deposited in the cemetery at Hayesville.

The usual resolutions of the Ashland county Historical and Pioneer society, of which he was a member, were adopted, concerning his decease.

DR. JACOB W. KINNAMAN

was born in Ellsworth, Trumbull county, Ohio, October 18, 1815. He spent his youth in that locality, and commenced the study of medicine when eighteen years of age, and attended lectures at Jefferson Medical college, in Philadelphia, in the winter of 1833. He commenced practice in Ellsworth, and remained there some years. In 1836 he married Miss Harriet Carson, a cousin of the celebrated Kit Carson, the explorer. In 1847 he graduated in Cleveland Medical college, and removed with his family to Ashland. He opened an office, and continued to practice until 1849, when he caught the gold fever, and went to California, his family remaining in Ashland. He returned in 1851, and again engaged in the practice of medicine. In 1854 he again went to California, intending to remain several years, leaving his practice in the hands of his brother, Dr. Lawrence Kinnaman; but, a little more than a year after his arrival in California, learning the dangerous illness of his brother, he returned to attend him, but arrived a short time after his decease. He again engaged in practice, and continued until his last illness. In 1871, leaving his practice in the care of his son, Dr. R. C. Kinnaman, he went to California to recruit his failing health, and remained one summer, failing to receive any direct relief. He returned, and remained feeble, until July 18, 1874, when he deceased, at the residence of his son-in-law, Mr. Henry Carter, at Lancaster, Ohio. His remains were brought back and interred in the cemetery of Ashland.

Dr. Kinnaman was reticent, but frank and honorable in his profession. He was a member of the Ohio State Medical society, and also a member of the Academy of Natural Sciences, at Cleveland. He was an attentive student, and possessed an extensive knowledge of medicine. He left a large family.

DR. ISAAC L. CRANE

was born in Akron, Ohio, May 7, 1825. His parents having died when he was quite young, he was compelled to depend upon his own industry and energy for success. He learned the trade of a tailor, and, by economy and close application, earned sufficient to warrant an attempt to study medicine. He became a student of Dr. L. Firestone about the year 1850, and graduated in the Western Reserve college, in the session of 1853-54. He soon after located in Ashland, and drew around him many warm and devoted friends. He was a careful practitioner, and unremitting in his attentions to his patients, and evinced a good deal of skill as a physician. In 1861 he was commissioned in the three months' service as surgeon in the Twenty-third regiment Ohio militia. After the expiration of his service he was again commissioned, for three years, in the Sixty-third regiment Ohio volunteer infantry, October 17, 1861, and served until January, 1864. During his service he acted for some time as medical director in the army of the Tennessee. He acquitted himself with honor to the profession and his friends.

Full of zeal for the dignity and honor of the medical profession, few of his age have done more to dignify it. He became president of the county medical society upon its organization, in 1864, and was a member of the Ohio State Medical association.

During his arduous services in the war, he greatly impaired his constitution, and gradually became more feeble, until his lungs became involved, and drained his vitality. He died June 12, 1867, of pulmonary consumption. The County Medical society and the Masonic fraternity, of which he was a member, paid him their last honors in accompanying him to his final resting place in the cemetery at Ashland. His wife resides in Iowa.

DR. SAMUEL GLASS

was born in Wayne county, Ohio, April 14, 1818. In early life he possessed no advantages of education beyond the district schools. The first eighteen years of his life were occupied in clearing the forests and in farm labor. Wages were low, and it took a long time to accumulate sufficient money to enter upon a course of study. He grew up in habits of industry and frugality, and these habits became a part of his maturer years. His first effort was at school teaching. In 1840, he commenced the study of medicine with Dr. Harrison Armstrong, of Hayesville, in this county, and in 1842 attended medical lectures at Cincinnati. In 1843, he opened an office in Mifflin, of this county, where he remained three years. In April, 1845, he married Miss Amanda A. Armentrout, of Hayesville, and opened an office in that place. In the winter of 1847-8, he attended a second course of lectures at Jefferson Medical college, Philadelphia, where he graduated. Shortly after his return, Dr. H. Armstrong retired from practice, and his son, Dr. David Armstrong, and Dr. S. Glass entered into partnership. This continued until the decease of Dr. Armstrong, which occurred in 1852. Dr. Glass continued in practice, a part of the time with Dr. Yocum, until he was elected State senator in 1861-2. He again resumed practice and continued until 1865, when he removed to Ashland, and formed a partnership with Dr. D. S. Sampsell in 1866, with whom he continued until his last illness. In the meantime he became a member of the Ohio State Medical association, and president of the Medical society of Ashland county. He died of congestion of the brain, February 26, 1873. Dr. Glass was a large, well-developed man, full six feet high, and would weigh about two hundred pounds. He had a large brain, a strong will, and tremendous endurance. He performed an uncommon amount of labor, in his practice, which was always quite extended. He accumulated a handsome fortune, and was esteemed a very thorough and successful physician. He was childless. His widow resides in Ashland.

DR. OLIVER C. McCARTY

was born in Lycoming county, Pennsylvania, December 29, 1816, and moved with his father, Job McCarty, to New Lisbon, Columbiana county, Ohio, when young, and resided there until 1826, when they settled in Dalton, Wayne county, Ohio. He began his medical studies in 1829 with Dr. Joseph Watson, of Massillon, Ohio, and continued there until 1833, and then located at Albion, now Ashland county, Ohio, where he continued in practice until 1841, when he attended a full course of lectures at the Ohio Medical college at Cincinnati, and graduated at the Hudson Medical college, Cleveland, in 1846. He continued in practice at Polk, Ohio, until 1863, at which time he was commissioned as assistant surgeon in the army, by Governor John Brough, and remained in the service until the close of the war. At the close of the war, he was examined and commissioned for five years in the regular United States service as surgeon; but declined to remain, and returned to his former locality and again entered into active practice. He has, with the exception of his absence in the army, practiced medicine over forty years in Jackson township, in this county. He is an attentive observer, a close student, and a successful physician. He possesses inventive talents of a high order, and has patented a number of inventions for the benefit of agriculturists. He has strong tastes for natural science, and has repeatedly delivered a course of lectures before the students of Vermillion institute, of Hayesville. He married Miss Eleanor B. Pancoast, daughter of Hezekiah Pancoast, of Wayne county, in 1836. His family consists of his wife, self and five children, all of whom survive but one son, H. W. McCarty, who died in the army. The doctor is quite vigorous, and may survive many years.

MAJOR R. P. FULKERSON

was born in Somerset county, New Jersey, February 11, 1807. In his youth he attended the country schools of that State, and made fair progress in the elementary branches. At the age of eighteen he was apprenticed to learn the trade of a blacksmith. He also learned, at the same time, the art of making augers. In 1829 he married Miss Sarah Ann Wicoff, and in the spring of 1830, removed to Ashland, Ohio. Upon his arrival he opened a shop and commenced business. In addition to country work, such as shoeing horses, repairing and fitting plows, he ironed many road wagons and carriages, and repaired guns. Being remarkably ingenious in working iron, he was able to turn his hand to many branches of the art. When gas was first introduced into Ashland, he engaged in fitting and preparing burners, pipes and other fixtures, and his books contain drawings showing the labyrinths concealing gas throughout most of the leading buildings and private residences of Ashland. In 1860 he retired from the toil and worry of his trade and entered upon the horticultural business, for which he had strong tastes and many qualifications. He was fond of the study of botany, and his green-house gave evidence of his fine taste in the floral kingdom. He also succeeded in introducing many fine varieties of fruit, flowering shrubs, and plants. He was industrious in his researches into the habits of the honey-bee, and in fact, took a lively interest in everything that could contribute to the prosperity and happiness of his race. He was extremely fond of the sport of hunting, and generally kept a "pointer" or "setter" of the best blood. Few of the best hunters could excel him in shooting quail or pheasants on the wing. He was particularly successful in ensnaring, in the spring time, wild pigeons, and in taking ducks. He was buoyant in spirit, and a great favorite with his associates. There were but few subjects that he could not illustrate and explain. In 1875, when the State Archæological society was formed at Mansfield, he became a member, and about the same time he became a member of the Pioneer and Historical society of Ashland county. He took a deep interest in the topics discussed in those organizations. His tastes were strongly military, and in his younger years he was promoted from a company officer to be major of a regiment. He is said to have been a good drill officer, and could he have been educated at an institution such as West Point, would have made an accomplished officer in the engineer department.

He was a strong friend of the school system of Ohio, and when the old academy was under the superintendency of the lamented Lorin Andrews, gave his time and attention to the encouragement of that institution. He was frequently a member of the Ashland council, and was acting as such at his decease. He was also a trustee of the cemetery association and aided in preparing that beautiful site for the dead.

In 1873 his excellent lady deceased, since which time he resided with the younger members of his family.

In 1876 he visited the Centennial at Philadelphia, and upon his return, expressed his gratification and astonishment over the wonders in art and invention beheld by him on exhibition on that occasion.

Early in the winter he was attacked with pneumonia and other complications, and gradually failed until he died, May 21, 1877. He was buried in the cemetery at Ashland.

The usual resolutions were adopted by the obituary committee of the Historical society, of which he was a member.

HON. JAMES E. CHASE

was born in Stark county, Ohio, October 19, 1824. He was educated in the common schools of the neighborhood, and grew up a farmer. His ancestors were Scotch-English. His father, Seth Chase, was born in Massachusetts, and his mother, Syena Wood, in Vermont. Bishop Chase, and Salmon P. Chase, of Ohio, were a branch of the same family. Seth Chase removed, with his family, to Massillon, Ohio, in 1825, and remained one year, but finding his health greatly impaired by the malaria of that region, returned to Vermont, and in 1836 again came to Ohio and located in Massillon. Here he died in 1852, aged fifty-eight years. His wife died in 1856, aged fifty-six years. His family was composed of James E., Emily V., wife of Jacob Colopy, Laura T., single. James E. Chase became an active farmer, and in 1857 was elected, by the Democracy, a member of the Ohio legislature, and was re-elected in 1859. In 1861 he sold his farm and removed to Jackson township, Ashland county. In 1869 he was again elected, by the Democracy of Ashland county, to the Ohio legislature, and was re-elected in 1871. In 1873 he was elected treasurer of Jackson township, and again in 1874. He has been regularly a delegate to State conventions for over twenty years. He married Mrs. Jane Baughman, of Stark county. Their children are James B., Orlan D., Sherwood M., Nelson H., Mary I., wife of Jacob Moor, of Illinois, Ellen S., wife of David Wise, of Ashland county, and Samantha, single.

ROBERT NEWELL,

a native of Washington county, Pennsylvania, is believed to have located in the east part of Montgomery township in 1811. He had resided for two or three years on White Eyes plains, near the present site of Newcomerstown, in Tuscarawas county, Ohio. He is believed to have erected the first cabin in Montgomery township. It was situated on what has since been known as the Hugh McGuire farm, some five miles southeast of Ashland. In the fall of 1812, after the Ruffner–Zimmer–Copus tragedies on the Black fork, the cabins of Mr. Newell, Mr. Cuppy, and Mr. Fry, further up a branch of the same stream, were burned by the Indians, while the families of the above-mentioned pioneers sought safety at the fort or Jerome's place, now the village of Jeromeville. After peace had been declared, Mr. Newell re-erected a cabin and continued to improve his farm, which he finally sold to the late Hugh McGuire, and located one mile north of Olivesburgh, in Richland county, where he deceased in 1848, at an advanced age. When Montgomery township was associated with Vermillion township for civil purposes, from 1814 to 1816, Mr. Newell, from Montgomery, and James Wallace, from Vermillion, were elected justices of the peace. Upon the organization of Montgomery in 1816, Mr. Newell lost his office. He is represented as having been a clever, whole-souled pioneer, but in point of education quite illiterate. He could not write, and consequently kept no docket. There was but little litigation in those days, and it was the habit of Squire Newell to appoint a day and cite the plaintiff and defendant to appear before him. When the parties had assembled, he required them to state, under oath, the nature of their claims, and having partially heard both sides, required an equitable and peaceable adjustment of the dispute. It is related, that on some occasions, money being exceedingly scarce, and whiskey being a "legal-tender," it was decided that a gallon of that article should be provided by the winning party for the crowd, and the case be dismissed, with the injunction that in the future the litigants should be neighbors and friends. Mr. Newell was a very liberal officer. He rarely charged for his services. Constable Kline, who served under him, being a poor man, had to exact his fees.

The sons of Mr. Newell were: Absalom, Franklin, Samuel, Zachariah, and Jesse. The daughters were two—Mrs. Jonathan Edy and Mrs. Lloyd Edy, of Richland county. The sons all moved west, most of them to Iowa, where some of them yet reside. Like Robert Newell, their father, they were all large, rugged men, and preferred the rough and tumble of a new country. Like the Lattas, the Mackleys, the Uries, and hundreds of others of the early settlers, they were formidable men at a military muster, a cabin raising, a political meeting or any other gathering where physical force was brought into question. The days of the giants are no more! The race of backwoodsmen has departed. Feebler men occupy their places.

JACOB H. GRUBB.

Jacob Grubb was born in Union county, Pennsylvania, October 18, 1800. His ancestors were Franco-German. In his youth he attended the schools of his neighborhood, and obtained a fair knowledge of the English branches. After arriving at the age of about sixteen years, he served an apprenticeship to learn the trade of cabinet-maker. After completing his trade, he married Miss Hannah Robison, daughter of David Robison, of Union county, Pennsylvania. In 1823 he removed, with his wife and infant daughter Mary, now wife of David J. Rice, to Uniontown, now Ashland, Ohio. At that time the village was quite small. He rented a small log cabin of Christopher Mykrantz, situated in the rear of what is now the town hall, where he resided and worked at the cabinet-making business; he was the second cabinet-maker who settled in Uniontown, the late Alexander Miller being the first. After residing there some years, he removed to his late residence, on the north side of Main street, where he continued to work at his trade. He carried on business continuously for nearly fifty years, and retired from active labor some four or five years since. Many of the pioneers yet possess bureaus made by him more than forty years ago. His work was of the most substantial character and finish, and was noted for its durability.

Mr. Grubb stood high among his fellow-townsmen in consequence of his integrity and moral worth. In 1823 he and his excellent lady assisted in the organization of the first class of the Methodist Episcopal church of Ashland. The class long met at the residence of John Smith, which stood on the lot subsequently occupied by the residence of the late Christopher Mykrantz. His membership in the Methodist Episcopal church of Ashland was, therefore, continuous for a period of fifty-four years, during which he adorned his profession by an upright and exemplary Christian life. He passed through all the inconveniences and hardships of pioneer Methodism; having for many years worshipped in a cabin, and in the great assemblies in the forest, known as camp-meetings, and freely expressed the opinion that the plainness of primitive Methodist manners was greatly conducive to true piety. Mr. Grubb and all the members of his family possessed fine musical taste, and delighted to join in the exercise of singing, as well as to take part in instrumental music.

The family of Mr. Grubb consisted of five sons—John, Frank, Burr, and two deceased; and six daughters—Mary, wife of D. J. Rice; Lorilla, wife of Samuel Davis; Rosanna, wife of Henry McCormick, and three deceased, and his aged wife, Hannah. He died January 9, 1878, of paralysis, aged seventy-seven years, two months, and twenty-one days.

CAPTAIN ALANSON WALKER.

He was born in Allegheny county, Pennsylvania, March 4, 1804, and emigrated to Uniontown, now Ashland, Ohio, in 1822. Shortly after his arrival he apprenticed to Robert Ralston, jr., of Orange township, to learn the trade of a carpenter, and served about four years. Upon the completion of his trade, in January, 1827, he married Esther Robison, of Clearcreek township, and located in Ashland, where he has continued ever since as a carpenter. In the earlier years of his pioneer life, he endured all the privations and hardships incident to the settlement of new countries. He retained a vivid recollection of the early settlers, and their adventures, to the last. Very few of the early mechanics attended more house raisings, log rollings, corn huskings, and early military trainings, than he. From a native forest, he lived to see the site of Ashland develop into a prosperous and handsome county seat. Of the first inhabitants of the town, he retained a very clear recollection, and could relate many anecdotes concerning their social habits and customs.

In the palmy days of the old militia, he was elected captain of a company that more than forty years ago trained at Mansfield, and the prairie west of the town of Mifflin. When the war of the Rebellion broke out, though well advanced in years, he volunteered and was attached to the Eighty-second Ohio regiment, where he served until he was accidentally injured, by having the wheel of one of the baggage wagons run over his foot, which so disabled him that he asked his discharge.

Of late years, he quietly pursued his trade, and was noted for his industry and inoffensive habits. It was quite a treat to hear him relate the rough-and-tumble habits of the pioneers, their feats of strength and personal courage, and insist that we would never see their like again; for all countries have but one set of pioneers, and, when they disappear, new men, and new manners, succeed them. The hardy men that prostrate forests, construct roads, build cabins and log barns, and add wealth to communities, soon seek other localities for a renewal of old excitements, or die early.

In politics Captain Walker had settled opinions and adhered faithfully to the party of his choice, though he never pressed his claims to official promotion. He had no affinity for the tricks of political office-seekers, and concurred in the idea that a man should evince as much integrity in office as in the private stations of life.

On the morning of his decease, May 7, 1878, he felt it to be his duty to engage, as usual, at his trade. He had just ascended to the roof of a one-story building, near the shop of Mr. Fasig, between Second and Third streets, to make some change in the roof, when he was noticed to be somewhat confused in manner, and, by the time aid reached the roof, he had become unconscious. He was assisted to the ground, and carried home—only a short distance—but never rallied. In about four hours from the attack (apoplexy), he died in great distress, aged seventy-four years, two months and four days.

He was the father of eleven children, seven of whom survive—David, Mary, Hannah, Belle, Esther, Nora, and William.

His excellent lady yet retains a good deal of physical and mental vigor, though she is far advanced in life, and saw Ashland county when it was mostly forest.

JAMES DOTY.

Mr. Doty was born near Wheeling, West Virginia, in 1802, and was of Scotch-Irish descent, his ancestors having settled in that region prior to the close of the American Revolution. His father, Abraham Doty, experienced many of the terrors of Indian invasion during the border wars from 1780 to 1795, Fort Henry at Wheeling, being a point for attack by the *Shawnees* and *Wyandots*.

In 1815 Abraham Doty removed with his family to what is now Milton township, Ashland county, then in

Richland county, and settled about four miles from Uniontown, now Ashland, on an unimproved farm in the woods. There were at that time but few settlers in Milton and Mifflin townships, and the pioneers had to endure many hardships. Here James and other members of the family grew up amid the wilds of the new country.

The war of 1812 had ended propitiously, and emigrants began to flow into this region, and the woodman's axe could be heard in every direction, leveling the forests in the preparation of log cabins, and in preparing fields for culture.

The institutions of the older settlements were rapidly planted in these wilds. The log school-house and hewed log church ere long were found wherever new settlements appeared. The minister followed the adventurers, and for a time, organized congregations, that met and worshipped in the cabins of the pioneers. About 1817, Abraham Doty assisted in the erection of "Old Hopewell," one and a half miles west of Ashland, and was soon elected and ordained an elder of the church. James, and other members of the Doty family, attended this church for several years, though residing nearly four miles from it, in the south part of Milton township.

Abraham Doty gave his influence in the erection of school-houses, for the spread of education, and intelligence among the rising generation, and instructed his own children that intelligence, morality and integrity gave all men influence among their companions and neighbors; and society prospered in proportion to its support of these maxims and ideas.

In 1834, James Doty, having grown to manhood amid the wild forest scenes around him, and having obtained a fair knowledge of the English branches, concluded to engage in preparing a future home for himself. He married Miss Sarah Croninger, daughter of Leonard Croninger, of Mifflin township, and settled on an unimproved farm near the present home of Joseph Charles. He improved his homestead, and soon was elected to a number of minor township offices by his neighbors. He also was elected justice of the peace three successive terms. He often related an amusing circumstance that occurred when justice. At one time a young man and lady called at his cabin desiring him to perform the marriage ceremony. He did so, after which the young man stated that he had no money, but would see that the 'squire should be paid for his services. The 'squire said it was all right. Several months after this occurrence the 'squire was greatly surprised to see the aforesaid party appear at his office with a fine puppy, declaring that he could not rest contented while he owed so sacred a debt as that held by the 'squire, and begged him to accept the puppy in lieu of the money, and thereby remove the debt. As the 'squire was a generous man, and good dogs were useful in expelling wild animals, he accepted the puppy, and his friend departed in the best of spirits.

In 1846, Ashland county was erected principally out of territory belonging to Richland county. The first officers were nominated from all parties, by common consent, and elected and served for six months, or until their successors were elected and qualified. Mr. Doty was elected sheriff in the spring, and re-elected at the October election for two years. He was, therefore, the first sheriff of Ashland county. His deputies were Matthew Clugston and Isaac Stull. Mr. Gates became his successor. Mr. Doty made an accommodating and pleasant sheriff. He declined a nomination for his second term, and retired to his farm, where he remained until 1856, when he disposed of his home, and removed to Plymouth township, Richland county, since which time he has lived the agreeable life of a farmer. The personal appearance of Mr. Doty is well remembered by many. In disposition he was genial and kind. His weight was near two hundred and fifty pounds in his prime. In business, he was regarded as above reproach, and was much respected by all. In religious opinion he was a Presbyterian in sentiment and practice. He was one of the useful and solid pioneers, and will long be remembered by his old neighbors. He was the father of ten children, seven sons and three daughters, eight of whom (five sons and three daughters) survive him. The pioneers of Ashland county sincerely condole with his numerous relatives, in the loss of so valuable a friend and relative. He died near Plymouth, Richland county, Ohio, January 4, 1879, aged seventy-seven years.

JOHN CHARLES

was born in Lancaster county, Pennsylvania, July 13, 1802. He was the youngest of a family of three children. His early educational opportunities were quite limited. At the age of twenty-four, he came over to Ohio, and settled in Mifflin township. He married in Lancaster. Mr. Charles was engaged for many years in farming. He owned the farm upon which Martin Ruffner had settled in 1812, consisting of one hundred and sixty acres, near the village of Mifflin. He exchanged this property, a few years since, for the Kauffman mill property on the Black fork, some three miles southwest of Mifflin. This is one of the best water-mills within the county, and is kept in constant motion. Mr. Charles has a large circle of friends, and has been repeatedly elected to township offices by the citizens of Mifflin. He has served as justice of the peace, and acquitted himself to the satisfaction of all. He was originally an old line Whig; but on the disbandment of that party after the campaign of 1852, he became an upholder of the principles of the Democratic party. He has passed through all the scenes of the early pioneers, and retains a vivid recollection of the "rough and ready" habits of the early settlers of the Black fork. He has aided scores of the settlers in the erection of cabins—in rolling logs—at corn huskings, and other gatherings. He has assisted in opening and improving most of the highways in the north part of the township. He is genial and agreeable to all, and a friend to the poor. He is the father of six children, four of whom still survive, three residing in Mifflin township, and one daughter in Indiana. Mr.

Charles is a member of the Pioneer and Historical society of Ashland county. He is yet vigorous and cheerful.

JOHN LAMBRIGHT

was born in Frederick City, Maryland, January, 1778. In 1802 he married Anna C. Smith, and in 1811, removed to Harrison county, Ohio, and in the spring of 1812, located in Mifflin township, Richland, now Ashland county. In the fall of 1812, the cabin of Frederick Zimmer, a neighbor, was attacked by the Indians, and the son of Mr. Zimmer hastened to inform James Copus and Mr. Lambright of their presence, and the desire of Martin Ruffner and the Zimmers for their assistance. Messrs. Copus and Lambright hastened to the cabin, and arrived in the earlier part of the night, finding all silent in and about the premises. They returned to their respective cabins, took their families and fled to the block-house of Jacob Beam, on the Rocky fork. Here he remained three weeks, and fled to Lancaster, Fairfield county, Ohio. While there, Mr. Lambright was drafted, and served in the northwest, about four months. He and his family remained near Lancaster three years, and then returned to his deserted cabin on the Black fork, where he continued to reside until November 9, 1832, when he deceased. Some members of his family yet reside in the township. Mrs. Joseph Doty is a daughter.

For a full description of the Ruffner, Zimmer, and Copus fights, and the part Mr. Lambright took, see articles on that subject in the historical part of this volume.

JOSIAH THOMAS

was born in Somerset county, Pennsylvania, March 9, 1804. His father, George Thomas, of Welsh descent, removed to Harrison county, Ohio, and located near Cadiz, in 1807. He was a tailor by trade, and followed his business there until 1817, when he emigrated to the village of Petersburgh, now Mifflin, Mifflin township, Ashland county. He, George Thomas, remained there several years engaged at his trade, and in keeping a hotel, the village being on the main line of travel from Canton, Wooster to Mansfield, and the west part of the State. Jacob Beam being a brother-in-law of Mr. George Thomas, and an uncle to Josiah, his two older brothers, Henry and Peter, had visited Mr. Beam, to see the country prior to the removal of the family. In 1824 George Thomas, with his family, removed to Orange township, and located upon the present homestead of Josiah Thomas. Josiah attended the common schools of the neighborhood, and adopted farming as an occupation. In 1828 he married Miss Eliza Zimmerman. His family consists of seven children—George, Henry, Warren, Mary, Elizabeth, Freelove, and Harriet. George, Henry and Elizabeth are married. Mr. Thomas is a quiet, industrious and exemplary farmer. He has never been an office-seeker; yet, against his protests, the people of his township have elected him trustee fifteen or sixteen times. When Ashland county was organized in 1846, Mr. Thomas was appointed commissioner for the short term, and elected in October, for three years, and served until 1850. He has been a member of the Disciple church about twenty years. In 1879 he was elected president of the Historical and Pioneer society of Ashland county, which office he yet holds.

HON. JOHN DOUGHERTY

was born in Washington county, Pennsylvania, October 10, 1819. His father, Daniel Dougherty, was born in Ireland and emigrated to the United States in 1806, and landed at Baltimore, and thence removed to Washington county, Pennsylvania. He emigrated with his family to Milton township, now Ashland county, in 1822, where he died. Mrs. Dougherty and her children removed to Vermillion township in 1832. Here John grew to manhood, attending the schools of the neighborhood. At an early age he took an active part in politics, and being a fluent speaker, he was regarded as the leader in his township. He voted with the Democracy. He rarely asked official promotion for himself. When the gold fever of 1850 spread over the land, he joined in search of the hidden treasure in California. His venture proved a success, and he returned in 1854. In 1858 he again visited the Pacific slopes, and remained until 1863. He prospected in the mines of Idaho, Washington and British Columbia with success, and returned to his old home in Ashland county. In 1861, prior to his return, he was elected a member of the California legislature, and served one session, and resigned. Having visited nearly all the mines of the Pacific slopes, he is of opinion there is plenty of gold in the Black Hills, which fact is being concealed by the Indian ring and other speculators. In 1872 he again returned to California, in the hope of restoring his declining health, and remained eleven months, to no advantage. His malady is chronic rheumatism, with which he has been tortured for several years. He now resides near Jeromeville. He has been twice married. He is an exemplary member of the Catholic church. He is a high-toned gentleman.*

Z. T. PAULLIN

was born in Greensburgh, Pennsylvania, August 24, 1822, and emigrated with his father's family, in 1823, to Wayne county, and in 1824 to Vermillion township, now Ashland county. They located near Daniel Porter on Beall's trail. Mr. Isaac Paullin, sr., had a description of the country from Mr. Porter, who passed up the trail in 1812. Isaac Paullin was a shoemaker, and the first practical workman in that part of the township. He was also the first gunsmith. His sons Z. T. and Daniel learned the shoemaking business of their father, and continued to manufacture shoes. In 1835 Isaac Paullin

---

* Mr. Dougherty died in 1878.

JOSIAH THOMAS.

MRS. JOSIAH THOMAS.

Josiah Thomas, the subject of this sketch, was born in Somerset county, Pennsylvania, March 9, 1804. His parents, George and Mary Beam Thomas, were natives of Pennsylvania. The ancestors of his father came from Wales, and those of his mother from Germany. George and Mary Thomas, with their family, removed to Brooke county, Virginia, in about 1807, and remained there about one year, when they came to Ohio and settled in Harrison county. Mr. Thomas was, by trade, a tailor, and followed that business until old age compelled him to relinquish it. From Harrison county the family came to Mifflin township, in the present county of Ashland, about 1817, and after about seven years again removed in 1824, this time to Orange township, where he purchased the farm now owned by his son, Josiah Thomas. Here he died at the age of eighty-two years. His widow survived him some five years, and died aged eighty-five years. They had a family of eleven children, of whom but two representatives now remain: Mrs. Elizabeth Jaques, in Illinois, and Josiah Thomas, the youngest son, on the old homestead.

Josiah Thomas worked on the farm of his father during his boyhood and youth, doing his part toward redeeming the wilderness, clearing, log-rolling, rail-splitting, building fence, and other hard manual labor, until his brothers and sisters, having left the farm, died, or married and made homes for themselves, when, by will, he inherited the property, after paying certain sums to the other heirs. He was married September 2, 1830, to Eliza Zimmerman, who was born in Union county, Pennsylvania, December 25, 1809. Her father died when she was small, and she came to Ohio with other members of the family, when about twenty years of age. To them have been born ten children, two of whom died in early childhood: Sanford, at the age of three years, three months and seven days; Jefferson, aged one year, seven months and three days. Adeline died aged seventeen years and one month. Those now living are: George, Henry C., Warren R., Mary, Elizabeth, Freelove, and Harriet, all of whom are now married except Warren and Harriet, who remain at home with their parents.

Mr. Thomas was one of the first commissioners of the present county of Ashland, in which office he served three years and six months, when he declined to further serve. He has also held the office of township trustee some seventeen years. He has never been an office-seeker, but the people of his township, appreciating his worth, have continued him in office. Both himself and his wife are members of the Disciple church, with which they have been connected some thirty years. His first vote was cast for Andrew Jackson, and he has ever since adhered to the principles of the Democratic party. He has a good home in the southern part of Orange township, comprising the old homestead of one hundred and sixty acres.

and family settled on the present site of the village of Mohicanville. Here he deceased. Z. T. Paullin is the only son remaining in Mohican township. He has accumulated a comfortable property, and has a pleasant family. We obtained many valuable reminiscences from him concerning the early settlement of Vermillion and Mohican townships.

PETER HUFF

was born in Virginia, December 25, 1798, and when a child accompanied his parents to Beaver county, Pennsylvania, where he remained until 1825, when he came west and located in Lake township. He settled on the west side of the Lake fork in the forest, and soon erected a cabin and began to improve his land. Those residing on the west side of the stream were George Marks, John C. Young, John Emerick, Enoch Covert, Abraham Blue, Jabez Smith, Emer Akins, and Nathan Dolby. Mr. Huff has a fine property south of Mohicanville. He is quite vigorous and retains all his faculties. He has two sons, Samuel and William. The former resides in Mohicanville and carries on a large woollen manufactory, and the latter resides on the homestead. Mr. Huff stays with his son.

WESLEY COPUS

was born in Green county, Pennsylvania, August 15, 1804, and immigrated, with his father's family, to Mifflin township, Richland, now Ashland county, in the spring of 1809. In reaching their wilderness home, they passed through the Indian village of Greentown, and followed a trail to the south part of what is now Mifflin township, and erected a camp cabin of poles about one mile northeast of what is now Charles' mill, near a run subsequently named Zimmer's. They resided in this cabin about fifteen months. In the meantime, the family cleared a few acres and planted corn. It was frosted in July, and much injured. Mr. Copus had moved his family in a cart, with a good yoke of oxen; and also brought two or three milch cows, which fed, during the summer, on sedge grass and pea-vines. In the spring of 1810, he commenced the erection of a more substantial log cabin near a fine spring, about one mile south of his pole cabin, and removed to it during the summer of 1810. The old Greentown trail passed near the spring, and Mr. Copus was often visited by the Greentown Indians, during the spring and summers of 1809–10–11–12. Thomas Armstrong, the chief, and his sons Silas and James, and Tom Lyons, Bill Dowdee, Billy Montour, Abram Williams, and others, frequently came to the cabin, and were quite friendly. James and Silas Armstrong, then boys, often came to the sugar camp and ran races and wrestled with the Copus boys. For over three years the intercourse continued in harmony, and not until after the disgraceful surrender of General Hull at Detroit, in August, 1812, were any apprehensions of danger from the Greentown Indians felt. Fears were then entertained that they might be corrupted through British influence, and attack the defenceless settlements along the branches of the Mohican.

As a means of safety the State authorities ordered the removal of the Jerome and Greentown Indians to Piqua, after which, a number of Greentown Indians, who had, prior to that time, fled to Upper Sandusky, returned and assassinated the family of Frederick Zimmer and Margaret Ruffner, and, a few days afterward, attacked the cabin of James Copus, father of Wesley, and killed him, and several soldiers near the cabin. Wesley, then nine years old, with the balance of the family, was in the cabin during the assault, and saw his father fall and expire. He retained a vivid recollection of the terrific screams of the savages as they riddled the walls of the cabin with bullets.

After this tragedy, his mother and children returned to Guernsey county, where they remained until the fall of 1814, when they came back to the old cabin, where, some forty years afterward, Mrs. Copus deceased. At that time the family consisted of Henry, Nancy, Sarah, James, Wesley, Nelson, and Anna.

Wesley Copus continued to reside in the vicinity of the old homestead. For several years his health had been gradually failing. It had been apparent for some time that he could not survive a great while. Having been somewhat exposed to the inclemency of the weather, he was attacked with pneumonia, and expired February 14, 1876.

During his youth his educational advantages were limited, and his entire schooling consisted of about three months; but, by observation, a retentive memory, and good judgment, he had acquired a fund of information, and was a very interesting conversationalist.

He was twice married. His first wife survived only six months. By his second wife he had ten children, six of whom survive—John W., Madison, Eliza J., Sarah, Mary, and Nancy E., all of whom are married.

Mr. Copus was a member of the United Brethren church for thirty-five years. As a citizen, he was industrious, conscientious, and the opponent of all shams and vices. He was buried at the old cemetery near Charles' mill, where many of his kindred sleep. Mr. Copus being enrolled among the pioneers, the obituary committee of the Pioneer and Historical society, of Ashland county, adopted the customary resolutions.

Only two of the James Copus family now survive—Mrs. Sarah Vail, of Mifflin, and Mrs. Anna Whitmer, of Wood county, Ohio.

FREDERICK W. COFFIN

was born in Washington county, New York, January 6, 1809. He learned the trade of a cabinet-maker in Vermont. On reaching manhood he married Mary Waters, of Bennington, and located in Troy, New York, in 1833. In 1845 he removed to Mohicanville, Ashland county, where he remained two years, and removed to Ashland, where he still resides. He is of English descent, and the family trace their ancestry back to the invasion of the conqueror William, of Normandy. The Coffins settled in Worcester, Massachusetts, as early as 1642. At one time the Coffins were the proprietors of Nantucket.

Mr. Coffin is an excellent mechanic, and a gentleman of high integrity. He is the parent of twelve children, part of whom are deceased. In December, 1875, he held a family reunion; those present were: the father, Frederick W. Coffin, aged sixty-seven; the mother, Mary Coffin, aged sixty-two; Mrs. L. J. Sprengle, Mrs. F. H. Smith, Mrs. M. Jennings, Mrs. E. L. McIlrath, Thaddeus Coffin, Arthur W. Coffin, Eugene Coffin, Harry T. Coffin, and Edward Coffin. These, with relations by marriage, and offspring, numbered in all thirty-two souls. If the mother of Mrs. Mary Coffin, who resides in Troy, New York, aged eighty-six, had been present, there would have been five generations under the same roof.

The Coffins are noted for their musical endowments, and when all together make an interesting family concert.

THOMAS SMITH SUTHERLAND

was born in Washington county, Pennsylvania, November 4, 1816, and removed with his father's family to Richland (now Ashland,) county, in 1833. He became a farmer by occupation, and married Martha Sheets, daughter of the late Joseph Sheets, one of the pioneers of Montgomery township. Mr. Sutherland purchased from his father's estate part of the homestead one and a half miles south of Ashland, and more recently the balance of the home farm, from the heirs.

He was a man of industrious and economical habits, and noted for his integrity and strict honesty. He possessed an excellent judgment, and was honored by being selected to fill several township offices.

On the third day of May, 1876, Mr. Sutherland was fatally injured while assisting in the removal of a neighbor. Being in advance of other teams, in a small wagon, one of the teams became alarmed at a hog who jumped up by the road side, and commenced to run. Mr. Sutherland turned aside to permit the team to pass, but was run into, breaking his wagon to splinters, and in passing over him, the wheels crushed two or three ribs. He survived until the fifth, and deceased. The melancholy termination of his life produced a feeling of sadness throughout the township. He left a widow and one daughter, the wife of Mr. Jameson. A large concourse of friends and neighbors followed him to his final resting place in the cemetery at Ashland.

NATHANIEL HASKELL

was born in Windsor county, Vermont, October 3, 1792. He emigrated to Ohio in 1817, and located in Cleveland. In July, 1818, he removed to Wooster, Wayne county, where he remained three years, and located in Loudonville, Richland, now Ashland, county. Soon after his arrival, he erected a carding-machine and fulling mill, which for several years was a great neighborhood convenience. In April, 1823, he married Hettia A. Skinner, the daughter of a pioneer, who erected the first grist-mill in the vicinity of Loudonville. Mr. Haskell was a thrifty business man and accumulated property quite rapidly. He laid out an addition to Loudonville, and, by his business energy and strict integrity, contributed to the growth of the town. He was long engaged in the mercantile business, and possessed tact and energy in its management. He took a deep interest in the school system of Ohio, and was always liberal in forwarding the interests of education. He was, for many years, an active member of the Masonic fraternity, and noted for his genial disposition and love for that ancient order. In his later years—1868—he became the principal stockholder and owner of the Haskell bank, of Loudonville, which was an institution of deposit and exchange, and was managed by him. In 1855 his excellent wife deceased. September 30, 1871, Mr. Haskell deceased, leaving his bank interest to a nephew, he having died childless. The institution was conducted by the nephew until 1875, when he deceased.

DANIEL BEACH

was born in Warren, Litchfield county, Connecticut, March 16, 1785. In 1805 he came on foot to Canfield, Mahoning county, Ohio, and worked one year, then returned and married Lorinda Sacket, January 1, 1810. He purchased two hundred acres of wild land in what is now Summit county, Ohio, to which he removed in 1811, coming the entire route with a yoke of oxen and one horse. In 1812 he was drafted in the military service, and served near Fort Croghan six months. In 1823 he disposed of his farm and accompanied Bradford Sturtevant in search of a new home to Ruggles township, Huron, now Ashland county, and purchased, of Jessup & Wakeman, of Connecticut, one mile square of land in section three, he taking the west and smallest part. He returned, and in July, 1823, removed with his wife and five children—Cyrus, Reuben, Cordelia, Harriet, and Daniel, to his new home in the forest, about one mile west of what is now known as the corners. The paths in the forest were narrow, and required quite an effort to get over by teams. He had two yoke of oxen to haul his goods. He encamped one night in Medina county, and one night at Sullivan center. A man—Mr. John Soles—piloted him thence by way of New London. He encamped one night on the route in what is now Troy, and again at New London, and was just one week in reaching his forest home. Their first supper was cooked at the fire of a deserted Indian camp on the premises. The forest was dense, and it required years of unremitting toil to prepare the lands for culture. Mr. Beach was accompanied in his removal by Eleazer Sacket, a brother-in-law. He built a pole cabin, ten by fifteen feet, in which he resided until he built a log cabin. By fall he had cleared five acres, which he put in wheat. Other pioneers began to select lands, and Mr. Beach's cabin was frequently visited. In the winter of 1824 he hired hands, and cleared the timber from one hundred acres. In the spring he and Bradford Sturtevant returned to Tallmadge and purchased apple-trees for new orchards, some of which yet bear fruit. Mr. Beach, by industry and economy, accumulated a handsome property. In 1854 he divided his homestead between his two sons, Wakeman and William, and removed to Kent county, Michigan. Mrs. Beach died on a visit to Ruggles, at the residence of her son, Cyrus Beach, in November, 1856. Mr. Beach subsequently married Mrs. Frances Peck, widow of Tylor Peck. He died at his residence in Ruggles in May, 1862. He was remarkable for his habits of industry and enterprise. He was exact and careful in all his business transactions, and his integrity was never questioned. His children were Cyrus S., Reuben K., Harriet L., married to Rollin Curtiss, Daniel, deceased, Wakeman J., and Cordelia M., married to Isaac Cowell. Most of the family reside within Ruggles township, and are noted as farmers and stock growers. Wakeman Beach, born January 11, 1825, is believed to have been the first child born within the township. He resides on the old homestead west of the corners. I am indebted to him for the foregoing sketch.

BRADFORD STURTEVANT

was born in Litchfield county, Connecticut, March 16, 1786. January 1, 1809, he married Sarah Carter, and removed to Richfield, now Summit county, Ohio, in June, 1816. Here he improved a small farm, which he sold in 1823, and purchased, in company with Daniel Beach, one section in Ruggles township, then in Huron county. In August, 1823, he erected a cabin, and removed with his wife and children in September. He removed with ox teams, taking along twelve head of cattle and twenty sheep. The following winter he returned to Richfield and purchased a lot of stock hogs, and drove them through the woods to Ruggles. July 4, 1824, three of the four pioneer families of Ruggles celebrated independence at the cabin of Mr. Sturtevant. They had a dinner, and in the evening, for fire-works, attempted to blast a white-wood tree, but failed. In 1836 he removed to the village of Milan, Erie county, to give his children the educational advantages of the place. In 1844 he returned to Ruggles, and deceased in May, 1871, aged about eighty-five years. He was a man of fixed purposes, highly conscientious in his moral ideas, and a most successful farmer. He engaged largely in raising fine stock, and by good management accumulated a handsome homestead. Like his New England ancestors, he was a Puritan in his religious opinions, and possessed the confidence and esteem of all his neighbors and acquaintances. His children were— Carleton H.; Marcia, married to B. Ashley, of Milan; Harriet, deceased; Sarah, married to Dr. Galpin, of Milan; Isaac G., who resides on the homestead; Martha, married to Horace Taylor, a missionary to India; and William B. Martha was the first female child born in the township—May 17, 1825. Isaac G. Sturtevant, from whom we obtained the foregoing particulars, married Adelaide Carter. Carleton H. married Lydia Peck, and William B. married Anna Wolcott. He also states that the first school-house was built in 1824, half a mile west of the residence of Bradford Sturtevant, and was taught by Miss Betsy Sacket, sister of Harvey Sacket. The school was supported by subscription. The scholars were of the families of the Beaches, Sturtevants, and from Greenwich township, adjoining Ruggles. The first church organization was in 1827. It was Congregational, and Rev. E. T. Woodruff was the first minister. At that time the pioneers attended mill at Cold creek, in Erie county, some forty miles away. They reached the mill on pack-horses, by winding paths through a dense forest, finding but few settlers on the way. Two or three years after the arrival of Bradford Sturtevant, the little colony was increased by the arrival of Jacob Roorbach, Harvey Sacket, Justus Barnes, Taylor Peck, Solomon Weston, Aldrich Carver, Norman Carter, James Poag, Abraham Ferris, Albert Buell, George W. Curtiss, Reuben Fox, and others. Isaac G. Sturtevant is a model farmer and stock-grower. He resides about half a mile west of the corners. Adorned by tasteful buildings, select fruit orchards, and good fences, his homestead furnishes proof that the lessons of economy, neatness, and business tact, enforced by the father, are carefully followed and adhered to by the son. He is a genial and intelligent gentleman.

HARVEY SACKET,

was born in Warren, Connecticut, December 24, 1791. He came to Tallmadge, Ohio, with his father in 1811. In 1812 he was drafted, and served six months in the army of the northwest. In 1816 he returned to Connecticut and married Thalia Eldred, and located in Tallmadge until 1825, when he removed to Ruggles township, on lot eleven, section three. He removed with ox teams, and owing to sparseness of settlers, and the narrow forest paths, was eight days on the way. Mr. Sacket died August 11, 1875. He was twice married. His family by his first wife was: Dimmes, wife of Mr. Smith; Erastus and Erasmus M.; Irena, wife of C. Curtiss. His first wife died in 1843, and in 1844 he married Mrs. Mary Van Vranken, widow of Garrett Van Vranken. He had one son, Justus H. Sacket, by his second wife. Justus resides on the homestead. Mr. Sacket was long a member of the Congregational church, and was an excellent citizen. He was the first justice of Ruggles. Most of the family reside in Ruggles township.

ALDRICH CARVER

was born in Tolland county, Connecticut. He came to Huron county in 1818. In 1819 he assisted in capturing some Indian murderers, who were subsequently hung at Norwalk. In 1821 he returned to Cayuga county, New York, and married Amy Kniffin. In the fall of

1822 he settled in Greenwich, Huron county, Ohio, and in the spring of 1825 on lot ten and eighteen, section four, in Ruggles. Mr. Carver served as justice of the peace in Ruggles, and as commissioner and auditor of Ashland county. He was a shrewd politician, and a man of good native abilities. He died of cancer of the face in 1870, aged about sixty-five years. His family consisted of Fanny, wife of Daniel Huffman; Phebe, wife of Jacob Huffman, and John, who resides on the homestead. Mr. Carver was one of the petitioners for the organization of the township in 1826. It was called Ruggles, after Judge Almon Ruggles, who surveyed the Fire Lands. At the first election, held January 2, 1826, there were twelve votes cast: Perry Durfee Harvey, Sacket, Norman Carter, Truman Bates, Reuben Fox, Bradford Sturtevant, Jacob Roorback, Abraham Ferris, Justice Barnes, Daniel Beach, Ezra D. Smith, and Aldrich Carver. The officers chosen were: E. D. Smith, clerk; Jacob Roorback, D. Beach, and A. Carver, trustees; Bradford Sturtevant and Harvey Sacket, overseers of poor; J. Barnes and A. Ferris, fence viewers; Reuben Fox and Perry Durfee, appraisers of property; N. Carter, constable; J. Bates, supervisor, and Harvey Sacket, treasurer. There were thirteen offices and twelve voters.

At the April election, the vote was increased by the names of C. Sanders, A. Bates, T. Hendrix, D. J. Parker, and S. A. Nott. Harvey Sacket was chosen justice of the peace.

JAMES POAG

removed into Ruggles from Clearcreek in 1827. He died April 9, 1854. He was twice married, and left by the two marriages some seven or eight children, part of whom reside in the township.

NORMAN CARTER

was born in Warren, Connecticut, January 23, 1802, and came to Ruggles in 1824, and located on lot twenty-six, section four. He labored some three years, part of the time for Daniel Beach, and returned to Connecticut in 1827, and married Lavina Hopkins; and in 1828 removed to Ruggles, where he has since deceased. His family consisted of Huldah Adelaide, wife of Isaac G. Sturtevant, and Sarah Lavina, married to William Gault. They all reside in Ruggles.

ABRAHAM FERRIS

was born in Columbia county, New York, June 16, 1788. He served in the war of 1812, and married Marinda Philips, and removed to Ruggles township in 1824. He voyaged up the lake from Buffalo to Sandusky in a schooner, and after being delayed by a lake storm, reached Ruggles, by way of New London, and located on lot seventeen, section three, having erected a cabin. His family, at his decease, which took place August 13, 1850, consisted of Laura, Philetus, Samuel, Sarah, Lois, Erastus, Elias, Jesse and Elmira. His wife died September 17, 1850. Several members of the family are now deceased.

JACOB ROORBACK

was born in Maryland, February 27, 1795, and his parents removed to Yates county, New York, where he was drafted and served in the war of 1812. He married Amy Sutherland in 1821, and in 1823 purchased four hundred acres of land in section two, in Ruggles, to which he removed in 1824. He died March 21, 1850. His wife deceased shortly afterward. He had but one child, Sarah, who married A. W. Purdy, of the same township.

JAMES GRINOLD

was born in Washington county, New York, May 26, 1814. Removed to Belleville, Richland county, Ohio, in company with his brother Thomas, in 1828. Resided there until 1830, then located in Berlin, Huron county, and in 1836 removed to Ruggles Corners, where his brother had settled a few months prior. He married Sarah Taylor in 1837. He is a cooper by trade, but is now a farmer. He is an active Democratic partisan, and takes an influential part in the party. He was deputy sheriff from 1852 to 1854. Thomas became justice of the peace in 1836, and was defeated in 1839, political lines being closely drawn. He deceased, of consumption, in October, 1846. James at present resides at the Corners. He has no children.

GEORGE W. BOWERICE

was born in Frederick county, Maryland, November 15, 1818, and came with his father, Christian Bowerice, to Orange township, Richland (now Ashland) county, in 1829. He removed to Troy township in 1845. He married Eva Stober, daughter of Jacob Stober, of Clearcreek. Christian Bowerice, his father, also settled in Troy, and deceased September 3, 1866, aged seventy-three years. Mrs. Bowerice died in October, 1869, aged seventy-two years. George W. is their only son. His family consists of six boys and three girls. Mr. Bowerice is an intelligent farmer, and may be regarded as one of the pioneers of Troy.

ROSWELL WESTON

was born in Litchfield county, Connecticut, July 28, 1811. He removed with his father, Salmon Weston, to Ruggles township, Huron (now Ashland) county, in the spring of 1826. His father died in 1864, aged about seventy-six years. He left two sons, Phineas and Roswell, the subject of this sketch. Roswell died May 21, 1875, aged sixty-four years. He resided two miles east of the center. His family consisted of one daughter, Lucy, who married Milton N. Campbell, who resides at Mt. Pleasant, Iowa, and one son, Clarendon, who resides with his mother on the homestead. Phineas Weston resides in Ruggles, two miles east of the center, adjoining the homestead of Roswell.

JOSEPH McCUTCHIN

was born in Lancaster county, Pennsylvania, August 3, 1803. He resided a short time, in his youth, in Maryland, where he attended school. In 1815 his father's family removed to Westmoreland county, Pennsylvania, where he served an apprenticeship of three years at the hatter's business. In 1828 he married Nancy Stem, and removed to Pittsburgh. In 1835 he came to Orange township, Richland (now Ashland) county, and, in 1845, removed to Savannah, where he still resides. His wife died in 1843, and, in 1845, he married Mary Ann Freeborn, daughter of one of the pioneers of Clearcreek.

Mr. McCutchin has been in the mercantile business for many years. He connected with the Methodist Episcopal church in 1818. He became a member of the Masonic fraternity in Pittsburgh—Miller lodge, No. 165—in 1830, and of Western Star lodge, of the Odd Fellows, No. 24, in 1832. He has been notary public about seventeen years; mayor of Savannah four years; postmaster eleven years, and township treasurer six years. He is the father of a large family, part of whom are married, and part deceased.

Mr. McCutchin is a quiet and undemonstrative citizen. In politics he acts with the Democratic party, though not proscriptive in his opinions.

CHARLES S. VAN ARNAN

was born in Columbia county, State of New York, April 5, 1814. He lost his parents in infancy, and is a self-educated man. He became a professional teacher in early life. He came to Clearcreek township as early as 1838, where he taught school. In 1839 he located in Ashland, where he taught several sessions. In 1843 he acted as deputy sheriff under Sheriff Kerr, of Richland county. After the erection of Ashland county, he served a number of years as constable for Montgomery township, and as superintendent of the county infirmary. He studied law with Gates & McComes, and was admitted in 1853. He married Eunice Cornell, of Elyria, in 1842. He removed to Troy in 1854, and became a farmer-lawyer. During the war of 1861-5, he served in Tennessee. Since his return he has been elected justice of the peace. He is now farming one mile southeast of the center. He is the parent of three girls and two sons, one of whom fell in the late war. The other members of his family are married. As the name denotes, Mr. Van Arnan is a descendant of the original Hollanders, of New York.

NATHANIEL CLARK

was born in the State of New York, March 10, 1792. In 1799 his father removed to Seneca county, New York. In 1812 he was drafted and served in the war. After peace he married Elizabeth Phelps, of the same county. In 1832 he moved to Troy township and settled amid the forests. He located north of the center, where he still resides on lot eighteen, upon an improved farm of ninety-nine acres. His family consists of but two children, both of whom are married. His honorable wife is a sister of Mrs. Parker, of the same township. At this time, 1876, he and his aged wife are in the enjoyment of good health. They are members of the Methodist Episcopal church.

SAMUEL RICHARDS

was born in Jefferson county, Ohio, December 23, 1803. When a young man he located in Orange township, of this county, and removed to Troy in 1857. The township was at that time thinly settled. It was densely timbered, and the pioneers performed a prodigy of labor in removing the forest and preparing fields for culture. His family consisted of six sons and six daughters. Four—two boys and two girls—are dead. The balance are married and reside mostly within this county. His wife deceased in 1875. He resides at present with a son at Troy center. He is a member of the Methodist Episcopal church.

HENRY SMITH

was born in Pennsylvania in 1796, and located in Columbiana with his parents after the war of 1812. He moved thence to Clearcreek township, where he resided until 1846, when he purchased a farm and settled in Troy township. He cleared and improved a valuable homestead. He died in 1865, aged about sixty-nine years. His family were: John, Adam, Samuel, Joseph, Elizabeth Biddinger, Susan Stentz, Mary Ann Beymer, and Caroline Barrack. The family are considerably scattered.

THOMAS DUNLAP

was born in the north of Ireland in 1772, and in infancy came with his father's family to Westmoreland county, Pennsylvania, about the beginning of the war of the Revolution. Upon reaching manhood, he married Margaret Blair, and in the spring of 1809, removed to Tallmadge, Portage county, Ohio. He remained there until November, 1830, when he located in Ruggles township, Huron (now Ashland,) county. When he entered the township he found the following settlers, who had preceded him some years: Daniel Beach, Bradford Sturtevant, John Jameson, Aldrich Carver, Harvey Sacket, Justus Barnes, Norman Carter, Reuben Fox, Salmon Weston, Taylor Peck, G. Ferrier, Mr. Murphy, Andrew

Clark, James Poag, Enoch Taylor, Benjamin Green, Joshua Frost, Samuel Monroe, David Blair, John Hall. Samuel Monroe, David Blair, and Enoch Taylor were shoemakers, and Benjamin Green and Joshua Frost, blacksmiths.

John Dunlap, oldest son of Thomas Dunlap, came on and worked for Daniel Beach, prior to the removal of the Dunlap family, and died at the cabin of Mr. Beach.

Thomas Dunlap died in 1847, aged seventy-five years, and his wife in August, 1872, aged eighty-six. The family were: John, who died at the cabin of Mr. Beach, William, Thomas, Nancy, wife of W. McMeekin, Alexander, David, Samuel, Solomon, Amos, James, Joseph, and John F. All are now dead except David, William, and James. David resides in Wood county, Ohio; William in Michigan; and James in Sullivan, Ashland county, Ohio. He has been commissioner of Ashland county six years, and is at present conducting a hotel. He married Minerva Myers, daughter of Jacob Myers, of Clearcreek. He has four boys and four girls.

The Dunlap family was noted for tremendous physical power. All the sons, but two, were full six feet in height, and averaged about one hundred and eighty pounds in weight. As axe-men, log rollers, and pioneer delvers in the forest, it would be difficult to find another equally vigorous class of brothers. Like their Scotch-Irish ancestors, they were all frank and generous.

SAMUEL ROBERTSON

was born in Washington county, Pennsylvania, May 20, 1797. His father, James Robertson, of Scotland, settled in that county about 1794. He removed, with his family to Cross Creek township, Jefferson county, Ohio, in 1798, where he died. Samuel Robertson, grew to manhood in Jefferson county, and in 1817 visited Milton, Montgomery, and Orange townships, in what is now Ashland county. The Burgetts and Montgomerys, of Milton township, were friends and acquaintances. In 1817 he worked most of the spring and summer for George Burgett, assisting him in clearing his lands, and in cutting and preparing timber for a new barn. He returned to Jefferson county and remained during the winter. The next spring he was accompanied by Alexander Morrow, a brother-in-law of the late Patrick Elliot, of Clearcreek. Their route was from Cadiz to Coshocton, thence up the Walhonding, to and up Owl creek to Mt. Vernon, thence to Mansfield. For nearly twenty miles south of Mansfield he found only an occasional cabin, and from there to Burgetts an almost unbroken forest. In the fall of 1818 and spring of 1819, he and John Grimes assisted Isaac Charles in preparing a race and dam for a grist- and saw-mill one and a half miles south of the present site of Olivesburgh, on the Black fork. Wages were very low and money very scarce at that period. The pioneers were crowding into Montgomery and the surrounding townships. Cabin raisings and log-rollings were the chief occupation of the new settlers. A wonderful amount of energy and self-sacrifice were expended in assisting the incoming pioneers. The woodman's axe could be heard ringing in every township. Mr. Robertson states that wild game at this period was very numerous, particularly deer and turkey. The leading hunters were Solomon Urie, John McConnell, James Clark, Christopher Mykrantz, and a Mr. Wheeler. In the spring of 1824, he resided in what is now Seneca county, and worked that summer for Mr. Gibson, father of General William H. Gibson, and remembers the organization of the county, and the location of the seat of justice at Tiffin. There was an Indian reservation within the limits of the county and the *Senecas*, or more properly, *Cayugas*, were quite numerous, though generally friendly and harmless. He remained there about one year. When he entered the county, in 1824, he is of the opinion that there were only about a dozen or twenty white families in that region, among whom were the Gibsons, Welshes and H. C. Brish, Indian agent. He reached the county by way of Beall's trail, New Haven and Fort Ball. In 1833 he located in the north part of Wayne county, where he cleared a small farm which, in 1837, he sold, and purchased lot one hundred, in Sullivan township, Lorain, now Ashland, county. It was densely covered with tall timber. He cleared and resided upon this farm about eighteen years. He then purchased a new homestead in Orange township, known as the Linard farm. Here his wife, with whom he had lived very happily for many years, deceased. He afterward sold his farm, and now (1876) resides in Ashland. His family consisted of James, who died in the hospital in United States service in 1863; John, who resides in; Michigan Margaret, wife of Thomas Miller; Rebecca, wife of John Welsh; Mary, wife of Michael Stentz; Isabel, wife of James Campbell, and Sarah Jane, wife of John Crawford. Mr. Robertson has passed through all the pioneer scenes of the county, and still possesses a good deal of physical vigor. His memory seems to be unimpaired, and he may survive many years. Mr. Robertson died about 1878, in Orange township.

PATRICK ELLIOTT

was born in Donegal county, Ireland, in 1788, and emigrated with his parents, and located in Washington county, Pennsylvania, in 1803. He grew up in that county, and married Nancy Morrow, of Jefferson county, Ohio, in 1813, and removed to Clearcreek township, Richland county, and located on the southwest quarter of section twelve, in the spring of 1817. He resided on his farm until 1826, when he deceased. He was a member of the Episcopal church from his youth. At his death his family consisted of his wife, Sarah, Mary, Elizabeth, Hugh, Jane, George, and Moses, of whom only Hugh and Moses survive. Mrs. Elliott died in 1847, aged about sixty years.

Mrs. Elliott is believed to have taught the first subscription school, in her own cabin, in Clearcreek township, in 1817, the parties sending scholars assisting Mr. Elliott to clear his land in payment for tuition. Noble woman!

Hugh, the oldest son, fifty-six years of age, and Moses, the youngest, reside on the old homestead.

ALLEN OLIVER

was born in Washington county, Pennsylvania, in 1757, and in 1810 removed from Beaver county to the Clear fork of the Mohican, now in Ashland county, and, in February of the same year, located on the farm upon which his son, Lewis Oliver, now resides, on the Black fork, about one mile east of the present site of Perrysville. His family consisted of three sons—John, Daniel, and Lewis—and four daughters—Mrs. Mary Tannehill, Mrs. Sarah Tannehill, Mrs. Elizabeth McMahan, and Mrs. Margaret Quick.

He forted in his double log cabin in 1812, during the Indian excitement, and remained undisturbed until the close of the war. The Greentown Indians, Thomas Lyons, Billy Dowdee, James Armstrong, Jonacake, and others, often visited him after the war.

Mr. Oliver died in 1823, aged about sixty-four years. His wife died in 1827, aged sixty-seven years. Mrs. Mary Tannehill, wife of Charles Tannehill, died in 1854, aged fifty-nine years; Sarah Tannehill, wife of Melzer Tannehill, jr., still survives, aged about seventy-four years; Mrs. Elizabeth McMahan and Mrs. Margaret Quick, died in 1872, aged, respectively, seventy-six and seventy-one years. Daniel Oliver resides one mile northeast of Loudonville, and is about eighty-four years of age; John deceased on his homestead, three miles below Perrysville, in 1854, aged sixty-four years.

John Chapman had a nursery of fruit trees on the farm of John Oliver, from which sprang nearly all the early orchards of Green township.

Mr. Oliver was an agreeable conversationalist, and a steadfast friend. His family continue to reside on the old homestead. We have given a sketch of Lewis Oliver elsewhere.

GEORGE W. CURRY

was born in Tompkins county, New York, May 20, 1812. He attended school and remained there until 1838, when he married Ava Ann Smith, and removed to Clarksfield, Huron county, and resided there five months, and located in Clearcreek, Richland, now Ashland, county, where he farmed four years, and in 1842 settled in the north part of Ruggles, and in 1849 sold to Mr. Peck, and purchased the farm formerly owned by Geo. Eaton, where he now (1876) resides. Mr. Curry was a very active anti-slavery man, during the palmy days of that institution. He is now a Democrat. He has been a member of the Baptist church, of Savannah, a number of years. He is the parent of thirteen children, nine of whom are deceased. The living are John B., Geo. W., Lucretia A., and Francis J.; all married. Mr. Curry is noted for his skill and industry as a farmer, and his zeal in whatever he regards as right and honorable.

COLONEL GEORGE W. URIE

was born in Washington County, Pennsylvania, February 22, 1806, and emigrated with his father's family to Orange township, Richland, now Ashland county, Ohio, in November, 1815. For many years he has been a citizen of Ashland. His tastes are strongly military. Under the old State organization, he was promoted through the various grades, from captain to colonel, of his regiment of independent rifles. When mounted on horseback, properly caparisoned, he was a fine looking officer, being tall and finely proportioned. With an unusually piercing black eye, he was every inch a soldier, in address and appearance. In the fall of 1845 he was elected treasurer of Richland county, and upon the erection of Ashland county, in 1846, he resigned, and was elected the first treasurer of the new county, which office he held two terms. Being bitten by the gold fever in 1851, he spent one year in California, reaching that region by way of Panama. In 1853 he was elected a member of the State board of equalization from the district composed of Ashland and Richland counties. In 1857 he was appointed deputy United States marshal for the northern district of Ohio, and in 1860 aided in taking the census. In 1865 he was elected recorder of Ashland county, and held the office until 1874. In the spring of 1874 he was elected mayor of Ashland, and held the office two years. Colonel Urie is a member of the Presbyterian church, and noted for his integrity and uprightness. He is a son of the late Solomon Urie, noticed elsewhere. The family of Colonel Urie consists of four daughters, Mrs. Mary J. Porter, Mrs. Alice A. Beer, Mrs. Libbie H. Anderson, and Mrs. Sadie A. Beer, and a son who died young. Mrs. Porter deceased in September, 1875.

JOHN CHAPMAN.

[The oddest character in all our history was John Chapman, *alias* Appleseed, who was discovered in Knox county as early as 1801.   A. B. NORTON.]

John Chapman, sometimes called "Johnny Appleseed," because of a penchant for planting apple seeds, and the cultivation of nurseries, was born in Massachusetts, as is believed, in the year 1770. Nothing is known of his ancestry, except that they were genuine Yankees, poor, enterprising, and restless. His name was not "Jonathan," as it is generally printed in pioneer sketches, but plain John Chapman; hence, he is generally called, among the early settlers of this region, "Johnny Appleseed."* It is remarkable he never communicated his

---

*This fact is gathered from a letter addressed to the Fort Wayne *Sentinel*, by Hon. J. W. Dawson, author of a history of Allen county, Indiana, dated October 11, 1871. He found "John Chapman" to be his true name, in looking over the papers of his estate, which was settled in the probate court of Allen county. For instance, two notes were filed against his estate, one dated at Franklin, supposed to be on the Great Miami river, in Ohio, February, 1804, payable to Nathaniel Chapman, one year after date, for one hundred dollars—"in apple trees or land;" the other, one hundred dollars, payable to some minor children named Rudde, of the commonwealth of Massachusetts, when they became of age, both of which were signed by John Chapman. A better evidence of his name was found in the purchases of land, which

real history to his most intimate friends, and was equally reticent concerning his youth and school days. We have only a glimmer of his early instruction, and even there, but a single ray of light bursts through the clouds that hover over and about his boyhood. All agree that he was a good reader—eloquent at times—and that in conversation, when discoursing upon fine fruit, and the spiritual theories of his beloved Swedenborg, his dark eyes would flash with peculiar intelligence, while he discussed his favorite topics. It was clear to all that his education had not been neglected, for he possessed a fair fund of information upon many subjects not connected with his fruit enterprises.

The time when, and the reason why, he bade adieu to the sterile hills of New England, were never communicated to any one, so far as we have been able to learn. Whether the acceptance of the life of a recluse sprang from disappointment in a love affair, or was voluntary and a matter of choice, will never be known. As early as 1796-7, he was seen in the autumns, for two or three successive years, along the banks of the Potomac, in eastern Virginia, visiting the cider mills where the farmers were pressing cider, picking the seeds from the pumice. When he had collected a sufficient quantity of seeds for his purpose, they were carefully packed in linen or leather sacks, and carried on his shoulders or by an old horse procured for that purpose, across the mountains, to the territories west of the Ohio river. He generally had with him an axe, a hatchet, and a Virginia hoe, with which he cleared and dug in loamy or rich soil, along the banks of a stream, a few rods of ground, around which he erected a brush fence, and then planted his apple seeds. His first nurseries were planted, as near as we can learn, along the Tuscarawas, the Muskingum, the Licking, and Walhonding and its branches, Vernon river, the Lake fork, and the Jerome and Black forks. He probably passed up the Licking two or three years before he ascended the Walhonding, which took place about the year 1800. When the Butlers ascended Vernon river to the present site of Mt. Vernon in 1801, they found the eccentric John Chapman at the cabin of the wild, rollicking pioneer, Andrew Craig. He planted a number of nurseries along the banks of the Walhonding, and several along the Vernon river as high up as Mt. Vernon. These nurseries were placed at eligible points in the region of good farm land; and when the pioneers began to pour in, young fruit trees in abundance awaited their arrival.

It is not well ascertained when Johnny Chapman commenced planting seeds within the present limits of Ashland county, but from the fact that most of the territory along the Black fork belonged to Knox until 1813, we incline to the opinion he may have passed up the Black fork as early as 1808-9, for he had a very fine nursery one and a half miles west of Mifflin as early as 1811-12, and had, in 1809, obtained a small piece of ground for a nursery from Alexander Finley, near the present site of Tylertown, in Mohican township. Here he was ready with his choice apple-trees as soon as the woodman's axe began to echo through the forest. Besides the nurseries at Finley's and west of Mifflin, he planted one on the farm subsequently owned by the late John Oliver, in Green township, and a fine one on the bottom, near the present site of Leidigh's mill in Orange township, and sundry smaller ones in the east and west parts of the county, along the small streams, where the early settlers procured trees for a trifle. Ever restless, Johnny kept moving from point to point. His nurseries were not neglected, for he frequently returned and pruned them so as to make the trees symmetrical. His nurseries were scattered along the streams for hundreds of miles, and he consumed many months during the year traveling from place to place. Sometimes he would be gone several months, and then suddenly appear among the pioneers, all tattered and bruised by the briars and brambles, ready to give them fresh news right from Heaven. His usual charge for young trees was a "fip-penny-bit" apiece. As money was extremely scarce, Johnny was very accommodating; and if the pioneer could not pay the money he would sell in exchange for old clothing, and if he could not get such articles he would kindly close the contract, in a business way, by taking a note payable at some future period, and if he ever got his pay he was very much gratified, and if he never got it he seemed equally content and happy.

In the year 1811 he extended his operations into Richland county, planting several nurseries there, and probably one or two within the present limits of Crawford county. During the war of 1812-15, he often visited Mansfield, Mt. Vernon, Clinton, and the settlements along the forks of the Mohican and the Walhonding. When these sparsely settled regions were threatened by Indian invasion, he hastened from cabin to cabin notifying the pioneers of approaching danger, and conjured them to flee for their lives to the block-houses and places of safety. He was well known among the Indian tribes; and from his harmless demeanor, was regarded as a "great medicine man;" and never incurred the hate and suspicion of the warriors. Thus, he was enabled to glide through the forests from settlement to settlement on errands of mercy, in entire safety. From Richland county, after the close of the war, he passed through Crawford to Upper Sandusky, and as early as 1825 into the present limits of Defiance county, and along the Maumee. In 1826 he visited John H. James, a leading lawyer at Urbana, concerning a nursery that he had planted sometime prior to that year, in Champaign county, and which had passed into the hands of a third party, owing to the neglect of the man from whom he had permission to plant it, to reserve the interest of Chapman. He doubtless had planted nurseries in Delaware county prior to 1826. From 1815

---

he made in Allen county, as well as in Adams and Jay counties, Indiana. The muniments of title, which he held, were in the name of John Chapman. He had a sister in Adams or Jay county, married to a man by the name of Broom, who was probably living at his death. This estate of Johnny was in litigation about ten years. So he did not die as poor as most people suspected.

This sister of Johnny, alluded to by Hon. J. W. Dawson, was Persis, her husband's name was William Broom. They at one time resided on the farm now owned by William Cowan, in Green township, a mile north of Perrysville, on the road to Ashland. Broom had the care of one or two nurseries (owned by Johnny), in Green township.

JOHNNY APPLESEED.

to 1843, when he made his last visit, he often returned to Ashland county, at which times he usually passed down the Black fork, among the Copuses, the Irwins, the Coulters, the Tannehills, the Rices, the Olivers, and the Priests. From thence, he passed over to Finley's; then up the Jerome fork, among the settlers along that stream, until he reached Jacob Young, Patrick Murray, and the Fasts and Masons, at his nursery, near Leidigh's mill—rarely stopping in the villages—though occasionally he called in Mifflin, at the Thomas hotel—in Ashland, at Slocum's; and in Mansfield, at Wiler's. When he did so, he always slept on the floor of the bar-room.

The precise period when he ascended the Maumee and entered the territory of Indiana is left in doubt. It is probable he had reached Fort Wayne as early as 1826; for in 1830 he was seen on the Maumee seated in a section of a hollow tree, which he improvised for a boat, laden with apple-seeds, and which he landed at Wayne's fort. Thus, as the pioneers infringed upon the location of his nurseries, he passed on, and continued to plant seeds in advance of the settlements, until death, that waits for no one, called the old man from his toil.

When interrogated on the subject of grafting, he would dilate on the evils of such a custom with as much earnestness as most surgeons would the operation of separating an arm or a limb from a human being, insisting that the true way to obtain good fruit was to let it grow upon ungrafted trees, because the native growth produced the finest fruit. How often he visited the cider mills in the east is not known; but the practice must have been kept up to a late period in his life, for he visited the pioneers of Green township as late as 1843, looking very much as he did a quarter of a century before. The old man generally traveled alone, and rarely had lodgers at his primitive camp-fires. We hear an occasional instance of parties, desiring to purchase trees, tarrying all night at his solitary hut.

It is a matter of surprise to many how he survived so long, while roaming through the forests, without defensive weapons, illy clothed and half famished for healthful food during the inclement seasons of the year. He always refrained from taking the life of animals—never, if possible, even disturbing their lairs or haunts. So, he never procured sustenance in that way. His food was generally meagre, and consisted of berries, nuts, vegetables, and a little corn-bread or mush made from meal given him in exchange for trees, or as a matter of charity. He carried with him a few cooking utensils—a tin pan, which served the double purpose of a hat and a mush-pot, when he had no other head-gear. He would rarely eat at a table with families—and never until he felt sure there would be enough left to satisfy the hunger of the children, always manifesting a great affection for young people, especially little girls, for whom he always had some little keep-sake, consisting of a piece of ribbon or calico. This peculiarity throws a faint explanation over his monomania for the life of a hermit. The shadow of some bright little lady of New England still clung to the heart of this strange man.

When he remained any length of time about a nursery he erected a pole hut, over which he placed a bark roof after the manner of the Indians. He then gathered leaves and made a very comfortable bed upon which he slept, while the wolves and other wild animals gave him a sort of rude welcome to their precincts by assembling in the vicinity of his slumbers and giving him nightly serenades. He often slept on the ground in the midst of the forest near a small fire, erected to cook his scanty meal and protect him from freezing, if the weather was cold. At other times he reposed upon the leaves beside a log, with his pan and other traps by his side, and seemed to be the object of special interest and regard of both wild animals and savages, for he always escaped injury from both. In his tenderness for every sentient creature he was a greater humanitarian—or if you please, "animaltarian," than even the famous Bergh, of New York city; for it is related that more than once he suffered the chill night air and winds of autumn rather than singe the wings of the mosquito by his camp-fire. In this respect the affection he possessed for the brute creation seems to have been fully reciprocated, for the fiercest animals and Johnny Chapman seemed to have had a truce. He avoided them and they avoided him.

His dress was a marvel of scraps and tatters. It consisted, invariably, of cast off, badly worn garments, given him by the pioneers in exchange for young apple-trees. He always seemed thankful for such small favors, and by the aid of such articles—ill-fitting, patched and shabby—he protected himself against the wintry blasts. Upon his head he generally wore a crownless hat, much dinged and limbered with rough usage, which he often ran his hand through and carried on his arm. Sometimes he turned his tin pan over his crownless hat, in the top of which rested a testament and a well-worn volume of Swedenborg, which he declared was an infallible protection against snakes, wild animals, Indians, and all other evils. At other times he wore a pasteboard hat, with an enormous rim, which he conceived protected his face from the scorching rays of the sun.

His feet were generally covered, in the winter season, with old shoes, or one shoe and a boot; sometimes one foot was bare, undergoing, in most rigorous weather, a sort of penance for some imaginary violation of Johnny's religious whims. At other times, he wrapped his feet in old rags or bark, and tied on a sort of wooden sandal, which protected the bottoms of his feet against thorns and rough stones. Sometimes he was seen slowly advancing through the snow, with one foot entirely naked, breaking the crust with the other, on which he wore an old boot or brogan, which he had picked up at some cabin. Being asked why he favored one foot more than the other, he replied that the one with the boot on had once been bitten by a rattlesnake, and had suffered more than the other, and deserved to be favored.

While clothed in such habiliments he presented a most ludicrous appearance, and it was hard to repress a smile on meeting him; yet such was the regard of the pioneers for this strange old man, that even the children of the cabins greeted him respectfully when he entered and craved the privilege of lying upon the floor a short time to give them fresh news, right from Heaven. "Almost the first thing he would do when he entered a house, was to lie down on the floor, with his knapsack for a pillow, and his head toward the light of a door or window, when he would carefully take out his old worn books, the exponents of the beautiful religion that Johnny so zealously lived out. We can hear him read just now, as he did that summer day, when we were busy quilting up-stairs, and he lay near the door, his voice rising and thrilling, strong and loud, as the roar of the waves and winds, then soft and soothing as the balmy airs that stirred and quivered the morning glory leaves about his gray head." *

His charitable impulses were such, that when he met a poor emigrant going west, shoeless and penniless, he would part with his last shoe and penny to help the stranger and his family on their way. Rude and uncouth as to appearance, he was not without sensibility and modesty; and often excused himself from entering the cabins of the settlers, "because his clothing was not fit." In conversation, he was attentive, polite and chaste in all kinds of company. He was a small man, rather bony and sinewy, about five feet nine inches high, with dark eyes, thin beard, and dark hair, which he generally wore long. Sometimes he could be induced to clip his beard, which rather improved his appearance, for his face was more round than bony, and was rather pleasant in expression, when he engaged in conversation.

His religious sentiments were as remarkable as his other traits. He was a devout and ardent disciple of the great Sweedish seer, Emanuel Swedenborg; and always carried portions of his works. Whenever an opportunity presented, he entered upon the discussion of the peculiar doctrines of Swedenborg, upon which he expatiated with great warmth and eloquence. Sometimes he carried a volume of Swedenborg beneath his waistband, from which he distributed fragments whenever he could get a reader, until a volume had disappeared. His ideas upon marriage were as eccentric as upon other topics. He excused himself from entering that state on the ground that he had a vision, in which two angelic ladies visited him to encourage his single blessedness, by the assurance that if he held out in this world, he would secure two wives in the world to come! While relating this circumstance, a wag took the liberty of interrogating Johnny as to the occupation of people in the other world. Johnny seemed to think people would recognize the marriage state there, and pursue much the same occupations they did here. The wag said:

"So you think men will follow the same occupations in Heaven?"

Johnny—"I really do."

Wag—"Do people die in Heaven?"

Johnny—"I think not."

Wag—"Then my occupation is gone; for I am a grave-digger!"

Johnny seemed somewhat quizzed by this argument,

* Recollections of Johnny-Appleseed by Rosella Rice, contributed to Knapp's History, page 32.

but still consoled himself on the idea of having two wives in the spiritual land of Swedenborg. His theological tenets taught him it was wrong to deprive any creature of life; and he carried this doctrine so far as to refuse even to kill a rattlesnake, after it had bitten him. His kindness to horses was such, that when he found an old or worn down animal turned out to die, by pioneers, he would always conduct it where it could get food, or hire some one to feed it. From some intimations dropped by him at Mansfield, and other points, it is believed that he was regularly ordained by the disciples of Swedenborg, and sent west as a missionary. Some expressions of his when Rev. Adam Paine, a sort of Lorenzo Dow, was once preaching on the public square in Mansfield, confirm this impression. In winding up an eccentric discourse on the sin of pride, Paine called out: "Where now is your barefooted pilgrim on his way to Heaven?" Johnny, holding up his bare pedals, exclaimed: "Here he is." A repetition of all the anecdotes concerning this strange wanderer would fill a volume. He was just as happy in the solitudes of the forest, communing with the author of all, as he lay gazing at the stars, where he could almost see the Angels, as in the midst of his nurseries or among the pioneers.

How, and where did he die? He died at the house of William Worth, in St. Joseph township, Allen county, Indiana, March 11, 1845. Some days prior to his decease, information was conveyed to Johnny, who was some fifteen miles distant from Mr. Worth's, near where he had a nursery, that some cattle had broken into it; and he immediately started. When he arrived he was very much fatigued, having exhausted his strength in the journey, which being performed without intermission, and on foot, was too great a task for the poor old man. He laid down that night never to rise again; for he was attacked with pneumonia, which baffled medical sk..." and in a few days he passed into the spirit land. Mr. Fletter, a neighbor of Mr. Worth, who laid out the body of Johnny, states, he had on when he died, next to his body, a coarse coffee-sack, with a hole cut in the centre, through which he passed his head. He had on the waists of four pairs of pants. These were cut off at the forks, ripped up at the sides, and the front thrown away, saving the waist-band attached to the hinder part. These hinder parts were buttoned around him, lapping like shingles, so as to cover the whole lower part of his body; and over all these were drawn a pair of what was once pantaloons. In this garb he died as he had lived*.

He was buried in David Archer's graveyard, two and one half miles north of Ft. Wayne, near the foot of a natural mound, and a stone set up to mark the place where he sleeps. He remained a firm believer in the doctrines of Swedenborg. His calm and resigned manner attracted the attention of his physician, who enquired about his religious tenets, asserting that he never saw a patient so resigned†. Johnny Chapman was a

*Hon. J. W. Dawson's letter to the Fort Wayne *Sentinel*, 1871.

†Letter of Richard Worth to the *Shield and Banner*, of Mansfield, describing the last hours of Johnny Appleseed. William Worth, at whose house he died, has been dead several years.

good man. He possessed many virtues. He was honest—upright, and harmless. He seems to have been specially fitted by Providence to prepare the wilderness for the reception of emigration and civilization.

The lovers of choice fruit in Ohio and Indiana owe him a monument to be erected over his remains, as a token of their high regard for the cheerful sacrifices he made, to contribute to the comfort and happiness of those seeking homes in the western wilds.

APPLESEED JOHN.

Old Johnny was bent well-nigh double
With years of toil and care and trouble,
But his large old heart oft felt the need
Of doing for others some kindly deed.

"But what can I do?" old Johnny said;
"I, who work so hard for daily bread?
It takes heaps of money to do so much good,
I am far too poor to do as I would."

The old man sat thinking deeply a while,
Then over his features gleamed a smile;
While he clapped his hands with a childish glee,
And said to himself: "There's a way for me!"

So he went to work with might and main,
But told to none the plan in his brain.
He took stale apples in payment for chores,
And carefully cut from them all the cores.

When he filled his bag, he wandered away,
And no man saw him for many a day.
With the well-stuffed bag o'er his shoulder flung,
He marched along and whistled or sung.

He seemed to roam with no object in view,
Like one who has nothing on earth to do;
But, rambling thus o'er prairies wide,
He paused sometimes and his bag untied.

His sharp-pointed cane deep holes would bore,
And in every hole he placed a core;
He covered them well, and left them there,
In keeping with sunshine, rain, and air.

Sometimes for days he waded through grass,
And saw never a living creature pass;
Though oft, when sinking to sleep in the dark,
He heard owls hoot and prairie dogs bark.

But sometimes butterflies perched on his thumbs,
And birds swarmed round him to pick up his crumbs.
They knew he carried no arrow or gun,
And never did mischief to any one:

For he was tender to all dumb things
That crept on the earth or soared on wings;
He stepped aside lest a worm should die,
And never had heart to hurt a fly.

Sometimes an Indian, of sturdy limb,
Came striding along and walked with him.
Whichever had food, shared with the other,
As if he had met a hungry brother.

When the Indian saw how the bag was filled,
And noticed the holes that the white man drilled,
He thought to himself 'twas a silly plan
To be planting seed for some future man.

Sometimes a log-cabin came in view,
Where John was sure to find jobs to do,
By which he gained stores of bread and meat,
And welcome rest for his weary feet.

He hilled potatoes and hoed the corn,
And mended shoes that were somewhat worn;
He taught the babies to use their legs,
And helped the boys to hunt for eggs.

He was so hearty at work or play
That every one urged a longer stay;
But he replied: "I have something to do,
And I must go on to carry it through."

The boys, who were sure to follow him round,
Soon found what it was he put in the ground;
So, as time passed, and he traveled on,
All the folks called him "Apple-seed John."

When he used up the whole of his store,
He went to cities and worked for more;
Then off he marched to the wilds again,
And planted seeds in prairie and glen.

In cities some said the man was crazy,
Others said, No; he was only lazy.
But he took no notice of jibes and jeers;
He knew he was working for future years.

He knew that trees would soon abound
Where once a tree could never be found;
That a flickering play of light and shade
Would make dancing shadows on the glade.

That blossoming boughs would form fall bowers,
And sprinkle the earth with rosy showers;
And the little seeds his hands had spread
Would form ripe apples when he was dead.

So he kept on traveling, far and wide,
'Till his old limbs failed him and he died.
He said, at last: "'Tis a comfort to feel
I've done good in the world, though not a great deal."

Weary travelers, journeying West,
In the shade of his trees find pleasant rest;
And often they start with glad surprise
At the rosy fruit that around them lies.

And if they inquire whence came such trees,
Where not a bough once swayed in the breeze,
The reply still comes, as they travel on,
"These trees were planted by Appleseed John."
—LYDIA MARIA CHILD.

THOMAS SPROTT

was born in Newville, Cumberland county, Pennsylvania, March 4, 1766. His parents were of Irish birth, from county Downe, in Ireland, and emigrated to America in the year 1764. When Thomas Sprott was a small boy his parents moved to the region now known as Allegheny county, and settled on the banks of the Youghiogeny river, where they remained a short time. Owing to the sparseness of the settlers and the hazards of Indian invasion, they deemed it best to change their location. The father of Thomas selected a new home, twelve miles west of Pittsburgh, and four south of the Ohio river, which at that point runs nearly west. Here he erected a strong log cabin after the manner of the pioneers, and commenced to prepare a farm for culture. The Wyandot and Delaware Indians made frequent incursions among the border settlers, capturing the children of the pioneers, killing and scalping whole families, and conveying away horses and other property. These expeditions were so frequently repeated that the Government deemed it best to establish forts within the Indian territory. Accordingly, General McIntosh was ordered to construct a fort near the junction of the Beaver with the Ohio river, in the spring of 1778. It was built of strong stockades, furnished with bastions, and mounted one six-pound cannon. The fort was called McIntosh, after the general. A strong garrison was placed within the fort to protect the settlements. The ferocity of the northwestern Indians continuing, and many incursions being made by them into the border settlements, General McIntosh was ordered to conduct an expedition, consisting of one thousand men, to Upper Sandusky to punish the warriors. Prior to setting out, he erected Fort Laurens, on the Tuscarawas, and proceeded on his expedition, the result of which is narrated in the history of the times.

The pioneers of the border were generally rough, rugged and fearless men. They taught their sons the art of border defence, and it was not unusual to find boys at the age of twelve or fifteen years fine woodsmen and unerring marksmen. The sons of Mr. Sprott, like the Wetzels, the Shepards, the Zanes, and others, were early taught the use of the rifle, that they might aid in repelling the savage red-skins in their attempts at capturing or murdering the settlers. At the age of seventeen Thomas Sprott was sufficiently skilful to become an effective scout and spy, and was induced by Brady to enter the service.*

In 1779 General Broadhead was ordered to Fort Pitt with his regiment, and Samuel Brady, who had been at the siege of Boston, and was a lieutenant at the massacre of the Paoli, accompanied the regiment. A short time prior to this, his father and brother had fallen by the hands of Indians, and Brady had sworn to avenge their murder; and was full of relentless hate. He was selected by General Broadhead, upon the suggestion of General Washington, as a suitable officer to proceed to Upper Sandusky to ascertain the number of British and Indians in that region. He was appointed captain of the spies, and furnished a rude map of the country in which the Indians were supposed to be located. He was accompanied by four *Chickasaws*, and some eight or ten select woodsmen and Indian hunters, as spies. They were all dressed and painted in true Indian style, and looked so much like Indians that it was really difficult to distinguish them from the genuine article. Brady was versed in the wiles of Indian strategy, and was well acquainted with their languages and mode of warfare. He led his band in safety through the deep, dark forests, across streams and over marshes and bogs to the Sandusky. On the way, his *Chickasaws* deserted him, and suspecting treachery, he was doubly on his guard. On his arrival at Sandusky, he concealed his men, and stealthily approached the Indian town in company with a select spy, where from his concealment he saw about three thousand Indians engaged in the amusement of the race-ground. They had just returned from Virginia and Kentucky with some fine blooded horses. After watching the Indians some hours, he and his companion returned to the place where he had concealed his spies and they turned their faces homeward. On the homeward trip to Fort McIntosh, Brady and his men had several startling adventures. He returned to Fort Pitt and made due report to General Broadhead, and was saluted as a hero.

In 1789 a line of spies and scouts was formed to patrol the borders from Fort Henry, now Wheeling, to Fort Le Bœuff on Lake Erie, of which Samuel Brady was captain. Thomas Sprott, Samuel Sprott, Alexander McConnell, Lewis Wetzel, George Foulks, Adam Poe, Andrew Poe, and some eight or ten other active border hunters were members of the company, which was regularly organized. About this time Captain Brady concluded to enter the Ohio wilderness and proceed in the direction of Upper Sandusky, in the hope of discovering an encampment of the Indians, who were constantly harrassing the border settlers. In company with George Foulks, Thomas Sprott, Samuel Sprott, McConnell, a young man by the name of Grant, and five or six others, whose headquarters were at Fort McIntosh, Captain Brady ascended Big Beaver to the mouth of the Mahoning and encamped over night. During the ascent of Beaver, one of the company shot a very fat young bear, a part of which they roasted and cooked for supper. They all eat heartily of the meat, and during the night young Grant was taken suddenly very sick; in the morning he was unable to proceed. After consultation, it was agreed that he should return to Fort McIntosh. He was unable to go alone. Lots were drawn to determine who should accompany him. The task fell upon a young man who was very anxious to continue with the expedition, and he refused to go back. The lot then fell upon Thomas Sprott, very much to his regret, because he was desirous of advancing. He and Grant descended the Beaver in a canoe, and landed safely at the fort.

Captain Brady and his men continued up the Mahoning to about the present site of Youngstown, where they left the stream and traveled through the forest in a southwest direction, until they reached Sugar creek, some twelve miles below the present site of Wooster, where they found a camp of Indians, one of which they shot, while another fled into the forest. The escaping Indian appeared to be a chief, and fled across the creek with the fleetness of a deer, and disappeared. From this point they traveled a westerly course until they reached a stream now known as Apple creek, where they found a camp with one man, a woman and a boy. They shot the man and woman, and the boy being some distance from the camp, and hearing the guns, cautiously approached, dodging from tree to tree; and when he had come within speaking distance, one of Brady's men told him to come in, as his father and mother were safe. The boy became alarmed and attempted to escape; but one of the sharp-shooters shot him through the bowels as he ran, and so disabled him that he was easily caught. On examination it was found the wound would be fatal. It was then determined to dispatch him. The poor little fellow understood what was to be his fate, and clung to the legs of one of the scouts, begging him to

---

* Captain Samuel Brady was born in Shippensburgh, Cumberland county, Pennsylvania, in 1758. He entered the army of the Revolution at an early age, and was in several battles. In 1779 he was ordered to Fort Pitt, under General Broadhead, where he became noted as an Indian hunter and spy. He was a brave and reckless man. Those who were best acquainted with him say he was, morally, quite unscrupulous.

Maj. G. W. Urie

COLONEL GEORGE W. URIE

was born in Washington county, Pennsylvania, February 22, 1806, and in 1815, when nine years of age, accompanied his father's family to Ohio, making a home in Orange township, in the present county of Ashland. In his boyhood he was an adept in the sports of the day, jumping, wrestling, running foot races, etc., in which he was able to hold his own with the best. His father was a great deer and bear hunter, and he generally accompanied him to assist in bringing in the trophies of the chase. In these expeditions he learned the intricate details of woodcraft, and became as expert with the rifle in securing game as his father.

When a young man he learned the trade of millwright, which called him some distance from his home. He also worked at the carpenter trade for more than twenty years—at that time very hard work, as mechanics were obliged to go into the woods, cut suitable trees, juggle, score and hew down the timber to a proper size, after which it was hauled by ox teams to the place designed for the building, where it was mortised and framed. Very many of these strongly framed houses and barns are now standing where they were built fifty or sixty years ago, and bid fair to remain another half century.

Colonel Urie possessed strong military tastes, and with his commanding figure and erect bearing was a prominent character at drill and general muster. Under the old State militia law he passed through the various grades from captain to colonel of a regiment of independent rifles. At the breaking out of the war with Mexico he still commanded this regiment, and made all his arrangements to accompany his comrades in support of the honor of the American flag, but having recently recovered from a severe attack of sickness, he was advised by his physician that if he followed his inclination in the matter it would very likely prove fatal to him. He therefore reluctantly decided to remain at home, and leave the honors that might be won to other officers of the regiment.

In the fall of 1845 he was elected treasurer of Richland county, and upon the erection of Ashland county in 1846, he resigned, and was elected the first treasurer of the new county, which office he held two terms.

In 1851 he was seized with a desire to seek a fortune among the gold mines of California, and entered the "golden gate" by way of the isthmus of Panama. He remained in California but one year, and finding his golden dreams contained more dross than pure metal, he returned. In 1853 he was elected a member of the State board of equalization from the district composed of Ashland and Richland counties. In 1857 he was appointed deputy United States marshal for the northern district of Ohio, and aided in taking the census of 1860. He was elected recorder of Ashland county in 1865, and held the office until 1874, when he was elected mayor of Ashland, which office he held two years.

Colonel Urie has been a resident of Ashland many years. As is evinced by the numerous places of trust he has filled, he has the confidence of the people of the county in which he lives. He was twice married, and by his first wife raised a family of four daughters—Mrs. Mary J. Porter, Mrs. Alice A. Beer, Mrs. Libbie H. Anderson, and Mrs. Sadie A. Beer. A son died young. Mrs. Porter died in September, 1875.

An extended sketch of the life of Solomon Urie, father of Colonel George W. Urie, will be found on page 189 of this work.

save his life, and take him along. A blow from a tomahawk soon silenced his cries, and his body was left as food for wild beasts.

From 1781 to 1791 during the Indian hostilities, Fort McIntosh was the principal headquarters of Brady and his men. Here the Sprotts, McConnells, Wetzels, Poes and Dickinsons often met for consultation. From 1783, the close of the Revolutionary war, until the defeat of Harmar and St. Clair, the border settlements were comparatively secure from Indian invasion. Brady and his men often passed up the Beaver to the Mahoning, and once or twice to the Cuyahoga where, on one occasion, Brady made a celebrated leap to escape from his pursuers. His trips with the spies frequently extended to Fort Laurens on the Tuscarawas.

In 1793-4 Thomas Sprott was employed by the Government to carry the mail from Fort Legionville, the winter quarters of General Wayne, to Fort Franklin on the Allegheny. His route was along an old Indian trail, without bridges or means of crossing streams, which he was compelled to wade, many times when flooded with ice. The trip was beset by many dangers, yet he delivered his precious packages promptly.

In 1795, after the treaty of Greenville, Thomas Sprott crossed the Ohio and located a tract of land near the present site of the village of Darlington, in Beaver county, Pennsylvania. About this time he married Mary Woodburn, of Allegheny county, and moved upon his farm, which consisted of four hundred acres. The disastrous defeat of the combined tribes, at Fallen Timbers, by General Wayne, and the large cession of territory made the United States by the tribes at the treaty of Greenville, completely humbled the warlike leaders, and a peace of fifteen years between the Indians and pioneers of Ohio prevailed.

The transition from Indian scout to the peaceful occupation of agriculturist was easy and agreeable to Thomas Sprott. He soon became noted as a quiet and careful farmer. To the day of his death he took great pleasure in narrating the adventures and hairbreadth escapes of Brady and his men, and proudly contended that the great State of Ohio was indebted to such leaders and men for the expulsion of the merciless savage, who had so often desolated the borders of Pennsylvania and Virginia.

Mr. Sprott remained on his farm in Beaver county until 1821, when his excellent wife deceased. In 1823 he purchased a farm in Clearcreek township, Richland, now Ashland, county, and with his family, consisting of four sons and four daughters, located thereon—James, his oldest son, remaining in Beaver County.

When Mr. Sprott arrived in Clearcreek it was but sparsely settled. The *Delawares* and a few of the *Wyandots* returned annually to make sugar and hunt. They were then harmless and annoyed no one. Mr. Sprott had but little intercourse with them, and was never disturbed. He had seen enough of the red-skins on the eastern border of the State; and the sight of a tomahawk and an Indian hunter brought unpleasant memories of the past.

In 1839 Mr. Sprott deceased, and according to a desire expressed sometime before his death, was buried on a favorite Indian mound a few hundred yards northeast of his residence, where his son William was also buried in 1845. The location of the mound is very striking. It was built upon an upheaval of drift deposited during the glacial period, something over ninety feet high, with a circular base some three hundred yards in diameter. This natural upheaval or deposit of drift was slightly flattened on the top, where the Indians erected two mounds, each of which possessed a diameter, at the base, of about twenty-five feet, and a height of about five feet. From the top of this mound a grand view is presented. The observer can take in a landscape of five or six miles, exhibiting as fine a valley of land as can be seen on the globe. Here, Thomas Sprott, the brave old scout and pioneer, rests from his toils, with a reputation unsullied, and a consciousness of having done his duty as a citizen, a soldier, and a Christian.

Mr. Sprott raised an excellent family of sons and daughters, who are much scattered: Thomas, jr., aged seventy-two, resides on the old homestead; Samuel, aged seventy-one, resides in Auburn, Indiana; John, aged sixty-seven, resides at Bryan, Ohio; Jane married Colonel Samuel Russell, and resides in Seattle, King county, Washington Territory; Martha resides in Savannah, Ashland county, Ohio; Mary married Samuel Sprott, a cousin, and resides in Leseur City, Minnesota.

SOLOMON URIE

was born in Bedford county, Pennsylvania, near Bloody run, in 1769. He was in Williamson's campaign against the Moravian villages, on the Tuscarawas, in 1782, and was at the massacre of the Christian Moravians, and saw the burning of their houses. He was then quite young, but large of his age. Colonel David Williamson was a brother-in-law, and for that reason he was induced to accompany the expedition. He always disapproved that barbarous act, and often stated to his sons, that Williamson yielded a reluctant consent to the perpetration of that dreadful tragedy, being unable to control the violence of his soldiers, who were border volunteers, and had suffered much from Indian raids and depredations.

In the year 1810, Solomon Urie and his brother Thomas went on a hunting excursion across the Ohio and established a camp about midway between the present sites of Cadiz and New Philadelphia. They hunted together some days, and finally, in one of their trips through the forest in search of game, became separated. Thomas, having killed a bear, in the evening was conveying the skin toward the camp, which he had nearly reached, when he was shot and killed by Indians, who had taken possession of it, and were in ambush, watching his arrival. Solomon, at the same time, was approaching the camp from another direction, driving before him his horses, which had been belled and hoppled. When almost in sight of the camp, he heard a double crack of guns, and, fearing his brother might have been assailed by Indians, considered it prudent to leave his horses and carefully guard against surprise. When he came in sight of his camp, he saw two Indians plundering it, while a third was acting as sentinel. He raised his rifle to shoot the Indian guard, when his brother's dog began to bark, which pointed out his position to the Indian. Mr. Urie comprehended the position at a glance. There were three Indians. To press forward might be fatal. In his rear was a swamp. To retreat in that direction would be folly. Summoning all his energies, he made a bold dash in the direction of the Indian sentinel. The Indian became alarmed and retreated, dodging behind trees to escape his white assailant. Mr. Urie pressed boldly forward, discovering as he went, the body of his brother Thomas. He successfully escaped the Indians, who pursued him some miles to the verge of a precipice, down which he plunged, and on descending to the bottom, discovered that he had broken the breach of his gun, the lock being uninjured. The Indians were amazed at the leap, and abandoned further pursuit. Mr. Urie continued his flight in the direction of the Ohio river, and, much to his surprise, came upon a camp formed of Captain Samuel Brady and other hunters. The next morning he and a number of others returned to his late camp and found Thomas covered with the skin of the bear he had shot the day before. The Indians had carried away one of his moccasins and a leggin. His body was pierced with two bullets, and scalped. A grave was dug with wooden shovels, into which his body was deposited, enclosed in a coffin made of puncheons. The Indians had departed with the horses, forty deer, ten bear, and ten beaver skins, and the entire stock of provisions and traps. Mr. Urie offered all the property to his new comrades if they would join him in the pursuit, capture and punishment of the Indians. It was regarded as too hazardous an undertaking, and he was reluctantly compelled to leave the murder of his brother unrevenged for the present.

He returned to his home in Washington county, resolved to retaliate on the red fiends of the Ohio forests at no distant day. When the war of 1812 was inaugurated, he and his son Samuel served three months on the borders of Canada, and rendezvoused at Black Rock. In the summer of 1814, Mr. Urie visited Orange township, and located a quarter section of land, and a quarter section in Montgomery township, and erected a small cabin and cleared a few acres of ground, and in the fall of 1815 removed to it with his family, which consisted of seven sons—Samuel, Thomas, David, Solomon, John, George W. and James; and two girls—Susannah and Elizabeth.

In the fall of 1815, he erected a blacksmith shop on his land, being the first one in Orange township, he being a blacksmith and gunsmith by trade. The first winter after his arrival, he killed forty deer, eight large black bears, a great number of wolves, and other game. On one occasion, there being considerable snow on the ground, he took an old horse and rode two or three miles north in the forest, hitched to a sapling, and, proceeding a short distance, shot a fine deer. Returning to the horse, he rode it through the undergrowth to the deer, tied a rope around its neck, fastened the other end to the tail of the horse, mounted, and rode home, dragging the deer after him. He had reached his cabin but a few minutes, when, as he was engaged in skinning the deer, a gang of hungry wolves, following his trail, appeared in the vicinity of his cabin. His dogs set up a furious barking and commenced an attack upon the wolves, when they soon fled into the forest. It was a narrow escape; for they were half famished for food. He was very successful in trapping wolves. He usually made a sort of triangular pen, arranging a large trap, so that the wolf would have to pass over it in reaching a piece of fresh meat which he placed in the narrow end, covering the trap with leaves. Having bent and trimmed a small sapling, he fastened the chain of the trap to it in such a manner that when the wolf attempted to back out, it would tread upon the trap, set it off, be caught by the hind legs, and elevated by the sapling. In this way, he captured a great many, a reward being offered for their scalps. Soon after the erection of his shop, Tom Lyons, Jonacake, Catotawa, and other Wyandot and Delaware Indians, came to have their tomahawks and guns repaired. They frequently brought bent gun-barrels to be straightened. Passing the barrel between the logs of his shop, he used sufficient force to spring it back, until the bend was out; then, taking a bow with a thong of deer sinews, he passed the thong through the barrel, and, springing it until it was tense, he could see whether any kinks were left in the barrel by sighting through the bore; and if any were discovered, he removed them by a wooden mallet, by laying the barrel on the end of a square block and striking on it, occasionally looking through the bore at a piece of white paper, to see if all the kinks were out. The Indians watched the operation very closely, insisting that he would "spoil gun." After completing the work, Mr. Urie would challenge the Indians to shoot at a mark with him. Being a fine shot, always shooting off-hand, "Old Peel," as he called his rifle, was sure to cut the paper. The Indians, being accustomed to shoot with a rest, made poor shots off-hand. When they were about to shoot, Urie, who was always brimful of fun and tricks, would stand close to his competitor, saying, "Indian stir mush," "Cooza," "No go," when the Indian, becoming very nervous, would miss the mark, and Urie would laugh heartily. In this way, when he bet he won most of their furs and skins.

After the murder of his brother, Mr. Urie never entertained a very cordial feeling for the red race; and, on his hunting excursions along the Black river, from 1815 to 1825, though reticent on the subject, it is believed he more than once avenged the death of his brother.

Mr. Urie died in Montgomery township, July 7, 1830, aged nearly sixty-two years, and Mrs. Elizabeth Urie, his wife, in June, 1842, aged about seventy-three years. Colonel George W. Urie is the only one of the family in this county. Thomas* and David† are in Iowa; and

---

* Thomas Urie died in Iowa, September 8, 1875, aged eighty-two years.

† David Urie died in Iowa, March, 1874, aged seventy-eight years.

James is in Indiana. All the others are gone to their final resting place.

STERLING G. BUSHNELL, SR.,

was born in Hartford county, Connecticut, in 1770, and emigrated to Trumbull county, Ohio, in 1806. He left Connecticut in December, 1805, and journeyed on sleds with his wife and five children. On the route he was joined by a number of other families. The most of the route was through the forests of eastern and northern New York. He passed directly to Albany, and thence to near Buffalo, on the lake. He and his traveling companions generally camped by the wayside at night, scraping the snow aside and erecting a sort of tent or screen of bed quilts to protect their families against the storms and cold. The forests were infested by large numbers of ferocious wolves. To protect himself against these animals, he generally encamped near a dead tree, which he set on fire. When they reached the Hudson, the ice was somewhat weakened by a thaw. Fearing to cross it with his teams, he took the sled and children and hauled it by hand to the western side, leaving his wife and horse to follow. After he had landed, she mounted and followed, and when about midway of the stream, the ice broke with a tremendous roar. He stood appalled at the sight, expecting to see his wife and horse disappear beneath the floating ice. Fortunately, she floated on a large piece of ice which drifted to the western shore, some distance below him. Watching its approach to land, when it touched the bank, she applied her whip vigorously to the sides of the horse upon which she was seated, and aided by this stimulus, it gave a great leap, fastened upon and ascended the bank in safety. Great was his joy over the providential escape. From near the city of Buffalo the whole party kept up the lake shore. By examination they found the ice was sufficiently strong to bear their teams, and hence, followed it until they reached the northwest corner of Pennsylvania, when they learned from an old Indian chief of the *Senecas* where they were, and the proper route from there to Trumbull county, Ohio. When he arrived at the residence of his brother, William Bushnell, who had preceded him one year, his wife gave birth to a child about two hours after his arrival—Jonathan Bushnell. Mr. Bushnell resided in Trumbull county about fifteen years. His occupations were various. Part of the time he taught school—acted as justice of the peace and county surveyor. In his late residence, he engaged in the mercantile business and carried on a tannery and a farm. He also made two trips to New Orleans, with flat-boats, loaded with the productions of Trumbull county—principally butter and cheese. He launched his boat on a small stream emptying into Big Beaver, and passed down it to the Ohio, and thence down the Mississippi, where he sold his commodities at good prices, and returned on horseback, passing through the Indian nations, *Choctaws*, *Cherokees* and *Chickasaws*, carrying his money in a portmanteau. While crossing a stream, he got his money—bank bills—wet, and stopped with a chief of the *Chickasaws*, who entertained him kindly and helped dry his bank bills, and directed him on his way. This venture proved very profitable, and upon returning home, he resolved to make a second trip loaded as before. In passing down the Ohio, he became ice-bound until the opening of the spring thaw, and when he arrived at New Orleans, his goods were greatly damaged from the climate—his butter melted and cheese spoiled. The trip proved a failure, and he was ruined financially. He was gone about six months, returning by the Gulf and Atlantic to New York city, and thence by private conveyance home.

During the war of 1812 a regiment was raised in Trumbull county, Richard Hayes being colonel, Sterling G. Bushnell adjutant, and an eminent pioneer preacher, Father Badger, chaplain. This regiment made a forced march up the lake shore to Sandusky, where Sandusky City now stands. The regiment was, for some time, at Fort Avery, and near Fort Meigs. While near the mouth of Huron, Adjutant Bushnell assisted in the exchange of prisoners between Malden and Huron. While stationed here he became possessed with the malaria of that region, and was discharged on account of disability, and his widow, forty years afterward, was awarded a pension, which was continued until her decease.

In May, 1821, he emigrated to near the present site of the town of Hayesville, in Vermillion township. When he arrived he was fifty-one years old. The township was sparsely settled, and he entered upon pioneer life in earnest, purchasing eighty acres of land, upon which his son, Thomas Bushnell, now resides, of Joseph Lake, of Wooster, for forty dollars. It proved to be a fine bargain. He commenced improvements upon it by the erection of a comfortable log cabin, in which he resided for many years.

Being a good mathematician, and a practical surveyor, he soon began to retrieve his southern losses. His experience as a business man gave him an opportunity to acquire a knowledge of legal proceedings in justices' courts, and he soon became expert as a country attorney. Many anecdotes are related of him in his capacity as a lawyer, some of which evince a good deal of shrewdness. On one occasion, three young men, of Vermillion township, went on a little frolic to cut a bee tree on the premises of a watchful farmer. After securing the honey, the secret was divulged to a comrade, who told the farmer of his loss. A suit was brought to secure the value of the tree, before a justice of the peace. The young men consulted Mr. Bushnell as to the best method of escape. They related the circumstances—said the tree was on a ridge—which fact they had stated. Bushnell desired to learn whether the precise locality had been stated. They said it had not. Mr. Bushnell told them to return with part of the honey and comb, and cut another hollow tree on the same ridge in the adjoining township, and fill the crevices of a large limb with the comb, and smear it over with honey, and leave the balance to him. The young men agreed to pay him fifteen dollars—five each—if he would clear them. The trial came, and it was shown that a tree had been cut on the ridge, but the exact point was in uncertainty. After examining the witnesses, Mr. Bushnell stated that his clients did not deny cutting a tree on the ridge, but the tree was in the adjoining township, and the present court had no jurisdiction. Witnesses for the defence had testified that they had seen the tree, and it was as stated. The plaintiff had, therefore, failed to fix the cutting of the tree upon the young men, as charged in his affidavit. Mr. Bushnell, therefore, demanded the discharge of his clients, which the justice granted without further delay. For fees he received thirty silver half-dollars, and returned triumphantly to his own cabin.

Mr. Bushnell died at his homestead in Vermillion township, August 16, 1846, aged seventy-four years. He was the father of eleven children—five sons and six daughters—Betsy, wife of Sylvester Bucher; Laura, wife of Tully Crosby; William, an eminent surveyor of Mansfield, Ohio; Collins, who built the first hotel in Hayesville, and died in Louisiana in 1832 leaving three sons—Judge Tully C., Sterling G. (a justice of the peace), and Collins W. (probate judge); Sedelia, wife of James Connolly, of Iowa; Jothan, deceased; Huldah, wife of Stephen Tanner, of Illinois; Rosella, wife of Jonathan W. Sloan, of Mansfield; Homer, of Mercer county, Ohio, deceased; Olive, wife of Dr. David Snively, of Xenia, Ohio; and Thomas, of Hayesville, who resides on the old homestead, and is noted for his zeal and success in agriculture and horticulture.

ELIAS SLOCUM

was born in Rodman township, Jefferson county, New York, August 11, 1784. In June, 1817, he came west to select a home, and arrived in Uniontown, now Ashland, in July, after a long and toilsome journey. After examining the country in and about Montgomery township, he concluded to make the vicinity of Uniontown his residence. In October he returned east for his family. In this trip he was accompanied by George W. Palmer, a Mr. Lucas and a Mr. Butterfield. In the meantime the families of the foregoing pioneers remained in the vicinity of Black Rock, somewhat noted in the Indian wars and the war of 1812, and in January, 1818, after having attempted to make a passage up the lake, but having been driven back by the tempestuous storms then prevailing, commenced their journey overland, and arrived in Uniontown in March, after continuous travel of near two months, over rugged hills, down narrow valleys, along winding paths, often crossing deep streams. Mr. Slocum purchased of George Butler, one of the sturdy pioneers, one hundred and six acres of land, two miles east of Uniontown, on section sixteen, and also jointly with Alanson Andrews, and George W. Palmer, who accompanied him with his family, three acres on Montgomery's run, in Uniontown, and erected a distillery, an institution prior to that time unknown in Uniontown. His family resided in a cabin on the farm, to which Mr. Slocum returned from his daily toils at the village of Uniontown. At that time there was not a physician in the present limits of Ashland county; and school-houses were equally rare. "Old Hopewell," Presbyterian, one mile west of the village, was the only church in this region. Log cabins were the order of the day, and Mr. Slocum, like other pioneers, often spent the whole week at cabin-raisings, and log-rollings, traveling several miles from home to do so. All were anxious to increase the number of settlers, and great exertions were made to aid in raising cabins and preparing lands for culture. When Mr. Slocum settled on section sixteen wild animals, such as deer, bear and wolves, were quite numerous, while the latter proved quite destructive to sheep and hogs. Wild turkeys were also very plenty, and an expert hunter could easily procure an abundance of wild meat.

Mr. Slocum, at a later period, purchased a lot and house where the town hall now stands, and removed into it, and kept hotel a number of years. He accumulated property quite rapidly, and was very shrewd in money matters. At an early day he became quite expert in legal disputes, and was the principal attorney in this region, although never regularly admitted to the bar. Many anecdotes evincing unusual sharpness in practice, are related of him. At an early day he had a suit before 'Squire Solomon Sherradden, who resided where James Newman now lives. It was for the price of a certain "crow-bar," which had disappeared from a quarry two and a half miles east of Ashland; and was in possession of a certain citizen. The ownership was in dispute, and the question of identity was to be raised by the defendant. On the morning of the trial Mr. Slocum visited the residence of the justice, and finding him absent, obtained permission from Mrs. Sherradden, who was at a spring a short distance from the cabin engaged in washing, to go to the house and examine the bar, as he was the attorney for the defendant. Having done so, he replaced it beneath the bed where he found it, and returned at the hour of trial. He was confronted by the late Silas Robbins, jr., as attorney for the plaintiff. The trial proceeded regularly until proof was made that the bar in question was new, unmarked, and of the usual style. After cross-questioning the witnesses sharply, to avoid equivocation, Mr. Slocum requested the production of the bar in court. It was drawn from under the bed, and upon examination was found, not to be smooth and unmarked; but on the contrary, was deeply indented. Mr. Slocum demanded judgment for the defendant, and the court readily granted it, to the great chagrin of Mr. Robbins and the plaintiff. The facts were, that on the examination in the morning, Mr. Slocum had taken the bar to the shop of Mr. Sherradden, who was a blacksmith, and made the indentations that defeated the claimant. These tricks, then perfectly allowable among country attorneys, constituted a large proportion of the strategy of litigation.

The relation of these incidents of practice furnished a good deal of amusement to those outside the quarrel. He often met Mr. Sterling G. Bushnell, of Hayesville, as a country practitioner in legal contests in justices courts. Mr. Bushnell had the reputation of being decidedly sharp—was fluent, extremely sarcastic, and untiring in his efforts in behalf of his clients.

Before the establishment of the county of Ashland, Mr. Slocum often conducted appeals in the courts at Mansfield with considerable ability and success. In person, he was commanding in appearance, was about six feet in height, hair light brown, eyes a bluish gray and very expressive. In disposition he was kind and rather disposed to conciliate; but when aroused, exceedingly sarcastic and unyielding. As a business man he was very shrewd, insinuating, and successful. He was a good judge of values, and was not easily overreached in his purchases and exchanges. He arrived in Montgomery when it was sparsely settled, and lived to see it the most populous and thrifty township in the county. He passed through all the struggles from a poor and humble pioneer to that of thrift and wealth, and at the advanced age of seventy-eight years, April 17, 1862, deceased at his residence in Ashland, and his remains now rest amid the tombs of his pioneer neighbors, who passed away before him.

He was twice married, having lost the wife of his youth in 1829. He had no children by his second wife. His family consists of Sarah, married to John Lafferty, of Stark county, Illinois; Mary, married to Joseph Palmer, of Galesburgh, Illinois; Elizabeth, married to Daniel Carter, of Ashland; Lyman, deceased; Wealthy, married to the late David Bryte, of Ashland; Ephraim, who resides on the old homestead, near Ashland; Willard, an attorney, who resides in Ashland; Mahala, married to Johnson Carson, of Galesburgh, Illinois; Eli, of Ashland; Alfred, near Ashland; and Cordelia, deceased. His descendants are all thrifty, intelligent, and influential people.

CAPTAIN PIPE,

whose Indian name was "Hobacan," belonged to the Monsie or Wolf tribe of the *Lenni-Lenape* or *Delawares*. This famous war chief, in his later years, appears to have resided on the upper branches of Mohican, the head branches of Black river, the Vermillion and the Cuyahoga. It is believed that some time between 1793 and 1795, he made his headquarters at Jerometown, an Indian village about three-fourths of a mile southwest of the present site of Jeromeville, and erected a cabin on the old site of Mohican Johnstown. This village was surrounded south, east and north by alder swamps that were impassable by cavalry, and difficult of penetration by infantry.

A brief outline of the career of this noted chief of the *Delawares*, may be interesting to the reader.

He was born, as near as can be learned, on the banks of the Susquehanna river, in Pennsylvania, about the year 1740. Though undoubtedly a member of the royal or ruling family of his tribe, his youth seems to have been remarkably obscure. This obscurity may have arisen from the fact that all Indian youths were taught to show deference to age and experience. It is believed that Pipe and other *Delawares* located at the junction of the Sandy and Tuscarawas rivers as early as 1758. His first appearance on the historic page was among the warriors at a conference held at Fort Pitt, July, 1759, between the agent of Sir William Johnston, Hugh Mercer, the *Iroquois*, *Delawares* and *Shawnees*.

Pipe was then probably about nineteen years of age, and much too young to be conspicuous. He is next mentioned in an agreement with Charles Frederick Post, the eminent Moravian missionary, in the year 1762. Post had visited the junction of the Sandy and Tuscarawas rivers, in 1761, and obtained the consent of King Beaver, a Delaware chief, to erect a cabin for a school and mission house. When he returned in 1762, with John Heckewelder, then nineteen years old, as an assistant to teach the young *Delawares*, he located in the cabin, and commenced to mark out a small field for corn. The Indians ordered him to desist. A council was held, in which the Indians expressed fears that a fort would soon appear at that point if they permitted Post to go on with his clearing. On being assured by Post that their fears were groundless, they consented to allow the missionaries a spot of ground—fifty steps each way—for a garden or field, in which to raise corn or vegetables for their support. Accepting these terms, "Hobacan"—Captain Pipe, a young Delaware chief—was ordered to step off the boundaries, and drive stakes at the corners. Pipe seemed very suspicious of the mission, because his people had suffered many wrongs at the hands of the British in Maryland, Delaware and Pennsylvania, and never failed, in a sly way, to urge his tribe to be cautious of the whites and the new missionaries.

In 1764 Colonel Henry Bouquet led an expedition to the Muskingum river against the Indians. When his army reached Fort Pitt, now Pittsburgh, Pennsylvania, he delayed his march a few days. Some ten Indians appeared on the north bank of the Ohio river during the time he was at this fort, and asked to have a talk. Part of them crossed the river and entered the fort, and not being able to explain their object in coming to the settlement, were detained as suspicious characters or spies. One of these proved to be young Pipe, the *Delaware*, who, two years prior, had marked out Post's garden spot. He was detained at Fort Pitt until Colonel Bouquet returned from the Muskingum, where he dictated terms of peace and a treaty with the *Delawares* and *Shawnees*. The transaction soured the temper of Captain Pipe, and he resolved upon a relentless course in the future against the "Long Knives," as he called the colonists.

Captain White Eyes, "Coquethagechton," chief of the Turtle tribe of *Delawares*, unlike Pipe, was friendly to the missionaries, and opposed him in his hostility towards the settlers in western Pennsylvania. Although Pipe's tribe repressed their hate, with few exceptions, until 1780, he entertained a bitter feeling toward the colonists. In 1765 he attended a conference at Fort Pitt, at which about six hundred chiefs and warriors and many women and children were present. In 1768 he again met in conference at Fort Pitt, George Croghan, the sub-agent of Sir William Johnston, and over one thousand *Iroquois, Delawares, Shawnees, Wyandots* and *Mohegans*. In the meantime Pipe and White Eyes became rivals for ascendancy in the councils of the *Delawares*. White Eyes was a frank, manly and courageous chief, and had the sagacity to see that to make war upon the border settlers was to invoke incursions into the Indian territory, and bring ruin upon his people. Pipe was haughty and ambitious, and detested the "Long Knives," and longed for the time when it would be safe for him to take the hatchet. His young warriors very generally seconded his warlike ferocity, and a large number of the Turtle tribe were deeply affected by his intrigues.

In 1771 he sent a speech to John Penn, the governor of Pennsylvania, in which he made complaints against white aggression and wrong. Not being relieved of the complaints in 1774, Pipe, White Eyes, and others, met the agent of Governor Dunmore, John Connelly, at Pittsburgh, in conference, in regard to recent aggressions on the Indian territory, and the unprovoked murder of the relatives of the noted Mingo, Logan. At this conference strong efforts were made to pacify the Indians and prevent war. The effort was in vain, for a great battle was fought at the mouth of the Kanawha, in October. It is not known how many of the *Delawares* participated in that battle.

In 1778 a conference was held at Fort Pitt between Andrew and Thomas Lewis, United States commissioners, and Captains White Eyes, Killbuck, and Pipe, deputies and chiefs of the *Delawares*, concerning the wrongs inflicted by the "Long Knives," and the retaliation of the Indians.

The long-impending separation of Pipe and White Eyes soon after this took place. Pipe made an effort to overthrow White Eyes. Seeing the effect of the intrigues of Pipe upon the Turtle tribe, Whites Eyes summoned a council, and declared that if they determined, in spite of his remonstrances, to go to war, he would lead the warriors himself and die with his tribe. This heroic proposition turned the scale, and his people remained the friends of the colonists. Pipe, and the warlike members of his tribe, departed from the Tuscarawas and located on the Walhonding, about fifteen miles above the present site of Coshocton, and attached himself to the British, who furnished his warriors blankets, tomahawks, guns, and ammunition, in exchange for human scalps.

In the midst of the revolution (1780) Captain Pipe and his warlike *Delawares* removed from the Walhonding to the Sandusky, on Tymocktee creek, and united his forces with the *Wyandots, Senecas*, and other savages favoring the British cause. While he resided in this region he organized an expedition (1781) for the removal of the Moravian *Delawares* from the Tuscarawas. He was accompanied by three hundred warriors, two distinguished chiefs, and the notorious Captain Elliott, then active in the British service. After the removal, Colonel Williamson and a large number of border ruffians from western Pennsylvania, made an expedition to the deserted villages on the Tuscarawas, barbarously murdered all they could find, and burned their houses and bodies.

In 1782 followed the unfortunate expedition of Colonel William Crawford. Captain Pipe has been censured for the cruelty inflicted upon Colonel Crawford and the other captives. We are apt to think, notwithstanding ingenious attempts have been made to excuse that wicked expedition, that it was the deliberate intention of Crawford and Williamson, and the barbarous persons who accompanied the expedition, to first assault and destroy the Moravian settlements, and then finish their work of blood and death upon the *Wyandots*.

The barbarities of the men who accompanied the new expedition on the Tuscarawas, led Pipe and his people to believe that no Indian would be spared. The *Delawares, Wyandots*, and *Shawnees*, were ready to meet the invaders and give them a hot reception. They were not non-resisting Moravians. They fully appreciated their position, and, like brave men, met their enemies and put them to flight. The subsequent tragedies were such as Crawford and his men should have expected when Williamson and his men failed to show mercy even to praying women and innocent children.

Yet Williamson was actually a candidate to lead the new expedition, and some writers are surprised that the historians of that day should entertain the idea that the expedition contemplated the destruction of the remaining Moravians. Pipe was relentless. It was a contest of life and death. Crawford had to die, because he would have killed Pipe and his people, and burned their towns. Retributive justice is severe, but generally overtakes bad enterprises.

Captain Pipe appeared before the British authorities at Detroit, as a witness against the Moravians, and finally excused them against the false accusations of Girty and others; and expressed a determination to treat the captive missionaries better in the future. In December, 1781, he appeared before the same British officer, Colonel Arentz Schuyler DePeyster, and reported the result of his military enterprise against the colonists, and bitterly reproached that officer for seducing the Indians into a war, in which they were acting the part of a hunter's dog, which, being hissed to the attack, received all the injuries inflicted by the ferocious beasts of the forest. At the same time he expressed a determination to withdraw from their service by returning his war tomahawk. In 1785 he was present at the conference at Fort McIntosh, and signed the treaty of that date. His name, by the interpreter, was affixed to that treaty, as "Wobocan," and signed. At this period, it is evident, he made frequent trips up and down the Muskingum, and possibly to his old residence at Sandy. We next hear of him at the mouth of the Big Miami, below Cincinnati, at a treaty with the *Shawnees* and others, as late as 1786. He was not a party to the treaty, however, but was present, and signed the document as a witness. One year after this, according to Zeisberger, the missionary, he attached himself to the tribes friendly to the United States, but in a short time violated his new engagement.

In 1788, when the pioneer settlers landed at what is

now Marietta, they found Captain Pipe and about seventy warriors encamped in the neighborhood. At that time General Harmar described him as a "manly old fellow, and much more of a gentleman than the generality of the frontier people." Colonel John May, during the same spring, says: "Here (at the residence of General Harmar) I was introduced to 'Old Pipe,' chief of the Delaware Nation, and his suite, dressed like the offspring of Satan." Here he is described as "Old Pipe." According to the most reliable accounts, Captain Pipe was then about forty-eight years of age.

When we consider the fact, that Blackhoof, and perhaps Thomas Lyon, each lived over a century, Captain Pipe was then in his prime. This leaves Captain Pipe quietly navigating the Muskingum and its branches, hunting and making annual trips, at the proper season, to exchange furs and peltry for such goods and supplies as were needed by himself and people. Whether he visited Marietta at a later period than 1790 does not seem quite clear, though it is possible he may have done so.

It seems to be conceded, very generally, that Captain Pipe took an active part in the campaign against Harmar in the fall of 1790. It is urged, however, by some authorities, that he did not freely second the wishes of the *Delawares* in that campaign; and that he was opposed to entering the struggle against Harmar; but that he was overruled and yielded a reluctant consent to enter the contest. Pipe was no coward. He was rash and vindictive. His wishes for peace in this instance were pretended. He entertained no scruples about entering the campaign against General St. Clair in 1791. It is related that he boasted of slaughtering the soldiers of that unfortunate expedition until his arm was weary. That was the temper of Pipe when roused to vengeance. He was a merciless foe.

In the campaign of General Anthony Wayne in 1794, we are of opinion Captain Pipe was one of his bitterest foes. We are also of opinion he was engaged in the battle of Fallen Timbers, and was even present at the treaty of Greenville in 1795, though it is asserted that he died in 1794. His name is not attached to that treaty. Why is this? Captain Pipe was in disgrace. He had betrayed his friendship for the United States; brought ruin upon his people by his alliance with Little Turtle and other leaders in that war. The *Delawares* were left in a state of anarchy. They had warred against the United States by the advice and aid of Captain Pipe, and ruin and disorganization had overtaken them. Pipe, with a few of his friends, skulked away, and came down to the branches of the Mohican.

A late writer says "he died a few days previous" to the battle of Fallen Timbers, in 1794. Where and under what circumstances? "Upon the Maumee River." Where? In the presence of whom? Who first gave circulation to the story of his death? "Joseph Brandt," a Mohawk, who desired to pacify the trembling Moravians. Why did Heckewelder, Loskiel, and other Moravians not hear of and mention the circumstance? They had had bitter experience under the rule of Pipe, and would have been rejoiced to be liberated from his surveillance and dictation. Heckewelder, who is so frequently assailed as a romancer, would have been but too happy to have penned a criticism on his old accuser and foe. Heckewelder passed down these valleys many times between 1794 and 1810, and could have thrown much light on the decease of Pipe, and the incidents connected with his last hours. He is silent. So is Loskiel and others; and Zeisberger doubtless based his statement on a rumor, and subsequent writers have simply repeated that rumor.

Now for the reason. About the year 1795, John Baptiste Jerome, a French trader, who had married a Delaware woman, on the Auglaize river, about 1790 or 1791, located with his wife and daughter, then some four or five years of age, upon the present site of Jeromeville, and after whom the village was called. The stream passing said village also received his name, and has ever since been called the Jerome fork of the Mohican. When the earliest settlers came into that region, in 1808-9, Jerome had a good cabin, and some thirty or forty acres of land cleared and in a tolerable state of cultivation. About three-fourths of a mile southwest of his cabin, across the Mohican, was located the ancient Mohican Johnstown, then inhabited by *Delawares*, and near which old Captain Pipe, Hobocan, located about the same time. Is there any mistake about that? The identical spot of his wigwam is yet known. From whom was this information gleaned? From John Baptiste Jerome, the French trader, who accompanied Captain Pipe to this region, and who knew him well. Jerome often related to the pioneers the circumstances connected with the battle of Fallen Timbers, the utter amazement and terror of the Indians over the movements and victory of "Mad Anthony." According to his statement, Pipe was in the battle of 1794, although it was his opinion that Pipe was not present at the treaty. He often stated to pioneers, yet living in this county, that after the treaty of Greenville Captain Pipe began to see that his diplomacy had brought distress upon his people, and though accepting the terms of peace, bitterly regretted that he had not refrained from identifying himself with the allied tribes and the British. In a vain endeavor to correct the errors of the past, he left the region of the Maumee, and quietly sought repose on the Mohican.

Captain Pipe resided on the Mohican in 1809-10-11 and 1812, and when the Finleys, Carters, Warners, Chandlers, Coulters, Olivers, Rices and Tannehills, most of whom still survive, settled on the branches of the Mohican. He continued to reside in a wigwam, about a mile southwest of the present site of Jeromeville, until the spring of 1812, when he and most of his people quietly disappeared from that locality and never returned.

In the fall of 1811 a great feast took place at Greentown, an Indian village on the Black fork of the Mohican, about ten miles southwest of Jerometown. Captain Armstrong, chief of the Turtle tribe, and his people, resided in Greentown. There were present between three and four hundred *Delawares* and other Indians. Among the number of chiefs was Captain Pipe, of

Jerometown. The whites present were the Rices, the Coulters, Tannehills, and the Rev. James Copus, and a few others. Some of these are yet living. They all describe him as "Old Captain Pipe." Armstrong, then sixty-five or seventy; Thomas Lyon, seventy-five or eighty, and other aged Indians, were present. In the opinion of nearly all the white persons present, the majority of whom have furnished statements, Captain Pipe is represented as being quite advanced in years, in fact, "Old Captain Pipe." Captain Pipe, when last seen at Jerometown and Greentown by the pioneers, appeared to be about seventy years of age, was tall, straight, dignified, and very imposing in appearance. He always dressed as an Indian. This corresponds with the description of Mr. Adams.*

This was the Pipe of Crawford, Richland, Ashland, Summit, Knox, and Muskingum counties, and was none other than "old Captain Pipe," the executioner of the unfortunate Colonel Crawford. The Pipe, of Pipestown, south of Upper Sandusky, was too young to be "old Captain Pipe" in 1812. He was about the age of Silas Armstrong, who resided at Greentown, with whom Wesley Copus, and other pioneers yet surviving, ran races and wrestled in their boyhood in sugar camps along the Black fork of Mohican. Armstrong, the father of Silas, was never seen in this region after the war of 1812; neither was young Pipe nor the old captain, his father. Young Pipe could not have been over twenty-two or twenty-three years of age at that period.

In 1814, after the close of the war, Captain Pipe, Killbuck, and White Eyes, and thirteen *Delawares*, signed a treaty in the presence of William Walker, a Wyandot interpreter—General Harrison, and Governor Lewis Cass, being commissioners of the United States. This was probably young Captain Pipe, son of old Captain Pipe; and the Killbuck and White Eyes here mentioned were evidently the sons of the chiefs of that name, who were then deceased. It is supposed by an old author that the elder Captain Pipe survived until 1818, when he visited Washington city on business connected with the Mohican reservation. He is probably mistaken in the identity of the parties, for young Captain Pipe was then a half chief. Old Captain Pipe probably died some time between 1812–14, perhaps in Canada. There is a shade of mystery covering his later years. His son was half chief

---

*In 1807, Seth Adams, father of W. A. Adams, of Covington, Kentucky, settled on the present site of Dresden, Ohio, and opened a store to trade with the Indians. His customers were principally *Delawares*, from the branches of the Mohican. They exchanged peltries and furs for ammunition, blankets and cloths. Among the leading Indians were "Old Captain Pipe" and his wife, from Jerometown. Mr. Adams says he was a tall, aged, and fine looking chief. He and his squaw, on one occasion, took supper with Seth Adams, on which occasion he gave utterance to the following sentiments. Mr. Adams said: "Captain Pike, I notice you do not drink whiskey like the other Indians." Pipe said: "You are mistaken; I love whiskey, but refuse to drink because it sets a bad example. Among gentlemen I drink." Mr. Adams, at the table, handed the captain a bottle and a glass, and he drank the health of all, remarking: "We Indians have a saying which is good. It is, 'Captain Whiskey is a brave warrior; you fight him long enough and he is sure to get your scalp.'"—*Reminiscences of the early settlements on the Muskingum, by W. A. Adams, of Covington, Kentucky.*

---

with Silas Armstrong, son of old Captain Thomas Armstrong, who ruled the Turtle tribe at Greentown, in Ashland county. The younger chief, or sub-chief, Captain Pipe, never married. He removed with his tribe to Kansas, and died in 1839 or 1840, aged about fifty-five or sixty years.

It will be seen at once that in 1808–12 he was too young to be called "old Captain Pipe." He was too young to be called "old Captain Pipe" at Wakkatomica, at Mohican Johnstown, and at Greentown. "Old Captain Pipe" was generally accompanied on these occasions by his wife. The young captain had no wife. The distinction is marked. There can be scarcely a doubt, then, that after the disastrous battle at Fallen Timbers, Captain Pipe and a remnant of the Wolf tribe located at Mohican Johnstown, on the Jerome fork, with John Baptiste Jerome, wife and daughter, where he was residing when the pioneers of Mohican, Lake, Green, and Mifflin townships commenced to erect cabins and open up farms in 1808–9.

To confirm this opinion, we now offer an authority often quoted as reliable, and of undoubted weight in Indian tradition and history. We mean the late Governor William Walker, of Wyandotte, Kansas. In a letter on the subject of Pipe and the *Delawares*, addressed to the author some months prior to his death, he says:

WYANDOTTE CITY, November 10, 1873.

"DEAR SIR:—Yours of the twenty-seventh ultimo I received yesterday. I regret, deeply, that owing to certain untoward circumstances, I have been prevented from attending to and complying with your request earlier. And now, being able to do some clerical work at short intervals, I cheerfully proceed to give you what little information I am in possession of, though I fear you will be disappointed on reading my meager details. To begin then: I am not an Ohio, but a Michigan Wyandot, came to Ohio after General Harrison's campaign into Canada. That winter, 1813 and 1814, I saw several of the *Delawares* and *Mohegans* at the Indian agency (my father then an officer of the Indian department) from what they called Greentown. Among these were a very aged man named Lyons and his son George Lyons, Billy Montour, Solomon Jonacake, Buckwheat, Monnis Dalledoxis, Jim Jerk. At the head of these Indians as ruling chief, it seems, was a white or part white man named Armstrong. I never saw him, as he died that winter or the following spring. He was succeeded by Captain Pipe, jr., and Silas Armstrong, son of the deceased. Silas died of smallpox in Washington city, in the winter of 1817. The elder Armstrong left eight or nine children. Among these were James, Mrs. Margaret Hill, Silas, Joseph, Tobias, Robert, and two or three younger. These were all smart, stirring men, jovial, fond of fun and frolic. James, if living, resides in Canada. They are all dead except Tobias, who is somewhere down South. The following summer, 1814, I was west on the borders of Indiana, and on my return a part, if not all, of these people had settled on the Sandusky river, five miles south of Upper Sandusky. This settlement took the name of "Pipetown." At the treaty of Maumee, held in the summer of 1817, at the instance of the Wyandot chief, a party to the treaty, a reservation of a township, to include "Pipetown," was made to these people. When the colonization of Indians in the west, under General Jackson's administration, went into operation, they, with other Ohio tribes, ceded their domain and went west and rejoined their kindred from Indiana, under the leadership of Captain Pipe, their surviving chief. The elder Captain Pipe could not have died as early as 1794, for he certainly was at the treaty of Greenville, when the pacification took place in the following year; and Howe, in his pictorial history, says the Delaware Indians had a settlement at or near Jeromeville, which they left at the beginning of the war. Their chief was old Captain Pipe, who resided near the road running to Mansfield, one mile south of Jeromeville. When young he was a great warrior, and the implacable foe of the whites. He was in St. Clair's defeat, where, according to his own account, he distinguished himself, and "slaughtered white men until his arm was weary with the work." I can not learn where he died. I can gather no reliable information about him from the present generation of Wyandots. The late Captain Pipe was undoubtedly the son of the former, and the only son. He died in this country in 1839 or 1840, leaving no children. I do not think he ever married. He was a man of fine natural abilities, good-natured and genial in disposition, and popular with his people. I do not know whether I have answered all of your questions or not. Most of my papers are in Kansas City, Missouri, where I reside. If I can add more, will cheerfully do so. I expect to return south the last week in this month to attend the great Okmulgee council, which will meet simultaneously with Congress, to organize the prospective Indian Territory, determine the question whether the Indians will organize their own government, or Congress. The former, I opine, will be the *finale*. I thank you warmly for the papers you were so kind to send me. They interest me a good deal.

Very respectfully, WILLIAM WALKER."

This would seem to be conclusive as to the existence of "old Captain Pipe" after the year 1794, as well as his residence on the branches of the Mohican, as late as 1812. There is not a scintilla of evidence that the younger Pipe fought against Harmar and St. Clair, as well as Wayne. The story of John Baptiste Jerome concerning the last battle, and the part Pipe and himself took in those campaigns, confirms his identity, and renders his presence on the branches of the Mohican as definitely certain as any human event, not recorded at the time of its occurrence, can be.

ABRAHAM HUFFMAN

was born in Brooke county, Virginia, November 19, 1785. In 1813 he enlisted with the Brooke county soldiers to serve in the northwest part of Ohio; but before seeing active service the war closed. He entered the east half of section thirty-one, in Clearcreek township, Richland county, in the spring of 1815, and came on with a hand and erected a small open cabin, and returned about the middle of the summer, after having prepared a few acres of new ground for corn, and brought his family. His was among the first families who located in Clearcreek— the families of Robert McBeth, James Haney, John and Richard Freeborn, and William Shaw having arrived about the same time. When Mr. Huffman first landed he found large numbers of Delaware and Wyandot Indians encamped along the stream, engaged in hunting and trapping. After a few weeks they returned to Sandusky. In the fall they came on again. A large and well worn trail passed near his cabin. The hunters passed up and down this trail on their way to Wooster and Pittsburgh, on their trips to exchange furs and peltry for lead, powder, tomahawks, knives, clothing, and "white men's fire-water." There were two burial spots on the farm of Mr. Huffman, one near the modern site of his barn, and where one Mr. Mykrants erected a residence, east of the Savannah road. In their hunting excursions along the streams of Clearcreek, they frequently stopped at these cemeteries, and seemed to mourn the departed. Mr. Huffman was careful not to disturb the last sleeping place of their braves. It was his custom to feed the Indians when they called at his cabin, and by doing so he won their esteem. They never disturbed him, although they passed in large numbers until about 1822. Mr. Huffman was a large, energetic and thoroughgoing man. His land contained a splendid sugar camp, and the second year he made enough sugar to complete his payments on his farm. It sold at the trading points at eighteen cents per pound, in cash. For three or four years his toil was constant, for, when not engaged in leveling the forests on his own premises, his services were freely given to aid his neighbors in erecting cabins, rolling logs and the like. The timber of the native forests of Clearcreek was very dense and exceedingly tall. To prepare fields for tillage, therefore, required much hard labor and toil for a number of years. Mr. Huffman, in his prime, possessed uncommon endurance. In a few years he had a model farm, and was surrounded by all the comforts of the thrifty agriculturist. He resided on his homestead until his family had grown up and became somewhat scattered. He had been foremost in encouraging the common schools of the township, in erecting public highways and in support of houses of worship. He was always ready to aid the needy, and was the foe of every species of vice. In his intercourse with his neighbors, he was frank and outspoken. He was an active member and official of the Methodist Episcopal church for over fifty years. He removed to Ashland in 1848, disposing of his farm, and died October 19, 1860, at the age of seventy-five years. Mrs. Huffman died in 1862, aged seventy-three years. The family consisted of Zachariah, Susan, Abraham, Benjamin, John, William, Mary Ann, Sarah Jane, Daniel, and Perrin. Zachariah, Abraham, John, William, and Sarah are dead, and the balance of the family are very much scattered.

JOSIAH GALLUP,

born at Leadyard, Connecticut, in 1793, came to Uniontown, now Ashland, in the winter of 1817. He obtained a good English education, including mathematics and surveying, in the schools of his native village. In the winter of 1817, in company with a cousin, Jabez Gallup, he came west in a one-horse wagon, and at the end of six weeks travel, over rough roads and amid wintry storms, landed at Cleveland. Here his cousin remained, and Mr. Gallup concluded to locate in Uniontown. His personal appearance in 1817 is remembered by a number of the pioneers. He was a reticent young man, of prepossessing manners, and noted for his intelligence, love of order, and gentlemanly bearing. He taught school five or six successive winters in and about the neighborhood of Ashland. In the summer season, having the implements of a surveyor, he was extensively employed in what are now Ashland and Richland counties, in running lines for the pioneers, surveying and locating new roads and the like. In 1822 he married Miss Vilata Pomeroy, and built a house not a great way from the present site of the jail in Ashland. While residing here he opened the first Sabbath-school in Uniontown—quite a novelty at the time. The people of the village then attended "Old Hopewell," about one mile west on the Olivesburgh road.

After disposing of his Uniontown property, Mr. Gallup purchased what is now known as the Fulton farm, south of Mr. Andrews, on the Mansfield road, where he resided until his death, in March, 1833. He aided in the survey of a road from Richland county to Detroit, Michigan, about the year 1825-6, and was extensively employed in surveying in every part of Richland county. About the year 1824 he was elected one of the justices of the peace for Montgomery township, and it is believed was re-elected three terms. As a justice he is well remembered. At that period in the history of Montgomery township, there were a great number of rugged, rollicking, fun-loving pioneers. Corn whiskey was very cheap, and was freely used on all public occasions. In fact, there were but few cabins that were without it. It was deemed essential in cold weather to keep up animal heat, and proper in warm weather to keep it down. On election days and other village gatherings, there being *only* three distilleries in and about town, many of the pioneers became excessively patriotic, and it was not uncommon to see half a dozen well contested pugilistic battles in the streets, and hear any amount of profanity. It is reported that after Squire Gallup got his court fairly organized, he set to work to reform the obstreperous pugilists. He commenced with moderate fines, and if the same parties reappeared he doubled the amount each time, until fighting became an expensive luxury. In this way he succeeded in checking the noisy fellows who assembled on Saturday evenings to have a spree and a few innocent (?) fights, and go home. Mr. Gallup had served a short time in the year of 1812, in Connecticut; and during his residence in Richland, now Ashland, county, he served as brigade inspector of the militia. He was about forty years old at the time of his death. His widow re-married. She resides at Ottawa, Putnam county, Ohio. Her second husband's name is J. R. Clark. Most of these particulars were obtained from Hon. M. E. Gallup, his son, who resides in Strongsville, Ohio, and was born in Ashland.

PATRICK MURRAY

was born in Ireland, March 17, 1755, and emigrated to America in 1782. He located at Harrisburgh, Pennsylvania, where he married Mary Beattie, also of Irish descent. He remained at Harrisburgh until 1806, and then removed to Greensburgh, Pennsylvania. About the year 1809, he located in Stark county, Ohio, where he continued to reside until 1815. In the fall of 1812, Mr. Murray volunteered in the brigade of General Reasin Beall to go to the defence of the border settlers in the northwest. His son James, then thirty-five years of age, also entered the same brigade. While quartered at Fort Meigs, the army became much distressed for want of rations. The roads to the settlements were long, rough and in poor condition, passing mostly through dense forests and across marshes and bogs. The quantity of forage consumed by the cavalry, as well as the supply of the quartermaster's department for the troops, made it difficult to furnish the necessary rations at the proper time.

For a time, the rations were reduced to but a few ounces per meal, and the half starved soldiers began to murmur over their hardships. The weather was inclement, and their sufferings were regarded as almost unbearable. General Harrison deeply sympathized with the half famished troops; and was urgent in regard to immediate supplies; but "red tape" made many delays in forwarding and distributing food. In the midst of the general distress, the privates began to remonstrate with their officers, and threaten retaliation if their hunger was not soon alleviated. Little knots of clamoring soldiers continued their discussions, notwithstanding the guard-house menaced them.

Among those who were particularly active and persistent, was Patrick Murray, who took it upon himself to enter the marquee of General Harrison, to expostulate with him concerning the distribution of food. On entering the general's tent, Mr. Murray was asked by one of the aides-de-camp what he desired, and how he dared enter without permission?

Mr. Murray—"May it plase your honor, I am very hungry, and wish to know whin our rations will be increased?"

General Harrison—"I am sorry to learn that the troops are suffering for food. We have been urgent for an increased supply, which we hope will be here in a few days."

Mr. Murray—"But, gineral, in the manetime we may all starve. We can't stand it much longer, sur."

General Harrison—"You will have to be patient. We are doing the best we can."

Mr. Murray—"Do you think, gineral, a man would commit a great sin to steal, rather than starve?"

General Harrison—"That is a hard question. I would not like to starve so long as I could obtain food."

Mr. Murray—"I thank you, gineral, you are right, and, as there seems to be a spare loaf or two here, I will begin at headquarters to supply meself."

Mr. Murray approached the larder, and, taking a large loaf of bread, commenced to devour a part of it, intending to take the balance to his comrades. An officer in the general's tent ordered him to put it back.

Mr. Murray—"The gineral has relaxed the moral law that he might not starve; and I decline to depart from the same principle, sur."

At this response the general laughed heartily, and ordered the officer to permit Mr. Mrrray to return to his company.

For this act of generous forbearance Mr. Murray always remembered General Harrison, and declared that he was "a brave officer, a patriot and gintleman."

I have preserved this reminiscence, because it is characteristic of Mr. Murray, who was never known to be without a reply, and wit enough to escape the sharp repartee of an adversary.

After Beall had returned, Mr. Murray and his son served a second enlistment, and were at the battle of Fort Meigs. In that contest Mr. Murray was separated from his company, and the grass being very tall, it was presumed, by his comrades, that he had been killed and scalped by the Indians. After a few hours, he appeared in the camp amid the cheers of his companions at his safe return. Upon the expiration of his term of service, he returned to his home in Stark county, where he remained until 1815, and then removed to what is now Orange township, in what was then Richland county. The members of his family at that time were James, Edward, Catharine, Susannah, William, John, Mary, Elizabeth, Alice, Sarah, Rebecca, George, and Hester, and, in 1816, Hugh.

Mr. Murray was a tailor by trade, and worked at that occupation in Harrisburgh and Greensburgh, Pennsylvania, and in Stark county, Ohio. He was a "live Irishman" in company—full of wit and original humor. Although his education was defective, he had a very retentive memory, and, if now living, would relate a volume of exploits and border achievements. On the fourth of July, the year he was ninety-nine years of age, he rode to Ashland in a buggy, walked about one mile during the day, and returned home, some three miles, in the evening. He was enthusiastic, like all his countrymen when they have become Americanized, on the observation of the natal day of American Indepedence. Mr. Murray voted for ten different Presidents of the United States. He died at his farm in Orange township, July 23, 1854, aged ninety-nine years and nearly four months. His wife had preceded him to the grave a short time.

James Murray studied medicine, and resided for a time in Cincinnati, where he died. John studied surveying, and afterwards became treasurer of Richland county for two terms, and then removed west, where he died. Of his numerous family, all have deceased, except three married daughters, who do not reside in the county.

JOSEPH MARKLEY,

from Somerset county, Pennsylvania, purchased the Trickle farm in Montgomery township, and moved to the cabin, a twelve by twelve structure, early in the spring of 1815. When he arrived, there was a camp of Indians on the present site of the residence of Jerry Fulkerson, in South Ashland, and two or three camps down the stream about half a mile, all of which contained about fifty Indians, including their squaws and pappooses. They were engaged in hunting and making sugar, and had twenty or thirty ponies, and a number of dogs with them. They left early in the summer. Mr. Markley's family consisted of himself, wife, and seven sons—Jonathan, John, Matthias, Moses, Aaron, Horatio, and Solomon; and two daughters, Matilda and Frances. They left four sons, grown, in Pennsylvania—Philip, Peter, David, and Joseph. They came by Canton and Wooster. They brought seven horses, and a fine covered wagon, and six milch cows. The forests were filled with grass, pea-vines, and shrubbery, upon which the cattle and horses fed.

The first summer, Mr. Markley, wife and two daughters slept in the little cabin, and the boys in and under the covered wagon. Conrad Kline, who had purchased the Carter farm (since owned by John Mason), and John Heller, were kind enough to supply Markley and family with corn-meal at a neighborly price, until they could purchase corn and get it ground at one of the mills. Aaron Markley, the only member of the family in this county, says: "Corn-bread, hominy, a little pork, and a tin of good milk constituted their luxuries the first summer and winter."

The old gentleman, aided by his seven sons, soon prepared a few acres of corn, which they cultivated with care, and which yielded a tolerable crop. Their next care was to put up a hewed log cabin. It was completed and ready to be occupied early in the fall.

When winter began to approach, Mr. Markley went to Mansfield and purchased three large hogs, for which he paid eighty-four dollars and fifty cents. This constituted the winter meat for the family. Jonathan and Horatio took five horses with pack-saddles, and following the Indian paths proceeded to Owl creek, the "Egypt" of northern Ohio, for corn. They purchased five loads of shelled corn, and went to Shrimplin's mill to get it ground; but the mill having given out, they brought it home, and it was crushed in the hominy block by pounding. After this process, it was sifted, and the coarse fragments being separated, were converted into hominy, and the balance into corn-bread. Thus the winter of 1816 passed with the Markleys.

The Markley family soon became famous for their uncommon size and strength. The old gentleman weighed two hundred and sixty pounds, the old lady two hundred and forty, and the boys, when grown, averaged about two hundred and fifty, while Aaron, the runt of the family, weighs two hundred and thirty. The boys, with the exception of Aaron, averaged about six feet three inches in height—Aaron being about five feet seven. It is asserted by the early settlers that David, the third son, could lift by the chimes a barrel of sugar water, and drink from the bung-hole. It is rare that such a family of giants is found in a new country. No one had the temerity to contend with David. Samuel, Thomas, and Solomon Urie, all six feet high, and very stout, sometimes had a little tilt with the Markleys, but rarely won a laurel.

Aaron Markley now (1880) resides on the old homestead, is seventy-nine years of age, and is the only member of the family in this county.

Joseph Markley, sr., died in 1831, aged sixty years, and his wife soon followed him to the tomb. Most of his sons went west, where several of them have risen to posts of honor.

VACHEL METCALF.

One of the first settlers in the township of Orange was Vachel Metcalf, originally from Washington county, Pennsylvania. When quite a young man, Mr. Metcalf joined the expedition of General Anthony Wayne, which organized at Pittsburgh, and drilled for some time at Legionville, about thirty miles below that city, on the banks of the Ohio river. When Wayne's legion descended the Ohio to Fort Washington, now Cincinnati, Mr. Metcalf accompanied it, as a private in a Pennsylvania company. He went with the army to the northwest, and participated in all the skirmishes, until the final contest at Fallen Timbers in 1794. After the treaty he returned with the Pennsylvania troops.

During the great battle of Fallen Timbers Mr. Metcalf and four comrades, in a charge, became separated from their company in the forest, and were immediately pursued by the savages. They were unable to rejoin their company without a terrible conflict, in which all might lose their lives. In this crisis they struck out boldly through the forest, making a circuit of some four miles to reach the rear-guard of the army. They made the best time possible, and being strong and active, kept at a safe distance in advance of their pursuers. Although shots were frequently exchanged, none of the party were wounded; but all were much fatigued by the race for life.

In the spring of 1810 a number of families from western Pennsylvania and Virginia located in Mohican, then Killbuck township, Wayne county. Mr. Alexander Finley had settled at a point now known as Tylertown, in the spring of 1809, being the first pioneer in the township. Mr. Metcalf entered a farm in what is now known as the "Bunn settlement." He selected a fine quarter section in the forest, put up a cabin, and commenced to clear a field. He was a man of strong will, full of courage, of much physical power, and of unshrinking determination when he had formed a resolution. He looked forward to a time when he would have an excellent farm and valuable improvements, to reward his toil and privations. He was a man of peace, and loved good neighbors. He was astonished, however, to find that tricky neighbors envied his choice of land, and were laying schemes to dispossess him.

The fact was, Mr. Metcalf had failed to secure his certificate of entry before commencing improvements on his new farm. This became known to a few, and a meddlesome neighbor resolved on securing the title. The sly neighbor, in order not to excite suspicion, employed a young man to visit the land office at Canton, and enter the land.* In doing so, he rode past the cabin of Mr. Metcalf in the day time, and, on enquiry, Mrs. Metcalf strongly suspected from his evasive answers, the object of his trip. She hastened to her husband, who was chopping some distance from the cabin, in the forest, and related the circumstance. Mr. Metcalf was convinced that all was not right. He requested his wife to return to the cabin, make two small linen bags into which he might put his hard money; and also to put up for lunch some cold corn-bread and pork. By the time this had been done, he reached the cabin, lunched, and taking the two "money-bags," containing each one hundred dollars in silver, he started down a path leading by the

*James Bryan, who subsequently moved to Wood county, Ohio, and deceased in 1861.

present site of Wooster, and thence, in the direction of Canton, the location of the land office. Sometime in the early part of the night he reached a point where, for several miles, at certain seasons, the trail was very swampy and difficult to pass on horseback. He found a cabin, and learned that his adversary had not yet passed that point. He was much fatigued by the weight of his dangling money-bags, and his thighs were considerably bruised and his arms wearied. By permission of the occupants, he took a supper of mush and milk with them, and slept on the floor. Early in the morning, the footsteps of a horse were heard approaching the cabin, in the direction of the swamp. Mr. Metcalf hastily arose, took some refreshments, and learned that at the swamp, a new road had been cut around it, increasing the distance one or two miles. He again took his money-bags, and hastened down the path; and on reaching the swamp, found that the man on horseback had gone around. He kept straight ahead, and trusted to luck.

On arriving at the opposite side of the swamp, where the new road intersected the old trail, he found, to his joy, that he was again in advance. With renewed energy, he pressed rapidly on, while his adversary, apprehending no danger, rode leisurely and securely. On approaching the Tuscarawas, he discovered an old friend, by the name of Brady, who often ferried emigrants across the stream. He aided Mr. Metcalf, and informed him that he was the first traveler who had passed in that direction that day. He hastened onward, and arrived at Canton, after a journey of some thirty hours on foot, with limbs stiffened, and arms bruised by his dangling money-bags, and piled his coin on the table, in the presence of the register, and requested a certificate of entry to be issued as soon as convenient, for the reason that he had traveled a long distance, and desired to return without delay. The money was counted, and the certificate filed with a description of the quarter of land desired. Mr. Metcalf received, and carefully placed it among his papers, and retired from the office. It was, to him, a great victory, and he felt exultant. He was now safe. About two hours after this scene, the young agent rode leisurely up to the register's office, to learn that the coveted farm was in legal possession of its rightful owner. Upon his return home, his officious neighbor was greatly chagrined.

After the surrender of General Hull, at Detroit, in 1812, the Indians of the northwest assumed a hostile attitude toward the border settlements in Ohio. The Indians at Jerometown and Greentown were ordered, by the State authorities, to be removed from their villages to Urbana, as a means of safety, until peace should be restored. A few weeks after the removal of these Indians, a number of them returned, when the Ruffner-Zimmer tragedy took place near the Black fork. This affair was speedily followed by an attack on the cabin of James Copus, by some forty savages. The settlements were greatly alarmed, and means of defence adopted as rapidly as possible. There were some six or eight families in the vicinity of Mr. Metcalf, among whom were those of William Bryan, James Conley, Elisha Chilcote,

Benjamin Bunn, James Slater and James Bryan. These met in council at the cabin of Mr. Metcalf, when it was determined that a fort should be built. The building was to be two stories high, the walls of the second story to project two feet beyond the first, on all sides; the floor and sides of the second story to be pierced with port-holes. The pioneers gathered with their ox-teams, and axes, and the logs were cut and rapidly gathered; and the building soon completed. The lower story, with strong doors, securely fastened, was to be occupied by the women and children, while the men, with their trusty rifles, were to occupy the second story, in hours of danger and alarm. About one acre of ground was cleared around the fort, and enclosed with a palisade twelve or fourteen feet high, with a strong gate; and all the families of the neighborhood were gathered into the fort, and the horses and cattle inside the palisade. Mr. Metcalf and his neighbors remained, most of the year, in the fort, occasionally visiting their cabins to see that they were safe, and to cultivate their corn and vegetables, with pickets to guard against surprise by the Indians. This fort was about two miles below the present site of Jeromeville, and stood on an elevated spot, on the lands of Mr. Metcalf.

In the spring of 1814, Vachel Metcalf and Amos Norris moved into what is now Orange township, and purchased lands adjoining the present village of Orange. They are believed to have been the first settlers in the township, although several other families arrived within that year, among whom were those of Jacob Young, Martin Mason, Jacob Mason, Martin Hester, Joseph Bishop, Solomon Urie, and John Bishop, single. The cabin of Mr. Metcalf stood not a great way from the present site of the tannery of Mr. Smurr, on a knoll. Mr. Metcalf had an excellent piece of land, though it was heavily timbered, and required much labor to fit it for cultivation. Being a man of fine physical powers, and of determined purpose, he soon cut away the forest and prepared a desirable homestead. At that day, the pioneers traveled many miles to aid each other in the erection of cabins, in rolling logs and clearing. Mr. Metcalf willingly attended all gatherings of this kind. In fact, the unselfish character of the pioneers was one of the most striking features of the times. Each settler volunteered his aid and good wishes to forward the enterprises and interests of all new comers. They aided each other in the distribution of seed, and in harvesting their crops. In other words, the "latch-string was always out."

Mr. Metcalf was a very active member of the Methodist Episcopal church, and the organization of the first class was probably the result of his zeal. The first church was built about the year 1830, and he was one of the first class-leaders and official members, and is understood to have been one of the speakers. In the erection of the present church, in 1853, he was prominent as a member and class-leader. He was a lover of peace and good neighborhood, and his influence went far toward attaining such a condition of society.

When Orange township was organized, in 1818, Mr. Metcalf was chosen as justice of the peace, and John Bishop as constable. Mr. Metcalf was, we believe, elected justice of the peace three times. In politics he was a Whig, and, during the heated campaigns of 1828 and 1832, his party fell into the minority, and remained so during most of the balance of his life.

Mr. Metcalf died in 1858, aged about seventy-nine years. He is remembered as a good neighbor, frank and straightforward in his business transactions, and a lover of truth and integrity.

His sons, William and Vachel, removed to Illinois, and John to Michigan. None of his family remain in Orange township.

THOMAS SMITH

was a native of Sussex county, State of Delaware, and was born January 12, 1780. His parents being quite poor, he was compelled at an early age to enter the employ of strangers to procure a living. When a mere boy he became a sailor, in the coast trade, on the Delaware bay. For many years he followed a seafaring life, during which he became well versed in the vocabulary of that branch of human enterprise, and obtained from "Jack" a wonderful store of anecdote and song. He was vivacious, brave, and uncommonly active, and prided himself on being an experienced sailor and hardy seaman. In the meantime, he acquired a fair knowledge of the English branches taught in the schools of Delaware, wrote a fair hand, and concluded to abandon the sea and seek a home in the far west. In 1805 he married, and in 1806, with his wife and father's family, emigrated, by the usual route, to Fairfield county, Ohio. In 1813 he was drafted to serve in the army in the northwest part of Ohio, and was out twenty-one days, when peace was declared and he discharged. In March, 1818, he emigrated to Milton township, and located for a short time on what was then known as the Jonathan Markley farm. He subsequently purchased the farm on which his aged widow now resides, near Burns' school-house, to which he removed. Mrs. Smith thinks his nearest neighbors then were: Nicholas Rutan, John Owens, John Taylor, Jacob Foulks, William Houston, Benjamin Montgomery, Boston Burgett, John Crabbs, David Crabbs, Andrew Burns, Robert Nelson, Frederick Sulcer, John Bryte, and a few others, very much scattered.

At the April election, in 1819, Thomas Smith was elected a constable for Milton township. At the April election of 1820 he was elected one of the trustees for Milton township. In 1821 he was re-elected. In 1823 he was elected appraiser of property. In 1824 he was re-elected appraiser of property. In 1825 he was elected lister and appraiser of property. In 1826 he was elected supervisor for his quarter of the township. In 1827-8 he was elected overseer of the poor of the township. In 1829 he was elected treasurer of Milton township. In 1830 he was elected justice of the peace, and was re-elected the six succeeding terms, making a continued service of twenty-one years. During his official career as justice of the peace he was repeatedly elected township treasurer, trustee and road supervisor. Very few officials anywhere had a stronger hold upon the confidence of the public. In the midst of his official duties, in 1837, he taught a district school, and acquitted himself to the satisfaction of his employers.

It may be proper, in this connection, to speak more fully of the popularity of the squire. He was benevolent to a fault. He rarely permitted a plaintiff to distress a debtor, always endeavoring to prevent the accumulation of cost, by giving the party notice prior to commencing an action. His docket shows that after judgment had been rendered he often neglected to exact the full payment of his own costs. This act of mercy, though it ill rewarded him for his time and worry, made him many friends among the poor pioneers. Again, he was free with his money, social and remarkably shrewd. He could tell a good story, sing a pioneer or sailor song, and was the central figure at a log-rolling, house-raising, corn-husking, or at an election. It was his custom, on election days, to treat his friends. For many years saloon keepers from Ashland were in the habit of sending beer and gingerbread to the polls in Milton township, at the elections. When Squire Smith was in his prime he often purchased a keg of beer and treated his political friends, and to wind up the sport, took a large roll of gingerbread under each arm, and passing through the crowd, permitted those who desired to do so, to pluck off a large slice. This produced much amusement among the young men, and the mirthful voters joining in, the scene was decidedly rich. In the meantime the voting quietly progressed, and Squire Smith was always elected. In the days of old corn whiskey, he was expected to treat with a stronger stimulant than beer. In his familiar moods, he would take a tumbler of whiskey, put in sugar, and stir it with his finger, and invite his friends to drink health and prosperity. To abstinence people this may seem objectionable; but church members, as well as all others, by the customs of those days, were regarded as uncivil unless they treated their visiting friends.

The long official services of Mr. Smith show that he retained the confidence and respect of the people of his township to the last. He was emphatically an honest man. As a politician he was frank and firm. He declared he was a Democrat after the Jeffersonian and Jackson school.

His death occurred July 18, 1851. Being exceedingly fond of fruit, he climbed upon a rail fence, near his residence, to gather cherries from a tree, and his foothold being insecure he fell upon his head and shoulders, dislocating his neck, and expired before he was discovered. He was about seventy-two years of age at his decease. His widow, now (1875) eighty-seven years of age, still survives, and possesses a clear recollection of the past, though physically quite frail. Mr. Smith was the father of eleven children—seven sons and four daughters: Robert, Henry, John, Mitchel, Charles, William and Thomas, and Ardilla, Catharine, Margaret and Malinda, all of whom are married, and some of whom reside in other parts of the State.

ROBERT NELSON

was a native of Northampton county, Pennsylvania, and born June 29, 1769. He was educated in the common schools of his native county. He taught school, when a young man, and was regarded as a fine English scholar and a successful teacher. When about forty-six years of age he purchased the tract of land known as the Andrew Heltman farm, in Milton township, being Virginia military land; and in 1815, came to the township and erected a sort of camp-cabin, and cleared and cultivated a small field about it. He had his bread prepared by Mrs. Conrad Kline, who resided some distance east of the present site of Ashland, and camped each day to labor at his new home.

He resided in Beaver county, Pennsylvania, from about the year 1801, where he married Miss Emalie Bonham, and where were born to him seven of his eleven children.

In the spring of 1816, he removed to his cabin with his family. From near New Lisbon, he passed up Beall's trail, the common route, to within about one mile of his cabin, and then cut a path. He resided there a short time, and then exchanged his land for a new homestead, where Scott Nelson now resides, where, by the aid of his neighbors, he erected a new cabin, removed into it, and continued to reside until his decease. When he landed with his family, there were but few settlers in Milton township. His nearest neighbors are believed to have been: James Kingsal, Frederick Sulcer, Peter Lance, James Kelly, and Abraham Doty.

At the time of his arrival, and for many years afterward, the neighborhood was infested by wolves, which destroyed the sheep, and, when hungry, would frequently attack young calves and pigs. Mrs. Nelson was often compelled to build a fire at night near the pen where she secured the young calves, to keep the wolves from destroying them. Mr. Nelson obtained meal and flour at Beam's mill for a number of years, until mills began to be more numerous.

In 1816, July 6, Milton township was organized, prior to that time being under the control of Mifflin for civil purposes. The petition was drawn by Robert Nelson, the best scholar and penman in the township, and duly acted upon by the court of common pleas of Richland county, and the request of the petitioners granted. The petition displays considerable ability and readiness of composition, and is an honor to the author. Its history runs thus:

"Now it came to pass when men began to multiply on this side of the river westward toward the lake, even the great Lake Erie, and the inhabitants of Milton township, became numerous and strong, that they said one to another, go to, let us separate ourselves from Mifflin township, to which they aforetime had been attached; for why should we be oppressed by our brethren, and costs multiplied on us in carrying us before strangers? Let us select a goodly number from among our brethren, that shall bear rule over us. And they prayed the court in Mansfield, and their request was granted. Milton was organized, and became a free and independent

BARBARA CULLER.

township. This happened in the year of our Lord one thousand eight hundred and sixteen."

The selfishness of our race is apparent in the foregoing document, in that, while Milton became "free," her jurisdiction continued over Clearcreek four years after the important event narrated by Mr. Nelson.

Upon the erection of Milton, it is believed Robert McBeth was elected the first justice of the peace. Mr. McBeth resided in the territory now composing Clearcreek township, which circumstance evinced a disposition on the part of the electors of Milton to divide honors with her neighbor.

In 1819 Robert Nelson was elected a justice of the peace, and served until 1822. In 1817, at the spring election, David Crabbs was elected township clerk, and Benjamin Montgomery, Elijah Charles and Robert McBeth, trustees, and David McKinny, fence viewer, and John Ferrell, appraiser of property, and Abel Montgomery and William Houston, listers; supervisors, William Houston, Frederick Sulcer, and George Burget; and John Freeborn and Jacob Montgomery, constables; and Jacob Foulk, treasurer.

In 1818 Robert Nelson was elected township clerk, and was re-elected in 1819-20. After the expiration of his term as justice, in 1822, he was re-elected; and was repeatedly elected trustee and constable after that time.

He is said to have been an upright and popular officer, and could have retained office for many years; but had no ambition to seek office and public favor in that direction.

When the congregation of "old Hopewell" organized in 1817, Robert Nelson, Abraham Doty, Daniel McKinny, William Houston, David Pollock, Jacob McClusky, and Abel Montgomery, Samuel Burns, David Burns, William Andrews, Alexander McCrady, and their wives, in Milton township, became members of the new congregation. Robert Nelson and Abraham Doty were elected and ordained elders. Mr. Nelson remained an elder until advanced age caused him to retire.* He died August, 16, 1844, aged seventy-five years; and his widow survived until May 31, 1862, when she deceased, at the age of eighty years.

Mr. and Mrs. Nelson were the parents of thirteen children: Mary, James, Eliza, Rachel, John, Samuel, Sophia, Nancy, Margaret, Scott, Robert, Jane and Milton, all of whom survived Mr. Nelson, he being the first member of the family that deceased. John and Scott and three sisters remain in Milton, five of the family are dead, and three are in other localities.

Mr. Nelson served in the war of 1812, and his widow received a land warrant for his services.† John and Robert, sons of Nelson, served in Mexico in the war of 1846; and Scott Nelson, another son, served in the war of 1861-5 in the South.

Mr. Nelson was an influential and upright citizen.

---

*In the war of 1812, he went as a substitute and was elected orderly sergeant, and served at Erie, Pennsylvania. His brother William Nelson was in the same company and died.

†At the proper place a history of the organization of "old Hopewell" or the "Montgomery church," as it was originally called, will be given.

His education and fine judgment qualified him to fill the highest public stations in the county. As a member of the Presbyterian church he was much respected. Diffident and unselfish, he found more real pleasure in being a quiet farmer than in public display and official promotion. Devoted to his church and the elevation o fsociety, his example, all through life, was in the direction of good order, obedience to law, and the precepts of religion; and when he had run his course, he passed over the dark stream without fear or regret.

JAMES ANDREWS

was another leading citizen of Milton township. He was a Pennsylvanian by birth, and in 1800 emigrated to Columbiana county, Ohio, where he resided until 1816, when he entered a farm in the south part of Milton township, and removed to it with his family. He served in the war of 1812, as a captain in the Second regiment, Second brigade of Ohio militia, and was promoted, during his service, to brigade inspector, and obtained a warrant for his services in 1854. After the organization of Milton township, he served as trustee, constable, supervisor, and justice of the peace, and acquitted himself to the satisfaction of the electors of his township.* He died in the fall of 1863, and was buried in the cemetery in the south part of the township. He was about eighty-five years old at his decease. He left several members of his family, none of whom, we are informed, remain in the township. Mr. Andrews, like his pioneer neighbors, passed through many hardships in preparing his farm for culture. He lived to surround himself with many comforts, and was highly respected. The settlers of his day have nearly all disappeared, and soon there will be none left to tell the story of pioneer life amid the wilds of this region.

MICHAEL CULLER,

of Mifflin, purchased the Zimmer farm in 1815. Having come from Frederick county, Maryland, by way of Charleston (now Wellsburgh), Virginia, through Cadiz, Ohio, to Wooster, he proceeded thence, by way of Mr. Gardner's (now Windsor), to Mansfield, where he met Philip Zimmer, whose father, mother, and sister, had been killed at the Zimmer cabin on the Black fork, in the fall of 1812, and purchased the farm. To have the deed properly executed, he accompanied Philip to Circleville, Pickaway county, Ohio, to the residence of George Zimmer, a brother. Here the deed was signed by Philip Zimmer, May 6, 1815, the original patent being made to him, and signed by James Madison, President, and Edward Tiffin, commissioner of the land office, October 2, 1812. Zimmer was the German name of the family. While Mr. Culler was there Philip married a Miss Ballentine, and removed west. In 1826 he returned to visit

---

*Mr. Andrews was, for many years, a member of the Seceder church. Like his Scotch-Irish ancestors, he accepted, in good faith, the doctrines and discipline of that church.

the grave of his father, mother, and sister, on the old farm, since which time he has resided in the west. Mr. Culler cultivated his land for two or three years, stopping most of the time with John Lambright, who was a relative.

Returning to Maryland, he married, about the year 1818, and moved to the Zimmer farm, where he has resided ever since. He lived two or three years in the old Zimmer cabin, which still showed marks of the tragedy of 1812. He was in Circleville in 1812, when the Zimmer murder took place, and is conversant with the whole affair, having heard all its details repeatedly from John Lambright and Philip Zimmer. He says:

"Martin Ruffner was a stout, frolicsome sort of man, and went to Zimmer's more to capture the Indians and have a little fun, than to bring on a fight, and believes that if Philip had remained at home, instead of going for James Copus, the whole disaster would have been averted, for Philip was a very rugged and active young man, and the two would have deterred the Indians from the attack."

Mrs. Culler died in the summer of 1873. Mr. Culler died at his residence in Mifflin township, July 28, 1874, aged eighty-four years, four months, and three days. Two or three of his sons reside in this county.

Mr. Culler was benevolent and kind to the poor, and his donations to religious and benevolent institutions very liberal. He was regarded as quite wealthy, but was always humble, and seldom referred to his worldly possessions, believing it better to lay up his treasures in Heaven, where moth and rust doth not corrupt. He was followed to his last resting place by a large number of people, who said in their hearts, "Blessed are the dead who die in the Lord."

JOHN McCONNELL,

brother of Mrs. Solomon Urie, located in Orange township about the same time that the Uries came. He was an accomplished backwoodsman and Indian fighter. He was a relative of the famous Alexander McConnell, of Washington county, Pennsylvania, and also a relative of Colonel Williamson. He had many encounters with the Indians in the border wars, and in the Miami and Wabash country; and is believed to have settled a number of accounts with the Green and Jerometown Indians after he came to this county. Being a bachelor, while a resident of Orange township, he spent a good deal of time in his forest camps, hunting deer, bear, wolves, and other game. He had lost many dear friends in the border wars; and hence had no very strong attachments for his red neighbors. He never hesitated, when threatened with danger by the Indians, as he roamed through the forest, to face his foe, and resent impending attacks; particularly when he met savages who had made themselves conspicuous in murdering the border settlers.

Some thirty-five years since, when game had grown scarce in this region, McConnell sought a new home in the wilds of Wood county, where he remained a few years, and then located in Eaton county, Michigan, where he died.

Hardy, frank and fearless, he seemed to enjoy a lonely hut in the wilderness, like Boone and Kenton, more than the restraints of civilized society.

FREDERICK SULTZER

was born in Green county, Pennsylvania, July 25, 1762. From the time he was ten years old, he was compelled to handle fire-arms. From the period of his childhood, until the close of the war of 1812-15, the border settlers of western Pennsylvania were menaced by Indian raids. He became very expert as a backwoodsman, and when a deer, a bear, or any other species of game, came within range of his rifle, it was sure to fall a victim to his unerring aim. He visited what is now Milton township, in the fall of 1815, and located the tract of land upon which he settled. In the spring of 1816, he brought a covered wagon and four good horses, with a plow and other farming utensils. He slept four months in the wagon, doing his cooking in a sort of camp hut. In the fall, after having put up a cabin and secured his crop of corn, he returned to Pennsylvania and brought on his wife. At that time, the Indians were quite numerous along the Black fork, engaged in hunting, though they were harmless. The next spring they encamped near him and made sugar. Mr. Sigler, who married Mr. Sultzer's daughter, informs us that the old gentleman retained his vision and his steadiness of aim to the last. When he was ninety-two years old, he shot a hawk, offhand, on a very high tree, near his residence, to convince Mr. Sigler that his sight and aim were as accurate as in the days of his prime. He never wore glasses. He was a cousin of the famous Louis Wetsel, and in his boyhood often hunted with Wetsel, who tried to teach him how to run and load his gun. He never became a proficient in that mode of loading. He possessed much admiration for the achievements of his noted cousin as a border warrior and spy. He was a man of very even temper, genial, and warm in his attachments. Mr. Sultzer voted for Washington and the ten succeeding presidents. In his later years, he became a member of the denomination known as Christians. He died childless, at his farm, on the Mansfield road, in Milton township, March 30, 1857, aged nearly ninety-six years. His wife died in 1843. Mr. Sultzer had drawn a pension of ninety-six dollars per annum, for many years prior to his death, as a compensation for his border services in western Pennsylvania in his youth. He was the last of the border men in this county, and deserved the esteem of his countrymen.

JOSEPH SHEETS

was born in New Jersey, about thirty miles below Philadelphia, Pennsylvania, January 21, 1792. He learned, in his native village, the trade of tailor, which he followed for many years. When he had completed his trade he went to Philadelphia and sought employment a short time, and then, in 1811, passed over the mountains to Steubenville, Ohio, where he remained at his trade for about six years. Being a young man of good habits, he soon began to accumulate money. In the meantime he formed the acquaintance of Miss Nancy Harper, daughter of William Harper, of Fairfax county, Virginia, who had settled in Jefferson county, Ohio, about the year 1806. They were married. The result of the marriage was, that Mr. Harper and family concluded to accompany Mr. Sheets and his wife to, and locate in, Richland, now Ashland county. In the spring of 1817 these families started across the country, through the forest, over rough roads, for their new homes. After a fatiguing journey of several days they arrived safely at Uniontown. Mrs. Sheets states they first put up in a very inferior cabin that stood somewhere near the northeast corner of what is now known as Kellogg square, there being only three or four other cabins in town, one of which was that of Mr. Montgomery, and the other that of Mr. Groff, the tanner, where the old residence of George Swineford formerly stood. Early in the spring they resided for a short time with Mr. Montgomery, where the hardware store of Stull & Charles now stands. Mr. Sheets put up a house nearly opposite, known now as the Weisenstine building, for a small store and tailor-shop, and moved into it. This was the first store. Mr. Harper located about one mile northwest of the present site of Hayesville, where he lived until 1832, when he was accidentally killed by his team, near Plymouth, Richland county. Mr. Sheets continued to occupy his new home some years, engaged at his trade, keeping a house of entertainment, and making himself useful as a citizen. He finally disposed of his Ashland property, and purchased of Mr. Montgomery the ninety acres of land upon which South Ashland was subsequently laid out. About the year 1847 Mr. Sheets sold this tract of land to a corporation known as the South Ashland company, and removed to Vermillion township. About the year 1864 he returned to Ashland to reside on a part of his old property, and died March 6, 1866, aged seventy-four years. Mrs. Sheets still survives, aged seventy-nine years. Her memory is unimpaired, and very few persons of her age possess a more acurate recollection of the pioneers and their times. William Sheets, her oldest son, is believed to have been the first male child born within the limits of Ashland. Mrs. Sheets states that William was born January 1, 1819.

Mrs. Sheets says during the time they resided in the village it was a very lively place, especially on public days and Saturday evenings. She states it was not uncommon in those days to see five or six fights in an evening. The strong armed pugilist who could "tan two or three dog skins," claimed high honors. On one occasion, Mrs. Sheets states, the clans had gathered for a little settlement, and prior to opening the ball, visited the distilleries to fit and prepare them for the task. In their absence, just after dark, Mrs. Sheets, butcher knife in hand, visited all the hitching posts, and cut the horses loose. She says that in fifteen or twenty minutes the village was cleared of roughs. She thinks it was a "little rough," but a work of necessity.

ALANSON ANDREWS.

Mr. Andrews was born in Massachusetts in 1784. He emigrated to Ohio in the spring of 1817, and located in the village of Uniontown, now Ashland. His cabin stood near the spring west of Center street, in the rear of the present residence of David Whiting. Mr. Andrews resided there but a short time, and then completed a new cabin about where the Whiting blacksmith-shop now stands, and moved into it. He resided in that locality two or three years, and carried on a distillery just below the present residence of David Whiting, in company with a Mr. Palmer. During his residence in this cabin, Lorin Andrews, the second male child of Ashland, was born. This event took place April 1, 1819. A short time after, Mr. Andrews purchased the farm of David Markley adjoining Ashland on the southwest, and moved upon it. Mr. Andrews was a good farmer, and soon had an abundance of this world's goods to reward him for his toil. He put up a fine residence, barn, and other out-buildings at an early day, and his orchard, fields, fences, and improvements indicated thrift, good judgment, and industry.

He was a man of fair education, close observation and of strict habits. Like all New England people, he was the friend of educational institutions, and took a deep interest in the establishment of advanced schools in the village of Ashland. He was one of the founders and props of the old academy, where so many young men commenced a career of usefulness and honor. He was a warm patron of the school from its commencement, and every member of his family passed through its various grades of classification. Mr. Andrews stood high among his neighbors for his truthfulness, integrity, and personal worth.

It has often been remarked in the presence of the writer of these sketches, that being one of the best judges of the value of personal and real estate, that he had, perhaps, assisted in the appraisement of more estates than any other citizen in the township.

In politics he was a Whig, and always cast his influence in favor of the prevalence of the principles of that party. He never sought office of any kind, although his fitness was admitted by his neighbors.

He was tall and well formed; his face, though not handsome, impressed itself upon the recollection. In the general way he was reticent, and rarely revealed his plans. In temper, he was decidedly firm and resolute. All in all, in his intercourse with his neighbors, he was pleasant, and noted for his hospitality and kindness to the poor. He died after a brief illness, May 11, 1850, and sleeps in the cemetery west of Ashland. His widow and numerous family reside in the west. But three of his sons reached manhood—Lorin, Lyman, and Levi. Lorin is deceased, Lyman resides in Indianapolis, Indiana, and Levi in California. His widow, at an advanced age, resides with a daughter in Geneseo, Illinois.

FRANCIS GRAHAM

was born in Delaware county, Pennsylvania, in 1792. He removed with his parents to Erie, Pennsylvania, in 1805. Here he entered a mercantile establishment and learned the business, and remained until the close of the war. In 1815 the firm for which he was employed was left in possession of a large stock of unsold goods. Hard times followed the war, and the firm concluded to transport a part of their goods to Detroit, in the hope of finding a readier sale. In November, 1815, the company dispatched Mr. Graham overland with five large sled loads of goods. He and those who accompanied him passed leisurely up the southern shore of Lake Erie, until they reached the mouth of Huron. Here they were stopped by the melting of the snow, and compelled to abandon the trip to Detroit. The goods belonged to Sanford & Reed, of Erie, Pennsylvania, a firm that has since accumulated its millions. Mr. Graham was compelled, under the circumstances, to rent a house at Huron and open a store there. He succeeded well in the sale of the goods, and one of the partners visiting him, sanctioned all that he had done. He remained here four years. In 1819 he settled in Sandusky City, prior to that time known as Ogontz's town and Portland. In 1821 Mr. Graham arrived in Uniontown, from Sandusky City. He rented and occupied the room where Joseph Sheets had had a small stock of goods, and boarded with Mr. Sheets. This lot was what is now known as the Weisenstine property. Mr. Graham conducted business in this establishment some time, and then put up a store-room where Millington's drug store since stood, now the Schneider bakery. He continued to do a thrifty business until the financial crash of 1837 to 1844, when, owing to the pernicious effects of the credit system, he was compelled to wind up his affairs. For years he had done an extensive business, and exerted himself to find a market for all the surplus products of this locality. Financial panics are remorseless. Many a good man has been crushed that would have survived if time had been given. Although he had furnished a market for nearly everything, many times against his own interest, when hard times came, the unfeeling grip of the law seized the little that had been left him, and left him in distress. He never recovered from the blow.

Shortly after opening his store the necessity of a post-office was felt. Mr. Graham sent a petition to Judge Sloan, the member of Congress from this district, asking the erection of a post-office at Uniontown. The post-office directory showed that there was already a post-office by that name in Ohio. The name was then changed to Ashland, and the village with it, after the home of Henry Clay, and the office created; and Mr. Graham was made the first postmaster.

Mr. Graham, some years since, after his retirement from business, was elected justice of the peace of Montgomery township, and acquitted himself ably.

In September, 1875, when the Pioneer and Historical society of Ashland county was organized, Mr. Graham was elected the first president.

He is now about eighty-three years of age. He resides in a comfortable little home, and, in company with his excellent lady, is spending the evening of his days reflecting calmly upon the past and preparing to pass to a better and a happier land.

WILLIAM HAMILTON

was born in York county, Pennsylvania, in 1777, and about the year 1800 removed to Washington county, Pennsylvania, where he remained until December, 1820. He was of Irish descent. He married in Fayette county. In 1820 he purchased, of his brother Hugh Hamilton, the northeast quarter of section three, in Perry township, Wayne county, Ohio, and removed to it. He erected a cabin and other buildings, and improved his farm. At that period, the Delaware Indians made annual visitations during the seasons for making sugar and hunting. They were harmless and friendly, and often exchanged the products of the chase for corn and other food. Game was abundant in the forests, and the wolves were very destructive upon sheep, young swine and poultry. A premium was offered for scalps at the county offices in Wooster, and large numbers of wolves were caught in traps. By industry, economy and care, Mr. Hamilton soon surrounded himself by all the comforts that result from agriculture. In the year 1834 he undertook the erection of a valuable farm-house, and in excavating for the cellar, dug down an Indian mound which stood upon the spot selected. An oak tree grew upon the top of it, which was some two feet in diameter. When the greater part of the mound had been removed they came upon a triangular stake, the upper part of which had decayed. It was embedded in a grayish sand, which Mr. Hamilton proceeded to remove. When he had dug down some two feet, he came upon an Indian skeleton. Continuing to excavate, he soon reached another. Proceeding, he soon came upon a third one of unusual size, which was almost entire. Near it was found a lot of red paint, and a bluish stone somewhat like a scythe stone, highly polished. The thigh bone of the giant was much longer than that of the tallest man in the neighborhood. The inferior maxillary or lower jaw bone would pass over that of the largest person. Here relics were kept several years. There was also another small mound a little east of the former, which was never thoroughly examined. Northeast of these mounds, about one mile, was an ancient intrenchment, square in form, which contained something near an acre of land. It was upon the highest point of land in the neighborhood, and overlooked the valley. It was not a great way from the Muddy fork of Mohican. These reminiscences of an extinct race are quite interesting, and evince the fact that the occupants of this region not only understood the arts of military defence, but honored their braves by a monument of earth erected over their remains. Mr. Hamilton survived long enough to see his family comfortably situated in life. He was the friend of the Ohio school system, and gave his children

J. P. CULLER.

SAMUEL CULLER.

all its advantages. He was an active member of the Presbyterian church for over a half century, and was the uncompromising opponent of every demoralizing vice. He deceased in 1850, at the ripe age of seventy-three years. His family consisted of Ann, John M., William H., Joseph, Daniel K., Mary J., Rebecca J., Alexander and Louisa. Of these, Ann, John M., William H., Joseph and Rebecca, are deceased. The balance of the family reside in Wayne and Ashland counties.

RICHARD WINBIGLER

was born in Frederick county, Maryland, near Frederick City, in 1782. He grew to manhood and married in his native State. In 1818 he concluded to cast his lot among the pioneers of the branches of Mohican, in Ohio, where many other Marylanders found homes. He emigrated with his family, and located about two miles southeast of Jeromeville. Mr. Winbigler deceased some twenty years since, over seventy years of age. At his decease, his family consisted of Mary Anne, Henry, Elizabeth and William, all of whom are dead, except Henry.

Henry Winbigler was born in Frederick county, Maryland, June 4, 1808. He accompanied his father's family to Mohican township in 1818, and has a very distinct recollection of the pioneer days of that township. He attended the common schools of that period, and obtained a fair knowledge of the elementary branches. In 1832 he married Jane, daughter of John Hootman. He has filled several township offices in Mohican, and been elected justice of the peace four times, or twelve years. Mr. Winbigler is a gentleman of intelligence and undisputed integrity. His family consists of Richard M. and Elizabeth, wife of Josephus Newbrough, of Jackson county, Michigan. Mr. Winbigler is an industrious farmer, and in possession of a valuable homestead, where he lives quietly and contentedly.

HON. GEORGE W. BULL.

One of the leading pioneers of Hanover township was Hon. George W. Bull. He was born in the city of Hartford, Connecticut, September 7, 1799. His father was the owner of two or three vessels which were constantly on the ocean, engaged in the West India trade. When only eleven years old, young Bull was placed on one of his father's vessels to learn the art of a sailor. He continued on the ocean until about the year 1816, when, owing to commercial difficulties, and the dangers attending ship owners in the trade with the West Indies, the line was discontinued, and his father's family located in Canton, Ohio.

About the year 1818 George W. Bull visited the site of the flourishing town of Loudonville. It was then a mere village, having been laid out by James Loudon Priest and Stephen Butler, four years prior to that time. He remained but a short time. In his brief apprenticeship in the West India trade he formed a strong attachment for a life on the ocean. The rugged hills of Hanover township were destitute of novelty and excitement. His mind dwelt continually upon his maritime adventures of other days. He soon became restive, and longed to renew his seafaring exploits and excitements. By the permission of his father he went to the city of New York and engaged as supercargo on a commercial vessel (packet Canton), commanded by Captain Jack Wheaton. This merchant vessel sailed between the city of New York, and Liverpool. He remained in the employ of Captain Wheaton about three years, during which time his ardor for a life on the ocean had been somewhat cooled; and he resolved to retire from the dangers and uncertainties attending such an occupation. In 1821 he again visited Loudonville, and found that during his absence many new settlers had located in and about the village. The town began to show signs of future growth and improvement. The great stage line from New Lisbon, Canton, Wooster, Mount Vernon, and Columbus, passed through Loudonville. At that period there was a good deal of travel by stage, as well as by road wagons, and the village hotels, and the few dry goods establishments in the town, were busy.

Mr. Bull determined to make Hanover township his future home. He purchased a quarter section of land adjoining the village, and commenced to improve it. At that time there was a surplus of grain, hogs and cattle raised in Green and Hanover townships, which, owing to the want of a suitable market, commanded but low prices. Mr. Bull had sufficient New England sagacity to perceive that if these surplus articles could be conveyed to a market, the enterprise would be remunerative. He had been tossed upon too many rough seas to shrink from a vigorous encounter with pioneer life; so he determined that while he could find a market that would profit himself, he could, at the same time, be a benefactor to his neighbors. In 1821, a short period after his return, he constructed a flat-boat, and loaded it with wheat, corn, pork, whiskey, and cherry lumber, and passed down the Black fork to the Walhonding; thence, into the Muskingum; thence, down the Ohio and Mississippi, to New Orleans, where he sold his cargo and boat for cash. He returned on foot to Nashville, Tennessee, by the main road, where he purchased a horse, and from thence made the balance of his journey on horseback. The trip to New Orleans and return took about three months, and was attended with many hazards. The river travel and trade gave employment to a hardy and daring class of men. The boatmen and gamblers on the river at the time were proverbial for recklessness and contempt of danger. The bowie-knife and the pistol were the chief weapons of defence, and were often called into requisition. Mr. Bull was a large man, and possessed uncommon strength and activity, and was as courageous and fearless as he was athletic. The rough boatman that courted an encounter with him generally became satisfied before he got through, that he had met a man, in all respects. While thus capable of defending himself against the assaults of the wild and reckless boatmen of the Ohio and Mississippi, he was genial, whole-souled and courteous, and never provoked ill-will or sought a quarrel with any one. The trip he took to New Orleans in 1821 is believed to have been the first attempt at navigating the Black fork and the Walhonding. He subsequently conveyed two or three other flat-bottomed boats, similarly laden, to New Orleans, returning on foot by Nashville, and from thence homeward on horseback, in each instance consuming about three months to the trip.

In 1822 Mr. Bull married Miss Mary Farquher, daughter of Amos Farquher, who resided near Fredericktown, Knox county, Ohio; and located on his farm near Loudonville. In 1825 he constructed a keel-boat one hundred and twenty feet long, which he named the "Ben Franklin." He freighted this boat with the surplus products of the country, and conveyed it down the same streams to Louisville, Kentucky, where he met a ready market, and procured a load in exchange, which he brought to Cincinnati and sold at a profit. These trips were occasionally renewed until about the year 1832, when he abandoned the business and gave his attention to farming. He was very industrious as a farmer, and few could surpass him in endurance. He was of a class of men who always make an impression, and seem born to lead. In his intercourse with men he was frank, outspoken and independent. His spirit of candor always made him liberal and charitable. In 1839 he was elected one of the justices of the peace for Hanover township; and was subsequently re-elected to the same position four times. While acting as justice, many characteristic anecdotes are related of him. He had a strong dislike for that class of the legal fraternity known as "pettifoggers." He regarded such fellows the pests of society, because their occupation led them to encourage strife and litigation. Some years after his election two neighbors engaged in a heated suit before him, urged on by such legal gentlemen, that they might obtain a fee. The fact was, the neighbors should have refrained from litigation; but a lawsuit was a novelty, and pride of opinion, apparently, unconquerable. Quite a crowd of spectators gathered to see the fun, as it was understood a lawyer from Mansfield, and one from Millersburgh, were to take the lead in the case. A number of witnesses were examined, during which all sorts of technical difficulties were raised and discussed by the attorneys. Thus several hours were consumed, much to the annoyance of the justice, in a wordy legal combat; and the patience of the 'squire was severely tried. The examination of witnesses was finally concluded, and 'Squire Bull turned to his docket and made a brief entry, and again faced the attorneys. The plaintiff's attorney proceeded to make a long, wordy, foggy argument, in which he belabored the defendant's witnesses and concluded that the cause should be given to the plaintiff. The defendant's attorney followed in an equally diffuse address, criticising the plaintiff's claim, the character of his witnesses, and the attainments of his attorney. At the conclusion of the arguments, there was a profound silence in the court-room, during which the rival attorneys fixed their eyes on the justice. After some time, one of the lawyers said:

"Squire, as this seems to be a case involving some intricate legal questions, I have no doubt you will desire a few days to investigate, and decide it."

The justice promptly responded: "Not at all, gentlemen. The case was decided more than three hours ago."

The attorneys were amazed, and demanded to know why he had permitted such extended arguments.

The justice said: "Gentlemen, you appeared anxious to hold a discussion, and I was not averse to hearing it. No harm is done—the case is decided."

At the organization of Ashland county, in 1846, Mr. Bull was elected a representative to the Ohio legislature, and served one session. He was then elected to the senate one term. When the new constitution was adopted, the district was changed, and he declined to be a candidate. The senatorial district, at his election, was composed of Ashland and Wayne counties. As a member of the house and senate, Mr. Bull acquitted himself with ability. He was an ardent Democrat of the Jeffersonian and Jackson school, and attracted much attention in the senate by the independent utterance of his principles. He was a large man—full of courage—outspoken and manly in his address. He possessed a warm heart and a clear head. He detested every species of hypocrisy, time-serving and political cowardice. Full of humor and pleasant in his general deportment, he made many warm friends wherever he went. Although not a member of any church, from his earliest intercourse with the people of Hanover, his table was often spread for the pioneer preachers, whom he treated with courtesy and kindness.

In the vigor of manhood Mr. Bull was prostrated with paralysis, and, after lingering a few months, deceased December 13, 1852, aged about fifty-three years.

Mr. Bull was an honest man—frank even to bluntness—of undaunted courage, and possessed mental powers of a high order. As a citizen, an officer, and a business man, he was conspicuous. He is worthy of a high place in the history of his township and county.

Mrs. Mary Bull, wife of Colonel George W. Bull, died March 8, 1877, aged seventy-seven years, seven months, and twenty-five days. She had been sick about three weeks with acute bronchial inflammation.

The remaining members of the family are: John W. and George Franklin, of Loudonville; Mrs. Sarah J. Slutz, of Cleveland; Mariah, Mary, and Phebe, of Loudonville; Emily Hazlett, wife of Thomas M. Hazlett, of Howell, Michigan.

LORIN ANDREWS, LL. D.

Lorin Andrews was born in Uniontown, now Ashland, April 1, 1819, and was the second male child born within the present limits of the town. Alanson Andrews, his father, resided in a small log cabin, about thirty-five or forty feet south of Main street, on the lot on which the office of M. H. Mansfield is now located. Here it was that Lorin Andrews first saw the light, learned to lisp the name of his parents, and began to give evidence of that talent for which he became, in after years, so noted. When quite young, his father purchased of David Markley, the farm adjoining Ashland on the southwest, and located thereon. Lorin attended the district schools of the village, and made rapid progress in the branches taught at that period. He was much beloved by his schoolmates, because of his amiable disposition, sprightliness of manner and acuteness.

When he was about seventeen years of age, he was regarded as one of the foremost youths of the village. In the year 1836, the patriotic fires of the Revolution were still kept blazing on the altars of the country. It was resolved to celebrate the natal day of our freedom in a becoming manner. To this end, after several village meetings, it was agreed that the people would assemble in Carter's grove, about one and a half miles east of Ashland, on the fourth of July, for that purpose; and that Michael Ritter, who kept a hotel on the premises now known as the Finley property, be invited to prepare a dinner; and that Lorin Andrews be requested to prepare and deliver the oration. When the time for assembling arrived, the procession was formed at Ashland, with Alexander Miller as marshal of the day; and the people were escorted to the grove, headed by a band, composed of Jacob Grubb as drummer, Pierce Robinson fifer, Joshua H. Ruth and John K. Billings with flutes. Young Andrews delivered the oration with a coolness and self-possession that astonished the assemblage. His address had been carefully prepared, well studied, and delivered with an ease of manner and grace of gesticulation that was pronounced admirable. The dinner and toasts followed. And the festivities of the occasion are yet referred to by many of the pioneers with much pride.

A copy of the address of young Andrews was published in the *Ohio Globe*, a little paper, then edited by our late townsman, Joshua H. Ruth.

A bright future was predicted for the young orator; and his father was induced to send him where his ambition, as a student, could have a better field and be more fully gratified. He at once entered the grammar school of Gambier college, where he commenced a thorough course of instruction. He remained in the grammar school about two years, and entered college, but during his junior year, in 1840, owing to financial embarrassment, was withdrawn from college. He returned to Ashland, and after a few months, by invitation of the trustees, took charge of the Ashland academy as principal, aided by several able assistants, in the male and female departments. Under his superintendence the school was in a most flourishing condition; students from every part of the State, and from distant States, came in by the hundred and enrolled their names. Not having completed his collegiate course, Professor Andrews was compelled to continue his studies in private, to keep in advance of his students. He applied himself with uncommon industry, and distanced the most advanced classes; he evinced a knowledge of the branches taught, and a readiness in recitation that was really surprising. His manner, as an instructor, was agreeable and well calculated to win the esteem of the student.

He had a peculiar faculty of enlisting the sympathy, respect and confidence of all with whom he was brought in contact. He was frank and pleasing in his address, and a student met but to love and honor him. When compelled to enforce, with apparent severity, the rules governing the academy, it was done in such a way that the student respected him for his impartiality and evident intention to do justice. The writer of this sketch has seen Professor Andrews, scores of times, after reprimanding a hot-headed student for some gross violation of the rules, while yet smarting under the reproof, and blinded by rage and resentment, approach him at the black-board in the most friendly manner, take the chalk and give him a statement, and frequently solve the problem. Such treatment would soften the resentment of any young man of reflection, and secure his respect. In this Professor Andrews evinced his deep insight into human nature, and often succeeded in taming the ferocity of the worst students, and changed the whole current of their lives. With him "kind words could never die."

Professor Andrews was a fluent conversationalist, was very kind and gentlemanly in his manner; and egotism was an element that could not be detected in his intercourse with his students or society. In fact, he was the least selfish public man I ever knew. The result was that while he always had a flourishing school, and was popular among the students and the people, he was always financially distressed. If he found a student struggling to obtain an education, teaching in the winter and attending the academy in the summer, he would not exact tuition, but insist that his pupil should go ahead, and pay him when he could. This was often equivalent to no pay.

As a speaker, Professor Andrews was not an orator, unless we define oratory to be the ability to please and hold an audience. His addresses at school institutes, and lectures before his classes, were all delivered in conversational style. He talked remarkably well, and could hold an audience or an institute for hours. There was a fascination about his manner that invariably made his audience feel friendly toward him, while the lucidness of his ideas enlisted their whole attention. As a lecturer before institutes, he was widely known throughout the State; and he exercised as much or more influence, perhaps, than any other teacher in the west.

In consequence of his success as a teacher, in 1846, the honorary degree of A. M. was conferred upon him by Kenyon college.

In 1850 the union school system was adopted in many parts of the State. The trustees of the schools at Massillon solicited Professor Andrews to become superintendent. In an unfortunate hour the people of Ashland permitted him to retire from the academy, an institution which had been an ornament to the town, and a source of profit to our people. The academy speedily passed away, and the buildings were merged into the union schools.

Professor Andrews remained at the head of the Massillon schools about three years, during which time he was nominated by the Whig party, under the new constitution, for commissioner of common schools for the State. He failed, by a small vote, to secure his election. Under his management the schools of Massillon were very efficient and popular.

In December, 1854, he was invited to accept the presidency of Kenyon college, with which request he complied. He was the first lay member of the Episcopal church who had been invited to fill that position. To be selected to preside over such an institution was indeed a flattering compliment. His high educational attainments, added to his purity as a man, made him the worthy recipient of such an honor. His presence in the college acted like magic—his friends from every part of the State began to look toward Kenyon as an appropriate place to educate the young men of the country. The college received new life; and energy and prosperity were diffused through every department. Students began to fill the classes, and everything betokened a prosperous future for the institution.

Some months after Professor Andrews had been inaugurated president of Kenyon college, the honorary degree of LL. D. was conferred upon him by Princeton college, New Jersey. This was a high distinction and well deserved, because of his remarkable success as an educator.

In 1861, in the midst of his success as president of Kenyon, the rumbling sounds of discontent were borne from the south, and a sanguinary civil war seemed to be imminent. In February, believing the war to be inevitable, President Andrews offered his services to the governor of Ohio. In April he raised a company in Knox county, which reported to the governor, and he was appointed colonel of the Fourth Ohio regiment. Soon after his regiment was ordered into West Virginia, where it remained on duty during the summer. In September Colonel Andrews, in consequence of exposure, was attacked by a malignant form of typhoid fever, that fell destroyer of so many northern soldiers, and, although able to reach his home in Ohio, was so much prostrated that the friendly efforts of the physician, and all human aid, failed to avert his impending end. The sentiment—

> Our life is a dream,
> Our time like a stream
> Glides swiftly away,

was fully illustrated. He died September 18, 1861. Just prior to his departure with his regiment to Virginia, fearing some disaster might overtake him, he, accompanied by his wife, went into the cemetery at Gambier, and selected the spot where he desired to be buried in case of his death in the army. His wishes were complied with, and his honored remains now rest in sight of the institution he loved so well during his active and useful life.

Much surprise was manifested among many of his old friends when it was learned that he had abandoned the presidency of Kenyon college to accept a place in the army. It was believed that his true field was that of letters, and that his tastes all ran in that direction. When a student under his instruction in the old Ashland academy, years prior to the war, while translating Homer, Virgil, Xenophon, Livy, Cicero, and the orations of Demosthenes, the military spirit could be plainly detected in his comments upon the strategy of the heroes of that age. At the mention of Achilles, "swift of foot"—"Peleus' godlike son"—"Mighty Agamemnon, king of men" —the venerable "Nestor"—the achievements of the Scipios, Alexander, Cæsar, Hannibal and Pompey, his enthusiasm exhibited itself in a forcible manner. There can be but little doubt if Colonel Andrews had survived the war he would have reached an elevated position as a military man, and acquitted himself as bravely as a Morgan, a McPherson, and a Sheridan. He was very ambitious to excel in everything he undertook, and his spirit, like—

> "An eagle soared
> On restless plumes to meet the imperial sun."

His motto was "conquer, never cower at, opposition." Hence he was always making progress in the line of his profession. His theory was—

> "Rest not! Life is sweeping by;
> Go and dare before you die.
> Something mighty and sublime
> Leave behind to conquer time."

Right well he performed his part in the drama of the world. He was only about forty-two years old at his decease. Few men have accomplished more. From a cabin, by the force of his genius, he elevated himself to the presidency of one of the best colleges in the west before he was thirty-five years of age, and proved himself one of the first educators of the times.

In person President Andrews was about five feet eight inches high, would weigh about one hundred and thirty-five pounds, hair inclined to be curly and sandy, a broad forhead, a clear gray eye, a manly face full of benevolence; in his manners, courteous and gentlemanly; in his gait, very erect and quite sprightly in his movements. Such was President Andrews, one of the noblest sons Ashland ever sent forth, and whose career is worthy the emulation of all her future sons.

JOHN SPRINGER

was born in Allegheny county, Pennsylvania, October 27, 1794. He was of German descent, his ancestors having come from that country prior to the American Revolution. He grew to manhood amid the border scenes of his native country, and learned the story of the cruelties of the savage red men. His education, in consequence of the newness of that region, was confined to the elementary branches. At the age of twenty, in the year 1814, he visited Richland, now Ashland county, Ohio, and selected the homestead, where he deceased. His father, Michael Springer, had entered three quarter sections of land at the office in Canton, in Montgomery township, upon one of which he built a cabin, while John selected another tract. On this trip he was accompanied by Jacob and William Figley and his son John. They all camped together by the side of a large log, against which they erected a shed-roofed camp-house. They built the first cabin for Jacob Figley, who moved to it first, and made the farm the homestead, where he died many years since. In raising the cabin, they invited John and Charles Wheeler, Conrad Cline, Jacob Heller, Jesse Newell, Jacob Cline, and the late Daniel Carter and son, they being pretty much all the settlers in the township. Provisions were growing very scarce. Michael Springer and the Figleys had brought along a few bushels of corn-meal, some potatoes, and a little salt meat on a pack-horse; but when the cabin was ready to be raised their food had become almost exhausted. In preparation for the raising, John Springer took his gun and hunting dog the day before the frolic, and scoured the forest in search of wild meat. When he arrived near Beall's trail, some two miles south of their hut, his dog treed a large and very fat raccoon, which he shot, and upon arriving at home dressed and boiled it with potatoes for dinner on the day of the raising. He obtained from some of the pioneers a little flour, which was mixed in a sugar trough and baked into an ash-cake for the same occasion. With a degree of merriment Mr. Springer informed the writer that the hands all thought it a very fine dinner and relished it very much, washing it down with parched corn coffee boiled in a brass kettle. This was in December, 1814, just sixty-four years ago. That region of Montgomery township was then a dreary and dense forest, inhabited by wolves and other wild animals. The war of 1812 was drawing to a close. They had been six weeks preparing Mr. Figley's cabin and were glad to retrace their steps to Allegheny county. The party returned by way of Wooster, then a mere village, staying one night at a little hotel kept by a Mr. Jones.

Mr. Jacob Figley, who was a brother-in-law of Mr. Springer, returned to Ohio in 1816 and occupied his cabin; while John Springer did not permanently locate until 1818. He came out and cleared a fraction of the land prior to that time, making his home part of the time at the hotel of William Montgomery, then located where the hardware store of Mr. Stull now stands, and often went deer hunting with the late George Swineford to supply their quota of wild meat—he also boarded at the same log hotel. About this time he married Elizabeth, daughter of the late Daniel Carter. When Mr. Springer located he was of the opinion his neighbors were William Dwire, Solomon Sherradden, John Owens, Peter Swineford, George Butler, the Wheelers, Clines and Newells; and in 1820 Henry Springer, Elijah Smith, Jesse Callihan, who married Rachel Carter, and the Figleys, William and Jacob.

Mrs. Springer deceased about 1847, since which time John Springer has resided with his children. His family, at his decease, consisted of five sons and five daughters, all grown: William, John, Lorin, Augustus and Herbert, Susan, Matilda, Rachel, Elizabeth and Irsula, all living.

Mr. Springer lived a harmless and exemplary life. For nearly fifty years he was strongly attached to the doctrines of the Methodist Episcopal church, though of late years, from the distance of his residence from the church, he was compelled from the infirmities of age, to remain at home most of the time.

At the organization of the Pioneer and Historical society of Ashland county, he became an enthusiastic member, and was always in attendance at the regular meetings. It is a remarkable fact that Mr. Springer was never known to have been sick until his last illness, which was but of a few days' duration. He died at the residence of Samuel Thornburg, in Montgomery township, Thursday, December 5, 1878, aged about eighty-four years, of general debility.

He was followed to the grave, the final resting place of all, by a large number of neighbors and friends. He was buried at the Carter cemetery beside his wife and kindred. Peaceful is the rest of the good and true.

THE McGUIRES.

The grand-parents of the Ashland county McGuires, of Irish extraction, appear to have located near the Potomac, in Virginia, as early as 1771. About the close of the Revolution, three brothers—Francis, Robert, and John—appear to have located in what is now Washington county, Pennsylvania, where Francis and Robert attached themselves to Brady's patrol, and became famous as Indian fighters and scouts. Francis died in Brooke county, Virginia, in 1825, aged about seventy-eight years. Robert lost his life in Cross creek, in a skirmish, in 1794. John died in 1831. Thomas and Hugh were sons of John.

Hugh first visited this county in 1810, in company with Robert Newell, and others, on a hunting excursion. In 1811 Mr. Newell entered the farm in Montgomery township, which subsequently became the property of Hugh McGuire. Hugh emigrated in 1841. He was a fine mathematician and a polished gentleman. He filled the office of township trustee for a number of years, and, after the erection of the county, was infirmary director. He was averse to holding office, and asked no promotion. He was an influential and leading citizen, and exerted that influence in behalf of his friends. He died September 13, 1867, aged eighty-one years. This family are all dead, but two daughters.

Thomas McGuire settled in Vermillion township in 1831, and died in the spring of 1849, aged seventy-two years. He was a man of fine native abilities, but could not be induced to accept an office. When in his prime, he wielded more political influence than any citizen of Richland county, and often controlled an election.

Thomas and Benjamin, nephews of Thomas and Hugh, settled in Green township, in 1837. They are influential and leading citizens. Thomas is seventy-five, and Benjamin about sixty-four years of age.

JOSEPH STRICKLAND

was born in the State of New Jersey, January 4, 1804, and removed with the family of his father, Joseph Strickland, sr., to Jefferson county, Ohio, prior to the war of 1812, and thence to Vermillion township, now Ashland county, a few years subsequent to the close of that war. His father had served honorably as a soldier from New Jersey in the war of the Revolution, and died in Seneca county, Ohio, at the advanced age of eighty-six years, in 1850. In 1826 Joseph Strickland, jr., the subject of this sketch, purchased and removed to the farm on which he deceased, in the northwest part of Vermillion township. He improved his homestead and made it a valuable property. He connected with the Methodist Episcopal church early in life, and was an exemplary Christian for over fifty years, and several times a leader in the church. He was noted for his domestic worth, and kindness to his family. His affection and goodness of heart had a cheerful influence over his children, all of whom revered, honored and followed his counsel. As a citizen, he was quiet and unobtrusive. His integrity and uprightness fitted him for public promotion. He was frequently called upon by his neighbors to fill offices of trust in his township. He served as trustee, justice of the peace and infirmary director, and retired from the latter position, some years since, because of a paralytic attack, which disabled him, and prevented an active discharge of public duties. In politics he was a Democrat, and had been from his arrival at manhood. He was noted for his benevolent and kindly feelings, and made an excellent infirmary director. He has gone home to rest with the just and the pure. May his example as a Christian and a man have its influence upon those who remain to conduct the affairs of their fellow citizens.

Mr. Strickland died at his residence in the northwest part of Vermillion township, Sunday, October 8, 1876, after a long and painful attack of paralysis, aged seventy-two years, nine months, and one day.

At a meeting of the obituary committee of the Historical and Pioneer association, of Ashland county, appropriate resolutions were adopted regarding his decease.

JOHN PORTER

was born in Virginia, October 15, 1799, and removed with his father's family to Westmoreland county, Pennsylvania, in 1810. In 1824 he removed to Vermillion township, now Ashland county. He located near what is known as Smith's mill, near Beall's trail and camping ground. His brother Daniel and several acquaintances had been in Beall's expedition in 1812, and finally located in the same neighborhood. Mr. Porter's neighbors were John Johnston, Thomas Roe, Uriah Johnston, George Eckley, Eli Finley, George Keene, Isaac Vail, Robert Finley, Lemuel Bolter, and John Farrer, and shortly afterwards Isaac Paullin.

Mr. Porter improved his farm and resided on it until January 20, 1860, when he deceased. His widow still survives. His sons are David, deceased, William O., and Daniel.

William O. Porter has filled a number of township offices, and been sheriff four years. He possesses a good education, and has recently studied law, and been admitted. He resides on the old homestead.

EDWARD METCALF

was born in Washington county, Pennsylvania, August 5, 1783, and removed to Mohican (then Killbuck,) township, Wayne county, in the spring of 1815, and located on what is now known as he Robert Glenn farm. He cleared and improved his land, and resided on it for many years. He deceased in 1856, at the age of seventy-three years. His family consisted of three sons, John, Vachel, jr., and Daniel; and three daughters, Julia, Nancy, and Rachel. The family have all removed to other localities, except John, who resides in the vicinity of Mohicanville. He is by occupation an industrious farmer.

THOMAS METCALF,

brother of Edward, was born in Washington county, Pennsylvania, January 9, 1797. He grew to manhood in his native county. In June, 1818, he married Miss Nancy Durbin, of Washington county. In September, having heard much of the richness of the valleys of Mohican, he and his lady traveled on horseback to the residence of his brother, Edward, in the wilds of the valley, and tarried a few weeks, until he erected a cabin. His father had entered a piece of land three miles south of the present site of Jeromeville, upon which Thomas Metcalf settled.

He passed through all the struggles of pioneer life, and resided about fifty-eight years on the same farm. In 1868 he had the misfortune to lose the wife of his youth. Since that occurrence, his hours have passed slowly. In 1875 he became partially paralyzed; February 9, 1876, he deceased, at his old homestead, aged seventy-nine years and one month. His family consisted of Drusilla, Rachel, Maria, Eliza, and Sarah; all married.

WILLIAM LATTA

was born in Westmoreland county, Pennsylvania, in 1777. He settled in the east part of Montgomery township, in the fall of 1815. His nearest neighbors were John Carr and Robert Newell. Mr. Latta had some trouble in procuring hands to aid in erecting his cabin. In doing so he had to go as far south as the present site of Jeromeville. When his rude house had been completed, his next difficulty was to procure food. He travelled through the forest, along Indian paths, to Shrimplin's mill to procure corn, and when converted into meal, carried it home on a pack-saddle. He also made many trips, with horse and pack-saddle, to Stibbs' mill, near Wooster. These trips were toilsome and not devoid of danger. Mr. Latta was a large, rugged man, and met the dangers and toils of pioneer life with undaunted fortitude. He prepared an excellent farm, and, in his old age, lived comfortably. He was a member of old Hopewell Presbyterian church. He died February 2, 1849, aged seventy-two years. His family consisted of Lewis, John, William, Moses, and Jackson. Moses owns the homestead; John and Jackson reside in Iowa, and Lewis and William are dead. These sons were noted for their remarkable size and vigor. Moses is a good business man, and has been twice elected infirmary director for the county, and a number of times township trustee.

MOSES LATTA.

Mr. Latta was born in Westmoreland county, Pennsylvania, January 20, 1815, and removed with his father, the late William Latta, to Montgomery township, Richland, now Ashland, county, in the fall of 1815. He attended the common schools of the neighborhood, and obtained a fair knowledge of the elementary branches. When his father settled on Catotaway his neighbors were few and far between, and in the erection of cabins and other buildings, it was the custom of the pioneers to go many miles to assist the new settler. In the earlier history of Montgomery township the Lattas were noted for their industry, energy and physical vigor, all the sons being large men, and constitutionally clever. William Latta, the father of Moses, was of Scotch-Irish descent, and like his ancestors, was strongly attached to the doctrines of the Presbyterian church. He was, for many years, a member of "Old Hopewell" in Ashland, and his sons were impressed by the same faith. Upon the decease of William Latta, in 1849, Moses became possessed of the homestead, where he has resided the major part of the time ever since. He was a man of good business habits and of unquestioned integrity, and was frequently elected to act as school director, township trustee, and twice an infirmary director for Ashland county. He was a large, energetic, hard working man, and had accumulated quite a fortune. His general health began to give way early in the summer, and continued to fail until he became prostrated, and gradually approached the hour of dissolution, which occurred on Saturday, November 11, 1876. His remains were interred in the cemetery at Ashland, on Tuesday, November 14. Mr. Latta leaves a widow to mourn the loss of a most excellent husband. During his late sickness, he connected with the Presbyterian church of Ashland.

He was also a member of the Masonic fraternity and the Pioneer and Historical society of Ashland county.

As a citizen, neighbor and business man, he stood deservedly high, and will be much missed and lamented in the circle of his past and present associations. Peace to his ashes.

JOHN S. NELSON

was born in Allegheny county, Pennsylvania, December 10, 1812, and moved with his father's family to Milton township, Richland, now Ashland, county, in the spring of 1816. He was the oldest son of Robert Nelson, one of the leading pioneers of Milton township, and saw it clothed in its primitive forest. When a boy he roamed amidst its wilds, and often saw the wild deer, bear and wolves. A serenade of wolves was very common, and the pioneers were compelled to enclose young calves, sheep and swine to prevent capture by wild animals. He grew to manhood in Milton, attending log-cabin schools, helping to remove the forest, erect cabins, cutting highways, and making other improvements. When his father entered the township the Delaware Indians, in their hunting excursions, often passed down Beall's trail, and hunted along the streams of this county, but never interfered with the citizens of Milton. But a few families preceded Robert Nelson in Milton. John Nelson, in a personal interview with the writer, said he remembered the following: James Gunthel, Peter Lance, James Kelley, Frederick Sulcer, John Anderson, Obediah Ferrell, Alexander Reed, Edward Wheeler, Allen Lockhart, William Lockhart, Henry Wetzel, George Myers, David Teal, John Kane, Abraham Doty, David Pollock and Laban Conley.

In 1846 he volunteered from the State of Illinois, to serve during the Mexican war, and with his company was in several battles, one of the most noted of which was the battle of Buena Vista. He was in Colonel Clay's regiment, and assisted in carrying that gallant young officer from the field after his fatal wound. His company was attacked in this engagement by a squadron of lancers, and Mr. Nelson was wounded twice; once by a ball in the hand, and afterward by a lancer, who struck him in the breast with his lance. He shot and killed the Mexican and secured the lance-head, which he brought home as a trophy.

Like all those from the north who entered the Mexican army, he became a victim of chronic disease, resulting from dysentery. For many years he has been too feeble to labor, and constantly a sufferer. Many years since he became a member of the Lutheran church, and adorned his faith by an upright walk. The immediate cause of his decease was a fall, in which he fractured his hip-bone. He failed rapidly, and after three or four days of pain he expired January 28, 1877. His remains were interred in the cemetery at Ashland, Tuesday, January 30, 1877. He was also a member of the Ashland County Historical and Pioneer society. Suitable resolutions were passed by the appropriate committees touching his decease and life.

JACOB FREES,

of English-German descent, was born in Uniontown, Pennsylvania, November 22, 1808, and he came to Wayne county, Ohio, in November, 1822, and to Wayne township, with his father's family. He remained there until 1857, then removed to Smithville, same county, and, in 1864, removed to Ashland county. He learned the trade of a shoemaker, and carried it on in Wayne county, with a shoe-store, until he came to Ashland county. He attended common schools, and became a member of the Lutheran Reformed church in 1825. He is now a member of the English Lutheran church of Ashland, and has been an elder six or seven years. When he came to Ashland he became one of the proprietors of the steam saw-mill until 1870, and then retired. His family consists of two sons and four daughters.

JOHN VAN NEST

was born December 1, 1814, in York county, Pennsylvania. He attended common schools, learned the trade of a saddler in 1831-32, came to Wooster, Wayne county, in 1838, and worked until 1839. He married Miss Sarah Wiley, of Smithville, Wayne county, May 2, 1839, moved to Rowsburgh the same month, and has carried on business ever since. He has served as a justice of the peace six terms. He was elected commissioner in 1864, and served two terms. He has been a member of the Lutheran church since 1849. His ancestors were from Holland, and located in New Jersey. His father, John Van Nest, located in York county, Pennsylvania, and came to Wayne county in 1838, and died in Millbrook, in 1862, aged eighty-seven.

John Van Nest is the father of ten children—two dead, eight living.

JESSE CHAMBERLAIN

was born in Windom county, Vermont, September 27, 1794. In June, 1815, he married Betsy Mann, of the same county. In 1817 he accompanied what is known as the Parmely colony as far as Medina, where he remained until 1819, when he settled in Sullivan, now Ashland county. The colony traveled from the east with six teams, one yoke of oxen, and sometimes the addition of one horse to each wagon. The wagons were covered and contained beds, cooking utensils, and provisions for the trip. They also brought along a number of cows, which supplied milk on the way. They came by the way of Buffalo, New York, and were many weeks making the journey. These aged people yet (1876) retain considerable physical vigor. They are quite lively, and their mental powers seem to be unimpaired. They had three children—Adeline, wife of Mr. Rice, Alzina, deceased, and Miranda, deceased. Whitney and Richard Chamberlain, brothers of Jesse, settled in the township with the mother who died in 1843. They are deceased.

ASA S. REED

was born in Lynn, Massachusetts, December 22, 1817. His father, Josiah Reed, came to Westfield, Medina county, Ohio, in the spring of 1829, and died February 18, 1830. He left his family in limited circumstances. Asa was apprenticed to a farmer until he was twenty years of age, to be instructed to the rule of three in arithmetic, and in spelling, reading and writing. In 1834 he hired as a farm hand at twelve dollars per month, and unfortunately wounded his limb, which had to be amputated near the knee. He suffered many months, and being unable to labor was reduced to the necessity of being aided by charity. As soon as he could regain sufficient strength, he engaged in various enterprises to recruit his fortunes. In 1835 he taught school three months. His chief occupation until 1844 was that of teacher. He then undertook to learn the trade of a tailor, and sewed three months in Jeromeville with John D. Jones. In 1846 he was elected recorder of Ashland county for the short term of six months, and was re-elected continuously the three following terms. He acted at the same time as notary public nine years. He then taught one term in the Union school at Ashland. He has been remarkably successful as a teacher, and has taught more terms than any teacher within the limits of the county—in the aggregate amounting to near fifteen years. In 1859 he removed to Sullivan, and became a successful farmer and teacher. He married Priscilla Smalley, of Perry township, by whom he had three sons—George W., John F., and Oliver. George is dead. In December, 1872, Mrs. Reed deceased, aged fifty-one years. April 29, 1873, he married Charlotte Forbes, of Ashland, an experienced teacher, and a resident of Ashland for about forty-two years. Mr. Reed and his former and present wife were and are exemplary members of the Christian church. He possesses a neat and valuable homestead, and is another illustration of what can be accomplished amid all embarrassments by industry, perseverance, integrity and an upright life. Few in early life have undergone more trials, and few have been more successful in mastering all obstacles.

MARTIN MASON, SR.,

was born in Germany in 1742, and emigrated with his parents to America in 1745, and settled on the south branch of the Potomac river, in Virginia. When he was about thirteen years of age, in 1755, he was captured by the Indians. This occurred about two weeks after the disastrous defeat of General Braddock, when on his way to attack Fort DuQuesne. Young Mason was taken by the Indians to the fort, and thence, by Niagara, to Canada, where he was purchased by a French officer at Montreal. When General Wolfe captured Quebec, in 1759, young Mason was ordered, by his master, to conduct the family to a neighboring swamp for safety during the battle. Four years after the surrender of the city to the English, in 1763, he was liberated and returned home, after an absence of about eight years, where he remained until his marriage. He subsequently removed to what is now Fayette county, Pennsylvania, and located land by "tomahawk right," which consisted in blazing trees around the tract selected and having it surveyed and recorded, all of which cost but a trifle. This was four or five years after the Dunmore war, when with his neighbors, he was greatly harrassed by the Indians for a number of years. Mr.

Mason died at an advanced age on the old homestead of the late Jacob Mason, in Orange, in 1838, aged ninety-six years, leaving nine children: Elizabeth, Barbara, Margaret, Abigail, Mary, John, Martin, Charles, and Jacob. Martin and Jacob located in Orange township, Ashland county, and Charles in Columbiana county, Ohio. He was born in Fayette county, Pennsylvania, February 16, 1780, and died in Columbiana county, in April, 1869, aged about eighty-nine years. He had four sons, John, Martin, Jacob, and Lewis. Martin emigrated to Ashland county in 1844, and settled on a quarter of land purchased by his father in 1814. He was born April 12, 1817. He still resides on the homestead. His children are a son, W. A. Mason, and two daughters, Emila and Mary.

REV. JOSEPH SEELEY PARKER

was born in South Salem, Westchester county, New York, May 10, 1795. When seventeen years of age, he went as a substitute in the war of 1812, four months. In 1813 he was drafted for three months in the same war. In his first tour he was in the battle of Queenstown. After the war he resided in Columbiana county, Ohio, two years, to which he removed in 1826, and then in Austintown five years, and in 1833 removed to Troy township, now in Ashland county, and located amid a dense forest on lot three of surplus lands. Upon his arrival he found Benjamin Moore, David Mason, David Carrier, Ralph Phelps, Nicholas and Christian Fast and their families. At that time Francis Granger, of New York, owned nearly all the lands of the township, and the primitive forest covered the same. Two years after his arrival, the township was organized, and he thinks, at the first election, there were seven votes cast for the following officers: Benjamin Moore, justice of the peace, J. S. Parker, treasurer, Sanford Peck, David Mason and Ralph Phelps, trustees. He is unable to name the constable. The return was made to Elyria. The first school was a little south of his present residence, and was taught by Ralph Phelps. It was in a cabin, which was sometimes used as a church for the earlier preachers. Mr. Parker and his venerable lady became members of the Methodist Episcopal church as early as 1813-14, and he was licensed as a local preacher nearly sixty years ago. The first class was organized by him at his cabin a short time after his arrival in the township, from which has grown the fine structure in Troy center. He states that the Baptists erected a small building and had a few members at an early day, but the organization went down. He and his lady, now (1876) about eighty-two years of age, are quite vigorous, and their mental powers seem to be unimpaired. When they arrived, and for a few years afterward, the *Wyandots* from Sandusky hunted in the neighborhood. A number of huts were found a little northwest, near a deer lick. He found on and about his premises great numbers of flint arrow points, stone axes and fleshers, some of which he has presented to the Historical and Pioneer society. He is drawing a pension of ninety-six dollars annually for his services in the war of 1812, and takes a deep interest in the prosperity of the country. His wife's name before marriage was Eunice Phelps. She is a sister of the wife of the venerable Nathaniel Clark, of Troy, another soldier of 1812. Their children are Alonzo, Elisha, Samuel, Joshua, Nathaniel, Mary Ann, Julia and Hannah. They are somewhat scattered. All are married, except Samuel, who died many years since. Mr. Parker could never be persuaded to travel on a circuit. For over fifty-five years he has been a speaker and zealous advocate of the doctrines of the Methodist Episcopal church. In his earlier years he was a fine singer and a fluent speaker.

REV. R. D. EMERSON.

Richard Dumont Emerson was born in Fairfax county, Virginia, near the city of Alexandria, August 14, 1794. His mother was a highly educated French lady, whose maiden name was Louis, a branch of the royal family, and his father also of French birth. A brother of his mother accompanied General Lafayette to this country, and fell in the battle of Brandywine, during the Revolutionary war.

In his youth, Mr. Emerson attended school near Alexandria, and acquired a fair English education.

When about eighteen years of age he entered the army of the war of 1812, as a volunteer, and was at the battle of Crany Island, where he was honorably mentioned for his conduct on the field, and promoted to captain. At the close of the war he returned to Alexandria, and engaged in business as a manufacturer and dealer in shoes and boots.

In 1824-5, when General Lafayette visited Alexandria and Mt. Vernon, Captain Emerson was one of the marshals who commanded the guard that received and conducted the general to that "Mecca of American freemen," the tomb of George Washington. He was a fine horseman, and was highly complimented by General Lafayette for his fine military bearing on that occasion.

While a young man he became an active membe rof, and local minister in, the Methodist church. In 1840 he removed to Guernsey county, Ohio, and became a Lutheran minister. He subsequently removed to Ashland county, and preached for Lutheran congregations at Rowsburgh, Hayesville, Mifflin, and Orange. He was regarded as a forcible and fluent speaker, and made a fine appearance in the pulpit. In 1852 he was elected a member of the Ohio legislature from Ashland county, and served one term, declining to be a candidate for re-election. In 1854 he was appointed postmaster at Hayesville, and retained the position to the close of the administration of Franklin Pierce. In 1860 he removed to Missouri, but subsequently located and took charge of a Lutheran congregation at Bardstown, Kentucky, where he remained until May, 1876, when he removed to Clark county, Missouri, where he deceased after a lingering illness, September 10, 1876, at the advanced age of eighty-two years and twenty-seven days. Mr. Emerson had served his church, as minister, about forty-six years, and was regarded as an able and influential exponent of the creed and teachings of Martin Luther, the great German reformer.

He was enrolled among those who drew pensions for services in the war of 1812, and it may be truly said, "he served his country as a patriot, and his church as a Christian."

Mr. Emerson was above medium in size, very erect, had black hair, large gray eyes, and was impressive and dignified in his bearing. He was exceedingly fond of fine horses, and rode with all the grace of a marshal of France. His tastes were largely military, and if he had been reared in a country like France, he would have risen to distinction in military life.

He was married three times. His family consisted of Rev. William A. G. Emerson, of Kentucky; Colonel Richard D. Emerson, of Iowa; John Emerson, deceased; Mrs. Martha White, of Kansas; Mrs. Elizabeth Davis, of Canal Dover, Ohio; Mrs. Virginia Crellen, of Missouri; and Mrs. Caroline Ewing, of Illinois.

REV. SAMUEL MOODY.

The Rev. Samuel Moody, of Scotch-Irish descent, was born in Northampton county Pennsylvania, February 14, 1801, in the vicinity of the mission station of David Brainard, among the Indians. His parents being Presbyterians, he was at an early period of his life indoctrinated in the tenets of that faith. His youth was marked by morality and sobriety. When about fifteen years of age he was greatly impressed by the preaching of Rev. Robert Finley, D. D., of New Jersey. At the age of eighteen he removed to Beaver county with his father's family. When about twenty-three years of age he attached himself, by profession, to Mill Creek church, in Beaver county. Prior to that time he had attended the common schools of the neighborhood. Having thoughts of preparing for the ministry in the fall of 1824, he commenced the study of Latin with his pastor, Rev. George Scott. He continued under his tuition for about three years, and then entered Washington college, Pennsylvania. When in his senior year, the college was temporarily closed by the removal of the president. Still ambitious to become a scholar, he entered Jefferson college, where he graduated in September, 1829, being twenty-eight years of age. He then taught one year, and entered the Western Theological seminary in 1830, at Allegheny City. On the third of October, 1833, he was licensed to preach by the presbytery of Washington. He preached a few months at Upper Ten Mile, Wolf Run, and Unity churches in Washington presbytery, and in 1834 located at Big Spring, in Carroll county, Ohio, and remained about eight years. He was ordained by the presbytery of Steubenville, July 5, 1837, and installed pastor of the Big Spring church. In 1843 he was invited to Hopewell, in Ashland, and Orange churches, and accepting the call, removed to Ashland, July 9, 1843. He continued as pastor of Hopewell and Orange about thirteen years. His ministry was characterized by an exemplary and devout life, and during his residence at Ashland he won the esteem of all. Owing to an unfortunate division arising among his people concerning church music, and a separation of a number of members from the parent church, for the establishment of the First Presbyterian church of Ashland, the number of members in Hopewell was not largely increased during the labors of Mr. Moody. In April, 1856, Mr. Moody and some members of his family visited western Pennsylvania. While crossing the Ohio on the 24th of April, near Wellsville, in a skiff with his little daughter, the ferryman and three others, the skiff being moored to the ferry-boat, on approaching the Ohio shore, became separated from the barge and overturned by the violence of the current, and he and his daughter thrown into the stream. Mr. Moody soon disappeared beneath the turbid current and was drowned, while his daughter floated, being supported by her clothing, and was saved. The remains of Mr. Moody were recovered on the fifth of May, eleven days after the fatal accident, in the vicinity of Steubenville, and brought to Ashland for interment. His funeral was preached by Rev. John Robinson of the First Presbyterian church of Ashland. We are indebted to him for the following summary of the habits and character of Mr. Moody:

Brother Moody's traits of character are easily sketched for they were apparent to all his acquaintances.

First—He was unobtrusive, quiet; not as easily known as some, and most highly appreciated where most intimately known. He was a man of tender attachments, disposed to contribute in every practicable way to the comfort of those about him, and exceedingly careful not to give pain by word or act.

Second—He was a man of correct judgment. He carefully weighed matters presented for his consideration, and seldom failed to reach a conclusion which commended itself to others. Associated with him from our earliest ministerial life, we have rarely known him to mistake in transacting ecclesiastical business. Calm, thoughtful, and under the influence of sterling principle, his judgments were to be relied upon in all matters pertaining to the interests of Christ's kingdom.

Third—He was very conscientious. This may be illustrated by a fact in his college life. Washington college closed temporarily when he was a senior half-advanced. The other members of his class received diplomas, as if they had graduated. He felt that he was not strictly entitled to a diploma, and, therefore, took a certificate and went to Jefferson college, and after a summer term of study, graduated. Now the last term of the senior class is generally passed, mostly in review and preparation for the commencement. So that he had little to gain by this course, as far as mere learning is concerned. But then his diploma never disturbed his conscience by asserting what was not literally true. And this trait ran through all his conduct, in all his relations.

Fourth—He was very uniform in his temper and manners. During an acquaintance of nearly sixteen years, we have scarcely ever seen him either manifestly depressed or elated. He was seldom irritated or fretted, or unduly buoyant. He seemed to live realizing the great truth that the Lord reigns, and that "he doeth all things well." More than almost any man we have known, he fully filled the poet's description:

> "The good man lays his hand upon the skies
> And bids the world roll on, nor heeds
> Its idle way."

Mr. Moody was married February 17, 1840, and had five children, three sons and two daughters, all of whom survive. Mrs. Moody, his widow, and most of her family, reside in the village of Savannah, Ashland county.

REV. JOHN ROBINSON, D. D.,

was the son of Henry and Elizabeth (Harkness) Robinson, of Westmoreland county, Pennsylvania. His grandparents—James Robinson and his wife, of Lancaster county, Pennsylvania, and William Harkness and his wife, of Westmoreland county, Pennsylvania—all immigrated to this country from the north of Ireland, about the year 1765. He is, therefore, of Scotch-Irish descent. He was born January 27, 1814, in Westmoreland county, Pennsylvania. When about two years of age his parents removed to Stark county, Ohio, settling about seven miles south of where Massillon now stands. Thus, when he was eight years old his father died, and four years afterward, his mother, with her three sons, of whom he was the oldest, one having died meantime, returned to Westmoreland county, Pennsylvania. During the five following years he labored as a hired farm hand, to help in the maintenance of the family in the summer time, and attended school each winter. When he was seventeen years of age he went to Cadiz, Harrison county, Ohio, as an apprentice to the tin-plate business. His employers were Presbyterians, and as his early training had been in the Associate Reformed church, he readily formed the habit of attending the Presbyterian church, joined the Sabbath-school, and, under the labors of the pastor, Rev. John McArthur, soon united with the church. When about half of his time as an apprentice had expired, his employers ceased business and gave him his indenture. He at once obtained employment at his trade for so much of his time as was needful to earn his food and clothing, spending the rest of his time in study, under the instruction of his pastor. His studies were directed with a view to the gospel ministry. This he continued until he completed the ordinary college curriculum as far as the close of the junior year. Then he entered Franklin college, located at New Athens, Harrison county, Ohio, and graduated there in October, 1837. He immediately went to the Western Theological seminary at Allegheny City, Pennsylvania. Here he remained three terms, not attending the fourth term, which was the prescribed course, because of his suffering from a slight bronchial affection.

He was licensed to preach the Gospel by the Presbytery of Steubenville, April 8, 1840. He was at once engaged to supply the pulpits of the adjacent churches of Corinth and Monroeville, the former in the eastern edge of Carroll county, the latter in the northwestern corner of Jefferson county, Ohio. From these churches he received a call for permanent settlement as pastor in the fall of that year, and on the second day of March, 1841, he was ordained to the full work of the ministry and installed as pastor of those churches by the Presbytery. On the twenty-second day of October, 1840, he married Miss Mary W. Willson, daughter of William Willson, Esq., of Pittsburgh, Pennsylvania. He had a prosperous pastorate of nearly three years in this field. In the autumn of 1843 he was invited to take charge of the Presbyterian church of Ashland. He removed to Ashland and commenced labor there on the first Sabbath of February, 1844. In April following he received a formal call to the pastorate of that church, and in June was installed as pastor by the presbytery of Richland. In that charge he still remains near the close of the thirty-second year of his labor. The membership of the First Presbyterian church has been greatly increased under his pastorship, and now numbers nearly three hundred. The exemplary life of the pastor, added to his care for his flock, has aided in bringing about so desirable a result. He is a pleasant speaker, and well versed on theological topics. As a scholar, his attainments are of a high order. In June, 1871, the honorary degree of doctor of divinity was conferred upon him by Washington and Jefferson college, Pennsylvania. By long service in the ministry, accomplished scholarship, and a profound knowledge of theology, he had fairly won his promotion. He is now in fair health, and may survive many years to carry out the great mission upon which he entered in early life.

His family consists of his wife and eight children. One is not. Five are sons and three were daughters. John F., the oldest, resides in Mankato; William W., the second, James A., the fifth, and Etta B., the sixth, reside in Cleveland; Henry M., the third, at home; Samuel N., the fourth, in Dakota; Mary E. in Van Wert, Ohio; all of whom have had good educational advantages and training.

WILLIAM A. G. EMERSON

was born near Alexandria, Virginia, July 12, 1816. He grew to manhood in Fairfax county, Virginia. In 1836 he came to Ohio, having married Miss Catharine Atkins in 1835, when he was but nineteen years of age. His father, Rev. Richard Dumont Emerson, had preceded him to Ohio, and exercised great influence over him. In the meantime his father had connected as a minister with the Lutheran church. William, although from boyhood a member of the Methodist church, and recently licensed as a local preacher, was urged also to unite with the Lutheran church, which he finally did in 1845. He evinced a talent that at once attracted attention, and was soon employed to preach at Bridgeport, Wayne county, and from thence, about 1847, came to Ashland, Ohio, and was employed to preach at the Lutheran church, a little frame, on the corner of Third and Orange streets. He was then thirty-one years old, and possessed all the enthusiasm of youth, and an imagination and zeal that glowed with fervid eloquence. We remember, right well, his appearance in the pulpit. He attracted a great deal of attention, and exerted a wonderful power as a young but gifted minister in the Lutheran church. It will be remembered that many of the leading young lawyers—General John S. Fulton, Professor John Rankin, James Sloan, and many of the brightest students from the old academy, were accustomed to crowd into the little frame church on the corner, on Sunday evenings, to hear the eloquent young preacher. This little church had been purchased from the Universalists about 1842, and the membership was quite feeble. In a few years such had been its increase in members under the preaching of this remarkable young man, that the place of meeting had to be changed, and resulted in the erection of the present church on Third street, which was built in 1852. Mr. Emerson laid aside his robes, and toiled like a day laborer to secure the completion of the church. His salary was small, yet he contributed, in toil and money, as much as many wealthy members toward the work. Often have we seen him with one horse and wagon, clothed like a laborer, engaged in hauling bricks and mortar for the work. It went rapidly forward, and in due time was dedicated.

Soon after, for some unknown reason, he was permitted to engage his ministerial services to the congregation at Wooster, where he remained until 1854. In 1855 he removed to Hayesville, where he preached about one year, and was then employed by the congregation at Mt. Zion, Richland county, where he remained until 1859, and then preached one year at Newville. From thence he went to Independence and Bellville until 1861, when he returned to Ashland, where he was appointed chaplain of the One Hundred and Twentieth regiment of Ohio independent militia, and was at Vicksburgh, Mississippi, during the winter of 1862-3, and in consequence of enfeebled health, returned to Ashland, and in the fall of 1863, was elected probate judge of Ashland county. His election was contested, and early in 1864 the court awarded the office to the contestant. The contestor and contestant have now removed the case to that court where neither judge nor jury err, and where equal and exact justice will be awarded all men.

In 1855-56 he remained in Ashland, frequently preaching to his friends in various parts of the county. In 1866 he was employed by the Lutheran congregation at Brookville, near Dayton, as their pastor, and remained there about two years. In 1868 he removed to Florence, Kentucky, and connected with the Methodist conference of that part of the State, and was assigned to a circuit, where he preached two years. In 1869-70 he preached upon a circuit at Germantown. In 1870 he was assigned a circuit at Bryantsville for one year, and, at the expiration of that time, removed to Mercer, where he remained until 1872, and, in 1873, was sent to a station at Augusta, where he labored two years, and, in 1875, worn down with hard work, enfeebled in health, and much discouraged, he returned to Ashland, where he made his home at the residence of his favorite daughter, Irene, and son-in-law, Mr. Daniel Folk, where he died on Tuesday, November 11, 1879, of acute pneumonia, aged sixty-three years and five months. Mrs. Folk and her husband did all they could to render his situation comfortable, peaceful, and pleasant. He passed away without a struggle, so calmly, sitting upon a chair and resting his head upon the back of another, that it was some moments before it was noticed that he had departed. He looked so natural that it was difficult to realize that he slept not. In his last conversations, he expressed a readiness for the change. The case was indeed a sad one. His whole life had been full of turmoil, disappointments and hardships. The storm is now over, and he has gone home, where critics and censorious people can no longer add a pang to his grief. God is just and will reward.

Mr. Emerson was not well adapted to the accumulation and retention of wealth. The science of finance was no part of his study. He had not a venal breath in his whole nature. He was genial, and moved by the warmest impulses. In his address he was earnest and amiable. He loved his friends and treated all men kindly and courteously. He spoke truly to the poor, and never shunned them in their distress. In his last days his wardrobe was greatly neglected. Naturally fastidious and tidy in his dress, he felt this apparent neglect most keenly, and had nearly disappeared from a curious public. He was unable to toil as a common laborer, and too much prostrated physically and mentally, to labor in the pulpit; in his extreme sensitiveness and humiliation, he said to the writer, a short time before his decease: "I am very poor—have always been poor. I never had money to give the rich. I always labored for the poor, and when my work is done, I hope, like the poor man mentioned in Sacred Writ, I may find a place of rest in the paradise of God." He was naturally hopeful and buoyant in spirit, and every expression of cheerfulness and genialty was criticised and turned to his injury. This was all wrong. True, a minister should be careful and guarded in his intercourse and conversation, but we are too apt to be severe in our criticisms. A preacher is but a man, and often has to govern his own frailties. It is certainly proper that a minister cultivate a cheerful, hopeful, and sprightly habit, casting aside the gloomy deportment of the hermit. His usefulness largely depends upon his friendliness, sympathy, and his cheerfulness. The Saviour did not hesitate to dine and associate with sinners. He did so because he could the better impress his character and teachings upon his hearers. Many remarkable teachers have been crushed or pushed into obscurity by a fault-finding and captious public.

Mr. Emerson had none of the early advantages of collegiate training, neither was he permitted to spend years of study in some theological seminary. Nature had done all for him. He was endowed with fine ability, and an uncommon versatility in the use of words. He never hesitated, even during the glowing flights of imagination, for words to fitly, fully, and elegantly express his ideas. When addressing an audience, the spirit of genius awakened his whole countenance. Tall in person, spare in form, with a voice musical and impressive, and great earnestness and energy in the delivery of his discourses, he always spoke with the utmost effect. He threw such a force and power into his sermons, that the magic of his address seemed to electrify the hearer as if touched by sacred fire. His clear, strong voice and energetic manner carried an audience along, and moved it to pity or thoughtfulness. He was sympathetic in manner, and clothed his words in beautiful images, and painted to the mind and heart the wonderful majesty and goodness of the Supreme Father of all. Large audiences crowded to hear him in the South, and the presence of so many faces seemed to electrify him, and call forth his wonderful powers as a pulpit orator. He is gone, and we shall never hear his eloquent voice again. He has gone home until the summing up of all things. It will be a long time before the impress of his preaching will fail to be remembered in this and other communities.

Mr. Emerson was of French descent, and possessed many of the genial traits of that most polite and remarkable people. He had eight children, four boys and four girls, all grown and married.

His friends secured him a nice metallic case, in which his body now reposes, in the Lutheran cemetery lot. A funeral discourse was delivered at the church by Rev. Wilhelm, and brief addresses made by Revs. John Robinson, Miller and Moody, after which he was conducted by Captain Finger and company to the cemetery, and buried with military honors, Thursday afternoon, November 13, 1879.

MR. ENOCH TAYLOR

was born in Litchfield, Connecticut, May 21, 1793. In his youth he served an apprenticeship at the trade of a shoemaker.* He married in his native county, in April, 1814, and removed to Ruggles township, Huron county, Ohio, in 1828. He erected a cabin north of the corners, in the midst of a dense forest. He cut away the trees in the vicinity of the cabin, and made a garden for vegetables. When he entered the township there were but about a dozen families in it. Wild game was quite plenty, so much so, that he often shot deer in the vicinity of his cabin. Wild turkeys were uncommonly numerous, and fed upon beach-nuts and acorns. Wild hogs often approached the cabin. He obtained his meal and flour from a mill in the vicinity of Savannah, often carrying a few pecks of corn along the paths on his shoulders. Like his pioneer neighbors, he underwent, for many years, all the hardships incident to the early settlement of this county. When he erected his first cabin there were few to aid him. The settlement of the township at that time was greatly embarrassed by eastern speculators, who owned and refused to part with the lands at a fair price. Mr. Taylor, in his lifetime, expressed the opinion that he had made the first pair of boots in the center of the township. He followed his trade for many years, in connection with the cultivation of a small farm, and by the joint result of both occupations raised and educated his family. In person he was of medium size, pale, nervous and full of genuine Yankee vivacity. He could not resist the perpetration of a joke even to the last. He was a man of excellent habits. He had been a member of the Congregational church for a long series of years, and adhered with much firmness to its doctrines. In 1875 he lost the wife of his youth, with whom he had lived over half a century in great happiness. In September, 1875, he attended and became a member of the Pioneer and Historical society of Ashland county, and expressed much gratification over the organization of such a society. He was then in feeble health, and expressed the opinion that he would never meet the pioneers again. He died of general debility, February 15, 1876. His family consisted of two sons, Clark Taylor, of Iowa, and George Taylor, of Ruggles, who resides on the old homestead, and two girls, Sarah, wife of James Grinold, of Ruggles, and Mary, wife of Argalious Peck, now deceased.

*Mr. Taylor served three years in the war of 1812, in Connecticut when about nineteen years of age.

JACOB HELBERT

was born in Montgomery county, Pennsylvania, June 1, 1794. His parents were of German descent. During his youth he attended a German school in his native county, and became a fair scholar in that language, which he talked fluently. In 1814, in September, he volunteered to serve in the war against Great Britain. He entered a company commanded by Captain George Hartman, and was stationed about twenty-five miles northwest of Philadelphia. He saw no active service. In December, 1814, he was discharged and returned home. He now (1876) draws a pension of ninety-six dollars per annum for his services during the war of 1812. In 1812 he married in his native county. His wife was two years his senior, and survived until 1872, when she deceased at the advanced age of eighty years. Mr. Helbert removed to Mohican township, Wayne, now Ashland, county, in 1835, and located adjoining the village of Mohicanville, where he purchased a farm. In connection with his enterprise as a farmer, he engaged in selling dry goods in the village, for a number of years. He now resides with a daughter—Mrs. Wachtell—and is quite frail in body, though his memory of the past is quite perfect. He is an upright citizen; a conscientious and courteous old gentleman, and much respected by all his acquaintances. His family consisted of eight sons, Jacob, Michael, Peter, Henry, Levi, Edmond, John, and one deceased; and five daughters: Mrs. John Newman, Mrs. Charles Cosner, Mrs. Henry Wachtell, and two deceased. His children all reside within the limits of Ashland county, and are noted for their industry and intelligence.

ABRAHAM DOTY

was born in West Virginia, in 1779, and in 1816, removed with his family to Milton township, Richland (now Ashland,) county, where he located a farm, and remained eight years, and then sold and located a larger tract, which he improved and remained upon until his decease, in 1843. He was one of the pioneer Presbyterians of Milton township, and assisted in the organization of "old Hopewell church," of which he became an elder and leading member.

At his decease his family consisted of James Doty, the first sheriff of Ashland county, Peter, Elizabeth, John, Joseph, Martha, Jackson, Samuel, Mary, Sarah, and Jane. They are all living but Sarah, who married Joseph Hill, of Hayesville.

Joseph Doty was born in West Virginia, August 2, 1812, and accompanied his father's family to Milton in 1816. In 1835 he purchased his homestead in Mifflin township; and in 1838, married Rachel Lambright, daughter of John Lambright, who had located in Mifflin township prior to the Ruffner–Zimmer–Copus tragedies in 1812.

The family of Joseph Doty consists of six girls and three boys, all of whom survive but one girl, the wife of Joseph Staffer, of Ashland; and are all located in Ashland county, but two married daughters, who reside in Indiana. The Doty family have long been attached to the Presbyterian faith.

Mr. Doty has creditably filled several township offices, but prefers the plain life of a farmer to the duties and criticisms of a public officer. He has been a life-long Democrat.

REV. WILLIAM HUGHES,

of Green township, was born in Beaver county, Pennsylvania, May 20, 1802. He attended a primary school and academy, at Darlington, and graduated at Jefferson college, Cannonsburgh, Pennsylvania, and studied theology at Princeton, New Jersey, and was licensed to preach June 24, 1829. He came west in August, and, having preached a few trial discourses in September, 1829, it was arranged for him to preach steadily at Perrysville, and in Lake township, now in Ashland county. He occupied the pulpit, in Perrysville, from 1829 to November 17, 1866, a period of over twenty-seven years. He retired in consequence of failing health. He is now disabled by chronic rheumatism. During his pastorate, at Perrysville, he preached at several places in the south part of this county; some of them statedly, on Sabbath evenings and week days.

When he settled in Green township, in 1829, there were no church buildings in either Green, Hanover, or Lake townships. The larger part of that territory was then covered with a primitive forest, unbroken, save where were found the scattered cabins of the pioneers. The preachers of that era met their congregations in the cabins of the new settlers, or in log schoolhouses. Mr. Hughes has lived to see the forests leveled, and hundreds of farms opened and improved where wild game resorted forty years ago. The sons of the pioneers have productive farms and fine improvements, and comfortable residences, and are blessed with abundance. Great has been the change. Dozens of school-houses, neat and comfortably furnished, are now to be seen, where fifty years before the red man had scarcely ceased to hunt. Then there were no churches. Now we find one Methodist, one Presbyterian, one German Reformed, and two Baptist churches in Green; and one Methodist, one Baptist, one Presbyterian, one German Reformed, and one Catholic church, in Hanover; and one Lutheran, one Presbyterian, and one German Reformed in Lake; in the aggregate, containing several hundred members.

Mr. Hughes now resides on his farm in the vicinity of what is known as Meanor's mill, on the Loudonville road, in the east part of Green township, where, when not engaged in the active service of his congregation, he performed, for many years, a good deal of manual labor in the improvement of his farm. He is very comfortably situated.

He was married in 1830, and has had seven children, six boys, and one girl. Of the sons, one is a farmer, the other a physician, three are ministers; and an only daughter, the wife of a minister. The others are deceased.

It will be seen, therefore, that Mr. Hughes can be congratulated upon his effort to educate and prepare his children for usefulness. Few men have accomplished as much. He died in July, 1880.

JOSEPH SHEETS

was born in New Jersey, about thirty miles below Philadelphia, Pennsylvania, January 21, 1792, and came to Steubenville, Jefferson county, Ohio, about 1806, where he worked at his trade as tailor for seven or eight years. He came to Uniontown, now Ashland, in 1817, and was among the earliest tailors in the place. About the time of his location, he married Miss Nancy Harper, daughter of William Harper, who removed from Steubenville in 1815, and settled in Vermillion township, then of Richland, but now of Ashland county, where he remained with his family until 1832, when he was unfortunately killed by his team, while hauling wheat to Milton, near Plymouth, aged sixty-eight years. Mr. Sheets survived until March 6, 1866, when he died, aged about seventy-four years. At his decease, he had the following family: Elizabeth, Joseph (dead), William, Mariah, Martha, Samuel, Alfred (dead), Mary and Sarah. Mrs. Sheets still survives. She was born in Fairfax county, Virginia, June 12, 1796, and is over eighty-four years old, and yet possesses a clear intellect, and is quite active for one of her age. Mr. Sheets originally owned the eighty acres of land upon which South Ashland was laid out.

Mrs. Sheets lives on the south margin of town, where a large number of the old settlers of Ashland and vicinity assembled, to celebrate her eighty-fourth birthday. The old lady had been kindly invited by Mrs. Judge Kenny, to spend the afternoon with her, tea included; and while the time was passing, ladies assembled in multitudes, took possession of her house, and like busy bees went to work preparing supper. Ere Mother Sheets was aware of what was being done, all was ready, and the good old lady invited back to her own house, to be entertained there. The attendance was large, numbering, perhaps, nearly one hundred. Besides a large number of her friends and neighbors of the long ago, in the pioneer age, many of her present neighbors were there to share in the festivities, as well as to do her honor by their presence and encouragement. Mother Sheets came to this county in 1817, and was, of course, one of the earliest settlers of Montgomery township. The tables were furnished abundantly with all the good things that the market supplied, and the ladies maintained their well-deserved reputation, which has become proverbial for excelling the world in the getting up of choice viands.

Mr. John Harper, of Vermillion, one of the oldest settlers of that township, and brother of Mrs. Sheets, was present, and although he bears the burden of ninety years, still appears hale and hearty. He came to Vermillion in 1816. Mrs. Polly Strickland, widow of Joseph Strickland, was also present; a fine appearing lady who bears the weight of seventy-five years well. Francis Graham, esq., ex-president of the Pioneer association, of Ashland county, was present, and although somewhat feeble, and carrying eighty-eight years, was still able to do justice to a well-filled table, and without doubt hopes to live many years, and enjoy many another agreeable meeting with old friends. Many others were there also, old and venerable, their gray hairs and wrinkled visages showed them to be toilers of years; and though aged they still had not forgotten how to enjoy themselves. Among the ladies a list was obtained of names and ages, but some, being so much older than any one dared to dream, while others were so much younger than hope ever whispered, it is deemed best not to publish the list without unanimous consent. It may not be best to individualize when all did so well, or tell tales out of school, still it was a warm day, and Mr. McNulty's ice-cream tasted so good that it cannot well be avoided in this instance.

Mrs. Sheets desires that her thanks be publicly expressed to her friends and neighbors for their kindness and thoughtfulness in remembering her in the loneliness of age, and that her blessings will follow them in their journey of life, and that it will be long remembered as an epoch in her life.

Rev. Persons introduced Rev. Dr. Robinson, who closed the services with prayer.

Thus has passed another of our profitable and interesting pic-nic sociables, and it is hoped they will continue to be held from time to time, as long as a single pioneer is left.

REV. THOMAS BEER

was born in Northampton county, Pennsylvania, March 22, 1807. His father removed to Allegheny county the same year, and settled on a farm on the north side of the Ohio river, on which the flourishing town of Sewickley now stands, twelve miles below the city of Pittsburgh, Pennsylvania, until his twenty-third year. He enjoyed the advantages of a common school education, such as it was. In 1823 he commenced a classical course of study at an academy in Allegheny City, Pennsylvania. In 1825 he entered the Western university of Pennsylvania, graduating in 1827, with a class composed of seven, all of whom afterward became ministers of the gospel. In the fall of the same year he, with three other young men, entered the Western Theological seminary of the Presbyterian church, located in Allegheny City. Mr. Beer's name stands at the head of the roll, and he is the only survivor of the class. Leaving the seminary in the fall of 1830, under the auspices of the Home Missionary society of the Presbyterian church, he took charge of four small churches in the northwestern portion of Wayne county, Ohio. A few years later his labors were given to the two churches, Congress and Mt. Hope. From the spring of 1834 until 1859 he resided at Mt. Hope, Wayne county, now Ashland county. In the fall of 1859 he located on a farm three miles southwest of Ashland, where he still resides. In 1861 he took charge of the Presbyterian church in Jeromeville, where he labored until near the close of 1871, since which time, on account of the infirmities of age, he has had no parochial charge.

His family consisted of thirteen children, two of whom died in infancy—eleven lived to maturity. Dr. John Cameron, deceased 1865; Rev. Robert, of Valparaiso, Indiana; Judge Thomas, of Bucyrus, Ohio; Adeline, an invalid; Ashbel G. who lost a leg in the battle of Stone River, and for several years post-master at Ashland, and at this writing engaged as hardware merchant in Ashland; Henry M., lieutenant, and now physician at Valparaiso, Indiana; James A. died at Cumberland Gap; William N., captain, attorney at law, Iowa deceased in 1874; Charles E., deceased 1864; Richard C. and Mary L.

Feeling that his own education had been deferred too long, Mr. Beer has been assiduous in educating his family. The result is very gratifying. His children, upon arriving at the age of maturity, have entered upon the business of life with energy, and have attracted the good opinion of the public because of their integrity, efficiency and manhood.

JOHN ROBISON

was born June 16, 1791, in what was then Chester county, Pennsylvania, and upon arriving at the age of manhood married Miss Mary Hawk, who died in Pennsylvania about 1831. Mr. Robison came to Montgomery township about 1834, with his children, and stopped at the residence of David Robison, sr., his father. Soon after his arrival, July 4, 1836, Michael Ritter got up and prepared a dinner in Carter's grove, east of Ashland some two miles, where the youthful Lorin Andrews was the orator of the day. Mr. Ritter kept a hotel at that time where Finley's now stands. Mr. Robison was a carpenter by trade, and made paterns, etc., for the Penn foundry, in Northumberland, now Union county, Pennsylvania, where he was employed for many years. David Robison his father, came to Montgomery township in 1824, and died in 1842, aged about eighty years, and his wife about 1847, aged about eighty-four years. David Robison, jr., who served as justice of Montgomery township, removed to Indiana where he died many years ago. His family consisted of Wallace, Wilson, Willard, Fernandez, Hannah, Lucia, Aurilla and Rebecca.

His death resulted from a fall at the hardware store of Messrs. Stull & Charles, of Ashland, about the third of May 1880. The old gentleman was desirous of being weighed and passed into the store room with Mr. Charles to learn his weight, stating that he felt unusually well that morning, and on reaching the stairway stumbled and fell heavily upon the floor, striking his shoulder and fracturing it. He was rendered immediate assistance, and the injury dressed, when he was taken home, where he remained in a feeble condition until his death. He did not seem to rally from his wound, but did not appear to suffer much from it, and died on the evening of June 10, 1880.

At the time of his death Mr. Robison's surviving children were Percifer and Hannah.

He retained a fine memory to the last, and knew his friends at each visit. He was an honest, upright man, and always noted for punctuality and prompt dealing among his neighbors. We believe that he was respected by all, and had no enemies in the world. May he rest in peace.

HUGH DAVIS

was born in Franklin county, Pennsylvania, June 23, 1802, and died in Ashland, Ohio, June 13, 1876, aged seventy-four years.

Martha S. Davis was born in Franklin county, Pennsylvania, December 12, 1803, and died at Ashland, Ohio, April 8, 1870, aged sixty-six years, three months, and twenty-four days.

Hugh Davis came to Knox county, Ohio, about 1820, and returned to Pennsylvania in 1821, where he completed the trade of tanner, after which he married Martha S. Morrow, in 1829, and returned to Mount Vernon, Knox county, Ohio, and lived some months, working for James Loverage and Samuel Trimble, at the tanning business, and about 1829, located in Ashland upon the property now owned by Justus W. Davis, his son. He erected and carried on a tan house upon this lot, commencing business about 1830. Himself and the late George Swineford were the only tanners in the village. Mr. Swineford had purchased the property of George Croft, where the machine works of D. Whiting are now located, and carried on business, while Mr. Davis, as a rival, erected property on the east end of Main street.

The family of Mr. Davis consisted of Morrow H., Lester Finley, Justus Wilson, Sylvester Curtis, Josephine Agnes, Ilgar Vanleer, and Martha Estelle. The two girls are dead. The boys are all living and married.

Justus W. was born April 13, 1833, in Ashland county, and married Miss Catharine Jane Trimble, of Carlisle, Pennsylvania, daughter of Thomas Trimble, November 11, 1857, at Mount Vernon, Ohio. Their children are: Horace Urie, Thomas Trimble, and Mary Ellen.

Mr. and Mrs. Davis were originally members of the old Hopewell Presbyterian church, and, upon its sale and transfer to the Catholics, never united with the First church.

JOHN SWINEFORD

was born in Northumberland county, Pennsylvania, March 25, 1795. His father, Peter Swineford, located with his family in Fairfield county, Ohio, in 1807, and remained there until 1819, when he removed to Montgomery township, then in Richland, but now in Ashland county, and settled one mile and a half southeast of Ashland, then Uniontown. In February, 1823, Mr. Swineford married May, daughter of the late Jacob Young, and having erected a cabin, commenced to improve his farm. He remained on the homestead until 1857, when he moved into Ashland, where he now resides. Mr. Swineford gives the following statistics:

The first grist-mill in Montgomery township, one mile north of Ashland, by Thomas Oram, in spring of 1816.

First saw-mill, two miles from Ashland, in Milton township, by Allen Lockhart.

First church, Methodist Episcopal, at Eckley's, now Smith's mills, in Vermillion township, 1819, and Old Hopewell, in Milton, 1817.

First dry goods store in Uniontown, Joseph Sheets, succeeded by Francis Graham.

First blacksmith, Ludwick Cline, on Wooster road, two miles east of Ashland.

First cabinet-maker and undertaker, the late Alexander Miller.

First carding-machine, stood where Smiths' mill now is in Vermillion township, built by Andrew Newman; the next by the late Andrew and Uriah Drenub, in Ashland.

The first tannery stood where Whitings agricultural works now stand, built by John Croft, and subsequently owned by the late George Swineford.

The first wagon-shop, where Barkholder's saw-mill now stands, and was owned by Henry Wachtell.

The first blacksmith in Ashland was the late Samuel Urie.

The second cabinet-maker in Ashland, the late Jacob Grubb.

The family of Peter Swineford, father of John, consisted of George, John, Anthony, Samuel, and A. C. Swineford. They are all deceased, except John and Abram C., who reside in Ashland. Peter Swineford, sr., died January 30, 1849, aged seventy-eight years, and Samuel died January 13, 1862, aged sixty-two years. The family of John Swineford consisted of Abraham (dead), Lib (dead), Hannah, Mary, Nancy, and Austin. The family of Samuel Swineford consisted of Luther, Alfred P., James, Curtis, Sarah, Elsa, Jane and Emily.

HULBERT LUTHER.

He was born in Lanesborough, Berkshire county, Massachusetts, March 14, 1809, and attended the common schools of the neighborhood until he was fifteen years of age. In 1825, he emigrated to Lewis county, New York, and remained there until the spring of 1830, when he emigrated to Ashland, Ohio, where an older brother (Dr. Joel Luther) had located and entered upon the practice of medicine, some fourteen years before.

At that time, Dr. Luther and John P. Rezner were in company in the mercantile business, and Mr. Luther entered their employ as clerk. In 1831, he formed a partnership with John P. Rezner, and continued the same some six or eight years; and dissolved the arrangement, and formed a new firm with Jacob Crall, known as Luther & Crall, which continued until 1854. In 1849, the firm established a hardware store, under the management of George H. Topping, and the new firm was known as that of H. Luther & Co. In 1851, Luther, Crall & Co. established a bank of deposit and exchange in Ashland, which continued until 1864, when the same stockholders, under a law of Congress, established the First National Bank of Ashland, and Mr. Luther became its president, and Jacob O. Jennings, cashier; and retained the position until 1870, when he withdrew his stock, and Jacob O. Jennings became president. At that time, Mr. Luther purchased a farm in Milton township, in this county, and for about five years gave his attention to agriculture. Some time prior he owned and conducted the steam flouring mills of South Ashland, and was one of the principal proprietors of the woollen factory connected with it. In 1874, he engaged in the sale of ready-made furniture, and continued to carry on the business until his decease.

For a period of forty-nine years he has been actively engaged as a business man in Ashland. When he arrived it was a mere village. His business career, and his bearing as a citizen, have been influential and honorable. He has done as much as any other citizen to promote the growth and prosperity of the place. He was for a long time postmaster of the town, and was very influential in securing the location of the county-seat at this point. At a period when the markets were distant, and the transportation of the surplus products of the country exceedingly expensive, he paid the farmers and producers liberally for their products. In this respect, the interests of the farming portion of the community were promoted, and those of the merchant enhanced. In habits, Mr. Luther was retired, and, though reserved in manner, in conversation he was fluent and agreeable.

Though chronically dyspeptic, he was regarded as a well preserved man of his age, and his prospects of long life were thought to be fair. His sudden demise, unexpected, enables us to realize that in the midst of life we are in death, and what shadows we are and what shadows we pursue.

Mr. Luther was an exemplary member of the Disciple or Christian church for a number of years.

Mr. Luther married Miss Lydia E. Wicoff, of Ashland, February 17, 1835. His family consisted of his wife and three children—Joel H., and two daughters—Helen, wife of John Holland, of Cleveland; and Emily, wife of Andrew J. Burns, of Ashland.

Mr. Luther died Saturday evening, March 15, 1879, aged seventy years and one day, after a brief illness. The remains of Mr. Luther were deposited in the cemetery of Ashland, on Tuesday, March 18, 1879. May he rest in peace.

The circumstances attending the last illness, and decease of Mr. Luther, though generally known in this community, may be repeated in this connection. On Saturday, March 1st, he had gone into the garden for some purpose, when he found his strength failing him, and at once attempted a return to the house. Finding he could not succeed in this, he called to his daughter, Mrs. Burns, who sat by a window near by. Before that lady could reach him, however, he had fallen to the ground, and lapsed into unconsciousness. By the time aid had been summoned, and his removal to the house had been effected, sensibility returned, and towards evening the heart had resumed its normal condition. From this time until the middle of the following week he gradually rallied, and hopes were entertained of his recovery. But on Thursday he grew rapidly worse, to rally slightly the day following, and to relapse again and pass peacefully away Saturday afternoon. With the exception of one short moment of unconsciousness when he was first stricken, he retained his senses until the last moment, conversing easily with his family and friends until death took him.

THOMAS COLE, SR.,

was born in Baltimore county, Maryland, March 20, 1796. His grandfather, Aquilla Cole, came from England and settled near Baltimore about 1760. After the close of the Revolutionary war, when the lands of Kentucky came into market, he started on a journey to that region with the intention of purchasing a large tract of land and finally locating there. On his way through Ohio, while traveling along "Zane's trace," from Wheeling to the present site of Zanesville, in crossing the main stream of Wills creek, his horse became entangled in driftwood, the stream being full and deep, and he was drowned. His traveling comrades all escaped, and recovered and buried his remains near where he met his melancholy death. His estate, under the old English law, fell to his oldest son. His sons were Thomas, Elijah, Aquilla, Salathiel, Mycagy, and Stephen. They all removed to Kentucky but Thomas and Stephen. Thomas finally located in Washington county, Pennsylvania, while Stephen removed to Fairfield county, Ohio, about the year 1809. Stephen was twice married in Maryland, prior to his removal. He died in Fairfield county, leaving the following family: Stephen, Salathiel, Thomas, Charles, who died in infancy, Abraham, Mycagy, John, Eleanor, Mary, Richard, Charles, Wesley, Elijah, and Eliza. Stephen and Thomas came to Jackson township, Wayne county, now Ashland county, in August, 1819. Thomas had married in 1816, and had one child at the time of his removal. On his route from Fairfield he came by Newark, Mount Vernon, Bellville, Greentown, Jeromeville, and over the east part of Montgomery township to the forest home of William Bryan, south of the present site of Polk, where he remained until he and his brother cut a path to section eight, southeast and southwest quarters. When they selected a site for a cabin their wives stitched a number of linen sheets together and a tent was erected, in which they lived until the cabin could be erected and prepared for occupation. The third day was Sunday, and with the night came a heavy rain. His child was sick, and the rain beat through the tent. The bed became wet, and Mr. Cole sat upright with the quilt over his head to protect his sick child. Fortunately the next morning his child was better. He retains a vivid recollection of that introductory storm, and his altitude as "center-pole." Salathiel, with a team, accompanied them to their wilderness home, and returned to Fairfield by the path he came. When the cabin was raised, Mr. Cole states that most of the hands were from the present vicinity of the village of Orange. He squared his house to the meridian by observing the section line, setting up and plumbing a stake and watching when the sun shadow pointed due north.

Upon his arrival he found the following families in the north half of the township: Rev. John Hazzard, John Mason, Mr. Morton, Thomas Green, Josiah Lee, Jesse Matthews, Laffler, and James Durfee, and in the south half, Noah Long, Jonas H. Gierhart, James A. Dinsmore, John Jackson, Michael and Matthias Rickel, William Bryan, Charles Hoy, and John Davault. A number of other families arrived during the fall of 1819. Stephen and Thomas Cole brought a number of milch cows and young cattle, and two or three head of horses. A favorite mare escaped and attempted to return to Fairfield, but was pursued and captured, after a lively chase of several hours in the south part of the township. Wild grass was abundant in the forest, and cattle thrived upon it. Mr. Cole, by industry, and the assistance of his pioneer neighbors, soon prepared fields for culture. There were no schools or churches at his arrival in the township. Rev. Mr. Hazzard was a gentleman of good English education, and soon volunteered to instruct the children of the pioneers. He resided in the northeast part of the township, on section eleven. In 1822-3 Mr. Hazzard also established the first class of the Methodist Episcopal church, of which he was leader and teacher. He became a local preacher of the Methodist Episcopal church. The class was established in what has since become the village of Perrysburgh—known sometimes as Albion, the name of its post-office. The first class contained about ten members; Josiah Lee was at one time a leader. Mr. Cole became a member in 1825, and about 1830, a leader and exhorter, and in 1840 was licensed a local preacher and still retains his license. The Rev. Mr. Hazzard died in 1870 and was buried on his homestead. Mr. Cole, and we believe, Mr. Hazzard also, was licensed by that venerable and much loved pioneer minister, Rev. Elmer Yocum. Mr. Cole is now (1876) deprived of his vision, having been afflicted some years with opacity of the crystalline lens, or cataract. His general health is good, and his disposition quite cheerful. Mrs. Cole, his excellent wife, who shared his pioneer toils, deceased May 8, 1870, aged seventy-four. His children are: Thomas Cole, jr.; Elizabeth, wife of Chester C. Matthews; Rebecca, wife of Joseph C. Bolles; Mary, wife of Jacob Plice; Rachel, wife of Isaac Gordon, deceased, and Ruthie, wife of James Campbell, of Iowa. Mr. Cole has forty-six grandchildren, and twenty-five great-grandchildren. Most of his children reside in Ashland county.

Rev. Thomas Cole died of paralysis, May 17, 1880, aged eighty-four years, one month, and twenty-seven days.

This sketch was written in 1876, when Mr. Cole was in fair health. His infirmities of vision gradually grew worse, until his decease on the 17th.

HENRY BROTHERS

was born in Beaver county, Pennsylvania, December 11, 1804. When a babe, his parents removed to Stark county, this State, where he resided until the year 1827, when he removed to this county, where he resided until his death, making him a resident of Ashland county for over fifty years.

On May 20, 1825, he was married to Miss Mary Duffy. The fruits of this union are eleven children, seven of whom are still living: Nathaniel, Mary, Ruth, John, Elizabeth Ann, Ursula, and Franklin. The ones deceased were: Catharine, Hannah, Nancy, and Jonas. They were all born in this county but Nathaniel; and all that are living are married but one, Franklin C.

Mr. Brothers settled in Rowsburg, at a time when there were but one or two houses in the place, as well as in Ashland. At that time Ashland was called Uniontown. He used to often recall the many hardships and privations that he, together with others, had to contend with, that the present as well as future generations will never know or experience.

He never professed religion, but always tried to live an upright life. Although he had his faults as well as virtues, and which the human family are all heir to, his friends have the satisfaction to know he enjoyed the respect and esteem of those in the community where he resided, and have their sympathy in their sad bereavement.

Mr. Brothers died at his late residence, May 14, 1880. We commend his spirit to Him who gave it, and trust his ashes may rest in peace.

WILLIAM RAMSEY

was born in Maryland and removed to Jackson township, Wayne county, in 1823, and has resided in Jackson township about forty seven years. When he located the original settlers were Charles Hoy, John Baker, John Russell, Noah Long, John Jackson, William Bryan, Elisha Chilcote, John Tucker, John Davault, John Swaney and Robert Crawford, who owned a horse-mill, and finally went to Missouri. He owns a good farm and has it under fine cultivation, with fine buildings. Mr. Ramsey is now about eighty-two years of age.

MICHAEL RIDDLE, SR.,

son of George and Mary Riddle, was born August 21, 1793, in Maryland. His father was of Scotch-Irish descent, and his mother was a native of Maryland, and of Welsh descent. His father died and was buried on Crows' Island, when the subject of this sketch was but ten years old; and at the age of sixteen he came into Fayette county, Pennsylvania, and engaged to serve an apprenticeship at blacksmithing, with a Mr. Peter Herdsack, for a term of five years. But a short time before the expiration of said term, and in the fall of 1812, the Ruffner, Zimmer, and Copus assassination on the Black fork of Mohican took place, by the Indians.

Volunteers from western Pennsylvania were called out to defend the border settlers in Ohio. He entered the service as one of the volunteers, for a term of six months, under General Robert Crooks, and passed over the territory now constituting Ashland and Richland counties, en route for Upper Sandusky; was at all the principal points along the rivers and lakes, from Fort Meigs, on the Maumee, to Toledo, Detroit and Cleveland, under General Harrison. He became acquainted with Col. Richard M. Johnston, of Kentucky; and was finally detailed to take charge of the sick on Put-in-Bay and South Bass islands, where he remained most of the time for which he had enlisted.

He stood by and saw James Bird shot for deserting Perry's fleet; and in the spring of 1813 he returned to Fayette county, Pennsylvania, worked at his trade, and in the fall, September 11, 1814, married Miss Barbara Ann Franks, daughter of George and Abigail Franks, of Fayette county, Pennsylvania. The result of said marriage was eleven children, nine sons and two daughters. George W., was born in Fayette county, Pennsylvania, June 5, 1815; Aaron, born in same county, February 10, 1817. And in the spring of 1818, he removed with his little family to Applecreek, Wayne county, Ohio, at which place his daughter Abigail was born, December 31, 1818. And in the spring of 1820, he located on eighty acres of military school land, four miles northeast of Ashland, then Uniontown, on the Cleveland road, it being then in Richland county, and there he erected his little log cabin in which to live, surrounded by a dense forest of tall oak and hickory, as well as beech and maple. And in the fall of the same year, November 28, 1820, his son, Samuel was born. Then Michael, jr., born October 28, 1822; John R., born April 12, 1824; Jacob, born January 12, 1826; Cornelius, born December 8, 1827; Jesse, born August 3, 1830; Mary Ann, born January 9, 1832; and William Patterson, born October 31, 1834; of these, Jacob, Jesse, Cornelius, Aaron, and Mary Ann are dead.

Aaron married Miss Delia Ann Alexander, February 15, 1838, who died August 17, of the same year. George W., married Miss Ruth Alexander, October 23, 1838, who also died, May 31, 1839; George's second marriage, to Miss Jane Scott, March 31, 1842, by whom he has eleven children—John S., dead; Sarah, Cornelius F., Ira A., Jane Irene, dead, Samantha Ann, Sophia S., Eliza E., Rebecca A., Flora and Dora, twins. Of these Samantha Ann, Sophia S., and Eliza E., are school teachers. Aaron's second marriage was with Miss Elizabeth McCammon, November 1, 1843. They have had four children—three boys and one girl: Marshall W., dead; Almon G., dead; Judson B., in the far west; and Lucy Jane, school teacher, wife of Joseph Welch, a farmer. Aaron died November 17, 1851, aged thirty-four years nine months and seven days. Abigail remains single.

Samuel married Miss Margaret Dally, of Mohicanville, November 16, 1843. The result of said marriage was nine children, three boys and six girls.

Michael, jr., married Miss Catharine Hatfield, of Doylestown, Ohio, February 1, 1849. Result of marriage, six children, two boys and four girls.

Mary Ann was married to James A. Hazlett, and had seven children, three boys and four girls; Willie, dead; John, Ellie, Ettie, Lucy, Phoenie, and James Franklin.

William Patterson married Kate D. Stents, December 10, 1861, and has three children—Orwell, Emma, and Norman. Two of his sons, Samuel and Michael, turned their attention somewhat to the subject of education, and attended the Ashland academy, under the superintendence of the Fultons and Lorin Andrews. After teaching school each several terms, the former turned his attention to the study and practice of medicine; the latter, to the ministry of the Gospel. The other members of the family are farmers, and live on and near the old homestead.

Mr. Riddle was noted for his habits of industry, economy, and self reliance. He was an excellent farmer, and experimented largely in choice varieties of fruits, and is believed to have manufactured the first wine in Montgomery township, from the catawba grape. In his earlier years he was an active member of the Baptist church; he and his wife were baptized by Elder John Rigdon, who was then a pioneer preacher, living in Clearcreek township, Richland county; but when Alexander Campbell began to publish his views of church doctrine and government, in what was called the *Christian Baptist*, first published in 1823, Mr. Riddle embraced the doctrine of the Disciples, and assisted Mr. Rigdon and others in organizing a church in Ashland. Many years, however, before the little church-house was built which stands on Orange street, of which he was one of the original trustees, he opened his own house for public worship; he made it the home of all the old pioneer preachers, as they passed through from place to to place; and not unfrequently they held protracted meetings at his house. He entertained on many occasions from forty to fifty people at a time, giving largely of his means to support the ministers, besides. He was for a long time the only elder of the church, but in after years, others were appointed to assist him.

He unfortunately received a mortal injury in a fall from an apple tree, October 28, 1857, from which he expired in a few hours, aged sixty-four years two months and twenty-seven days. His wife died June 15, 1880, aged sixty-seven years five months and seven days.

He was a life-long Democrat, of the Jeffersonian and Andrew Jackson school, and was never known to vary his vote in any case.

PETER VAN NORDSTRAND, SR.,

was born in New Jersey, and, after the close of the Revolutionary war, emigrated to Westmoreland county, Pennsylvania. His ancestors were from Holland. In

1816 he came to Clearcreek township, Richland (now Ashland) county, and located on section thirty-five, where he deceased, in 1817, aged about fifty years. He had been a neighbor to the Baileys and Brytes in Westmoreland county, and was induced to settle in the wilds of Clearcreek because of their emigration to that region. A brother-in-law, Archibald Gardner, located in Mifflin, on the present site of Windsor, in the spring of 1811, and forted at Ream's in 1812.

Mr. Van Nordstrand's sons were: John, who subsequently removed to, and deceased, in Iowa; Isaac, who also located in Iowa, and Peter, who continues to reside in Clearcreek township. The daughters were: Elizabeth, wife of Abraham Bebout; Anna, wife of William Andrews; Rachel, wife of David Urie; Effie, wife of Alexander McCready; Eleanor, wife of James McCool; Margaret, wife of Michael Shoup; Mary, wife of David Bryte, and Sarah, wife of John Mykrants.

Peter married Nancy Shaw, and is now about seventy-two years of age. He states that when his father landed in Clearcreek, there were but eight or ten families in the township. The first school-house in his part of the township was a little cabin of round logs, erected on the farm of the late Abraham Huffman, in 1817. The children of the following householders attended, Mr. Robert Nelson being the first teacher: Abraham Huffman, John Brown, Andrew Stevison, Robert Ralston, Widow Trickle, David McKinny, Rev. William Matthews, Levi and Thomas Brink, Widow Mary Van Nordstrand, and the children of Robert Nelson. The country was in its primitive condition, game was plenty, and the Indians from Sandusky hunted annually in the forests of Clearcreek for a number of years after the arrival of the first settlers. They were harmless, and rarely visited the cabins of the pioneers, except when they were driven to do so from pinching hunger.

Peter Van Nordstrand, jr., occupied the old homestead until about 1872, when his wife deceased. He is now residing with a son-in-law. He has been an exemplary member of the Christian church for over thirty years. His wife was also a devoted member of the same church. It is rarely that men, in a single community, witness the changes that have taken place within this county in the last sixty years. From an almost unbroken forest, the hills and valleys of this county have been reduced to cultivation, and every township teams with abundance. Schools, villages, and towns have sprung into being, as if by magic. From a few hundred the inhabitants of the county have multiplied until our population reaches over twenty-three thousand. The Indian that roamed over the hills and along the fertile valleys of this county, has long since removed to the far west, and his race will, ere long, become extinct.

THE MERCERS.

Abner E. Mercer was born in Virginia, January 19, 1810. He emigrated with his family to Jackson county, Ohio, in 1812. From that county his father, Levi Mercer, served as a soldier in the war of 1812, in the northwest. In 1824 he removed with his family to Milton township, Richland, now Ashland, county, where he entered a half section of land in section six. He deceased in 1850, and his wife in 1853; he at the age of seventy years, and she at seventy-three. They left a numerous family—thirteen children—Sabra, Elizabeth, Levi, Maria, Hale, Abner, Sarah, Mary, Jackson, Franklin, Mohada, Washington, and Caroline, and about one hundred grandchildren.

Ebner E. was the sixth member of the family, and has resided on a part of the home farm since arriving at manhood. He attended the common schools of the township, and learned the trade of a plasterer. He married Miss Thankful Crabbs, daughter of John Crabbs, near Olivesburg, Richland county, February 17, 1834. In 1835 he became a member of the Disciple church, and adorned his faith by an upright walk. In 1844 he became the elder of Bryte's church, and was devoted to his faith.

Mr. Mercer was also a farmer of industrious habits and admitted integrity and uprightness. When he entered the township, in 1824, it was largely in its primitive condition. The native forest had been comparatively undisturbed by the woodman's axe. At that period cabin-raising, log-rolling, and wood-cutting were the principal occupations of the pioneers, who cheerfully volunteered their aid to assist those who sought a home amid the forests. Great have been the changes since the Mercers entered the township. Mr. Mercer, for the last six or seven years, had been greatly enfeebled by that fell destroyer, consumption. The immediate occasion of his last illness was pneumonia, of which he deceased February 23, 1877, and was interred at Bryte's church on the 24th.

He was the father of fourteen children—Jefferson, John, Levi, Polly, Madison, Abner, Sarah, Darius, Benjamin, William, Silas, Jacob, Nancy, and one unnamed. His funeral was attended by a large number of his neighbors, the members of his family, and fourteen grandchildren. Mr. Mercer still survives and is aged about sixty years.

Thus, one by one, the pioneers are being gathered home by the great reaper, and soon the funeral chime will have tolled the knell of the last early settler.

SOLOMON MARKEL

was born in Westmoreland county, Pennsylvania, December, 1813, and came with his parents to Congress township, Wayne county, in 1837. The name of his father was Solomon Markle, sr., who died in 1852, at the age of fifty-two years; his mother died in 1850, aged seventy-two years. Solomon located on section sixteen, Orange township, in 1837. He had married Miss Hannah Howman, of Congress, Wayne county, prior to locating in Orange. Their family consists of five boys, Jacob, Israel, Aaron, Franklin and Lewis C., and four girls, Mary, Margaret, Elizabeth and Hannah J. The children are all married but Lewis C. They are much scattered, living in the new States. Mr. Markel possesses a fine homestead of one hundred and sixty acres of well-improved land, on section sixteen, Orange township.

Israel Markel was born in Westmoreland county, Pennsylvania, February 7, 1819, and came with his father's family to Congress township, Wayne county, in April, 1835, where he remained until 1839, and married shortly after settling on section sixteen, in Orange township, Miss Mariah Ricket, in 1839. Mr. Markel has been a justice of the peace two terms, a constable two terms, and a coroner of the county one term, in 1846. He now resides in Ashland, but retains one hundred and seventy acres of his homestead in Orange township, on sections sixteen and nine. His family consists of six boys: Jacob W., George A., Samuel D., Israel C., a physician, Isaiah F. and Henry A., lawyer, and four daughters, Eliza, Rachel, Lucia A. and Artha M. Like the family of Solomon, they are much scattered in the west and in this State.

ELI W. WALLACK

was born September 3, 1828, in Tuscarawas county, Ohio, from whence, at the age of twenty years, he removed to Ashtabula county, Ohio, and remained until 1848, when he located in Ashland. At first he formed a partnership with J. W. Harman in the provision business, which lasted about two years, when he formed a partnership with R. and J. Freer in the same business. About this time he married Miss Anne Faws, who deceased in 1873 aged thirty-nine years. He afterward married Mrs. Caroline Campbell in 1876. Mr. Wallack has been an active business man in Ashland for thirty-two years, and is one of the oldest business men of the town. He has met many business reverses. The failure of the Citizens' Bank in 1877, greatly shook his confidence in men. The destuction of his store rooms, by fire, in June, 1880, was a sad disaster and a great loss. He is now in company with W. C. Frazee in a furniture establishment on Main street, Ashland. Mr. Wallack has often been called to fill the office of treasurer for Montgomery township, and has many friends who respect him for his undoubted integrity and honor.

WILLIAM C. FRAZEE

was born December 10, 1841, in Alleghany county, Maryland, and came to Ashland county, Ohio, in 1863, and taught school two winters and labored one summer on a farm, after which he formed a partnership with John Rebman in the provision business about one year, and then entered the same business with Joseph Stoffer, during which time he was elected clerk of the court of common pleas for Ashland county from 1870 to 1876. Since his time as clerk has expired he formed a partnership with E. W. Wallack in the bed spring business, and subsequently in the furniture and undertaking business in Ashland. He married Miss Nancy Swineford, daughter of John Swineford, December 26, 1864, by whom he had two children, one of whom yet survives.

THE RALSTONS,

originally Scotch, fled from Scotland to the north of Ireland during the persecution of the Presbyterians, and from that branch of the family descended the American Ralstons, who emigrated to Lancaster county, Pennsylvania, about the year 1760. From Lancaster they removed to Washington county in 1786.

Robert Ralston, sr., served in the war of 1812, in a regiment from western Pennsylvania. On the way to the Maumee, he passed over the territory now constituting Ashland county; and being pleased with the appearance of the country, sold his farm in Washington county on his return from the army, and came to Montgomery township, Richland (now Ashland) county, in 1814, and settled two miles north of Ashland, where he resided until 1830. He became one of the justices of the peace at the first election, after the organization of Montgomery township, his commission being in the possession of his son James.

He married Jane Woodburn; he died October 26, 1854, aged eighty-six years. Jane, his wife, died September 3, 1862, aged eighty-six years, five months.

Their children were: Robert, jr., who died November 17, 1871, in Clinton county, Iowa, aged seventy-four years; James, of Plymouth, Richland county, Ohio, aged seventy-seven years; Jane Hall, oldest daughter, resides in Nevada, Wyandot county, Ohio; Margaret Hall resides in Orange township, Ashland county; Nancy Gribben, in Plymouth, Richland county; Alexander, in Franklin county, Tennessee; Samuel W., in Auburn, Indiana; Maria Dickson, in Crawford county, Ohio; David, in Clinton county, Iowa; and Julia Bodley, in Whitley county, Indiana. Robert was the father of the late W. C. Ralston, of San Francisco, California.

James, the second son of Robert, sr., the oldest living member of the family at this time (1876), was the millboy during the first few years of their residence in Ashland county. With a horse and pack-saddle, with a sack of corn or wheat, he often traveled by new-cut roads and Indian trails to Shrimplin's mill, in Knox county, the journey occupying three or four days, to obtain a grist. In these trips, he often forded swollen streams, and encountered many dangers and difficulties.

Robert, jr., was a house carpenter, and constructed many of the first buildings in Ashland and Montgomery township. He removed from his farm, north of Ashland, to Plymouth, Richland county, in 1829; and from there to Brooke county, Virginia, in 1832; and from there to Wellsville, Ohio, in 1836; and to Clinton county, Iowa, in 1853, where he died.

Alexander represented Richland county in the Ohio legislature two terms, and served as justice of the peace a number of years, prior to his removal to Tennessee; he was also a carpenter by trade.

The Ralstons, like their Scotch-Irish ancestors, are warmly attached to the Presbyterian faith, and have all been noted for their intelligence, frugality, industry, and moral integrity.

ADAM LINK

was born November 14, 1763, in Washington county, Maryland. His father, Jacob Link, was a native of the same State, while his mother was born in Switzerland. When Adam was about six years old his mother died. His father married again, and moved to the frontier, and located some seven or eight miles from Wheeling, Virginia, where he secured by "tomahawk right," six hundred acres of land, four hundred in Virginia and two hundred in Washington, then Westmoreland, county, Pennsylvania. At the breaking out of Indian hostilities he had already made a good deal of progress in clearing and fitting up his farm, and had a number of horses, cattle and hogs, and determined to remain in his cabin and defend his property, taking the precaution, however, of sending his wife and smaller children back to the settlements before the approach of the savage *Shawnees* and their allies. In August, Mr. Link sent Adam and an older brother, Jonathan, with horses laden with provisions to his family. After the departure of his sons, the same evening, two strangers hunting strayed horses stopped at the cabin of Mr. Link for the night. A nephew of Mrs. Link by the name of Miller also remained at the cabin. When the strangers arose the next morning Mr. Link cautioned them not to go out, as the dogs had been uneasy all night. Paying no attention to his warning, they opened the door and went out to wash, and were immediately shot by Indians, who were concealed near the cabin. Link and Miller gathered up the guns and retreated to the second story of the cabin, drawing up the ladder. The Indians rushed into the building, but finding the stairway safely guarded by rifles pointing down, retreated. After exchanging shots for an hour without effect, a painted white man came forward with a flag of truce, and said if they would give up their arms and come down they would not be hurt, otherwise they would set fire to the cabin and burn them out. Finding further resistance to be useless, they handed down their guns, descended, and their hands were tied. They were marched some distance into the woods, where the Indians halted and held a council, there being some thirty in the gang. The consultation related to the fate of the prisoners. At the conclusion, Mr. Link was tomahawked and scalped, and his body left. Mr. Miller was a sad witness of the fate of his friend. The Indians then moved forward, marching, as he observed, in a circle. That night they had a scalp dance, after which Miller was fastened by raw-hide cords to a large Indian to sleep. The Indians being tired, soon slept profoundly. As soon as it was safe Mr. Miller commenced to gnaw the thongs from his wrists. After much perseverance he finally succeeded. He then carefully removed the cord that encircled his wrist, arose to his feet, seized a good gun and passed into the forest; but had made little progress before the Indian awakened, and with a yell, aroused his companions. Miller continued his flight, and finally reached the settlement. On the morning before the fight took place at the cabin, Adam and Jonathan, who had accompanied their step-mother to a neighboring settlement, were requested to remain part of the day to cut wood. Adam remained, but Jonathan returned. There were several families on the route. On his way Jonathan rode up to a cabin where the owner was making a trough, and asked him if he was not afraid of Indians. He replied—"the d—d redskins are afraid to come about here." Jonathan had not proceeded over one hundred rods when he found himself in the middle of a large body of savages, who were watching the cabin he had just passed. They ordered him to surrender, but he fled. The Indians pursued—his horse became frightened—the saddle turned; he cut the girth and fled in the direction of his father's cabin. When he came in sight of it he found it and the barn in flames. He returned by a circuitous route to the fort. In a few hours Adam followed his brother, and met a stranger on horseback, who told him to turn back, "for the Indians were as thick as yellow jackets in Hawkin's bottom."

After these adventures, the family of Jacob Link became scattered, until the close of the Revolutionary war. Some returned to the vicinity of Baltimore, where the father of Mrs. Link resided. At the conclusion of the war, Adam located adjoining the old homestead in Washington county, Pennsylvania. The old farm passed from the possession of the family, and Adam became a common laborer. He was a young man of great endurance, and could thresh, with a flail, sixty bushels of wheat per week, and make as many rails as any man of his weight in the border settlements.

At the age of twenty-eight he married Miss Elizabeth Link, a relative, and settled in Washington county. He purchased, improved and sold a number of small farms in that county. He saw no active service in the war of 1812. In 1818 he walked from his home in Pennsylvania to Uniontown, now Ashland, Ohio, and located in the southwest quarters of sections one and eleven in Milton township, built cabins, and in the following spring removed with his family, consisting of four sons and five daughters. He located on section one, and afterward sold it to William Lockhart, and removed to section eleven, which, in his seventy-fourth year, he sold to a son, and then improved a small farm on section fourteen, and then removed to Crawford county, and resided with his son-in-law, Mr. Rashton Markley, until August, 1864, when he deceased, at the age of one hundred and one years.

Mr. Link was a peculiar man. His habits are worth notice. In height he was five feet ten inches. His weight was about one hundred and sixty pounds. He was compact in muscle, and possessed great strength and endurance. He was never sick, and never suffered pain. He retained his soundness of constitution until he had nearly reached the age of ninety years. As his limbs began to grow stiff and unwieldly, he was accustomed to say "the machinery is wearing out." From early life he attended the Presbyterian church, but always contended that "all men would be saved after being beaten with few and many stripes, according as they had sinned in this life. That having paid the penalty of sin, they would eventually be saved with the just." Although nearly all his life a border settler, he was well versed in the history of the times. He was an interesting conversationalist, and in narrating the adventures of the border settlements of Pennsylvania and West Virginia, he was accurate in incident, and often eloquent in description. In politics he was a Jeffersonian Democrat. He had a strong preference for military presidents, and is believed to have supported General W. H. Harrison, General Zachariah Taylor and General Scott, for president. As a farmer, he was peculiar. For a period of nearly sixty years he never used or owned a wagon. He always attended market with a sled, and packed his wheat to mill on a horse. He was equally singular in his diet. His standard living was bread, meat, eggs, potatoes, butter, sugar and coffee. No fruit or milk. He was a hearty meat eater. He regarded two goose eggs as a medium breakfast, combined with a little bread and meat. When he was eighty-seven years old, having used whiskey freely all his lfe, he became convinced that the modern modes of its manufacture were pernicious, by reason of the deleterious drugs entering into the new compound, and abandoned its use. Here, then, are two problems for solution: 1. Did his diet contribute to the preservation of his health to so advanced an age? 2. Is it true that the use of pure spirituous liquors, as a common beverage, shortens life by enfeebling the physical and vital powers?*

JOHN BISHOP.

To preserve the memory and hold in respect the deeds and services of the pioneers who have devoted their lives and energies to leveling the forest and taming the wild luxuriance of a new country, must ever be grateful to those who survive. While this is true, in regard to the world's great men in military life, it is equally true in all discoveries of science, as well as in building up of new communities, in prosperity, intelligence, virtue, and wealth. It has often been the case, that in the age in which the pioneer lives, his invaluable services fail to be appreciated, yet those who survive, have generally made liberal amends for any apparent neglect. The present generation is under lasting obligations to those who encountered the dangers, and endured the hardships of our new settlements to prepare the way for the advance of the standard of civilization, where hitherto the wild native roamed free and unmolested. We should long remember these fathers and mothers for such incalculable services in the cause of human improvement; for they deserve to be held in remembrance in all coming time as public benefactors. This sentiment, we

*Note—Jonathan Link built a block-house on Middle Wheeling creek, in 1780, near the present town of Triadelphia. He was killed in it by the Indians in the fall of 1781.

trust, actuates all the members of the Pioneer society of Ashland county.

John Bishop was born January 22, 1793, in Frederick county, in the State of Maryland. At the age of thirteen years, his parents removed to Green county, Pennsylvania. His father, being in moderate circumstances, John was hired to work for a neighbor named William Estel, for ten shillings per month, and having amassed sufficient means, came to Licking county, Ohio, during the war of 1812. That county was then sparsely settled, and the pioneers had to endure many privations in the midst of war. Here he found employment for one year. He was then twenty years old, and remained one year. In 1814 he returned to Pennsylvania and induced his father's family to accompany him to Licking county. At the close of the war, in 1815, he came to Orange township, then Richland, now Ashland, county. He found the pioneers of that region few and greatly scattered. It was not uncommon to meet the red men in the woods, who were friendly to the whites, and often hunted in our forests. His first work consisted in digging the foundation of a new mill erected by Martin Mason, on the present site of Mr. Leidigh's mill in the west part of Orange township. There were then no villages in the township and none in the county. The mill was put in running order, to do a small business in 1816. In 1820, he aided in the erection of the first school-house in the township in the Hiffner settlement. In 1819, March 9, he married Miss Catharine Hiffner, daughter of Jacob Hiffner, a revolutionery soldier, who died about 1849. This lady was the choice of his youth, and he lived in great peace with her until about 1876, when she left earth for a happy home prepared for all the good. Mr. Bishop could exclaim with the poet:

She's the star I missed from heaven,
Long time ago,

and has now gone to join her in the happier land, never more to part.

There were ten children when the Bishop family arrived in Ohio. There are still living: Jacob, Catharine Weedman, and Elizabeth Young, all of whom now reside in the State of Illinois. Mr. Bishop leaves several members of his family in Ashland county. He resided about sixty-four years in this county, most of the time on his late homestead north of Orange.

Mr. Bishop had always been an industrious, unpretending farmer, and, by economy and uprightness had acquired a good property, which he divided among his children. As a citizen, socially and morally, he occupied a high place in the respect of his neighbors. He was among the earlier pioneers of the township—the Metcalfs, the Fasts, the Norrises, the Youngs, and the Uries. He helped to clear its forests, make its roads, erect its school-houses, and aid the pioneers by his kind offices. As a citizen he was kind and gentle in his manners, and, as a Christian, exemplary among his neighbors. He was a faithful member of the Methodist Episcopal church for more than half a century, and deemed death but gain for the true Christian. Although regarded as a member of the Pioneer and Historical society of the county, advanced age and exposure prevented his meeting with his pioneer associates frequently.

Mr. Bishop died, after a brief illness, March 12, 1879, aged eighty-six years, one month, and eighteen days. His work is done, and he has gone to rest. May he find the reward of the good and true.

JOHN CORY

was born in Washington county, Pennsylvania, May 17, 1800. His father, Aaron Cory, was born in New Jersey in 1772, and came to Washington county when a young man, in 1793, and married Miss Elizabeth McGuire, sister of the late Thomas and Hugh McGuire. He and his family, consisting of his wife and children, removed to what became Tuscarawas county, Ohio, in 1802. That region had been the home of the Delaware Indians prior to the expeditions of Williamson and Colonel William Crawford, in 1781-2, and was long a favorite resort for Indians of that nation, after the Corys came into the country. The *Delawares* were much attached to the preaching and teaching of the Moravian missionary, Rev. John Heckewelder, and visited Goshen in memory of the past. Here the Corys and Carrs became acquainted with many leading Indians, among whom were George Hamilton and Philip Ignatius, who participated in the fight with General Wayne at Fallen Timbers in 1795, and often spoke of the wonderful manner in which he conducted the campaign. These Indians, with others, often visited Mr. Cory in Perry township, Wayne county, after his removal in subsequent years. In the year 1814 Aaron Cory located two quarters of land in Wayne and Richland counties, one in section twenty-nine in Perry, and one in Montgomery township, known as the old Andress farm, at the land office at Canton. In 1817 Aaron Cory and his son John, the oldest member of his family, visited Perry township with the view of improving his land. They cleared about ten acres, and Mr. Cory returned to Tuscarawas county. John remained, and continued the improvements in the summer season, for two years, returning home during each winter. In the spring of 1819, Aaron Cory and family, consisting of his wife and eight children, John being the oldest, removed to the farm in Perry township. Mr. Cory remained about eight years, and then purchased a new home, and located in Crawford county, where he died in 1834, aged about sixty years. John took possession of the home farm in Perry township, and married Miss Elizabeth Cantwell, sister of the late Colonel James Cantwell, who fell at the second battle of Bull Run, during the late war.

John Cory continued to reside on the old farm until 1867, when he sold it and purchased in Morrow county, whence he removed. Here he had the misfortune to lose, by death, the wife of his youth, in 1872, aged about sixty-five years. He felt the separation most keenly, and was never fully reconciled to her death. Mrs. Cory was an excellent lady, and possessed of great firmness, good judgment, and Christian forbearance, in a large degree. Of late years Mr. Cory has resided in Sandusky township, Richland county, at the residence of a daughter, Mrs. Stevens, where he died.

His family consists of Anne Mariah, wife of Peter Spangler, of Evansport, Defiance county, Ohio; Aaron F. Cory, of Hixville, Defiance county, Ohio; Sarah, wife of Dr. J. McKune, of Marion county, Ohio; Martha J., wife of George Palmer, of Marion county, Iowa; William W. Cory, esq., of Ottumwa, Iowa; John F. Cory, of Hixville, Defiance county, Ohio; and Rhoda A., the wife of Lewis Stevens, of Richland county, Ohio. The members of the family above enumerated are all living, and were generally present at the funeral of Mr. Cory.

The Corys, on the mother's side of the house, were French, and on that of the father's and grandfather's, of Scotch descent, and originally settled in New Jersey, some time before the American Revolution. Mr. Cory, at the time of his decease, possessed a Bible printed in France in 1727, which is said to have been originally the property of his great-grandfather, Joseph Freeman. The Bible was purchased in France about the time his ancestors settled in New Jersey.

Mr. Cory often, in his conversation, dwelt upon the early reminiscences of settlement in Perry township, the wildness of the forest, the hardships of the pioneers, the difficulty of procuring milling, and the thinness of the settlements. He related, with much merriment, the experience of himself and father during the first summer, whilst engaged in making their first improvements. They erected, against a large log, a camp cabin, eight by ten feet, of small logs or saplings, and covered it, the roof all sloping one way, by clapboards, to keep out the wet. It had no floor, and was open in front. A fire was built a few feet from the front, to keep off the wolves, which at night were quite numerous. The only furniture of the cabin consisted of a rifle, two axes, two or three knives, a fork or two, two or three pewter plates, one or two tin cups, an iron pot for cooking, a skillet for frying meat, and two or three home-made stools. They slept on their blankets spread on leaves in their cabin. In this solitary home they were often joined by the late John Carr, sr., who lived a few miles away, in their work. One evening, while preparing supper, Mr. Cory had the misfortune to upset the skillet in frying meat. The oil immediately took fire, and with a great blaze was, with the meat, consumed. The fragrance of the consuming fat was wafted on the evening breeze, and snuffed by the hungry wolves, which speedily gathered in the distance, and commenced a hideous serenade, not daring to approach, having great fears of the fire. In this manner, Mr. Cory began his improvement in Perry, about sixty-two years ago. Such has been the change that has, almost imperceptibly, gone on in a single life time.

It may be remarked that Mr. Cory was an intelligent, honest, and kind-hearted gentleman. He was noted for his Christian bearing and generous impulses. In his politics, as in his religious views, he was firm and fixed, and never shrank from the issue. For a long series of years he was a most exemplary member of the Methodist Episcopal church. He met the dread monster, Death, fearing not, but conscious that his work was well

J. H. McCombs

JOHN H. McCOMBS

was born June 14, 1813, in Washington county, Pennsylvania. He had two brothers, one, James A. McCombs, died at the age of four years. Andrew M. McCombs was a member of Captain Barber's company, and died in the service on the thirtieth of April, 1862, at Ashland, aged forty-seven years and five months. His mother, Ann McClean, was married to his father, Matthew McCombs, on the twenty-third day of April, 1812. His father served six months in the war of 1812, under General Harrison, and died, from the effects of the service, in the year 1822. His mother died at Ashland February 18, 1867, in the eighty-second year of her age.

Mr. McCombs' grandfather, on the father's side, was born in Ireland, and emigrated to, and bought a farm in, Washington county, Pennsylvania, and lived to about the age of eighty years, and his wife to near the same age. Mr. McCombs' grandfather, on the mother's side, Andrew McClean, died on his farm in Washington county, Pennsylvania, Smith township, at the age of eighty-five years, and his wife at the age of sixty-seven years. Grandfather McClean was born near Fort Deposit, Maryland, was a Revolutionary soldier, who died at a ripe age, full of years and full of faith, being an elder in the Presbyterian church of Raccoon. He performed an important part in procuring the liberties we now enjoy. He was in the battles of Brandywine, Long Island, Germantown, Monmouth, Stony Point, etc., serving five years, and enlisted at the age of seventeen. He saw and participated in the mighty event which, under Providence, ended in the permanent independence of this country, and died enjoying the confidence and esteem of all his neighbors. Mr. McCombs was left to the care of his mother, who brought him up and early taught him self-independence. He taught school in his neighborhood at the early age of sixteen. He commenced to acquire a liberal education at Florence academy, Washington county, Pennsylvania, then attended Washington college, and after a course of over five years was graduated at Franklin college, in Harrison county, Ohio, in the class of 1839. He then read law with the Hon. T. M. T. McKennan, who was Secretary of the Interior under General Taylor, and his son, William McKennan, now United States district judge for northwestern Pennsylvania, and he was admitted to the bar in Washington, Pennsylvania; when he came to Ohio and resided in Richland county one year; came to Ashland, Ashland county, Ohio, before the county was erected, and assisted in procuring the county-seat, where he has ever since resided and engaged in the practice of the law. He was married to Sarah A. Wright, a native of the State of New York, December 29, 1846. They had three children—S. Anna, Mary B., and John. The youngest, John, remains with the parents; Anna is married to S. W. Andrews, and Mary to James Whyte.

done, and he had nothing to regret, but was ready to go. Just as the morning of the fourth of July, 1879, commenced to dawn, the good old pioneer was ushered into the presence of all those who had long since departed to a better and, we trust, a happier world. May he rest in peace.

JOHN CARR, SR.,

was born in Maryland, and came to Washington county, Pennsylvania, about 1790, and married Margaret McGuire, sister of the late Thomas and Hugh McGuire, and during the border wars acted as an Indian spy a short time, when the Bradys, the Poes, as well as Frank McGuire, Robert McGuire, and the Wetsels, scouted along the western border of Pennsylvania. From Washington county, Pennsylvania, John Carr removed into Tuscarawas county, Ohio, where he remained until about 1810, when he came to Mohican township, then in Wayne, now in Ashland, county, with his family, and settled on what is now known as the Chessman farm, about half a mile northwest of Jeromeville, which he subsequently sold to John Ewing, sr., and purchased what is now the Horn farm, on the east line of Montgomery township, where he died in 1837, aged about sixty years. Mrs. Carr died there also. His children were: Thomas, Nicholas, Nancy, Hugh, Joshua, Benjamin, John, Samuel, Margaret, Aaron, Susan, and Curtis, by his first wife, and Aquilla and David by the second wife. When the people became alarmed in Mohican, in the fall of 1812, because of the menacing conduct of the Indians, Mr. Carr and his family took refuge upon the Tuscarawas, until all danger and threats had been so far removed as to warrant a return to his cabin. Mr. Carr is understood to have been on friendly terms with the Indians of Mohican township, many of whom had resided in other days, at Goshen, on the Tuscarawas. In fact, it has often been suggested, that so warm was his attachments for many of the Jerome Indians, and so deep their regard for Mr. Carr, that he probably would have remained unmolested in his cabin, near the fort, had he chosen to do so, during the war. The Indians often called on him, after the war, in their hunting excursions in Mohican. He was a good man.

JAMES CLARK

was born in Chambersburgh, Pennsylvania, October 7, 1790, and in youth attended the common schools of his neighborhood. In 1797 his parents removed to Washington county, in the same State, where he grew to manhood. War having been declared against Great Britain in 1812, by the United States, all those capable of bearing arms in the contest were either drafted or volunteered for the service. Washington county during the Revolution and subsequent struggles, had suffered severely by the incursions of the red men from Sandusky and the Scioto. From the temper evinced by the mother country, it was apprehended that so far as her agents could corrupt and inflame the passions of the tribes of the northwest against our people they would do so. Her agents secretly gave to the fierce red men ammunition, blankets, and arms, as the price of human scalps. They regarded the Americans as rebels in rebellion, and in a relentless war expected to subdue our people. The border settlers were aroused, and a most determined effort was put forth to turn back the red fiend, headed by British bayonets, and thus parry every attempt to subdue our country a second time. The young men of Washington county, in 1813, of the proper age, were drafted into the service. Mr. Clark was among those who drew a place in the service, and was soon enrolled. The heroic victory on Lake Erie, by Commodore Perry, and the brave conduct of Captain Crogan, turned back the red hordes of the northwest, headed by British bayonets, and thus repelled invasion, by lake and land, and by the time the troops of western Pennsylvania had reached Pittsburgh, a lull in the contest soon caused a declaration of peace, and Mr. Clark and his comrades were discharged without further service. He was in no battle, but evinced his readiness for the fray.

In 1814 he entered, at the land office, his late home in Orange township. When he visited his land he came by way of Wheeling, Zanesville, Coshocton, up the Walhonding, the Lake and Jerome forks, by Finley's, to the blockhouse on Jerome's farm, and thence up the stream by what became the home of Jacob Young, to his own location northwest of what is now the village of Orange, on the waters of Mohican. In 1818 he built a small cabin on his land, and kept bachelor's hall during the summer season, doing his own cooking, grubbing, chopping, and preparing his land, and in the fall returned home and engaged in teaming to "old Pitt." In this manner he continued to labor on his land, each summer, for seven successive years. When he came out in 1818, he was accompanied by his brother John, and stayed all night at Uniontown, now Ashland, at the cabin hotel of Joseph Sheets, just opposite the present hardware store of Mr. Stull, on the north side of Main street. Mr. Sheets deceased several years since; but Mrs. Nancy Sheets, the former landlady, resides in South Ashland, possessing a good deal of energy, and quite a vigorous mind, for an aged lady. For some time after his arrival wild game was abundant. Mr. Clark was a good marksman, and easily procured plenty of venison, wild turkeys, and occasionally a black bear. These he dressed and cooked according to his taste. Wolves were very numerous and bold. He related that on several occasions, having no door to his cabin, wolves ventured in during the night and actually carried away meat and other articles. On one occasion he killed and dressed a large, fat turkey, expecting to enjoy the luxury of roasting and eating the same. On going to bed he hung it up in his cabin; but when he arose next morning he found that during the night some howling, hungry wolf had carried it away and devoured it while he slept.

He was repeatedly visited by bands of Delaware Indians, from the Fire Lands, during their encampment and hunts in the neighborhood. These Indians were very poor, and miserably clad. They were always apparently hungry, and in a begging humor. They often got corn-meal and other food from him, and agreed to pay him in deer skins and peltry for it, but invariably forgot to remember the agreement. Mr. Clark, in his prime, was fully six feet high, and would weigh one hundred and eighty pounds. He was very resolute in his manner, and frank in his interviews with the Indians, and hence was never uncivilly treated by them. These Indians had a number of wigwams, or bark huts, three-quarters of a mile northwest of him, in what is now Troy township. Old Tom Lyons, Jonacake and his squaw, Catottawa, and other Indians, often came to his cabin, on their hunting excursions. He was also visited on several occasions by the eccentric, but harmless, Johnny Appleseed, who was engaged in planting, on Mason's run, a nursery in advance of the pioneers.

These were solitary times; but Mr. Clark often stated that, being busily engaged in clearing and preparing his farm, time passed rapidly, and he really enjoyed himself working, and occasionally traversing the wild forests in search of game. When he entered the township, he was of the opinion there were not over sixteen or seventeen families in it. Joel Mackerel, John Bishop, and Peter Biddinger were his nearest neighbors. Mr. Biddinger was a blacksmith, and also repaired guns and tomahawks for the Indians.

At that time two shillings a day, and twenty-five cents a hundred for cutting and splitting twelve foot rails, in trade, was the customary price. He often traveled five miles on foot, to help roll logs or raise a cabin, and was really glad to assist in this manner all new settlers. There were no improved roads; all was new, and no road fund to repair highways. The willing hands and stout arms of the resolute pioneer had it all to do, and right cheerfully did they perform the task. It was some years before the advantages of good schools were enjoyed by the rising generation.

Mr. Clark dwelt on the reminiscences of the past, the growth of the country in population, intelligence and wealth, and regarded the change that had occurred in this region, as simply wondrous in the last sixty-one years. In 1830 he married Miss Charlotte Myers, daughter of Jacob Myers, of Clearcreek, by whom he had four sons: Josephus, John, M. L., and James M. Clark, and two daughters, Mary A. McBride and Mrs. C. Sharrick. Mrs. Clark died in 1841, and Mr. Clark subsequently married a Miss Marshall, who, at an advanced age, survives her husband, and resides at the home of James M. Clark, on the old homestead. Mr. Clark and his aged lady enjoyed the filial attentions of the family, and esteem of all his pioneer neighbors, and life ebbed quietly away, and at eighty-nine years he became gradually feeble, and gently passed over the dark river to a better and happier land July 7, 1879.

A deep veneration for the memory of these fathers and mothers of a new country pervades the rising generation. In the last twelve months we have parted with over twenty-five of the pioneers of the county, who have been gathered to their fathers. Ere long the last will disappear from among us. It is a grateful duty we owe them to smooth their departing hours by kind and respectful attention, ere we are called upon to enjoy the fruits of their toil and valor.

JAMES KILGORE

was born in Cumberland county, Pennsylvania, December 21, 1795. He removed, with his parents, to Fairfield county, Ohio, in December, 1809, when about fourteen years of age. In 1810, his father located in Franklin county, on Alum creek, about two miles east of the present site of Columbus. He resided in a cabin, at this point, when the city of Columbus was surveyed and numbered in lots, and helped erect the first cabin, in 1811. This cabin was owned by Adam Hare, and stood on the corner of Broad and High streets. The Kilgores helped cut the trees and roll the logs on Broad and High streets, and hauled the stone for the foundation of the old capitol building from Black Lick, nine miles east of Columbus.

In 1812, after the surrender of General Hull at Detroit, a great panic took place in the county of Delaware, and extended to Franklin, resulting from what was then known as Drake's defeat, in the southern part of what is now Marion county. Captain Drake was leading a new company of pioneer settlers from Delaware county, to recruit some advanced station near Upper Sandusky, to prevent surprise by the Indians, then largely in the interest of the British. By way of testing the courage and steadiness of the new troops, after the company had encamped, and placed a guard about the camp, and retired to rest, the captain managed to send out a few soldiers, who were to return from the forest in a short time, crying, "Indians! Indians!" and fire in quick succession, and thus arouse the soldiers from their slumber. In due time the false alarm took place. The new soldiers were greatly terrified, many taking the back track, and giving the alarm all along the road to Delaware, while the settlers immediately became panic-stricken, and, almost in a body, fled toward the settlements in Franklinton and Chillicothe. John Brickel, who was engaged on the upper branches of the Scioto, six miles above Columbus, in the milling business, and others in the neighborhood, fled to Franklinton, then the capital of the State, to the stockade. A requisition was immediately made for the service of all able-bodied men and youth, who were notified to report for duty at the stockade. James Kilgore, then about seventeen years of age, took his father's old gun and obeyed the call. In crossing the Scioto, at a ford near the site of the present National bridge, he overtook a woman and three children on their way to the stockade. He remained at the stockade a few weeks on guard duty, and when the excitement over the Drake stampede had subsided, southern Ohio and Kentucky having sent forward a large number of troops, to recruit the army of the northwest, he returned home. At the close of the war, the Kilgores reoccupied their old cabin on Alum creek, and continued their improvements for six or eight years.

After Columbus became the fixed capital of the State, the growth of the new city was quite rapid. The Kilgores participated in its improvement, and Mr. James Kilgore often stated that he saw the erection of the first cabin, in what is now the most valuable part of the city, and if nature had endowed him with a sufficient foresight, he might have owned some of the most valuable locations. Like General Cass (when asked how he made so much real estate in Detroit, responded: "Buy a farm, young man, and have them build a city on it"), he long since felt that the only mistake was that he did not purchase in the city, instead of in Ashland county. In 1818, he located in Stark county, where he married in 1821. In 1827, he purchased a half-quater of land, then in Richland, but now of Ashland county, and removed to it, and continued to reside there until his decease.

In 1873 he had the misfortune to lose, by death, his excellent lady. She deceased at the age of seventy-six years. At the time of her death their family consisted of one son and five daughters. One son fell in the battle of Chickamauga, in the war of 1862-5. The other, Silas, lives on the homestead, and with whom the old gentleman resided at the time of his demise, July 4, 1878. Mr. Kilgore is believed to have been a member of the Presbyterian church for more than fifty years. In politics he was an old time Whig of the strictest order. He was in full possession of all his faculties to the last, and was very fond of relating his pioneer experiences. Upon the organization of the Ashland County Pioneer and Historical society he became an active member, and retained a high regard for the society. Thus, one by one, the pioneers pass away. May their exemplary lives and great sacrifices long impress the rising generation. Peace to their ashes.

SYLVANUS PARMELY

was born in Wilmington, Vermont, March 31, 1784. He was the oldest son of John Parmely, of English descent. He married Miss Louis Gould, in Somerset, Vermont, where he resided several years. In 1816 he came to the Western Reserve to select a home. He traveled the entire distance on horseback. At that time the lands of the Reserve townships were being surveyed into lots and sections. Mr. Parmely assisted in surveying Sullivan township during that season. The surveying party camped in the forest, and procured food from Harrisville during the period of the survey, by means of pack-horses. In the fall he returned to Connecticut, and in the spring of 1817 removed his family, accompanied by six other families, to Sullivan center. These families were his father, John Parmely, his brother, Asahel Parmely, his brother-in-law, Thomas Rice, James Palmer and their families. A few months later this little colony was joined by Henry, Benjamin and Khesa Close and their families. The first mentioned families came in ox-teams, with the exception of Mr. Rice, who drove a span of horses. From Harrisville to Sullivan center, a distance of ten miles, they cut a road through the forest, to enable their teams to pass. They arrived August 28, 1817. The log hut, enclosed on two sides and one end, which had been erected and occupied by the surveyors the year before, was given to Mr. and Mrs. James Palmer to occupy, while the rest of the families slept in their wagons about three weeks, until cabins could be erected for their accommodation. Two hewed log houses were built near the center of the town. Mr. Palmer went to the village of Wooster, on foot, by paths through the forest, to obtain glass for his windows. The nearest mill was also that of Stibbs, near Wooster, to which the new settlers in Sullivan resorted for their grists. Mr. Parmely and others soon conceived the idea of erecting a horse-mill in the center. The people, far and near, came there to have their grinding done, after staying all night. Mr. George Mann was the next pioneer. When it became necessary to establish a post-office in the Center, about the year 1820, Mr. Parmely was made the first postmaster. In 1822 he removed to Elyria, and Mr. John Gould was appointed postmaster. In 1833 Mr. Parmely returned to Sullivan and reoccupied his old farm. In company with Alexander Porter, he erected a large steam grist- and saw-mill, and established a dry goods store at the Center.

In 1843 he was elected representative from Lorain county to the legislature. After the expiration of his term he attended at Columbus as lobby member several years, to procure the erection of a new county, of which Sullivan was proposed to be the seat of justice. It was believed by him that ample territory could be procured from the surrounding counties to erect such a county. A counter project was set on foot by rival interests, culminating in the erection of Ashland county in the winter of 1846. This unexpected result terminated the legislative efforts of Mrs. Parmely. He returned to the routine of business, and conducted his store until advancing age required his retirement. He was noted as a thoroughgoing, energetic and upright business man. He was exceedingly industrious, and during his pioneer life labored early and late. His axe was heard ringing amid the wilds. He felled the lofty forest trees, and soon made "the wilderness blossom as the rose." He was strictly honorable in business, mild in disposition, genial and kind to all. He was a friend to the struggling pioneer, and always ready to lend a helping hand to worthy enterprises. He was an earnest member of the Christian church, and a diligent student of the scriptures. He was, for many years, a member of the Baptist church, which was established at an early day in Sullivan. Upon hearing the doctrines advocated by Alexander Campbell, he became warmly attached to that reform, and helped organize the first Disciple church in Sullivan. For a period of nearly seventy years his name was enrolled as a member of the Baptist and Disciple churches. He died January 23, 1874, aged nearly ninety years. Mrs. Louis Gould Parmely, his wife, was born January 31, 1789, and died April 12, 1873, about nine months prior to the decease of her husband. Her ancestors were also English, and settled at Newburyport, as early as 1644. She was a Christian lady, and much beloved by her children and acquaintances. Her house was the minister's home, and many pilgrims were sent on their way rejoicing by the ministrations of this excellent woman. Eight of her nine surviving children were at her funeral. "The memory of the just is blessed."

The children of Sylvanus Parmely were—Manning, Louis, Louisa, Rosetta M., Sylvia P., Ellesworth, Jane L., Celia D., Melvin B., and Sarah A. Louisa married Robert B. Campbell, of New Orleans; Rosetta M., John P. Mann, of Sullivan; Sylvia P., John L. Campbell, of Cincinnati; Jane L., John M. Gorham, of Ashland; Celia D., James Pritchard; Sarah A., Stephen Doughton. Ellesworth resides in Wisconsin, and M. B. in Dayton, Ohio.

The whole number of families arriving in 1817 was nine. There were but twenty-seven families there in 1824, and in 1825, about twenty-nine. Jesse Chamberlain and Betsy, his wife, are the only heads of families now (1876) living, of the original pioneers, Aretas Marsh having deceased May 2, 1876, aged seventy-seven years. Whitney Chamberlain is eighty-two years old, and his wife, Maritta, is eighty years old.

Many of the children of the first settlers reside in Sullivan township. Ashley Parmely, son of Asahel Parmely, born February 21, 1818, was the first birth in the township. He is now (1876) living on the farm first purchased by his father in Sullivan. Mrs. Sylvia Parmely Campbell was the second birth in the town, June 3, 1818, She was the daughter of Sylvanus and Louis Parmely. John Parmely was the first death in the township, in the spring of 1818.

The Baptist church reorganized in 1834. A new house of worship was erected in 1839. The Methodists had a small church in 1833. The church of Christ was organized in 1837. The Methodist Episcopal church has gone down. The others possess a good membership.

JACOB CROUSE.

Among the early pioneers of Montgomery township, Jacob Crouse occupies a high place in the esteem of his neighbors, by reason of his good sense, frugality, intelligence and integrity. He was born in the State of Maryland, near Antietam, September 10, 1775. When a young man, in 1799, he sought and obtained employment in Fayette county, Pennsylvania. At this period the settlements adjoining the Ohio river were just beginning to recover from a long continuance of the Indian wars. Very few families had wholly escaped the tomahawk and gleaming scalping-knife. The frightful scalp-halloo and shrill shriek of the red warriors had sent terror into thousands of cabins. A few of the most hearty frontiersmen ventured to locate west of the Ohio river; and about the year 1807 Jacob Crouse and wife located a cabin home in Columbiana county, where a few of their neighbors and acquaintances had removed.

That region was often traversed by the humble red men after their disastrous route by General Wayne, in the northwest. In fact, their path leading to "old Pittsburgh" ran through that part of the newly-organized State of Ohio, and it was not uncommon to see hundreds of *Delawares* and *Wyandots* loaded with peltry on their way to Fort Pitt, to purchase blankets, cloths and ammunition in exchange for furs.

In 1801 Mr. Crouse married Rebecca Reifsnyder, of Fayette county, Pennsylvania, who willingly accompanied him to the wilds of Ohio, and endured the privations incident to pioneer life, that she and her husband might in the future become the happy possessors of a homestead.

In 1812, upon the surrender of General Hull, at Detroit, and the assassinations upon the Black fork, Mr. Crouse was drafted, with many of his neighbors, to assist in defending the helpless pioneers of the northwest against the savage incursions of the *Wyandots* and *Delawares*. He was enrolled in the company commanded by Captain Foulks, and made ensign, and the company entered the regiment of General Beall, and marched to the village of Wooster, where a block-house was erected and part of a company stationed, and from there a wagon-trail was cut to the place of John Baptiste Jerome; (now Jeromeville) where another block-house was built and a part of a company stationed; thence, they cut a trail, (now known as Beall's trail), across the north part of what is now Vermillion, the south part of Montgomery, and the middle part of Milton townships, and thence west across the northern part of Richland county, in the direction of Fort Meigs. He served six months, and was discharged in the spring of 1813, and returned to Columbiana county.

In January, 1814, Martin Mason and Jacob Young visited the regions of Jeromeville, Loudonville, Mansfield, Ashland, and Orange township, with the view of locating wild lands. Their report of the new country was so flattering that they concluded to enter a number of tracts, at the land office in Canton, and return, with others, and put up cabins. In August, Martin Mason, Jacob Mason, Jacob Crouse, Martin Hester, Lot Tod, and Peter Biddinger returned and erected six cabins on lands since owned by the respective parties, and cut and cured a lot of prairie hay, and made preparations to bring on their families, and returned. In October, 1814, Martin Mason, Jacob Crouse, Jacob Young, Joseph Bishop, and their families, removed to their new cabins on the branches of the Mohican. The new colony, including old and young, numbered thirty-one. The route was along the old army trail to Jerome's block-house, and the home of John Carr, now the Nailor farm, where they rested one night, in his cabin, having slept or tented in the air, the entire distance. From thence, they cut a wagon-path up the east side of the Jerome fork, across lands now owned by Joseph Chandler, and thence, across Catotawa, to the cabin formerly owned by Daniel Mictey, now by Andrew Mason, to the cabin of Jacob Young, some distance west of the present Crouse school-house, where they all rested one night. The next morning Jacob Crouse moved into his own cabin, near where the residence of John Doty now stands. He had leased one hundred and sixty acres, being of the Virginia military lands, for ninety-nine years, and began to prepare a field to plant corn in the succeeding year. His first field was where the Doty orchard now is.

Like all good and intelligent pioneers, the first thought, after preparing a cabin for the reception of their families, and a field for culture, the new colony turned attention to the necessity of training youth in lessons of Christian culture and civilization. Mr. Crouse proposed to donate one acre of land on his north boundary, for school purposes, and to be used as a cemetery. The proposition was accepted, and a comfortable log house was erected about where the present school-house stands, and dedicated to the culture of the youthful mind. The first school was taught there in the winter of 1815-16, by John Swigart. Ever since that time, that temple of knowledge has been known—and justly too—as the "Crouse school-house." Let it always retain that name.

A year or two after the expiration of the term of 'Squire Robert Newell, the pioneers of Montgomery elected Jacob Crouse a justice of the peace, and he served three years, and then declined re-election. His manner was modest and retiring, and official life had no charms for him.

He took a deep interest in the prosperity of common schools, and one of his sons, Jonas H., became a very energetic and noted teacher.

He and his lady connected with the Lutheran church, in Fayette county, Pennsylvania, and remained zealous and leading members nearly fifty years. Mr. Crouse died of pulmonary disease, September 14, 1839, aged sixty-four years and four days; his wife survived him until 1850. They sleep in Crouse's cemetery.

His family living at his decease, consisted of Catharine, wife of John Proudfit, Isaac, Benjamin, Jonas H., Isaiah, Mariah, wife of Martin Wolf, and Anna, wife of Thomas Urie, jr.; all are now deceased.

JACOB YOUNG,

of Orange, was born in Hardy county, Virginia, January 1, 1773. His parents were natives of Bavaria, Germany, and immigrated to America about the year 1743. The Youngs settled in Virginia, and the father and mother of Jacob Young (the mother's name was Cox), landed in New York, and subsequently settled in Virginia, where Andrew Young, father of Jacob, married into the Cox family. When Jacob Young was four or five years old his father removed to Washington county, Pennsylvania, then considered part of Virginia, and located near Ten Mile creek. He subsequently served some two years as teamster in the Revolutionary army, and died on his homestead about the year 1807, at an advanced age.

Jacob grew to manhood in Washington county, and married Mary Mason, of Fayette county, Pennsylvania, June 7, 1795, and, in 1804 removed to and located in Columbiana county, in the newly admitted State of Ohio, where he remained until October, 1814, when he removed to Orange township, then in Richland, but now in Ashland county, Ohio, where he had erected a cabin the preceding year. Prior to his removal he had entered, at the office at New Lisbon, a number of tracts of land, one of which is now (1878) owned by John Crivelin, one by the heirs of the late George Hall, one by Isaac Mason, one by William Rhone, and another by Rev. William Sattler. His route to his new home was by the old army trail to Wooster, thence by Beall's trail to Jerome's Place and block-house, now Jeromeville, and thence up the Mohican, by a new path passing near where Andrew Mason now resides, and thence to his cabin on the present Sattler farm. But few settlers had preceded him, and his cabin was in the midst of an almost unbroken forest. It was a lonely home, and he was soon serenaded by wolves and the screams of other wild animals. As soon as he had arranged for winter he set to work upon the rich alluvial bottoms to prepare ground for culture the next year. The forests were of stupendous growth, and required much toil to cut and remove them. During the winter his family lived upon corn-bread, milk, and such wild meat as he could secure by means of his trusty rifle. The hominy block was brought into requisition, and such corn as could be procured in Columbiana county and in the vicinity of Wooster, was prepared for use. His nearest neighbors were Solomon Urie, Vachtel Metcalf, Amos Norris, Patrick Murray, and Jacob Crouse, to whose number others were soon added.

An old Delaware and Wyandot trail ran near his cabin, and Indians from Sandusky frequently passed along, with furs and skins to Pittsburgh and returned with new blankets, ammunition, and such other articles as they received in exchange for peltry; but were then quite civil. They occasionally called at his cabin, in small numbers, for something to eat, and always were served by Mrs. Young when she had anything to allay their hunger. After 1817 they rarely visited the cabin, when off their reservation, which was situated in what is now Marion county, Ohio. They generally hunted in the forests along Black river and in Huron, Lorain and Medina counties. They finally disappeared about 1824, and went west in 1829. In his hunting excursions he often met small parties of *Delawares* in the northern forests. On one occasion, in attempting to pass silently to a resort for deer—a sort of lick—he came quietly upon an old *Delaware* seated upon a log, soundly asleep, and apparently very much exhausted from fatigue and want of food. Upon his approach the Indian was very much frightened; but Mr. Young advanced, showing by signs that he intended no harm, and, upon discovering the real situation of the Indian, drew from the pocket of his hunting shirt a corn cake, which he tendered to his red friend, which was eagerly accepted. The Indian kneeled down in token of thankfulnesss, at the same time pointing toward the heavens, as if to intimate that the Great Spirit would reward him for generously feeding the hungry.

In 1833, when the great stellar shower took place, when it seemed as if the universe were coming to an end, Mr. Young was hunting in the north woods along the banks of the Black river, and slept of nights in a rude hut or wigwam covered with bark. The singular appearance of the heavens amazed him, and fear that some great evil might befall his family seized upon him, but upon his return he was happy to discover that his apprehensions were baseless. The heavens had again become calm, and the fiery torches that blazed through the limitless regions of space had disappeared, and all nature seemed at rest. It was not a matter of surprise that he should have been alarmed, for philosopher and divine alike trembled at beholding the phenomenon, and were uncertain as to its final termination.

Mr. Young succeeded in raising a few acres of corn the first year; but was compelled to depend largely upon the chase for meat. His neighbors were few and far between, and he was often requested to assist in erecting cabins for new settlers, to roll logs, and do other acts of good neighborhood, to all of which he responded, often boarding himself in addition to services rendered, and at the same time furnishing seed corn to the newcomer. Indeed, though industrious, economical, and careful, he found it difficult to protect himself and family from suffering, until he had succeeded in raising a few crops. Nevertheless, short as was his home supply, he was noted for his generous aid to all comers, even to squandering his own profits by helping parties who were subsequently unable or unwilling to pay him in return. His wife often related that they had, not unfrequently, been so short of meat, for the first year or two, that Mr. Young depended almost wholly upon his gun, from day to day, for a supply; and often returned, hungry and weary, without game, and made a supper upon milk and pone. In his hunting excursions, during his earlier years, he often met, in the northern forests, that skilful and successful woodman and hunter, Solomon Urie. He often found signs of bear, and frequently succeeded in capturing bruin, of whose flesh he was very fond. Deer were very common, and turkeys often made havoc with cornfields, in the fall of the year. Wolves were also numerous, and very destructive on sheep; their scalps commanded a fair price in money.

Mrs. James Kerr, daughter of Jacob Young, has in her possession a family Bible purchased by her father, with wolf scalps, in Columbiana county, over sixty-five years ago. It was a book duly venerated by Mr. Young, during his life. He made a conscientious effort to follow its precepts.

In July, 1815, John Whittaker, a surveyor of Columbiana county, was employed by William Montgomery to survey the original plat of the village of Uniontown, now Ashland, Ohio, and boarded at the cabin of Jacob Young, while so doing; for the site of the new village was covered by the original forest, and had no boarding houses or hotels for the accommodation of travelers.

In 1815 he helped erect the first school-house in Orange township, near his residence, in which John Swigart taught the first school, in the winter of 1815-16, and married Barbara Young, about the close of his school, which is supposed to have been the first wedding in Orange township. The ceremony was performed by 'Squire Newell, of Montgomery township, at the cabin of Jacob Young.

Mr. Young became a member of the Evangelical Lutheran church at the age of seventeen years, in Washington county, Pennsylvania, and continued faithful until his decease, which occurred in 1862, at the age of eighty-nine years, a period of about seventy-one years.

It is a sufficient panegyric upon the life and character of Mr. Young to say, that he never had a quarrel with any man; that he never sued any man; that he was never a defendant in a law-suit; that he was generous to all men; and that, while he was born under the dominion of King George III., he lived to see the independence of the American Republic, the establishment of the Union, and the prosperity and greatness of the States.

His wife, Mrs. Mary Mason Young, was a member of the same church from 1800 until her decease in 1865, being about ninety years and six months old.

The family of Mr. Young consisted of twelve children, two boys, John, who died in Van Wert county, Ohio, in 1851, and Abraham, who died in Missouri in 1877; and ten girls—Elizabeth, wife of the late Joseph Bishop; Barbara, wife of John Swigart; Mary, wife of John Swineford; Christiana, wife of Samuel Baughman; Phebe, wife of Rhinehart Allaphela; Sarah, wife of Abraham Marks; Amy, wife of John C. Kerr; Hannah, wife of Robert McKee; Nancy, wife of Jacob Marietta; and Margaret, wife of James Kerr. All survive but Mrs. Bishop.

The entire family, learned at an early day, lessons of industry, economy and morality, and lived to honor the parents that gave them birth. The loom was their parlor organ, and the busy hum of the spinning-wheel kept time with the music of the shuttle as it shot to and fro among the warp. All made intelligent, exemplary mothers, and faithful wives.

HOMER PECK

was born at Kent, Litchfield county, Connecticut, March 3, 1820. In April, 1826, his father, Taylor Peck, and family, consisting of his wife and four children, started in a wagon for Ohio; on arriving at Albany, New York, they took boat passage on the canal, to Buffalo. They found the route pleasant and cheap. At Buffalo they took passage on a schooner, and, after enduring a rough and tempestuous journey, arrived safely at Sandusky City. At that point Taylor Peck hired a team to remove his family and goods to Ruggles township, Huron, now Ashland, county. The trip occupied three days. The streams were full, and had to be forded at some risk. The road, a mere path cut through the forest, was rough and full of chuck holes. Upon reaching the center Mr. Peck and family were kindly received and sheltered under the hospitable roof of Daniel Beach, who had preceded him some three years to Ruggles township. When Mr. Peck arrived, there were about eight families in the township. He purchased one hundred and fifty-seven acres of land, in lots twenty and twenty-seven, section three, and went to work to clear the same; and by the aid of his neighbors soon had comfortable buildings and other improvements. Mrs. Jerusha Peck died in 1835, and Taylor Peck, the husband, died September 24, 1855. Homer Peck, a son, and subject of this sketch, married in 1845. His family consisted of four daughters, three of whom survive. Mr. Peck has lived to see the last of the pioneers pass away—being Harvey Sacket, who died August 11, 1875. He has been justice of the peace five terms. He is a member of the Congregational church, a Republican, and a reputable citizen.

ABRAHAM ARMENTROUT

was born near Harrisonburgh, Rockingham county, Virginia, December 15, 1797. In his youth he attended a subscription school and studied the elementary branches. In 1812 he volunteered, and served three months in the company of Captain William Harrison, under Colonel Spangler, at Richmond and Camp Bottom's bridge. After the expiration of his service he was apprenticed and learned the trade of a carpenter and house joiner. About the year 1817 his brother George, and family, removed to Worthington township, Richland county, and located near the present site of Newville. He was also a carpenter.

In December, 1818, Abraham Armentrout, then a single young man, journeyed on foot from Rockingham county, Virginia, through Cumberland, Maryland, along the pike which had been completed to Wheeling, where he crossed the Ohio river, and continued along Zane's trace to Zanesville, thence up the Licking to Newark, and thence to Mount Vernon, and, by the path leading through Clinton, to Lewis' block-house, on the Clear fork, where he found his brother. He married Miss Priscilla Wade, and worked at his trade until about 1821, when he became a farmer, and continued at that occupation until 1840, when he located at Hayesville, in what is now Ashland county. After his arrival in this county he kept a hotel about fourteen years, and, in 1854, became postmaster, and retained the office to the close of the administration of President Buchanan.

In September, 1863, Mrs. Amentrout deceased, since which period he has resided in the family of his son, Wade Armentrout, of Hayesville. He is in fair health, and possesses a good deal of physical vigor for a man of his age. The ancestors of Mr. Armentrout were English and German—on his father's side German, and on his mother's English. They settled in Rockingham county about the year 1690. His grandfather, Henry Armentrout, died there in 1792, at an advanced age. His father died in the same county in 1804.

George Armentrout located in Worthington township, Richland county, in 1817, and Philip Armentrout, another brother, in Knox county, near Mount Vernon, and Jacob in Cedar county, Iowa. The descendants of these brothers are quite numerous. The family retain a number of relics of the olden times. Abraham Armentrout has in his possession a copper tea-kettle, highly finished, which was imported by the family, on the mother's side, from England, about one hundred and fifty years ago. It is in good state of preservation, and quite a curiosity.

The family of Mr. Amentrout consisted of seven children, three sons and four daughters. Four yet survive—Mrs. Amanda Glass, wife of the late Dr. Samuel Glass, of Ashland, who was born in a little log cabin, twelve by twelve feet, in Worthington township, Richland county, and rocked in an humble cradle; Alpheus, of Windsor, Richland county; Anseville, wife of Judge John J. Gurley, of Mt. Gilead, Morrow county, and Wade, who resides in Hayesville.

HENRY CHURCH

was born in Suffolk, England, in 1750, and came as a British soldier in the Sixty-third light infantry, and served under Lord Cornwallis in the memorable campaign in Virginia, in 1781. A short time prior to the surrender of Cornwallis, at Yorktown, while on a scouting party between Richmond and Petersburgh, he was captured by the troops under Lafayette, and sent a prisoner to Lancaster, Pennsylvania. He remained there until peace was proclaimed; but the general amnesty brought no freedom to him. He was soon after captured by the meek eyes of a Quaker maiden, and forgot his loyalty to King George, and bowed his neck to the gentle yoke which he wore with exemplary patience for a period of about eighty-one years.

Hannah Keine, the lady that held him so long a captive, was born in Chester county, Pennsylvania, in 1755, and survived to the advanced age of about one hundred and five years. Mr. Church survived until 1863, when he died at the great age of one hundred and eleven years. He located near Burton, West Virginia, after the close of the Revolutionary war, and continued to reside there until his decease. The fruits of his union with the meek Quaker maiden were eight children, the oldest of whom, Anne, died at about sixty years of age; William, the next, lived to be about ninety-six years of age; James, the third member of the family, removed to Milton township, Ashland county, about the year 1817, and yet survives at the age of eighty-five years; Elsey, the fourth child, lived to be fifty-five; Henry, who still survives, is eighty years old; Elizabeth lived to be seventy-five; Hannah lived to be seventy, and Sarah, the youngest, still survives at the age of sixty-eight years. In 1859 an excursion party of artists, with some members of the British Legation at Washington city, visited Father Church at his humble home near Boston, and made drawings of his residence, himself and members of his family. A young English soldier, who had been decorated for gallant conduct on the bloody parapits of the Redan, was introduced to Mr. Church. The old gentleman extended his hand mechanically, but his dull-dim eyes gave no sign. "Bring here the bugle," said a member of the company. It was produced, and one of the martial airs of old England was sounded. Private Church, then one hundred and eight years old, stood up as if his blood had been warmed with wine, and his aged face flashed with intelligence. "I know—I know it. An Englishman and a soldier, did you say? Ay, a brave lad, I'll warrant." The scene was indeed touching. The old man, eighty years before, had landed on our shores an armed invader to aid in crushing out the spirit of revolt. With the sound of the martial bugle he, in imagination doubtless, heard the roll of musketry and the thunders of the deep-mouthed cannon. With his dim eyes he again called up and saw the scarlet battalions of his king marching towards the camps of Washington, Lafayette and Lee. What memories must have crowded upon his brain! He survived until 1863, and left his countrymen again in a death struggle to preserve the liberties and institutions bequeated by his fathers.

James Church, of Milton, born in 1791 in West Virginia, now 89, is in possession of all his faculties, though his bodily vigor is greatly impaired by reason of age. The longevity of the Church family is quite remarkable, and arises, no doubt, from their plain and simple diet.

Mr. Church has been twice married. His children by his first wife were Elsey, Henry, William, Hannah, wife of Henry Speece, Amanda, Mary, Elizabeth and Caroline.

JACOB CRALL

was born near Harrisburgh, Dauphin county, Pennsylvania, December 16, 1811. He is of German descent. He attended the common schools of his neighborhood until he reached manhood, and emigrated, in 1835, to Ashland, Ohio, and became a clerk in the store of R. B. Campbell & Co., where he remained about one year. In 1836 he became the partner of John P. Reynor in the mercantile business, and continued until 1838, when he separated from Reynor and formed a partnership with Hulbert Luther, under the name and style of Luther & Crall, and continued as a member of the firm until 1854. In 1851 he also, in company with Mr. Luther, opened a hardware store, which subsequently became the property of Crall and Topping. In the fall of 1851 he became a stockholder and one of the directors in the establishment of a bank of exchange and deposit in Ashland, and continued in the same until 1864. In 1864 the First National Bank of Ashland was organized under a law of Congress, and the stockholders of the bank of Luther, Crall & Co. transferred their interest to the new institution, and Mr. Crall became one of the directors, and still acts in that capacity. In the fall of 1855 he was elected treasurer of Ashland county, and held the office two years. In 1861 he was appointed postmaster of Ashland by the administration of Abraham Lincoln, and retained the office four years. He has been a member of the town council two years. He was elected mayor of Ashland in 1876. He is at present largely engaged in the purchase and sale of coal. As a business man he has always sustained an unblemished reputation. Very few men in this region have taken a deeper interest in the improvement of the county. He was among the foremost in procuring the location of a railroad at Ashland, and was engaged in its construction. He has been a member of the Methodist Episcopal church for a number of years. He married Miss Elizabeth M. Melsheimer, of Ashland, June 27, 1837. His family consists of three sons—George, of Virginia City, Nevada; Oscar F. of Ashland, and Charles, of California; and one daughter, Helen J., who resides with her parents.

JACOB O. JENNINGS

was born in Dauphin county, Pennsylvania, January 21, 1819; he is of English-German descent. His father deceased when he was a child. He attended, in his youth, the common schools of his neighborhood, near Middletown, Pennsylvania; and when about fourteen years of age, removed with his mother and family to Perry township, Wayne (now Ashland) county, where he attended district school. In the spring of 1834, he entered the store of Michael D. Row, at Row's corners, as a clerk, and remained about one year; then entered the employ of Joseph Naylor, as clerk, at Jeromeville, where he stayed until the fall of 1835. He then entered the employ of Crawford & Crites, merchants, at Wooster, and continued in their employ until 1838. In the spring of 1838, William Hatfield, then of Wooster, purchased a stock of goods at Loudonville, but circumstances preventing his going there himself, he employed Mr. Jennings to go and take charge of the store. In the fall of 1838, Mr. Hatfield and G. H. Stewart formed a partnership, and Mr. Jennings remained for, and in the interest of, Mr. Hatfield until August, 1842, when he returned to Jeromeville, and entered the employ of Robert McMahon. Soon after, he became a partner, and continued to do business until the spring of 1848. In the meantime, the county of Ashland was erected; and in March, 1847, Mr. Jennings was appointed clerk of the court of common pleas. In 1849, he removed with his family to Ashland. His term as clerk expired on the adoption of the constitution of 1851, and he retired in the winter of 1852. In the fall of 1851, the bank of Luther, Crall & Co., an institution of discount and deposit, was organized, and Mr. Jennings was elected cashier. In the fall of 1855, he was elected clerk of the court of common pleas of Ashland county, and held that office three years, at the same time conducting the affairs of the bank, as cashier. In 1864, the bank of Luther, Crall & Co. disbanded, and the First National Bank of Ashland was organized, under the laws of the United States, as a bank of issue and deposit, and Mr. Jennings was elected cashier by the stockholders, which position he held until 1870, when he was elected president, Mr. Joseph Patterson becoming the cashier. Mr. Jennings (1880) still continues president of the bank.

In the fullest sense of the term, he is a self-made man. In the death of his father, he was left without means to acquire a finished education. By close application, attention to business, and unquestioned integrity, he surrounded himself by friends, and made constant advancement in public confidence. Energetic, exact and upright in all his dealings with men, he commands the respect of the poor, as well as the thrifty. He has been twice married; his children are all deceased. He has been a member of the Presbyterian church, of Ashland, since 1856.

ARTHUR CAMPBELL, JR.,

was born in Washington county, Pennsylvania, January 19, 1810, and emigrated with his parents (Arthur Campbell, sr.,) to Perry township, Wayne, now Ashland, county, Ohio, in May, 1815. They came in two wagons, by the way of Steubenville, Canton, and Wooster, then villages, and followed Beall's trail. Mr. Campbell visited his land, which was entered at Canton, in 1814, in the fall of that year, and built a small cabin, stopping with John Raver while doing so. He located on section twenty-three, just southeast of what is now the village of Rowsburgh. When he landed, the pioneers of Perry are believed to have been John Raver, Henry and John Pittinger, David and Daniel Williams, Henry Worst, Cornelius Dorland, Benjamin Emmons, Thomas Johnston, and Samuel Chasey. Joseph Chandler, sr., and two sons, John Cory and father, and John Carr and family, had been in the township a short time prior to the war of 1812, but had returned to the east part of the State, where they remained until the close of the war, and then re-occupied their improvements. The settlers next succeeding Mr. Campbell, are believed to have been: William Adams, John Adams, Hugh Adams, Richard Smalley, Isaac Smalley, John Smalley, Henry Worst, James Dickason, Samuel White, Abraham Ecker, John Keiser, Michael Row, Jacob Shinnabarger, and perhaps others. The spring of the arrival of the family of Mr. Campbell, the Sandusky Indians came down and made sugar near what was afterwards the Hoy farm, at Red Haw, and a few of their poll huts, covered with bark, were left standing. The sap was gathered in bark vessels and boiled in copper kettles. The Indians were then quite peaceable. From 1815 until about 1820, they passed down the old trail once a year, in large numbers, to draw their annuities at Canton. The trail came by the Vermillion lakes, near the residence of the late Jacob Young, in Orange, and ran a southeast course to the cabin of John Raver, half a mile southeast of what is now Rowsburgh, passing by the cabin of Mr. Buckingham, in Montgomery, and thence to the cabin of John Premer, in Chester township, Wayne county, by the cabins of Judge Goodfellow and Adam Shinnaman, Yankee Smith, and across Killbuck, near Wooster. The trail was opened and traveled many years as a wagon road for the pioneers, though destitute of bridges.

The first year Mr. Campbell was compelled to visit Knox county, by pack-horses, for corn. The first trip was made in company with Benjamin Emmons. They followed Indians, directed by a small pocket compass, and camped out two nights, serenaded by immense packs of wolves, but were not harmed. After procuring a few sacks of corn it was ground at Shrimplin's mill and carried on pack-saddles, through the forests, to their cabins. Mr. Campbell was greatly mortified to learn, upon his arrival, that his family could not eat the meal. He was compelled to return to Washington county, with a wagon and three horses, to procure flour enough to last until his first crop had been harvested. In the spring of 1816 John Raver erected a small log mill with nigger-head stones, which did some business in the way of cracking corn. He afterwards added horse power, but the mill did not come up to his expectations. The major part of the pioneers obtained their grists at Stibbs' mill, one mile east of Wooster, until John Pittinger erected, in 1820, what afterwards became the Ecker mill, east of the village of Rowsburgh.

The people were destitute of the means of carrying on schools, but managed, by subscription, to gather their children into a log cabin for instruction, two miles northeast of the present site of Rowsburgh, at a point known as Mt. Hope graveyard. The first teacher was Alexander Smith, and the first school in 1816. The scholars were, John Allison, Alexander Allison, Peter Pittinger, Betsy McMillen, Robert Hillis, William Hillis, John Hillis, Peggy Hillis, Ellen Hillis, John Somerton, Tabor Somerton, Mary Campbell, Charles Campbell, Arthur Campbell, Henry Worst, Lydia Pittinger, and Mary Allison. Very few of these remain. Arthur Campbell speaks well of the school.

The first preaching was in the same school-house, and the first preacher Rev. Cole, about 1817. The first Sabbath-school was organized about the same time, at the same place. The children brought a lunch and remained all day, and were instructed and catechised. It was under the control of the Presbyterians, and Mr. Campbell took a deep interest in it. The congregation and school were small, but increased and flourished for many years.

Arthur Campbell, sr., was the first shoemaker in the township. He generally prepared shoes for his own family, and occasionally made brogans for his neighbors, though not having learned the trade in a regular way. Samuel Neal was the first tanner, and his establishment was carried on near Mt. Hope. A blacksmith arrived in the person of Thomas Andrews. The shop was located in the northwest part of the township, near what is now known as the Hance Hamilton farm. The shop was much frequented; and Mr. Andrews was not only a useful tradesman, but also acted as the first township clerk.

In the erection of the first cabins, almost any pioneer could prepare the clapboards, hew the logs or puncheons, and carry up a corner; but cabins began to improve as the farmers acquired means. Isaac Smalley, about 1817, became the first regular carpenter. He followed the business many years, and instructed a number of apprentices in the art.

In the absence of fulling mills and eastern manufactories, the good mothers made the spinning-wheels hum, night and day, until the flax and wool were prepared for the weaver. Henry Brown was the first wheelwright, maker of looms and chairs. He carried on his trade as early as 1817. The woollen goods thus woven were carried to a fulling mill, at Stibb's, near Wooster, fulled and dressed for winter wear.

Justice was first administered by 'Squire Thomas Johnston, who resided in the west part of the township. on what is now the Davault farm. Mr. Johnston, like 'Squire Newell and others, was not noted for his legal lore, but made a good practical officer, dispensing with the dry chaff of forms for the real substance.

The forests abounded in wolves, bear, deer, and other game. The wolves were destructive to sheep, and a premium was offered for their scalps, at Wooster. Mr. Campbell relates that a few weeks after the arrival of his father, in neglecting to shelter his sheep, he lost his whole flock in one night, by the wolves. Their throats were cut in the most scientific manner.

The most noted hunters in Perry were John Jackson and Thomas Pittinger; they ranged the forests for many miles, and killed annually hundreds of bear, deer, wolves and turkeys. They were very successful in trapping wolves, and often visited Wooster to obtain the result of their scalps.

In constructing new roads the pioneers traveled many miles, and were able to do but little more than cut a narrow wagon path. The construction of bridges at public expense was impossible, so that in times of heavy rains and freshets, the larger streams were, for weeks, impassable.

Mr. Campbell relates that some two years after their arrival, Mr. Robert McBeth and family, on their way to Clearcreek township, was delayed by the overflowing of the Muddy and Jerome forks, about three weeks, at his father's cabin.

The first deaths in Perry were Henry Johnston, son of Thomas Johnston, in 1814, of cancer of the lower jaw; James Campbell in 1814, of rheumatism in the foot; and the third death, a son, seven years old, of John Raver, frightened to death by a mouse under his pantaloons leg; he died in spasms some hours after the occurrence.

Arthur Campbell, sr., was killed, August 19, 1819, by the falling of a tree, at the age of forty-five years. A neighbor, Alexander Allison, was present when the accident happened. It was on the premises of John Pittinger. Messrs. Pittinger and Campbell were sitting near a tree conversing, when an oak tree in the clearing, which had been several hours burning, commenced falling. Mr. Allison noticed the falling tree, and instantly notified Campbell and Pittinger of their danger; Pittinger dodged behind a tree near by, but Campbell was struck in the act of rising, by a heavy limb, on the back causing instant death. He left a widow and seven children: Mary, Charles, Arthur, Margaret, Daniel, John, and William. These grew up in Perry township, and the living are Margaret, William, and Arthur. Mrs. Campbell died in 1865, aged eighty-three years.

Arthur Campbell, jr., married Lydia, daughter of Dr. Abram Ecker, by whom he had eleven children. Mrs. Campbell died in 1871. He married Mary, widow of James Scott, in 1877, and resides in Rowsburgh. Mr. Campbell came into the possession of the home farm, and has been a leading agriculturalist for many years. His children are nearly all grown, some of whom occupy the old homestead near Rowsburgh. He is a large, well-developed man, and would weigh about two hundred pounds, is full six feet high, and is in a good state of preservation, mentally and physically.

JOHN H. McCOMBS

was born June 13, 1813, in Washington county, Pennsylvania. He had two brothers, one James A. McCombs, died at the age of four years. Andrew M. McCombs was a member of Captain Barber's company, and died in the service on the thirtieth of April, 1862, at Ashland, aged forty-seven years and five months. His mother Ann McClean, was married to his father, Matthew McCombs, on the twenty-third day of April, 1812. His father served six months in the war of 1812, under General Harrison, and died, from the effects of the service, in the year 1822. His mother died at Ashland on the eighteenth of February, 1867, in the eighty-second year of her age.

Mr. McCombs' grandfather, on the father's side, was born in Ashland, and emigrated to, and bought a farm in. Washington county, Pennsylvania, and lived to about the age of eighty years, and his wife to near the same age. Mr. McCombs' grandfather, on the mother's side, Andrew McClean, died on his farm in Washington county, Pennsylvania, Smith township, at the age of eighty-five years, and his wife at the age of sixty-seven years. Grandfather McClean was born near Fort Deposit, Maryland, was a Revolutionary soldier, who died at a ripe age, full of years and full of faith, being an elder in the Presbyterian church of Raccoon. He performed an important part in procuring the liberties we now enjoy. He was in the battles of Brandywine, Long Island, Germantown, Monmouth, Stony Point, etc., serving five years, and enlisted at the age of seventeen. He saw and participated in the mighty event which, under Providence, ended in the permanent independence of this country, and died enjoying the confidence and esteem of all his neighbors. Mr. McCombs was left to the care of his mother, who brought him up and early taught him self-independence. He taught school in his neighborhood at the early age of sixteen. He commenced to acquire a liberal education at Florence academy, Washington county, Pennsylvania, then attended Washington college, and after a course of over five years was graduated at Franklin college, in Harrison county, Ohio, in the class of 1839. He then read law with the Hon. T. M. T. McKennan, who was secretary of interior under General Taylor, and his son William McKennan, now United States district judge for northwestern Pennsylvania, and he was admitted to the bar in Washington, Pennsylvania;

when he came to Ohio and resided in Richland connty one year; came to Ashland, Ashland county, Ohio, before the county was erected, and assisted in procuring the county-seat, where he has ever since resided and engaged in the practice of the law. He was married to Sarah A. Wright, a native of the State of New York, December 29, 1846. They had three children—S. Anna, Mary B., and John. The youngest, John, remains with the parents; Anna is married to S. W. Andrews, and Mary to James Whyte.

WILLIAM TAYLOR AND SONS.

Among the early settlers of what is now Ashland county was William Taylor, who emigrated from Pennsylvania in the year 1822, with his wife, eight sons and one daughter. He arrived at Mansfield in the month of June and remained there until autumn, when he removed on a farm which he had purchased, situated on what is called Honey creek, in Green township, Ashland county, but at that time belonged to Richland county. He brought with him from Pennsylvania eleven head of horses, three wagons and a set of blacksmith tools, and quite a number of farming utensils. In 1830 he was elected commissioner, and for several years filled the office of justice of the peace. After a great many years of hard labor he became the owner of nearly a thousand acres of land, and on which he quite extensively carried on farming and stock-raising. Mr. Taylor was born in Bucks county, Pennsylvania, in the year 1774, and died in 1851. Jane, wife of William Taylor, was born in Huntingdon county, Pennsylvania, in the first year of American independence, and died in 1832. William, their eldest son, in 1828 located in Findlay, Hancock county, Ohio, where he embarked in merchandising, and became quite a prominent business man. He at one time represented his county in the State legislature. Thomas, the second son, was a farmer, and settled in Wood county, where he remained until death. Levi followed his brother to Hancock county. He began active life on a farm, but was afterwards elected treasurer of his county. James foresaw Horace Greeley's advice, and emigrated to Oregon in 1844. He was with the first train that crossed the Rocky mountains in search of gold, and at one time he was territorial treasurer of Oregon. He has been successful in business and has amassed quite a fortune. He is at the present time in retired life on the banks of the Columbia river. Daniel is a farmer, and at present resides in Richland county, Ohio. He is a man of energy and enterprise, and has been successful in life. He was commissioner of his county during the building of the new court house. Andrew J. took up his abode in Putnam county, Ohio, and for several years was clerk of the court, and filled the office of probate judge for six years. He now resides in Paulding county, Ohio. Sarah J. McGuire, the only daughter, resides in Green township, near the old homestead. Judge John, the only son in this county, has most of his life lived on a farm, and always dealt more or less in stock, and in an early day, before railroads in this county, drove a great deal of stock across the Alleghany mountains. He served as justice of the peace for his township for many years, and was elected to the State legislature in 1859, and re-elected in 1861; and in 1875 was elected probate judge, and re-elected in 1878, and holds that position at the present time.

JUDGE DANIEL W. WHITMORE

was born in the town of Leicester, county of Livingston, and State of New York, March 2, 1823. His father was quite an extensive farmer when Daniel was a small boy. He was the oldest of his father's children. Mr. Whitmore remained with his parents, worked on the farm, and attended to his father's business, until he was about eighteen years of age, when he became afflicted with sciatic and inflammatory rheumatism, and, consequently, could do but little labor on the farm. Up to this time he had attended a common district school, only two or three months each winter, which was one and a half miles from his father's residence. He could imperfectly read, write, and cipher a little, which was about the extent of his education. Being an invalid, and knowing, from the condition of his physical organization, that he would not likely ever be able to perform hard manual labor, and possessing an ambitious disposition to be, or do, something in the world, with the influence of his mother he obtained the consent of his stern father to let him go to a select school at Perry center, three terms, in all nine months. In the estimation of his father, nearly all professional men were, more or less, contaminated with one, or all, of the following vices: Intemperance, recklessness, and dishonesty, and the laziest man made the best fiddler, and the next laziest would come in as a country school-teacher.

School-teaching he had chosen as his profession. As a student, his full determination was to know the principles of his studies. All the time he attended the select school he did not lose an hour, sometimes studying until midnight. To be a good and successful school-teacher, was his aim. To that end he spared neither pains nor expense. After the close of the last term of the select school, he returned home and attended a graded school taught by Professor Nuland, a graduate of the normal school at Albany, New York. In the autumn of 1845 he made application to Mr. Crosby, town superintendent, for a certificate to teach school, and draw public money for his services. He had no difficulty in procuring a school, as he had a recommendation from the professor and superintendent. He taught a term of four months, and, at the close of the term, he received for the services he had rendered, sixty-four dollars. He never had so much money at one time before. He states that he would have been well recompensed if he had not received a dollar, for he never passed a more agreeable winter. The following summer he attended the district school at home, three months, which was taught by a thorough and practical teacher, and studied the remainder of that summer at home. The winter following he engaged as assistant teacher in a graded normal school. The following summer, his health being poor, he visited the sulphur springs, at Avon, New York.

In the month of September, 1847, he came to Ashland, Ohio, on a visit; and a long one it has proven, for it has lasted thirty-three years. He had not been thirty miles from home before. His first night in Ohio was passed in Oberlin. In the coach that carried him from Oberlin to Ashland, he met a tall, elderly gentleman, who was very jovial and communicative. A couple of days after arriving at Ashland, he was informed that there was an interesting lawsuit in progress at the Stone church, then used as a court-room, to decide whether Ashland village should remain the county-seat of Ashland county. There, to his surprise, stood the tall, spare man, who came in the coach with him, pleading in the interests of Ashland village. Upon enquiry, he found the interesting speaker to be Reuben Wood, the great expounder of law, from Cleveland.

A few days after arriving at Ashland, he became acquainted with one of Ohio's most gifted and talented sons—one of the most energetic, generous, scholarly and self-sacrificing of men, and who did everything in his power for the advancement of the rising generation; that man was Lorin Andrews. Being informed where Mr. Whitmore formerly resided, and that he had taught school, and that he was familiar with the methods employed in the common and graded schools in the State of New York, Mr. Andrews strongly urged him to remain in the county and teach school, and help him and other teachers in the cause of education. He informed him that he had a district school in view, that wanted to engage a school-teacher, and was willing and able to pay the highest wages to a teacher who would teach them a good school and give general satisfaction; he was fully convinced it was a difficult school to govern. Mr. Whitmore took Professor Andrews' advice, and made application for the school referred to.

After several interviews with Mr. James Anderson, one of the school directors, Mr. Whitmore engaged to teach school for fifteen dollars per month of twenty-four days, and to receive his board in the homes of his pupils. He was admonished that the school would be a difficult one to manage. He believed that good order was the first and leading principle in successful school-teaching. He commenced his school on the day agreed upon, and had a much larger number of pupils at the commencement than he expected. He distinctly recollects this, his first day of school-teaching in Ohio. The most of his pupils on this day were from five to fifteen years old, and in appearance robust and healthy, with sparkling eyes and anxious countenances, and in their behavior quiet and mannerly. The second day a few more came, and his school continued to so increase through the winter that his average daily attendance was over forty. His school-room was considered to be one of the best in the township, and was of peculiar structure and greatly in contrast with what he had been accustomed to see and use in the east. It was constructed of logs, nearly twenty feet square, about seven feet high to the eaves, and roofed with oak shingles. Yet it let in water and snow when the storms were violent. The chimney was built on the outside; the foundation was built of stone, brick and clay mortar. Mr. Whitmore found, after he had taught a few days, that he had the material for a good school, provided he could get the parents and householders to purchase their children suitable school books. This he finally accomplished after much persistent effort. He persuaded Professor Andrews to visit his school and give the parents of the pupils a lecture upon the subject, which had a wholesome effect. Mr. Whitmore offered to purchase school books for the pupils of such parents as could not afford to buy them then, and wait until they could repay him.

An effort was made, just before holiday time, by some of the older pupils, lead on by young men not members of the school, to have Mr. Whitmore agree to treat the scholars, after the usual custom that then prevailed. The teacher refused to agree to anything of the kind, much to the chagrin of some of his pupils; but after the time had passed, and all hope of a treat had been given up, he surprised his school with a most liberal distribution of fruit and palatable delicacies. Mr. Whitmore relates the following:

In one school district, a teacher was barred out, because of his refusing to treat, and wanted possession of his school-room. His scholars were all in, and had the doors and windows well fastened. The teacher, expecting to be barred out, had prepared himself for the emergency. He got a ladder, and ascending to the top of the house, dropped sulphur down the flue into the stove, where there was a good fire. It ignited so quickly that the room soon became filled with a strong sulphurous odor, and the scholars were obliged to open the doors and windows to breathe, putting the teacher in victorious possession.

In another district the case was similar, but the scholars were more shrewd. After the teacher had ascended the ladder to the cone of the house, and was trying to smoke his scholars out, by covering the top of the chimney, one of the boys crawled out of a window, and took the ladder down, leaving the gentleman teacher on the top of the house, with the cutting wind whistling around, to keep him cool and bring him to time. He begged to have the ladder replaced, but the boys would not unless he would consent to treat. After a couple of hours of shivering meditation, he came to the conclusion that he had better treat than freeze, or kill himself by jumping down. The contract was not considered binding unless it was in writing, so one of the boys took a long pole, and, tying the agreement to be signed and a pencil to the end of it, reached them up to him, when he signed the agreement and threw it down. The boys replaced the ladder, and he came down nearly frozen. So they compelled the teacher to treat, and had a jolly good time.

It was not customary for the householders to take part in the treating business, but let the children and teacher fight it out. One of the parties would generally back down or give up in a few days, or the school would be entirely closed for that term.

Mr. Whitmore had marked success with his first school; and public funds being lacking, money was raised by subscription, and he was invited to teach a summer school in the same district, and was employed again for the winter session. His further experience as a teacher extended over a number of years, and it is to be regretted that sufficient space cannot be given to recount the many interesting facts and events connected with his school-teaching days. His contribution to education in the county of Ashland was very great.

The text-books then used were the elementary spelling-book, McGffeuy's readers, Mitchell's geography, and atlas, Green's grammar and analysis, Adams' new arithmetic, and Colburn's mental arithmetic; and a good deal of writing was done. They had no steel or gold pens, and no writing-books with plated copies. After arriving at the school-houses in the morning and making a fire and sweeping the room, Mr. Whitmore's next task was to write copies and make pens out of geese quills, and sometimes his pupils would bring turkey quills as a substitute when geese quills could not be conveniently had. Their ink was mostly made by his pupils or their parents out of the water which maple or chestnut bark had been strongly boiled, then putting in coperas and boiling it with the liquid to its proper thickness, and then straining. It made a very good black ink.

The following principles were a guide to Mr. Whitmore in his educational labors, and he endeavored to have his pupils governed by them: 1st. That it is no disgrace to perform manual labor, but an honor, a credit and a benefit to themselves, to the community, and to their country. To be industrious, economical and saving should be the aim of all, and that physical and mental exercise are necessary to fulfill nature's laws; and that they should not forget the old adage, that "idleness is said to be the mother of crime." 2d. The sure way to success was for them to depend upon themselves, and that self-reliance, with proper exertions, would enable them to accomplish whatever they might reasonably undertake, and that it is all within their own power to have or not to have the confidence and respect of their fellowmen, and a person without friends is a miserable being. Wirt says, and it is true, that every person is the architect of his own fortune. 3d. That they should be honest in all their business transactions, tell the truth on all occasions, and they would be well rewarded for their uprightness and truthfulness; that they should never forget, but always follow, the precepts of that good old maxim: "Honesty is the best policy." 4th. That they should at all time reverence and treat their parents with respect and kindness; be civil, quiet and mannerly, and not forget the golden rule, but practice it: "Do unto others as you would have others do unto you." Much other good advice he gave to his pupils.

Mr. Whitmore had determined to follow farming for a livelihood, but in the spring of 1857 he was elected township treasurer, and the following spring moved back to Milton township, in this county, and in the autumn of 1858 was elected real estate appraiser for the township of Milton, and assessed the value of the realty the following summer. In the spring of 1861 he was elected justice of the peace. At the expiration of three years he declined a re-election, but was elected again in the spring of 1866, and was re-elected again in the spring of 1869, and in the month of October, 1869, was elected probate judge for Ashland county, and three years thereafter re-elected probate judge for the second term, which expired in February, 1876; since that time he has employed himself in farming.

JACOB GIBSON

was born in York county, Pennsylvania, March 31, 1797. In 1804 his parents removed to Allegheny county, where his father died, and in 1810 his mother removed to what was then Jefferson county, Ohio, and settled near the village of Cadiz, in what is now Harrison county, where his mother died, in 1814. He then learned the clothier business, serving three years at the trade. He then returned to York county, Pennsylvania, and remained there until 1817, and then went to Washington county, where he worked at the trade until 1819, and in 1823 married Miss Mary Gault, removing to Ohio county, Virginia. In 1825 he came to Belmont county, Ohio, where he built a fulling-mill, and carried it on until 1836, when he removed to Clearcreek township, then Richland, now Ashland, county, and located one and a quarter miles west of Haneytown, now Savannah, on the Vermillion river, in 1836. Here he built a fulling-mill, a carding-machine, and a saw-mill, and purchased the farm upon which he now resides, one hundred and sixty acres. He carried on his mills about twenty years, in the meantime operating his farm. For the last twenty-eight years, 1851 to 1879, he has devoted his time wholly to his farm. When he came the leading pioneers of his region were the Freeborns, the Fords, the Baileys, Joseph Davis, James Gribben, Jacob Myers, Thomas Cook, John Gault, John Haney, and others. At that time the Indians had all disappeared, though there was much talk about them. The story of the captivity of Christian Fast was often related, and he often met Mr. Fast at his mills. When clearing some ground on the bottom, east of his house, he came upon the remnants of an Indian village, where the *Delawares* had often encamped and cooked. He found hearths, or pot-holes, of boulders, where fires had been built, and large amounts of charcoal had been burned. The boulders had been so frequently heated that they were much stained and reddened by the fire. After Mr. Fast came, the Indians had a feast at this place. The sugar trees were much hacked, by the Indians, in tapping to make sugar, before the whites came, all over the bottom. Mr. Gibson died in 1874, of heart disease, aged seventy-six years. The family of Mr. Gibson consists of John, William, and Robert. William lives in Cleveland, and Robert in the State of Indiana. His daughters were, Malinda, wife of James Chambers; Margaret Jane, deceased; Lucina, wife of Dr. William Shaw, deceased; Malissa, wife of Levi Shiply, a widow, and Leticia, single. Mr. Gibson has been an exemplary church member for many years. In 1878 he became a member of the Ashland County Pioneer society, in which his name has been enrolled for future reference. He is now, 1879, in his eighty-third year, and possesses a fair share of vigor, for a man of his age. His memory is clear and retains past events, and rehearses pioneer times with much interesting detail.

John Gibson, son of Jacob Gibson, resides on the adjoining farm in Clearcreek township, which is under a good state of culture, and quite valuable. His family is small, and they own a pleasant home.

MARTIN HENRY MANSFIELD

was born in the city of New York, December 1, 1821, and left an orphan by the death of his father and mother when quite young. There were but two children, Martin H. and William, who by the intervention of friends, succeeded in finding desirable homes in Pennsylvania. Martin found a place at the home of the father of Senator Patterson, at Mifflintown, Juniata county, where he grew to manhood and learned business habits. He early developed a talent for mechanical pursuits, and devoted his time in perfecting machinery to aid the agriculturist. He never had any training by practical machinists, and his mechanical ideas were all born with him, and of a wonderful cast. About 1846 he began to evince his peculiar talent for invention, and letters patent were granted by the office in Washington for improvements in clover hullers; his object being to enlist the farmers in raising clover for the purpose of saving the seed, and enhancing the price of both clover and seed, and in making it a valuable crop as a fertilizer of failing lands, and a good feed for stock. When patented his original huller was visited by many farmers, and looked upon as an effort that would aid in saving the seed, and increase a disposition to raise and save increased crops wherever introduced. He visited several States with a view to interesting farmers in the enterprise, and selling territory. He met with some encouragement, but not such as the merits of his invention warranted, and finally turned his attention to Ohio, where his invention attracted a good deal of attention, and finally settled in Mifflin township, in Richland county, where he commenced the manufacture of his huller in 1848.

His original object was to enlist mechanics who would engage in making this huller. His shop was at first in Mifflin, in Juniata county, Pennsylvania. He procured two horses and a wagon, and with one of his hullers and cleaners commenced to canvass, hoping to encourage the growing of clover, but met with little success in selling machines and patents. It was then in the fall and winter, when clover could be procured to exhibit the machine by hulling and cleaning the seed. The weather was generally stormy, with rain or snow, arresting the hulling and cleaning. It was not pleasant work exhibiting the machine. The roads became very bad, and he could hardly travel.

In the winter of 1848 he made a trip to Ohio and made an effort to sell the patent, and operated among the farmers of Richland and Ashland counties, but without sales. In Ashland he put up at the hotel kept by the late James McNulty. While at his hotel he drove out to the farm of the late Isaac Davis, near the Mifflin line, and states that by that time "he was flat broke" in finances. He remained with Mr. Davis about two weeks, and sold one machine to Isaac Roland and Jacob Hoover, for fifty dollars—about half-price—getting twenty-four dollars cash and a note for the balance. He found that in his travels it would be better to sell machines than patents. So he determined to come to Ohio and engage in manufacturing his huller and cleaner, and never again offer a patent right for sale. Before leaving he went to Mansfield and partly arranged with Messrs. Hall and Allen, then proprietors of the Mansfield Machine Works, to assist in making his huller. Leaving Ashland county, he returned to Juniata county, Pennsylvania, receiving from Roland and Hoover twenty-four dollars, balance due on a machine, which carried him safely through the mountains, there then being no railroad for conveyance to Ohio. About six weeks after, being in December, 1848, he arrived at his old home. It is proper to state that Mr. Saiger, a brother-in-law, accompanied him on his former trip. In a good covered spring wagon, with curtains, and a pair of good horses and about eight hundred pounds of goods and clothing, and in February, 1849, his wife, Mr. Saiger and himself started for Ohio. The roads were then frozen and were smooth, much resembling a plank floor all the way to Mansfield, where he rented a house from Dr. Teegarden, and lived in it until April, 1849. Having failed to complete a contract with Messrs. Hall & Co., to manufacture machines, and becoming scarce of money, he concluded to settle in Mifflin township, near Mr. Isaac Davis, and start a shop of his own, furnished by Mr. Steinhour, who lived near, and with his assistance, he being a mechanic, made hullers. On the first of April, 1849, he moved near Mr. Davis, and commenced making clover hullers in a small way. He made five that spring and summer, and sold them all in the fall. He remembers that George Stillwagon and Daniel Koogle, near Mifflin, bought machines and gave him a friendly recommend among the farmers, which aided him very much, these gentlemen having done a good deal of hulling during that fall and winter. Mr. Mansfield regarded this act as very kind to the day of his decease, and attributed his success to the aid of such friends. It was the means of selling a number of hullers that fall and winter, and was the cause of many other sales in Ashland county. By this means he had accumulated a small amount of money by April 1, 1850, when he removed to Ashland and settled in an old frame building opposite the house of the late Captain A. Walker, on Third street, in which he lived and used as a shop for two years.

The demand for hullers was very great, and it became necessary to procure more room. So he purchased outlot number sixteen, of Joseph Wasson, in South Ashland, where he built a shop, where Robert McMurray subsequently built a residence. The shop was twenty-four by sixty feet, two stories high, one of which was converted into a dwelling, where Mr. Mansfield lived, having moved into it, until the spring of 1852. A short time after he attached a foundry, and made plows and other farm implements, having a blacksmith shop, with steam engine. The demand for hullers kept increasing from year to year—some years running as high as one hundred—until he was compelled to enlarge his facilities, and, in the summer of 1853, Mr. D. Whiting built him a residence, where he resided, which gave him all the room he needed for the hullers. In 1856 he entered into partnership with D. Whiting, who built a shop on ground formerly owned by the late George Swineford, as a tannery and residence, and now occupied by Messrs. Whiting & Shearer for the manufacture of agricultural implements. After he and Mr. Whiting formed a partnership they increased their facilities for manufacturing. He sold one-half of the undivided interest in his patents to Mr. Whiting, after having conducted a thriving business four years, being limited to that time. In January, 1860, he sold his interest in the machine works to Mr. Whiting. On the fourth of January, 1861, he purchased lot number thirty-five, on the south side of Main street, in Ashland, from William Skilling, and commenced again to make hullers, during the year, in an old building on the lot. He seems to have been destined to wear out in improving and making clover machinery.

In 1862 he built the brick building that now stands upon the lot opposite the *Times* office, and in 1866, put up the rear brick. The front part is about twenty-eight by seventy-five feet, two stories high, with a basement. The rear is thirty-eight by seventy-five feet, with same number of stories as front. It is now occupied by F. E. Myers & Brother as an agricultural implement store-room. These buildings were built for the manufacture of clover hullers; also with a view to other employments.

Previous to 1864 the clover hullers and cleaners made in Ashland were not like the ones made at the present day. They hulled and cleaned the seed from the clover heads after the straw was first removed by a separate machine, or by a wheat threshing machine, or in some other manner. In 1858 Mr. John Birdsall, then of New York State, obtained a patent for combining in one machine, a cylinder to thresh the heads, from the straw, and a cylinder to hull the seed, with separating and cleaning apparatus. These were called double-cylinder machines. Other manufacturers immediately commenced to make the two-cylinder machines. Mr. Birdsall brought suit in the United States court against several parties for infringements upon his machine. In order to compete with Mr. Birdsall, and not to infringe upon his patents, Mr. Mansfield constructed in the fall of 1863, a machine with only one cylinder to do the same work as that done by the Birdsall two cylinder machine. To the surprise of quite a number of manufacturers he was successful, and succeeded in obtaining a patent for his machine in 1864, 1866, and in 1871, with additional improvements. In 1875 he retired from business, and granted a license to Messrs. Russell & Co., of Massillon, Ohio, and since then retired from the business altogether, in consequence of ill health, and being affected with a bronchial trouble, brought on by being exposed to the clover dust by experimenting, setting up and starting clover hullers for the past thirty years.

Since the Mansfield machine was invented, and introduced among the farmers of this part of Ohio, the production of clover has been largely increased, the acreage being more than five times as great as formerly. The land has been greatly improved by raising the crop, the old adage that "he that causes one blade of grass to grow, where it had not previously grown, must be regarded a benefactor of his race," is literally true. It was Mr. Mansfield's pride, not only to be a successful inventor, but to aid the farmer in producing a valuable crop. In this respect, his value to the agriculturist cannot easily be determined. He has now done his last work, and been called home to rest. He died April 4, 1880, and was buried April 6, 1880.

As a mechanic, he was very successful; in fact, he may be regarded as a genius in invention. He was methodical and unassuming in manner, and deemed a very generous and conscientious manager of his business. Employes speak of him only in a spirit that evinces true affection. They carried him, with many tears, to his last resting place in the cemetery, accompanied by hundreds of citizens, who had learned, by long association, to love and respect him.

Mr. Mansfield was married to Miss Anna Saiger, of Mifflintown, Juniata county, Pennsylvania, February 1, 1848. Of this union there were eleven children, seven boys and four girls; two boys died young, and five survive. Two members of the family are married, William and Anna Belle.

GEORGE SWINEFORD

was born in Northumberland county, Pennsylvania, September 22, 1797, and came to Ashland county with his parents in 1819. He married Miss Rosa Ewing, of Mohican township, in 1820. She was a daughter of John Ewing, one of the pioneers of that township. Mr. Swineford was a tanner by trade, and one of the first mechanics of Ashland. His tan-yard stood where the agricultural works of David Whiting were built. Mr. Swineford continued in business until about 1850, when he removed to his farm in the country, some two miles east of Ashland, on the Wooster road. Mr. Swineford was for several years in feeble health, and died in 1866, aged sixty-nine years. His family consisted of nine living children, and three deceased, at his death. They were— Mahala, Sopharus, Anthony, Harriet, John, Lewis, Ellen, Almira, Rosa; and the dead, Rosa, George and William.

Mrs. Swineford survived until April 15, 1878, when she deceased, aged seventy-two years.

WILLIAM W. ILGAR

was born in Berks county, Pennsylvania, June 27, 1813, and came to Ashland in 1836. He had learned his trade at harness making and as a saddler in Pennsylvania. When he first came to town he worked in the shop of the late Hugh Davis about three years, and started a shop of his own, and has continued in business since the year 1839. For the last ten years he has been engaged in carriage trimming, at which he is a fine mechanic. He was married to Miss Mahala Swineford, daughter of George Swineford, in 1842. His family consists of Charles, George, and Clara, and three boys dead. Charles, Clara and George are married. Mr. Ilgar is much respected as a citizen, and has frequently been elected to the town council and other offices.

MICHAEL MYERS

was born January 24, 1814, in Germany, and came to America with his parents and settled in Lebanon county, Pennsylvania, in the fall of 1814. From there his parents removed to Dauphin county, where they lived about eight years, and then removed to Center county, where they resided until 1832, when they removed to Columbia county, where they remained about two years, and then emigrated to Richland county, Ohio, in 1836, and settled near Savannah, then known as Haneytown, in Clearcreek township.

Here he became acquainted with and married Miss Anne Mason, daughter of Martin Mason, and then resided about two years in Ruggles township, Huron county, after which he removed to Montgomery township, and purchased his present homestead. The fruits of his marriage have been sixteen children, fourteen of whom still survive. His sons are Charles, Alonzo, John, Martin, Joseph, Frank, and George; the girls are Mary Anne, Lucia, Elizabeth, Irene, Ella, Ida, and Maggie; all married but two boys and one girl.

Mr. Myers came in 1836, and has been a resident of Montgomery township forty-four years, and, all the time, he has been a practical farmer. He has been a member of the Methodist Episcopal church ten years. He now attends all Protestant churches, miscellaneously. Mr. Myers owns a good farm, which is in an excellent state of cultivation, and yields an abundance to reward him for his toil. He has quite an interesting family who have been raised to habits of industry and economy, and are respected as useful and exemplary citizens.

DANIEL VANTILBURG, SR.,

was born in New Jersey, in 1781, and with his father's family settled in Jefferson county, Ohio, about 1809 or 1810, where he served as a soldier under General R. Beall, in the war of 1812, in the Sandusky campaign. He located one hundred and sixty acres of land, one and one-half miles south of Ashland, on the Hayesville road, which he cleared up and improved, and where he died, August 4, 1866, at the ripe old age of eighty-five years. He married, in 1813, in Jefferson county, Ohio, Miss Margaret Clinton, by whom he had six children, three boys and three girls. The boys were: Henry, who died in 1843; John, who died in 1846; and Daniel, who died in 1877. Mrs. Vantilburg died in 1864, aged about seventy-one years.

Daniel Vantilburg, jr., died in May, 1877, aged fifty-six years. His family consisted of Margaret, John, William, and George. Margaret married Dr. Charles Campbell, and died in 1879. Mrs. Vantilburg's name before marriage was Clarissa Myers. She was born January 22, 1828, and was married to Daniel Vantilburg, jr., January 3, 1846.

JOHN RAMSEY

was born in Maryland, near Baltimore, February, 1790, and came into Wayne county, Ohio, about 1822, and afterward settled on his homestead in section thirty-five, in Orange township. His father located in Jackson township, and by his assistance cleared up the farm which came into the possession of John, after the death of his father, whose name was William, and who died at the age of eighty-six years. Mr. Ramsey passed through all the early pioneer scenes, such as cabin-raisings, log-rollings, corn-huskings, attending the first mills, or in the use of hominy blocks, which were in extensive demand, flax-pullings or scutchings, and the evening dances on such occasions. These were regarded as occasions of much fun by the young people. Those days are all gone. Age gradually comes on, and many of his associates of fifty years ago have been gathered to their long home. Mr. Ramsey has a fine estate, and has always lived on agreeable terms with his neighbors, and does not know of a single enemy in the world. He states that he has always obeyed the dictates of conscience, and treated all men kindly, and believes when his time is at an end, the Good Being will reward his actions in a better world. He has always lived a single life, believing that he would have less trouble and be quite as happy as those who married. He has one hundred and sixty-six acres of land in Orange township, and ninety in Jackson, and thinks he is in no danger of coming to want. William Ramsey, of Jackson, is a brother. He is eighty-two years of age. Mr. Ramsey resides with a widowed sister on his one hundred and sixty acre lot in Orange township. The widow is the wife of the late Samuel Tilton, and aged about seventy-two years. Mr. Ramsey is quite cheerful and is perfectly contented and happy, and may live to see his hundredth anniversary.

EPHRAIM WELCH

was born November 27, 1800, in Washington county, Pennsylvania, and came to Orange township, Richland, but now Ashland, county, in February, 1828. The farm upon which he located, and which he cleared up and improved, section two, southeast quarter, had been entered by his father, and some timber girdled prior to his improving it. He married Miss Jane McAdoo, of Scotch-Irish descent, October 2, 1827, in Washington county, Pennsylvania, who came with him when he

J. W. SMITH.

put up his first cabin, and submitted to all the hardships of pioneer life. The union was blessed by four sons, James, John, Johnson, and Rankin, and two daughters, Catharine, married to Dr. Bailey, and Mary Jane, married to Levi Mason, of Ashland.

Ephraim Welch deceased April 1, 1874, aged about seventy-four years. Mrs. Welch resides in district number one, and remembers many of the early teachers. She mentions among their number: Isaac Stull, Clarissa Rising, Shadrach Bryan, and others. Mrs. Welch has one hundred and sixty acres of land in the old homestead, which is well improved and valuable. She states that her earliest neighbors were, John McConnell, William McConnell, Thomas McConnell, George McConnell, all from Washington county, Pennsylvania; Jacob Ridenour, Robert Walters, Thomas Donley, John Bishop, Samuel Mackeral, Robert Culberson, Peter Biddinger, Robert Mickey, James Clark, John Sibert, John Haun, and Jacob Hiffner. Mrs. Welch is a member of the United Presbyterian church, of Savannah, and has been for fifty years. She is at this time in good health, and seems to possess a clear recollection of former events in Orange township.

DANIEL SUMMERS

was born in Westmoreland county, Pennsylvania, May 27, 1788, and came to Orange township, Richland county, Ohio, in 1818, and located on section ten, where he died, August 15, 1863, aged seventy-five years and seventeen days. During his pioneer life, he passed through many hardships incident to the times, such as cabin-raisings, log-rollings, corn-huskings, flax-scutchings, and the like. For the first few years, he and his family met with many privations; but he met all bravely, and was employed often in assisting his neighbors to improve their lands, and in erecting cabins. Mr. Summers married in Lancaster county, Pennsylvania, December 5, 1815. At his decease his family consisted of seven girls and four boys: Barbara, Mary, Catharine, Margaret, Susan, Eliza, Hannah, Henry, Adam, Daniel and Jacob. Four of the girls, Susan, Catharine, Eliza and Barbara, are dead; the boys are all living.

The first settlers, Mrs. Summers states, were: Philip Fluke, James Clark, Peter Biddinger (the first gunsmith), Thomas Donley, Robert Mickey, Mr. Wheeler and sons, William Patterson, John McConnell, William McConnell, George McConnell and others, now nearly all gone. Mrs. Summers also states that the earliest teachers in that district remembered, were: Isaac Stull, Sage Kellogg, Elijah Banning, and many others not now remembered.

Mrs. Summers is a member of the German Reformed church, and has been for the past sixty-four years. She remains on the old homestead, and taught her children lessons of industry, morality and economy.

JAMES W. SMITH, ESQ.,

was born March 2, 1818. His father, John V. Smith, then resided three miles east of Wooster, Ohio, and owned what was known as Smith's mill, situated on Apple creek. In 1824 he built a mill in Cedar valley, six miles northwest of Wooster, where he lived until 1841, after which he continued to reside in Wooster until his death, January 24, 1852.

James W. was the fourth son, and was one of a family of thirteen children by the same parents. At an early age he manifested a strong desire for education, and soon acquired a knowledge of all the branches then taught in the common schools. At the age of fifteen he left the paternal home and engaged in a drug store, with Dr. J. P. Coulter, of Wooster, but, after an experience of about one year, he was engaged by his eldest brother, V. C. Smith, as a clerk in his dry goods store at Congress (then Waynesburgh), where he remained another year, when his brother sold out and quit business there. It was then that he fully determined to engage in literary pursuits, and not being satisfied with a common school education, he and his brother, William Harrison Smith, shouldered their bundles of clothing, and, for want of a better mode of travel, footed it across the country to the then famous Norwalk academy, in two days, a distance of fifty miles, where he remained until 1835, when the academy building burned down. The school was temporarily suspended, and Mr. Smith returned to Wooster, and became a clerk in the store of V. C. Smith & Co., the firm consisting of his brother and father.

In 1837 he, in company with his friend, the late Samuel Hemphill, esq., of Wooster, took passage on a canal-boat at Canal Fulton, for the Ohio university, at Athens, Ohio, and, having reached Lancaster, they were compelled to foot it across to Athens, a distance of forty-five miles, there being neither stage-coach, canal, or railroad, between the towns at that time. Hope then boomed, and the prospect was fair for a classical education, but, after studying the languages and higher mathematics for a year or more, he was induced to suspend the collegiate course, and entered the law office of the late Judge Cox, of Wooster, and, in the month of October, 1841, was admitted to practice as an attorney and counsellor-at-law, at Millersburgh, Ohio. He first commenced practice at Bucyrus, Ohio, but, on the death of Silas Robbins, esq., an old lawyer well known to the older settlers of this county, Mr. Smith located at Ashland, in July, 1842, and opened a law office with his late preceptor, Judge Cox, as his partner.

Ashland county had no existence at that time, but was part of Richland county, and, in this connection, it is worthy of note, that having experienced the great inconvenience of practicing law away from the county-seat, and feeling that the growing demands of the time for a new county must give Ashland the superiority over all other localities, at the suggestion of the late I. P. Reznor, Mr. Smith took measures to call the first new county meeting that was ever held in Ashland, by giving notice in person to the citizens of the town to meet at the counting-room of Luther & Crall, at a time named, to consider the question of a new county, with Ashland as the county-seat. The meeting was accordingly held, and he was made chairman of the committee, and actually drafted the notice and petitions to be signed by the citizens, and presented it to the legislature, fixing the boundaries of the proposed new county. In the winter of 1845-46, being the second session of the legislature after the enterprise began, it was successful, and the county of Ashland began its own independent existence, and thus became historic.

In the month of October, 1843, James W. Smith was married to Miss Augusta Burnham, who was then attending the Ashland academy as a pupil, residing with her sister, the late Mrs. T. W. B. Hibbard. She was born at Rumney, New Hampshire, September 29, 1823, where she lived until she came to Ashland, at the age of eighteen; and having been born and raised beneath the shade of the granite mountains of her native state, and possessed of more than an ordinary share of the graces of her sex, with admirable health and personal attractions, she found it no hard task to capture the young Buckeye lawyer, and to this day it is said he still entertains the opinion that she has lost none of the qualities that so much ennoble and dignify woman in all the relations of life.

The children consisted of two sons and two daughters. The two youngest, Charlie and May, died in childhood, the former at seven, the latter at two and a-half years old.

George B. Smith was admitted to the bar as an attorney at law in the year 1867, and has been his father's law partner ever since. He was elected prosecuting attorney of the county in 1878, and was married to Miss Jessie Sutherland, daughter of the Hon. J. W. Sutherland, of St. Louis, Missouri, on the 29th day of May, 1879.

Belle H. Smith was married December 1, 1869, to Frederick S. Hanford, esq., an educated and talented young lawyer of Akron, Ohio, who died January 29, 1879, of congestion of the lungs, after a brief illness, leaving two little daughters, Ethel and Grace Hanford, the fruits of said marriage.

Mr. Smith has been in the active practice of law since his settlement in Ashland, and by close application to the business of the profession, careful and thorough investigation and preparation of cases confided to him, and a strict regard for the interests of his clients, prompt attention and honest and fair dealing in all matters of business, has secured to him a larger share of public confidence as a lawyer, and a greater number and variety of cases than fall to the lot of most lawyers, which, together with his temperance principles and Christian character, entitles him to the confidence and respect of all men as a citizen, and place him as a member of the legal profession in a position worthy of the emulation of the fraternity. During his long residence he has been identified more or less with all the enterprises and business interests of Ashland, has at various times been placed in nomination by his party for office, in earlier times for prosecuting attorney and state senator, and later for judge of the court of common pleas of the sixteenth judicial district, third sub-division, composed of Ashland, Richland and Morrow counties; but being a Republican in politics, although in the latter instance he ran five hundred votes ahead of his ticket, it was not enough to overcome the Democratic majority of his judicial district, and therefore was not successful.

SOLOMON VANCE

was born in Richland county, Ohio, April 1, 1828, and when two years of age went with his parents to Allegheny county, Pennsylvania, where he remained ten years, and returned with his parents, and settled on section five in Orange township, then in Richland, but now of Ashland county, upon the farm upon which he now resides. He attended the early schools of that township, where he obtained a knowledge of the English branches as then taught. He married Miss Eliza Richards, daughter of Samuel Richards, of Troy township, by whom he has had eight children, all of whom are living, five girls and three boys. One daughter is married and lives in Nebraska, and another in Troy township; and one son, married, resides with Valentine Vance, his grandfather, in Orange township, upon a part of the old homestead, which contains one hundred and thirty acres.

Mr. Vance is in prosperous circumstances as a farmer, and much respected by his neighbors. He is a member of the Christian Union church, as well as his lady.

Valentine Vance was born December 18, 1797, in Lancaster county, Pennsylvania, and when seventeen years of age, came with his father, Valentine Vance, to Canton, Ohio, and from thence to near Mansfield, in Richland county, Ohio, where he resided as a pioneer, and then sold his land.

He married Mrs. Eliza Chapman in July, 1827. She was a widow, and had been married to Mr. Chapman in Harrisburgh, Pennsylvania, by whom there is yet living one son.

Mr. Vance, after selling his land near Mansfield, returned to Allegheny county, and remained there several years, and finally returned to Richland county, and located on section five in Orange township. His first neighbors were John Krebs, Robert McLaughlin, William Murray, William Patterson, Henry Hiffner, Edward Murray, Jacob Krebs, and Philip Biddinger. The country was new and the times were hard.

Mr. Vance is the father of eight children, four boys—Solomon, Job H., David and George; and three girls—Fannie, Rachel and Matilda D.; Rachel and Matilda D. are deceased; and David died young; the rest are all living and married. Mr. and Mrs. Vance belong to the Christian Union church. Mr. Vance is now eighty-three years of age, and quite feeble. Mrs. Vance was eighty years old June 14, 1880, and seems to have excellent health and a clear mind. Mr. Solomon Vance now owns the old homestead, and seems solicitous to render the old people happy and comfortable, while they journey in the valley of trials and troubles.

COLONEL JOHN BERRY

was born in Center county, Pennsylvania, July 2, 1807, and emigrated with his father's family (Jacob Berry) to Huntingdon county, in 1803, where he remained till the spring of 1819, in May, when his father and family came to Perry township, Ohio, and located on what was known as the old Peter Berry farm (section sixteen), and resided there until 1821, when he located on section sixteen in Jackson township, then in Wayne county, Ohio. When his father landed in Jackson the settlers in the north part were: James Durfee, Josiah Lee, John Measor, James McBride, Thomas and Stephen Cole, Thomas Green, Lawrence Swope, John Hazzard, Hankey Priest, Charles Hoy, and perhaps a few others. A few Delaware Indian hunters yet remained on Black river, but were quite harmless. "Billy Dowdee" had often hunted on a run that now bears his name. A *Delaware* by the name of "Wolf" also hunted there—a run bears his name. John Measor had bored for salt water some time before Mr. Berry and father arrived, but found it in insufficient quantity to be profitable, and continued to boil the water but a short time when the works were abandoned. Mr. Berry attended school but a part of a winter after his parents settled in 1823, to James Durfee, teacher. It was a little subscription affair in a cabin house. Rev. John Hazzard, John Rigdon, Charles Rigdon, Sidney Rigdon, and Thomas Cole held occasional meetings at that time in the cabins of the settlers. The first doctor called to Jackson is believed to have been Dr. Ecker, of Rowsburgh, and Dr. Church, from Jeromeville, who made frequent visits to the township. Game was then quite plenty, such as deer, bear and turkey. Wolves and wild cats were also very common, and quite destructive on sheep and hogs. Mr. Berry was elected lieutenant, and afterward captain, and finally promoted adjutant and colonel, and finally made brigade inspector under the old militia system, while Jackson township was yet in Wayne county. After the erection of Ashland county, in 1845, Mr. Berry served six years as justice of the peace, and prior to that time served as constable continuously for fifteen years, and also as township clerk and supervisor a number of times. He was elected commissioner of Ashland county seven years, two terms, and served one year by appointment, in lieu of Robert Cowan, who removed west. Colonel Berry married Mary Smith, of this county, October 22, 1833, by whom he had the following children: Leander S., Allen J., Robert J., and Mary J., Josephine and Emma, and two deceased when quite young. Allen J. was accidentally killed by being thrown from a vicious horse in November, 1876. The rest of the family are believed to be all living. The colonel possessed much military enthusiasm and made a fine officer. As commissioner of the county he was watchful and prudent in the expenditure of the people's money, and stands high as a man of integrity and uprightness.

JACOB BERRY

was born in Reading, Pennsylvania, June 5, 1789, and married Miss Elizabeth Herring in 1806, and emigrated to Wayne county, Ohio, in 1819, and settled on section sixteen, in Jackson township in 1821. His wife deceased about 1866, after which he resided with Colonel John Berry, a son, where he deceased, March 31, 1874, aged about eighty-five years and ten months. His family consisted of John, Philip, Jacob, Christena, Henry, Margaret, Peter, William, Susannah, and Elizabeth, all of whom are believed to be living except Philip, William, and Elizabeth.

Philip, Jacob, and Peter removed to Richland county, Illinois, and Henry to West Salem, Wayne county, Samuel and John remain in Jackson township, and Christena, wife of Samuel Landis, and Margaret Fast, of Eli, in Ruggles township.

Jacob Berry and his wife were for many years members of the Lutheran church.

As one of the reminiscenses of the past, it may be remarked that Jacob Berry was a very successful hunter, and often averaged over one hundred deer during season. Colonel John states, that he and his father killed large numbers of deer as well as other game. John also states that he has seen his father shoot a wolf and kill it a distance of one hundred and ninety yards. There was a nest of wolves in a hollow log, near the spot where he killed the wolf, and the next morning he and his sons returned and killed four half-grown cubs. The bounty, at that time, was twelve dollars for old ones, and six dollars for young ones. He received thirty-six dollars for the job, at Elyria, in the county where he had killed them, being in Homer township, Huron county.

ISAAC STULL

was born in Green county, Pennsylvania, January 13, 1810, and removed with his parents to Jefferson county, Ohio, in 1818. In December, 1820, his father and family removed to Orange township, then in Richland, but now in Ashland county, and located near the farm of Jacob Young, on lands now owned by Mr. Saddler.

Isaac continued to reside with his parents until he became of age, and then he learned the trade of a millwright, from Colonel John Murray. At the conclusion of his apprenticeship, he worked at the trade for several years, and then purchased a farm and made farming his occupation, until about 1865, when he removed to Ashland and purchased a homestead, and opened a shoe store. He carried on the shoe furnishing business for some four years, then sold out; and purchased a hardware store with his son-in-law, Mr. Joseph Charles, with whom he is at present engaged in active business.

Mr. Stull gives the following reminiscences of the early settlement of Orange township:

The first road was from Rowsburgh to Jacob Young's, on the Jerome branch of the Mohican, along the old Indian trail, and thence to Savannah lakes.

The other road was known as the Cuyahoga road, and passed

through the present site of Ashland, then Uniontown; after which it was known as the Harrisville and Cuyahoga road.

The first school-house, in 1820, was on the old Crouse farm, built of logs, and taught by the late Sage Kellogg.

The first four blacksmiths were Solomon Urie, 1816, and Peter Biddinger, 1818, Robert Lincoln, 1818, and John King at a later period.

Robert Ralston, sr., was the first carpenter and cabinet-maker, in 1820. Alanson Walker and Robert Russell, leading citizens, learned the trade of him.

The first wheelwright was George Hall, in 1822.

The first wagon-maker was Jacob Young, in 1815.

The first grist-mill was erected on the present site of Leidigh's, by Martin Mason, in 1815.

The first Methodist Episcopal church, at Orange, was a frame structure, built in 1829; by Robert Williamson and John P. Anderson. The church was erected under the preaching of Rev. Haney and Hazzard, local preachers.

The first Presbyterian church was the old Hopewell west of Ashland one and one half miles. Rev. Matthews and a few members built the church. There was also occasional preaching near Philip Flukes', in Martin Hester's house, in 1828.

The first Baptist church was at the house of Christian Fast, in the west part of Orange township, by John Rigdon, in 1825.

The first turner in wood was Jacob Fast, in 1817.

The first coopers were Thomas and Solomon Urie and John Y. Burge, who also made wooden moldboards for plows, as well as plows themselves, from 1820 to 1830.

The first regular wagon-maker in Orange was Fred Nichols, in 1829.

The first doctors in Orange were: John Hannah, 1834; William Deming, 1836; Dr. Alden, 1839; John Lambert, 1848; A. McClelland, 1850; J. Deal, 1862; J. Hahn, 1865; and Dr. Crowell, 1871–'80.

The first stores. Isaac Cutter, 1828; Cutter, Metcalf, Norris & Co., 1829; Thomas Smurr & Co., 1833; Charles R. Deming, 1835; George W. Urie and Daniel Campbell, 1841.

The first tanners were: Christian Rugh, 1834; Philip Fluke, jr., 1838; Isaiah Crouse, 1840 to 1845.

The first postmaster at Orange was Vachtel Metcalf, in 1828.

The first tailor in Orange was Brown, in 1829, who made buckskin breeches, moccasons, etc., and Mrs. John Murray, who also made gloves and moccasons of deer skins.

The first shoemakers were C. Biddinger and Philip Biddinger, in 1820–21.

The first gunsmith was Peter Biddinger, who had a shop north of Orange two to three miles, at Culberson's corners. He had worked in the United States armory at Harper's Ferry, and it is related that he received his pay in United States continental money, just prior to the great depreciation of that currency. He paid forty dollars for his supper, and the morning before leaving, sixty dollars for his breakfast, so great had been the depreciation in a few hours. Mr. Biddinger died at his old home in Orange township in 1842, and was buried at St. Luke's church in the west part of the township, where many of his relatives rest in peace.

Mr. Stull was married in 1832 to Miss Susan Kail, who deceased March 8, 1879, aged seventy-one years and five months. Mr. Stull had lived happily forty years with this lady, and they were blessed by three children; one son, Mahomet H., and two daughters, Jane A. and Mary Estelle. Mahomet H. died at the residence of his father in South Ashland, aged thirty-three years and twenty-seven days. He had been afflicted over three years, but bore all with unusual patience and resignation. He was a young man of rare intellectual endowments, of most amiable manners, and of unblemished reputation. If his physical powers had been equal to his mental faculties he would have made a large figure in the world, in almost any department of learning or mechanics; but the fell destroyer had marked him for his own, and neither the ties of friendship nor medical skill could rescue him from an early grave. Few parents possess such a son, and few sisters a kinder brother. His loss creates a great change in his father's house, and many a tear of deep sorrow will be shed over his departure; and often around the family circle, in evening's silent hour, will his memory be called up, and his goodness of heart, the many pleasantries of his life, and his unselfish nature be rehearsed. In their irreperable loss his parents and sisters have the sympathy of all their neighbors and friends. "So die the good and the pure." Peace to his ashes.

Jane A. married Mr. Orville Pershion, and Mary Estelle, Mr. Joseph B. Charles, now business partners with Mr. Stull in the hardware business, in Ashland.

FRANCIS GRAHAM

was born in Delaware county, Pennsylvania, October 14, 1792. His father removed to Crawford county, in 1797. In 1812 Francis was in Erie county, and in 1814 entered the establishment of Reed & Sanford, dry goods merchants, as a clerk, in the village of Erie. In 1815, Reed & Sanford being overstocked with goods from the war, sent him west with a stock of goods intended for Detroit. These goods were transported on sleds, and when he reached Huron, Ohio, the snow disappeared and he was obliged to open a store there. He spent four years in the service of Reed, Sanford & Co., at Huron. The stock being disposed of Mr. Graham entered a new store in Portland, now Sandusky City, as a clerk for William Townsend, where he continued until October, 1821, when he purchased a new stock of goods, and located at Uniontown, Richland, now Ashland, Ashland county. He rented a room of the late Joseph Sheets (died in 1866), which contained a small stock of goods, owned by Mr. Sheets, and of which he had sold, prior to the arrival of Mr. Graham. He boarded with Mr. Sheets, at one dollar a week, for some time. He continued actively in the mercantile business until about 1844, when financial panics compelled him to wind up his business. Since that period he has been miscellaneously employed. He has served two terms as justice of the peace in the meantime. He yet (1880) possesses considerable mental and bodily vigor, and is spending his remaining days in domestic quiet. At the organization of the County Pioneer Association, September 10, 1875, he was unanimously elected its first president, and served one year. He was married to Amelia Shepard, March 13, 1823. The family consisted of Francis A., Franklin S., Helen S., Henry C., John P., Augustus C., and Alice E. Amelia A., Helen S., Henry C., Augustus C., and an infant, are dead. Mrs. Graham, although well advanced in years, retains all her bodily strength, and much mental clearness. There are only three members of the family living: Franklin S., of Illinois; John P., of Ashland, and Alice E., married to Mr. J. H. Black, a merchant of Mansfield, Ohio.

Mr. Graham gives the following early incidents of the village when he landed:

The first grist-mill in Uniontown, now Ashland, was owned by Henry Wetsel, and was a log building, and had one run of stones, "niggerhead."

The first saw-mill was erected by Seth Cook, on the creek, at the west of town, near what is now the cemetery.

The first school was kept by Mr. Williamson, a cripple, in 1821 and 1822.

The first church was erected by the Methodists, on the lot where the court house now stands, and was of stone.

The first blacksmith was the late Samuel Urie. The shop stood where the citizens' bank was built, on Main street.

The first cabinet-maker and undertaker was the late Colonel Alexanander Miller, who resided on the Daniel Gray lot.

The first tinner was John Croft, who was secured by the late George Swineford, on the lot where the agricultural works of Whitney & Co. now are. The next, the late Hugh Davis, at the east end of town.

The first carding-machine was owned by the late Andrew Drumb, associated with his brother, the late Uriah Drumb.

LABAN BURGAN

was born in Westmoreland county, Pennsylvania, near Mount Pleasant, August 13, 1806. He was the son of Joseph Burgan, who came to that State from the east (originally from England,) at an early day. When about eight years of age, in 1814, his father removed to Wayne county, Ohio, and settled near Wooster, where he continued to reside until 1832, when he removed to Medina county, where he lost his wife, by death. From there he removed to Michigan in 1853, and died in 1860, aged about seventy-seven years. Mrs. Burgan died in Medina about 1840, aged about fifty years. Laban Burgan lived at Wooster from the time he was eight years old. He learned the trade of a tailor, and worked, when a young man, in Canton, Ohio.

He came to Ashland in 1829, and returned to Wooster and married Miss Jane Chubb in 1830. She survived until 1874, aged nearly sixty-seven years. Mr. Burgan continued in Ashland, as a merchant tailor, until 1856, often going to the Indian country in the west, and purchasing large quantities of Indian dressed buffalo robes, which he sold annually, from 1849. He remembers the early days in Wayne county very distinctly. He states that the pioneers had hard times, owing to the sparseness of the settlers and the newness of the country. At the period he came it was the custom of the pioneers to navigate the Killbuck in keel-boats, to convey to Coshocton and Zanesville surplus grain, whiskey, sugar, etc.

The Delaware Indians often visited the settlements to trade, and were harmless. Their old trail passed a little south of the village, and crossed the Killbuck near the old Warner farm, west of Wooster.

Owing to the scarcity of flesh, it was the custom of Joseph Burgan, his father, to hunt wild deer and turkey in the forest; skin the deer killed during the day, hang up the carcass upon a sapling out of the reach of wolves, and carry home the skins and other game at night, and return the next morning with Laban and his pony to carry the game home. After being loaded he turned the pony homeward, and continued to hunt at a distance of six or eight miles. In this manner he obtained all the flesh needed to supply meat. Laban, then about nine years of age, made many trips with the pony, who always landed him safely at his father's cabin. Mr. Burgan remembers that the waters of the Killbuck were often very high and dangerous in the spring of the year, owing to the floods and freshets. At one time he remembers a keel-boat was crushed in its downward trip by large quantities of driftwood, and the owners landed on an island, where they could only get to shore by being reached by a canoe; in fact, some of the parties saved themselves from being drowned by clinging to trees leaning over the water.

It is a common observation that all the streams supplied more water at that period, and are gradually becoming smaller as the country becomes cleared up, and the forests disappear.

Mr. Burgan says, in addition to a great abundance of game of every kind, the forests abounded in large quantities of wild honey, which was easily obtained.

In 1858 Mr. Burgan entered into the erection of the lightning rod business, and continued until 1876, when he removed to Findlay, where he now is. His family consists of Isaiah, married to Miss Hogan; Mary, single; Edmund, married to Miss Kriss; Frances, married to C. P. Lewis; and Flora, married to Frank Reynolds; five in all, two boys and three girls.

Mr. Burgan is now in delicate health, owing to a chronic condition of stomach and liver. He is credited with ringing the old academy bell upon the announcement of the passage of the legislative bill erecting Ashland county, in the spring of 1846. The old man was bound to make a noise over that notable event. The old bell still rings our children to their lessons in the new school-room. May it continue to ring another half century. Many endearing memories cling around that old school-room. Lorin Andrews, a name always dear to Ashland, is still held in grateful recollection.

WILLIAM FAST

was born in Greene county, Pennsylvania, March 24, 1794, and went to school until he was sixteen years old. He came to Orange township when about twenty-one years old, and entered three hundred and twenty acres of land for himself and father, and moved out in the spring of 1814. The family were Martin, Nicholas, Jacob, William, Christian, David, Francis, George, John, Margaret, Barbara, Betsy, and Christena, married to a cousin in Fayette county, Pennsylvania.

William Fast married Elizabeth Fast, a cousin, in Fayette county, Pennsylvania, in 1817. His wife lived until July 1869, when she died, aged seventy four. Their children were: Frances, Elizabeth, Christena, Sarah, Levi, Jesse, John V., William, Jonas, Joshua B., and one who died in childhood. Five of these are also dead: Frances, Elizabeth, Christena, John N. and William. Levi, Jesse and John live in Michigan; the rest in Ashland county.

The mental faculties of Mr. Fast seem to be well preserved, and he possesses fine physical powers for one of his age. The old gentleman often relates incidents in relation to Tom Lyons, Jonacake, and other *Delawares* with whom he was acquainted in his youth. He knew many of the Green and Jerometown Indians.

JUDGE EDMUND INGMAND

was born at Lancaster, Fairfield county, Ohio, February 9, 1806, and removed with his parents to a farm about two miles southeast of Jeromeville, Ashland county. At an early age he fully realized the responsibilities of life, and strove to avail himself of every opportunity. He performed with due respect to his parents the routine of light and arduous duties of a boy's life, exerting every possible effort to secure a home.

The trials and vicissitudes incident to pioneer life prevented young Edmund from giving vent to his natural inclinations, hence he and his sister Mary (she is now Mrs. Joshua Carr, of Bowling Green, Ohio,) received nothing more than the instructions given at common schools, the educational advantages at that time being quite limited. Part of his time was occupied in school-teaching, and at odd times did carpenter work, which trade he pursued with great success, the knowledge of which came from his own ingenuity. Thus, by his ambitious disposition and industrious habits thus formed, he devoted every hour to doing good. At the age of eighteen he united with the Methodist Episcopal church, to which helm he clung with unwavering steadfastness till the death sentence reached his ear, "Come up higher!" In his twenty-sixth year he was married to Miss Mary Kinsey Naylor, an amiable young lady of eighteen. Miss Mary being of a very retiring and modest temperament, as well as loving and agreeable, she adorned the home of her affianced in the most becoming manner; so mild and gentle was this " gude wife " that one of her daughters avers that she never heard her mother laugh aloud.

Though Mrs. Ingmand was delicate in constitution, yet she shared the lights and shadows of " early days, " which were destined to surround her husband with a great degree of pleasure and patience.

Mr. and Mrs. Ingmand located on a farm given them by his father, which was situated one mile southwest of Jeromeville. Mr. Ingmand clerked in a dry goods store one year previous to his marriage, and two years following that event, most of his mercantile life being spent in Waynesburgh (now Congress), Wayne county.

This youthful pair's home in the forest, of course, required a vast amount of labor to change its rude appearance to that of ease and comfort, as well as profit and pleasure.

A family of eight children was reared on this farm—Almira, the eldest, dying in the year 1851, in her twenty-first year. The other seven—Samantha A. (now Mrs. J. D. Axe), of Ashland; William, Alva, Joseph, Edmund H., Hattie A. and Leslie survive.

On the twelfth of June, 1860, Mrs. Ingmand exchanged worlds, after suffering the most excruciating pain for nearly one year, previous to her death.

Mr. Ingmand being a man of sterling qualities and unexcelled business capacity, he was chosen many times to settle differences of minor, as well as of great, importance. He was appointed administrator of fifty estates, besides protecting the affairs of many orphans. For twenty years previous to his demise he made entries in his journal of each day's proceedings, and at the close of each respective year knew the exact outlay and income of his farm and household. He was a true friend of the needy and afflicted; none went from his door hungry, or in need of comfort. His willing and beneficent hand was endeared in every circle in which he moved. In disposition he was remarkable for the cheerfulness and geniality which he possessed, and from one of his oldest children comes the pleasant reflection, that she has often heard him say, that several consecutive months had passed in his life without the least inclination to become angry.

After five days of extreme suffering from paralysis, after enjoying nearly sixty years of uninterrupted good health, he closed his eyes on earthly things on the twenty-seventh of March, 1866, to open them in Heaven.

LUKE INGMAND

was born on Carroll's manor, in Frederick county, Maryland, and, a few years afterward removed to Berkeley county, Virginia, where he resided a number of years, and, at the age of twenty-six years, was married to Miss Elizabeth Hay.

About the year 1805 he removed to Ohio, locating in Amanda township, Fairfield county. A few years later he removed to Wayne (now Ashland) county, near Jeromeville, where he resided until two years previous to his decease, which occurred at the residence of his son, Judge E. Ingmand, in Ashland, at the advanced age of ninety-two years.

Of him it may be said that he was an honest man, in every sense of the word, greatly abhoring any base principle in the character of his fellow-men. Being reared under Quaker discipline, he was extremely plain in his dress, and exceedingly courteous in his address. His plainness of speech, and marked eccentricities, called forth many peals of laughter, wry faces, and at times, perhaps, a slight degree of ill-feeling; his intentions, however, were of the purest character, disliking the idea of coming in contact with those he could not salute cordially. He possessed an unusual jovial disposition and affable bearing, which gained for him hosts of friends wherever he went. He was a great favorite with the children, and was often besieged to relate anecdotes of long ago. Among the writer's happiest hours were those spent at the feet of "grandfather," pleading him to tell a story, when he very often replied, jestingly: "Why, no child, I'd rather tell the truth than a story."

Thirteen years of loneliness was allotted this venerable man before he was called to join Mother Ingmand in the spirit land. Nearly seventy-five years he adorned the Christian profession, being a member of the Methodist Episcopal church most of his life.

His last days were not victimized by disease, but was merely the wearing out of life's machinery, and, on the morning of June 25, 1865, the white-haired patriarch was called to swell the holy ranks above.

It would be injustice to bring before the public eye the history of this noble pioneer without mentioning the commendable qualities of his amiable companion, who shared the privations and trials of pioneer life with such marked Christian patience and fortitude.

Her parentage was of the highest rank and culture, being fortunate to receive as good an education as advantages would permit, which, in addition to their dignified bearing and mature judgment, placed them on an equality with the most respectable.

About the time Mrs. Ingmand moved to this State her brother, John Hay, moved to Kentucky, where he became a neighbor and intimate friend of the late Abraham Lincoln. The two families, Hay's and Lincoln's, soon after removed to Illinois. As Mr. Lincoln had chosen the legal profession, as did also a son of Mr. Hay, the two became fast friends, and entered into the practice of law together.

Grandmother Ingmand was equally as lively disposed as uncle Lukey, as her husband was familiarly called. Hence their home and society were often sought after, when in quest of pleasure. This dear old lady spent sixty-five years in this world, and on the seventh of June, 1853, was transplanted to a higher, holier clime.

LOUIS JEFFERSON SPRENGLE

was born in Frederick City, Maryland, January 26, 1824. His father, David Sprengle, was born in York county, Pennsylvania, in 1796, and died in Frederick City, Maryland, in 1832, of cholera. Captain David Sprengle was a soldier in the war of 1812, entering the army at Baltimore, in 1814, at the age of eighteen years. He was a direct descendant of the same family from whom Dr. Kurt Sprengle, the celebrated German botanist, of Halle university, descended. The family emigrated from Prussia, Germany, to this country about the year 1760, and settled in that part of Pennsylvania known as York county. His father served as a private soldier in the Revolutionary army for American independence. His mother, Caroline M. A. Ruth, was of German descent. Her grandfather, Jacob Medart, was one of the staunchest supporters of the American Revolution, and his hotel, in Frederick, Maryland, at that critical period, was the rendezvous of the patriots of that trying time. General Washington always made his hotel his stopping place, when passing through Frederick. He furnished the army of the Revolution with many thousand dollars of supplies, taking his pay in continental money, and leaving several barrels of it as a legacy to his children. Her father was in the war of 1812, and rose to the rank of captain. Having, during his early boyhood, attended a select school in Frederick City, our subject came to Ohio, unto his parents, in 1835, and settled in Ashland. Until 1839 he was employed as a clerk in a store. In the public schools and in the Ashland academy he finished his education. He then learned the trade of a cabinet-maker, and worked at it subsequently in Ashland, Mansfield, and Pittsburgh, Pennsylvania. While at Mansfield keeping up his studies, he walked over to Ashland each Saturday for the purpose of reciting to Professor Lorin Andrews, afterwards professor of Kenyon college. While working at Pittsburgh, during the year of the great fire in that city, in 1845, all his books, about three hundred volumes, educational and miscellaneous, were burned. Returning to Ashland, he there worked at his trade for two years. He was then appointed agent for that county for the old Protection Fire Insurance company, of Hartford county, in which position he remained until that company ceased to do business. He then, in connection with J. O. Jennings, Abraham Huffman, Joseph Wasson, G. W. Urie, Joseph Musgrove, Peter Resser, Hugh Burns, J. B. F. Sampsel, and B. B. Clark, on the eighth of February, 1851, as incorporators, procured a special charter from the legislature of the state of Ohio, and organized the Ashland County Mutual Fire Insurance company, of which he was elected secretary, and has retained that position ever since, and for the last six years also performing the duties of treasurer. Up to 1869 he also performed the duties of general agent and adjuster. Under his management this company has been very successful, its business being done on what is known as the twenty per cent. plan, and without making any assessment on the premium notes. For twenty-five years they took none but the safer kind of risks, and this practice has been but slightly departed from. Recently a few of the better class of special hazards are written up by the company for small amounts. The accumulated assets of the company, July, 1880, amount to six hundred thousand dollars, while the risks have been so carefully selected that their losses have not exceeded fifteen thousand dollars a year.

In 1853 Mr. Sprengle began the publication, at Ashland, of a weekly newspaper in the interests of the old Whig party, called the Ashland *Times*. This he continued with the assistance respectively of the Hon. William Osborn and Josiah Locke, until the spring of 1857, when he assumed the entire control of the paper as editor and proprietor, until June, 1876, when he sold the property to his son-in-law, Joseph E. Stubbs. Under Mr. Sprengle's management the paper became one of the most influential and prosperous weeklies in the State, and was the first paper printed on a Hoe power press, and by steam, between Cleveland and Columbus. He was the author of the agents' hand-book of insurance, of which an edition of over ten thousand copies was sold to the underwriters of the different States; also of the manuscript reader, for the use of schools and academies, printing offices and the counting-room. Its object was to learn the pupil to read readily any manuscript. Pages of manuscript for this novel work were contributed from Professor Spencer, President Andrews, of Kenyon college, President Andrews, of the Virginia university, Horace Greeley, Rufus Chote, and other eminent scholars of the day. He was also associated with all the enterprises of the place, acting as secretary of the Ashland union mills for the manufacture of flour and woollen goods; also as president of the Ashland machine company, manufacturers of agricultural implements and clover threshers and hullers, as well as an independent manufacturer of other useful implements having an extensive sale throughout the world. He had but one brother, Henry Clay Sprengle, present treasurer of Washington county, Kansas, and a prominent citizen of that State. Also two sisters, Frances S. Locke, wife of Josiah Locke, of Indianapolis, a poetess and a lady of rare talent, and Mrs. I. P. Coates, of Chicago, Illinois. On the first of January, 1852, Mr. Sprengle married Miss Sophia W. Coffin, of Ashland, Rev. Dr. John Robinson performing the ceremony. Of this union six children, all living, have been the issue, viz.: Ella A., wife of Joseph E. Stubbs; Jessie F., wife of William G. Stubbs; May Caroline, William Marston, Mattie F., and David S. During the war for the union, he was a strong supporter of the government, and a member of the safety or military committee for Ashland county. In 1862 he was appointed by President Lincoln provost marshal, with the rank of captain, which position he held until 1863. During the war his pen was eloquent in defence of the flag, and the union of the States.

WILLIAM BEER

was born in Northampton county, Pennsylvania, near the New Jersey line, in 1794. His father, Thomas Beer, served as a soldier in the American Revolution, and brought home from New Jersey a relic highly prized by his children, and exhibited by Mr. Beer with especial interest. It was an English bayonet, and had the words, "29 reg. 5 division, King George III," engraved on it. It had evidently been left by one of the British soldiers, who fled or was killed during the battle. His father removed with his family to Allegheny county, Pennsylvania, in the year 1800, where he resided twelve miles below Pittsburgh, about thirty years. Mr. Beer was of Irish descent.

In 1825 he married Miss Mary Mann, and removed to Montgomery township, Richland (now Ashland) county, in 1832, and located on a quarter of land adjoining his brother Richard. Here he resided about forty years, and cheerfully submitted to all the toils of a pioneer in clearing up and preparing his homestead. In 1867, he had the misfortune to lose, by death, his excellent lady. His family consisted of Thomas, Quincy, Henry, Calvin, Serena, Sherman W. and B. F. Beer. Mr. Beer died October 3, 1879. The entire family, except Sherman W., preceded Mr. Beer to the grave.

Mr. Beer possessed, to the last, all his mental faculties. He was noted as retaining a most retentive memory for dates and events, and loved to dwell upon the border scenes of seventy or eighty years ago. From the gravity of his manner and personal dignity, he was familiarly called "Judge." Indeed, he was much more worthy such a promotion than many "limbs of the law," who preside over our courts. He had long been a zealous and worthy member of the Presbyterian church, and illustrated the goodness of his heart by many acts of kindness to the poor and the orphan. Though called suddenly to bid adieu to time and the scenes of earth, we cannot doubt his fitness for another and, we trust, a better world. His cheerful face and kind words will greet us no more, but be embalmed in memory. The tide waits for no man. Soon the bell will toll a last farewell to the aged pioneers. May they rest in peace.

JAMES ALBERSON

was born in Harrison county, Ohio, July 7, 1822, and moved with his parents, Thomas Alberson and wife, to Orange township the fourth of April, and landed April 7, 1837. He attended school at eight square, district five, until seventeen years of age. His father died about 1856, aged about fifty-nine years. His mother died in November, 1870, aged seventy-six years. Her name before marriage was Fanny Campbell. There were four boys and three girls—Mary, James, Sarah, Anne, William C., Elizabeth, Robert W., and T. C. They are all living except Elizabeth Somers, wife of Jacob. Mr. Alberson was married to Rachel Andrews, December 10, 1844. She died June 4, 1853. He again married, January 10, 1854, Miss Susan C. Bowlby. His first wife had W. T. Alberson and A. N. Kelso; his second wife, Alice C. and J. K., son and daughter. Mr. Alberson is serving on his eighth term as justice of the peace, having been elected in October, 1854, and again in October, 1861, and continuously since then. His term will expire in 1882. He also served as constable several terms. He now resides within one mile of where he settled in 1837.

CHARLES WILLSON

was born in Baltimore county, Maryland, August 10, 1795, and came to Perry township, Wayne county, Ohio, in 1810. In 1819 he married Mary Anderson. He has two sons, William and Joseph, and four daughters including Mrs Z. Greenwald. When a youth he resided with his parents in Jefferson county, Ohio, eight years, from whence he came to Perry township, and thence to Montgomery.

RICHARD BEER

was born in Northampton county, Pennsylvania, November 21, 1796. His father, Thomas Beer, of Irish extraction, settled in that county in 1764. In 1800 he located in Allegheny county, where he resided, engaged in farming, twenty-one years. During this time he aided in clearing the Ohio river of drift, and other obstructions, to the mouth of the Beaver. In 1821 he located in Montgomery township, about two miles southwest of Uniontown, now Ashland. He was accompanied by a cousin, Richard Aten. He and Mr. Aten kept bachelor's hall about six years, doing their own cooking and housework. In the meantime, he made considerable improvements on his homestead, by erecting a comfortable dwelling, a barn and out-buildings, and clearing some forty acres of land.

In 1827 he married Miss Jane Anderson, by whom he had seven children: Emma, Adeline, William A.,

JOHN DONLEY.

SARAH A. DONLEY.

John Donley was born near Orange village, Ashland county, March 20, 1817. His parents, Thomas and Susan Donley, came to Ohio from Washington county, Pennsylvania, in February, 1817, and when he was two weeks of age, located on the farm where they passed the remainder of their lives, and where the subject of this sketch lived and died. John Donley attended the first subscription school in the township, which was taught by Elijah Banning, in a log cabin situated on a corner of the Donley farm. This school was established in 1830. He grew to manhood on the farm, in early life partaking of the hardships of pioneer life, and lived to see fruitful farms take the place of the rugged forests of his boyhood days.

March 11, 1845, he was married to Miss Sarah A. Alberson, and soon after marriage removed to Nashville, Holmes county, where they remained one year, when they returned to Ashland county, and for the four succeeding years lived on a farm at that time owned by Major George W. Urie. In 1850 Mr. and Mrs. Donley removed to the old home farm in Orange township, where they ever after lived, and where he died June 26, 1880, of general debility, at the age of sixty-three years, three months and six days.

A family of eight children was the result of this union, of whom seven are now living, as follows: Calvin, Susan, Edward, Jennie, Rachel, Lizzie, and Carrie. Frances died when a small child.

John Donely was a man of strict integrity, and one who loved his family well. No one with whom he had business or friendly association ever had cause to charge him with double dealing. He was honest to a fault and scorned deception. He was widely known as a man of more than ordinary ability and intelligence, with strong likes and dislikes, but when apologies were offered, was ever ready to forgive. His life was that of a Christian, and he died with a Christian's hope. For many years he had been a leading member of the Orange Presbyterian church, and for the past fourteen years held the responsible office of ruling elder. Through storm and shine he went to his beloved church, and never faltered in its support. In the course of his life he amassed a comfortable competence, which was acquired by his own hard labor, seconded by that of his wife, who has proved for him a helpmeet indeed. The greatest prize he left his family was that of a pure character, an unblemished reputation and an unsullied record. These by his family are more prized than all else.

Thomas and Fannie Campbell Alberson, the parents of Mrs. John Donley, were born in Pennsylvania—he in the city of Philadelphia, and his wife, Fannie Campbell, in Westmoreland county. The Campbell family removed to Harrison county, Ohio, in 1817, and about the same time Mr. Alberson came to the same place, where they were married in 1819. They moved to Ashland county in 1837, and settled in Orange township, where they passed the remainder of their lives. Mr. Alberson was a ruling elder of the Presbyterian church, and by occupation was a farmer.

Sarah A. Alberson was born in Archer township, Harrison county, February 12, 1825, and was married to John Donley, March 11, 1845. She became a member of the Presbyterian church of Orange in 1853, and has since remained in its communion. Since the death of her husband, she has occupied their old home with her five daughters and son, William Edward. Another son, Thomas C., is married, and lives on the adjoining farm.

Amanda, Thomas M., James, and Kate. James was killed in Virginia during the late war. The remaining members of the family, most of whom are married, reside in the vicinity of Ashland.

When Mr. Beer arrived, in 1821, his nearest neighbors were Michael Thomas, C. Wheeler, Benjamin Shearer, Henry and Daniel Vantilburg, Joshua Brown, and Daniel Carter. Log-rollings, cabin-raisings, corn-huskings, flax-pullings, and scutchings, as well as linsey-woolsey clothing, corn-bread, pork, and venison, were the occupations, the clothing and the food, of the hardy pioneers. It was not uncommon, the first few years, to be so occupied five or six days each week at such gatherings. The nearest mill was Newman's, on the Black fork, to which Mr. Beer often resorted. He occasionally visited a mill, subsequently owned by Armstrong Meaner, in Green township. For many years wheat was cut with a sickle, and all the pioneers were expert in its use. In fact, it was not uncommon to find women in the field using the same instrument. In those days the fields were carefully gleaned and very little grain was left standing. When the stumps began to disappear, sickles were invaded and were gradually substituted by the grain-cradle. Mr. Beer says he owned the first grain cradle used in Montgomery township, over fifty years ago, on the farm of Joseph Sheets, where South Ashland now stands. It created quite a sensation among the old reapers, because he could cut a swath, equal to that of three reapers, with much ease. The surplus grain of this region was hauled to Milan for a market until about 1861, when the New York, Pennsylvania & Ohio railroad was completed, and a home market furnished.

Mrs. Beer died in 1859, and Mr. Beer, now (1875,) aged seventy-nine years, resides in Ashland. He is quite vigorous; his mind is clear and vivacious; he loves a joke and abounds in humor. Like all his Scotch-Irish ancestors, he is much attached to the Presbyterian church, of which he is a member.

JOHN DONLEY

was born in Orange township, March 20, 1817, on the old Wertz farm, and married Miss Sarah A. Alberson, March 11, 1845. He then removed to near Nashville, Holmes county, where he remained one year and came back to Ashland county. He moved to his present home in 1850, and has resided there ever since—thirty years. He was the father of eight children. Seven of them, Calvin, Susan, Edward, Jennie, Rachel, Lizzie and Clara are living. Francis died when but a small child.

In 1830 the school-house was built in Donley's district, and he and his brother Thomas were the first scholars; Elijah Banning the first teacher.

The principal old citizens in the district were the McConnells, the Clarks, the Flukes, the Hesters, the Murphys, the Mackerels, Robert Mickey, Peter Biddinger, William McConnell, Thomas McConnell, John Burge, Isaac Mickey, Daniel Summers, Thomas Donley, Robert Culberson, John Bishop and Jacob Hiffner.

John Donley died June 26, 1880. He was a man of strict integrity, and a man who loved his family. No man, with whom he associated, ever had cause to charge him with double-dealing. He was honest to a fault, and scorned deception. He was widely known, for he was a man of more than ordinary ability and intelligence. He had strong likes and dislikes, but when apologies were made none forgave more quickly. His life was that of a Christian. For many years he had been a leading member of the Orange Presbyterian church, and for the past fourteen years has been a ruling elder. Through storm and shine he went to his beloved church, and never faltered in its support. He amassed a good competency by his own hard work. But the greatest prize he left was that of a pure character, an unblemished reputation and an unsullied record. These, to his sorrowing wife and children, are far more prized than all else. He was followed to his last resting place by all his neighbors and friends, who thus testified their appreciation of his goodness and worth. Funeral services were conducted by Rev. Kelly, of Savannah, assisted by Revs. Cummings and Jones. Peace to his ashes.

THOMAS DONLEY

was born in Washington county, Pennsylvania, in 1780, and deceased, on his homestead in Orange township, Ashland county, Ohio, October 21, 1850. He came to the township in 1817, and resided there until his decease. His first wife died before he did, when he married, in 1844, Miss Mary McKinney, of Milton township, who still survives at an advanced age, supposed to be near one hundred years, there being no record of her birth. Her health is good, and she retains a good memory of the past. Her sight and hearing are gradually failing. Her father, Patrick McKinney, died when she was young, in Cumberland county, Pennsylvania. She emigrated with her mother and Ross McKinney to Milton township, 1816, and resided near the old Hopewell church, where she deceased and was buried many years ago.

CAPTAIN ROBERT BEER.

In the correspondence of the Pittsburgh *Herald*, we find the following concerning Captain Beer, who accompanied the expedition of Colonel Robert Crooks, in the war of 1812, to Upper Sandusky. The captain died about May 4, 1880, aged nearly ninety years.

I've just had a conversation with Captain Robert Beer, one of our oldest and most respected citizens, who served his country in the war of 1812. In answer to my inquiries, he gave the following account of his trip from this city to Upper Sandusky, Ohio, and his return on foot the following winter of 1812-13:

"About the first of November, 1812, the Government advertised for volunteer teamsters, having some thirty carriages (without cannon, however) and forty covered wagons to supply with drivers. As soon as a volunteer would sign the roll, he was ordered to go into a large yard, on Garrison alley, and bridle four horses. I was among the volunteers, being then an unsophisticated country boy of twenty years. (You will observe that I am now old enough to vote.) I was directed to hitch a team to a cannon-carriage, and drive over to the ground where the western penitentiary now stands. Here we were encamped for three weeks before we were ready to start. The road wagons were loaded with cannon-powder, clothing, and all kinds of government stores. These wagons were drawn by five, and sometimes by six, horses. All being in readiness, we started for General Harrison's winter quarters, at Upper Sandusky, Ohio. Colonel James Anderson was wagon-master; James McHenry, a bricklayer of our city, assistant wagon-master; Paul Anderson, forage-master; and Captain Gratiot had command of the train. To guard the teams and property, we had Captain Johnson and his company, from Greensburgh, now called Darlington, and half a company from Beaver county, under command of Lieutenant Walker, who was subsequently killed by the Indians.

"The journey was through an almost unbroken wilderness, and its difficulties cannot be appreciated by the people of to-day. Ten miles was considered a good day's travel, and when the route was bad, as was frequently the case, we did not make more than six miles. It took us three days to go through Hahn's swamp, and had hard work to do it in that time. We would often stop for a day, and, mounting our horses, go miles away along paths, there being no wagon road, and return with our horses loaded with forage.

"At Canton we lay a whole week, repairing the wagons, shoeing the horses, and giving them much needed rest, and procuring a supply of foliage.

"From Canton to Wooster it was thirty-five miles. At the latter place we found the first picketed fort. Mansfield, it may be said, ended the settlements in this direction. The only buildings were a fort, one tavern, one store, and one private house. We remained three days in Wooster to recruit our horses, repair damages and gather forage. Between Wooster and Mansfield we had a good deal of new road to cut, the old one being impassable for the train. This was slow work, as you can judge.

"We were about two months on the road, and finally reached Upper Sandusky on New Year's day—and as cold a day, by the way, as I ever experienced. We never saw a fire from sunrise till sunset, and to make the matter worse, we were but thinly clad at best. On our arrival we were ordered to ungear our horses and start with them for a small town on the Scioto river, called Franklinton, just across the river from Columbus. Corn was plenty and cheap in that neighborhood, and they wanted their horses to recruit there for the spring service.

"Next day we started back to Upper Sandusky to get our money and be discharged from the service. There was no money there to pay us with—not a dollar in the treasury—so they furnished us with tents and rations. We pitched our tents just outside the military lines, and for three weeks had nothing to occupy our time but eating and sleeping. At the end of this time Colonel Piatt, of Cincinnati, who was treasurer of the army, gave us our discharge and an order for our pay at the barracks in Pittsburgh. We hadn't a dollar towards paying our way home. They gave us rations to put in our knapsacks, but they got stale and unfit for use.

"Of course, after we left our horses at Franklinton, we did all our traveling on foot. I cannot tell the distance from Franklinton to Upper Sandusky, but from the latter place to Mansfield was thirty-five miles. We all arrived in Pittsburgh safe and well, after a very fatiguing journey.

"The Captain Gratiot I have mentioned was one of the engineer corps of the regular army, and an officer of high standing. Captain Wheaton was the paymaster; and a cross old chap he was. He carried a canteen of brandy slung round his neck, and sometimes he absorbed the brandy too freely.

"I suppose I am entitled to a pension for my services in 1812, but I have not yet applied for one. I observe that some are drawing pensions whose term of service lasted only fourteen days. In 1856 I got a land warrant for one hundred and sixty acres of land."

During a great part of his life he was engaged in building and running steamboats, and it is hardly necessary to say that his long record was spotless and unblemished. He retired from active business several years ago, and since then devoted his time to his private affairs.

JOHN SMITH

was born in Columbiana county, Ohio, October 1, 1822. He learned the trade of a carpenter in Stark county, in 1843-4. In 1845 he married Rebecca Fettehoff, and in 1849 removed to Troy township, Ashland county, and purchased a small farm. He became a farmer-mechanic for some years, and finally abandoned his trade to become an agriculturalist.

Mr. Smith is of German descent. His father, Frederick Smith, came from Germany in 1821. He died in Stark county, Ohio, in 1854, at an advanced age. His children were: Frederick, who died in Troy township, Ashland county, in 1864; John, of Troy; Savilla, wife of Jacob Hipp, of Troy; Mary, wife of Michael Auer, of Indiana; Christian and Andrew, of DeKalb, Indiana.

The family of John consists of Elizabeth, wife of Michael Merkel, of Michigan; Jacob F., married to Sephrona Fast, of Huron county, Ohio; James Smith; Hannah, wife of Oran Chapman, of Lorain county; and Mary, William, Loretta, Pheba, Lydia, and Emma, unmarried.

Mr. Smith is a good business man, and noted for his strong common sense and frankness. He has been elected trustee of Troy township five times, although the party with which he affiliates is in the minority. At the spring election of 1876, he was elected a justice of the peace. He is very active in propagating his political ideas, though always courteous to his political opponents.

When he entered Troy township, the primitive forest, with here and there a small clearing, and a few cabins, covered the township. It is now greatly improved.

MR. SAMUEL SMITH

was born in New Milford township, Litchfield county, Connecticut, May 23, 1800. At the age of fifteen years he was apprenticed to learn the trade of carpenter and house joiner, and served six years. At the expiration of his apprenticeship he married, and followed his trade for ten years, in his native State. In 1832 he removed to Lorain county, Ohio, where he again resumed his trade. While a citizen of Lorain county, he took an active part in military organizations, and was elected captain, and subsequently promoted to lieutenant colonel, and finally colonel of his regiment. In 1837 he located in Milton township, Richland, now Ashland, county. While a citizen of Milton, he served twelve years as justice of the peace, and acquitted himself to the satisfaction of his friends. Milton was largely Democratic, and Colonel Smith was an old Whig. His integrity and uprightness elevated him above party bias, rendered him personally popular, and hence, he was re-elected to the same position twice. In 1860 he disposed of his farm and removed to Ashland, where in 1863, his excellent lady deceased, aged sixty-three years. He again married. Mr. Smith for many years was an active and influential member of the Presbyterian church. His family consisted of Orlow, Riley, Charles, Nelson, Augustus, Lemon and three daughters. Orlow served in the late war, and was promoted to brigadier-general. Nelson fell at the sanguinary battle of Chickamauga. The rest of the family, we believe, all survive.

Mr. Smith died September 22, 1876. The funeral

services were conducted by Elder N. P. Lawrence, of the Disciple or Christian church, at the late residence of Colonel Smith, South Ashland, at two o'clock p. m., Sabbath, September 24th, when his remains were conducted to and deposited in the cemetery of Ashland.

ISAAC DAVIS

was born in New Holland, Lancaster county, Pennsylvania, August 10, 1802. When quite young he was apprenticed to learn the art of weaving. In consequence, his education was neglected, and he could neither read nor write. At the age of nineteen years he went to Juniata county, where he remained some years working at his trade. In the year 1823 he married Miss Fanny Stoner, of that county. That lady survived until 1876, when she deceased, aged about eighty years. In 1834 Mr. Davis came to Mifflin township, then in Richland county, and purchased a farm of eighty acres in section one, of Benjamin Hershey. The land at that time was nearly all in its native forest. He and his sons in after years cleared the land and reduced it to a state of excellent culture. Mr. Davis made weaving a business for many years. In this respect he was a useful citizen. He was a good weaver, and by his industry and skill made sufficient to support and educate his sons and pay for his farm. When he arrived at Mifflin township he found John Hewey, William Hewey, Henry Roland, Peter Brubaker, John Brubaker, Solomon Wertman, Abraham Doty, James Andrews, Leonard Croninger, Benjamin Hershey, and Father Gongwer, who had preceded him as pioneers. Nearly half a century has passed since he arrived. Great changes have taken place. Nearly all these pioneers have paid the debt of nature. Only one or two of his old neighbors yet live. For several months the health of Mr. Davis has been gradually failing, and finally terminated in consumption of the lungs. In his prime he weighed about three hundred pounds. He became greatly emaciated before death. He was a member of the River Brethren church, about thirty-five years, and was an exemplary Christian. He died on Friday, evening, December 18, 1879, and was buried at the Mennonite church, in Mifflin township, on Saturday, December 20th.

The family of Mr. Davis consisted of nine children—Susannah, single; Samuel, married to Catharine Roland; Mary, wife of Dillman Switzer; George, single; John, married to Margaret C. Day; Isaac, married to Sarah Hilburn; Abraham, married to Mary Kagey; William, married to Rebecca Sechrist, who is deceased, and again to Barbara Callen; Fanny, married to Jacob Hetler. Mr. Davis had forty-four grandchildren, and nine great-grandchildren.

SAMUEL CORDELL

was born in Loudoun county, Virginia, October 15, 1793. During his boyhood, war was declared against Great Britain. The English forces were beleaguering the city of Baltimore, and the coasts of Maryland and Virginia. When invading Maryland, volunteers were called upon to defend the capital at Washington and other points. Mr. Cordell, youth as he was, entered the army and served in the defence of Baltimore. For this service he recently obtained a pension. He was in the company commanded by Captain George Huff, Virginia militia, regiment of Colonel Mason, of the brigade of General Douglas, in the war of 1812. Upon his discharge he returned to Loudoun county, Virginia, where he married Miss Catharine Carnes, and in 1833 removed to Orange township, Richland, now Ashland, county. Here he remained one year upon the farm of John Mason. He then removed to Milton township and lived about two years upon what was subsequently the McDonald farm, one mile west of Ashland. He then purchased the Hoover farm, where he lived until his decease, a period of about forty-six years. During this time he was recognized as a quiet, prudent, and industrious man. He was a plain farmer, fully devoted to the culture of the soil, in which he succeeded in accumulating enough of this world's goods to render himself and family comfortable. In 1859 he had the misfortune to lose, by death, the wife of his youth, aged about sixty years. Since then he has resided with his family. He and his wife united with Rahobeth Methodist Episcopal church, in Loudoun county, Virginia, about 1831, since which time he has remained a faithful member. His family consisted of eleven children, nine of whom survive: Emeline, wife of Samuel Doty, of Crawford county; Cornelia, wife of Rev. Jacob Fry, deceased; Anne Elizabeth, wife of Ezekiel Moore, of Lake township; Mary Margaret, who resides at home; Washington, deceased; Catharine, wife of George Hall; John Francis, deceased; James L. and Jane L., twins, the latter the wife of Dr. Harkins, deceased; Rebecca, wife of Cyrus Plank, of Ashland; Cordelia, wife of John W. Oswald, of Toledo.

Mr. Cordell took but little interest in politics. He was an original Whig, and elected to the office of trustee of Milton, two or three times, and school director occasionally. He was a strong friend of the school system, and was always desirous of giving proper instructions to the rising generation. He often related an incident that occurred to him in Loudoun county, Virginia. Some years before he left, one day an old colored man came and made an appeal to his feelings. He said, "Mr. Cordell, I think you are a friend of mine. I have to be sold to a stranger, and go south. I want you to buy me." Mr. Cordell said, "I would do so, but I am too poor to spare the money at present." "I pledge my honor, said the colored man, if you will do so, I will hunt a master who will keep me in Virginia, and treat me kindly." Mr. Cordell's feelings were touched, and he consented to buy him. This deed of kindness was fully reciprocated. The colored man in due time found a new master, and kept his word with Mr. Cordell. That was the only time he ever owned a colored man, and he often stated "his conscience approved of what he had done." He passed through much pioneer experience in Ashland county—was always found kind and obliging to his neighbors, and courteous to all men. May the sods of the valley rest lightly upon his manly breast, till the summing up of all things. Mr. Cordell died April 19, 1879, and was buried in the cemetery at Ashland.

PETER BRUBAKER

was born in Lancaster county, Pennsylvania, February 20, 1795, and was the son of John Brubaker, of German descent. He grew to manhood and married in his native county. He married Miss Mary Brubaker, though of no relation, in 1818, and remained in Lancaster until the year 1823, when he came to Milton township, Richland, now Ashland, county, Ohio, and settled upon the farm upon which he died, adjoining that of Joseph Charles. When he entered the land, he found it covered by an almost unbroken forest of large timber. By long-continued labor, he subdued the wild luxuriance of nature, and made a desirable farm for his homestead. When he settled in the wilds of Milton, he found that the Croningers, John Hazlet, James Andrews, and others had preceded him. At that early period, wolves, deer, wild turkey, and an occasional bear, ranged the forests of the township. Mr. Brubaker lived to see a great change in the appearance of the native forests of the township, his neighbors, like himself, having by industry and economy accumulated a desirable property.

In 1870, his wife, aged about seventy-five years, deceased; since which time Mr. Brubaker resided on his homestead, near Mr. Charles, until his death, April 21, 1879. He had been a member of a branch of the Tunker church, known as the River Brethren, about forty-five years, at Chestnut grove, near his home, where he was buried.

At his decease, his family consisted of ten children, all grown: Susan, wife of Henry Rowland; Mary, wife of Christian Rowland; John; Elizabeth, wife of Nathan Stirewalt; Maria, wife of John Gongwer; Fannie, wife of Jacob Barr, deceased; Benjamin; Nancy, wife of William Stauffer; Lydia, deceased; and Christian. These all reside in Ashland county. It is estimated he had sixty-eight grandchildren at the time of his decease.

Mr. Brubaker was known among his neighbors as an industrious, economical, conscientious Christian, always desirous of peace and good will among men. "By their fruits ye shall know them." A good man has gone to his rest, and his works will follow him. Funeral services were conducted by the Rev. J. D. Parker, assisted by Rev. H. Davison.

WILLIAM WESTHEFFER

was born in Lancaster county, Pennsylvania, in 1794, and, when twenty years of age, removed to Cumberland county, in the same State, where he married Miss Young, about 1823. She deceased in 1834, in the same county.

In 1844 Mr. Westheffer emigrated to Montgomery township, then Richland, now Ashland county, Ohio, and purchased a farm in section two. Since the death of Mrs. Westheffer he has remained single, and has resided with members of his family on his late homestead. His occupation was that of a plain farmer. He was warmly attached to his family, and was an exemplary Christian—having been a member of the Lutheran church for sixty years. One year ago (in 1878) he became a member of the Ashland County Pioneer and Historical society, and took a deep interest in the attempt, by his fellow members, to record the incidents of the past and preserve the memory of those who cleared and improved our beautiful county. Now, he too has been called over the great river to join the millions who have been summoned home, having died April 21, 1879. He was a quiet, industrious, Christian gentleman, and we trust his account will be found approved by the Great Author of our being.

The members of his family consisted of five children, all grown: George, Mary M., wife of Daniel Ambrose, of Montgomery; Elizabeth, wife of James McDermot, of Iowa; Sarah, wife of Daniel Kramer, of Iowa; and Margaret, wife of Jeremiah Deardorf, deceased, of Indiana.

Mr. Westheffer was buried at the White church, six miles east of Ashland, and his funeral sermons were preached by Revs. Roseberry and Keiffer. May he rest in peace.

MICHAEL THOMAS

was born in Somerset county, Pennsylvania, in the year 1802, and was of German descent. When about eighteen years of age he married Elizabeth Myers, and in the spring of 1821, he and his brother-in-law, Samuel Myers, removed to the southeast quarter of section thirty, in Montgomery township, then of Richland county, but now of Ashland county, Ohio, where he purchased, and since improved the farm upon which he resided until his death.

When he erected his first cabin there were but few settlers in that part of the township, and he states that of those present, he remembers Daniel Carter, sr., Joshua Brown, Mr. Wheeler, Joseph Sheets, David Markley, Captain Andrews, Henry Gamble, and possibly Richard Beer, and a few others, including Samuel Myers, his brother-in-law, who was to occupy the same cabin, a double one.

When he and Mr. Myers came on they stopped a few days in Uniontown (now Ashland), where they became acquainted with the late Henry Gamble, Joseph Sheets, and the Markleys.

He cut a path to his land, wide enough to permit his wagon, a covered one, and four horses to pass, and obtained rye straw of Mr. Gamble to feed his horses until they could live on wild grass, and sprinkled a little salt on it as an "appetizer." Of nights, the horses were tied around the wagon, exposed to the cold rains until he could cut logs, and by the aid of pioneers erect a stable. At first the only floor in his cabin was provided by nature—the bare ground. It snowed freely a night or two after he and his family entered the new cabin, and melted quite rapidly, flooding the floor, when, to procure a dry resting place, he cut a lot of brush, and piled it up a bed in the middle of the cabin. Being remarkably rugged, and ambitious to have a home, he set to work at once to remove the forest, and prepare for planting his first crop of corn, and succeeded in raising a small field the first summer.

Near where he and Mr. Myers erected their cabin, was a fine mineral spring, a resort of deer as a lick. Near this an Indian had erected and deserted a neat wigwam or pole cabin, which was still standing, covered with bark. He was of opinion that the hut had been built by the noted Indian hunter, Jonacake, who often visited the pioneers of the township.

At that time, his music consisted of almost nightly serenades by the wolves, which were quite numerous, but dangerous only to the small flocks of sheep brought on by the pioneers.

Mrs. Thomas, though formerly occupying a comfortable home in Pennsylvania, consented to accompany him to the wilds of the new country, that they might obtain a property of their own, and entered heartily into the task of assisting him in the preparation of a log cabin home in the forest, consenting to encounter all the privations incident to such an undertaking, and survived to share his toils and anxieties until 1863, when she deceased at the age of sixty-two years. Mr. Thomas subsequently married Barbara Myers, a sister of his first wife. His death occurred August 9, 1878.

Mr. Thomas was an honest, hard-working farmer, and by his strict integrity and thrift, had accumulated a fine fortune, which he shared with his children. He had experienced many privations in early life, but submitted to them like a brave man, that he might enjoy better things in the future.

When a young man he became a member of what is now known as the Dunkard or Brethren church, and was an exemplary member thereof about fifty-four years, and at his decease expressed a willingness to die and go home to a better world.

The members of the family consisted of six sons and six daughters. The surviving sons are: Jonathan, Philip, Michael, jr., and John; the daughters, Sarah, wife of David Bolyeat; Elizabeth, wife of Jesse Vanosdall; Fannie, wife of Jacob Bolyeat; Nancy, wife of David Arter; and Catharine, wife of John Benigoff. The majority of the foregoing reside in Ashland county.

The obituary committee of the Ashland County Historical and Pioneer society upon learning the death of Mr. Thomas adopted the usual resoutions.

Thus, in a few years, at most, the last of the pioneers will have been gathered home. We are indebted to them for having penetrated the forest wilderness of Ashland county, and for rescuing it from its original occupants. Let us honor them for what they have accomplished, and preserve their memory by continuing the improvements they began.

ROBERT CULBERSON

was born in Huntingdon county, Pennsylvania, March 19, 1796, where he grew to manhood, attending the common schools of his neighborhood; and married Miss Elizabeth Sharp, December 13, 1818, and removed to Harrison county, Ohio, where he remained about five years, and then purchased his homestead in Orange township, then in Richland, but now in Ashland county, upon which he located in the fall of 1824, and resided until his decease, being a period of about fifty-five years.

When he landed, Orange township was covered by its native forest. A few Delaware Indians from the Fire Lands, on the Western Reserve, continued to hunt annually in the township, and often visited the cabins of the settlers, and were then thought to be an inoffensive and harmless race. Mr. Culberson, with other neighbors, at one time became somewhat alarmed for the safety of Mr. Biddinger, a gunsmith, up the stream, who had unfortunately offended some of the *Delawares*. A noted hunter, named Jim Jirk, was observed to be skulking in the settlement. Mr. Culberson and others were put on the alert, but no harm resulted from the Indian.

The ancient trail leading from Mohican Johnstown, near Jeromeville, to the Canesadooharie or Black river, passed near the residence of Mr. Culberson. It is supposed that the captive, James Smith, was led up this part in 1755, by his Delaware captors, on his way to Lower Sandusky. The route was a favorite one of the ancient *Mohegans* in 1765, to the close of the border wars, and many tragic scenes have, doubtless, occurred along this trail.

Mr. Culberson improved his fine homestead, residing there over half a century, and was much respected by the old pioneers, and always regarded as a kind-hearted, Christian gentleman, ever ready to reciprocate the kind acts of his neighbors. In 1843 he was elected justice of the peace for Orange township, and acquitted himself so well that, in 1846, he was re-elected for another term.

At the organization of the Presbyterian congregation in Orange, in 1832, Mr. Culberson became one of the ruling elders, and was one of the early members who survived to the present time. He was always esteemed as an exemplary, high-minded, Christian gentleman, ever living with his neighbors in great peace and contentment, and conforming to the requirements and usages of his church, and presiding in his family in an humble, Christian spirit; and his death evinced the fact of his readiness to depart to the better land, the home of the Christian.

In 1875, he became an active member of the Ashland County Pioneer and Historical society, and took much pleasure in relating the early scenes and occurrences of his part of the county.

He died February 23, 1880. The wife of his youth had preceded him to the grave about one year. Two sons, Joseph and John, had also gone home. The surviving members of his family were four daughters and one son, Thomas, who resides on the homestead.

PETER STENTZ

was born in Green township, Columbiana county, Ohio, November 14, 1807. His father, Daniel Stentz, emigrated to Fayette county, Pennsylvania, when he was six months old.

In 1829 he was united in marriage to Mary Ranshaw. In 1832 they moved to New Lisbon, Ohio, and from thence to Orange township, Ashland county. He purchased the premises owned respectively by Edward Wheeler, Jacob Cline, and John Richards. He enjoyed the acquaintance and friendship of Daniel Summers, James Clark, Samuel and John Richards, Joseph and George Fast, Henry Heiffner, Philip Biddinger, and others, whom he esteemed very highly.

Mr. Stentz was the father of nine children, all of whom are living, except one, and are settled in life. He also had two brothers and three sisters—all but one have left the shores of time.

Mr. Stentz was, for many years, a member of the Presbyterian church in Savannah, Ohio; subsequently he united with the Methodist Episcopal church at Troy center, and, as far as circumstances would permit, attended the means of grace at that place.

In his last sickness his sufferings were intense, but he endured as seeing Him who is invisible. A short time before his death, when asked in reference to his spiritual enjoyment, he said: "I am trusting and resting in Jesus." He gave clear evidence to the last that the messenger of death found him prepared and ready to depart in peace. The funeral services were conducted by Rev. George W. Walker, assisted by Rev. S. Z. Kaufman, in the Methodist Episcopal church at Troy. After the services his remains were laid by the side of kindred forms, in the cemetery north of that place.

> "Let me go; my soul is weary
> Of the chain which binds it here;
> Let my spirit bend its pinion
> For a brighter, holier sphere.
>
> "Earth, 'tis true, has friends to bless me,
> With their fond and faithful love;
> But the hands of angels beckon
> Me to brighter climes above."

PETER BURNS

was nearly a hundred years old at the time of his death. Upon visiting him in 1879, the following notice was published in the Ashland *Press:*

"THE OLDEST MAN IN ASHLAND COUNTY.

Some days since we had the pleasure of visiting, perhaps, the oldest man in Ashland county, in the person of the venerable Peter Burns, of Milton township, at the home of Mrs. John Brindle, near the Black fork. Mr. Burns was born in Frederick county, Maryland, in July, 1782, just before the termination of the American war of independence. His father resided about twenty-eight miles west of the city of Baltimore, and died near Gettysburgh in 1815, aged about eighty-seven, and his mother near the same place at an advanced age. His father was from Scotland, and his mother of German descent. Mr. Burns had reached the age of about thirty years when the war of 1812 was declared between the United States and Great Britain. He was enrolled in the Maryland militia, and served in the company commanded by Captain William Derbins, in the defence of Baltimore and North Point, as well as Fort McHenry. About the middle of August, 1814, the British fleet passed up the Chesapeake with about six thousand troops, under the command of General Ross, destined for the capture of Washington city. It landed on the Patuxant, twenty-five miles from its mouth, five thousand men, and marched across to the Federal city, by way of Bladensburgh, where Commodore Barney confronted the British army, but failed to repel their march, General Winder, at the head of three thousand raw militia having made but a feeble stand, fleeing to Washington city, pursued by the exultant British, who burned the capitol, the president's house, and other public buildings, and then fled to their shipping. General Ross was greatly elated over this achievement, although the act was denounced in the English House of Commons, and by all civilized Europe. It was regarded as the act of a marauder and a vandal. General Smith prepared to meet Ross at Baltimore. General Strickler rallied the militia, numbering about fifteen thousand, and prepared to defend the town. Ross landed eight thousand soldiers at North Point, fourteen miles from the city, and part went up the Patapsco to bombard Fort McHenry. General Strickler repelled the advance of General Ross in a heavy skirmish, in which Ross was killed, and after his army continued to bombard the garrison for many hours the enemy withdrew, and the body of Ross was carried, as reported, to England in a hogshead of rum to be buried. After the withdrawal of the British, Mr. Burns and other soldiers from Frederick county, returned to their homes.

About 1825 Mr. Burns commenced to learn the trade of a stonecutter and bricklayer, at which he informs me he worked industriously until he was over ninety-one years old, a period of nearly sixty years. During that time he worked in Baltimore, Little York, in Virginia, and in many parts of Maryland and Pennsylvania.

About the year 1845 he came to Ashland county with his wife, and was joined by his son-in-law, the late John Brindle, who settled on the farm where the surviving members of his family now reside, near the Black fork. Mr. Brindle continued to reside there until 1877, when he deceased, aged about sixty-two years. Mr. Burns and his lady, being well advanced in years, became a part of the family of Mrs. Brindle. Mrs. Burns died at the residence of her daughter on Christmas day, 1878, aged about eighty years. Mr. Burns is the father of four living children Emanuel, Samuel, Jacob, and Susan, wife of the late John Brindle.

Mr. Burns has been drawing a pension of ninety-six dollars, since 1872, for services performed in the war of 1812. His mind is quite clear, though his powerful frame is greatly broken by hard work. He is now content with ordinary exercise. In his prime he weighed about two hundred and ten pounds. His average weight is now about one hundred and eighty pounds, and his height, about six feet two inches. He eats and sleeps well, though at this time he is harassed by a bad cough. His remarkable age must be attributed to a fine constitution. His mother and father died at advanced ages. In fact, longevity has been characteristic of his family, and he may survive to reach one hundred years. He has never been compelled to pay many doctor bills. Temperate eating and living have done more than medicine to give him long life and vigor. Though his sight is failing, his senses remain unimpaired. He has always been a man of peace, and strongly attached to justice and integrity, and opposed to the desolating march of war and internal strife. May his remaining years glide peacefully away, and happiness crown his eventful days."

Mr. Burns died March 16, 1880. He retained his usual health until near his decease. He had lived under the old colonial government, and met many of the fathers of the Revolution He has now gone to his rest, where we trust he will find the peace of a patriot and a just man. Soon we will see the last of the patriots of 1812. All honor to them.

The remains of Mr. Burns were buried in the cemetery of Ashland, on Thursday, March 18th, by the company of Captain Finger, with military honors. With the exception of the late Patrick Murray, who lacked a few months of one hundred years of age, Mr. Burns was probably the oldest man in the county, and near the last of the 1812 soldiers.

PHILIP FLUKE.

MARY FLUKE.

Philip Fluke was born in Bedford county, Pennsylvania, in 1791. In about 1810 he was married to Mary Summers, who became his companion for a lifetime. They raised a family of eleven children, seven sons and four daughters, as follows: Henry, Lewis, Samuel, Philip, Catharine, Jacob, David, Eliza, Lucinda, Margaret, and John. Some few years after his marriage he emigrated to Ohio, and settled in what is now Orange township, Ashland county,—in that day a wilderness of heavy timber, with few if any settlers. Hard work was to be done, as was expected, before a comfortable home could be had, but neither Mr. nor Mrs. Fluke were persons to flinch from an undertaking they had commenced. The first work to be done was the erection of a small log cabin to shelter the family from the storms and protect them from the attack of wolves and other wild animals, which nightly prowled about the lonely cabin. As soon as a home was built, the sturdy father made an onslaught on the forest, and every blow of his ringing axe accomplished something toward removing the heavy timber and preparing a place where could be planted corn and the future subsistence of the family provided for. In time, the land was cleared and improved, but during the most of his long life there was still hard work to be done.

As soon as Mr. Fluke had improved the land included in his first purchase, he added to it acre by acre, until he possessed eight hundred acres of valuable lands. His family gradually increased, but soon the elder children became his assistants, and as they grew to maturity and desired to have homes of their own, he gave to each son one hundred acres of improved land, on which to commence life. His aim in life had been accomplished, and his children would never be compelled to begin, as he had done, in an unbroken wilderness. He departed this life in 1876, surviving his beloved wife but six weeks. Both sleep their last sleep side by side in St. Luke's cemetery, their names and virtues being held in loving remembrance by their children and other relatives who are left behind.

Henry Fluke, the eldest child of Philip and Mary Fluke, was born in Pennsylvania in 1811, and when a small boy accompanied his parents to their new home in Ohio, where he grew to manhood, and performed his part in the pioneer work of the county. He was married in 1836 to Margaret Switzer, and raised four children: Mary Ann, Wilson, Amanda and Enos, all of whom left the parental roof except the elder son, Wilson. He was an energetic, industrious and frugal man, esteemed by all who know him. He died in December, 1875, leaving his widow and his son Wilson, who cares for his mother in her declining years, on the home farm in Orange township.

Lewis Fluke was born in 1813, and died at the old home, unmarried, in 1844.

Samuel Fluke was born in 1814, and lived in the vicinity of his father's family until 1874 or '75, when he removed to Iowa, where he now resides.

Philip Fluke, jr., was born in 1816, and removed to Indiana about 1845, when that State was new and almost unsettled. He was by trade a tanner, and in that business accumulated a good property, but is now retired, and still lives in Indiana.

Catharine Fluke was born in 1819, April 1st, at the old homestead, where she lived until the time of her marriage to Abraham Fast, January 23, 1840, when she removed to his home on the Troy and Ashland road, where she now resides with her son Byron, who manages the farm and cares for his mother. She raised a family of three sons and two daughters, who are now living: Wilson A., Jennie E., Judson L., Byron F., and Mary B. The daughters are married and live in the west. Judson lives in Nevada, unmarried, and Byron remains at home, also single. Three other children of Mrs. Fast—Melissa A., James I., and Rollin,—died in infancy. Mr. Fast, her husband, died November 28, 1862, aged forty-six years.

Jacob Fluke was born in 1820, married, and lives on the farm adjoining his brother John's, in Orange township.

David Fluke was born in Orange township in the year 1822, and lived on the home farm until his marriage, in 1845, to Miss Hannah Stine. They had five children: Lucinda, Celia Ann, Laura Jane, Perry M., and a son who died in infancy, unnamed. Mr. Fluke died in the fall of 1866, and his widow remains on the farm with her children, Laura and Perry, who care for their mother in her declining years.

Eliza Fluke was born in Orange township in 1825. She married David Campbell, and now lives in Iowa.

Lucinda Fluke was born in 1826, at the old Fluke homestead. She married Lewis Mason, and after a few years deceased.

Margaret Fluke was born in 1829. She married John Sherick, and lives in Orange township.

John Fluke, the youngest member of the family, was born in 1831. He remained with his parents, caring for them until their death. November 24, 1864, he was married to Elizabeth McDowell, by whom he had three children: James S., Mary S., and Esther C. Mary died when five years of age. The wife and mother died February 15, 1879, and Mr. Fluke was a second time married to Freelia A. Thomas, February 5, 1880. They live on a part of the home farm, where they have a good home.

DAVID FLUKE.

HANNAH FLUKE.

HENRY FLUKE

was born in Huntingdon county, Pennsylvania, December 20, 1811. His father, the late Philip Fluke, emigrated with his family to Orange township, Richland, now Ashland, county, in October, 1816. Mr. Fluke grew up on the old homestead, north of the village of Orange, married Miss Switzer, daughter of Jacob Switzer, and located a short distance south of the residence of his father, where he had been an active and prosperous farmer for many years. At the pioneer organization in September, 1875, at Ashland, he became a member of the society. When his father's family located on a branch of the Mohican, in Orange township, and for several years afterwards, it was the custom of the Delaware Indians, from Black river, and the Fire Lands, on the Western Reserve, to pass up and down the old trail, which ran near his father's cabin, with peltry and furs, on their way to Pittsburgh and other trading points, to exchange the same for blankets, amunition, and other necessaries. They often camped on the bottom, in the fall to hunt, and in the spring to make sugar. At that period they were harmless of any intent to injure their white neighbors. They occasionally poached upon the swine and fowls of the pioneers, but this was of rare occurrence. Mr. Fluke stated that on such visits it was the habit of his mother, on seeing the approach of the savages, to draw in the latch string of the cabin door, that no temptation to enter might be given the Indians. They were never disturbed in any way, except by the loss of a few fine shoats.

He died December 17, 1875. Mr. Fluke was a citizen of excellent habits, moral, intelligent, industrious, and upright. Though not a member of any church, no citizen sustained a better record for integrity and manly bearing than he. It will be difficult to fill the station in society vacated by his decease.

MICHAEL MORR

was born in Center county, Pennsylvania, October 10, 1796. He was of German descent. He resided in his native county until manhood, when he married, and in the year 1827, with his wife and one child removed to section seven, in Perry township, Wayne (now Ashland) county, Ohio, where he continued to reside until his decease, which occurred Sunday, June 10, 1877, at the advanced age of eighty years and eight months. The immediate cause of his death was dropsy, of which he suffered for many months.

When he landed in the woods, his neighbors were: Charles Wilson, William Lash, Jonas H. Gierhart, William Latta, Samuel Sheets, James Boots, Frederick Wise, Jacob and Benjamin Myers, Hugh Carr, William Shisler, and Jacob Onstott; most of whom have long since been called home to rest.

He entered the forest as a pioneer, cleared a farm of ninety acres, and erected substantial and valuable buildings thereon. He passed through all the hardships and privations incident to the settlement of all new countries. He performed a full share of the toil expended in opening highways through the dense forests, in log-rolling, erecting cabins, school-houses and churches, and lived to see his township and county thickly populated, and dotted with villages, towns and happy homes.

He assisted in the erection of the first Lutheran church, on the old Meng farm, east of Jeromeville, as far back as 1833, and attended the same until about 1840, when a small class of the Evangelical church was formed in his neighborhood, and occasional preaching took place at the houses of the members for six or seven years.

In 1845 he lost, by death, his excellent and much beloved wife, who was a member of the new class.

About the year 1847, steps were taken for the erection of the Evangelical church located in the neighborhood of Mr. Morr, and he became an active member of the same, and has ever since sustained his professions by a devout life.

He was an industrious, frugal, honest, exemplary Christian, and died in great peace. The members of his family consist of four sons: George, Michael, Jacob, and Henry; and four daughters: Julia Ann, wife of William Clapper; Sarah, wife of Reuben Kramer; Harriet, wife of William Holmes; and Christena, wife of John Clouse.

The remains of Mr. Morr were deposited in the cemetery attached to the Evangelical church, of which he was a member, and the funeral services were conducted by the pastor, Rev. Crouse.

JOHN McCLAIN,

son of Samuel McClain, was born in Washington county, Pennsylvania, August 20, 1796. He attended the common schools, and grew to manhood in his native county. The McClains were of Irish extraction, and all large, tall men. They were Protestants, and, like most of the Scotch-Irish, were Presbyterians in faith and practice.

Mr. McClain married Miss Mary Lash, of Washington county, Pennsylvania, and removed to, and located in, Perry township, then in Wayne, but now in Ashland county, in 1817, and settled near the present site of the village of Rowsburgh. He has, therefore, resided in Ashland county about sixty-two years. When he entered Perry township, it was almost an unbroken forest, abounding in large numbers of deer, wolves, and other wild animals. The Delaware Indians, former inhabitants of Greentown and Jerometown, still continued to return to the township in the spring and fall, to make sugar and hunt. The township at that time was but sparsely settled, and Mr. McClain was often solicited by pioneer neighbors to assist in the erection of cabins, at log-rollings, and to prepare fields for culture, and most cheerfully responded to all such invitations. He resided in Perry township for many years, and saw it gradually change from a dense forest to cultivated fields, and blessed with an industrious and intelligent population. Being remarkably ingenious in working wood, though never having learned a trade, he could frame a building, construct a saw- or grist-mill, make the woodwork of a plow, or do almost any other species of work needed by the early farmers of his neighborhood. Naturally industrious, his services were often brought into requisition by the pioneer farmers of Perry and Mohican townships.

In 1844, he had the misfortune to lose the companion of his youth by death. He subsequently married Margaret Noble, who still survives to mourn his loss.

He resided some time at Jeromeville, and then removed to a farm in the south part of Montgomery township, where he continued to reside for some years, and then sold out and removed to his late residence in Ashland.

Of late years his habits have been retiring; but his tall form, erect, and apparently, until of late, quite vigorous, with long flowing beard, white as snow, made him noticeable on the streets or at his place of public worship. He was always diffident, and never sought the emoluments or distinctions of office. He was careful and conscientious as a voter, and desired to cast his suffrages for honest and competent officers.

In religious opinion and faith Mr. McClain was an exemplary and devoted member of the Presbyterian church. He became a member of that denomination in his younger years, and was often chosen to fill leading positions, such as deacon and elder. Up to the close of his life, it was rare that his venerable form was not seen in his pew, at the proper hour, on the Sabbath.

He was in possession of all his faculties to the close of life. On Tuesday morning, the day of his decease, he was quite cheerful and walked to and from the post-office, as was his daily custom. After the middle of the day he engaged for a short time in preparing wood, and as is supposed, became faint and attempted to return to his room, but fell, and after a renewed struggle, entered the kitchen gasping for breath, attracting the attention of Mrs. McClain, who hastened to his aid; but died in a few moments without uttering a word. His decease occurred February 12, 1876.

Mr. McClain was an honest man, a good neighbor, and a sincere Christian. He has passed over the dark river, we hope, to a happier land, the home of the good and the pure. He died childless; and leaves but the companion of his riper years to mourn his loss; but not without hope of joining him in that eternal home prepared for the righteous.

The funeral services were preached at the residence of Mr. McClain by Rev. John Robinson, D. D., and some reminiscences of the deceased were related by Rev. Thomas Beer, A. M., and his body borne to the grave by the deacons and elders of the Presbyterian church, February 14, 1876, followed by his neighbors and friends.

JOSEPH BECHTEL

was born in Lancaster county, Pennsylvania, August 28, 1811, and came with his father's family, Peter Bechtel, sr., to Milton township, Richland, now Ashland, county, in 1824. His father located on the southeast quarter of section eighteen. There were but fifty or sixty families in the township at that time. The mother of Joseph Bechtel died in 1822 in Lancaster county, Pennsylvania, and his father remained single. He died in 1861, aged about eighty-five years. His family consisted of Joseph, Barbara, wife of Jacob Storer, and Jacob, who resides in Indiana. Joseph married Magdalena Bauer in 1831, by whom he had the following children: Susannah, Peter, Mary, Catharine, and two sons and one daughter deceased. One son died in company K, One Hundred and Second regiment, Ohio volunteer infantry, in the late war. When the Bechtels located in Milton wild game, such as deer and turkeys, was abundant. There was an occasional black bear to be found, and the shrill shriek of the panther was frequently heard in the forest. Wolves were plenty, and very destructive upon sheep. Wild hogs, springing from the domestic race, and escaping from their owners in search of mast were quite numerous, and when disturbed, very ferocious. Mr. Bechtel states that about 1830 he was pursued in the night season through the forest by a panther, and it did not desist, although he carried a torch a good part of the way, until he was safely in his father's cabin. He had, also, a fight in which he was severely wounded in the knee by a frantic boar, and will carry the scar to his grave. He is now sixty-five years old and quite vigorous. He states, in 1829, while wild game was yet plenty, he offered Frank Graham, then the principal merchant in Ashland, sixty pounds of good wheat for one-fourth of a pound of powder, and was refused. Wheat had no market, but ammunition was cash. About the same time, he hauled twenty-four bushels of good wheat, with a wagon and three horses, to Portland, now Sandusky, and was gone seven days, and stuck in the mud eight times, and obtained but three shilling—thirty-seven and one-half cents per bushel for his wheat. About 1870 he sold his homestead and removed to Ashland, where he now resides. He has been an active member of the United Brethren church about twenty-two years. As a citizen, he is industrious, frugal and upright. He has passed through all the stages of pioneer life, and is now ready to be garnered with his fathers. In 1879 Mr. Bechtel and lady removed to the State of Kansas to reside with a married daughter, and are enjoying fine health at the present writing, 1880.

HENRY SHELLER

was born in the city of Philadelphia in 1760. His parents were of German and English descent. When sixteen years of age, he was apprenticed to an uncle in Lancaster county to learn the trade of a shoemaker. After the close of the Revolutionary war he located in Westmoreland county, where he remained until 1805, in the meantime marrying. In that year he removed with his family to Columbiana county, Ohio, where he remained until 1814, when he removed to Canton, Stark county, and in 1820 located in Mifflin, Richland county,

Ohio. Here he deceased in 1845, aged about eighty-five years. His family consisted of Samuel, who enlisted in the war of 1812, and was captured at the surrender of General Hull, and taken to Montreal, and never returned; Jacob, who died in 1838; John, who resides in Vermillion township, Ashland county; and three daughters.

John Sheller was born in Westmoreland county, Pennsylvania, March 4, 1805, and was an infant when his father removed to Columbiana county. He has passed through all the pioneer scenes of the early settlers of this county, and is remarkably vigorous for a man of his age. He is a prosperous and thorough-going farmer. His homestead is valuable, and he is surrounded by a thrifty community. He is a man of few words, unflinching in his integrity, and inflexibly opposed to prevarication and shams. His family consists of three sons—William, Henry and Manuel; and three daughters, Ellenora, Sarah and Mariah—all married but the youngest daughter. His wife had been married to John Brubaker, who deceased. She became the wife of Mr. Sheller in 1840.

MRS. SARAH H. ANDREWS

was born in Massachusetts in August, 1796. She was the daughter of Levi Gates, one of the early families of that State. She married Mr. Andrews, having lost a former husband, when quite young. She accompanied her husband to Ohio in 1817, and located in Uniontown, now Ashland, in the spring of that year. When they arrived the present site of Ashland was nearly covered with the primitive forest, there being but about five houses in the town. It is remembered that the owners or occupants of these residences were Joseph Sheets, nearly opposite the present hardware store of Isaac Stull, on Main street; William Montgomery, near where Mrs. Wages resides; David Markley, where the town hall now stands, and John Croft, a tanner, who resided just south of that point. These constituted the population of Uniontown. Mrs. Joseph Sheets, we believe, is the only person of this number known to be alive, and present at the funeral of her old and esteemed friend, on the fourteenth of February, who was brought to Ashland to be interred beside her husband, Alanson Andrews, who died May 20, 1850.

During the lifetime of Mr. Andrews, he and his family resided on what was formerly known as the David Markley farm, bounding Ashland on the southwest, having purchased the same from Mr. Markley. Some time in 1830, Mr. Levi Gates, father of Mrs. Andrews, became a citizen of Ashland, residing with his daughter, and died September 6, 1837, aged about seventy-two years. Her mother died in Massachusetts, some years prior to his decease. Mrs. Andrews was the mother of the gifted and scholarly Lorin Andrews, who died president of Kenyon college, and is believed to have been the second child born in Ashland, in 1819. Some years since Mrs. Andrews removed to Geneseo, Illinois, to reside with a relative, all her children having sought homes in the west.

It has been about sixty-two years since Mr. and Mrs. Andrews landed in the wilds of this region, very few suspecting, at that time, that the little village in the woods might in the future become a large town and county-seat. How great the change. In lieu of the rugged settlers who cleared the forests, erected cabins, and constructed our highways, and caused the country to blossom as the rose, a new people now cultivate our fields and possess the homes of the hardy pioneers who have been gathered to the tomb. Here and there may be found a surviving pioneer, with tottering gait and trembling hand, frosted with years, to remind us that all must bid adieu to the scenes of time sooner or later.

Mrs. Andrews died at Geneseo, Illinois, February 9, 1879. She had many friends in Ashland, and their sympathies are extended to those who have been bereaved in her death. She was an exemplary member of the Presbyterian church for many years, and evinced due preparation and fitness for another and better world. Her death brings to remembrance many reminiscences of the past. The remaining pioneers in this region, in her departure, call to recollection the scenes of other days, and their early experiences in the forests of this county. In her decease they are reminded of the certainty of death, and preparation that fits all mankind for another and better world, where all pain and trouble shall cease.

JUDGE WILLIAM OSBORN

was the third son of Ralph and Catharine Osborn, late of the city of Columbus, at which place he was born May 1, 1821, and was fifty-eight years old at his decease.

His father, Ralph Osborn, was a native of Waterbury, Connecticut, who, after studying law at Litchfield, Connecticut, and Albany, New York, moved to the west in the year 1806, and at first settled in Franklinton, but afterward removed to Jefferson, then county-seat of Pickaway county. He was elected clerk of the house of representatives of the Ohio legislature, in the session of 1810, and consecutively until 1814; and during the winter succeeding, he was elected auditor of State. This office he held until the winter of 1833–4, when he was succeeded by the late John A. Bryan.

The mother of Judge Osborn was of the family of John Renick, of the south branch of the Potomac, in Hardy county, Virginia, who moved to Ohio and settled upon the rich lands of Pickaway county, lying west of the Scioto river, about the year 1803 or '4. The family of which Judge Osborn was a member, consisted of four sons and four daughters. After the death of his mother, his father was married to Mrs. Jane Turney, of Columbus, the widow of Dr. Daniel Turney, a very eminent and skilful physician of that city. By his second wife, he had three daughters.

Judge Osborn received his earlier academical instruction at Blendon, Franklin county, under the teaching of the late Rev. Ebenezer Washburn. After that, he was sent to the Ohio university, at Athens, Ohio, and spent three years in study, under the direction of the late Alexander McGuffey, then president of the university, and with whom the student was upon more friendly and intimate relations than are usual between students and their teacher. After quitting the university, Mr. Osborn had partially made up his mind to enter upon a purely business career, as distinguished from a professional one. For this purpose he entered the dry goods store of his brother, the late James D. Osborn, of Columbus, and was in this employment about one year. The details of this kind of business were not congenial. Though of very soft and winning manners, and likely to be popular with customers, he could not brook the confinement and tedium of measuring cloth by the yard-stick, or of tying up parcels neatly, or of putting up goods from counter to shelf. Besides this, his constitution, never very robust, was not likely to be improved in the confined employment of a store. Of a reflecting and studious habit, he preferred the companionship of books, and when deeply immersed in the logic or narrative he had in hand, he was apt to become quite oblivious to events about him. He became convinced that his future success in life, and his own tastes and comfort, would be much more promoted in a professional life, than in the drudgery of business. Accordingly, he determined to commence the study of the law.

His elder brother, John R. Osborn, then of Norwalk, was in the practice of the law in Huron and other counties, and occasionally extending to Richland. He offered the young man a place in his office, as well as a home in his family.

In the course of the first winter after commencing, and while young Osborn was pursuing his studies, he felt that he could do something in the way of support by teaching school. It was not long after this determination was known that he obtained a good school in Bronson, five miles south of Norwalk. This school was in the immediate neighborhood of Alexander McPherson, a prominent, leading citizen of Huron county, and afterwards a member of the legislature from that county. Mr. McPherson took the teacher into his own family. He was a Scotchman, intelligent, industrious, quick-witted, and devout. There grew up between the two a warm friendship, which continued through life. Mr. McPherson was some years the senior of Judge Osborn, and died about two months after the latter was buried. The school lasted about four or five months. Mr. Osborn continued the study of the law in his brother's office for a period of something over two years, perhaps two and a half years, and was admitted to the bar at the session of the supreme court in Huron county in the year 1846.

The county of Ashland was organized in the year 1846, and was composed of parts of Richland, Huron, Lorain, and Wayne counties.

It was in the year 1847 that, pondering and considering the field of his future employment, he determined to locate at the village of Ashland, then recently made the county-seat of the new county. The Hon. R. C. Parsons, now of Cleveland, had been spending about a year or so at Norwalk. The young men were nearly of the same age, and together they started out from Norwalk to Ashland. They took up quarters at Mr. Slocum's, and young Osborn soon found a room for an office, and hung out his shingle.

He was ex-judge of the court of common pleas for this district, and one of the most highly esteemed men of northern Ohio. He died at his home on Center street, Wednesday, February 11, 1880, at two o'clock. His illness was of brief duration, dating from Monday, the second instant, when he was confined to his room by an attack of acute pneumonia. On the day previous he had attended church, both morning and evening, evincing more than usual enjoyment of the communion services which distinguished that day.

At an early period of his illness he gave evidence that he had little hope of his recovery. While his suffering was not extreme, there was a feeling of utter weariness and desire for rest that shadowed the coming of the hour when he should "enter into that rest." The death of Judge Osborn was such as every good man might wish to die, and such as only a noble man could die. The last hour of his mortal life was a fitting close to a long, useful and honorable career. On Wednesday morning he refused to take any medicine whatever, seemingly conscious that the time of his departure was at hand. At an early hour his life-long friend, A. L. Curtis, was sent for to draw up a will. After this was done he appeared very much exhausted, and rested quite a while before making any effort to speak. At last rousing himself he reached out his hand to his daughter, who was sitting at the bedside, and said: "I must leave you, good-bye." As the grief-stricken family gathered around the bedside he gave each an affectionate farewell, and then, in a tone of peaceful assurance, said: "It is right, I should go before." Thus fell asleep William Osborn in the fifty-ninth year of his age; honored in public and private for the graces and virtues of character that ennoble human nature. "Mark the perfect man and behold the upright for the end of that man is peace."

The following sketch of Mr. Osborn's life is taken from the Ashland *Times*, under the cover of the signature of J. E. S.:

William Osborn came of good New England stock. He was the third son of Ralph and Catharine Osborn, and was born in Columbus, Ohio, May 11, 1821. He received his collegiate education from the Ohio university, at Athens, when that institution was enjoying its greatest prosperity, taking his degree about the age of twenty-one. Thence he went to Norwalk, Ohio, and entered the law office of his brother, Hon. John Osborn, now of Toledo. Having in due course of time accomplished his legal studies and been admitted to the bar, he decided to begin his practice in Ashland, then a small village of large expectations. He came to this place in 1846, and prepared for the practice of his chosen profession. In 1853 he entered into copartnership with L. J. Sprengle to publish the Ashland *Times*, Mr. Osborn's name appearing as editor. From this position he retired at the end of three years in order to devote all his time to the practice of law. In 1846, soon after locating, he entered into law partnership with Willard Slocum. In 1858 he formed a copartnership with A. L. Curtis. The firm of Osborn & Curtis had a large and flourishing practice for many years. The firm was dissolved in 1866, when Mr. Osborn was elected judge of the court of common pleas. After retiring from the bench, in 1871, he resumed practice at the bar. January 1, 1875, he associated P. S. Grosscup, esq., with himself over the name of Osborn & Grosscup. Owing to the rapid growth of their office business Mr. C. J. Kenny was admitted to the firm last year, and the firm name changed to Osborn, Grosscup & Kenney.

As a lawyer, Judge Osborn ranked very high in this section of the State. His was a mind of mental grasp and power. He was an acute thinker, a clear, conclusive reasoner. If his physical strength had been commensurate with his intellectual ability, his reputation and influence would have extended far beyond the limits of northern Ohio. He was especially distinguished for the ability of his pleadings, and an extensive knowledge of the principles and practice of law. He was, in a pre-eminent degree, a wise and conscientious counsellor, enjoying the confidence and patronage of many corporations, commercial houses, and capitalists, to whom he held the relation of legal adviser.

From early manhood Mr. Osborn was a man of affairs, devoting much time and money to promoting worthy public enterprises. Every good cause received his support, and for over thirty years he has been identified with the industrial, commercial, and moral growth of Ashland. The years have been few in which he has not been serving his fellow-citizens in some place of public trust with marked zeal and fidelity. As a member of the board of education, he has had much influence in building up our public schools. As a public-spirited citizen, he has been identified with all public improvements. At the time of his death he was president of the Ashland County Mutual Insurance company, a position which he held for ten years. He has been a member of the board of directors for a period of twenty years. He was also a director and stockholder of the First National bank.

In politics, Judge Osborn was an ardent and consistent Republican, loved by his party associates, and esteemed by his political opponents. He was a skilful party organizer, and trusted party leader to the day of his death; yet in the hottest political campaigns no breath of slander, or taint of dishonor, ever touched him. His name was always above reproach. In his death the Republican party of Ashland county has sustained an irreparable loss.

But if in public and professional life he was conspicuous for ability and nobility, with how much more brilliant lustre does his name and character shine in private life, distinguished as he was for unostentatious benevolence and generous helpfulness, especially to young men struggling to secure a foothold in a chosen business or profession. A man of abstraction in thought, he was yet a careful observer and lover of the young. There are young men who owe a lifetime of success to the counsel and substantial assistance rendered by Judge Osborn, at a time when the only security they could offer was that of personal honor. As long as gratitude springs up in the human breast, so long will the memory of this sainted lawyer be kept green in the hearts of many who have had the blessing of his confidence and counsel. The memory of this just man "blossoms in the dust." His deeds of benevolence were done so quietly, that not even nearest friends knew how constant and frequent were the acts which have distinguished his private life. "Those who knew him best loved him most."

Few men have been so happy in their home life, and few have infused such a spirit of love and happiness in the domestic circle as this husband and father, whose attention was so constantly engrossed by public and professional duties. In all the plans and pleasures of home he was a participant. The little things, which enter so largely into home life, were never overlooked. That ready sympathy which made the friend of the young in business, here found its freeest expression. Judge Osborn, especially at home, was a genial companion. His conversation abounded in practical observations of men and things, set off in a delightful way, by the kindly humor which pervaded all that he said. Mathematical studies had great attraction for him, and he took much pleasure in solving new problems as he formed them. I had a wide and familiar acquaintance with standard literature, and kept abreast with the best current thought and investigation of the day.

At an early period of his professional life Judge Osborn united with the Presbyterian church, and at once took his place as a Christian worker. His loss will be especially felt in the Sunday-school, where he has been engaged as a teacher or superintendent for almost thirty years. No part of the Sunday-school escaped his attention, and many poor children have been provided with clothing, that they might attend Sunday-school, without knowing that the means were provided by one who had seen their need. This was a characteristic feature of his benevolent spirit; he avoided observation and comment in his charitable work.

Even from our imperfect sketch it will be seen that the life and character of Judge Osborn was exceptionally noble and exalted. There was in him a rare combination of the higher qualities of human nature. He has demonstrated that a noble Christian life is compatible with the practice of law and the discharge of political duties; that it is possible to be an active participant in public life, and yet keep "oneself unspotted from the world." Pure and above reproach he passed through thirty-four years of public life, a distinguished example of the highest type of Christian manhood. It was indeed befitting, that when the mortal remains of William Osborn were passing to their last resting place, that business should be suspended and the public schools closed as a tribute of respect to his memory. He rests from his labors and his works do follow him."

W. T. ALBERSON

was born in Orange township, Ashland county, Ohio, September 17, 1846. He entered the auditor's office as clerk, March 14, 1870; was elected auditor in October, 1874, by eight hundred and thirty majority, and re-elected, in October, 1876, by seven hundred and sixty-one majority. He and W. G. Heltman purchased the Ashland *Press*, July 17, 1879, of which paper Mr. Alberson is editor.

The following letter the author inserts in this place:

MINE LAMOTTE, April 15, 1876.

MR. GEORGE W. HILL, ESQ.:

I was absent when your letter arrived, which accounts for it not being answered sooner. Your first query is, "where did Jerome settle on Mohican." When we came to the county he was living at Jerometown, in a small cabin, a short distance apart from the Indian houses. He cultivated some six or eight acres of land; kept a few horses, cattle, and swine; he also kept a house of entertainment. He and the Indians did not get along very well. They wished him to divide the products of his farm with them; this he refused to do, the consequence was, when they had whiskey they whipped him. When the Indians left he said he gave his squaw the privilege of going or staying with him. She chose to go with the Indians. He then bought land where Jeromeville now stands, but sold to Mr. Deerduff. He soon after settled at Huron, in Huron county, and married a white lady, and died shortly after. Jerome commenced trading with the Indians when seventeen years old, but how long he continued a trader I do not know. He was with the Indians in Wayne's campaign, but whether he was with them in Harmar's and St. Clair's, I do not know. You enquire how much cleared land the Indians had. I never saw their field, but it was situated out of sight of the village; I think only a few small patches. The cleared land around the village was a lawn well set with blue grass with an occasional tree and a few shrubs, perhaps amounting to six or eight acres. I was in the village during the residence of the Indians, some three or four times. The village consisted of some five cabins, about sixteen or eighteen feet, one story high. The council-house, I think, was a temporary building, built lodge fashion. I do not recollect ever having seen it. I did see Pipe, and his wigwam was in Jerometown. I have no recollection of wife and children. He appeared to be fifty years old; a tall, dark, straight Indian. I never talked with him; perhaps father did, but I think not much, as Pipe was a surly, unrelenting foe of the whites, and had but little intercourse with them. I think he left with the other Indians. I have no knowledge of Captain Pipe, junior. The Captain Pipe the author speaks of must have been some other Captain Pipe. I know that an Indian by that name resided at Jerometown in the years 1809, 1810 and 1811. I believe there were more Captain Pipes than one. I think Jerome said the Indians had been on Mohican about ten or twelve years previous to the white settlement, but of this I am not positive, but it was not very long.

Very respectfully yours,
JAMES FINLEY.

Dr. Hill's Centennial Address.

DELIVERED AT ASHLAND, OHIO, JULY 4, 1876.

FELLOW-CITIZENS:—This is the natal day of our independence. We have assembled to review the progress of a century. How amazing has been the change in these valleys. At the close of the Revolutionary war the territory now constituting the great State of Ohio was in the possession of the red men of the forest, the *Wyandots*, the *Ottawas*, the *Mohegans*, the *Senecas*, the *Delawares*, successors to the fallen *Eries*, owned and hunted upon the headwaters of the Mohican.

In 1755, just prior to the defeat of General Braddock, James Smith, a Pennsylvania youth, was captured and brought to the Indian village of Tullehas, on the Lake fork of the Mohican, and adopted by the *Mohegans*. He afterward ascended what has since been known as the Jerome fork of the Mohican, and passed over what are now the townships of Lake, Mohican, Montgomery, Orange, and Sullivan, to the headwaters of the Canesadooharie or Black river. He was, probably, the first American who penetrated these wilds.

In 1760, after the surrender of Canada to the English by the French, Major Robert Rogers, of the Royal army, was ordered to take charge of the western forts, one of which was situated at Detroit. On his return east, he passed around the southwestern border of Lake Erie, by the Maumee and Sandusky, down the old trail across what are now the counties of Crawford, Richland, Ashland, Wayne, Holmes, and Tuscarawas, to Fort DeQuesne, now the city of Pittsburgh. He tarried and hunted one day at Mingo village, probably where Jeromeville now stands, in January, 1761. He and his red-coated soldiers were the first armed men who penetrated these valleys.

From memorials preserved by Rev. John Heckewelder, the Moravian missionary, it is presumed that sometime between 1750 and 1760, Mohican John, with a remnant of the old Connecticut *Mohegans*, from near Montreal, Canada, founded a village on a branch of the Walhonding, on section eighteen of what is now Mohican township, and gave name to all the streams of this county.

In 1782, the disastrous military expedition of Colonel William Crawford passed over this county *en route* for Upper Sandusky. The story of that ill-fated movement is too well remembered to need repetition. Many of his defeated, dejected, scattered, fugitive troops, as they hurried through the forests of Richland and Ashland counties, fell a prey to the tomahawks and scalping knives of the exasperated red men. Thus, on the branches of Mohican was avenged the bloody work of Williamson and his men on the Tuscarawas.

In 1783 the Indian village of Greentown, on the Black fork of Mohican, was founded by an American tory from the blood-stained valley of Wyoming. After that sanguinary slaughter, Thomas Green, who had aided the fierce *Mohawks* to murder his countrymen, fled to the wilds of Ohio with Jelloway, Armstrong, Billy Montour, Tom Lyons, and others. The village received the name of the white fiend, and was called Greentown.

In 1791-2, the *Mohegans* and *Delawares* of these valleys joined the *Wyandots, Shawnees* and *Miamis* in repelling the invasions of Harmar and St. Clair, and disaster met our arms at every point. The *Delawares*, of Greentown, were led by their chief, Thomas Armstrong, while the *Dslawares* upon the Sandusky and the Huron were led by Captain Pipe. In 1794, these confederate tribes met the vigilant and unconquerable Wayne, at Fallen Timbers, and were signally routed, while their military ardor was forever crushed, and their power broken.

In 1795, the treaty at Greenville gave the United States the fertile valleys, streams and forests of northern Ohio. Reservations were assigned the conquered, and they ceased to depredate upon the border settlements. The territory thus acquired was erected into one county, perhaps the largest in the world, and received the name of the hero that wrested it from the proud-spirited red man, Wayne. Soon after the treaty, Captain Pipe and a remnant of the wolf tribe of the *Delawares*, with a Frenchman by the name of Baptiste Jerome, joined the *Mohegans* at their village, in what is now Mohican township.

In 1806-7, the territory of this county was surveyed into ranges, townships, sections and quarter-sections, by deputy United States surveyors; and a land office was established at Canton, and subsequently at the village of Wooster, for the entry of wild lands. Very soon the primitive forests of Wayne and Richland counties were penetrated by the enterprising pioneer.

On the fifteenth of April, 1809, Alexander Finley and family, from near Mt. Vernon, Knox county, Ohio, settled and erected an humble cabin on the present site of Tylertown, in Mohican township. About the middle of May, he was joined by William and Thomas Eagle and John Shinnabarger, and their families. Their nearest white neighbor was John Baptiste Jerome, a French trader, who had married a squaw, and lived in a cabin on the present site of Jeromeville, a village that was named after him. He had cleared thirty or more acres of land, had horses, cattle and swine, and was attached to the band of Captain Pipe, who resided near the Indian village.

In March, 1809, James Copus and family passed

through the Indian village of Greentown, on the Black fork of Mohican, and located, in a pole cabin, near the present site of the John Charles mill. Upon his arrival he found near the Indian village, a wild, rollicking, West Virginian, and his wife, who fancying the nomadic habits of the Indians, had settled in their midst and hunted with them.

From 1809 to the spring of 1812, as near as now can be ascertained, the following families located within the present limits of this county; On the Clear fork: Samuel Lewis, James Cunningham and Peter Kinney. On the Black fork: Henry McCart, Thomas Coulter, Allen Oliver, George Crawford, David Davis, Edward Haley, John Davis, Melzer Charles, and Bazel Tannehill, Joseph Jones, Ebenezer Rice, Joseph Hill, Lewis Hill, Calvin Hill, Harvey Hill, Moses Adzit, Jeremiah Conine, Sylvester Fisher, Otho Simmons, Frederick Zimmer, John Lambright, Martin Ruffner, Melzer Coulter, John Coulter, and Abraham Baughman. On the Lake and Jerome forks: James Loudon Priest, William Greenlee, Thomas and Joshua Oram, Mordecai Chilcote, Vachtel Metcalf, Jacob Lybarger, William Bryan, James Conley, Benjamin Bunn, James Slater, James Bryan, Elisha Chilcote, James Collyer, George Eckley, Jonathan Palmer, James Wallace, Ezra Warner, John Carr, David Noggle. And in what is now Montgomery township: Robert Newell, Daniel Carter, Jacob Fry, Benjamin Cuppy, and Christopher Trickle. These families, by reciprocal aid, had succeeded in erecting comfortable cabins and in clearing and cultivating a few acres in Indian corn, the first year of their settlement.

Early in the spring of the year 1812 the Indians on the branches of the Mohican began to be uneasy, and frequent visits to Sandusky and Detroit were made. It was noticed when they returned they were in possession of new blankets, guns and tomahawks. The seductive influence of British agents was brought to bear, and the demeanor of the *Delawares* evinced their readiness for the fray.

In June the United States declared war against Great Britain. The events of the Revolution forcibly constrained her to admit the independence of the colonies; yet she refused to execute the treaty in good faith, and availed herself of every equivocation to justify her perfidy. She refused to vacate the western forts, and paid a price for human scalps in the campaigns of Harmar, St. Clair and Wayne, and claimed the right to impress our sailors and seamen into British service.

Governor Meigs, of Ohio, was required to furnish twelve hundred militia for the defence of the northwest and the border settlements. These, with other troops, were placed under the command of Brigadier General William Hull, of Dayton, Ohio, and marched to the Maumee, and thence to Detroit, where, without a struggle, on the sixteenth of August, he surrendered his army to the British commander, Major General Isaac Brock. The army of Hull contained about twenty-five hundred men, well armed, with an abundance of fixed ammunition, and plenty of rations. The circumstances attending the surrender were of the most suspicious character. Hull, stupefied from intoxication, was believed to be a venal coward, and was doubtless bribed with British gold. The surrender was execrated by the brave officers and men who had thus been treacherously betrayed into the hands of the enemy.

Upon the reception of the news of the surrender, alarm and consternation spread throughout the border settlements of Ohio. It was apprehended that Tecumseh, with his red fiends, flushed by the late disaster, would immediately begin a war of extermination upon the defenceless people of this region. By order of the governor, the citizens of the border counties were enrolled in the home guards, to defend their firesides against invasion from the relentless savage. In a few days General Payne and Colonel Johnson arrived at Dayton with two thousand Kentucky militia, and were joined by Tupper and Winchester with one thousand regulars, who hastened forward and held Tecumseh and his bloodthirsty bands in check. In the meantime, Colonel Samuel Kratzer, from Mt. Vernon, received orders to remove the Jerome and Greentown Indians to Urbana, where they could be restrained from joining the hostile Indians under British influence.

A few days after the removal of the Greentown Indians, the cabin of Frederick Zimmer, near the Black fork, was attacked, and he and his wife and daughter, and Martin Ruffner, killed and scalped by a band of hostile Greentown Indians, from Sandusky; and on Tuesday morning, September 15th, the guard at the cabin of James Copus was surprised and he and a part of the guard killed. Immediately thereafter there was a general flight of the pioneers to the block-houses at Beam's, on the Rocky fork; Samuel Lewis's, on the Clear fork; James Loudon Priest's, on the Lake fork; Jerome's Place, on the Mohican; Clinton, in Knox county, and to Wooster. In a few days most of the pioneers of Green township returned, and a block-house was prepared on the lands of Thomas Coulter, and another of the cabin of Allen Oliver, in which several families quartered during apprehended danger. In the meantime a stockade was erected by James Loudon Priest, in Lake, and another by Vachtel Metcalf, in Mohican, and a cabin defence by John Shinnabarger, to which several families retreated for safety.

During the panic there were many adventures and amusing occurrences. We have room for but one or two: The family of Alexander Finley sought safety at Wooster, which was about eleven miles away. Arranging his cabin, and concealing such articles of value as could not be carried along, he and his family crossed the Mohican and proceeded as rapidly as possible along the Indian paths. Suddenly recollecting that he had several young calves in a pen, he returned to let them out lest they might starve in his absence. Having done so he again turned toward the fort at Wooster; but supposing he could save distance, attempted to pass straight through the forest. He became confused, traveled in a circle, had to sleep upon the leaves and did not reach the fort until he had been out over thirty hours and serenaded by the wolves. Jacob Lybarger, a neighbor, also fled to the Wooster block-house. In his haste he gathered his only child from the cradle, wrapped in a blanket which he swung across his back, and started along the paths, directing his wife to follow. The shades of evening made the forest gloomy; Mr. Lybarger exerted himself lest night and darkness might prevent his escape. His wife followed for a time near by, but at last becoming quite fatigued hallooed to her husband: "Jake, Jake, are you afraid!" The brave husband, being somewhat nettled at the curiosity of his wife, exclaimed: "No, I am not afraid!" The journey was continued, and Mr. Lybarger failed to slacken his pace. In his haste along the winding paths he was considerably embarrassed by the brush and brambles. Suddenly stumbling upon the child, his wife again exclaimed: "Jake, you need not say you are not afraid—you have dropped Maria and did not know it!" The little daughter was speedily replaced, survived the war, and upon reaching womanhood became the wife of the late Justus S. Weatherbee.

Some weeks after the flight of the pioneers General R. Beall, with an army of about one thousand seven hundred soldiers, passed by Jerome's Place, and cut, on the old Wyandot trail, a wagon path through the townships of Vermillion, Montgomery and Milton, and thence over Richland county to Sandusky. This army was followed by General Robert Crooks, from Pittsburgh, with a large army train, and about two thousand two hundred soldiers. From Jerome's Place he cut a trail southwest by the Indian village of Greentown, known as the old Portage road, and quartered some weeks at the village of Mansfield. Troops from these armies were detailed at various points to defend the block-houses of the pioneers.

During the continuance of the war the following families quartered in the Priest stockade when menaced by danger from the savages: James L. Priest, William Greenlee, William Hendrickson, Nathan Odell, John Oram, Thomas Oram, Joshua Oram, and Mordecai Chilcote; at Shinnabarger's—William and Thomas Eagle, Jacob Laybarger, and Alexander Finley; at Metcalf's—William Bryan, James Conley, Elisha Chilcote, Benjamin Bunn, James Slater, and James Bryan; at the Jerome block-house—Robert Newell, Jacob Fry, Benjamin Cuppy, George Eckley, Jonathan Palmer, James Wallace, Christopher Trickle, James Bryan, Daniel Carter, John Carr, Ezra Warner, and David Noggle; but Messrs. Cuppy, Fry and Carter did not remain. Mr. Carter and family passed on to Tuscarawas county, and returned in a few months to their cabin in Montgomery, and again entered the fort, where Mrs. Carter died. Those who forted at Beam's, Lewis's, Coulter's, Oliver's, and Clinton's, were the Olivers the Coulters, the Tannehills, the Rices, the Chapels, the Crawfords, the Adzits, the Baughmans, the Kinneys, the Conines, the Lambrights, the Copuses, and the Hills. About eighteen of the Green township block-house pioneers, ranging from sixty-eight to eighty-three years of age, yet survive. Of those who gathered at the Priest fort, John Greenlee, and of those of the Jerome fort, Daniel Carter, jr., and Joshua Carr are believed to be the only survivors.

The inmates of the block-houses succeeded in cultivating vegetables and small fields of corn in 1813, while several families returned to their cabins and were undisturbed. Indeed, the danger was probably considerably exaggerated from the beginning. The treachery of the Indians and the disasters that befell our army in the northwest kept the border settlements constantly in a state of anxiety. By the aid of hominy-blocks and hand-mills the pioneers were enabled to provide, by the expenditure of considerable labor, for their families.

Upon the declaration of peace, the tide of emigration again set in, and hundreds of families pressed forward in search of homes in the wilderness. The woodman's axe re-echoed through the forests, and cabins sprang up in every quarter. A glance at the method of raising cabins, and the geniality of the pioneers may not be inappropriate. The first cabins were generally made of round logs, which were cut in suitable lengths and dragged by oxen to the spot selected for the erection of a house. The pioneers for miles around, gathered with ox-teams and hauled the logs as the axe-men cut them in proper lengths. While this was being done others were riving clapboards for the roof. A good axe-man was placed at each corner to notch the logs as the hands shoved them into position. When the main building had been erected the roof was rapidly constructed. A section of logs was cut out for a chimney, a door, and a small window, the floor being of huge puncheons or the ground. Having brought a lunch along, each hand exerted himself until the completion of the cabin, and then all congratulated the owner on his new home and dispersed. In such rude cabins hundreds of those present to-day lived fifty or sixty years ago. They were warm-hearted, whole-souled people, and though some of them possessed rough exteriors, they were noted for their hospitality and manhood. The log-rollings, corn-huskings, flax-pullings, road-making, ancient militia musters, bear and deer hunting need no detail at my hands. They will never be forgotten.

While the sturdy pioneer was thus cutting away the forest, and opening and fitting for culture a homestead, how were the mothers, wives and daughters of the pioneers employed? They, too, toiled, and were not clothed in costly garments. Woollens, calicoes, cottons, and other goods of eastern manufacture, were scarce and expensive. The deficiency was supplied by home industry. Attention was given to the coloring properties of roots, barks and berries, combined with alum, copperas, soda, and other alkalies used in dyeing flax and wool for domestic manufacture. Flax was extensively cultivated, and the hum of the spinning-wheel was heard in almost every cabin. When woven into linen, it was much used for shirting, pantaloons, sheeting, and other uses. When combined with wool, it was called "linsey-woolsey," and was very generally worn by both sexes. What were known as hunting-shirts, with a cape and belt, and beautifully fringed around the edges, were worn by the men. Almost every housewife of that era could spin and weave. The "bang, bang," of the ancient loom, and the magic shuttle shot to and fro under the threads of the warp, as the stout fabric grew under skilful hands, instead of the piano, made music for the cabin. These good mothers have long since gone to rest. Monuments and gratitude should preserve their memories.

The food of the early settlers was exceedingly plain, and consisted, for the first year or two, of hominy, cornmeal, and wild meat. The majority of the pioneers possessed one or two cows which fed on sedge-grass and browse. Milk was abundant, but sometimes tainted with wild onions and the buckeye. Mush and pone were the standard food. Almost every cabin was adorned by the primitive hominy block; the preparation of food by such instruments was tedious and quite laborious. The hand-mill, constructed of a bowlder, after the fashion of a coffee-mill, came into extensive use. The hopper was an inverted cone, with a cylinder of the same material exactly fitting the hopper, perforated by a shaft and regularly grooved, was placed on a pivot and propelled by the aid of a lever by one or two hands; this was a slow process. Horse-mills soon followed, and then water-mills, and, at a later period, the steam grist-mill. The first water-mill was built by Benjamin Cuppy, near Ashland, in the spring of 1816. The next mill was built by Martin Mason (now Leidigh's), in March, 1816; the next by John Raver, near the present site of Rowsburgh, in 1817; the next by Constance Lake, on what is now Goudy's run, in Vermillion township, in the fall of 1817. Prior to the erection of these mills, the pioneers obtained grists at Shrimplin's mill, on Owl creek, and at Stibbs', one or two miles below Wooster. The trip, by the Indian paths, was difficult and attended with danger, as several streams had to be forded, and the forests abounded with wolves, panthers, and other wild animals. The trip consumed from two to four days, and had to be made on the pack-saddle. Many of the mill-boys of sixty years ago are here to-day. How great the change in a single generation!

Organization seems to be the highest characteristic of the Anglo-Saxon. Wherever enough adventurers or pioneers are found to locate, the first prominent idea is to call a meeting and organize for self-government. In the midst of the war-like excitements of 1812-15, the pioneers of the branches of the Mohican, failed not to remember that self-government was the boon for which their revolutionary fathers contended. As rapidly as the population would permit, they began to organize townships and elect magistrates to enforce the laws and preserve order. In range fifteen, Lake township was organized in 1814, Mohican in 1812, Perry in 1814, and Jackson in 1819. In range sixteen, Hanover was organized in 1818, Green in 1812, Vermillion in 1814, Montgomery in 1816, and Orange in 1818. In range seventeen, Mifflin was organized in 1815, Milton in 1816, and Clearcreek in 1818. Of the Reserve townships, Ruggles was organized in 1826, Sullivan in 1819, and Troy in 1835. The earlier settlers after the war, on the north half of range fifteen were: John Carr, John Ewing, Joseph Chandler, Aaron Cory, John Raver, Benjamin Emmons, James Scott, Richard Smalley, Henry Worst, Arthur Campbell, Cornelius Dorland, Noah Long, John Chilcote, Isaac Lyons, John Jackson, John Davault, Charles, Hoy, Jacob Berry, Thomas and Andrew Cole, John A. Dinsmore, J. H. Gierhardt, Josiah Lee, Jesse Matthews, Michael and Matthias Rickel, John and William Hamilton. On range sixteen, north of Green, James Wallace, Robert Finley, Samuel Bolter, Jonathan Palmer, George McClure, William Harper, William Reed, William Ryland, Joseph Workman, George Eckley, Ezra Warner, John Scott, William Montgomery, Jacob Shaffer, Elias Slocum, Daniel Carter, John Springer, Jacob Figley, George W. Urie, George W. Palmer, Alanson Andrews, Samuel Urie, Joseph Sheets, David Markley, Henry Gamble, Joel Luther, Jacob Crouse, William Latta, Peter Swineford, Richard Beer, Michael Riddle, Vachtel Metcalf, Amos Norris, Jacob Young, Patrick Murray, Martin Mason, Lott Todd, Joseph and John Bishop, Christian Fast, Solomon Urie, Thomas Green, Mordecai Chilcote, Philip Fluke, Jacob Hiffner, Peter Biddinger, Rudolph Branderberry, and James Clark. In Hanover, Stephen Butler, William Burwell, Thomas Taylor, Robert Dawson, William Webb, Abner Winters, Abel Strong, John Burwell, George W. Bull, and Nathaniel Haskell. On range seventeen, John Lambright, David Braden, Leonard Croninger, Michael Culler, Daniel Harlaw, George Thomas, Jacob Keever, Alexander Reed, Robert Nelson, James Andrews, Peter Brubaker, John Clay, Frederick Sultzer, Henry Keever, Abraham Doty, Thomas Smith, Joseph Bechtel, Andrew Burns, John Hazlett, Andrew Stevenson, Joseph Charles, John Woodburn, J. Crawford, Robert McBeth, David Burns, John Richards, W. Freeborn, James Haney, William Shaw, Abraham Huffman, Peter Van Ordstrand, Isaac Van Meter, Patrick Elliott, Abel Bailey, John Bryte, and many others.

The earliest settlers in Ruggles, Troy and Sullivan were: Bradford Sturtevant, Daniel Beach, James Poag, Harvey Sackett, Aldrich Carver, Norman Carter, Reuben Fox, Jacob Roorback, Perry Durfee, Joseph Parker, Nathaniel Clark, Benjamin Moore, Christian Bush, David Mason, Ralph Phelps, Sanford Peck, Nicholas Fast, Philip Biddinger, Ashael Parmely, Jesse Chamberlin, Abijah Chamberlain, Thomas Rice, James Palmer, and one or two other families.

Next to the organization of townships came the founding of villages. The order of their survey and plat is as follows: Loudonville by James Loudon Priest, in 1814; Perrysville, by Thomas Coulter, in 1813; Jeromeville, by Christian Deardorf and William Vaughn, in 1815; Uniontown, now Ashland, by William Montgomery, in 1815; Petersburgh, now Mifflin, by William B. James and Peter Deardorf, in 1816; Savannah, by John Haney, in 1818; Orange, by Amos Norris and John Chilcote, in 1828; Hayesville, by Thomas Cox and Linus Hayes, in 1830; Perrysburgh, by Josiah Lee, in 1830; Mohicanville, by Simeon Beall and Henry Sherradden, in 1833; Sullivan, by Sylvanus Parmely, Joseph Palmer, Ira Palmer, and Joseph Carlton, in 1836; Rowsburgh, by Michael D. Row, in 1835; Lafayette, by William Hamilton and John Zimmerman, in 1835; Polk, by John Kuhn, in 1849; Troy Center, by Dr. Norris, in 1851; and Ruggles Center in 1860.

In the first settlement of this county, the interests of education were not forgotten. The earlier schools were taught in log cabins, and teachers paid by subscription. They received low wages for their services. Many of the pioneers, owing to the sparseness of the settlements, instructed their own children. The first school-houses were of the most primitive character. They had large fire-places, rude benches, and light was reflected through oiled paper, instead of glass. The earlier teachers were generally from New York, Pennsylvania, New England, and Ireland; the reading books were few, and spelling, reading, writing, geography and arithmetic constituted the course. Rigid rules were adopted and enforced, sometimes by birch. On the approach of the holidays, boys and girls expected to be treated by the teacher, and the expectation was generally gratified. Elizabeth Rice, subsequently Mrs. John Coulter, is believed to have taught the first school, near Perrysville, in 1814. She now resides at Congress, Wayne county. Asa Brown taught in 1816. Mrs. Nancy Elliott taught in Clearcreek, in 1817. Robert Nelson taught in Milton and Clearcreek, in 1817; Rev. John Hazard, in Montgomery township, in 1818; John Swaggart and Sage Kellogg, in Orange, in 1819; John G. Mosier, in Perry, in 1820; L. Parker, in Lake, in 1820; John Bryte, in Clearcreek, in 1823; William Irvin, in Vermillion, in 1823; Therygood Smith, in Ashland, in 1824; Chandler Foot, in 1825, and Daniel Austin, in Sullivan. Up to that period, all schools were paid by subscription. At a later day, a fund was collected by taxation, for the erection of schoolhouses, and to pay tuition; since which, school-houses and schools have kept pace with modern improvements.

In 1839 an academy was founded at Ashland and successfully conducted until about 1850, when it was merged into the union school system. It acquired an extended reputation under the management of the late lamented president, Lorin Andrews, than whom Ohio never produced an abler educator nor a more estimable citizen.

In 1845, Vermillion institute, at Hayesville, was chartered and authorized to confer degrees. It originated through the efforts of Rev. Lewis Granger, J. L. McLain and the citizens of the town. It has had, thus far, a career of varied success. It is handsomely situated and should command a liberal support.

In 1858 an academy was established at Savannah. It has had able teachers, and has sent forth many young men and ladies, who have made their mark, in various localities, as instructors.

In 1871 an academy was established at Perrysville, under the management of Professor J. C. Sample, an able educator. It is in a prosperous condition.

Believing that integrity, uprightness, courage, intelligence and morality should constitute the foundation of society, as well as the State, our fathers failed not, in their new homes, to inculcate those ideas. An occasional minister from the older settlements preached in the cabins of the pioneers or to people assembled in the forest. Religious societies were organized, and hewed log churches erected by the voluntary contributions of labor, prepared timber, and other materials. The first church was erected in the northeast part of Vermillion township in 1817, and was known as "Eckley's." It was free to all Protestant ministers, but was chiefly used by the Methodists. The Presbyterians, of Milton, organized in 1816, and erected "Old Hopewell" one mile west of Ashland, in 1819. "Hopewell" and "Eckley's," formed the nucleus from which Presbyterianism and Methodism radiated in this county. The German Reformed and Evangelical Lutherans began to organize congregations as early as 1825–30. The Baptists in 1824, the Disciples in 1830, the German Baptists in 1845, the United Brethren in 1848, the German Methodists in 1832, and the Congregationalists in 1838.

The leading ministers have been: Joshua Beer, William Matthews, Robert Lee, James Robinson, Robert Fulton, Samuel Moody, John Robinson, Thomas Beer, Samuel Baldridge, William Hughes, William Colmary, S. Diefendorf, T. B. Van Emmon, F. A. Shearer, W. C. Kniffin, A. Scott, J. R. McLain, J. Y. Ashenhust, W. T. Adams, S. T. Boyd, John Hazard, Fathers Goff and McIntire, H. O. Sheldon, Elmer Yocum, Elijah Yocum, Russell Bigelow, W. B. Christie, Edward Thompson, Thomas Barkdale, John H. Power, Adam Poe, J. McMahan, David Gray, John Mitchell, Jesse Warner, H. M. Shaffer, Rolla H. Chubb, P. B. Stroupe, A. L. Yourtee, W. J. Sloan, William Gilbraith, E. Eastman, J. J. Hoffman, W. A. G. Emerson, S. Ritz, Isaac Culler, A. H. Myers, W. J. Swick, M. L. Wilhelm, Francis Ruth, M. Hartsbarger, John Risser, D. R. Moore, H. H. Sanders, S. E. Matzinger, Richard D. Emerson, John Rigdon, Solomon Neoff, I. N. Carman, Mr. Tulloss, Mr. Wiley, Mr. Eddy, B. Y. Seigfried, John Cox, Lewis Granger, S. Stanley, Andrew Burns, James Porter, John Reed, Judson Benedict, L. Norton, S. E. Pearree, John Lowe, N. P. Lawrence, John Bryte, David Sprinkle, D. H. Rosenburg, E. B. Crouse, and E. F. Woodruff.

The healing art is the custodian of the highest interests of the people, and the educated physician, properly devoted to his profession, has it within his power to contribute largely to the health and elevation of society, for healthy minds must come from healthy bodies. Diseased bodies rarely contain minds that are not affected with eccentricities, depression, and melancholy; and so long as people place more value upon a horse or a cow than upon the life of a human being, mental deficiencies and bodily frailties will be transmitted. For the first six or eight years after these valleys began to be settled, the nearest physicians were at Mt. Vernon, Mansfield, and Wooster. The prevailing diseases were agues and bilious fevers, caused by the exhalations of decaying vegetable matter in marshes and ponds, during the summer and autumnal months. They rarely proved fatal. Butternut pills, bitters of wild cherry bark, boneset tea, and black alder, were freely used. "Blood-letting" was deemed a sovereign remedy for many ills. "Turnkeys" and the lancet were used by the surgically inclined pioneer. The earlier physicians were: Joel Luther, Joseph E. Cliff, Harrison Armstrong, E. B. Fuller, Thomas Hayes, William Deming, Abraham Ecker, Moses Owens, Thomas

Eagle, J. S. Irwin, Robert Irwin, John Hanna, George W. Paddock, Gustavus Oesterlin, W. C. Moore, O. C. McCarty, William Mead, William B. Young, J. L. McCully, Joseph Hildreth, and Constance Lake. The leading physicians of a later date are: Willard Slocum, N. S. Sampsel, Bela B. Clark, J. W. Kinnimam, I. L. Crane, J. P. Cowan, D. S. Sampsel, David Armstrong, Andrew J. Scott, James Yocum, Samuel Glass, John Ingram, John Lambert, S. Z. Davis, Amos B. Fuller, J. W. Griffith, J. Chandler, H. Buchanan, O. L. Andrews, George Weedman, George Gregg, A. B. Sampson, and many others.

The legislative act creating this county was passed February 24, 1846. It was formed of the territory of Richland, Huron, Lorain and Wayne counties. The fractional townships of Mifflin, Milton and Clearcreek, and the full townships, of Hanover, Green, Vermillion, Montgomery and Orange were from Richland county; while Ruggles was from Huron; and Sullivan and Troy, from Lorain; and the fractional townships of Jackson, Perry, Mohican and Lake, were from Wayne county. On the first Monday of April, 1846, the county-seat was located at Ashland by a vote of the electors. In 1847-8 the present jail was erected by O. S. Kinney, architect, and cost the county about fourteen thousand dollars. An old stone church, purchased on the site of the grounds selected for the erection of county buildings, was occupied some seven years as a court house. In 1851 the present court house was commenced by O. S. Kinney, architect, and completed in 1853. It cost about twenty thousand dollars. In 1849 Sylvester Alger and George W. Urie, architects, constructed the county infirmary in Vermillion township. It cost about four thousand dollars. Topographically, this county is admirably situated. It contains two principal slopes or water-sheds, one-half of the streams flowing north and the other south. The uplands, south of the dividing ridge, slope gently to the south, presenting fine views for residences, and are most desirable lands for culture. At many points a landscape of eight or ten miles sweeps before the vision, giving as lovely a view of valley, stream and gentle slope, dotted with farms and villages, as can be found on the globe. The soil is of clay, second bottom loam, and rich alluvium along the streams, giving every variety of soil. North of the dividing slope the lands are of stiff clay, and better adapted to grazing and stock; and many fine cattle are produced for the eastern market. It is also noted for its fine dairies, butter and cheese. The people north are from New England; south, from Pennsylvania, New York, New Jersey, Maryland, Virginia and Germany.

In 1812 the land constituting this county was valued at about three hundred and thirty thousand dollars. In 1876 the same lands, with their improvements, are valued at about seventeen million dollars.

In 1812 the chattle property would not exceed the meagre sum of six thousand dollars. In 1876 the chattle property of this county, appraised at its money value, will reach six million dollars.

In 1812 the population, as near as can now be ascertained, was about one hundred and fifty souls. In 1876 the entire population is estimated at twenty-six thousand five hundred and forty.

In the constitutional convention of 1851, delegates were elected by Ashland and Wayne counties as a district. Ashland county elected John J. Hootman; and Wayne, Ezra Wilson and Dr. Leander Firestone, and upon his resignation, John Larwill.

In the constitutional convention of 1873, each county elected the number of delegates to which it was entitled in the house of representatives. Dr. George W. Hill represented Ashland county.

The legal profession of Ashland county will compare favorably with the younger counties of the State. Our people are not noted for a tendency to litigation. Their occupation is mostly agricultural, and calculated to conciliate and encourage integrity and uprightness in dealing. Crime has been quite limited, and but one execution for a capital offence has taken place since the organization of the county—that of Charles Steingraver, for murder. The attorneys who have practiced at the Ashland bar are: Nicholas M. Donaldson, James W. Smith, Erastus N. Gates, John S. Fulton, Bolivar W. Kellogg, John H. McCombs, William A. Hunter, Jonathan Maffett, James Sloan, John W. Rankin, John Clark, H. H. Johnson, O. F. Jones, Willard Slocum, William Osborn, S. W. Shaw, J. Vincent, A. M. Fulton, A. L. Curtis, Alexander Porter, Thomas J. Kenny, George W. Geddes, William Henry, Thomas J. Bull, Amos Norris, George W. Carey, John J. Gurley, William Cowan, Francis Kenyon, N. Huber, John Scott, William B. Allison, George W. Hill, G. H. Parker, William B. McCarty, Robert Beer, John J. Jacobs, Robert M. Campbell, William T. Johnson, George B. Smith, H. S. See, H. S. Knapp, J. P. Devor, J. D. Jones, John McCray, Henry McCray, D. S. Sampsel, J. Hahn, William O. Porter, Peter S. Grosscup, Byron Stilwell, and Charles Dorland.

The bulwark of liberty is an enlightened press. Neither tyrants, venality, nor the frowns of the ambitious can put down an independent, high-toned journal. It is the vanguard of progress and civilization. It is the foe of corruption, the friend of truth and of science. As long as we have an incorruptible press, the rights of mankind will be safe.

The newspapers of this county have been the *Mohican Advocate and Journal*, at Loudonville, established in 1834, by Mr. Rogers; its career was brief. The Ashland *Herald* appeared in 1834, and was published by J. C. Gilkison; it lived about eight months. The *Ohio Globe*, by Joshua H. Ruth, appeared in 1836. It was a Van Buren organ, and survived about one year. The *Western Phœnix*, by Thomas White and Samuel McClure, appeared in 1840. It was a Harrison organ. It lived about ten months. The Ashland *Standard*, by R. V. Kennedy, appeared in 1849. It was for paper money, and lived about two years. The Ashland *Democrat*, by W. A. Hunter and Jonathan Maffet, appeared in 1846. H. S. Knapp succeeded as editor of the *Democrat* in 1848, and purchased and merged the *Democrat* and *Standard* into the *Ohio Union*. He was succeeded by

John Sheridan, he by Collins D. Bushnell, he again by H. S. Knapp, he by John J. Jacobs, he by J. M. & J. H. Landis, they by George W. Hill, and he by Benjamin F. Nelson and William H. Gates. The paper in the meantime having changed in name to *States and Union*, and the Ashland *Press*. The *Ashlander*, by William B. McCarty, appeared in 1850. It was a Whig journal. In 1852 it passed into the possession of L. J. Sprengle, and the name was subsequently changed to the *Ashland Times*. Mr. Sprengle was publisher and William Osborn editor. Mr. Osborn retired in 1855, and Josiah Locke became editor. In 1857 he retired, since which Mr. Sprengle remained editor and proprietor until November, 1875, when he sold the paper to J. D. Stubbs & Co., with J. E. Stubbs as editor. The *Independent* of Loudonville, by Robert Lockhart, appeared as a temperance organ in 1867, and ceased to exist in 1874. The *Loudonville Advocate*, by Joshua H. Ruth, appeared in 1872. It is neutral in politics. The *Hayesville Journal*, by J. B. Paine and E. T. Fairchild, appeared in 1875. It is also neutral in politics.

Of the brave soldiers of the Revolution, John Tilton, Jacob Hiffner, Jacob Shaffer, Frederick Sultzer, John Davis, and Adam Link, were citizens of this county. John Wheeler was killed in Orange township about 1819. Abraham Decker, of Milton township, died about 1828.

Of the soldiers of the war of 1812, who have resided in this county the following still survive: James Clark, James Compbell, Joseph Parker, Nathaniel Clark, Abraham Armentrout, Jacob Shopbell, R. D. Emerson, Francis Graham, James Kilgore, and E. Halstead. The balance of the list, one hundred and ten, have been gathered to their place of rest.

My friends, let us preserve these memorials while we may. Ere long the last of the pioneers will have been garnered by the relentless reaper. Even now they are rapidly departing, and soon the village bell will have tolled the knell of the last tottering frontiersman. The red men who met and welcomed them to these fertile valleys have long since gone to the great hunting-grounds, or now roam, old and feeble, toward the setting sun. Of the teeming millions that people this vast continent, not one will see the grand display of the centennial anniversary of 1976. At least three generations of man will have come and gone before the close of the second century of our independence. In the first, how grand has been our march in the paths of prosperity and greatness. Nothing but national suicide can arrest our onward career in all that renders a people free and happy. With pleasing emotions we look forward to the period when the Republic shall stretch all over the continent, and our banner wave triumphantly over one hundred capitals.

THE WELCH HOMESTEAD, MRS. JANE WELCH PROP'S.
ORANGE TP ASHLAND CO. OHIO.

THE HOMESTEAD 1827

Township Biographical Sketches.

GREEN TOWNSHIP.

NOAH CASTOR was born in Pennsylvania in 1764, and married Rebecca Matheny. He came to Ohio in 1814, and settled in Ashland county, on the farm now owned by Paul Oliver, and occupied by Mrs. Dewalt, where he raised a crop of corn. He then moved on the farm now owned by Benjamin McGuire, where he remained several years, and afterward moved on the farm now owned by Benjamin Castor, where he died July 26, 1829. In politics he was a Democrat. He was the father of nine children, viz.: Nathan, who married Freelove Castor; Susan, who was the wife of John McDole (both died in Indiana); Conrad, also deceased; Uriah, who married Betsy Hunter, and Rachel, wife of Joseph Guin, both died in Michigan; Sampson, died in St. Louis, Missouri; Ruth, wife of Datus Stutley, and Nancy, wife of Frederick Hardee, both died in Indiana. Benjamin, the only surviving member of the family, and the subject of this sketch, was born in Beaver county, Pennsylvania, in 1809, and came to Ohio with his father. In 1829 he married Elizabeth Van, who died in 1866. In 1869 he married Louisa Herr. He has followed farming all his life and has, by industry and economy, accumulated a nice fortune. He was a Democrat until Lincoln was nominated for president, when he became a Republican, and has remained one ever since. He is a member of the Baptist church, and a highly respected citizen. He is the father of seven children: Rachel, wife of John Zigler, of Ashland county; Noah, who married Harriet Clew, and lives in Ashland county; John, who married Mary J. Runion, and lives in Perrysville; Joseph, deceased; Allen, who married Susan Carnahan; Kate Monahan Castor, who married Thomas Burns, and lives in Spencerville, Allen county, Ohio.

CONRAD CASTOR, born in Beaver county, Pennsylvania, in 1790, came to Ohio in 1816, and first settled on the farm now owned by Thomas Castor, in Green township, where he cleared his own farm and built his own cabin, and followed farming all his life. In 1814 he married Anna McDaniel, of Beaver county, Pennsylvania. During the early part of their lives they were members of the Methodist Episcopal church, but later united with the Baptist church, and died in that faith. In politics he was an old time Whig, and from 1844 to 1857 he voted the Democratic ticket, and afterwards the Republican ticket. He died May 21, 1871. His wife died in 1868. He was the father of eight children, viz.: Tobias, who married Delia Hickox; Noah, who married and lives in Cleveland; Eunice, wife of Cyrus H. Goodell, of Lucas, Richland county, Ohio; Rebecca, deceased; Ruth, wife of Aaron Kindle, of Loudonville; Martha, wife of John Smith, who died in Colorado, and was afterwards the wife of David Snyder, of Indiana; Thomas, who married Louisa Webb, of Ashland county.

TOBIAS CASTOR, son of Conrad Castor, was born in Pennsylvania in 1815, and came to Ohio with his father. In 1849 he married Delia Hickox, of Portage county, Ohio, and has followed farming all his life. He has held the office of township clerk and constable several years, and is at present president of the Mutual Aid association of Jelloway, Knox county, Ohio, and adjuster of the Farmers' Home Insurance company, of Knox county. In politics he is a Democrat. He is the father of five children, viz.: Tobias, who married Catharine Hunt, and lives in Nebraska; Irene, wife of Levi Maurer, of Ashland county; Edmund R., who married Mary J. Boyd, and lives in Ashland county; Ida E., wife of W. H. Bushnell, of Perrysville, Ohio, and Bertie.

WILLIAM KINDLE, born in Maryland in 1801, came to Ashland in 1849, and settled on the farm now owned by Jacob Kittering, in Green township. He was a farmer and a member of the United Brethren church. He died in 1877. In 1824 he was married to Elizabeth Burrell, who still survives him. He was the father of ten children, viz.: Hiram, who married Elizabeth Oakes, and lives in Ashland county; Aaron, who married Ruth Castor, and lives in Ashland county; Mary A., wife of Timothy Everett, of Ashland county; Josiah, deceased; Susan, wife of James Plummer, who died in the army; Angeline, deceased; Eliza, wife of Jacob Goon, of Richland county, and Sarah A., wife of Daniel Hilderbrand, of Knox county.

AARON KINDLE, son of William Kindle, born in Tuscarawas county, Ohio, in 1828; came to Ashland county with his father. In 1853 he married Ruth Castor. He is one of the most energetic farmers of Green township, and has by industry and good management secured for himself a nice farm near the corporate limits of Loudonville. In politics he was a Democrat until 1860, when he became a Republican, and has remained one ever since. He is the father of two children—Edwin, deceased, and Emma.

JOHN COULTER, born in Washington county, Pennsylvania, in 1790, came to Ashland county in 1810, and settled on the farm now owned by J. N. Castor. He was the first constable and coroner of Richland county. He served two terms in the legislature, representing

Richland county, and was a member of the State board of equalization in 1856. In politics he was a Democrat. He was a member of the Methodist Episcopal church. In 1814 he married Elizabeth Rice, who was the first school teacher in Richland county, and opened the school in her own house. He died October 2, 1873. He was the father of ten children. At the present time only four are living, viz: Christopher, who married Mary Cary, and afterward married Nancy Farr, and lives in Ashland county; John N., who married Elsie Polock, and afterward Alice E. Skelly, and lives in Iowa; Elizabeth, wife of Dr. Strickler, and afterward wife of A. D. Zimmerman, and lives in Wayne county, Ohio; Nancy L., wife of Rev. Frank Eddy, who lives in Wayne county, Ohio.

CHRISTOPHER C. COULTER, born in Ashland county, and in 1840 married Mary Cary, who died January 12, 1872. In 1850 he went to California, and was very successful there in gold mining. When he came back he made the trip by water. January 7, 1878, he married Mary A. Tarr. He held the office of justice of the peace in Perry township for two years, when he resigned, and during the times of militia held the offices of captain and major. He is a farmer and storekeeper. In politics he is a Republican, and was a Jacksonian Democrat. He is an earnest Christian, and a respected member of society. He is the father of six children, viz: Artemicia, deceased; George Benton, who married Olive Ayers, and lives in Ashland county; Samuel J., deceased; Mary E., wife of Dr. James H. Christie, of Pennsylvania; John W., deceased; and Martha L.

GEORGE B. COULTER, son of Christopher C. Coulter, was born in 1845, and in 1867 married Olive M. Ayers, of Green township. He has held the office of councilman in Perrysville ever since it was incorporated, and has been in the dry goods business there since 1868, under the firm name of C. C. Coulter & Son, and by honesty and fair dealing has built up a large trade. He has been a member of the Methodist Episcopal church since he was eleven years old, and is highly respected by the community in which he lives. He is a member of the Masonic lodge at Loudonville, and a member of Odd Fellows lodge and Royal Arcanum, in Perrysville. He is the father of three children—Louis L., who died when about nine years of age; Claude C., who died when one year old, and Alfred.

THOMAS W. COULTER was born in Beaver county, Pennsylvania, in 1806, and came to Ohio in 1814, and married Elmira Hill, of Perrysville. He at one time, while living on the farm now owned by John Castor, near the Black fork, built a flat-boat, and loaded it with pork and set out for New Orleans, making the journey there in about a month, where he sold his stock of provisions and also his boat. It was a common way then, among enterprising men, to take provisions down to New Orleans—unless they sold out before they got there. Thomas Coulter was a tanner by trade, and bought out White, Colton & McBride, who built the first tannery in the county, where he carried on the business twenty-five years. He kept a farm, store, blacksmith shop, and harness shop, for ten years, and, after that, carried on a farm and was engaged in the dry goods business until the time of his death, which occurred in 1865. He held the office of justice of the peace for three years in succession, and it was offered him a fourth time, but he would not accept it. In politics he was a Republican. He was the father of eleven children, of whom five are living, viz.: Eliza E., wife of Joseph Hubbs, of Illinois; Jonathan, who married Lulie Peterson, and lives in Perrysville; Jennie, wife of Jacob Robinson, of Ashland county; Thomas W., and William H.

HARVEY HILL, father of Mrs. Thomas W. Coulter, was born in Vermont. He came to Ohio in 1812, and settled in Perrysville. The same year he married Abigail Coulter. He was a member of the Presbyterian church. In politics he was a Republican. He died in August, 1869. He was the father of eight children, six of whom are living, viz.: Angelina, wife of David Manor, of Kenton, Ohio; Ellmina, wife of Thomas Coulter, of Perrysville; Amanda, wife of George Turner, of Lima, Ohio; Clarendia, wife of James Segur, of Indiana; Eliza, wife of Stanton Myers, of California; and Thomas, who married Clarance Douglass, of Lynn, Massachusetts.

JONATHAN COULTER, son of T. W. Coulter, was born in Perrysville, in 1844. He received a common school education in Perrysville, and attended the Vermillion institute, at Hayesville, three terms. In 1867 he bought an interest in the store formerly known as the dry goods store of T. W. Coulter & Son, and, at the same time, was ticket and express agent of the Pittsburgh, Fort Wayne & Chicago railroad. In 1873 he purchased his brother's interest in the store, and sold a two thirds share to A. D. Zimmerman, and, at the end of two years, sold out to Zimmerman, and began to clerk in a hardware store for his brother, T. W. Coulter. At the end of one year he bought his brother's interest, and the following year purchased the stove and tin store of Leopold & Yarnell, and consolidated the two. On the fourteenth of April, 1880, his store, with all its contents, was destroyed by fire, but, not discouraged by his heavy loss, he erected a temporary building near his dwelling house, where he is doing a flourishing business. He has been councilman for three years; in politics is a Republican. In 1867 he married Ursula J. Peters, of Richland county, and to them have been born two children, Ettie E. and Esther L.

THOMAS JOHNSTON, born in 1809, came from Westmoreland county, Tennessee, to Ohio in 1827, and settled in Green township, on the farm now owned by William McIlvain. For twelve years he drove a stage, drawn by six horses, between Baltimore, Pittsburgh, Mansfield, Mt. Vernon, New Lisbon, and other points. In politics he was an old line Whig. He was a member of the Universalist church. He married Sarah A. Workman in 1833, and was the father of thirteen children, of whom only four are living, viz.: John F., who married Mary A. McCready, and lives in Ashland county; Harriet J., wife of William Armstrong, of Ashland county; Robert W., who lives in Galion; and Charles F., who lives in California.

JOHN F. JOHNSTON, son of Thomas Johnston, was born in Ashland county in 1834, and studied medicine with Dr. Glass, of Hayesville, Ohio, two years, and graduated at Jefferson college, Philadelphia. He commenced the practice of medicine in Perrysville, in 1858, where he still remains. In 1857 he married Mary A. McCready, who died in 1874. In 1877 he married Miss A. E. Ullman, and in 1879 married miss Florence Smith. He is a member of the Methodist Episcopal church; and in politics is a Republican. He is the father of five children, viz.: Florence E., wife of Norman Strickler, of Perrysville; Thomas V., in California; Mary D., Carrie, and Stewart, deceased.

JAMES M. POCOCK, son of Elijah Pocock, was born in Ashland county, Ohio, in 1850, in Mohican township. He studied medicine, and graduated at the Ohio Medical college in 1874, and the same year began the practice of medicine in Perrysville. In 1874 he married Sarah A. Harvey, and is the father of two children—Ruth and Mary.

MELZER TANNEHILL, born in Maryland in 1766, emigrated from there to Alleghany county Pennsylvania, and came to Jefferson county, Ohio, in 1805, and settled in Green township in 1811, on the farm now owned by N. McD. Coe, where he built his own cabin. He was one of the first county commissioners of Richland county, and the first justice of the peace in Green township. He held the office but a short time when he resigned. In politics he was an old line Whig. He married Eleanor Lisle, of Pittsburgh, in 1790, who died September 1, 1840. He died April 24, 1851. He was the father of ten children, of whom only three are living, viz.: Melzer, who married Sarah Oliver; Nancy, wife of Matthew Anderson, and afterwards wife of Adam Graber, and lives in Perrysville; and Sallie E., wife of Isaac M. Ayers, of Perrysville.

MELZER TANNEHILL, JR., was born in Butler county, Pennsylvania, in 1801, and came to Ohio with his father in 1805. They came in a flat bottom boat, called a broad horn, down the Allegheny to Pittsburgh, and then down the Ohio to Steubenville. In 1827 he married Sarah Oliver. He is a farmer, a member of the Presbyterian church, and in politics is a Republican. He is the father of five children, viz.: Elizabeth, wife of James A. Van Horn, and afterwards wife of Wilson Enos, of Richland county, Ohio; Charles L., in Arkansas; Nancy E., in Ashland county; Mary, and Letitia, wife of N. McD. Coe.

CHARLES TANNEHILL, born in Butler county, Pennsylvania, in 1792, came to Ohio with his father, and settled on the farm now owned by John Hunter, in Ashland county. He followed farming up to the time of his death, which occurred in 1876. He was a member of the Disciple church; and in politics was an old-line Whig, and afterwards a Republican. In 1814, he married Mary Oliver, sister of Lewis Oliver, of Ashland. She died in 1855. He was the father of twelve children, of whom only five are living, viz: John Q., who lives in Missouri; Clark L., who married Nancy Burwell, and lives in Indiana; Charles O., who married Sarah McNaull, and, after her death, married Rebecca Zigler, and lives in Perrysville; Mary J., wife of Joseph Kithcart, of Indiana; and Sarah M., wife of Dr. Cullum, of Missouri.

CHARLES O. TANNEHILL, son of Charles Tannehill, was born in Ashland county, May 6, 1830, and in 1854, married Sarah McNaull, who died in 1865. In 1866 he married Rebecca Zigler. He followed farming until the Rebellion broke out, and in October, 1861, enlisited in company G, Sixty-fifth Ohio, as a private. In November, he was promoted to second lieutenant, and in November, 1862, was promoted to first lieutenant. In March, 1863, he was promoted to captain, and, the same year, was recommended to Governor Todd to the rank of major; but Governor Brough changed the order of things by ordering that every man should be promoted according to rank, so his commission as major was countermanded. He took part in the battles of Stone River, Chickamauga, Resaca, Kenesaw Mountain, Peachtree Creek; was at the siege of Atlanta, and Perrysville, Kentucky, and at Pittsburgh Landing. At the close of the war, he engaged in the lumber business, from 1866 to 1874, when he went into the produce business. He has held the office of mayor ever since Perrysville was incorporated. In politics, he is a Republican. He is the father of four children : Frank G., who married Laura Grove, and lives in Perrysville; and Willie, Charles, and Minnie, who died in infancy.

DR. J. M. PERCIVAL, born in Clearcreek township, Ashland county, Ohio, in 1853, studied medicine with Dr. J. C. Bright, at Chatham, Ontario, Canada, and graduated at Long Island college hospital, in Brooklyn, New York, and began the practice of medicine in Perrysville in 1879. He is a member of the Methodist Episcopal church; and in politics is a Republican. In 1879, he married Miss Clara Skinner, of Detroit, Michigan.

SAMUEL BLACK was born in Allegheny county, Pennsylvania, in 1805, and came to Ohio in 183– and settled on the farm on which he now lives. In 1825, he married Rosanna Cashdollar, who died in 1855. He afterwards married Eliza Hilderbrand. He has been engaged in farming all his life; is a member of the Church of God, and in politics is a Republican. He is the father of eleven children, viz : Catharine, deceased, who married Samuel Conkle; Elizabeth, wife of Sylvester Huff, of Indiana; Philip, who married Margaret Rhinehardt, and lives in Loudonville; John, who married, and lives in Sandusky county, Ohio; Henry, who married and lives in Iowa; Sarah, wife of Henry Snyder, of Green township; Samuel, who married Caroline Ullen, and lives in Ashland; Joseph, who married Miss Sneer, and lives in Iowa; William, who died in Missouri; Daniel, who went to Tennessee, and the family have no farther knowledge of him; Lewis, who married Paulina Bartlett, and lives in Green township.

GEORGE BITTENGER, born in Franklin county, Pennsylvania, came to Ohio in 1827, and first settled on the farm now owned by Daniel Bittinger. He is a member of the Lutheran church; and in politics is a Democrat.

He married Susanna Derr, and is the father of eight children, viz: Elizabeth, wife of John Motes, of Ashland county; Daniel, who married Susanna Grimes and lives in Ashland county; Sarah, deceased, wife of Peter Wilkenson, of Indiana; Catharine, deceased, who was the wife of Peter Myers, of Bucyrus, Ohio; George, who married Polly Kidwell, and lives in Richland county, Ohio; Mary, deceased, who was the wife of Jacob Mathews, of Ashland county; Susanna, deceased, who was the wife of Samuel Brayton, of Richland county, Ohio; and Barbara, wife of William Cresswell, of Indiana.

DANIEL BITTINGER, born in Franklin county, Pennsylvania, in 1802, came to Ohio with his father, and has always lived on what is called the Bittinger homestead, and can truly be called one of the pioneers of Ashland county. In 1824, he married Susanna Grimes, of Frederick county, Maryland. He is a member of the German Reformed church, and contributes largely to its support. He is the father of nine children, three of whom are living, viz: Leah, wife of Michael Heffner, of Ashland county; Sarah and Anna.

BENJAMIN MCGUIRE born in Washington county, Pennsylvania, in 1824, came to Ashland county September 25, 1838, and settled on a farm a short distance from where he now lives. He has followed farming all his life, and has made wool-growing a specialty—has held the office of trustee in Green township three times, and was elected infirmary director in 1879; is a member of the Baptist church. In 1843 he married Rachel Gladden, and is the father of nine children, viz.: James G., who married Margaret Anderson, and lives in Ashland county; Elza W., who married Nancy J. Criswell, afterward married Mary Brown, and lives in Iowa; Orlin M., who married Mahala Budd, and lives in Ashland county; Elizabeth E., wife of James C. Andrews, of Holmes county, Ohio; Louzinski, who married Melinda Budd, and lives in Ashland county; Mary A.; Alva M., who married Lilly Earnest, and lives in Ashland county; Hugh D., and Willis.

THOMAS MCGUIRE, born in Washington county, Pennsylvania, August 28, 1808, came to Ohio in 1837, and settled on the farm on which he now lives. He has held the office of township trustee and treasurer for several terms; is a respected member of society, and is highly esteemed by all who know him. He has followed farming all his life. In 1839 he married Sarah J. Taylor, and is the father of seven children, viz.: William T. (now deceased), who married Melinda Laird; Electa J., wife of R. P. Wallace, of Ashland county; Diadama S., who married Nahamia Neptune, of Holmes county; John A., who married Eliza Armstrong, in Ashland county; James M., who married Patty Byall, and lives in Kansas, and Alice I.

DANIEL BUDD, born in Pennsylvania, came to Ohio in 1827, and settled in Ashland county, near Jeromeville. He was a carpenter by trade, and worked at that business exclusively. In politics he was a Democrat. He was the father of eight children, of whom but three are living, viz: Susanna, who became the wife of Caleb Edwards, and lives in Illinois; Thomas, who married Rebecca Black, and afterward married Clarissa Edwards, and lives in Ashland county; Samuel, who married Temperance Woodhull.

SAMUEL BUDD, son of Daniel Budd, born in Westmoreland, Pennsylvania, in 1821, came to Ohio in 1828, and in 1847 married Temperance Woodhull, and was the father of four children, viz.: Amanda, deceased, who became the wife of Samuel Dent; William S., who married Mary Hawks, and lives in Ashland county; Araminta, deceased; and Mahala, who became the wife of Orlin McGuire, of Ashland county.

WILLIAM S. WOODHULL, father of Mrs. Samuel Budd, born in New Jersey in 1799, came to Ohio in 1837, and settled in Ashland county, and followed farming all his life. In 1838 he married Mary Peterson. He was a member of the Baptist church, and in politics was a Republican. He died in March, 1879. He was the father of seven children, viz.: Temperance, wife of Samuel Budd; Joachin, who married Phebe Jones, and lives in Richland county; William, who married Martha Earnest, and lives in Ashland county; Mary E., wife of Benjamin Hughes, of Indiana; Sarah E., deceased; John, who married Elizabeth Cochrane, and lives in Ashland county; and Margaret, deceased.

JOHN MAURER, born in Pennsylvania, in 1818. came to Ashland county in 1833, and first settled on the farm now owned by William Moore, in Lake township. He was a farmer by occupation, and held the office of trustee in Green township for several years, also the office of constable, and was assessor one term. He was a member of the Baptist church, and in politics was a Democrat. In 1838 he married Miss Wachtel, who died in 1879. He died in 1870. He was the father of eleven children, of whom eight are living: Rebecca, wife of Mahlon Werrick, of Loudonville; Henry, who was elected clerk of Green township in April, 1880; Hannah; Mary M., wife of John Clugh, of Shreve, Wayne county, Ohio; Jacob; Levi, who married Irene Castor, and lives in Ashland county; Ellen, wife of Shannon McLeod, of Ashland county, and Phebe.

JOHN JONES, SR., born in Washington county, Maryland, in 1808, came to Wayne county, Ohio, in 1819, where he remained until 1847, when he settled in Ashland county, on the farm on which he now lives. In 1849 he married Susan Bowers of Wayne county. He has been engaged in farming all his life. He is a member of the Reformed church, and one of its main supporters. In politics he is a Democrat. He is the father of eight children, viz: Barbara, Catharine, Minerva, wife of William Carpenter, of Ashland county; Benjamin, who married Rebecca Dillier, and lives in Ashland county; Jane, Levi, who died when three years of age; John and Annie.

JOSEPH COWAN, born in Ireland in 1777, came to America in 1802, and first settled in Chester county, Pennsylvania. He came to Ashland county in 1831, and settled on the farm now owned by William Cowan. He married Eleanor Ellison in Ireland, who died in 1857. He was a member of the Disciple church, and belonged to the order of Jacksonian Democrats. He died in August, in 1857, at the age of eighty years. He was the father of nine children, six of whom are living, viz: George, living in Mercer county, Missouri; Sophia, wife of James Kelsey, of Missouri; Rachel, formerly wife of Alexander Calhoun, deceased, of Clark county, Ohio, now wife of Edward Lipsett, of Iowa; Mary, wife of Simmons Cornine, of Iowa; Sarah, wife of James Wood, of Holmes county, Ohio; and William.

WILLIAM COWAN, born in Chester county, Pennsylvania, in 1809, came to Ohio, with his father, and in 1855 married Mary Comer. He was admitted to the bar in Richland county, but was a farmer by occupation, only practicing law occasionally. He has been elected commissioner of Ashland county for six years, and has held the office of justice of the peace for nine years, and has also held the office of assessor. He has always voted for all the Democratic Presidents until Hayes' campaign, and for every Democratic governor until Allen was nominated for a second term. He is the father of three children, viz: Philip C., Jane N., wife of Hezekiah Boyd, of Ashland county, and Francis.

RICHARD GUTHRIE, born in Pennsylvania, came to Ashland county in 1814, and settled on the farm now owned by Benjamin Castor and Jacob Robinson. He bought his farm off the school lands. He was a distiller by trade, and built a distillery on his farm, which he run for about forty years. He was a member of the Presbyterian church, and in politics was a Democrat. He married Mary VanScoyoc of Pennsylvania, and was the father of thirteen children, viz: John, Margaret, Stephen, Sarah, George, Jane, Keziah, Lewis, Elizabeth, Hannah, William, Susan, and Simon.

GEORGE GUTHRIE, son of Richard Guthrie, was born in Ashland county, August 15, 1822, and April 20, 1848 married Ellen Dunbar. He has been engaged in farming all his life. He is the father of eight children— William D., who married Emeline Kindle; Edward, who married Harriet Drara—both live in Ashland county; Benjamin; Jane, deceased; George W., Isabella, and Lizzie.

JOSEPH JONES, born in Essex county, New York, in 1807, came to Ohio with his father in 1813, and settled on the farm now owned by Emanuel Millegan, in Green township, Ashland county. He has been engaged in farming all his life, and has by industry and economy secured a comfortable fortune, and is a respected member of society. He has always taken a deep interest in educational matters; is a member and firm supporter of the Baptist church, and assisted in the erection of the first Baptist church that was built in Green township. In 1830 he married Alcinda Bacorn, of Virginia, and is the father of eleven children, viz: Phœbe E., wife of Joachim Woodhull; Martha A., (deceased,) wife of Peter Vanscoic; Hannah V., wife of William Metcalf, and afterward wife of Gilbert Peterson, of Marshall county; Amasa B. who married Melinda Baker, and lives in Ashland county; William R., who died at Vicksburgh; Adelaide, wife of Joshua Lemart, who lives in Kansas; Alcinda L., deceased; Joseph M., who married Josephine Thompson, and lives in Ashland county; Mary C., wife of William Shelley, who lives in Kansas; Emma F., wife of Jacob Portz, of Ashland county; and Rebecca E., wife of John Hunter, of Ashland county.

JACOB BACORN, father of Mrs. Joseph Jones, was born in New Jersey, in 1785, and came to Ashland county in 1829, and settled on the farm now owned by Anderson Byers. He is a member of the Baptist church, and in politics is a Democrat. He married Phebe Harris, and is the father of eleven children, viz: Elizabeth, deceased, Mary, Sarah, deceased, Phebe Hannah, Nancy, Alcinda, wife of Joseph Jones, Jacob, deceased, Rebecca, William and John.

JOHN AREHART, born in York county, Pennsylvania, in 1815, came to Ashland county in 1840, and settled on the farm on which he now lives. In 1838 he married Elizabeth Senett; has followed farming all his life; is a generous, kind-hearted and strictly honest man, highly respected by all who know him; is a member of the Lutheran church; in politics he is a Democrat. He is the father of six children, viz: Sarah, wife of John Oswalt, of Perrysville; Columbus, who married Emeline Yates, and lives in Richland county; Susan, wife of Alfred Chew, of Ashland county; Jane, wife of Andrew Underwood, of Perrysville; Arsulia, wife or Martin Robinson, of Richland county; and John W., who married Olive Chew, and lives in Richland county, Ohio.

JAMES C. MOLTRUP, born in Shenango county, New York, in 1822, came to Richland county in 1840, and settled in Perrysville in 1844. He was a machinist, having learned his trade in Erie county, Pennsylvania. He opened a machine shop and foundry in Loudonville, and built the shop and foundry in company with Stephen Rust, on the ground now occupied by the English Lutheran church. In 1850 he sold out to Rust & Sons, and in 1852 came into possession of an interest in the same business, which he continued about two years, when he sold out to Tillson & Feik. In about three years he purchased Feik's interest and continued the business six years, when he sold out and went to Crawford county, Ohio, where he remained nine years, when he returned to Loudonville, and at present holds an interest in the machine shop, doing business under the firm name of Moltrup, Sons & Miller. While in Loudonville he held the office of councilman two terms. He is a member of the Methodist Episcopal church. He married Rosanna Rust, and after her death he married Hannah A. Russell. He is the father of fourteen children, of whom eleven are living, viz: Amanda, wife of J. W. Robinson, of Pittsburgh; William, who married Caliste Underwood, and lives in Perrysville; Helen; Ida, wife of Thomas Underwood, of Perrysville; Mary; Stephen; James T.; Rosanna; Walter; Jane; and Charles F. The following is a list of James C. Moltrup's inventions: In 1859 he invented a plow called Moltrup's patent. It was made of either cast-iron or steel, and is now in general use; a wrought-iron latch lever screw, used for cider presses; a drag-saw and horse-power attachment; a tire bender; a plaster dropper that can be attached to any corn planter now in use; a patent bobsled; a school-house seat; a machine for bending bobsled runners; a plow handle bender; an adjustable kettle ear; also the inventor of one of the best horse powers now in use; and manufactures four different styles of seats for school-houses, and can be considered one of the most ingenious men of the age.

ISAAC WOLF, born in Beaver county, Pennsylvania, in 1789, came to Ashland county in 1819, and settled on the farm now owned by Warring Wolf. He built the first house on the farm, and when built there was not another house within a mile of it. He was engaged in farming all his life, and, although not a mechanic, he manufactured wooden plows for all the people near there. He was a member of the Baptist church, and in 1813 married Nancy Small. He died in October, 1840. He was the father of ten children, eight of whom are living, viz: Warring, who married Sarah Peterson; Sylvester, who married Hannah Gladden, and lives in Indiana; Abrilla, wife of Henry M. Hoover, of Shelby county, Ohio; Milo A., who married Elizabeth Priest, and lives in Iowa; Boston F., who married Elizabeth Cotton, and lives in Barre county, Michigan; Aletha, wife of Jacob Rheinhardt, who lives in Morrow county, Ohio; Orsamus S., who married Pamela Fuller, and lives in Osceola county, New York; and Samantha A.

WARRING WOLF, son of Isaac Wolf, was born in Beaver county, Pennsylvania, in 1815, came to Ohio with his father, and, in 1841, married Sarah Peterson. He has been engaged in farming all his life, and has held the office of trustee for several years; has been justice of the peace for six years, and assessor for three years. He is a member of the Baptist church, and has been a deacon in the same ever since the death of his father, which occurred forty years ago. In politics he is a Democrat. He is the father of nine children, only four of whom are living, viz.: Mary A., wife of John L. Metcalf, of Ashland county; Isaac, who married Alice Freshwater, and lives in Ashland county; Margaret E., and John P., who married Annie Workman, and lives in Holmes county.

JOHN NORRIS was born in Huntingdon county, Pennsylvania, January 25, 1807, came to Ohio in 1823, and first settled on the farm now owned by Henry Cooper, in Mohican township. He held the office of supervisor several terms. He was a member of the Presbyterian church twenty-two years, but is at present connected with the United Brethren church. In 1829 he married Mary Smith, of Lake township. He was the father of six children, only two of whom are living, viz.: Mary A., wife of Darby Taylor, of Ashland county, and Joseph B., who married Phebe Lee, and lives in Perrysville.

JOSEPH B. NORRIS, son of John Norris, was born in Ashland county in 1848, and, in 1870, married Phebe I. Lee. He has been engaged in farming all his life, and is a member of the United Brethren church. In politics he is a Republican. He is the father of three children, viz.: Mary J., John L., and Joseph W.

WILLIAM NORRIS was born in Maryland in 1781, came to Ohio from Huntingdon county, Pennsylvania, in 1823, and first settled on the farm now owned by John L. Metcalf. In 1805 he married Mary Hornoc. He was a captain in the war of 1812. He was a member of the Methodist Episcopal church. In politics he was an old-line Whig. He was the father of twelve children, of whom five are living, viz.: John; Nancy, wife of George Miller, of Holmes county; Joseph, who married Susan Young, and lives in Ashland county; Matilda, who married Lemuel Burgh, and afterwards Thomas Urie, and lives in Michigan; and Margaret, wife of Hiram Watson, of Knox county, Ohio.

JOHN WELTMER was born in Wayne county, Ohio, November 22, 1829, and in 1852 married Phebe Moses. In 1857 he settled on the farm on which he now lives. He is a cabinet-maker and carpenter by trade, but is at present engaged in farming. He is a member of the Evangelical Association, and a class-leader in the church; in politics he is a Republican. He is the father of four children: Sylvania, deceased; Pinninnah, wife of Charles Scott, of Ashland county; Epraim, who married Mina Anderr, and lives in Ashland county, and Lenna L.

THOMAS KITHCART, SR., born in York county, Pennsylvania, in 1796, came to Ashland county in 1815, and entered a quarter section of land. He then returned to his native State, and in 1818 married Deborah Wright. In 1822 with his family, consisting of himself and wife and three small children, in company with Thomas Andrews, he returned to Ashland county and settled on his quarter section, and by perseverance and hard labor cleared, and had before his death one hundred and twenty acres of his farm under cultivation. A part of the farm is now owned by Thomas Kithcart. He was several times elected trustee of Green township; was a member and supporter of the Presbyterian church; was a Democrat in politics until the Republican party was formed, when he voted the Republican ticket. His wife died in 1853, and he died in 1860. He was the father of nine children, of whom but four are living, viz.: Joseph, who has been married three times (he first married Mary J. White, then Phebe Moses, and is now the husband of Mary J. Tannehill, and lives in Indiana); Thomas, who married Anna Ernst, and lives in Ashland county; Deborah; and Anna, who is the wife of Joseph Weltmer, and lives in Wayne county, Ohio.

THOMAS KITHCART, son of Thomas Kithcart, sr., was born in Ashland county in 1826, and in 1848 married Anna Ernst. He has been engaged in farming all his life; has held the office of trustee for two terms, and is a respected member of society; is a member of the Evangelical Association, and is a Republican in politics. He is the father of six children, viz.: Anna M., deceased, wife of Luther Finley, of Ashland county; Nathan, who married Emma Bucey; Newton, Lambert, Sherman, and Sylvia.

NATHAN STEARNS, born in Connecticut in 1788, came to Ohio in 1817, and settled in Green township, Ashland county, on the farm now owned by the McKinley brothers. It was then a wilderness. He was a shoemaker, and worked at his trade in connection with farming. In 1810 he married Mary Morehouse, who died in 1870. They were both members of the Baptist church. He died in 1851. In politics he was an old-line Whig. He was the father of seven children, viz.: Lucius S., supposed to have died in Cochactaw with cholera in 1832; Warren L., who married Jane McCreaden, and died in the army; Charlotte M., who married Phillman H. Phuner, and afterward married Lawrence Omera, of Loudonville; Horace L., who married Mary J. Veach; Norman L., deceased, who married Rebecca Smith, and died in Indiana; Milo E., who married Mary A. Calhoun, and lived in Tipton, Missouri.

HORACE L. STEARNS, son of Nathan Stearns, was born in Green township, Ashland county, Ohio, in 1821. In 1846 he enlisted in company A, Third regiment Ohio volunteer infantry, commanded by Captain William McLaughlin. The regiment was commanded by Samuel R. Curtiss, in the Mexican war. He went to Mexico, traveled as far as Matamoras, and was discharged in consequence of disability. In 1849 he began keeping the American house in Perrysville, Ohio, having bought out John Shaffer, and he remained in that business twenty-two years. In 1866 he went into the dry goods business in company with N. P. Reed. The partnership lasted but six months, and Mr. Stearns soon went into the same business alone, and is still engaged in it. He is a member of the Presbyterian church. In politics he is a Democratic prohibitionist. He has held the office of constable, township clerk and township treasurer. In 1844 he married Barbara N. O'Hara, who died in 1855. She had one child, Barbara A., who died when fifteen years old. In 1850 he married Rachel B. Huntsbury, who died in 1851. She had one child, Myron N., who was drowned in 1860, when nine years old. In 1855 he married Margaret Butteroff, who died in 1870. In 1871 he married Mary J. Veach, and by her had two children, Ora V., who died in infancy, and Mary V.

ALONZO N. STEARNS was born in Perrysville in 1827, and in 1851 married Mary J. Heath, of Loudonville. He was a carpenter and joiner by trade, having learned his trade of A. A. Quick. He followed that occupation twenty-six years, when he bought a saw-mill of Henry Feese, and has since been engaged in lumbering. During the late war he enlisted in company C, One Hundred and Twentieth regiment Ohio volunteer infantry, under Colonel French. He is a member of the Methodist Episcopal church, and in politics is a Republican. He is the father of five children, viz.: Matthias H., Myron N., Robey, Emma and Eva.

GEORGE W. CAREY was born in Ashland county, near Perrysville, in 1824. In 1847 he married Elizabeth Foster. He was both a lawyer and farmer; was admitted to the bar in Wayne county, Ohio. He was Republican in politics and took an active part in all political campaigns. He represented Ashland county in the legislature in 1864, and held the office of justice of the peace several years. He died in 1867. He was the father of four children: Thomas, who married Susan M. Parr, and lives in Richland county; Mary, wife of R. H. Goram, living in Richland county; George, who died in Rowsburgh, Ashland county, and Charles.

CHARLES CAREY, son of George Carey, was born in Ashland county in 1853, and in 1874 married Sarah E. Stull. He is engaged in farming, and lives on the old homestead; is the father of three children, viz.: George W., Lillie and Frank.

LUCIAN RUST was born near Binghamton, New York, and received a common school education. He began the study of law with George A. Elliot, of Erie, Pennsylvania in 1842, but his health failing, he was obliged to give it up in 1843, when he went south, but in 1844 returned to Erie and began clerking in a book store and express office. In 1846-47-48 he was book-keeper for Williams & Wright, who were in the dry goods business, and was afterwards with A. King, wholesale grocer, and with Boyd, Cook & Co., contractors on the Lake Shore railroad. In 1850 he went into partnership with Albert Becker, under the firm-name of Becker & Rust, general contractors, and constructed the railroad bridge across Walnut creek, on the Lake Shore railroad, in Pennsylvania; built the Akron branch of the Cleveland & Pittsburgh railroad, and commenced in 1853 the construction of the Hillsborough & Parkersburgh railroad, and in 1854-5 ballasted the Hillsborough & Cincinnati railroad. In 1855 took the contract for laying the Nashville & Northwestern railroad in Tennessee, but suspended operations on account of the approach of war. He soon returned to Erie, and in 1861 built the Carbon Oil company's refinery. In 1864 he built the Dale oil works, in Franklin, Pennsylvania. In 1867 he moved to Loudonville, and has since been employed by the Brundage Iron Bridge company, and in 1871 built the iron bridge over the Kentucky river, at Cogar's Landing. In 1873 he was appointed clerk in the treasury department, under Commodore Douglas, and held that position until July, 1875, when he returned to Loudonville and engaged in the clothing business. In 1849 he married Sarah Davis, of Washington county, New York. She died in 1856. In 1857 he married Francis A. Smith, who died in 1859. In 1861 he married Jeanette A. Whitney, of Chautauqua county, New York. He is the father of five children, viz.: Lucian, deceased; Helen, deceased; Frances H.; Sarah J. and Lucian.

STEPHEN RUST, born in Connecticut in 1790, came to Ohio, in 1840, and settled in Ashland county. He was a moulder by trade, and manufactured the first cast-iron plow that was cast in the United States; he was also the first patentee of the first wash-board that was ever manufactured in the United States. It was made of copper, sheet-iron, tin, and zinc. In 1845 he built the foundry in Loudonville, and started the first steam-engine that was ever used in a foundry in central Ohio, and in company with his sons, run the foundry thirty years. In 1812, at Onondaga Hill, New York, he manufactured from the ore, shot and shell for the United States army. In 1817 he married Hannah Wiard. He died in 1870. Was a Democrat in politics, and was the father of six children: Lucian, who married Sarah Davis, then married Francis Smith, and afterwards Jeanette Whitney, and lives in Loudonville; Morrell, deceased, who married Mary Smith, of Loudonville; Darius, who married Philena Priest, and afterward married Elizabeth Priest, of Ashland county; Halbert, who lives in Jeffersonville, Indiana;

Rosanna, deceased, wife of J. C. Moltrup, of Ashland county, and Helen, deceased.

DARIUS RUST, born in New York in 1824, came to Ohio with his father, and settled in Ashland county. He was a moulder by trade, and worked in the foundry with his father until 1874, when he went to Iowa and remained four years, when he returned to Ohio and settled in Loudonville, where he now lives, and where he has been township clerk, village recorder, mayor, member of council, and member of the school board. He is a member of the Disciple church, and in politics is a Democrat. In 1859 he married Philena Priest, who died in 1863. Afterwards he married Elizabeth Priest. He is the father of six children, viz.: Stephen and Francis, deceased; Fayette L., Jennie, Arquette and Nettie.

H. B. CASE is of Welch ancestry. His great-great-grandfather, Augustus Case, his great-grandfather, Joshua Case, and his grandfather, Augustus Case, were all born on Long Island, New York. The latter was born July 27, 1759, entered the army of the Revolution in 1777, married Elizabeth Bell in 1793, settled in Wayne county, Plain township, in 1803, and was the father of ten children—five sons and five daughters. The youngest son, Joshua, was born October 2, 1812, married Rebecca J. Phillips, and died March 18, 1845. He was the father of six children—Elizabeth E., wife of John Coleman, who died in Wayne county, Ohio; Mary Etta, wife of James Miles, who died in Richland county, Ohio; Henry B., who married Mina Horn, and lives at McKay; Sarah A., wife of Samuel L. Paramore, who died in Richland county, Ohio; Carrie J., wife of Joseph H. Hartuper, who lives in Loudonville; Joshua M., who married Mary A. Hissem, and died at McKay. H. B. Case, born in Plain township, Wayne county, Ohio, December 13, 1839, moved to Washington township, Holmes county, Ohio, in 1850, and to Green township, Ashland county, Ohio, in 1856. He worked at marble cutting, clerked in a store, and taught school until the spring of 1863, when he purchased the McKay store of A. B. Case, and married Mina Horn. He is the father of five children, four sons and one daughter, viz.: Dayton L., Albert P., Jessie, deceased, Frederick and Herbert. He continued business at McKay as merchant, postmaster, and notary public, until the fall of 1872, when he left the business in the hands of J. M. Case (who afterwards became his partner in the McKay store) to engage in the clothing business with J. C. Pell, of Loudonville, Ohio. In the spring of 1873 he moved with his family to Loudonville, and remained in the clothing business until 1879, when he returned to McKay to take charge of the store (his brother, J. M. Case, having died), where he still continues as merchant and postmaster.

JACOB FULMER, born in Elsos, France, in 1809, married Mary Hoffman, and in 1837 came to Ohio, and settled in Lake township, Ashland county, on the farm now owned by Mrs. Fulmer. Mr. Fulmer was a stone mason by trade, but followed farming all his life. He was a member of the Evangelical Association, and in politics was a Republican. He was the father of eleven children, three of whom died in infancy. Eight are living, viz.: Margaret; John, who married Lucretia Tipton, of Perrysville; Jacob, who married Jennie McMorrill and lives in Wayne county, Ohio; Catharine, wife of Abel Metcalf, of Lake township; Julia, wife of Levi Shut, of Lake township; Frederick, who married Amanda Workman and lives in Holmes county, Ohio; Daniel, who married Mary Sprang and lives in Perrysville; Mary, wife of William Steward, who lives in Mohican township.

DANIEL FULMER, born in Ashland county in 1855, married Mary Sprang in 1879. He carried on the business of queensware, groceries and bakery combined, in partnership with his brother, John Fulmer, doing business under the firm name of Fulmer Brothers. They have the largest and best selected stock in Perrysville. In 1880 he was elected clerk of the township, and in 1878 was appointed postmaster by President Hayes, which office he still holds. He is a member of the Evangelical Association, and in politics is a Republican.

JOHN FULMER was born in in Ashland county, Ohio, in 1846, and in 1871 married Lucretia Tipton. He is a baker by trade, and is engaged in business with his brother, Daniel Fulmer. He has held the office of marshal in Perrysville for two years. Mr. Fulmer is a member of the Methodist Episcopal church, and in politics is a Republican. He is the father of three children, viz.: Zella, Zada and Hattie.

WILLIAM H. VAN GILDER was born in Ashland county, Ohio, in 1842. He first learned the tinsmith trade, and followed that four years; then learned the carpenter's trade and worked at that eight years. He was then engaged in farming a few years, and is now engaged in the hotel business—at present is proprietor of the Commercial house, at Perrysville, the only hotel in the place. In the fall of 1861 he entered the quartermaster's department of the army of the Cumberland, and served there eighteen months. In the fall of 1863 he enlisted in the Fourth Ohio battery light artillery, under Captain Conkle, in battery D; was in the Atlanta campaign, Hood's raid into Tennessee, and took part in the capture of Wilmington and Fort Fisher, under General Thomas, and was discharged by special order of the war department in July, 1865. In 1865 he married Catharine Scott, and is the father of two children, viz: Lawrence and Byron

PHILIP LONG, son of George Long, was born in Lake township in 1844, and in 1870 married Paulina Murklinger. He learned the shoemaker's trade with Philip Bucher, and commenced the boot and shoe business with J. B. Long, in Loudonville, in 1867, and continued in partnership three years; he then sold his interest to J. B. Long, bought a new stock, and opened a store in Perrysville, the only boot and shoe store in that place, and has, by honest and fair dealing, built up a large trade, and gained the confidence of the public. He has been township treasurer three years, and still holds that office; and is one of the councilmen in Perrysville. He is a Democrat in politics. He is the father of four children, viz: Normanda A., Nora A., Mary A., and Emma A.

A. H. WILSON, born in Pennsylvania, came to Perrysville in 1873. He attended the Greentown academy three years, and taught school two terms; he then began the study of medicine with Dr. S. F. Griffith, but at the end of one year gave it up, on account of ill health. In 1877 he bought an interest in the Perrysville machine shops, with F. P. Grosscup and W. A. McCool. In 1878 he bought Grosscup's share, and the firm name at present is McCool & Wilson. They manufacture thirty-five styles of plow points, and ship them to nearly every county in Ohio, as well as to other States. They also manufacture wrought screws for cider presses, and a cast iron wad scraper, and are agents for the Griffith & Wedge steam engines, and the Massillon separator and engine. In 1878 A. H. Wilson married Ida J. Rice, of Perrysville. He is a member of the Presbyterian church, and in politics is a Democrat. He is the father of one child, viz: Kittie L.

WILLIAM CONDICK was born in Hampshire, England, and in 1866 married Jane A. Day; came to America in 1869, and first settled in Philadelphia, where he remained five years, clerking in a drug store. In 1874, he came to Perrysville, bought a stock of drugs and medicines, and opened a store in the room now occupied by the post-office, where he remained until 1878, when he bought a lot and erected a fine store-room, in which he is now doing business; he has the only drug store in Perrysville, and is doing a flourishing business, keeping for sale a general line of drugs, medicines, cigars, tobacco, notions and toilet articles. He is the father of four children: Harry, Mabel L., Minnie E., and William, who died in England.

JOHN EWALT, born in Pittsburgh, Pennsylvania, in 1780, came to Ohio in 1823, and settled in Lake township. He married Ann Todd, of Bedford county, Pennsylvania; was a farmer and followed farming all his life. He was trustee in Lake township several terms; was a member of the Presbyterian church; and in politics, a Democrat. His wife died in 1841, and he died in 1844; he was the father of seven children, only three of whom are living, viz: William D., who married Mary VanHorn, and afterwards married Margaret Perry; Harris, who married Annie Sheldon, and lives in Hannibal, Missouri; Rebecca, who married Harvey Reinhard.

WILLIAM D. EWALT, born near Pittsburgh, Pennsylvania, in 1813, came to Ohio with his father, John Ewalt, and in 1837 married Mary VanHorn, of Green township. She died in 1848, and in 1849 he married Margaret Perry. He is a farmer by occupation, and has held the office of trustee in Green township three years, and treasurer two years; he is a member of the Presbyterian church. In politics, he was a Democrat until the war broke out, when he became a Republican, and has voted the Republican ticket ever since. Two of his sons were in the army; they belonged to the Twenty-third Ohio volunteer infantry. He is the father of seven children: Eliza A., deceased, wife of William Byers, of Indiana; Elvina, wife of George W. Cline, of Indiana; John, who married Agnes Burger, and lives in Illinois; William, who married Catharine Chestnut, and lives in Ashland county; the other three children died in infancy.

JOHN B. GRETZINGER, born in Germany in 1809, came to Ashland county in 1843, and settled in Perrysville. In 1847, he moved to Erie, Pennsylvania, where he remained five years, when he with his family returned to Perrysville, and have remained there ever since; he is a tanner by trade, and at present is engaged in that business; is a member of the Evangelical Lutheran church. In politics, he was a Democrat until 1849, but since that time has voted the Republican ticket. He is the father of eight children: Harmon, William, Augustus and Frederick, who died in infancy; Charles, who married Rosella Workman; Matilda, who is the wife of Joseph McClure; and Emeline, who is the wife of Orville F. Ayres.

ADAM GRETZINGER, son of John B. Gretzinger, born in Philadelphia, Pennsylvania, in 1842, came to Ohio with his father, and in 1867 married Rachel Irvin. By trade he is a tanner, but is at present engaged in the livery business. In 1862, he enlisted in the First Baltimore light artillery, under Captain F. W. Alexander, and took part in the battles of Fredericksburgh and Winchester. Politically, he is a Democrat; and is a member of the Evangelical Lutheran church.

WILLIAM IRVIN, father of Mrs. Adam Gretzinger, was born in Butler county, Pennsylvania, in 1798, and came to Ohio with his father in 1811. They first settled in the Darling neighborhood, in Green township. Farming was his occupation all through life. The office of constable he held for several years, and was one of the parties who assisted in ridding the county of the outlaws, Driscoll and Brawdy. In politics, he was a Republican; and he was a member of the Presbyterian church. January 13, 1823, he married Rachel Tannehill. She died February 13, 1880; he died September 12, 1879. He was the father of eight children, only four of whom are living: Melzer, Robert, John, and Rachel, wife of Adam Gretzinger.

DANIEL YARNELL, a resident of Wayne county, Ohio, was born in Pennsylvania in 1787, and married Elizabeth Calhoun. He was a shoemaker by trade. He held the offices of sheriff, justice of the peace, and constable, in Wayne county, for a number of years. He died in 1864. His wife died in 1871. He was the father of eight children: David, who married Laura Henderson, and lives in Wayne county, Ohio; Aaron deceased, who married Margaret McMahon; Hannah and Ewing (deceased); Sarah, wife of G. G. Leopold, of Loudonville; Ellen (deceased), who was the wife of Jacob Everhart, of Wooster, Ohio; and Phebe (deceased).

AARON YARNELL was born in Wayne county, Ohio, in 1818, came to Ashland county about 1838, and settled in Loudonville. He was a tinner by trade, and was engaged in that business about ten years, when he sold to G. G. Leopold, and, in company with Thomas McMahon, opened a dry goods store, in which business he continued about six years. He died in 1877. He was married to Margaret McMahon, who died in 1878. They had three children: Mary E., who became the wife of Isaac Seigenthaler, and, afterwards, the wife of Timothy Osborn; John, who died in infancy; and Daniel R.

DANIEL R. YARNELL, son of Aaron Yarnell, was born in Loudonville April 3, 1846. He learned the tinner's trade of G. G. Leopold, in Loudonville, and February 27, 1867, in company with G. G. Leopold, opened a stove and tin store in Perrysville, the only store of the kind there, and remained in partnership twelve years, when they sold to Jonathan Coulter. At present Mr. Yarnell is engaged in milling, his mill being situated two miles south of Loudonville, on the Clear fork. It has three run of stone, and grinds on the new process. January 2, 1868, he married Miss L. L. Gladdon, of Richland county, Ohio. He has been trustee of Green township one term, and councilman ever since the town was incorporated. He is the father of four children: Oakley E., Guy G., Leon L., and Don G.

JAMES MCCOOL was born in Pennsylvania in 1822, came to Ohio in 1838, and settled in Green township, Ashland county. He is a miller by trade and occupied the old steam-mill in Ashland until 1861, when he was elected sheriff of Ashland county, and held the office two terms. In 1866 he bought an interest in John W. Springer's livery stable, and remained in partnership with him one year, when he sold his share to Springer, and bought out Helpman's stock of groceries, and was engaged in that business until 1875, when he sold his share to Springer, and went to Minneapolis, Minnesota, where he is engaged in milling. In 1845 he married Rhoda Swacick, and is the father of seven children, four of whom are living, viz.: James; William A., who married Elizabeth Denner; Henry C., of Perrysville; and Chas. W., of Ashland.

WILLIAM A. MCCOOL was born in Ashland county in 1850, and received a common school education. When he was fourteen years old he went to work for David Whiting, of Ashland, where he learned to be a machinist, and has always worked at his trade. He is now one of the proprietors of the Perrysville machine works. In politics he is a Democrat. In 1871 he married Elizabeth Denner, of Rowsburgh, Ashland county, and is the father of four children: Jesse M., who died in infancy; Howard S., William A, and Charles E.

ANDREW MUMPER was born in York county, Pennsylvania, in 1787, came to Ohio in 1837, and first settled in Ashland county on the farm now owned by Samuel Staffer. He was a farmer by occupation; a member of the Methodist Episcopal church, and in politics was a Democrat until the Whig party was organized, when he became a Whig. He married Margaret Dato, of York county, Pennsylvania, who died in 1861. Mr. Mumper died in 1860. They had a family of nine children, six of whom are living, viz.: Catharine, who married Michael Bender, of Pennsylvania; John, who married Leah Wonders, of Iowa; Andrew, who married Elizabeth Bryan, of Ashland county; Hannah, who married Vincent Daly, of Indiana; Jane, who married Samuel Shaffer, of Illinois; and Joseph, who married Christina Fleck, of Ashland county.

ANDREW MUMPER, SR., was born in York county, Pennsylvania, in 1816, and came to Ohio with his father in 1837. In 1836 he married Elizabeth Bryan, of York county, Pennsylvania. In 1838 he removed to Knox county, where he remained seven years, when he returned to Ashland county, and, in 1851, bought the farm on which he now lives. He has farmed all his life, and the last thirty-nine years has threshed. He commenced business with a small capital, and, by honesty and industry, has accumulated a large property. He is a member of the Methodist Episcopal church, and a respected member of society. He is the father of nine children, six of whom are living, viz.: William A., who married Susan Sanborn, and now lives in Holmes county; Frances, wife of Isaac Hunter, of Hanover township; Andrew, who married Hannah Hite, of Ashland county; Margaret, wife of George Lawrence, of Ashland county; Joseph, and Catharine.

ANDREW MUMPER, JR., was born in Knox county Ohio, in 1841, and came to Ashland county with his father in 1846. In 1861 he enlisted in company G, Sixty-fifth Ohio volunteer infantry, under Captain Orlow Smith, and served until July, 1862. In 1867 he married Hannah Hite. He is a farmer, has been school director for five years, and is deeply interested in educational matters. He settled on the farm on which he now lives in 1872. He has three children: Mary T., Harry O., and Katie.

ROBERT R. HUMPHREY, born in Ashland county, Ohio, in 1851, was engaged in farming and school teaching until 1874, when in company with J. R. Swartz he purchased A. D. Zimmerman's stock of dry goods, groceries and notions in Perrysville, and continued in partnership until 1878, when he purchased Swartz's share, and still continues business under the firm name of Humphrey & Son. April 14, 1880, their store and nearly their entire stock was destroyed by fire, but they immediately erected a temporary building adjoining their old stand, bought a new stock of goods, and still continue in business. They deal largely in country produce; their sales in all amounting to between twenty-five thousand and thirty thousand dollars per annum. In 1878 he married Jennie E. Wallace, and they have one child, Clyde.

ANDREW HUMPHREY, born in Ireland, came to America when only twelve years old, and afterward married Mary Humphrey, of Erie, Pennsylvania. He came to Ashland county in 1824, and first settled on the farm now owned by William Humphrey. He was a shoemaker by trade, but in the latter part of his life was engaged in farming. He was a member of the Disciple church, and in politics was a Democrat. He was the father of ten children, six of whom are living: William, who married Nancy McIlvaine; Rebecca, wife of Lewis Patterson, of Missouri; Nancy, wife of Alexander McS——; Catharine, wife of John Ramsey, of Iowa; John, who married Rebecca Toney, and lives in Ashland county, Ohio; and Jane, wife of James Laird.

WILLIAM HUMPHREY, born in Mifflin county, Pennsylvania, in 1814, came to Ohio with his father, and in 1842 married Mary McIlvaine. He is engaged in farming, and also in the dry goods business in Perrysville, and has the largest vineyard in Green township. He has held the office of trustee, clerk and treasurer for a number of years, and is an honored and respected member of society. He has eight children, viz.: James A., who married Mary Wachel, and lives in Ashland county; Mary, wife of Benjamin Fry, of Ashland county; Annie; Robert, who married Jennie Wallace, and lives in Ashland county; William, Jane, Sadie and Hattie.

BENJAMIN QUICK, born in Bedford county, Pennsylvania, in 1793, came to Ohio in 1812, and first settled in what was then Wayne county, but is now a part of Holmes county, and is called Washington township. He settled in Ashland county in 1839. He was a wagon-maker by trade, and worked at his trade all his life. He first married Clarissa Priest, and afterward married Susan Clough. He died in 1841. He was the father of eleven children, eight of whom are living, viz.: Harriet, wife of William Ayers, of Upper Sandusky; Daniel, who married Elizabeth Tannehill, and lives in Missouri; Olive; Aaron; Benjamin, who married Mary Jackson, and lives in Colorado; Isaac, who lives in Oregon; William in California, and Thomas in California.

AARON N. QUICK, son of Benjamin Quick, was born in Holmes county, January 8, 1824, and in 1848 married Catharine Darling. At first he worked at his trade, that of a carpenter and cabinet-maker; then he purchased his father's farm, about two miles south of Perrysville, and for the last twenty years has been engaged in farming and stock-dealing. In politics, he is a Republican. Seven children belong to his family: Ella; Franklin, who married Russia Robinson, and lives in Pittsburgh, Pennsylvania; Jonas B.; Drego A., deceased; Thomas, who lives in Pittsburgh; Jeanette, and Hattie.

HENRY COBLE was born in Northumberland county, Pennsylvania, May 19, 1798; came to Ohio with his father at an early date and settled in Wayne county, near Wooster, where he married Anna M. Harner in 1824. In 1823, he came to Ashland county, and settled in Lake township, and has always been engaged in farming. In politics, he is a Republican; and is a member of the Presbyterian church. February 28, 1880, his wife died. Six children constitute his family, viz; John, who married Sophia Kantzer, and afterwards married Rebecca Horn; Sarah, wife of John Norris, deceased; Rebecca, wife of Thomas Metcalf, living in Iowa; Daniel, who married Margaret Kantzer; Henry, who married Mary E. Young; Maria A., wife of Joseph Chesseroun.

ALLEN OLIVER was born in Sussex county, New Jersey, in 1760; came to Ohio in 1810, and first settled on the Black fork, in Ashland county, on the farm now owned by Lewis Oliver. The nearest neighbors were three miles distant, and the nearest mill was at Frederick, about twenty miles away. When he entered the farm, in 1809, it looked like a wilderness, and the Indians were quite numerous. Truly, he can be called one of the pioneers of the county. Though he had very little money, he accumulated a fair fortune and a comfortable home. During the Revolution, he manufactured salt for the soldiers; not as we manufacture it now, but by boiling down ocean water. Elizabeth Kinney, of Pennsylvania, became his wife. She died in October, 1828, at the age of sixty-seven years. Although not a member of any church, he contributed liberally to the support of the Gospel. In politics, he was a Democrat. In September, 1823, he died, the father of seven children, of whom only two are living: Daniel, who married Sarah Quick, and lives in Ashland county; and Lewis, who married Nancy Ravenscroft.

LEWIS OLIVER was born in Washington county, Pennsylvania, December 26, 1793, and came to Ohio with his father. May 6, 1824, he married Nancy Ravenscroft. In 1814, he entered the farm now owned by Mrs. Hill, in Loudonville. For two years he has been township treasurer, and is respected by all who know him. In politics, he is a Democrat. January 2, 1873, his wife died, at the age of seventy-seven years, leaving seven children, viz: William A., Paul, John; Rebecca J., wife of Amos A. Burwell, of Indiana; Elizabeth, wife of W. W. Martin, of Wisconsin; Malcolm, deceased; Margaret, wife of J. Rice, of Ashland county.

CEPHAS PARKER was born in Sangerfield, New York, in 1807, and came to Ohio with his father in 1816. They settled in Holmes county, on the farm now owned by John Priest; he was always engaged in farming, and was one of the most systematic farmers of his time. For one year he was constable in Washington township, Holmes county. A member of the Baptist church, he was an honorable and upright man. In politics, he was an old-line Whig. In 1867 he died, at the age of sixty years; his wife died in 1864, at the age of fifty-seven. Eight of his nine children are living, viz: Silas C., who married Christie N. Gibbon; Alonzo P., who married in Kansas; Calvin C., who married Catharine Traverse; William P., who married in Philadelphia; Elenora, wife of Harison Fisher; Clementine D., wife of Wilson Norris; Isaac D., who married Miss Mocherman; and James L., who lives in Sacramento, California.

SILAS C. PARKER was born in Holmes county, Ohio, in 1831, and took a course in the Loudonville academy and at Delaware university. He taught school twenty years, and was superintendent of the Perrysville union school two years, and of the union school in Lucas one year. He studied law with R. M. Campbell, of Ashland, and was admitted to the bar in Mt. Vernon, Knox county, Ohio, in 1876. In 1854 he went over the plains to California, and remained there four years, engaged in mining with fair success. In 1858 he returned to Ashland county, and engaged in farming and teaching until 1861. In 1862 he enlisted in the Thirty-second Ohio volunteer infantry, where he remained until the end of the war. He was a non-commissioned officer and division commissary sergeant, and color-bearer, and took part in the battles of Port Gibson, Raymond, Jackson, Champion Hill, where he was wounded; Vicksburgh, with Sherman on his Meridian expedition, at Atlanta, Peach Tree creek, Decatur, and took part in every action that took place with Sherman on his march to the sea, up to the time of Johnson's surrender; he then returned to Big Prairie, Wayne county, where he engaged in the mercantile business, and remained there until March,

1868, when he removed to Perrysville, where he is engaged in the practice of law. In 1876 he was elected justice of the peace of Green township, which office he now holds. He is a member of the Baptist church; and in politics is a Democrat. In 1860 he married Christie N. Gibbon, of Wayne county, Ohio, and is the father of seven children: Sallie L., deceased; Essa M., Edie J., Amasa C., Frank A., Lib. C., and Kary G.

LAKE TOWNSHIP.

GEORGE KANTZER, SR., born in Ellsos, France, September 27, 1792; came to America in 1840, and settled on the farm now owned by his son George. He was a shoemaker, but when he came to America he gave up his trade and engaged in farming. He married Saloma Schmidt, who was born August 12, 1797, in Ellsos, France. She died in January, 1879. He was a member of the German Lutheran church, and in politics a Democrat. He was the father of five children. George, who married Catharine Taber; Salmona, who is the wife of Peter B. Long; Sophia, deceased, who was the wife of John Coble; John, who married Barbara Reinhardt, and afterward married Sophia Shaffer; and Margaret, who married Daniel Coble.

JOHN KANTZER, was born in Ellsos, France, in 1832; came to Ohio with his father, and in 1855 married Barbara Reinhardt, who died in 1874. In 1876 he married Sophia Shaffer. He is a farmer. He has been township treasurer for three years, and justice of the peace for four years. He is a member of the German Lutheran church, and has been one of the trustees for two years. In politics he is a Democrat. He is the father of nine children, six of whom are living, viz: John B.; Salmona C.; Sophia M.; William B.; Walter and Bertha.

GEORGE KANTZER, JR., was born in Ellsos, France, December 22, 1824. He came to America with his father in 1840, and in 1849 married Catharine Taber, who was born in Ellsos, France, in 1825. He was a shoemaker by trade, but soon gave it up and engaged in farming. He is a prominent member of the German Lutheran church, in which he takes great interest, and has held every office except that of elder, and is at present one of the trustees, and contributes largely to its support. He is the father of ten children, viz: Catharine, wife of George Kreiffer, of Wayne county, Ohio; Saloma; John P., deceased; Emma M.; George F.; Annie B.; Matilda M.; Caroline; Helena; and Minnie I.

GEORGE B. WOLF, born in Ellsos, France, in 1838, came to America with his father in 1840, who settled in Ashland county, Lake township, Ohio. In 1860 he married Alla V. Myers, of Wayne county, Ohio. Mr. Wolf is a stone mason, having learned his trade of Michael Roth, but has been engaged in farming for several years past. He has held the office of township clerk for the past four years, and is the present incumbent. He is a member of the Lutheran church, and a highly respected member of society. His children are: Adeline M., Ida M., John M. and William S.

ROBERT RICHEY, born in county Armagh, Ireland, in 1797, came to America in 1804, and settled in Ashland county, on the Big Mohican, where he remained for a number of years, when he moved to Wayne county, Ohio, where he married Naomi Isabella in 1823. He then moved to Knox county, Ohio, where he remained one year, and then returned to Ashland county, and settled on a farm in Mohican township. At the end of the year he sold his farm and settled on the farm now owned by Francis J. Richey, in Lake township. He was a distiller by trade, and followed the business for several years, but in 1830 gave it up and was engaged in farming until the time of his death, which occurred August 2, 1863. He was deeply interested in educational matters, and was a school director for a number of years. He had but three months' schooling, and was determined that his children should, if possible, have better advantages. He was a firm believer in Universalism but never united with the church. He was the father of seven children: Joel, who married Rebecca Hoy and lives in Ashland county; Cordelia, who married Eliza Bunion; Emily, who died in infancy; Francis T., who married Elizabeth Crumlick; Newton, who married Sarah Finley; Louisa, who married Martin Tannehill, and lives in Illinois.

FRANCIS T. RICHEY was born in Ashland county on the farm on which he now lives, in 1835, and in June, 1857, married Elizabeth Crumlick, of Wayne county, Ohio. He has been trustee of Lake township for two years, school director for six years, and supervisor of roads for several years. He is engaged in farming. In politics he is of Democratic faith. He is the father of seven children, viz.: Mary C., Laura L. Florence M., Clement L., and Celestia. Frank L., and Dennis M., deceased.

JOHN WOLF was born in Ellsos, France, in 1803, and came to Ashland county in 1840, and settled on the farm now owned by J. J. Wolf, in Lake township. A weaver by trade, he followed his occupation six years after he came to Ohio, when he gave it up and engaged in farming, which he followed up to the time of his death, which occurred in 1861. He married Mary Peteas in Ellsos, France, who still survives him. He was a member of the Lutheran church. In politics he was a member of the Democratic party. He had five children: Mary, Catharine, Margaret, John J., and George B.

JOHN J. WOLF, son of John Wolf, was born in Ellsos, France, in 1835, and came to America with his father, and now owns the farm in Lake township upon which his father first settled. In 1858 he married Matilda Myers, of Wayne county, Ohio. He has been township trustee two terms, and assessor two terms, and in 1877 was elected county commissioner, which office he now holds. He is a member of the Lutheran church, and is highly respected by his neighbors.

JOHN BURD, born in Pennsylvania, came to Ohio, and first settled in Jefferson county in 1805, where he remained thirty years, when he came to Ashland county and settled near Savannah, in Ruggles township, on the farm now owned by Robert Pogue. In 1840 he moved to Illinois, where he remained until his death, which occurred in 1845, when his wife also died. He was the father of ten children, only three living, viz.: Sparks, who married Rachel Finley; John, who lives in Illinois, and Fannie, wife of Robert Cochrane.

SPARKS BURD, SR., born in Washington county, Pennsylvania, in 1796, came to Ohio with his father in 1805, and settled in Jefferson county, Ohio, where he remained nine years. He then went to Wayne county, Ohio, where he stayed four years, and then returned to Ashland county, and settled on the farm on which he now lives in 1818, and in 1820 cleared ten acres of land and sowed seven acres of wheat, and built a cabin. He then went back to Jefferson county, where he remained until the following spring, when he returned in company with his brother William, and they cleared off the farm on which he now lives, and can truly be called the pioneer of Ashland county. On March 28, 1833, he married Eliza Long, of Lake township, who had two children, and died June 23, 1835. In 1840 he married Charlotte Austin, who died in 1861, and in 1864 he married Rachel Finley. The two children were Sparks, who married Mary Finley, and Sarah A., who became the wife of Ithamer Covert.

SPARKS BURD, JR., was born in Ashland county, June 25, 1835, and received a common school education. He is a farmer and school-teacher, and has taught school twenty-five terms. In 1862 he enlisted in the Fourth Ohio volunteer infantry, under Captain D. R. Timmons, and served three years, when he was promoted to sergeant major of the battalion. He served under Burnside, Hooker and Meade, and took part in nearly all the battles of the army of the Potomac from Chancellorsville to Apamattox Court House, and was wounded at Spotsylvania. He was mustered out in 1865, and in 1870 moved to Kansas, where he remained until 1874. While there he was elected representative of Bourbon county, and served one term in the legislature. In April, 1874, he returned to Ashland county, Ohio, and in 1877 was elected justice of the peace of Lake township, and in 1880 was re-elected to the same office. On September 10, 1857, he married Mary Finley, who died April 13, 1870. On April 30, 1871, he married Mary Seiss. There are eight children, viz: Charlotte, Edwin S., John E., William, Sarah E., Norah, Frederick and Burton.

ITHAMER COVERT, was born in Lake township, Ashland county, Ohio, in 1832, and received a common school education. In 1855 he married Sarah Burd. He is engaged in farming, is a deacon in the Reformed church and contributes largely to its support. In politics he is a Republican. He is the father of eight children, viz: Cyrus B., Ithamer E., Emma E., Enoch I., Harvey S., John C., Eliza A., and Dayton.

JACOB DILLIER, was born in Germany in 1783, came to Ohio at an early day and married Elizabeth Staver, in Lebanon county, Pennsylvania. He came to Ohio in 1830, and first settled in Sugar Creek township, Wayne county, Ohio, and remained there nine years. In 1839 he settled in Lake township, Ashland county, Ohio, on the farm now owned by Henry Dillier and brothers. He was a carpenter, but after he came to Ashland county gave up his trade and became engaged in farming. He was a member of the Lutheran church during the early part of his life, but in later years joined the Reformed church, and died in that faith January 3, 1867. His wife died December 8, 1846. He was the father of seven children, viz: Joseph and David, both living in Ashland county; Hannah, who is living in Summit county, Ohio; Rebecca, deceased, who was the wife of George Creisbaum; Henry, who married Sarah Mowery, and afterward married Lucinda Covert; Mary, deceased, who was the wife of James Winebigler; Lydia, wife of George Bender, of Illinois.

HENRY DILLIER, son of Jacob Dillier, was born in Lebanon county, Pennsylvania, in 1820, and came to Ohio with his father in 1830; he is a farmer. He has held the office of trustee for several terms, and is deeply interested in schools and all things that pertain to the education of the young. He is a member of the Reformed church, and has held the office of elder since 1865. On October 21, 1841, he married Sarah Maurer, of Lake township, who died March 1, 1863. On October 10, 1867, he married Lucinda Covert; he is the father of six children, only three of whom are living, viz: Eliza, wife of Alfred W. Hall, of Indiana; Hannah, wife of Wesley Cusmore; and Rebecca, wife of Benjamin Jones, of Ashland county. Mr. Dillier has taken his grandson, Adam A. Long, son of his daughter Mary, deceased, to bring up.

PETER HUFF, born in Berkeley county, Virginia, in 1798, came to Ohio in 1825, and settled on the farm on which he now lives. It was then in the midst of a forest. He cleared off a small piece of ground and erected a log cabin, and by industry has cleared his farm and accumulated a nice fortune. He has held the office of supervisor for a number of years, and is overseer of the poor. He is a member of the Baptist church. In politics he was a Jacksonian Democrat, but since the organization of the Republican party has voted the Republican ticket. In 1825, in Beaver county, Pennsylvania, he married Rosanna Lower, and is the father of five children: Elizabeth, who married Samuel Shoup, and afterward married Anthony Stentz; Samuel, who married Annie Marks; William, who married May Horn; Sarah, who married Jacob Harker; and Martha A., who married George Riland.

WILLIAM LONG was born in Ashland county, December 11, 1846, and received a common school education. He learned the baker's trade, and in company with his brother, Samuel Long, opened a confectionery store and bakery in Napoleon, Henry county, Ohio, and stayed there five years, when he gave up the business, and has since been engaged in farming. In 1868 he married Annie Andrews, of Green township, Ashland county.

She died in December, 1876, and in December, 1878, he married Magdalena Weimer, of Holmes county. He was a member of the Lutheran church, but is now a member of the Evangelical Association. He is the father of four children: Peter, deceased; Maggie, Bertie A., and Harry.

ADAM LONG was born in Ashland county in 1838. He received a common school education, and in 1868 married Mary L. Dillier, who died in 1870. In 1871 he married Matilda D. Esselburn. He has held the office of township trustee two years; has been assessor two years, and still holds that office, and has also been justice of the peace for six years. He is a member of the Lutheran church, much respected and highly esteemed in the community in which he lives. He has four children: Adam A., Lewis A., William H., and Alice M.

GEORGE BRUBAKER, born in Dauphin county, Pennsylvania, in 1798, and came to Ohio in 1825, and settled in Lake township, Ashland county, on the farm now owned by John Garst. In 1819 he married Elizabeth Burkhart, of Bedford county, Pennsylvania. He was a mason, but after he came to Ohio gave up his trade and engaged in farming. He was a member of the Methodist Episcopal church, and in politics a Democrat. He died in 1862. He was the father of eleven children, six of whom are living, viz.: Joseph B.; Margaret B., wife of Abram R. Owen; George W.; Elias P., who married Diantha Rodgers, and lives in California; Mary E., wife of D. C. Kean, and Harrison A., who married Elizabeth Gilbert, and lives in Michigan.

GEORGE W. BRUBAKER, son of George Brubaker, was born in Bedford county, Pennsylvania, January 12, 1828, and came to Ohio with his father in 1834. He went to school in Lake township and attended the Vermillion institute in Hayesville two years and a half; has taught school twenty-two winters and one summer, and is one of the veteran teachers of the county. In 1856 he purchased the farm on which he now lives, and commenced with a very small amount of capital, but has by hard labor and economy accumulated a nice property. He has cut in one day with a cradle ten acres of wheat, and has several times cut eight acres, and frequently cut five acres of oats in a half day. He has held the office of justice of the peace in Lake township nine years, and has been clerk and trustee for several years. He is engaged in farming, and is a member of the Methodist Episcopal church. In 1852 he married Susanna Smith, of Green township, Ashland county, Ohio. She was born in Maryland. They are the parents of nine children, viz.: Emma E., wife of Abel Gowdy; Simpson, who died when three years old; Sophrona, wife of Harpster Cooper; Mary L., wife of Emer S. McKinley; Rosella R.; Dyantha J.; Edson O.; Anna B., and George W.

AUGUSTUS C. KEAN, born in Wayne county, Ohio, in 1838, received a common school education, and in 1869 settled in Ashland county on the farm on which he now lives. He is a member of the Methodist Episcopal church, and in politics is a Republican. In 1861 he married Nancy Brubaker, who died in 1877. They had five children: Alice E., Mary G., Gary W., and two who died in infancy.

HENRY MAURER was born in Pennsylvania, near Hollidaysburgh, in 1792. In 1833 he came to Ashland county, and settled on the farm now owned by George Brubaker, in Lake township; and was engaged in farming all his life. For several years he was justice of the peace, and also held the offices of trustee, clerk, and treasurer, and was highly respected in the community in which he lived. He first married Hannah Cautner, who died in 1856. In 1862, he married Mary A. Smith. In 1864 he died, the father of nine children, only two of whom are living, viz: Rebecca, wife of Daniel Metcalf; and Samuel, who married Mary J. Stow.

PETER SANDERS, SR., born in Lebanon county, Pennsylvania, in 1792, came to Ohio in 1829, and first settled in Stark county, where he remained six years. In 1835, he came to Ashland county and settled in Lake township, on the farm now owned by Peter Sanders, jr. By trade he was a weaver, and worked at that business as long as he lived; he was a member of the German Baptist church. In Lancaster county, Pennsylvania, he married Hannah Botenstat. She died in 1867; and he died in 1876, the father of ten children: Peter; Jacob, who married Mary Karns, and lives in Indiana; Fannie, wife of Fleetus Dow; Samuel, who married Sarah Wright; Hannah, wife of George Wolf; George, Henry and Susan, who died when young; Mary and John.

PETER SANDERS, JR., was born in Lancaster county, Pennsylvania, in 1820, and came to Ohio with his father. Mr. Sanders never married, but he lives on the old homestead. Though not a member of any church, he contributes liberally to all the churches in the vicinity, and takes a deep interest in all educational matters. For three years he has held the office of school director, and is an influential and respected member of society. In politics, he is a Republican.

JOHN ARTZ, born in Ellsos, France, in 1830, came to America in 1852 and settled in Upper Canada, where he remained two years. Then he came to Ohio and settled in Holmes county, where he remained three months, when he went to California and was there six years engaged in gold mining. In 1861 he returned to Ohio and settled in Knox county, where he remained seven years. At the end of that time he came to Ashland county, and bought the farm on which he now lives. The offices of supervisor and school director he has filled; is a member of the Lutheran church, in which he has been elder for two years. In 1863, he married Elizabeth Motz, of Knox county, who had one child, and died in 1864. In 1865, he married Louisa Schauncker, of Ashland county, who has had six children. Their names are as follows; John A., who died in infancy; Gustave A., John W., Annie M., Louis P., Frederick C. and George E.

JOHN WARENS was born in Pennsylvania, in 1800, came to Ohio at an early day, and settled on the farm now owned by the Warens heirs. When he first settled there it was like a wilderness. He cleared his own farm and built his own cabin, and was truly one of the pioneers of Ashland county. In 1830 he married Mary Ekes in Ashland county. He died in 1867, and his wife still survives him. He was the father of seven children, viz: William, who married Catharine Horn; John C., who married Magdalena Estwiler; Elizabeth, Mary E., Susan R., Martin, deceased, and one child who died in infancy.

JOHN C. WARENS was born in Ashland county, in 1837, and received a common school education. In 1866 he married Magdalena Estwiler. He is a farmer, and deeply interested in educational matters, and is now director of the school in his district. He is not a member of any church, but contributes largely to the support of the Reformed church. In politics he is a Democrat. He is the father of three children: Irvin A., Eliza E., and Mary E.

WILLIAM WARENS was born in Ashland county, on the farm on which he now lives, in 1835. He is a carpenter by trade, but is now engaged in farming. He has held the office of supervisor one year. In 1869 he married Caroline Horn, and is the father of five children, viz: Harvey I., Jacob N., Wallace A., William E., and one child who died in infancy.

GEORGE BENDER was born near Reading, Pennsylvania, in 1775. He came to Ohio in 1828, and first settled on the farm now owned by Martin Bender. He was a carpenter, but gave up his trade, and during the latter part of his life was engaged in farming. He was a member of the Reformed church, and in politics was a Democrat. He married Catharine Warens, of Pennsylvania, who died in 1847. He died in 1857. He was the father of seven children, of whom four are living, viz: John, who married Margaret Hauntz; Martin, who married Barbara Hauntz; Catharine, and George, who married Lydia Dillier, and lives in Illinois.

MARTIN BENDER was born near Carlisle, Cumberland county, Pennsylvania, in 1811, and came to Ohio with his father, and settled on the farm on which he now lives. He is a farmer—a member of the Reformed church, in which he has been an elder seven years. He married Barbara Hauntz, and is the father of twelve children: Matthias, who married Horretta Everhart; Eliza, who married Philip Snyder; Catharine, Sabina, who married Michael Snyder; Barbara A., Clementine, Caroline, Mary, deceased, and four others who died in infancy.

JOHN BENDER was born in Pennsylvania, in 1806. He came to Ohio with his father, and in 1839 married Margaret Hauntz, of Ashland county. In 1840 he settled on the farm on which he now lives. He has held the office of supervisor several years, and is a respected member of society. He is a member of the Reformed church, and has held the office of deacon and elder ever since St. Jacob's church was built. He is the father of eight children, of whom only five are living, viz: Martin, who married Lydia Durk, and lives in Kansas; Elizabeth, wife of Alonzo Workman, of Holmes county, Ohio; David, John, and Francena.

JOHN EMERICK, born in Berks county, Pennsylvania, in 1781 came to Ohio in 1821, and settled on the farm now owned by Lewis Chesroun. He was a wagon-maker and blacksmith by trade, and followed that business about twelve years in Ohio, when he gave it up and was engaged in farming until the time of his death, which occurred in 1874. He married Mary Troutman, of Somerset county, Pennsylvania. For several years he held the office of trustee in Lake township, and although not a member of any church, contributed largely to the building and support of all the churches in his vicinity. He was the father of nine children, six of whom are living, viz.: Drusilla, wife of William North; Mary, wife of George Cornell; Christina, wife of Simon Topper; George, who married Sarah Guthrie; Rebecca, wife of Michael Otto; and Alexander, who married Mary A. Yocum.

ALEXANDER EMERICK was born in Ashland county in 1825, where he received a common school education, and studied medicine with Dr. Blatchly, of Blatchlyville, Wayne county, Ohio, three years. Then he went to Cleveland, and finished his course at the Western Reserve college, where he remained one year. In 1848 he went to Waterloo, Michigan, where he practiced medicine four years. At the end of that time he settled in Lake township, Ashland county, Ohio, where he has practiced medicine ever since. For four years he has been coroner of Ashland county. He married Mary A. Yocum, a native of Cumberland county, in 1849, and is the father of ten children, of whom six are living: Lewis N., who married Hannah Abert, and afterwards married Martha Harpman, and lives in DeKalb county, Indiana; Washington E., who married Alice Spade; Charles Xenophon; Clement L. V.; and Ella.

JOHN G. LONG, born in Ellsos, France, in 1798, came to America in 1828, and first settled in Stark county, Ohio, where he remained ten years. Then he came to Ashland county, and settled in Lake township, on the farm now owned by Peter B. Long. All his life he was engaged in farming. He was a member of the old Lutheran church, in which he was elder twenty years. He married Catharine Barnhart in Ellsos, France. She died in 1875. In 1868 he died. He was the father of five children: George, who married Margaret Murklinger; Peter, who married Saloma Kantzer; John; Adam, who married Barbara Wyemer; and one child who died in infancy.

GEORGE LONG was born in Ellsos, France, in 1822, and came to America with his father. He is engaged in farming, and has held the office of supervisor and school director for several years. He is a member of the old Lutheran church, in which he has been deacon for thirty years. In politics he is a Democrat. In 1843 he married Margaret Murklinger, and is the father of six children, viz: Philip, who married Paulina Murklinger; George A., who married Christina Priest; John D.; David, who married Caroline Hipp; Simon P., and Catharine, who became the wife of John Peter.

EZEKIEL MOORES, born in Jefferson county, Ohio, in 1805, came to Ashland county in 1850, and bought the farm on which he now lives, from the Webster heirs. He has held the office of supervisor and school director in the township from time to time, and although seventy-five years of age, is still able to superintend his farm. In politics he is a Republican, and is a highly respected citizen. August 6, 1829, he married Mary James, of Jefferson county, Ohio, who had ten children, and died October 4, 1864. In 1865 he married Ann E. Cordell. The names of his children are: Sarah, who married Andrew Lybarger; Elizabeth, who married James H. Dunfee, deceased; Margaret, who married George M. ———————, of Illinois; Mary Ann, and James, who are deceased; Effie, who married Webster Orum, of Illinois, now deceased; William, who was killed at Gettysburgh; Ezekiel, who married Lydia Smith; Alfred, who married Minnie Smith, and John, who married Mary Lorentz.

EZEKIEL MOORES, JR., was born in Monroe county, Ohio, in 1842, and came to Ashland county with his father, in 1850, where he received a common school education. In 1861 he enlisted in the Sixty-fifth Ohio volunteer infantry, under Captain Orlow Smith, as a private, but was appointed corporal, and afterwards was promoted to first sergeant in the same year, and, for meritorious conduct at the battle of Stone River, was promoted to the rank of first lieutenant January 1, 1863. On July 10, 1864, he was promoted to the rank of captain, which place he held until his discharge, which occurred on the El Paso plains, in Texas, in 1866. He was engaged in the battles of Pittsburgh Landing; Iuka, Mississippi; Perrysville, Kentucky; Stone River, Chickamauga, Missionary Ridge, Rocky Face Ridge, Resaca, Dallas, Muddy Creek, Kenesaw Mountain, Peach Tree Creek, Atlanta, Jonesborough, Lovejoy Station, Spring Hill, Franklin, and Nashville. In 1866 he married Lydia Smith, of McKay, and in 1867 moved to Jefferson county, Illinois, where he remained ten years. While there he was county commissioner for three years, deputy clerk of the supreme court of the southern district of Illinois eighteen months, and also held several minor offices. In 1877 he returned to his old home in Lake township, Ashland county, Ohio, where he still remains, and is engaged in farming. In 1880 he was elected township trustee, and appointed census enumerator. In politics he is a Republican. He is the father of three children: Adella, Nettie, and Charles.

JOHN FINLEY was born in Knox county, Ohio, in 1806, came to Ashland county with his father in 1809, and settled on the farm now owned by Seibert & Austin, in Mohican township. In 1827 he married Sarah Baird, of Plain township, Wayne county, Ohio. He was engaged in farming all his life. In politics he was an old-line Whig until the Republican party was organized, when he became a Republican, and voted with the party until his death, which occurred in 1865. His wife still survives him, and resides with her son, Luther C., in Lake township. John Finley was the father of seven children, viz.: Abner, who married Elizabeth Smith; Elizabeth, who married Isaac Rainey; Lusette, wife of Wesley Chesroun; Mary, deceased, who was the wife of Sparks Burd; Luther, who married Ann Plank, and afterwards married Anna M. Kithcart, and then Eliza J. Hootman; and Sarah, the wife of N. Richey.

ABNER FINLEY, son of John Finley, was born in Ashland county in 1830, on the farm now owned by his mother; he received a common school education, and has always been engaged in farming. In 1856, he married Elizabeth Smith, of Green township, Ashland county. One year he was township trustee; and in politics is a Republican. The names of his eight children are as follows: Thomas A., who married Effie L. Lybarger, of Wayne county; Frank S., James B., Clinton, Luella, John, Mark and Howard.

JACOB FULMER, born in Ellsos, France, in 1805, came to America in 1845, and the same year settled in Lake township, Ashland county. By trade he was a mason, but after he came to America he gave up his trade and engaged in farming. He was a member of the Evangelical Association; and died in 1862. In 1839, he was married to Mary Huffman in Ellsos, France, who still survives him. Of his family of eleven children, but eight are living: Margaret; John, who married Lou. Tipton; Catharine, wife of Abraham Metcalf; Julia, wife of Levi Shutt; Jacob, who married Jane Morrell; Frederick, who married Amanda Workman; Daniel, who married Mary Spreng; and Mary, wife of William Stewart.

JOHN WOLF was born in Ellsos, France, in 1789, and married Margaret Spak, in Ellsos. She was born in 1798. June 14, 1853, he came to America, and settled in Lake township, Ashland county, on the farm now owned by John Artz, where he engaged in farming all his life. In 1860 he died; he was a member of the old Lutheran church, and while in Ellsos was elder in the church sixteen years. A hard-working, honest, industrious man, he was much respected in the community in which he lived. In September, 1874, his wife died. Only three of his five children are living, viz: George, who married Hannah Sanders; Michael, who married Mary Spack; and Mary, wife of Jacob Breckhisen.

GEORGE WOLF, born in Ellsos, France, in 1824, came to America with his father in 1853, and purchased a farm in Ashland county, Ohio, in company with his father. In 1848 he married Mary Cross, who died August 1, 1869. She was the mother of seven children. In 1870 he married Hannah Sanders. After the death of his father he sold the old homestead and purchased the farm on which he now lives, and has accumulated a nice fortune. He has held the office of school director for six years, and has been supervisor several terms. He is a member of the old Lutheran church, in which he has been elder for twelve years, and is a highly respected member of society. In politics he is a Democrat. He had seven children: John, who married Matilda Kayler; Mary, deceased, who was the wife of John Keik; Margaret, wife of Jonathan Tobe; Catharine, George, Caroline and Jacob.

HENRY KAYLER, born in Ellsos, France, in 1790, came to America in 1829, and first settled in New York, where he remained seven years, when he moved to Holmes county, Ohio, where he bought a farm and remained until his death, which occurred in 1843. He was the father of eight children, all of whom are living.

JACOB KAYLER, son of Henry Kayler, was born in

Ellsos, France, in 1823, and came to America with his father, and first settled in Ashland county in 1846. He was a distiller by trade and was engaged in that business twenty years, but gave it up on account of the Rebellion, and has since been engaged in farming. In 1842 he married Charlotte Hans, a native of Baier, Germany. He has been township trustee two terms, supervisor four terms, and school director fourteen years; is a member of the old Lutheran church, in which he has been trustee for ten years. When he commenced life he had comparatively nothing, but by industry and economy, has accumulated a large fortune and is highly respected by all who know him. In politics he is a Democrat. He is the father of ten children, viz.: Jacob H., who died when twenty-three years old; George, who married Sallie Long; Matilda C., who is the wife of John Wolf; John, who married Sarah Rominger; Daniel, who died when six years old; Emeline, Adam, Solomon, (deceased), Charlotte M, Jonas P. (deceased).

MICHAEL WOLF, born in Ellsos, France, in 1837, came to America in 1852, and first settled in Hanover township, Ashland county, Ohio, on the farm now owned by Adam Young. In 1863 he sold it and purchased the farm on which he now lives, from David Workman. The farm contains two hundred and twelve acres; and he has built on it one of the largest brick houses in the county. When he first came to America he had to borrow ten dollars of his brother in Cleveland in order to reach Loudonville, and since that time (only about twenty-seven years), by industry and economy, has accumulated a nice fortune, and has secured for himself one of the best places in the county. He is a member of the old Lutheran church, in which he has been trustee for nine years, and to which he contributes largely. He married Mary Spack in Hanover township. She was a native of Ellsos, France. Mr. Wolf is the father of eight children, all living at home, viz.: John, George, Mary, Martin, Henry, Margaret, Michael and Charlie.

JOHN COBLE, born in Wayne county, Ohio, in 1825, came to Ashland county with his father when four years old. He learned the blacksmith trade with John Moulter, in McZena, and worked at his trade seven years. In 1850 he went overland to California, where he remained about a year, engaged in gold mining. He met with success, and during the year cleared about fifteen hundred dollars. Then he returned to Wayne county, Ohio, where he bought fifty acres of land. He remained there three years, and was engaged in blacksmithing. In 1854 he came to Ashland county, and purchased eighty acres of land—the same now owned by John and George Smith—and remained there about two years and a half, and then went to McZena, where he remained three years and worked at his trade. Then he returned to Wayne county and purchased one hundred acres of land, and at the end of six years again returned to Ashland county and purchased one hundred and twenty-two acres of land—the same now owned by Jacob Kayler—and at the end of two years bought the farm on which he now lives, from Calvin Parker. For twelve years he has held the office of school director, has been township trustee two years, and supervisor several years. He is director of the Washington township, Holmes county, fire and lightning insurance company. In politics he is a Democrat. In 1851 he married Sophia Kantzer, who became the mother of seven children, and died in 1875. In 1876 he married Rebecca Horn, who is the mother of two children. The names of his children are: Samuel, deceased; infant, deceased; Margaret, Saloma, Sophia C., John G., Clementine, Elza A., and an infant, deceased.

ELIAS HORN was born in Germany, in 1840, and first settled in Pennsylvania in 1820. He came to Ohio, and settled in Lake township, Ashland county, on the farm now owned by Jacob Kayler, and was engaged in farming all his life. He was a member of the German Baptist church, and in politics was a Democrat. He married Mary Foreman, of Pennsylvania, and after her death married Eve Mercer, of Pennsylvania. He died in 1823. He was the father of eight children, of whom only three are living, viz: Frederick, Jacob, and Susanna.

JACOB HORN was born in Pennsylvania, in 1810, came to Ohio with his father and settled on the same farm, and has been engaged in farming all his life. He has been trustee of Lake township two years, and school director several years. He is a member of the German Reformed church, and a respected member of society. In 1837 he married Catharine Hans, and is the father of nine children, viz: Daniel, George, who married Sarah E. Harner; David, who married Mary Otto; Caroline who became the wife of William Worms; Mary, wife of William Huff; Rebecca, wife of John Coble; Barbara, wife of Solomon Easly; and Emeline.

PETER WICOFF was born in New Jersey, and came to Ohio in 1815; he first settled in Harrison county, where he remained five years, when he moved to Ashland county, and settled on the farm now owned by William Wicoff. For several years he was a school director; was a member of the Presbyterian church; and in politics was an old-line Whig. September 26, 1841, he died. He married Elizabeth Bruce, in Pennsylvania, who died in 1849. Four of his ten children are still living, viz: John, who lives in Indiana; William; Philura, who lives in Kansas; and Eleanor, who lives in Indiana.

WILLIAM WICOFF, born in Crawford county, Pennsylvania, in 1811, came to Ohio with his father and settled on the same farm. In 1831, he married Sabrina Oram. The office of justice of the peace of Lake township he has held for twelve years in succession, and was trustee for several years; he is a member of the Methodist Episcopal church; and in politics is a Republican. The names of his five children are: Nancy J., wife of Andrew Stewart; Jasper; Newton, who died when nine years old; Delphinia, wife of Silas Smith; and Emma S., wife of Uriah McFarlan.

ENOCH COVERT was born in Northumberland county, Pennsylvania, in 1781, and married Elizabeth Hannon, of the same place. In his young days, he was engaged in lumbering on the Susquehanna. In 1818, he came to Ohio, and first settled near Wooster, where he remained one year, and in 1819 came to Lake township,

Ashland county, and settled in what was then a wilderness, on the farm now owned by William Covert. At that time, there were only three families within a radius of four miles. While in Ohio he was engaged in farming. For several years he was an elder in the Presbyterian church, of which he was a member, and was an earnest Christian; he contributed largely to the support of the church, and was respected by all who knew him. In 1861 he died, aged eighty years; his wife died in 1879, aged eighty-four years. Ten of his eleven children are living: John E., who married Esther Hanbey; William, who married Hannah Ewalt, and afterward married Rebecca Smith; James M., who married Martha Martin; Esty T., who married Elizabeth Byers, of Indiana; Susan, who married Matthew Leach; Lucinda, who married Henry Dillier; Matilda; Ithamer, who married Sarah A. Burd; Sarah A.; and Nancy, who married David Leach.

JOHN E. COVERT was born in Pennsylvania in 1817, and came to Ohio with his father, and settled in Ashland county. In 1847 he went to the State of New York, where he followed the carpenter and joiner's trade nine years. He then returned to Ashland county and settled on the farm on which he now lives. He has held the office of school director and is deeply interested in all educational matters; is a member of the Reformed church, and in politics is a Republican. When he first began business he had only a small capital, but by industry and economy has accumulated quite a fortune and a very comfortable home. May 13, 1844, he married Esther Hanbey, of New York, and is the father of one child, James Enoch.

GEORGE EASLY, born in Baden, Germany, in 1810, came to America in 1829, and settled in Loudonville, Ashland county, Ohio, in 1832. He was a jeweler by trade, and the first jeweler in Loudonville. When he first began he carried clocks on his back and sold them through this and adjoining counties. He followed his trade until his death, in 1859, and accumulated a nice fortune. In early life he was a member of the Catholic church, but in after years became a member of the Lutheran church, and died in that faith. His wife still survives him. He was the father of ten children, six of whom are living, viz.: Henry, who married Arsulia R. Bender, of Loudonville; John J.; Julius S., who married Barbara Horn; Emeline E., wife of John J. Vance, of Holmes county, Ohio; George, and Adeline A.

JULIUS S. EASLY was born in Loudonville in 1845, and in 1876 married Barbara Horn. He has always been engaged in farming; has been township treasurer two years, supervisor one year, and school director one year. He is a member of the old Lutheran church. In politics he is a Democrat, and is a highly respected member of society. He is the father of four children: Augustus E. and Charles O., deceased, and Amanda E. and Andrew A.

JOSHUA EBERHART, born in Huntingdon county, Pennsylvania, April 16, 1816, came to Ohio in 1839, and first settled in Wayne county, where he remained until 1855, when he came to Ashland county, and settled on the farm now owned by Michael Shelby. He was a cooper by trade, but when he came to Ohio engaged in farming. In 1841 he married Isabel Myers, of Wayne county. He was a member of the Lutheran church, and in politics was a Republican. He died in 1868. His wife still survives him. He was the father of six children: Eliza; John, who married Rebecca Young; Abraham; Lewis, who married Alice Hazen, and lives in Missouri; Harriet, wife of Matthias Bender; Albert, who married Margaret Jobes.

JOHN EBERHART, born in Wayne county, in 1843, is at present engaged in the lumber business. In 1862 he enlisted in company C, One Hundred and Twentieth Ohio volunteer infantry, under Captain McKinley, and took part in the battles of Chickasaw Bluffs, Arkansas Post and Port Gibson. At the last battle he was wounded in the left lung, and was discharged at Trenton, New Jersey, in August, 1865, when he returned to Lake township, and in 1867 married Rebecca Young, and is the father of six children, viz: Harvey, Emmit, Gamelza, Charles, Montford, and Clyde.

JOHN C. YOUNG, born in Virginia, came to Ohio in 1817, and settled in Lake township, Ashland county, on the farm now owned by George Wolf. He was a cooper by trade, but while in Ohio was engaged in farming until his death, which occurred in 1851. During his residence in Lake township he was justice of the peace eleven years and township treasurer several years. He was a member of the Presbyterian church, and in politics was a Democrat. He married Rebecca Mathews, of Virginia, who died in 1845. He was the father of seven children, five of whom are still living, viz: Drusilla, wife of John Megary, of Richland county, Ohio; Eliza, wife of Reuben Hill; James, who married Eliza Stoner; Lucinda, wife of Elias Snowbarger; and John, who married Louisa Myer.

JAMES YOUNG was born in Virginia, in 1815, came to Ohio with his father, and in 1836 married Eliza Stoner. He is a member of the Reformed church, and in politics is a Democrat. His wife died in September, 1879. He is the father of nine children, only five of whom are living, viz.: Catharine, wife of Tobias Wessel; Mary E., wife of Henry Coble; Rebecca, wife of John Eberhart; and Sarah A., wife of Truman Cross.

JACOB EMRICK was born in Pennsylvania in 1806, came to Ohio in the year 1820, and settled on the farm now owned by Lewis Chesroun, in Lake township, where he was married to Sallie Green. He has been county commissioner of Ashland county for six years, and has also held the office of constable, trustee, and treasurer. He was a member of the Masonic order in Loudonville for several years, and was an honored and respected member of society. He died in 1864. His wife still survives him. He was the father of ten children, viz.: Noah, who lives in Arizona; Jacob, who married Elizabeth Chapman, and lives in Indiana; Sarah, wife of James Swain, of Ashland county; John, who married Catharine McFillen, and lives in Indiana; Elizabeth, wife of Jacob Sprang, of Kansas; Rebecca, wife of Philip Bucher, of Michigan; Mary, deceased, who was the wife of Peter Homer, of Holmes county,

Ohio; Jackson, who married Caroline Dirrim, and lives in Indiana; George, who married Caroline Crumlick; and Anna, wife of Jacob Garst.

GEORGE EMRICK was born in Lake township, Ashland county, Ohio, in 1843, and is engaged in farming. In 1864 he married Caroline Crumlick. He has been township trustee two years, and is now school director. In politics he is a Democrat. He is the father of seven children, viz.: Lillian, Philora, Thurman (deceased), Noah, John, Dora, and Cloid.

HANOVER TOWNSHIP.

JAMES LOUDON PRIEST was born in Massachusetts, in 1769, and married Paulina Channey; he moved from Oneida county, Massachussetts, to Onondaga county, New York, and then to Crawford county, Pennsylvania. He came with a large family down the Ohio river in a dug-out canoe, and settled in Holmes county, on the Lake fork, about two miles from Loudonville, on the farm now owned by Jacob Schauweker. May 10, 1810, with Stephen Butters as his partner, he laid out the town plot of Loudonville; wrote all the first titles of the town lots, and the village was named in honor of him. He was a farmer and dealt extensively in real estate; was a prominent Free Mason and a Royal Arch Mason; was a Whig, and during the war of 1812, he built a fort on his farm, and kept guard there two years. He was an active member of the Baptist church. He died in 1822, at the old homestead, and was buried with Masonic honors. He was the father of fourteen children, of whom only two are living, viz: John, who married Barbara Workman, and lives in Ashland county; and Alonzo, who became the husband of Rhoda Clark, and lives in Holmes county.

JOHN PRIEST, son of James Loudon Priest, was born in Crawford county, Pennsylvania, in 1807, and came to Ohio with his father in 1810, and settled in Holmes county. In 1835 he married Rebecca Workman, and in 1870 came to Ashland county. He is engaged in farming and stock dealing. In politics he is Republican. He is the father of eight children, viz: Melissa, who became wife of B. F. See, and lives in Wood county; Elizabeth C., Normanda, wife of L. S. Culver, of Loudonville; Columbus D., who married Elizabeth McCrary, and lives in Loudonville; Josephine, who became the wife of James A. Hackett, and lives in Massillon; Morgan A., Ida M., and Agnes L.

DAVID QUICK, grandfather of Jacob L. Quick, was born in Bedford county, Pennsylvania, and came to Holmes county, Ohio, in 1814, and settled on the farm now owned by Jacob L. Quick. He was the father of ten children, of whom only one survives, Mrs. Mirah Ligett, who lives near Nashville, Tennessee. Isaac Quick, father of Jacob L. Quick, was born in Bedford county, Pennsylvania, and came to Holmes county, Ohio, in 1814. In 1834 he married Elizabeth Lybarger, of Lake fork, Ashland county, Ohio. He was one of the prominent men of Holmes county, having held the office of justice of the peace and trustee for a number of years, and being also connected with the public schools. He was a member of the Methodist Episcopal church, and an honored and respected member of society. In 1860 he died in Holmes county. He was the father of nine children, only four of whom are living, viz.: Jacob L., who married Ella Barker, and lives in Ashland county; David, who married Jane Layman, and lives in Ashland county; John, who married Emma Ross, and lives in Indiana, and Cyrus, who married Barbara Workman.

JACOB L. QUICK was born in Holmes county, Ohio, in 1837, on the farm he now owns; came to Ashland county in 1866, and settled in Loudonville. In 1868 he married Louisa Sprague, who died in 1871. In 1874 he married Ella Barker. From 1866 to 1868 he was superintendent of the public schools in Loudonville, when he severed his connection with the schools and went into the Loudonville bank as cashier, and has remained there up to the present time. He is a member of the Methodist Episcopal church, and has served as Sunday-school superintendent for the past eight years; he is a Republican in politics. The Quick family, as far as they can be traced, were Jacksonian Democrats.

N. H. BARKER was born in Caledonia county, Vermont, in 1814; came to Ohio in 1836, and in the same year married Roxanna Price. He is a Methodist minister, and in 1840 became a member of the North Ohio conference; was first stationed at Mansfield, and was agent of the Mansfield Female college one year, and was afterward stationed at the following places: Roscoe, East Union, Chesterville, Kenton, New London, Mt. Vernon, Shelby, Clyde, Fredricktown, Orange, Congress, Wadsworth, Ontario, West Salem, and Loudonville. His health failing, he was obliged to abandon the ministry, and for the past five years has been engaged in the boot and shoe business in Loudonville. He is a Republican in politics, and the father of four children, only one of whom is living, Ella M., now the wife of Jacob L. Quick, of Loudonville.

E. B. FULLER, father of Dr. Amos B. Fuller, was born in New York, in 1799, and married Sarah Culver, in Tioga county, Pennsylvania. In 1831 he first settled in Loudonville, and began the practice of medicine; was a doctor of the old school; was a member of the Methodist Episcopal church. In politics he was a Democrat—one of the liberal kind, bitterly opposed to the fugitive slave law. In 1856 two fugitives came to his house early in the morning. He fed them and sent them to Robert Wilson, where they were cared for and taken beyond the reach of United States marshals, blood-hounds, etc. He was the father of ten children, only four of whom are living: Catharine, who became the wife of Gilbert Pell, afterward married Calvin Hibbard, and lives in Ashland county; Susan, who married J. W. Hildebrand, and lives in Columbus; Content, who married J.

W. Stacker, of Ashland county; Amos B., who became the husband of Mary E. Stewart, and lives in Loudonville.

Dr. Amos B. Fuller was born in Ashland county, in 1842; studied medicine with his father, and began to practice in 1862. In 1867 he graduated from Jefferson Medical college in Philadelphia, and in 187– took the degree at Bellevue Medical college, New York. In 1868 he married Mary E. Stewart. He has built up a large practice, and is respected by all who know him; is a member of the Methodist Episcopal church, and the father of four children, viz.: Mary M., Grace, Gertrude B., and Stewart E.

John Schauweker came from Strasburgh on the Rhine, and settled in Loudonville in 1855. He was a tanner by trade, and carried on that business in Loudonville for six years, under the firm name of John Schauweker & Son. In 1861 he bought the farm now owned by Jackson Strausbaugh, moved on it, and lived there until his death, which occurred in 1871. He was a Democrat in politics, and a member of the German Lutheran church. He was the father of seven children, viz.: Godfrey, who married Sarah Ullman, and lives in Loudonville; Caroline, who became the wife of Michael Ullman, and lives in Holmes county; Louisa, who became the wife of John Arts, and lives in Ashland county; William, who married Louisa Wise, and lives in Marseilles, France; Gustavus, who married Mary Long, and lives in Columbus; Frederika, who married Gotlieb Myer, and lives in Danville, Illinois; Julia, who became the wife of John Faulkhaber, and lives in Fort Wayne, Indiana.

Godfrey Schauweker was born at Strasburgh on the Rhine, in 1830, and came to America with his father in 1852. In 1855 he married Sarah Ullman and settled in Loudonville, where he has held the offices of town clerk and councilman for several years. In January, 1876, he commenced the business of banking, and is still engaged in it, besides having a tannery in Loudonville and holding a share in a tannery in Columbus, Ohio, doing business under the firm name of Schauweker & Brothers. The Schauweker family, as far back as they can be traced, were tanners. Godfrey is a member of the German Lutheran church, a Democrat in politics, and the father of seven children: William F., Julia, Mary, Edward, Frank, Herman and Frederick.

Abiather Stockman, came from Essex county, New Jersey, and first settled in Delaware county, Ohio, and lived there seven years. He came to Ashland county in 1814, and settled in Loudonville, trading with Hatch and Eddy for the American house which he kept twelve years, when his son John took possession of it. Mr. Stockman was a member of the Dunkard church, a Democrat, and the father of nine children, five of whom are living, viz: John, who married Mary A. Campbell, and resides in Loudonville; Hiram, who married Mazey Barrow, and lives in Ashland county; Marritt, who lives in California; Harvey, who married Minnie Leopold, and lives in Ashland county; Francis A., who became the wife of Jerry Moster, and lives in California.

John Stockman, was born in New York city, and settled in Ashland county, in 1841. In 1855 he married Mary A. Campbell, and followed the hotel business; has held the office of councilman two terms in succession. His wife died in November, 1878, leaving one child, Allen L. Stockman.

Dr. Joseph Deyarmon, father of Christian Deyarmon, was born in Pennsylvania. At an early day, he came to Ohio, and settled in Wayne county, about five miles from Wooster; he was a doctor of the old school, and practiced medicine as long as his health would permit. He was a member and class-leader in the Methodist Episcopal church; and a Republican. In 1851 he died. But three of his eight children are living, viz: Sarah, who became the wife of Dr. Peters, and afterward the wife of Rev. J. P. Davis, and is now living in Illinois; Christian, who married Caroline E. Harris, and lives in Loudonville; and Joseph, who lives in Holmes county, Ohio.

Christian Deyarmon was born in Halifax, Pennsylvania, in 1820, and came to Wayne county, Ohio, with his father, in 1827. In 1842 he settled in Loudonville, and in 1844 married Caroline E. Harris. By trade he was a cabinet-maker, and followed the business for eight years, when he was obliged to give it up on account of ill health. Then he began farming, and in 1857 went into partnership with Nathaniel Haskell in the grain business, and followed that five years. In politics he is Republican; has held the office of mayor for two years, and councilman three terms. He is a member of the Methodist Episcopal church; and has raised six children: Mary A., now deceased, who married Philip Kelser, and settled in Summit county, Ohio; John D., who lives in Holmes county, Ohio; Joseph A., who lives in Ashland county; Zoe C., who became the wife of Augustine Leopold, and lives in Loudonville; Jessie E. and Kate E., who live in Ashland county.

Asa Harris, father of Mrs. Christian Deyarmon, came from Troy, Vermont, and settled in Loudonville in 1838. By trade he was a carpenter and joiner, and followed that business all his life. He was a member of the Congregational church, and an old-line Whig. He married Mary Houghton, of Brattleboro, Vermont, and five children were born to them: Solomon H., who married Tabitha Knights, and lives in Massachussets; Orison W., who married Jacintha Darling, and lives in New Hampshire; William H., who married Sarah Hickox, and lives in Huron county, Ohio; Mary A., who became the wife of John Legget, and lives in Fulton county, Ohio; Caroline E., who became the wife of Christian Deyarmon, and lives in Loudonville.

Thomas Gaines, father of John Gaines, was born in eatern Virginia, in 1811, and came to Ohio in 1833. He settled in Knox county, near Danville, and married Susannah Buckholder, of Virginia. In politics he is a Democrat; and has been a member of the Christian church for the last forty years. He is the father of eight children, viz.: Jacob B., who married Leah Elgenfritz, and lives in Knox county; John C., who married Elizabeth Robinson, and lives in Loudonville; Sarah H., wife of H. Workman, who lives in Knox county; Josie H., wife of H. H. Greer, who lives in Knox county; Mary E., wife of Dr. A. J. Hyatt; Robert S., who married Bell Baker; Louisa, who married Harmon White; Thomas, who married Ellen Bradfield, all living in Knox county, Ohio.

JOHN C. GAINES, son of Thomas Gaines, was born in Knox county, Ohio, in 1835, and married Elizabeth Robinson in 1857. They settled in Ashland county in 1869. In June, 1876, he was admitted to the bar in Ashland, and began the practice of law in Loudonville the same year. He was elected to the office of justice of the peace in 1874, and again elected in 1877. He is the only Republican who ever held that office in Loudonville. He is the father of four children, viz.: Irena, Loren A., Walter S., and Clara L., deceased.

WILLIAM REED, SR., was born in Washington county, Pennsylvania, came to Ashland county in 1829, and settled on the farm now owned by Frederick Frank. For sixteen years he held the office of justice of the peace in Loudonville, and was a Jacksonian Democrat. At the organization of the Republican party he became a Republican and remained one until his death. He was a consistent member of the Presbyterian church in Perrysville. He married Rosanna Lyle, of Washington county, Pennsylvania, and six children were born to them, viz.: James O., who married Nellie Allison, and lives in Louisiana; Sarah J., who lives in Loudonville; Joseph R., who married Jeanette Dinsmore; Elizabeth, wife of D. A. Newell, who lives in Mercer county, Pennsylvania; William R., who married Rebecca Robinson, and Rose, all living in Ashland county.

WILLIAM R. REED, JR., was born in Ashland county, in 1846, and in 1870 married Rebecca Robinson. In 1874 he began business in Loudonville as a hardware merchant in company with Joseph H. Hartupee. He is a Republican and the father of five children: Ralph, Edgar, Marion, Annie, and an infant daughter.

JEREMIAH SANBORN was born in Chichester, New Hampshire, in 1795; and came to Ohio, in July, 1837, and settled in Loudonville. By trade he was a carpenter and joiner. He was a member of the Swedenborgian church, and in politics was an old line Whig. He married Clarissa Smith, and died on September 14, 1846. His wife survived him and died in 1866. To them four children were born, viz.: Gilman S., and Jeremiah L., who are living in Colorado; Joseph H., who married Clara Smith, and lives in Loudonville, and Charles H., living in Nevada.

JOSEPH SANBORN was born in New Hampshire and came to Ohio with his father in 1837. In 1864 he married Clara Smith, and for some time made clerking his business. He was in the employ of N. Haskell, afterwards with Taylor & Larwille, of Loudonville. He has been ticket agent in Loudonville for the Pittsburgh, Ft. Wayne & Chicago railroad for the last twenty-two years, and has held the office of town clerk for two terms. He is a consistent member of the Presbyterian church, an exemplary man, honored and respected by all. In politics he is a Republican. He has had four children: Haven L., Mary A., Clarissa L. (deceased), and Gilman S.

PHILIP J. BLACK was born in Allegheny county, Pennsylvania, and came to Ohio in 1832, and settled on the farm now owned by his father; was apprenticed to a baker in Tiffin, and at the close of his apprenticeship, in the spring of 1851, opened the first bakery in Loudonville, in the building now owned by Michael Derrenberger, jr. Eight years he followed the business, and at the end of that time sold out to S. W. and J. Black, and commenced the manufacture of dulcimers—the only establishment of the kind in Ohio. On the breaking out of the Rebellion, he closed out his business and opened a grocery at Shreve, where he remained two years. Then he opened a grocery and bakery in company with J. F. Redd, and, at the close of three years, sold out to Mr. Redd and went into the produce business, which he is still engaged in. The first year's business amounted to nine thousand dollars, and in eight years had increased to eighty-five thousand dollars. He is a member of the Methodist Episcopal church, and a Republican in politics; has held the office of coucilman and mayor. In 1852, he married Margaret Reinhardt, and to them three children have been born: Josephine, Mary A., and Minnie A.

DANIEL SIGLER was born in Mifflin county, Pennsylvania; came to Ohio in 1833 and settled on the farm now owned by Jacob Speidel, in Green township, Ashland county. By occupation he is a farmer; in politics, a Republican; and is a member of the Presbyterian church. Mr. Sigler married Elizabeth Mathews, who died January 2, 1856; he died September 30, 1865. Four of his seven children are living, viz: Clarissa, who became the wife of William Hannawalt, and lives in Wisconsin; Edward, who married Sarah Campbell, and lives in Loudonville; Isaiah, who married Elleithier Campbell, and lives in Ashland; Sarah A., wife of John Much, living in Williams county, Ohio.

EDWARD SIGLER was born in Pennsylvania in 1823; came to Ohio with his father and settled on the farm with him. By occupation he is a farmer. In 1848 he married Sarah Campbell, and is the father of four children: Margaret, wife of Randolph Barron, who lives in Ashland county; Clementine and Ida, deceased; and Sherman, born June 13, 1864.

JAMES REDD, father of J. F. Redd, was born in Pennsylvania, came to Ohio at an early day, and married Lydia Nettles, of Wayne county. By trade he was a carpenter, and in politics was an old-line Whig. He died in 1840, leaving but one child, a son, John F. Redd, who was born in Wayne county, in 1836, came to Ashland county in 1840, and lived there with George Ream for three years; then went to Holmes county and stayed three years, when he returned to Ashland county and stayed until he was eighteen years old. He then settled in Loudonville, and learned harness-making of J. T. Henderson; worked at the trade thirteen years, and, at the end of that time, went into business for himself, and worked three years more. In 1867 he bought the grocery store of P. J. Black, and has continued in that business up to the present time. He is a member of the Methodist Episcopal church. In 1858 he married

Louisa Reinhardt. Two children were born to them—Charles M. and Cora B.

JACOB REINHARDT was born in Ellsos, France, in 1799, came to America in 1833, and first settled in Green township, on the farm now owned by Calvin Pell. By trade he was a carpenter, but, after coming to Ohio, was engaged in farming; was a member of the German Lutheran church. In 1822 he married Catharine Millhime, who died December 5, 1877. Mr. Reinhardt was the father of six children, viz.: John J., who married Alethea Wolf, and lives in Mt. Gilead, Morrow county, Ohio; Catharine, who became the wife of George Feit, and lives in Wayne county, Ohio; Margaret, wife of Philip Black, who lives in Loudonville; George, who married Sarah Hunter, and lives in Green township; Mary, wife of Peter Wygait, of Loudonville; Louisa, wife of J. F. Redd, of Loudonville.

CLAUDE PETOT was born in Venare, France, in 1827, came to America in 1854, and first settled in Pittsburgh, Pennsylvania, where he remained three years. In 1857 he removed to Loudonville, Ohio, where he has since been engaged in the boot and shoe business, having learned the shoemaker's trade in France. Twenty years ago he commenced to deal in ready-made boots and shoes. In 1852, in the city of Paris, he married Catharine Speack. He is a member of the English Lutheran church; in politics is a Democrat; holds the office of councilman, has been township trustee for two terms, and is also a member of the school board. He is the father of six children, viz.: Alfred, who married Mary Selix, and lives in Loudonville; Josephine, wife of Henry Stentz, of Loudonville; Mary L., Frank M., Lizzie, and Charles E.

N. H. BAILEY was born in Orange county, New Jersey, in 1823, and married Henrietta Meade in 1846. They came to Ohio in 1863, and in 1865 settled in Ashland county. At one time he lived in Crestline, Ohio, and while there had charge of the office of the Pittsburgh, Fort Wayne & Chicago railroad. In politics he is a Republican. He is an elder in the Presbyterian church, and the father of two children, both deceased, viz: Georgiana and Ida V.

WILLIAM McCRARY was born in Ireland, and came to America in 1815. He settled in Ashland county in 1847. He was a farmer and stock raiser, and was a member of the Disciple church. In politics he was a Democrat. He was the father of eight children, all living except one: William, who married Margaret Gibbs, and lives in Ashland county; Thomas Y., who married Mary E. Barnhill, and lives in Ashland county; Grace A., wife of Martin T. Fast; and John T., who married Minerva Craft—both are living in Ashland county; Henry L., who married Enrietta V. Shaw, and lives in Loudonville; Lewis J., who married Almyra Fast, and lives in Ruggles; Joseph A., who married Miss Gates, and lives in New York city.

HENRY L. McCRARY, son of William McCrary, was born in Washington county, Pennsylvania, in 1845, and came to Ohio with his father. He studied law with T. Y. McCrary, of Wooster, Ohio, and was admitted to the bar July 6, 1866, and began the practice of law the same year, in Wooster, with his brother. He remained there four years, going from there to Ashland, where he stayed two years. At the end of that time he settled in Loudonville, and was elected town clerk in 1874. He held the office of councilman one year, and in 1880 was elected mayor. He once run for State senator, but was defeated. In politics he is a Democrat. In 1869 he married Enrietta V. Shaw, and four children have been born to them, viz: Benjamin W., Maud M., Henry A., and Charter O.

P. A. REINHARD, was born in Neidernbergh, Bavaria, Germany, in 1827; came to Ohio with his father in 1832 and settled in Columbus, where he learned the trade of gun-smith with Cornelius Jacobs, and began that business in Columbus in 1872, following the same for seven years. In 1849 he came to Loudonville, and there opened a shop for the manufacture of target rifles, the first and only establishment of the kind in the county, and in order to perfect his trade and gain accuracy in making target guns, in 1856 he closed his place of business and went to Rochester, New York, and served an apprenticeship with William Billinghurst, the celebrated gun-maker of the world. At the close of his apprenticeship he returned to Loudonville, where he again commenced business, and proved to his patrons that his rifles, with the Billinghurst improvement, were the best. His guns have been tested at the following ranges and carried off first money: At South Vernon, Vermont; at the National shoot, when twenty-eight States were represented; at Dayton, in 1877, he won the first prize, together with seventy-five dollars in gold; at Fort Wayne, Indiana, in the same year, he won the first prize and fifty dollars in gold; at Tiffin, Ohio, in 1878, he won a lady's gold watch and three twenty dollar gold pieces, and in the same year at Warren, Ohio, in company with L. W. Rodgers, of Tiffin, Ohio, won over one hundred dollars in gold. At a private match with John W. Adams, of West Virginia, for one hundred dollars, he won the money; shot forty rods, ten shots, string measure, measured from center to center; Reinhard's string measured eleven and one-fourth inches. At the National shoot, forty rods, ten shots, string measure, from center to center, Reinhard's string measured ten and one-fourth inches. At another, in Wheeling, West Virginia, with John W. Johnson, he won one hundred dollars. In 1849 he married Catharine Clee, who was born in Minster Meiseldt, Prussia, in 1827; came to America with her father in 1840, and settled in Delaware county, Ohio. P. A. Reinhard was the father of eight children, only five of whom are living, viz: Josephine C., Martha A., William H., Mary T., and Frank A.

JOHN LEE BURWELL'S ancestors came from England as early as 1639 and were descendants of a royal family. They first settled in what was then called New England, and were the first pioneers of America. They took an active part in the organization of the government of New England, and were faithful subjects to their mother country until the days of the Revolution, when they with one accord severed their ties with King

George and took up arms for the defence of the land of their adoption. They withstood the trials and privations of the Revolution, and in the war of 1812 they were among the first to answer to the call of the President for troops. Their voices have been heard in the halls of Congress and in several State legislatures, also many minor offices, the mention of which would only take up space in this work. Suffice it to say, that they have been an exemplary family, not one of the name ever bringing disgrace upon it. William Burwell, father of John Lee Burwell, was born in Hunterdon county, New Jersey, in 1780, and came to Ohio and settled in Ashland county, on the farm now owned by A. J. Mumper, jr.. In 1817 he married Elizabeth Weldy, daughter of George Thomas. On March 12, 1868, he died. He was the father of five children: Jacob, John Lee, Hannah, Lydia and Elizabeth Miller. John Lee Burwell was born in Hanover township, Richland county, March 23, 1820. In 1843 he married Louisa Greenlee, who died in 1866. In 1867 he married Clarinda Kemp. By trade he was a blacksmith, and served an apprenticeship with Mayor R. P. Fulkerson, and followed the business until 1868, when he began the business he is now engaged in, viz., a dealer in millinery and fancy goods, under the firm name of Mr. and Mrs. J. L. Burwell. He is a consistent member of the regular Baptist church, a Republican in politics, and the father of six children, three living and three dead, viz.: Herbert, who married Emma Kellog, John L. and William G., living; Minor S., Mack and George W., deceased.

JOHN STRONG was born in Onondaga county, New York, in 1814; came to Ohio in 1825, and settled in Loudonville, and in 1835 married Catharine A. Danner. He was the first clerk of Loudonville, and held the office of constable two years, and in 1865 was mayor of the village. In 1861 he was appointed postmaster by Abraham Lincoln, and has held the office ever since, with the exception of four months and a half, when it was held by George Honeybarger, who was appointed by Andrew Johnson. In politics he is a Republican. He was the father of twelve children, of whom ten are living, viz.: Selah, who married Cynthia Bishop and lives in Loudonville; Henry, who married M. E. Doty; Elmina, wife of A. C. Moore, of Mt. Vernon, Ohio; James, who married Annie E. Critchfield and lives in Richland county; Louisa, wife of J. S. Ramsey of Chicago, Illinois; Rhoda, wife of William Geiselman, of Loudonville; Mary E., wife of W. A. Churchfield, of Loudonville; John E., who married Margaret Rosensteel, of Loudonville; Harvey, and Anna. Martha and Laura died in infancy.

GEORGE C. HASKELL was born in the State of Vermont in 1836; came to Ohio in 1870 and settled in Loudonville, and went into the bank with his uncle, Nathaniel Haskell, where he continued until his death, which occurred January 15, 1876. He was a member of the Universalist church, and in politics was a Republican. In 1871 he married Lucy E. Hayes, of Holmes county, Ohio, and to them two children were born—Charles C., who died, and Mary I.

JOHN G. HERZOG was born in Buffalo, New York, in 1854; came to Ohio and settled in Loudonville in 1878. He served an apprenticeship in a printing office with Silas Folsom in the Attica, New York, *Atlas* office, when only fourteen years old, and afterwards worked in the Attica *News* office with C. F. Malloy; he also worked in the Buffalo *News* office. When only twenty-one years old was elected to the office of sealer of weights and measures in Attica, New York, and held that office two years, and was publisher of the first directory of Attica. In February, 1879, he started the first political paper in Loudonville, with a circulation of over nine hundred subscribers. At present he is a member of the school board, and a member of the German Lutheran church; in politics is a Democrat. He married Maggie Lorentz of Loudonville, August 27, 1874, and to them three children have been born, viz.: Cora C., William G., and Walter C.

SAMUEL HESS was born in Bucks county, Pennsylvania, in 1817, and came to Ohio in 1837; settled in Ashland county in 1839. He was a cooper by trade, and carried on that business for some time. In 1869 he began the grocery and provision business and in 1879 took W. C. Hamlin as partner, and is doing a thriving business, their sales amounting to about twenty thousand dollars per annum. He is a member of the English Lutheran church, and in politics is a Republican. He married Parmelia Johns of Ashland, Ohio, and is the father of eight children, viz.: Christopher C., who was taken prisoner at Chickamauga, and died in Andersonville prison; Mary J., wife of John H. Cutle, Alliance, Ohio; William H., who is deceased; Sarah E., wife of Jonathan Nebil of Loudonville; Samuel E., who married Miss Travirs, and lives in Mansfield; Jonathan E., who died; George A., who married Martha Honeybarger; Olive E., who married William C. Hamlin.

SIMON BOLLY was born in Beriniger, Switzerland, in 1827, and came to America in 1851. He remained in New York one year and a half, and in Pennsylvania one year; and came to Loudonville in 1853, and began working on the railroad and worked there one year and a half; at the end of that time he began work in Jefferson Bull's foundry and worked there seven years, and then went into partnership with Joseph Lyons in the foundry business. At the end of two years and a half he sold out and opened a grocery and restaurant, and continues in that business. He has held the office of township clerk two terms, and was at one time township treasurer and is now one of the councilmen. In 1854 he married Mary Young of Holmes county, Ohio, and is the father of seven children; Mary, who married Ezra Swier of Loudonville; Maggie, Josephine, Amanda, Julia A., Elizabeth, and Emil.

JACOB BRECKEISER, SR., was born in Ellsos, France, and came to America in 1853, and settled in Ashland county, on the farm he now lives upon, situated about one mile north of Loudonville. In politics he is a Democrat; and is a member of the German Lutheran church. In Ellsos, France, he married Mary Wolf, and to them seven children were born, five of whom are living: Mary, who became the wife of George Lugend, and lives in

Ashland county; Margaret, who married Jacob Breckeiser, of Ashland county; Jacob, who married Barbara Pfiester, and lives in Ashland county; and John and George.

JACOB BRECKEISER, JR., born in France in 1847, came to Ohio with his father and settled in Ashland county. In 1869 he married Barbara Pfiester, of Knox county, Ohio, and in 1873 erected the building in which he now carries on the grocery and provision business; he deals extensively in country produce. At present he is a member of the German Lutheran church, and is the father of five children: Mary E., Jacob E., Emma L., George F. and Charles.

ALEXANDER AKINS came from Lancaster county, Pennsylvania, in 1811, and first settled in Belmont county, Ohio, where he remained two years and a half. In 1814 he moved to Lake township, Ashland county, then a part of Wayne county, and settled on the farm now owned by Jacob Eckey and Jacob Horn. Mr. Akins married Elizabeth Sloam, and was the father of four children, but two of whom are living: Emer, who married Druselda Metcalf; and Alexander, who married Christina Shipp.

ALEXANDER AKINS, JR., was born in Lancaster county, Pennsylvania, in 1808; came with his father and settled in Ashland county, and married Christina Shipp; and is engaged in farming. In politics he is a Democrat. Three of his five children died in infancy; the other two are: William, who married Sarah Miller, and in 1847 went to Indiana; Albert, who married Sarah Shumaker in 1867, and lives in Loudonville.

PETER HIGH STAUFFER was born in Berks county, Pennsylvania; and in 1875, at Milford, Berks county, Pennsylvania, he opened a printing office and began the publication of a paper called *Our Home Friend*, which he published there two years, and one year at Quakertown, in connection with a job office. In 1878 he came to Loudonville and purchased the *Advocate* office, and began the publication of the Loudonville *Advocate*, in connection with *Our Home Friend*, the latter having a circulation of nine thousand and the former nine hundred. In 1875 he married Augusta, daughter of Jacob Miller, of Vermillion township. Mr. Stauffer is a member of the Mennonite church, and is the father of two children: Gilman and Clara.

C. L. BUCKWALTER was born West Lebanon, Wayne county, Ohio, in 1845, and studied medicine with Drs. Fuller and Wirt. In 1872 he graduated from the Medical Department of the University of Wooster, in Cleveland, Ohio, and, in the same year, began the practice of medicine in New Washington, Crawford county, Ohio, where he remained six years. In 1878 he gave up the practice of medicine and engaged in dentistry, having studied with Dr. O. Buckwalter, of Millersburgh, Ohio. In 1879 he opened an office in Loudonville, where he deals in all the modern improvements, and is steadily building up a large practice. In 1874 he married Maggie H. Stewart, daughter of Judge George H. Stewart, of Loudonville, and is the father of two children, viz: Xenophon O. and Ware J.

HENRY GILBERT was born in Cornwall county, England, in 1825, came to America in 1843, and first settled in Coshocton county, Ohio, where he served an apprenticeship with Jacob Wagner, cabinet-maker; came to Loudonville in June, 1849, and opened a furniture store on Spring street, where he still remains. Mr. Gilbert has been elected councilman, and member of the school board, for several terms, and is a member of the Baptist church. In 1851 he married Elizabeth Sprague, and is the father of ten children, of whom nine are living, viz.: Henry, who married Hattie Scott, of Loudonville, John F., William J., Clement G., Thomas B., Lew H., George, Jesse, and Joseph N.

JAMES P. BARRON was born in Center county, Pennsylvania, in 1835, and settled in Ashland county in 1859. He attended the Vermillion institute, in Hayesville, four years, and went from there to Jefferson college, Pennsylvania, where he graduated in 1864, after which he taught in Canaan academy, Wayne county, Ohio, and, afterwards, in Buckhannon, West Virginia, and while there organized the first union school in that place, of which he was superintendent for three years. He first married Libbie Mullins, of Buckhannon, who died in 1869. In 1869 he was admitted to the bar at Harrisonville, Missouri, and practiced in Pleasant Hill, Missouri, nine years. Mr. Barron came to Loudonville in 1878, where he is building up a good practice. In 1870 he married Mary A., daughter of Thomas H. Galloway, and is the father of one child—Francis J.

MICHAEL DERRENBERGER, was born in Holmes county, Ohio, in 1847, and settled in Loudonville in 1872, where he bought a half interest in a restaurant with Simon Bolly, and remained three years. At the end of that time he sold his share to Bolly and formed a partnership with J. H. Burris in the same business. At the end of a year he sold to Burris, and at the end of another year he bought out Burris, and is still engaged in the business of keeping a restaurant. He is a member of the German Lutheran church. In 1874 he married Lizzie Ullman, of Loudonville.

JOHN C. LARWILL, was born in Wooster, Wayne county, Ohio, in 1824. He first settled in Loudonville April 1, 1846, and engaged in milling. At the end of three years he sold to A. A. Taylor, and on the thirteenth day of April, 1848, bought out Nathaniel Haskell's stock of dry goods in partnership with A. A. Taylor, with whom he continued in business twelve years, when he bought A. A. Taylor's share and continued in business alone five years. He then took W. S. Fisher into partnership, and continued that partnership fifteen years, when the partnership was dissolved and J. C. Larwill has since continued the business alone. He is a dealer in dry goods and groceries, and has the largest and best selected stock of goods in Loudonville. When he began he had comparatively nothing, but by honesty and fair dealing has built up the largest trade of any merchant in the town, if not in the county, his sales averaging about fifty thousand dollars per year. In 1856 he married Norma Workman, who died in 1869. In 1876 he married Susan L. Moore, of Newark, Ohio, and is now the father of one child, viz: Arthur Larwill.

SAMUEL GARRET, the father of William Garret, was born in New Jersey in 1782, and came to Ashland county, Ohio, in 1822. He first settled on the farm now owned by his son, William Garret, and was a manufacturer of woollen goods. In 1830 he erected a factory on the Black fork, and continued in the business until his death, which occurred in 1868. His factory was the first woollen factory in the county. He also built a sawmill on the farm now owned by the Yarnell heirs. He married Catharine Vaness in New Jersey, and was the father of two children, viz: Catharine, who lives in New Jersey, and William.

WILLIAM GARRET was born in New Jersey in 1810, came to Ashland county in 1836, and settled on the farm which he now owns. He is a blacksmith by trade, but since he came to Ohio, has been engaged in farming and in the lumber business. He is vice-president of the Loudonville Banking company, and has held the office of justice of the peace nine years; has been trustee and clerk of the township, and is highly respected. He married Dense Jennings, of New Jersey, and is the father of six children, two dead and four living, viz: Jane, wife of Daniel C. Priest, afterwards of Washington Hyatt, of Knox county; Charlotte, wife of Dr. Scott, of Loudonville; Sophia, wife of J. M. Myhart, who lives in Knox county, Ohio; Anna, wife of James Ross, of Knox county; and Virginia and William, deceased.

CHARLES OPENHEIMER was born in Steinbach, Germany, and came to America in 1852, and settled in Cincinnati, Ohio, where he remained six years, when he came to Loudonville and opened a clothing store, bringing his stock of goods from Cincinnati. In 1873 his building was destroyed by fire, but he saved his stock, and in the same year erected the fine brick building which he now occupies. In politics he is a Democrat. In 1868 he married Carrie Hirsch, and is the father of five children, viz: Jennie, Blanche, Isadore, Emanuel and Elias.

WILLIAM BARRON was born in Muskingum county, Ohio, in 1817. When eighteen years of age he went to Knox county, Ohio, and in 1863 went to Ashland county, Ohio, and settled on a farm near Loudonville, which he now owns. At present he is proprietor of the American house, in Loudonville, Ohio, having bought out John Stockman in 1878. He is a member of the Wesleyan Methodist church, and is a Republican in politics. In 1844 he married Mary A. Hall and seven children have been born to them, viz.: James, who was killed at the battle of Chickamauga in 1863; Randolph, who married Margaret Sigler; Libbie, wife of Herman Bauscher; Ella, Carrie and William.

NATHAN W. SMITH was born in Wayne county, Ohio, in 1835, and came to Ashland county in 1856 with his father, who settled on the farm now owned by John Richey, in Vermillion township. In 1866 he married Maggie E. Lair, of Wilmington, Clinton county, Ohio. He learned photography in Wooster, Ohio, with Walter Jones, and has since been located in Hayesville, Monroeville, Fostoria and Upper Sandusky, and is now located in Loudonville. In politics he is a Republican, and is the father of three children, viz.: Lulu, Olive and Mildred.

HUGH SCOTT was born in Pennsylvania in 1785; came to Ohio in 1827, and settled near Steubenville, where he died May 22, 1827. In 1807 he married Catharine Humphries. In the year of his death she removed to Ashland county, and settled on the farm now owned by William Humphrey, in Green township. In the following spring she moved into Vermillion township on the farm now owned by O. H. Scott. She died while on a visit to her old home in Mifflin county, Pennsylvania, November 21, 1854. Mr. Scott was the father of eight children, of whom Thomas, Jane, James, Francis, and Winfield are dead. William married Margaret Sigler, and lives in Ada, Hardin county, Ohio. Oliver H. married Eliza J. Tawney, and lives in Vermillion township.

ANDREW J. SCOTT, the subject of this sketch, was born in Ashland county in 1827; attended school at the Ashland academy while Loren Andrews was proprietor, and also at Vermillion institute at Hayesville, under Lewis Granger, Rev. McClain, Rev. W. W. Colmery, and others. For two years he taught in the Loudonville academy, and studied medicine with E. B. Fuller and is also a graduate of Buffalo university. He is a doctor of the old school, and has the largest practice of any physican in Loudonville; has held the office of mayor of Loudonville for several years, and was at one time a member of the school board, and has always taken a deep interest in educational matters. In 1852 he married Miss S. M. Fuller, who died in 1854. In 1856 he married Anna Fuller, who died in 1864. Then, in 1867, he married Charlotte Garret. In politics he is a Democrat. He is the father of four children, viz.: L. Content, Charles B., S. Hattie, wife of Henry W. Gilbert, of Loudonville, and Idella A.

DANIEL GEISELMAN was born in Stark county, Ohio, in 1846; came to Loudonville in 1868, and in 1876 married Alice Webster, of Mohican township, Ashland county, Ohio. By trade he is a harness-maker, and carries on the largest line of that busines in Loudonville. He is also proprietor of the most extensive livery stable in Loudonville. In politics he is a Democrat.

WILLIAM H. WIRT was born in Summit county, Ohio, in 1841, attended college in Hillsdale, Michigan, two years, and then began the study of medicine with Drs. Fuller and Scott, in Loudonville, Ohio, where he remained three years. In the spring of 1869 he graduated at Rush's Medical college, Chicago, Illinois, and the same year began the practice of medicine in Dundee, Tuscarawas county, Ohio, where he remained one year, when he returned to Loudonville and formed a partnership with Dr. A. B. Fuller, with whom he remained in partnership five years. In 1875 he dissolved partnership, and continued in business alone until the fall of 1879, when he took Dr. O. W. Schwan into partnership, and is now practicing medicine under the firm name of Drs. Wirt & Schwan. He is a physician of the regular school, and has built up a large practice. In 1872 he was elected member of the school board, and has been re elected every term since, and has held the offices of president and clerk of the board; was also chief of the fire department for one year. In 1879 he received the nomination of representative on the Republican ticket, but, owing to the large majority on the other side, was defeated, but greatly reduced that majority. He is a member of the Methodist Episcopal church, and contributes largely to its support. Mr. Wirt is a man who has gained the esteem and confidence of the community, and is honored and respected by all who know him. In 1869 he married Clementine L. Smith, of Loudonville, and is the father of two children—William G.; and Rush, who died when about four months old.

GEORGE H. STEWART, was born in Alexandria, Huntingdon county, Pennsylvania, October 9, 1809. When a boy in his teens he went to Amagh, Pennsylvania, and clerked in a store two years, during the time of making the Pennsylvania canal and Portage railroad over the Alleghany mountain. From there he went to clerk at Junction Forge, and got a contract on the canal on the Juniatta, but gave up canaling and went to Pittsburgh, where he got a position as book-keeper in a wholesale store at a salary of five hundred dollars per year, then considered a large salary. In 1832 his salary was raised to six hundred dollars per year, then among the highest in the city. In the summer of 1833 he bought a stock of goods and started west to find a location to sell them; tried to get a house to put the goods in, but there was none to be had, except Stuart's bar-room at the Phœnix hotel, then considered too far out of the business part of town, so he hired a horse of Stuart at twenty-five cents per day to come to Loudonville, then in Richland county, a small village with about one hundred inhabitants. He commenced the mercantile business in August, 1833, at a time when the people were talking about building a canal up the White-woman and Mohican. Stewart, having had experience in canaling, took an active part in procuring a law for a State canal to Loudonville, and the law was passed while General William McLaughlin, of Mansfield, was our State senator, and it was through his untiring labor in the legislature that the bill was passed and the canal was located to Loudonville, and advertised for letting, but before it was commenced the legislature abolished all State works not commenced, and they failed to get a canal. In 1835-36, when the question of organizing Ashland county was agitated, he took an active part in bringing it about, and was sent to Columbus several times to lobby for the undertaking, spending his time and paying his own expenses. In 1845-6 his efforts were rewarded, and in 1845 he was appointed associate judge for Ashland county, which office he held seven years. From 1846 to 1850 he took an active part in the construction of the Pittsburgh, Fort Wayne & Chicago railroad, for which he secured the right of way through Holmes, Ashland, and a part of Wayne and Richland counties, and in 1851 purchased a tract of land of David Foltz in Wayne county, and laid out what is now called Shreve, a station on the railroad above mentioned. He was employed by the railroad company as station-agent for ten years. He has been township trustee and treasurer of Hanover township at various times, and has also held the office of councilman in Loudonville. In politics he is a Republican. In 1837 he married Emeline Cappels, of Loudonville, and is the father of eight children, viz: Charlotte A., who lives in Loudonville; Eliza T., wife of Amos Culver, in Dacotah Territory; Mary E., wife of Dr. Fuller, of Loudonville; Satira and James, deceased; George, who married Katie Cassel, and lives in Zanesville; Xenophon C., who lives in New York city; and Margare H., wife of Dr. Buckwalter, of Loudonville.

CALEB CAPPELS was born in Vermont, and came to Ashland county in 1814, and settled near Loudonville, on the farm now owned by Thomas Whitney, where he built the first frame barn that was erected in Green township. He was a carpenter and joiner by trade, but after he came to Ohio he engaged in farming. In politics he was an old-line Whig. In 1834 he died. He was the father of six children, all now deceased except Emeline, wife of George H. Stewart of Loudonville.

DANIEL HONEBARGER was born in Bavaria, Germany, in 1793, and married Catharine Baum, of Bavaria, and in 1836 came to America and settled in Stark county, Ohio, where he engaged in farming. He was a member of the German Reformed church, and died in 1839. In 1871 his wife died in Indiana, at the age of seventy-nine years. He was the father of six children, four of whom are still living: Elizabeth, who married George Wiselogal, of Michigan; Harriett, who married Adam Kremick, and lives in Michigan; Catharine, who married George Gache and lives in Fulton county, Ohio, and George, who married Ann Goodman.

GEORGE HONEBARGER was born in Bavaria, Germany, in 1828, and came to America with his father and settled in Stark county, Ohio, where he remained two years, and then went to Wooster, where he remained one year, and in the spring of 1841 came to Ashland county, and settled in Loudonville. By trade he is a painter, but, owing to ill health, he was obliged to give up his trade. Then he clerked in a dry goods store for Adam Kunrick six years, after which he engaged as clerk in a grocery store for John Sheet. In 1852 he married Ann Goodman, of Loudonville. He has been treasurer of Hanover township thirteen years, and also treasurer of Loudonville village for several years; township assessor four years; also councilman four years, and member of the school board. He is a member of the German Reformed church, and in politics is a Democrat. He is the father of seven children: Emeline, wife of Lyman Parish, of Loudonville; Charles, living in Michigan; Harvey, who married Lillie Marietta, of Loudonville; Martha, wife of George Hess, of Loudonville; Franklin, Luella and Joseph.

MICHAEL CROWNER was born in Bucks county, Virginia, in 1798; came to Ohio in 1810 and settled in Belmont county; but in 1828 moved to Richland county, Ohio. He was a farmer; and held the office of trustee of his township for many years. In establishing the schools he took an active part, and was deeply interested in all educational matters. He was a member of the Catholic church, and died in 1861. In 1821 he married Nancy Nesbit, of Pennsylvania, who still survives him; he was the father of eight children, viz: Margaret, who became the wife of James McNoll; William, who married Catharine Vance, and afterwards married Elizabeth Baum; John, who married Elizabeth Whistler, and lives in Kansas; Rachel, wife of Jacob Lax, and afterwards wife of Mr. Ross; David, who married Elizabeth Hoover; Sarah, wife of Clemons Osfelt; Jackson, who lives in Kansas; and Thomas, who married Nancy Vance, and lives in Kansas.

WILLIAM M. CROWNER was born in Belmont county, Ohio, in 1826, and in 1853 married Catharine Vance, who died in 1873. In 1875 he married Elizabeth Baum. In his younger days he taught school in the winter and superintended his farm in the summer; he is now wholly engaged in farming. He first settled in Ashland county in 1853, and has held the office of assessor for at least twelve years; was superintendent of the infirmary one year, when he resigned; was elected county commissioner in 1871, and served six years; was elected land appraiser in 1869; and also in 1879; in 1877 he was elected justice of the peace, which office he now holds. In politics he is a Democrat; he is the father of four children: Agnes, wife of Edward Baum; Madison, Jennie and Cora.

VERMILLION TOWNSHIP.

HARRISON MCCRARY was born in Vermillion township, Ashland county, Ohio, July 3, 1840. His grandfather, John McCrary, was among the pioneers of this section of Ohio, having removed from Jefferson county, Pennsylvania about 1812, and settled on the Black fork, and soon after sold his farm there and came to Vermillion township, and purchased the tract of land where the subject of this sketch now lives, and where he was born. His father, David McCrary, was a young unmarried man at that time; and engaged in the hardships of those early times, and assisted in clearing the land. When Harrison was a small boy his father died, and his mother built the house in which he now lives; she died September 30, 1876. In October, 1863, Mr. McCrary was married to Miss Elizabeth Sackett of Montgomery township, Ashland county. They have had nine children, one of whom is dead; the eight living are at home with their parents. Mr. McCrary gives his farm his whole time. It is one out of many of the farms that has been held by members of the same family for over sixty years. In politics he is a Republican, but his ticket is cast in every case, for the man who, in his judgment, is best fitted to fill the office to which he is chosen, regardless of political name. Mr. and Mrs. McCrary are members of the Presbyterian church at Hayesville, Ohio.

JAMES B. SMITH was born in Trumbull county, Ohio, November 18, 1815. When a little more than one year old, his parents moved to Ashland county and located in Vermillion township, about three miles south of Hayesville, on land entered by Mr. Smith's grandfather. This section of the country was unimproved, and they had to endure the hardships that only these hardy pioneers could. James, the subject of this sketch, grew up among these scenes, in which he took part, until he reached manhood. March 3, 1840, he married Lydia Workman, and at once emigrated to the State of Illinois, where he expected to remain; but in the fall of the same year his father's death decided him to return to the scenes of his childhood, and, after closing up the affairs of his father, he settled down where he now resides, and determined to remain here. From that time to the present, Mr. Smith has seen the many changes that have taken place. Where the old forest trees swayed to and fro, waving fields of grain and grass now fill the heart of the owner and passer-by with thankfulness to Him who ruleth the destinies of mankind. The old log cabins, with their spacious fire-places, have gone, and in their place are beheld beautiful and convenient houses, brick and frame, and large barns filled with the abundant harvest. The ox team, and the ungainly cart with its wooden wheels, we see no more, but, in its stead, the prancing steed, in light, but durable harness, moves rapidly over a smooth road, with a four-wheel vehicle that would have been a thing of wonder to our venerable forefathers. Mrs. Smith died February 3, 1845. They had four children. One child, a daughter, and the first of the family, died at the age of two years. The others are: Lydia Amanda, who was the wife of John VanDeren, and died in March, 1874, in Kansas; Ruth Ann, wife of Dr. Cole, of Crestline, Ohio; and Stephen S., who is married and lives in Jasper county, Missouri. April 15, 1847, Mr. Smith married Martha Jane McClure. To them have been born five children, two sons and three daughters. Wilber F. died May 29, 1854. Of the remaining four, one son is married and the three daughters remain with their parents. Mr. Smith has served as justice of the peace for six years, and although a Republican since the existence of that party, he was elected to the office in a township which was strongly Democratic. Mr. and Mrs. Smith are members of the Methodist Episcopal church at Hayesville.

LAFAYETTE PAXTON was born in Vermillion township, February 21, 1849. His father, Hugh Paxton, was born in Washington county, Pennsylvania, and came to Ohio in 1819, and located in Wayne county. In 1833 he moved to Vermillion township, and purchased a tract of land, one mile west of the village of Hayesville, Ohio. Here he remained the balance of his life. He was a very industrious and energetic man. To the breaking out of the Rebellion he was a Democrat, but he at that time changed to a strong Republican, which principles he adhered to until his death, which occurred January 23, 1878. Lafayette, the subject of this sketch, is the only heir, and has charge of his invalid mother, who is a great care. September 28, 1873, he married Miss Ellen

Himes, of Richland county, Ohio. They have one child, Hugh, born May 19, 1876. Mr. Paxton is a Democrat in politics.

JACOB EICHELBERGER was born in Vermillion township March 21, 1831. On September 4, 1851, he married Susannah, daughter of Samuel and Elizabeth Conn, early settlers of Ashland county, both of whom are dead. They have had children as follows: Louisa, born July 22, 1852; Elizabeth, born November 29, 1854; Mary, born November 6, 1856; Rosanna and Barbara, born May 25, 1858; Samuel, born November 12, 1861; Clara, born April 9, 1863; Elmer E., born May 4, 1866; Benjamin, born May 22, 1871. Of these, two are dead—Elizabeth, who died February 17, 1864, and Benjamin, who died November 5, 1872. Louisa is the wife of Cyrus Miller, and lives in Mifflin township. They were married in 1870, and have three children. Rosanna is the wife of Henry Daubenspeck, and lives in Vermillion township. They have three children. The other four are at home assisting the father on the farm, and the mother in the household duties. In politics Mr. Eichelberger is a Democrat, but in home elections casts his vote for the man he considers most worthy of the confidence of the public, and best fitted to take care of their interests, regardless of political views. He is not connected with any church, but recognizes the importance of churches and schools as a public benefit, and the contents of his purse are used to their benefit many times.

WILLIAM McNAULL was born in what is now Montgomery township, Ashland county, Ohio, about four miles east of Ashland, November 18, 1816. His parents came to Ashland county in 1815, and may well be classed among Ashland county's pioneers. They teamed from the State of Maryland, and entered land in what was at that day a wilderness. Here they went to work in good old fashioned pioneer style. They raised a family of six children, all of whom lived to maturity. William, the subject of this sketch, remained with his parents until he was about twenty-three or four years of age, when his disposition led him to investigate distant countries, States, and territories, which he continued to do for several years, occasionally returning to the scenes of his childhood, and in March, 1865, he was married to Miss Elizabeth Adams of Vermillion township. They have no children. The place where they now live has been their home since their marriage. The farm was cleared almost entirely by Mr. McNaull or under his directions. He has a good farm and it is well improved. He is a Democrat in politics, and is a good neighbor, highly esteemed as a literary man, far superior to many who have had equal privileges. Mrs. McNaull is a member of the Presbyterian church at Hayesville, Ohio.

WILLIAM TANGEMAN was born in the kingdom of Hanover, Germany, December 31, 1831. In 1851 he left Germany with the determination of trying the new world, and upon his landing here went directly to Cincinnati, Ohio, and remained engaged in the wholesale tobacco trade, until 1855, when he moved to Mansfield, Ohio. In April he married Miss Margaret Schiedt. In Mansfield he remained two years in the tobacco business, when he disposed of his business in Mansfield and returned to Cincinnati, where he remained eight years, and in 1865 he purchased a farm near Loudonville, Ashland county, Ohio, and in 1867 sold this farm and bought and removed to where he now resides, about one mile west of Hayesville, Ohio. They have eight children—three sons and five daughters, all except the oldest son being at home and single. Mr. Tangeman has served his township as trustee, and his school district as director. In politics he is a Democrat, but is a man with many friends in both parties. Mr. Tangeman and wife are members of the German Evangelical church in Vermillion township. The oldest son, Charles W., is in Mansfield, Ohio, practicing medicine.

SOLOMON ARNOLD, proprietor of the Vermillion hotel at Hayesville, Ohio, was born February 18, 1841, in Vermillion township. He remained and worked on the farm until he was twenty-seven years of age, and married Miss Harriet Vangilder, of Vermillion township, November 9, 1859. His father died May 31, 1874, and his mother died May 16, 1860. In 1870 Mr. Arnold moved from the old farm home to Hayesville, Ohio, and kept a livery stable, and in 1872 he took possession of the Vermillion house, and has managed it for the past eight years in connection with the livery business.

JOHN M. RITCHIE was born where he now resides, January 28, 1840. His parents emigrated to Ohio from Pennsylvania in 1835. They purchased a farm that has been their only home in this State for a period of forty-five years. The parents names are Samuel and Elizabeth. Mr. Ritchie died February 13, 1844, at the age of thirty-one years and nineteen days. Mrs. Ritchie is still living, at the advanced age of about seventy-five years. The exact age cannot be given, on account of the family record having been destroyed by fire when she was a child. She is quite smart, and says she is young, or at least feels as young as she did years ago. She, with her daughter, Miss Martha Jane Richie, occupy the home with John and his family. The old home is now owned by Miss Martha and her brother John, the subject of this sketch. In addition to his share of the old home, John owns a tract of land of forty acres which he purchased some years ago of Philip Smith. On September 2, 1875, Mr. Ritchie was married to Miss Mary A. Robinson, of Richland county, Ohio. They have two sons—Samuel N., born October 7, 1876, and Charles E., born October 18, 1877. Mr. Ritchie is a farmer. He has served the people of Ashland county as director of the infirmary. In politics he is a Democrat. He makes no profession of religion, but recognizes churches and schools as very necessary to the well being of any community, and supports them liberally. His aged mother is a member of the Presbyterian church at Hayesville Ohio.

MR. J. H. BOYD was born in Washington county, Pennsylvania, May 20, 1810; came to Ohio with his wife and three children in 1850. Mr. Boyd's father accompanied him, and located near where Mr. Thomas Stafford now lives, his mother having died May 26, 1827, at the age of thirty-eight years. The subject of this sketch located on a tract of land a short distance from where he now lives, where he remained about twenty-five years. In connection with his farm Mr. Boyd has owned and operated a flouring mill, which he kept in operation about twenty-three years. His father died in the spring of 1869, at the advanced age of eighty-five years, and even at that age was quite active, showing very little the weight of so many winters. They seem to be a long-lived people, as an uncle of Mr. J. H. Boyd is still living in Washington county, Pennsylvania, at the wonderful age of one hundred years. Mr. Boyd has given his time entirely to farming, with the exception of the mill just mentioned. January 31, 1839, he was married to Miss Elizabeth Burns, of Ohio county, Virginia. She died February 18, 1861. By this union there were three children—Rebecca Mary, born April 3, 1840; James T., born September 9, 1843; Emeline, born July 6, 1845, all of whom are living, married, and have families of their own. Rebecca, the wife of Alva Ingman, a farmer of Mohican township, has two children. James lives on the old home farm, and has three children; and Emeline is the wife of Porter Craig, and lives in Lawrence county, Illinois, and has two children. February 26, 1863, Mr. Boyd married Miss Kesiah Nailor, of Mohican township. They have one child, Edward E., born May 24, 1864. He is at home with his parents. Mr. Boyd is a Republican in politics; and is a member of the Presbyterian church at Hayesville, Ohio. He has been connected with the Presbyterian church for over forty-five years. Mrs. Boyd is a member of the same church.

MICHAEL SHEMBERGER was born in York county, Pennsylvania, January 28, 1823. In 1828 he came to Ohio with his parents, who located in Vermillion township. They bought a farm, a short time after they landed in the township, adjoining the place where their son Michael, the subject of the sketch, now lives. The old home also belongs to him. The parents remained here until their death. His father died December 17, 1870, and his mother March 15, 1879. On January 22, 1850, the subject of this sketch was married to Miss Rowanah Bennett, daughter of Peter and Sophia Bennett, who came from Maryland at an early day and settled on the Black fork, in Mifflin township. They remained here but a short time, when they bought a farm in Vermillion township and moved there, and about 1857 sold their property, and moved to DeWitt county, Illinois, where they died a few years later. The family of Michael Shemberger and wife consists of five boys and one daughter, all of whom are living except Mary Ann, the sixth child who died at the age of five years, four months and twenty-two days. Those now living are all single, and are at home with their parents. In politics he is a Democrat, as also are his three sons. He and his wife are members of the English Lutheran church at Petersburgh, Ohio. Mr. Shemberger is not an office-seeker, though he has served his neighbors as supervisor, and is held in high esteem by all who know him. The public welfare of the county gets his share of encouragement at all times.

JAMES M. ECHELBARGER was born in Vermillion township, October 17, 1846, and was married January 12, 1871, to Arminda Kyle, daughter of Samuel and Elizabeth Kyle, of Vermillion township. They have four children: Nellie Jane, born November 19, 1871; Cora Almina, born September 17, 1874, died October 23, 1876; Hiram Martin, born April 22, 1876; Ralph, born April 14, 1880. Mr. Echelbarger is a farmer; he has sixteen acres of his own, and farms about forty acres on shares for Martin Kramer. In politics, he is a Democrat.

ROBERT WILSON was born in Washington county, Pennsylvania, May 3, 1816, and came to Ashland county with his parents in 1820, his father having purchased eighty acres of land where Robert now lives. At the time they came to this place there was an abundance of game, turkey and deer principally. Indians were numerous, but peaceably inclined toward their white brethren. They were true pioneers, and as such are quite well remembered by the old settlers in the community at the present time. They began the improvement of their land, and by perseverance and hard knocks, such as our grand old forefathers and mothers could endure, the old forests gave way and the waving fields of grain took their place. Robert, the subject of this sketch, remembers quite well the privations and hardships of those early days. In 1839, November 14th, Mr. Wilson married Martha Jeannette Roison, who came from Westmoreland county, Pennsylvania, with her parents when she was about three or four years of age. They had seven sons and one daughter. Two sons died in infancy; one son, James, the oldest of the family, died in the army; he was a private in the One Hundred and Twentieth Ohio volunteer infantry, and served as such from the date of his enlistment to the time of his death, which took place at Milliken's Bend, Louisiana, February 11, 1863. Three sons and one daughter are married, and doing for themselves. The youngest child, Robert, jr., remains with his father. Mrs. Wilson having died Mr. Wilson afterwards married Anna E. Greenwood, widow of Charles Greenwood, of Holmes county, Ohio. To them have been born one child. Mr. Wilson is one of the best known men in this section of the county. In politics he is a Republican. Both himself and wife are members of the United Presbyterian church at Hayesville, Ohio.

ADAM BAUN was born in York county, Pennsylvania, February 25, 1819, and came to Ohio before he was married, about the year 1839, and worked in the gristmill for Mr. Daniel Smith, by the year; here he worked six years and a half, and purchased a tract of land of Hugh Finley; he then worked for Andrew Newman and Joseph Boyd a period of ten years, in the mill still owned by Mr. Boyd, but not now in operation. In the fall of 1843 he returned to Pennsylvania and married Miss Rebecca Lechman, of York county. She died June 28, 1857. They had two children, one son and one daughter. The son, Adam, jr., was a soldier in the late war, in the One Hundred and Second Ohio volunteer infantry, company B, and after a service as a soldier almost three years, and a prisoner six months at Castle

Thunder, at Cahoba, Alabama, while on his way home at the close of the war, April 25th he was lost on the boat Sultana, near Memphis, Tennessee. This came with crushing weight on father and sister, and many who knew him well in the neighborhood where he was raised. February 25, 1859 Mr. Baun was married again, this time to Miss Ruby Ann Snyder, whose parents lived in Crawford county, Ohio. She died April 7, 1878. By this union there were three sons—Allen C., the oldest, is in the west; Lewis A. and Edward I. are at home; they are all single. Sarah J., born April 14, 1845, is at home, filling the place that only daughter and sister can. She takes entire management of the household cares and duties. Mr. Baun has a fine farm and manages it to good advantage, as the appearance about his farm is proof. He has bought and sold stock for many years, having many times driven over the mountains. When he first came to Ohio he had but twenty dollars, since which, by hard work and good management, with a small amount he received from his father's estate, he has a competence. In politics he is a Republican. Mr. Baun is not a member of any church, but is a liberal supporter of all such institutions.

WILLIAM GLENN was born, in 1822, in Mohican township, Ashland county, Ohio. His father Joshua Glenn emigrated from Harford county, Maryland, in 1818. He was one of the pioneers of Ashland county. His home was a log cabin, and was surrounded on all sides by forest. Here the subject of this sketch was born. He remained and labored on the farm until he was over thirty years of age, and many an old oak fell beneath the heavy blows of his axe. The forest gradually gave way and in its place waving fields of grain were to be seen. On September 23, 1852, Mr. Glenn married Miss Caroline Ewing, daughter of William Ewing, of Vermillion township, another of Ashland county's pioneers, having come from Pennsylvania to Ohio in 1813 and located in Mohican township on the 17th day of March, 1853. William and his wife moved to Green township, on a farm owned by his father. Here they remained four years, when he purchased a farm in Milton township, and moved there. He sold this farm some two years later and returned to his mother's farm in Mohican township. After a year's stay there he bought a farm in Mohican township and lived there five years, at the end of which time he sold and moved to a farm owned by his father-in-law, in Montgomery township. At the end of one year he bought and moved where he now lives. This, in all probability, will be his future home. They have four children. One daughter and three sons. One son is married and lives on his father's farm. Mr. Glenn has never sought public office. He is a Republican in politics. His wife and daughter are members of the English Lutheran church at Jeromeville. Mr. Glenn does not belong to any church, but is in hearty sympathy with the truths of the Bible. The son is a member of the Presbyterian church at Hayesville.

MR. SAMUEL ECHELBARGER was born in Vermillion township, October 23, 1843. His parents emigrated from Westmoreland county, Pennsylvania, about the year 1823 with their parents. His father was then a boy about fifteen years old, and his mother a girl of thirteen summers. They were married on the seventeenth day of May, 1829. They moved at once to a farm in Vermillion township owned by his father, and which is now owned by Mr. William Goard. This farm fell into his possession at the death of his parents for the care he had of them in their old age. This farm, which consisted of forty acres, he traded by giving some boot money for eighty acres known as the Ferry farm. About the year 1850 he sold this farm and purchased the farm on which Samuel and his mother now live. On July 9, 1877, Mr. Echelbarger died. Mrs. Echelbarger is still living with her son Samuel, aged seventy years. On February 9, 1868, the subject of this sketch was married to Miss Eliza Ann Kyle. She died May 10, 1877. They had four children—three daughters and one son. The son is all the child now living. One daughter died in infancy, one at the age of fifteen months and one at the age of four years. On December 3, 1878, Mr. Echelbarger married Miss Elizabeth Endinger, a sister of Mrs. N. D. Ryland. By this union there have been no children. Mr. Echelbarger is a Democrat in politics.

N. D. RYLAND was born in Knox county, Ohio, February 19, 1846. His parents came to Ashland county about the year 1850, and bought a farm about a mile and a half south of Hayesville, where they remained until the fall of 1857, when they sold the farm and emigrated to Randolph county, Missouri. In the fall of 1861 they returned to Ohio, and bought a farm one mile south of Hayesville. The next spring he sold his farm and removed to the farm of James Ewing, and, at the end of two years, bought a farm adjoining the one owned by N. D. Ryland, where they lived some ten years, when they concluded they would leave the farm, and try town life. They rented the farm and moved to Hayesville, where they now reside. The subject of this sketch, N. D. Ryland was married April 6, 1871, to Eliza, daughter of John and Barbara Endinger, of Mohican township. In 1874 they purchased the farm on which they now live. They have two children, one son and one daughter—Willis Howard, eight years old, and Effie Blanche, four years old. In politics Mr. Ryland is a Democrat, but is a man who does not allow politics to interfere with his business affairs or his association with neighbors. With the exception of running a threshing-machine four years, his whole time has been given to his farm. Mr. and Mrs. Ryland are members of the Presbyterian church in Hayesville. They have bright prospects before them, as both are young and hard workers, and are highly respected by the community in which they live.

SAMUEL CRAIG was born in Allegheny county, Pennsylvania, December 25, 1814. In 1834 he came to Ohio with his parents, and located where William Craig now lives. Samuel was twenty years of age at the time. On November 22, 1837, he was married to Miss Jemima, daughter of James and Rebecca Stafford, of Vermillion township. They moved into a house on Mr. Craig's farm, where they remained most of the time until 1846. Mr. Craig then bought the farm in section sixteen, Vermillion township, on which they now live, and which has been their home ever since, and is likely to be the remainder of their lives. They have had nine children, seven of whom are living; two died when quite young—a boy and a girl; two sons and one daughter are married: James S., who married Miss Barbara Mosser, of Vermillion township; Daniel, who married Miss Lydia Youngling, of Vermillion township; Rebecca Jane, who married William Sites, and now lives in Mifflin township, Richland county; Albon, Mary Ann, Elizabeth and Ella are at home. Mr. Craig has a fine farm, and gives it his undivided attention. He has been assessor and trustee a number of years, and has been elected to other township offices, which he declined to fill, as his farm required his whole time. He is a man with many friends in the community that has been his home so many years. He is a hard worker and a good manager. Mr. Craig is a Democrat in politics, though at home elections leaves politics out of the question, and votes for the man he considers best fitted to do credit to the trust conferred by the people. He belongs to no church, but is a liberal supporter of religious and educational institutions, and considers them necessary for the well being of any community.

THOMAS CRONE was born in Mifflin county, Pennsylvania, October 27, 1800; and married Fannie Starkey February 18, 1823. In 1840, with his wife and seven children, he came to Ohio, and located in Mohican township; where he remained one year, when he moved to Perry township and remained three years. Then he moved to Chester township, Wayne county, remained four years, and returned to a farm adjoining the one he first located on. There he remained until the spring of 1877, when he moved to the farm on which he now resides. All his life he has been a farmer, and has now one of the best farms in this section of the county. Mrs. Crone died April 16, 1865. One son, James, was a soldier in the One Hundred and Second Ohio volunteer infantry, and served till the close of the war, a term of nearly three years; he is now married, and lives in Green township. The children, with the exception of three daughters, are married and live in Ashland county. One married daughter lives in Clinton county, Indiana. Mr. Crone is yet bright in mind, and as active as men of his age can expect to be. In politics he is a Democrat; and he has been township trustee. He is a member of the United Presbyterian church, at Hayesville, Ohio.

WILLIAM DAVIS was born in Mifflin township, August 28, 1836. He is a son of Isaac and Francis Davis, who are among Ashland county's early settlers, a sketch of whose lives will be found elsewhere in this work. The subject of this sketch remained with his parents and worked on the farm until he was eighteen years of age, when he left home to learn the carriage making trade with Ames & Leach in Ashland. Here he remained about two years and a half, when he, in company with John Burnett, went to Iowa and worked at his trade and on a farm, and in about eighteen months returned to Ohio and worked at his trade some three years and a half, when he enlisted August 14, 1862, as a private soldier in the First Ohio independent battery, and remained and served his country until the close of the war, and was discharged on the twenty-sixth day of June, 1865. He was faithful in the discharge of a soldier's duties, as he was only excused from service about two weeks during the whole term. At Cloid mountain and many other places he saw hard fighting, and engaged on severe raids and hard marches, and with many others of his comrades withstood the necessary privations and hardships of a private soldier. On October 5, 1865, he was married to Miss Rebecca Sechrist, of Richland county, Ohio. He remained one year with his father, when they moved to Vermillion township and commenced life for themselves. They have ever since made this their home, his whole time being given to the steam saw-mill, at what is known as Steam Corner, in the northwest corner of Vermillion township. They have three children—two daughters and one son. Mrs. Davis died May 14, 1874, and on the nineteenth day of November, 1874, he married Mrs. Barbara Callin, widow of Hugh Callin, of Montgomery township. They have no children.

WILLIAM H. STRICKLAND was born December 8, 1824, on a tract of land located by his grandfather as early as 1815. The Stricklands are well known as a pioneer family of Ashland county, a sketch of whose lives will be found elsewhere in this work. William H., the subject of this sketch, when a babe, left his birthplace, his parents moving to a farm near the northeast corner of Vermillion township, where he remained until he was a man of twenty-two years of age, when he married Mary, daughter of Jacob Eichelbarger. Mrs. Strickland died March 21, 1848. They had one child, a daughter, now the wife of George Kelley, of Vermillion township. February 19, 1850, Mr. Strickland again married, Elizabeth, daughter of Henry Hough, of Montgomery township. They had two children, one son and one daughter—the son is at home and is single, and the daughter married David Hostetter, of Richland county, Ohio. Mrs. Strickland died June 29, 1871. April 1, 1873, he married Catharine E., daughter of Jacob Smith, of Vermillion township. They have one child, a son, now four years old. Mr. Strickland owns the farm on which he first saw the light, which he purchased about five years ago. It is a fine farm, and will, probably, be his home the remainder of his life. He has acted as supervisor and school director a number of years; is a good neighbor and a kind husband and father, and a hard, earnest worker. In politics he is a Democrat, and he and his wife are members of the English Lutheran church at Jeromeville, Ohio.

JOHN BELL was born in Wayne county, Ohio, October 3, 1827, and settled in Ashland county in April, 1836. He was married June 12, 1849, to Elenor McCrary, daughter of J. D. S. McCrary, of Ashland county, Ohio. Their children were: Sarah A., born March 10, 1850; William H., born January 17, 1852; D. W., born November 9, 1853; Mary I., born September 3, 1855; G. W., born July 12, 1857; Nancy J., born July 7, 1859;

Emma L., born June 22, 1863; Elizabeth M., born July 4, 1865; Flora, born September 23, 1867; Hatty M., born August 18, 1869; Lilly, born August 22, 1874; an infant born June 27 1861; an infant born May 8, 1862; two infants died, one on June 29, 1861, and one September 11, 1862. In politics Mr. Bell is a Republican. Both himself and his wife are members of the United Presbyterian church.

BENJAMIN S. McKINLEY was born in Juniata county, Pennsylvania, July 31, 1825. In 1835, he came to Ohio with his parents, and settled in what is now Mohican township, Ashland county. September 10, 1848, he was married to Sarah Ryland, daughter of William and Catharine Ryland, who were among Ashland county's early settlers. Mr. and Mrs. McKinley's parents are dead. They have four children, two sons and two daughters: Judson, Lillie Alice, Emer, and Sadie Agnes. Lillie Alice is the wife of Abraham Hossler, who owns a farm adjoining his father-in-law. Emer married Mary Brubaker, of Mohican township, and owns a farm adjoining Mr. Hossler. Judson owns a farm adjoining his father's place, but as he is yet living in single blessedness, he makes his home with his parents. Sadie Agnes is yet unmarried and lives at home. Mr. McKinley is one of the most thorough, go-ahead farmers of Vermillion township, and is a neighbor highly respected by all who know him. Though a very hard worker for a man of his age, he is genial and companionable. He loves a good horse, and has the gratification of having some that he has raised on his own farm. In politics he is a Democrat. Both himself and wife are members of the Presbyterian church at Hayesville, Ohio.

ANTHONY R. SIGLER was born in Jeromeville, Mohican township, Ashland county, February 14, 1821. At a very early day his parents came from Pennsylvania and may well be classed among Ashland county's early settlers. The subject of this sketch remained with his parents until he was married, July 4, 1848, to Miss Eliza Duncan, daughter of Joseph and Catharne Duncan, who came to Ashland county at an early day, and located in what is now Vermillion township. To this couple have been born three children—all boys. The oldest, Willard Dexter, died at the age of eight months. Joseph H. and John Marion are still living, both married and doing for themselves. Joseph H. married Miss Julia Ann Vangilder, and John M. married Miss Zentippa A. Humbert. John lives with his parents, and Joseph lives on an adjoining farm. Mr. Sigler, the subject of this sketch, is a man of many friends. Having spent his whole life in Vermillion township, he may well be called one of its prominent farmers. He has many times served as a trustee of the township, and but for his positive refusal, could at the present time hold that office or a better one. He is a Democrat in politics, but in home elections gives his vote for the man he considers most worthy of the trust of the people, without regard to politics.

CONRAD FOX was born in Bavaria, Germany, June 18, 1829, and at the age of three years, in company with his parents, brothers, and sisters, he left the old world for a home in the new. Soon after the arrival of the Fox family in America they came to what is now Vermillion township, Ashland county, and here the children have lived and prospered by their own good management and hard work. Conrad, the subject of this sketch, remained with his parents until he was married. April 16, 1852, he married Miss Gertrude Hirshler, daughter of Henry and Christena Hirshler, who died in Germany when she was about eight years old. When she was sixteen years old, in company with her brothers, John and Henry, she came to Ohio. Immediately after they were married they bought the farm on which they still live, nearly three miles northwest of the village of Hayesville. They have two children; Adolph, born April 16, 1854, and Amanda, born February 21, 1859. Adolph is married and lives on his father's farm. Amanda is single and remains at home with her parents. Mr. and Mrs. Fox are members of the German Lutheran church, near where they live. Mr. Fox is a Democrat in politics, and is a man highly esteemed by his neighbors. He has one hundred and forty-two acres of land in one of the most fertile sections of Vermillion township. He is a good farmer, and his family and farm have his whole time.

H. J. HOUGH was born in Ashland, Ohio, January 24, 1847. William Hough, his father, was an early settler in Ashland, and in 1848 removed to Crawford county, Ohio, where he died in 1862. H. J. remained with his parents until after the death of his father, when he went to different parts of the State to see how other people live, and in 1864 enlisted in the service of his country, and served till the close of the war. In 1875 he returned to his native county, and located in the village of Hayesville. January 24, 1877, he married Miss Elizabeth, daughter of Daniel Smith, of Vermillion township. They have one son, born September 4, 1878, and named Daniel Leslie. January 4, 1878, Mr. Hough engaged in the hardware, tin and stove business, under the firm name of Hough & Boyd. December 31st the partnership changed to Hough & Maag, who are at present doing a thriving business, enjoying the respect of all who patronize them.

JOHN BECK, son of Jacob Beck, one of Ashland county's pioneers, and a sketch of whose life will be found elsewhere in this work, was born May 11, 1850. February 15, 1870, he married Miss Amanda Aby, of Mifflin township. They have four children, all daughters: Nettie Celesta, Rella May, Alice Arvilla, and Catharine, an infant. Mr. Beck is a Democrat in politics.

WILLIAM BECK, son of Jacob Beck, one of the prominent pioneers of Vermillion, was born November 9, 1846, and was brought up to hard work on the farm, where he learned industry and perseverance. August 18, 1870, he was married to Miss Mary Ann Helbert, daughter of Jacob and Catharine Helbert, of Vermillion township. They have four children, three sons and one daughter—William Sylvester, Lewis David, Arabella, and Jacob, who is but one year old. Mr. Beck is a Democrat in politics. He gives his whole time to farming.

MRS. KELLY, widow of Patrick Kelly, is a daughter of John and Rosa McNaull, who were among Ashland county's pioneers. Her father has been dead about twelve years, and her mother is living with Mrs. Kelly, and is upwards of eighty years of age. Mr. Kelly came to Ohio from Pennsylvania when he was a boy, and saw many of the privations of the early settlers. June 20, 1839, Mr. and Mrs. Kelly were married, and commenced life in earnest for themselves. They bought land in Vermillion township, and by perseverance, secured an elegant home in the northwest portion of the township. They have nine children—Rosa, Mary, Susan, John, James, Sarah, Emily, William, and Michael; of these eight are living; Susan, the third child, died at the age of eight years and nine months. Mary is the wife of John Harper, son of Thomas Harper, of Vermillion township—they live in Abilene, Kansas; Sarah is the wife of Henry Sheller, of Vermillion township; the six unmarried children are at home, or at least recognize their mother's house a welcome home, when business does not call them elsewhere. Mr. Kelly died February 18, 1859. Since his death Mrs. Kelly has managed the farm, and as her children grew to an age to be of assistance, they cheerfully took their part. They certainly deserve much credit for good management. Mrs. Kelly now owns over two hundred and fifty acres of well improved land in Ashland county.

JOHN K. CRONE was born in Juniata county, Pennsylvania, December 23, 1823, and at the age of sixteen years he came to Ohio with his parents and located in what is now Mohican township, Ashland county, Ohio. He remained at home until he was thirty-five years of age, with the exception of a few years in which he lived with his aunts, the Misses Starkey, sisters of his mother, and during which time he rented and worked the Daniel Pocock farm in Mohican township. In August, 1868, he was married to Mrs. Greenlee, widow of John Greenlee, of Lake township, Ashland county. They have had four children, one of whom died at the age of two years. Mrs. Crone, after her marriage to Mr. Crone, had a daughter who died at the age of eleven. Three children are yet living—John Alvie and Mary Alma, are twins. George Walter is six years old. Mr. Crone is a farmer and a man held in high esteem as a neighbor and friend. He is a Democrat in politics, though in home elections he allows his judgment to decide as to the man most fitted to fill the trust conferred by the people, with little thought as to politics. He is one of the township trustees, and has enterprise sufficient to fill any office creditably that may be entrusted to him.

ROBERT SIGLER was born in Vermillion township, Ashland county, Ohio, January 4, 1823. His father, Henry Sigler, was one of Ashland county's pioneers, having emigrated from Lancaster county, Pennsylvania, at an early day. Here the subject of this sketch was reared in pioneer style, and assisted in reducing the wilderness to the lovely country we now find it. Robert was the fifth of a family of twelve children. He remained at home until he was married in April, 1865, to Miss Catharine Graber, who was born in Germany. They have had four children, two of whom are dead. One died in infancy, and one at the age of thirteen years. Willis and Maudy are living. Willis is seven and Maudy two years old. Mr. Sigler is a good neighbor and a hard worker, giving his whole time to his farm and his family. He is a Democrat in politics. Mrs. Sigler is a member of the Church of God in Vermillion township, about one mile from Mr. Sigler's residence. Mr. Sigler does not seek public office, but has the interests of his county at heart, and never fails to support any public improvements.

JACOB BECK was born in Germany, December 4, 1808, and came to America in 1835, making the trip from Amsterdam to New York in a sailing vessel in seventy days. It was a discouraging voyage, and the hearts of the passengers would sometimes sink; and when they were at last permitted to set foot on land in this free America, their hearts went up in thankfulness to the good being for His preserving care. Mr. Beck remained about five years in Philadelphia, Pennsylvania, and on the twenty-fourth day of January, 1841, he was married to Barbara Schilling, of that city, and in September of the same year, with all his earthly effects, consisting of a bed and what they could pack in two chests, they started for the west with a covered wagon and one horse; and soon after arriving in what is now Vermillion township, he purchased a tract of land, on which was a log cabin, and went to work in earnest to improve his land. Many a giant oak fell to the ground from the heavy strokes of the axe swung by his strong arm. Those were times that tried men's souls, and Mr. Beck and his good wife endured their hardships and privations as only the sturdy pioneers could. Mr. Beck has the satisfaction, in his old days, of seeing good improvements about him, where once was a howling wilderness, and his children in good circumstances. He is a man highly esteemed by his neighbors as a trustworthy Christian man, who has done well his part to make Vermillion township what it is—one of the finest townships in the State. He now owns over three hundred acres of excellent land, in a good community, with excellent school and church privileges. Ever since he came to this county, he has been a member of the German Lutheran church. On the ninth day of April, 1880, his wife died, and his three sons are all married, and he is alone in the home in which he has seen many pleasant days and some sorrows.

DR. E. V. KENDIG was born is Westmoreland county, Pennsylvania, January 11, 1838. He came to Ohio in 1861 and located in Hayesville, Ashland county. Shortly after arriving in Hayesville he commenced the study of medicine with Dr. Samuel Glass of that village. Here he remained and prosecuted his studies with unflinching determination, and in March, 1864, graduated from University Medical college of New York city. Returning at once to Hayesville, he enlisted as assistant surgeon in the Second Ohio heavy artillery, and served his country faithfully in this position for a period of one year, when the war closed, and he again returned to Hayesville and began the practice of medicine. September 21, 1865, he married Miss Mariah Kauffman of Richland county, Ohio. They have three sons, Harry, Willard, and Ralph. The doctor, by his untiring energy and ability, has secured a very large practice. As a physician Dr. Kendig ranks high, and by his kind manner is much beloved by his many patients.

WILLIAM CRAIG was born in Allegheny county, Pennsylvania, September 28, 1812, and removed with his parents to Vermillion township, March 28, 1833. The family then consisted of father, mother, and ten children. The subject of this sketch was the oldest but one, and was then twenty-one years of age. Immediately after their settlement here William left home and began work at his trade, that of blacksmithing, near where the infirmary now stands. Here he remained fourteen years, and worked earnestly at his chosen trade. In November, 1837, he married Miss Barbara Whittington, daughter of James Whittington, of Vermillion township, one of Ashland county's old pioneers. He died September 30, 1846. Mr. Craig boarded with the Whittington family about four years prior to his marriage, and doubtless his energy and ability as a workman won the heart of the woman who has been his helpmate these many years. In 1849 Mr. Craig moved to Hayesville, and worked at his trade till 1855, when he purchased the old home farm and moved there, and took the management of the farm. His mother having died in 1847, his father remained with his son until he died in May, 1871. Mr. Craig has served the people of Vermillion township as trustee six years, and the county as infirmary superintendent. Aside from this public service he has given his time to his farm, which is a good one. This aged couple are members of the Methodist Episcopal church at Hayesville, and have been for a period of thirty-six years. He is a Democrat in politics, but has many warm friends in both parties. He is a man of kind heart, a good neighbor, and a man well known in every township in the county. He was defeated by only ten votes in 1874 for nomination for the office of county commissioner. They have ten children, all living, eight daughters and two sons. All but one are married. The youngest son, William, jr, is single.

GEORGE W. LONG was born in Canton, Stark county, Ohio, February 22, 1831; came to Ashland county with his parents when he was about seven years old, and settled on a farm in Lake township, Wayne county, now Ashland county. Here he remained and worked on the farm until he was about eighteen years old, when he went to Mohicanville and learned the boot and shoe trade. This trade he followed until the spring of 1852, when he started for the gold fields of California, and engaged in mining. He went by overland route, and in 1856 returned to Ohio by water, and in the same year, September 30th, was married to Miss Catharine Mohre, daughter of Jesse Mohre, of Lake township, Ashland county. Mr. Long had sent money from California and purchased a farm about two miles from his father's place, and soon after he was married moved and began improving his own farm. For a period of ten years they lived here, when they sold their farm in Lake township and purchased the farm on which they now live. They have six children—three sons and three daughters. The oldest daughter married Mr. John Eighinger, of Vermillion township. She was married September 30, 1879—just twenty-three years after her father and mother. Mr. Long has been township trustee a number of terms in Vermillion township, and was trustee one term in Lake township previous to coming to Vermillion. Both himself and wife are members of the English Lutheran church. In politics he is a Democrat, but is a man highly esteemed by both parties, as he is moderate in his views, and gives his best time to his family and farm.

EMANUEL SHELLER is a son of John Sheller, who came to Ohio from Pennsylvania in a very early day. He has raised a family who are all grown and doing for themselves. Emanuel, the subject of this sketch, was born in Mifflin township, Richland county, Ohio, in 1848, February 5th. December 28, 1875, he married Miss Susan Swoveland, daughter of Peter Swoveland, of Mifflin township, Richland county, an early settler there. They have but one child, Stella, born November 28, 1876. Mr. Sheller farms the old home place, and is an industrious, energetic man, and a good neighbor.

HENRY SHELLER was born in Richland county, Ohio, December 23, 1844. He remained with his parents, and worked on the farm until he was thirty years of age. January 25, 1875, he married Miss Sarah M. Kelly, daughter of Patrick Kelly, one of Vermillion township's early settlers. She was born March 7, 1850. The subjects of this sketch moved to where they now reside soon after they were married, on a farm owned by Mr. Sheller's father. Mr. Sheller and wife have spent almost their entire life in Vermillion township. They have one child, Emily Almina, born December 13, 1878. Mr. and Mrs. Sheller are descendents of pioneer blood, and are well calculated to meet the perplexities of life, and be useful members of society. Mr. Sheller is a Democrat in politics. He and his wife are members in good standing of the English Lutheran church.

W. G. GALLOWAY was born in Mifflin county, Pennsylvania, November 3, 1815. His father, John Galloway, moved to Ohio October 23, 1830, and settled in Vermillion township. In 1816 he came to Ashland county, and took up a tract of land, near where he afterwards settled, and then returned to his home in Pennsylvania, where he remained until 1830, and, of course, forfeited the claim of 1816. The subject of this sketch remained with his parents until he was twenty-seven years of age, and worked on the farm. In May, 1842, he married Miss Ann Bradley, daughter of John Bradley, who died when she was a child, in the State of Delaware. She came to Ashland county with her mother a short time before the settlement of the Galloway family. They have had seven children; two sons died when quite young; the other five are living. They are all married but one son. Mr. Galloway has served the people of Ashland county six years, in the capacity of infirmary director, and has been justice of the peace nine years. Mrs. Galloway died December 3, 1877. Mr. Galloway is a man highly respected. In politics he is a Democrat, though he has many friends in both parties.

T. C. HARVEY was born in Green township, Ashland county, in 1842. At the age of ten years he removed with his parents to Vermillion township, two miles south of Hayesville. In September, 1867, he left the farm and entered the drug store of J. Kinninger, at Hayesville, as clerk. In 1869, in company with Mr. J. R. Swartz, he purchased the stock and commenced business for himself. The firm then being Swartz & Harvey; this partnership was dissolved in 1872, and Mr. Harvey continued the business alone. In 1879 Mr. Swartz returned from Toledo, Ohio, and again entered business with Mr. Harvey, under the firm of Harvey & Swartz, and at present they are doing a thriving business. Industry and ability have their reward. In the fall of 1870, Mr. Harvey was married to Miss Sarah J. Armstrong, daughter of Dr. Armstrong, one of the pioneers of Ashland county. They have no children living.

JOHN HARVEY was born in Bedford county, Pennsylvania, in 1810. William Harvey, his father, moved with his wife and three children to Ashland county, Ohio, in 1835, and located at Hayesville, where the subject of this sketch kept a tavern for about four years, when he bought a farm in Green township, known as the Kent farm, and moved there. After residing there ten years he removed to his present home, two miles south of Hayesville. This farm he has improved handsomely, and now, in the seventieth year of his age, lives in ease, and, in his declining years, has but little care. William, his oldest son, is married, and lives in Johnson county, Missouri, and was one of Ashland county's brave soldier boys, having served his country a little over three years; Thomas, Wilson, and Sarah Ann live in Ashland county; Frank, the youngest son, is practicing medicine in Mansfield, Ohio. Mr. Harvey was married to Miss Ruth Culbertson, of Wayne county, in 1838. Mrs. Harvey was born in 1814, and is quite active.

THOMAS STAFFORD was born September 15, 1815, in Jefferson county, Ohio. Nathan Stafford, his father, moved from Jefferson county in September, 1820, and bought a tract of land from Ephraim Palmer, where he remained until his death, in September, 1847. The subject of this sketch made his father's house his home until he was married, March 5, 1839, to Phebe, daughter of David and Betsy Stevens, who came to Vermillion township in 1832, and located on a tract of land adjoining Mr. Stafford's farm, where they lived the remainder of their lives, Mr. Stevens to the ripe age of nearly eighty years, having deceased in 1866. Mrs. Stevens died in 1877, aged eighty-two years, ten months, and six days. Mrs. Stafford says, that though her father and mother lived to such an advanced age, yet their minds were bright, and they were not childish, as most persons are at that age. The parents of Mr. and Mrs. Stafford, the subjects of this sketch, were surely pioneers, and are remembered by many who are much younger. They have four children, one son and three daughters, three of whom are married and have gone to try the realities of life for themselves. Amanda M. was born in December, 1839, and is the wife of J. N. McClanahan, an attorney-at-law at Chariton, Iowa. They were married in September, 1872, and have three children—Arvilla, the second child, who was born in 1842, and remains with her parents; David L., who was born in August, 1846, and was married February 13, 1873, to Miss Martha E. Heiser, of Mohican township, Ashland county, and has three children; the youngest child is the wife of T. C. Nelson, married in December, 1876, and lives in Hayesville—and has one child. Mr. and Mrs. Stafford still live on the farm that was their first purchase about thirty-four years ago. They have a fine farm, and seem quite contented, as they well may, to make it their home the balance of their days. Mr. Stafford has served the interests of his township as supervisor, and has, for many years, held the office of school director. They are cheerful, and are well calculated to await old age without regret for the past. Mrs. Stafford died at the age of eighty-two years and a few days, about three days previous to the death of Mrs. Stevens. The mother of Mrs. Thomas Stafford purchased in Green township, in 1844, and remained there about two years and a half, when they purchased their present home.

JOHN C. WOLF was born in Germany, March 20, 1848, and emigrated to America, when he was but four years of age, with his parents. They located in Richland county, Ohio; here he remained until 1854. November 16, 1878, he was married to Elizabeth Vesper, daughter of Michael and Mary Vesper, residents of Orange township, Ashland county. In April, 1879, Mr. Wolf was chosen by the people of Ashland county as superintendent of their county infirmary; and he is a man well calculated to fill such a position to the satisfaction of the people. He is of a sociable and pleasant disposition, though he possesses sufficient firmness to manage the affairs of his office in such a manner that the people appreciate and are fully satisfied with their choice. He has many warm friends among those who are intimately acquainted with him. No children, as yet, have come to vex or cheer this young couple.

HENRY F. REES was born in Brooklyn, New York, December 16, 1848. In 1852 he came with his parents to Vermillion township, Ashland county, and located on land adjoining the farm of Clark A. Barton. His father died in 1862, and his mother in 1879. The subject of this sketch was married to Barbara Baumann, of New York city, June 14, 1877. They have one child, a daughter, born September 7, 1879. Mr. Rees is farming the old homestead place. He is a man of literary taste, is a good neighbor, and a man well calculated to make a neighborhood what it should be.

DAVID CIPHERS was born in Vermillion township, Ashland county, Ohio, March 12, 1842, about half a mile north of Hayesville, on the farm he now owns. The old log cabin, in which he was born, still stands just across the road from his present residence, and is a fair sample of the homes of the hardy pioneers. Were it not that we can occasionally see one of these old landmarks, it would be hard to believe that this now beautiful and well improved country was once the scene of hardship, where only the sturdy and determined pioneer could abide. The subject of this sketch is the son of David and Catherena Ciphers, who came to Ohio from Bedford county, Pennsylvania, in 1835. Mr. Ciphers was married June 4, 1868, to Eliza Latimer, daughter of John Latimer, of Mifflin; her mother died in Wayne county, Ohio, a number of years ago. Mrs. Ciphers died January 5, 1877, leaving two daughters, who are the cheer of their father in his loneliness. Mr. Ciphers gives his whole time to his farm, and deals quite extensively in cattle. He is a model farmer, and a man highly esteemed as a neighbor and friend.

MICHAEL CULLER, jr., is the son of one of Ashland county's pioneers. His father, Michael Culler, from Frederick county, Maryland, made a trip to this part of Ohio in 1814, but did not purchase land till about 1815, or 1816, when he made another trip and purchased a quarter section of land of Phillip Zimmer, the story of whose life and adventure as a pioneer and Indian hunter is familiar to nearly every boy and girl in Ohio. Mr. Culler at that time was not married, and would come to Ohio and improve his farm during the spring and summer, and in the fall return to his home in Maryland. In the fall of 1819 he married Miss Barbara Thomas, a resident of Frederick county, Maryland, and moved at once to his new home in Ashland county, Ohio. The subject of this sketch was born February 1, 1822, and remained and worked on the farm with his parents until he was married in 1858, April 6. He married Miss Michal Swearingen, daughter of Nicholas Swearingen, a resident of Vermillion township. After marriage they returned to the farm, where they now reside. They have had five children, four sons and one daughter. Two sons died in infancy. The two sons and one daughter now living are all at home. Mr. Culler has been justice of the peace, and is a man held in very high esteem by his neighbors.

CLARK A. BARTON was born in Wayne county, Ohio, October 16, 1844. In 1854 he came to Ashland county with his parents, and located in Milton township, about three miles southwest of Ashland, December 20, 1866. He was married to Miss Maggie E. Christy, daughter of Robert Christy, an old pioneer of Chester township, Wayne county, Ohio. They have two children, one son and one daughter, Grace M., born October 12, 1873, and Charles W., born August 19, 1877. Mr. Barton was infirmary director six years. He gives his undivided attention to his farm, which in appearance ranks second to none in Vermillion township. Mr. Barton is a genial, companionable friend, and a man highly esteemed by his neighbors. In 1867 they moved on the farm in Vermillion township, where they now reside, and commenced life in earnest for themselves.

JOHN RISSER was born in Bavaria, Germany, February 4, 1825, and emigrated to America with his parents, Jacob and Mary Risser, in 1834. His parents located in Vermillion township, on a tract of land adjoining the farm where the subject of this sketch now lives. On January 10, 1850, Mr. Risser married Miss Catharine Grabill, of Vermillion township, daughter of Joseph and Hertzler Grabill, who resided on the farm now owned by Mr. Risser. They have seven children, three sons and four daughters. Two daughters are married and live in Ashland. Amelia is the wife of E. S. Briggs, a boot and shoe merchant; Mary, married Uriah S.

Shelly, a minister of the Mennonite church, but on account of poor health was compelled to quit the ministry and is at present engaged as clerk in his brother-in-law's boot and shoe store. The other children are all single, and live at home with their parents. Mr. Risser gives his time entirely to his farm, and deals largely in fine draft horses.

JOSEPH R. SWARTZ was born in Perry township, Ashland county, Ohio, in 1843. His father, Jacob Swartz, was one of Ashland county's old pioneers, having removed, when a young man, from Bucks county, Pennsylvania. Joseph R. remained on the farm until he was fourteen years old, when he left home and engaged as a clerk in the dry goods store of C. C. Coulter, of Rowsburgh. Here he remained eighteen months, then accepted a position in the same business with M. A McHose, just across the street from Coulter's place of business, remaining there, with the exception of a few months, until he enlisted in the Forty-second Ohio volunteer infantry in September, 1861. He served his country for a period of three years and two months as a private soldier, engaging in more than a dozen hard fought battles, coming out of the war at the expiration of his term of enlistment, after all the hardships and privations to which a soldier is exposed, without a scar, but with the satisfaction of knowing he had served his country faithfully, and that the old flag waves over a free people. On May 14, 1868, he married Miss Samantha Ciphers, of Vermillion township. They had two children, one son and one daughter. In 1864 Mr. Swartz engaged in the dry goods business with J. Kinninger, at Hayesville, as clerk, and in 1867 he was surprised to find Mr. Kinninger had recognized his ability to such an extent, that without solicitation on Mr. Swartz's part, the firm was changed to Kinninger & Swartz. In 1869, in company with T. C. Harvey, he purchased the stock, and the firm was changed to Swartz & Harvey. This partnership continued till 1872, when Mr. Swartz left Hayesville and engaged in business at Toledo, Ohio. In 1879 he returned to Hayesville, and again engaged in business with Mr. Harvey, where he is at this writing, the firm being Harvey & Swartz.

MR. MCCLURE DAVIS was born in Westmoreland county, Pennsylvania, February 23, 1825. In 1833 his father, Ephraim Davis, moved to Ashland county, and located in Vermillion township on a farm adjoining the farm now owned by the subject of this sketch. His father died in 1864, and his mother died in 1840. Mr. Davis worked with his father on the farm until he was twenty-one years of age, and then engaged in teaching, mostly in winter, for a period of about nine years. In 1853, March 10th, he married Miss Mary Jane Baker, daughter of Zachariah and Edee Baker, who were among the pioneer families of Ashland county. Her father died in 1863, but her mother is still living at the advanced age of seventy-nine years. They have five children, three sons and two daughters. The oldest daughter is the wife of Thomas Budd, of Vermillion township. The other four still live with their parents. Mr. Davis has filled either township or county offices for a number of years. He was justice of the peace six years, and twice elected county commissioner, in which position he is now serving.

FREDERICK FOX was born in Bavaria, Germany, October 28, 1822, and emigrated to America with his parents in 1833, August 28th; they arrived in Vermillion township, Ashland county, after a tedious journey of twenty days from New York city. Vermillion township has been the home of Mr. Fox ever since. Mr. Fox left home to learn the saddler and harness trade in Mansfield, Richland county, at the age of nineteen. On September 6, 1849, he was married to Miss Eliza Jane Blackburn, of Green township, Ashland county; she came from Bedford county, Pennsylvania, with her parents in 1832. Mr. Fox worked at his chosen trade in Hayesville continuously about sixteen years, at the end of which time he moved to his farm, where he worked winters at his trade and summers tilled and improved his farm. At the end of four years he returned to Hayesville, stayed about two years, when he again returned to the farm, where he has remained ever since. They have had ten children, eight sons and two daughters; nine of whom are living. Charley died at the age of seventeen months, January 25, 1868. Joseph Benton, born August 7, 1850; Lewis B, born December 24, 1852; Justice, born November 3, 1854; Curtis Buchanan, born January 10, 1857; Lillie Irene, born May 5, 1859; Franklin, born July 28, 1861; Conrad C., born February 3, 1864; Coates, born August 11, 1866; Morris, born January 24, 1869; Mary Margreta, born August 20, 1872.

MR. H. BUTCHER was born in Jefferson county, Ohio, in 1837. At the age of fifteen he left home and learned the blacksmith trade, at which he worked about twenty years. Mr. Butcher came into Hayesville, Ashland county, Ohio, in 1859, and was married June 9, 1867, to Miss Amanda Smalley, of Ashland. In 1862 he hired to the government as a mechanic. In about six weeks after he was promoted to the superintendency of the Franklin shops at Nashville, having under his control about twelve hundred men. This position Mr. Butcher held one year, when he was appointed by Captain Irvin, acting assistant quartermaster, as store-keeper for the government at Nashville, holding this position until Lee's surrender. After the war closed Mr. Butcher remained in Nashville one year, and worked at his trade. For four years he has been mayor of Hayesville, justice of the peace three years, and postmaster four years, which position he still occupies. A daughter, aged eight years, is the only child.

JACOB MILLER was born in Bavaria, Germany, in 1824. In 1830 he emigrated with his parents to America, and located in Wayne county, seven miles northeast of Wooster. Michael Miller, his father, died in 1842, July 30th. In March, 1858, his mother died. In 1850 Mr. Miller married Miss Mary Risser, daughter of Jacob Risser, of Vermillion township, Ashland county, Ohio. In the spring of 1860 he moved to the farm formerly owned by his father-in-law in Vermillion township, Ashland county, Ohio, where he now lives. They have had seven children, two of whom are dead. One son and one daughter live in Philadelphia, Pennsylvania. One daughter lives in Loudonville, Ohio, and one son and one daughter live at home.

GEORGE BUCHANAN was born in Washington county, Pennsylvania, in 1800. In about 1831 he came to Ashland county, Ohio, and located in Vermillion township, on a farm near Hayesville. In 1829 he married Miss Elizabeth Bragg, and has one son living in Newton, Iowa. Mrs. Buchanan died September 5, 1833. February 27, 1840, Mr. Buchanan was married to Mrs. Rosena Miles. They have seven children—three sons and four daughters. Two sons and three daughters are married. Mr. Buchanan taught school in Alabama a number of years previous to locating in Ashland county, since which time his business has been that of a farmer. He has served in the capacity of justice of the peace.

MARGARET ISAMAN, widow of Jacob Isaman, was born in Mifflin township, Ashland county, Ohio, February 5, 1824. Philip Pressler, her father, came to Ohio from Pennsylvania in 1822, and erected a log cabin in the woods, and, by untiring energy and the assistance of his good wife, the old forest trees gave way, and in their stead it was not long until he had the pleasure of seeing waving fields of grain. Mrs. Isaman relates to the writer that her good mother, in order to assist her husband in clearing a spot to raise some garden stuff, would bend some saplings and tie a sheet to them, and place her babe in this as a cradle. But this is the kind of stuff our forefathers were made of, and to their hardships we are indebted for the appearance of this lovely country. Mrs. Isaman was twice married; first time, July 22, 1847 to Jacob Stoufer, who died in 1852. They had three sons, two of whom are married. The youngest, Samuel, is single. October 29, 1857, she married Jacob Isaman, by whom she had three children, two sons and one daughter. Mr. Isaman died September 2, 1877. Mrs. Isaman has a beautiful farm, containing over one hundred acres, and with the help of her boys keeps it in good shape. They are good, industrious young men, and are well calculated to take good care of their mother in her declining years.

DAVID FOX was born in Bavaria, Germany, near the river Rhine, in 1819. In 1833, he emigrated with his parents to America, locating in Vermillion township, Ashland county, Ohio. Conrad Fox, his father, died July 28, 1872, and his mother died January 10, 1851. 'Squire David Fox learned the harness business in Hayesville, and worked at it continuously about eighteen years, when he turned his attention to the hotel, farming and stock raising business. At the end of sixteen years he quit hotel keeping, and gave his whole attention to farming, with the exception of serving the community for a number of years in different official positions. In 1868 he was elected justice of the peace; re-elected in 1877, and again in April, 1880. At the advanced age of sixty-one years, he is active, industrious and cheerful. In December, 1840, he was married to Matilda Watson. They have five children, four sons and one daughter. The oldest son, a physician, died in Kansas in 1877.

Mr. Fox studied law and was admitted to the bar in Mansfield, Ohio, in 1874. He has had the advantage of but three months schooling in America.

JOHN S. GRABILL was born in Bavaria, Germany, in 1818. In the fall of 1833 he left Germany in company with his parents and arrived in America Christmas week of 1833, spending the holidays of that year in Philadelphia. In January, 1834, they left Philadelphia for Ashland county, Ohio, traveling some five or six weeks by team, and located in Vermillion township. Mr. Grabill was fifteen years old when he arrived in Ashland county, and has resided in Ashland county ever since. His father died in 1845, and his mother at a later date. Mr. Grabill has given his whole time to farming, and by industry, economy and good management occupies a front rank among the best farmers of Ashland county. On August 21, 1845, he married Miss Nancy Harper, of Vermillion township. They had one son, Samuel, born August 29, 1846, who was married March 13, 1877, to Miss Anna Ewing, by whom he has two children. Father and son live in the old house happily. In 1877 Mr. Grabill made a southern tour, visiting Atlanta, Jacksonville, St. Augustine, Charleston, and many other cities, returning by the way of Washington city.

JOSEPH BENTON FOX was born in Hayesville, Ashland county, Ohio, in 1850. He worked with his father on the farm until he was seventeen years old, when he learned the harness business, at which business he continued two years. In 1869 he returned to the farm, teaching school winters, and in 1876 engaged in the dry goods business with T. C. Harvey, at Hayesville, in which position we find him working earnestly, doing a little business outside of the mercantile in the way of a broker, buying and selling paper. Mr. Fox is an earnest business man. On September 11, 1879, he married Miss Christiana Wallace, of Vermillion township, Ashland county, Ohio.

O. H. SCOTT was born in Mifflin county, Pennsylvania, in 1821, and came with his parents to Jefferson county, Ohio when he was three years old. Hugh Scott, his father, died in Jefferson county, soon after, and, at the age of six years, Mr. Scott came with his mother to Ashland county, stopping about six months in Green township, when they moved to Vermillion township, where he now lives, and located in the woods, in a small log cabin. Mr. Scott had five brothers, at that time, somewhat older than himself, who were quite a help to their mother, and from their willing hands the old forest gradually gave way to waving fields of grain. At the age of twenty-one Mr. Scott learned the carriage-making business in Hayesville, and worked about ten years at the business, when he determined to try his luck in the gold fields of California. His trip over the plains was one of interest, though full of perils and hardships. After an experience of about three years, mostly as a miner, he returned to his old home in Vermillion township. His mother died in 1855. Mr. Scott was married to Miss E. J. Tawney, of Ashland county, in 1858. They have nine children, three sons and six daughters. Two little boys died when about a year old.

JOHN M. LONG was born September 24, 1834, in Canal Fulton, Stark county, Ohio. When he was about three years old his parents removed to Lake township, Ashland county, where he remained and assisted his father on the farm until he was twenty years of age, when he went to California, by water, via New York and the isthmus of Panama, and engaged in mining in company with his two older brothers, George and Peter. By strict attention to business, at the end of four years he was able to return to the old home, and purchased the farm he now lives on. On May 12, 1859, he married Mary Jane Laird, of Vermillion township. They have five children, four sons and one daughter, all at home cheerfully doing all in their power to make home the most desirable place on earth. Mr. Long has filled township offices two different times, and is held in high esteem by his neighbors. He now owns a farm of one hundred and forty-two acres.

CLEARCREEK TOWNSHIP.

LOUIS COWIE, was born in Scotland, in 1814, came to America in 1842, and settled in Ashland county. In 1849 he was married to Christiana Copland, by whom he had seven children, four of whom are living. He remained in the country but three years, when he returned to Scotland, remaining there nine years. He again returned to America, and is now residing in Clearcreek township. His wife died in the year 1869. He is a consistent member of the Presbyterian church, and is a citizen esteemed for his integrity and worth.

HUGH B. MCKIBBEN was born in Beaver county, Pennsylvania, May, 1804. His wife's maiden name was Isabella Chambers. He came into Ashland county in 1828, and settled in Clearcreek township, four miles northwest of Savannah. He was the father of eight children: William C., Elizabeth Jane, Mary, Sarah, James A., Robert, Hugh, and Martha Belle. Mary, married James Brinkerhoff in 1849, and died in September, 1854, leaving one daughter. James A. died May 16, 1858. The father died September 26, 1868, his wife surviving him until the year 1879, November 14th. Both were earnest members of the Presbyterian church, and were industrious and worthy people. Robert was married to Mary P. Platt, March 31, 1864. Their children are one son and one daughter. Robert still occupies the old homestead.

JOHN G. BROWN was the second son of William Brown, and was born in Ireland, in the year 1818. In 1835, he came to America and settled in Ashland county (then Richland county), near Savannah. When he arrived at the age of thirty, he was married to Sarah Calhoun, September 26, 1848. Their children's names are: Maggie J., Mary C., and Alexander M., all of whom are living. The oldest of the family was the census enumerator in 1880, for Clearcreek township, and accomplished the work creditably, and with dispatch. Mr. Brown commenced life as a school teacher and was successful in getting together a sufficient sum to purchase a farm of one hundred acres. The land was covered with a dense forest, and after building himself a cabin, he set about clearing up the farm. By hard labor and a wise economy, Mr. Brown has grown from poverty into one of the substantial farmers of Clearcreek township. He and his family are all members of the church, and are recognized everywhere as estimable and worthy people.

DANIEL HUFFMAN, a native of Virginia, was born in Brooke county, March 9, 1793, and came to Ohio in 1818. He was first married May 20, 1815, to Nackey Holmes, by whom he had thirteen children, seven sons and six daughters. Three sons and four daughters are still living. His first wife died May 20, 1837; he married for his second wife Barbara Wagner, whose maiden name was Stoner, January 10, 1838, by whom he had two children—John Q. and Martha E.; the latter is deceased. Daniel Huffman died November 18, 1876. He was a worthy old man, and enjoyed the confidence and esteem of all who knew him.

ISAAC COLEMAN was born in the year 1832, and with his parents came to Ohio in 1840, and settled in Orange township, three miles north of the town of Orange. April 10, 1856, he was married, and farmed the old homestead for his father for fourteen years. Then he moved to Montgomery township, and, after a short residence there, went to Iowa. After remaining there a brief time, he came back to Richland county, and, finally, to the old home, which he purchased of his father. This he sold, and removed to Clearcreek township, and bought the old Shaw farm. He is the father of five children: Arabella, Jennie, Eva, Charles, and Emma. At the age of two, Eva was killed by a log falling upon her. The loss was a severe one to the fond parents. The other children are all living. Mr. Coleman is a man of enterprise and industry.

GEORGE SHRIVER, son of David Shriver, was born in what is now Ashland county in 1833. In June, 1858, he was married to Laura McCook, by whom he had five children: Loren J., deceased; John E., Willard C., Albert H., and one son dying in infancy unnamed. The Shrivers are an old family, and fuller sketches of their ancestors will be found elsewhere in this work.

J. R. SHRIVER, son of an early pioneer, was born in Richland county in the year 1837, June 4th. June 17, 1866, he was married to Jennie Mercer, by whom he has had two children: Martha Olena and Frona Belle. He resides, at present, in Clearcreek township, three and one-half miles southwest of Savannah, near the old homestead.

ISAAC BUCHANAN is a son of James Buchanan, and was born in Ashland county in the year 1839. He lived on the home farm until 1868, when he was married to Miss Anna M. Wilson. He is an esteemed citizen, and at present one of the trustees of his township.

T. W. HUNTER is the second child of George and Rosannah Hunter. He came to Ashland county about the year 1864, from Indiana, and settled in Clearcreek township. The greater part of Mr. Hunter's early life was given to teaching school, which he followed with success and profit. He made his home with his father until his marriage, June 9, 1870, to Miss Addie J., daughter of James Wharton, an early settler in Milton township. They have two children, Estella and Pearl. Mr. Hunter purchased of his father the farm where he now resides. His means being limited this incurred a heavy debt, and although meeting with a severe reverse in the loss of his house by fire, he has by industry and hard work cleared his farm of all incumbrance, and is now enjoying that independence which comes of easy circumstances. Mr. Hunter is one of the young and enterprising farmers of Clearcreek township, and both he and his lady who comes of old pioneer stock, are highly respected by all those who know them.

E. R. BUFFENMIRE was born in Ashland county in 1843. March 12, 1861, he was married to Sally Ann Myers, by whom he has had three children, Jennie B., Todd, and Blanche. Shortly after his marriage he left his young bride and enlisted for three years in the army. He was engaged in sixteen different battles, the severest of which was the siege of Vicksburgh. He was a brave soldier, and served his country faithfully and with honor until he was discharged, December 2, 1864.

GEORGE MACKEY was a native of Scotland; he was born in the year 1801. In 1835 he came to America, on the "Lady of the Lake," and settled in Ashland county, near Savannah. He was married in 1838. He has adopted three children, and cares for them as his own. He is a man of charity and integrity, and he and his aged wife still live near the town of Savannah.

PETER VANNORSTRAND came to Richland, now Ashland county, as early as 1816, and settled four and one-half miles south of Savannah, in Clearcreek township. He was born in Westmorland county, Pennsylvania, in 1807, and May 24, 1832, was married to Nancy Shaw, by whom he had seven children, three sons and four daughters: John, George, Jesse, Elizabeth, Mary, Ellen, and Delilah. Jesse, Elizabeth, and Delilah, are the only ones living. George died in the army. Mrs. Vannorstrand died June 24, 1872.

WILLIAM FERRELL, son of Obediah Ferrell, was born in Beaver county, Pennsylvania, in 1812. He came to what is now Ashland county, with his parents in August, 1816. On April 18, 1844, he was married to May Huffman, a daughter of an old pioneer family. To them have been born eleven children, six sons and five daughters. One daughter died in infancy, and Obediah on February 15, 1868, at the age of twelve. All are settled in life, except Daniel, George W., Lilly and Lewis, who live with their parents on the old homestead. Mr. Ferrell is a prominent citizen of Ashland county, and is honored and respected by all who know him.

ROBERT J. SIMANTON was born in Northampton county, Pennsylvania, May 1, 1835, and settled in Montgomery township, in 1851. He remained one year, and then removed to Clearcreek township, where he has since resided. In 1858 he was married to Miss Elizabeth Vannorstrand, daughter of an old pioneer family. They have had three children—Alda, George, and Todd—all of whom are living, but George. He has been a man of energy and thrift, and enjoys the esteem of his neighbors and friends.

ALBERT SHRIVER was born in Ashland county, Ohio, on the old homestead now occupied by his parents, in 1843. On September 3, 1872, he was married to Mary I. Burns, by whom he had five children—Edna D., Alice M., Albert W., William, and an unnamed who died in infancy. Mr. Shriver is one of the thrifty farmers of the county, and resides near the old home farm.

THOMAS BRYTE, son of John and Elizabeth (Ford) Bryte, was born January 28, 1830. In 1855 he went to California, where he engaged in a grape-vine and dairy business, which he followed for sixteen years. Then he returned to Ashland county and purchased the farm known as the old John Eaton homestead, where he still resides. On the southern borders of this farm are evidences of an ancient fort, a description of which is given elsewhere in this work. Mr. Bryte's father was an old pioneer, an extended sketch of whom is found elsewhere.

ALEXANDER CALHOUN was born in Ireland, November 4, 1796. He was married to Margaret Morehead, by whom he had eight children. In 1831 he sailed on the steamer Colossus for America. First he settled in Ashland county, where he purchased a quarter section of land in Orange township, known as the old John Patterson homestead, and resided there until his death, in 1870. Matthew, the elder son, resides in Clearcreek township, and was married June 21, 1848, and had three children. Mr. Calhoun is a prominent farmer and worthy citizen of the township.

BENJAMIN EMMONS was born in 1780, and came to Ohio in the spring of 1812 and settled at Wooster, where he remained two years. Then he removed to Rowsburgh, where he purchased a quarter section of land, which he owned and had possession of until 1817. He then sold out to Michael Rowe, and he and his wife, the spring following, loaded what furniture they had in an old Pennsylvania wagon bed, and started life anew in the woods two miles north of Ashland, on what is now known as the Savannah and Ashland road. While the cabin was building they were obliged to sit around the campfire for a period of six weeks, at night taking shelter in the wagon box. By hard toil he succeeded in clearing up almost every acre of his farm. Upon this farm he resided until his death in 1852. His wife's maiden name was Ann Adams, of Jefferson county, Ohio. They had eight children—Jane, Henry, John, Benjamin and Isaac, twins, born on Christmas day, 1820; Sarah, Ann and Hugh. All are living save Jane, John, Ann and Hugh. Isaac, the only representative of the family living in Clearcreek, was married in 1853 to Susan Harriet Wertman, by whom he has had eight children—Hugh, John, Clara, Abby, George, Harry, Hattie and Jay—all unmarried save Hugh.

JOHN CUPPY was born in the State of Virginia, 1797. In 1816 he made a visit to Ohio, but did not make a permanent settlement until the following fall, when he came to Ashland county, erected for himself a rude log cabin in the woods in Clearcreek township. In 1817 he was married to Malinda Wheeler, of Baltimore, Maryland. They had seven children—Susan, Eleanor, Mary A., Caroline, Edwin, Abraham, and Wesley. Abraham, the only son living, has possession and resides upon the old homestead. October 2, 1860, he was married to Margaret Eaton, by whom he had seven children. Mr. Cuppy is a prominent citizen of Clearcreek township, and a son of one of its pioneers. September 6, 1876, his father died, at the age of seventy-nine years; and his mother died May 1, 1869, at the age of sixty-nine years.

DAVID HART came into Ashland county from Washington county, Pennsylvania, in 1831, and settled in the woods, one mile and three-quarters northwest of Savannah. Immediately after his arrival he set about erecting for himself a cabin. In 1835 he was married to Miss Anna McCorkle. Robert, who is the only living representative of this family living in this State, resides on the old home farm, which he inherited from his father. On September 18, 1861, he was married to Jennie Gault. To them were born four children, all of whom are living, viz.: Mary, Charles, John, and Wylie. Mr. Hart is an extensive wool-grower, and a prominent farmer in this county. David, his brother, was a member of the Twenty-third regiment Ohio volunteer infantry, and died in two months after returning home, from disease contracted in the army.

MOSES COOK PERCIVAL, son of Milton and Hannah Percival, was born in Cuyahoga county, Ohio, moved to Ashland county in the fall of 1850, and settled three miles south of Savannah, on the Olivesburgh road, where he still resides. He has been twice married—first to Mary Wright, by whom he had five children: Hannah, Sophia J., Adeline M., Moses Cook, and J. Milton. Moses Cook died July 19, 1878, after having served about five years in the ministry. Mrs. Percival died June 3, 1857, and, on January 11, 1859, Mr. Percival married Margaret Ann Scott, by whom he has had three children—James Gates, Grace D., and Alice Scott. Mr. Percival is a man of intelligence and a great reader.

WILLIAM J. VERMILYA was born in Delaware county, New York, in the year 1803. January 21, 1829, he was married to Ruth W. Benson, by whom he had nine children: Frances, Emily, Phila, Eliza, Sidney, Elkanah, Chancey, John and Albert. In 1838 he came to Ohio, and settled in Ruggles township, three miles north of Savannah. He died at the age of seventy-six. But two sons survive. John was married January 2, 1868, to Mary Frizzel, and resides near Ashland. In the fall of 1879 he was elected justice of the peace, his father having held the office a number of years before he died.

WILLIAM KIRKTON, in company with his wife and an intimate friend, George McKay, came to America in 1835, bidding farewell to his native Scotland. They sailed in the "Lady of the Lake," which was soon after lost. He settled in Clearcreek township, but afterward removed to Ruggles township, where he purchased eighty acres of land, but sold this soon and bought one hundred and forty acres in Clearcreek township. They have had nine children, six of whom are living. Mr. Kirkton still resides in Savannah, in apparently good health for one of his years, being seventy-six years old.

WILLIAM BURNS, son of David Burns, was born in what is now Ashland county in the year 1821. In the fall of 1849 he was married to Miss Jane McKibben, by whom he had six children: Mary B., Tirzah L., David M., J. Bartlett, Maggie C., and Ida M., all of whom are living but J. Bartlett and Maggie C. Mary married Albert M. Shriver. Tirzah L. married William C. Shriver, and lives in Iowa. David Burns died at the ripe old age of seventy-three years in 1863.

DAVID SHRIVER was born February 25, 1808. In the year 1833 he moved into Ashland county, and settled about three miles southwest of Savannah, where he still resides. January 24, 1833, he was married to Rebecca Scott, by whom he had eight children—George, Elizabeth, Ebenezer, Mary Ann, Albert, William, Harvey W., Silas Elmer.

ELIJAH F. BRYTE, son of John Bryte, who was an early settler of Ashland county, was born in this county, in 1834. In 1862 he was married to Martha Ekey, by whom he has had five children—Elmore S., Thomas T., Ada B., Artie, dead, and one daughter dying in infancy, unnamed. Mr. Bryte lives about four miles southwest of Savannah. He is a prominent farmer and a worthy citizen.

GEORGE BURGETT was born in Germany about the year 1766. He emigrated to America and settled in Washington county, Pennsylvania. Here he married Miss Fannie Rodgers, June 25, 1791, by whom he had nine children, all of whom are deceased but Joseph, Eliza and Susannah. George, the youngest son, came to Ohio in the spring of 1813, and settled in what is now Ashland county, about three miles west of Ashland. At this time but one lone log cabin made up the town of Ashland, or as it was then called Uniontown, and so dense was the forest, they were compelled to cut a way for the teams. He lived but three years after his settlement here, and his wife died seven years later. All the hardships common to pioneer life, they experienced. Joseph is the only living representative of this family now in the county. He was married June 12, 1829, to Ann Rayburn, by whom he had six children—J. R., Fannie, Eliza J., George F., Sally, and Melissa, all of whom are living but Fannie and George. Two of the daughters, Eliza and Sally, married ministers, Melissa married George B. Masters, with whom Mr. Burgett makes his home; he has reached the ripe old age of seventy-nine years, and is in the full possession of his faculties.

WILLIAM GREGG came to Ashland county in 1829; he is a native of Ireland, and was born May 12, 1826. March 15, 1855, he was married to Martha Jane Tenant, by whom he had four children, three of whom are living. March 10, 1862, his wife died. He was married again September 11, 1862, to Martha Graham, by whom he had five children.

D. H. COLEMAN, a native of Northumberland county, Pennsylvania, came through by wagon in the spring of 1839, and settled in Orange township. In the year 1855 he was married, and was the father of six children, four sons and two daughters: Mary D., Margaret A., Joseph S., John, Oscar E. and William. Joseph S. and Margaret A. are deceased. Mr. Coleman is a worthy citizen.

JOHN FERRELL, son of Obediah, was born in Beaver county, Pennsylvania, in 1816. When he was but three months old, his father moved to Ohio and settled in Ashland county, three miles northwest of Ashland, on a farm adjoining Mr. Burgett. They commenced life in a log cabin, he remaining with his parents until the death of his father in 1844; his mother lived three years longer and died in 1847. The subject of this sketch was married in 1850, to Eliza Gries, by whom he had five sons and five daughters. Mr. Ferrell now resides in Clearcreek township, with his family around him, enjoying the reward that energy and industry are sure to bring.

JOHN LEISTENSNIDER emigrated to this country from Germany in the year 1836, and first located at Harrisburgh, Pennsylvania, where he worked at his trade, that of tailoring, until 1839. He was then married to Catharine Schwartz, and at once moved to Lewisburgh, York county, Pennsylvania, where he started in business for himself, which he carried on successfully for thirteen years, and by hard labor and constant toil he accumulated a little fortune of about two thousand and four hundred dollars, which he took with him to Savannah, Ashland county, Ohio, in 1852, and invested it in a farm just west of the village. Here he again opened a merchant tailoring establishment, a business he followed for twenty-one years. He then disposed of his stock and removed to the farm where he now resides. Mr. Leistensnider is the father of ten children: Mary, Henry, Philip, Caroline, Julia, Emma, Martha, Theodore (who died in infancy), one died in infancy, unnamed, and George, who resides on the home farm. Our subject has labored under more than ordinary disadvantages and is entitled to a great deal of credit for the success he has attained. Born of poor parents with but little opportunity for schooling, he has raised himself by dint of hard toil, industry, and good management, from a poor boy with but nine coppers in his pocket when he landed at Baltimore in 1836, to one of the most substantial and leading citizens of Clearcreek township. Although suffering somewhat from the effects of his long continued toil "on the board," he now lives in easy circumstances in one of the pleasantest homes to be found in the county. Mr. Leistensnider is a man of good judgment, independent in thought and action, hospitable and courteous, and highly regarded by his neighbors.

JAMES CHAMBERLAIN was born December 8, 1796, in Pennsylvania, and settled in Ashland county in the year 1823. On June 22, 1826, he was married to Sarah Peterson, who was born December 8, 1806, by whom he had ten children: John, Mary, William, Josiah, Elizabeth J., James, Washington, H. Harrison, Weden, and Abraham. His first purchase of land was made when John Beebout was living. Both were members of the Disciple church. He was one of the party who laid out the old roads that ran from Ashland to Norwalk. He was an industrious man and possessed of a good mind. A. N. Chamberlain, his son, was born in this county October 15, 1846. December 14, 1867, he married Mary Stout, a daughter of one of Ashland's pioneers, by whom he had two children: Tuly J., born January 16, 1869, and Cloah A., born July 14, 1871. He is a farmer of prominence and resides near the old homestead.

JACOB STONER was a native of Pennsylvania, where he was born in the year 1775. He was twice married. In the year 1835 he moved into Ashland county from Pennsylvania. He died in 1856. John, the youngest child by his first wife, was married in Somerset county, Pennsylvania, in 1833, to Judith Miller, by whom he has had eleven children: Jacob, Philip, William, Christian, John, Abraham, Hannah, Elizabeth, Eliza J., Minerva, and Iona Annetta. Four of Mr. Stoner's sons were brave soldiers in the late war: Philip, William, Christian and John. Philip lost an arm at Fort Donelson, and Christian gave up his life at the battle of Winchester. He was supposed to have fallen into the hands of the rebels, and was never heard of. Philip was in the service ten months. William served a little more than four years. He received several slight wounds. John was in sixteen months and was mustered out at the close of the war. Abraham is the resident minister of the Reformed church at Norristown, Pennsylvania. All his children are married but two. He is one of the most substantial and respected farmers in Clearcreek township, and is familiarly known as "Uncle John Stoner."

THE SHIVELY FAMILY were early settlers in Ashland county, and were formerly from Pennsylvania. They settled on the farm where Walton Hafer, a grandson, now lives. They raised but one child, Elizabeth, who married Levi Hafer. She lived with her mother until the latter's death, which occurred January 15, 1880. Susan Shively was born in the year 1803, and was a woman of great energy. She retained the use of her faculties up to the time of her death. The daughter, Elizabeth, was married about the year 1855, and had two children: Walton, born October 16, 1856, and Dora E. who died at the age of three. Mr. and Mrs. Hafer now reside at Shiloh, Richland county, Ohio. Walton, who occupies the old homestead, was married October 24, 1878, to Miss Carrie Beelman, a native of Richland county. She is the mother of one child, Clyde L., born August 30, 1879. She is a member of the Winebrenerian church. Mr. Levi Hafer served two years in the late war, and was a good soldier.

CHRISTOPHER MYKRANTZ was a native of Westmoreland county, Pennsylvania, and was born in the year 1788. At the age of twenty he was married to Catharine Poorman, who was his senior by six days only, and by whom he had three children: Betsey, who was born in 1808, and died April 19, 1880; John, who was born in 1810, and died in 1870; Jacob, who was born December 8, 1819, and is the only living representative of the family. The father made the trip to Ohio in wagons in the year 1822, and settled in Ashland, when he engaged in the hotel business, which he followed for a period of six years, when he purchased the Lawrence farm, a short distance from Ashland, where he resided for thirteen years, when he again returned to Ashland, where he resided until his death, in April, 1872. His wife died three months previous. Jacob married, first, Susan McLaughlin, by whom he had eight children. She died November 26, 1868. On March 1, 1870, he was married to Rachel Minker, by whom he has had one son, George M. Mr. Mykrantz resides in Clearcreek township, three miles northwest of Ashland, and is one of the foremost men of the township.

MICHAEL LEHMANN was born in Germany, near the city of Worms, February 8, 1804. In the year 1829 he was married to Susannah Krehbiel, emigrated to Ohio in 1845, and in the spring of 1846 settled in Ashland county, two miles southwest of Savannah. Jacob, his son, still resides on the old homestead. On August 27, 1863, he was married to Elizabeth Shriver, by whom he has had three children—John A., who was born July 11, 1864; Mary, who was born September 20, 186.; Susannah, who was born February 5, 1871. The father died March 21, 1879; the mother, September 3, 1867. Jacob is one of the most successful farmers in the township, and a prominent citizen.

JOHN CUBBISON, a native of Pennsylvania, was born in the year 1794. On October 25, 1821, he was married to Jeannette Glenn, by whom he had eight children. He came to Ohio in the fall of 1837, and settled two miles northeast of Savannah, and here resided until his death, which occurred March 23, 1852. His wife survived him but three weeks. In this same year John, Alexander and Jeannette died, all within a few days of each other. Mary died in the year 1863; Hugh resides in Kansas; Margaret in Belmont county, Ohio; Sarah in Ruggles township; and Joseph on the old homestead. The latter was married to Margaret Marshall, December 31, 1862, by whom he has had three children. He is a prosperous farmer and a good citizen.

JAMES LAWSON was born in Scotland in the year 1778. He married Margaret E. Lamond, by whom he had seven children. They emigrated to America in 1834, and setted in Savannah, where he resided until the following spring, when he purchased a farm of fifty acres three miles southwest of Savannah, on which he resided until he died in 1861, at the ripe old age of eighty-three. His wife survived him but one year. His son James married Mary A. Gault, June 7, 1876, and still owns and occupies the old homestead. Both are faithful members of the Presbyterian church, and he is one of those sturdy honest Scotchmen, a number of whom reside near Savannah.

L. FRIZZEL was born in the State of Maryland in the year 1815, and came to Ohio prior to the organization of Ashland county, and settled near Olivesburgh, where he remained about two years. When he landed at Olivesburgh he had three one-half dollar pieces in his pocket, and all of his baggage, beside the suit of clothes he wore, tied up in a handkerchief. He removed from Olivesburgh to Savannah, and engaged with an old pioneer by the name of Smith, at fifty cents per day to take charge of and drive his team. When twenty-one years old, his employer started him on a trip to Baltimore with one hundred and sixty bushels of clover and timothy seed. In this venture he was successful, and it was the beginning of a career that has proved to be a successful and prosperous one. He soon after married the daughter of his employer, and has, by industry, perseverance and pluck, amassed a good fortune, and is one of the leading members of the Methodist church, and a prominent man in the township.

MIFFLIN TOWNSHIP.

NEWTON A. HART was born September 2, 1811, and his wife, Elizabeth, was born April 11, 1818. To them have been born fourteen children, as follows: Mary, born December 18, 1836, married Christian Leiter, and lives in Morrow county, Ohio; James, born July 17, 1838, married Lucy Myers, and lives in Ashland; Alfred, born July 17, 1840, married Mary Eighinger, and lives in Ashland; John, born December 22, 1841, and died February 21, 1851; Margaret, born January 1, 1844, married Peter Stutz, and lives in Ashland; Amanda, born December 21, 1845, and died December 25, 1874; Catharine, born January 3, 1848, married Benjamin G. Rahl; Newton A., born December 27, 1849, died February 11, 1850; Barbara, born November 26, 1850; Abram, born January 23, 1853, married Ellen Clark; Irene, born January 26, 1856, married Charles Cook; Elijah, born January 19, 1858; Samuel, born May 13, 1860; and Fian, born September 10, 1863.

HARRISON HOOVER was born in Mifflin township, Ashland county, October 4, 1833, on the farm he now owns, which was entered by his father, Joseph Hoover, who came here in an early day. He is the only living child; there were two other children, one of whom died in infancy, and Daniel W., who was younger, but is now deceased. In 1852 his father died, and his mother died in 1870. Mr. Hoover was married May 20, 1875, to Sarah E. Mourey, who was also born in the same county. They have reared two children, both of whom are living: William Harrison, born March 28, 1877; and Ollie May, born July 7, 1879.

JOSEPH MOUREY was born in Pennsylvania, April 3, 1825. When about three years old, his parents removed to Ohio and located in what is now Ashland county. Mr. Mourey has always lived here. May 16, 1851, he was married to Hester Shull, who was born in Richland county. They have had five children, all living and married: Mary A., who married Robert McCracken; Sarah E., who married Harrison Hoover; Nannie, George McClenan, and Charles Curtis.

JOHN WESLEY VAIL was born in this township, on the Copus farm, September 13, 1849, where he has always resided. He is a grandson of Mrs. Vail, whose father was a Copus, and was killed by the Indians at an early day, as is mentioned elsewhere. He was married September 5, 1871, to Miss Ellen Bochelden; she was born in December, 1849. They have reared a family of two children, both of whom are living. They are Lawrence Wade and Hattie May. Lawrence W. was born October 9, 1872, and Hattie M. was born May 14, 1875.

DANIEL KAUFFMAN was born in Lancaster county, Pennsylvania, June 30, 1810. He is the fifth child of Dr. John and Anna Kauffman, who were also born in Lancaster county, Pennsylvania. His father was born August 22, 1764; his mother, May 28 1768. They resided in Pennsylvania until the year 1827, when they removed to this county and located in Mifflin township, Richland county, a part of this township before Ashland county was formed, where they lived until their deaths. His father died June 16, 1845, aged eighty years nine months and twenty-four days; and his mother died September 7, 1849, aged eighty-one years three months and nine days. Daniel Kauffman came here with his parents and made his home with them until he was married, which was on March 25, 1841, since which time he has resided in this township. He was married to Miss Linda Cronninger, who was born in this township, August 21, 1818. She is the fifth child of Leonard and Elizabeth Cronninger, of whom mention is made elsewhere in this work. The fruits of this union are seven children—Maria M., who was born January 12, 1842, and was married to a Mr. Stephen M. Cole, March 14, 1870; Elizabeth C., born October 23, 1843, and married to Samuel C. Fry, April 21, 1871; Anna B. born February 7, 1847, and married to Milton Charles, September 20, 1866; Sarah D., born January 12, 1853; Alice G., born December 21, 1857, and married to B. B. Hout, October 20, 1878. The ones deceased were John F. and Henry C. John F. departed this life January 4, 1869, aged twenty-three years eleven months and twenty-one days; Henry C. died March 17 1879, aged twenty-four years and twenty-four days. Mr. Kauffman is a millwright by trade, and made that business a specialty for a period of thirty years; but for the past twenty years he has paid all of his attention to farming. Mr. Kauffman's grandfather was also born in Lancaster county, Pennsylvania; his great-grandfather was born in Switzerland, and came to Lancaster county, Pennsylvania, in 1717.

LEVI B. LAMBRIGHT was born in Pennsylvania, January 5, 1810. When a babe his parents removed to this State and located in this township. He was married May 3, 1860, to Miss Sarah Copus, who was born in this county and township, January 10, 1837. They have reared a family of eleven children, ten of whom are living: Mary, born June 15, 1861; Margary, born September 22, 1862; she is married to Adam Miller; Rachel J., born April 5, 1864; William W., born November 5, 1865; Sarah Catharine, born September 19, 1867; Levi Curtis, born October 22, 1872; Harriet N., born August 1, 1873; N. A., born October 16, 1877. Margaret I. was born July 1, 1869, and died August 4, 1870. Mr. Lambright is numbered among the old settlers of his township; has always paid his attention to farming, and now owns one of the best farms in this part of the county. His wife is also identified with the earliest settlers of the county. Mr. Lambright's eyes have been affected for the past fourteen years; he was totally blind for about four months. But since he had them operated upon he can see just enough to get around. Cataract is the trouble.

JAMES W. LEMON was born in Mifflin township, February 16, 1852. He is the second child of John and Harriet Lemon, of whom mention is made elsewhere in this work. He was married February 24, 1874, to Miss Harriet Brubaker. The fruit of this union is one child, named May U. Mr. Lemon has been in the mercantile business since he became of age, and prior to that he clerked for his father together with farming. He is now engaged in the mercantile business at Mifflin.

GEORGE W. MILLIGAN was born in Vermillion township April 30, 1836. For six years he has lived in Mifflin township. In 1861 he was married to Nancy E. Copus, who was born August 17, 1840. They have had five children, all of whom are living: William H., who was born July 10, 1862; Frances Marian, born April 8, 1867; Anna S., born July 3, 1872; Mary A., born March 20, 1874; George B., born September 11, 1878. Mr. Milligan has always farmed from boyhood, and now carries on the farm of his mother-in-law, Mrs. Margerrie Copus, who is identified with the early history of the county.

SAMUEL HECKMAN was born in Stark county, Ohio, April 17, 1840, where he resided until the age of about eight years, when he went to Wayne county to live with his uncle, Jacob Arnold, his parents, Abraham and Mary Heckman, having died prior to his going there; his father died when he was about eighteen months old, and his mother died just previous to his going to live with his uncle. He remained with his uncle until he was fourteen years old, when he went to live with another uncle, named Philip Hoover, in the same county. With him he remained three years, when he went to work for a man by the name of Fulk, and with him went to the State of Illinois. After remaining there six months, he returned to Wayne county, Ohio, staying this time about eighteen months, when he went back to Stark county again, where he remained about seven months, when he came to Ashland county and located in Mifflin township, where he has since resided. February 27, 1862, he was married to Catharine Brubaker, who was born on the farm Mr. Heckman now owns, October 15, 1838. She is the only living daughter of John and Catharine Brubaker, of whom mention is made elsewhere in this work. The fruits of this union are two children. One is living—Lester, who was born March 30, 1867; the one deceased was Franklin, who was born March 11, 1865, and died July 17, 1865, aged four months and six days. Mr. Heckman has never turned his attention to political matters, although he has served his township as trustee.

DAVID S. BENNIGHOF was born in Mifflin township, this county, March 22, 1856. By occupation he is a school teacher; and he also carries on a farm. He is the seventh child of Jacob and Mary L. Bennighof, who came to this county about forty-four years ago. They came from the old country in 1832 and located in Wayne county, then came to this county. Mr. Bennighof's father died April 2, 1877, aged seventy-two years and some months. His mother is still living. There were eight children in the family—John, Jacob, Elizabeth, Lucilla, Charlotte, Peter, David and Benjamin, who are all living. Only two are living at home—David and Benjamin.

LEWIS P. YEATER was born in Mifflin county, Pennsylvania, November 29, 1838, where he resided until 1854, when his parents removed to this county and located in Mifflin township. October 19, 1865, he was married to Miss Amelia Wertsbaugh, who was also born in Pennsylvania, twelve miles from Chambersburgh, in Cumberland county. The fruits of this union are five children, four of whom are living: William P., who was born November 27, 1867; Henry A., born August 26, 1873; Maud, born March 30, 1876; Mary, born October 1, 1878. The name of the one that died was Norma A.—departed this life October 22, 1874, aged four years, five months and thirteen days.

EDWIN PARKES was born in England, December 25, 1835, where he resided until he was twenty-seven years old, when he came to this country and located in Cincinnati, where he remained one year, and then went to Louisville, Kentucky, and remained there a short time, when he removed to Mt. Vernon, and from there to Mansfield, where he remained fifteen years, when he came to this county and located in Mifflin township, where he has charge of and runs a tannery. He also owns a tannery in Mansfield, and has run that for a period of fifteen years, the tanner and currier business being his trade. On August 10, 1857, he was married to Mary Ann Borham. She was born October 1, 1834. The fruits of this union are eleven children: Julia N., who was born in England, May 15, 1858; Emily M., who was born October 5, 1859; George P., who was born April 13, 1861; Edwin J., who was born February 13, 1863; Frank, who was born October 24, 1865; Harry, who was born December 25, 1867; John William, who was born October 19, 1869; Howard, who was born October 14, 1872; Edna R., who was born April 12, 1874; Arthur L., who was born September 8, 1876; and Walter L., who was born December 2, 1878. The first four named were born in England, six were born in Richland county, and one in this county. Mr. Parkes has never paid much of his attention to political matters, although he claims to support the Democracy.

JOHN LUTZ was born in Lancaster county, Pennsylvania, January 18, 1836, where he resided until the age of fourteen years, when his parents removed to this county and located in Milton township. He lived there ten years, when he was married and returned to Richland county, where he lived three years when he removed back to this county, and located in this township (Mifflin), where he has since resided. He was married November 10, 1860, to Eliza Keever, who was born in this county June 26, 1839. They have had three children. Henry, who was born November 25, 1861; Amanda, J., born September 4, 1863; and Alice C., born July 21, 1871.

MRS. NANCY J. PETTERSON is the widow of the late J. A. Petterson, who was born in Vermillion township, this county, June 19, 1846. He died March 27, 1878. Mrs. Petterson was born in Allegheny county, Pennsylvania, April 1, 1848, where she resided until the age of nine years, when her parents removed to this county. She was married April 5, 1868. The fruits of this union are six children. John F., born June 4, 1869; Nettie M., born March 29, 1872; Almira, born June 1, 1874; Grace A., born April 6, 1878. The ones deceased were Lester, who died in March, aged about three months; and the other, one who died in infancy.

ENOCH COUN was born in Mifflin township September 11, 1849, where he has always lived, with the exception of seven years when he resided in Mifflin township, Richland county. October 17, 1871, he was married to Sarah Eby, who was born in Mifflin township, Richland county, September 21, 1849. The fruits of this union are four children, three of whom are living: William Curtis, who was born October 9, 1872; Byron O., who was born July 15, 1874; Amos L., who was born July 3, 1879. The one deceased was named Allen G. Thurman, and was born July 1, 1876. His death was caused by his clothing catching fire, burning him so badly that he only lived from Tuesday until Thursday; he died April 8, 1880. Our subject, Mr. Coun, has run a threshing machine for the last seventeen years. When not in the season for threshing, he pays his attention to the carpenter trade.

JACOB S. BLACK was born in Ashland county, May 27, 1834. In the late war, he was a member of company B, Forty-eighth Illinois volunteer infantry; he enlisted September 2, 1861, and participated in all the battles the regiment engaged in, until he received an injury at the battle of Fort Donelson, Tennessee, February 15, 1862. Soon after, he was honorably discharged on accounts of wounds received, which disabled him from performing duty as a soldier. He is the second child and only son of James and Nancy Black, who came to this county at an early date. His mother has lived here since 1830. His father came here about 1804. He came from Maryland when about two years old. He is among the early settlers, as mention is made elsewhere. He died October 12, 1835. His widow survives him. Jacob S. was married July 9, 1867, to Miss Agnes Hogarth, who was born in Edinburgh, Scotland, April 1, 1858. She was only two years old when she came to this country. She has resided in this township eleven years, coming from Illinois here with her husband. The fruits of this union are five children: James C., who was born June 4, 1868; Benjamin William, born July 9, 1870; Homer A., born September 22, 1872; Edward Jacob, February 24, 1874; Thomas Ross, born August 17, 1876. Mr. Black is a shoemaker by trade, and is constable of his township.

ISAAC H. MATTHEWS was born in Vermillion township, this county, February 18, 1853, where he resided until the eighth year of his age, when his parents removed to Jeromeville, where they resided four years. Mr. Matthews was married March 24, 1875, to Miss Harriet Barr, who was born in Mifflin township, Richland county, where she resided until she was married. She was born January 8, 1858. The fruits of this union are two children, Ira O. and an infant. Mr. Matthews is constable of his township. He carries on all kinds of blacksmithing in all its branches, having worked at that trade since he was a small boy.

JOHN SCOTT was born in Columbiana county, Ohio, July, 6, 1817, where he resided until the age of seventeen years, at which time his parents removed to this county an located in Vermillion township. Mr. Scott has always lived in the county, with the exception of two years spent in Hancock county. He has lived in this township twenty-three years. Andrew Scott, his father, was born in Washington county, Pennsylvania, in 1769. His mother was born in Allegheny county, Pennsylvania, in 1785. They reared a family of twelve children, all of whom lived to maturity. Their names were: Margaret, Elizabeth, Jane, Sarah, Mary, John, Duncan, Andrew, Joseph P., Alexander, David, and Jason. All are living but Elizabeth, Sarah, and Duncan, and all are married but Jason. John is the sixth child, and was married April 25, 1837, to Miss Julia Ann Arnold, who was born in Vermillion township. The fruits of this union are twelve children, ten of whom are living: Catharine A., who was born May 24, 1842; John F., who was born March 6, 1844; Harriet Jane, who was born December 22, 1845; Calista C., who was born October 25, 1847; Julia I., who was born March 12, 1850; Mary Amanda, who was born April 7, 1852; Joseph P., who was born January 19, 1857; James R., who was born January 7, 1860; Ann E., who was born November 16, 1862; and Arizona, who was born October 5, 1868. All are married but three—Joseph P., James R., and Arizona. One child died in infancy, and Andrew departed this life July 2, 1841, aged fifteen months. Mr. Scott is a farmer. He run a threshing-machine for twenty-eight years in succession, and from time to time since, but, for the past six years he has paid all his attention to his farm and stock. Arizona, the youngest, is the only child living at home.

PETER ZEHNER was born in Mifflin township, this county, October 29, 1836, and was married January 24, 1861, to Hannah Boyer, who was born in Butler county, Pennsylvania, March 15, 1839. When six months old her parents removed to this county, since which time she has resided here. The fruits of this union were eleven children, nine of whom are still living: John I., who was born February 1, 1862; Sarah Ann, who was born June 23, 1863; William H., who was born September 20, 1864; F. and G. Nety, who was born October 12, 1866; Leah, who was born February 12, 1868; Joseph, who was born March 7, 1870; Hannah S., who was born November 9, 1871; Malinda, who was born April 17, 1876; and Peter, born December 14, 1877. Those deceased are: Leonora, who died September 7, 1875, aged about twenty months; and Caroline, who died February 20, 1880, aged three months. Mr. Zehner is a carpenter and contractor, to which business he pays all his attention, his sons carrying on the farm. In connection with his carpentering business, which he has followed for over twenty years, he has carried on the undertaking business for the past five years.

JOHN K. AMEND was born in Lancaster county, Pennsylvania, August 15, 1837. In 1843 his parents removed to this township. He is the fourth child of John and Elizabeth Amend. There were six children, as follows: Nancy and Frances, who were twins; Jacob and John K., our subject, also twins; Louis and Isaac; one named Leah died while in Pennsylvania; all the others are still living, and all are married. Mr. Amend's father departed this life December 13, 1863, aged sixty years, five months and seventeen days. His mother died June 14, 1870, aged sixty-seven years, five months and ten days. He was married October 10, 1871, to Miss Lovina Stoner, who was born August 21, 1845, in Richland county, where she resided until the age of twelve years, when her parents removed to Williams county, this State. They remained there until she was twenty-three years old, when she came back to Richland county, where she remained until she was married. The fruits of this union are five children, named respectively Allen O., who was born September 18, 1871; Amanda M., born June 9, 1873; Celia M., born September 18, 1875; Lorella J., born April 30, 1877; and William A., born May 10, 1879. Mr. Amend is by occupation a school teacher, as well as a carpenter and farmer, but has turned all of his attention to his farm for the past fourteen years. He now owns a good productive farm of one hundred and twenty acres in this township. He served his township as clerk one term.

GOTLIEB KOCH was born in Wayne county, this State, December 15, 1823, where he resided until the age of ten years, when his parents removed to this county, and located in Mifflin township, where our subject lived until he was twenty-three years old, when he went to the State of Indiana. He remained there twenty-nine years, when he came back to this township, where he has since resided. He is the oldest child of John and Barbara Koch, who came to this county at an early day. His father died in March, 1871. His mother died in December, 1825 or 1826. Our subject, Gotlieb, was married December 13, 1846, to Miss C. Hault. They have reared a family of fifteen children, ten of whom are living, and named: Christian, born February 3, 1848; George W., born September 18, 1852; Josiah, born January 23, 1854; Mary J., born January 11, 1856; Louisa, born August 31, 1857; Martin Luther, born September 15, 1861; Amanda, born May 27, 1864; Isaiah, born October 31, 1866; Simon R., born February 2, 1869; Lida Ann, born March 17, 1871. Those who are dead were Joseph, born August 12, 1849, and died September 21, 1849; John, born April 30, 1851, and died October 3, 1851; Levi, born April 15, 1859, and died December, 1874; Barbara, born March 7, 1860, and died October 9, 1860; and Rosa Ann died when about six weeks old. Mrs. Koch was born in Germany, August 29, 1827. She came to this country at the age of five years. Mr. Koch has paid his attention to farming from boyhood, which vocation he still follows, and now owns one of the best productive farms in his township, containing three hundred and twenty-six acres.

NICHOLAS MATTHEWS was born in Milton township, this county, November 3, 1833, and this county has always been his home. He was married March 24, 1852, to Miss Angeline Sigler. She died March 24, 1874, aged forty years. The fruits of this union were eight children, all of whom are living; Isaac H., Mary S., Isabel, Clara, Elseya, Charles M., Benjamin H., and Jennie. Mr. Matthews is a blacksmith by trade, and is proprietor of his shop in this place; he has carried on this business since 1850.

JOHN BAKER was born in Cumberland county, Pennsylvania, September 2, 1830; when about seven years of age his parents removed to this State and located in Wayne county, where they remained about eighteen months, when they came to this county. He was married April 18, 1852, to Margaret Conn, who was born in the township December 9, 1832. The fruits of this union are ten children, eight of whom are still living. They are Elizabeth, who was born July 16, 1852; Lorenda, born May 6, 1854; Flora, born December 27, 1855; Samuel S., born August 10, 1858; John D., born July 16, 1862; Sherman G., born September 2, 1866; Robert G., born August 28, 1868; and Semildia, born August 9, 1873. The ones deceased were Tula B., born in May, 1868, and died when about seventeen months old; and Alfreta, who died in March, 1861, aged five weeks. Mr. Baker is by trade a blacksmith. He now carries on a shop in this place, and has his share of public patronage.

GEORGE CONN was born in Washignton county, Maryland, August 13, 1823. When at the age of seven years his parents, Samuel and Elizabeth Conn, removed to this county and located in Mifflin township, where our subject has since resided. His father died in 1833, three years after he came here; his mother survived him, and died November 19, 1879, aged eighty years eight months and seventeen days. Mr. Conn is the seventh of eleven children. He was married May 31, 1848, to Miss Phebe Sunday. They have reared a family of eight children, one of whom died in infancy. Seven are living, as follows: Enoch, born September 11, 1849; Susan, born April 22, 1852; Mollie Ann, born October 22, 1855; Belinda, born June 10, 1858; John, born November 30, 1861; Morris, born February 10, 1866; Emma L., born February 4, 1870. Mr. Conn has seven grandchildren living. One of his grandchildren, a little boy, named Allen Thurman Conn, while playing with a bonfire was burned so badly that he died April 8, 1880. Mr. Conn has always paid his attention to farming.

JACOB STAMAN, SR., was born November 5, 1812, in Lancaster, Pennsylvania, and in 1824 came with his father to Mifflin township. He died in 1866 on the old farm, near what is known as Staman's mill, aged about fifty-three years. He left four sons, William, Abraham, Curtis J., Francis L., and five daughters, Anny, Mary M., Fanny B., Harriet E., and Elizabeth H. The sons are all married but one, Francis L., and all the daughters but Elizabeth H. Mrs. Fanny Staman, formerly Miss Fanny Lantz, married Mr. Laman in 1842, in Richland county.

WILLIAM A. BACHELDER was born in Mifflin township, this county, November 22, 1855, and has always lived in the township. During life he has paid the most of his attention to hunting and trapping, together with farming; but, for the past few years, he has turned all of his attention to the timber business. Now he is general dealer in all kinds of timber, such as walnut, cherry and oak.

JOHN LEMON was born in Paisley, Scotland, May 8, 1803, and came to Philadelphia in 1816, and worked in the factories and attended the first two power looms ever used in that city, two years. From thence he came across the mountains in 1818, and located one mile west of the present site of Hayesville. It was then called Hayes' cross-roads. In 1839 he located in Mifflin township. William Lemon, his brother, had been doing business with John Scott prior to that time. In coming across the mountains he remembers that he met a man on horseback going east to purchase goods. Mr. Lemon ate dinner with him. McClenchy was his name, and he was doing business at Mansfield, Ohio. Mr. Lemon has been in the mercantile business since 1840, and has sold goods with the late John Scott in Hayesville seven years, from 1855 to 1862. Twice he has been married; the first time to Jennie Stewart, who died about 1843, and to Harriet Keffer in 1858. By the first wife his children were one daughter, Mrs. Dr. Yocum, now dead; and four sons by his second wife—William W., James W., John R. and Henry F., all living. Mr. Lemon by close application and upright dealing has acquired a good property. He is now in the mercantile business in Mifflin.

ROBISON KEFFER was born November 12, 1804, in Dauphin county, Pennsylvania, and came to Ashland April 18, 1834, where he worked at the trade of boot and shoe making about fifteen years. About 1857 he commenced keeping tavern in Mifflin, and in 1865 to 1868 kept store and gave up the hotel in 1874. About 1878 he returned to his present residence, and a son engaged in the hotel business. In 1820 he was married to Sarah Dyer, by whom he had seven children—three boys and four girls (and two who died), all grown and married. Mr. Keffer is not now engaged in regular business. He possesses good health and seems to have a good memory. He has had much experience as a hotel keeper, and made many acquaintances.

WILLIAM J. WILSON, JR., was born in Vermillion township, this county, June 4, 1852, where he resided until the age of twenty-three years, when he came to Mifflin township, where he has since resided. He was married July 5, 1875, to Margaret Jarvis. She died sixteen months after marriage. His second and present wife was Miss Rebecca Agnes Boon. They were married July 31, 1877. The fruit of this union is one child, whose name is Eva May. She was born December 17, 1879, and is still living. Mr. Wilson has followed farming from boyhood, and expects to make that his vocation in the future. He now carries on the farm owned by his father.

SAMUEL MOORE, SR., was born in Lancaster county, Pennsylvania, July 15, 1806. He resided in Pennsylvania until the year 1834, when he came to this State and located in this county and township. It was then Richland county. He was married in May, 1827, to Miss Rebecca Dissinger. The fruits of this union are eleven children, ten of whom are still living, and named Mary, Moses B., Amanda, John H., Lucy, Joseph, Samuel, Catharine, Elizabeth, and William C. The one deceased, Rebecca, died February 19, 1874, aged twenty-eight years and some months. All the children are married, and all but four born in the county. Mary, Moses B., Amanda, and John H. Mary was married to John Burke; Moses, to Miss Mary Hunter; Amanda, to Henry Burke; John H., to Mary Reding; Lucy, to Joseph Miller; Joseph, to Sarah Hershy; Samuel, to Mary E. Ohl; Catharine, to Martin Kagey; Elizabeth, to George Buchanan; William C., to Bessie Morgan; Rebecca, to Samuel Rollen. Mr. Moore has thirty-three grandchildren living, besides nine who are dead, and has five great-grandchildren now living. He always paid his attention to farming, but of late years he has lived a retired life. His son, Samuel, jr., carries on the farm, and has for the past ten years.

DAVID WERTMAN was born in Mifflin township, this county, on the old Squire Doty farm, December 5, 1831, where he resided until the year 1869, when he removed to this township. He was married December 15, 1853, to Miss Rachel Garver, who was also born in Mifflin township April 22, 1832. The fruits of this union are nine children, eight of whom are still living, as follows: Agnes, who was born January 21, 1855; Josiah F., born April 17, 1857; John W., born March 30, 1859; Oscar A., born April 19, 1861; Anice C., born February 21, 1864; Leah, born March 29, 1866; Jennie, born June 25, 1869; George, born November 5, 1873; Nora, born March 9, 1875. John W. departed this life December 16, 1863, aged four years eight months and seventeen days. Agnes and Josiah F. are married; Agnes to Frank Vantelburg, and Josiah to Elizabeth Stofer. Agnes has two children, named Arthur and Olive E. Josiah has one child, a babe. Mr. Wertman is by trade a carpenter, and followed that vocation until the late war broke out; but since that time he has paid all of his attention to farming, which he still follows. He never meddled much in political matters, but always cast his vote for the Democracy; and has served his township as trustee for three terms.

BENJAMIN BRUBAKER was born in Milton township, this county, June 10, 1835, where he resided until the year 1864, when he removed to Vermillion township, where he lived one year. From thence he removed back to Milton township, remaining four years, when he came to this township, where he has since resided. He was married, March 17, 1859, to Lydia Roland, who was also born in the county. They have reared a family of seven children, four of whom are still living, as follows: Daniel, Annie, Reuben, and Mary E. Those who died were Sarah, Samuel, and Almira. Mr. Brubaker is the sixth child of Peter and Mary Brubaker, of whom mention is made elsewhere in this work.

JOHN W. WHISLER was born in Jackson township, this county, February 1, 1853, where he resided until the age of ten years, when his parents removed to Milton township. From thence they removed to Mifflin township in 1873, where Mr. Whisler has since resided. He is by profession a school teacher, but of late years, having been superintendent of the Louisville school, his health has failed him and he had to resign his charge, since which time he has paid his attention to farming, but expects to resume his profession. He was married, March 29, 1877, to Miss Martha E. Baker. To them has been born one child, Orson L.

DILLMAN SWITZER was born in Somerset county, Pennsylvania, April 1, 1827. When at the age of two years, his parents removed to Wayne county, this State, where he resided until the year 1848, when he removed to this county, and has since resided here, with the exception of four years, when he resided in Medina county, Ohio. He is by profession a school teacher and a carpenter, and has followed both as his vocation for the past twenty-five years, and prior to that time he worked at farming. He was married August 1, 1849, to a Miss Mary Davis. They have reared a family of nine children, seven of whom are still living, and named respectively, John D., Susan F., Rufie A., George H., Hannah M., Fannie, and Adam A. The ones deceased were Amos D. and Howard S.

MARTIN KAGEY was born in Shenandoah county, Virginia, on December 14, 1801; emigrated to Mifflin township, then in Richland county, in 1825, and located on his farm in 1827. He married Nancy Charles in 1828. He has resided on his farm ever since. Mrs. Kagey died in March, 1869, aged seventy years. His family consists of five boys and two girls: John, Christian, Daniel (died in army, 1863), Martin, and Henry; Mary, wife of John Landis, and Annie, single.

SAMUEL KAGEY was born in this township, December 24, 1835, and has always resided in the township. March 10, 1859, he was married to a Miss Ester Croninger, who was also born in this township August 1, 1833. The fruits of this union are eight children, all of whom are still living, and named, respectively, Martha Ann, Mary, Daniel, Austin, Flora C., William A., Ester, Elizabeth, and Martin B. Mr. Kagey is the fifth child of Martin and Nancy Kagey, of whom mention is made elsewhere in this work. Mr. Kagey has, by economy and industry, made for himself and family a good home.

CHRISTIAN KAGEY was born in this township, October 24, 1833, and has always lived in the township. March 26, 1857, he was married to a Miss Hannah Ballich, who was born in Richland county, August 13, 1837. They have reared a family of eight children, six of whom are still living, and named, respectively: Rufus L., born December 21, 1857; Sarah Ann, born July 29, 1859, Harriet J., born May 18, 1862; Mary B., born November 5, 1863; Jacob E., born August 15, 1866; and Olla M., born April 13, 1873. The ones deceased are Jennie, who died January 29, 1873, aged three years, eleven months and twenty-four days; and one who died in infancy. Mr. Kagey has always paid his attention to farming, which vocation he still follows. To political matters he never paid much attention, although he has represented his township as trustee for several terms, as well as assessor, and is land appraiser for this year. He is the fourth child of Martin and Nancy Kagey, who settled in the county in 1827, and who is mentioned elsewhere. By industry and good management he has made for himself and family a good home.

JOSEPH ZEHNER was born in Richland county, July 4, 1833. When a babe his parents removed to Ashland county, and settled in Mifflin township. He is the tenth child of Samuel and Christiana Zehner. His father died in 1854, aged sixty-seven years. His mother died in 1867, aged about sixty years. He has always lived in the county, with the exception of about eleven years he spent in California and Nevada territory. He was married, January 9, 1872, to Miss Annie Apple, in this county. The fruits of this union are four children, named respectively: David, who was born December 9, 1873; Minnie, born December 7, 1874; Irene, born January 5, 1876, and Bertha, born January 19, 1879. Mr. Zehner has always paid his attention to farming, with the exception of the time he spent in the west, at which place he turned his attention to speculating and mining. He now owns a good farm and intends to make that and the raising of stock his future business. He is comfortably situated in regard to this world's goods, and together with his family, are respected by all who know them.

WILLIAM LATIMER was born in Stark county, this State, April 8, 1815. He is the youngest child of James and Elizabeth Latimer, who came here when our subject was ten years old, in April 1825, and settled on the farm he now owns, and where he has since resided. His father departed this life about thirty years ago; his mother about twenty years ago. Mr. Latimer was married in January, 1839, to Miss Sarah Nutter, who was born in Virginia, January 18, 1815; her parents came to this State at an early day, and located in Richland county, and she lived there until her marriage with Mr. Latimer. The fruits of this marriage are nine children; two are dead. The oldest, James, died while in the late war, aged about twenty years; and Sarah died June 5, 1850, aged three years nine months and five days. Seven are still living, named: Elizabeth, who was born March 16, 1842; Nancy Jane, who was born September 8, 1843; Harriet, who was born December 3, 1844; John, who was born December 4, 1845; William St. Clair, who was born April 13, 1851; Martha Amanda, who was born January 1, 1853; and Zachariah, who was born January 20, 1857. He has nine grandchildren. Mr. Latimer has always paid his attention to farming, and he has, by industry and economy, saved a good home, and enjoys the respect and esteem of all in the community where he resides.

JOSEPH MILLER was born in Union county, Pennsylvania, November 11, 1828, where he resided until the year 1841, when his parents, Jacob and Catharine Miller, removed to Clarion county, Pennsylvania, in the northwestern part of the State, where they remained two years. From thence they removed to Wayne county, this State, where they remained one year, and then they removed to Ashland county, where our subject has since resided. November 24, 1859, he was married to Lucy Ann Moore, who was born in this county, where she has always lived. Samuel Moore, her father, is one of the oldest surviving settlers in the county. The fruits of this union are two children, both of whom are still living, and named Catharine J., who was born July 24, 1861, and Rebecca E., who was born March 18, 1871. Mr. Miller is by trade a carpenter as well as a cooper, and has always followed both of those vocations from boyhood first; the cooper trade, and later he paid his attention to the carpenter trade until the past year, since which time he has been farming. For a period of thirty-six years he has lived in this county, and is considered by all who know him to be an upright citizen and neighbor.

C. F. ENGLE was born in Nassau, Germany, March 11, 1841, and at the age of seven years his parents removed to this country and settled in New York city, where they remained one year, when they came to this State and located in Vermillion township, this county, where our subject remained until the year 1861, when he removed to Mifflin township, where he has since resided, with the exception of the time he spent in the late war. Mr. Engle followed farming as his vocation previous to the war, but since that time he has been engaged in the mercantile business at this place. He is also postmaster, and has been since 1875. He was married July 28, 1867, to Miss Mary Hart. They have reared a family of three children, two of whom are still living, and named respectively, Walter M. and Emma. The one deceased, Charles H., departed this life July 21, 1871, aged one year, two months and eleven days.

ABRAHAM BARR was born in Richland county, this State, August 13, 1845, where he resided until the year 1861, when he removed to this township, where he has since lived. He has been twice married; first, June 21, 1855, to Carlina Baum. She died March 2, 1873. He was married to his second wife, Miss Martha A. Gochnauer, March 18, 1880. She was born in Wayne county, December 9, 1841. Mr. Barr has one child, Benjamin F. He has always paid his attention to farming, which avocation he still follows on the farm he now owns in Mifflin township.

J. F. BENNIGHOF was born in Germany, February 27, 1830. When at the age of seven years, his parents, John and Charlotte Bennighof, emigrated to this country, and located in Vermillion township, where they lived three years. They then removed to Mifflin township, where the subject of this sketch has since resided. He was married, January 8, 1856, to Miss Susan Young, who was born in Huntingdon county, Pennsylvania, January 8, 1829. Her parents removed to this county in 1836, and she has since lived in the county. The fruit of this union are eight children, six of whom are still living, and named respectively, John D., born April 30, 1858; Mary C., born November 15, 1859; Susannah, born December 4, 1861; Hannah, born August 5, 1863; Allen J., born March 18, 1865, and William H., born December 11, 1868. The ones deceased are Jacob and one who died in infancy. Jacob died December 18, 1870, aged four years and three days. Mr. Bennighof is by trade a carpenter and a painter, and has followed those avocations, principally the carpenter trade, from his boyhood. Politically he is a Democrat, and has represented his township as justice of the peace for nine years, and has been a member of the board of education for twenty-five years, being its presiding officer twenty-three years. He has helped build every schoolhouse in the township. By good management and industry he has made for himself a good home, and is considered by all who know him, to be a gentleman whose character cannot be impeached.

SAMUEL CULLER was born in Frederick county, Maryland, in the village of Jefferson, November 26, 1809. When at the age of fifteen years, his parents removed to this county and township, where Mr. Culler has since lived. He is the oldest child of Philip and Mary Culler. His father died in 1855, and his mother in 1845, on the farm in the southeast quarter of section thirty-six, where they settled one month after they came here. Samuel was married March 22, 1849, to Sarah A. Blust. The fruit of this union are twelve children, all of whom are living, as follows: Philip M., who was married March 11, 1880—he was born June 13, 1810; Henry D., born September 17, 1851, who is now practicing law in Mansfield, Ohio, he being attorney for Aultman, Taylor & Co; Margaret L., born July 24, 1853; William H., born August 7, 1855; John F., born December 23, 1856; Mary S., born September 27, 1858; Sarah A., born June 3, 1860; Thomas J., born August 8, 1861; Laura E., born May 23, 1863; Almira V., born April 25, 1865; Samuel S., born April 4, 1867; and Joseph E., born April 6, 1872. Mr. Culler is among the early settlers of this county, and is identified with the Seymour, or more properly the Zimmer and Culler families of the township. He relates many incidents pertaining to pioneer life that are not only interesting but instructive to any one who may be fortunate to hear him. He remembers at one time when a boy his father sent him to Sandusky City with some grain to buy salt and other things for family use. His father gave him all the money they had, which was ten cents. He went to Sandusky alone, and came back without spending the money. He also recalls many hardships and privations that at that time all had to endure, that the present as well as the future generations will never know or experience. His great-grandfather on his mother's side was in the war of the Revolution, and was commissioned by General Washington as captain. His great-grandfather on his father's side was in the war at the time Braddock was defeated by the French and Indians at Bloody Run, Pennsylvania, as well as in the Revolutionary war. His grandfather was born in this country, and several of his sons participated in the war of 1812. His uncle Henry held a commission as second lieutenant at first, and when discharged was first lieutenant. Samuel Culler is what is termed a self-made man, never having had the advantages of a common school education. But to-day he is justice of the peace, and has held that office from time to time for nearly twenty-one years, as well as various other offices of trust in his township. He votes the Republican ticket, and his township is Democratic fully three to one.

SEBASTIAN CULLER, is the eighth child of Michael and Barbara Culler, who was born in Mifflin township, May 6, 1833, and has always resided there, on the old homestead farm. He has always followed farming from boyhood, and now owns the farm his father bought of Philip Zimmer, which contains one hundred and sixty acres. The deed for the land was signed by Philip Zimmer. Michael Culler died July 28, 1874, aged eighty-six years. His wife died July 16, 1873, aged seventy-nine years.

JOHN P. CULLER was born on the Seymour farm, or what is better known as the Zimmer farm, in this township, in the house in which Zimmer was killed, July 3, 1820, and Mifflin township has always been his home. He is the first child of Michael and Barbara Culler, of whom mention is made elsewhere in this work. Mr. Culler was married February 22, 1865, to Amanda Keffer, who was born in this township July 29, 1842. Her father and mother came to this county at an early day, as is mentioned elsewhere. Her parents, together with Mr. Culler's parents, were among the earliest settlers of the county, and have a very prominent part in this work. Mr. Culler has always farmed it from boyhood, and now makes that his vocation.

JOHN SUNDAY was born in York county, Pennsylvania, September 29, 1797, and came to Mifflin township, Richland county, in the fall of 1818. He was married to Miss Leah Gardner, November 7, 1822. She was the daughter of William Gardner, who was a justice of the peace for Mifflin twenty-one years, and died in June, 1855, aged seventy-nine years. Mr. Gardner settled in Mifflin township in April, 1810, but again returned to Fairfield county, Ohio, having sold his farm to Andrew Newman in 1812. He then purchased what is now known as the Simpson farm, in 1812, upon his return from Fairfield county, upon which there were some improvements. Mrs. Gardner baked bread for Martin Ruffner during the summer of 1812. Ruffner had built a cabin and was clearing his land, aided by a bound boy named Levi Berkinhizer, and doing his own cooking, keeping a sort of bachelor's hall, Mrs. Gardner doing his baking, as before stated. His wife came on a short time before Hull's surrender; but she returned soon to friends near Utica, Licking county. Mrs. Sunday knew young Berkinhizer quite well, and often played and romped with him. Martin Ruffner was a stout, broad-chested man, and perfectly fearless. Young Berkinhizer brought word from Zimmers of the prowling Indians, and Ruffner immediately went to the relief of Zimmers, not expecting to bring on a fight, believing that the Greentown Indians were his friends. Berkinhizer remained in the cabin all night alone. Ruffner and the old gentleman, the old lady and Catharine Zimmer, were all found dead the next day, and only conjecture told the story of their fate. They were buried in two graves not a great ways from the cabin of Zimmer. Frederick Zimmer and wife returned to Licking county almost crazed by the murders, when he committed suicide, by shooting himself. Philip Zimmer, and his wife Elizabeth, subsequently quit-claimed their land to Michael Culler, who had purchased the old farm. Levi Berkinhizer, if still alive, resides about one mile from Norwalk, Huron county, where he located after the war. William Gardner was present at the burial of the Zimmers and Martin Ruffner. Mrs. Sunday was born April 25, 1804, in Fairfield county, and has been in Mifflin nearly seventy-six years. Her memory is quite good, and the old lady may reach eighty-five years of age. Her venerable husband is now eighty-three, and seems quite active and sprightly. They have several grown sons and daughters, some of whom are married. They possess a good property and will not want in the future. John and Leah Sunday have raised a family of seven children, five of whom are still living. They are Mary, Phebe, Joseph, Harrison A., and Leah. William and Belinda died in infancy.

JOSEPH SUNDAY was born in Mifflin township, September 25, 1830, where he has always resided. November 13, 1853, he was married to Miss Margaret Zeitler, who was born in Germany, near the river Rhine, February 24, 1834. The fruits of this union are four children, three of whom are living, as follows: Samantha E., who was born August 5, 1854, and married William C. Winters September 29, 1875; Lizzie, who was born September 2, 1860; Celina, who was born October 20, 1862. The other died in infancy. Mr. Sunday has always paid his attention to farming. He is the fourth child of John and Leah, of whom mention is made elsewhere, they being among the early settlers of the county.

ANDREW SUNDAY was born in Mifflin township, July 11, 1835, and has always resided here. By trade he is a carpenter, and follows that as his vocation. March 14, 1858, he was married to Miss Ida M. Edwards. The fruits of this union are nine children, five of whom are living, as follows: Mary H., Susan I., Annie, Wade H., and Margaret A. The ones deceased were Ella, Cyrus, and Nettie, and one that died in infancy.

JAMES FRANKLIN BUSH was born in Bucyrus, Crawford county, Ohio, February 27, 1845, where he resided until he was nineteen years old. When at the age of sixteen, he commenced working at the trade of carriage painting, at which he remained about three years, when he removed to Tiffin, Ohio. In Tiffin he remained about two years, and from that time until 1875 he has been doing business in different places throughout the State. Since 1875 he has been carrying on business in Ashland. During the late war, Mr. Bush enlisted as a member of the One Hundred and First Ohio volunteer infantry, but, owing to his youth, he was rejected. October 17, 1867, he was married to Miss Rosa E. Swineford, who was born in this county, October 15, 1850.

The fruits of this union are five children, three of whom are still living, and named, respectively, Clarence F., who was born November 25, 1869; George O., born August 31, 1874; and Zoa, born May 7, 1879. The ones deceased are Ida, who departed this life October 27, 1878, aged six years, eleven months and thirteen days; and Field, who died October 23, 1878, aged two years. Mr. Bush is now engaged in the manufacturing of carriages and buggies; and he also makes carriage and sign painting a specialty. He is considered proficient at his business, and aims to please every one, and with good success.

PERRY TOWNSHIP.

S. P. COUNTRYMAN, second son of Christian and Barbara Countryman, was born in Perry township, Ashland county, Ohio, in the year 1847. He resided with his parents until the time of his marriage, in 1871, to Miss Selina Myers, daughter of a pioneer family. To Mr. and Mrs. Countryman were born two children, both sons. Mr. Countryman is one of the most substantial and enterprising young farmers of Perry township. Mrs. Countryman is an earnest member of the Albright church, and has always assisted in its support. While Mr. Countryman is not associated with any church organization, he is a firm advocate of law and order. By dint of hard labor, frugal habits, and wise economy, he is now the possessor of quite a nice property.

WILLIAM W. HARRIS, eldest son of James G. and Rachel Harris, was born in Wayne county, Ohio, near Orrville, and there resided with his parents until the time of his marriage, in the year 1840, to Miss Catharine Crites, daughter of an early pioneer family, The fruit of this union was ten children, two sons and eight daughters. Their names are as follows: Mary E., Rachel A., Sarah J., Eliza, James W., Louisa, Lucy, George, Irvin, Minerva, and Theresa; all of whom are living. Our subject came to Perry township in the spring of 1841, and purchased a small tract of land, on which he resided for a period of five years; he then purchased the farm on which he now lives, and settled immediately in the woods; here he reared and educated his little family. Mr. Harris is one of the most industrious and prosperous farmers in Perry township. Mrs. Harris is an actve member of the Lutheran church, and has always been one of its most liberal supporters, and while Mr. Harris is not associated with any church organization, he is a firm advocate of law and order. His aged mother is yet living, at the astonishing age of ninety-one years, and is a remarkably well preserved old lady for one of her advanced years. His father lies sleeping at the old Morr cemetery.

ANDREW JACKSON, the seventh son of Henry and Hannah Jackson, was born February 28, 1828, in Mohican township, Ashland county. He resided with his parents until the time of his marriage, March 21, 1850, to Miss Maria Swiegart, of Wayne county. To them were born nine children, four sons and five daughters. Their names are as follows: Catharine, John, Elizabeth, Melissa, William H., Mary, Andrew, Calista, and Amasa. Those deceased are John, William Henry, Calista, and Amasa. John died at the age of twenty-three; the others in early childhood. Andrew Jackson purchased the farm on which we now find him, in Perry township, in the year 1856. Both himself and his wife are active members of the Reformed church, and have been among its most liberal supporters. He has served in all the various positions of honor and trust. For two terms he served as infirmary director of the county, as justice of the peace in his township two terms, and repeatedly acted as township trustee, thus bespeaking for him the full appreciation of the people in his faithfulness and ability. He also served for eight different terms as director of his school district. His father and mother lie buried side by side in the old Meng cemetery.

MR. J. MYERS, second son of Abram and Susannah Myers, was born in Cumberland county, Pennsylvania, in 1822. He lived with his parents until he had reached his majority. In 1847 he was married to Miss Elizabeth Miller. To them have been born eight children, five sons and three daughters, as follows: Abraham, Augustus, May Isabel, George F., John J. S., Elizabeth L., David E., Catharine E., and Elmore Oscar, all of whom are living but Abram and Elmore, who died in early childhood. He came to Ohio in the fall of 1866, having previously purchased the farm on which we now find him—a beautiful tract containing one hundred and sixty-six acres. Although Mr. Myers is not an early settler, he has one of the most comfortable homes in Perry township. Both himself and his wife are earnest members of the Albright church, to which they contribute liberally in its support.

JOSEPH EICHELBERGER, third son of Adam and Susan Eichelberger, was born in Pennsylvania in 1836, and came to Ohio in company with his parents in 1840, and resided with them until the time of his marriage, in the year 1858, to Mary Myers. He lost his wife in 1872, and was again married, in 1874, to Miss Sarah Wise. Mr. Eichelberger and his wife are earnest members of the Albright church, and have been among its most liberal supporters. He is a hard-working, industrious, and frugal citizen, and, by dint of hard labor, careful judgment, and wise economy, he has accumulated quite a handsome property.

ELIZA MORR, daughter of Jacob Myers, of Ashland county, Ohio, was born in Center county, Pennsylvania, October 31, 1829, and removed with her father's family to Ohio when a child. Her father settled on the farm that is now owned by his son George, on which but a rude log cabin stood. Mrs. Morr was married October 18, 1855, to Emanuel Morr, son of John Morr. By this union four children were born, viz.: George Milton and Harvey P., both of whom reside at home; and two who died in infancy. Mr. Morr was a member of the Evangelical church at Perry, and was a consistent and devout Christian man; he took a very active part in the interests of both church and school, and was a liberal contributor to all enterprises tending to promote the common interests of the vicinity in which he lived. His was a well spent life, his aim being to gain a competence that would leave his family in affluent circumstances. He departed this life January 24, 1877, and was much esteemed and respected by all who knew him. Mrs. Morr is a most estimable lady, and, with the support of her two sons, still carries on the business of the farm on which the kind father and husband had for many years devoted his labors. George M. was born April 31, 1859, and Harvey P. was born July 26, 1867.

HENRY WORST was born in the year 1775, in the State of Pennsylvania, Berks county. In the year 1799 he was married to Miss Barbara Donet, and came to Ohio in the year 1814 and settled immediately in the woods on the farm now owned by his son Samuel. The farm showed no signs of improvement whatever, to give evidence of civilization or advancement. Here he reared and educated a family of eleven children—seven daughters and four sons. Their names are as follows: Catharine, Elizabeth, Mary, Sarah, Margaret, Henry, Susan, Jacob, Samuel, Nancy and George, six of whom are dead—Catharine, Elizabeth, Mary, Margaret, Sarah and Nancy. Our subject died in the year 1869, surviving his wife for a period of twenty years. This aged couple lie buried side by side in the Mount Hope cemetery. Few pioneers are more deserving of a kind remembrance than Mr. and Mrs. Worst.

SAMUEL WORST, the subject of this sketch, was born in the year 1817, on the farm now owned by him, and the old Worst homestead. Mr. Worst was thrice married, first in the year 1838, May 3d, to Miss Mary Martin. The fruit of this union was nine children—five sons and four daughters: Elizabeth, John, Margaret, Nancy, George, Mary, Samuel, David and William. John, the eldest son, died in early childhood. Mr. Worst lost his wife in the summer of 1868. In the year 1878 he was again married to Miss May Facker. She died eighteen months later, in the month of October, 1879. Again he was married to Miss Lucy Besecker. Himself and wife are earnest members of Jerome Baptist church.

DANIEL SHIDLER was born in Washington county, Pennsylvania, in the year 1787. In the year 1831, he came to Ohio, bringing with him his wife and five children—four sons and one daughter, and made a settlement in Orange township, on a farm which he had previously entered. Here he resided for a period of one year, and left for Holmes county, where he remained for eight years, when he returned to Perry township, and located permanently on the farm now owned by his son Hartman. In the meantime, he had two daughters born to him, making seven in all. Here he remained until the time of his death, in 1864. His wife survived him until January 31, 1867. Both lie buried side by side in the old Lucas cemetery. Hartman, the third son, and the subject of the following sketch, was born in Washington county, Pennsylvania, September 13, 1826. Now he owns and resides on the old Shidler homestead, in Perry township. In the year 1852, he was married to Miss Susannah Shutt. The fruit of this union was six children—one son and four daughters, as follows: Charles W., Laura A., Cordelia E., Ida I., Jennie M., and one who died in infancy, unnamed. While Mr. and Mrs. Shidler are not associated with any church, their most earnest sympathies are with the Christian church. Our subject has served as trustee of his township, and has always taken an active part in the educational interests of his neighborhood. Mr. Shidler has always been a hard working, industrious man, and, by the aid of a kind father, wise economy, and careful judgment, he has acquired quite a handsome property, and his acres now number, in total, three hundred and eighty-seven and one-half, all well improved.

ADAM EICHELBERGER was born in Lancaster county, Pennsylvania, in 1801, and was married, in 1827, to Miss Susannah Westheffer. The fruit of this union was seven children, five sons and two daughters, viz.: Simon, William, Joseph, Catharine, Adam, David, and Susan, all of whom are living. Mr. Eichelberger came to Ohio in the year 1839, and settled near Wooster, Wayne county, where he resided for one year, when he removed to Perry township, and purchased a tract of land containing one hundred and forty-eight acres. His settlement was almost surrounded with timber, with no improvements save a rude log cabin to give evidence of his having had a predecessor. This aged couple yet reside on the old homestead, and both have passed their three score and ten. Simon, the eldest son, and subject of the following sketch, was born in Cumberland county, Pennsylvania, in 1828, and resided with his parents until he arrived at the age of nineteen, when he learned the trade of carpenter and joiner, which occupation he industriously pursued for a period of eight years. He was married in 1852 to Miss Sarah Ambrose. To them have been born five children, four sons and one daughter, viz.: Agnes, Horace, Henry, Elmore, and Newton. The latter died at the age of eleven years. Himself and wife are members of the Evangelical Association. His present home is what is known as the old Ambrose homestead.

ANDREW WIREMAN was born in Petersburgh, Adams county, in 1806, came to Wayne county in the fall of 1827, where he located, and for the first twelve months followed chopping for a livelihood. He then learned the trade of a mason, which occupation he industriously pursued for almost fifty years. Mr. Wireman was married in 1831 to Miss Sarah Baker. To them were born twelve children, four sons and eight daughters, viz.: Sevilla, Margaret, Samuel, Elizabeth, John B., Sophronia, John K., Sydna H., Orline, Irena, Minnie, Etta, and Barton Leroy. Three are deceased—John B., Elizabeth, and Sydna H. Elizabeth died when just budding into womanhood, the others in early childhood. The subject of this sketch came to Perry township March 15, 1854. Himself and wife are members of the Lutheran church.

MICHAEL MORR was born in the State of Pennsylvania, in the year 1796, October 10th. He was married to

Miss Christinie Stover. To them were born eight children—four sons and four daughters. Their names are as follows: Julia Ann, George, Michael, Sarah, Harriet, Jacob, Henry, and Christinie, all of whom are living. In the year 1828, May 22d, he came to Ohio, and made permanent settlement in Perry township, immediately in the woods, with no improvements save a rude log cabin and a barn of the same to show traces of his having a predecessor. Here he raised his little family. The wife and mother departed this life December 9, 1845, leaving a family of eight children and a fond husband. The husband survived his companion until the year 1877, June 10th. Mr. Morr was a man who had always taken an active part in educational and church affairs, was a kind parent, and a citizen respected and esteemed wherever known. This worthy couple lie side by side in the old Mokle cemetery.

GEORGE MORR, the eldest son of Michael Morr, and the subject of the following sketch, was born in the year 1829, February 10th. He resided with his parents until the time of his marriage, in the year 1853, December 15th, to Miss Mary A. Frankhouser. The fruit of this union was eight children—five sons and three daughters: William P., Elmore, Emma, Martin, Ellen, Celia, Arthur and Franklina. Two have died—Ellen and Celia—both of a fever, and but four days intervening between their departures. They died in early childhood, in the year 1871. At the age of nineteen Mr. Morr learned the trade of carpenter and joiner, which occupation he has industriously and very successfully pursued for more than thirty-three years, and has been the most extensive contractor that ever operated within the limits of his county. Himself and wife are earnest members of the Evangelical Association.

MICHAEL MORR, JR., second son of Michael and Christinie Morr, and subject of the following sketch, was born in the year 1831, February 15th, and resided with his parents until the time of his marriage to Miss Mary Ann Stover, in the year 1854, December 30th. The fruit of this union was four sons—Hiram H., John P., George W., and David V., all of whom are living. He and his wife are members of the Evangelical Association.

MICHAEL WISE was born in Center county, Pennsylvania, October 25, 1820. His father, George Frederick Wise, emigrated to Ohio in 1822, locating in what is now Perry township, Ashland county. Seven years previous to his coming he entered one hundred and sixty acres of land, and to this tract he brought his family, consisting of his wife and seven children—four sons and three daughters. They erected a log cabin in the dense forests, and at once began the improvement of his chosen home. These were times that required sinews and perseverance, and this they brought in abundance from their eastern home. This was his only home. As it improved it naturally became more and more attractive to them. There were born in this Ohio home six children—two sons and four daughters, making a family of thirteen children. By earnest endeavor, father and sons soon had the satisfaction of seeing the sturdy old forest trees give way, and in their stead waving fields of grain. Mr. Wise lived to the age of eighty-eight years, and had it not been for a sad accident he might have lived many years longer. He fell on the frozen ground and fractured his thigh which caused death in about six days. Mrs. Wise is still living on the old homestead. She is ninety-one years of age, being the oldest person now living in Perry township. Well may we call them pioneers, for such they certainly are in every sense of the word. Michael, the subject of the following sketch, was not two years old when his parents removed to this county, and he grew up in pioneer style, learning well the lesson to earn his bread by the sweat of his brow. He made his home with his parents until he was married to Sarah Weaver, daughter of Thomas and Julia Ann Weaver, of Perry township. To them have been born eight children, three sons and five daughters: David, Mary M., Sarah, Rebecca, Emma, Harriet E., John A., and George Morgan. David, Rebecca and Sarah, are married, and all live in Perry township. The other five are at home with their parents. Mr. Wise is a good farmer, and has one hundred acres of fine land. He is a man highly esteemed as a neighbor and friend. He is forward in improvements that tend to elevate the character of the people, though his time is principally given to his family and his farm.

ELIAS MORR, third son of Andrew and Elizabeth Morr, was born in Pennsylvania in the year 1825, and came to Ohio with his parents, with whom he resided until he reached his majority, when he learned the trade of carpenter and joiner, which occupation he industriously pursued for twenty years. He was married in the twenty-seventh year of his age to Miss Sarah Myers, daughter of one of Ashland county's pioneers. The fruit of this union was eight children—six sons and two daughters: Oliver F., Emma J., Albert A., John P., Daniel L., Benjamin W., Harvey M., and Maggie Anna, all of whom are living. Mr. and Mrs. Morr are both earnest members of the Evangelical Association, and have always been among its most staunch supporters.

DANIEL MYERS, fourth son of Jacob and Mary Myers, was born in the State of Pennsylvania in the year 1836, and came with his parents to Ohio when but an infant. He resided at the old homestead until the time of his marriage, in January, 1861, to Miss Elizabeth Felgir, of Wayne county. To them were born three children, one son and two daughters. Their names are as follows: Lily U., Melvin S., and Artie A., all living. Mr. and Mrs. Myers, and also the eldest daughter, Lily, are members of the Evangelical church. Our subject has repeatedly been elected to the office of trustee, thus bespeaking for him the full confidence of his people.

ADAM EICHELBERGER, JR., fourth son of Adam and Susan Eichelberger, was born in the State of Pennsylvania in the year 1840, and came with his parents to Ohio when but an infant, and with them resided until his marriage, in 1862, to Miss Jane McFadden. To them have been born five children, three sons and two daughters, all living: Laura, Clinton, Carrie, William F., and Ira. Himself and wife are members of the Evangelical Association.

GEORGE EICHELBERGER was born in the State of Pennsylvania, in the year 1797. He was married in the year 1827, to Miss Lanah Humer. To them were born five children, two sons and three daughters: Sarah, Susan, Louisa, John, and Adam. Two are deceased; Susan, who died in early infancy, and Adam, who died in childhood. Our subject came to Ohio with his family in the year 1870, and settled in Orange township, and resided with his son John for part of the first year, after which he removed to Perry township, and made his home on a farm owned by his son John, where he resided for four years, after which he made his home with his son until the time of his death, in 1876, July 14th. He now lies sleeping in the old Morr cemetery. His worthy widow still survives him, at the age of seventy-two years, and is a remarkably well preserved lady for one who has seen the frost of so many winters. She makes her home with her son, John, who feels it a duty to protect and care for her in her declining years.

JOHN EICHELBERGER, eldest son of George Eichelberger, and subject of the following sketch, was born in Pennsylvania, in the year 1838. He came to Ohio in the fall of 1862. He was married in the year 1865, to Miss Catharine Myers. His first purchase of land was in Perry township; he afterwards made several purchases, and we now find him on a beautiful farm near Rowsburgh. To Mr. and Mrs. Eichelberger have been born five children, one son and four daughters: George Elmore, Mary Zeulima, Clara Virginia, Minnie Bell, and one who died in infancy, unnamed.

HENRY SEALER, the eldest son of George and Amanda Sealer, was born in Lebanon county, Pennsylvania, in the year 1843. He resided with his parents until in his nineteenth year, when he left the parental roof, and went out in the service of his country. He served as a valiant soldier for eighteen months, and remained until the war was over, when he returned to his home uninjured and crowned with all the honors to which our brave boys were justly entitled. He then learned the trade of a carpenter and joiner, which occupation he industriously and successfully pursued for a period of nine years. He came to Ohio in the year 1867, and settled near Wooster, Wayne county, where he made his home for six months; he then operated in Medina county for a short time, and afterwards in Smithsville, and thence came to Perry township, to the place where we now find him. He was married in 1868 to Christiann Garn. To them have been born three children, two sons and one daughter; their names are as follows: Amanda Nora, Henry Melvin, and Uebrtis, all living. Mr. Sealer purchased the beautiful farm on which he now resides in the year 1876.

MATTHIAS CAMP was born in the State of Pennsylvania, Westmoreland county, in the year 1744. He came to Ohio in the year 1815, and made his home with his brother Anthony, in Baughman township, Wayne county, where he followed clearing and chopping until the time of his marriage, in 1821, to Miss Sarah Evans. He then rented a cabin of his brother, where he remained for one year, when he purchased a quarter of land in Perry township, Wayne county, and began settlement immediately in the woods with no implements whatever. Here our hero commenced life in earnest. He at once set about the erection of a house in which to shelter his little family. His structure was a rude cabin with stick chimney, puncheon floor, and greased paper for windows, and with nothing for a door but a quilt or coverlet, and when all was completed he looked upon it and called it good. To him were born eleven children, seven sons and four daughters. Their names are as follows: Silas, James, John, Anthony, Mary, Evans, Wesley, Margaret, Sarah, Agnes and Matthias. Three are deceased: Margaret, Anthony and Matthias. Here, in this pioneer home, our subject reared his family, situated as he was, directly in the forest. It required a strong will and earnest determination to conquer, and as evidence the wilderness was soon made to give way, and waving fields of grain told that his labors had not been unrewarded, and each year as he was prospered he continued improving his farm until it now compares favorably with the best farms in the county. By dint of hard labor, careful judgment, and wise economy, this pioneer father has acquired quite a handsome property, sufficient to carry him through his old age. Silas, Anthony, and Matthias all served in the war of the rebellion in company C, Forty-fourth regiment. Matthias died of disease at Louisville, Kentucky, and Anthony died at the battle of Lookout Mountain, from a mortal wound, surviving but for two hours. Their brother Silas brought them home, and they both lie side by side in Wayne county. Silas remained until the close of the war, receiving a slight wound, but nothing serious. Frank W. Eckerman, of the same company, was mortally wounded at Dallas, Georgia, the wound proving fatal, July 4, 1864, at Chattanooga. He now lies buried in the sunny south in an unknown, but not an unforgotten, grave.

JOHN CAMP, third son of Matthias Camp, was born in 1826 in Perry township, Wayne county, and resided with his parents until the time of his marriage, in 1853, to Miss Ellen Campbell, daughter of one of Ashland county's early pioneers. The fruit of this union was eleven children, five sons and six daughters: May C., Margaret J., Alice Emma, Lydia A., Warren C., Matthias G., Arthur E., John W., Sarah E., Eunice E., and one who died in infancy unnamed. Eunice E. also died in infancy, and Matthias died in early childhood. Mr. Camp now resides in Perry township, on the farm adjoining the old homestead. He and his wife are active members of the Methodist Episcopal church, and have always been among its most liberal supporters.

C. S. MCFADDEN, sixth son and twelfth child of John and Catharine McFadden, was born in Wayne county, Ohio, in 1832, and resided with his parents until the year previous to his marriage, December 6, 1856, to Miss Lydia Fry. To them were born four children, one son and three daughters, viz.: Sarah, Ellen, Emma, and Aldie. One died in infancy, unnamed. Sarah E. died at the age of twelve years. The wife and mother died in May, 1878, leaving two little daughters and a fond husband. Mr. McFadden was married again, in December,

DR. I. F. MARKEL

is a son of Israel Markel, of Ashland, and was born on his father's farm in Orange township, October 3, 1850. His boyhood and youth were spent on the farm, where he remained until he was eighteen years of age, attending the district schools during the winter months, and thus laying the foundation for an education. At eighteen he attended the Savannah academy for two years, after which he taught district school for two years in Troy and Orange townships. About this time his father removed to Ashland, and he commenced the study of medicine with Drs. Cowan & Myers, with whom he remained eighteen months, when he attended a first course of lectures at Jefferson Medical college, Philadelphia.

At the close of the session he returned to Ashland, and in the fall of 1875 attended a second course of lectures at the same college, from which he graduated in March, 1866, receiving a prize offered by the demonstrator of anatomy, for the best dissection in the anatomical rooms. In May of the same year he opened an office for the practice of medicine in the village of Mifflin (or Petersburgh, as it is generally known), where he still remains. He is a close student, and by giving careful attention to the details of his profession, has built up an extensive practice, and gained the confidence of the community in which he lives. September 14, 1876, he was married to Miss Anna Hill, who was born near Olivesburgh, Richland county, November 6, 1852. Dr. Markel has a fine collection of Indian antiquities, consisting of stone hammers or tomahawks, fleshers, arrow and spear points, and other articles, to which he is constantly adding.

1878, to Miss Sarah Jane Greenlee, daughter of one of Ashland county's pioneers, a sketch of whose life appears elsewhere in this volume. Mr. McFadden is a retired farmer, living at his ease in Rowsburgh, this county. He comes from pioneer stock, his parents settling in Wayne county at a very early period. They came to Ashland county in the spring of 1853, and remained here until the time of the death of his father, September 12, 1860, his mother surviving her husband about four years. The subject of our sketch came to Wayne county a poor man. Commencing life immediately in the woods, he had, by dint of hard labor, careful judgment, and wise economy, accumulated quite a handsome property. Mrs. McFadden is an active member of the Disciple church, and has been one of its liberal supporters.

LUDWICK FRIDLINE, third son of Conrad and Sarah Fridline, was born in Pennsylvania, in 1821, came to Perry township with his parents when an infant, and is now the owner of the old homestead, where his parents lived until the time of their death, his mother dying in 1844, and her husband surviving her until the year 1870, living to the ripe old age of seventy-eight years. He was a man respected and esteemed wherever known, and his loss was deeply felt among his friends and acquaintances. Ludwig, the subject of our sketch, was married in the year 1859 to Miss Elizabeth Boffenmyer. To them have been born thirteen children, viz.: Henry H., Irvin, Sarah E., Jacob, Mary A., U. S. Grant, Alvy, Elsura, Emma, Noah E., Elizabeth, Alma, and Clara.

RICHARD S. SMILIE, second son of John A. and Catharine Smilie, was born in Chester township, Wayne county, Ohio, in the year 1841. With his parents he came to what is now Perry township, Ashland county. After moving about several times his father finally made a permanent settlement in Vermillion township, and there remained until the time of his death, in 1867, surviving his wife about fourteen years. Mr. Smilie was a man esteemed wherever known. Richard, the subject of our sketch, was married in the year 1866 to Miss Frances Dorland. The fruit of this union was three children— one son and two daughters. Their names are as follows: Jessie, J. Paul and Millie. Mr. Smilie lost his wife December 12, 1879, leaving him with three little children. He served as clerk of his township for one term, and is an active member of the Methodist Episcopal church, and has always been one of its most liberal supporters. Mr Smilie enlisted in the service of his country August 25, 1862, for a period of three years, and was taken prisoner in the spring of 1864, and discharged July 7, 1865, as a prisoner of war, and came out without a scar, although he was not without his hairbreadth escapes, at one time having his pipe and tobacco knocked out of his mouth by a shot from the enemy.

C. C. FUNK, eldest child of Hugh and Elizabeth Funk, was born in Wayne county, in the year 1831, and there resided with his parents until the time of his marriage, April 19, 1854, to Miss Mary Jane Foltz, daughter of an early pioneer family. Immediately after marriage, Mr. Funk came to Perry township, where we now find him, and purchased a beautiful farm of one hundred and eight acres. To Mr. and Mrs. Funk were born three sons. Their names are as follows: Harvey H., Walter W. and Leroy L., all living. While Mr. F. has not aspired to official position, the citizens of Perry elected him to the office of trustee at three different times. As a soldier, he went forth in the discharge of his duties, occupying the position of first lieutenant. He enlisted as one of the hundred day men, and served for one hundred and thirty-two days, returning to his home and family uninjured, and crowned with all the honor to which he and his rank were entitled. Mr. and Mrs. Funk are both active members of the Disciple church, and have been among its most liberal supporters. His life has been devoted to school teaching, and that of farming. The schools he taught number fifteen in all, and, as proof of his ability and success, they were all within a mile and a half of his home. By the aid of a kind father and his own energy and perseverance, he is now the possessor of one of the finest homes in the county. Mr. Funk is also a dealer and breeder of thoroughbreds and high grades of cattle. Mr. Funk has in his possession a most valuable dog, that has been doing all the churning until the last eight years, churning in that time over fifteen thousand pounds of butter. The name of this member of the family is Shep, and is now in the twelfth year of his age.

SAMUEL FRIDLINE, fifth son of Conrad and Sarah Fridline, was born in Perry township, Ashland county, then Wayne county, in the year 1826, on the farm where his brother Ludwick now lives. He made his home with his parents until the time of his marriage, which was in the twenty-fourth year of his age. He was twice married; first to Miss May Ann Harpster, by whom he had one child, who died in infancy, unnamed. Immediately after his marriage he and his young wife moved to Mohican township, where he purchased a small farm of sixty-two acres. His wife died thirteen months after. He was married again May 9, 1854, to Miss Rachel Zimmerman. To them have been born nine children, eight sons and one daughter. Their names are as follows: Francis M., Eli, May E., William, Elsy, Samuel, Harvey, William Henry, and one who died in infancy, unnamed. Mr. Fridline resided in Mohican for a period of twelve years, when he returned to Perry township and purchased an additional tract of sixty-seven acres near the old homestead, and now owns two hundred and fourteen acres. Mr. Fridline was a soldier in the service of his country, going out when the call for one hundred days' men was made. He served out his time and came to his home without a scar. He lost two brothers in the war. Jacob died at Paducah from a wound received at Vicksburgh, and Harrison died from disease at Baltimore. They were both brought to their homes, and lie buried in the Meng cemetery in Perry township.

ISAAC ZIMMERMAN, the eldest son of Eli and Elizabeth Zimmerman, was born in Westmoreland county, Pennsylvania, in the year 1830, and came to Ohio in company with his parents in the fall of 1838. On the organization of Ashland county, he came to Perry township. His father resided here until the year 1865, when he removed to Mohican, and to-day is one of the largest landholders in the county. Isaac, the subject of our sketch, purchased the old Zimmerman homestead in Perry township, and has added many noticeable improvements. He was married in the year 1859 to Miss Susan Ely. To them have been born five children, three sons and two daughters. Their names are as follows: Judson A., Zenas W., Isadore, John E., and Etta May, deceased, who died in early childhood. So great is his ambition to improve, advance, and reach the zenith in farming, that he has purchased fine specimens of wheat at the enormous price of fourteen dollars per bushel, sowing the present season forty-eight different specimens. By dint of hard labor, wise economy, and careful judgment, Mr. Zimmerman has accumulated an extensive property, being the possessor of three hundred and fifty-three acres of land. Mrs. Zimmerman is one of the staunch members of the Reformed church, and has always been one of its most liberal supporters, and while Mr. Zimmerman is not associated with any church organization, he is a firm advocate of law and order.

JOHN SNYDER and family emigrated from Adams county, Pennsylvania, October 20, 1833, and arrived at Jeromeville on the above mentioned date, with but one shilling in his pocket, which was expended on the following morning for one pound of butter. Fortunately for him, his services were much needed, he being a carpenter. He at once contracted to erect a barn on what is now known as the Glass farm, and by the aid of his four willing sons, Levi, Jeremiah, H. K., and William, his task was soon completed. In the spring of 1836 he leased the Meng farm, and for a period of three years he combined cabinet-making with farming. After the expiration of his lease, he made several removals, when he finally returned to Perry township and settled on the Schwartz farm, where he remained until the death of his wife. Two years after this sad occurrence he and his family, with the exception of Henry, moved to LaGrange county, Indiana, where he followed cabinet-making and contracting, meeting with severe losses by fire. Yet, with all his trials and reverses, he lived to the ripe old age of eighty-four years, retaining his full vigor and strength of mind. Henry, the subject of this sketch, and the only representative of the Snyder family residing in Ashland county, was born in the State of Pennsylvania, in the year 1817. He came to Ohio with his parents, and now resides in Perry township. He was twice married—first, in the year 1837, to Miss Anna Meng. To them were born five children, four sons and one daughter, as follows: Andrew Phillip, John H., Jacob M., Samuel, and May Margaret Ann, all of whom are living but Samuel, who died at the age of eleven years, from an injury received from the kick of a horse; the daughter also died in early childhood, at the age of two years. The wife and mother died in the year 1875, leaving a family of three children. Mr. Snyder was again married, in the winter of 1879, to Elizabeth Meng. He is an earnest member of the Reformed church, and has always been one of its most liberal supporters.

ADAM MISH, seventh son of John and Magdalene Mish, was born in the year 1808, in the State of Pennsylvania, Franklin county, near Strasburgh. In the year 1832 he was married to Miss Elizabeth Colsmith. The fruit of this union was nine children—six sons and three daughters. Their names are as follows: John A., Washington, Sarah, William Augustus, Ann, Jeremiah, Adam, Mary, and Simon, all living but Washington, who died in early childhood. In the year 1845 he emigrated to Ohio and purchased a beautiful tract of land, containing one hundred and five acres. Here he began life in earnest, immediately in the woods, with no improvements whatever, save a rude log cabin, and a rickety barn of the same mould. But he was determined to conquer; and with a corageous heart and positive will, the forest was soon made to give way. Here he reared and educated his family. The wife and mother died in the year 1874. Three of Mr. Mish's sons volunteered in the war of 1861—William, Jeremiah, and Adam—serving hororably their full time, and returning to their home uninjured, and crowned with all the honors to which our brave sons were entitled. He is an earnest and active member of the Lutheran church, and has always been one of its most liberal supporters.

CHRISTIAN COUNTRYMAN, fifth son of Peter and Rosanna Countryman, was born in the State of Pennsylvania, in the year 1817, and came to Ohio in the year 1847, and leased the farm on which he now lives. Here he began life in earnest immediately in the woods. He was married in the year 1844, to Miss Barbara Kline. To them have been born eight children, two sons and six daughters; all are living. Their names are as follows: Elizabeth, Jacob, Nancy, Simon Peter, Ann Maria, Mary Ellen, Sarah J., Lettie Levina; all married but Jacob and Levina. All were born in this State but Elizabeth, who was born in Pennsylvania. Both himself and his wife are earnest members of the Lutheran church.

GEORGE MYERS, second son of Jacob and Mary Myers, was born in Pennsylvania in 1822, and came to Ohio with his parents in 1836. He lived with his parents until the twentieth year of his age, when he went to Ashland to learn wagon- and carriage-making, which occupation he followed for a period of twenty-two years. He was married, in the fall of 1858, to Miss Elizabeth Morr, daughter of a pioneer family. To them were born nine children, viz.: F. E., Celena, Philip A., Miranda M., Sevilla E., Alvah N., George D., Minnie, and Effie Centennie—all living but Minnie. Both Mr. and Mrs. Myers are members of the Evangelical Association, and have been among its most liberal supporters. He was elected to the office of infirmary director in 1870, which position he occupied six successive terms, and has repeatedly served as trustee of his township.

ALFORD SCOTT, third son of James and Mary Scott, was born in Ashland county, then Perry township, Wayne county, in the year 1840, and lived with his parents until the time of his marriage, in the year 1860, on Christmas day, to Miss Mary Margaret Meng. To Mr. and Mrs. Scott have been born three children—one son and three daughters, as follows: Laura, Ellen, one dying in infancy, and Elmore D., the only surviving heir; Laura died in early childhood. While he is not associated with any church organization, he is a firm advocate of law and order. For a period of four years he served as trustee of his township. His father and mother are both deceased, and lie buried in the Jeromeville cemetery.

WILLIAM SCOTT, the eldest son of James and Mary Scott, was born in Ashland county, then Wayne, in the township of Perry, in the year 1828. He resided with his parents until he became eighteen years of age, when he went forth in the world to care for himself. He learned the trade of carpenter and joiner with George Irwin, which occupation he industriously pursued for a period of eighteen years. In the meantime, he purchased a lot at Golden Corners and erected a home. Afterwards he purchased eighty acres of land situated in Kane township, Wayne county, and there resided for a period of five years. During that time, he met with a severe loss by fire, yet he withstood all these reverses, determined to conquer. Then he moved to Plain township, and bought a farm of one hundred and fourteen acres of land, which he cultivated for five years. Then he sold it and returned to Perry township, and located on a beautiful home, where we now find him. Twice he was married; first, in the year 1850, to Miss Mary Ann Young. To them were born two children, both daughters: Sarah Jane, and Maria M. In 1859 his wife died, leaving two children. In the year 1862, he was again married, to Miss Elizabeth Garbrerich. The fruit of this union was eight children—four sons and four daughters. Their names are as follows: Simon A., Fietta L., Henry M., Albertos, Emma E., Elsie Eugene, Arminda, Eva May, all of whom are living but Henry, who died in early childhood. Himself and wife are earnest members of the German Baptist church, and have always been among its most liberal supporters. His father and mother are deceased, and lie buried side by side in the Jeromeville cemetery.

JONATHAN MYERS, eldest son of Joseph and Mary Myers, was born in the State of Pennsylvania in the year 1821, and came to Ohio in company with his parents in the year 1836. He made his home with his parents until the time of his marriage in 1848 to Miss May Spangler, daughter of a pioneer family. To Mr. and Mrs. Myers have been born twelve children, seven sons and five daughters, as follows: Jacob, Mary, Henry, Emma, Jane, William, Elmore, Katie, Clemont, and Holbert; all of whom are living. His first permanent settlement was on the farm on which he now resides. While our worthy subject is not associated with any church, he is a firm advocate of law and order. His father and mother are both deceased, and lie buried side by side in Zion cemetery. He has always been a great man for hunting and recreation. In fact, he is a man who believes in pleasant employment.

WILLIAM N. SHISLER was born in the State of New Jersey, Sussex county, in the year 1794, and came to Pennsylvania in company with his parents about the year 1816. He was married in the twenty-fourth year of his age, to Miss Margaret Townsend. The fruit of this union was eight children, four sons and four daughters, as follows: Henry, Lydia, Hylandreth, Sophia, Theresa, Elizabeth, William Wheeler, and Townsend. Three are deceased: Theresa, William W., and Hylandreth, who died in early infancy. Our subject came to Ohio in the year 1822, and made a settlement in Perry township, Wayne county, now Ashland. His first purchase was eighty acres, on which he resided for four years, and which he also improved. He then sold, and bought a quarter near by, where he lived until his death in the year 1857, January 24th. His wife survived him until the year 1870, March 4th. This worthy pioneer couple lie sleeping side by side in the old Morr cemetery. The only representatives of the Shisler family residing in Perry township are Townsend and Henry, the subject of the following sketch. He was born in Washington county, Pennsylvania, in the year 1818, January 8th. He came to Ohio with his parents in the year 1822, and lived with them until the time of his marriage, August 26, 1841, to Miss Christina Morr. To them were born six children, four sons and two daughters: Harriet, born August 23, 1843—died at the age of three years and six months; William A., born February 14, 1848; Similda Ann, born March 4, 1851; Oliver L., born June 17, 1853; Enoch H., born November 21, 1858; Stephen A., born November 10, 1862. Our subject located on the farm on which we now find him, immediately in the woods, with no improvements whatever to give evidence of civilization or advancement. Here he reared his little family. He has repeatedly been elected to the office of trustee, thus bespeaking the full confidence of his people. He and his family are members of the Evangelical Association, and have been among its most liberal supporters. Those of the family who are married are William, who was twice married, first to Miss Malinda Falk. His second companion was May Rosswiler. He is in the ministry. Similda married William Rittenhouse, and resides on the farm adjoining her old homestead. Oliver T., who was married to Miss Sadie May Rickle, is living on the farm of her father.

ANDREW MORR was born in the State of Pennsylvania, Center county, in the year 1794. He was married to Miss Elizabeth Stover in the twenty-fourth year of his age. To them were born twelve children, seven sons and five daughters: Jacob, Catharine, Christinie, Harriet, Andrew, Adam E., Elizabeth, Samuel, Philip, Henry, Enoch, and Julia Anna, all living but Andrew. He came to Ohio May 22, 1828, and settled on the farm now owned by his son Jacob. This worthy pioneer departed this life in the year 1858, in the sixty-fourth year of his age. The wife and mother survived him until the year 1877, dying at the age of eighty years. Jacob, who now resides on the old homestead, was born June 22, 1817. He lived with his parents and aided his father until the time of his marriage, in the year 1840, August 27th, to Miss Sarah Dundore. The fruit of this union was seven children, four sons and three daughters. Their names are May E., Andrew P.,

Malinda, Adaline, Benton S., Jacob W., and Stephen A., all living but Adaline and Benton, who died in early childhood. Those married are, Mary to David Weiker; Andrew to Mary Jane Weikre, who died after five years of married life—he was afterward married to Miss Mary R. Ambrose; Malinda to Lemon Schnaders. The other members of the family reside at their father's home. Mr. Morr and his family are members of the Trinity church, and have been among its most liberal supporters. Andrew, the pioneer father of the Morr family, was one of the organizers of the Trinity church of Perry township, and was leader and exhorter in the church for over twenty-five years. His wife was born in 1797.

DAVID WEYANT, eldest son of Jacob and Margaret Weyant, was born in the State of Pennsylvania, Washington county, in the year 1815; he made his home with his parents until after he had reached his majority; he then left the parental roof, and came to Ohio in the year 1838, and took up his abode in Doylestown, where he purchased property, and there resided until the spring of 1848. He was married in the year 1838, September 26th, to Miss Rachel Nowland. To Mr. and Mrs. Weyant were born five children, three sons and two daughters; their names are as follows: Margaret A., Jacob H., Martha S., Noah I., and Harvey I.; all of whom are living and married—Margaret, to Henry Morr; Jacob, to Lizzie Scott; Martha, to Solomon Mouser; Noah, to Lizzie Fridline; Harvey, to Catharine Jackson. Our subject is grandparent to eleven grandchildren. Mr. Weyant lost his wife in the year 1864, February 26th. She left a family of five children. Our worthy subject was married again September 27, 1866, to Miss Rosanna Gallwitz. Himself and wife are earnest members of the Evangelical Lutheran Church General Synod, and have always been its staunch supporters; he has been repeatedly elected to the office of trustee. His parents are both deceased; his mother is buried at Ginger Hill, Pennsylvania, and his father sleeps in the old Meng cemetery in Perry township. He has been elder in his church for almost forty years, and never shrank from what he thought a duty.

JOHN RUDY was the eldest child of Frederick and Elizabeth (Smith) Rudy, of Dauphin county, Pennsylvania, and was born October 18, 1806. His father died when John was but a boy of seven years. His widow survived him, and was married again, to Jacob Jennings, by whom she had two children. One, a son, is one of the wealthy and prominent men of Ashland, and is engaged in the banking business. After the death of his father, John was "put out" by his guardian, and served his first master two and one-half years, when he again returned to his mother. His guardian then bound him out the second time, to a man to learn the weaving trade, as that was then a paying business. He remained at this until he was eighteen years old, when he again returned to his mother, where he lived until he was thirty-two years of age. He was then married to Sophia Spangler, by whom he has had four children, two boys and two girls, as follows: Elizabeth, Jacob S., who died in infancy, Jennie, and John Edward. Two only are living—Elizabeth and Jennie, both married, leaving both the old people alone. John Rudy, our subject, removed to Ohio in the year 1833, and first settled on the farm now owned by Murray & Ewing. His first purchase of land was one hundred and thirty-seven acres. This he traded for a farm of ninety-one acres, upon which a saw-mill was located. This business he followed successfully for twelve years, when he exchanged it for the fine property on which he now resides. Although not a member of any church organization, his sympathies and inclinations are with the Church of God, of which his wife is an earnest and consistent member. Mrs. Rudy is a lady of very youthful appearance for one of her years, and has withstood the ravages of time, and although having worked hard all through life, she shows but few traces of it. Mr. Rudy is a staunch Republican, and firm advocate of the party measures and principles. Although well advanced in years he has kept pace with the times, and is a farmer of advanced ideas. Mrs. Rudy has been a kind and judicious mother and loving wife. This old couple live in a pleasant home, surrounded by every comfort, and can look back over the past with satisfaction at what they have accomplished. Every one has a good word to say of "Uncle John Rudy," as he is familiarly known. He is one of Perry township's most respected citizens.

ALEXANDER ALLISON, second son of James and Elizabeth (Smith) Allison, was born in Washington county, Pennsylvania, in 1805, and emigrated to Ohio with his parents in 1809. They first settled in Jefferson county, Ohio, on a rented farm, where he remained for a period of nine years, when he again started with his little family to seek a more desirable home, which he found on coming to Ashland (then Wayne) county. He made a permanent settlement in Perry township, where he remained until the time of his death, in 1839, surviving his wife about thirteen months. Their children were: Jane, Catharine, and Alexander. The only representative of the family is Catharine, who resides in Wayne county, near Wooster, performing a duty that seems to her a pleasure, that of caring for the orphan children of her deceased sister. Alexander, the subject of this sketch, was twice married, first to Miss Alice Firestone, in 1830, and settled on the farm where we now find him, adjoining the old homestead of his father. His home, at that time a rude cabin, was situated almost in the woods, with no improvements whatever to give any token of civilization. Here he reared his little family, and the dense forest that so closely surrounded him was soon made to yield to his strong will, and waving fields of grain soon gave evidence that his determination had been earnestly put into execution. In fact, the means with which he purchased his pioneer home he earned by clearing and chopping. To Mr. and Mrs. Allison were born seven children, two sons and five daughters, viz.: Nancy, Elizabeth, John F., Rachel, Mary Ann, Eliza J., and Alexander C.—all living but Eliza J., who died just after developing into womanhood—John F. died in infancy. The wife and mother was taken from her earthly home

July 9, 1844, at the age of thirty-one years. Mr. Allison married for his second wife Miss Elizabeth White, in 1851. To them were born six children, three sons and three daughters, viz.: William W., John P., Alice Catharine, Ann Isabel, Margaret Edith, Thomas B.—all living but Margaret Edith, who died at the age of one year and ten days. Mr. Allison still resides on the old home place. He is a gentleman advanced in years, but is in his full strength and vigor, and a man remarkable for his memory and accuracy. Scarcely too much can be said of this worthy pioneer. Himself and wife are consistent members of the Presbyterian church, and have always been among its most liberal supporters.

LEVI H. KIPLINGER was born February 12, 1832, in Jackson township, Ashland county, and was the fourth son of Henry and Elizabeth (Switzer) Kiplinger, who were natives of Pennsylvania. They moved to Ohio about the year 1825. By trade he was a blacksmith, and worked at his trade the greater part of his life, although he combined farming with it. His experience was similar to that of all other pioneers of that day. He could remember when the entire cash capital of the community was a half-dollar piece, which was sometimes in his possession, and then in others. In his trade he was an expert, and was sought out by people far and wide to do their work. In the year 1872 he died, in his eightieth year. His wife survived him two years, and died at the age of eighty years. Our subject lived with his father until sixteen years of age, when he learned the cabinet trade, which he worked at for fifteen years, when he went into the army, and had the honor of serving under that gallant commander, General James A. Garfield. He served with honor and distinction until he lost his arm at the battle of Thompson Hill. He went all through the fight until about four o'clock in the evening, when the fight had just about closed, when he received the shot that cost him his arm. He received the wound the first day of May, 1863. A complete record of the fight is given in a history of the Forty-second regiment. Mr. Kiplinger was married to Lucinda Deibler, September 29, 1853. To them have been born seven children—five boys and two girls. He has led at active life, and since his discharge from the service of his country he started in the mercantile business, which he has carried on successfully. He has served his county as sheriff one term, he being the first and only Republican sheriff ever elected in the county, carrying the election by the bare majority of four votes. He is an ardent Republican and a staunch supporter of its principles and measures. He served his county as he did his country—with honor and distinction. He has been a faithful officer, a conscientious and law-abiding citizen, and a man who enjoys the confidence and esteem of all his neighbors and citizens. He is well preserved, and being comfortably situated in a pleasant home, he is freed from the cares and anxiety of business; and he can look back with satisfaction and contentment to his record of the past, which has been full of activity and danger as well as honor. To men of his character our country owes a debt of gratitude, and they should ever be held in remembrance for the deeds they have accomplished. Too much cannot be said in their praise. He has been postmaster of Redham ever since the expiration of his term as sheriff.

AMOS FUNK was born in Franklin county, Pennsylvania, February 5, 1823, and was the oldest son of Benjamin and Elizabeth Funk. They both removed to Wayne county, Ohio, in the year 1831, where he lived until his removal to Indiana, where the father died in 1873. His son Amos, and the subject of our sketch, moved into Ashland county about the year 1850. Previous to his removal from Wayne county, he was married to Matilda Jane Kramer, of Ashland county, May 23, 1844. To him have been born eight children, five of whom are living: Elizabeth, deceased; Benjamin; John, who died in infancy; Christian, who died in infancy; William F., Lewis A., Stanzie E., and Abner W. Mr. Funk's first purchase was twenty acres of land, where he now lives. He has increased his possession now until he is the owner of a tract of one hundred and forty-four acres. Mr. and Mrs. Funk have been consistent members of the Church of God, and have been liberal supporters of the same. Mr. Funk is one of the substantial farmers of Perry township. He is a man of a very strong physical organization, and has been able to endure the great labors that have been necessary for him to undertake. In connection with his farming, he carried on a saw-mill, which he has operated successfully for twenty-five years. Mr. Funk generally acts with the Republican party, and is a firm advocate of its measures and principles. For one of his years, he is a well preserved man, and is surrounded by a family of intelligent children, and in a pleasant home.

DAVID BUFFENMIRE, fifth son of Henry and Mary Buffenmire, was born in Lancaster county, Pennsylvania, in the year 1814, and emigrated to Ohio in 1826, in company with his parents and their family of ten children, coming in a wagon with five horses. Mr. Buffenmire first made a settlement two miles south of Rowsburgh, immediately in the woods. Here he soon erected a rude log cabin in which to shelter his little family, and here he began life in earnest. The forest which completely surrounded him was soon made to give way to his determined will. Here Mr. Buffenmire reared his family and remained until the time of his death in the spring of 1849. His wife survived him until the year 1867, when she, too, was taken from her earthly home, leaving seven children. David, the subject of this sketch, cared for his aged mother through her declining years, from and after the death of his father. He was twice married, first in 1835, to Miss Phebe Ann Meng, by whom he had four daughters: Mary Ann, Amanda, Elizabeth and Annetta. The wife and mother died in the spring of 1838. Mr. Buffenmire married for his second wife, Miss Sarah Otto. To them have been born five children, three sons and two daughters, as follows: Franklin, Emma, Harvey, E. Stanton, and Martha. Franklin died in infancy, and Emma in early childhood. Mr. and Mrs. Buffenmire are members of the Lutheran church. Mr. Buffenmire, by careful management, wise economy, and sound judgment, has acquired quite a fine property.

ELIJAH EBERT, third son of Joseph and Leah Ebert, was born in Wayne county, Ohio, in the year 1848, March 11th. He lived with his parents until the time of his marriage, in 1866, to Miss Christiann Sweitzer. The fruit of this union was five children, four sons and one daughter—Ira, Irvin, Oscar, Alonzo, and Dora D.; all living but Alonzo, who died in early childhood. Mr. Ebert came to Ashland county in the year 1863, and located on a farm near Lafayette, where he resided until the year 1867, when he came to the town of Lafayette, and there established himself in the general mercantile business, making boots and shoes a specialty. He is one of the enterprising business men of the county; respected and esteemed. A valiant soldier in the war of the Rebellion, he went forth in the discharge of his duty to his country. In August, 1864, he enlisted with Captain George Streby, of Wayne county. He served until the war closed, when he was honorably discharged, and returned to his home in Ashland county, and since that time his life has been taken up in business pursuits.

WILLIAM MAURER was born in Lycoming county, Pennsylvania, April 30, 1813, and was the son of John and Barbara (Rotharmal) Maurer. They removed to Ohio in 1822, and took up a piece of land containing eighty acres, on which they built a rude log cabin, where they commenced pioneer life, and many are the incidents that can be related of these early times that were common to the lot of the pioneer. Wild game abounded, and the forests were filled with deer and other animals. The beautiful fields of Perry township, now teeming with the rich waving grain, were then covered with a dense forest of trees, out of which must be carved a home for our pioneer settlers. With courage and fortitude they entered upon their work, and to-day their posterity are reaping the benefit of the labors of these hardy old pioneers. The wife and mother lived to the remarkable age of one hundred years and a few months. She was a woman of great endurance, remarkable for her courage and fortitude, and possessing her faculties up to within a few years of her death. She was the mother of eight children, five boys and three girls, whom she reared with care. Three only have survived her—Isaac, who lives in Fremont; Mrs. Jackson, and William, the subject of this sketch, both of whom reside in this county. William Maurer lived with his parents until he became a man, and then took it upon himself to care for his aged parents. Now that they have passed away, the dutiful son can look back to it as a duty pleasant to have been permitted him to perform. He was married to Catharine Garn, a native of Guilford, Franklin county, Pennsylvania, who moved to Ohio in 1872, and settled in Ashland county. Here her father died upon the old homestead, the mother having died before their removal from Pennsylvania. The marriage of Mr. Maurer occurred March 12, 1839. To them were born four children, three boys and one girl—William G., Adam R., John D., and Mary A., who died when just blossoming into womanhood. This loss was a severe stroke to the fond parents. She was the only daughter, and much beloved by all who knew her. Mr. Maurer's occupation has been that of a farmer, and has followed it successfully. Although he has passed the age allotted to man he is still well preserved, and presents a hearty and rugged appearance, and seems able to withstand many years more the ravages of time. Both Mr. and Mrs. Maurer have been for over thirty-five years consistent members of the German Reformed church, and have been faithful followers of the teachings of the Holy Scriptures. He has never aspired to political position, although he has served his township in various capacities. He has been an honest and industrious man, commencing life in poverty, and, after meeting with reverses, he has steadily pursued his course through life, and has now surrounded himself with every comfort necessary to his happiness. The oldest son has been driven to the far west by the breaking down of his health. He is a young man of more than ordinary business abilities, and has occupied many positions of trust. Mrs. Mauer has been a fond and judicious mother, loving her children as only a mother knows how, and has been a loving companion to her husband for forty-one years. This old couple are pleasantly located in a nice home, and enjoy the esteem and good will of all who know them. He is one of Ashland county's pioneers.

ARTHUR CAMPBELL, JR., is the oldest son of Arthur and Lydia (Ecker) Campbell, and was born September 20, 1833, in Perry township. Mr. Campbell commenced his trade, that of carpenter and joiner, when he was twenty years of age, and has followed it continuously up to the present time (1880). On December 9, 1856, he was united in marriage to Elizabeth Swartz, of this county. The fruits of this union are eight children, six living: Cassius Clay, Elmer (dead), Minnie May, Clara, Jane twin of Laura E., who is dead, Owen Grant, Arthur Herman, and Elizabeth L. Mr. and Mrs. Campbell are earnest and consistent members of the Methodist Episcopal church. He is a firm advocate of the principles and measures of the Republican party, and his vote is generally cast for the men who represent it. He has been trustee of his township one term, and notwithstanding the township is strongly Democratic, he was elected to fill that office by the aid of Democratic votes, who broke away from party and voted for the man. Mrs. Campbell is a careful and judicious mother and loving wife. They are pleasantly situated in a comfortable home near the town of Rowsburgh. Mr. Campbell still continues at his trade, besides cultivating a farm of eighty acres.

JOHN A. CAMPBELL was the only son of John and Agnes Campbell, and was born in Somerset county, Pennsylvania, June 21, 1803. He removed to Ohio with his father in 1833, and settled on the farm where his widow still resides. Previous to his removal to Ohio he was married to Margaret Clark, of Somerset, Pennsylvania. The year 1849 brought to him a great affliction, in the loss of his father, adopted son and wife. He and his father had never been accustomed to a life on the farm, having devoted their time, while in Pennsylvania, to business matters, and, although not understanding much of the manual labor that is common to the lot of a farmer, the father and son carried on farming extensively. The mother died in 1835. There was a family of six children: Ann, Margaret, Isabella, Jane, Matilda, and John A., whose name is at the head of this sketch. The only surviving member of the family is Matilda, who is well preserved and has an astonishing memory for one of her years. She has reached the age of seventy-nine, and is a highly esteemed old lady. She came from a family noted for their longevity and hardy constitutions. Our subject was married the second time to Mary Jane Hamilton, a native of Green county, Pennsylvania, whose father came to this county in 1820. This event took place November 4, 1852. To them have been born two children: Josephine M., who married Henry Dorland, and Walter H., who resides with his mother. Mr. Campbell died June 21, 1866, after a brief illness. He and his wife were earnest, consistent members of the Presbyterian church. He was a man of delicate constitution, of large experience, of a genial and social disposition, a worthy citizen, and highly esteemed as a citizen and a Christian man.

BENJAMIN FUNK is the oldest son of Amos and Matilda Funk, a sketch of whose life will be found elsewhere in this work. Our subject was born May 1, 1847, in Wayne county, Ohio. At the age of twenty-one, he attended school at Smithville, and there completed his education. Following this, he taught two terms of school in his home district. After working a part of his father's farm on shares for three years, he was married to Eliza E. Foltz, a native of Wayne county. This event occurred April 10, 1873. To them have been born three children, all boys: Captain Perry, Adelbert R., and Charles H. Mr. Funk is a young and promising farmer, of good habits, is industrious, enterprising, and pleasantly situated in a nice home, and is very happy in his family. Upon his place he has put a nice and commodious house, and his farm is well improved. In religious belief, his sympathies are with the Church of God, that branch of the church best exemplifying his view of the Christian religion. In politics he is a staunch Republican, and an advocate of its measures and principles. Mr. Funk devotes his attention to the breeding of a superior grade of stock, making a specialty of the Berkshire pig. Besides this, he owns a fine stock of sheep, and devotes some attention to the raising of grain. He is a farmer of advanced ideas, careful and prudent, and thorough in everything he undertakes. Mr. Funk served his country during the war a term of four months, going out to its aid at the early age of seventeen. His children will ever look back with pride at this part of their father's career in life. He was a member of the One Hundred and Sixty-third Ohio volunteer infantry.

SAMUEL SHEETS was born September 9, 1796, in the State of Maryland, and came to Ohio in the year 1805, and settled in Columbiana county, where he resided until he reached his majority. Soon after arriving at man's estate he was married to Miss Elizabeth Wolf, in the year 1819. The same year he moved to Congress, Wayne county, Ohio, where he lived until the spring of 1832, when he again moved to Montgomery township, Ashland county, and began settlement immediately in the woods, with no improvements whatever save a lonely rude cabin. By earnest labor and perseverance, Mr. Sheets was soon able to erect a more commodious home in which to place his little family. By economy, industry and good management, he succeeded in acquiring quite a fine property. He died in the year 1872, at the ripe old age of seventy-five years eleven months and twenty-three days, leaving a wife and seven children. The wife and mother survived him six years, when she was called away. Both Mr. and Mrs. Sheets were earnest members of the Lutheran church, and strong advocates of the cause of Christ.

JACOB SHEETS, fourth son of Samuel Sheets, was born in Wayne county, Ohio, December 12, 1829. In 1832 he came with his parents to Ashland county, and remained with them until the year 1868. In 1860 he was married to Miss Emeline Jacoby. He is one of the most substantial farmers of Perry township; is a prominent citizen, respected and esteemed. He served as trustee for four terms. Both himself and his wife are members of the Lutheran church.

JACOB KREADY was born in Lancaster county, Pennsylvania, in the year 1819, and immigrated to Ohio in the year 1855, and settled in Perry township, Ashland county, where he purchased a beautiful farm of one hundred and sixty-nine acres, which he at once set about to improve. Afterwards, he bought seventy acres, comprising in all two hundred and thirty-nine acres. Twice he was married. First, in the twenty-fourth year of his age, to Miss Nancy Musser, by whom he had six children—three sons and three daughters: Lizzie, May, Henry, Benjamin, and Frances, one dying in infancy, unnamed. In the year 1851 his companion was taken from him, leaving four affectionate children. Mr. Kready was married again in the year 1855, to Miss Rachel A. Baird, of Adams county. The fruit of this second union was six children—three sons and three daughters: Alikasiah, William Clayton, Laura E., Edward B., Tratia Ann, and Samuel F., all living but Alikasiah and William Clayton. Mr. Kready still lives on the old homestead where he first made settlement.

JOHN P. SMALLEY is the youngest son of John and Elizabeth (Bradfield) Smalley, and was born on the place where he now resides, June 28, 1823. His father was a native of New Jersey, and his mother was a Virginian by birth. The father was a soldier of the war of 1812, and endured many of the hardships that were common to the lot of the soldiers of that war. He was married in Jefferson county, Ohio, in the year 1807. He was born in the year 1777. He was one of the early settlers of Ashland county, then Wayne county, coming here as early as the year 1819, when the beautiful fields we now see in Perry township were covered with a dense wilderness. His experience was similar, and his hardships the same, as those endured by the pioneers of that early day, graphic accounts of which we read elsewhere in this volume. John P., the subject of this sketch, lived with his parents until his marriage to Sarah A. Davis, a native of Delaware county, New York. This event took place December 23, 1847. To them have been born eleven children, eight of whom are living: John A., Matthew R., Lindsley H., Frank E., and Charles A.; McClellan, who died in early childhood; Sarah E., who died in childhood; Anna M., Harriet E., Lottie and Sanidda, died in infancy. Mr. and Mrs. Smalley have been earnest, consistent members of the Methodist Episcopal church for the past twenty years—that branch of the Christian religion best exemplifying their beliefs. He has been recording steward for the last nine years. He has served his county two terms as county commissioner, and was a careful and faithful officer. Mr. Smalley has, by dint of hard work and careful management, accumulated a fine property. Commencing in poverty, he is now surrounded by a nice family of children and has one of the pleasantest homes in the township. Mr. Smalley is one of Ashland county's most highly respected citizens. He is noted for his careful habits and good judgment in all matters of a public or business nature. He is spoken of by his neighbors and citizens as one of Perry township's substantial farmers, and is well regarded by all who know him. He has held the office of township clerk nine years in succession, and was land appraiser as far back as 1860. He held this position in 1870 and also assisted in 1880. He has never aspired to official position, but has been sought out by his fellow citizens, and the office has ever sought the man.

J. N. McFADDEN, the only son of John and Susan McFadden, was born in the year 1837; he resides with his widowed mother in Perry township. In the year 1877 his father died, leaving two children and a faithful and devoted wife. The subject of our sketch is one of the substantial and enterprising farmers of Perry township, and the owner of a pleasant home.

THOMAS OSBORN was born in England, near Southampton, in the year 1785, May 27th, and emigrated to Ohio in the year 1829, and first made a settlement in Perry township, where his widow now resides. In the year 1831, August 18th, he was married to Margaret Campbell, a daughter of one of Ashland county's early pioneers. To them were born nine children, four sons and five daughters. Their names are as follows: Ann E., Matilda J., Arthur, William, Margaret, Lydia, Susan, Thomas, and an infant who died, unnamed. Thomas also deceased in early childhood. The husband and parent died in the eightieth year of his age, leaving a kind and devoted wife and seven children. He settled immediately in the woods, and by dint of hard labor, careful management and wise economy, left his widow nicely provided for. Mr. Osborn was a kind husband and an endearing father, and his loss was irreparable. The wife and mother, together with her two daughters, Margaret and Susan, still reside on the old homestead, the daughters caring for their aged mother in her declining years. For the last thirty years she has been an earnest member of the Lutheran church, and has always been one of its most liberal supporters. At the age of twelve he left his home and followed the sea for eight years, when he came to New Jersey, and remained one year, and thence to Pennsylvania, where he lived until the year 1829, when he came to Ohio.

R. V. SMALLEY, fourth son of Richard and A. Smalley, was born in Montgomery township, Ashland county, in the year 1847. He resided with his parents until the time of his marriage, in the year 1876, to Miss Barbara Jane Golbert. While he is not associated with any church organization, he is a firm advocate of law and order.

EMANUEL KAUFMAN, the only son of Rudolph and Elizabeth Swartz Kaufman, was born in Wayne county (now Ashland), July 31, 1824. In the year 1822, his father immigrated to the State of Ohio, from Lancaster county, Pennsylvania, and made settlement on the farm now owned by his son Emanuel, and there resided until the time of his death, on March 24, leaving his only child and a devoted wife. Mrs. Kaufman was married again, February 3, 1828, to Jacob R. Swartz. The fruit of this union was six children—three sons and three daughters: Henry, Elizabeth Ann, Amanda, Catharine, Owen and Joseph, all living but Henry and Amanda. Emanuel was married, June 10, 1851, to Miss May Webster. To them were born twelve children—six sons and six daughters: Errin C., Henry W., Emma A., Elmore B., David N., Mary E., William S., Della M., Ora E., Sarah V., Emanuel G., and one who died in infancy, unnamed. Mr. Kaufman and his wife are both earnest members of the Lutheran church. The names of those who died are: Elmore, who died in early childhood, at the age of seven; Mary, who died at the age of three years; Della, who died in infancy, and Henry, who died just before reaching his majority. His loss was deeply felt by the fond parents.

JACOB ECKER, third son of Abraham and Elizabeth Ecker, was born in Wayne county, Ohio, in the year 1820. In 1837, he came to Ashland county, then Wayne, in company with his father, and settled in Perry township, residing here until the time of his father's death, November 11, 1859, his mother surviving until the year 1872. Abraham Ecker was one of Ohio's early pioneers, coming to the State as early as the year 1818. He left a family of ten children, the only representatives of the household now living in the county being Mrs. Barbara Bringolf, Mrs. Susan Tolbert, and Jacob, who resides on a farm adjoining the old homestead. Jacob Ecker was married first to Anna Garver, in the year 1845. To them were born three children, one son and two daughters. Their names are as follows: David Newton, a twin, his twin sister dying in infancy, unnamed, and Mary Elizabeth. David grew to manhood, enlisted in the war of 1861, and never returned, losing his life by disease at Clarksburgh, Tennessee, in 1863. Having always been a dutiful son, his loss was deeply felt by the fond family. Mr. Ecker lost his wife May 14, 1848, and was left with two affectionate children. September 17, 1854, he married his second wife, Ann Ellen Brandt. The fruit of this union was six children, one son and five daughters: Emma Viola, Nora

Ann, Mary Ellen, Lulu Loretta, Lillie May, and Charles Wesley. Two are deceased, Emma and Lulu, one dying in infancy, and the other in early childhood. Mr. Ecker is one of the most substantial farmers of Ashland county. He has served repeatedly as treasurer of his township, thus bespeaking for him the confidence of the people. Both himself and wife are earnest members of the Methodist Episcopal church, and have been among its most liberal supporters. For twenty-four years he operated successfully a fine grist-mill, making a handsome fortune therefrom; but he has now retired, and the old mill has been torn away.

WILLIAM WEIKAL, third son of Daniel and Mary Weikal, was born in Columbia county, Pennsylvania, in the year 1817. At the age of seven years he accompanied his parents to Venango county, where he resided until the twentieth year of his age, after which he made his home with his brother Samuel until the time of his marriage to Miss May Ann Ketner, June 13, 1841. He then purchased fifty acres of land, and erected a fine and commodious house, and there began life in earnest. There he lived for a period of twelve years, when he disposed of his farm to his brother Samuel, and removed three miles distant to a quarter of land owned jointly by himself and his brother, whose interest he afterward bought. Here he again made settlement immediately in the woods, with no traces whatever to give evidence of civilization and advancement. By his strong will and earnest determination to succeed, he soon erected good buildings, and waving fields of grain soon gave evidence that his intentions had been fully executed. Here he reared his family of fourteen children, seven sons and seven daughters. Their names are as follows: John Aaron, David, Isaac Newton, Margaret Malinda, Ellen Jane, Albert K., John Milton, Ann Eliza, Uriah D., Emma Ann, Isa Alice, Hattie May, William F., and Dora, all of whom are living but John A., Isaac Newton, Ann Eliza and Dora. Mr. Weikal immigrated to Ohio in 1865, and settled in Perry township, where he purchased a farm of two hundred and ten acres, known as the old Row farm. Both himself and his wife are earnest members of the Evangelical church. Mr. Weikal's family are much scattered, but four remaining at home. David, the eldest son living, resides in Pettis county, Missouri. Mr. Weikal has always made it a rule in his family, to give to each child on leaving the parental roof, two thousand dollars, which always comes at a time when most needed. Few parents are more deserving of honor and remembrance. Mr. Weikal has other sons in the different western States, whom he has also equally aided. To him his children owe a deep debt of gratitude. Albert K. is living in the town of Newton, Iowa, following his occupation, that of painter. John M. and Uriah D. are living in Edwards county, Kansas, where they are located on good farms.

WILLIAM OSBURN, second son of Thomas and Margaret Osburn, was born in Wayne (now Ashland) county, September 15, 1839. He resided with his parents until he attained his majority, in the spring of 1861, when he enlisted in the service of his country for three months, and, before the time expired he re-enlisted for a period of three years, serving his full term. He was engaged in almost every serious engagement, and, with the exception of several slight injuries, he returned to his home crowned with all the honor to which the faithful are entitled. In 1867 he was married to Miss Lydia Lucas. To them have been born six children, viz.: Jacob, Thomas, Channing, Lydia, Miriam, and Alice. The subject of our sketch is the possessor of three separate tracts of land, containing in all one hundred and twenty-three acres. He comes of pioneer stock.

DAVID MCCONNELL, fourth son of William McConnell, was born in the State of Pennsylvania, Mercer county, January 15, 1813. He emigrated to Ohio in the year 1815, in company with his parents, and lived with his father in Wayne county, where he first settled, until the twenty-third year of his age, when he was married to Miss Matilda Firestone. He then rented his father's farm, which he superintended for three years. Then he came to Ashland county and purchased a little farm of fifty acres in Perry township and began life in earnest, immediately in the woods, with no improvement whatever, save a rude log cabin, to give any traces of civilization or advancement. To Mr. and Mrs. McConnell were born eleven children, four of whom were born in the pioneer home. Through his strong will and earnest determination the forest was soon made to give way, and waving fields of grain soon gave evidence that his intentions had been fully executed. Here he reared and educated his little family, and as Heaven prospered him he was able every few years to add more acres to his pioneer farm, and to-day has one of the most pleasant and comfortable homes in Perry township. The names of his children are as follows: James, who lives in Missouri; Sarah, who lives at home; Rachel Flora, who resides in Seneca county; Nancy, who lives at home; Annis Shonnaker, who resides in Seneca county; John, who is superintending the home place; David, who makes his home in Ashland; Alice Spotts, who lives in Wayne county; and Florence, Burzilla and Rebecca, deceased. Mr. McConnell is one of the most substantial pioneer farmers in the township. Mrs. McConnell is an earnest member of the Lutheran church, and has always been one of its most liberal supporters, while the husband is not associated with any church organization. He is a strong advocate of law and order. James enlisted in the Forty-second regiment, company C, September 25, 1861, and served three years under T. C. Bushnell, and was in the fight at Vicksburgh and various other engagements, and was captured by the enemy at Champion Hill and kept in custody for about three weeks, when he was paroled. He was exchanged about three months later, when he again joined the army.

DAVID WEILER, youngest child of Joseph and Rosanna Weiler, was born in Chester county, Pennsylvania, in 1825, and emigrated to Ohio in company with his parents in 1834. They first made a settlement in Wayne county, where his father rented for a period of five years, and afterwards purchased a quarter section of land near Smithville, where he resided until the time of his death, in 1858 or 1859, surviving his wife but eight years, and leaving a family of ten children. The only representatives of the Weiler family residing in the county are Mrs. Sarah Van Nest, who resides in Rowsburgh, and David, the subject of our sketch, who lives one mile west of Rowsburgh. David purchased the farm where we now find him, in the year 1856, and he at once set about improving his home. In 1849 he was married to Miss Anna Eberly. The fruit of this union was six children, two sons and four daughters, viz.: Tillitha J., George W., Ida May, William Sherman, Lora E., and Mary F. Those living are Lora and Mary, the others having died in infancy. Mr. Weiler is one of the most substantial farmers of Perry township, and is a worthy and respected citizen. He has served in the various township offices, thus bespeaking for him the full confidence of the people. His wife died in the summer of 1879. Mr. Weiler was one of the valiant soldiers of the Rebellion, serving in company I, of the One Hundred and Sixty-third regiment, one hundred days' men.

RICHARD SMALLEY was the eighth child and fifth son of Richard and Catharine (Emmond) Smalley. The father was a native of New Jersey, and the mother of Virginia. Their first settlement in Ohio was in Jefferson county, where our subject was born. They moved into Ashland county about the year 1820, and settled on the farm which is still in the possession of their son, Richard. A half-section of land was his first purchase, on which he built a log cabin and commenced his pioneer life in earnest. At this time, the now beautiful fields of Perry township were a dense wilderness, and it took courage and a brave heart to face the hardships they had to undergo. Our subject left home before reaching his majority, and worked as a farm hand for Captain Andrews, of Ashland, continuing at this ten or fifteen years. Then he bought a farm of one hundred and sixty acres, near Olivesburgh. After making several purchases of land, and as often changing his residence, he was married to Ardilla Vantilburg, of this county, in the year 1840. To them have been born nine children, five of whom are living. Their names are as follows: Henry C., who was a soldier in the hundred-day service; John W., who was a brave soldier, and died in St. Louis in the service of his country, and now lies buried in his native county; Daniel, who was a soldier, and was killed at Athens, his remains now lying somewhere in the "sunny south," in an unknown, but not forgotten, grave, his body never having been found; Richard V.; Jacob, who died in infancy; Silas W.; Dr. Benjamin F.; one, an infant, unnamed; and William E. Two only live at home —William and Silas. Although not members of any church organization, Mr. and Mrs. Smalley are peace-loving and law-abiding citizens. By dint of hard work, industry, and a wise economy, Mr. Smalley has risen from a poor man to be one of the thriftiest and most substantial farmers of Perry township. Both Mr. and Mrs. Smalley come from old pioneer stock, and to them posterity will look with mingled pleasure and pride for the results they have achieved.

JOHN G. BRINGOLF, the only son of Jacob and Catharine Bringolf, was born in Lancaster county, Pennsylvania, in the year 1824. He came to Ohio in 1846, and settled in Ashland county, and for the first twelve months pursued his trades of blacksmith and carpenter. He then commenced clerking, which he followed for a period of two years, after which he engaged in farming, which he followed for ten years. At this time he began the practice of dentistry, which he followed successfully for another decade. He then settled in Rowsburgh, where we now find him, and erected a handsome and substantial home and business rooms, in which he engaged in the retail grocery business. He is also postmaster, which appointment he received in August, 1879. On July 14, 1847, he was married to Miss Barbara Ecker. To them were born two children, a son and a daughter, Joseph E. and Deborah A. The daughter died in early childhood, at the age of four years. Our subject is one of the prominent and substantial business men of Perry township. Both himself and his wife are earnest members of the Lutheran church. Mr. Bringolf has served his township two terms as justice of the peace, two terms as clerk, and two years as treasurer, thus showing that he enjoys the confidence of the people for his faithful discharge of the trusts bestowed upon him.

TROY TOWNSHIP.

ADAM SMITH, son of Henry and Leah Smith, was born in Columbiana county, Ohio, May 3, 1831, and came to Ashland in the year 1846 with his parents. He has been a resident of the county ever since, with the exception of about three years that he spent in California. He was twice married; first, on July 18, 1859, to Elizabeth Richards, daughter of Wesley and Jane Richards, who was born in Wayne county, July 5, 1840. The fruit of this union was seven children, as follows: Loren C., Leah J., Willis J., Lewis H., John W., Martin R., and Nora E., all of whom are living. Mrs. Smith died July 9, 1877. Mr. Smith was married July 30, 1879, the second time, to Miss Jennie Pickard, second child of John and Mary A. Pickard, born November 16, 1850. Both Mr. and Mrs. Smith are members of the Methodist Episcopal church. When Mr. Smith came to Ashland county the farm he now owns was all woods. Mr. Smith served in the office of trustee of Troy township one term. When Mr. Smith went to California he went by the way of New York; from New York he went to Aspinwall; from there crossed the isthmus to Panama; from there to Gargonia, Mexico; and from there to San Francisco, and then to Sacramento, and took the steamer up the river to Red bluff, in Chasta county, and from there to Trinity county, and footed it forty miles over the mountains to work in the mines. He remained there three years and four months, and by this time he had made a good start and returned home.

ELISHA P. PHELPS, sixth child of Elisha and Weighty Phelps, was born in New York State, May 6, 1804. About the year 1848 he emigrated to Lorain (now Ashland,) county, Ohio, and was a resident of Ashland county up to the time of his death, which occurred November 5, 1867, at the age of sixty-three years and six months. The subject of our sketch was married to Miss Jane Kniffin, who was born in Ulster county, New York, July 4, 1811, and was married February 3, 1831. The fruit of this marriage was three children—Charles W., George W., and John D., all living. Mrs. Phelps is still on the farm, which is cultivated by her son, John D. Phelps. She is an earnest member of the Methodist Episcopal church, and is one of its most liberal supporters.

GEORGE W. BOWERIZE, second child of Christian and Elizabeth Bowerize, was born in Frederick City, Maryland, November 15, 1818, and emigrated to Richland (now Ashland,) county, Ohio, with his father, about the year 1829. Mr. Bowerize's sr., was the thirteenth family of old Orange. The township was all in woods at that time, and running full of wild deer. Mr. Bowerize moved to Troy township, December 18, 1845, and has been a resident of the township ever since. October 17, 1844, he was married to Eve A. Stober, daughter of Jacob and Catharine Stober, who was born in Lebanon county, Pennsylvania, April 31, 1821. The fruit of this marriage was nine children—William W., Ephraim C., Louisa K., George H., Sarah E., John F., Eliza E., Hiram J., and Charles C.; all living. At present four of the sons and one daughter are still at home. Both Mr. and Mrs. Bowerize are members of the German Reformed church.

JOSEPH L. PARKER, eldest child of Josiah and Elizabeth Parker, was born in Westchester county, New York, May 10, 1795. March 11, 1814, he was married to Miss Eunice Phelps, daughter of Elisha and Weighty Phelps, who was born in Seneca county, New York, November 23, 1797. To them were born eleven children: Wesley, Ceoleous E., Nelson, Charlotte, Mary A., Julie A., Elisha, Josiah, Hannah, Samuel, and Nathaniel. Of these, four are dead and seven living. About two years after the subject of our sketch was married, he moved to Pennsylvania, and remained in the State about four years. From there he moved to Columbiana county, in the year 1825, and from Columbiana county he moved to Mahoning county, then Trumbull, and thence to Ashland in the year 1832, and has been a resident of the county ever since. Both Mr. and Mrs. Parker are earnest members in the Methodist Episcopal church.

JOHN PARMENTER, JR., second child of John and Sally Parmenter, was born in Cortland county, New York, June 4, 1814. In the year 1836 he emigrated to Wayne county, Ohio, with his father, and remained there until the year 1852, when he moved to Richland county, and remained there two years, and in 1854 moved to Ashland county, where he has since resided. February 28, 1843, he was married to Miss Sarah, daughter of John and Rachel McDonald. To them have been born eight children: Frances E., John D., Rachel A., William Z., Lancaster W., Mary C., Linneus C., and one who died in infancy. The children have all left the parental roof but one, Linneus C. Mrs. Parmenter is an earnest member of the Methodist Episcopal church.

E. C. BRANDEBERY, son of Abraham and Sarah Brandebery, was born in Columbiana county, Ohio, August 28, 1831, and removed to Ashland county in October, 1834, with his father, where he has ever since lived. January 31, 1855, he was married to Miss Elizabeth Bailey, daughter of Joseph and Rebecca Bailey, who was born in Clearcreek township, Ashland county, February 13, 1838. To them have been born six children, as follows: Mary L., Albert E., Alletha A., Gertrude, Elias, Q. V., all of whom are living but one, Mary L., who died at the age of four weeks. Mr. and Mrs. Brandebery are members of the Methodist Episcopal church. The subject of this sketch started out in the world with nothing, and by hard work, wise economy, and careful management he is the possessor of a good farm.

CORNELIUS BISHOP, second child of John and Catharine Bishop, was born in Orange township, Ashland county, Ohio, July 16, 1821. In 1845 he moved from Orange to Sullivan township, and remained there twelve years, and in the year 1858 he came to Troy township, where he has since resided. August 21, 1845, he was married to Miss Sarah Hazel, daughter of Hugh and Ruth Hazel. To them were born five children, as follows: Mary J., Louisa, Albert W., Ida and John. Two of the children are still at home, two are residents of Troy township, while Albert W. is a minister of the gospel in Missouri. Mr. and Mrs. Bishop are members of the United Brethren church. The subject of our sketch is one of the prominent farmers of his township, and has at various times been elected to township offices. He is a class-leader in the church, and superintendent of the Sunday-school.

ALVIN CRITTENDEN, son of Medad and Sarah Crittenden, was born in Ruggles township, Ashland county, Ohio, October 1, 1855, and moved into Troy township in 1877, where he now lives. February 7, 1877, he was married to Miss Ida E. Ford, daughter of Laban and Sarah Ford. They have one child, Sarah A., born March 18, 1878. Both Mr. and Mrs. Crittenden are members in the church, Mr. Crittenden belonging to the Congregational and his wife to the Methodist Episcopal church.

JOEL BRUCE, oldest child of Josiah and Betsey Bruce, was born in Windsor county, Vermont, February 16, 1815. In the year 1837 he removed to Ashland county, Ohio, and in 1838 settled in Troy township. He was married twice; the first time to Caroline Smith, August 24, 1836. To them were born two children, Mary M. and Alden. Mrs. Bruce died in October, 1866. For a second wife he married Mrs. Julia A. Jacobs, widow of Hiram Jacobs, September 5, 1867. A short time after he settled in Troy township, he was elected to the office of constable, in that township, and served in that capacity for nine years. Afterward he served five years as trustee. During his service as constable, he became accustomed to auctioneering goods, and followed that occupation for eighteen years. Since that time he has been engaged in farming.

C. D. FAIR, son of Jacob and Eve Fair, was born in Somerset county, Pennsylvania, February 17, 1825, and moved to Holmes county, Ohio, with his father about the year 1832. About 1850, he came to Ashland county, and has been a resident of the county ever since. February 7, 1847, he was married to Sarah Richard, daughter of David and Nancy Richard, who was born in Holmes county, February 7, 1829. To them were born twelve children, as follows: Jacob W., Susan, Israel, Margaret, Sarah J., Daniel R., George W., James M., Nancy E., Jonah H., Harvey W., and one who died in infancy. Susan and Margaret are also dead.

GEORGE BECK, son of Leonard Beck, was born in the province of New Brunswick, February 24, 1815, and emigrated to Harrison county, Ohio, with his mother, five sisters, and two brothers, about the year 1830, and, in 1847, removed to Sullivan township, Ashland county, where he remained until 1865, when he removed to the farm where he now lives, in Troy township. He was married December 26, 1839, to Miss Delilah Miller, daughter of Peter and Catharine Miller, who was born in Somerset county, Pennsylvania, December 16, 1817. To them were born eight children, viz.: Martha J., William H., Titus F., David, George, Mary E., Eliza C., Ollie S., and Enoch G., but five of whom are now living. William, the oldest son, died in the service of his country, having been a member of company K, One Hundred and Forty-second regiment, Ohio volunteer infantry. Both Mr. and Mrs. Beck are members of the United Brethren church.

ORLANDO CRITTENDEN, son of Medad and Sarah Crittenden, was born in Ruggles township, Ashland county, February 18, 1849. He moved to Troy township December 2, 1869, and has been a resident of the county ever since. He was married to Miss Ellen J. Stratton, daughter of Alexander and Isabelle Stratton, July 1, 1869. To them were born two children—Wanda E. and Immer O.—both living.

JACKSON TOWNSHIP.

JOHN H. ELDRIDGE, son of Henry and M. Eldridge, was born in Jackson township, Ashland county, December 9, 1840. He was married to Lucy A. Matthews, oldest child of Chester C. and Elizabeth Matthews, October 12, 1865. He was a soldier in the late war, in battery D, First Ohio veteran volunteer light artillery, for four years. Both Mr. and Mrs. Eldridge are members of the Methodist Episcopal church.

SAMUEL BERRY, son of Jacob and Elizabeth A. Berry, was born in Jackson township, Ashland county, December 16, 1823, and has always resided there. He was married to Miss Malinda Shutt, daughter of Philip and Elizabeth Shutt, February 27, 1851. They have had nine children, as follows: Lure, Newton, Myrtle C., Margaret C., Olive J., Alma M., Charles V., Franklin W., and one who died in infancy. Margaret died at the age of twelve years. Both Mr. and Mrs. Berry are earnest members in the Methodist Episcopal church. Mr. Berry has held the offices of treasurer and trustee of Jackson township three terms each.

SAMUEL EICHER, son of Abraham and Esther Eicher, was born in Westmoreland county, Pennsylvania, November 21, 1830. He came to Wayne county, Ohio, with his mother, in the year 1852, and there remained until the year 1856, when he removed to Ashland county, and remained in the county two years. He then moved to Medina county, remaining there five years, and in the year 1861 moved back to Ashland county, to the farm where he now lives. He was married to Miss Mary J. Keller, August 16, 1854. The fruit of this union was six children: William A., Quincy L., Ida F., Salena J., and two who died in infancy. Mr. and Mrs. Eicher are both earnest members in the Methodist Episcopal church.

BENJAMIN BUZZARD, son of Jacob and Hannah Buzzard, was born in Center county, Pennsylvania, March 8, 1816, and in the year 1840 moved to Wayne county, Ohio. January 12, 1845, he was married to Miss Mary Mellinger, third child of George and Catharine Mellinger, who was born in Cumberland county, Pennsylvania, November 26, 1822, and came to Ohio, Wayne county, with her parents, when at the age of four years. Mr. and Mrs. Buzzard are members of the Brethren church.

JACOB KIPLINGER, son of Jacob and Barbara Kiplinger, was born in Pence valley, Pennsylvania, March 22, 1808, and emigrated to Ashland county, Ohio, in about the year 1824, and settled on the farm where his son Emanuel now lives. In the fall of 1832 he was married to Lizzie Keen, daughter of John Keen, sr. The fruit of this union was seven children—Polly, Emanuel, John, Rebecca, Hannah, and two who died in infancy. Polly, John and Rebecca are also dead. Emanuel was born February 5, 1840, and has lived in Ashland county since his birth, with the exception of about eight months that he lived in Medina county, Ohio. Emanuel Kiplinger was married August 23, 1866, to Miss Peggy A. Landis, daughter of Samuel and Christinie Landis, who was born in Ashland county, Jackson township, December 28, 1845. They have had seven children—Ida E., Alice L., Christina E., Rosa J., Viola M., Charlie F., and Harvey E., all living but Alice and a baby who died in infancy. Although Mr. Kiplinger is a member of no church, he is a strong advocate of law and order.

MICHAEL STENTZ, son of Philip and Polly Stentz, was born in Dauphin county, Pennsylvania, February 20, 1828, and came to Wayne county, near Wooster, with his father, when he was but two years old, and moved from Wayne county to Richland, now Ashland county, in February, 1837. He remained in Ashland county until the year 1855, when he moved to Illinois, and remained until 1864. In that year he came back to Ashland county to the farm where he now lives. March 18, 1852, he was married to Miss Mary Robertson, daughter of Samuel and Alice Robertson. The fruit of this union was nine children—John R., Alice M., James F., Ellen J., Florence J., Denton E., Cela L., and two who died in infancy. Florence also died March 25, 1864, aged two years. Both Mr. and Mrs. Stentz are members in the Methodist Episcopal church.

DAVID ESHLEMAN, son of Joseph and Margaret Eshleman, was born in Wayne county, Ohio, February 24, 1843, came to Ashland county in 1864, and has lived in this county ever since, with the exception of about six years that he lived in Wayne and Lorain counties. He was married June 20, 1867, to Harriet, daughter of Samuel and Christena Landis, who was born in Ashland county, June 5, 1848. They had six children, viz.: Rosella M., Christena, Lovenia E., Sophronia G., Alberta, and one who died in infancy. Christena is also dead.

HENRY MYERS, JR., son of Henry and Margaret Myers, was born in Center county, Pennsylvania, in 1781, and about the year 1830 emigrated to Jackson township, Ashland county, Ohio, and settled on the farm on which his son now lives. He was married to Barbara Foreman, daughter of Michael and Elizabeth Foreman. They had nine children, viz.: George, John, Rebecca, Daniel, Susan, Eliza, William, Henry, and Reuben—all living but Daniel and Henry. William, the seventh child, is still on the old home place. He was born in Center county, Pennsylvania, September 24, 1830, and was married March 31, 1866, to Mary, daughter of Peter and Elizabeth Miller, who was born in Lancaster county, Pennsylvania, June 4, 1848. They have raised three children, viz.: Corren, Orlando, and Henry P. But one of the three is now living—Henry P. Mr. and Mrs. Myers are both earnest members in the Evangelical church, and are among its most liberal supporters. Mr. Myers still lives on the old home place, his mother living with him. She has reached the ripe old age of eighty-four years. Henry Myers, her husband, died in March, 1861, aged seventy-two years. They were among the earliest settlers of Ashland county, and were respected and esteemed by all who knew them.

LEVI HOUSEHOLDER, son of Michael and Martha Householder, was born in Huntingdon county, Pennsylvania, May 21, 1815. In April, 1848, he came to Ashland county, where he has since resided. Twice he has been married; his first wife was Hester Hamer, widow of William Hamer, to whom he was married in March, 1836. The fruit of this marriage was five children: Mary A., Michael A., Abraham, Caroline and Oliver. Mr. Householder lost his first wife July 27, 1864. The second time he was married August 17, 1865, to Margaret J. Patterson,, daughter of James and Barbara Patterson, who was born in Westmoreland county, Pennsylvania, April 28, 1822. Both himself and wife are members of the Presbyterian church.

JAMES E. CHASE, only son of Seth Chase, was born in Stark county, Ohio, October 19, 1824. Nine years after the death of his father he removed to Ashland county, where he now lives. For two years he served as representative from Stark county, and two terms from Ashland county. In the year 1851, he was married to Jane Doty, of Stark county, and to them have been born eight children: Mary J., Eleanor S., Samantha, James B., Orland D., Sherwood M., and Nelson H., all living, and Franklin, deceased. Mrs. Chase is a member of the German Reformed church. Mr. Chase has held the office of treasurer of Jackson township two years, and has served as school director for twenty-five years; and he says that in the last ten years he has had an estate on his hands continually, showing the confidence people have in him.

MICHAEL BOWERS, son of Ulrich Bowers, was born in Germany March 25, 1814, and was but four years old when his father died. In 1830 he left Germany and settled in New York State, where he remained eighteen months. From there he moved to Columbiana county, Ohio, and remained there six years. Then he moved to Wayne county, and lived there twelve years. From there he removed to Ashland county, in 1852, where he now lives. Both himself and wife are members of the German Reformed church.

JACOB FAST, son of Martin Fast, was born in Ashland county, Ohio, September 12, 1821, and is living on the homestead at this writing. Mr. Fast was married twice, his first wife was Elizabeth Plice, to whom he was married September 7, 1848. To them were born four children, as follows: Irene T., Joseph E., Mary S., Samuel C.; all of whom are living but Samuel C. Mr. Fast married, for his second wife, Melissa M. Burlingame, July 20, 1865. The fruit of this marriage was two children—Edwin F. and Cora E. Mr. and Mrs. Fast are members of the Disciple church. Mr. Fast has held the office of justice of the peace since 1852, with the exception of one term.

JOHN KEENER, JR., was the first son of John Keener, sr., and was born in Pennsylvania, December 5, 1801. In April, 1820, he came to Ashland county with his father, and settled in Mohican township, and in 1828 moved to Jackson township. He has been twice married. First to Margaret Worst, on October 16, 1828. The fruit of this marriage was twelve children, six living, and six dead. He was married the second time to Sarah Fast, on the eighteenth day of February, 1872. Mr. and Mrs. Keener are both members of the Disciple church. Mr. Keener has held the office of constable and supervisor of Jackson township for several years.

JOSEPH WEIKEL, son of Daniel Weikel, was born in Venango county, Pennsylvania, February 25, 1829. On January 2, 1866, he came to Jackson township, Ashland county, to the place where he now lives. On October 25, 1849, he married Margaret Long, in Venango, Pennsylvania. The fruit of this marriage was nine children—Henry T., Mary J., Margaret M., George W., Joseph A., Leah E., Emma, Joseph U. G.; four of whom survive—Mary J., George W., Emma, and Joseph A. being dead. Mr. and Mrs. Weikel are both members of the Evangelical Association.

MICHAEL MAY, son of Jacob May, was born in York

county, Pennsylvania, February 25, 1823. In April, 1833, he removed to Wayne county, Ohio, with his parents. In the year 1858, he left Wayne county and came to Ashland county, to the farm where he now lives. On the twenty-fifth of March, 1858, he was married to Miss Mary B. Gout. The fruit of this marriage was three children: John, Melissa, and Jane—all living. Mr. and Mrs. May are both members of the Disciple church. With a little assistance from his father, hard work, and careful management, Mr. May has got as well improved farm as you will find one in Ashland county.

RANKIN F. WELCH, son of Ephraim Welch, was born in Orange township, Ashland county, December 13, 1833, one and a half miles west of the place on which he now lives. Twice he was married, his first wife being Druzella A. Frink, to whom he was married in February, 1867. The fruit of this marriage was one child, Gilbert P., who is still living. His second wife was Mary L. McDonald, to whom he was married May 1, 1879.

THOMAS MILLER, son of Thomas Miller, sr., was born in York county, Pennsylvania, April 7, 1823, and came to Orange township, Ashland county, in the year 1835, and in the year 1837 moved to Jackson township, where he now lives. In April, 1845, he was married to Miss Margaret Robertson. Their children were nine in number, as follows: Alice, John, Pierce, Rachel, Orville, Otis, Ada, and George M., all of whom are living. Although Mr. Miller is a member of no church, he is a strong believer of right and law. He is the largest landholder in Ashland county.

JOHN WELCH, son of Ephraim Welch, was born in Orange township, Ashland county, Ohio, February 7, 1830. October 1, 1861, he moved to the old Bryen place, in Jackson township. He was married to Miss Rebecca Robertson, December 6, 1853. To them were born four children, Vernon H., Alice B., Bernie E., Leclair S., all of whom are living. Mr. Welch is one of Ashland county's largest landholders.

THOMAS DEARMON, son of James DeArmon, was born in Ashland county, June 22, 1839, on the farm lying north of that on which he now lives. He was married to Augusta L. Fluke, of Ashland, May 7, 1868. They have six children: Annie, Winfield, Francis, Edwin, Guy, and Ernest, all of whom are living. Mr. DeArmon has filled the office of justice of the peace of Jackson township one term.

WILLIAM BERRY, son of Jacob Berry, was born in Wayne (now Ashland) county, Perry township, July 14, 1821. January 8, 1846, he was married to Miss Margaret Shutt. To them were born thirteen children, as follows: Philemon F., Mary M., Susannah E., Emma J., Lydia E., Milton M., Katie M., Wilson C., William C., Alice C., Lola B., Orville E., Lewis E., all of whom are living but Wilson, Philemon, William and Lola. Mr. Berry died September 15, 1873, leaving a widow and nine children. Mr. and Mrs. Berry were members of the German Reformed church. Mrs. Berry, assisted by her son, still manages the farm. At the time of his death, William Berry was justice of the peace in his township, which office he had held for nine years.

C. C. MATTHEWS, son of Jesse Matthews, was born in Trumbull county, Ohio, March 18, 1815, and came to Wayne, now Ashland county, when but three years old, with his father, ever since remaining on the farm on which his father first settled. December 19, 1839, he was married to Elizabeth Cole, and raised fourteen children: Lucy A., Harriet E., Rebecca J., Emma C., Athaliah, Mary N., Joseph E., Thomas L., Martha S., Sarah M. C., Jessie I. O., Newton E., Ettie C., and John E., all of whom are living except Martha S. Both himself and wife are members of the Methodist Episcopal church. He has served three terms as constable in Jackson township. In speaking of the early days, he says he has heard wolves howling around his house many a night.

JOHN IRWIN, son of Jacob Irwin, sr., was born in Franklin county, Pennsylvania, October 15, 1804, and moved to Stark county, Ohio, with his father in the fall of 1816. In 1826 he removed to Holmes county, and in 1838 moved to Jackson township, Ashland county, to the farm where he yet lives. In January, 1844, he was married to Hannah Mast, of Holmes county. They have had six children: Sarah, Archibald M., Amanda, Lucinda, Louisa, and Ellenora, all of whom are living except Ellenora.

JOHN BYERS, son of Frederick and Annie Byers, was born in Franklin county, Pennsylvania, March 11, 1803. He emigrated to Ashland, now Wayne county, Ohio, July 8, 1836. Before leaving Pennsylvania he was married to Miss Francis Ditwiler, March 6, 1827. They have raised a family of six children: Edward, Anna E., William, Frederick, Jane, and Catharine, all living but Edward and Anna E. Mrs. Byers died February 25, 1879, aged seventy-three years and six months. Mr. Byers served in the office of township treasurer three years.

GEORGE POORMAN, son of Matthias Poorman, was born in Lancaster county, Pennsylvania. From there he emigrated to Stark county, Ohio, at about the age of twenty. He was there married to Nancy Oberland in 1830. The fruit of this union was five children, as follows: Hiram, Catharine, John, Jeremiah, and Elesan, all living but Elesan and Catharine. In the spring of 1862 Mrs. Poorman emigrated with her little family to Ashland county, Jackson township, to the farm where she now resides. Her husband, George Poorman, died February 27, 1846, leaving his wife with the care of a family upon her. Mrs. Poorman is a member of the German Reformed church, and is one of its most liberal supporters. By wise economy and careful management, Mrs. Poorman has supplied each of her sons with a farm.

HENRY SWITZER, son of David Switzer, was born in Jackson township, Wayne, now Ashland county, June 11, 1833. In 1851 he moved to Wayne county, and remained there five years. He then moved back to Jackson township, where he now lives. He was married to Anna E. Landis, September 2, 1856, and has one child, Amanda J., still living. Mr. Switzer is a member of the German Reformed church, and his wife is a member of the Evangelical church. He has held the office of trustee six years; he also served as land appraiser ten years ago, and is in that office again.

ANTHONY KLINE, son of John Kline, was born in Franklin county, Pennsylvania, April 10, 1832, and emigrated to Wayne county, Ohio, in the year 1842, with his father, and, in 1859, removed to Jackson township, Ashland county, about two miles east from the place where he now lives. In the fall of 1861 he married Susan Kane. The fruit of this marriage was six children, viz.: George E., Jeremiah W., John F., James, Clarence, Ettie J., and Ira—the last named being dead. Elizabeth Kane, mother of Mrs. Kline, lives with her daughter. She has reached the ripe old age of seventy-seven years. She is an earnest member of the Evangelical church, and is one of Ashland county's pioneers. Mr. and Mrs. Kline are members of the Evangelical church, and are among its most liberal supporters. He has filled the office of trustee two years in Jackson township.

HERMAN KANE, son of J. C. and Elizabeth Kane, was born in Schenectady, New York, December 15, 1840, came to Ohio in the year 1857, with his father, and settled on the farm where he now lives, in Jackson township, Ashland county, Ohio. In 1859 he was married to Mary Kane. The fruit of this marriage was eleven children: William, Eugene, Ernest, Edna, Minnie, Florence, Maud, Guy C., Bertrand, Kenneth, and Louie—all living but William.

JAMES A. DINSMORE, SR., was born in York county, Pennsylvania, March 20, 1788. January 3, 1828, he entered a tract of land of three hundred and twenty acres, and in the year 1833 moved his family to Ashland county, then Wayne, to the farm where his widow and two of his children still live. On the fourteenth of March, 1826, he was married to Miss Grizell Collins. The fruit of this union was seven children: Catharine A., Tabitha M., David C., Jewett E., Andrew A., Rachel M., and James R. W., all of whom are living. Mr. Dinsmore and wife, and all the family that belong to any church, belong to the Presbyterian church. When Mr. Dinsmore became possessor of his farm of three hundred and twenty acres, there were but fourteen acres cleared. To protect his family from the wild beasts of the forest, he erected two log cabins. When Mr. Dinsmore came to Ashland county, he brought an agent with him. They had but one horse, and they would do, as the old saying is, "Walk and hitch." After a great deal of hard labor to prepare something for his family, that they need not suffer, he departed this life January 7, 1863, at the ripe age of seventy-five years. His son James still superintends the old home place. David Dinsmore, first son of James A. Dinsmore, is practicing medicine in Iowa, while Andrew S. is a preacher of the Gospel in Philadelphia. Tabitha M. married Rev. Beer, of Ashland; he is now a judge in Bucyrus. Jewett E. married J. R. Reed; they now reside in Council Bluffs, Iowa. Catharine A. was married twice; first, to Augustine M. Hay, the second time to William Collins, in Green county, Ohio. Rachel is still at home with her parents.

SIMON CLOUSE was born in Fayette county, Pennsylvania, February 14, 1815. Mr. Clouse, with his father, moved to Wayne county, Ohio, about the year 1820, and about the year 1852 moved to Ashland county, to the farm where he now lives, in Jackson township. He was married to Sarah Newcomer, of Wayne county, March 30, 1841. The fruit of this union was seven children: Mary, Jasper, Lewis, James M., Jacob, Leander, and Oliver. Of these, four are living: Mary, James M., Leander, and Oliver, the other three being dead. Mr. Clouse and wife are members of the Evangelical church, and are among its most liberal supporters. When Mr. Clouse came to the place where he now lives, it was all in woods. The first thing for him to do was to erect a log cabin, in which to shelter his family. Then he set out to clear and cultivate the soil. Now he has a well improved farm in Jackson township.

JACOB PLICE, oldest son of Jacob F. and Mary B. Plice, was born in Pennsylvania, March 4, 1821, and came to Ohio about the year 1830, with his father, who settled in Orange township, and about the year 1832 moved into Jackson township, where he has remained up to this date. Jacob Plice was married to Miss Mary Cole, sixth child of Thomas and Atheliah Cole, August 20, 1846. She was born in Ashland county, December 9, 1827. The fruit of this union was six children—George E., Thomas V., William A., Mary R., John, and Samuel V. Of these, four are living—Thomas V., Mary R., John, and Samuel V. Mr. and Mrs. Plice are members of the Methodist Episcopal church. He has served as constable of Jackson township.

ANDREW MOGLE, son of Valentine Mogle, was born in Center county, Pennsylvania, June 13, 1825. He moved to Ohio with his father in the year, 1835, and located in Montgomery township, Ashland county. He was married March 27, 1851, to Miss Nancy McFadden, daughter of John and Catharine McFadden, who was born April 22, 1820. Mr. Mogle is a member of the Albright church, and one of its most liberal supporters.

JONAS WILTROUT, son of Jacob Wiltrout, was born in Somerset county, Pennsylvania, January 21, 1825. He came to Ohio with his father in the year 1836, to Jackson township, Ashland county. He was married to Miss Eliza Priest in February, 1846. The fruit of this marriage was eight children, Edward, Jane, Erastus, Estella, Lincoln, Myron, Libby, and Elmore, all of whom are living. Both Mr. and Mrs. Wiltrout are members of the Methodist Episcopal church.

DAVID HEIFFNER, the only living representative of his father's family, came to Orange township in company with his parents, in the year 1817. He now owns and occupies the old Heiffner homestead. His father and mother are both deceased, and lie sleeping side by side, in the family cemetery. In the year 1828 he was married to Miss Margaret Hartman, and to them were born fourteen children, five sons and nine daughters. Mrs. Heiffner died in the year 1852. Mr. Heiffner was again married in 1856, to Mrs. Sophia Marks. The fruit of this second marriage was one son, Richard. Mrs. Heiffner was the widow of George Marks, by whom she had five children. He and his wife are earnest followers of the Christian religion, and have always been staunch supporters of the cause of Christ.

PHILIP FLUKE was born in the year 1791 in the State of Pennsylvania, Bedford county. He married in or about the year 1810, to Miss Mary Summers. To them were born eleven children, seven sons and four daughters—Henry, born 1811; Lewis, born 1813; Samuel, born 1814; Philip, born 1816; Catharine, born 1819; Jacob, born 1820; David, born 1822; Eliza, born 1825; Lucinda, born 1826; Margaret, born 1829; John, born 1831. He came to what is now Orange township, and made permanent settlement immediately in the woods with no traces whatever of civilization. Here he began life in earnest. He immediately set about the erection of a rude log cabin, in which to shelter his little family. This done, he at once proceeded to clear up and improve his pioneer home, and by his strong will and earnest determination to conquer, the forest was soon made to give way, and waving fields of grain soon told that his intentions had been fully executed. Here he reared and educated his family, and each year, as he was prospered, he kept constantly adding more acres to his first purchase, until he had accumulated eight hundred broad acres of valuable lands, and as each son left the parental roof, the father presented him with a farm of one hundred acres. Our subject departed this life in the year 1876, surviving his wife but six weeks. This worthy aged couple now lie sleeping side by side in the old St. Luke cemetery, and are deserving of a kind remembrance.

JOHN FLUKE was born in Orange township in 1831, on the farm now owned and occupied by him, being the old Fluke homestead. He resided with his parents until the time of their death, caring for them in their declining years. November 24, 1864, he married Elizabeth McDowell. The fruit of this union was three children, one son and two daughters, viz.: James M., Mary S., and Esther C.—all living but Mary, who was a bright little daughter of five summers, and the loss to the fond parents was irreparable. The wife and mother died February 15, 1879, leaving a broken family of two affectionate children and a kind and devoted husband, who had ever been ready to share alike with her all the cares and disappointments that are so common in life's pilgrimage. Mr. Fluke was married again, February 5, 1880, to Freelia A. Thomas, daughter of one of Ashland county's early pioneers. He is one of the most substantial and enterprising farmers of Orange township, his home denoting more than ordinary thrift. By dint of hard labor, careful judgment and wise economy, he is now the possessor of one of the most pleasant homes in Orange township. Both Mr. and Mrs. Fluke are earnest followers of the Christian religion, and have always been staunch supporters of the cause of Christ. They are surrounded by almost every comfort that a gracious Heaven could confer, and, as they pass along life's journey, they can look back without regret upon a well spent life.

PHILIP STENTZ was born in the State of Pennsylvania, where he was married to Mary Hoover. To them were born seven children, three sons and four daughters: Mary and Susan (twins), John, Michael, Catharine, Simon, and Sarah, who died in early childhood. He came to Ohio about the year 1831, and first made a settlement in Wayne county, four miles north of Wooster. There he purchased a tract of land and resided seven or eight years. Then he came to Clearcreek township, and remained until the time of his death, in 1870; he survived his life's companion eleven years. They were buried in the old Herb cemetery, in Clearcreek township.

JOHN STENTZ, the oldest son of Philip Stentz, was born in Pennsylvania, December 10, 1823. He resided with his parents until the year 1843, when he was married to Delilah Fast. The fruit of this union was seven children, five sons and three daughters. Their names are as follows: Madison, Irvin, Philip M., Wilson D., Perry C., Isabel and Augusta E. Madison and Isabel are deceased. The wife and mother departed this life March 17, 1864, leaving a broken family of six affectionate children and a kind and devoted husband. Mr. Stentz was again married February 22, 1866, to Margaret Culberson, daughter of one of Ashland county's early pioneers. To them was born one child, who died in infancy, unnamed. Mr. Stentz is one of the most substantial and enterprising farmers of Orange township, his home and surroundings denoting more than ordinary thrift. Both himself and wife are members of the Reformed church, and have always been among its most liberal supporters.

JOHN BISHOP was born in Frederick county, Maryland, January 22, 1793. At the age of thirteen years he went with his father to Green county, Pennsylvania. His father being very poor, John was obliged to earn for himself a livelihood, and he at once engaged with a man by the name of Estell for the small pittance of ten shillings per month, and remained faithful to his first employer until in his twenty-first year. In the year 1814 he came to Licking county, Ohio, remaining one year, when he returned to his father's home, and upon his suggestion the family also came to Ohio, in the spring of 1815, and settled in Licking county, John coming through to Orange township, Ashland county, then Richland. He was married in the year 1819, March 9th, to Miss Catharine Heiffner. To them were born eleven children, six sons and five daughters: Jacob, Cornelius, Elizabeth, Mary Ann, Hannah, John, Mahala, Isaac N., Joseph, Sarah J. and Henry. The first purchase made by Mr. Bishop was a tract of land containing eighty acres, almost completely covered with timber, with no improvements whatever save a rude log cabin to give evidence of his having a predecessor. His motto was "excelsior," and his earnest determination was to conquer. Possessed of a great amount of energy and in the full vigor of manhood, many were the mighty oaks that yielded to this worthy pioneer. The dense forest was rapidly cleared away, and waving fields of grain soon told that his intentions had been fully executed. After improving his home he sold and purchased different other tracts, owning at one time two hundred and eighty acres of valuable lands. He died in the year 1878, March 12th, at his home in Orange township, surviving his wife about two years. This aged couple were esteemed and respected wherever known, and to them Ashland county owe a deep debt of gratitude.

JOSEPH BISHOP, the fifth son of John Bishop, was born in Orange township in the year 1838, May 3d. He lived with his parents until the time of his marriage, in 1860, to Miss Eleanor Smith. The fruit of this union was one son, Charles G. Mr. Bishop is one of the most substantial and energetic farmers of Orange township. By dint of hard labor, careful judgment, and wise economy, he is now the owner of quite a pleasant home. Both himself and his wife are active members of the German Reformed church, and have been among its most staunch supporters. His son, Charles, is a member of the Methodist church.

STEPHEN BARRICK, the eldest son of George and Sarah Barrick, was born in Columbiana county, Ohio, in the year 1826. He came to Ashland county in company with his parents in the year 1834, and with them made his home until the time of his marriage, in the year 1850, to Miss Catharine Chilcote. She died in the year 1866. Mr. Barrick was married again in the year 1868 to Miss Martha A. Chilcote. To them have been born one son, George W. Mr. Barrick is one of the most substantial and enterprising farmers in Orange township. At the age of nineteen he learned the trade of carpenter and joiner, which occupation he industriously and successfully pursued for more than twenty-five years. He was elected to the office of assessor three successive times, 1871-2 and '73. He was elected as commissioner of his county in the fall of 1875, and re-elected in 1878, thus bespeaking for him the full confidence of his people. Himself and wife are earnest members of the Methodist Episcopal church.

HENRY FLUKE was born in the State of Pennsylvania in the year 1811, and came to Ohio with his parents when but a small boy, and resided with them until his marriage in 1836, to Margaret Switzer. The fruit of this union was four children, two sons and two daughters. Their names are as follows: Mary Ann, Wilson, Amanda and Enos, all of whom have left the parental roof, except the elder son, Wilson. Mr. Fluke died in December, 1875. Esteemed and respected wherever known, his loss to family and friends was one irreparable. Mrs. Fluke has been an active and earnest member of the Methodist Episcopal church for almost forty years. Being an energetic, industrious and frugal man, Mr. Fluke, by dint of hard labor, careful judgment, and wise economy, acquired quite a fine property. His widow resides at the old home in Orange township, with her son Wilson, who superintends the farm, and cares for his mother in her declining years.

DAVID FLUKE was born in the State of Ohio, in the year 1822, and resided with his parents until the time of his marriage, in 1845, to Miss Hannah Stine. The fruit of this union was five children—two sons and three daughters, as follows: Lucinda, Celia Ann, Laura Jane, Perry M., and one son who died in infancy, unnamed. Mr. Fluke died in the fall of 1866. Mrs. Fluke resides at her home in Orange township, with her children, Laura and Perry, who superintends the farm and cares for his widowed mother, in her declining years. Both Mr. Fluke and his wife were members of the Reformed church.

THOMAS S. CULBERSON, the eldest son of Robert and Elizabeth Culberson, was born in Harrison county, Ohio, in 1824. He remained with his parents until the time of his marriage, in the year 1851, to Jane Jackson. They raised a family of eleven children—eight sons and three daughters, as follows: Elizabeth M., Joseph J., John W., Robert S., George S., Oscar P., James E., Thomas C., Anna M., Mary M., and Frank B., four of whom are deceased—Elizabeth, Robert, James and Anna. Mr. Culberson resides on the old homestead. He and his wife are earnest members of the Presbyterian church.

JOHN RICHARDS, second son of Leonard and Elizabeth Richards, was born in Jefferson county, Ohio, in the year 1806. In the fall of 1813 he came with his father's family to Wayne county, and there resided until the time of his marriage, in the summer of 1828, to Miss Sarah Riddle. They had a family of eleven children, six sons and five daughters, as follows: Elizabeth, Samuel, Harriet, William, Allen, James, John, Margaret, Mary, Jane, and Bownan, three of whom are deceased—Harriet, who died at the age of forty-two; and James and William, who enlisted in the war of 1861. James died of disease contracted while in the service, at his father's home in Orange township. William died in hospital at Murfreesborough, and lies sleeping in the sunny south, in an unknown but not an unforgotten grave. They were both brave soldiers and dutiful children. Mrs. Richards died in 1867, and he was again married in 1869, to Miss Barbara Summers, who died in the spring of 1879. Mr. Richards is a consistent member of the Methodist Episcopal church, and has always contributed liberally to its support.

G. W. MILLAR, fourth son of Thomas and Rachel Millar, was born in Orange township, Richland county (now Ashland), in the year 1838. He made his home with his mother until the time of his marriage, in the year 1863, to Caroline Porter. To them were born three children, two sons and one daughter, as follows: Ermine, Denton, and John, all of whom are living.

JOHN RITCHEY was born in the State of Virginia, in 1801, and in 1804 came with his parents to Ohio, and settled in Columbiana county. In 1824 he was married to Lucinda Wolf, by whom he had eight children, five sons and three daughters: Samuel, Jesse, Simon, Jacob, Sarah Ann, Phebe, and Catharine, and one son who died in infancy, unnamed. In 1833 Mr. Ritchey came to Orange township, and in 1839 his wife died. In 1839 he was married again, to Fannie Millinger, and had ten children, four sons and six daughters, as follows: William, Joseph, James, George, Mary, Elizabeth, Fannie, Rebecca, Lucinda, and one who died in infancy, unnamed. While not associated with any church, he is a firm advocate of law and order.

ALFRED MCFADDEN, second child of Daniel and Margaret McFadden, was born in Green township, Wayne county, September 25, 1833, and moved to Orange township, Ashland county, with his father, when quite small. He has been a resident of the county since that time. He was married August 13, 1857 to Elizabeth Richard, daughter of D. and Nancy Richard, who was born in Holmes county, Ohio, September 23, 1834. To them have been born five children, as follows: Dianna, Pierce, Oliver, Leander, and Essa, all living. Four of the children are still at home. Although Mr. and Mrs. McFadden are members of no church, they are both strong advocates of law and order.

JAMES HEIFFNER, third child and second son of Henry and Elizabeth Heiffner, was born in Orange township, Ashland, then Richland county, July 15, 1824, and has been a resident of the township ever since. He was married to Elizabeth Shaw, daughter of William and Elizabeth Shaw, April 27, 1847. To them have been born three children: Ira, and two who died in infancy. Ira is still living and a resident of Troy township. Although Mr. Heiffner is a member of no church, he is a strong advocate of law and order. When Mr. Heiffner started out in the world his father gave him but a small start, but by hard work, wise economy, and careful management, he is now the owner of two fine farms.

JOHN CREVELING, fifth child of John and Charity Creveling, was born in Columbia county, Pennsylvania, October 22, 1810, emigrated to Ashland county, Ohio, October 5, 1837, and has been a resident of the county ever since. On March 23, 1837, he was married to Sophia, daughter of William and Sophia Roseberry, who was born in Columbia county, Pennsylvania, July 4, 1817. To them have been born five children, as follows: William N., Isaiah F., John W., Philip, and Moorress. Of these but two are living, Isaiah F. and William N., the latter being still at home. Both Mr. and Mrs. Creveling are earnest members of the Methodist Episcopal church, and are among its most liberal supporters.

DAVID R. HALL, fourth child of George and Margaret Hall, was born in Orange township, Ashland county, Ohio, August, 30, 1832, and has since resided here. He is a single man, and living with his aged mother, and one sister.

ISAAC MASON was born in Columbiana county, Ohio, December 7, 1813, moved to Orange township, Ashland county, in October 1833, and settled on the farm where he now lives. On March 10, 1836, he was married to Eunice, daughter of Henry and Eunice Miller, who was born in Union county, Pennsylvania, June 11, 1814, and came to Ohio, with her parents, about the year 1830. To them have been born ten children, viz.: Levi P., William H., Sarah E., Emily, Parvin L., Angeline, Helen J., Callie, and two who died in infancy—Emily also died at the age of two years. Both Mr. and Mrs. Mason are earnest workers in the Methodist Episcopal church.

DAVID SMITH, JR., was born in Perry township, Wayne county (now Ashland), Ohio, December 4, 1824, and moved to Orange township about the year 1839, where he has since resided. He was married to Rossetta, daughter of John and Anna Bails, who was born in Wayne county, April 11, 1834. They have had a family of eight children, as follows: Iva A., John B., James N., Maggie E., Emmit H., Stewart S., Etta M., and Emma C., all living but James N. and Stewart S. Four of the children are still at home. Mr. Smith and wife are earnest members of the Presbyterian church.

HENRY WERTZ was born in Somerset county, Pennsylvania, April 17, 1817, and came to Ohio with his father and mother, Henry and Magdalene Wertz, who settled in Holmes county when Henry was quite small. In the spring of 1858, he moved to Ashland county and has been a resident of the county ever since. On October 3, 1843, he was married to Sophia Rudy, daughter of Abraham and Elizabeth Rudy, who was born in Lancaster county, Pennsylvania, March 5, 1819. Mrs. Wertz is a member of the Brethren church. Mr. Wertz is a member of no church, but respects the religious convictions of others. He has served in the office of trustee of Orange township three terms, the last coming in the year 1874.

THOMAS W. RICHARDS, son of Wesley and Mary Richards, was born in Maryland, September 5, 1827. He came to Ohio with his parents when two years of age. They settled in Columbiana county, and after some years removed to Ashland. He was married to Miss Mariah Bowlby, daughter of Samuel and Elizabeth Bowlby, December 2, 1846. To them have been born eleven children as follows: Irene, Louisa, Ira C., John A., Susan, Hattie, Mary, Elizabeth, Lydia, James, and Minerva. All are living but Louisa, who died June 10, 1879; aged twenty-eight years. Both Mr. and Mrs. Richards are members of the Methodist Episcopal church.

GEORGE W. BARNHILL, second child of Robert and Eliza Barnhill, was born in Jefferson county, Ohio, July 30, 1843. The family came to Ashland county in the year 1853, and he has since been a resident of the county. His wife was Miss Alice Fluke, daughter of Samuel and Catharine Fluke, to whom he was married January 27, 1869. They have had four children, as follows: Leffie E., Thomas Y., Gertrude, and one who died in infancy. Mr. and Mrs. Barnhill are both earnest members of the Methodist Episcopal church, and are among its most liberal supporters. Mr. Barnhill is a class leader, and fills the office of trustee, also, in his church.

CHARLES E. BARNHILL, third child of Robert and Eliza Barnhill, was born in Carroll county, Ohio, October 10, 1850, and moved to Ashland county in 1853, where he has resided ever since. October 26, 1876, he was married to Helen M. Wallace, daughter of William and Christiana Wallace. They have one child, Mary E. They are both members of the Methodist Episcopal church.

ROBERT BARNHILL, fourth child of Robert, sr., and

Elizabeth Barnhill, was born in Jefferson connty, Ohio, March 3, 1813. The family moved from Jefferson to Carroll county, and remained nine years; then moved to Ashland in the spring of 1853, since which time he has been a resident of the county. March 4, 1841, he was married to Eliza Jackman, daughter of George and Margaret Jackman, who was born in Jefferson county, August 6, 1819. They have three children: Mary E., George W., and Charles C. They now live with their son, George. Both are members of the United Brethren church.

JERIAH JOHNSON, oldest child of John and Mary Johnson, was born in Wayne county, Ohio, January 5, 1827. In the spring of 1857, he came to Ashland county, and was a resident of the county up to the time of his death, which occurred February 23, 1872. May 20, 1852, he was married to Lydia Hoover, daughter of Philip and Catharine Hoover, who was born in Stark county, Ohio, January 13, 1830. They had a family of eight children, as follows: Sylvester, Harris L., Wilbert H., Clement H., Mary A., Jerusha A., Emma C. and one who died in infancy. All the others are living except Sylvester. Mrs. Johnson is a member of the Presbyterian church; and, with the assistance of her three sons, does the farming on the old place.

MICHAEL VESPER, youngest child of Christian and Magdalene Vesper, was born in Bavaria, Germany, July 4, 1819. In the year 1833 he immigrated to Pennsylvania, and remained there until May, 1835, when he came to Ashland county, where he has since resided. January 16, 1848, he was married to Mary Sattler, daughter of Lewis Sattler. To them have been born twelve children, as follows: Catharine, Margaret, Elizabeth, Franz, Michael, Magdalene, Christian, Susan, Minnie, George P., David, and Theodore A., all living. Mr. Vesper and wife are both earnest members of the German Reformed church. In 1879 he was elected trustee of Orange township, but, on account of sickness, he had to resign.

JONAS FAST, son of William and Anna C. E. Fast, was born in Ashland county (then Richland), April 10, 1836, and has always lived in this county. October 6, 1864, he was married to Mary A., daughter of Elias and Sarah Marshall, who was born in Ashland, July 8, 1845. Their children are: Clement L. V., Cladean, Ida B., William E., John L., Edea M., and one who died in infancy. Mrs. Fast and wife are members of the Disciple church.

DANIEL RICHARD, son of Frederick and Madeline Richard, was born in Alleghany county, Maryland, April 4, 1818, and came to Ashland county in the year 1851. May 31, 1830, he was married to Miss Marcy Markel, daughter of Jacob Markel. To them have been born ten children, as follows: Jacob, Sarah, Margaret, Elizabeth, Israel, Daniel D., Nancy, Solomon, Mary A., and Samuel; of whom seven are living and three are dead. Mrs. Richard died March 25, 1872. Both were members of the Presbyterian church. Since the death of his wife he has been living with his daughter and son, Samuel. His son Daniel, was born in Holmes county, December 10, 1839, and came with the family from Holmes to Ashland county, April 14, 1851. December 23, 1862, he was married to Jane A., daughter of William and Mary Murray. They have three children Clement L., Israel H. and Leana I. Mr. and Mrs. Richard are members of the Christian Union church.

WILLIAM PETERS, only child of Daniel and Mary Peters, was born in Lebanon county, Pennsylvania, December 8, 1823. In April, 1837, he came to Richland (now Ashland) county. He was twice married, his first wife being Rebecca, daughter of Edward Murray, to whom he was married November 2, 1845. To them were born eleven children—John, Edward, Levi, William, George, Mary J., Catharine, Louisa, Mertle, and two who died in infancy. Of these but two are living, William and Catharine. His second wife was Mary Murray, sister of his first wife, to whom he was married February 24, 1870. Mr. Peters lost his first wife July 20, 1869, at the age of forty-two years one month and twenty-nine days.

HARVEY ROBERTS, fourth son of Aaron and Matilda Roberts, was born in Dearborn county, Indiana, December 25, 1826. When he was eighteen months old, his parents emigrated to Ohio and located in Orange township, near the village of Orange, in Ashland county. The land had some improvements, such as our pioneer fathers were accustomed to make, and all they expected in those early days. The family consisted of five children, four sons and one daughter, when they came to Ohio, as follows: John, Ezekiel, Lewis, Sarah Ann, and Harvey. Two daughters were born in Ashland county, Hannah and Amanda. The pioneer father, Aaron Roberts, died March 17, 1834, aged forty-three years five months and six days. Mrs. Roberts died October 24, 1873, at the age of seventy-nine years nine months and seven days. Two sons of this family are dead, John and Lewis. Ezekiel left home in 1840, bound for New Orleans. The family received one or two letters from him, since which time no word has come, and the supposition is that he died in a southern clime of yellow fever or some of the contagious diseases that are so common in the south. Amanda is the widow of Jacob Young, and lives in Colorado. Her sister, Sarah Ann, is unmarried, and makes her home with her widowed sister. Hannah is the wife of Ephraim Fast, and lives in Huron county, Ohio. Harvey, the subject of the following sketch, now owns and lives at the old homestead. February 8, 1855, he was married to Mary Risher, of Tuscarawas county, Ohio. They have had seven children, two of whom died in infancy, George Winfield, and Clark. Those living are John Lambert, James Adison, Howard Milton, Horace Allen, and Leora Loveda. John is married and lives in Clearcreek township, Ashland county. James Adison is a carpenter, and works at his trade in Richland county, but makes his father's house his home. The other three children are at home, assisting the father on the farm, and the mother in her household duties. Mr. Roberts owns in addition to his farm, two and a half acres improved land in the town of Ashland, which will in all probability be his home in his old age, should a kind Providence permit him to remain here. In politics he is a Republican, and is a man highly esteemed by his neighbors in the community in which he has lived so many years.

WILLIAM PATTERSON was one of Ashland county's pioneers. He was born in Ireland, but at the age of four or five years his parents emigrated to America, locating in Brooke county, Virginia. At the age of about twenty-six, in the year 1815, he came to Clearcreek, Ashland county, Ohio, and entered a tract of land which was not to his liking, and in 1818 he entered another tract consisting of one hundred and sixty acres of land in the same township, which he improved, and continued to live upon the remainder of his life. In 1819 he was married to Jane Freeborn, daughter of William Freeborn, who was among the first settlers in Ashland county. The Patterson family consisted of eleven children, six of whom are still living. Freeborn and John are married and live in Steuben county, Indiana. Mary Jane, Sarah, Clark and Alexander, occupy the old homestead in Orange township, Ashland county. They have added seventy-six acres to the original farm, making one of the finest farms in the township. Mr. Patterson died May 13, 1867. Mrs. Patterson died March 19, 1857. To record the lives of these pioneers on the sacred pages of history is a pleasant task, as they well deserve the gratitude of coming generations for the sacrifices and hardships they were compelled to endure in reducing the wilderness to the beautifully improved condition we now find it. Mr. Patterson was a Democrat in politics, and his four sons adhere to the same views.

THOMAS BROWN was born in Ireland, and came to America when a young man in company with his mother, one brother and three sisters. After remaining a short time in Philadelphia they came to Ohio, and, soon after arriving Mr. Brown purchased a tract of land in Orange township, Ashland (then Richland) county. In 1841 he married Jane, daughter of Charles and Catharine Stewart, of Richland county. At the time he bought the farm in Orange township there was a log cabin on it, and part of the land was cleared, so that by building a log barn they were pretty well prepared to farm. The day after they were married they took quarters in their new home, where they lived ever after, and where we now find Mrs. Brown living pleasantly with her three sons and one daughter. Mr. Brown died February 6, 1858, leaving Mrs. Brown with five small children, the oldest, a son, being about fifteen years old. Prior to the death of Mr. Brown they had lost, by death, three children. Since his death, the mother, with the assistance of her children, has added eighty acres to the original farm, and they now own two hundred and twenty-five acres of excellent land, with good improvements, in one of the most fertile sections of Ashland county. Mrs. Brown is a kind neighbor, and well deserves the respect and admiration of those who know her, for the manner in which she has managed the family affairs. She is a woman of good judgment, and though she has seen the hardships that early settlers could not shun, she is as active and bright as many who have not seen such trials. In politics Mr. Brown was a Democrat, and the sons adhere to the same party principles. Mrs. Brown and her four children are members of the Presbyterian church at Savannah.

WILLIAM SHIDLER, only son of Jacob Shidler, was born in Orange township, Ashland county, Ohio, September 2, 1847. His father came to Ashland county from Holmes county with his parents when he was a young man; Ashland county was ever after his home. The farm on which William now lives, and which he owns, is the farm his father purchased when he was married, and where he raised his family, consisting of William, the subject of this sketch, and his sister, now the wife of Hugh Murry. Mr. Shidler died October 3, 1866, and Mrs. Shidler died February 5, 1877. November 5, 1872, William Shidler married Elizabeth Myers, daughter of John and Barbara Myers, of Clearcreek township. The fruit of this union was three children, Maud, Lloyd and Charley Jay. Maud, the oldest, died at the age of fifteen months. Mr. Shidler is a Democrat in politics, is an industrious farmer, and is a companionable man, much respected by his neighbors. He has been for six years assessor in Orange township. His farm is considered one of the best grain farms in the township.

DAVID BIDDINGER was born in Orange township, Ashland county, Ohio, August 3, 1823, his parents being among Ashland county's pioneers. Philip Biddinger, his father, is still living in Troy township, at the advanced age of eighty years; his mother died four years ago. 'Squire David Biddinger made his home with his parents until he was married, January 16, 1848, to Fannie Peck, daughter of Jacob and Lydia Peck, of Orange township. They setted in Troy township, on a tract of land owned by Mr. Biddinger prior to his marriage. Here they resided eight or nine years, when they moved to Orange township, on Mr. Peck's farm, and remained about ten years, when they bought the farm on which they have now resided some fourteen years. They have four children, all of whom were born in Troy township: Lydia A., Sarah Adaline, Mary Jane, and John Willard. Lydia is the wife of Gilbert M. Clark, and lives in Huntington township, Lorain county, Ohio. Sarah married Edmond U. Pollinger, and lives in Richmond township, Huron county, Ohio. Mary Jane is the wife of Jacob F. Singer, and lives on a farm adjoining Mr. Biddinger's. John W. married Lizzie Tedrow, of Harrison county, Ohio, and lives in the same house with his father, working the farm in common with him. 'Squire Biddinger is an industrious farmer, and highly esteemed by all. He is now serving his fourth term as justice of the peace; he has also been trustee a number of years, as well as school director and road supervisor, which shows his ability and enterprise in local affairs. In politics he is a Democrat. Both himself and wife are members of the church of the United Brethren in Christ, at South Troy union chapel, but a short distance from where they now reside.

JOHN GEIER was born in Bavaria, Germany, April 21,

1825. May 3, 1848, he left his native country in the ship Birmingham, and after a tedious voyage of sixty-five days they were overjoyed to behold New York city, in our free America. Tongue cannot describe the fears and anxieties of passengers in those early days, when the trip across the ocean required so many days and even weeks and months. He came at once to Pennsylvania, and lived for five years in Beaver, Washington and Allegheny counties, and then came to Ohio and engaged as miller for John Ralston, in Orange township, Ashland county, where he remained about one year. April 6, 1854, he was married to Elizabeth Heiffner, daughter of Valentine Heiffner, of Orange township, who was an early settler in Ashland county. To them were born six children: Henry, Stephen, Mary, John W., and James A. The third child, a son, died in infancy; Mary died at the age of four months and nineteen days. The four sons are living with their parents, assisting in making home pleasant. Mr. Geier for many years gave his attention to the milling business, a trade he learned in Germany. During the past nine years he has devoted his time to his farm. He is a man who takes a live interest in county and township affairs, having served as supervisor and school director a number of years. He loves his chosen trade, that of milling, but his health will not permit of his following it. He is a very competent man in a mill, and holds a certificate from Germany. In politics he is a Democrat. Both himself and his wife are members of the Christian Union church located in Orange township, near where they now live.

HUGH MURRAY, third son of William and Mary Murray was born in Orange township, Ashland county, Ohio, September 29, 1834. William Murray came to Ashland county when he was a small boy, about the year 1812. Mrs. William Murray, who came about the same time, at the age of twelve years, is still living with her son Hugh, at the advanced age of eighty years. The Murray family are well known in all parts of the county as one of the first families to settle here after the war of 1812 closed. These heroes of Ashland county deserve to be remembered by coming generations, as it was to their hardships and privations that the present and coming generations owe a debt of gratitude. William Murray was married November 1, 1825, to Mary Chilcote, daughter of Mordecai and Ruth Chilcote, another family that came to Ashland county as before mentioned. After their marriage they lived in different portions of Orange township, and in 1834 they moved to the farm on which mother and son now live, in section five, near range sixteen, the northwest corner of the township. Mrs. Murray says she well remembers the log cabin days when quilts were often used as doors. When they came to this farm it was a wilderness, and it required plenty of nerve and will to cope successfully with the hardships necessary to provide bread and clear the land. For Ashland county these hardships are the things of the past, and to record the names of these good pioneers on the sacred pages of history is a pleasant duty. They had a family of eleven children, but five of whom are living. George fell at Stone River, near Murfreesborough, Tennessee, while defending the American flag. He was a private in company H, Thirtieth Indiana volunteer infantry. James was one of Michigan's calvary boys. Hugh was a member of the One Hundred and Second Ohio volunteer infantry, company K. He returned after a service of three years to the old home in Ashland county. On September 25, 1870, he was married to Jane Shidler. They have two boys—Guy B. and Harold Fay. He owns the old homestead, consisting of one hundred and sixty acres, and has added eighty acres, making one of the most desirable farms in the township. The scenes of his childhood, no doubt, still linger in his mind, the more so as he has the pleasure of associating with his good mother, a pleasure that few men of his age are allowed. In politics Mr. Murray is a Democrat, and is a man of many friends, and as a neighbor is highly esteemed.

SAMUEL LEIDIGH was born in Lebanon county, Pennsylvania, February 17, 1801. In 1836 he came to Ohio and purchased eighty acres of land near Little Pittsburgh, Wayne county. Here he resided about one year, when he sold his farm and moved three miles east of Wooster, on the Canton road, where he rented the Henry flouring mill, and operated it for a period of three years, when he bought the Stover mill and fifty acres of land, two miles west of the village of Orange, in Orange township, Ashland county (then Richland), where he has remained ever since, and is well known in the county. They have had a family of seven children—five sons and two daughters, five of whom are living. The youngest son, Reuben, was lost on the boat "Sultana," when on his way home from the war, as an exchanged prisoner, after a service of nearly three years as a private soldier in the One Hundred and Second regiment, Ohio volunteer infantry. This was indeed a sad bereavement to the family, and such an one as many of Ashland county's good families were called upon, in those days of bloodshed, to realize. Elizabeth, a daughter, aged thirty-six years, died in May, 1869. Isaac and Samuel are married, and Mary Ann is the wife of Jacob Kissell, a farmer of Orange township. Isaac farms his father's land, and Levi, Israel and Samuel manage the mill. Mrs. Leidigh died April 16, 1879. The mill, under the management of the three sons, is in a very prosperous condition, running to its full capacity. They ship by rail from Nankin, a station about three miles east of the mill. In 1868 Mr. Leidigh built a new mill, as the old one had not sufficient capacity. He has also added to his land, until he now owns three hundred and ten acres of excellent land, all in Orange township, not far from his residence.

A. C. FAST came to Ohio from Pennsylvania when a small boy with his parents, who located in Orange township, Ashland county, on a tract of land, where the widow of the subject of this sketch now lives in as pleasant a home as is to be found in the county. Mr. Fast purchased this place, after the death of his father, from the other heirs, subject to his mother's dowry; she died about two years later. January 23, 1840, he married Catharine Fluke, daughter of Philip and Mary

Fluke, who were among the early settlers of Ashland county, a sketch of whose lives will be found elsewhere in this work. Immediately after their marriage they moved to the place that proved to be their home ever after. Mr. Fast died November 26, 1862. They had eight children; three died in infancy, and five are still living, all grown, and doing for themselves. Their names are as follows: Wilson, Judson, Jennie, Byron, and Mary B. Wilson is married, and is a successful law practitioner in Sedalia, Missouri. Judson is unmarried, and lives in Kelton, Utah, where he is a successful railroad man. Jennie is the wife of Mr. James Jacoby, and lives on a farm in Dakota. He is quite a stockman. Byron is unmarried, and lives with his mother at the old homestead. He is one of the most successful farmers in Orange township, and is a young man highly respected as an intelligent, go ahead man, such as any comunity might well be proud of. Mary B. is the wife of William Alger, and lives in Villisca, Iowa, where he is engaged in the banking business. To place the record of such a family on the sacred pages of history is a pleasant duty. Wilson Fast was a soldier for a period of nearly three years, in the One Hundred and Second Ohio volunteer infantry. He was on board the fated boat "Sultana" on his way home, and was one of those who successfully battled with the waves and miraculously made his way to land after a severe struggle, and reached home, and was warmly welcomed by a fond and anxious mother, and brothers, and sisters, and friends. The loss of a number of his comrades on board the boat from which he made his escape touched his sympathetic nature, and destroyed considerably his anticipated pleasure on reaching the home of his childhood.

MILTON TOWNSHIP.

Henry Keever, one of the early settlers of Milton township, was born in Frederick county, Maryland, in the year 1803. He was the oldest child of Andrew and Margaret Keever. Both of his parents died when he was but a lad. He then went to live with his grandfather, and moved with him to Ohio, in the year 1811, and first settled in Harrison county; here the grandfather died, and Henry, who was then a young man of sixteen, removed with his grandmother and sister to Milton township, Richland county, now Ashland county. His first purchase was a tract of land in Milton township, where he still resides. His settlement in Ashland county dates back to about the year 1819. In 1832 or 1833 he was married to Caroline Baum. They have had ten children—Eliza, Mary, Philip, Sarah, Henry P., Aaron, Susan A., Caroline, Franklin and John; all of whom reside within the State. He and his wife have lived together for nearly a half century, upon the same place where they first set up housekeeping, and both are well preserved, and in the full possession of their faculties. A grubbing hoe, a horse, and one dollar and fifty cents comprised his capital, when he first started in life. He is now one of the substantial farmers of Milton township. His life has been a frugal and industrious one, and he enjoys the esteem of his fellow citizens.

Robert Nelson, who was born in the year 1769, came from Northampton county, Pennsylvania, in the year 1816, and settled in Milton township, Ashland county, then Richland county. In the year 1801 he was married in New Jersey, and brought with him to Ohio his wife and nine little children. He experienced all the trials and hardships common to the life of an early pioneer, and died, after a useful and well spent life, at the age of seventy-five years, in the year 1844. His wife survived him until the year 1862, when she died at the ripe old age of eighty. At the time of her death there were eleven children living, four sons and seven daughters. The only ones now residing in Ashland county are Scott, Sophia and Nancy. After the death of his father, Scott purchased from the heirs the old homestead and there resides to this day (1880). In the year 1854 he was married to Rosanna Wells, by whom he had two children—James B. and Miranda. The latter married Alonzo Poff. James lives with his aged father at the old home. Mr. Nelson has been a prominent and worthy citizen, and is one of the leading men of Milton township.

Christian Roland, born in Pennsylvania in the year 1823, came to Ohio with his parents about the year 1833, and settled in Milton township. In the year 1844 he was married to Mary Brubaker, whose parents were early settlers in Ashland county. Their children are: Moses, Henry, Maria, Sarah, and Ann; all of whom are living. After an active and useful life, he died May 23, 1876. He was a preacher of some considerable note, and followed his calling up to the time of his decease. His widow still survives and lives upon the old homestead, surrounded by her children. He was a man esteemed for his worth and integrity, and an earnest man in the church.

Lance Ferrell is a native of Milton township, and was born August 19, 1829. August 20, 1849, he was married to Susan Nelson, daughter of a pioneer family of Ashland county. To them were born eight children, seven daughters and one son: Sarah E., who was born September 14, 1850, and died in early womanhood, four years after her marriage to Amos Jameson; Laura A., born September 7, 1853; Ella E., born January 14, 1856; Forrest A., born May 20, 1859, died April 4, 1863; Nettie A., born February 28, 1861, died March 26, 1862; Cora B., born July 8, 1864; Minnie E., born November 30, 1866; and Zettie, born January 24, 1871. Mr. Ferrell lives on what is called the Short farm, near the old homestead. Both himself and wife are members of the Lutheran church.

Henry Vantilburg was a native of New Jersey, where he was born December 8, 1779. September 6, 1810, he was married to Jane Shaw, in Jefferson county,

Ohio, where he lived till the year 1819, when he moved with his family to Ashland county, Montgomery township, where he resided until his death, in 1863, at the advanced age of eighty-four. He was the father of ten children: Julia Ann, Jane, Nathan, Mary, Henry, Matilda, Elizabeth, Sarah, Siniaette, and Franklin A. His wife survived him until the year 1874. Prior to her death, three of her married daughters died—Mary Holbrook, Sarah Shannon, and Siniaette Goudy. The representatives of the family living in the county are Julia Riley and Franklin A. The latter owns and occupies the old homestead. He was born in 1829, and in 1855 married Mary Shipley, by whom he has had four children, one son and three daughters: Ida, who married Franklin Masteis; Jennie, Delbert and Luzettie. Soon after Mr. Vantilburg's settlement in Ashland county, he commenced the erection of a barn, in which to store his grain, and encountered many difficulties. It is related that he would load two of his horses with wheat, and carry it a distance of seven miles to Jeromeville; where he would exchange his grain for wrought nails, giving one bushel of grain for two pounds of nails. He was a conscientious and law-abiding citizen, avoiding strife and contention. The only lawyer's fee he was ever called upon to pay was five dollars for the preparation of his will. His was an honorable name to be placed on the list of Ashland county pioneers.

ADAM FIKE was a native of Lancaster county, Pennsylvania, and came into Milton township in 1835, with his wife and three little children. At the age of thirty, he was married to Elizabeth Lutz. The names of their children were: Susan, Emanuel, C. L., and Adam, the last dying in early childhood.

C. L. FIKE was born in Pennsylvania, October 2, 1823, and came to Ohio with his parents in 1835. Twice he has been married; the first time to Mary Ann Buckley, who died in June, 1869, leaving a family of three children. Mr. Fike re-married August 24, 1872, to Amanda McQuait, by whom he has had two sons, Joseph Leander and Henry. He has led an industrious and honorable life, and is looked upon by all who know him as one of the most influential farmers of Milton township.

WILLIAM G. IMHOFF, is the youngest of the seven children of William H. and Susan Imhoff, and was the only son of the family born in Ohio. His father moved into this State about the year 1834, and settled upon the farm in Milton township, where his son now resides. There were seven children, and only one, William G., now resides in the county. One son, Alexander, is a Lutheran minister of some reputation, and resides in Urbana. The father died in 1872, and the mother in 1876. William G. was born April 16, 1840, on the place where he still resides. October 17, 1861, he was married to Martha Brown, of Richland county, by whom he has had six children: Albert R., William W., Susan D., Maggie R., Mattie A., and Elvero. Mr. Imhoff lives upon a farm of two hundred and forty acres, which denotes more than ordinary thrift and enterprise on the part of its owner, the buildings ranking with some of the best to be found in the township. He is an enteprising and thrifty farmer. Both he and his wife are members of the Lutheran church.

JOSEPH POLLOCK, a native of Virginia, born in 1801, came to Ohio with his father in 1816, and settled in Milton township. They were obliged to camp out in the wilderness until they could erect a cabin. During the time it required to construct a house, Mr. Pollock learned the art of cooking jonacakes, which were regarded as quite a luxury in early pioneer times. When summer was ended he had his cabin completed, and he then returned to Virginia for his wife, and the following spring they made the trip to their new home in wagons. The old original log cabin is still standing on the farm now owned by his son Robert. The children of Joseph and Nancy (McKenzie) Pollock were: David, James, Sarah, and Robert—all of whom are living, save James. Robert, the only living representative residing in Milton township, was born in 1834, and in 1865 was married to Freelove Gates, by whom he has had six children: Joseph Ellsworth, Sarah Nina, Harry Lee, J. Scott, and A. Z. Two are dead—Joseph E. and one dying in infancy. He is a prominent farmer and a worthy citizen.

SAMUEL URIE was born in Washington county, Pennsylvania, in 1792, and moved into Ashland (then Richland) county, in 1814. In the fall of 1815 he was married to Rachel Stephenson, by whom he had nine children: Thomas, Samuel, Andrew, John, George, Elizabeth, Mary Ann, Rachel, and Nancy. Elizabeth, John, and Andrew are dead. At the age of fifty-six, in the year 1848, Mr. Urie died. His wife still survives him. Samuel Urie was born in 1826, and was married in 1849 to Henrietta Nelson, by whom he has had five children: Elizabeth, Arabella, Loren, Ellsworth, and Willis. Arabella is deceased. Mr. Urie is a quiet, inoffensive man, of good habits, and a worthy and much esteemed citizen, and lives in full view of the old homestead.

JAMES HAZLETT, first son of John Hazlett, was born September 27, 1830, in Milton township, on the place where he now resides, and which is the old homestead of his parents. His father settled in the woods, occupying an old log cabin, but by hard toil, industry, and the aid of his eldest son, he cleared away the forest and carved out for himself a pleasant home. James was married in the year 1852, April 27th, to Miss Mary Ann Riddle, by whom he had seven children: Elmira, William Loren, Rosetta, John, Lucy, Mary, Ophenia, and Frank. William Loren died in infancy. May 3, 1866, Mrs. Hazlett died, and for his second wife he married Sarah J. Horn, by whom he has had one son, Christopher. He and wife are consistent members of the Disciple church, and liberal supporters of that branch of the Christian religion.

GEORGE W. HAZLETT was the second son of John Hazlett, and was born May 21, 1842. He lived with his father, and aided in clearing up the farm, until 1862, when his father died. Seven years later, in 1869, he was married to Libbie Thomas, who was born June 22, 1840. Both are earnest Christians, and members of the Disciple church.

ZEPHANIAH H. EKEY, a native of Jefferson county, Ohio, a son of James Ekey, was born April 26, 1827, and January 1, 1851, was married to Jane McClelland. The following March he moved into Ashland, and purchased the farm where he now resides, on which he erected the very commodious dwelling which he still occupies. They have had a family of four children: James M., William S., Elizabeth J., and one son who died in infancy, unnamed. Elizabeth died March 31, 1875, after a brief illness, at the age of eleven years and a few months. On the sixth day of November, 1877, William was married to Adelia McMillan. He and his brother James reside upon and cultivate the home farm. In politics, Mr. Ekey has generally acted with the Democratic party. He and his wife are members of the Methodist Episcopal church. He is a farmer of frugal and industrious habits, and in comfortable circumstances.

JOSEPH NELSON, a native of Pennsylvania, came to Ohio about the year 1847, and the following year was married to Margaret Nelson, a sister of Scott Nelson. He has given twenty-six years of his life to his trade, that of plasterer and stone-mason, besides carrying on his farm. He has been the father of five children, but Robert is the only one living. His first wife died in January, 1876, and in February, 1880, he was again married, taking for his second wife Susan Iceman. He is a member of the Presbyterian church, of Ashland, and acts with the Democratic party. He has been frugal and careful in his business, and has accumulated a nice property.

JOHN BRIGLE came to Ohio in 1840 from Cumberland county, Pennsylvania, and settled in Milton township. He was born January 11, 1797, and April 22, 1822, was married to Catharine Lininger, by whom he had twelve children: Elizabeth, who died in infancy; George, John, David, Barbara, who died in infancy; Catharine, Elizabeth, Barbara, Mary, Rebecca, Sarah A., and one unnamed. Elizabeth, Mary, Rebecca and Sarah, are the only living ones. Elizabeth, married Philip Smith, and is a widow; Mary married J. P. Russell, Rebecca married James O'Brien, and Sarah married David Rumph. Mr. Brigle has spent his life upon the farm, and has been a hard-working and industrious man. His wife died March 30, 1873, after having been a faithful companion to her husband for over half a century. She was a kind and loving wife and judicious mother, and bore bravely her share of the toil that fell to the lot of these two old people. Both were faithful members of the Church of God, and have lived consistent lives. Mr. Brigle is still living at the ripe old age of eighty-three, and is in the full possession of his faculties. He is an honest and well meaning old gentleman, and an earnest Christian man.

JOSEPH PIFER moved in from Wayne county about the same year that Mr. Brigle came into Ashland county. He was the sixth child of Henry and Polly Pifer, and the date of this birth was October 20, 1811. He was born in Berks county, Pennsylvania, and came to Ohio in 1835. He afterward moved to Indiana, but remained there but a short time. In 1837 he came to Wooster, Ohio, when he was married to Mary Ann Shuey, April 27th, of the same year. The Shuey family can trace their ancestry back for over three hundred years. They originally came from France. Mrs. Pifer was reared at the original homestead where the first Shuey family located in this country. Mr. Pifer by trade is a carpenter. He followed it for about eighteen years, but now devotes his attention to farming. He is the father of two children—Henry and Emeline. The former married Rebecca Grosscup; the latter is the wife of E. J. Grosscup, the present auditor of Ashland county. He has been an earnest and consistent member of the Reformed church for over fifty years. He has been a hard-working, energetic man, and has led an active life. He is one of the substantial farmers of Milton township, and a large landholder.

ANDREW HELTMAN came to Ohio with his father in 1836, and settled in Milton township. He was born in Pennsylvania, September 13, 1820, and is the oldest son of Joseph and Catharine Heltman. On May 12, 1842, he was married to Barbara Campbell, of this county. They have had four children, but none are living. Joseph Heltman died September 12, 1873. In 1851 Andrew went to California, where he engaged in the mining business. In 1857 he again returned to Ohio and engaged in the dry goods business, being one of the partners of Whitner, Myers & Co., and afterward the firm became Heltman & Myers. He followed this for seven or eight years, when he retired to his farm, where he still resides. He has led an active and busy life, and has accumulated a fine property, and to-day is one of the substantial men of the county.

JAMES WELLS moved into Ashland county about the year 1835. He was a native of Pennsylvania, and drove through in a wagon, with his wife and six children. In fording the Ohio river he came near losing his life and the lives of his family, who were with him. The water was much deeper than he supposed, and the attempt to ford it brought them into serious danger. He first settled on the farm where Mr. Brown now lives, but not being accustomed to farm life, he soon became weary of it and homesick, and urged his wife to return with him to Pennsylvania. This she refused to do, and he started back alone on horseback, so strong was his desire to see his native place. He soon returned, however, and never again expressed a desire to return to the old home. In January, 1879, his death occurred, at the ripe old age of eighty-two; his wife died in 1851. They had seven boys and four girls, but four of whom now live in Ashland county.

JOSEPH WELLS was born May 13, 1831, and was married November 25, 1855, to Catharine Greiner, a native of Lancaster county, Pennsylvania. Her ancestors moved to Ashland when it was but a small hamlet. Mr. Wells has spent most of his life in Ashland county, save a residence of nine years in Iowa. They have had six children: Lucinda, Loyal M., Clarissa M., Tempty E., Iley M., and Dora B., all of whom are living at home. They are both members of the Lutheran church, and enjoy the confidence of their friends and neighbors.

HENRY WELLS, the oldest living son of James and Mary Wells, was born October 29, 1829, in Somerset county, Pennsylvania, and was married to Catharine Mandey, September 28, 1871. He resided with his father most of the time until he went to California, in 1859, where he remained ten years; he then returned to Ohio, and has ever since devoted his attention to farming. The farm he now occupies he purchased from his father, and he gives his time to the raising of stock and grain. The ancestors of his wife were among the early settlers of Ashland county. Both himself and wife are members of the Disciple church, and enjoy the respect and esteem of all.

JOHN BRINDLE came to Ashland county about the year 1850. He was the second son of George and Elizabeth Brindle, and was born in Pennsylvania in 1815. He married Susan Burns, by whom he had twelve children, eleven of whom are living: Elizabeth, Mary C., Amanda, Martha A., George W., John M., Samuel E., Emily, Josephine, William H., Charles E., and Alice. Amanda is dead, and Elizabeth and Martha are married. Mr. Brindle was a man of thrift and intelligence, and his death, which occurred November 15, 1876, removed from Milton township a worthy man and a good citizen. His widow, with the help of her sons, carries on the farm.

HENRY PIFER, the only son of Joseph Pifer, was born in Wayne county, Ohio, in 1838, and in 1861 he was married to Rebecca Jane Grosscup, whose ancestors were pioneers. Nine children have been born to them: Mary M., Leandra, Joseph C., Henry L., Myrta, Charles, Shuey, Leander, Samuel A., and Alma. All are living except Mary and Leandra. Both Mr. and Mrs. Pifer are members of the United Brethren church. He is a young farmer of thrift and intelligence, and his premises denote a good deal of taste and care.

PETER BURK came into Ashland county with his father in 1834, and settled in Milton township, but afterwards removed to Mifflin township, where his father died, in 1838. He followed the carpenter and joiner trade for nineteen years, but he afterwards joined farming to this occupation, and has been successful. He was born in Lancaster county, Pennsylvania, July 9, 1818, and was married January 23, 1842, to Mary Landis, by whom he had six children. She died February 23, 1857, and he married Elizabeth Figley, July 4, 1859, by whom he had one child—Margaret L. Mr. Burk is of German-Irish extraction—his great-grandmother was a German, and his great-grandfather had the warm blood of a Celt in his veins. He has been a hard-working, industrious man and has met many reverses and endured many hardships. He is well posted in the early history of the township, and has a good memory for facts and dates. Mrs. Burk comes of old pioneer stock. Her grandfather lived to be one hundred and ten years old.

ROBERT W. SMITH was a native of Vermont, and the eldest son of Elisha and Amy Smith. He was born December 1, 1799, and with his parents moved to the State of New York, and from there to Ohio, in the year 18— and settled first in what is now Plain township, Wayne county, but shortly afterwards moved to Mohican township, Ashland county, where he made his permanent residence until his death. He died at his home, about three miles southeast of Jeromeville. He married for his first wife Priscilla Hatch, by whom he had eight children: Wilbur R., Julia A., Adelia, Elisha, Lydia, Asa, Edmund P., and Harriet. All are dead except Edmund P. His first wife died, and for his second wife he married Mrs. Isabella Cliffs, who still survives, and now resides in Iowa with her son, Dr. D. B. Cliffs, a prominent physician of that State. She has reached the advanced age of eighty years. He suffered from a severe hemorrhage of the lungs at the age of twenty-five, and was never considered a strong man physically from that time until the day of his death. He was, however, a very active, energetic, man, and possessed of a good mind, and rare business qualifications. He gave his attention to the buying and selling of stock, which he followed with good success. The pursuit of this business necessitated his leading much of his life on horseback, and this, no doubt, was the means of prolonging his life. He was a man of good judgment, and careful business habits, and accumulated a handsome property. Our subject experienced all the hardships and privations that were common to the pioneers of that day. He was a resident of Ashland county when it was a howling wilderness, and but one house was to be found between Jeromeville and Ashland. He made several trips to the mouth of the Huron river to get a barrel of salt, that being the nearest point at which it could be procured. He narrowly escaped with his life, one night, on his way home with provisions he had procured for the household. The wolves followed him for a long distance, he keeping them back with a stick he carried. They followed him even to the door of his cabin, and by the time he reached his home had become so bold as to almost defy his frequent attacks upon them with his club. His father Elisha was born February 18, 1873, and died January 29, 1851. His mother was born April 7, 1778, and died August 22, 1856. The only surviving member of this family is Edmund P. Smith, of whom we cannot refrain from saying just a word. He is a genial, courteous gentleman, and highly esteemed by the citizens of his native county. He was born August 31, 1834, and was married November 24, 1857, to Miss Ellen E. Hoy, who was born August 28, 1835, and is the daughter of one of the early settlers of Ashland county, a sketch of whom will be found in another place, of this volume. To him has been born one child, Julia M., August 10, 1858. Mr. Smith served a term of nearly three years in the late war, on General Garfield's staff, as quartermaster seargent. He is a staunch Republican, and an earnest advocate of his chosen party's measures and principles. Independent in thought and action, he is esteemed by members of both parties alike for his convictions upon all matters of a public nature.

GEORGE MILLER was born June 25, 1820, and February 20, 1845, he was married to Charity Elliott, by whom he has had six children—Mary Ellen, William, Albert, Joseph (deceased), Charles, and Jennie. He is a well-to-do farmer, and resides one mile and a quarter northwest of Ashland. He is the son of George and Mary (Stephenson) Miller, who was born in Ireland, in the year 1769. He emigrated to this country, and first settled in Washington county, Pennsylvania. About the year 1813 he moved into Wayne county, and died there in 1842, at the age of seventy-two years. His wife died in the year 1849.

STEPHEN OHL was the fourth son of George Ohl, and was a native of Pennsylvania. In the year 1831 he came to Ohio with his father, and they commenced life in the woods. The father purchased a quarter section of land on which were a rude log cabin and barn. Here they lived until 1862, the time of their father's death. Stephen and George are the only representatives of the family living in the county. Stephen was married in the year 1834, to Mary Schwarz, by whom he has had twelve children—Samuel, John, George, Stephen, Francis, Lavina, Mary Ann, Alice, Amanda, Malinda, Emma, and Kittie. Ann died in infancy. Mr. Ohl resides on the old homestead, and is a good farmer and a good citizen.

BENJAMIN WENRICK came into Ashland county from Pennsylvania, where he was born in Berks county, September 17, 1821, and settled in 1850 in Milton township. He has been twice married. First to Mary E. Coup, October 2, 1852, by whom he has had four children; and next to Harriet Williams, September 8, 1859, by whom he has had one son. He served nine years as justice of the peace, to the full satisfaction of the people of Milton township. He has filled the office of township trustee and treasurer at various times. He was a valiant soldier in the war of the Rebellion, being in a number of severe engagements, and was with Grant during the siege of Vicksburgh, but escaped unhurt, and returned to his home with all the honors to which he was entitled. By his fellow citizens he is highly esteemed for his integrity, and is looked upon by all who know him as a worthy citizen.

HENRY HARTMAN was a native of Germany, and emigrated to this country at an early age, and first settled in Pennsylvania; he removed to Ashland county in 1840, and settled in Milton township. In 1842 he was married to Barbara Albert, daughter of a pioneer family. To them have been born five children—George, Catharine, Elizabeth, Henry, and Abraham. The latter died in infancy. Mr. Hartman died in 1871, leaving a wife and four children to mourn his loss. The children are all residents of the county, and two remain with the mother at the old home, Henry and Elizabeth, who care for their aged mother, and carry on the home farm. On this farm stands a very rude log school-house, that must have been built at a very early day.

HYMAN L. HEIFNER, was the third son of John and Margaret Heifner, who were early residents of Orange township, and was born November 25, 1841. He lived with his father until his marriage to Sarah Lutz, November 15, 1874, when he came to Milton township to live. He has been a carpenter and joiner, but has now adopted farming, and gives it his whole attention. They have three children: Laura A., Bertha A., and Ida B.

Mr. Heifner generally acts with the Democratic party; he came from old pioneer stock; he had a great grandfather who was a Revolutionary soldier, and he is a peaceable and law-abiding citizen, and well respected. Mrs. Heifner is the daughter of John and Sarah Lutz. The father was a careful, industrious, and frugal man, and died July 2, 1873. His widow survived him until May 11, 1875.

JAMES WHARTON was born in the State of Pennsylvania, November 30, 1817, and came to Mifflin township, Richland county, but now Ashland, and settled in the woods, with no improvements whatever save a rude log cabin and a barn of similar construction, and a few apple trees scattered about the house. April 4, 1844, he was married to Nancy Williams, whose ancestors were early settlers in Ashland. They have had nine children, as follows: Adaline, Mary, Ebenezer, Malinda, Loren, John, Reumfried, Willard, and Grant. All are living but Mary and Loren, who died in childhood. Adaline married T. W. Hunter, a thrifty young farmer of Clearcreek township. Ebenezer married Lillie McClusky, and resides in Milton township. Mr. Wharton resides upon the old homestead, and his dwelling is one of the best to be found in the township. He is one of the largest landholders in the county, and the improvements to be seen on his lands denote more than ordinary thrift and tact on the part of the owner. He has held various township offices, and is a prominent man of enterprise, thrift, and intelligence, and highly esteemed by all who know him.

THOMAS WHARTON was born in Ashland county, March 7, 1835, and resided with his parents until his marriage to Eliza Butt, December 27, 1860. They have had four children: Henry, Charles, Frank and Anna Bell; Henry died in early childhood. Mr. Wharton has held various offices, and is at present treasurer of the township. A substantial farmer, he enjoys the esteem of his fellow citizens.

HENRY BUTT came to Ashland county in 1837; he was born in 1800, in Lancaster county, Pennsylvania. The maiden name of his wife was Nancy Gish; she died February 29, 1872. Both were earnest Christians. He now resides at the old homestead, with his son-in-law, Thomas Wharton.

EBENEZER WHARTON is the oldest son of James Wharton, of whom mention is made elsewhere in this volume. He was born September 6, 1849, and lived upon the home farm until his marriage to Lizzie McClusky, November 17, 1874. They have had two children, James and Charles. He is an energetic and enterprising young man of intelligence and thrift.

JOHN WHARTON was born January 2, 1789, in Pennsylvania. When a young man he married Nancy Fultz, who died August 15, 1830. In September, 1831, he was married to Anna McMillen, of Richland county. To them were born ten children, as follows: Sarah, Susannah, Alvina Jane, Robert, Martha and Minerva, deceased; Thomas, Hulbert, B. F. and Clara, who are living. John Wharton died February 7, 1860, aged sixty-five years and five days; his widow survives him.

SULLIVAN TOWNSHIP.

HENRY M. CLOSE was born in Connecticut, December 26, 1785, and married Eliza Knapp in New York, residing there until the time of her death. She was the mother of two children, who also died in New York. Then he married Mary Moe, who died October 5, 1849. In 1817 he came to Ohio, and settled in Sullivan township, Ashland county, on the farm now owned by Stephen Coats. He was the first justice of the peace of that township, and held the office for several years. He was a member of the Congregational church, and in politics he was an old-line Whig. August 10, 1846, he died. His second wife was the mother of eight children, five of whom are living: Esther, wife of Pierce C. Grannis, of Williams county, Ohio; Henry M., who married Betsey McConnell; Benjamin, who married Elzina Dyer, afterward married Harriet L. Brown, and lives in Illinois; Susan, wife of George W. Houghton; and Roderick, who married Rosetta Mann, and lives in Ashland county, Ohio.

RODERICK M. CLOSE was born in Ashland county, Ohio, on the old homestead, where he now resides. He is engaged in farming and stock-raising, and deals largely in blooded stock; he is also a breeder and extensive shipper of fancy fowls. For seven years he taught school, and has held the office of trustee of Sullivan township several years, and been justice of the peace one term. In politics he is a Greenbacker, and is one of the three who first voted that ticket in Ashland county. In 1860, he married Rosetta Mann, and is the father of three children: Esther A., Rosetta D., and Henry M.

BERNARD HOLBROOK was born in Vermont in 1798, and, in the same State, married Sallie H. Millet, who died in 1863. In 1833, he came to Ohio, and settled on the farm he now occupies, where he is engaged in farming. In politics, he was an old-line Whig; and is highly respected in the community in which he lives. He is the father of four children: Abner, Franklin, Charlotte and Clinton, Franklin being the only one now living.

WILSON WHITCOMB was born in Brattleborough, Vermont, in 1799, came to Ohio in 1832, and settled in Sullivan township, Ashland county, on the farm now owned by W. W. Whitcomb. He was a blacksmith by trade, and built a shop on his farm, and followed his trade in connection with farming nearly all his life; his was for many years the only blacksmith shop within a radius of twenty miles. In politics he was an old-line Whig. He married Olive Rugg, of Vermont, who died on December 4, 1853. He then married Betsey Davis, of Vermont, who died June 10, 1871. He died in 1875. He was the father of six children: Clarissa, wife of L. J. Fairchild, afterward wife of Alonzo Doolittle, of Ashland county; Horace N., who married Jane A. Toms, and lives in Ashland county; David R., who married Hattie N. Chase, and lives in Cleveland; Oren J., who married Susan Crissinger, and lives in Michigan; Minnie P., deceased, who was the wife of A. L. Firman, of Oberlin, Ohio; and Willie W., who married Rose Wirts, and lives in Ashland county, Ohio.

HORACE N. WHITCOMB, was born in Vermont, in 1824, and came to Ohio with his father, where he received a common school education. In 1844 he married Jane A. Toms, and has been engaged in farming. He has been school director several years, and takes a deep interest in educational matters. He has held the office of township trustee two years, and was district clerk twenty-one years. He is a member and one of the trustees of the Baptist church, and contributes liberally to its support. He is a highly respected member of society, and in politics is Republican. In 1864 he enlisted in company E, One Hundred and Twenty-eighth Ohio volunteer infantry, under Captain J. R. Sanford. He was a non-commissioned officer, and was discharged July 17, 1865. He is the father of four children, viz: Lottie, wife of George McConnell, of Ashland county, Ohio; Curtiss I., who married Melvina Bailey, and lives in Ashland county; Eugene C., who lives in Cleveland, and Carrie M., wife of Samuel Bennett, of Ashland county, Ohio.

JOSEPH JOHNSON was born in Vermont in 1782, and married Lovina Blake in New York. She died in May, 1836, in Summit county, Ohio. She was the mother of twelve children. He then married Mrs. Osborn, in Portage county, Ohio, and, after her death, he married Betsheba Ogden, who now resides in Michigan. Mr. Johnson came to Ohio in 1822, and first settled in Portage county, where he remained twenty years, and then moved to Ashland county, and settled on the farm now owned by his grandson, Joseph Johnson. He was engaged in farming all his life, and was a member of the Baptist church. He took part in the war of 1812, and, in politics, was an old-line Whig until the Republican party was organized, when he became a Republican. He died in 1866. Mr. Johnson was the father of twelve children, only four of whom are living, viz.: Ambrose B., who married Mary Van Wagnor; Nancy, who became the wife of William Sherwood, and afterwards wife of Sterling Acker; Lovina, wife of Gideon R. Bowker, of Dakota; and Elizabeth, wife of Jonathan Chase, of Maryland.

AMBROSE B. JOHNSON was born in the State of New York in 1811, came to Ohio with his father, and recieved such an education as the district schools of that time afforded. He married Mary VanWagnor, in Portage county, Ohio, and came to Ashland county in 1842, and settled on the farm on which he now lives, where he is engaged in farming and dairying. In politics he is a Republican. He is the father of eight children, viz.: Joseph O., who married Ann E. Parker, and lives in Ashland county; Cyrus W., who married Sarah S. Ogden, and lives in Lorain county; Henrietta, wife of Marcus De Moss; Harriet, wife of Leonard A. Coles, afterwards wife of Isaac N. McHose; Mary E., formerly wife of Ransom Persons, now wife of Rufus De Moss; Garret A., who married Mary E. Baldwin; George W., who married Helen Drake; Charles E. who married Alice Hewitt.

JONAH DEMOSS was born in Bath county, Virginia,

April 3, 1787, and in 1815 married Jane Kelly, a native of Clarksburgh, Virginia. In 1809 he came to Ohio, and first settled in Perry county, where he remained twenty years. While there he enlisted, and served six months in the war of 1812, in Major Tupper's regiment; he also served under General Harrison, at Fort Meigs, in 1829. He came to Ashland county and settled on the farm now owned by his son, Marcus DeMoss. He was one of the original members of the Baptist church —the first church of any denomination in the township; he helped build it, and contributed liberally to its support. In politics he was an old-line Whig, but became a Republican. In 1862 he died, and his wife died the same year. He was the father of ten children, four of them now living: James, who married Henrietta Campbell, and lives in Michigan; Nancy, wife of Elijah St. Freeman, in Indian Territory; Jonah, who married Sarah Sprague, and lives in Michigan, and Marcus, who married Henrietta Johnson. Jane Kelly, wife of Jonah DeMoss, was formerly the wife of Henry Battan, who died in Somerset, Perry county, Ohio, by whom she had five children, viz: Mary, now wife of H. Wadden, of Iowa; Annie, wife of Benjamin Van Osdell (deceased), of Medina county, Ohio; John, who married Rebecca Biggs (deceased), of Ashland county, Ohio; Sarah, who married Charles Crosby (deceased), of Michigan, and Isaac (deceased), who married Eliza Webster, of Ashland county.

MARCUS DeMoss, son of Jonah DeMoss, was born in Ashland county, Ohio, in 1832, on the farm on which he now lives. He received a common district school education, and taught school four years. At present he is engaged in farming and stock raising. In 1859 he married Henrietta Johnson, and in 1861 enlisted in company C, Forty-second regiment Ohio volunteer infantry, under Captain Bushnell, the (regiment was commanded by Colonel, now General, Garfield); he served sixteen months, and was with the regiment during the Big Sandy and Cumberland Gap campaign, and was discharged on account of disability. He has been trustee of the township, and was justice of the peace nine years, also constable, and in 1880 was appointed census enumerator. He is a member of the Congregational church, and has been clerk of the church for the past ten years. He is a highly respected member of society, and in politics is a Republican.

CHESTER DRAKE was born in East Windsor, Connecticut, in 1782. He married Percy Strong, and after her death, married Susan Cook, of Connecticut. He moved from Connecticut into the State of New York, where he remained about two years, when he came to Ohio, and first settled in Wayne county, where he remained about one year. In 1837 he came to Ashland county, and first settled on the farm now owned by his widow. He was engaged in farming all his life. He was a member of the Baptist church, and in politics was an old-line Whig until the organization of the Republican party, when he became a Republican. In June, 1876, he died, respected by all who knew him. He was the father of ten children, six of whom are living, viz: Simeon L., who married Martha Cummings; Lydia L., now wife of Levi Turner, of Iowa; Joshua L., who married Helen Swan, and lives in Minnesota; Henry H., who married Eliza Parker, and lives in Iowa; Mary E., wife of Thomas Webster, of Iowa; and Percy P., who lives in Ashland county.

SIMEON L. DRAKE was born in Madison county, New York, December 16, 1816, where he received a common school education; he came to Ohio with his father, and in 1842 married Martha Cummings, of Ashland county. He is a farmer and stock raiser, and for the past four years has been engaged in raising Durham cattle, but at present is dealing in Holstein cattle; he is a Republican in politics, and is the father of eight children, five of whom are living, viz.: Wilber C., who married Jennie Dunlap; Willard, who married Josephine Persons; Helen M., wife of George W. Johnson; Henry, and Silas; all living in Ashland county.

CHAUNCY GOODYEAR was born in Genoa, Cayuga county, New York, in 1807, and received a common school education. He came to Ohio in 1843, and first settled in Fitchville, Huron county, where he remained about one year, when he came to Ashland county, and first settled on the farm now owned by George French; he has held the office of township trustee four years, is a member of the Congregational church, in which he holds the office of deacon, and contributes liberally to the support of the church, and is respected by all who know him. His first wife died in 1844. She was the mother of three children. After her death he married Sophronia Webb, of Homer, Courtland county, New York, who has one child; but of the four children only two are living, viz.: William F., who married Sylvia L. Biggs; and Sarah S., wife of George E. French, of Ashland county.

WILLIAM F. GOODYEAR was born in Cayuga county, New York, in 1841, and came to Ohio with his father, where he received a common school education, and taught school in Ashland county, two terms. At present he is engaged in farming. In 1863 he enlisted in company E, One Hundred and Twenty-eighth Ohio volunteer infantry, under Captain Junius R. Sanford, and served until July 17, 1865. In 1865 he married Sylvia L. Biggs. In politics, he is a Republican, and is highly respected by all who know him. He is the father of two children: Clinton L. and Timothy T.

JOHN GOULD was born in Massachusetts, July 29, 1775, and married Mary Stearns, of Massachusetts, who was born June 10, 1777. In 1824 he came to Ohio, and first settled in Ashland county, on the farm now owned by the Gould heirs. He held the office of justice of the peace eighteen years, and was postmaster several years. In politics, he was an old-line Whig, and was commander of the militia in the State of Vermont. He died May 2, 1851, and his wife died January 21, 1851. He was the father of six children: Olive, who was the wife of John M. Madison, of New York; Enos, who married Philena Rice, of Ashland county; Brittania, wife of Levi Mitchel, of New York; Rufus, who married Mary E. Fletcher; Hannah, wife of Clement March, of

Ashland county, and Lucretia S., wife of Norman Mellen, of New York. The children are now all dead except Lucretia, wife of Norman Mellen.

RUFUS GOULD was born in Ontario county, New York, in 1810, came to Ohio with his parents in 1824, and received a common school education. On October 17, 1832, he married Mary E. Fletcher, in Medina county, Ohio, and was engaged in farming and stock-raising. He held the offices of township trustee and constable for a number of years, and in politics was a Republican. On December 5, 1871, he died. He was the father of one child—John T., who married Charity Riggs, and lives in Ashland county.

JOSEPH CURRY, father of Mrs Luther Gould, was born in Pennsylvania, came to Ohio, in 1838, and first settled on the farm now owned by Jacob Barrick, in Lake township, Ashland county. He married Jane Archbold, of Pennsylvania; was a member of the Methodist Episcopal church, and in politics was a Republican. He was the father of ten children, six of whom are living, viz: Thomas, who married Nancy Hayton, and lives in Iowa; William, who married Nancy Wright, and lives in Illinois; David, who first married Mary Thompson, and, after her death, married Sorinda Cady, and lives in North Amherst, Ohio; John, who lives in New Orleans; Jane, wife of David Barrick, of Ashland county; and Sarah, wife of Luther Gould, of Ashland county.

JOSEPH W. SPENCER was born in Maryland, in 1796, where he received his education. In 1816, he came to Ohio, and first settled in Harrison county, where he married Biddy Archbold. While there he was elected justice of the peace four terms. In 1845, he came to Ashland county, and settled on the farm now owned by John A. Spencer; and was here elected justice of the peace two terms. For about fifty years he was a member of the Methodist Episcopal church, and died in 1864, his wife surviving until 1878. Seven of his nine children are living, viz: David, who married Margaret Ferrill; Sarah A., wife of William A. Beck; John A., who married Margaret Summers; Mary J., wife of Valentine Piper—all living in Ashland county; Joseph W., who married Susan Bemer, and lives in Iowa; Elizabeth, wife of Frederick Housman, of Ashland county; and Daniel, who lives in Michigan.

JOHN A. SPENCER was born in Harrison county, Ohio, in 1822; came to Ashland county in 1845, and settled on the farm where he now lives, and has been engaged in farming and stock raising. In 1852 he went by way of the isthmus to California, where he engaged in mining for fifteen months, with good success. In 1853 he returned by the Nicaraugua route. In 1849 he married Margaret Summers, of Ashland county, and is the father of seven children: Devilla, who lives in Montana; Addie, Herschel, Biddy, Milton, Christina, and Mary, all of whom live in Ashland county. For three years he has been constable in Lake township; he is a member of the Methodist Episcopal church, and in politics is a Democrat.

WHITNEY CHAMBERLAIN was born in Dover, Vermont, in 1786, and married Lauretta Turner, of the same place. He came to Ohio in 1817. He first settled on the farm now owned by Joseph Chamberlain, and was engaged in farming and stock raising, and held the office of township trustee for a number of years. He was a member of the Baptist church, and helped build and organize the first church in Sullivan township. He was clerk of the church for many years, and always contributed liberally to its support. In politics he was a Republican. He died in 1861. His wife died in 1864. He was the father of seven children—five living: Lucy, wife of Perus Rice, of Ashland county; Joseph, who married Samantha Barker; Olive, wife of Charles Riggs, afterward wife of James Van Wagnor, of Michigan; Lewana, wife of John Farmer, of Michigan; and William, who married Lydia Farnsworth, of Ashland county.

JOSEPH CHAMBERLAIN was born in Vermont in 1814, and came to Ohio with his father when only three years old. He received a common school education, and taught school one term in Sullivan township, in the district in which he now lives. In 1838 he married Samantha Barker, of Sullivan township, and is engaged in farming and dairying. He has been elected township trustee several terms, and is a member and deacon of the Baptist church, and in politics is a Republican. He is the father of one child, Edsell W., who married Mary E. Spencer, and lives in Ashland county.

RICHARD ROGERS was born in Connecticut, in 1779, married Louisa Maynard in Connecticut, and came to Ohio in 1835, settling in Huntington township, Lorain county. By trade he was a blacksmith, but after he came to Ohio gave his time to farming. He was a deacon in the Baptist church, and in politics was a Republican. He was the father of ten children, viz.: David, deceased; Betsy; Richard, deceased; George; John, deceased; Ann; Nathan P.; Louis, deceased; Samuel, and James.

NATHAN P. ROGERS was born in Shenango county, New York, in 1811, where he received a common school education, and learned the hatter's trade. He married Pauline Park, of Chenango county, in 1835; came to Ohio in 1836, and settled in Sullivan center, where he opened a hat factory and store, and followed that business about six years, when he gave it up and has since been engaged in farming. He has been constable one year, and township clerk several years; is a member and deacon of the Baptist church, and in politics is a Republican. He is the father of nine children, viz.: Henry M., who married Olive Rice, and Edgar L., who married Ruvinia Rice, both of Ashland county; Frances D.; Allsetta M., who married Marques Sage, and lives in Michigan; Theodore J., who married Lydia J. Lewis, and lives in Ashland county; Nathan R., who married Dollie Safford, and lives in Lorain county; Carrie, wife of Carlton Safford, of New York; Merritt J., who married Fannie Mann, and lives in Ashland county; Arthur A., who married Theresa Myers, and lives in Ashland county.

ABIJAH MARSH was born in Massachusetts in 1757, and in 1783 married Beershia Snow in Vermont; was a weaver by trade, and worked at his trade some time after he came to Ohio. He came to Ohio in 1817 and settled in Medina county, where he remained two years. In 1819 he came to Ashland county and settled on the farm now owned by William W. Whitcomb. In politics he was an old-line Whig. He died June 14, 1840. He was the father of fifteen children, all now dead but two, Chester and Azuba.

ARETES MARSH, son of Abijah Marsh, was born in Vermont in 1799, where he received his education; he came to Ohio with his father. He married Ruth Rice, who became the mother of five children, and died March 18, 1838. After her death he married Evangeline Toms, who had three children, and who died March 27, 1879. He was engaged in farming all his life, and was elected township trustee several years; he was a member of the Congregational church, and in politics a Republican; he died May 2, 1876. He was the father of seven children, viz.: Orlando, (deceased), who married Anna Miller, and lived in Michigan; Alva, who married Jane M. Dulittle; Laurette, the wife of John H. Hyde, of Illinois; Maria, who died in Ashland county; Almira, the wife of Daniel C. Gibbs, of Iowa; Lafayette, who died when three years old; Cromwell, who married Rachel McConnel; and Aretas, who died in Clarksville, Tennessee; he served in the One Hundred and Second Ohio volunteer infantry.

ALVA MARSH was born in Sullivan township, Ashland county, Ohio, in 1825, where he received a common school education. He taught school three terms—one in Ohio, one in Illinois, and one in Michigan. In 1851 he married Jane Dulittle, in New York, and returned to Ohio, where he remained three years; then he went to Michigan, and staid four years, when he returned to Ohio and settled in Sullivan township, on the farm now owned by George Mays. He is a farmer and stock raiser, and in politics is a Republican. He is the father of four children: Alta R., Lilia A., and Effie A., all deceased, and Rosabell.

DAVID G. SPENCER was born in Harrison county, Ohio, in 1819, where he received a common school education. In 1840 he married Margaret Ferrell, and came to Ashland county and settled on the farm now owned by John Spencer, in Sullivan township. He is a farmer and stock raiser, and has been trustee of the township several years, and still holds that office. He is a member of the Methodist Episcopal church, and in politics is a Republican. He is the father of four children: Mary E., wife of E. W. Chamberlain; Joseph W., who married Laura J. Bolles; Charles F., who married Alice Close, all living in Ashland county, and one child who died in infancy.

HORACE RIGGS was born in Franklin county, New York, in 1822, and came to Ohio with his father in 1835, and settled in Holmes county, where he received a common school education. In 1844 he came to Ashland county and settled in Sullivan township, on the farm which he now owns. In 1845 he married Susan C. Pierce, of Sullivan township. He learned the cooper trade, and is at present engaged in that business, in connection with farming. In politics he is a Republican, and is the father of three children, viz.: Wadsworth, who married Caroline Holbrook; Charity, who married John Gould, all living in Ashland county, and one child who died in infancy.

DEAN PIERCE was born in Massachusetts in 1794, and married Susanna Chase, of the State of New York. In 1840 he came to Ohio, and the same year settled in Ashland county, on the farm now owned by Mrs. Horace Riggs. By trade he was a cooper, which business he was engaged in all his life. He was a member and deacon in the Free Will Baptist church, and in politics was a Republican. In 1845 his wife died, and he died in 1857. He was the father of six children, only two of them living, viz: Susan, wife of Horace Riggs, and Harriet.

MOHICAN TOWNSHIP.

E. F. EBRIGHT was born in Plain township, Wayne county, October 2, 1845. His father, A. B. Ebright, was born in Perry county, Pennsylvania, March 27, 1818, and came to Ohio, locating in Wayne county, in 1833, where he has since been engaged in farming. His wife was Tamer Frees, a daughter of David and Hannah Frees, of Wayne county, to whom he was married April 2, 1841. They raised a family of seven children: Frances, Artie L., E. F., Melville, Ulala T., George J. and John L. E. B. Ebright, the subject of this sketch, was married September 2, 1869, to Miss M. M. Miller, of this county. To them have been born three children: Artie B., born July 29, 1869; Lewis C., born October 12, 1872; and Melville W., born November 7, 1874, and died September 22, 1875. Mr. Ebright is a farmer and stock dealer, and owns a well-improved farm of eighty acres, lying along the Perryville road, one-half mile west of Lake fork. He served as a soldier in the One Hundred and Sixty-ninth regiment, Ohio volunteer infantry during the hundred days' service, enlisting May 1, 1864, and was mustered out September 17th, of the same year, after participating in several battles. Both himself and his wife are members of the Methodist brother Melville read law with Mr. Rauch, at Wooster, Episcopal church. In politics he is a Republican. His and graduated from Ann Arbor law school in 1877. He was admitted to the bar at Ashland, and soon after commencing practice died.

J. W. SELBY, son of Jefferson and Elizabeth Selby, was born in Perry township, Ashland county, April 21, 1852, and was married November 11, 1878, to Mary J. Houser, of the same county. They have one child, Clyde C., born March 26, 1879. He is a farmer and stock dealer, and lives on the home place, formerly called the Naylor farm, three-fourths of a mile east of Jeromeville. His father was born October 5, 1808, in New Lancaster, Ohio; his wife was Elizabeth Instey, of Green county, Pennsylvania, who came to Ohio with her parents when quite young. They raised a family of six children, of whom Joseph W. was the youngest. They were named: Phebe, Catharine J., Millen H., Enoch G., Sophronia, and Joseph W. Mr. Selby, sr., died October 22, 1878, aged seventy years and seventeen days. Mrs. Selby is still living, and makes her home with her son, Joseph W., who began life for himself when but sixteen years of age. In politics he is a Republican.

JOSEPH AUSTIN was born in England, near Seven Oaks, county of Kent, April 7, 1802, and was a subject of King George III. In 1821 he, together with his father and one brother, came to this country, and located in Mohican township, this county, where he lived on a farm until 1832; he then engaged as a salesman in a store at Ashland, where he remained about one year, when he went back and took charge of his father's farm, where he has since lived. His father died in 1843, and his mother in 1849. March 11, 1850, he went with a wagon-train the overland route to California, where he remained a little more than a year, when he returned, via San Francisco, by water, and bought his brother's share in the old homestead. In April, 1854, he was married to Catharine Heichel, and by this union had seven children, five of whom died in infancy. Two are still living: Josephine A., who was born July 12, 1860; and Lucy, born June 15, 1874. Mr. Austin and family now live a quiet life on the old homestead farm, near Jeromeville. Both himself and wife are members of the Lutheran church.

NEWTON RICHEY was born in Lake township, Ashland county, October 26, 1844, and is a son of Robert and Naomi Richey, to whom were born seven children, six living and one dead. Our subject was the seventh child. He is now located in Jeromeville, and is doing a large and extensive business. He has been in the wholesale and retail carriage manufacturing and undertaking business for about fifteen years. By fair dealing he has gained the good wishes of all his patrons. He was married to Sarah Finley, August 11, 1868, and by this marriage was born one child, named B. Myrtle, who was born June 6, 1869. Mrs. Richey was born in Lake township.

J. D. KARNS was born in Allegheny county, Pennsylvania, on the seventeenth day of April, 1812, and in March, 1832, he came to Wayne, now Ashland, county, where he now lives. February 4, 1834, he was married to Mary Hale, daughter of Joseph Hale, and by this marriage had eight children; Amelia, Lydia, Eliza Jane, Jasper; Joseph, who died August 12, 1847; Emily, Susan and Joel. October 10, 1860, his wife died, and on October 15, 1861, he was married to Catharine Leidigh, daughter of Peter Leidigh. Mr. Karns has held the offices of township trustee and assessor. By occupation he is a farmer, and in politics is a Democrat.

JAMES OFFINEER was born in Hardy county, Virginia, November 19, 1796. On April 25, 1825, he was married to Catharine, daughter of George and Mary Grimm, of the same county, who was born March 2, 1805, and was the third in a family of nine children. Mr. and Mrs. Offineer came to Ohio November 29, 1829, on which date they arrived on the farm now owned by William Brian, and from thence removed to the farm on which she now lives. They had a family of nine children—George, born September 24, 1821, married Miss Woods, and lives in Jeromeville; Nancy, born August 15, 1828, married William Metcalf, and died in Kosciusko county, Indiana; Mary, born July 7, 1830, died September 20, 1833; Susan, born January 2, 1833, married G. W. Roe, and lives near Mansfield, Ohio; James, born August 29, 1836, married Lydia Whissimore; Catharine, born January 4, 1839, married D. B. Cliffe; John, born April 17, 1841, died January 27, 1842; Francis Marian, born May 1, 1846, married Rachel Wolf, and lives in Crawford county, Iowa; Mary Elizabeth, born January 3, 1843, married Frederick Endinger, and lives near Lafayette, Perry township. Mr. Offineer was one of the early settlers of the township, arriving when the country was mostly covered with timber, and neighbors were few and far between. Wild game was plenty, but the still wilder Indians had just left the country. March 29, 1868, he died, having done his part in clearing and improving the farm he left to his family. He was a member of the Disciple church in Jeromeville, of which he became a member in September, 1838. In politics he was a Democrat, and cast his first vote for James Monroe. Mrs. Offineer now lives with her son-in-law, D. B. Cliffe. She is also a member of the Disciple church, which she joined at the same time as her husband. She is now in the seventy-sixth year of her age.

NANCY BOTDORF was born in Carroll county, Ohio, September 15, 1826. She is a daughter of George and Mary Ream, who came to this county in 1835, and located on the farm a half mile east of Mohican, which still bears their name. They raised a family of six children, of whom Nancy was the third. They were Lucinda, Elizabeth, Nancy, Margaret, Catharine, and Sarah, all of whom are living with the exception of Catharine. Nancy Ream was married March 21, 1847, to George Botdorf. To them was born one child, Dayton, born March 3, 1857. They moved to their present farm in 1858, where Mr. Botdorf died November 25, 1866. He was born in Pennsylvania, August 30, 1807, and came with his parents to Ohio in 1828. Mrs. Botdorf and her son live on the old farm one-half mile north of Mohican, where he attends to the farm work and raises stock. He was married August 4, 1876, to Catharine Leech, daughter of Robert Leech. To them have been born three children, of whom one died in infancy, unnamed: Charles J. was born April 17, 1878, and Asa G. was born March 27, 1880. Mrs. Nancy Botdorf became a member of the Methodist church at Mohican in 1856; her husband was also a member of the same church. In politics he was a Jacksonian Democrat.

C. S. SEIBERT is the son of Samuel and Mary Seibert, and was born in March, 1834. His parents came from

Virginia to Ohio, and settled on the farm on Lake fork, on which Mr. Seibert now resides, and where he owns three hundred acres. He was married in the spring of 1862 to Sophronia Finley, daughter of Abram Finley. To them were born three children: Bennett, born May 7, 1865; Mollie, born December 27, 1856; and Zen, born August 10, 1870. Mr. Seibert is a Republican in his political belief.

WILLIAM DAVIS was born in Westmoreland county, Pennsylvania, June 1, 1838. His father and mother were born in the same State, where they were married, and had a family of twelve children, as follows: Elizabeth, Rebecca, Hannah, Catharine, Eliza, Jesse, Mary, Jonathan, Susan, Clementine, William, and Charles. William came to this State with his parents and their family, and was married, April 22, 1841, to Maria Wilson, who was born January 29, 1818. Her parents were born in Ireland. To them were born two children: Samuel Z., born June 6, 1842, and Eliza Jane, born January 17, 1845. Samuel was married June 24, 1869, to Mary E. Aultz, daughter of Robert Aultz, and is engaged in the practice of medicine, and in the charge of a drug store at Jeromeville. Eliza Jane was married May 1, 1862, to Elder R. Winbigler, and also lives in Jeromeville. Mr. Davis lives one-half mile from Lake fork, on the Jeromeville road, where he is engaged in farming. He has many times been called on to act as administrator of the estates of his neighbors and friends, and has had no less than thirty-one trusts of this character to attend to, in which he has given universal satisfaction. He has also served as assessor in his township. Both himself and his wife are members of the Disciple church, of which he has been a deacon for some ten years. He became a member of the church at Jeromeville in 1840, and his wife joined some thirteen years later. In politics he is a Republican. His first vote was cast for Henry Clay.

ELMER D. MORR is the son of George and Mary Morr, who raised a family of eight children, as follows: William P., Elmer D., Emma, Martin, Ella, Celia, Arthur and Frank. Mrs. Morr's maiden name was Mary Frankhouser, and she was born in Pennsylvania. Elmer learned the trade of carpenter with his father, and afterwards bought a half interest in the dry goods store of Brubaker Brothers, at Jeromeville, in the winter of 1879-80. He is a young man, but has the confidence of those who deal with him. In politics he is a Democrat.

DAVID D. BOTDORF, son of George and Nancy Pinogle Botdorf, was born August 2, 1833. They had a family of eight children, as follows: Catharine, Samuel, Sylvester, John, David D., Sarah, Eliza and Dayton. David D. Botdorf was married in September, 1858, to Arabella N. Cliffe, and to them were born six children: George Daniel, Joseph Dayton, Zaidee Alice, Effie Virginia, Samuel Valentine, and Mary Margaretta. Mr. Botdorf lives on the road leading from Jeromeville to Mohican, on the farm which he occupied in 1859, where he owns eighty acres of land. In politics he is a Jacksonian Democrat, and has served as township trustee.

E. H. INGMOND, son of Judge Ingmond, was born January 4, 1844. His father was a native of Fairfield county, and his mother was born in the State of Maryland. She died when he was quite small, his father living one mile from Jeromeville. On the eleventh day of September, 1861, he left home and went to Cleveland, where he enlisted in the Second Ohio cavalry. After thirteen months' service, he was transferred to the Twenty-fifth Ohio independent artillery, which was stationed in Missouri and Arkansas, and was engaged principally in skirmishing with the enemy. During this service, he took part in the battle of Prairie Grove, Arkansas. February 15, 1863, he was mustered out at Little Rock, Arkansas, and immediately re-enlisted. He was in Captain Julius M. Hadley's company, and served under Generals Sill, Davidson and Raynolds. During his service he was an orderly, then third duty sergeant, and finally orderly sergeant. He was mustered out of service at the close of the war, on September 17, 1865. Immediately after his discharge he came home, and was married September 25, 1866, to Elizabeth Pocock, daughter of Elijah and Mary Pocock. To them were born five children: Charley Clifford, born September 3, 1867; Frank Willard, born April 16, 1869; William Walter, born December 26, 1870; Howard Ashley, born March 11, 1873; and Mary Grace, born September 24, 1877. He now owns the farm formerly the property of Elijah Pocock, which is situated two miles southwest of Jeromeville, and contains one hundred and sixty-three acres. Both himself and his wife belong to the Lutheran church in Jeromeville, of which he became a member in 1868. At that time his wife was a member of the Presbyterian church, but transferred her membership to the Lutheran. In politics he is a Republican, and believes in the theory of Abraham Lincoln: "All men are, and of a right ought to be, free and independent."

SAMUEL HUFF, son of Peter and Rosanna Huff, was born in Lake township, Ashland county, May 30, 1830, and was married to M. A. Marks, of the same county, October 26, 1854. They have had six children, as follows: Mary, born November 18, 1855, died January 7, 1859; George W., born May 18, 1858; William, born February 7, 1862; James C., born July 8, 1863; Rosanna, born March 5, 1866; Ella, born June 24, 1871. Mr. Huff worked his father's farm four years after 1854, when he removed to this place, and run a steam engine for three years. Then he purchased the fulling factory of Major Tyler, in 1861, and has since that time made the fulling of cloth his business. He has added improved machinery, and by energy and hard work has established a good trade. He is a self-made man, having worked hard in earning his property, and deserves credit for the success he has attained.

LEVI METCALF was born in Lake township, Ashland county, August 27, 1845. He is a son of Zebulon and Sarah Metcalf, and was married in 1867 to Sarah E. Leech, also of Ashland county. They have had three children, as follows: Mary Gertrude, born September 1, 1870; Eliza Lee and Elsa Maree, twins, born May

14, 1876. Elsa Maree died May 24, 1876. Mrs. Metcalf is a daughter of Gilbert and Sarah Leech, and was born July 12, 1840. Both Mr. and Mrs. Metcalf are members of the Reformed church. In politics he is a Democrat.

HENRY WACHTEL was born in Plain township, Wayne county, Ohio, June 16, 1829, his parents being Jacob and Marie Wachtel. His mother died when he was ten years of age, and he lived with his sister until he was seventeen years of age, when he went out and worked by the month wherever he could find employment at farming and carpenter work. On the second of October, 1851, he was married to Sarah Hulbert, daughter of Jacob and Elizabeth Hulbert. To them have been born seven children, as follows: Mary E., born January 5, 1852; Jacob M., born June 6, 1861; John W., born September 12, 1862; George E., born December 23, 1863; Hattie E., born September 5, 1866. Jacob M. died in infancy, and Charles H., who was born May 18, 1868, died March 14, 1871. An infant died unnamed. Mr. Wachtel went to California in 1852, and remained seven years, returning May 31, 1859, and settling in Mohicanville, where he engaged in general merchandise and produce. This business he has continued to the present time. He has been a member of the German Reformed church for eighteen years. In politics he is a Jacksonian Democrat.

B. F. PAULLIN, son of Z. T. and Hannah Paullin, was born October 9, 1847, in Mohicanville, where he was married to Martha A. Maurer, September 26, 1871. They have had two children, of whom the eldest died in infancy, unnamed; the other, William Ray, was born July 23, 1876. Mr. Paullin engaged in business shortly after his marriage; by trade he is a saddle and harness maker, and trimmer, which business he has been engaged in for the past thirteen years. He has a large shop for manufacturing these articles, in Mohican, and turns out the best quality of work. Both himself and wife are members of the Reformed church, to which they have belonged since 1873. In politics he is a Jacksonian Democrat, and has held the office of township clerk four years. His father was born in Greensburgh, Pennsylvania, August 24, 1822, and came to Ohio with his parents in 1824. He was married in 1844 to Hannah Hayes, a cousin of President Rutherford B. Hayes, and raised a family of nine children, of whom B. F. was the second.

J. H. STEELE, son of J. L. and Margaret M. Steele, was born October 6, 1853, on the farm known as "Evergreen Home," four miles west of Massillon, where his father was also born. He remained with his father until the fall of 1871, when he entered Heidelberg college, at Tiffin, Ohio, from which he graduated, and received the degree of A. B. in 1876. Then he entered the seminary of the same college and pursued a theological course, and in 1878 received a call to the ministry in Mohican, charge of Tuscarawas classes. In his youth he became a member of the Reformed church. After completing his studies, he was married to E. Allie Chapman, daughter of T. W. Chapman, who was born in Bethlehem, Stark county, Ohio. They have one child: James Chapman, born December 4, 1879. Mr. Steele has occupied the Mohican charge since he first commenced preaching. His wife attended Glendale academy, and afterwards studied at Heidelberg college, where she received lessons in painting, drawing, and music. Both have the confidence and love of their congregation, and of the people among whom they live.

WILLIAM NOGGLE was born January 23, 1841. Both his father and mother were born in Franklin county, Pennsylvania, whence they came to Ohio in 1828. He enlisted in the army in the first call for three months' volunteers, and at the close of his enlistment was mustered out of service and returned to his home. Soon after he went to Idaho territory, where he followed mining, ranching, and freighting, for three years and a half, when he returned, and was married October 31, 1867, to Nancy Craig, daughter of William Craig, of Vermillion township. She was born July 2, 1838. They have two children: Barbara Eldera, born December 7, 1868, and William Howard, born September 23, 1873. Mr. Noggle was born on the farm now belonging to Eli Zimmerman, which was, at that time, owned by his father, who afterwards sold it and bought the Noras farm, consisting of three hundred and four acres, and now owned by William Noggle, the subject of this sketch. Mr. Noggle is one of the largest grain and stock raisers in Ashland county, his wheat crop amounting to from six hundred to fifteen hundred bushels annually, as well as from fifty to one hundred bushels of cover seed, and from thirty to fifty acres of corn. He has a good farm, which he knows how to manage, and, in 1879, built himself a good house a mile south of Jeromeville, on the bank of the Jerome fork. Mrs. Noggle is a member of the Methodist church. In politics Mr. Noggle is an ardent Democrat.

JAMES McFADDEN is a son of Edward and Elizabeth McFadden, and was born December 11, 1841. November 12, 1863, he was married to Sarah Garus, of this county. They have had a family of seven children, as follows: Flora B., born August 21, 1864; Edward L., born August 7, 1866, died November 22, 1871; Clara B., born April 18, 1868; John W., born June 6, 1870, died December 2, 1871; Melvin L., born September 5, 1872; Elizabeth M., born July 6, 1875; and James E., born December 19, 1878. Mr. McFadden has a farm of one hundred and eighty acres, situated a mile from Jeromeville, on what is known as the Mansfield and Wooster road. When he was eighteen years of age, he commenced farming on the place known as the McFadden place, and has, by hard work and perseverance, accumulated a good property. For twelve years, he has been a leading member of the Reformed church, during eight of which he has held the office of deacon. Every member of his family belongs to the same church. In politics he is a Democrat.

EMANUEL TREACE is a son of George and Maria Treace, and was born on the farm on which he now resides June 25, 1846. May 15, 1870, he was married to Christie A. Kahl, of this county. To them have been born four children, as follows: Ada B., born June 20, 1871; Byron, born January 2, 1873; William K., born September 21, 1874; Zenas E., born September 26, 1877. The father of Mr. Treace was among the early settlers of this township, and raised a family of eight children, of whom all but one are living, Adeline, who died in 1868. Emanuel Treace is a farmer, and by hard work has provided for his family a comfortable home. Both himself and his wife are members of the United Brethren church, of which he has been superintendent and class steward. In politics he is a Republican. His father was born May 13, 1815, and died March 3, 1877; his mother was born September 22, 1817, and died February 23, 1870.

JAMES P. WINBIGLER is a son of Perry and Mary Winbigler, and was born in Ashland county, Ohio, January 10, 1841; his parents died when he was young, leaving himself and two sisters to depend on their own resources. At nineteen years of age he commenced life for himself. On April 16, 1868, he was married to Annie E. Morris by whom he had six children, but three of whom are now living. They were Edmund K., born June 30, 1868, and who died October 10, 1870; Mary C., born January 1, 1870; John D., born March 15, 1872; Louis A., born October 3, 1873; and twin boys, who died in infancy, unnamed. Mrs. Winbigler died February 12, 1875, and he was again married, June 20, 1876, to Mrs. Margaretta Glenn, widow of James R. Glenn. They have had one child, who died in infancy. Mrs. Winbigler is a daughter of James and Annie Hammett, and was married to her first husband August 10, 1854. By him she had two children, Sadie E., born September 23, 1863; and Mary A., born September 10, 1865, and who died June 29, 1868. Both Mr. and Mrs. Winbigler are members of the Presbyterian church. In politics he is a Democrat.

DANIEL FICKES is the son of John and Elizabeth Fickes, and was born in Stark county, this State, in 1849. He is the seventh of nine children. In 1871 he was married to Sylvia A. Eley, who was born in this county, which place has always been her home. The fruits of this union are four children, all of whom are living, and named respectively: David, born April 15, 1872; Clara Bell, born September 22, 1874; Mary J., born February 24, 1877; and John, born October 6, 1879. Our subject is a farmer by occupation, which vocation he has followed from boyhood. He, together with his wife, are members of the Methodist Episcopal church, and are alike respected for their Christian virtues.

WILSON LUTZ was born December 29, 1848, near Jeromeville, Ashland county, Ohio, within a few rods of where he now resides. His father, Martin Lutz, was born in Franklin county, Pennsylvania, and came from thence in 1836. His mother, Matilda Wilson Lutz, was born in Center county, Pennsylvania, and came from thence the same year. On the seventeenth day of October, 1869, Wilson Lutz was married to Nettie Robb, adopted daughter of Isaac and Sallie Robb, of Jeromeville, Ashland county, Ohio. She was born at Orange, Ashland county, Ohio, October 12, 1852. Their children are: Willie, born March 11, 1871; Bertha, born January 20, 1873; Charlie, born November 11, 1875; Johnny, born July 25, 1877; and Nora, born March 24, 1880.

E. F. SHELLEY, son of John and Catharine Shelley, was born in Wayne county, Ohio, October 22, 1853. His father was born in Pennsylvania, and his mother in Ohio. They raised a family of five children, as follows: E. F., Emma, Amasa, Allie, and Maud. E. F. Shelley obtained an education at the schools at Wooster and Smithville, after which he taught school two terms, and then bought the farm formerly owned by Nathan Glenn, which comprises one hundred and thirty acres. June 9, 1879, he was married to Tamazon Cornell, daughter of Jason and Rachel Cornell, of Shreve, Ohio. To them was born one child, Tot, whose birth occurred November 4, 1876. Mr. Shelley raises large quantities of wheat, averaging twelve hundred bushels per year, since he owned the place. Mrs. Shelley became a member of the Christian church in the winter of 1878, during a revival. In politics he is an ardent Democrat, as was his father before him. He is one of the charter members of the Royal Arcanum lodge at Jeromeville, in which he still retains his membership.

JOHN SPRENG, son of Jacob and Margaret Spreng, was born in Clinton township, Wayne county, May 14, 1845, and was married September 23, 1866, to Matilda B., daughter of Alfred and Elzan Baird, by whom he had four children: Alfred A., born August 12, 1867; Isaac E., born March 23, 1869; one who died in infancy, unnamed; and Mary, born October 21, 1875. Mr. Spreng is a member of the United Brethren church, in which he has held the most important offices, as well as having been class-leader and superintendent of the Sunday-school.

STEPHEN EWING is a son of John and Catharine Ewing, and was born in Mohican township, where he was married to Barbara Husser, who died December 28, 1871, leaving a family of five children, as follows: Isaac, born September 2, 1858; Thomas E., born October 25, 1863; Clara E., born June 17, 1865; Harvey, born October 1, 1867; Asa, born June 25, 1868. Another died in infancy, unnamed. Harvey died October 31, 1871. Mr. Ewing was a second time married January 16, 1873, to Melissa J. Mowry, by whom he has had three children—Mary J., born February 15, 1874; Alverdy A., born September 6, 1877; Rice M., born October 7, 1879. Mr. Ewing has been located on his present farm since his first marriage, and has one hundred acres of land, situated in the valley east of Jeromeville. In politics he is a Democrat, and held the office of township trustee from 1875 to 1877. Both himself and his wife are members of the United Brethren church, in which he has been trustee, steward and class-leader for many years.

LEVI FLICKINGER, son of Jacob and Christena Flickinger, was born in Londonderry township, Bedford county, Pennsylvania, July 24, 1817; he came to Ohio in 1838, and settled in Mohican township, Ashland county, where he has since resided. May 9, 1839, he was married to Annie Newman, of this county. They have had eight children as follows: Amanda A., born December 13, 1840, died February 14, 1841; Delilah, born February 18, 1842; Nathaniel, born March 26, 1844, died March 22, 1864; Daniel T., born April 7, 1847; Charlotte, born December 10, 1848; Elias, born November 22, 1851; and two who died in infancy, unnamed. Mrs. Flickinger died September 26, 1856, and he was again married February 26, 1857, to Eliza Wolever. They have had seven children, as follows: Levi W., born December 10, 1857; Samuel L., born August 22, 1859; Ida P., born January 31, 1861; Isaiah C., born July 5, 1863; Eliza L., born June 6, 1865; George E., born January 10, 1868, died June 3, 1878; Maggie, born October 9, 1869. Mr. Flickinger is a member of the United Brethren church, in which he has been a trustee for many years. In politics he is a Republican.

JOHN B. RIDGLEY, son of Wesley and Rebecca Ridgley, was born April 8, 1844, at Jeromeville, Ashland county, Ohio. In 1823, shortly after their marriage, his father and mother came from Frederick county, Maryland. The father worked at the trade of shoemaking, which he learned in Maryland; he was also an auctioneer of considerable renown. In 1847 he died, leaving the subject of our sketch to the care of his mother and elder brothers. At the age of eighteen he was apprenticed to his brother Leonard to learn harness and saddle making, at which he continued for eight years, when he accepted an agency of the Domestic Sewing Machine company. But, meeting with poor success, he abandoned the business after having worked at it for two and a half years, and next engaged in the grocery and produce business, at which he has met with success, and in which he is still engaged. As a business man, Mr. Ridgley is lively and energetic. December 17, 1867, he was married to Emma, daughter of John and Margaret Hoffman, and has two children: Anna, born November 10, 1867, and Willie, born October 19, 1871.

L. P. ZIMMERMAN was born in Wayne county, August 29, 1847, his parents being A. D. and Catharine Zimmerman, who came from Pennsylvania in 1833. During his boyhood he remained with his parents, and while still young commenced clerking for Mr. Thompson, in Perryville. Some two years later, his father moved to Perryville, and purchased Thompson's stock of groceries, which they disposed of after two years to Rouse & Fullmer. They still continued in trade in the Cotter store for two years, when they again sold out and removed to Orrville. Here L. P. Zimmerman remained in the grocery trade one year, when he came to Lake Fork and purchased the dry goods stock of Eddy & Harvey, where he still remains. In December, 1873, he was married to Ella Applegate, and has had three children: Zella, born in January, 1875, and an infant. Another infant died, unnamed.

ENOS TRYON was born in Plain township, Wayne county, in the year 1835, July 30th, and was a son of John and Lydia Tryon. His father was born in Otsego county, New York, March 8, 1794, and his mother was born in New York, March 12, 1799. They had twelve children, ten sons and two daughters. Enos was the ninth child. His father and mother were married in 1817. There children were: Moses, Matthew (died), Christopher, Daniel, Titus (died), Juna (died), Rufus (died), Rebecca, Enos, Nathan (died), John W., Elmor (died). Enos was married in October, 1857, to Maggaline Lorance, and by this union they had two children: Maria, born April 18, 1859, and died September 10, 1863; Ulysses W., born January 15, 1865. He moved to Indiana, and lived there until the death of his wife, which occurred November 12, 1865, when he moved back to Wayne county, and lived with his father until he came to Ashland county, in 1869, and settled in Mohican township. On November 17, 1868, he was married to his second wife, Sarah Metcalf, by whom he had one child, who died in infancy. Mr. Tryon is a farmer, and a member of the Methodist Episcopal church. In politics he has always been a Republican.

JOEL RICHEY, son of Robert and Naomi Richey, was born in Butler township, Knox county, Pennsylvania, December 18, 1825. January 1, 1851, he was married to Maria Harms, in Ashland county. To them was born one child, who died in infancy. Mrs. Richey died August 26, 1852, and he was married a second time, April 20, 1854, to Rebecca Hoy, of Clinton township, Wayne county. They have had four children: Melvin, born November 6, 1856; Alvaretta, February 5, 1858; Emmarilla, born November 14, 1863; and an infant, who died unnamed. The father of Mr. Richey came to America in 1805 and settled in Pennsylvania, and, in 1812, enlisted as private soldier in Captain Gill's company, and was among the prisoners captured by the British at Hull's surrender of Detroit. After the close of the war he came to Ohio and settled in Ashland county, where he worked in a still-house until 1830, when he engaged in farming, at which he continued until his death, August 2, 1863. His widow survived him, and now lives with her son Joel, who in his early days followed the trades of making wagons and painting. He now owns a farm of seventy acres near Jeromeville. In politics he is a Democrat; he is a member of the Masonic fraternity, and is strictly temperate in his habits.

PETER CHESROWN was born May 7, 1841, in Ashland county, Mohican township, where he now lives. His father was born in Pennsylvania April 11, 1811, and his mother, Elizabeth, was born in Washington county, Pennsylvania; she died January 26, 1879. Our subject started for himself in the fall of 1862, working on a farm and teaching school. In August, 1862, he went to Indiana, and resided there four years, when he came back to Ohio and went on his father's farm, where he has since lived. Mr. Chesrown is a stock-dealer and farmer, and is the owner of the thoroughbred stallion, Star Hambletonian. He lives on a well improved farm of one hundred and twenty acres, situated near Mohicanville. May 2, 1863, he was married to Eliza Emrick, and has three children: Emma J., born January 10, 1864; John W., born September 5, 1866; Stella, born July 25, 1869. In politics he is a Democrat.

BENJAMIN F. SEIBERT was born in Wayne county, Ohio, February 28, 1837, and removed to Ashland county when ten years of age. Samuel Seibert, his father, was born in Berks county, Pennsylvania, and his mother, Mary Mong, was born in Berkeley county, Virginia. They came to Ohio in 1824. Benjamin Seibert enlisted in company B, Sixth squadron of Ohio volunteer cavalry, under Major McLaughlin, and served over four years as a private and non-commissioned officer; and he was through the campaign of eastern Kentucky under General Garfield, and through the campaign and siege of Knoxville, eastern Tennessee, under General Burnside. January 10, 1864, he re-enlisted, and participated in the campaign from Chattanooga, Tennessee, to Atlanta, Georgia, under General Sherman. He was captured on the Stoneman raid, near Macon, Georgia, July 28, 1864, and went through the prisons at Andersonville, Charleston and Florence. After being a prisoner nearly seven months, he was exchanged about February 20, 1865, and rejoined the command near Greenborough, North Carolina, just before the surrender of General Johnston; and was mustered out of service October 30, 1865. Early in 1867, he was married to Julia A. Hassinger, of Richland county, Ohio, daughter of Abraham and Sarah Hassinger. They have five children: Daisy, born December 15, 1867; Charley, born February 14, 1869; Minnie, born August 28, 1871; Frank, born October 6, 1872; and Ross, November 14, 1876.

JOSEPH HEICHEL was born in Middleton, Dauphin county, Pennsylvania, November 5, 1819, and emigrated to this State in October, 1832, to Mohican township, where he has since resided; he was married April 27, 1843, to Ann Rebecca Bassford, daughter of G. W. Bassford, sr. By occupation he is a farmer. In early life he was a member of the Lutheran church, but about the year 1856 he united with the United Brethren church, and entered the ministry of that church in 1860, in which he traveled from 1862 until about 1866. By Mr. Herchel's marriage was born nine children, Sarah Jane, born March 14, 1844; Elizabeth Ann, born January 28, 1845; Francis Marion, born February 10, 1847; John Luther, born May 6, 1851; George W., born July 7, 1854; Henry, born November 14, 1857; Mary Anne, born May 3, 1860; Cassey, born July 21, 1862; Malinda Viola, born April 19, 1865; he has held the office of trustee, assessor, and justice of the peace, which office he holds at this time.

JOHN SPRENG, son of Jacob and Margaret Spreng, was born in Clinton township, Wayne county, Ohio, May 14, 1845, and was married September 23, 1866, to Matilda B. Baird, daughter of Alfred and Elzan Baird. By this union were born four children: Alfred, born August 12, 1867; Isaac E., born March 23, 1869, who died in infancy; Mary Maud, born October 21, 1875. Mr. Spreng has always followed farming; he served as supervisor in his district in 1870. He joined the United Brethren church in 1862, of which he has been a prominent member up to this date, and in which he has held the principal offices of the church. Besides being superintendent in their Sunday-school for a number of years, has served as class-leader at least ten years.

MICHAEL OTTO was born in Bedford county, Pennsylvania, March 8, 1818, and is a son of Matthias and Ann Elizabeth Otto. Our subject came to this county when he was about five years old, and has lived here since that time. He was one of the first settlers in this county, where he came with his father and mother, who had twelve children, our subject being the eleventh child. He started out in life for himself when he was fourteen years old, working on a farm at five dollars and fifty cents per month. At the age of sixteen years he commenced work at his trade as blacksmith, and made that his business for fourteen years, when he went to farming, at which he has since continued. He was married to Rebecca Emerick, February 22, 1838. By this marriage were born ten children, as follows: John E., born February 2, 1839; Cornelia, born January 17, 1844; Harmon, born January 4, 1846; Mary E., born October 27, 1848; Elvira A., born September 24, 1850; David A., born August 30, 1852; Cyrus, born November 19, 1854; Laura, born October 18, 1856; Michael, born October 24, 1859; George, born January 16, 1863. John E., died September 13, 1875. Mr. Otto is now living on his own farm, near Lake Fork, where he owns two hundred and sixty acres. He is now leading a quiet, retired life, and has held the office of trustee, and served one term as constable. Mrs. Otto is a member of the United Brethren church. In politics he is a Jacksonian Democrat.

S. J. CRITES was born April 26, 1850, in Green township, Wayne county, from which place his parents removed to Ashland county, where he remained until he was fourteen years of age, when they returned to Wayne county. He attended school at Smithville, and after two terms of study he engaged in school teaching in Chester township, Wayne county. After teaching some time he returned to Smithville, and continued his studies for another year. He again taught school a few terms, and then entered the Hayesville school for a year, since which time he has been engaged in teaching. On January 20, 1876, he was married to Alvaretta Richey. His father, P. L. Crites, was born September 7, 1822, and died May 11, 1876; his mother was born February 26, 1825, and died in January, 1873.

JACOB SPRENG, son of John and Catharine Spreng, was born in Alsace, Germany, October 8, 1813. His father and mother were born at the same place in 1774 and 1777, respectively, and raised a family of seven children, all of whom came to America in 1831. Jacob Spreng was married May 12, 1838, to Margaret Faber, by whom he had thirteen children: Philip, Barbara, Catharine, John, Jacob Frederick and George Christian, twins, Isaac, Otto, Enos, Mary Amma and Lydia Anna, twins, Martha Matilda and E. Albert. He has one grandchild, John Calvin Smith, son of Barbara, who lives with his grandfather, his mother having died when he was an infant. Mr. Spreng is a member of Hope Evangelical church.

D. F. POCOCK, son of Daniel and Sarah Pocock, was

born September 26, 1842. His father was born in Harford county, Maryland, in 1814, and came to this State in 1826; his mother was born in Ashland county, Ohio, in 1815, and was the daughter of Alexander Finley. Mr. Pocock enlisted in the army August 29, 1862, in company H, Forty-second Ohio volunteer infantry, and was engaged in the Chickasaw and Arkansas Post battles. After being in this regiment twelve months, he was mustered out at Vicksburgh, Tennessee, and came home; he then enlisted in the one hundred day service, in company I, One Hundred and Sixty-third regiment. He was mustered out at Columbus, Ohio, and came back home. April 2, 1868, he was married to Miss S. C. Glenn, daughter of Robert Glenn, of Hayesville, Ohio; she was born March 25, 1845. They have had three children: G. D., born March 29, 1871; D. D., a son, born December 3, 1875; and an infant, not named, June 14, 1880. Mr. Pocock lives on the old farm, on the road leading from Hayesville to Lake Fork, two and one-half miles east of Hayesville. The farm consists of one hundred and fifty-five acres, in the Pocock valley. Mr. Pocock became a member of the Presbyterian church in Hayesville in 1867; his wife was a member at the same time. For the past six years he has been a elder, and is still a leading member. He is a staunch Republican, and an active worker in the party.

MATTHIAS BENDER is a son of Martin and Caroline Bender, and was born September 8, 1847. His wife was Harriet Ebehart, of Wayne county, who has borne him three children: Viola, born September 20, 1869; Harriet, born March 8, 1875; and Ruth B., born November 11, 1876. Mr. Bender engaged in the undertaking and cabinet-making business at the age of twenty-two, and has built up an extensive trade. The water from a spring near by runs the machinery in his shop, which is located at Mohicanville, and is known as the Bender works. In addition to this business, he makes Bender's cough balsam and Bender's life liniment, which have a considerable reputation as medicines where they are used.

JOHN HEICHEL is a son of Michael and Catharine Heichel, and was born in Mohican township, Ashland county, April 17, 1836. When he was but sixteen years of age his father died, leaving him to battle his own course through the world. He engaged with Mr. Austin on a farm for one year, when he returned to the old homestead, where he has since resided. On September 3, 1863, he was married to Maria Hammett, daughter of James H. and Anna Hammett. They have five children, as follows: William E., born April 14, 1864; Thomas J., born September 9, 1865; Jennie B., born July 31, 1867; and Annie May and James Ray, twins, born May 23, 1878. Both himself and his wife are members of the Christian church, with which he has been connected twenty years, and has held the offices of deacon and elder. In politics he is a Democrat.

SAMUEL MCCLURE, son of Samuel and Elizabeth McClure, was born in Plain township, Wayne county, October 23, 1837, where he resided until the year 1878, when he removed to this county and located in Jeromeville, Mohican township, at which place he has since resided. He was married February 18, to Miss Jane Alexander, and has reared a family of nine children, eight of whom are still living. Mr. McClure now keeps the hotel at Jeromeville. The names of the children are: Eva A., born February 1, 1863; Thomas A., born August 22, 1864; Calvin W., born December 11, 1865; William W., born September 22, 1867; Mary C., born October 11, 1869; Elizabeth L., born June 4, 1872; Cleveland, born March 20, 1875, died April 19, 1876; Sadie E., born June 4, 1877; Madie M., born August 17, 1880.

THOMAS GLENN was born in 1834, and was married February 14, 1865, to Elizabeth Crailey, who was born June 24, 1841. They have a family of seven children—Anna B., born April 11, 1866; Opha A., born July 19, 1867; John W., born August 2, 1869; Harry LeRoy, born December 27, 1870; Emma J., born September 15, 1872; Branden B., born October 28, 1877; and Thomas R., born February 13, 1875. The father of Thomas Glenn was born in Harford county, Maryland, November 11, 1794, and died May 14, 1868; his mother was born December 1, 1800, and died May 30, 1841. They were among the early settlers of Ashland county. Mr. Glenn was descended from Irish stock. He became a soldier during the war of 1812, and participated in the battle of North Point. His relatives were southerners, and before the late war, were slaveholders. Thomas Glenn, the subject of this sketch, enlisted in 1864, at Jeromeville, in company I, One Hundred and Sixty-third, Ohio national guards, and was with his regiment during the hundred days' service, in Virginia, and participated in the three days' battle at Petersburgh. He was fourth sergeant in his company, and was mustered out of the service at Columbus, Ohio, September 10, 1864. Both himself and his wife are members of the Presbyterian church. In politics he is a Republican.

SAMUEL KEISER is a son of Joseph and Susannah Keiser, and was born in Paint township, Wayne county, Ohio, October 22, 1820. His parents were born in Pennsylvania, came to Ohio in 1803, and settled in Jefferson county, where they lived for fifteen years, when they moved to Wayne county, where our subject was born. He started out for himself at the age of sixteen, and in 1844 engaged in the mercantile business, which he followed until 1858; since that time he has followed farming up to the present time. June 16, 1846, he was married to Mary A., daughter of George and Elizabeth Harpster, of Mohican township, Ashland county, where they now reside. Mr. and Mrs. Keiser are members of the Disciple church. In politics he is a Democrat.

MILLISON EBERT was born in Perry township, Ashland county, December 5, 1835. His father, Valentine Ebert, was married in October, 1817, to Julia Ann Winbigler, and in 1819 emigrated from Maryland to Ohio. The subject of this sketch was married February 3, 1859, to Martha Selby, daughter of Thomas and Phebe Selby, and they have had four children: Isaac Newton, born November 6, 1859; Wilbur F., born September 10, 1861; Edson C., born February 23, 1863; and Mary J., born

November 9, 1867. Mrs. Ebert died from consumption August 14, 1872, and January 1, 1874, he was again married, to Elvira D., daughter of Felix and Matilda Lee. They have two children: Ethel E., born June 25, 1875, and Myrtle M., born January 7, 1877. Mr. Ebert has been a member of the Disciple church since 1852, and has held all the offices of the church, as well as superintendent of the Sunday-school. In April, 1865, he removed to Edgerton, Williams county, Ohio, and, after four years, he went to Kendallville, Indiana, where he remained one year. He then lived two years in La Grange center, when he again returned to Ohio, and settled at Jeromeville, where he now resides. By occupation he is a farmer. A few years ago he received an accident while working a threshing-machine, which rendered him a cripple.

CHRISTY M. ELLIOTT was born in county Donegal, Ireland, May 17, 1857, came to America in 1877, and settled in Ashland county, Ohio, in June of the same year. He taught school in district number six, Mohican township for four consecutive terms, ending in June, 1880. He became a member of the United Presbyterian church in May, 1879. He studied three years in Vermillion institute. George Elliott, his father, went to Michigan in the spring of 1880, together with the family, except one girl and two boys. The family consists of ten children—seven boys and three girls.

D. F. HEISER, son of John and Sarah Heiser, was born in Mohican township, Ashland county, Ohio. His father was born in Pennsylvania in 1808, came to Ohio in 1816, and located on the Tidd farm,, on which D. T. Heiser now lives. His mother was born in Pennsylvania in 1813, her father's name being William Otto. By their union were born eight children: Catharine, Sarah A., E. I., Mary A., D. F., Elizabeth, Martha E., and Emma E. D. T. Heiser was married to Lucy Harris, of Perry township, February 13, 1873, by whom he had two children: Ida Estella, born November 28, 1874, and Rutherford Roy, born April 25, 1877. Mr. Heiser lives three miles from Jeromeville, in the Mohican valley. Both himself and his wife became members of the Methodist church at Hayesville, in March, 1876. They afterwards transferred their membership to Jeromeville, where he is one of the trustees of the church, and also a parsonage trustee. In politics he is an ardent Republican, always working for the success of the party.

BENJAMIN FRY, son of John and Catharine Fry, was born March 5, 1848. At the age of twenty-one he went to the west, but did not like the country and soon returned, and worked at farming. In 1867 he again started for Idaho, and after reaching Nebraska City he turned back, concluding it was not the country he wished for a home. He returned to Indiana and worked for a time at the carpenter trade, and then came on to Ohio, when he followed the same business. On October 16, 1866, he was married to Mary Jane, daughter of William Umphrey, of Perrysville, Ohio. Of his father's children there were nine. Josiah went to California in 1852, and engaged in gold mining; he died January 11, 1869. George went to California in the same year, and is now engaged in the dairy business in Lawson county. John also went to California in 1856, and engaged in mining. While returning home on the Golden Gate, the vessel was burned. He buckled his money about his waist and clung to a rope until it was burned off, when he jumped into the water with two children he was bringing to New York. The others were Benjamin, Mary Ann, William, Harvey (who was killed by fragments of the balance wheel of a machine while sawing wood), Franklin and Catharine. The brothers, William and Benjamin, live on and own the old homestead, consisting of one hundred and seventy-eight acres, on the road leading from Jeromeville to Mohicanville. Both are Democrats. Benjamin and his wife are members of the Reformed church in Mohican.

WESLEY CHESROWN is the son of Lewis and Elizabeth Chesrown, and was born in Washington county, Pennsylvania. When quite young, he came to Ohio with his parents, and settled in Mohican township, Ashland county, one mile east of Mohicanville. In 1858, our subject bought a farm, and has ever since made farming and stock-raising his occupation. He is the owner of two fine stallions; one a draft horse, and the other a thorough-bred roadster, four years old. Mr. Chesrown lives near Jeromeville, and has a well-improved farm of one hundred and four acres. May 28, 1857, he married Lucetta Finley, and has had eight children, six of whom are living. They were: Luca, born March 28, 1858; Zeo, born January 3, 1860; Charlie W., born September 26, 1861, died in 1863; L. V., born November 29, 1864; M. M., born December 18, 1866; Harry, born February 16, 1870, died April 3, 1876; Gertrude, born February 18, 1873; and Belle, born September 14, 1875. Mr. Chesrown is a Democrat in politics, and has held different township offices, but of late years has declined them. His family are members of the Lutheran church.

MONTGOMERY TOWNSHIP.

WILLIAM C. MOORE was born in Ashland county, August 31, 1851, and has always resided here. In 1864 he entered a store at this place, in the capacity of clerk, which he followed until the year 1873, when he associated himself as partner with M. V. Kagey, the firm name being Kagey, Moore & Co., and has since been in the mercantile business, his partner now being Mr. Reiser. They have, by fair dealing, built up for themselves a large trade. They are general dealers in all kinds of groceries and provisions, Yankee notions, etc. Our subject was married, November 2, 1879, to Bessie E. Morgan.

MARTIN B. MASON is the sixth child of Martin and Elizabeth Mason, who came to this county at an early day, and of whom mention is made elsewhere in this work. Our subject was born October 11, 1810, in

JACOB BRUBAKER

was born in Mifflin township, Ashland county, October 19, 1843. His parents, John and Catharine Brubaker, came from Lancaster county, Pennsylvania, to Ohio, in 1832, and made a home in the woods, where they improved a farm and raised a family of eight children, as follows: Joseph, Henry, Elizabeth, John, Catharine, David, Jacob, and Polly. Of these, Joseph, Elizabeth, John and Polly are deceased. Henry studied medicine in Mansfield under Dr. Page, and was in active practice for twenty-five years in Indianapolis and other places, and at the present time is in the store of his brother Jacob, at Ashland. Catharine married Samuel Heckman, and lives on the home farm. David is in the store of his brother Jacob, and, besides this, attends to other business. Polly and Elizabeth died young. John died at Chattanooga while a soldier in the Rebellion, and Joseph died at his home in Indiana in 1875.

Jacob Brubaker, the subject of this sketch, obtained an education in the common schools of Mifflin, and remained on the farm until about twenty years of age, attending school during the winter season. He then came to Ashland and was in the employ of J. Cahn, as clerk, for one year, after which he clerked for B. Palmer six months. With this experience, he engaged in a partnership business, the firm name being J. P. Graham & Co., with which he was connected about two years. In 1865 he formed a partnership with his brother David; the partnership has several times been changed, and within the past two years he has conducted the business without partnership relations. He was married June 12, 1866, to Agnes R. Humrickhouser, and has two children: Ora J., born in 1874, and Guy H., born in 1879.

Mr. Brubaker has depended on his own unaided exertions for his start in life, and all that he has is due to his untiring industry, energy and pluck. In his business, he has achieved a good degree of success, and now stands as the leading dry goods dealer of Ashland, and one of the solid business men of this town.

Columbiana county, this State. When at the age of four years, his parents came to this county, and located in Orange township. But, for the past ten years, he has resided in this township. January 10, 1833, he was married to Sarah McMeeken, who was born in Washington county, Pennsylvania, August 12, 1812. At the age of ten years, her parents removed to this county, then Richland county, and located near Savannah. By this union have been born nine children, six of whom are still living, and named, respectively: Jane, who was born September 26, 1835, and was married to R. N. Hershey, April 15, 1856 (her husband died March 20, 1863; he served as county treasurer one term, and part of another, and died while holding that office); James P., born March 19, 1839, and who was married April 7, 1868, to Mary Gollady; William, born September 22, 1841, and who married Eliza Ross, in 1864; Harriet L., born March 19, 1846, who married Thomas Lilly, in 1873; Izra T., born July 23, 1848, who married Belle Sanders; Martin Poe, born May 17, 1852. The ones deceased are: Elizabeth, who was born December 2, 1833, and died in December, 1855, aged twenty-two years; John E., born December 22, 1843, and died at the age of six years. The other, a daughter, died in infancy, aged ten days. Mr. Mason is one of the oldest surviving pioneers of Ashland county, and can recall many hardships and privations that he, together with others, had to contend with, that the present, as well as the future, generations, will never know nor experience. He has, by industry and paying strict attention to business, made for himself and wife a good home. One year he raised over two hundred bushels of wheat and oats. It is conceded by all that he has raised more wheat than any other man in Ashland county. Joe Williams took wheat up after Mr. Mason for twenty-one successive years, the latter swinging the cradle.

JONATHAN DOTY was born in Westmoreland county, Pennsylvania, March 27, 1821, where he resided until the year 1851, when he removed to this county, which has since been his home. Prior to this time he spent one and one-half year in Illinois. On September 25, 1851, he was married to Martha J. McCune, who was also born in Westmoreland county, Pennsylvania, May 9, 1827. To them have been born seven children, four of whom are still living: Alexander, born January 11, 1857; Margaret Doty, born January 8, 1861; Clark Doty, born April 8, 1864; Martha J., born August 14, 1866. The ones deceased were two who died in infancy, and Nathaniel, born February 16, 1854. Mr. Doty's vocation, since his residence in this county, has been that of a farmer, but, prior to that, he sold fanning-mills, and run a saw-mill while in Illinois.

PHILIP SHEARER was born in Fayette county, Pennsylvania, October 7, 1829, where he resided until 1837, when his parents removed to this State and located in Montgomery township, where he has since lived, with the exception of two years he spent in Iowa. Mr. Shearer is the eighth child of Solomon and Susannah Shearer, who raised a family of thirteen children, ten of whom are still living, and all married but one. His mother is also living, but his father died some thirty-eight years since, soon after coming to this county. The subject of our sketch was married March 26, 1857, to Martha L. McCulley, who was born near Hayesville, this county, April 21, 1825. To them have been born seven children, only three of whom are living: Tully A., who was born December 17, 1863; Kittie, born October 4, 1866; and David F., born February 8, 1869. They also have one child whom they adopted, named Elizabeth H., who was born January 23, 1859. Those who are deceased all died in infancy. Mr. Shearer is one of the firm of Shearer, Kagey & Co., doing business at Ashland.

JOHN C. KAGEY, the subject of this sketch, is the third child of Martin and Nancy Kagey, of whom mention is made elsewhere in this work. February 19, 1863, he was married to Elizabeth Kohler, who was born June 19, 1842, in this county, which was then Richland county. To them have been born five children, four of whom are still living, and named respectively, Cora B., who was born February 6, 1865; William M., born July 18, 1867; John Tulley, born September 6, 1870; and Frederick, born July 9, 1874; all were born in this county. Mr. Kagey is one of the firm of Shearer, Kagey & Co., in the saw- and planing-mill, sash, door, blind, and bracket factory; also, general dealers in all kinds of lumber.

DAVID SHEARER was born in Fayette county, Pennsylvania November 29, 1834; when three years of age his parents removed to this State, and located in Ashland county, since which this place has been his home, with the exception of about two years he spent in the State of Iowa. March 17, 1859, he was married to Miss A. Furnish, who was born in Stark county, this State. The fruits of this union are six children, five of whom are still living, and named respectively: Ida F., who was born February 14, 1860; William T., born December 10, 1861; Susan B., born March 21, 1864; Hattie H., born April 26, 1866; Margaret M., born June 24, 1871. The one deceased was born December 11, 1875, and died August 11, 1876. Mr. Shearer is a carpenter by trade, but for the past seven years he has been associated as one of the firm of Shearer, Kagey & Co., in the saw- and planing-mill, and business connected therewith. Prior to that event he paid his attention to his trade and as a contractor.

MARTIN V. KAGEY was born June 26, 1840, and is a son of Martin Kagey, of Mifflin township, one of Ashland county's pioneers, of whose family a detailed account is given elsewhere in this work. Our subject is now one of the partners of Shearer, Kagey & Co. in the saw- and planing-mill, sash, door, blind and bracket factory at Ashland. November 27, 1862, he was married to Miss Catharine Moore, a daughter of Samuel Moore, also of Mifflin township, and of whom mention is made elsewhere in the family history. The fruits of this union are two children, both of whom are living. They are Emma, who was born February 14, 1864, and Martin Herbert, who was born August 14, 1873.

CYRUS ZIMMERMAN, the subject of this sketch, is the fourth child of Peter Zimmerman, of whom mention is made elsewhere in this work. He was born in Montgomery township, March 15, 1842, and Montgomery township has always been his home. He was married March 8, 1866, to Miss Amanda Irwin, who was born in Holmes county, Ohio, October 3, 1848. To them has been born one child, who is living, and named Elizabeth. She was born November 13, 1869. Our subject is a farmer by occupation, and has followed that as his vocation from boyhood.

E. C. LEACH was born in Unadilla, New York, August 1, 1821, and came to Ashland September 28, 1844, where he has been engaged in the carriage manufacturing business during the past thirty-six years. He was married July 31, 1844, to Miss Sarah E. Ashley, of Tallmadge, Ohio.

JACOB J. KAUFFMAN was born in Canton, Stark county, Ohio, June 20, 1839, where he resided until the year 1858, when he removed to Hancock county, Ohio, where he was engaged in the dry goods business for three years. From thence he entered the United States army. In the late war he was a member of company D, Ninety-ninth Ohio volunteer infantry. He enlisted August 2, 1862, and was mustered out of the service July 19, 1865, since which time his home has been in Ashland. His business here has been in the stove and tin trade for eight years. But for the past six years he has paid all of his attention to the bed spring bottom trade. He is one of the firm of Kauffman & Beer, and they are doing a very extensive business. Our subject was married November 9, 1865, to Miss Annie E. Willis, who was born in Stark county, October 17, 1840. To them have been born three children, all of whom are still living, and named respectively: Elizabeth C., born November 17, 1866; Edward S., born in September, 1871; and Harry, born June 30, 1873.

REV. JOHN ROBINSON, D. D., was born in Westmoreland county, Pennsylvania, January 27, 1816. At the age of two years he was brought to Stark county, Ohio. From thence, at the age of eight years, after the death of his father, he returned to the place of his birth. When about seventeen years old he went to Cadiz, Harrison county, Ohio, and became an apprentice to the tin plate working business. Before the expiration of his apprenticeship, the gentleman with whom he was engaged ceased business, and gave him his indenture. He at once entered upon a course of study, graduating at Franklin college, Ohio, in the fall of 1838. He studied theology at the Western theological seminary, and was licensed to preach on the eighth day of April, 1840, by the presbytery of Steubenville. On October 22, 1840, he was married to Mary W. Willson, of Allegheny City, Pennsylvania, and on the second day of March, 1841, was ordained to the full work of the ministry, and installed pastor of the churches of Corinth and Monroeville. In January, 1844, he was released from that charge and removed to Ashland, Ohio, and on the first Sabbath of February, 1844, took charge of the Presbyterian church of Ashland. In June, of that year, he was installed as pastor of that church by the presbytery of Richland. In that charge he remains now, after a service of thirty-six and a half years. His family consisted of five sons and two daughters. The oldest and fourth son are deceased. The third is residing in Greeley, Colorado, the fourth in Akron, Ohio, the fifth in Cleveland, Ohio. His oldest daughter resides in Van Wert and the youngest in Cleveland, Ohio.

JACOB KRICHBAUM was born in Betal township, Center county, Pennsylvania, May 27, 1809. When a small boy, his parents, John and Elizabeth Krichbaum, removed to this State, and located in Betlam township, Stark county, where he resided until 1830, when he removed to Ashland county, where he has since resided. July 17, 1834, he was married to Eva Ohl, who was born in Wespen township, Schuylkill county, Pennsylvania. To them have been born six children, two of whom are still living: George L. and Francis. The ones who are not living are: Louisa, William, and two who died in infancy. October 20, 1875, his wife died; and he was married again November 9, 1879, to Mrs. Elizabeth Cup, a sister of his first wife. Mr. Krichbaum is a cabinet-maker and undertaker by trade, and has followed that vocation since 1825, and since 1830 he has been established in that business in Ashland. He has lived in this county now nearly two generations; and while he owns a farm joining the incorporated village of Ashland, he pays all of his attention to his business.

LEVI GARDNER was born in Lancaster county, Pennsylvania, June 25, 1841, where he resided until the year 1853, when his parents removed to Ashland county, Ohio, where he has since resided. March 12, 1863, he was married to Susan J. Thompson, who was born in Chester county, Pennsylvania, October 31, 1838. To them have been born four children, three of whom are living; Martin M., who was born January 28, 1864; Elizabeth A., born November 13, 1872; George A., born November 17, 1874; the one deceased was Edwin T., born June 20, 1866, died April 5, 1871. Mr. Gardner's vocation has always been that of a farmer and thresher, but for the past five or six years he has paid all his attention to the farm. By strict economy and hard work, he has placed himself and family in very good circumstances.

MICHAEL RIDDLE, JR., was born in Montgomery township, Richland county, October 28, 1822. At the age of twelve years he became a cripple from a partial dislocation of the head of the femur bone. He continued in a district school until he was sixteen, when he attended the famous Ashland academy, taught by S. McClure, the Fultons, R. Sloan, and the celebrated Lorin Andrews and William Johnson, where he received a good English education, with some knowledge of Latin. Resorting to teaching, he taught in different portions of the county, as a means to assist himself in attending the academy. Wages were low, and public funds did not always reach, householders paying in proportion to the number they sent to school. He was once called upon to take a fall school in the Wilson district, Mifflin township. They had no money and he agreed to take wheat, at a fixed price, delivered at a barn in the vicinity, which he hauled to Milan and sold at a profit. On the fifth day of June,

1841, he was baptized by Elder C. E. Vanvoorhis, in the stream near his birthplace, and one-half mile from his farm. He united with the Church of Christ, on Orange street, in Ashland. Soon his gifts were called into use, and he began to exhort, receiving trip tickets to go with ministers to aid them, this continuing for some years. In 1846-47 he sold six hundred books called "Universalism Against Itself," by A. Hall, in Ashland and Wayne counties. The Universalists have not organized a church in these two counties since. He frequently lectured on that subject. On the first of February, 1849, he was married to Miss Catharine Hatfield, of Chippewa township, Wayne county, Ohio. She was born May 12, 1829. Their son, William Almon, was born in Chesterville, Morrow county, January 16, 1851, and died January 27th; Salina Delucia was born December 8, 1852, in Chesterville, Morrow county; Celestia Jane was born December 24, 1854, in Montgomery township, Ashland county; John Allen was born January 27, 1856, in Montgomery township, Ashland county; Mary Catharine was born in Lafayette, Madison county, January 11, 1860; Martha Marinda was born February 14, 1861, in Montgomery township, Ashland county. Salina D. and John Allen died January 3, 1859, two hours apart; Celestia Jane died January 11, 1859—all with malignant scarlet fever. After his marriage he removed to Chesterville, Morrow county, and engaged in the practice of medicine for three years, and continued public preaching. In October, 1852, he returned to his farm in Montgomery township, and has continued on it ever since, with a single year's exception. Michael Riddle was ordained as an evangelist in 1853 by Elder A. Burns, and others, by the laying on of hands, fasting and prayer, in Ashland. His certificate was written by Elder I. Errett, of Cincinnati. He then gave his whole time to evangelizing. In Union county he gave his time to four congregations for five years, traveling from his home in his buggy, over rough and muddy roads, going as far as one hundred and thirty miles, filling regular appointments. In 1859 he moved to Lafayette, Madison county, dividing his time between three congregations. In 1861 he removed to his farm. He was then engaged by the State Missionary society, and for ten years, constantly traveling, labored for it and the district societies. He has organized nine new congregations, and laid the foundations for as many more, re-organized seven more, and ordained many elders and deacons. In one year he preached four hundred times—had two hundred additions, and one hundred and eight by baptism. He had two thousand additions to the church, preached in all of the counties of the west half, and middle and southeastern parts of Ohio, held meetings in northern Michigan, adding one hundred; preached one year in Hillsdale county, Michigan, and some on the borders of Pennsylvania, West Virginia, and Indiana. He yet continues to preach some, and work on the farm. Thus, for about forty years, he has occupied his time, and he is still able, and ready, for active work.

WILLIAM PATTERSON RIDDLE was married December 10, 1861, to Kate D. Stentz, who was born in Ashland county, October 31, 1843. To them have been born three children, all of whom are living: Orwell, who was born March 25, 1863; Emma, born August 7, 1866; and Norman, born November, 1869.

GEORGE W. RIDDLE was born June 5, 1815, in Fayette county, Pennsylvania. March 31, 1842, he was married to Jane Scott, and to them were born eleven children: John S., who was born December 28, 1842, and died September 25, 1851; Sarah, born April 6, 1845; Cornelius F., born March 15, 1847; Ira A., born January 25, 1849; Jane I., born November 20, 1851, and died July 21, 1861; Anna S., born February 13, 1854; Sophia S., born December 28, 1855; Ella E., born April 11, 1858; Rebecca A., born May 20, 1860; Flora and Dora, twins, born April 27, 1865.

ALBERTUS FREER was born July 8, 1845, in Ashland, Ohio, where he has since resided, with the exception of the time he served as a soldier in the Rebellion. He was in company G, Twenty-third Ohio volunteer infantry, President Hayes' regiment. January 17, 1866, he was married to Ellen C. Plumb, who was born in Montgomery, Michigan, March 10, 1843. They have one child, Jessie W., born November 17, 1867. By occupation he is a farmer.

ELI SLOCUM was born in Ashland county, August 26, 1824, and attended school at Ashland academy until about seventeen years of age. In 1847 he took a trip to Iowa with John Clark, with whom he clerked six months in Iowa City, and then went to Canton, Illinois, and joined the Canton Tea company, and crossed the plains with T. S. Sutherland, William Sheets, John Charles, Jacob Myers, Ambrose Drum, J. D. McCammon, John Andrews, and others, and landed at Placerville, California, August 12, 1850, where two Frenchmen were hung for stealing, and ever since it has been known as Hangtown. He and his partner bought one hundred and sixty acres of land where the capital of the State now stands. The gamblers' and squatters war sprung up November 15, 1850, and he went to mining, which vocation he followed about one year, when he located his land and followed farming and dealing in stock. He remained at that business for about one year, when he went to the Wocolomy river and engaged in the stock and dry goods business until 1852, when he started for Ohio. Prior to that time he took a small schooner and went to the mouth of Columbia river, and took a steamer and went to Portland, where he bought one hundred head of hogs —the first that had been shipped down the coast of California to the Sacramento valley—and also twelve crates of chickens for the same market, probably the first ever brought to the State. He realized upon his hogs a fine profit, and upon his chickens a fair profit. He remembers that the news of their arrival created a great excitement, and many persons desired to purchase. The Indians partook of the curiosity, and called to see the little bantams, and were much amused at hearing them crow, and Captain John laughed heartily at the performance. Mr. Slocum sold his stock and fowls and returned to Ohio, and in the spring of 1853 bought a lot of milch cows and work horses, and returned by the overland route, losing only one head out of four hundred and forty-seven. He arrived in Sacramento September 20, 1853. On his second trip the party consisted of John Charles, Joseph Charles, Martin Gibbs, G. Daulia, John Moody, John Goodwin, Hiland Carter, Alfred King, John Yule, William Springer, L. G. Andrews, John Markley and Jacob Myers. Of this number seven returned. The others got married and settled in the State. There were forty-seven in all, but a great many from other parts of the State and counties. Mr. Slocum has made three trips across the plains. His last was for the purchase of sheep. On passing the plains he overtook Kit Carson at Fort Laramie, with a drove of seven thousand head of Texan sheep, small of frame, and almost destitute of wool. Mr. Carson sold his sheep readily in California at remunerative prices. Slocum got through with his enterprise all safely. Mr. Slocum found that the sheep speculation would not pay, and returned to Ohio, and now resides in a quiet way in Ashland, trading in stock, and dealing in real estate. His health for the past few years has been impaired, and requires attention. April 10, 1855, he was married to Miss Mary A. Hunter. The fruits of this marriage are Frank F. and William A., who reside at home.

GEORGE M. STONE, the subject of this sketch, was born in Jefferson county, this State, September 19, 1840, and when at the age of ten years, his parents removed to this county, where he has since resided. His mother died January 7, 1873; his father is still living. April 2, 1868, our subject was married to Emily Carter, who was born in this county. The subject of this sketch has always been a farmer, and now owns a good productive farm in this township.

FRANK S. JAMISON was born in Maryland August 11, 1844, where he resided until the year 1864, when he removed to this county and located in this township. May 12, 1869, he was married to Elizabeth Sutherland, who was born in this county, November 6, 1848. To them have been born four children, all of whom are living and named respectively, Martha A., who was born August 19, 1869; Lewis S., born October 16, 1871; Agnes L., born December 5, 1874; and Josephine H., born June 21, 1877. Our subject is by trade a harness-maker, and has also been in the mercantile business, but for the last few years he has paid all of his attention to the farm.

TOBIAS S. CRONE was born in Juniata county, Pennsylvania, October 16, 1825, where he resided until the year 1838, when his parents removed to this county, where he has since resided. December 1, 1853, he was married to Eve Molott, who was born in Fulton, Pennsylvania, September 17, 1831. To them have been born eight children, all of whom are living, named: George E., Thomas A., Mary J., Francis C., William M., James L., John L., and Harry T. Mr. Crone is a farmer, and has followed that as his business from boyhood.

REV. JOHN R. TALLANTIRE was born in England, March 15, 1807, where he resided until the age of nineteen years, when he came to this country and followed his calling—that of a minister—in Maryland and Pennsylvania, and also in South Carolina. But, for the past forty years, he has been a resident of Ashland county. In August, 1838, he was married to Eleanor Robison, who was born in Brooke county, West Virginia, July 15, 1812. To them were born seven children, three of whom are now living, as follows: Ann, John R. and Howard. The ones deceased are Ebenezer S.; George, who died in Andersonville prison during the late civil war; Amos J., and Elizabeth M. Our subject has, for the past forty years, paid his attention to his farm. John R., jr., his son, who carries on the farm, was born on the place he now occupies, May 2, 1843, and was married, April 6, 1873, to Emma M. Burdick, who was born in Wisconsin September 22, 1853. The fruits of this union are five children: Eleanor M., Arthur H., who died October 5, 1874, while in Kansas, aged three months and twenty-two days; Edith F., Anna L., and George B.

DANIEL STONE was born in Jefferson county March 13, 1839, where he resided until 1850, when his parents removed to Ashland county. He was married March 7, 1867, to Mary Folk, who was born in Crawford county, this State, February 12, 1843. To them have been born five children, three of whom are living, as follows: Estella A., John A., and Martha E. The ones deceased were: Adella E. and Elza E. The former died at the age of five weeks, and the latter at the age of twenty-three months. Mr. Stone has been a farmer from his boyhood.

FREDERICK SHEPPARD, the subject of this sketch, was born in England, September 5, 1844. He came to this country in the year 1849, and located in Ashland county, where he has since lived. He was married July 3, 1866, to Sarah E. Vanosdall. To them have been born six children, four of whom are living, and named Ida J., Ada and Frederick, twins, and Elsie A. The deceased are: William E. and Hattie B. Our subject is by profession a brick mason and contractor, and has contracted for and built more business houses and private residences in this and adjoining counties than any other contractor in this part of the State. Among some in Ashland that he erected is the First National bank building, S. W. Black's store and residence, the *Times* office, Presbyterian church, public school building, the Ashland college and buildings in connection, and many others.

CAPTAIN HENRY H. EBERHART was born in Blair county, Pennsylvania, January 26, 1838. When two years of age, his parents removed to this State and located in Plain township, Wayne county, where he resided until 1861, when he enrolled himself as a soldier in the late war, first entering the three months' service, in the first call for troops, as a member of company C, Sixteenth Ohio volunteer infantry. He was a member of company I, same regiment, where he served for a period of ten months, when he, through gallantry, received a commission from the governor of the State as first lieutenant, and was transferred to the One Hundred and Twentieth Ohio volunteer infantry, in which he served until they were mustered out of service. The regiment was consolidated with the One Hundred and Fourteenth regiment, which was afterward called the One Hundred and Fourteenth Ohio volunteer infantry until the time of service of that regiment expired, when the remaining members of the One Hundred and Twentieth were consolidated with the Forty-eighth Ohio veteran volunteer battalion, and were mustered out of service as such, and our subject came out of the war with the rank of captain. In all, his service amounted to four years and six months. He participated in all the numerous battles the regiment engaged in, except during twenty-two months when he was a prisoner, as the records show. December 24, 1865, he was married to Mary J. Webster, who was born in this county May 16, 1842. The fruits of this union are three children, two of whom are still living: William Webster, who was born March 19, 1867, and Francis L., born September 23, 1869; the one deceased died in infancy. Since April, 1866, the captain has been a resident of Ashland county, and has followed farming for his vocation, and, by industry and good management, he has made for himself a good home.

CAPTAIN WILLIAM S. MARTIN was born in Warren county, Virginia, May 28, 1837, where he resided until 1866, when he removed to Ashland county, where he has since resided, with the exception of four years he spent in Tennessee. During the late war he was captain of company D, in the Forty-ninth Virginia infantry, where he served during the war. He participated in all the numerous battles his regiment was called upon to engage in. January 1, 1867, he was married to Almena Sweeney, who was born in Montgomery township, which was her home, with the exception of the time spent with her husband in Tennessee. She departed this life November 28, 1877, aged thirty-two years seven months and twenty-one days. By this union were born six children, four of whom are still living, and named respectively, Benjamin Franklin, who was born November 24, 1868; Alice, born February 13, 1870; Charles, born August 27, 1872; and Emma, born August 31, 1874; the ones deceased are Edward, who died at the age of five months, and Arthur who died at the age of three months. Since the death of our subject's wife he has not devoted himself to any one vocation, living more of a retired life.

SAMUEL L. ARNOLD was born in Milton township, Ashland county, Ohio, August 26, 1846. He spent his youth on the farm, and in 1876 commenced to read law with J. D. Jones, of Ashland. Although he was considered by all to be perfectly competent to be admitted to the bar, and was earnestly urged by his friends to do so, he repeatedly declined to make the application. In 1878 he gave up his studies, and associated himself as a partner with G. S. Frantz in the boot and shoe business. In the winter of 1880 he bought out his partner, and is now sole owner of the stock. From 1870 to 1876 he was deputy probate judge, and filled the office with great credit to himself and friends. April 4, 1871, he was married to Amanda M. Bryte, who was born in Montgomery township, April 6, 1848. By this union three children have been born, two of whom are still living, and named, respectively: John E., who was born April 13, 1872, and Emma S., born December 5, 1873. The one who died was named Ross, who departed this life August 2, 1877, aged two months and twenty-three days.

ALFRED O. LONG was born in Green county, Pennsylvania, March 16, 1838, and moved to Orange township, Ashland county, Ohio, in 1844. He was raised on a farm until 1855, when he came to Ashland and apprenticed to the carriage firm of Ames & Leach to learn the carriage trimming trade, at which he worked most of the time in Ashland, until the breaking out of the civil war in 1861, when he enlisted in company G, Twenty-third Ohio volunteer infantry. He served in the regiment in all its marches and battles in the mountains of western Virginia, and was engaged in the battles of Carnifax Ferry, West Virginia, Cotton Mountain, Fayetteville, Rolla Court House, Giles Court House, and Pack's Ferry. In 1862 the regiment was ordered to Washington city to reinforce McClellan's army in its retreat from Richmond in 1862. He was engaged in the battle of Frederick City, Maryland, and again in the battles of South Mountain and Antietam, Maryland. He was wounded in the battle of Antietam, September 17, 1862. He served in the regiment until July 5, 1864, at which time the regiment was mustered out of service at Columbus, Ohio, and he returned to Ashland and went to work again for Ames & Leach at the carriage trimming trade. He was married to Mary E. McCauley August 31, 1869. In 1875 he embarked in the shoe business, buying out E. W. Wallack. He was elected one of the city council in the spring of 1879, and was appointed by President R. B. Hayes as postmaster of Ashland, July 16, 1880. He was a patron of Masonry, joining Ashland lodge No. 151, Free and Accepted Masons, September 2, 1868, and also Ashland chapter, Royal Arch Masons, No. 67, in 1870, and Mansfield Commandery Knights Templar, No. 21, in 1879.

JEFFERSON MONROE MCILVAIN was born in York county, Pennsylvania, March 21, 1826. When about nine years of age his mother removed to this State (his father having died prior to that event), and located in Mansfield, where he resided until the year 1849, when he removed to this county, where he has since resided. He was married March 22, 1848, to Rebecca Robbins, who was born in Wayne county, September 3, 1827. To them have been born eleven children, four of whom have departed this life. The seven who are living are: Harvey, Cynthia, Martha, Sarah, Julia E., Edward and Charles. Mr. McIlvain is by trade a molder, but for the past sixteen years has paid his attention to raising fruit and vegetables, and is a general dealer in ice. The facilities he has for preserving ice cannot be surpassed. His ice-house is sixty by thirty-six feet, and his intentions are to enlarge it this coming season to ninety by thirty-six feet. He has in connection an artificial pond near the ice-house where he can get enough ice to furnish the town. He was the first person in Ashland who established the ice business, his first ice-house being eight feet square, and he has kept increasing the dimensions from year to year until it has reached its present capacity. He intends to make the ice business a specialty in the future. He owns twenty-acres of land, all of which is inside of the incorporated village of Ashland, except three acres.

SAMUEL D. MORR was born in Center county, Pennsylvania, February 15, 1829, where he resided until the year 1833, when his parents removed to this county, where he has since resided. He is the oldest child of Daniel and Eve Morr. Daniel, his father, was born in Pennsylvania in 1801, and died in 1867. His mother, Eve, was born in Pennsylvania in 1807, and died in 1867, aged sixty years, after raising a family of thirteen children. Our subject was married February 6, 1851, to Mary Myers, who was born in the same county he was, December 25, 1831. She was the daughter of Benjamin and Margaret Myers. Her father died in 1851, but her mother is still living, now aged seventy-three years. To them have been born five children, all of whom are living: Melinda, who was born in November, 1852; Mary M., born in 1854; Amanda, born in 1857; A., born in 1859; and Marion E., born in 1865. The two oldest are married. By trade Mr. Morr is a carriage- and wagon-maker, and followed that as his business until his marriage, since which time he has devoted all his attention to farming and stock-raising; but for the past few years, his health being somewhat impaired, he has retired from all manual labor. By hard work and good management, he has made for himself and family a good home.

SAMUEL TAYLOR was born in Ireland in the year 1808. When ten years of age his parents removed to this country and located in Plymouth township, Richland county, Ohio, where he resided until he became fifteen years of age. While there he attended school. He then went to Milan, Erie county, where he learned his trade, that of foundryman, and after his trade was completed he worked as journeyman for a few years, when he made a trip to New Orleans, going the entire distance in a flat-boat, starting from Wellsville, Ohio. The next season he returned to Milan, where he worked at his trade for a period of two or three years, when he went to Maumee. There he remained two years, when he returned to Milan and remained about two years. He then went to Clarksfield, Huron county, where he remained about one year, and then came to Ashland county, which has since been his home. He was married in 1835, to Miss Harriet Wilmarth, who was born near Jamestown, New York, in about 1810 or 1812. She died in 1860. The fruits of this union are six children, five of whom are still living, as follows: Gustavus W., Harriet M., William H., Francis H., and Mary. The one deceased was Samuel, who died at the age of sixteen years. All who are living have been married, with the exception of William H. Mr. Taylor has three grandchildren living, and one deceased. He has always paid his attention to the foundry business, and now owns and carries on a foundry at this place.

JOHN SHEPPARD was born in London, England, October 21, 1819, where he resided until the age of thirty years, when he came to this country, and located in Montgomery township, this county, which has since been his home. October 8, 1843, he was married to Jane Jones, who was also born in England, in Kent county, in 1829. They have had a family of eleven children, seven of whom are living. They are: Frederick, born in England September 5, 1844; Edward, born in England in 1847; Benjamin, born in this county and township about 1853; Richard, born in this township in the fall of 1855; Albert H., born in this township in 1858; William, born in this township in 1864; Charles, born in this township in 1866. The ones deceased are: Charles, who died in England; as also did Jane; John and O. were born in this township, and died here. Mr. Sheppard is a brick manufacturer, and has followed that business since he came to this country. He has furnished brick to build the most of the business blocks and dwellings in this place, Ashland, and the surrounding country. He has, by fair dealing, and by paying strict attention to his business, made for himself and family a good home.

JOSIAH M. CLOSSON was born in Jefferson county, this State, December 20, 1820. When two years and two months of age, his mother removed to this county, his father having died prior to that time. He is the youngest of eight children of John and Jane Closson. The oldest child was Elizabeth, who married Samuel Rolland; Samuel, who married Mary Long; William, who married Mary Hamilton; John A., who married Susan Loper; Isaac, who married Henrietta Updegraff; Julia Ann, who married Thomas Hamilton; and Bezaleel D., who remained single. When his mother first came here, she located in this township in a log school-house, with a clapboard roof, puncheon floor; the loft was split boards, clapboard door six feet long, one window, with two cross sticks and a greased paper for light. The chimney was built of logs and sticks, together with nigger-head stones for jambs and back wall. His mother married in this house (the second time) David Mann, when our subject was about eighteen years old. September 6, 1870, his mother departed this life, aged eighty-six years and seven months. Mr. Closson recalls the many hardships and privations that himself and others had to contend with, that the present, as well as future, generations will never know or experience. June 23, 1878, he was married to Sophia C. Bentz. In the late war he was a member of company B, Sixteenth Ohio volunteer infantry, and re-enlisted in company G, Twenty-third Ohio volunteer infantry, President Hayes' old regiment. From there he was transferred to the Seventh regiment, Veteran Reserve corps, on account of disability, and was finally mustered out of the service the eighth of October, 1864, on account of inability to perform his duty as a soldier. He entered the service April 25, 1861, making him a soldier for a period of over four years. He is now totally blind, which was caused from exposure and disease contracted in the service. He is justly pensioned by the government, and will be during life; but this is a small compensation for his irreparable loss. Mr. Closson is among the old surviving settlers of the county. He, together with his wife, are members of the Methodist Episcopal church, and are comfortably situated, financially. Above all, they both enjoy the respect and esteem of all in the community where they reside.

THOMAS OGDEN was born in Wayne county, Ohio, November 15, 1832, where he resided until the age of eighteen years, when he worked at his trade, as wagonmaker, in different places, finally settling down at Wadsworth, Medina county, Ohio, about the year 1854, where he accepted a position as foreman, which he filled with credit for ten years, for the firm of Beach & Traver. Then he associated himself as a partner of the firm, the firm name being H. J. Traver & Co., and was such until the year 1868. During his connection with the firm, he was superintendent. They had a very extensive trade. In 1868 he sold out and came to Ashland, where he established a carriage and buggy shop, since which time he has carried on that business. Mr. Ogden commenced to work at this business at the age of fourteen years, and is considered very proficient in all its departments. The facilities he has here for making first-class work can not be surpassed in the State. He generally employs about fifteen men the year around. He was a perfect stranger when he first came to this place, and, by paying strict attention to business, turning out first-class work, and dealing honestly with every one, he has built up for himself a large trade.

SAMUEL S. DAVIS was born in Juniata county, Pennsylvania, December 26, 1826, where he resided until the age of nine years, when his parents removed to the present county of Ashland and located in Mifflin township. Our subject resided in that township until the year 1865, when he removed to Ashland, where he has since resided. January 7, 1850, he was married to Catharine Roland, who was born in Lebanon county, Pennsylvania, January 6, 1827. At the age of six years her parents removed to this State and located in Milton township. To them were born eight children, all of whom are living, as follows: Harriet, who was born November 8, 1850, and married Walter S. Gantz; Franklin P., born August 6, 1852; Amanda, born June 25, 1856; Reuben A., born December 4, 1858; Lovina, born July 14, 1861; Sarah, born March 5, 1863; Harvey J., born April 1, 1866; Samuel C., born May 9, 1868. Mr. Davis during his life has paid his attention to farming, until he removed to Ashland in 1865, since which time he has been a jobber and contractor, which business he still follows, but in the near future he intends to quit his present business and engage in the hotel and livery business, for which he is now having one of the finest barns in Ashland built for that purpose, and good facilities for keeping a first-class farmers' hotel. His aim will be to please all.

FREDERICK JONES was born in the county of Kent, England, February 22, 1809, where he resided until the age of forty years, when he came to this country and located in Ashland county, this township, where he has since resided. He was married January 1, 1826, to Miss Eliza Pickett, who was also born in Kent, England, March 9, 1810, where she resided until 1850, when she came to this country to join her husband. To them were born two children, who are still living, and named Jane, who was born in 1827—she married John Shepard in England, but they now reside here; Harriet, who was born in England also, in 1829, and married there, but now resides here. Mr. Jones has sixteen grandchildren and fifteen great-grandchildren. He is a brick and tile manufacturer, which business he has followed since his residence here. He paid some attention to the farm, but for the past few years has turned all of his attention to manufacturing tile, and he is considered proficient at his business and his aim is to please every one with work and low prices.

GEORGE SCHNEIDER was born in Knox township, Holmes county, this State, December 31, 1843, where he resided until he was twenty-three years old. From that place he removed to Loudonville, this county, where he resided three years, when he came to Ashland, where he has since resided. December 4, 1873, he was married to Miss Louisa Kuntner, who was born in the city of New York, December 15, 1856. To them has been born one child, who is still living—Magdalena K.—who was born November 8, 1878. Mr. Schneider spent the early part of his life on the farm with his father, but for the past fifteen years he has been in the confectionery and baker business, which vocation he still follows, and now has a store located at this place.

DR. J. E. ROOP, the subject of this sketch, was born September 25, 1828, in Carroll county, Maryland. The names of his father and mother were Joseph and Susannah Roop, both of whom were of German extraction. There were eleven children as the result of this marriage, nine boys and two girls, as follows: Josiah, David, Ephraim, Isaac, Israel, John, Eli, Jonas E., Mary, Elizabeth, and Joseph N., all of whom lived to maturity save Eli, who died when only two weeks old. Having a large family to provide for, they sold their farm in Maryland, and moved to Ohio in the summer of 1838, locating in the eastern part of Montgomery township, Ashland (then Richland) county, having purchased what was known as the Pratt farm. Here Dr. J. E. Roop was raised, doing general farm work and attending the district school during the winter terms, when he could be spared from the work on the farm, for at that time much of the wheat was threshed by putting it on the barn floor, and then tramping it out by riding horses over it until all the wheat was rubbed out of the heads. Thus his summers and winters were passed until 1848, when he spent one year at the academy at Republic, Seneca county, Ohio, until he was compelled to leave school for want of money. He taught his first school in Adams township, six miles north of Republic. In the spring of 1849 he entered the office of Dr. J. N. Waddell, of Jeromeville, with whom he remained until 1857. He then moved to Lucas county, Ohio, where he engaged in the practice of his profession until the next spring, when he joined Captain Dorland's party for California. The company left Rowsburgh on the eighteenth of March, 1852, and encountered many hardships. They went to the Ohio river and took passage on the steamer John Adams, for St. Louis, Missouri. There ox teams were bought, and the journey commenced in real earnest. After a long and tedious journey he arrived in Shasta City, California, on the ninth of September, lacking nine days of being six months on the march for the golden shores. He located in Shasta City, and engaged in the practice of his profession. He was also deputy postmaster. He remained until June, 1853, when he went to San Francisco. After arriving in that city he fell in company with parties going back to Ohio, whom he joined, and returned home in the month of July. He went with his father to Iowa that fall, and the next spring returned to Ohio and married Margaret Allen, of Lucas county, Ohio, with whom he became acquainted just previous to going to California. They returned to Iowa, where he practiced medicine for seven years, and by the persuasion of his father-in-law he returned to Ohio to live, and graduated from the Physio-medical institute of Cincinnati, Ohio. After a few years he was elected to the chair of botany, chemistry, and chemico-legal analysis in the Physio-medical institute in Cincinnati. After filling this chair for two years he was elected to fill the chair of obstetrics and diseases of women and children in the same college, which chair he filled for eight years, when he was compelled to resign his professorship in said college, on account of the failing health of his son Harrie, and take him to the country, thus compelling him to leave Cincinnati. Knowing Ashland to be a healthy locality, and as his people, the Tunkers, were about to build a college at that place, he decided to move back to his old home. Here he is engaged in the practice of medicine in partnership with Drs. M. E. Dunham and H. P. Nelson. They have a large and growing practice. Dr. Roop had born to him five children, as follows: George Joseph, Edward Allen, Jonas Wilber, Cora Bell, and Harrie Tait. Edward died when six months old, of cholera infantum; Jonas Wilber at two weeks, of general weakness; Cora Bell at ten months, of cholera infantum and difficult dentition; and George Joseph was drowned on the first of June, 1868, aged thirteen years, two months and fifteen days. Dr. Roop's father was one of the early pioneers of the Dunkard church in this county. By his energy ministers of that church were brought to this county. James Tracy was among the first preachers thus brought, and by energy a successful church was established, out of which has grown a large membership.

Dr. Hugh P. Nelson was born November 14, 1849, in Iberia, Morrow county, Ohio. His father, William L. Nelson, was a native of Pennsylvania, who removed to this county while young, and settled near Perrysville. His mother, Nancy, was born and reared on what is known as the old Moore farm, in the southeast part of Montgomery township. The family consisted of eight children—Hugh P., John M., Susan, Julia A., Mary F., Dillmon, Melissa, and William E.; three of whom died while young—John M., Dillmon and Melissa. The subject of this sketch being the oldest, the labors of providing for the wants of the family fell heavily upon him, so that his chances for obtaining a thorough education were almost impossible, as his time was occupied with his farm duties during his youth and early manhood. He attended district school during the winter; but being of a studious turn of mind, he succeeded in this way in obtaining a fair common school education. In the fall of 1868 he entered the academy at Hayesville, remaining a part of the time until 1874. During the summer of that year he attended school at Perrysville. For several years Dr. Nelson figured highly as one of Ashland county's most energetic and successful teachers. In the winter of 1876-77 he commenced the study of medicine, placing himself under the instructions of Professor J. E. Roop, then residing in Cincinnati, Ohio, and remained with him until the fall of 1878, when he attended medical lectures at the Medical Department of Wooster university, Cleveland, Ohio; resuming his studies again in the spring of 1879 under his former preceptor, who had in the meantime removed to Ashland. He attended lectures the following winter at Cincinnati, Ohio, and graduated with second honor from the Physio-medical college, March 2, 1880. Returning home he located in his native town, entering as partner with the well known practitioners, Roop & Dunham. Dr. Nelson is an earnest, hard student, ever searching after the best and most safe means of alleviating the sufferings of his fellow beings.

Neal McCoy Sweringer was born in Juniata county, Pennsylvania, May 13, 1842. When about three years of age, his parents removed to this State and located in Wayne county, where he resided until the year 1871, when he removed to Ashland county, where he has since resided. February 18, 1864, he was married to Rachel C. Thompson, who was born in Chester county, Pennsylvania, November 6, 1838. When at the age of twelve years, her parents removed to this State and located in Tuscarawas county. Ashland county has been her home the most of the time since her residence in the State. By this union seven children have been born, all of whom are living: William T. A., who was born in Wayne county, November 29, 1864; Alvi A. W., born in Wayne county, February 17, 1867; Effie E. E., born in Wayne county, July 24, 1869; George F. E. born in Ashland county, June 15, 1871; Edward T. D., born in Ashland county, June 4, 1873; Robert J. R., born in Ashland county, May 10, 1875; and Samuel N. R., born in Ashland county, July 7, 1877. Our subject was a farmer until ten years ago, since which time he has been running an engine, and is now an engineer by occupation. He, together with his wife, are members of the Christian church.

Dr. Abram L. Sherick was born in Ashland county, Ohio, June 19, 1856. David Sherick, his father, was a native of Pennsylvania, removing to this county while young, and settling near Hayesville. Amanda, his mother, was also born in Pennsylvania, and reared near West Salem, Wayne county, Ohio. The family consisted of ten children: Mary J., Matilda, Catharine, Almira, Amanda, William W., Abram L., Weldaw, Alice, and Lillie; two of whom, Amanda and Lillie, died while young. The subject of this sketch was the seventh child. His chances for obtaining a thorough education were quite good, and during his youth his time was occupied in attending district school during the winter season, and working on his father's farm during the summer months. But his father being desirous of having him attain a thorough education, he moved off the farm in 1873, to Lodi, where he attended school two years, after which he became somewhat tired of school life, removed with his father to the farm, and, after remaining there a short time, again resumed his educational pursuits, attending the academy at Burbank for some considerable length of time, and gradually rising in mental culture, until he became qualified to attend college. He then attended Baldwin university at Berea, for about two years. He being studious, energetic and enthusiastic, turned his attention to the subject of medicine. Dr. Thomas S. Hunter, his preceptor, accepted him as a student in the year 1877, and, after studying under him about nine months, he attended the Toledo School of Medicine one session, when he returned and remained with his preceptor for a short time, after which he continued the study of medicine in New York city, where he attended the Bellevue Hospital Medical college for two years, and was graduated with the class of 1880, with the highest honors. He then returned to his native county town (Ashland), where he formed a partnership with Dr. Hunter, for the practice of medicine, which he began the eighth of April, 1880. The doctor has—in this short period—by industry, and paying strict attention to business, built up for himself a good practice.

ORLANDO MARKLEY was born in this township (Montgomery), September 10, 1844, and has since resided in the county, with the exception of one year he spent in the State of Illinois. November 14, 1867, he was married to Kate C. Michael, who was born in Germany, June 22, 1846. At the age of twelve years her parents removed to this country, and located in this county and township, and this place has since been her home. They had nine children, five of whom died in infancy. The ones who are still living are: Sadie J., who was born October 24, 1869, while her parents were in Illinois; Mary L., born December 29, 1875; George C., born April 17, 1878; and Orlando V., born March 9, 1880. In the late war our subject was a member of company G, Twenty-third Ohio volunteer infantry. In 1863 he entered the service, and was discharged in 1865. By reason of injuries received while performing his duty as a soldier, the government grants him a pension, but this consideration is nothing to good health, as his health has been impaired ever since the war, which has disqualified him from performing any hard labor, and his vocation has been, since that event, that of a gardener. Mr. Markley and wife are both members of the United Brethren church, and are respected by all who know them.

JOHN KELLER, son of John and Mary (Johnson) Keller, from Northampton, now Monroe county, Pennsylvania, who removed to Ashland county, Ohio, then Richland county, in the fall of 1829, was born October 12, 1823, in Northampton county, Pennsylvania. John Keller, sr., was among the pioneer settlers, and did much toward clearing up this section, being a farmer by occupation. He was the sixth in a family of nine children, consisting of four brothers and four sisters, and was married December 2, 1852, to Abby Maria, daughter of Simon Wertman of Ashland county. To them have been born four children, viz: Orlando W., John, George W., and William H., three of whom are living at home; John S. residing east of Ashland some three miles. Mr. Keller is a farmer, owning eighty acres of land. In politics he is a Democrat. Mr. and Mrs. Keller joined the Lutheran church of Ashland in 1859, and their sympathies are still with that body. Mr. Keller is now, and for some time past has been, quite indisposed from attendance upon the sick and hard labor, though he still manages his farm.

BENJAMIN EMMENS, son of Benjamin and Anna Adams Emmens, was born December 25, 1820. His parents removed from Jefferson county to Wooster in the year 1812, to Rowsburgh in 1814, and to Montgomery township, Ashland county, Ohio, in 1818. He is a twin brother (in a family of eight children), of Isaac Emmens, and was married February 14, 1860, to Sarah Matilda, daughter or Samuel Wertman. To them were born six children, viz: Orra, Cora, Tully, Mattie, Simon and Ralph, all of whom are living. Mr. Emmens has made a life business of farming, and has forty acres of fine land. He is a Republican in politics. Mrs. Emmens is a member of the Methodist Episcopal church of Ashland. Mr. Emmens is a member of the grange of Ashland, and is a well preserved man of sixty years.

SAMUEL ROWLAND, son of Joseph and Christina (Lane) Rowland was born in Maryland, near Hagerstown, March 29, 1802. Some few years subsequently he, with his family, comprising some seven children, removed to Pennsylvania, and in the year 1818 removed to Ohio, landing in Orange township, July 12th of that year, coming with wagons, a distance of two hundred miles, all of the way. He first settled on the Burgess farm, which was then a wilderness. Here they began the life of pioneer farmers, clearing the first lands and cutting the first timber, built a rough log house with puncheon floor, clapboard roof, and wooden chimney. Here he remained some two years when he removed to Montgomery township, on what is now known as the Roseberry farm. Joseph, the father of our subject, died at Wyandot, at the age of ninety-five years. The mother died previously, aged sixty years. Our subject was married in 1825, to Elizabeth, daughter of John Closson. To them were born seven children, viz.: Mary Jane, Joseph, deceased; Reznor, deceased; Washington, and Christina, and others who died in infancy. Mr. Rowland settled about three and one-half miles east of Ashland, entering the farm of eighty acres as school lands which was in the woods, building the first house and doing other work incident to pioneer farming. Here he reared his family, and improved his farm to a high state of cultivation. Mrs. Rowland died in the year 1856. Two years thereafter Mr. Rowland married Rebecca Isman, by whom he has one child, and moved immediately to the place where he now resides. Mr. Rowland is a member of the church of Disciples, and Mrs. Rowland is a member of the Presbyterian church, both of Ashland. In politics Mr. Rowland is a Democrat, being a staunch member of that party. He cast his first presidential vote for Jackson, in 1824. Mr. Rowland is a well preserved man of seventy-eight years, the family being noted for their longevity.

ANDREW PROUDFIT was born in York county, Pennsylvania, May 26, 1809, and was the eighth in the family of ten children of Andrew and Mary Marshall Proudfit, who were natives of that State. The ancestry on the father's side dated back to Ireland; that of the mother to Scotland. The father of Andrew Proudfit, with his family, removed to Fairfield county, Ohio, in 1810 or 1811, where they remained some six or seven years, and then sought a home in Ashland county, where they entered three hundred and twenty acres of land in an almost unbroken wilderness, for which they paid two and one-half dollars per acre. They remained until the date of their death. Andrew, sr., died at the age of seventy-one, and his wife at sixty-six years of age. Our subject was married May 14, 1835, to Phebe Artman, by whom he had three children: John, Mary and Augusta, John being the only survivor. Mrs. Proudfit died January 29, 1865. He married for his second wife Rebecca Dininger, daughter of John Decker. He has made a life business of farming, and now owns two hundred and forty acres of very fertile land. In politics he is a Democrat; and has served his township as trustee some three or four terms, and in other positions, although not an office-seeker. He is of large physique, weighing some two hundred and eighty pounds, and is well preserved.

H. I. STEPHENS was born in Morrow county, Ohio, October 19, 1852, but for the past eleven years his home has been in Ashland, Ohio. By profession he is a tinner, and now carries on a store at this place, and is considered to be very proficient at his business. January 20, 1876, he was married to Clara Campbell. To them have been born two children, one of whom died in infancy; the other, Thad. C. S., died at the age of five months.

PHILIP R. ROSEBERRY was born near Bloomsburgh, Columbia county, Pennsylvania, Mary 19, 1821, and was the youngest in the family of ten children of William Roseberry and Sophia Reese, who were natives of New Jersey, and removed to Pennsylvania about 1808, and thence with their family to Ashland county, in the spring of 1837, where they remained until the dates of their death. William Roseberry died May 4, 1854; his wife died January 16, 1863. Both were members of the Methodist Episcopal church some fifty years. Our subject was married August 10, 1847, to Elizabeth, daughter of Nicholas and Catharine Jones, of this county. The result of this union was two children, viz.: Catharine S., and Sophronia E., the former the wife of Dr. James Frauenfelter, and the latter residing at home with her parents. Mr. Roseberry joined the North Ohio conference in 1845, but became indisposed and returned to his home, where he followed farming some two years, when he became recruited and again resumed the ministry, his fields of labor being principally in Ashland county, in the Methodist Episcopal church. He also manages his farm, it being the old homestead of his parents. The farm is highly improved, and composed of fine fertile lands, comprising one hundred and five and one-half acres. In politics he is a Republican.

MICHAEL MOWRY, son of Michael Mowry and Nancy Rough, was born October 15, 1836, in Wayne county, Ohio, and was the fifth child in a family of eleven children, consisting of five brothers and six sisters. November 23, 1863, he was married to Mary Steward, daughter of Samuel and Polly Steward, of Wood county, Ohio. By this union was born four children: Harvey A., Willard L., Cora A., and Jessie L. Our subject has a farm of one hundred and twenty-eight acres, finely improved, and with fine buildings; he has made a life business of farming and dealing in stock. In the fall of 1872 he removed from Wayne county to Ashland county. In politics he is a Republican. Both he and his wife are members of the Lutheran church, of Ashland, Ohio.

EMANUEL SWINEFORD, son of Jacob and Sophia Clays Swineford, was born September 16, 1814, in Union county, Pennsylvania. He was the fourth child in a family of eight, consisting of four brothers and three sisters. In the month of May, 1838, Mr. Swineford was married to Margaret, daughter of Thomas Hamilton, born in 1818, in the same county, and in August of the same year removed to Ashland, Ashland county, Ohio, and entered into a partnership with John Cairns in the distilling business, where he remained some six months, when he engaged in the same business as an employe of Michael Smith, remaining two and one-half years. He then purchased an oil and sawing mill near the present homestead, and remained in this business some thirteen years, and subsequently purchased one hundred and sixty acres with William Sheets, finally purchasing the whole tract, Mr. Sheets selling to his father. Mr. Swineford is now owner of a finely improved farm of two hundred and forty acres. Mr. and Mrs. Swineford came from their home in Pennsylvania with a team and wagon, being fourteen days on the road; took their dinners each day, except one, on the commons, and the last one was taken on their present farm at the close of their journey. Their nights were spent at the taverns along the route. To Mr. and Mrs. Swineford were born seven children, three of whom are living, viz: William H., Curtis and Henry. Those deceased are: Peter, Mary, Elizabeth, Catharine, Sophia, and Thomas Emerson. A grandchild, Harriet Elizabeth, now fills the place of those who have attained the years of manhood. Mr. and Mrs. Swineford have nine grandchildren. In politics he is a Republican, casting his first vote as a Whig, but upon the formation of the Republican party became a staunch and earnest supporter of its principles. Mr. and Mrs. Swineford and their family are all members of the Lutheran church of Ashland, Mr. Swineford having been elder for many years. It should be said of Mr. Swineford that as time advanced his thoughts of committing an error gradually forced itself upon his mind until he concluded to go out of the distilling business, and has ever since followed other avocations, which have proved profitable, and with a clear conscience. Mr. and Mrs. Swineford are both well preserved, have a home beautifully located, and seem to enjoy to the fullest extent that which has been their fortune to acquire through industry, and a close adherence to the principles of right. Mrs. Swineford is the youngest of a family of nine, and the only surviving member, including parents.

DANIEL CARTER was born in Baltimore county, Maryland, December 25, 1776, and was of English extraction, his father having come with Lord Baltimore's colony and settled in Maryland, he being the youngest of a family of three, viz: John, William and Daniel. Daniel was married February 14, 1797, to Ann Snyder, by whom he had eight children, viz: John, William, Daniel, Rachel, Elizabeth, James, George, and Anna. Mrs. Daniel Carter died September 25, 1813, and he married for his second wife Ruth Warner, March 9, 1814. To them were born seven children, viz: David, our subject, Sarah, Mary, Miranda, Samuel, Milton and Charles. Daniel died February 25, 1854; Ruth died June 18, 1862.

DAVID CARTER was born March 18, 1815, in the township of Montgomery, Ashland county, Ohio, within five rods of his present residence, in a rude log cabin erected by his father, the latter being a pioneer and the first settler, and living in camp during the first summer. Our subject was the first child born in Montgomery township. His youthful days were spent at school in the winter and assisting his father on the farm during the summer. He was married to Elizabeth Griffith, daughter of Benjamin Griffith, of Chester county, Pennsylvania, December 26, 1837. By this union was born three children, all of whom died in infancy. Mr. and Mrs. Carter are both members of the Methodist Episcopal church of Ashland. In politics Mr. Carter is a Democrat, having been a strong supporter of the principles of that party, though formerly he was an old-line Whig. Mr. Carter was commissioned by Thomas Corwin, in 1841, as first lieutenant of the Ashland guards, which commission he held some ten years, and was subsequently quartermaster sergeant, and latterly an aid-de-camp to General Meredith. Mr. Carter is a man of military bearing, and is a well preserved man of sixty-five years. Although over age, Mr. Carter enlisted in the war of the Rebellion October 28, 1861, for three years; was mustered in; joined the Sixty-fourth Ohio volunteers; went to Bardstown, Kentucky, where he was taken sick; returned home in April, 1862, with orders to remain and await his discharge, which he has never as yet received.

ISAAC PLANK, son of John Plank and Anna Zook, was born September 17, 1813, in Lancaster county, Pennsylvania, and remained at home until twenty-seven years of age, occupied at farming. February 6, 1840, he was married to Lydia, daughter of Evan Lewis, of Chester county, Pennsylvania, and to them were born four children: Lewis, Morris Dickenson, Hannah Ann, and Lydia Frances. Lewis died in infancy. In the spring of 1853, Mr. Plank removed to Montgomery township, Ashland county, on the farm now owned by Widow Whitwer. After residing there one year, he removed to Perry township, Ashland county, where he remained eleven years, then returned to Montgomery township, where he has followed agricultural pursuits until the present time. Both himself and wife have for years been members of the Baptist church of Ashland. In politics he was an old-line Whig until the formation of the Republican party, when he became an earnest supporter of its principles. Mr. Plank is the owner of some ninety-one acres of land in Montgomery and Orange townships. His father died in Pennsylvania at the age of seventy-four; his mother came to Ohio in 1849, where she remained, and died at the advanced age of eighty-three. Morris D. married Elizabeth Boots, and resides in Orange township. Hannah A. married Lorin Boots, and lives in Montgomery township.

JOHN SHIDLER, son of Peter and Catharine (Horn) Shidler, was born December 5, 1820, in Washington county, Pennsylvania, and was the third child and third son in a family of ten, consisting of four brothers and six sisters, of whom three sisters are deceased, and one brother, Morgan, died in August, 1878. John Shidler first came to Ohio with his father, in 1839, to look at some land previously entered by the father; then returned home. In 1842 he settled in Orange township, upon one hundred and sixty acres of land, which in 1845 was divided between him and his brother, George. October 13, 1844, he was married to Sarah Ann, daughter of John Myers, from Maryland, and to them were born four children: Hannah Ellen, Demas, Mary Isabelle (died in infancy), and John. In politics he is a Democrat, though of the hard currency kind. Both himself and wife are members of the German Baptist church, of Ashland. Mr. Shidler has a finely improved farm in Montgomery, Clearcreek and Orange townships, comprising three hundred and ninety acres, his residence being in Montgomery township. He has done much towards clearing up Ashland county, and making it what it is to-day. He believes in doing everything well, and in speaking his honest convictions. He contributed one thousand dollars, being the first subscription, toward the building of the Ashland college; also two hundred dollars for the building of the Atlantic and Great Western, now the New York, Pennsylvania and Ohio railroad, and, in fact, has been one of the foremost in all enterprises tending to promote the interests of Ashland county.

SIMON BRINDLE was born in Franklin county, Pennsylvania, July 6, 1808, and was the eldest child in the family of eight children of George and Elizabeth (Menich) Brindle, who were natives of Pennsylvania. Simon Brindle was married June 8, 1837, to Jane, daughter of William McKesson, and to them have been born seven children: William, John, Samuel, Martha, George, James, and Mary. William, Samuel and John are deceased, the latter being killed at Port Gibson during the war of the Rebellion. Mr. and Mrs. Brindle removed from their native State with their family in 1847, and settled in Wayne county, Ohio, where they remained one year, when they removed to their present homestead, purchasing sixty-two acres; he now owns eighty-seven acres. Both himself and wife are members of the Lutheran church, of Ashland, with which denomination they have been connected some fifteen years. In politics he is a born Democrat, casting his first vote for General Jackson. Mrs. Brindle's father was a soldier in the war of 1812. The children of Mr. and Mrs. Brindle are all married and reside in Ohio.

ISAAC ROSEBERRY, brother of P. R. Roseberry and son of William Roseberry, whose history appears with P. R. Roseberry's sketch, was born February 27, 1813, in Hemlock township, Columbia county, Pennsylvania. Here he remained with his parents until twenty-two years of age, when he removed to Medina county, Ohio, where he remained some two years. He then removed to Ashland county, Montgomery township, where he rented a farm some fourteen years, and then purchased one hundred and twenty acres where he now resides, it being the old homestead. He was married February 21, 1839, to Elizabeth Wolf, daughter of John Wolf, of Montgomery township. To them were born nine children, as follows: Elijah, Emanuel W., Mary Sophia, Sarah Catharine, Elizabeth Jane, Isaac, John Philip, Irene Isabella, and Christina Margaret, of whom all are living but Elijah and Isaac. Sarah C. married James Powell; Emanuel married Sarah Ellen Kahl; Elizabeth married George P. Biggs; Irene I. married James M. Sadler. Mr. Roseberry was formerly an old-line Whig, and is now a Republican.

STEPHEN WOLF was born in Butler township, Columbiana county, Ohio, June 19, 1814. He was the eighth in a family of ten children, of Jacob and Mary M. Mason Wolf. The father was a native of Maryland, and for many years was a resident of Virginia. He was of German descent. He, with his family, removed to eastern Ohio about the year 1807, and to Ashland county in the spring of 1832, where he died in December, 1856; the mother died in June, 1858. Our subject remained with his parents, following farming until he was thirty-three years of age, when he was married to Elizabeth Heifner, daughter of Frederick Heifner, from Pennsylvania. By this union were born seven children, four of whom are living, namely: Mary, Jane, Rebecca, and Lewis M. Those deceased are, George S. and infant twins. After his marriage our subject built a house on the farm where he still remains, which is the old homestead. Both Mr. and Mrs. Wolf are members of the Baptist church of Ashland. In politics Mr. Wolf is a Conservative, having formerly been a Democrat; but in Vallandigham's day cast a Republican vote and has since voted for whom he considered the best man. In 1847 Mr. Wolf was appointed deputy sheriff of Ashland county, and soon after was elected justice of the peace for one term. He served as deputy sheriff in Richland county under David Bright.

JOHN MCNAUL, a native of Ireland, emigrated from that country to America and settled in Pennsylvania sometime prior to the war of 1812, and subsequently, about the year 1815, removed to Ashland county, Ohio, and settled upon one hundred and sixty acres of land, the same being the homestead farm, now owned by his sons James and Michael. Here he erected a log cabin and proceeded to clear, cultivate and improve the land. He was married to Rosa Donner a short time before entering the lands. To them were born six children, viz: William, Sarah, James, Michael, John, and Mary, five of whom are living. John died some twenty years ago; Mary married Mr. McFadden and now resides in Missouri; the others reside in the vicinity of the old homestead. Mr. McNaul died some fourteen years since at the age of eighty-six years; Mrs. McNaul is living with her daughter Sarah, wife of Patrick Kelley. James McNaul was born August 10, 1820, in Montgomery township, Ashland county, and has made farming a life business. He was married to Margaret Crowner, October 12, 1847. To them have been born eight children, as follows: John, William, Michael, Agnes, James, Alfred, Rosa, Thomas Shannon, and Elmer, all of whom are living. In politics he is a Democrat, and is a staunch supporter of the principles of his party, and has never missed being present to cast his vote at election. Both Mr. and Mrs. McNaul are members of the Methodist Episcopal church. He served as infirmary director some twelve years since. The land he owns, comprising eighty acres, is part of the old homestead. Mr. McNaul is a man of fine physique, weighing over two hundred pounds, and is well preserved for one who has done so much toward clearing up and improving his section of country.

JAMES GIBSON was born in York county, Pennsylvania, October 26, 1807. He was the youngest child of James and Elizabeth (Mull) Gibson. The mother was of English-German descent, and the father was a native of Philadelphia, Pennsylvania. They removed to Ashland county in the spring of 1835, coming all the way with wagons, and settled on the farm now owned by the subject of this sketch. The father died in 1851 or 1852, aged eighty-five years; the mother died in 1853, aged eighty-six years. James, jr., was married to Margaret, daughter of Henry Spafford, in January, 1853. To them have born four children, three of whom are still living, viz.: John, Laura, and Catharine, who reside at home. Elizabeth died in 1865, aged six years. Mr. Gibson has followed the vocation of farming and has a finely improved farm of one hundred and eighty-eight acres, with fine buildings. In politics he is a Democrat; has been supervisor twice, and school director twice. He is a well-preserved man of seventy-three years.

JACOB LINN, son of Adis and Elizabeth (Rowland) Linn, was born in Bedford county, Pennsylvania, March 13, 1820, and when fifteen years of age removed with his father's family to Stark county, Ohio, settling there in the spring of 1835, and, in the fall of the same year removed to Ashland county, and purchased one hundred and sixty acres of land where Jacob Linn now resides, and where he and his wife spent the remainder of their days. Adis died in 1844, and his wife survived him about twenty-one years. The subject of our sketch was married in November, 1847, to Anna McGuire, daughter of Hugh and Mary McGuire, of Ashland county. To them have been born seven children, six of whom are living: Lorin H., Melissa J., Cornelius R., Hannibal, Lincoln, Alice, and Nettie May. In politics he is a Republican, having been formerly an old-line Whig. Mr. and Mrs. Linn are both members of the Methodist Episcopal church, with which body they have been connected about fifteen years. Mr. Linn is the owner of the original tract settled by his father, and also eighty-four acres additional. He has a very productive farm, and fine buildings, and is now erecting a fine barn near his residence.

JOHN L. THOMAS, son of Leonard Thomas, from Frederick county, Maryland, and Ellen Hough, from Westmoreland county, Pennsylvania, was born August 16, 1833, in Montgomery township, Ashland county, Ohio, on the homestead where he now resides. The father's family consisted of five children, three of whom are living: John L., Henrietta, and Eliza Jane. Mr. Thomas and his sisters inherited the property of their father, consisting of one hundred and twenty acres, located in the southeast portion of Montgomery township. In politics he is a Democrat, being an earnest supporter of the principles of that party. Mr. Thomas has never married. His sisters remain with him at the old homestead and attend to the duties of the household.

REV. WILLIAM SADLER was born in Fayette county, Pennsylvania, January 16, 1829. His parents' names were Joseph and Elizabeth. He moved with them to Wood county, Virginia, and from there back to Greene county, Pennsylvania. At the age of twelve years he had attended school three months. Near that time his mother died, and he found a home with Jonathan Miller, where he resided until after the age of twenty-one years. In the fall of 1849 he attached himself to the German Baptists or Brethren (commonly known as Dunkard Baptists), with whom he has been ever firm. Miller, on his death bed, requested him to take care of his stock until sold. He attended school nine months at Greene academy, Pennsylvania, and taught school sixteen months in the district in which he formerly lived. In the spring of 1854 he emigrated to Licking county, Ohio, and engaged in teaching, obtaining his first certificate in two hours after entering the examination room. In all he taught forty-four months. In the fall of 1856 he was united in marriage bonds with Miss Emeline Wolf, of Liberty township, Licking county, Ohio. The names of her parents were Joshua and Susannah. He was called to the ministry in 1859, and in 1865 moved with his family of two children to Ashland county, where he now resides, having a family of four children—two sons and two daughters, three of whom are members of the church. His youngest son is only four years old. He was one of the charterers of the Ashland college, and is now one of the trustees. The congregation in which he resides numbers nearly one hundred members.

DANIEL WERTMAN was born in Columbia county, Pennsylvania, November 2, 1824, and was the oldest child in a family of eight children, of Simon Wertman and Abigail Rohn, both natives of Pennsylvania. Mr. Wertman removed with his father's family to Ashland county, then Richland, in 1837, where Simon and his father, John Wertman, purchased one hundred and sixty acres of land in the south portion of Orange township, the property now owned by Mrs. Mary Kendig, an aunt of our subject. Mr. Wertman remained with his father until his death, which occurred in 1844, about which time our subject commenced to learn the trade of saddler with W. W. Ilger, of Ashland, where he remained three years. He then returned to the farm and took charge, he being the oldest child. In 1858, March 9th, Mr. Wertman was married to Mary, daughter of John Keller, of Montgomery township. To them have been born six children, all of whom are living, viz.: Perry S., Ida S., Hattie L., Augusta A., Sarah N., and Jennie B. Mr. Wertman owns one of the finest farms of Ashland county, comprising two hundred and fifteen acres, and located one mile north of Ashland, on the Troy road. It has fine buildings and all the conveniences of a nice home. In politics he is a Democrat. Mr. and Mrs. Wertman are both members of the Lutheran church of Ashland. Mr. Wertman has from time to time occupied positions of trust within the gift of the people, and has proved an able and efficient officer, and worthy of the trust imposed in him.

JACOB RUMBAUGH is the tenth child of Adam and Elizabeth Rumbaugh, and was born October 22, 1835, in Chester township, Wayne county. He was first married June 9, 1859, to Mary A. Mowrey. By this union were born three children, all of whom are living, as follows: Sarah Ann, born November 10, 1860, and who was married September 19, 1877, to L. A. Ash, who carries on our subject's farm in Wayne county; Priscilla E., born October 14, 1864, and Ira G., born August 4, 1871. Mr. Rumbaugh's first wife died October 28, 1875, aged thirty-six years, ten months and two days. August 12, 1878, he married his present wife, Mrs. Jennetta A. Latta. She was born in this county November 16, 1841. She is a granddaughter of Mrs. Wise, of Perry township, of whom mention is made elsewhere in this work. Our subject owns a very fine and valuable farm in Chester township, Wayne county, the old homestead where he was born, and where he lived for a period of forty-three years. In 1878 he removed to this county and located in this (Montgomery) township in 1878. Aside from his farm in Wayne county, he owns very valuable lands in Brown county, Kansas, in the county-seat, Hiawatha. He also owns ten acres of land near the depot at Ashland. His great grandfather served in the Revolutionary war. In 1819 his grandson, Adam, our subject's father, removed to Chester township, Wayne county, Ohio, settling on the farm now owned by Jacob Rumbaugh. He removed from Westmoreland county, Pennsylvania, making the journey in a wagon drawn by three horses, bringing his family, consisting of his wife Elizabeth, his two children, Isaac and John, and their household goods and farming implements. This was in March, and our subject has often heard his mother recall the many hardships they had to contend with on the route. The snow, at times, was from ten to fourteen inches deep. As they brought with them two cows, his mother had to wade through the snow to drive them, and to save their team from giving out.

GEORGE SAAL was born in Germany, and came to the United States in 1859, first settling in Wayne county, from whence he removed to Ashland in 1866. His parents, Peter and Eva Wise Saal, were natives of Hesse Darmstadt, where they were married about 1829, and raised a family of nine children, as follows: Mary, Peter, Henry, John, Jacob, George, and Leonard, besides two who died. Of these five are in this country. In 1869, George Saal went to Wooster and there married Louisa Young, returning to Ashland the following year. Her parents were also natives of Germany. They have two children—Mary Eliza, born in 1871, and Henry born in 1874.

FRANK KNOTH was born in 1834, his parents being Nicholas and Barbara Knoth, who were natives of Bavaria. They had three children—Charles, who died in 1872; Frank; and Henry, who is in business in Ashland. Frank Knoth was married April 22, 1857, to Kittie Snyder, a native of Hesse Cassel, Germany, who was born September 20, 1836. They have had eight children—Mary, born October 14, 1858; Katie L., born October 28, 1860; Cordelia M., born January 28, 1863; Hattie, born April 7, 1866; Frankie, born May 14, 1868; Willie, born September 22, 1872; Amelia, born August 4, 1870, died in 1873; another child, a son, died in infancy. The Knoth family came to America, and settled in Ashland county, in October, 1852, where our subject learned the tinner's trade, and has since been engaged in the stove and tinware business for himself, most of the time. He is now associated with Henry J. Pille. Mr. Knoth enlisted in February, 1865, and served in the Twenty-third regiment band until the close of the war. His brother Charles came to the United States soon after the rebellion of 1848 in Germany, and located in Ashland, which was the cause of the remainder of the family coming to the same place. He is still living in Ashland.

A. J. BURNS was born March 28, 1840. His parents were Hugh and Athaliah Rutan Burns, who were married in March, 1836, and raised a family of six children, as follows: A. J., Mary M., Barna, George W., Hugh R., and Sadie M. Hugh Burns, sr., was the first auditor of Ashland county, in 1846. The grandparents of A. J. Burns were natives of county Donegal, Ireland, whence they came to this country in early life, and were married in Little York, Pennsylvania. They had a family of six children, five of whom lived to maturity. A. J. Burns was the first man to enlist in Garfield's regiment (the Forty-second Ohio volunteer infantry). He enlisted in company H, November 15, 1861, and served with his regiment until he was mustered out in the spring of 1866, with the rank of first lieutenant. At the siege of Vicksburgh, in 1863, he was wounded by a minnie ball, which passed through his right lung, but, as soon as his wound was healed, he returned to his regiment. In the fall of 1866 he went to Missouri, where he remained something more than four years, when he returned to Ashland, and was married to Emily Luther, by whom he has one child, a son, Charles L., born in 1871.

E. J. GROSSCUP was born in Milton township, Ashland county, June 17, 1842. His parents were Daniel and Fiana Grosscup, who were natives of Westmoreland and Lancaster counties, respectively. They raised a family of four children—E. J., Daniel, Fiana, and Mary A. The early life of E. J. Grosscup was spent at trading and farming until 1863–64, when he was engaged in the mercantile business, at Mansfield, Ohio. December 24, 1863, he was married to Emma Pifer, and in the spring of 1865, removed back to Milton township, near the western line, where he engaged in farming. Early in 1866 he again removed to a farm two and a half miles west of Ashland, where he remained until March, 1878. In 1868 he was elected township treasurer, which office he held until 1878. In April, 1875, he was appointed by Judge D. W. Whittmore school examiner for the county, which office he held for three years, and was re-appointed in 1878. From the time of his appointment he has acted as secretary of the examining board. In June, 1878, he was nominated by the Democratic party as a candidate for the office of county auditor, to which he was elected in the fall of the same year. His children are: Mary G., born August 21, 1869, and Ella M., born September 6, 1873.

HERMAN M. RIESER was born June 4, 1842, in Buchau, Wurtemberg, Germany. He was apprenticed to a large dry goods house of his native city, for the term of two years, his father paying one hundred florins for the privilege. He was obliged to study so as to be able to correspond in English, French, and German, and little later took up Latin and Hebrew, besides drawing and other studies. At the close of his indenture he had to pass a tedious examination in all the branches of book-keeping, foreign and home correspondence, etc., which lasted from morning until evening, when he received his diploma as a merchant, with the privilege of conducting business in his own name. When sixteen years of age he was established in a successful wholesale business at which he continued for six years. At twenty years of age he paid eight hundred florins for a substitute in the militia, but owing to the unsettled condition of the country and the possibility of being called into the service at any time, he responded to the earnest solicitation of his brother Samuel, and came to the United States and engaged with him in the dry goods business at Oil City, Pennsylvania. They continued in business several years, and established a branch store at Pontiac, Michigan, soon after which they sold their Oil City business, and subsequently their Pontiac business. He was married in Franklin, Pennsylvania, November 11, 1867, to Miss Mathilde Weil, of Gorlinger, Grand Duchy of Baden. Soon after his marriage he came to Ashland and engaged in the millinery business, at which he has since continued. His father, Marx Rieser, died at

Franklin, Pennsylvania, March 20, 1871, nearly seventy years of age. His mother is still living with him and is nearly seventy-six years of age. Mr. Rieser has a family of six children: Albert, Jennie, Mollie, Isabella, Max, and Deborah.

CLARENCE S. MARTIN was born in Montgomery township, December 26, 1854. He was married September 26, 1876, to Elizabeth S. Myers, who was born in Cumberland county, Pennsylvania, June 8, 1862. By this union have been born two children—Ada E., who was born September 26, 1877, and John A., who was born September 5, 1879. Mr. Martin is a farmer by occupation, and has followed that from boyhood. By good management he has made for himself and family a comfortable home.

WILLIAM W. GIBSON was born in Harrison county, Ohio, March 17, 1826, where he resided until the age of fifteen years, when he with his mother removed to this county, his father having died prior to that time. Mr. Gibson is now living with his fourth wife. He has buried three wives and seven children. His present wife's maiden name was Hannah C. Maxwell, who was born in Wayne county, Ohio, May 17, 1837, but this county has been her home from infancy. She was married to Mr. Gibson May 23, 1877. Our subject is by trade a blacksmith, and has followed that as his vocation from boyhood until the past few years, since which he has paid his attention to his farm, and intends to make that his future business. By good management he has made for himself a comfortable home.

RUGGLES TOWNSHIP.

THADDEUS ANDREWS was born in Ellington, Connecticut, in 1778, and married Lydia Russell, of the same place. In 1808 he came to Ohio, and settled in Rootstown, Portage county, where he died, in 1845; his wife died in 1843. He was engaged in farming all his life; was a member of the Presbyterian church, and was deacon in the church for over forty years. In politics he was an old-line Whig. He was the father of nine children, five of whom are still living, viz: Thaddeus R., who married Axie Richardson, and lives in Portage county, Ohio; Lydia, wife of Harvey Shutliff, of Portage county; Romanta N., wife of Emby Norton, of Portage county; Roxey M., wife of Cyrus Norton, and afterwards wife of Cyrus Austin; and Orsamus L., who married Elvira Bassett.

ORSAMUS L. ANDREWS was born in Portage county, Ohio, in 1815, and received a common school education in Portage county; went to school at Randolph academy in Ravenna, and at Farmington, Trumbull county, Ohio, and then returned to Portage county and began the study of medicine with Dr. Bassett, where he remained three years, and during that time attended lectures at Willoughby, Ohio. In 1837 he married Elvira Bassett, and, in 1838, began the practice of medicine. In 1842 he moved to New Washington, Crawford county, Ohio, where he opened an office and remained six months, when he moved to Greenwich, where he went into partnership with Dr. Norton, and remained one year. In 1843 he removed to Ruggles and entered into partnership with Dr. Paddock, where he remained two years, when he sold to Dr. Paddock, and moved to New London, where he practiced medicine twelve years. While there he was elected justice of the peace for two terms, served as township clerk seven years, and township assessor three years. In 1856 he returned to Ruggles, where he engaged in the practice of medicine until 1868, when he gave it up and turned his attention to farming, in which business he is still engaged. He has been elected justice of the peace of Ruggles township for one term, has served as township clerk several years, and as township trustee one term; was appointed postmaster during President Pierce's administration, and held the office during nearly all of President Buchanan's administration; is a member of the Congregational church, and in politics he is a Republican. He is the father of ten children, six of whom are living, viz.: Lydia, wife of Robert Vanwranken, of New London; Orsamus L., who married Marion Beach, and lives in Ruggles; Lucy E., who married Wakeman E. Beach, of Ruggles; Bassett; George W., who married Lilly Vangorder, and lives in Illinois; and Emma, wife of John Weddell, of Ashland county.

Additional Biographies and Other Historical Facts.

JUDGE JOHN D. JONES.

Judge Jones was born in Shippensburgh, Cumberland county, State of Pennsylvania, June 25, 1815. He learned the trade of a tailor in Chambersburgh, Franklin county, and, after working at his trade in different towns of his native State for some years, came to Ohio in April, 1838, and stopped at Wooster, Wayne county, six months, and then located in Jeromeville, now in Ashland county, and carried on his trade, in which, being a good workman, he was always successful. In 1842 he married Louisa, daughter of Henry Andress, who was born in Maryland, and came to Ohio about the year 1830, and died about seven years since. Mr. Andress prided himself as a teamster, having a very-fine six-horse team with bells, and the best styled wagon; he was constantly engaged in hauling the produce of the west to Pittsburgh, Philadelphia, and Baltimore, and returning loaded with merchandise. He possessed all the pride of the old-time teamsters, among whom he was regarded as a hero; he was a man of excellent character, benevolent, upright and exemplary. His widow, Mary Andress, survived him about five years. Mr. Jones was appointed deputy sheriff under Isaac Gates, and removed to Ashland in 1849, carrying on a merchant tailor and clothing business until 1852, when he was elected sheriff, and served two terms. In 1857 he was elected probate judge, and served two terms. In 1860 he was elected justice of the peace, and has since been three times re-elected. In 1857 he became a member of the Methodist Episcopal church, being one of its official members, but that which he seems most to delight in is his connection with the Sabbath-school, of which he has been a teacher ever since he united with the church. For more than twenty years he has been an attorney at law, and has made probate business and collecting a specialty. He and his family reside at Ashland, having had five children, two of whom—Sumner Pixley and Mary S. M. Landis—have died. Those still living are: H. D. Jones, of the firm of Freer & Jones; Samuel R. Jones, and Anna Alsdorf.

JAMES CAMPBELL.

Mr. Campbell was born on the ocean while his parents were on the way to the United States, October 2, 1793. They were from Scotland. They settled in Dauphin county, Pennsylvania, where James grew to manhood and learned the trade of a weaver, which he followed for many years. In his earlier years, the old-fashioned double coverlets, as well as single ones, were in general use. He was a volunteer in the war of 1812, and went to Baltimore just after Ross was killed. At that time he was with other Pennsylvania troops quartered at Little York, and could hear the cannon at Baltimore during the battle. He served three months, and was discharged at Baltimore city. In 1817 he came to Ohio in company with Edward Murray, who was also a weaver, and settled in Orange township, adjoining the late Patrick Murray, who had preceded him about eighteen months. Mr. Campbell remained in the family of Edward Murray until 1862, in November, when the latter died, and James became a member of the family of William Peters, a son-in-law of Mr. Murray. Mr. Murray and wife and Mr. Campbell were for many years members of the Dunkard church. Mr. Campbell is now eighty-seven years of age, and among the few soldiers of the war of 1812 living.

HON. THOMAS M. BEER,

son of Richard Beer, was born on the second day of March, 1837, in Montgomery township, Ashland county, Ohio. He helped to clear the home farm and did all kinds of farm labor. He attended school in the winter and worked in the summer. When seventeen years old he taught school three months, and used his wages to pay his tuition at Vermillion institute, where he finished his education and graduated at Iron City Commercial college. He commenced the hardware business in December, 1865, and was a successful hardware merchant. In 1872 he was elected mayor of Ashland one term. In 1877 he was elected senator for the district composed of the counties of Ashland, Richland, Medina and Lorain, and re-elected in 1879. He was made chairman of the committee on finance. He is regarded as an energetic and capable member of the senate. He is a hard worker when in the assembly, and his friends place much reliance upon his integrity. He married Alice A. Urie, and his family consists of his wife, Lizzie, Frank and Harry, three children. He is about forty-three years of age, and possesses a fine physical development.

WILLIAM G. HELTMAN.

Mr. Heltman, the subject of the following sketch, was born near Mill Hall, Center county, Pennsylvania, June 1, 1835. When one and a half years old his parents

---

* These sketches were received from the author at too late an hour for insertion under the biographical department, hence their appearance here at the close of the volume.

THOMAS SPROTT.

removed to Ashland county, Ohio, then Richland county, and settled on a farm in Milton township, one and a half miles west of Ashland. Here he was raised and learned the art of farming, attending school in winter until nineteen years of age, when he taught a common school. Afterwards, in 1856 and 1857, he taught two terms in his own district, instructing those with whom he had been raised and most intimately acquainted. In 1857 he accepted a clerkship in the Mansfield post-office, under Jacob Reisinger, and acted in that capacity as chief clerk for two years, when, by reason of prolonged sickness, he gave up his place. In 1859 he was employed by E. W. Wallack, in his grocery and queensware store, in Ashland, and while there engaged, was three times elected clerk of Montgomery township—in 1861, 1862 and 1863. In 1860 he was married to Mary T. Rebman, an estimable young lady, whose parents resided on an adjoining farm to his father's, from early childhood. By this union there have been eight children, six of whom are living. In 1863 he was the Democratic candidate for clerk of the court of common pleas of Ashland county, and elected by a majority of about two hundred and fifty votes, and served as such clerk for three months, when, by the return and counting of the soldier vote, this result was changed by a few votes. In 1865 he was nominated by the Democracy of Ashland county for treasurer, and elected by a large majority, and re-elected in 1867, filling the position for two terms, with credit to himself and to the entire satisfaction of the community.

He is a member of the order of Free Masons, and has filled the chair as master of Ashland lodge for a number of terms, with marked ability and honor to the lodge. From 1871 to 1873, he was engaged in the dry goods trade successfully; then sold out his stock, and in 1874 engaged in the grocery and queensware trade in Ashland, in which occupation he continued till 1880, when he lost his stock of goods by fire, at the burning of the town hall. At present he is one of the publishers of the Ashland *Press*; has always been a Democrat, and a staunch advocate of the interests of the laboring class. By birth he is a German, and makes his influence felt more by acts and deeds than words. A thoroughly trained, self-made business man, his rule in life is strict and square dealing with his fellows; and while he values his word as sacred as his bond, he expects the same of others. In forming his judgment he is deliberate, but when he arrives at conclusions it is seldom he surrenders them. His intimate association with all sorts of people from boyhood renders him an excellent judge of human nature, and he is seldom deceived. In the family and social relations he is warm-hearted and charitable, and none ever confide in him in vain. His friendships are as steadfast and enduring as his dislikes are firmly grounded. Now in the vigor of life and sturdy manhood, his future will be felt in business relations and in the State alike.

SAMUEL LEIDIGH.

Mr. Leidigh was born February 17, 1801, in Lebanon, Pennsylvania, where he grew up and learned the trade of a miller, which he followed in Pennsylvania until 1835. He married Elizabeth Neff in 1826. He removed to Wayne county, Ohio, in the spring of 1835, and carried on the milling business three miles east of Wooster, at Henry's mill, about three years, and then removed to and purchased the old Mason mill in Orange township, then in Richland, but now in Ashland county, where he still resides and carries on business. His family consisted of five boys: Levi, Isaac, Israel, Samuel, and Reuben, who was blown up in the steamer "Sultana" during the war of 1863, and one girl, Elizabeth. His children living reside in Orange township, near the old homestead. He is a member of the Lutheran church. Mrs. Leidigh died April 16, 1879. The health of Mr. Leidigh is now good. The old mill is removed and a new one built—steam, which cost sixteen thousand dollars. He has been a miller since he was fifteen years old, and has followed the business sixty-two years. He has been a man of good business habits, and has accumulated a fine property. The Leidigh mill does a fine business and has a large patronage.

THOMAS SPROTT, JR.

Mr. Sprott was born in Beaver county, State of Pennsylvania, June 9, 1802, and emigrated with his father's family to Clearcreek township, Richland county, but now Ashland county, in the month of October, 1823, and settled on section twenty-five, where he has remained ever since. He never married, but, after the death of his father, about 1830, an aged sister kept house for him many years, until her death, some three years since, when he leased his farm to Mr. Boffenmyre, and has resided with him, and died at his residence. He experienced much trouble of late years, which seems to have shortened his days. Thomas Sprott, sr., his father, served as a scout in the war in 1790, with the celebrated Captain James Brady, a border scout, and a terror to the Wyandot and Shawnee Indians. He died in Clearcreek township about 1830, and now rests in the cemetery in Savannah. He was a Seceder in faith, and Thomas Sprott, jr., always held to the same belief. He was an honest man. He became a member of the Pioneer society which organized September 10, 1875. He died at his homestead in Clearcreek township, August 13, 1880, of general debility, aged seventy-eight years and two months, and was buried in the cemetery at Savannah. Peace to his ashes.

JOSEPH D. STUBBS.

Mr. Stubbs was born January, 6, 1820, in the village of Middletown, Dauphin county, Pennsylvania. His father was of pure English stock, and his mother of

French extraction. In 1828, when he was a lad of eight years, his mother moved to Ohio, and settled in Wooster. At the age of fifteen years he was apprenticed to Messrs. Spear & Beistle, furniture manufacturers, of Wooster, to learn the trade. At the expiration of his apprenticeship in 1839, he moved to Loudonville and engaged in the furniture trade for himself. In 1840 he was married to Mary Jane Gray, daughter of Rev. David Gray, a well known and highly esteemed Methodist Episcopal minister of Wooster. In 1843 he removed with his family to Ashland, where he has resided ever since. He first engaged in the cabinet business, having his shop and warerooms in a building on the corner of Second and Church streets, which, until within a few years, was one of the old landmarks. While engaged in business, he studied law as a means of self improvement, and was admitted to the bar during the sitting of the first supreme court in Ashland. In 1850 he engaged in the boot and shoe trade with Mr. Joseph Wasson, the firm name being Wasson & Stubbs. He continued in this business until 1859. In response to the call of Governor Dennison at the outbreak of the war, he offered his services and was accepted. He was commissioned lieutenant and regimental quartermaster of the Forty-second Ohio volunteer infantry, at the very beginning of the organization of that regiment, under Colonel James A. Garfield and Lieutenant Colonel L. A. Sheldon. He served with his regiment until November, 1862, when he was appointed captain and assistant quartermaster, for meritorious services, and ordered to report to General Garfield in Washington city. Soon after he was ordered to report to General Rosecrans, and was assigned to duty at Nashville, Tennessee. In 1864 he was ordered to establish a depot at Johnsonville, on the Tennessee river, where he remained until March, 1865, when he was transferred to the department of North and South Carolina, and assigned to duty at Raleigh, North Carolina. Soon after he was made superintendent of military railroads, with headquarters at Newbern, North Carolina, and continued in that responsible position until the roads were transferred to their owners. As a recognition of his services during this time, Captain Stubbs was brevetted lieutenant colonel, and in 1866 was assigned to duty, with this rank, as chief quartermaster of the Department of the South. In 1877 Colonel Stubbs was appointed to duty, in charge of the work of locating and improving the soldiers' cemeteries throughout the southern States. Under his direction cemeteries were established at Newbern, Raleigh, Saulsbury, and Wilmington, North Carolina, and at Florence and Port Royal, South Carolina. The cemeteries at Marietta and Andersonville were improved under his direction. Colonel Stubbs' time of service covers a period of seven years. His record as a faithful and efficient officer is a highly honorable one, as is evident from the sketch of his long service, even after the war had closed. Like many other soldiers, Colonel Stubbs found himself without a business when he returned home in 1868. He soon obtained a position, however, as general agent of the Ashland County Mutual Fire Insurance company, a position which he holds at present. Colonel Stubbs is a man of untiring energy, and a public spirited citizen, and holds an esteemed place among his fellow citizens. His family consists of four sons and two daughters. The eldest daughter, Elizabeth, is the wife of J. I. Dorland, of Ashland; the oldest son, David D. Stubbs, is secretary of the Oriental and Occidental Steamship line, and resides in San Francisco, California; the second son, John C., is general freight agent of the Central Pacific railroad, and resides in San Francisco, California; the third son, Joseph E., is editor of the Ashland *Times;* the fourth son, William M. G., has charge of the mechanical department of the *Times* office; the second daughter, May, is a teacher in the public school of Ashland.

JOHN McCONNELL.

Mr. McConnell was born in Washington county, Pennsylvania, and settled in Orange township, Ohio, in 1818. He settled near his brothers, William and Thomas. During the war of 1812 he served three months and was a brave defender of the cause, for which he received a land warrant about 1856. Mr. McConnell had been a border scout from 1790 to Wayne's great victory at Fallen Timbers in 1794. He became famous as a hunter and Indian fighter. At the hands of the red men he had lost many friends, and felt bitter toward the whole race, and never let an opportunity to avenge his wrongs pass. The *Delawares, Miamis, Shawnees* and *Wyandots* often fell before his unerring rifle. He ranged the forests far and near on his hunting excursions, and was as much feared as Brady, Sprott or Poe. He became quite famous as a hunter, and often camped in the forests along Black river and the Mahoning for weeks, and when the settlers became numerous, like Kenton and Wetsel, he became restless and pushed off to northwest Ohio, and finally sought a home in the forests of Michigan, where he could indulge his tastes in pursuing the wild deer and other game. His fame as a hunter still followed him as he ranged the forests. Often he camped out during the hunting season, weeks at a time. Finally the old man, weary of hunting, was gathered to his fathers about 1863, aged about eighty years.

Thomas McConnell was not so noted as a hunter. He was a lover of fine horses, and was fond of caring for that noble animal. He settled in Michigan, choosing the wild scenes of that country, like John, in preference to the more thickly settled parts of Ohio, where he survived until he had arrived at the age of seventy-five years.

William died when about forty-five years of age, and left a young family. Hon. George McConnell, the oldest son of William, resides in Orange township. He is a thrifty farmer, and by good management and industry has accumulated a valuable homestead of nearly eight hundred acres. For the last few years he has dealt largely in sheep. He is a leading farmer in his part of the township. In politics he is influential, and has been twice commissioner of the county, and made an efficient and prudent officer, guarding well the treasury of the people. During the war of 1861-5 he was elected a member of the legislature, and sustained his reputation as a careful and discreet member of that body. He was born in Washington county, Pennsylvania, March 15, 1811, and married Miss Narcissa Cox about 1850. They have two living sons, Elza and John.

JAMES A. OFFINEER.

Mr. Offineer was born near Yellow Creek lake, in Kosciusko county, Indiana, June 23, 1849. His parents were of French and German descent. His father followed carpentering and saw-milling until the war of the Rebellion, and in 1864 was drafted, at which time the family was scattered, a sister and brother going to Ashland county to live with their grandfather, James Offineer, sr., until the return of their father from the army. James A. and his mother lived in Indiana until the spring of 1865, and then went to Michigan, where his mother was employed as chief cook by John B. Dumont, the owner of a large mill and lumbering establishment at Allegan, and he worked as chore boy and shingle-edger, and at the latter occupation he became quite expert, having at one time edged twelve thousand five hundred shingles in five hours. In November, 1865, they met his father in Allegan, Michigan, and a few days later, returned to Ashland county, and, with his brother who had remained there, settled in Mohicanville, where his father worked at carpentering and shingle-making until James became of age. He then attended school three and one-half terms, when his health became impaired and he was obliged to give up study for the time being. On the fifth of November, 1871, he was married to Anna B. Carmack, of Perrysville, James Monroe and Mary Esterbrook being married at the same time. The ceremony was performed at the house of J. S. Carmack, by Rev. O. Webster, of the Methodist Episcopal church of West Salem. The winter following his marriage he went to Fulton county, Indiana, accompanied by his wife, where he taught one term of school with good success. In the spring they returned to New Salem, Ohio, where he engaged as book-keeper and superintendent for J. S. Carmack, who conducted a brickyard, a farm, and did plastering. It did not prove a good move as his employer failed and he lost the amount due him for nearly six months labor. January 1, 1873, they removed to Jeromeville, where he attended a select school, and in the spring engaged in carpenter work and shingle-making. In October, 1875, he again attended school for a year, in order to prepare himself for teaching. At the close of a year he again commenced teaching, attending select school during vacations, and now makes school teaching his business. In 1870 he joined the Disciple church at Jeromeville, and in 1872 his wife was transferred to the same church from the Baptist church at Perrysville, which she had joined in 1870. They have three children: Mary Orrilla, born January 1,

1873; Theresa Laura, born December 27, 1874; and George Arthur, born September 18, 1878.

JACOB FAST,

son of Martin Fast, the oldest son of Christian Fast, the Delaware captive, was born in Jackson township, Wayne county, State of Ohio, Sepember 12, 1821. His father owned the farm upon which he (Jacob) has resided since his birth. Martin Fast, his father, unfortunately lost his life June 13, 1838, at the age of fifty-six years. Like his father he was remarkably venturesome. At the time of the fatal accident he was attending a barn raising at the home of Mr. Hankey Priest, a neighbor. During the day a hive of bees swarmed and escaped. Mr. Fast and one or two others followed them until they settled on a tall tree. He ascended and hived them in a pillow case, and while in the act of descending, accidentally placed his foot upon a dead limb which gave way, and he fell to the ground, and was so injured that he survived but a few minutes. He had great fondness for bees, and could handle them without exciting their resentment. At the time of his death he possessed one hundred hives. This accident deprived his son Jacob, than seventeen years of age, of many advantages he otherwise would have had. He was compelled to remain on the homestead as a laborer, and his opportunities to attend school were limited. In 1844, by industry, he had acquired sufficient means to attend Ashland academy one session. He returned to his farm, and in 1852 was elected township clerk, and has held the office ever since. In the fall of the same year he was elected justice of the peace, and re-elected five times, serving until 1870. In the fall of 1873 he was again elected a justice of the peace, and in the fall of 1875 re-elected; so that, if he survives to the end of his present term, he will have acted as justice twenty-four years. Mr. Fast is noted for his integrity, sobriety, and intellectual worth. He is a member of the Christian church.

THE BULL FAMILY.

HEZEKIAH BULL, born in Dublin, Ireland, came to America before the Revolution, and first settled in Hartford, Connecticut. He served one year in the Revolution, and after the Revolution engaged in business in Hartford, Connecticut, and became the owner of a vessel in the West India trade, in which business he continued until 1815, when he sold out his business, and in 1816 came to Canton, Ohio. Here he remained one year, then moved to Massillon, where he settled on the farm now owned by Kent Jervis, or his heirs, where he died in 1818. He married an English lady, and was the father of eight children, seven of whom came to Ohio. Caleb on the Spanish main; Hester, Maria Louisa, Jefferson and G. W. settled in Loudonville; Hoyland, in Tennessee, and Emily in California.

G. W. BULL was born in Hartford, Connecticut, in

1799, and there received his education. When only eleven years old he went to sea, and followed a sailor's life about ten years, with an interval of one year. In 1820 he gave up a sea-faring life and came to Ohio, and settled on a farm for a short time. In 1821, with Thomas Taylor, he built a flat-boat, loaded it with pork, hams, bacon and whiskey, then the products of the country, and started for New Orleans from a point near the iron bridge across the Black fork in Loudonville. The round trip took about three months. These trips he continued to make at intervals until 1832, when he abandoned the business, and settled on the farm now owned by Hon. J. W. Bull, in Hanover township, where he held the office of justice of the peace fifteen years, and was township trustee, clerk, and treasurer for a number of years. In politics he was a Democrat. In December, 1852, he died. In 1822 he married Nancy Farrquhr, who died in 1877. He was the father of ten children, seven of whom are still living, viz: John W., who married Nancy Watson, afterwards married Eliza J. Pippit; George F., who married Ann Menor, and lives in Ashland county, Ohio; Sarah J., wife of Abner Stutes, living in Cleveland, Ohio; Hester M. and Nancy E., both living in Ashland county; Emily U., wife of Mr. Hazelett, living in Michigan; and Phebe E., who lives in Loudonville.

HON. JOHN W. BULL was born in Loudonville, Richland county, Ohio, August 16, 1824, and received a common school education. He worked on a farm until his twenty-seventh year, when he accepted a position as route agent on the Bellefontaine & Indiana railroad, and traveled between Galion and Indianapolis for nearly two years, when, in 1854, he was transferred to the Ohio & Indiana road, and traveled between Crestline and Chicago for four years. In 1861 he resigned his position as route agent, to accept the appointment of passenger conductor on the Pittsburgh, Ft. Wayne & Chicago railroad. This position he resigned to take charge of the Meyer house, in Ft. Wayne, Indiana. He gave up this business on account of the ill health of his wife, and in 1872 returned to Loudonville. In 1872 he served as mayor of the village, and as justice of the peace. He was elected to the Sixty-third general assembly by a majority of six hundred and seventy-two. He has always been an ultra Democrat, and from present indications will die in that faith. In 1847 he married Nancy Watson, of Loudonville, who died in 1851. In 1859 he married Eliza J. Pippet, and is the father of two children—one died in infancy, and Anna E. died when two years old.

GENERAL WILLARD SLOCUM

was born near Ashland, then in Richland county, State of Ohio, April 8, 1820. He remained on a farm with his parents until the death of his mother, which occurred in January, 1828, when he went to live with a married sister, Mrs. Palmer, with whom he lived, going to school and assisting Mr. Palmer in farming pursuits. After he left his sister he spent part of his time at home, and a part working for other persons, up to the spring of 1833, when he was taken by Dr. Willard Slocum, with whom he lived until the spring of 1838, going to school winter seasons, and working during the summer months. In the spring of 1838 he was sent by his father to Kenyon college. He remained there up to the spring of 1840, when he was called home. In the winter and spring of 1845 he taught school in the district where he had been raised.

He took a very active part in the presidential campaign of 1840, though not a voter. He was active and firmly fixed in the principles of the Whig party, and devoted the summer and fall to its interests. In the spring of 1841 he entered the law office of the late Judge Sherman, as a law student, in company with his brother John, now Secretary of the Treasury. Passing the routine duties of a law student for three years, he was regularly admitted to the bar of Richland county. At the time of his examination and admission there was a class of seventeen, among whom were Samuel J. Kirkwood, now United States Senator from Iowa, and John Sherman, now Secretary of the Treasury. In the fall of 1844 General Slocum returned to Ashland and commenced the practice of law, with C. T. and J. Sherman as his partners. The partnership continued up to the fall of 1847, when it was dissolved by mutual consent. The most kindly feeling existed in the Sherman and Slocum families at that time, and which has never been disturbed in any particular.

In the fall of 1847 General Slocum associated himself with the late Judge William Osborn. They continued the practice of law up to January, 1855. General Slocum was married on the tenth day of November, 1847, to Caroline A. Carr, of East Union, Wayne county, Ohio, and is now the father of seven children living and two dead. Among the living are: R. V. Slocum, C. W. Slocum, Lida S. Slocum, Willard McK. Slocum, Martin B. Slocum, Oliver J. Slocum, and Howard E. Slocum, but one of whom is married. In January, 1855, he continued in his profession, doing a very lucrative business, principally in the line of collecting for eastern houses.

In June, 1860, he attended the Republican National convention, which met in the city of Chicago, and nominated Abraham Lincoln. Though sent there under instructions to support Governor S. P. Chase, of Ohio, which he did up to the third ballot, he was among the first of the Ohio delegation to drop Chase and vote for Abraham Lincoln.

After the nomination was made he was chosen by the Fourteenth congressional district to represent it in the Electoral college, the Republicans being successful in the election, he met with the Electoral college in Columbus, and cast the vote of the Fourteenth district for Lincoln and Hamlin for President and Vice-President of the United States. Prior to the inauguration of President Lincoln, the country was thrown into intense excitement by the secession of many of the States of the Union, in which every Union loving man could not refrain his utter abhorrence of the political condition of affairs, which soon culminated in open rebellion against the United States government.

When President Lincoln called for seventy-five thousand men to suppress the rebellion, General Slocum was among the first to encourage enlistments.

In the year 1861 the President called for three hundred thousand more men, for three years' service. The proclamation was received on Thursday. General Slocum, though doing a lucrative business and having no one to take care of it, transferred it to his late partner, William V. Sloan, and converted his law office into a recruiting station. On Tuesday he left Ashland with one hundred men, among whom were many of its best citizens. Arriving at Columbus the same day, they were escorted to the basement of the State house, where they remained until the next morning. They were provided with a very fine article of straw for a bed, and ate their first army meal. The next morning he marched his men to Camp Chase, four miles west of the city, and reported to Colonel Rosecrans, who was then organizing the Twenty-third Ohio volunteer infantry. General Slocum here received his first military title, by being unanimously elected captain of company G. On June 7th the first man was recruited, and on the eleventh of the same month the company was mustered into service, being the first company recruited in the State of Ohio for three years' service, and the first mustered into the service of the United States. Soon after the complete organization of the company, Colonel Rosecrans was promoted to brigadier general, and Colonel Scammon, of Cincinnati, appointed in his place. Soon after Colonel Scammon assumed command, a serious difficulty arose between the colonel and Captain Slocum, growing out of a proposed change of orderly sergeant in company G. The order of the colonel was disobeyed in every particular. Captain Slocum was informed by Major R. B. Hayes that the colonel had prepared charges against him, and was about to convene a court-martial for the purpose of dismissing him from the service for disobedience.

To escape being dismissed from the army by order of a court-martial, he acted upon the advice of Major Hayes and Lieutenant Colonel Stanley Matthews, and resigned, thus freeing himself from the power of the colonel. The order of Colonel Scammon was never enforced, fearing the demoralizing effect it would have, not only on company G, but on the entire regiment. Here terminated Captain Slocum's connection with the men he had recruited and with the Twenty-third regiment, which to him was a subject matter of great regret. Having disposed of his law business, and being intent on giving his time and service to the Government until the close of the war, his dismissal from the army would forever preclude him from again entering the military service as an officer. Leaving Camp Chase on the third of July, 1862, he went immediately to Washington city and called on the President, to whom he made known all the circumstances connected with the trouble with Colonel Scammon, at the same time requesting an appointment in the military service. The President took the matter under consideration, and, after consulting Hon. Salmon P. Chase, who was then Secretary of the Treasury, and Hon. John Sherman, then a member of Congress, he offered him a captain's commission as quartermaster in the United States army. In the meantime he had, through the personal influence of Mr. Sherman, received an appointment in the interior department, which he held up to November 24, 1862, when he again called on the President and declined his generous offer, preferring active field service to that of quartermaster in the army, and again requested some appointment that would place him in the field. The President replied by saying, "that all appointments below the rank of brigadiers in the volunteer service were made by the governors of States," and referred him to Governor Dennison, of Ohio. Calling on Governor Dennison, and presenting the letter of President Lincoln, he at once expressed a willingness to appoint him provost marshal, and assign him to duty in the city of Columbus.

As soon as David Tod was inaugurated governor of Ohio he applied to him for a commission which would send him to the front. With a fair promise from Governor Tod to do so he returned home, awaiting the results. In April, 1862, he was called home from Columbus to attend the funeral of his father. Being detained for some time attending to business pertaining to the estate, he did not return to Columbus until sent for by Governor Tod. On arriving in Columbus the governor handed him a commission of first lieutenant, and detailed him as adjutant to organize the drafted men in Camp Buckingham, near Mansfield, Ohio, where he reported to Colonel C. G. Sherman, then in command of the camp, for duty. He at once entered upon that laborious work. The One Hundred and Second and One Hundred and Twentieth Ohio volunteer infantry regiments were then organized. The drafted men were mostly assigned to the older regiments and sent to the front. On the organization of the One Hundred and Twentieth he was again commissioned as adjutant, and assigned to that regiment, with which he left the State and went to the front, leaving Camp Buckingham in October, 1862, with Colonel French in command, and M. M. Speigle lieutenant colonel, and John Buckman as major. The regiment joined the main army at Memphis, Tennessee, and was assigned to the Thirteenth army corps. With the exception of Colonel French and Lieutenant Colonel Speigle, the regiment had never seen service. They participated in the assault on Vicksburgh from the Yazoo river. After laying in the swamps around Haines' bluff four days, participating in all the charges and battles of the campaign, he was ordered to take the regiment out to the front line and lay on their arms for the night. At two P. M. he received an order to retire the regiment and cover the retreat of the army to the Yazoo river, a distance of four miles. On returning back to their original lines he was surprised to find the entire army had left, leaving the One Hundred and Twentieth Ohio volunteer infantry to cover the retreat and guard four batteries of artillery. On arriving at the Yazoo he found the commanding officers of the regiment safely on transports, ready to follow the army back to the Mississippi river.

Before the regiment reached the river the picket of the army had crossed the bayou in force, and was following the retreating army. Soon after sunrise they approached near enough to commence firing. The First division of the Thirteenth corps were on transports in the Yazoo, and mainly out of sight of the advancing enemy. General Slocum hurried forward and informed General Osterhaus of the danger surrounding him. The artillery was hurried forward and put into position, and several batteries taken from the transports were put in enfilading position masked by the One Hundred and Twentieth, and held their position until the enemy advanced near enough, when the regiment filed to the rear of the guns, when they opened on the advancing enemy with grape, canister, solid shot, and shell. They were driven back with severe loss. Colonel French assumed command and marched the regiment on to the transport destined for Arkansas Post.

On the fifth of January, 1863, the entire army under General Grant, moved on transports against Arkansas Post, and, on the tenth of January, the fleet disembarked. On the following night they completely invested the entire fortification, behind which the enemy had about five thousand men. The attack was commenced on the morning of the eleventh, and was stubbornly resisted by the enemy. At four o'clock in the afternoon a charge was ordered on the left. The One Hundred and Twentieth occupying the extreme left, charged up the river bank directly upon the fort. As soon as the charge began the enemy opened fire on the advancing column. When within fifty yards of the fort Colonel French ordered the regiment to lie down. Adjutant Slocum being on the extreme left of the advancing column, did not hear the order of the colonel and pushed the left forward until he saw the right wing of the regiment flat on the ground. The colonel again commanded "Lie down!" I venture to say that no child ever embraced a parent with more affection than the officers and men of the One Hundred and Twentieth embraced mother earth on that occasion—one soldier (weighing at least two hundred pounds), literally flattened himself, with his head protected by a mullen stalk not more than one inch in diameter. While in this position the bullets of the enemy passed from three to four feet above them, and as long as they remained there were comparatively secure, as the sharpshooters on the right kept the enemy down, so that they dare not compress their guns to fire into the regiment.

Colonel French ordered Adjutant Slocum to go to the rear, and ask General Osterhaus to relieve the One Hundred and Twentieth. The adjutant replied by saying if he went back he would get shot in the rear, and that the regiment was safe in their present position, and if they got up to retire, every man of them would be shot. The order was made imperative, so the adjutant crossed back along the line of the men, for some distance, when the cry went up "see the adjutant craw-fishing." Finally he sprang to his feet, and in a zig-zag course reached General Osterhaus, who expressed surprise in seeing him deserting the regiment, and inquired into the cause of it. Instead of communicating the request of Colonel French to General Osterhaus, he informed the general that the rebel sharp-shooters were in the two wooden buildings inside the fort, shooting through the crevises, picking off our officers, and if he would order up two sections of artillery, and knock the buildings down, it would be the means of saving the lives of many of our officers and men. Four twenty-pound rifled guns were advanced and opened fire on the buildings, after a few shots the houses were knocked into splinters, and fell. Very soon thereafter the fort surrendered with five thousand prisoners.

At ten P. M. of the same day Adjutant Slocum received an order from army headquarters to report in person forthwith on board the transport Illinois. After reading the order, the Camp Chase difficulty flashed through his mind. He said to himself: " Here is another case of disobedience to the orders of a superior officer." Fearing to take counsel, lest he might commit himself, he started in company with the orderly for headquarters. On arriving on board he saw General Sherman with all the corps commanders sitting around a table. He advanced to General Sherman, laid down the order, and reported in person. After a number of questions were answered touching the matter, he was told to report back to his command. He heard no more of the matter until the eighteenth day of March, 1863, when he was informed that he had been promoted to major of the regiment for meritorious conduct in the field at Arkansas Post, jumping ten captains in one promotion, Colonel French resigning the same day.

On the eighth day of September, 1863, he was promoted to lieutenant colonel of the regiment. After the surrender of Fort Hindman and Arkansas Post the army returned to Young's Point, in front of Vicksburgh. Here Colonel Slocum was put in charge of digging out one section of the famous canal, to lead the waters of the Mississippi across the country in order that the transports might more safely pass the water batteries defending the city of Vicksburgh, a work that was never accomplished nor never intended to be. In March, 1863, the army of the Mississippi crossed the river below Vicksburgh on transports that had run the blockade. Colonel Slocum participated in all the battles in the rear of Vicksburgh—battle of Raymond, Thompson's Hill, Jackson, Champion Hill and Big Black. He led the right wing of his regiment in the charge on Vicksburgh on the eighteenth day of May; again on the twenty-second of May. On the seventh of June, 1863, he received an order of detail from corps headquarters, assigning him to duty as inspector general of the Thirteenth army corps, from which duty he was not relieved until after the surrender of Vicksburgh on the fourth of July, 1863. On the morning of the fourth he was left in command of three divisions of the Thirteenth corps at Big Black river, twelve miles in the rear of Vicksburgh, the superior officers all having gone down to witness the surrender.

At one P. M. of the same day, an order was sent out by General Grant to move all the forces at Big Black river upon Jackson. The order was received by Colonel Slocum, and at once put into execution by calling the forces into line. By four P. M. the entire command had crossed the river, while the advance was four miles on in the direction of Jackson. At five P. M. the advance column was attacked by General Breckenridge's command, which was retreating to Jackson, Mississippi. The engagement lasted but a short time, when the advancing column bivouacked for the night, the absent officers rejoining their respective commands before morning. On the sixth of July, Colonel Slocum's regiment led the advance of the Thirteenth on Jackson, and formed the base line, directly in front of the enemy's breastworks, and here he was engaged from the tenth to the seventeenth of July, the day the rebel authorities capitulated. Colonel Speigle there received a very severe, but not dangerous, wound in the hip, which disabled him until about the month of February, 1864, when he returned and assumed command of the regiment. After the siege of Jackson, Colonel Slocum returned to Vicksburgh, with but one hundred and eight effective men in the regiment.

In August, 1863, Colonel Slocum received an order from department headquarters, to proceed by transport to Port Hudson, on the Mississippi river, and there to await further orders. On the third of September, 1863, they disembarked and went into camp at Port Hudson, for what purpose no one seemed to know. After remaining there eight days, their rations and forage were consumed, and no means of supply. The command consisted of the One Hundred and Twentieth Ohio volunteer infantry and one battery of six-pound guns. On the twelfth day of September, Colonel Slocum ordered the battery to the bank of the river to bring to the first transport that went down the river. On the evening of the twelfth a transport was sighted and brought to by the battery. The regiment and battery were taken on board and landed at Carlton, ten miles above New Orleans. Colonel Slocum at once reported to army headquarters in New Orleans his action in the premises, which was approved by the commanding officer.

The regiment having been reduced to a mere skeleton by sickness and death, Colonel Slocum was placed on detached duty at department headquarters, as judge advocate. Soon thereafter he was ordered to Texas to organize a court-martial at Brownsville and one at another point. While there he received an order to report to Columbus, Ohio, on recruiting service. He took an ocean steamer for New Orleans, arriving at Carlton, where he was joined by the sergeants of the regiment, all of whom reached Columbus in December, 1863. In April, 1864, the colonel and his sergeants returned with one hundred and seventy-four enlisted men, and joined the regiment in Louisiana. He then re-organized the regiment by assignment of officers. The winter months had been conducive to the health of the men, and many who had been sent home on sick furlough had returned, besides many who had been in hospital.

On the first of May, 1864, the regiment was ordered to join General Banks' army, then operating up Red river in Louisiana. The regiment embarked on the steamer "City Belle," with six hundred and eighty effective men, Colonel M. M. Speigle in command. Arriving at the mouth of Red river in the evening, they laid over until the next morning to await a convoy of gunboats. In early morning they steamed up the river for some distance. Reaching Fort DeRuser, the officers of the navy reported shallow water, and they could proceed no further. Colonel Mudd, of the Second Illinois veteran cavalry, Colonel Blontz, bearer of dispatches, Colonel Bassett, and Colonel Slocum were called in council. A majority opposed going further without the protection of the navy, but Colonel Speigle, a brave officer, determined otherwise, and steamed up the river. Colonel Slocum and one hundred and fifty men took their position on the hurricane deck, not only as a guard, but to observe, if possible, any signs of the enemy. They had proceeded but a short distance until a negro woman was seen running in the direction of the transport, waving a handkerchief, saying that the rebels were around the bend. Colonel Speigle's attention was called to this demonstration by Colonel Slocum. He still persisted, saying there was no serious danger, but alas for Colonel Speigle and many brave boys! the warning proved to be more than true.

The river was very narrow but deep, with sharp curves. As the boat rounded Snaggy Point, a battery of their masked guns opened a vigorous fire on the frail transport, each shot taking effect; one killing the pilot, and one going through the machinery, cutting the steam pipe and on through the cabin. Scarcely had the sound of the last gun died away, until another battery opened in front. General Majors, with a brigade of infantry, emerged from behind a cover, and poured a murderous fire into the side of the transport. The infantry on the hurricane deck kept up a continuous fire, but of little effect. Colonel Speigle was among the first killed; Colonel Slocum hastened to the cabin, saw Colonel Speigle with many others, lying on the cabin floor, with pools of blood surrounding them. Colonel Slocum spoke to him; his only reply was "I am gone this time." He raised his head up while Colonel Mudd placed a knapsack under it. As Colonel Mudd raised up he was shot in the left temple. Colonels Basset and Blontz were also killed, and died instantly. The boat was then drifting down with the current; Colonel Slocum ordered the boat surrendered, and put fire to the state-room containing the mail for General Banks army. As soon as the boat was surrendered Colonel Slocum ordered every man ashore with his gun. The boat had neared the shore when the men began jumping and throwing their guns. Taking advantage of the situation, Colonel Slocum with one hundred and fifty-five officers and men reached the shore in safety, and sought shelter in a dense wood. Those who failed to reach the bank were either drowned or shot in the water attempting to reach shore. The remainder of the regiment were either killed or captured. The steam and hot water escaping from the boilers, drove all who were on the boiler deck into the river, many of them so badly scalded that they afterward died. This occurred about four P. M. Colonel Slocum called the men into line, and marched them some distance back from the river, where they were organized in squads, with a commissioned officer at the head of each. On examination it was ascertained that there were seven rounds of servceable ammunition to each man. Both officers and men supposed, from the dangers surrounding them, that they would be marched down the river under the protection of the gun-boats, but Colonel Slocum changed the direction and marched up the river in the direction of Alexandria, where General Banks had his headquarters.

Many were the complaints and murmurs of the men at this sudden and unexpected change in their destination—but to no avail. The march was a hazardous one at best, but Colonel Slocum best understood the situation, and pushed forward through an unbroken wilderness of pine, nothing to direct their course but drift from Red river. At sundown a plantation was reached. In a field some distance off a man was discovered unhitching a team from a plow. Lieutenant Vanness was directed to bring him in. He proved to be a negro man, and a slave of a man named Grimes. The negro was closely examined by Colonel Slocum as to distance, routes, and the general topography of the country. He gave the distance to Alexandria as twenty-eight miles, and three routes or ways of reaching the place, one being a mule path through the timber, and three miles shorter than either of the traveled roads. The negro was put under charge of Lieutenant Vanness, with a promise that if he piloted them through safely he would be rewarded, but if he led them into the enemy's lines, on another route, he would be shot. They then proceeded to the residence of Mr. Grimes, who met them with a stern rebuke for appearing on his premises with his slave in charge. Colonel Slocum placed a guard around his house, with instructions to let none of the inmates pass out. The men were nearly exhausted, having had nothing to eat since an early breakfast, and it became necessary that Mr. Grimes supply their wants. He became quite angry, and declared that no provisions could be given the men; he made severe threats as to what he would do if anyone attempted to enter his house in search of provisions. Colonel Slocum stepped on the porch and presented the old man two navy revolvers, which brought him to submission. In a few minutes the men had plenty of corn-meal, side pork, and sour milk, and a number of fires lighted in the yard, cooking their supper—baking their corn batter on boards, and frying their meat in anything they could find that would grease. When all were supplied they formed in line for the long, dark, and tedious march of the night. Mr. Grimes, unaccustomed to Yankee visitors, failed to bid them good-night. After marching through a wilderness country all night, they reached Red river at daybreak, eight miles below Alexandria. Th ... od station on the river and an old log house. Colonel Slocum, with a few trusty men, approached the house and called to the inmates to come out. The first to appear was the owner of the premises, who appeared surprised to see Federal soldiers in his locality. A guard was placed around his house, and Colonel Slocum inquired of him if there were any Confederate soldiers near. He was informed, after some hesitation, that one mile back from the river there were two regiments of rebel cavalry, and, looking across the river, we could see the rebel out-posts, or their horses.

Colonel Slocum determined to cross the river at this point, but on inquiry there were no skiffs nor boat of any kind. A picket line was extended back some distance from the house. A wood-rack was made into a skiff by laying boards in the bottom; then twenty or twenty-five men would take off their clothing, put them on the skiff, with their guns on top, and the men in the water started diagonally across the stream. When the shore was reached the skiff was towed up the river and sent back. In this way by ten A. M. the entire command crossed in safety. Major McKinley was among the first to cross, and took charge of the men as they arrived. Colonel Slocum, before calling in his pickets, cautioned the old man to remain quiet, as there was danger in his communicating with the enemy. They then took possession of the skiff and crossed the river, leaving the skiff to the mercy of the stream. Before the colonel was fully dressed, two transports, loaded with infantry, accompanied by two gunboats, were seen descending the river. The colonel made every effort to stop them, that he might warn them of the danger below; but they pushed onward and reached Snaggy Point, and fell into the same trap, and all were captured. The rebel pickets still occupied their post. Not knowing the exact force of the enemy, the colonel determined to put on as bold a front as possi!· He prolonged his line a great distance, with battle flag in front and regimental colors in the center, and marched upon the levee—the river and levee bending off in the direction of the rebel post.

When within a few hundred yards of the rebels' advanced line, they mounted their horses and galloped off like so many frightened wolves, thus allowing the colonel, with his handful of men, to pass through to Alexandria without firing a gun. On arriving at Alexandria the colonel reported in person to General Banks, who at once ordered all necessary provision to be made for the comfort of the men. After remaining in Alexandria a few days the remnant was temporarily consolidated with the Forty-second Ohio volunteer infantry, Colonel Slocum's regiment being again reduced by death and capture to less than a major's command. Owing to severe and permanent injuries received by Colonel Slocum while making his escape from the "City Belle," he was rendered unfit for field service. Before leaving the boat he had his left shoulder strap shot off. He was put on detached duty as chief of staff and provost marshal of the Thirteenth army corps, General M. K. Lawler commanding.

Here practically terminated Colonel Slocum's connection with the One Hundred and Twentieth. The regiment was reduced by death, disease and capture to a mere skeleton, yet it kept its distinction up to November 17, 1864, Major John McKinley in command.

On the thirteenth day of May General Banks commenced his memorable retreat from Alexandria to the Mississippi at Chaneyville. The retreating columns of General Banks were attacked in force by the enemy. Colonel Slocum, with the Fourth brigade, took an active part in that engagement, as he did in the battle at Willow bayou, crossing the Atchafalaya, arriving at Morganza bend on the twenty-first of May, 1864, where the army went into camp for reorganization.

On the twenty-fifth of May, 1864, Colonel Slocum was appointed provost marshal of the trans-Mississippi, with headquarters at Morganza, Louisiana. Much importance was attached to this new duty. It involved the trade and commerce of the river for one hundred and eighty miles front and eighty miles back. All the products of the country, destined for market or shipment, had to pass through his hands. This duty he continued to perform as long as the army remained at Morganza, and the entire country west of the Mississippi had been abandoned by rebel authority.

The monotony of the military post at Morganza was broken on the sixteenth day of November, 1864. Prior to this date, General Lawler spoke of his having a birthday on the sixteenth, and proposed to celebrate it. Mrs. Breed, a widow lady from New Hampshire, a visiting friend, was married on the sixteenth of November. Mrs. Slocum, the wife of General Slocum, proposed that they all join in celebrating the event, it being the anniversary of their marriage. Mrs. General Reynolds wished to join in. General Lawler directed General Slocum to take the headquarters boat and go to New Orleans, and lay in a supply for the occasion, and extend an invitation to a number of officers and citizens of New Orleans to join them and partake of their hospitality. About sixty invited guests were in attendance, many of them from New Orleans. An elegant dinner was prepared for the occasion, and the table spread in the cabin of the headquarter boat. There were old and young, citizens and soldiers, all commingling together. After dinner they had music and dancing, in which all engaged. The presents brought up from New Orleans were quite profuse. The whole affair was enjoyed by all, and by none more than the citizens present. The next day General Slocum sent the headquarter boat to the city with all who desired to go down.

On the tenth day of January, 1865, General Slocum was honorably mustered out of the service, when he returned to Ashland. The results of the war had so effectually revolutionized the business of the country, that the practice of law was not at all desirable. In the winter of 1865-6, he returned to Louisiana with the view of purchasing property and making that State his future home.

After spending some time in different localities, he saw from the impression left on the minds of the ex-confederates, that it was unsafe for any northern man to remove to that locality with his family, so he returned to Ohio in the spring of 1866, and engaged in civil pursuits.

On the thirteenth day of March, 1865, he received from the President of the United States a brigadier general's commission by brevet, "for meritorious service in the field." This promotion was given him without solicitation on his part. On the first day of March, 1867, he received a telegram from the treasury department, wishing to know if he would accept an appointment as assessor of internal revenue for the Fourteenth district of Ohio. The general called a few of his Republican friends together, and made known to them the contents of the dispatch. Among the number was Captain S. M. Barber, a one-legged soldier. After some consultation, he offered to decline the offer himself, if Captain Barber would accept it. The captain considered the matter until the next morning, when he declined, for the reason that he was receiving, as superintendent of the public school, an equal salary. So the general accepted, and on the sixth of March he was confirmed by the Senate, and his commission forwarded. He held the office up to June 22, 1872, when the office of assessor was abolished by law. Two years thereafter his accounts with the treasury department were balanced, and a treasury draft for thirty-six dollars and eighty-five cents sent him, as his due. Since 1872 he has been actively engaged in the practice of law.

General Slocum from early manhood has taken an active part in the politics of the country. He was identified with the old Whig party, and commenced his political career before he became a voter, in the campaign of 1840. Though always living in a strong Democratic locality, he would enter each succeeding campaign to win. He has for years represented his county in State conventions, and been twice a delegate to Republican National conventions. In August, 1866, the loyal Union men of the southern States called a convention in the city of Philadelphia. To give to their efforts and manifestation of nationality a hearty recognition, the governors of all the northern States appointed two delegates from each congressional district to meet their southern brethren in convention. Hon. Martin Welker, then a member of Congress from the Fourteenth district, and General Slocum, were appointed by Governor Brough as delegates to that convention, which in magnitude and grandeur was the most imposing convention ever held in America. Up to the present writing General Slocum is regarded as one of the leaders of the Republican party in central Ohio.

An incident not particularly connected with this sketch, though one of peculiar historic account, occurred under his observation and direction. Nine days after Colonel M. M. Speigle had been killed, the major of the Second Illinois cavalry, and General Slocum, sought to recover the remains of their colonels. On General Banks' retreat down Red river, General Slocum and the major, (whose name is not remembered) went down to Snaggy Point in search of the colonels, and found them both buried in the same grave. General Slocum mounted his horse and rode seven miles up the river, where the fleet was tied up, boarded a quartermaster's boat, saw the officer, and requested him to stop his boat at the place of disaster, and throw off two coffins, for the purpose stated. When the fleet moved down the river the coffins were taken ashore, the major remaining there with his men to place the remains in the coffins, and ship them to the mouth of the river, or to the Atchafalaya. Some of the detail reported to General Slocum that the quartermaster's boat was crowded into the river before the coffin containing the remains of Colonel Speigle could be put aboard, and consequently left it on the banks of the river. General Slocum procured a detail of twenty men and an ambulance, and sent them down to bring up the coffin, which they did, under the fire of the enemy on the opposite shore. The detail reported that they had placed the coffin in the ambulance, and it had gone forward to join the ambulance corps. On the night of the battle of Willow Bayou, General Slocum received the following note:

HEADQUARTERS THIRTEENTH ARMY CORPS,
NEAR SIMSPORT, LOUISIANA, May 18, 1864.

"COLONEL: I have the honor to request that you will make arrangement with some transport in the Atchafalaya to convey the body of Colonel Speigle. It is getting so much decomposed that we *cannot* carry it in an ambulance any further, or keep it in the train. I know your anxiety to preserve it, and will contribute all in my power toward it.

Very respectfully, your obedient servant,
G. B. DULLEM, Chief Clerk,
COLONEL SLOCUM, One Hundred and Twentieth Ohio volunteer infantry.

On the receipt of the above note, General Slocum hurried forward, in advance of the corps, and reached the Atchafalaya, where he found the fleet awaiting the army, to convey it across the stream. He at once made arrangements with the dispatch boat to carry the remains of Colonel Speigle to Cairo, and from there forward them to Millersburgh, Ohio. On making inquiry at headquarters, where the ambulance could be found containing the remains of Colonel Speigle, he was informed by the chief clerk that the surgeon of the department had ordered it to be taken from the ambulance and run back in the woods. After getting a suitable box made for the coffin, the general, with a detail of men, went to bring in the remains, and place the same on the transport. Finding the wagon a hundred rods or more back from the road, in the woods, the coffin was taken from it. It appeared unusually light, and grave suspicions were aroused that the body had been taken from the coffin. The coffin was opened in the presence of at least twenty men, and no corpse had ever been in it. The inside was clean, and contained the shavings of the undertaker. This fact was communicated to the officers at headquarters, who appeared incredulous, and thought they must be mistaken. To satisfy themselves, each examined the coffin, and could see no mark or evidence that it had ever been used. In October following, General Slocum, for the purpose of getting the facts in the case, went to Burwick bay, in southwest Louisiana, where the Second Illinois cavalry were on duty, and there saw the major who had been left in charge at Snaggy Point. He informed General Slocum that when the fleet went down the river, the quartermaster ran his boat to the shore and threw off two coffins, in one of which they put the remains of Colonel Mudd, and carried on board the other coffin, which was too small to receive the remains of Colonel Speigle, so they placed him back in the grave, and covered him over, leaving the empty coffin on the bank of the river, where his remains repose to this day. The medical department at headquarters even went so far as to say that the stench arising from the decomposed body of Colonel Speigle was creating sickness, and thus ordered out of the ambulance, and sent in an open wagon back in the woods. It has often been wondered by General Slocum if this astute medical corps were not yet inhaling the stench arising from the imaginary decomposed body. They certainly labored under an extreme hallucination of mind.

THE PIONEER SOCIETY.

September 10, 1875, the pioneers met at the court house in Ashland, and organized a pioneer and historical society, adopting a constitution and by-laws for the government of the society. The first officers elected were: Francis Graham, president; George W. Urie of Montgomery, James Kilgore of Orange, Hamilton Porter of Sullivan, Henry Summers of Troy, Jacob Hershey of Ruggles, John Bryte of Clearcreek, Hugh Burns of Milton, Thomas Cole of Jackson, Joseph Chandler of Perry, Henry Winbigler of Mohican, Allen Metcalf of Lake, Thomas Bushnell of Vermillion, Daniel Kauffman of Mifflin, C. C. Coulter of Green, and John Bull of Hanover, vice-presidents—one from each township; Dr. P. H. Clark of Ashland, secretary; Dr. George W. Hill of Ashland, historian; Isaac Stull of Ashland, treasurer. The election of officers for the society takes place annually. The successive presidents have been: Colonel George W. Urie, 1876; Andrew Mason, 1877; Josiah Thomas, 1878; and Hugh Burns, 1880. The same secretary and historian have been elected annually from the organization of the society. The following honorary members have been elected: Isaac Smuker, esq., Newark; General L. V. Bierce, Akron; Dr. J. P. Henderson, Newville; President Diefenorf, Hayesville; Professor Sample, Perrysville; Rev. John Robinson, D. D., Ashland; Dr. J. P. Clark, Ashland; Dr. George W. Hill, Ashland; and M. Ebright, esq., Ashland.

THE LOCUSTS.

Those little pests, the seventeen-year locusts, a great phenomena in their way, made their appearance again in June, 1880. An old settler says they appeared in 1813, 1829, 1846, and 1863 in Ohio, and remained each time about thirty or thirty-five days, doing much damage to young timber and fruit. It was noticed that in 1813 there was a plain "P" on their wing; in 1829, 1846 and

1863, a "W" in the same place, meaning, according to theory, war. They may be expected to return in 1897.

ASHLAND CITY CHURCH. *

The Ashland city church of the Brethren (Dunkard) was organized May 22, 1879, with S. Z. Sharp as elder in charge, and S. H. Basher assistant in the ministry. J. H. Worst was also called to the ministry on the day of organization and J. N. Roop and E. J. Worst, deacons. The number of members enrolled at the time of organization was forty-three, which has increased since to sixty-five. The congregation worships every Sabbath in the chapel of Ashland college, and has a Sunday-school of one hundred members. The *Gospel Preacher*, having a circulation of about five thousand, and *Our Sunday School*, a juvenile weekly, having nearly six thousand subscribers, are published in Ashland under the auspices of the Brethren church.

ASHLAND COLLEGE. †

For many years the church of the Brethren (Dunkards) had under consideration the propriety of establishing an institution for the higher education of the sons and daughters in that denomination, and had made a number of attempts in this direction, at Berlin, and at Plum Creek, Pennsylvania, and at Bourbon Indiana, all of which efforts had failed, but the friends of the movement in northeast Ohio, undaunted by previous reverses, determined to make their enterprise a success, and solicited S. Z. Sharp, then professor in Maryville college, Tennessee, to sever his connection with that institution and throw his entire energy into this new enterprise. After several refusals he at last consented, and in June, 1877, made a tour through a part of this State, in search of a suitable location. The choice of himself and friends was nearly unanimous in favor of Ashland, and when this was well discussed by the friends of the movement, the matter was laid before some of the most influential citizens of Ashland, who at once caught the spirit, called a meeting in the city hall, where an unusually large and enthusiastic audience was addressed by the present president of the college, S. Z. Sharp, who set forth the object of the founders to be to establish a college equal to any in the State. That it would be under the care of the church of the Brethren to the same extent that other colleges were under the care of other religious bodies.

That among the prominent features of the institution would be thorough scholarship and the cultivation of a sentiment among students to appreciate solid worth rather than vain show, and that plain neat attire and a richly stored mind were better than a gaudy dress and an empty mind. After hearing the plans and aims of the proposed institution, the citizens of Ashland unanimously endorsed the project, and at once raised ten thousand dollars toward the erection of the college building. The most beautiful site in this part of the State was selected. A campus of twenty-seven acres of land was bought for six thousand three hundred and thirty-three dollars, and a building erected, which is at this writing nearly completed, and will cost, including material, work, supervision, furniture, apparatus and cabinet, sixty thousand dollars. The college building is one hundred feet front, one hundred deep, four stories high, built of brick, roofed with slate, and for substantial construction and convenience, has few equals. There is also a boarding hall one hundred and ten feet long, forty feet wide, and four stories high, which, when completed, will cost between ten thousand and eleven thousand dollars.

A charter was obtained February 22, 1878, by which the institution is placed under the care of the Church of the Brethren, and put upon an equal footing with any other college in the State. The charter provides for the following courses of instruction: Classical, philosophical, normal and commercial. The college was formally opened September 17, 1879, with a full corps of instructors, as follows: Elder S. Z. Sharp, A. M., president and professor of mental and moral philosophy; L. Huber, A. M., professor of Latin and modern languages; J. E. Stubbs, A. M., professor of Greek language and literature; David Bailey, A. M., professor of mathematics; Jacob Keim, Ph. B., professor of natural science; J. C. Ewing, professor of music; Mrs. C. P. Chapman, teacher of painting and drawing.

The first term closed December 24, 1879, with one hundred and twelve pupils enrolled, and was regarded as a decided success in every respect.

EARLY EVENTS.

FIRST BIRTH.

Of the first birth in Ashland, Mr. Knapp says, on page 203:

"William Sheets, now residing about two miles east of Ashland, was the first male child born within the town, who lived to reach manhood, Lorin Andrews, president of Kenyon college, and late a colonel in one of the Ohio volunteer regiments, was the second child who attained maturity, born in Ashland."

This takes the advantage of other deserving pioneers born in the township. Messrs. Sheets and Andrews were born a few weeks apart in the spring of 1819, while David Carter, yet living on the old Carter homestead, two and one-half miles south of Ashland, was born March 18, 1815, about four years before either. He has no children, but resides with his lady at the old Carter home, with good mental and physical preservation. Let justice be done, and the truth of history be preserved.

NEW SETTLERS.

Within the six or eight years succeeding the war, John, Henry, and Reuben Newkirk, James Gray, Thomas Ba-

---

* This article is a revised sketch of this church, received for publication after the author's short notice elsewhere published in this volume had been put in type.

† A revised sketch, received after the author's first account of the college was published.

ker, Peter Wicoff, John Emerick, John Riddle, J. C. Young, William Green, John Ewalt, George Marks, Asahel Webster, Elijah Oram, John Weatherbee, John Smith, Robert Chandler, the Cornells, Metcalfs and others settled in Lake township. These settlers located principally east of the Lake fork, and were from the States of New York, Pennsylvania, Maryland and Virginia. The lands west of the Lake fork remained unsettled for many years after the first pioneers came into the east part of the township. From 1820 to 1830, the tide of emigration was continuous; and at this period, 1875, very few townships within the limits of this county can exhibit finer farms, better dwellings and more costly bank barns. The valley of the Lake fork for richness of soil and well cultivated farms, cannot be excelled. The lands west of that stream are mostly owned by sturdy farmers from Pennsylvania, and produce an abundance of wheat, oats and corn.

THE FIRST MILL.

John Greenlee is of the opinion that the first mill, known as Odell's, was erected in the spring of 1813, and not in 1812, as stated by Mr. Knapp, the nearest mills at that period being those of Shrimplin, on Owl creek, Knox county, and Stibbs, east of Wooster, where the settlers obtained their grists and grain the first and second years after they arrived. These mills were poor concerns—made of hewed logs, with one run of stones. That of Odell was also of hewed logs, an undershot wheel, one run of stones, and was a mere corn cracker. Nearly all the settlers used hominy blocks, and perforated deer skins for sieves. In this way their meal and hominy were separated. About the year 1820, Jabez Smith erected a saw- and grist-mill about half a mile south of Mohicanville. He continued to own and use those mills for a number of years, and then sold to Robert F. Chandler, who occupied the premises until the spring of 1875, when the mills accidentally took fire and were wholly consumed. The Rochester mill, so-called, was erected at a point some three miles southeast of Mohicanville, on the Mohican, where William Green had a saw-mill, in 1836. The site was purchased by Hanvey & Smith, from Rochester, New York, and the present large mill erected. These parties carried on the mill for some time, when it passed into new hands. It was called the "Rochester mill," from the locality from which they came in New York.

FIRST JUSTICE OF THE PEACE.

Mr. Greenlee states that the first justice of the peace elected in Lake township was James Loudon Priest, who was chosen in 1812, for three years. He was succeeded in 1815 by John Weatherbee, father of the late Justus S. Weatherbee, and he, in 1818, by John Newkirk. The records of the township have been lost or destroyed, and the statement of Mr. Greenlee is presumed to be correct on that subject.*

FIRST SCHOOL.

The first school-house was built on the lands of Mr. Greenlee, in 1817, and the first teacher was John Newkirk, afterward justice of the peace. The second school-house was erected on the lands of John Weatherbee, near the old fort, a year or two later.

FIRST CHURCH.

The Presbyterians put up a small church on section sixteen, in 1826, at which there was occasional preaching. Prior to that, meetings were held in the cabins of the pioneers. The Revs. Graham and Warner, were the earliest Methodist preachers in Lake.

DOCTORS.

For many years there was no physician in Lake. In cases demanding skilful medical treatment, physicians from Mansfield or Wooster were called. The principal diseases were fever and ague, and bilious disturbances, and rarely fatal. A good constitution, a little dieting, a decoction of bitter herbs, cherry bark and whiskey, constituted the principal home remedies. Mrs. James L. Priest and Mrs. Nathan Odell possessed a great deal of fame as doctors and nurses among the pioneers. Their system of practice is now called the Eclectic among anti-mineral practitioners.

BOATING ON THE LAKE FORK.

About the year 1823 Robert Crawford, a rugged pioneer from Orange township, conceived the idea of building a long flat-boat on the Lake fork, to be loaded with cherry and walnut lumber for New Orleans. He possessed a fine team, and a strong Maryland wagon, with which he gathered logs to the various mills between Ashland and the Lake fork, to be cut into lumber. He constructed a flat-boat about one hundred and twenty-five feet long, and launched it near what is now the Rochester mill, and collecting his lumber, placed it on board. All being ready, he passed down the Lake fork into the Walhonding, the Muskingum, the Ohio, and the Mississippi to New Orleans, where he made sale of his lumber and returned. It is believed that the Wachtel brothers accompanied him on his voyage. This is the only instance in which a flat-boat descended the Lake fork from that region. Many of the early pioneers, however, ascended the stream in small boats or pirogues as high as what is now known as Tylertown or Finleys.

[For a further account of the pioneers of Lake, see chapter on the erection of block-houses and stockades.]

---

*The impression is created by Mr. Knapp that Joshua Oram, of that part of Lake now in Clinton township, Wayne county, was a justice of the peace in 1814, and consequently the first justice. Mr. Greenlee says Joshua Oram was never a justice in Lake, nor elsewhere so far as he knows. William Wicoff who is a relative of Mr. Oram, confirms the foregoing statement.

Additional Township Sketches.

Professor S. Z. Sharp, A. M., first president of Ashland college, Ohio, was born in Airy Dale, Huntingdon county, State of Pennsylvania, where his father, Solomon Sharp, also was born. He began teaching school in the year 1855, and afterwards attended the Pennsylvania State Normal school at Millersville, where he graduated in 1860. He became principal of Kishacoquillas seminary in 1861, assistant professor of languages in the Pennsylvania State Normal school in 1866, and in 1868 took charge of New Providence Normal school in the State of Tennessee. In 1875 he accepted a professorship in Maryville college, Tennessee, and in 1878 was elected president of Ashland college. His wife, Salome Z. Sharp, was the daughter of Shem Zook, a citizen of note and an extensive contributor to the agricultural department at Washington. She was born March 31, 1839, at Reedsville, Mifflin county, Pennsylvania. The children of the above are: Annie L., born April 9, 1865; Theodore S., born August 15, 1869; and Maurice, born March 17, 1874.

George B. Smith was born in Ashland, Ohio, December 5, 1844. He received his education at the Ashland union schools, and at Kenyon college, Gambier, Ohio. He was admitted to the bar at Ashland in 1867, after reading the required time and course in the office of his father, J. W. Smith, and soon after was taken into his father's business as partner, which partnership still exists. He was also admitted to the circuit court of the United States for the Northern district of Ohio, at Cleveland, in 1874. In 1879 he was married, at St. Louis, to Miss Jessie Sutherland, of that city, daughter of Hon. J. W. Sutherland, a former well known Ashland county boy. In 1878 he was elected to the office of prosecuting attorney of his county, being elected thereto by the Democratic party, of which he is an active working member. At the end of his first term he was again renominated for the same position.

Henry J. Pille emigrated to the United States in 1853, when but fourteen years old. His parents, Werner H. H. and Margaretta Pille resided in the Grand Duchy of Oldenburgh, Germany, where they both died at the advanced age of seventy-four years. The family consisted of nine children, six boys and three girls. The latter died when young. The boys are still living, of whom four are in the United States. One, Francis H., is in Cincinnati; Herman H. is in Massillon, Ohio; Henry J. is in Ashland, and his twin brother, John H., in Dayton, Kentucky. Henry J. Pille came direct from Germany to Massillon Ohio, where he resided for six years, and while there learned the trade of a tinner. He worked in several large cities in the United States, and in 1859 went to Illinois, where he resided for nearly six years, working at his trade. During the late Rebellion he enlisted in the One Hundred and Thirty-second regiment, Illinois volunteer infantry, and while in the service contracted disease, and was sent home on sick furlough, but did not join his regiment again, on account of his disease. The regiment was discharged from service at Chicago, Illinois. From this disease he has suffered more or less since that time. In 1866 he came to Ashland, Ohio, where he has resided ever since, working at his trade occasionally, as his health would allow. In the spring of 1867 he went into business with F. Knoth, and carried on the stove and tin trade for nearly four years, when he sold out, and in 1877 went into business again with Mr. F. Knoth, in which they are still engaged. In 1868 he married Fredericka Wendling, a native of the Rhine Province of Bavaria, Germany. They have three children, one boy and two girls. The oldest, Henry E., is eleven years of age; Josephine F., ten, and Carrie K., five. In religion, he is a member of the Catholic church, and in politics is an adherent to the Democratic principles.

William Hunter, born in Franklin county, Pennsylvania, in 1780, died in Ashland county, Ohio, September 8, 1863. In 1808 he was married to a Miss Ray, by whom he had four children: Eleanor, Elizabeth, William R. and Martha. His wife dying in 1824, he married Jane McCrelia in 1826, and by her had seven children: Mary, Isabelle, Anna, Rachel, Thomas S., Rose and Jennie, all of whom are living but Jennie, who died February 27, 1874. Before the war of 1812, he moved from Franklin county to Westmoreland county, Pennsylvania, and from there entered the army in that war, in Captain Jack's company of Pennsylvania militia. In 1834 he removed with his family to Vermillion township, Ashland county, Ohio, where he resided to the day of his death, and was buried in Ashland cemetery. His widow resided in Vermillion township until April, 1880, when she moved to Milton township, one mile west of Ashland. She was born April 2, 1800, and is at this time in the enjoyment of tolerable health. Two unmarried daughters are still living with her—Isabelle and Ann. Eleanor married Eli Keslar and reared a large family, and at present lives in Westmoreland county, Pennsylvania, where she has always resided. William R. also resides in Westmoreland county, Pennsylvania, where he married a Miss Wirsing, of that county. They have had eleven children, of whom ten are still living: Elizabeth, married Jesse Weddle, by whom she had one son. Mr. Weddle died, and she afterward married William Mann, and raised six children with him. At present they live in Wooster, Ohio. Martha married Michael Bourses, and resides in Butler, Indiana. Mary married Moses Moore, and has five children living; they reside in Ashland, Ohio. Rachel married Henry Hurmichouser, September 30, 185-, and immediately afterwards moved to Plymouth, Indiana, where they have resided ever since, having had two sons: Willie, who died August 3, 1879, aged twenty years; and Harry, who is still living, aged thirteen years. Thomas S. was born December 12, 1839, at the old home in Vermillion township, and attended the common school until the age of fifteen, when he went to Vermillion institute, then under the care of Dr. Diefendorf, for whom he has great reverence. At the age of sixteen he commenced teaching, and continued attending school and teaching until 1861. In the spring of 1861, he went to Indiana, and worked there till autumn, when he came home with the noted "Indiana shakes," which lasted nearly eighteen months. In the summer of 1863 he read medicine in Wooster, Ohio, with Dr. Robison and his partner, where he continued untill May, 1864, when he went out as hospital steward in the One Hundred and Sixty-ninth regiment Ohio volunteer infantry, but soon acted as assistant surgeon. In the fall of 1864 he returned, and went to attend medical lectures at Jefferson Medical college, where he graduated in March, 1866. He came home and was married April 3, 1866, to Kate Blocher, of Wayne county, Ohio, daughter of John Blocher, deceased, of Canaan township, Wayne county. He then located in Ashland for the practice of medicine and surgery, where he has remained ever since. They have a son, born June 3, 1867, and a daughter, born January 2, 1877, comprising all their children. His wife, Kate Blocher, was born December 23, 1839, in Canaan township, Wayne county, Ohio.

OWEN TOMPKINS was born in Chester county, Pennsylvania, February 7, 1839. His parents were John Tompkins, who was also born in Chester county, Pennsylvania, and Mary, his wife, who was a native of Montreal, Canada. They had a family of eight children, as follows: Elizabeth, Emily, Mary, Margaret, Peter, John, Naomi and Owen. Soon after the birth of the latter his mother died. He remained with his father and the other members of the family until he became of age. In 1861 he enlisted as a soldier in the war of the Rebellion for the term of three months, and at the end of that time was appointed as second lieutenant in the Eighty-second Pennsylvania volunteers for the three years service. During that time he was promoted from second to first lieutenant, and became adjutant of the regiment. In 1864 he was commissioned as captain of the company he first entered as lieutenant. After the close of the war, in 1867, he was commissioned by the Secretary of War as a second lieutenant in the regular army, but from force of circumstances did not serve. He held a civil position under the State government of Pennsylvania five years, and in 1872 went to Columbus, Ohio, and in 1876 came to Ashland, where he has since been engaged in business. In 1863 he was married to Prudence A. Russel, by whom he has one child, William M., born in August, 1866.

WILLIAM H. H. POTTER, the subject of this sketch, was born in Columbia township, Lorain county, Ohio, May 7, 1816. When an infant his parents removed to Medina county, Ohio, where he resided until eight years of age, when his father died, and he went to live with Franklin Wells, where he remained until the age of twenty-one years. Until he was fifteen years old he followed farming as his vocation, but from that time until he was of age he worked in a store, and at the trade of cabinet making. From that time until the year 1849 or '50 he carried on the cabinet making business himself in Lorain and Ashland counties. After that date he engaged in the book and drug business at this place, Ashland, until 1867, since which time he has carried on and owned the gas works and has furnished Ashland with gas. He was married October 27, 1841, to Miss Catharine Peabody, who was born in New York State, July 21, 1819. By this union have been born nine children, five of whom are still living and named respectively, Emma F., who was born July 11, 1844; William H., born January 20, 1851; Charles W. H., born July 13, 1853; George E., born September 1, 1855; and Edgar A., born June 20, 1858. The ones deceased were Nancy Alice, born August 11, 1842, and died November 12, 1873; Mary Florence, born June 9, 1847, and died June 21, 1849; William C., born July 29, 1849, and died March 20, 1851; Frank Irwin, born July 2, 1861, and died October 8, 1862. William H. was married September 16, 1878, to Miss Julia Young. Samuel Y. Potter, our subject's father, was born in New Haven, Connecticut, about the year 1795, and he together with his brother, came to this State at an early day, and located in Lorain county. From thence he removed to Medina county, where he died. At the time of his death he was sheriff of the county. He was married to Miss Sallie Pritchard, who died in 1849. She was also born in Connecticut, and removed with her parents to Ohio at an early day. Mr. Potter used to hear his parents recall the many hardships and privations that they together with their pioneer associates had to contend with, incident to pioneer life, that the present as well as the future generations will never know nor experience. Mr. Potter has, by industry and good management, made for himself and family a good home. He and his family enjoy the respect and esteem of all in the community where they reside or where they are known.

SAMUEL GATES WIEST was born in Adams county, Pennsylvania, June 28, 1850. His parents are Jacob Wiest, his father, born November 24, 1825, and his mother, Margaret Wiest, born March 22, 1828. They still live in Pennsylvania, where they have raised a family of seven children, as follows: Samuel G., M. L., Emma S., Ellen B., Charles E., Ada Kate, and Anna L., of whom all but two live in the county of their birth. M. L. is in Ashland, and is a member of the firm of Bahnley & Co., marble cutters. Samuel G., the subject of this sketch, came to Ashland in June, 1873, and immediately engaged in the drug business with J. P. Harley.

He afterwards took the old stand of W. K. Foltz, one door east of the Miller house, where he continued in business by himself until 1880, when he associated with himself E. W. Reaser, and still continues in the drug business. S. G. Wiest was married September 4, 1876, to Belle Mansfield, daughter of M. H. Mansfield, of Ashland, and has one child, John M., born February 4, 1879.

P. H. CLARK, M. D., was born August 3, 1819. His grandparents and parents were among the early settlers of Ohio, arriving in this State in 1817. Dr. H. M. Clark, his father, was a native of Connecticut, and was born in 1789; he served as surgeon in the navy during the war of 1812–15. His mother was Laura Downs Clark, who was born in Connecticut in 1798. Their children were: P. H., Leander, Hannah M., and Theo. F. Both Leander and Theo. are in Tama county, Iowa; Hannah is the wife of Professor J. C. Bryant, of Bryant's Mercantile college, Buffalo. All of the above named children were born in Wakeman, Huron county, Ohio, whence the parents moved from Connecticut. The grandparents settled in Medina, where they lived and died. Dr. P. H. Clark, the subject of this sketch, studied at Oberlin college, and attended his first course of lectures at Willoughby Medical college, in the winter of 1839–40. He then moved to New Haven, Indiana, where he practiced medicine six years. December 12, 1845, he was married to Sarah Jane McDougall, of that place. She died December 6, 1846, and after her death he removed to Ozaukee, Wisconsin, where he practiced his profession four years. He was again married May 18, 1847, to Elizabeth Clark, daughter of B. B. Clark, M. D., of Ashland; she was his first cousin. In June, 1850, they came to Ashland, where he has since been engaged in the practice of medicine, with the exception of two years, when he served as assistant surgeon in the war of the Rebellion. In the winter of 1861–2 he attended his second course of lectures at the Buffalo Medical college, from which he graduated in March, 1862. He was elected secretary of the Ashland County Pioneer Historical society, September 10, 1875, and still retains the office. He has been president of the Ashland Cemetery association several years; and has been a member of the Ohio State Medical association since June, 1862, and has been United States pension examining surgeon since December, 1862.

M. R. GODFREY was born in Huron county, Ohio, August 3, 1842. His father, William A. Godfrey, was born in New York State; his mother was also a native of the same State. They raised three children: Zera, who lives in Michigan; Elizabeth, who lives in Huron county; and Michael R., the subject of this sketch. The latter enlisted in the Sixteenth Ohio volunteer infantry for the three months' service. In October, 1864, he was married to Miss Deloras Everet, and the day following his marriage he enlisted in the Twenty-ninth Ohio volunteer infantry, in which he served until the close of the war. To them have been born five children, as follows: Cora E., Ida May, William A., Charles and Mabel.

ALMER R. CAMPBELL was born May 19, 1853. His grandparents were of Scotch and Irish ancestry, and came from Pennsylvania to Ashland county, where his father, James Campbell, was born, May 19, 1828. His mother, Isabel Campbell, was born in the same county, and is now living in Bowling Green, Wood county, Ohio, his father having died February 9, 1875. They had five children, three of whom died in childhood. Laura E. is the wife of Titus Beck, of Bowling Green. Almer R., the subject of this sketch, received his education at Baldwin university, Berea, Ohio, after which he taught school until 1875, when he commenced reading law with his uncle, R. M. Campbell, esq., of Ashland, with whom he was a partner one year. In 1877 he was elected justice of the peace for Montgomery township, which office he held for three years.

BENJAMIN GROSSCUP, son of Paul and Rebecca Grosscup, was born in Westmoreland county, Pennsylvania, September 15, 1818. Benjamin's father was born in Berks county, Pennsylvania, in 1784, and his mother, whose maiden name was Rebecca Shearer, was born in Franklin county, Pennsylvania, in 1786, and died in 1859. They were married in 1810. Paul Grosscup removed to Milton township, Ashland county, Ohio, in 1830, with his family, consisting of five sons and two daughters, of whom two are now living—Benjamin and Daniel. Benjamin owned the farm in Milton township, which he helped to clear, until 1872, when he removed to Ashland. He was married in 1843 to Susannah Bowermaster, who was born October 14, 1821, and came to Milton township with her parents in 1842. Frederick Bowermaster, her father, was born in Lancaster county, Pennsylvania, in 1782, and was married to Catharine Mohler, of Cumberland county, Pennsylvania, who was born in 1782 and died in 1857. They raised a family of four children, one son and three daughters. Mr. Benjamin Grosscup has had four children: Lehman, who died; Peter S., born February 15, 1852; Frederick P., born April 5, 1854; Benjamin S., born October 14, 1858.

JACKSON S. WERTMAN was born March 13, 1845. His grandparents were from Columbia county, Pennsylvania, where his father, William Wertman, was born about 1817. In 1837 the family came to Ohio and settled in the present county of Ashland. His father came to Ashland about 1840, where he married Susannah Stahl, in 1844. She was a native of Harrisburgh, Pennsylvania, and was born about 1821. She died in 1859, after raising a family of four children: J. S., Z. T., E. P., and Virginia. The father was again married about 1862, to Keziah Culbertson, by whom he had two children, one of whom died in infancy. The surviving one, Ida L., is now living in Ashland county. J. S. Wertman, the subject of this sketch, completed his education in Wittenberg college in 1869. After leaving college he occupied himself with teaching for a time, and then engaged in surveying and engineering. In 1873 he commenced reading law at Indianapolis, Indiana, in the office of B. F. Davis. From thence he came to Ashland county, in 1877, where he has since practiced his profession. He was married to Sara Kilgore, of Indianapolis, June 16, 1875, and by her has had two children, of whom one died in infancy. The other, Shields K., was born May 9, 1877. The grandfather of J. S. Wertman, settled on the farm now owned by William Wertman, where our subject and his brothers and sisters were born.

JOHN DAMP was born in England, May 15, 1834. His father, James Damp, died in England; his mother died at Cuyahoga Falls, Ohio. They raised a family of six children, of whom Samuel lives at Olmsted Falls; William at Akron; Elizabeth at Olathe, Kansas; Edward at Olmsted Falls; and Joseph at Randolph, California. John Damp learned the trade of milling in England, where he served four years, and afterwards worked one year at the business. When twenty years of age he came to this country, and remained at Cuyahoga Falls from 1856 to 1865, when he removed to Ashland, where he has since resided, with the exception of three years, when he was engaged in milling at Mansfield. His mill at that place was destroyed by fire, and in the fall of 1869 he returned to Ashland. Since that time he has been engaged in milling at this place, with different partners, and has been associated with E. T. Drayton since 1877, under the firm name of Damp & Drayton. He was married February 20, 1861, to Fannie Palmer, of Cuyahoga Falls, by whom he has had five children. Three of the children died in infancy. Those now living are Albert Grant, born December 31, 1863, and Anna Bell, born October 6, 1874.

NELSON THOMAS was born June 6, 1831. His father was a native of Wales, where he was born about 1786; he died near Jeromeville, Ohio, in 1853. His mother, Anna Thomas, was born in New Jersey, about 1806. They had a family of five children, of whom Jane died in Kosciusko county, Indiana; Elizabeth, who married J. M. Hess, and lives in Cass county, Missouri; Amanda, who married Thomas Norris, and lives in Fulton county, Indiana; Sarah M., who married Joseph H. Page, and lives in Cass county, Missouri. Nelson Thomas, the subject of this sketch, was married when twenty-one years of age, to Sarah Keister, of Hayesville, Ohio. They have had six children, five of whom are living. One son, Franklin, died October 30, 1877, at the age of nineteen.

H. K. MYERS was born in Carroll county, Maryland, December 21, 1834. His father, John Myers, was a native of the same county, as was his mother, Hannah Myers, both of whom died in Ashland county, after raising a family of eight children, as follows: Eliza, David, Mary A., Israel, Sarah A., Lydia, Henry K. and Julia A. Henry K. Myers, the subject of this sketch, came to Ohio in the fall of 1839, with his parents and their family, and settled in Orange township, Ashland county. He remained at his father's for some years, working a part of the time in the saw-mill owned by his father. While there he was married to Anna Shoemaker, of Chester township, Wayne county, Ohio, by whom he has had five children, one of whom, Allen Gilbert, died in infancy. The others are John W., Mary E., David N. and Bertha B. Mr. Myers remained in Orange township until 1865, when he moved to Ashland and engaged in the lumber business. In 1874 he went into the milling business with partners, the firm name being H. K. Myers & Co. The partners were Christian Cabel and J. T. Engel. The partnership still continues, the lumber business being conducted under the firm name of Cabel, Myers & Co., the third partner being Jesse Cabel, son of Christian Cabel. Mr. Myers is also interested with J. J. Shoemaker in the grocery business in Ashland.

FRANK E. MYERS, son of George and Elizabeth Myers, was born March 16, 1848. His father was a native of Pennsylvania, whence he came with his parents when a youth, and settled on the homestead in Perry township, and his mother was born in Wayne county, Ohio. There they were married, and raised a family of nine children: Frank E., Celena, P. A., Mary M., Elizabeth S., Alvah N., George D., Minnie V., and Effie. Frank E. Myers, the subject of this sketch, lived at home working on the farm, and attending school during the winter months, until he arrived at maturity, when he left home and entered the dry goods store of M. B. Parmely, at Ashland, with whom he remained about a year, when he returned to the farm. He again came to Ashland and worked for the Ashland Machine company, where he continued four years, until 1875, when he opened a local agency for agricultural implements, and in 1879 associated with himself his brother, P. A. Myers, who had until then been employed by him. In 1878 the increasing demand of his business required him to move to the large building now occupied by himself and his brother. During all the time since 1875, he has been general traveling agent for Bucher, Gibbs & Co., of Canton, Ohio, for Ohio and the eastern States. January 18, 1872, he married Alvesta, daughter of S. Hohenshil, of Rowsburgh. They have had five children: Mamie E., George J., Charley, John C., and Laura E.

MEIGS S. CAMPBELL was born June 8, 1825, in Danville, Knox county, Ohio. His father, Silas Campbell, was a native of Virginia (now West Virginia), and his mother was born in Maryland. They raised four children—Meigs S., Thornton W., James M., and D. R. Meigs S. Campbell, the subject of this sketch, learned the hatter's trade, at Coshocton and Mt. Vernon, living in the latter place from 1846 to 1851, when he removed to Ashland. While living in Ashland he has been engaged in the livery business and the hat and cap trade, the most of his time being devoted to the latter, in which he is still engaged December 25, 1850, he was married to Clara Hall, of Mt. Vernon, Ohio, by whom he has had three children, as follows: W. Fletcher, born in 1851, married and living in Laramie City, Wyoming territory; Mary B., born about 1853, married Maurice Vallant, and lives in Cleveland; Clara, born about 1856, married Harry Stevens, and lives in Ashland.

E. T. DRAYTON was born at Canton, Ohio, September 30, 1825, his parents being Thomas A. Drayton, a native of Massachusetts, and Margaret Drayton, a native of Pennsylvania. They had six children, two of whom died in infancy. Those living are Elizabeth, Sarah Jane,

Amanda M., and E. T., the subject of this sketch, who came to Ashland in 1842. He spent three years in learning the harness trade, after which he was engaged in various mercantile pursuits until 1877, when the firm of Damp & Drayton was formed, for the purpose of carrying on the milling business, at which they still continue in Ashland. He was six years clerk of the county court, from 1862 to 1868, and was elected as a Republican in a county which is strongly Democratic. He has been twice married, his first wife being Sophia Sloan (daughter of Rev. John Sloan, of Orange township), by whom he had one child, Mary S., who lives at home in Ashland. His second wife was Emma Bean, niece of Judge Wick, of Greenville, Pennsylvania, to whom he was married June 5, 1860. He is a member of the Presbyterian church, and has been superintendent in the Sunday-school of that church for the past eight years. In politics he is a Republican.

DIEBOLD GUTH was born in Uhrweiler, Alsace, Germany, October 17, 1824. His father, Jacob Guth, a native of Alsace, came to the United States in 1849, and remained in New York until his death in 1875. His mother, Catharine Guth, was born in Alsace in 1810, and died there in 1829. Their children were Diebold and Margaret. After the death of his first wife, Mr. Guth was again married and had two children, Jacob and John. The latter is in the commission business in New York. Diebold Guth emigrated to the United States in 1841, and settled in Knox county, Ohio, where he remained until 1843, when he removed to Loudonville, Ashland county. In the fall of 1847 he returned to his native land, and in the fall of 1848 came back to this country, bringing with him his parents. In October, 1848, he was married in Mohicanville, to Margaret Wolf, also a native of Alsace. She died March 17, 1851, leaving one son, John Jacob, who was born December 24, 1850. Mr. Guth was again married in 1857, to Adeline Craig, who died without issue. For his third wife he married Augusta Long, February 10, 1870. She was born August 21, 1841, in Wurtemberg, Germany. By this union there were five children—Amelia J., born August 17, 1871, and died November 28, 1873; August Diebold, born February 18, 1873, died February 28, 1873; Henry W., born January 14, 1874; Frederick G., born May 20, 1875, died August 15, 1875; and Augusta M., born June 28, 1876. Mr. Guth is at present engaged in the grocery business in Ashland, in which he has been engaged since he removed from Loudonville in 1863.

THEO. TEEPLE was born November 29, 1835. His father, S. P. Teeple, was born in New York State and died in Iowa about 1840. His mother, Sarah Teeple, is also a native of New York State. After the death of her husband she was married to John Baker, and lives in Wooster, Ohio. To Mr. and Mrs. Teeple were born two children, Theo. and Ralph. Theo. Teeple, the subject of this sketch, was born in Pennsylvania. When young his parents removed to Iowa, where his father died in a few years. When about ten years of age his mother removed to Ohio. In 1862 Mr. Teeple was married to Jennie S. Bingham. They have had three children, one of whom died in infancy. Those who are living are J., born in 1863, and Albert, born about 1865. Mr. Teeple learned photography in 1861, and has since followed that business. In the fall of 1879 he removed to Ashland. Previous to that time he lived in Cincinnati from 1872 until 1876, and the remainder of the time until he removed to Ashland, was located at Wooster. He now has a photographic studio in both Wooster and Ashland.

J. A. HISEY, D. D. S., was born in 1849. His father and mother were natives of Columbiana county, in which his mother still lives. Their children were Wilson, Clara, Hannah, Cyrus, Sylvanus, Jonathan A., Leonard, Joseph, Charles, Kate and Milton. Jonathan A. Hisey, the subject of this sketch, commenced the study of dentistry in Columbiana, Ohio, in 1867. After completing his studies he commenced practice in that town, where he remained until 1873. March 12, 1869, he was married to Lucretia Hinkle, of the same town, and in 1873 removed to Ashland, where he opened a dental office, and has since been in continuous practice. They have three children—Walter H., born June 19, 1870; Austin E., born August 4, 1872; and Nora M., born September 17, 1874.

JOSEPH B. CHARLES was born in Ashland (then Richland) county, April 21, 1833. He lived on a farm until fifteen years of age, when he learned blacksmithing and edge-tool making. In the spring of 1853 he walked across the plains to California, and was there eight years. He returned from there in 1861 and volunteered in battery D, First regiment of Ohio Light artillery, in which he served three years. In 1864 he was promoted by the War Department from sergeant in his regiment, to captain in the First regiment of United States colored troops. In 1866 he was brevetted major of artillery, and was mustered out in April of the same year. He was married January 30, 1866, to Mary E. Stull, of Ashland, at that time being home on a furlough for thirty days, and, on his return was accompanied by his wife. Mrs. Charles returned to Ohio, leaving Chattanooga, Tennessee, March 5, 1866, and arrived at home three hours after the burial of her brother, of whose death she had not learned. From 1867 to 1871 he sold boots and shoes, and in April of the latter year he engaged in the hardware business, and has since been engaged in that and the shoe trade, associated with his father-in-law, Isaac Stull.

GEORGE A. ULLMAN was born at Loudonville, his parents being Adam and Barbara Ullman, both of whom were born in Alsace, Germany. Each came to the United States when about two years of age, and were married in Holmes county, Ohio. They raised a family of eight children, as follows: Caroline, who married Michael Scheff, and lives in Richland county; George A.; Minnie, who married W. S. Fisher, and lives in Loudonville; Maggie, who died about 1864; Mary, who married F. Arnold, and lives in Loudonville; Adam, Adolph, and Amanda, who also live at Loudonville. George A. Ullman clerked in his father's store in Loudonville until

August, 1878, when he took the office of county treasurer, to which he had been elected the fall previous. He was married to Anna Rebecca Merklinger, of Loudonville. In 1870 he became associated with his father in his store, in which he still retains an interest. He is the father of two children: Joseph A., born January 2, 1870, and Anna A. B., born September 9, 1874.

WILLIS L. EDWARDS was born June 27, 1843, near Bucyrus, Ohio, and at the early age of six months was adopted by Rev. William Hutchison, his mother dying July 3, 1843. His parents were Dr. L. M. Edwards, a native of Pennsylvania, who died near Kenton, Ohio, in 1876, and Susan Edwards, a native of Wales. They had a family of eight children, as follows: Wellington, Caroline, Rachel, Cortland, Valumnia, Adaline, Willie, and Willis B. Rev. William Hutchison went to Tennessee with his family in 1846, and remained until the spring of 1860, when they returned to Bucyrus. Mr. Edwards commenced learning the art of photography in 1861, and in 1862 he enlisted in the Eighty-sixth Ohio volunteer infantry, in which he served four months. He then returned and again commenced the work of photography, which he has since followed. He worked one year at Mansfield, and in 1864 came to Ashland as operator for Budtorf & McCormick. From 1864 until 1870 he followed this art in Ravenna, Wooster and Mt. Vernon, and in the latter year opened a studio in Ashland, where he has since remained. In the fall of 1864 he was married to Mary J. Sauer, of Ashland, by whom he had three children—Ida May, born in September, 1865; Charles F., born in September, 1867; and Milton L., born in September, 1869. Mrs. Edwards died August 25, 1873, and two years later he was married to Mrs. Mary A. Heifner, of Ashland county.

FRANK MONEYSMITH was born in Auburn, Indiana, in July, 1852. When a child his parents removed to Perrysville, Ashland county, where he was raised. His father, William H. Moneysmith, was a native of Pennsylvania, and died in Michigan in 1858. His mother, E. J. Moneysmith, was born in this State. She was the mother of four children—Cordelia, who married H. Ridgeley, and lives in Ashland; Dora, who married A. B. Comins, and lives in Mt. Gilead; W. H., who lives in Kansas; and Frank, the subject of this sketch. When a youth he attended the Vermillion institute, from 1865 to 1868, and in the latter year he came to Ashland, where he learned the cigar business, at which he worked until 1875, when he went west. He returned early in 1880, and is now engaged in the cigar business in Ashland.

MRS. KATE OTTA was the daughter of John and Barbara Mecael, natives of Germany, where he died, leaving two children: John, who still resides there, and Catharine, the subject of this sketch, who was born in Germany, February 26, 1823. Some time after the death of her husband, Mrs. Barbara Mecael was a second time married, to Nicholas Knoth, by whom she had three children: Charles, Frank, and Henry. Catharine Mecael was married January 22, 1846, to John Haelbrond, and in 1847 came to this country, locating in Ashland. By this union were born six children, one of whom, a girl, died in infancy. The others were John, born September 8, 1847, who lives in Ashland; Charles, born July 17, 1849, who also lives in Ashland; Jacob, born April 23, 1852, who lives in Fremont; Frank P., born August 1, 1854, who lives in Wyoming territory; Clara Catharine, born November 28, 1856, and died January 13, 1859; A. Cordelia, born November 2, 1860. Mr. Haelbrond died August 17, 1860. His widow was married October 22, 1862, to Frederick Otta, a native of Prussia. They have one child, Daniel William, born February 27, 1863, who lives at home in Ashland. Mr. Otta died January 17, 1874. He had been engaged in the brewery business until within some four years of his death, when he disposed of his brewery on account of ill health. After his death Mrs. Otta opened a restaurant and boarding house on Third street, where she still remains.

S. W. BLACK, son of S. M. and Rosanna Black, was born in Green township, Ashland county, Ohio, March 3, 1834. His parents were natives of Pennsylvania, and had the following children born to them: Catharine, who married Samuel Conkle, and died about 1865; Elizabeth, who married Sylvester Huff, and lives in Indiana; P. J., who lives in Loudonville, Ohio; John, who lives in Burgoon, Ohio; Sarah, who married Henry Snyder, and lives in Ashland, Ohio; S. W., the subject of this sketch; Henry and Joseph, who live in Iowa; William, who died in Missouri in 1878; Daniel; and Lewis, who lives in Ashland county. Mr. Black, sr., is now living in Green township, Ashland county, his wife having died about 1855. S. W. Black lived at home until the age of seventeen, when he went to Loudonville to learn the bakery and confectionery business with his brother, P. J. After finishing his apprenticeship he worked at his trade in various places for three years, and in the fall of 1856 returned to Loudonville, where he worked for his brother for several months, when he bought him out and continued there in business for about four years. Mr. Black went to Ashland in the fall of 1861, remained there three years, and returned to Loudonville, where he stayed one year. In 1866 he again removed to Ashland and opened a bakery and confectionery store, in which business he is now engaged. In 1857 Mr. Black was married to Caroline Ullman, of Loudonville, by whom he has had two children—Henry, born February 15, 1858, and James A., born July 17, 1867.

GUTELIUS I. YERICK was born in Mifflinburgh, Pennsylvania, August 11, 1834. When a small child he removed with his parents to the eastern part of Ashland county, then a part of Wayne county, Ohio, and when seven years of age went to live with Jacob Berry, on whose farm he worked for two years, and afterwards resided with Samuel Landis, doing farm work for about the same length of time, and for John Russell one year. At the age of twelve years he was apprenticed to John Goodwin, to learn the wood turning and painting business, serving two and one-half years, when he removed to Ashland and worked at his trade about three years. About the year 1852 he went to western Ohio and Indiana, where he continued to work at his trade until the spring of 1855, when he returned to Ashland and engaged in the furniture business, which he carried on until the spring of 1860, when he sold his interest in the business to J. B. Stubbs. From 1860 to 1869 he was engaged in the real estate and collection business, and in the latter year was elected treasurer of Ashland county, in which office he served four years, when he again resumed the real estate and collection business. In 1874 he bought out the interest in the livery stable of Peter Fitzgar, of the firm of Thomas & Fitzgar, but gives his chief attention to the real estate and collection business, Mr. Thomas conducting the livery business. Mr. Yerick's father, Peter Yerick, was born in Pennsylvania, in 1796, and his mother, Catharine Yerick, was born in Mifflinburgh, Pennsylvania; both are still living. They had the following children born to them: Elvina, who married John Goodwin, and lives in Findlay, Ohio; Henry E., who lives in Washington, Iowa; Elizabeth, who married John Shott, and lives in Wayne county, Ohio; Gutelius I.; Caroline, who lives in Toledo, Ohio; Rebecca, who died when about sixteen years of age; Catharine, who married John Switzer, and is a widow, living in Iowa City; Samuel W., who lives in Burlington, Iowa; Mary Ann, who married John Lane, and lives in Crete, Nebraska; F. E., also in Crete, Nebraska; John, who lives at Atlantic, Iowa; Joseph, who lives at Toledo, Ohio; and Simon, who lives in Nebraska.

LIZZIE WEISENSTINE was born in Germany March 31, 1837, and came to this country with her mother when seventeen years old, and located at Mansfield, Ohio, where she lived until the age of twenty, when she was married to Jacob Weisenstine, of Ashland, where she then removed. Mrs. Weisenstine had the following children by this marriage: Lizzie, born March 30, 1859, and died January 9, 1862; Mary, born August 23, 1861, married E. W. Rogers, and lives in Missouri; Jacob E., born October 28, 1863, and died August 29, 1865; Joseph F., born October 15, 1865; Louise, born September 24, 1869; and Frank S., born June 27, 1873. Mrs. Weisenstine's parents, Jacob and Clara Houtz, were natives of Otterberg, Rhine Phaltz, Germany; her father died in Germany, and her mother died in Mansfield, Ohio, in 1878. Mr. and Mrs. Houtz had children as follows: Frank, who died in Germany in 1877; Jacob, who lives in Mt. Vernon, Ohio; Catharine, who married David Miller, of Mansfield; Charlotte, who married Jacob Wentz, and lives in Mansfield; Louise, who married Philip Lawrence; and Lizzie.

Jacob Weisenstine was born in Wertemberg, Germany, June 12, 1833, and came to this country in 1853, stopping in New York. The following year he came to Ashland, and worked at his trade of shoe-making for Stubbs and Wasson for several years. In 1858 he married Miss Lizzie Houtz. Mr. Weisentine was engaged in the shoe, grocery, and restaurant business for some time previous to his death, which occurred January 8, 1876. Mrs. Weisenstine now carries on the business.

BENJAMIN MYERS was born in Perry township, December 21, 1841, and is the son of Jacob and Mary Myers, natives of Pennsylvania. His father was born in Center county, of that State, May 25, 1788, and died in Ashland county, Ohio, August 4, 1857. His mother was born in the same county as his father, and died in Perry township, Ashland county, September 12, 1878. His brothers are Jonathan, George, Jacob, and Daniel, all residents of Perry township, except Jacob, who resides in Kansas; his sisters are Margaret, Eliza, Mary, and Catharine, all living in this county, except Mary, who is deceased. Benjamin Myers resided with his father in Perry township until 1860, doing farm work in the summer time and attending district school in the winter time. In 1861-62 he attended the Vermillion institute at Hayesville, but, in 1862, offered his services in defence of his country, enlisting in company F, One Hundred and Twentieth Ohio volunteer infantry. In July, 1865, he returned home from the war and resumed his studies at the institute. In 1866 he began the study of medicine at Wooster, Ohio, in the office of Drs. Robinson & Weaver. In 1867 he attended upon a course of medical instruction in the Jefferson Medical college of Philadelphia, graduating from that college in 1869. In June of the same year he formed a partnership with Dr. J. P. Cowan, and began the practice of medicine at Ashland, Ohio. November 29, 1879, he was united in marriage with Samantha Cowan, his partner's daughter. His children are: Rena M., born November 19, 1871, and Emma C., born September 14, 1873. Mrs. Myers died November 21, 1878. In 1873 Mr. Myers was elected to the Ohio legislature, and re-elected in 1875, serving in all four years.

LEO WERTMAN, son of Simon and Abagail Wertman, from Columbia county, Pennsylvania, was born August 7, 1829, at the old homestead in Pennsylvania. He removed with his father's family to Ohio, and settled in the present county of Ashland, in the spring of 1839. Here he remained on his father's farm, comprising one hundred and fifty-nine acres, most of the time until eighteen years of age, when he started to learn the trade of cabinet-maker with Stubbs & Coffin, of Ashland. He completed his trade, and for some time carried on the business, when in the year 1859 he changed his business to the pursuits of agriculture, purchasing one hundred and five acres of the original tract purchased by his father. Here he has remained, continuing to improve and add to, until it can be said that he has one of the finest improved farms of Ashland county. Mr. Wertman was united in marriage in the year 1852 to Allada S. Simonton, daughter of Henry Simonton, of Pennsylvania. To this union were born two children, both of whom are living, viz: Abbie Belle and Simon Henry. Mrs. Wertman died in the spring of 1859. Mr. Wertman chose for his second partner Mary Ann, daughter of Henry Walburn, from Maryland. To them was born one child, viz: George Richard, now residing with his parents. In politics Mr. Wertman is a Democrat, casting his first presidential vote for Franklin Pierce.

BYRON M. SWINEFORD was born in this township (Montgomery), this county, March 6, 1850, and this county has always been his home. His vocation through life has been that of a salesman in different stores, and he has been engaged in the furniture business, as also the bed spring bottom business. He has also paid some attention to farming, in which business he is now engaged in. He was married April 8, 1878, to Miss Libbie Gates, who was also born in this county, August 27, 1856. They have one child, named Susie May, who was born May 3, 1880. She is still living.

ISAAC KILHEFNER was born in Lancaster county, Pennsylvania, January 28, 1850, he being one of eleven children of Henry Kilhefner. In the year 1854, his parents, with their family of then three children, moved from Lancaster county, Pennsylvania, to Ashland county, Ohio. They bought a small farm four miles east of Ashland, moved upon it, and lived there some twenty odd years. During this time Isaac remained with his parents upon the farm. In the winter of 1870 he was married to Miss Amanda Kahl. In the following spring (1871,) he moved upon the farm of Mr. Samuel Horn, taking charge of it. In the year 1872 he united with the German Baptist (or Dunkard) church. In the year 1875 he was elected to the ministry by the church, and in the year 1877 was duly licensed as a minister of the Gospel. He is the father of one child: Edwin L. Kilhefner.

J. P. DEVOR was born January 15, 1822, near Roxbury, Franklin county, Pennsylvania, and was married to Mary A. Hassler, near Grindstone Hill, same county and State, February 1, 1849, and removed to Ashland, Ohio, April 25, 1849, where they have since resided. To them have been born ten children—seven are still living. Their names are Charles A., Alice A., John R., Jacob P., jr., Horace L., Mary A., William J., Edgar J., Harry H. and Samuel H. The last named, Samuel H., died at the age of fifteen years, five months and seven days, of typhoid fever, a bright and intelligent boy. The other two died young. John, at the age of two and one-half years, of scarlet fever; the other thirty-three days old, of cholera infantum. Mr. Devor is of Scotch-Irish descent. In the fall of 1856 he was elected justice of the peace, and continued in said office by re-election for three terms. By profession he is an attorney at law, and by applying himself strictly to his profession he has built up for himself a large practice.

JOSHUA L. DEVOR was born in Plymouth, Indiana, July 14, 1859. When he was four years of age he removed with his mother to Ashland county, Ohio, which has since been his home. His father died in the army during the war of the Rebellion. Mr. Devor was married May 22, 1879, to Miss Leanette Rowland, a native of Ashland county, having been born in Montgomery township July 30, 1860. Mr. Devor, though he has had a brief experience as a school teacher, has given his chief attention to farming, in which pursuit he has been very successful.

EPHRAIM SLOCUM was born in Stillwater, Livingston county, New York, March 19, 1818, and was brought to Ohio by his parents the year of his birth. They settled a mile and a half east of Ashland, where Mr. Slocum now lives. His education was limited to the subscription schools of the day, and two winters in the district schools of New York. When twelve years of age he went to the mouth of Black river and there clerked two years, when he returned to his home. Soon after he went to Onondaga county, New York, where he also remained two years. On his return from Buffalo to Cleveland the vessel on which he sailed narrowly escaped wrecking, and was obliged to return to port. Another start was made, and after rough sailing for a day and a half they arrived at Cleveland. From that point he walked the entire distance to Ashland, through an almost unbroken forest. In 1837 he went with a team to Illinois, and down the river from Peoria to Danville, Kentucky, in a boat, from which point he walked to his home. May 14, 1840, he was married to Eliza Freer, by whom he had nine children—E. W., Harriet, Melissa, Annice, Albert, Ida, Emma, Alfred and Fred. Mrs. Slocum died November 4, 1855. August 20, 1856, he was again married to Martha P. Carter. Mr. Slocum and his brother Eli bought the homestead several years before the death of their father. Ephraim still retains his purchase, but Eli sold his some years since.

CAPTAIN EMANUEL FINGER was born in Orange township, Ashland county, November 6, 1834. He has served as auditor of the county two terms, in addition to six months to which he was appointed by the county commissioners. At the present time he is the commanding officer of company C, in the Seventeenth regiment of Ohio National Guards, of Ashland, which, under the drill of himself and the junior officers of the company, has reached a high degree of proficiency. The following is a list of the officers and members of company C: captain, Emanuel Finger; first lieutenant, John Vantilburg; second lieutenant, William Drumheller; sergeants, William H. Ambrose, Peter Bechtel, Allen Thomas, J. P. Kosht, M. L. Wiest; corporals, Frank Whitmore, John McCombs, Reuben Davis, Ralph Smith, J. W. Brown, George Urie, Martin Grindle; privates, George Brown, Edward Campbell, Daniel Buchler, Collins Bushnell, Charles Cook, George Downs, Lewis Drum, Henry Edy, William Fullington, William Gribbins, E. J. Hard, George Horn, Parvin Kosht, Charles Knapp, W. A. Lockart, Wesley Miller, Milton Miller, Lyman Marietta, D. A. Phillips, J. M. Pry, Hiram Sloan, C. C. Saner, Charles Smalley, Lewis Satler, William Whitmore, Matthew Williams, Ed. Widgeon, Elmer Woods, Eli Stark, D. S. Youngblood.

JAMES FERGUSON was born in Beaver county, Pennsylvania, June 31, 1830. In 1867 he removed to Ashland county, where he now resides. He has three children—Ruth, James, and William P. His first wife, and the mother of his children, died and he has been a second time married.

JESSE WERTMAN was born in Columbia county, Pennsylvania, May 18, 1810, and there lived until 1838, when he came to this county. He was married December 19, 1833, to Ann Pursell, who was a native of the same county, where she was born June 30, 1810. To them have been born twelve children, two of whom died in infancy. Those living are Charles N., William F., Mary E., Maria C., Daniel, Harriet, Jacob, Sarah M.,

John and Simon. Mr. Wertman has devoted his life to agricultural pursuits.

WILLIAM WERTMAN was born in Columbia county, Pennsylvania, May 28, 1815. In 1837 he came to Ohio and remained in Stark county one year, after which he removed to this county, where he has since resided. By trade he is a saddle and harness maker, which business he followed for many years, but of late has devoted his time to his farm in Clearcreek township. He was married in October, 1845, to Susannah Stott, by whom he had four children: Jackson S., Zacharay T., Eugene T. and Sarah V. Mrs. Wertman died in 1860, aged about forty-five years. He was a second time married, November 24, 1862, to Keziah Culbertson, who has borne two children: Ida L. and Arthur J. The latter died March 29, 1865.

BENJAMIN STAMAN came from Lancaster county, Pennsylvania, to Ohio, in about 1827. In 1830 he was married to Anna Kauffman, who came with her parents from the same county at about the same time. She was the daughter of Dr. John Kauffman, who was a physician of good reputation, both in Pennsylvania and after his settlement in this State. To Mr. and Mrs. Staman were born five children, two of whom died in infancy and childhood, and one, Jacob B., died when twenty years of age. The two now living are John K. and Christian C. Mr. Staman built a saw-mill on his property, which has since been several times repaired and added to, and is yet in use. His wife died in 1877, and he now lives with his son John K. After he had been here some time he bought a portion of the Zimmer or Seymour place, which he still retains. John K. Staman, his son, was born March 8, 1833, and was married February 25, 1869, to Elizabeth A. Grabill. They have had five children: Anna E., Clara B., Cyrus B. (who died when seven months of age), Willard and Frank. Christian C. Staman was born June 25, 1838, and was married in 1862 to Elizabeth Croninger. They have had two children, Nettie and Huldah. The latter died in infancy. Both John K. and C. C. Staman have fine collections of Indian antiquities and geological specimens.

JACOB WERTMAN, of Clearcreek township, died on November 26, 1873, aged seventy-six. Mary Wertman, his wife, died July 11, 1865, aged about sixty-five. Their sons, Jesse and William, live on the old homestead, and Enoch in Milton township. They are all farmers by occupation, and influential men in the county.

GEORGE FAST was born in Fayette county, Pennsylvania, June 4, 1807. He removed with his parents, Christian and Barbara Fast, to Orange township, then Richland, but now in Ashland county, in the spring of 1815, and has remained upon the homestead then entered and purchased for his father ever since, and has always been a hard working farmer. Upon reaching manhood, he married Miss Sarah Brink, who was born December 12, 1807, and deceased in 1875, aged about sixty-eight years. By this union there were ten children, of whom Nancy A., Jonathan M., Hannah J., Delia, George W. and William survive. In October, 1877, he married Hannah Rubenau. Mr. Fast has resided on the homestead about sixty-five years, and is one of the oldest pioneers in the township. He has always been a plain farmer, and possess a valuable property. He is yet vigorous in mind and body. He was the eleventh child of the late Christian Fast, the old captive, who formerly lived with the Delaware Indians, and of whom mention is made elsewhere in this volume.

SUSANNAH C. HOFFMAN was born on the thirteenth of March, 1815, in Jefferson county, Ohio, and died August 24, 1880, in Ashland, Ohio. At the time of her birth her father was clearing up the farm now occupied by Edward Wallace in Clearcreek township, whither the family soon moved. She spent her entire life of over sixty-five years in this immediate vicinity. When about twenty years of age she united with the Methodist Episcopal church, which then worshipped in the old stone house on Court square. Her life has been one of quiet, intelligent, consistent piety. Infirmity, resulting from disease more than age, has kept her closely at home for some years. But she has been cheerful, though much alone and often afflicted.

MRS. NANCY SHEETS, whose name before marriage was Nancy Harper, was born in Fairfax county, Virginia, June 12, 1796. Her parents emigrated to Jefferson county, Ohio, in the summer of 1812. While residing there in November, 1814, she married Mr. Joseph Sheets, and removed to Uniontown, now Ashland, in November, 1817, where she has resided almost continuously ever since. It was then a mere village, and had but three families residing in it. These were the families of William Montgomery, David Markley and John Croft. Mr. Markley owned a small stock of goods, Mr. Montgomery had a small tavern, and Mr. Croft a small tannery where Whiting & Shearer's manufactory now stands. Its population did not exceed one dozen. Since that time great changes have taken place, as this was sixty-three years ago. The human mind can hardly comprehend it. Yesterday, a wilderness full of wild animals and red men, now the Indian has gone, and luxuriant fields occupy his place in the forest. Mrs. Sheets lived through the administration of seventeen presidents, from Washington to Hayes. At her birth we had thirteen States in the Union, and a population of three and a half millions; now we have thirty-seven States and a population of fifty millions in this great republic. Its internal improvements: canals, railroads, pikes, telegraphs, and the like, fill the land. The red man that often visited our village then, now finds a home in the far west; well cultivated fields are now found where the native forest then was. Ashland, with slight variations, is what the pioneers have made it, and will continue through the generations to come, until, by some catastrophe, chaos and the wilderness shall return again. These things attracted the attention of Mrs. Sheets during her lifetime, and she often recapitulated them in her clear way. She often dwelt upon the times of the pioneers and their hardships, and seemed to take a deep interest in the welfare of their posterity.

She possessed a clear mind to the last. On the afternoon of June 12, 1880, her eighty-fourth birthday, many of her old neighbors assembled at the residence of Mr. Samuel Sheets and congratulated her upon her great age and fine health. Fears were expressed that it would be the last meeting of many of her aged friends. The party proved to be a very cheerful assemblage, and was very gratifying to the old lady. She again met the pioneers at their meeting August 19th, and was in her usually cheerful temper. It was not then supposed that she would never meet with the society again, but in less than a week she was borne to her grave. She died after a brief illness at the residence of her son, Mr. Samuel Sheets, in Ashland, August 26, 1880, aged eighty-four years, two months and fourteen days.

Mrs. Sheets was a Christian lady. She had many friends among the pioneers. She had been a member of the Presbyterian church since 1816, and lived an exemplary life. Her funeral was preached by Rev. John Robinson, D. D., assisted by Rev. Mr. Persons. The members of her family were: Elizabeth, Joseph, William, Maria, Martha, Alfred, Samuel, Mary and Sarah; all living but Joseph and Alfred, who died young.

Peace to her ashes.

D. B. GRAY was born in Columbia county, Pennsylvania, July 9, 1813. In 1847 he came to Ohio and settled in Ashland, from which point he run a stage line to Mansfield, Wooster, Oberlin, New London, and Shelby, for some twenty years, during the same time conducting a livery business at Ashland, at which he is still engaged. He was married in 1849 to Catharine Stentz, of Ashland county, and has raised a family of seven children, all of whom are living. They are Mary, Hattie, Nellie, Jennie, Will, Burr, and Addison. Two are married—Hattie, who lives in Texas, and Mary, who lives in Illinois. Will is a telegraph operator.

MICHAEL MILLER was born in Alsace, France, September 18, 1818, and came to this country in 1840, locating at Wooster, where he remained until 1846, when he came to Ashland. For several years he followed the bakery and confectionery business, and in 1853 built the hotel known as the "Miller House" in Ashland, over which he has since presided, with the exception of one year. In 1873 he was elected treasurer of Ashland county, and held that office two terms. March 20, 1845, he was married. His wife, Mrs. Susan Miller, was born in York county, Pennsylvania, August 10, 1825. They have raised a family of four children, Hulbert, Charles, Snyder, and Delia. Hulbert was a soldier in the regular army three years, and during that time contracted rheumatism and was discharged. He never recovered his health, and died from this disease. Charles is also deceased.

DON F. TAYLOR, son of Judge John Taylor, was born July 6, 1849, in Green township, Ashland county. He obtained an education at Greentown academy, and read law in 1873 with Andrew Stevenson of Mansfield, completing his studies with R. M. Campbell, of Ashland. In 1875 he was admitted to the bar in Henry county, and soon after formed a partnership with Mr. Campbell, which continued about one year. At the time he was admitted to the bar he was a candidate before the county convention for the office of prosecuting attorney, but did not secure the nomination. At the termination of his partnership with Mr. Campbell he went to Perrysville, where he had an office for a short time, but his father being elected probate judge of the county, he returned to Ashland and became probate clerk, which position he now fills. He was married to Normanda F. Robinson, and has a family of three children—May Belle, Don R., and an infant.

ROBERT W. SMITH was born near Sudbury, Vermont, December 1, 1799, and went with his parents, Elisha and Amy Smith, first to the State of New York, and afterward moved to Ohio about 1817 or 1818, first settling on the farm of Major Tyler in what is now Plain township Wayne county, Ohio.

Elisha and Amy Smith were natives of the State of Massachusetts, and Asa Smith, father of Elisha, was in the French war and Revolution, at the battle of Bunker Hill, etc.

Robert W. was the oldest son of a family of eleven children, and the first winter, on coming to Ohio, his father being sick, and unable to do anything, the care of the family and all the heavy labor fell upon him. During the first fall and winter he and his brother, Asa, a lad of fourteen, cut off, cleared and fenced twenty acres of heavily timbered land, and also with a few neighbors' help, built and covered a double log barn. About this time Elisha, his father, entered a quarter section in Mohican township, Ashland county, Ohio, some three miles from their home, and all extra time was improved to first build a hut where the men could cook and sleep while clearing, and building a cabin for the family to move into a few years later. This was the homestead to which the family moved, and where Elisha and Amy Smith lived and died; the first in January, in 1851, and the second in August, 1856.

Elisha Smith, father of Robert W., was born February 18, 1773, and Amy Smith, his mother, was born April 7, 1778. They had the following children: Mary, born March 4, 1796; Electa, born January 17, 1798; Robert W., born December 1, 1799; Rachel, born October 29, 1801; Asa, born September 21, 1803; Hervey, born August 17, 1805; William R., born July 14, 1807; Willard, born May 11, 1809; Daniel P., born May 19, 1811; Elisha F., born February 19, 1815, and Daton, born May 31, 1817.

Robert W. Smith was married to Priscilla Hatch about January, 1823. She was a native of New York, born March 25, 1799, and died March 3, 1837. The family consisted of eight children: Wilbur R., Julia A., Elisha, Adelia, Lydia, Asa, Edmund P., and Harriet Smith, all deceased, save Edmund P. Robert W. Smith's life was full of the hardships, privations and dangers of pioneer life. At one time returning late to his hut with provisions, and night overtaking him, he was chased a long distance by a pack of hungry wolves, and only escaped by throwing a ham of fresh pork to them as he sprang into the hut which was opened and quickly closed by a comrade inside. He was full of energy, and amongst his first successful enterprises, was buying cattle and oxen, and driving them to Detroit, Michigan, to sell, passing through "Black Swamp" where there were twenty miles without a habitation, and often compelled to return to his starting point at night for accommodations for himself and horse. In later years his son, Edmund P., often accompanied him to Michigan to buy cattle to bring home to graze and fatten on his farms. He bought horses, and travelled them to New York city to sell, and sold dry goods in the town of Mohicanville. The latter business proved very unprofitable, but he died worth a handsome competence, leaving a name of stainless integrity to community, and a sacred memory of unfailing tenderness and affection for his family and friends. He died July 16, 1862. About 1844 he married a worthy and estimable lady, Mrs. Isabella Cliffe, a native of Scotland, who still survives at the ripe age of eighty years. She passes her declining years with her son, Dr. D. B. Cliffe, of Franklin, Tennessee, a very prominent physician, and noted during the civil war for his unwavering devotion to the Union.

JUDGE TULLY C. BUSHNELL was born in Vermillion township, Ashland county, May 5, 1826. His grandfather, Sterling G. Bushnell, was one of the early pioneers of this county; a sketch of his life will be found in another part of this work. His father, Collins Bushnell, lived in Vermillion township during his life. In 1832 or 1833 business called him to New Orleans, where the cholera was raging; he was attacked by the disease, and died at Fort Adams on his return trip. Collins Bushnell left a widow, Eliza Potts Bushnell, who afterward married Mr. Janette Purdy, and died in 1842. She was the mother of three children by her first husband: Tully C., Sterling G., and Collins W.

Judge Tully C. Bushnell obtained an education at the old Ashland academy, under the instruction of Lorin Andrews, and before reaching his majority in 1846, engaged in the mercantile business, which he followed until the breaking out of the war. In August, 1861, he entered the service as captain of company C, Forty-second Ohio volunteer infantry, General Garfield's regiment. He was also largely instrumental in recruiting company H of the same regiment. He was in the service fifteen months, and in the Cumberland Gap campaign planted the first flag on the enemy's works. He was in several engagements, and was specially mentioned by the commanding general, George W. Morgan, for gallant conduct in resisting the attack of General Stevenson's division for two hours, with but forty men under his command. On account of disability he was discharged from the service, and returned to his home in Ashland, where he was confined to the house for nine months. After his recovery he entered the quartermaster's department at Nashville, as chief clerk, and remained at that post some six months. In November, 1866, he was appointed by Governor Cox to fill the unexpired term of Judge Ingmand, as probate judge of the county, and was afterwards elected to fill the balance of the short term, and one full term of three years, on the Republican ticket, in a strong Democratic county. Since the expiration of his term in the probate office he has been engaged in mercantile pursuits and the produce business, and at present, attends to the wool trade. He was married January 4, 1848, to Nancy C. Willson, and has raised a family of five children—one son and four daughters. The eldest, Allie W., married S. D. Willson; Frank T. C. married Miss Ollie Corbus; Garie married Daniel Smith; Emma Grace and Nettie Maud remain at home.

CHARLES HOY, SR., was a native of Washington county, Pennsylvania, and settled in Stark county, Ohio, some time prior to the war of 1812, in which he served as a soldier three months. In May, 1817, he came to Jackson township, then in Wayne county, in company with John Mason, and located on section two, in the forest. His family consisted of his wife and son Joseph, then a child, now of New Orleans, Louisiana. The first settlers in the township who had preceded him were: Isaac Lyons, John Jackson, Daniel and John Davault, and Noah Long, with their families. Of these, Noah Long is believed to have located as early as 1816. These pioneers are all deceased. In 1819 Mr. Hoy purchased a quarter in section twenty-seven, upon which he raised a cabin. It was built in the winter and had at first a ground floor, and was not daubed with clay. A tent was put up within the building to protect Mrs. Hoy and the children from the cold. Mr. Hoy felled a large tree out of which he split and prepared puncheons for a floor. Mrs. Hoy assisted him in conveying them to their place in the cabin. These were hard times, yet Mr. Hoy often stated that they were the most agreeable of his life. The settlers for many miles around willingly assisted each other in raising cabins, rolling logs, and clearing fields for culture. At this time the forests abounded in game of every kind, and the Delaware and Wyandot Indians often camped and hunted all around him. They were, at that time, a harmless people, and never disturbed him or his property; in fact were honest and trusty as neighbors. Mr. Hoy was a full cousin of Adam and Andrew Poe, and was a stout, vigorous man. His weight was about two hundred pounds, and his height about six feet; hence, he feared no man, red or white, in a personal contest, though always noted as a man of peace. In 1821 he was elected a justice of the peace, but declined to serve, not desiring to fill any office, though eminently qualified. He was ambitious only to be a successful farmer. He cleared and improved his fine homestead and engaged largely in improving and raising fine stock, at which he was very successful. His home farm was valuable and handsomely located, and the toil thus spent on it rendered him comfortable and independent as old age approached. In the fall of 1867 he visited friends in the State of Illinois, and while there he became suddenly ill, and deceased aged seventy-eight years. His remains were brought to Ashland and deposited in the cemetery, where they now repose. His family consisted of Joseph, of New Orleans; Charles, of Coshocton; Dawson, of Jackson township; Mrs. E. P. Smith, of Ashland, and Mrs. Rachel, wife of Rev. Lyons. Mrs.

Mary Hoy survived until August, 1871, when she died aged seventy-seven years, and was buried in the cemetery at Ashland, beside her esteemed husband.

DANIEL FOLK, the subject of this sketch, was born in Crawford county, Ohio, March 6, 1845. When about ten years old, his parents removed to this (Ashland) county, where he has since resided. He was married February 20, 1866, to Miss Virginia I., daughter of Captain W. A. G. Emerson, of whom mention is made elsewhere in this work. Mr. Folk's occupation is that of saddle and harness making, having been engaged at that business for the past fourteen or fifteen years, and he is considered by all to be a very proficient workman in all the different branches pertaining to the trade. For the past few years he has been foreman for the firm of J. W. Davis, at Ashland.

JACOB P. COWAN, M. D., was born of Scotch-Irish parents, in the village of Florence, Washington county, Pennsylvania, March 20, 1823. He attended the schools of that place until thirteen years of age, when he removed with his parents to Steubenville, Ohio, in 1835, and was engaged in manufacturing until 1843, when he commenced the study of medicine and removed to Jeromeville, Ashland county, Ohio, in 1846, and engaged in the practice of his profession; attended lectures and graduated at Starling Medical college, in Columbus; was elected a member of the State legislature in 1855, and re-elected in 1857. At the expiration of his term in 1859, he removed to Ashland and engaged in the practice of his profession. In 1874 he was nominated and elected to Congress from the Fourteenth district, composed of the counties of Ashland, Holmes, Richland, Wyandot, and Crawford. While a member, he served on several standing committees and was chairman of the committee on militia. The doctor was married in June, 1846, to Miss Mary J. Hooker, of West Virginia. He has had, by this union, nine children: Randolph and Darwin S.; Dr. Frank, of Jeromeville; Samantha (Mrs. Dr. Benjamin Myers), William F.; Lucy and Edgar; Harry and Emma. Of these, Mrs. Myers, Harry and Emma, Randolph and Darwin Stanton, are deceased. In political opinion the doctor is a Democrat. At present he is the senior member of the medical firm of Cowan & Myers, of Ashland, Ohio.

LIST OF SUBSCRIBERS FOR DR. HILL'S HISTORY OF ASHLAND COUNTY.

MONTGOMERY TOWNSHIP.

1. J. O. Jennings,
2. Joseph Patterson,
3. J. D. Jones,
4. E. J. Grosscup.
5. G. A. Ullman,
6. John Taylor,
7. W. T. Alberson,
8. J. Crall,
9. H. K. Myers,
10. P. S. Grosscup.
11. Wallack & Frazee,
12. Stull & Charles,
13. W. H. Gates,
14. P. H. Clark,
15. S. G. Weist,
16. M. Miller,
17. J. P. Cowan,
18. R. C. Kinnaman,
19. S. W. Beer,
20. E. T. Drayton,
21. Joseph E. Stubbs,
22. George B. Smith,
23. J. S. Wertman,
24. D. Guth,
25. Thomas S. Hunter,
26. G. W. Urie,
27. D. W. Whitmore,
28. L. Jeff. Sprengle,
29. Ephraim Slocum,
30. J. W. Smith,
31. Thomas & Yearick,
32. W. Slocum,
33. H. J. Pille,
34. J. A. Hisey,
35. M. S. Campbell,
36. John Damp,
37. M. R. Godfrey,
38. John Keller,
39. B. Emmens,
40. S. Z. Sharp,
41. P. R. Roseberry,
42. William Sheets,
43. A. R. Campbell,
44. F. E. Myers,
45. Daniel Wertman,
46. Emanuel Swineford,
47. David Carter,
48. M. Mowrey,
49. Frank Knoth,
50. George Saal,
51. John Shapperd,
52. N. M. Swearingen,
53. A. L. Sherick, M. D.
54. H. P. Nelson, M. D.
55. J. Brubaker.
56. J. P. Devor,
57. John Swineford,
58. Prof. J. E. Roup, M.D
59. Samuel Sheets,
60. Isaac & R. H. Gates,
61. T. C. Bushnell,
62. I. N. McElvain,
63. Eli Slocum,
64. A. O. Long,
65. T. M. Beer,
66. S. L. Arnold,
67. W. C. Moore,
68. Thomas J. Kenney,
69. E. Weisenstein,
70. S. W. Black,
71. George Dougherty,
72. Herman M. Rieser,
73. W. T. Heltman,
74. Catharine Otta,
75. Benjamin Myers,
76. P. J. Stoner,
77. George W. Spruce,
78. Laban Burgan,
79. George Snyder,
80. D. B. Gray,
81. Thomas Ogden
82. E. C. Leach,
83. J. T. Evans,
84. H. I. Stevens,
85. J. J. Kauffman,
86. S. Riddle,
87. M. D. Kagey,
88. Daniel Shearer,
89. J. G. Kagey,
90. Levi Gardner,
91. Samuel D. Morr,
92. Andrew Mason,
93. J. R. Riddle,
94. M. Riddle,
95. G. W. Riddle,
96. Philip Shearer,
97. M. R. Mason,
98. Owen Tompkins,
99. S. D. Gault,
100. F. P. Moneysmith,
101. B. F. Nelson,
102. L. Wertman,
103. H. Ames,
104. Simon Brindle,
105. Isaac Roseberry,
106. J. W. Davis,
107. James McNaul,
108. James Gibson,
109. Mrs. W. S. Reed,
110. John Thomas,
111. A. J. Burns,
112. W. L. Edwards,
113. T. Teeple,
114. J. F. Bush,
115. Samuel Taylor,
116. Josiah J. Closson,
117. Newton A. Hart,
118. Frederick Jones,
119. Orlando Markley,
120. S. S. Davis,
121. C. and J. Vantilburg,
122. Michael Myers,
123. P. and J. Thomas,
124. George Moherman,
125. George M. Stone,
126. Frank S. Jamison,
127. William McNulty,
128. Tobias Crone,
129. Daniel Stone,
130. John R. Vallentine,
131. Emanuel Finger,
132. Fred Sheppard,
133. Albertus Freer,
134. H. H. Eberhart,
135. Cyrus Zimmerman,
136. William H. Gibson
137. Jacob Rumbaugh,
138. C. S. Martin,
139. W. H. H. Potter,
140. Isaac Kilhefner,
141. Joshua L. Devor.

ORANGE.

1. Josiah Thomas,
2. Solomon Vance,
3. James Alberson,
4. David Heiffner,
5. John Fluke,
6. John Stentz,
7. J. W. Bishop,
8. Jane Welch,
9. George McConnell,
10. S. Barrick,
11. Margaret Fluke,
12. Hannah Fluke,
13. Thos. S. Culbertson,
14. Mrs. S. A. Donley,
15. John Richards,
16. Johnson Welch,
17. G. W. Miller,
18. J. M. Welch,
19. John Richey,
20. David Biddinger,
21. John Geier,
22. Hugh Murray,
23. Alex. Patterson,
24. Mrs. Jane S. Brown,
25. William Shidler,
26. Samuel F. Leidigh,
27. G. W. Fast,
28. Catharine Fast,
29. W. A. Mason,
30. L. H. Mason,
31. Harvey Roberts,
32. Henry Fluke,
33. James Heifner,
34. Elizabeth McFadden,
35. John Creveling,
36. D. R. Hall,
37. Isaac Mason,
38. William Saddler,
39. David Smith,
40. Henry Wertz,
41. C. C. Barnhill,
42. T. W. Richards,
43. George W. Barnhill,
44. Michael Vesper,
45. Jonas Fast,
46. Daniel D. Richards,
47. William Peters,
48. Jesse Wertman.

MILTON.

1. L. Ferrell,
2. Scott Nelson,
3. Samuel Urie,
17. Hugh Burns,
18. John Brigle,
19. Joseph Pifer,

4. F. A. Vantilburg,
5. George Miller,
6. James Sloan,
7. Benjamin Wenrick,
8. James Wharton,
9. Thomas Wharton,
10. Robert Pollock,
11. C. L. Fike,
12. Z. H. Ekey,
13. Joseph Nelson,
14. Henry Wells,
15. E. E. Wharton,
16. E. P. Smith,
20. Henry Keever,
21. Joseph Charles,
22. Susan Brindle,
23. Stephen Ohl,
24. James Hazlett,
22. G. W. Hazlett,
26. H. Pifer,
27. H. A. Hartman,
28. W. G. Imhoff,
29. Joseph Wells,
30. H. L. Heiffner,
31. Peter Burk,
32. A. Heltman,
33. Mrs. Susan Roland.

CLEAR CREEK.

1. William Gregg,
2. Robert McKibben,
3. Lewis Cowie,
4. Abel Bailey,
5. Jacob Gibson,
6. John Gibson,
7. William Kirkton,
8. George Mackey,
9. J. B. Vermilya,
10. Jacob Huffman,
11. Peter Van Nordstrand,
12. R. J. Semanton,
13. D. R. Buffenmire,
14. Thomas Sprott,
15. John Stoner,
16. D. H. Coleman,
17. Jacob Mykrantz,
18. J. R. Shriver,
19. Elizabeth Bryte,
20. J. R. Burgett,
21. John Ferrell,
22. D. Shriver,
23. M. C. Percival,
24. A. N. Shriver,
25. J. B. Lehmann,
26. I. Buchanan,
27. A. Cuppy,
28. Barbara Huffman,
29. William Ferrell,
30. T. W. Hunter,
31. Isaac Emmens,
32. J. S. Cubbison,
33. Matthew Calhoun,
34. Robert Hart.
35. L. Frizzell,
36. James Lawson,
37. George Shriver,
38. Isaac Coleman,
39. E. F. Bryte,
40. A. N. Chamberlain,
41. Maggie J. Brown, jr.,
42. John Leistensneider,
43. W. B. Hafer,
44. William Wertman.

RUGGLES.

1. O. L. Andrews.

SULLIVAN.

1. R. M. Close,
2. Bernard Holbrook,
3. H. N. Whitcomb,
4. A. B. Johnson,
5. Marcus DeMoss,
6. S. L. Drake,
7. Mary E. Gould,
8. John A. Spencer,
9. William Goodyear,
10. Joseph Chamberlain,
11. N. P. Rogers,
12. Alva Marsh,
13. D. G. Spencer,
14. Horace Riggs.

PERRY.

1. George Gregg,
2. Arthur Campbell,
3. Jacob Sheets,
4. J. A. Harris,
5. Jacob Kready,
6. Richard Smalley,
7. Amos Funk,
8. Arthur Campbell, jr.,
9. John P. Smalley,
10. Mary J. Campbell,
31. C. C. Funk,
32. Samuel Fridline,
33. Isaac Zimmerman,
34. H. K. Snyder,
35. Adam Minsh,
36. George Myers,
37. Alord Scott,
38. William Scott,
39. Jonathan Myers,
40. S. P. Countryman,
11. L. H. Uplinger,
12. John Rudy,
13. B. Funk,
14. William Maurer,
15. Elijah Ebert,
16. David Boffenmyer,
17. J. G. Bringolf,
18. David Weiler,
19. David McConnell,
20. William Osburn,
21. William Weikal,
22. Jacob Ecker,
23. Emanuel Kauffman,
24. R. V. Smalley,
25. Margaret Osburn,
26. John Camp,
27. C. S. McFadden,
28. Ludwick Fridline,
29. R. S. Smilie,
30. C. Countryman,
41. Henry Shisler,
42. Jacob Morr,
43. William W. Harris,
44. David Weygant,
45. Andrew Jackson,
46. Joshua Myers,
47. Joseph Eichelberger,
48. Eliza Morr,
49. Samuel Worst,
50. Michael Morr, jr.,
51. Hartman Shidler,
52. Simon Eichelberger,
53. Andrew Wireman,
54. George Morr,
55. M. Wise,
56. A. E. Morr,
57. Daniel Myers,
58. A. Eichelberger,
59. John Eichelberger,
60. Henry Sealer,
61. J. H. McFadden.

HANOVER.

1. H. L. McCray,
2. J. G. Herzog,
3. John Stockmon,
4. J. C. Gains,
5. W. R. Reed,
6. P. A. Reinhard,
7. J. H. Sanborn,
8. Andrew J. Scott,
9. Peter H. Stauffer,
10. Lucy E. Haskell,
11. J. P. Barron,
12. G. Schauweker,
13. J. L. Quick,
14. A. Akins,
15. J. W. Bull,
16. H. Gilbert,
17. George H. Stewart,
18. A. B. Fuller,
19. John Priest,
20. John Strong,
21. Samuel Bolly,
22. Jacob Breckheisen, jr.,
23. C. S. Deyarmon,
24. P. J. Black,
25. J. F. Redd,
26. Claude Petot,
27. M. H. Bailey,
28. Samuel Hess,
29. C. L. Buckwalter,
30. Edward Sigler,
31. J. L. Burwell,
32. Michael Derunberger,
33. John C. Larwill,
34. C. Openheimer,
35. William Barron,
36. N. W. Smith,
37. William Garret,
38. William M. Crowner,
39. Daniel Geiselman,
40. William H. Wirt,
41. George Honebarger,
42. T. Y. McCray.

GREEN.

1. Silas C. Parker,
2. Melzer Tannehill,
3. Elmina Coulter,
4. J. M. Percival,
5. Horace L. Stearns,
6. C. O. Tannehill,
7. C. C. Coulter & Son,
8. J. P. Pocock,
9. J. F. Johnston,
10. S. M. Black,
11. Daniel Bittenger,
12. H. B. Case,
13. C. L. Carey,
14. William Cowan,
15. George Guthrie,
25. J. C. Sample,
26. A. M. Stearns,
27. John Weltmer,
28. Waring Wolf,
29. J. B. Norris,
30. Tobias Castor,
31. Thomas Kithcart,
32. Aaron Kindle,
33. D. Rust,
34. John Fulmer,
35. D. P. Fulmer,
36. W. H. Van Gilder,
37. Kate Gretzinger,
38. Benjamin Castor,
39. D. R. Yarnell,

16. H. D. Maurer,
17. John Jones, sr.,
18. Joseph Jones,
19. John Archart,
20. A. N. Quick,
21. O. McGuire,
22. James C. Mothrup,
23. Benjamin McGuire,
24. Thomas McGuire,
40. A. H. Wilson,
41. R. R. Humphrey,
42. William Condick,
43. Jonathan Coulter,
44. Philip Long,
45. William D. Ewalt,
46. A. Mumper, sr.,
47. William A. McCool,
48. Lewis Oliver.

JACKSON.

1. James E. Chase,
2. Michael Bowers,
3. Jacob Fast,
4. John Keener,
5. Joseph Weikel,
6. R. F. Welch,
7. Thomas Miller,
8. John Welch,
9. D. L. Travis,
10. Margaret Berry.
11. Thomas DeArmon,
12. C. C. Matthews,
13. John Irvin,
14. John Byers,
15. Nancy Bowman,
16. Henry Switzer,
17. A. Kline,
18. H. Kane,
19. Simon Clouse,
20. Jacob Plice,
21. Andrew Mogle,
22. Jonas Wiltrout,
23. John H. Eldridge,
24. Samuel Berry,
25. Samuel Eicher,
26. Benjamin Buzzard,
27. J. R. W. Dinsmore,
28. E. Kiplinger,
29. M. Stentz,
30. David Eshleman,
31. William Myers,
32. Levi Householder.

LAKE.

1. John Kantzer,
2. F. T. Richey,
3. George Kantzer,
4. Sparks Burd, sr.,
5. Ithanar Covert,
6. Henry Dillier,
7. Elizabeth Brubaker,
8. John Artz,
9. John C. Warens,
10. John J. Wolf,
11. Sparks Burd, jr.,
12. Peter Huff,
13. William Long,
14. Adam Long,
15. George W. Brubaker,
16. Peter Sanders,
17. Martin Bender,
18. John Bender,
19. Alexander Emrick,
20. George Long,
21. Ezekiel Moores,
22. Abner Finley,
23. George Wolf,
24. Jacob Kayler,
25. Michael Wolf,
26. John Coble,
27. Jacob Horn,
28. William Wicoff,
29. J. E. Covert,
30. J. S. Easly,
31. J. M. Eberhart,
32. G. W. Emrick.

MOHICAN.

1. Samuel S. McClure,
2. J. R. Wallace,
3. Wilson Lutz,
4. Daniel Fickes,
5. R. M. Winbigler,
6. Joseph Austen,
7. Thomas Glenn,
8. Enos Tryon,
9. Benjamin Sibert,
10. H. A. Sloane,
11. J. D. Karns,
12. C. M. Elliott,
13. S. J. Crites,
14. L. P. Zimmerman,
15. J. A. Offineer,
27. C. S. Seibert,
28. Joseph Heichel,
29. John Spreng,
30. Michael Otto,
31. E. F. Ebright,
32. Henry Wachtel,
33. John Heichel,
34. Samuel Huff,
35. Matthias Bender,
36. B. F. Paullin,
37. Rev. Jas. H. Steele,
38. Levi Metcalf,
39. Stephen Ewing,
40. M. Ebert,
41. Benjamin Frey,

16. Joel Richey,
17. N. Richey,
18. Joel Karns,
19. John B. Ridgley,
20. Elmer D. Morr,
21. William Noggle, jr.,
22. David D. Botdorf,
23. Jacob Spreng,
24. E. H. Ingman,
25. Catteanie Offineer,
26. Margaret Botdorf,
42. E. F. Shelly,
43. W. Chesrown,
44. Peter Chesrown,
45. William Davis,
46. D. F. Pocock,
47. Samuel Keiser,
48. Levi Flickinger,
49. Emanuel Treace,
50. D. F. Heiser.
51. J. P. Winbigler.
52. James McFadden,

53. J. W. Selby.

TROY.

1. Adam Smith,
2. Jane E. Phelps,
3. G. W. Bowerize,
4. George Beck,
5. Eunice Parker,
6. John Parmenter,
7. E. C. Brandebery,
8. C. Bishop,
9. Alvin Crittenden,
10. Joel Bruce,

11. C. D. Fair.

MIFFLIN.

1. Joseph Doty,
2. John K. Staman,
3. C. C. Staman,
4. Daniel Kauffman,
5. I. F. Markel, M. D.,
6. C. F. Engle, P. M.,
7. John Charles,
8. Sebastian Culler,
9. Dillman Switzer,
10. John W. Whisler,
11. Benjamin Brubaker,
12. Samuel Kagey,
13. Christian Kagey,
14. David Wertman,
15. Abraham Barr,
16. Joseph Miller,
17. Samuel Moore,
18. B. F. Beninghoff,
19. Jno. & Jos. Sunday,
20. William Lattimer,
21. W. Wilson, jr.,
22. Joseph Zehner,
23. J. W. Lemon,
24. David S. Beninghoff,
25. Lewis P. Yeater,
26. Samuel Heckman,
27. John Lutz,
28. Edwin Parks,
29. John W. Vail,
30. Samuel Cullen,
31. George W. Milligan,
32. Harrison Hoover,
33. Levi Lambright,
34. Enoch Conn,
35. Mrs. N. J. Peterson,
36. John P. Culler,
37. Isaac Matthews,
38. J. S. Black,
39. John Scott,
40. Peter Zehner,
41. N. Matthews,
42. John Baker,
43. Gotlieb Koch,
44. Jacob Staman.

VERMILLION.

1. J. W. Brant,
2. S. Diefendorf,
3. H. Armstrong, jr.,
4. David Fox,
5. T. C. Harvey,
6. J. B. Fox,
7. Dr. E. V. Kendig,
8. John Harvey,
9. John S. Grabill,
10. O. H. Scott,
11. J. M. Long,
12. William O. Porter,
13. H. Butcher,
14. F. Fox,
15. George Buchanan,
34. Henry Sheller,
35. William Davis,
36. Thomas Crone,
37. William H. Strickland,
38. William Glenn,
39. Adam Bahn,
40. J. W. Harper,
41. N. D. Ryland,
42. Samuel Craig,
43. Samuel Echelbarger,
44. William Harvey,
45. John M. Ritchie,
46. Joseph H. Boyd,
47. Solomon Arnold,
48. William Tangeman,

16.	Mrs. S. S. McNabb,	49.	Michael Shenberger,	25.	J. I. Armstrong,	58.	John Beck,
17.	J. R. Swartz,	50.	William McNaull,	26.	J. W. Stillwagon,	59.	William Beck,
18.	John Risser,	51.	James Echelbarger,	27.	Mrs. Margaret Isaman,	60.	J. Wilson Harvey,
19.	Clark A. Barton,	52.	Lafayette Paxton,	28.	David Ciphers,	61.	H. J. Hough,
20.	Henry F. Rees,	53.	Jacob Echelbarger,	29.	Thomas Stafford,	62.	John K. Crone,
21.	W. W. Armstrong,	54.	Robert Wilson,	30.	George W. Long,	63.	John Bell,
22.	B. F. Armstrong,	55.	James B. Smith,	31.	William Craig,	64.	Robert Sigler,
23.	McC. Davis,	56.	Harrison McCrory,	32.	W. G. Galloway,	65.	B. McKinley,
24.	Michael Culler,	57.	Jacob Beck,	33.	Emanuel Sheller,	66.	A. R. Sigler.

Akins, Alexander, Jr.	296
Alexander, Sr.	296
Alberson, James	254
W. T.	265
Allison, Alexander	330
Amend, John K.	318
Andrews, Alanson	205
James	203
Lorin, LL. D.	208
Orsamus L.	379
Sarah H. (Mrs.)	263
Thaddeus	379
Arehart, John	277
Armentrout, Abraham	237
Armstrong, Captain	130
David, Dr.	171
Harrison, Dr.	170
Arnold, Samuel L.	369
Solomon	300
Artz, John	286
Austin, Joseph	357
Bachelder, William A.	319
Bacorn, Jacob	277
Baker, John	318
Bailey, Abel	154
N. H.	294
Barker, N. H.	291
Barnhill, Charles E.	344
George W.	344
Robert	344
Barr, Abraham	321
Barrick, Stephen	342
Barron, James P.	296
William	297
Barton, Clark A.	308
Baun, Adam	301
Beach, Daniel	178
Beall, Reason (General)	142
Bechtel, Joseph	262
Beck, George	338
Jacob	305
John	304
William	304
Beer, Richard	254
Robert, (Capt.)	255
Thomas, (Hon.)	380
Thomas, (Rev.)	221
William	254
Bell, John	303
Bender, George	287
John	287
Martin	287
Matthias	363
Benninghof, David S.	316
J. F.	321
Berry, Jacob	249
John, (Col.)	249
Samuel	338
William	340
Biddinger, David	346
Bird, Sparks (see also Burd)	152
Bishop, Cornelius	337
John	229, 342
Joseph	343
Bittinger, Daniel	276
George	275
Black, Jacob S.	317
Philip J.	293
S. W.	398
Samuel	275
Bolly, Simon	295
Botdorf, David D.	358
Nancy	357
Bowerice, George W.	180
Bowerize, George W.	337
Bowers, Michael	339
Boyd, J. H.	300
Brandebery, E. C.	337
Breckeiser, Jacob, Jr.	296
Jacob, Sr.	295
Brigle, John	350
Brindle, John	351
Simon	375
Bringolf, John G.	336
Brothers, Henry	224
Brown, John G.	310
Thomas	346
Brubaker, Benjamin	319
George	286
George W.	286
Jacob	364B
Peter	258
Bruce, Joel	337
Bryte, David	154
Elijah F.	313
John	155
Thomas	312
Buchanan, George	309
Isaac	311
Buckwalter, C. L.	296
Budd, Daniel	276
Samuel	276
Buffenmire, E. R.	311
David	331
Bull, family	383
George W. (Hon.)	207
Burd, John	285
Sparks, Jr.	285
Sparks, Sr.	285
Burgan, Laban	251
Burgett, George	313
Burk, Peter	351
Burns, A. J.	378
Hugh	156
Peter	260
William	313
Burwell, John Lee	294
Bush, James Franklin	322
Bushnell, Sterling G., Sr.	191
Tully C., (Judge)	403

Butcher, H.	309
Butt, Henry	352
Buzzard, Benjamin	338
Byers, John	340
Calhoun, Alexander	312
Camp, John	326
Matthias	326
Campbell, Almer R.	395
Arthur, Jr.	239, 332
James	380
John A.	332
Meigs S.	396
Cappels, Caleb	298
Carey, Charles	279
George W.	279
Carr, John, Sr.	231
Carter, Daniel	375
Daniel, Jr.	159
Daniel, Sr.	148
David	375
Norman	180
Carver, Aldrich	179
Case, H. B.	280
Castor, Conrad	273
Noah	273
Tobias	273
Chamberlain, James	313
Jesse	214
Joseph	355
Whitney	355
Chandler, Joseph	148
Robert F.	151
Chapman, John	183
Charles, John	175
Joseph B.	397
Chase, James E.	339
James E., (Hon.)	173
Chesrown, Peter	361
Wesley	364
Church, Henry	237
Ciphers, David	307
Clark, Bela B.,(Dr.)	170
James	231
Nathaniel	181
P. H.,(Dr.)	170, 395
W. R. S.,(Dr.)	170
Cliff, Joseph E.,(Dr.)	167
Close, Henry M.	353
Roderick M.	353
Closson, Josiah M.	370
Clouse, Simon	341
Coble, Henry	283
John	289
Coffin, Frederick W.	177
Cole, Thomas, Sr.	223
Coleman, D. H.	313
Isaac	311
Condick, William	281
Conn, George	318
Copus, Wesley	177
Cordell, Samuel	257
Cory, John	230
Coulter, Christopher C.	274
George B.	274
John	273
Jonathan	274
Thomas W.	274
Coulters, the	146
Coun, Enoch	317
Countryman, Christian	328
S. P.	323
Covert, Enoch	289
Ithamer	285
John E.	290
Cowan, Jacob P., (M. D.)	404
Joseph	276
William	277
Cowie, Louie	310
Craig, Samuel	302
William	306
Crall, Jacob	238
Creveling, John	344
Crites, S. J.	362
Crittenden, Alvin	337
Orlando	338
Crone, John K.	305
Thomas	303
Tobias S.	368
Crouse, Jacob	234
Crowner, Michael	298
William	299
Cubbison, John	314
Culberson, Robert	259
Thomas S.	343
Culler, John P.	322
Michael	203
Michael, Jr.	308
Samuel	321
Sebastian	322
Cuppy, John	312
Curry, George W.	183
Joseph	355
Damp, John	396
Davidson, Dr.	169
Davis, Hugh	222
Isaac	257
McClure	308
Samuel S.	371
William	303, 358
DeArmon, Thomas	340
Deming, William N., (Dr.)	169
DeMoss, Jonah	353
Marcus	354
Derrenberger, Michael	296

Devor, J. P.		400
Joshua L.		400
DeYarmon, Christian		292
Joseph, (Dr.)		292
Dillier, Henry		285
Jacob		285
Dinsmore, James A., Sr.		341
Donley, John		254B, 255
Thomas		255
Doty, Abraham		219
James		174
Jonathan		365
Dougherty, John, (Hon.)		176
Dowdee, Billy		153
Drake, Chester		354
Simeon L.		354
Drayton, E. T.		396
Dunlap, Thomas		181
Eagle, Thomas		145
William		145
Easly, George		290
Julius S.		290
Eberhart, Henry H., (Capt.)		368
John		290
Joshua		290
Ebert, Elijah		332
Millison		363
Ebright, E. F.		356
Echelbarger, James M.		301
Samuel		302
Ecker, Jacob		334
Edwards, Willis L.		398
Ekey, Zephaniah		350
Eichelberger, Adam		324
Adam, Jr.		325
George		325
Jacob		300
John		326
Joseph		323
Eicher, Samuel		338
Eldridge, John H.		338
Elliott, Christy M.		364
Patrick		182
Emerick, Alexander		287
John		287
Emerson, R. D., (Rev.)		215
William A. G.		217
Emmens, Benjamin		373
Emmons, Benjamin		312
Emrick, George		291
Jacob		290
Engle, C. F.		321
Eshelman, David		339
Ewalt, John		281
William D.		281
Ewing, Stephen		360
Fair, C. D.		338
Fast, A. C.		347
Fast, Christian, Sr.		133
George		400
Jacob		339, 383
Jonas		345
William		251
Ferguson, James		400
Ferrell, John		313
Lance		348
William		311
Ferris, Abraham		180
Fickes, Daniel		360
Fike, Adam		349
C. L.		349
Finger, Emanuel, (Capt.)		400
Finley, Abner		288
Alexander		143
John		288
Flickinger, Levi		360
Fluke, David		343
Henry		261, 343
John		342
Philip		260B, 342
Folk, Daniel		404
Ford, Elias		164
Foulks, Elizabeth		138
George		138
Fox, Conrad		304
David		309
Frederick		309
Joseph Benton		310
Frazee, William C.		227
Freer, Albertus		367
Frees, Jacob		213
Fridline, Ludwick		327
Samuel		327
Frizzel, L.		314
Fry, Benjamin		364
Fulkerson, R. P., (Major)		172
Fuller, Amos B., (Dr.)		292
Ephraim B., (Dr.)		167
E. B.		291
Fulmer, Daniel		280
Jacob		280, 288
John		280
Funk, Amos		331
Benjamin		333
C. C.		327
Gaines, John C.		293
Thomas		292
Galloway, W. G.		306
Gallup, Josiah		197
Gardner, Levi		366
Garret, Samuel		297
William		297
Gates, Isaac		159
Geier, John		346
Geiselman, Daniel		297
Gibson, Jacob		243
James		376
William W.		379

Gilbert, Henry	296
Glass, Samuel, (Dr.)	171
Glenn, Thomas	363
William	302
Godfrey, M. R.	395
Goodyear, Chauncy	354
William F.	354
Gould, John	354
Rufus	355
Grabill, John S.	310
Graham, Francis	206, 250
Gray, D. B.	402
Greenlee, John	150
William	162
Gregg, William	313
Gretzinger, Adam	281
John B.	281
Grinold, James	180
Grosscup, Benjamin	395
E. J.	378
Grubb, Jacob H.	173
Guth, Diebold	397
Guthrie, George	277
Richard	277
Hall, David R.	344
Hamilton, William	206
Harris, Asa	292
William W.	323
Hart, David	312
Newton A.	315
Hartman, Henry	352
Harvey, John	307
T. C.	306
Harvuot, Joseph	160
Haskell, George C.	295
Nathaniel	178
Hazlett, George W.	349
James	349
Heckman, Samuel	316
Heichel, John	363
Joseph	362
Heiffner, David	341
James	344
Heifner, Hyman L.	352
Heiser, D. E.	364
Helbert, Jacob	219
Heltman, Andrew	350
William G.	380
Herzog, John G.	295
Hess, Samuel	295
Hiffner, Jacob, (Sr.)	164
Hildreth, Joseph, (Dr.)	168
Hill, George W., (Dr.)	126
Harvey	274
Hisey, J. A., (D.D.S.)	397
Hoffman, Susannah C.	401
Holbrook, Bernard	353
Honebarger, Daniel	298
George	298
Hoover, Harrison	315
Horn, Elias	289
Jacob	289
Hough, H. J.	304
Householder, Levi	339
Hoy, Charles, Dr.	403
Huff, Peter	177, 285
Samuel	358
Huffman, Abraham	197
Daniel	311
Hughes, William, (Rev.)	220
Humphrey, Andrew	282
Robert	282
William	282
Hunter, T. W.	311
William	393
Ilgar, William W.	245
Imhoff, William G.	349
Ingmand, Edmund, (Judge)	252
Luke	252
Ingmond, E. H.	358
Irvin, William	281
Irwin, John	340
Isaman, Margaret	309
Jackson, Andrew	323
Jamison, Frank S.	368
Jennings, Jacob O.	238
Jerome, Baptiste	127
Johnson, Ambrose B.	353
Jeriah	345
Joseph	353
Johnston, John F.	274
Thomas	274
Jonacake, Solomon	129
Jones, Frederick	371
John, Sr.	276
John D., (Judge)	380
Joseph	277
Kagey, Christian	320
John C.	365
Martin	320
Martin V.	365
Samuel	320
Kane, Herman	341
Kantzer, George, Jr.	284
George, Sr.	284
John	284
Karns, J. D.	357
Kauffman, Daniel	315
Jacob J.	366
Kaufman, Emanuel	334
Kayler, Henry	288
Jacob	288
Kean, Augustus C.	286
Keener, John, Jr.	339
Keever, Henry	348
Keffer, Robison	319

Keiser, Samuel	363
Keller, John	373
Kelly, Mrs. Patrick	304
Kendig, E. V., (Dr.)	305
Kilgore, James	232
Kilhefner, Isaac	400
Kindle, Aaron	273
William	273
Kinnaman, Jacob W., (Dr.)	171
Kiplinger, Jacob	338
Levi H.	331
Kirkton, William	312
Kithcart, Thomas	278
Thomas, Sr.	278
Kline, Anthony	341
Knoth, Frank	378
Koch, Gotlieb	317
Kready, Jacob	333
Krichbaum, Jacob	366
Lambright, John	176
Levi B.	315
Larwill, John C.	296
Latimer, William	320
Latta, Moses	213
William	212
Lawson, James	314
Leach, E. C.	366
Lehman, Michael	314
Leidigh, Samuel	347,381
Leistensnider, John	313
Lemon, James W.	316
John	319
Link, Adam	228
Linn, Jacob	376
Long, Adam	286
Alfred O.	369
George	287
George W.	306
John G.	287
John M.	310
~~Philip~~ Philip	280
William	285
Lucas, Jacob	164
Luther, Joel, (Dr.)	167
Hulbert	222
Lutz, John	316
Wilson	360
Lyons, Thomas	130
Mackey, George	311
Mansfield, Martin Henry	244
Markel, I. F., (Dr.)	324B
Solomon	226
Markley, Joseph	199
Orlando	373
Marsh, Abijah	356
Alva	356
Aretes	356

Martin, Clarence S.	379
William S., (Capt.)	369
Mason, Andrew	157
Elizabeth, (Mrs.)	157
Isaac	344
Martin, Sr.	214
Martin B.	364
Matthews, C. C.	340
Isaac H.	317
Nicholas	318
Maurer, Henry	286
John	276
William	332
May, Michael	339
McCarty, Oliver, (Dr.)	172
McClain, John	261
McClure, Samuel	363
McCombs, John H.	230B,240
McConnell, David	335
John	204,382
McCool, James	282
William A.	282
McCrary, Harrison	299
Henry L.	294
William	294
McCutchin, Joseph	181
McFadden, Alfred	344
C. S.	326
J. N.	334
James	359
McGuire, Benjamin	276
Thomas	276
McGuires, the	211
McIlvain, Jefferson Monroe	369
McKibben, Hugh B.	310
McKinley, Benjamin S.	304
McNaul, John	376
McNaull, William	300
Mercers, the	226
Metcalf, Edward	212
Levi	358
Thomas	212
Vachel	199
Millar, G. W.	343
Miller, George	351
Jacob	309
Joseph	321
Michael	402
Thomas	340
Milligan, George W.	316
Mish, Adam	328
Mogle, Andrew	341
Moltrup, James C.	277
Moneysmith, Frank	398
Moody, Samuel, (Rev.)	216
Moore, Samuel, Sr.	319
William C.	364
Moores, Ezekiel	287
Ezekiel, Jr.	288

Morr, Andrew		329	Paxton, Lafayette	299
	Elias	325	Peck, Homer	236
	Eliza	323	Percival, J. M., (Dr.)	275
	Elmer D.	358	Moses Cook	312
	George	325	Peters, William	345
	Michael	261,324	Petot, Claude	294
	Michael, Jr.	325	Petterson, Nancy, (Mrs.)	317
	Samuel D.	370	Phelps, Elisha P.	337
Mourey, Joseph		315	Pierce, Dean	356
Mowry, Michael		374	Pifer, Henry	351
Mumper, Andrew		282	Joseph	350
	Andrew, Jr.	282	Pille, Henry	393
	Andrew, Sr.	282	Pipe, Captain	193
Murray, Hugh		347	Plank, Isaac	375
	Patrick	198	Plice, Jacob	341
Myers, Benjamin		399	Poag, James	180
	Daniel	325	Pocock, D. F.	362
	Frank E.	396	James M.	275
	George	328	Pollock, Joseph	349
	H. K.	396	Poorman, George	340
	Henry, Jr.	339	Porter, John	212
	J.	323	Potter, William H. H.	394
	Jonathan	329	Priest, James Loudon	161,291
	Michael	246	John	291
Mykrantz, Christopher		314	Proudfit, Andrew	374
Nelson, Hugh P., (Dr.)		372	Quick, Aaron N.	283
	John S.	213	Benjamin	283
	Joseph	350	David	291
	Robert	202,348	Jacob L.	291
Newell, Robert		173		
Newman, Andrew		166	Ralstons, the	227
Noggle, William		359	Ramsey, John	246
Norris, John		278	William	224
	Joseph B.	278	Redd, James	293
	William	278	Reed, Asa S.	214
			William, Jr.	293
Oesterlen, Gustavus, (Dr.)		169	William, Sr.	293
Offineer, James		357	Rees, Henry F.	307
	James A.	383	Reinhard, P. A.	294
Ogden, Thomas		371	Reinhardt, Jacob	294
Ohl, Stephen		352	Rice, Ebenezer	162
Oliver, Allen		183,283	Richard, Daniel	345
	Lewis	160,283	Richards, John	343
Openheimer, Charles		294	Samuel	181
Osborn, Thomas		334	Thomas W.	344
	William, (Judge)	263	Richey, Francis T.	284
Osburn, William		335	Joel	361
Otta, Kate, (Mrs.)		398	Newton	357
Otto, Michael		362	Robert	284
			Riddle, George W.	367
Parker, Cephas		283	Michael, Jr.	366
	Joseph L.	337	Michael, Sr.	224
	Joseph Seeley, (Rev.)	215	William Patterson	367
	Silas C.	283	Ridgley, John B.	361
Parkes, Edwin		316	Rieser, Herman M.	378
Parmely, Sylvanus		233	Riggs, Horace	356
Parmeter, John, Jr.		337	Risser, John	308
Patterson, William		346	Ritchey, John	343
Paullin, B. F.		359	Ritchie, John M.	300
	Z. T.	176	Roberts, Harvey	345

Robertson, Samuel		182
Robinson, John, (D.D., Rev.)		217,366
Robison, John		221
Rogers, Nathan P.		355
Richard		355
Roland, Christian		348
Roop, J. E., (Dr.)		371
Roorback, Jacob		180
Roseberry, Isaac		376
Philip R.		374
Rowland, Samuel		373
Rudy, John		330
Rumbaugh, Jacob		377
Rust, Darius		280
Lucian		279
Stephen		279
Ryland, N. D.		302
Saal, George		378
Sackett, Harvey		179
Sadler, William, (Rev.)		377
Sanborn, Jeremiah		293
Joseph		293
Sanders, Peter, Jr.		286
Peter, Sr.		286
Schauweker, Godfrey		292
John		292
Schneider, George		371
Scott, Alford		328
Andrew J.		297
Andrew J., (Dr.)		167
Hugh		297
John		155,317
O. H.		310
William		329
Sealer, Henry		326
Seibert, Benjamin		362
C. S.		357
Selby, J. W.		356
Sharp, S. Z., (Professor)		393
Shearer, David		365
Philip		365
Sheets, Jacob		333
Joseph		204,220
Nancy, (Mrs.)		401
Samuel		333
Sheller, Emanuel		306
Henry		262,306
Shelley, E. F.		360
Shemberger, Michael		301
Sheppard, Frederick		368
John		370
Sherick, Abram L., (Dr.)		372
Shidler, Daniel		324
John		375
William		346
Shisler, William N.		329
Shively, family		314
Shopbell, Jacob		166
Shriver, Albert		312
David		313
George		311
J. R.		311
Sigler, Anthony R.		304
Daniel		293
Edward		293
Robert		305
Simanton, Robert J.		311
Slocum, Eli		367
Elias		192
Ephraim		400
Willard, (Dr.)		169,384
Smalley, John P.		333
R. V.		334
Richard		336
Smilie, Richard S.		327
Smith, Adam		336
David, Jr.		344
George B.		393
Henry		181
James B.		299
James W.		247
John		256
Nathan W.		297
Robert W.		351,402
Samuel		256
Thomas		201
Snyder, John		328
Spencer, David G.		356
John A.		355
Joseph W.		355
Spreng, Jacob		362
John		360,362
Sprengle, Louis Jefferson		253
Springer, John		210
Sprott, Thomas		187
Thomas, Jr.		381
Stafford, Thomas		307
Staman, Benjamin		401
Jacob, Sr.		318
Stauffer, Peter High		296
Stearns, Alonzo N.		279
Horace L.		279
Nathan		278
Steele, J. H.		359
Stentz, John		342
Michael		338
Peter		260
Philip		342
Stephens, H. I.		374
Stewart, George H.		298
Stockman, Abiather		292
John		292
Stone, Daniel		368
George M.		368
Stoner, Jacob		314
Strickland, Joseph		211
William H.		303
Strong, John		295
Stubbs, Joseph D.		381

Stull, Isaac	249	Warens, John	286
Sturtevant, Bradford	179	John C.	287
Sultzer, Frederick	204	William	287
Summers, Daniel	247	Weikal, William	335
Sunday, Andrew	322	Weikel, Joseph	339
John	322	Weiler, David	335
Joseph	322	Weisenstine, Lizzie	399
Sutherland, Thomas Smith	178	Welch, Ephraim	246
Swartz, Joseph R.	308	John	340
Sweringer, Neal McCoy	372	Rankin F.	340
Swineford, Byron M.	399	Wells, Henry	351
Emanuel	374	James	350
George	245	Joseph	350
John	222	Weltmer, John	278
Switzer, Dillman	320	Wenrick, Benjamin	352
Henry	340	Wertman, Daniel	377
		David	319
Tallantire, John R., (Rev.)	368	Jackson S.	395
Tangeman, William	300	Jacob	401
Tannehill, Charles	275	Jesse	400
Charles O.	275	Leo	399
Melzer	275	William	401
Melzer, Jr.	275	Wertz, Henry	344
Tannehills, the	163	Westheffer, William	258
Taylor, Don F.	402	Weston, Roswell	180
Enoch	219	Weyant, David	330
Samuel	370	Wharton, Ebenezer	352
William	165	James	352
William & Sons	241	John	352
Teeple, Theo.	397	Thomas	352
Thomas, John L.	377	Whisler, John W.	320
Josiah	176	Whitcomb, Horace N.	353
Michael	258	Wilson	353
Nelson	396	Whitmore, Daniel W., (Judge)	241
Peter	158	Wicoff, Peter	289
Tilton, John	165	William	289
Tompkins, Owen	394	Wiest, Samuel Gates	394
Treace, Emanuel	359	Williams, Abram	128
Tryon, Enos	361	Willson, Charles	254
		Wilson, A. H.	280
Ullman, George A.	397	Robert	301
Urie, George W., (Col.)	183,188	William, Jr.	319
Samuel	349	Wiltrout, Jonas	341
Solomon	189	Winbigler, James P.	360
		Richard	207
Vail, John Wesley	315	Wireman, Andrew	324
VanArnan, Charles S.	181	Wirt, William H.	297
Vance, Solomon	248	Wise, Michael	325
VanGilder, William H.	280	Wolf, George	288
VanNest, John	214	George B.	284
VanNorstrand, Peter	311	Isaac	278
Peter, Sr.	225	John	284,288
Vantilburg, Daniel, Sr.	246	John C.	307
Henry	348	John J.	284
Vermilya, William J.	312	Michael	289
Vesper, Michael	345	Stephen	376
		Warring	278
Wachtel, Henry	359	Woodhull, William S.	276
Walker, Alanson, (Capt.)	174	Worst, Henry	324
Wallack, Eli W.	227	Samuel	324

Yarnell, Aaron	281
Daniel	281
Daniel R.	281
Yeater, Lewis P.	316
Yerick, Gutelius I.	398
Young, Jacob	235
James	290
John C.	290
Zehner, Joseph	320
Peter	317
Zimmerman, Cyrus	365
Isaac	327
L. P.	361

www.ingramcontent.com/pod-product-compliance
Lightning Source LLC
Chambersburg PA
CBHW042350070526
44585CB00028B/2887